New Perspectives on

HTML, XHTML, and Dynamic HTML

3rd Edition

Comprehensive

New Perspectives on

HTML, XHTML, and Dynamic HTML

3rd Edition

Comprehensive

Patrick Carey

Carey Associates, Inc.

COURSE TECHNOLOGY
CENGAGE Learning™

Australia • Brazil • Japan • Korea • Mexico • Singapore • Spain • United Kingdom • United States

COURSE TECHNOLOGY
CENGAGE Learning™

New Perspectives on HTML, XHTML, and Dynamic HTML, 3rd Edition—Comprehensive
is published by Course Technology.

Managing Editor: Rachel Goldberg

Product Managers: Karen Stevens, Donna Gridley

Associate Product Manager: Emilie Perreault

Editorial Assistant: Shana Rosenthal

Marketing Manager: Joy Stark

Developmental Editor: Sasha Vodnik

QA Manuscript Reviewers: Chris Carvalho,
    Christian Kunciw, Burt LaFountain,
    Serge Palladino, Ashlee Welz Smith

Senior Production Editor: Catherine G. DiMassa

Composition: GEX Publishing Services

Text Designer: Steve Deschene

Cover Designer: Nancy Goulet

Cover Artist: Helmick & Schechter Sculpture

www.handsart.net

For product information and technology assistance, contact us at
Cengage Learning Customer & Sales Support, 1-800-354-9706
For permission to use material from this text or product, submit all requests online at **cengage.com/permissions**
Further permissions questions can be emailed to
permissionrequest@cengage.com

ISBN-13: 978-0-619-26748-3

ISBN-10: 0-619-26748-8

Course Technology
25 Thomson Place
Boston, Massachusetts 02210
USA

Cengage Learning is a leading provider of customized learning solutions with office locations around the globe, including Singapore, the United Kingdom, Australia, Mexico, Brazil, and Japan. Locate your local office at:
international.cengage.com/region

Cengage Learning products are represented in Canada by Nelson Education, Ltd.

For your lifelong learning solutions, visit **course.cengage.com**

Purchase any of our products at your local college store or at our preferred online store **www.ichapters.com**

Any fictional URLs used throughout this book are intended for instructional purposes only. At the time this book was printed, any such URLs were fictional and not belonging to any real persons or companies.

Some of the product names and company names used in this book have been used for identification purposes only and may be trademarks or registered trademarks of their respective manufacturers and sellers.

Printed in the United States of America
6 7 8 9 09 08

Preface

Real, Thought-Provoking, Engaging, Dynamic, Interactive—these are just a few of the words that are used to describe the New Perspectives Series' approach to learning and building computer skills.

Without our critical-thinking and problem-solving methodology, computer skills could be learned but not retained. By teaching with a case-based approach, the New Perspectives Series challenges students to apply what they've learned to real-life situations.

Our ever-growing community of users understands why they're learning what they're learning. Now you can too!

See what instructors and students are saying about the best-selling New Perspectives Series:

"First of all, I just have to say that I wish that all of my textbooks were written in the style of the New Perspectives Series. I am using these titles for all of the courses that I teach that have a book available."
— Diana Kokoska, University of Maine at Augusta

"The New Perspectives format is a pleasure to use. The Quick Checks and the tutorial Review Assignments help students view topics from a real-world perspective."
— Craig Shaw, Central Community College—Hastings

"We have been using the New Perspectives Series for several years and are pleased with it. Step-by-step instructions, end-of-chaper projects, and color screenshots are positives."
— Michael J. Losacco, College of DuPage

...and about New Perspectives on HTML, XHTML, and Dynamic HTML:

"For readability, no HTML title is in the same league as this one. I highly commend Carey for his writing and organizational styles and the way Course Technology formatted the materials."
—Zachary Wong, Sonoma State University, School of Business and Economics

www.course.com/NewPerspectives

Review

Apply

Reference Window

Why *New Perspectives* will work for you

Context

Each tutorial begins with a problem presented in a "real-world" case that is meaningful to students. The case sets the scene to help students understand what they will do in the tutorial.

Hands-on Approach

Each tutorial is divided into manageable sessions that combine reading and hands-on, step-by-step work. Screenshots—now 20% larger for enhanced readability—help guide students through the steps. **Trouble?** tips anticipate common mistakes or problems to help students stay on track and continue with the tutorial.

Review

In New Perspectives, retention is a key component to learning. At the end of each session, a series of Quick Check questions helps students test their understanding of the concepts before moving on. And now each tutorial contains an end-of-tutorial summary and a list of key terms for further reinforcement.

Assessment

Engaging and challenging Review Assignments and Case Problems have always been a hallmark feature of the New Perspectives Series. Now we've added new features to make them more accessible! Colorful icons and brief descriptions accompany the exercises, making it easy to understand, at a glance, both the goal and level of challenge a particular assignment holds.

Reference

While contextual learning is excellent for retention, there are times when students will want a high-level understanding of how to accomplish a task. Within each tutorial, Reference Windows appear before a set of steps to provide a succinct summary and preview of how to perform a task. Finally, each book includes a combination Glossary/Index to promote easy reference of material.

Student Online Companion

This book has an accompanying online companion Web site designed to enhance learning. Go to www.course.com/carey to find:

- Additional content for further exploration
- List of URLs from the book
- Student Data Files
- Links to software
- Student Edition Labs—These online interactive labs offer students hands-on practice and reinforcement of skills and concepts relating Web and Internet topics.
- Information about other Patrick Carey products

www.course.com/NewPerspectives

New Perspectives offers an entire system of instruction

The New Perspectives Series is more than just a handful of books. It's a complete system of offerings:

New Perspectives catalog

Our online catalog is never out of date! Go to the catalog link on our Web site to check out our available titles, request a desk copy, download a book preview, or locate online files.

Coverage to meet your needs!

Whether you're looking for just a small amount of coverage or enough to fill a semester-long class, we can provide you with a textbook that meets your needs.

- Brief books typically cover the essential skills in just 2 to 4 tutorials.
- Introductory books build and expand on those skills and contain an average of 5 to 8 tutorials.
- Comprehensive books are great for a full-semester class, and contain 9 to 12+ tutorials.
- Power Users or Advanced books are perfect for a highly accelerated introductory class or a second course in a given topic.

So if the book you're holding does not provide the right amount of coverage for you, there's probably another offering available. Go to our Web site or contact your Course Technology sales representative to find out what else we offer.

Instructor Resources

We offer more than just a book. We have all the tools you need to enhance your lectures, check students' work, and generate exams in a new, easier-to-use and completely revised package. This book's Instructor's Manual, ExamView testbank, PowerPoint presentations, data files, solution files, figure files, and a sample syllabus are all available on a single CD-ROM or for downloading at www.course.com.

How will your students master Computer Concepts and Microsoft Office?

Add more muscle and flexibility to your course with SAM (Skills Assessment Manager)! SAM adds the power of skill-based assessment and the award-winning SAM classroom administration system to your course, putting you in control of how you deliver exams and training.

By adding SAM to your curriculum, you can:

- Reinforce your students' knowledge of key computer concepts and application skills with hands-on exercises.
- Allow your students to "learn by listening," with access to rich audio in their training.
- Build hands-on computer concepts exams from a test bank of more than 200 skill-based concepts, windows, and applications tasks.
- Schedule your students' training and testing exercises with powerful administrative tools.
- Track student exam grades and training progress using more than one dozen student and classroom reports.

Teach your introductory course with the simplicity of a single system! You can now administer your entire Computer Concepts and Microsoft Office course through the SAM platform. For more information on the SAM administration system, SAM Computer Concepts, and other SAM products, please visit http://www.course.com/sam.

Distance Learning

Enhance your course with any of our online learning platforms. Go to www.course.com or speak with your Course Technology sales representative to find the platform or the content that's right for you.

www.course.com/NewPerspectives

About This Book

This book provides comprehensive instruction in basic to advanced concepts of HTML, XHTML, and Dynamic HTML using a practical, step-by-step approach.

- Teaches students HTML and XHTML using a simple text editor to create basic to complex Web sites. Advanced tutorials on DHTML help students to further their skills by learning and applying DHTML to make interactive features such as animated text, image rollovers, pull-down menus, drag and drop objects and dynamic Tables of Contents.
- Provides students with an interactive way to learn JavaScript and DHTML concepts through a companion CD of demo pages, ten of which are new to this edition.
- Contains a revised tutorial on web forms that includes new coverage of regular expressions and of passing data between Web forms.
- Includes expanded coverage of string objects, including number formatting and expanded coverage of form validation, including validating credit card data.
- Covers document nodes and the node tree in a new tutorial, in which students create a dynamic Table of Contents.
- Includes an enhanced Student Online Companion with additional material.
- Visit www.course.com/carey to find the latest information on best-selling Carey products.

Acknowledgments

I would like to thank the people who worked so hard to make this book possible. Special thanks to Sasha Vodnik for his excellent suggestions and ideas in developing this material and to Karen Stevens and Donna Gridley, the Product Managers who worked so hard in overseeing this project, keeping it on task and on target. Other people at Course Technology who deserve credit are Rachel Goldberg, Managing Editor; Emilie Perreault, Associate Product Manager; Cathie DiMassa, Senior Production Editor; and Quality Assurance Testers Chris Carvalho, Christian Kunciw, Burt LaFountain, Serge Palladino, and Ashlee Welz Smith.

Feedback is an important part of writing any book, and thanks go to the following reviewers for their ideas and comments: George Jackson, Collin County Community College; Allen Schmidt, Madison Area Technical College; Dorothy Harman, Tarrant County College; Cheryl Jordan, San Juan College; Lisa Friedrichsen, Johnson County Community College; and Mary Lee Herrmann, Hagerstown Community College.

Special thanks also go to the members of our New Perspectives HTML Advisory Committee: Dr. Nazih Abdallah, University of Central Florida; Liz Drake, Santa Fe Community College; Ric Heishman, Northern Virginia Community College, Manassas Campus; George Jackson, Collin County Community College District; David Jampole, Bossier Parrish Community College; Eric Kisling, Indiana University; Diana Kokoska, University of Maine Augusta; William Lomerson, Northwestern State University—Natchitoches; Lisa Macon, Valencia Community College; David Ray, Jones County Junior College; Lo-An Tabar-Gaul, Mesa Community College; Sandi Watkins, Foothill College; and Zachary Wong, Sonoma State University.

I want to thank my wife Joan for her love and encouragement, and my six children: John Paul, Thomas, Peter, Michael, Stephen, and Catherine, to whom this book is dedicated. In memory of my brother, Kevin.

—Patrick Carey

Brief Contents

HTML, XHTML, and DHTML

New Perspectives Series

Table of Contents

Level II Tutorials **105**

Read This Before You Begin **106**

Tutorial 3   **107**

Designing a Web Page **107**

Working with Fonts, Colors, and Graphics 107

Tutorial 4   **173**

Designing a Web Page with Tables **173**

Creating a News Page 173

Tutorial 7   347
Working with Cascading Style Sheets **347**
Creating a Style for Online Scrapbooks 347

Tutorial 10   521

Working with JavaScript **521**

Creating a Programmable Web Page
for North Pole Novelties 521

Additional Case 1   ADD 1

Creating a Company Web Site .... **ADD 1**

FrostiWear Winter Clothes ....ADD 1

Additional Case 2   ADD 11

Designing a Style for a Web Site .... **ADD 11**

Mayer Photography ....ADD 11

Tutorial 16

Working with Dynamic Content and Styles 895
Creating a Dynamic Table of Contents

New Perspectives on
HTML and XHTML

Read This Before You Begin: Tutorials 1–2

To the Student

Data Files

To complete the Level I HTML Tutorials (Tutorials 1 and 2), you need the starting student Data Files. Your instructor will either provide you with these Data Files or ask you to obtain them yourself.

The Level I HTML tutorials require the folders shown to complete the Tutorials, Review Assignments, and Case Problems. You will need to copy these folders from a file server, a standalone computer, or the Web to the drive and folder where you will be storing your Data Files.

Your instructor will tell you which computer, drive letter, and folder(s) contain the files you need. You can also download the files by going to www.course.com; see the inside back or front cover for more information on downloading the files, or ask your instructor or technical support person for assistance.

▼ **HTML**

    Tutorial.01

    Tutorial.02

To the Instructor

The Data Files are available on the Instructor Resources CD for this title. Follow the instructions in the Help file on the CD to install the programs to your network or standalone computer. See the "To the Student" section above for information on how to set up the Data Files that accompany this text.

You are granted a license to copy the Data Files to any computer or computer network used by students who have purchased this book.

System Requirements

If you are going to work through this book using your own computer, you need:

- **System Requirements** An Internet connection, a text editor and a Web browser that supports HTML 4.0 and XHTML 1.1 (for example, version 6.0 or higher of either Netscape or Internet Explorer). You may wish to run an older browser version to highlight compatibility issues, but the code in this book is not designed to support those browsers.

- **Data Files** You will not be able to complete the tutorials or exercises in this book using your own computer until you have the necessary starting Data Files.

Objectives

Session 1.1
- Review the history of the Internet, the Web, and HTML
- Describe different HTML standards and specifications
- Learn about the basic syntax of HTML code

Session 1.2
- Mark elements using two-sided and one-sided tags
- Insert an element attribute
- Create comments
- Describe block-level elements and inline elements
- Specify an element's appearance with inline styles
- Create and format different types of lists
- Create boldfaced and italicized text
- Describe logical and physical elements

Session 1.3
- Define empty elements
- Insert an inline image into a Web page
- Insert a horizontal line into a Web page
- Store meta information in a Web document
- Display special characters and symbols

Developing a Basic Web Page

Creating a Web Page for Stephen Dubé's Chemistry Classes

Case

Stephen Dubé's Chemistry Classes

Stephen Dubé teaches chemistry at Robert Service High School in Edmonton, Alberta (Canada). In previous years, he has provided course information to students and parents with handouts. This year, he wants to put that information on the World Wide Web, where anyone can access it easily. Eventually, he hopes to post homework assignments, practice tests, and even grades on the Web site. Stephen is new to this technology and has asked you to help him create a Web page for his class.

Student Data Files

You can find a complete listing of the associated files in the comment section of each HTML file.

▼ **Tutorial.01**

▽ **Tutorial folder**
  dube.jpg

▽ **Review folder**
  chemtxt.htm
  logo.jpg
  flask.jpg

▽ **Case1 folder**
  childtxt.htm
  newborn.jpg

▽ **Case2 folder**
  euler.jpg
  eulertxt.htm
  pi.jpg

▽ **Case3 folder**
  flakes.jpg
  frosttxt.htm
  runner.jpg

▽ **Case 4 folder**
  logo.jpg
  smith.jpg
  smith.txt

Session 1.1

Introducing the World Wide Web

Before you start creating a Web page for Stephen, it's helpful to first look at the history of the Web and how the HTML language was developed. To understand this history, we need to first become familiar with some of the basic features of networks.

A **network** is a structure linking computers together for the purpose of sharing resources such as printers and files. Users typically access a network through a computer called a **host** or **node**. A computer that makes a resource available to a network is called a **server**. A computer or other device that requests services from a server is called a **client**. Networks can be structured in many different ways. One of the most common structures is the **client-server network**, which is made up of several clients accessing information provided by one or more servers. You may be using such a network to access your data files for this tutorial from a network file server.

We can also classify networks based on their ranges. If the computers that make up a network are close together—for example, within a single department or building—then the network is referred to as a **local area network** or **LAN**. A network that covers a wider area, such as several buildings or cities, is called a **wide area network** or **WAN**. Wide area networks are typically built from two or more local area networks. The largest WAN in existence is the **Internet**.

In its early days in the late 1960's, the Internet was called the **ARPANET** and consisted of two network nodes located at UCLA and Stanford connected by a phone line. Today, the Internet has grown to include hundreds of millions of interconnected computers, cell phones, PDAs, televisions, and networks. The physical structure of the Internet uses fiber-optic cables, satellites, phone lines, and other telecommunications media, enabling a worldwide community to communicate and share information (see Figure 1-1).

Figure 1-1	Structure of the Internet

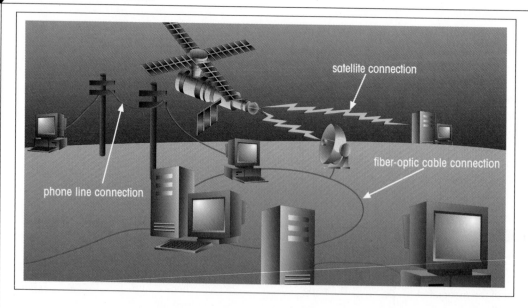

Most of the early Internet tools required users to master a bewildering array of terms, acronyms, and commands. Even navigating the network required users to be well-versed in both computers and network technology. Before the Internet could be accessible to the general public, it needed a simpler interface. This interface proved to be the World Wide Web.

The Development of the World Wide Web

The foundations for the **World Wide Web**, or the **Web** for short, were laid in 1989 by Timothy Berners-Lee and other researchers at the CERN nuclear research facility near Geneva, Switzerland. They needed an information system that would make it easy for their researchers to locate and share data, and which would require minimal training and support. To meet this need, they developed a system of interconnected hypertext documents that allowed their users to easily navigate from one topic to another. **Hypertext** is a method of organizing information that gives the reader control over the order in which the information is presented.

Properly used, hypertext provides quicker and simpler access to diverse pieces of information than traditional methods could. For example, when you read a book, you follow a linear progression, reading one page after another. With hypertext, you progress through those pages in whatever order best suits you and your objectives. Figure 1-2 illustrates the relationships of topics in linear and hypertext documents.

Linear versus hypertext documents ◄ **Figure 1-2**

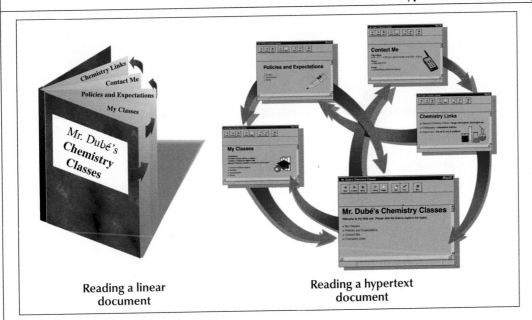

Reading a linear
document

Reading a hypertext
document

The key to hypertext is the use of **hyperlinks**, or **links**, which are the elements in a hypertext document that allow you to jump from one topic to another, often with a mouse click. A link may point to another section of the same document, or to another document entirely. A link can open a document on your computer or, through the Internet, a document on a computer anywhere in the world.

The hypertext approach was just what was needed to make the Internet accessible to the general public. The end user didn't need to know exactly where a document was stored, just how to get it. Since getting it was often no more difficult than clicking a mouse, access to any document anywhere was literally at every user's fingertips. The fact that the Internet and the World Wide Web are synonymous in many users' minds is a testament to the success of this approach.

An entire collection of linked documents is referred to as a **Web site**. The hypertext documents within a Web site are known as **Web pages**. Web sites have evolved from simple collections of text documents into complex sites where users can make purchases online, discuss a variety of topics, or access real-time stock market quotes. Individual pages can contain text, audio, video, and even programs that users can run remotely. While Web pages are primarily sources of information, they are increasingly becoming works of art in their own right.

Web Servers and Web Browsers

A Web page is stored on a **Web server**, which in turn makes it available to the network. To view a Web page, a client runs a software program called a **Web browser**, which retrieves the page from the server and displays it (see Figure 1-3).

Figure 1-3 | **Using a browser to view a Web document from a Web server**

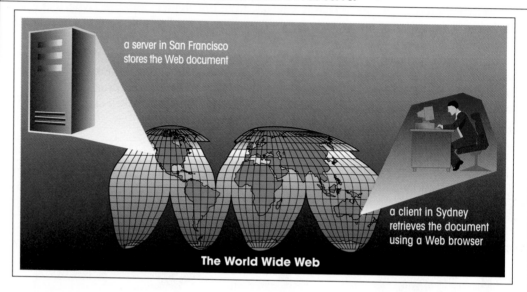

The earliest browsers, known as **text-based browsers**, were incapable of displaying images. Today most computers support **graphical browsers**, which are capable of displaying not only images, but also video, sound, animations, and a variety of graphical features. Cell phones can also connect to the Web to display sports scores or stock market tickers. Browsers can run on teletype machines, PDAs (personal digital assistants), Braille machines, and even information devices within a car. How does a Web page work with so many combinations of browsers and clients and devices? To understand, let's look at how Web pages are created.

HTML: The Language of the Web

A Web page is simply a text file written in a language called **Hypertext Markup Language** or **HTML**. We've already discussed hypertext, but what is a markup language? A **markup language** is a language that describes a document's structure and content. For example, if this tutorial were created using a markup language, that language would mark heading text, paragraph text, figure captions, and so forth.

Even though you can incorporate program code into an HTML file, HTML is not a programming language. HTML is also not a formatting language like those used by some desktop publishing programs. HTML does not necessarily tell you how a browser will display a document. If you want to format your document, the preferred method is to use styles. **Styles** are format descriptions written in a separate language from HTML that tell browsers how to render each element. We'll explore some of the basic styles as we create our first Web pages.

The History of HTML

Because the way HTML evolved impacts how you use it today, it's a good idea to review the language's history before going further into its details. The first version of HTML was created using the **Standard Generalized Markup Language (SGML)**. Introduced in the 1980's, SGML is a strong and highly flexible **metalanguage**, or a language used to create other languages. SGML is device- and system-independent, meaning that it can be applied to almost any type of document stored in almost any format. While powerful, SGML is also quite complex; for this reason, SGML is limited to those organizations that can afford the cost and overhead of maintaining complex SGML environments. However, SGML can also be used to create markup languages like HTML, which are tailored to specific tasks and are simpler to use and maintain.

In the early years after HTML was created, no one organization was responsible for the language. Web developers were free to define and modify HTML in whatever ways they thought best. While many rules were common, competing browsers, seeking to dominate the market, introduced some differences in the language. Such changes to the language were called **extensions**. The two major browsers during the 1990's, Netscape Navigator and Microsoft Internet Explorer, added the most extensions to HTML. These extensions were providing Web page authors with more options, but at the expense of complicating Web page development.

Web designers faced the challenge of determining which browser or browser version supported a particular extension, and creating a workaround for browsers that did not. By adding this layer of complexity to Web design, extensions, while often useful, diminished the promise of simplicity that made HTML so attractive in the first place.

Ultimately, a group of Web developers, programmers, and authors called the **World Wide Web Consortium**, or the **W3C**, created a set of **standards** or **specifications** that all browser manufacturers were to follow. The W3C has no enforcement power, but since a uniform approach to Web page creation is in the best interests of everyone, the W3C's recommendations are usually followed, though not always right away. The W3C also provides online tutorials, documentation, and quizzes that you can use to test your knowledge of HTML and other languages. For more information on the W3C and the services they offer, see their Web site at http://www.w3c.org.

Figure 1-4 summarizes the various versions of HTML that the W3C has released over the past decade. While you may not grasp all of the details of these versions yet, the important thing to understand is that HTML doesn't come in only one flavor.

Versions of HTML and XHTML ◀ **Figure 1-4**

Version	Date	Description
HTML 1.0	1989–1994	The first public version of HTML which included browser support for inline images and text controls.
HTML 2.0	1995	The first version supported by all graphical browsers. It introduced interactive form elements such as option buttons and text boxes. A document written to the HTML 2.0 specification is compatible with almost all browsers on the World Wide Web.
HTML 3.0	1996	A proposed replacement for HTML 2.0 that was never widely adopted.
HTML 3.2	1997	This version included additional support for creating and formatting tables and expanded the options for interactive form elements. It also supported limited programming using scripts.
HTML 4.01	1999	This version added support for style sheets to give Web designers greater control over page layout. It added new features to tables and forms and provided support for international features. This version also expanded HTML's scripting capability and added increased support for multimedia elements.
XHTML 1.0	2001	This version is a reformulation of HTML 4.01 in XML and combines the strength of HTML 4.0 with the power of XML. XHTML brings the rigor of XML to Web pages and provides standards for more robust Web content on a wide range of browser platforms.
XHTML 1.1	2002	A minor update to XHTML 1.0 that allows for modularity and simplifies writing extensions to the language.
XHTML 2.0	2004–	The latest version, designed to remove most of the presentational features left in HTML.

When you create your Web pages you'll have to keep in mind not only what the W3C has recommended, but also what browsers currently in use actually support. This may mean dealing with a collection of approaches: some are new and meet the latest specifications, while some are older but still widely supported. Older features of HTML are often **deprecated**, or phased out, by the W3C. While deprecated features might not be supported in current or future browsers, that doesn't mean that you can't continue to use them—indeed, if you are supporting older browsers, you may *need* to use them. Because it's hard to predict how quickly a deprecated feature will disappear from the Web, it's crucial to be familiar with these features.

Future Web development is focusing increasingly on two other languages. **XML (Extensible Markup Language)** is a metalanguage like SGML, but without SGML's complexity and overhead. Using XML, document developers can create documents that obey specific rules for their content and structure. This is in contrast with a language like HTML, which included a wide variety of rules without a built-in mechanism for enforcing them. Indeed, one of the markup languages created with XML is **XHTML (Extensible Hypertext Markup Language)**, a stricter version of HTML. XHTML is designed to confront some of the problems associated with the different and competing versions of HTML, and to better integrate HTML with XML.

Even though XHTML shows great promise for the Web, HTML will not become obsolete anytime soon. HTML and XHTML overlap considerably, and the World Wide Web is still full of old HTML documents. In addition, we need to support those Web users who are still using older versions of Web browsers. In this book, we'll discuss the syntax of HTML 4.01 and XHTML 1.1, but we'll also bring in deprecated features and browser-supported extensions where appropriate.

Where does all of this leave you as a potential Web page author? A few guidelines are helpful:

- **Become well-versed in the history of HTML**. Unlike other languages, HTML history impacts how you write your code.
- **Know your market**. Do you have to support older browsers, or have your clients standardized on a particular browser or browser version? The answer affects how you write the code for your Web pages. Become familiar with what different browsers can and can't do.
- **Test**. If you have to support several types of browsers and several types of devices, get them and use them to view your documents. Don't assume that if your page works in one browser it will work in an older version of that same browser. In addition, a given browser version might even perform differently under different operating systems.

Tools for Creating HTML Documents

Because HTML documents are simple text files, you can create them with nothing more than a basic text editor such as Windows Notepad. However, specialized HTML authoring programs, known as HTML converters and HTML editors, are available to perform some of the rote work of document creation.

An **HTML converter** converts formatted text into HTML code. You can create the source document with a word processor such as Microsoft Word, and then use the converter to save the document as an HTML file. Converters free you from the laborious task of typing HTML code, and because the conversion is automated, you do not have to worry about introducing coding errors in your document. However, HTML code created using a converter is often longer and more complicated than it needs to be, resulting in larger-than-necessary files. Also, it is more difficult to edit HTML code directly in a file created by a converter.

An **HTML editor** helps you create an HTML file by inserting HTML codes for you as you work. HTML editors can save you a lot of time and can help you work more efficiently. Their advantages and limitations are similar to those of HTML converters. In addition, while HTML editors allow you to set up a Web page quickly, you will usually still have to work directly with the HTML code to create a finished document.

In the next session, you'll start creating your first HTML document using a simple text editor.

Session 1.1 Quick Check

1. What is a hypertext document?
2. What is a Web server? A Web browser? Describe how they work together.
3. What is HTML?
4. How do HTML documents differ from documents created with a word processor such as Word or WordPerfect?
5. What is a deprecated feature?
6. What are HTML extensions? What are some advantages and disadvantages of using extensions?
7. What software program do you need to create an HTML document?

Session 1.2

Creating an HTML Document

It's always a good idea to plan out a Web page before you start coding. You can do this by drawing a planning sketch or by creating a sample document using a word processor. The preparatory work can weed out errors or point to potential problems. In this case, the chemistry teacher, Stephen Dubé, has already drawn up a handout that he's used for many years with his students and their parents. The handout lists his classes and describes his class policies regarding homework, exams, and behavior. Figure 1-5 shows the current handout that Stephen is using.

Figure 1-5 The chemistry class handout

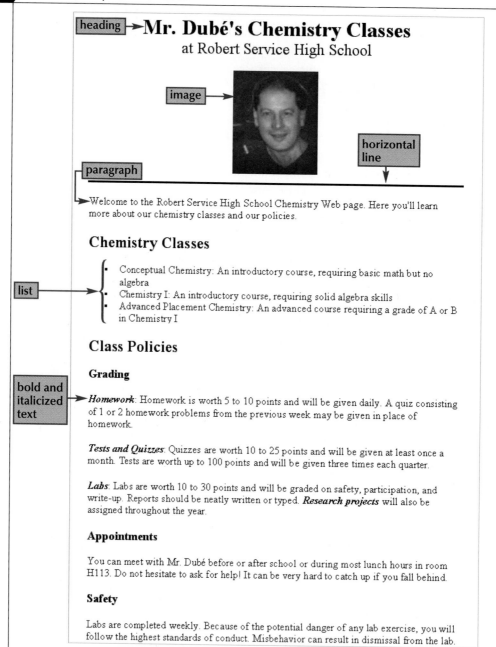

When we begin the planning process with a sample document, it can be helpful to identify the document's different elements. An **element** is a distinct object in the document, like a paragraph, a heading, or the page's title. Even the whole document can be considered an element. Stephen's handout includes several elements. A heading prominently displays his name, and beneath the heading, the document contains a photo and a horizontal line. The handout includes a brief introductory paragraph followed by two main sections: Chemistry Classes and Class Policies. The Chemistry Classes section lists the three classes he teaches. In the Class Policies section, three smaller headings list and describe his policies on Grading, Appointments, and Safety. We also want to take note of formatting features, such as text displayed in **boldfaced** font, and *italicized* text. As you recreate Stephen's handout as a Web page, you should periodically refer to Figure 1-5.

Marking Elements with Tags

The core building block of HTML is the **tag**, which marks each element in a document. Tags can be either two-sided or one-sided. A **two-sided tag** is a tag that contains some document content. The general syntax for a two-sided tag is:

```
<element>content</element>
```

where `element` is the name of the HTML element and `content` is any content it contains. For example, the following code marks the text, "Robert Service High School", with the <p> tag:

```
<p>Robert Service High School</p>
```

As you'll learn later, this indicates that a browser should treat "Robert Service High School" as a paragraph element.

In this book, the term "element" refers to an object in a Web page, and "tag" refers to the HTML code that creates the object. Thus we would say that we can create a p element in a Web page by inserting a <p> tag into the HTML file.

A two-sided tag's **opening tag** (<p>) and **closing tag** (</p>) should completely enclose its content. Earlier versions of HTML allowed designers to omit a closing tag if the surrounding code clearly indicated the tag's content, but this practice is no longer recommended. XHTML requires both an opening and closing tag.

HTML allows you to enter element names in either uppercase or lowercase letters. Thus you can type either <p> or <P> to indicate a paragraph. However, since XHTML strictly requires lowercase tag names, we will follow that convention here, and strongly recommend that you do likewise so that your Web pages will be consistent with current and future standards.

Unlike a two-sided tag, a **one-sided tag** contains no content. The general syntax for a one-sided tag is.

```
<element  />
```

where `element` is once again the element name. HTML also allows you to enter one-sided tags using the syntax <*element*> (omitting the space and closing slash). However, XHTML does not support this form, so we once again strongly recommend that you include the space and the closing slash at all times. Elements that employ one-sided tags are called **empty elements** since they contain no content. One example of an empty element is a line break, which forces the browser to display the next set of characters on a new line. To create a line break you would use the one-sided tag:

```
<br />
```

Reference Window

Unless a Reference Window item is labeled "Deprecated," it is compliant with XHTML 1.0 standards.

Inserting Two-Sided and One-Sided Tags

- To create a two-sided tag, use the syntax:
  ```
  <element>content</element>
  ```
  where *element* is the name of the HTML and *content* is any content it contains. Element names should be lowercase.
- To create a one-sided tag, use the syntax:
  ```
  <element />
  ```

Deprecated

- Many browsers also accept one-sided tags written as:
  ```
  <element>
  ```
  This syntax is not recommend because it is not supported by XHTML and will probably not be supported by future browsers.
- Some browsers allow uppercase element names. This technique is not recommended because it is not supported by XHTML and probably not by future browsers.

A third type of tag is the **comment tag**, which you can use to add notes to your HTML code. While comments are not required and are not displayed or used by the Web browser, they are useful in documenting your HTML code for yourself and others. The syntax of the comment tag is:

```
<!-- comment -->
```

where *comment* is the text of your note. The following is an example of a comment tag that could describe the page you'll be creating for Stephen Dubé:

```
<!-- Chemistry page created for Robert Service High School -->
```

A comment can also be spread over several lines as follows:

```
<!-- Chemistry Class Web Page
     Created for Robert Service High School
-->
```

Reference Window

Inserting a Comment

- To insert a comment anywhere within your HTML file, enter:
  ```
  <!-- comment -->
  ```
  where *comment* is the text of your comment. Comments can extend over several lines.

White Space and HTML

The ability to extend a comment over several lines is not unique to the comment tag. You can do this with any tag. As simple text files, HTML documents are composed of text characters and **white space**—the blank spaces, tabs and line breaks within the file. HTML treats each occurrence of white space as a single blank space. Thus, as far as HTML is concerned, there is no difference between a blank space, a tab, or a line break. When a browser encounters consecutive occurrences of white space, it collapses them into a single occurrence. The following code samples are equivalent as far as HTML is concerned:

```
<p>This is an example of White Space</p>
<p>This is an example  of    White      Space</p>
<p>This is an example
   of    White
   Space</p>
```

Even though browsers ignore extra white space, you can use it to make your HTML documents more readable—for example, by indenting lines or by separating blocks of code from one another.

Element Attributes

Many tags contain **attributes** that control the behavior, and in some cases the appearance, of elements in the page. You insert attributes within the tag brackets using the syntax

```
<element attribute1="value1" attribute2="value2" .../>
```

for one-sided tags, and the syntax

```
<element attribute1="value1" attribute2="value2" ...>content</element>
```

for two-sided tags, where *attribute1*, *attribute2*, and so forth are the names of the attributes, and *value1*, *value2*, etc. are the values associated with those attributes. For example, you can identify an individual element using the id attribute. The following code assigns the id value of "title" to the paragraph "Robert Service High School", distinguishing it from other paragraphs in the document.

```
<p id="title">Robert Service High School</p>
```

You'll learn more about the id attribute in the next tutorial.

You can list attributes in any order, but you must separate them from one another with white space. As with element names, you should enter attribute names in lowercase letters. In addition, you should enclose attribute values within quotation marks. While many browsers still accept attribute values without quotation marks, you can ensure maximum compatibility by always including them. XHTML requires quotation marks for all attribute values.

Reference Window

Inserting Attributes

- To add attributes to an element, insert the following into the element's opening tag:
     `attribute1="value1" attribute2="value2"`
  where *attribute1*, *attribute2*, and so forth are the names of the attributes, and *value1*, *value2*, etc. are the values associated with each attribute.

Deprecated

- Some browsers accept attributes without quotation marks, as well as attribute names in uppercase. This syntax is not recommended because it is not supported by XHTML or will probably not be supported by future browsers.

The Structure of an HTML File

Now that we've studied the general syntax of HTML tags, we'll create our first HTML document. The most fundamental element is the HTML document itself. We mark this element using the two-sided <html> tag as follows:

```
<html>
</html>
```

The opening <html> tag marks the start of an HTML document, and the closing </html> tag tells a browser when it has reached the end of that HTML document. Anything between these two tags makes up the content of the document, including all other elements, text, and comments.

An HTML document is divided into two sections: the head and the body. The **head element** contains information about the document—for example, the document's title, or keywords that a search engine on the Web might use to identify this document for other users. The content of the head element is not displayed within the Web page, but Web browsers may use it in other ways; for example, Web browsers usually display a document's title in the title bar.

The **body element** contains all of the content to be displayed in the Web page. It can also contain code that tells the browser how to render that content.

To mark the head and body elements, you use the <head> and <body> tags as follows:

```
<html>

<head>
</head>

<body>
</body>

</html>
```

Note that the body element is placed after the head element.

The first thing we'll add to the document's head is the page title, also know as the **title element**. A given document can include only one title element. You create a title by inserting the two-sided <title> tag within the document's head. Since Stephen wants to give his page the title, "Mr. Dube's Chemistry Classes", our HTML code now looks like this:

```
<html>

<head>
<title>Mr. Dube's Chemistry Classes</title>
</head>

<body>
</body>

</html>
```

The technique of placing one element within another is called **nesting**. When one element contains another, you must close the inside element before closing the outside element, as shown in the code above. It would *not* be correct to close the outside element before closing the inside one, as in the following code sample:

```
<head><title>Mr. Dube's Chemistry Classes</head></title>
```

Now that you've seen how to insert HTML tags, let's start creating the chemistry Web page. In addition to the above code, we'll also add a comment that specifies the page's purpose and author, as well as the current date.

To create an HTML file:

1. Ensure that you can access your data files from your file server, CD-ROM, or floppy disk drive.

   Trouble? If you don't have access to your data files, talk to your instructor. See the Read This Before You Begin page at the beginning of the tutorials for further instructions.

2. Create a new document with a text editor.

   If you don't know how to locate, start, or use the text editor on your system, ask your instructor or technical support person for help.

3. Type the following lines of code in your document. Press the **Enter** key after each line. Press the **Enter** key twice for a blank line between lines of code. Insert your name in place of the text *your name* and the current date in place of *the date*.

   ```
   <html>

   <head>
   <!-- Chemistry Classes Web Page
        Author: your name
        Date:   the date
   -->
   <title>Mr. Dube's Chemistry Classes</title>
   </head>

   <body>
   </body>

   </html>
   ```

4. Using your text editor, save the file as **chem.htm** in the tutorial.01/tutorial folder where your Data Files are stored, but do not close your text editor. The text you typed should look similar to the text displayed in Figure 1-6.

Initial HTML code in chem.htm   **Figure 1-6**

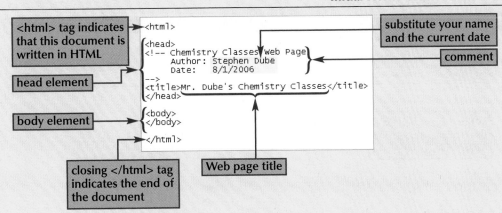

Trouble? If you don't know where to save your Data Files, ask your instructor or technical support person for assistance.

Trouble? Don't worry if your screen doesn't look exactly like Figure 1-6. The figures show the Windows Notepad text editor. Your text may look different. Take the time to ensure that you entered the text correctly.

Trouble? If you are using the Windows Notepad text editor to create your HTML file, make sure you don't save the file with the extension .txt, which is the default for Notepad. Instead, make sure you save the file with the file extension .htm or .html. Using an invalid file extension may make the file unreadable to Web browsers, which require .htm or .html as the file extension.

Trouble? If you are using Microsoft Word as your text editor, be sure to save your files as Web page files and not as Word documents.

Note that the extra space before and after the <body> tags is also not required, but it makes your file easier to read, especially as you add more code to the file.

Displaying an HTML File

As you continue adding to Stephen's Web page, you should occasionally view the page with your Web browser to verify that the file contains no syntax errors or other problems. You may even want to view the results using different browsers to check for compatibility. The steps and figures that follow use the Internet Explorer browser to display Stephen's page as you develop it. If you are using a different browser, ask your instructor how to view local files (those stored on your own computer rather than on the Web).

To view Stephen's Web page:

1. Start your browser. You do not need to be connected to the Internet to view local files stored on your computer.

   Trouble? If you try to start your browser and are not connected to the Internet, you might get a warning message. Click OK to ignore the message and continue.

2. After your browser loads its home page, open the **chem.htm** file that you saved in the tutorial.01/tutorial folder.

   Your browser displays the chemistry Web page, as shown in Figure 1-7. Note that the page title appears in the browser's title bar and not on the page itself.

Figure 1-7 | **Initial Web page viewed in Internet Explorer**

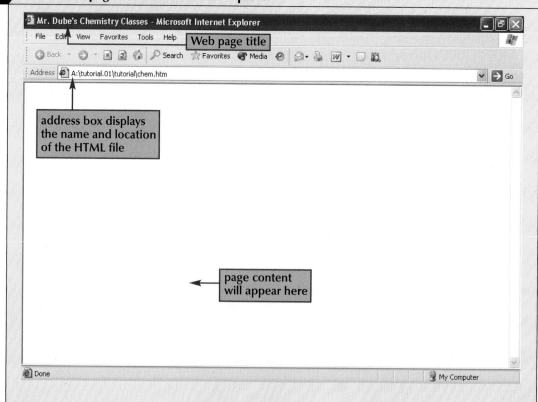

Trouble? To open a file in most browsers, click File on the menu bar, click Open, and click the Browse button to locate the file.

Trouble? Depending on the browser you're using, you may have to use a different command to open the file from your Data Files. Talk to your instructor or technical support person to find out how to open the file.

Trouble? If your browser displays something different, compare the code in your file to the code shown in Figure 1-6 and correct any errors. Save your changes, then return to your browser and click the Refresh or Reload button to view the new version of your Web page. So far, you have only entered a title for the Web page, which is why the main content area of the Web page is blank.

Working with Block-Level Elements

Now that you have created the basic structure of your document, you can start inserting the page's content. In a Web page, most content is marked as either a block-level element or an inline element. A **block-level element** contains content displayed in a separate section within the page, setting it off from other blocks. Paragraphs and headings are examples of block-level elements. An **inline element** is part of the same block as its surrounding content—for example, individual words or phrases within a paragraph.

Stephen's Web page includes several block-level elements. You will start adding page content by inserting the headings. You need to create a heading for the entire page and headings for each of two sections: Chemistry Classes and Class Policies. The Class Policies section includes three additional subheadings: Grading, Appointments, and Safety. You can mark all of these headings with HTML heading tags.

Creating Headings

HTML supports six heading elements, numbered h1 through h6. The h1 heading is reserved for the largest and most prominent headings, while the h6 element indicates a minor heading. The syntax for inserting a heading element is

```
<hy>content</hy>
```

where y is a heading number 1 through 6 and content is the content of the heading.

Figure 1-8 illustrates the general appearance of the six heading elements. Your browser might use slightly different fonts and sizes.

Figure 1-8	HTML headings

This is an h1 heading

This is an h2 heading

This is an h3 heading

This is an h4 heading

This is an h5 heading

This is an h6 heading

Reference Window | **Inserting a Heading**

- To define a heading, use the syntax
  ```
  <hy>content</hy>
  ```
  where y is a heading number 1 through 6, and `content` is the content of the heading.

Inserting an Inline Style

By default, the contents of a heading are aligned with the left margin of the page. You notice that some of the headings in Stephen's handout are centered. To use styles to control the appearance of an element, such as text alignment, you use the style attribute. The syntax for inserting the style attribute into an HTML tag is

```
<element style="style1: value1; style2: value2; style3: value3; …">
```

where `element` is the element's name, `style1`, `style2`, `style3` and so forth are the names of styles, and `value1`, `value2`, `value3` and so on are the values associated with those styles. Styles specified as attributes in a tag are also referred to as **inline styles**. As you proceed in your study of HTML, you'll learn more about different styles and the many ways to apply them. For now, we'll focus on the text-align style.

Reference Window | **Inserting an Inline Style**

- To add an inline style to an element, insert the following attribute into the element's tag:
  ```
  style="style1: value1; style2: value2; style3: value3; …"
  ```
  where `style1`, `style2`, `style3`, and so forth are the names of the styles, and `value1`, `value2`, `value3`, etc. are the values associated with those styles.

Applying the Text-Align Style

The text-align style tells the browser how to horizontally align the contents of an element. The style has four values: left, right, center, and justify; the value "justify" tells a browser to spread the content to touch both the left and right margins of the element. To display the text "Chemistry Class" as a centered h1 heading, you would use the following code:

```
<h1 style="text-align: center">Chemistry Class</h1>
```

Most browsers also support the align attribute. Thus, you could also write

```
<h1 align="center">Chemistry Class</h1>
```

However, because the align attribute is a deprecated feature of HTML, you should probably not use it unless you need to provide backward-compatibility with older browsers. HTML attributes such as the align attribute are known as **presentational attributes**, meaning that they specify exactly how the browser should render an element. Remember that one of the goals of HTML is to separate content from design. HTML should inform the browser about the content of the document, but you should use styles to inform the browser how to render that content. For this reason, almost all presentational attributes have been deprecated in favor of styles.

Aligning the Contents of an Element

- To horizontally align the contents of an element, use the style:
    ```
    text-align: align
    ```
  where *align* is left, right, center, or justify.

Deprecated

- You can also align the contents of an element by adding the following attribute to the element's tag:
    ```
    align="align"
    ```
  where *align* is left, right, center, or justify. Not all elements support the align attribute. It is often used with paragraphs and headings.

To add headings to the chemistry file:

▸ **1.** Using your text editor, open **chem.htm**, if it is not currently open.

▸ **2.** Place the insertion point after the <body> tag, press the **Enter** key to move to the next line, and then type the following lines of code:

```
<h1 style="text-align: center">Mr. Dube's Chemistry Classes</h1>
<h2 style="text-align: center">at Robert Service High School</h2>
<h2>Chemistry Classes</h2>
<h2>Class Policies</h2>
<h3>Grading</h3>
<h3>Appointments</h3>
<h3>Safety</h3>
```

Figure 1-9 displays the revised code. To make it easier for you to follow the changes to the HTML file, new and modified text in the figures is highlighted in red. This will not be the case in your own text files.

| Figure 1-9 | Entering heading elements |

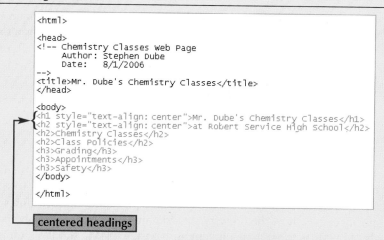

```
<html>

<head>
<!-- Chemistry Classes Web Page
    Author: Stephen Dube
    Date:    8/1/2006
-->
<title>Mr. Dube's Chemistry Classes</title>
</head>

<body>
<h1 style="text-align: center">Mr. Dube's Chemistry Classes</h1>
<h2 style="text-align: center">at Robert Service High School</h2>
<h2>Chemistry Classes</h2>
<h2>Class Policies</h2>
<h3>Grading</h3>
<h3>Appointments</h3>
<h3>Safety</h3>
</body>

</html>
```

centered headings

3. Save your changes to **chem.htm**. You can leave your text editor open.

Now view the revised page in your Web browser.

To display the revised version of the chemistry page:

1. Return to your Web browser. Note that the previous version of chem.htm probably appears in the browser window.

2. To view the revised page, click **View** on the menu bar, and then click **Refresh**. If you are using a Netscape browser, you will need to click **View** and then click **Reload**.

Trouble? If you closed the browser or the file in the last set of steps, reopen your browser and the chem.htm file.

The updated Web page looks like Figure 1-10.

| Figure 1-10 | Headings as they appear in the browser |

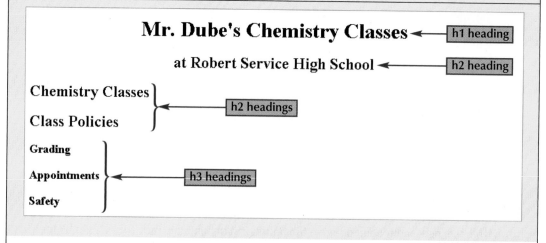

Creating Paragraphs

The next step is to enter text information for each section. As you saw earlier, you can insert a paragraph element using the <p> tag as follows:

```
<p>content</p>
```

where *content* is the content of the paragraph. When a browser encounters the opening <p> tag, it starts a new line with a blank space above it, separating the new paragraph from the preceding element. In earlier versions of HTML when standards were not firmly fixed, Web authors would often include only the opening <p> tag, omitting the closing tag entirely. While many browsers still allow this, your Web pages display more reliably if you consistently use the closing tag. Additionally, if you wish to write XHTML-compliant code then you must include the closing tag.

Creating a Paragraph

- To create a paragraph, use the syntax:
  ```
  <p>content</p>
  ```
  where *content* is the content of the paragraph.

To enter paragraph text:

1. Return to **chem.htm** in your text editor.

2. Place the insertion point at the end of the line that creates the h2 heading, "at Robert Service High School", and press the **Enter** key to create a blank line.

3. Type the following text:

```
<p>Welcome to the Robert Service High School Chemistry Web page.
Here you'll learn more about our chemistry classes and our policies.</p>
```

4. Press the **Enter** key to insert a blank line below the paragraph.

   Note that a blank line is not required for the text to display correctly in your browser. However, adding this space makes it easier for you to read the code by separating the first paragraph from the heading that follows. See Figure 1-11.

Inserting the first paragraph | **Figure 1-11**

```
<body>
<h1 style="text-align: center">Mr. Dube's Chemistry Classes</h1>
<h2 style="text-align: center">at Robert Service High School</h2>
<p>Welcome to the Robert Service High School Chemistry Web page.
   Here you'll learn more about our chemistry classes and our
   policies.</p>

<h2>Chemistry Classes</h2>
<h2>Class Policies</h2>
<h3>Grading</h3>
<h3>Appointments</h3>
<h3>Safety</h3>
</body>
```

paragraph

5. Save your changes to **chem.htm**.

6. Using your Web browser, refresh or reload **chem.htm** to view the new paragraph. See Figure 1-12.

Figure 1-12 ▷ **First paragraph in the browser**

Mr. Dube's Chemistry Classes

paragraph

at Robert Service High School

Welcome to the Robert Service High School Chemistry Web page. Here you'll learn more about our chemistry classes and our policies.

Chemistry Classes

Class Policies

Grading

Appointments

Safety

Next you need to add the three paragraphs under the Grading heading and the single paragraphs under both Appointments and Safety.

To enter the remaining paragraphs:

▷ 1. Return to the **chem.htm** file in your text editor.

▷ 2. Below the h3 heading "Grading," insert the following three paragraphs:

```
<p>Homework: Homework is worth 5 to 10 points and will be given
daily. A quiz consisting of 1 or 2 homework problems from the
previous week may be given in place of homework.</p>

<p>Tests and Quizzes: Quizzes are worth 10 to 25 points and will be
given at least once a month. Tests are worth up to 100 points and
will be given three times each quarter.</p>

<p>Labs: Labs are worth 10 to 30 points and will be graded on
safety, participation, and write-up. Reports should be neatly
written or typed. Research projects will also be assigned throughout
the year.</p>
```

Note that because of how HTML handles white space, you can insert additional blank lines between the paragraphs or line breaks within paragraphs to make your code easier to read. This does not affect how a browser renders the paragraphs.

▷ 3. Below the h3 heading "Appointments," insert the following paragraph:

```
<p>You can meet with Mr. Dube before or after school or during most
lunch hours in room H113. Do not hesitate to ask for help! It can be
very hard to catch up if you fall behind.</p>
```

▷ 4. Below the h3 heading " Safety," insert the following paragraph:

```
<p>Labs are completed weekly. Because of the potential danger of any
lab exercise, you will follow the highest standards of conduct.
Misbehavior can result in dismissal from the lab.</p>
```

Figure 1-13 shows the new code in the chem.htm file.

Inserting additional paragraphs | Figure 1-13

```
<h2>Chemistry Classes</h2>
<h2>Class Policies</h2>
<h3>Grading</h3>
<p>Homework: Homework is worth 5 to 10 points and will be given
daily. A quiz consisting of 1 or 2 homework problems from the
previous week may be given in place of homework.</p>

<p>Tests and Quizzes: Quizzes are worth 10 to 25 points and will be
given at least once a month. Tests are worth up to 100 points and
will be given three times each quarter.</p>

<p>Labs: Labs are worth 10 to 30 points and will be graded on safety,
participation, and write-up. Reports should be neatly written or
typed. Research projects will also be assigned throughout the
year.</p>

<h3>Appointments</h3>
<p>You can meet with Mr. Dube before or after school or during most
lunch hours in room H113. Do not hesitate to ask for help! It can be
very hard to catch up if you fall behind.</p>

<h3>Safety</h3>
<p>Labs are completed weekly. Because of the potential danger of any
lab exercise, you will follow the highest standards of conduct.
Misbehavior can result in dismissal from the lab.</p>

</body>
```

5. Save your changes to the file.

6. Return to your Web browser and refresh or reload **chem.htm** to view the new paragraphs. Figure 1-14 displays the revised version.

New paragraphs in the chemistry page | Figure 1-14

Mr. Dube's Chemistry Classes

at Robert Service High School

Welcome to the Robert Service High School Chemistry Web page. Here you'll learn more about our chemistry classes and our policies.

Chemistry Classes

Class Policies

Grading

Homework: Homework is worth 5 to 10 points and will be given daily. A quiz consisting of 1 or 2 homework problems from the previous week may be given in place of homework.

Tests and Quizzes: Quizzes are worth 10 to 25 points and will be given at least once a month. Tests are worth up to 100 points and will be given three times each quarter.

Labs: Labs are worth 10 to 30 points and will be graded on safety, participation, and write-up. Reports should be neatly written or typed. Research projects will also be assigned throughout the year.

Appointments

You can meet with Mr. Dube before or after school or during most lunch hours in room H113. Do not hesitate to ask for help! It can be very hard to catch up if you fall behind.

Safety

Labs are completed weekly. Because of the potential danger of any lab exercise, you will follow the highest standards of conduct. Misbehavior can result in dismissal from the lab.

Creating Lists

You still need to describe the three chemistry courses that the school offers. Rather than entering these in paragraph form, you'll use a list. HTML supports three kinds of lists: ordered, unordered, and definition.

Creating an Ordered List

You use an **ordered list** for items that must appear in a particular sequential order. You create an ordered list using the ol element in the following form:

```
<ol>
    <li>item1</li>
    <li>item2</li>
...
</ol>
```

where *item1*, *item2*, etc, are items in the list. Each <li> tag marks the content for a single list item. For example, if Stephen wants to list the three chemistry classes from the least difficult to the most difficult, the HTML code could look as follows:

```
<ol>
    <li>Conceptual Chemistry</li>
    <li>Chemistry I</li>
    <li>Advanced Placement Chemistry</li>
</ol>
```

By default, browsers display ordered lists as a series of sequentially numbered items. Based on the preceding HTML code, Stephen's list would appear in the following form:

1. Conceptual Chemistry
2. Chemistry I
3. Advanced Placement Chemistry

Reference Window

Creating an Ordered List

- To create an ordered list, use the syntax:
  ```
  <ol>
      <li>item1</li>
      <li>item2</li>
      ...
  </ol>
  ```
  where *item1*, *item2*, etc. are items in the list.

Creating an Unordered List

To display a list in which the items do not need to occur in any special order, you would create an **unordered list**. The structures of ordered and unordered lists are the same, except that the contents of an unordered list are contained within a <ul> tag:

```
<ul>
    <li>item1</li>
    <li>item2</li>
    ...
</ul>
```

By default, the contents of an unordered list are displayed as bulleted items. Thus, the code

```
<ul>
   <li>Introductory course</li>
   <li>No algebra required</li>
</ul>
```

would be displayed by a browser as

- Introductory course
- No algebra required

Creating an Unordered List

- To create an unordered list, use the syntax:
  ```
  <ul>
      <li>item1</li>
      <li>item2</li>
      ...
  </ul>
  ```
  where *item1*, *item2*, etc. are items in the list.

Creating a Nested List

One list can contain another. For example, it can sometimes be useful to combine two different types of lists, as in the following example:

1 Conceptual Chemistry

- Introductory course
- No algebra required

2 Chemistry I

- Introductory course
- Algebra required

3 Advanced Placement Chemistry

- Advanced course
- Requires an A or B in Chemistry I

You could create the preceding combination of ordered and unordered lists using the following HTML code:

```
<ol>
   <li>Conceptual Chemistry
      <ul>
         <li>Introductory course</li>
         <li>No algebra required</li>
      </ul>
   </li>
   <li>Chemistry I
      <ul>
         <li>Introductory course</li>
         <li>Algebra required</li>
      </ul>
   </li>
```

```
      <li>Advanced Placement Chemistry
         <ul>
            <li>Advanced course</li>
            <li>Requires an A or B in Chemistry I</li>
         </ul>
      </li>
   </ol>
```

Note that some of the list items in this code contain lists themselves.

Applying a Style to a List

If you don't want your list items marked with either numbers or bullets, you can specify a different marker by applying the following style to either the ordered or unordered list:

```
list-style-type: type
```

where *type* is one of the markers listed in Figure 1-15.

Figure 1-15 ▶ **List style types**

List-Style-Type	Marker (s)
disc	•
circle	○
square	■
decimal	1, 2, 3, 4, …
decimal-leading-zero	01, 02, 03, 04, …
lower-roman	i, ii, iii, iv, …
upper-roman	I, II, III, IV, …
lower-alpha	a, b, c, d, …
upper-alpha	A, B, C, D, …
none	*no marker displayed*

For example, to create the following list:

a. Conceptual Chemistry
b. Chemistry I
c. Advanced Placement Chemistry

you would enter the HTML code:

```
<ol style="list-style-type: lower-alpha">
   <li>Conceptual Chemistry</li>
   <li>Chemistry I</li>
   <li>Advanced Placement Chemistry</li>
</ol>
```

You can also substitute a graphic image for a list marker by using the style:

```
list-style-image: url(file)
```

where *file* is the name of an image file containing the marker. Figure 1-16 demonstrates how to use a graphic image named "flask.jpg" as a marker in a list.

Using a graphic list marker ◄ **Figure 1-16**

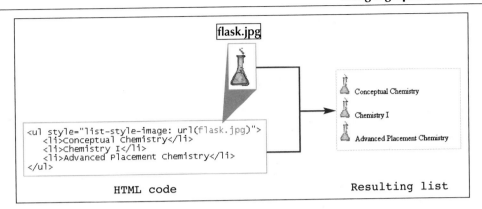

In this style, URL stands for Uniform Resource Locator. A URL is the standard method for specifying the location of a document or resource on the Internet. You'll learn about URLs in the next tutorial.

Each list item is itself a block-level element. By default, most browsers place each list marker outside of its corresponding block; however you can change this by using the following style:

```
list-style-position: position
```

where *position* is either "outside" (the default) or "inside". Placing the marker inside of the block causes the content of the list to flow around the marker (see Figure 1-17).

Defining the marker position ◄ **Figure 1-17**

markers are placed inside of the block and the content flows around the marker	• Conceptual Chemistry: An introductory course requiring basic mathematics but no algebra • Chemistry I: An introductory course requiring solid algebra skills • Advanced Placement Chemistry: An advanced course for students who passed Chemistry I with an A or B and who want to prepare for the AP Chemistry exam (which can count toward college credits)

`list-style-position: inside`

markers are placed outside of the block, away from the content (the default)	• Conceptual Chemistry: An introductory course requiring basic mathematics but no algebra • Chemistry I: An introductory course requiring solid algebra skills • Advanced Placement Chemistry: An advanced course for students who passed Chemistry I with an A or B and who want to prepare for the AP Chemistry exam (which can count toward college credits)

`list-style-position: outside`

The three previous styles can be combined in the following single style:

```
list-style: type url(file) position
```

where *type* is one of the marker types, *file* is the location of a graphic file that can be used for a marker, and *position* is either "inside" or "outside". Text-based browsers use the *type* value, while graphical browsers use the graphic file. For example the tag

```
<ul style="list-style: square url(flask.jpg) inside">
```

would create an unordered list with a square marker for text-based browsers and the flask.jpg image marker for graphical browsers. Whichever marker a browser uses appears inside of each list item.

For older browsers that don't support inline styles, you can use one of the presentational attributes that HTML provides for ordered and unordered lists. See the accompanying reference window for details.

Reference Window

Formatting a List

- To change the list marker, use the style:
    `list-style-type: type`
  where *type* is disc, circle, square, decimal, decimal-leading-zero, lower-roman, upper-roman, lower-alpha, upper-alpha, or none.
- To use a graphic image in place of a marker, use the style:
    `list-style-image: url(file)`
  where *file* is the name of the image file.
- To specify the location of the list marker, use the style:
    `list-style-position: position`
  where *position* is either inside or outside.

Deprecated

- You can also change the list marker by adding the following attribute to the <ol> or <ul> tag:
    `type="type"`
  For unordered lists, the *type* value can be circle, square, or disc. For ordered lists, *type* values are a (for lower-alpha), A (for upper-alpha), i (for lower-roman), I (for upper-roman), and 1 (for numeric).
- For ordered lists, you can specify the starting number of the first item in the list using the attribute:
    `start="number"`
  where *number* is the starting value. A start number of "2" starts the list with the second marker. For a numeric marker, this is the value '2', while for an alphabetical list, this is the letter "b" or "B".

Creating a Definition List

HTML supports a third list element, the **definition list**, which contains a list of definition terms, each followed by a definition description. The syntax for creating a definition list is:

```
<dl>
    <dt>term1</dt>
    <dd>definition1</dd>
    <dt>term2</dt>
    <dd>definition2</dd>
...
</dl>
```

where *term1*, *term2*, etc. are the terms in the list, and *definition1*, *definition2*, etc. are the definitions of the terms.

If Stephen wanted to create a list of his classes and briefly describe each one, he could use a definition list. The code might look as follows:

```
<dl>
   <dt>Conceptual Chemistry</dt>
   <dd>An introductory course requiring basic mathematics but no
       algebra</dd>
   <dt>Chemistry I</dt>
   <dd>An introductory course requiring solid algebra skills</dd>
   <dt>Advanced Placement Chemistry</dt>
   <dd>An advanced course for students who passed Chemistry I with an A
       or B and who want to prepare for the AP Chemistry exam (which can
       count toward college credits)</dd>
</dl>
```

Web browsers typically display the definition description below the definition term and slightly indented. Most browsers would display the definition list code shown above as:

Conceptual Chemistry
   An introductory course requiring basic mathematics but no algebra

Chemistry I
   An introductory course requiring solid algebra skills

Advanced Placement Chemistry
   An advanced course for students who passed Chemistry I with an A or B and who
   want to prepare for the AP Chemistry exam (which can count toward college credits)

Creating a Definition List

Reference Window

- To create a definition list, use the syntax:
  ```
  <dl>
      <dt>term1</dt>
      <dd>definition1</dd>
      <dt>term2</dt>
      <dd>definition2</dd>

      …
  </dl>
  ```
  where *term1*, *term2*, etc. are the terms in the list, and *definition1*, *definition2*, etc. are the definitions of the terms.

Now that you've seen how you can use HTML to create different kinds of lists, you'll add an unordered list of classes to the chemistry Web page. You decide to use a square marker for each item. By default, the marker is placed outside of the block.

To add an unordered list to the chemistry page:

1. Return to the **chem.htm** file in your text editor.

2. Below the line "<h2>Chemistry Classes</h2>" insert the following code, as shown in Figure 1-18.

```
<ul style="list-style-type: square">
   <li>Conceptual Chemistry: An introductory course, requiring basic
       math but no algebra</li>
   <li>Chemistry I: An introductory course, requiring solid algebra
       skills</li>
```

```
     <li>Advanced Placement Chemistry: An advanced course requiring a
          grade of A or B in Chemistry I</li>
     </ul>
```

You can indent the lines using either tabs or blank spaces. Remember that indenting has no effect on the appearance of the list in a browser.

Figure 1-18	Inserting an unordered list

```
<body>
<h1 style="text-align: center">Mr. Dube's Chemistry Classes</h1>
<h2 style="text-align: center">at Robert Service High School</h2>
<p>Welcome to the Robert Service High School Chemistry web page.
    Here you'll learn more about our chemistry classes and our
    policies.</p>

<h2>Chemistry Classes</h2>
<ul style="list-style-type: square">
    <li>Conceptual Chemistry: An introductory course, requiring basic
        math but no algebra</li>
    <li>Chemistry I: An introductory course, requiring solid algebra
        skills</li>
    <li>Advanced Placement Chemistry: An advanced course requiring a
        grade of A or B in Chemistry I</li>
</ul>
```

3. Save your changes to the file.

4. Using your Web browser, refresh or reload **chem.htm**. Figure 1-19 shows the latest version of the page.

Figure 1-19	An unordered list in the browser

Mr. Dube's Chemistry Classes

at Robert Service High School

Welcome to the Robert Service High School Chemistry Web page. Here you'll learn more about our chemistry classes and our policies.

Chemistry Classes

- Conceptual Chemistry: An introductory course, requiring basic math but no algebra
- Chemistry I: An introductory course, requiring solid algebra skills
- Advanced Placement Chemistry: An advanced course requiring a grade of A or B in Chemistry I

Using Other Block-Level Elements

HTML supports several other block-level elements that you may find useful in your Web pages. For example HTML supports the address element to indicate contact information. Most browsers display an address element in an italicized font. You can indicate long quoted passages by applying the blockquote element. A browser encountering this element typically indents the quoted text. Figure 1-20 describes additional block-level elements and shows how they look in most browsers.

Block Level Element	Description	Visual Appearance
<address> ... </address>	Identifies contact information	*Italicized text*
<blockquote> ... </blockquote>	Identifies a long quotation	Plain text indented from the left and right
<center> ... </center>	Centers content horizontally within a block. **Deprecated**	Plain text, centered
<dd> ... </dd>	Identifies a definition description	Plain text
<dir> ... </dir>	Identifies a multicolumn directory list; superseded by the ul element. **Deprecated**	Plain text
<div> ... </div>	Identifies a generic block-level element	Plain text
<dl> ... </dl>	Identifies a definition list	Plain text
<dt> ... </dt>	Identifies a definition term	Plain text
<hy> ... </hy>	Identifies a heading, where y is a value from 1 to 6	**Boldfaced text of various font sizes**
<li> ... </li>	Identifies a list item in an ordered or unordered list	Bulleted or numbered text
<menu> ... </menu>	Identifies a single column menu list; superseded by the ul element. **Deprecated**	Plain text
<ol> ... </ol>	Identifies an ordered list	Plain text
<p> ... </p>	Identifies a paragraph	Plain text
<pre> ... </pre>	Retains all white space and special characters in preformatted text	`Fixed width text`
<ul> ... </ul>	Identifies an unordered list	Plain text

You'll have a chance to apply some of these other block-level elements in the case problems at the end of the tutorial.

Working with Inline Elements

As you compare your Web page with Figure 1-5, you notice that Stephen's original handout contains several words formatted in boldface or italics. In order to apply this formatting to the chemistry Web page, we need to use a set of HTML's inline elements known as **character formatting elements**, which allow us to format text characters. Figure 1-21 describes some character formatting elements that HTML supports.

Figure 1-21	Inline elements

Inline Element	Identifies	Visual Appearance
`<abbr> ... </abbr>`	an abbreviation	Plain text
`<acronym> .. </acronym>`	an acronym	Plain text
`<b> ... </b>`	boldfaced text	**Boldfaced text**
`<big> ... </big>`	big text	Larger text
`<cite> ... </cite>`	a citation	*Italicized text*
`<code> ... </code>`	program code text	`Fixed width text`
`<del> ... </del>`	deleted text	~~Strikethrough text~~
`<dfn> ... </dfn>`	a definition term	*Italicized text*
`<em> ... </em>`	emphasized content	*Italicized text*
`<i> ... </i>`	italicized text	*Italicized text*
`<ins> ... </ins>`	inserted text	<u>Underlined text</u>
`<kbd> ... </kbd>`	keyboard-style text	`Fixed width text`
`<q> ... </q>`	quoted text	"Quoted text"
`<s> ... </s>`	strikethrough text. **Deprecated**	~~Strikethrough text~~
`<samp> ... </samp>`	sample computer code text	`Fixed width text`
`<small> ... </small>`	small text	Smaller text
`<span> ... </span>`	a generic inline element	Plain text
`<strike> ... </strike>`	strikethrough text. **Deprecated**	~~Strikethrough text~~
`<strong> ... </strong>`	strongly emphasized content	**Boldfaced text**
`<sub> ... </sub>`	subscripted text	Subscripted text
`<sup> ... </sup>`	superscripted	Superscripted text
`<tt> ... </tt>`	teletype text	`Fixed width text`
`<u> ... </u>`	underlined text. **Deprecated**	<u>Underlined text</u>
`<var> ... </var>`	programming variables	*Italicized text*

For example, if you wanted to mark a section of boldfaced text within a paragraph, you could enter the following HTML code:

```
<p>Welcome to our <b>Chemistry Classes</b></p>
```

resulting in the following paragraph in the Web page:

Welcome to our **Chemistry Classes**

To mark those same words as italicized text, you would use

```
<p>Welcome to our <i>Chemistry Classes</i></p>
```

If you want the phrase "Chemistry Classes" to be marked as both boldface and italics, you could use the code

```
<p>Welcome to our <b><i>Chemistry Classes</i></b></p>
```

which would be displayed as

Welcome to our ***Chemistry Classes***

Stephen's handout requires the use of character tags only in the Grading section, where he wants to highlight the name of each grading topic. You decide to use a combination of the `<b>` and `<i>` tags to display the key words in bold and italics.

To add character tags to the chemistry file:

1. Return to the **chem.htm** file in your text editor.

2. Type the <i> and <b> tags around the key words in the Grading section of the handout as follows:

   ```
   <p><i><b>Homework</b></i>:Homework is worth …
   <p><i><b>Tests and Quizzes</b></i>: Quizzes are worth …
   <p><i><b>Labs</b></i>: Labs are worth …
   <i><b>Research projects</b></i> will also be assigned …
   ```
   See Figure 1-22.

Inserting boldfaced and italicized text   **Figure 1-22**

```
<h2>Class Policies</h2>
<h3>Grading</h3>
<p><i><b>Homework</b></i>: Homework is worth 5 to 10 points and will be given
daily. A quiz consisting of 1 or 2 homework problems from the
previous week may be given in place of homework.</p>

<p><i><b>Tests and Quizzes</b></i>: Quizzes are worth 10 to 25 points and will be
given at least once a month. Tests are worth up to 100 points and
will be given three times each quarter.</p>

<p><i><b>Labs</b></i>: Labs are worth 10 to 30 points and will be graded on safety,
participation, and write-up. Reports should be neatly written or
typed.  <i><b>Research projects</b></i> will also be assigned throughout the
year.</p>
```

3. Save your changes to the file.

4. Using your Web browser, refresh or reload **chem.htm**. The updated Grading section of your page should look like Figure 1-23.

Displaying boldfaced and italicized text   **Figure 1-23**

> ## Class Policies
>
> ### Grading
>
> *Homework*: Homework is worth 5 to 10 points and will be given daily. A quiz consisting of 1 or 2 homework problems from the previous week may be given in place of homework.
>
> *Tests and Quizzes*: Quizzes are worth 10 to 25 points and will be given at least once a month. Tests are worth up to 100 points and will be given three times each quarter.
>
> *Labs*: Labs are worth 10 to 30 points and will be graded on safety, participation, and write-up. Reports should be neatly written or typed. *Research projects* will also be assigned throughout the year.

5. If you are continuing to Session 1.3, leave your text editor and browser open. Otherwise you can close them at this time.

Understanding Logical and Physical Elements

As you examine the tag list in Figure 1-21, you may notice some overlap in the way the content appears in the browser. For example, if you want to display italicized text you could use the <dfn>, <em>, <i>, or <var> tags, or if you want to italicize an entire block of text, you could use the <address> tag. Why does HTML support so many different ways of formatting text?

While HTML can control the way text appears, the language's main purpose is to create a structure for a document's contents. While some browsers render different elements in the same way, it's important to distinguish between how a browser displays an element and the element's purpose in the document. For this reason, page elements are therefore often organized into two types: logical elements and physical elements. A **logical element**, which might be created with tags like <cite> or <code>, describes the nature of the enclosed content, but not necessarily how that content should appear. A **physical element**, on the other hand, which you might create with tags like <b> or <i>, describes how content should appear but doesn't indicate the content's nature.

While it can be tempting to use logical and physical elements interchangeably, your Web pages benefit in several ways when you respect the distinction. For one, different browsers can and do display logical elements differently. For example, both Netscape's browser and Internet Explorer display text created with the <cite> tag in italics, but the text-based browser Lynx displays citation text using a fixed width font. Some browsers, like those that display Braille or convert HTML code into speech, don't even display formatted text. For example, an aural browser might increase the volume when it encounters emphasized text. In addition, Web programmers can also use logical elements to extract a page's content. For example, a program could automatically generate a bibliography from all of the citations listed within a Web site.

In general, you should use a logical element that accurately describes the enclosed content whenever possible, and use physical elements only for general content.

You have finished inserting the text of the chemistry Web page. In the next session, you will add additional elements to the page, including an image and a graphical line.

Review

Session 1.2 Quick Check

1. What are the two main sections of an HTML file?
2. What are empty elements?
3. What is the syntax for creating a centered heading 1 of the text, "Chemistry Classes"?
4. What is the difference between a block-level element and an inline element?
5. If you want to create an extra blank line between paragraphs, why can't you simply add a blank line in the HTML file?
6. What are presentational attributes? When should you use them?
7. What attribute would you add to the <ol> tag to display uppercase Roman numerals?
8. What attribute would you add to the <ul> tag to display the ball.gif image mark on the inside of the item block?
9. What is the difference between a logical element and a physical element? Which would probably be more appropriate for a non-visual browser, such as a Braille browser?

Session 1.3

Working with Empty Elements

In the last session, you worked exclusively with two-sided tags to create content for the chemistry Web page. Stephen also wants to add images and horizontal lines to the page. To create these objects, you use empty elements. We'll start by inserting a graphic into the Web page.

Inserting a Graphic

To display a graphic, you insert an inline image into the page. An **inline image**, which is another example of an inline element, displays a graphic image located in a separate file within the contents of a block-level element. While a variety of file formats are available for image files, inline images are most widely viewable in two formats: GIF (Graphics Interchange Format) or JPEG (Joint Photographic Experts Group). You can use an image editing application such as Adobe Photoshop to convert images to either the GIF or JPEG file format. To create an inline image, you use the img element as follows:

```
<img src="file" alt="text" />
```

where *file* is the name of the image file and *text* is an alternative text string that browsers can use in place of an image. It's important to include an alt attribute in all of your inline images. Some users run browsers that do not display images, meaning that you need to duplicate with text any information that an image conveys. HTML does not require you to use an alt attribute with your inline images, but XHTML does.

If the image file is located in the same folder as the HTML file, you do not need to include any file location path information along with the filename. However, if the image file is located in another folder or on another computer, you need to include the full location path along with the filename in the src attribute. The next tutorial discusses folder paths and filenames in more detail. For now, you can assume that Stephen's image file is located in the same folder that contains the HTML file.

The image file that Stephen wants you to use in place of the page's main heading is named **dube.jpg** and is located in the tutorial.01/tutorial folder on your data disk (see Figure 1-24).

Image for the top of the chemistry page ◀ **Figure 1-24**

Stephen wants you to center the image on the page. Since the img element is an inline element, it does not support an alignment attribute. In order to center it, we need to place it within a block-level element like a paragraph. We can then center the contents of the paragraph, which in this case consists only of the image.

To add Stephen's image to the Web page:

1. If necessary, use your text editor to reopen **chem.htm**.
2. Near the top of the file, select the two lines of code just below the <body> tag (from the <h1> opening tag to the </h2 > closing tag), and then press the **Delete** key. This removes the first two headings from the document.

3. Insert the following code directly below the <body> tag (see Figure 1-25):

```
<p style="text-align: center">
    <img src="dube.jpg"
     alt="Mr. Dube's Chemistry Classes at Robert Service High School"
     />
</p>
```

| Figure 1-25 | Inserting an inline image |

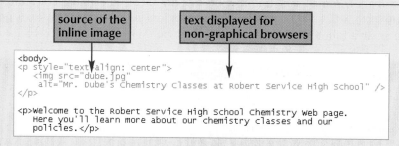

4. Save your changes to the file.

5. Open or refresh **chem.htm** in your Web browser. Figure 1-26 shows the placement of the image in the page.

| Figure 1-26 | Displaying an inline image |

Inserting Horizontal Lines

Stephen is pleased with the image's placement on the page. He would like you to add a horizontal line below the image, separating it from the page's text. To create a horizontal line, you use the one-sided tag

```
<hr />
```

To modify the line's size, you can use the styles

```
width: value; height: value
```

where *value* is a size measurement in pixels. A **pixel** is a dot on your computer screen that measures about 1/72" square. You can alternately specify a width value as a percentage of the page's width. The default width is 100% (the width of the Web page) and the default height is 2 pixels.

You can set a line's color using either of the two following styles:

```
color: color; background-color: color
```

where *color* is either the name of a color or an RGB color value. We'll study the issue of color in greater detail in a later tutorial. For now, know that browsers understand basic color names like red or blue or green.

While some browsers use the color style to assign a color to a horizontal line, other browsers use the background-color style. Therefore, if setting a line's color is an important aspect of your page's design, it's best to include both the color and background-color styles.

Inserting a Horizontal Line

- To insert a horizontal line, use the tag
  ```
  <hr />
  ```
- To change the color of the line, use the style
  ```
  color: color; background-color: color
  ```
  where *color* is either a recognized color name or an RGB color value.
- To change the width and height of the line, use the style
  ```
  width: value; height: value
  ```
  where *value* is the width or height of the line in pixels. You can also express the width value as a percentage of the page width. The default width is 100%, which is equal to the width of the Web page. The default height is usually 2 pixels.

Deprecated

- You can also format the appearance of your horizontal lines by adding the following attributes to the <hr /> tag:
  ```
  align="align" color="color" size="value" width="value"
  ```
  The align attribute specifies the alignment of the line on the page and can have the values left, right, or center (the default). The color attribute specifies the color of the line (Internet Explorer only). The size attribute specifies the height of the line in pixels. The width attribute specifies the width of the line in pixels.

For example, if Stephen wants to create a red horizontal line that is half the width of the page and 5 pixels high, he would enter the following tag into his HTML document:

```
<hr style="color: red; background-color: red; width: 50%; height: 5" />
```

The default rendering of a horizontal line is not standard across browsers. Typically the line extends across the complete width of the page at a height of 2 pixels. Some graphical browsers display the line in a solid black color, while others apply a chiseled or embossed effect. Text-based browsers display the line using dashes or underscores.

For the chemistry page, Stephen simply wants a red horizontal line, 2 pixels high. He'll let the line extend across the width of the page.

To add a horizontal line to the chemistry file:

1. Return to the **chem.htm** file in your text editor.
2. Below the paragraph containing the dube.jpg inline image, insert the following tag (see Figure 1-27):

   ```
   <hr style="color: red; background-color: red; height: 2; width: 100%" />
   ```

Figure 1-27	**Inserting a horizontal line**

```
<body>
<p style="text-align: center">
    <img src="dube.jpg"
      alt="Mr. Dube's Chemistry Classes at Robert Service High School" />
</p>
<hr style="color: red; background-color: red; height: 2; width: 100%" />
<p>Welcome to the Robert Service High School Chemistry Web page.
   Here you'll learn more about our chemistry classes and our
   policies.</p>
```

3. Save your changes to the file.

4. Using your Web browser, refresh or reload the **chem.htm** file. Figure 1-28 shows the new horizontal line.

Figure 1-28	**Displaying a horizontal line**

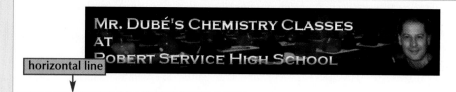

horizontal line

Welcome to the Robert Service High School Chemistry Web page. Here you'll learn more about our chemistry classes and our policies.

Most browsers still support several deprecated presentational attributes, which you can use in place of styles for your horizontal lines. See the "Inserting a Horizontal Line" reference window for more details.

Other Empty Elements

Other empty elements you may wish to use in your Web page include line breaks and meta elements. The <br /> tag creates a line break, which starts a new line within a paragraph. For example, the following code

```
<br />
<br />
<br />
```

creates three consecutive line breaks. You can use the <br /> tag to control the spacing of the different sections in your document.

Meta elements are placed in the document's head and contain information about the document that may be of use to programs that run on Web servers. You create a meta element using the one-sided <meta /> tag as follows:

```
<meta name="text" content="text" scheme="text" http-equiv="text" />
```

where the name attribute specifies the name of a property for the page, the content attribute provides a property value, the scheme attribute provides the format of the property value, and the http-equiv attribute takes the place of the name attribute for some Web servers. For example the following <meta /> tag stores the name of the Web page's author.

```
<meta name="author" content="Stephen Dube" />
```

Some Web sites, like Google, use search engines to create lists of Web pages devoted to particular topics. You can give extra weight to your Web page by including a description of the page and a list of keywords in <meta /> tags at the top of the document.

```
<meta name="description" content="Chemistry Class Web page" />
<meta name="keywords" content="chemistry, school, Edmonton, science" />
```

Note that a document's head can contain several meta elements.

Working with Special Characters

Occasionally, you will want to include special characters in your Web page that do not appear on your keyboard. For example, a page might require mathematical symbols such as β or μ, or you might need to include the copyright symbol © to show that an image or text is copyrighted.

Stephen's last name uses an accented letter, "é". His name appears three times in his Web page: in the title at the top of the page, again in the alt text for the inline image, and finally in a paragraph on making an appointment.

HTML supports the use of character symbols that are identified by a code number or name. The syntax for creating a special character is:

&*code*;

where *code* is either a code name or a code number. Code numbers are preceded by a pound symbol (#). Figure 1-29 shows some HTML symbols and the corresponding code numbers or names. The appendices include a more complete list of special characters. Some older browsers support only code numbers, not code names.

Special characters and codes — **Figure 1-29**

Symbol	Code	Name	Description
©	©	©	Copyright symbol
®	®	®	Registered trademark
•	·	·	Middle dot (bullet)
°	°	°	Degree symbol
			Nonbreaking space, used to insert consecutive blank spaces
<	<	<	Less than symbol
>	>	>	Greater than symbol
&	&	&	Ampersand

To add a character code to the chemistry page:

1. Return to the **chem.htm** file in your text editor.

2. Replace the **e** in Mr. Dubé's name in the page title, the img element, and the appointments paragraph with the code, **é** as shown in Figure 1-30.

Figure 1-30	Inserting a special character

character code
for the é character

```
<h3>Appointments</h3>
<p>You can meet with Mr. Dub&#233; before or after school or during most
lunch hours in room H113. Do not hesitate to ask for help! It can be
very hard to catch up if you fall behind.</p>

<h3>Safety</h3>
<p>Labs are completed weekly. Because of the potential danger of any
lab exercise, you will follow the highest standards of conduct.
Misbehavior can result in dismissal from the lab.</p>

</body>
```

3. Save your changes to the file.

4. Using your Web browser, refresh or reload **chem.htm**. Figure 1-31 shows Stephen's page with the accented é in his last name; you should also see the é in the page title in the browser's title bar.

Figure 1-31	Displaying a special character

Appointments

special character é

You can meet with Mr. Dubé before or after school or during most lunch hours in room H113. Do not hesitate to ask for help! It can be very hard to catch up if you fall behind.

Safety

Labs are completed weekly. Because of the potential danger of any lab exercise, you will follow the highest standards of conduct. Misbehavior can result in dismissal from the lab.

Now that you've completed the Web page for Stephen, you decide to print both the text file and the Web page as it appears in the browser for his review.

To print the text file and Web page:

1. Using your browser, carefully compare your Web page to Figure 1-32, which shows the entire page. If you see any errors, return to your text editor to fix them. When the page is error-free, use your browser to print the page.

Final Web page | **Figure 1-32**

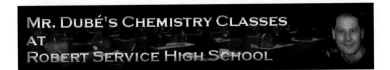

Welcome to the Robert Service High School Chemistry Web page. Here you'll learn more about our chemistry classes and our policies.

Chemistry Classes

- Conceptual Chemistry: An introductory course, requiring basic math but no algebra
- Chemistry I: An introductory course, requiring solid algebra skills
- Advanced Placement Chemistry: An advanced course requiring a grade of A or B in Chemistry I

Class Policies

Grading

Homework: Homework is worth 5 to 10 points and will be given daily. A quiz consisting of 1 or 2 homework problems from the previous week may be given in place of homework.

Tests and Quizzes: Quizzes are worth 10 to 25 points and will be given at least once a month. Tests are worth up to 100 points and will be given three times each quarter.

Labs: Labs are worth 10 to 30 points and will be graded on safety, participation, and write-up. Reports should be neatly written or typed. *Research projects* will also be assigned throughout the year.

Appointments

You can meet with Mr. Dubé before or after school or during most lunch hours in room H113. Do not hesitate to ask for help! It can be very hard to catch up if you fall behind.

Safety

Labs are completed weekly. Because of the potential danger of any lab exercise, you will follow the highest standards of conduct. Misbehavior can result in dismissal from the lab.

2. Using your text editor, print chem.htm, and compare it to the complete code shown in Figure 1-33. When you are finished, you can close your text editor and browser unless you are continuing on to the assignments.

Figure 1-33	Final HTML code

```
<html>

<head>
<!-- Chemistry Classes Web Page
     Author: Stephen Dube
     Date:   8/1/2006
-->
<title>Mr. Dub&#233;'s Chemistry Classes</title>
</head>

<body>
<p style="text-align: center">
   <img src="dube.jpg"
    alt="Mr. Dub&#233;'s Chemistry Classes at Robert Service High School" />
</p>
<hr style="color: red; background-color: red; height: 2; width: 100%" />
<p>Welcome to the Robert Service High School Chemistry web page.
   Here you'll learn more about our chemistry classes and our
   policies.</p>

<h2>Chemistry Classes</h2>
<ul style="list-style-type: square">
   <li>Conceptual Chemistry: An introductory course, requiring basic
       math but no algebra</li>
   <li>Chemistry I: An introductory course, requiring solid algebra
       skills</li>
   <li>Advanced Placement Chemistry: An advanced course requiring a
       grade of A or B in Chemistry I</li>
</ul>

<h2>Class Policies</h2>
<h3>Grading</h3>
<p><i><b>Homework</b></i>: Homework is worth 5 to 10 points and will be given
daily. A quiz consisting of 1 or 2 homework problems from the
previous week may be given in place of homework.</p>

<p><i><b>Tests and Quizzes</b></i>: Quizzes are worth 10 to 25 points and will be
given at least once a month. Tests are worth up to 100 points and
will be given three times each quarter.</p>

<p><i><b>Labs</b></i>: Labs are worth 10 to 30 points and will be graded on safety,
participation, and write-up. Reports should be neatly written or
typed. <i><b>Research projects</b></i> will also be assigned throughout the
year.</p>

<h3>Appointments</h3>
<p>You can meet with Mr. Dub&#233; before or after school or during most
lunch hours in room H113. Do not hesitate to ask for help! It can be
very hard to catch up if you fall behind.</p>

<h3>Safety</h3>
<p>Labs are completed weekly. Because of the potential danger of any
lab exercise, you will follow the highest standards of conduct.
Misbehavior can result in dismissal from the lab.</p>

</body>

</html>
```

Stephen is pleased with your work on his Web site and feels that it effectively captures the content of the original handout. You explain to him that the next step is to add hyperlinks to his Web page so that you can add contact information and create links to the interesting chemistry Web sites you've discovered. You'll do this in the next tutorial.

Tips for Good HTML Code

- Use line breaks and indented text to make your HTML file easier to read.
- Insert comments into your HTML file to document your work.
- Enter all tag and attribute names in lowercase.
- Place all attribute values in quotes.
- Close all two-sided tags.
- Make sure that nested elements do not cross.
- Use styles in place of presentational attributes whenever possible.
- Use logical elements to describe an element's content. Use physical elements to describe the element's appearance.

- Include the alt attribute for any inline image to specify alternative text for non-graphical browsers.
- Know your market and the types of browsers that your audience will use to view your Web page.
- Test your Web page on all relevant browsers and devices.

Review

Session 1.3 Quick Check

1. What is an inline image?
2. Why is it important to always include the alt attribute when inserting an inline image?
3. What code would you enter to display the inline image, logo.jpg, into your Web page? Assume that the alternate text for this image is "Chemistry Web Page".
4. What code would you enter to insert a blue horizontal line that is 200 pixels wide?
5. How does a text-based browser display a horizontal line?
6. How do you insert a line break into a Web page?
7. What tag would you add to your document to insert the meta information that the page author's name is "Diane Chou"?
8. What code would you use to insert the copyright symbol © into your page?

Review

Tutorial Summary

This tutorial introduced you to the basics of HTML. You learned about the history of the Internet, the Web, and HTML. You also studied the philosophy of HTML and learned how the language's standards and specifications were developed, and how they are maintained. You created your first HTML file through the use of two-sided and one-sided tags and learned how to use these tags to mark the various elements of your page, such as headings, paragraphs, and lists. You also learned how to use inline styles to provide formatting instructions for your browser. This tutorial also covered how to insert inline images and horizontal lines into a Web page. Finally, you learned how to use HTML to insert special characters and symbols.

Key Terms

ARPANET	Extensible Markup	inline style
block-level element	Language	Internet
body element	extension	LAN
character formatting	graphical browser	link
elements	head element	local area network
client	host	logical element
client-server network	HTML	markup language
closing tag	HTML converter	metalanguage
comment tag	HTML editor	nesting
definition list	hyperlink	network
deprecated	hypertext	node
element	Hypertext Markup	one-sided tag
empty element	Language	opening tag
Extensible Hypertext	inline element	ordered list
Markup Language	inline image	physical element

pixel	text-based browser	Web server
presentational attribute	title element	Web site
server	two-sided tag	white space
SGML	unordered list	wide area network
specification	W3C	World Wide Web
standard	WAN	World Wide Web
Standard Generalized	Web	Consortium
Markup Language	Web browser	XHTML
style	Web page	XML
tag		

Practice

Practice the skills you learned in the tutorial using the same case scenario.

Review Assignments

Data files needed for this Review Assignment: chemtxt.htm, flask.jpg, logo.jpg

Stephen has some time to study the Web page you created for him and has asked your help to make some additional revisions. In the Chemistry Classes section, he wants you to add a new class that he'll be offering next semester, and he would like the chemistry class names displayed in boldface. He also wants the list marker changed to a graphic image of a flask. He would like to you to indent the paragraphs on grading, office hours, and safety. He also wants you to add a numbered list in the Safety section listing his five main safety rules. He wants you to insert horizontal lines dividing the main sections of the page. Finally, he wants to add a whimsical sentence at the bottom of the site to let his students know that though he is serious about learning and safety, he wants his classes to be fun. He'd like the line to read: "Chemistry with Dubé is like medicine with a spoonful of $C_{12}H_{22}O_{11}$!" ($C_{12}H_{22}O_{11}$ is the formula for sugar.) Figure 1-34 shows a preview of the page you'll create.

Figure 1-34

MR. DUBÉ'S CHEMISTRY CLASSES
AT
ROBERT SERVICE HIGH SCHOOL

Welcome to the Robert Service High School Chemistry Web page. Read below to learn about our classes and policies.

Chemistry Classes

Conceptual Chemistry: An introductory course, requiring basic math but no algebra

Chemistry I: An introductory course, requiring solid algebra skills

Applied Chemistry: An introductory course requiring solid algebra skills and an interest in using critical thinking to solve real-world chemistry-related problems

Advanced Placement Chemistry: An advanced course requiring a grade of A or B in Chemistry I

Class Policies

Assignments and Grading

Homework: Homework is assigned after each class and is worth 5 to 10 points. A periodic quiz consisting of 1 or 2 homework problems may be given in place of homework.

Tests and Quizzes: Tests and quizzes are essential to check your understanding of the material. Quizzes are worth 10 to 25 points and will be given at least once a month. Tests are worth up to 100 points and will be given 3 times each semester.

Labs: Labs are worth 10 to 30 points and will be graded on safety, participation, and write-up. Your reports should be neatly written or typed.

Research projects: Research projects give you a chance to expand your knowledge beyond the classroom. There will be several research projects throughout the year.

Office Hours

You can meet with Mr. Dubé before or after school or during most lunch hours in room H113. Do not hesitate to ask for help! It is very hard to catch up if you fall behind.

Safety Rules

Because of the potential danger of any lab exercise, you will be held to the highest standards of behavior, and will be removed from the class if you pose a threat to yourself or other students.

1. Follow the instructor's written and oral directions carefully and immediately.
2. Never perform any procedure that the instructor does not specifically direct you to do.
3. No playful behavior is permitted in the lab.
4. You must wear safety equipment as directed at all times, even if you find it uncomfortable or unbecoming.
5. No food, drinks, or loose clothing are permitted in the lab.

Chemistry with Dubé is like medicine with a spoonful of $C_{12}H_{22}O_{11}$!

To complete this task:

1. Using your text editor, open **chemtxt.htm** located in the tutorial.01/review folder. Save the file as **chem2.htm** to the same folder.

2. Within the head element of the document, insert the Web page title, "Robert Service High School Chemistry". Also insert a comment that includes your name and the date.

3. Directly above each of the h2 headings (Chemistry Classes and Class Policies), insert a blue horizontal line that is 3 pixels high with a width equal to the width of the page.

4. In the unordered list section, after the line describing the Chemistry I class, add the following new list item:
   Applied Chemistry: An introductory course requiring solid algebra skills and an interest in using critical thinking to solve real-world chemistry-related problems

5. Display each of the four class names in the list in a boldfaced font. Change the markers to the graphic image found in the flask.jpg file in the tutorial.01/review folder.

6. Enclose the four paragraphs below the h3 heading, "Assignments and Grading" within a blockquote element (this will cause the text to appear indented in most browsers.) Also enclose the paragraph below the Office Hours heading and the paragraph below the Safety Rules heading in separate blockquote elements.

7. After the block quote describing Stephen's safety rules, create a numbered list with the following five list items:
   1. Follow the instructor's written and oral directions carefully and immediately.
   2. Never perform any procedure that the instructor does not specifically direct you to do.
   3. No playful behavior is permitted in the lab.
   4. You must wear safety equipment as directed at all times, even if you find it uncomfortable or unbecoming.
   5. No food, drinks, or loose clothes are permitted in the lab.

8. Enclose the numbered list you just created within a blockquote element.

9. Below the numbered list insert another blue horizontal line 3 pixels high and extending the width of the page.

10. Below the horizontal line, insert a centered paragraph containing the following text. (*Hint:* Use the <sub> tag to mark the numbers as subscripts and use a character code to display the character, é.)
    "Chemistry with Dubé is like medicine with a spoonful of $C_{12}H_{22}O_{11}$!"

11. Save your changes to chem2.htm.

12. Open your page in your Web browser and verify that it matches the page shown in Figure 1-34.

13. Submit your completed assignment to your instructor.

Case Problem 1

Apply

Use the skills you have learned to create a Web page for a childcare agency.

Data files needed for this Case Problem: childtxt.htm, newborn.jpg

ChildLink, Inc. You are an employee of ChildLink, Inc., a small, nonprofit agency in Las Cruces, New Mexico. ChildLink provides financial and emotional support for families with children who have newly discovered physical or mental disabilities. The agency received significantly more donations in the last year than expected, and it has decided to offer qualifying clients temporary help with housing and medical costs. The assistant director, Sandra Pauls, has asked you to post the eligibility requirements and application process on the Web. Figure 1-35 shows a preview of the page you'll create for ChildLink, Inc.

Figure 1-35

ChildLink of Las Cruces

A Loving Connection between Children with Disabilities and the Resources They Need

Temporary Financial Assistance Available

To be eligible for this program, you must meet the following criteria:

- Your child must have been diagnosed with a physical or mental disability within the last 6 months (the diagnosis can be prenatal or at any age)
- Your family must be at or below the State of New Mexico's poverty line

To apply, please complete the following steps:

1. Pick up an application from ChildLink (address below)
2. Assemble the following documents:
   a. Your completed application
   b. Doctor's record of your child's diagnosis
   c. Tax records or New Mexico Social Services certificate of your income level
   d. Your lease, mortgage, or medical bills, depending on which you need help with
3. Make an appointment with a ChildLink volunteer, available at the following times:
   a. Ida: MW 10:30 a.m. to 3:30 p.m.
   b. Juan: TR 9:00 a.m. to noon
   c. Chris: F 10:30 a.m. to 3:30 p.m.

ChildLink
1443 Cortnic Drive
Las Cruces, NM 88001
505-555-2371

To complete this task:

1. Use your text editor to open the file **childtxt.htm** from the tutorial.01/case1 folder, and save the file as **child.htm** to the same folder.
2. Within the head element, insert a comment containing your name and the date and insert the following Web page title: ChildLink Temporary Financial Assistance.
3. Within the body element, create an h1 heading containing the text "ChildLink of Las Cruces", and center the heading on the page.

4. Below the h1 heading, create an h3 heading containing the text "A Loving Connection between Children with Disabilities and the Resources They Need", and center the heading on the page.

5. Below the h3 heading, create an h2 heading containing the text "Temporary Financial Assistance Available", and center the heading.

6. Below the h2 heading, create an h4 heading containing the text "To be eligible for this program, you must meet the following criteria:" Leave this heading left-aligned.

7. Below the h4 heading, create a bulleted list with square bullets. Include the two list items shown in Figure 1-35.

8. Below the bulleted list, insert an h4 heading containing the text "To apply, please complete the following steps:" Leave this heading left-aligned.

9. Below the heading, insert an ordered list containing the three numbered items shown in Figure 1-35.

10. Within the "Assemble the following documents:" list item, create an ordered list containing the four items shown in Figure 1-35. Use the lower-alpha style to display a letter rather than a number next to each item.

11. Within the "Make an appointment" list item, create another ordered list containing the three volunteer names and times as shown in Figure 1-35; as in the previous step, display the items using letters rather than numbers.

12. Insert a horizontal line below the main numbered list.

13. Below the horizontal line insert the contact information shown in Figure 1-35 as an address element. Insert line breaks within the address, and display the word, "ChildLink" in a boldfaced font. Align the address with the right margin of the page.

14. After the h3 heading ("A Loving Connection…") near the top, insert a centered paragraph containing the inline image **newborn.jpg**. For text-based or non-visual browsers, display the alternative text, "We provide support for newborns".

15. Below this image, insert a horizontal line.

16. Save the file, view it in your browser, compare it to Figure 1-35, and then make any corrections necessary in your text editor. Submit your completed assignment to your instructor.

Explore

Broaden your knowledge and challenge yourself by exploring how to create a Web page for a mathematics department.

Case Problem 2

Data files needed for this Case Problem: euler.jpg, eulertxt.htm, pi.jpg

Mathematics Department, Coastal University Professor Laureen Coe of the Mathematics Department at Coastal University in Beachside, Connecticut is preparing material for her course on the history of mathematics. As part of the course, she has written short profiles of famous mathematicians. Laureen would like you to use content she's already written to create several Web pages that students can access on Coastal University's Web server. You'll create the first one in this exercise. Figure 1-36 previews this page, which profiles the mathematician Leonhard Euler.

Figure 1-36

Euler, Leonhard

(1707-1783)

The greatest mathematician of the eighteenth century, **Leonhard Euler** was born in Basel, Switzerland. There, he studied under another giant of mathematics, **Jean Bernoulli**. In 1731 Euler became a professor of physics and mathematics at St. Petersburg Academy of Sciences. Euler was the most prolific mathematician of all time, publishing over *800 different books and papers*. His influence was felt in physics and astronomy as well. Euler's work on mathematical analysis, *Introductio in analysin infinitorum* (1748) remained a standard textbook for well over a century. For the princess of Anhalt-Dessau he wrote *Lettres à une princesse d'Allemagne* (1768-1772), giving a clear non-technical outline of the main physical theories of the time.

One can hardly write mathematical equations without copying Euler. Notations still in use today, such as e and π, were developed by Euler. He is perhaps best known for his research into mathematical analysis. Euler's formula:

$$\cos(x) + i\sin(x) = e^{(ix)}$$

demonstrates the relationship between analysis, trignometry and imaginary numbers, in one beautiful and elegant equation.

Leonhard Euler died in 1783, leaving behind a legacy perhaps unmatched, and certainly unsurpassed, in the annals of mathematics.

Math 895: The History of Mathematics

To complete this task:

1. Using your text editor, open the file **eulertxt.htm** located in the tutorial.01/case2 folder, and save it as **euler.htm**.
2. Add the opening and closing <html>, <head>, and <body> tags to the file in the appropriate locations.
3. Within the head element, enter "Leonhard Euler" as the page title.

Explore

4. Also within the head element, enter two meta elements. The first should contain an author property set to your name. The second should contain a date property set to the current date.
5. Insert the inline image **euler.jpg** (located in the tutorial.01/case2 folder on your Data Disk) at the top of the body of the document, within a paragraph element. Provide the alternate text, "Image of Leonhard Euler" for non-graphical browsers.
6. Format the first line of the page's body, "Euler, Leonhard", as an h1 heading and format the second line of the page's body, "(1707-1783)" as an h3 heading.
7. Define the next two blocks of text as paragraphs.
8. Within the first paragraph, display the names "Leonhard Euler" and "Jean Bernoulli" in boldface. Identify the phrase "800 different books and papers" as emphasized text, and identify the phrase, "Introductio in analysin infinitorum" as a citation.

Explore

9. In the phrase "Lettres a une princesse d'Allemagne," use the character code à to replace the one-letter word "a" with an à, and identify the name of the publication as a citation.

Explore

10. In the second paragraph, italicize the notation "e" and replace the word "pi" with the inline image **pi.jpg**, located in the case2 folder on your Data Disk. Provide the alternate text "pi" for non-graphical browsers.

Explore

11. Place the equation in a centered paragraph element and italicize each occurrence of the letters "x", "i", and "e" in the equation. Display the term "(ix)" as a superscript.
12. Format the next two blocks of text as paragraphs.
13. Define the name of the course at the bottom of the page as an address element.
14. Add horizontal lines before and after the biographical information.
15. Save your changes to the euler.htm file. Submit your completed assignment to your instructor.

Explore

Go beyond what you've
learned in the tutorial
by exploring how to use
color and background
images in a racing
results Web page.

Case Problem 3

Data files needed for this Case Problem: flakes.jpg, frosttxt.htm, runner.jpg

Frostbite Freeze   You are on the organizing committee for the Frostbite Freeze, a fun but competitive event held each January in Butte, Montana. You've volunteered to publish the results for Montana's craziest running race on the Web. You talk about the format of the page with Matt Turner, the chairman of the committee.

Matt wants you to include a snowflake background behind the text, which you can do using a graphic image. Such backgrounds are called tiled-image backgrounds because the browser repeats, or tiles, the image to cover the background of the entire page. You can create a tiled-image background with an image in either GIF or JPEG file format. To add a background image to an element, you apply the following style:

```
background-image: url(file)
```

where *file* is the name of the image file. Matt has given you two JPEG files to use for this Web page: **flakes.jpg**, which contains a snowflake pattern, and **runner.jpg**, which shows a Frostbite Freeze racer. Figure 1-37 shows a preview of the page you'll create.

Figure 1-37

Frostbite Freeze

Montana's Craziest Footrace

The results are in ...

257 runners braved the -10° weather on January 19 and ran, in one fashion or another, the icy 5-kilometer course through downtown Butte. About half the runners sported costumes rather than serious running gear, and many runners posted good times (costumed or not). For many, this was the season's first run (not race – *run*), a motivational warm-up for the fun and work that lies ahead.

Awards were given for best time in four age categories for both sexes.

Girls 14-19
Jamie Harrington 19:33 · Sorcia Besay 20:06 · Rachel Stores 25:44

Boys 14-19
Bruce Bevin 18:55 · Endre Witthoeft 19:46 · Joe Wesevich 21:19

Women 20-39
Marie Sillers 17:45 · Denise Wortenhau 18:33 · Lorel Dwiers 18:56

Women 39-49
Jannie Gilbert 17:48 · Mia Saphi 19:23 · Dawn Severson 21:31

Women 50+
Julia Gent 21:09 · Mandy Reming 34:24 · Sung Bon 41:02

Men 20-39
Gary Cruz 17:11 · Lanny Sorla 18:40 · Kip Oestin 18:55

Men 40-49
Steve Jackson 18:50 · Jim Kostenberger 24:33 · Lee Whisten 27:18

Men 50+
Billy Tisa 18:22 · Alois Anderson 28:48 · Lyle Tolbor 35:46

To complete this task:

1. Using your text editor, open **frosttxt.htm** from the tutorial.01/case3 folder, and then save it as **frost.htm**.
2. Insert the <html>, <head>, and <body> tags in the appropriate locations.
3. Insert the Web page title "Frostbite Freeze Results" in the head element in the document and add a comment containing your name and the date.

Explore

4. Apply a style to the body element to add flakes.jpg as the background image.
5. Mark the text "Frostbite Freeze" with as an h1 heading and center it on the Web page.
6. Mark the text "Montana's Craziest Footrace" as an h2 heading and center it on the page.

Explore

Explore

Explore

7. Insert a purple horizontal line below the h2 heading that is 50% of the width of the screen and 5 pixels high.

8. Mark the text "The results are in" as an h3 heading tag, leaving the text left aligned.

9. Add an ellipsis (…) after the text "The results are in" so it reads, "The results are in…" Use the character code for the ellipsis symbol, which you can find in appendices.

10. Add a degree symbol after "-10" in the first line of the first paragraph. (Use the character code for the degree symbol from the appendices.)

11. Identify the first two text blocks as paragraphs (one starts with "257 runners" and the other starts with "Awards were given").

12. Near the end of the first paragraph, display the word "run" in italics (see Figure 1-37).

13. Mark each of the eight age-sex categories (for example, "Girls 14-19") and the winners as eight individual paragraphs. Insert a line break between the category name and the winners.

14. Display the names of the eight age-sex categories in a boldfaced font.

15. Insert a middle dot symbol between each of the three names in each of the eight age-sex categories. Insert three nonbreaking spaces at the start of each line containing the winners to make the line appear indented on the page.

16. Insert the inline image **runner.jpg** (located in the case3 folder of the tutorial.01 folder on your Data Disk) between the top two headings, as shown in Figure 1-37. For non-graphical browsers, display the alternate text, "Race Results Page". Center the image within a paragraph.

17. Save your changes and view the completed page in your Web browser. Submit your assignment to your instructor.

Create

Test your knowledge of HTML by creating a product page for Body Systems.

Case Problem 4

Data files needed for this Case Problem: logo.jpg, smith.jpg, smith.txt

Body Systems Body Systems is one of the leading manufacturers of home gyms. The company recently hired you to assist in developing their Web site. Your first task is to create a Web page for the LSM400, a popular weight machine sold by the company. You've been given a text file, smith.txt, describing the features of the LSM400. You've also received two image files: logo.jpg, displaying the company's logo and smith.jpg, an image of the LSM400. You are free to supplement these files with any other resources available to you. You are responsible for the page's content and appearance.

To complete this task:

1. Create an HTML file named **smith.htm**, and save it in the tutorial.01/case4 folder.

2. In the head element, include an appropriate page title, along with a comment describing the purpose of the page, your name, and the date.

3. Include at least one example of each of the following in the document:

   - a heading
   - a paragraph
   - an ordered or unordered list
   - a character formatting element
   - an inline image
   - a horizontal line
   - a special character
   - a block-level element that is not a heading, paragraph, list, or horizontal line

4. Demonstrate your understanding of inline styles by including at least two different examples of an inline style.
5. Use proper HTML syntax at all times. Close all two-sided tags. Properly nest all tags. Use lowercase element and attribute names. Enclose attribute values in quotes. Include alternate text for non-graphical browsers with inline images.
6. Write your code so that it will be easy for your supervisor to read and understand.
7. Save your HTML file, and then view the resulting Web page in a browser.
8. Submit your completed assignment to your instructor.

Review

Quick Check Answers

Session 1.1

1. A hypertext document is an electronic file containing elements that users can select, usually by clicking a mouse, to open other documents.
2. Web pages are stored on Web servers, which then makes those pages available to clients. To view a Web page, the client runs a software program called a Web browser, which retrieves the page and displays it.
3. HTML (Hypertext Markup Language) is the language in which Web pages are written.
4. HTML documents do not exactly specify the appearance of a document; rather they describe the purpose of different elements in the document and leave it to the Web browser to determine the final appearance. A word processor like Word exactly specifies the appearance of each document element.
5. Deprecated features and those features that are being phased out by the W3C, and which might not be supported by future browsers.
6. Extensions are special formats supported by a particular browser, but not generally accepted by all browsers. The advantage is that people who use that browser have a wider range of document elements to work with. The disadvantage is that the document will not work for users who do not have that particular browser, thus complicating the development process.
7. Because HTML documents are simple text files, you can create them with nothing more than a basic text editor such as Windows Notepad. However, specialized HTML authoring programs, known as HTML converters and HTML editors, are available to do some of the rote work of creating an HTML document.

Session 1.2

1. The head element which contains information about the document or instructions to the browser, and the body element which contains the content that the browser should render in the page.
2. Empty elements are elements that have no content. They are created using one-sided HTML tags.
3. `<h1 style="text-align: center">Chemistry Classes</h1>`
4. Block-level elements contain content that is displayed in a separate section within the page, such as a paragraph or a heading. An inline element is part of the same block as its surrounding content—for example, individual words or phrases within a paragraph.
5. HTML treats all white space (tabs, line breaks, blank spaces) as a single blank space and collapses consecutive occurrences of white space into a single occurrence. Thus, adding an extra blank line to your HTML file does not create an extra blank line in the rendered page.

6. Presentational attributes are HTML attributes that exactly specify how to the browser should render an HTML element. Most presentational attributes have been deprecated, replaced by styles. You should use presentational attributes when you need to support older browsers.

7. `style="list-style-type: upper-roman"`

8. `style="list-style-image: url(ball.gif); list-style-position: inside"`
   or
   `style="list-style: url(ball.gif) inside"`

9. Logical elements describe the nature of their enclosed content, but do not necessarily indicate how that content should appear. Physical elements describe how an element should appear, but provide little or no information about the nature of its content. Logical elements are more appropriate for a non-visual browser.

Session 1.3

1. An inline image is an inline element, used to display graphical images within the contents of a block-level element.

2. The alt attribute provides a text alternative to the image for non-graphical browsers.

3. `<img src="logo.jpg" alt="Chemistry Web Page" />`

4. `<hr style="color: blue; background-color: blue; width: 200" />`

5. Text based browsers display horizontal lines using dashes or underscores.

6. Use the `<br />` tag.

7. `<meta name="author" content="Diane Chou" />`

8. `&#169;` or `&copy;`

Objectives

Session 2.1
- Define links and how to use them
- Create element ids to mark specific locations within a document
- Create links to jump between sections of the same document
- Describe how to set and use anchors for backward compatibility with older browsers

Session 2.2
- List different types of Web site structures and how to employ them
- Create links between documents
- Create links to sections within a document
- Define absolute and relative paths

Session 2.3
- Interpret the structure and contents of a URL
- Link to a page on the Web
- Link to FTP servers, newsgroups, and e-mail addresses
- Open links in a secondary window
- Work with popup titles and access keys
- Create semantic links
- Create link elements

Developing a Basic Web Site

Creating a Chemistry Web Site

Case

Creating a Chemistry Web Site

In the last tutorial you created a basic Web page for Stephen Dubé, a chemistry teacher in Edmonton, Alberta. With your help, Stephen has made a few changes to the Web page, and he has ideas for additional content. Stephen notes that while the Web page's appearance reflects the course handout on which he originally based it, the Web page's layout is limiting. For example, students and their parents must scroll through the document window to find information about his classes. Stephen wants to make it as easy to navigate from topic to topic on his Web page as it is to scan the single-page handout.

Stephen also wants to put more information online, but he is concerned about making the original Web page too large and difficult to navigate. He'd like to list the ways students and parents can contact him (office hours, e-mail, phone numbers, and so forth). He would also like to share several helpful chemistry Web sites with his students.

Student Data Files

▼ **Tutorial.02**

▽ **Tutorial folder**
chemtxt.htm
conttxt.htm
linkstxt.htm
+1 graphical file

▽ **Review folder**
chemtxt.htm
conttxt.htm
glosstxt.htm
linkstxt.htm
+1 graphical file

▽ **Case1 folder**
links.txt
mpltxt.htm
+1 graphical file

▽ **Case2 folder**

glosstxt.htm
hometxt.htm
m1txt.htm
m2txt.htm
m3txt.htm
m4txt.htm
+8 graphical files

▽ **Case3 folder**

classtxt.htm
indextxt.htm
memtxt.htm
+1 graphical file

▽ **Case 4 folder**

about.txt
bench.txt
cable.txt
contact.txt
lpress.txt
products.txt
smith.txt
whybuy.txt
+5 graphical files

Session 2.1

Working with Links

Since the last tutorial, you and Stephen have made some modifications to the layout and have added new content to the chemistry Web page. However, because the page is too long to fit in a browser window, a user opening the Web page sees only a small portion of the document. Of the document's four sections (Classes, Grading, Appointments, and Safety), a user initially sees only the class logo, the welcoming message, and the beginning of the class list (see Figure 2-1). To view the additional information, a user must scroll through the document. Stephen would like users to have a quicker way to access that information.

Figure 2-1 | **Top of the chemistry Web page**

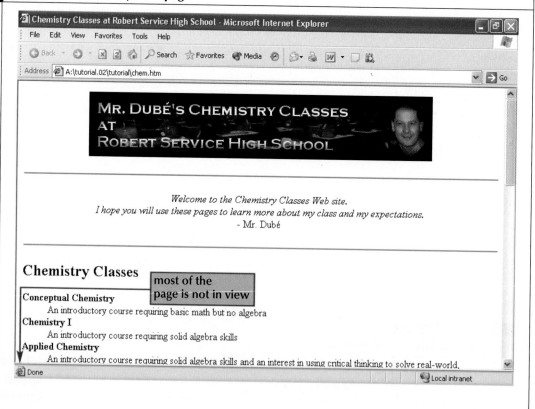

In the previous tutorial, you learned that a user can select a **link** in a Web page, usually by clicking it with a mouse, to view another topic or document, often called the link's **destination**. Stephen would like you to add links to his Web page that point to the different sections of the document. He would like you to list the four sections at the top of the page, and then format the names as links. When users open the chemistry page, they can click a link to move directly to the section of the page that interests them. You'll use the following steps to create these links in Stephen's page:

1. List the section names at the top of the document.
2. Mark each section in the HTML file using an id attribute. (You'll learn about this attribute shortly.)
3. Link the text you added in Step 1 to the sections you marked in Step 2.

Let's start by creating a list of the section names. We'll separate each section name with a • to make the text easier to read. You use the HTML character symbol · to create the • symbol.

To create a list of the section headings:

1. Use your text editor to open **chemtxt.htm** from the tutorial.02/tutorial folder. Save the file as **chem.htm**.

2. Enter **your name** and **the date** in the comment tag at the top of the file.

3. Directly above the first <hr /> tag, insert the following code:

```
<p style="text-align: center">
    Classes &#183;
    Grading &#183;
    Appointments &#183;
    Safety
</p>
```

See Figure 2-2.

Adding code for the text links | **Figure 2-2**

```
<body>
<p style="text-align: center">
    <img src="dube.jpg"
    alt="Mr. Dub&#233;'s Chemistry Classes at Robert Service High School" />
</p>

<p style="text-align: center">
    Classes &#183;
    Grading &#183;
    Appointments &#183;
    Safety
</p>

<hr style="color: red; background-color: red; height: 2; width: 100%" />
```

4. Save your changes to the file, but leave your text editor open.

5. Start your Web browser and open **chem.htm** to verify your change, as shown in Figure 2-3.

Figure 2-3 | **List of section heads**

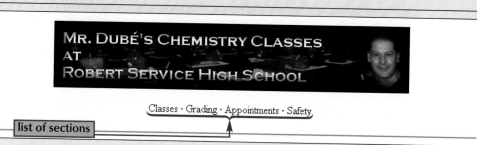

Creating Element ids

Now that you've listed the different sections of the Web page, you need a way to identify those elements in the HTML document. One way of doing this is through the id attribute, which uses the syntax:

```
id="id"
```

where *id* is the id name assigned to the element. For example, the code

```
<h2 id="classes">Chemistry Classes</h2>
```

assigns the id name "classes" to the h2 heading "Chemistry Classes". Note that id names must be unique. If you assign the same id name to more than one element in an HTML document, a browser will use only the first occurrence of the id name. In addition, if a browser finds duplicate id names in an XHTML document, it reports an error. Id names are not case sensitive, so browsers do not differentiate between ids named "classes" and "CLASSES", for example.

For Stephen's Chemistry file, you decide to add ids to the h2 headings Chemistry Classes, Grading, Appointments, and Safety. You'll assign these tags the id names "classes", "grading", "app", and "safety".

To add id names to the section headings:

▶ 1. Return to the **chem.htm** file in your text editor.

▶ 2. Locate the <h2> tag for the heading "Chemistry Classes" and add the id attribute **id="classes"** as shown in Figure 2-4.

Adding id names | **Figure 2-4**

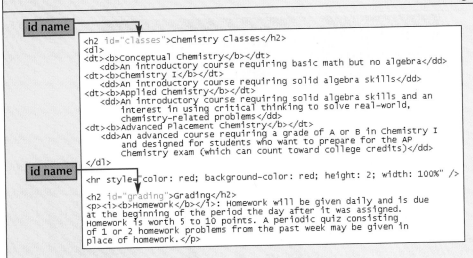

id name

```
<h2 id="classes">Chemistry Classes</h2>
<dl>
<dt><b>Conceptual Chemistry</b></dt>
    <dd>An introductory course requiring basic math but no algebra</dd>
<dt><b>Chemistry I</b></dt>
    <dd>An introductory course requiring solid algebra skills</dd>
<dt><b>Applied Chemistry</b></dt>
    <dd>An introductory course requiring solid algebra skills and an
        interest in using critical thinking to solve real-world,
        chemistry-related problems</dd>
<dt><b>Advanced Placement Chemistry</b></dt>
    <dd>An advanced course requiring a grade of A or B in Chemistry I
        and designed for students who want to prepare for the AP
        Chemistry exam (which can count toward college credits)</dd>
</dl>
```

id name

```
<hr style="color: red; background-color: red; height: 2; width: 100%" />

<h2 id="grading">Grading</h2>
<p><i><b>Homework</b></i>: Homework will be given daily and is due
at the beginning of the period the day after it was assigned.
Homework is worth 5 to 10 points. A periodic quiz consisting
of 1 or 2 homework problems from the past week may be given in
place of homework.</p>
```

3. Add the attribute **id="grading"** to the <h2> tag for the Grading heading (see Figure 2-4).

4. Add the attribute **id="app"** to the <h2> tag for the Appointments heading.

5. Add the attribute **id="safety"** to the <h2> tag for the Safety heading.

6. Save your changes to the file.

7. Using your Web browser, refresh or reload **chem.htm** and scroll through the page to confirm that it appears unchanged. The ids you placed in the document should not change the appearance of the Web page.

   Trouble? If you see a change in the page, check to make sure that you correctly typed the code for adding ids.

You've added ids to the document's four section headings. The next step is to create links to those sections.

Creating Links within a Document

For Stephen's page, you want to link the entries in the list you created earlier to the document's four sections. When a user clicks one of the linked entries at the top of the page, the browser will display the corresponding section of the document without requiring the user to scroll down. Figure 2-5 illustrates the relationships between the four links you want to create and the Web page's sections.

Figure 2-5 ▶ Links in the Chemistry page

Classes · Grading · Appointments · Safety

Welcome to the Chemistry Classes Web site.
I hope you will use these pages to learn more about my class and my expectations.
Mr. Dubé

> clicking a link in the list jumps the user to the correct heading in the page

Chemistry Classes

Conceptual Chemistry
An introductory course requiring basic math but no algebra
Chemistry I
An introductory course requiring solid algebra s
Applied Chemistry
An introductory course requiring solid algebra s and an intere n using cr al thinking to solve real-world, chemistry-related problems
Advanced Placement Chemistry
An advanced course requiring a grade of B in Chemistry I designed students who want to prepare for the AP Chemistry exam (which can count college credits)

Grading

Homework: Homework will be given daily and is due at the beginnin the peri day after it was assigned. Homework is worth 5 to 10 points. A periodic quiz consisting of 1 or 2 homewo oblems the past week may be given in place of homework.

Tests and quizzes: Quizzes are worth 10 to 25 points and will be at least a month. Tests are worth up to 100 points and will be given 2 or 3 times a quarter.

Labs: Labs are worth 10 to 30 points and are graded on safety ipation rite-up. Reports should be neatly written or typed.

Research projects: To explore other aspects of chemistry, s search s will be assigned throughout the year.

You must make up missed tests and quizzes the day you and you bmit missed homework assignments and labs within two days for every one day you missed. Failure t up wor these time frames will result in a 0 for that test or assignment.

Appointments

You can meet with Mr. Dubé before or after school or st lunch hours in room H113. Do not hesitate to ask for help! It can be very hard to catch up if you fall behind.

Safety

Labs are completed weekly. Because of the potential danger of any lab exercise, you expected to follow the highest standards of conduct. Misbehavior can result in dismissal from the lab.

- Follow the written and oral directions carefully and immediately.
- Never perform any procedure not specifically assigned in the lab.
- No playful behavior is permitted in the lab.
- Safety equipment must be worn as directed at all times, even if you find it uncomfortable or unbecoming.
- No food, drinks, or loose clothing are permitted in the lab.

To create a link within a document, you enclose the content that you want to format as a link in an <a> tag, and use the href attribute (short for "Hypertext Reference") to identify the link target. The general syntax is

```
<a href="#id">content</a>
```

where *id* is the value of the id attribute for the destination and *content* is the content in the document that you want to act as a link. For example, to format the text "Classes" as a link pointing to the element named class, you would enter the code:

```
<a href="#classes">Classes</a>
```

In this example, the entire word "Classes" is defined as a link. When a user clicks on any part of the word, the browser jumps to the link's destination—in this case, the element whose id name is "classes".

Reference Window

Inserting and Linking to an Id

- To add an id name to an element, insert the following attribute into the element's tag:
    id="*id*"
  where *id* is the id name assigned to the element.
- To link to an element with an id, use the syntax:
    <a href="#*id*">content</a>
  where *content* is the content in the document that you want to act as a link.

A link's content is not limited to text. You can also format an inline image as a link, as in the following example:

```
<a href="#classes"><img src="dube.jpg" /></a>
```

In general, a link should not contain any block-level elements. Thus, if you want to change an h1 heading into a link, you should nest the link within the heading as follows:

```
<h2><a href="#classes">View Class List</a></h2>
```

rather than placing the heading within the link:

```
<a href="#classes"><h2>View Class List</h2></a>
```

While some browsers may accept this second form, others will reject it. XHTML will not accept any block level element placed within a link. Nor can you place one link inside of another. However, you can place most inline elements, including character-formatting elements, within a link. When in doubt, a good rule is to not place anything other than text and empty elements, such as inline images, within a link. This will ensure that your code is acceptable to all browsers and to XHTML.

Now that you've seen how to create a link, change the entries in the section list to links pointing to the document's different headings.

To create links in the chemistry page:

▶ **1.** Return to **chem.htm** in your text editor.

2. Add opening and closing <a> tags to the list of sections at the top of the document as follows:

```
<p style="text-align: center">
    <a href="#classes">Classes</a> &#183;
    <a href="#grading">Grading</a> &#183;
    <a href="#app">Appointments</a> &#183;
    <a href="#safety">Safety</a>
</p>
```

See Figure 2-6.

Figure 2-6	Linking text to a destination

id name in the current document

```
<p style="text-align: center">
    <a href="#classes">Classes</a> &#183;
    <a href="#grading">Grading</a> &#183;
    <a href="#app">Appointments</a> &#183;
    <a href="#safety">Safety</a>
</p>
```

3. Save your changes to the file.

4. Using your Web browser, refresh or reload **chem.htm**. The headings should now be a different color and be underlined. This is the standard formatting for links in most browsers. See Figure 2-7.

Figure 2-7	Links in the chemistry page

links are displayed in a different color font and are underlined

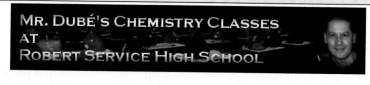

MR. DUBÉ'S CHEMISTRY CLASSES AT ROBERT SERVICE HIGH SCHOOL

Classes · Grading · Appointments · Safety

Trouble? If the headings do not appear as text links, check your code to make sure that you are using the <a> and </a> tags around the appropriate text, the href attribute within the tag, and the quotes and # symbols, as shown previously.

Before continuing, you should verify that the links work as you expect them to. To test a link, simply click it and verify that it jumps you to the appropriate destination.

To test your links:

1. Click one of the links. Your browser should display the section of the document indicated by the link. If it does not, check your code for errors by comparing it to Figure 2-6.

2. Click each of the other links, scrolling back to the top of the page after each test.

3. If you are continuing on to Session 2.2, leave your browser and text editor open. If you are not, you can close them at this time.

Trouble? The browser cannot scroll farther than the end of the page. Thus you may not see any difference between jumping to the Appointments section and jumping to the Safety section.

Creating Anchors

Older browser versions, such as Netscape Navigator 4.7 and Internet Explorer 4, do not support ids as link destinations. If you need to support these older browsers, you have to insert an anchor element into your document. An **anchor element** marks a specific location within a document. To create an anchor, you use the following syntax:

```
<a name="anchor">content</a>
```

where the name attribute provides the name of the anchor and *content* is the content (usually text) in the document that acts as the anchor. For example to add an anchor to the h2 heading, "Chemistry Classes", you could use the following HTML code:

```
<h2><a name="classes">Chemistry Classes</a></h2>
```

Since you create anchors with the same <a> tag you use to create links, anchor content can also include most inline elements and empty elements (like inline images); however, anchors cannot include block-level elements.

Once you create an anchor, the anchor's name acts just like an element id. Thus to link to the above anchor, you could create the following link:

```
<a name="#classes">Classes</a>
```

Inserting an anchor does not change your document's appearance in any way; it merely creates a destination within your document. Since anchors do not modify their content, you may be tempted to use them without content, as in the following example:

```
<a name="classes"></a><h2>Chemistry Classes</h2>
```

While many browsers will accept this form, some browsers expect every two-sided tag to contain some content and thus will reject this code. In practice, therefore, you should not create empty anchors.

Reference Window

Inserting and Linking to an Anchor

- To add an anchor to a document, use the syntax:
  ```
  <a name="anchor">content</a>
  ```
  where *anchor* is the name you want to give the anchor and *content* is the document content that will act as an anchor.
- To link to an anchor, use the syntax:
  ```
  <a href="#anchor">content</a>
  ```

You've completed your work adding links to the chemistry Web page. Stephen is confident that they will help his students and their parents to quickly navigate this lengthy page. In the next session, you'll learn how to create links to other documents on Stephen's Web site.

Session 2.1 Quick Check

Review

1. What is the HTML code for marking the h2 heading "Colorado State University" with the id name "csu"?
2. What is the HTML code for linking the text "Universities" to an element with the id, "csu"?
3. What is wrong with the following code?
   ```
   <a href="#info"><h3>For more information</h3></a>
   ```

4. What is the HTML code for marking an inline image, photo.jpg, with the anchor name "photo"?

5. What is the HTML code for linking the inline image button.jpg to an anchor with the name "links"?

6. When should you use anchors in place of ids for marking destinations within a document?

Session 2.2

Working with Web Site Structures

Stephen wants to add two more pages to his Web site: a page showing his contact information, and another listing his favorite chemistry links. Each page must contain links to the site's other pages, in order for users to be able to easily move around within the site. Figure 2-8 shows the three pages in Stephen's proposed site.

Figure 2-8 ▷ **The three chemistry pages**

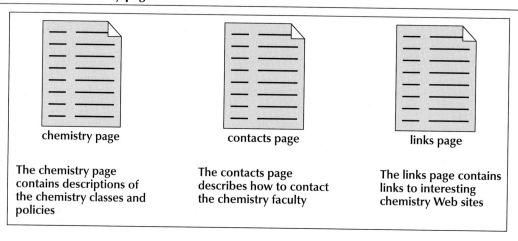

chemistry page

The chemistry page contains descriptions of the chemistry classes and policies

contacts page

The contacts page describes how to contact the chemistry faculty

links page

The links page contains links to interesting chemistry Web sites

Before you set up links to navigate a Web site, it's worthwhile to map out exactly how you want the pages to relate, using a common technique known as storyboarding. A **storyboard** is a diagram of a Web site's structure, showing all the pages in the site and indicating how they are linked together. Because Web sites use a variety of structures, it's important to storyboard your Web site before you start creating your pages in order to determine which structure works best for the type of information the site contains. A well-designed structure can ensure that users will able to navigate the site without getting lost or without missing important information.

The Web sites you commonly encounter as you navigate the Web use several different Web structures. Examining some of these structures can help you decide how to design your own sites.

Linear Structures

If you wanted to create an online version of a famous play, like Shakespeare's *Hamlet*, one method would be to create links between the individual scenes of the play. Figure 2-9 shows the storyboard of a **linear structure**, in which each page is linked with the pages that follow and precede it in an ordered chain. To read the online play, users move forward through the scenes (or backward if they wish to review the previous scenes).

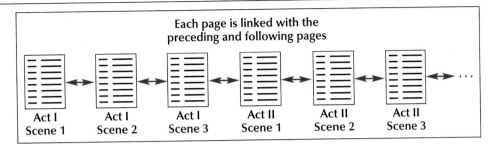

Each page is linked with the
preceding and following pages

Act I Scene 1 | Act I Scene 2 | Act I Scene 3 | Act II Scene 1 | Act II Scene 2 | Act II Scene 3

Linear structures work best for Web pages with a clearly defined order. However, they can be difficult to work with as the chain of pages increases in length. You can modify this structure to make it easier for users to return immediately to an opening page, rather than backtrack through several pages to get to their destination. Figure 2-10 shows this online play with an **augmented linear structure**, in which each page contains an additional link back to an opening page. In this case, each scene is linked to the preceding and following scene *and* to the first scene of the current act.

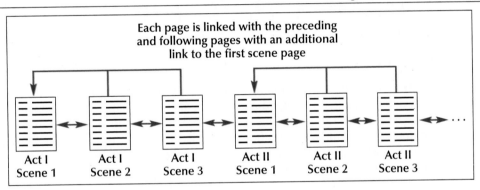

Each page is linked with the preceding
and following pages with an additional
link to the first scene page

Act I Scene 1 | Act I Scene 2 | Act I Scene 3 | Act II Scene 1 | Act II Scene 2 | Act II Scene 3

Hierarchical Structures

Another popular structure is the **hierarchical structure**, in which the pages are linked going from the most general page down to more specific pages. Those pages, in turn, can be linked to even more specific topics. In a hierarchical structure, users can easily move from general to specific and back again. In the case of our online play, we can link an introductory page containing general information about the play to pages that describe each of the play's acts, and within each act we can include links to individual scenes. With this structure, a user can move quickly to a specific scene within the page, bypassing the need to move through each scene in the play.

Figure 2-11 | **A hierarchical structure**

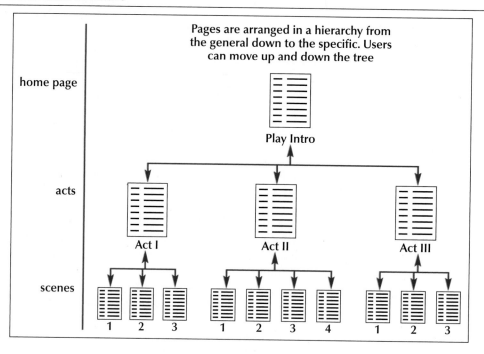

Mixed Structures
================

Mixed Structures

As your Web sites become larger and more complex, you often need to use a combination of several different structures. Figure 2-12 shows our online play using a mixture of different structures. The overall form is hierarchical, as users can move from a general introduction down to individual scenes; however, links also allow users to move through the site in a linear fashion, going from act to act and scene to scene. Note as well that each individual scene contains a link to the introductory page, allowing users to jump to the top of the hierarchy without moving through the different levels.

Mixed structure ◀ **Figure 2-12**

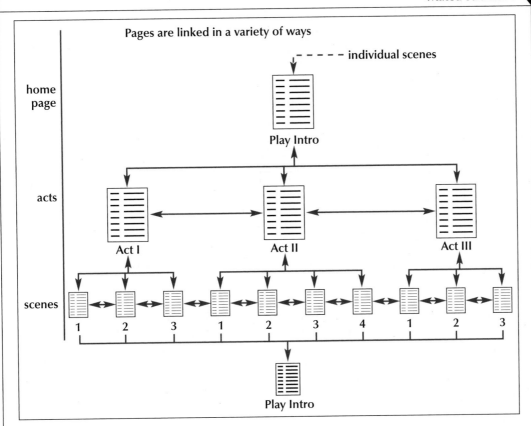

As these examples show, a little foresight can go a long way toward making your Web site easier to use. In addition, search results from a Web search engine such as Google or Alta Vista can point users to any page in your Web site, and they will need a way to quickly understand what your site contains and how to get at it. Thus, each page should contain at minimum a link to the site's home page, or to the relevant main topic page, if applicable. In some cases, you may want to supply your users with a **site index**, which is a page containing an outline of the entire site and its contents. Unstructured Web sites can be difficult and frustrating to use. Consider the storyboard of the site displayed in Figure 2-13.

Figure 2-13 ▶ Web site with no coherent structure

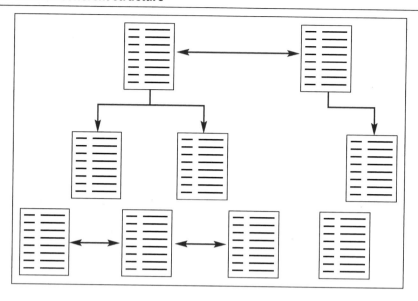

This confusing "structure" makes it difficult for users to grasp the site's contents and scope. The user might not even be aware of the presence of some pages because there are no connecting links (or the links only point in one direction). The Web is a competitive place and studies have shown that users who don't see how to get what they want within the first few seconds often leave a Web site. How long would a user hang around a site like the one shown in Figure 2-13?

Creating Links between Documents

Stephen wants students and their parents to be able to move effortlessly between the three documents in his Web site. To do that, you'll create links between each page and the other two pages. Figure 2-14 provides a storyboard for the simple structure you have in mind.

Figure 2-14 ▶ Storyboard for the chemistry Web site

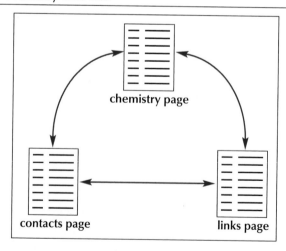

chemistry page

contacts page   links page

Stephen has given you the information to create the two additional HTML files for his site: conttxt.htm, a page containing his contact information; and linkstxt.htm, a page containing links to various chemistry Web sites that he has found particularly helpful to his students. These files are located in the tutorial folder in the tutorial.02 folder on your Data Disk. You should save these files with new names to keep the originals intact.

To rename the conttxt.htm and linkstxt.htm files:

1. Using your text editor, open **conttxt.htm** from the tutorial.02/tutorial folder. Enter **your name** and **the date** in the comment tag at the top of the file. Save the file as **contacts.htm**.

2. Using your text editor, open **linkstxt.htm** from the tutorial.02/tutorial folder. Enter **your name** and **the date** in the comment tag at the top of the file. Save the file as **links.htm**.

Linking to a Document

You begin by inserting links in the chemistry page to the contacts and links pages. To link to a page, you specify the name of the file using the href attribute of the <a> tag. For example, to link the phrase "Contact me" to the contacts.htm file, you enter the following HTML code:

```
<a href="contacts.htm">Contact me</a>
```

In order for the browser to be able to locate and open contacts.htm, it must be located in the same folder as the chem.htm file. You'll learn how to link to documents in separate folders shortly. Note that unlike creating links between elements on the same page, this process does not require you to create an id attribute or to set an anchor. The filename serves as the target.

Filenames are case sensitive on some operating systems, including the UNIX and Macintosh operating systems, but not on others, such as Windows and MS-DOS. For this reason, you may find that links you create on your computer may not work when you transfer your files to a Web server. To avoid this problem, the current standard is to use lowercase filenames for all files on a Web site, and to avoid using special characters such as blanks and slashes (/). You should also keep your filenames short, so that users are less apt to make typing errors when accessing your site.

To add links to the Contact and Links pages:

1. Using your text editor, reopen the **chem.htm** file that you worked on in Session 2.1 of this tutorial.

2. Locate the links you created in the last session, and then insert the following links at the top of the list, as shown in Figure 2-15.

```
<a href="contacts.htm">Contact Info</a> &#183;
<a href="links.htm">Chemistry Links</a> &#183;
```

Linking to other documents ◄ **Figure 2-15**

links to other documents

```
<p style="text-align: center">
   <a href="contacts.htm">Contact Info</a> &#183;
   <a href="links.htm">Chemistry Links</a> &#183;
   <a href="#classes">Classes</a> &#183;
   <a href="#grading">Grading</a> &#183;
   <a href="#app">Appointments</a> &#183;
   <a href="#safety">Safety</a>
</p>
```

3. Save your changes to the file.

4. Open **chem.htm** in your Web browser. The two new, external text links appear to the left of the four internal links, as shown in Figure 2-16.

Figure 2-16 ▶ Displaying links to other documents

links to other documents

Contact Info · Chemistry Links · Classes · Grading · Appointments · Safety

5. Click the **Contact Info** link to verify that the Contact page opens.

   Trouble? If the link doesn't work, check to see that chem.htm and contacts.htm are in the same folder on your Data Disk and that you've entered the HTML code correctly.

6. Go back to the Chemistry page (usually by clicking the Back button on your browser's toolbar), and then click **Chemistry Links** to verify that the Links page opens.

Next you'll need to add similar links in the contacts.htm and links.htm files that allow users to open the other two pages. In contacts.htm, this means adding links to the chem.htm and links.htm files; in links.htm you need to add links to the chem.htm and contacts.htm files. These links will complete the Web site's structure, allowing Stephen's students and their parents to open any page in the site, no matter what page they're on.

To add links in the Contact page to the Chemistry and Links pages:

1. Return to the **contacts.htm** file in your text editor.

2. Locate the first <hr /> tag in the document, near the top of the page, and then insert the following above it (as shown in Figure 2-17):

```
<p style="text-align: center">
   <a href="chem.htm">Home Page</a> &#183;
   <a href="links.htm">Chemistry Links</a>
</p>
```

Figure 2-17 ▶ Adding links to the contact.htm file

```
<p style="text-align: center">
   <img src="dube.jpg"
   alt="Mr. Dub&#233;'s Chemistry Classes at Robert Service High School" />
</p>

<p style="text-align: center">
   <a href="chem.htm">Home Page</a> &#183;
   <a href="links.htm">Chemistry Links</a>
</p>
```

3. Save your changes to the file.

4. Open **contacts.htm** in your Web browser. Your links should now look like Figure 2-18.

Links in the Contacts page ◀ **Figure 2-18**

Home Page · Chemistry Links

How to Contact Mr. Dubé

Office Hours

5. Test the two links to verify that the Chemistry and Links pages open.

Trouble? If the links do not work, check the spelling of the filenames in the href attributes of the <a> tags. Because some Web servers require you to match any capitalization in a filename, you should verify this in your attributes as well.

You need to follow similar steps for the Links page so that it links to the other two Web pages.

To add links in the Links page to the Chemistry and Contact pages:

1. Return to the **links.htm** file in your text editor.

2. Above the <hr /> tag near the top of the file, insert the following code (see Figure 2-19):

```
<p style="text-align: center">
    <a href="chem.htm">Home Page</a> &#183;
    <a href="contacts.htm">Contact Info</a>
</p>
```

Adding links to the links.htm file ◀ **Figure 2-19**

```
<p style="text-align: center">
    <img src="dube.jpg"
    alt="Mr. Dub&#233;'s Chemistry Classes at Robert Service High School" />
</p>

<p style="text-align: center">
    <a href="chem.htm">Home Page</a> &#183;
    <a href="contacts.htm">Contact Info</a>
</p>
```

3. Save your changes to the file.

4. Open the **links.htm** file in your Web browser. Your links should look like those shown in Figure 2-20.

| Figure 2-20 | Links on the Links page |

MR. DUBÉ'S CHEMISTRY CLASSES
AT
ROBERT SERVICE HIGH SCHOOL

Home Page · Contact Info

Helpful Links

Homework Aids

5. Verify that you can now move between the three Web pages by clicking the appropriate links.

Linking to a Location within another Document

Stephen also wants the contact and links pages to contain links to the various sections of the chemistry home page. The syntax for linking to a location within another document is

```
<a href="file#id">content</a>
```

where *file* is the filename of the document, *id* is the id or anchor name of the location in the document, and *content* is the document content to be changed into a link. The following sample code creates a link to the classes id or anchor within the chem.htm file:

```
<a href="chem.htm#classes">Classes</a>
```

Note that when you exclude the filename from a link reference, the browser looks for the location within the current document. You created this type of link in the last session.

To insert additional links into the contact and links documents:

1. Return to the **contacts.htm** file in your text editor.

2. At the end of the line containing the link for the chemistry links page, insert a space, followed by the symbol code **·**.

3. Press the **Enter** key and insert the following lines as shown in Figure 2-21:

```
<a href="chem.htm#classes">Classes</a> &#183;
<a href="chem.htm#grading">Grading</a> &#183;
<a href="chem.htm#app">Appointments</a> &#183;
<a href="chem.htm#safety">Safety</a>
```

| Figure 2-21 | Adding links to the contact.htm file |

links to locations in the chem.htm file

```
<p style="text-align: center">
    <a href="chem.htm">Home Page</a> &#183;
    <a href="links.htm">Chemistry Links</a> &#183;
    <a href="chem.htm#classes">Classes</a> &#183;
    <a href="chem.htm#grading">Grading</a> &#183;
    <a href="chem.htm#app">Appointments</a> &#183;
    <a href="chem.htm#safety">Safety</a>
</p>
```

4. Save your changes to the file and then reopen **contacts.htm** in your Web browser. Verify that the list of links appears as shown in Figure 2-22 and that the browser displays the appropriate target when you click each link.

Final link list for the Contacts page | **Figure 2-22**

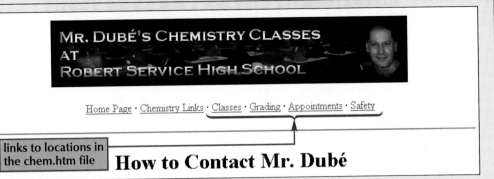

5. Go to the **links.htm** file in your text editor.

6. Enter the code indicated in Figure 2-23 (the same code you inserted into the contacts.htm file).

Adding links to the links.htm file | **Figure 2-23**

```
<p style="text-align: center">
   <a href="chem.htm">Home Page</a> &#183;
   <a href="contacts.htm">Contact Info</a>   &#183;
   <a href="chem.htm#classes">Classes</a> &#183;
   <a href="chem.htm#grading">Grading</a> &#183;
   <a href="chem.htm#app">Appointments</a> &#183;
   <a href="chem.htm#safety">Safety</a>
</p>
```

7. Save your changes to the file and reopen **links.htm** in your Web browser. Verify that the link list appears as shown in Figure 2-24 and that each link works appropriately.

Final link list for the Links page | **Figure 2-24**

8. If you are continuing on to Session 2.3, you can leave your browser and text editor open. Otherwise, you may close your files now.

Linking to Documents in Other Folders

So far, none of the links we have created have specified the location of the destination document. Browsers assume that if this information is not included, the destination document is located in the same folder as the document containing the link. However, these files are not always located in the same place. For instance, the files in a large Web site, which can number in the hundreds, are often organized into separate folders. To create a link to a file located in a different folder than the current document, you must specify the file's location, or **path**, so that browsers can find it. HTML supports two kinds of paths: absolute and relative.

Absolute Paths

An **absolute path** specifies a file's precise location within a computer's entire folder structure. Absolute pathnames employ the following syntax:

```
/folder1/folder2/folder3/... /file
```

where `folder1` is the topmost folder in the computer's folder tree, followed by `folder2`, `folder3`, and so forth, until you reach the file you want to link to.

Figure 2-25 shows a sample folder tree that might be used for the Web server at Stephen Dubé's school. In this case, the topmost folder in the tree is named faculty. The faculty folder contains a file named index.htm as well as two subfolders, named lee and dube. The lee folder contains a single file named bio.htm. The dube folder also contains a file named bio.htm, as well as a subfolder named class. The class folder contains the three files we've been working with in this session.

Figure 2-25	A sample folder tree

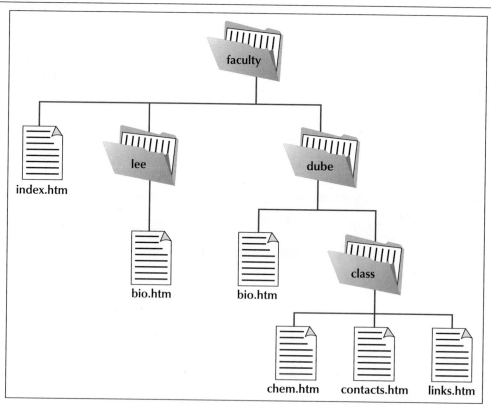

Folders aside, this tree contains six files. Figure 2-26 shows how we could express the absolute paths to each of these files.

Absolute paths in the sample folder tree | **Figure 2-26**

Absolute Path	Interpretation
/faculty/index.htm	The index.htm file in the faculty folder
/faculty/lee/bio.htm	The bio.htm file in the lee subfolder
/faculty/dube/bio.htm	The bio.htm file in the dube subfolder
/faculty/dube/class/chem.htm	The chem.htm file in the dube/class subfolder
/faculty/dube/class/contacts.htm	The contacts.htm file in the dube/class subfolder
/faculty/dube/class/links.htm	The links.htm file in the dube/class subfolder

If files are located on different drives as well as in different folders, you must include the drive letter as follows:

`/drive||/folder1/folder2/folder3/... /file`

where `drive` is the letter assigned to the drive. For example the chem.htm file located on drive C in the /faculty/dube/class folder would have the absolute path:

`/C|/faculty/dube/class/chem.htm`

Remember that you don't have to include a drive letter if the destination document is located on the same drive as the document containing the link.

Relative Paths

When many folders and subfolders are involved, absolute pathnames can be cumbersome and confusing. For that reason, most Web designers prefer to use relative paths. A **relative path** specifies a file's location in relation to the location of the current document. If the file is in the same folder as the current document, you do not specify the folder name. If the file is in a subfolder of the current document, you have to include the name of the subfolder (forward slash is not required) followed by the file name. If you want to go one level up the folder tree, you start the relative path with a double period (..) and then provide the name of the file. To specify a different folder on the same level, known as a **sibling folder**, you move up the folder tree using the double period (..) and then down the tree using the name of the sibling folder.

For example, Figure 2-27 shows the relative paths to the six files in the tree from Figure 2-25, starting from a file stored in the /faculty/dube folder.

Relative paths in the sample folder tree | **Figure 2-27**

Relative Path from the faculty/dube folder	Interpretation
../index.htm	The index.htm file in the parent folder
../lee/bio.htm	The bio.htm file in the lee sibling folder
bio.htm	The bio.htm file in the current folder
class/chem.htm	The chem.htm file in the class subfolder
class/contacts.htm	The contacts.htm file in the class subfolder
class/links.htm	The links.htm file in the class subfolder

You should almost always use relative paths in your links. If you have to move your files to a different computer or server, you can move the entire folder structure without having to change the relative pathnames you created. If you use absolute pathnames, however, you must revise each link to reflect the new location of the folder tree on the computer.

Changing the Base

As we've noted, a browser resolves relative pathnames by default based on the location of the current document. You can change this behavior by specifying a different base in the document's head. The syntax for specifying the base is:

```
<base href="path" />
```

where *path* is the folder location that you want the browser to use when resolving relative paths in the current document.

The base element is useful when a document is moved to a new folder. Rather than rewriting all of the relative paths to reflect the document's new location, the base element can redirect browsers to the document's old location, allowing any relative paths to be resolved as they were before. The base element is also useful when you want to create a copy of a single page from a large Web site on another Web server. Instead of copying the entire site to the new location, you can copy the one file, but have the base point to the location of the original site. Any links in the copied page will behave the same as the links in the original page.

You've completed your work creating links between the three files in Stephen's Web site. In the next session, you'll learn how to create links that point to documents and resources located on the Internet.

Review

Session 2.2 Quick Check

1. What is storyboarding? Why is it important in creating a Web page system?
2. What is a linear structure? What is a hierarchical structure?
3. What code would you enter to link the text, "Sports Info", to the sports.htm file? Assume that the current document and sports.htm are in the same folder.
4. What code would you enter to link the text, "Basketball news", to the location with the id or anchor name of "bball" within a different file named sports.htm?
5. What's the difference between an absolute path and a relative path?
6. Refer to Figure 2-25. If the current file is in the /faculty/lee folder, what are the relative paths for the six files listed in the folder tree?
7. What is the purpose of the <base />tag?

Session 2.3

Linking to Resources on the Internet

In the links.htm file, Stephen has listed the names of some Web sites that have proved useful for him and his students. He would like you to change these names into links, so that his students can quickly access those sites from their browsers.

Understanding URLs

To create a link to a resource on the Internet, you need to know its URL. A **URL**, or **Uniform Resource Locator**, specifies the precise location of a resource on the Internet. The general form of a URL is:

```
scheme:location
```

where *scheme* indicates the type of resource that the URL is referencing, and *location* is the location of that resource. For Web pages the location is a document stored in a folder on a Web server, but for other resources, the location could be an identifying name. For example, an e-mail URL would have a location pointing to an e-mail address.

The name of the scheme is taken from the protocol used to access the Internet resource. A **protocol** is a set of rules defining how information is exchanged between two devices. Your Web browser communicates with Web servers using the **Hypertext Transfer Protocol** or **HTTP**. Thus, the URLs for all Web pages must start with the scheme "http". This tells a browser to use http to communicate with the Web server you specify. Other Internet resources, described in Figure 2-28, use different protocols and thus have different scheme names.

Common communication protocols ◀ **Figure 2-28**

Protocol	Used to
file	access documents stored locally on a user's computer
ftp	access documents stored on an FTP server
gopher	access documents stored on a gopher server
http	access Web pages stored on the World Wide Web
mailto	open a user's e-mail client and address a new message
news	connect to a Usenet newsgroup
telnet	open a telnet connection to a specific server
wais	connect to a Wide Area Information Server database

Linking to a Web Page

The URL for a Web page has the general form:

```
http://server/path/filename#id
```

where *server* is the name of the Web server storing a specific file, *path* is the path to the file on that server, *filename* is the name of file, and if necessary, *id* is the name of an id or anchor within the file. A Web page URL can also contain specific programming instructions for a browser to send to the Web server, but we won't deal with that topic here. Figure 2-29 shows the URL for a sample Web page with all of the parts identified.

A sample URL for a Web page ◀ **Figure 2-29**

http ://www.mwu.edu /course/info.html #majors
protocol | server | path | filename | id or anchor name

You may have noticed that a URL like http://www.course.com doesn't include any path or file name. If a URL includes no path, then it indicates the topmost folder in the server's directory tree. If a URL does not specify a filename, the server searches for a file named "index.html" or "index.htm" in the specified location. This file is often the Web site's home page. Thus, a URL like http://www.course.com is equivalent to http://www.course.com/index.html.

Stephen has listed six Web pages that he wants students to be able to access. He's provided you with the URLs for these pages, which are shown in Figure 2-30.

Figure 2-30 ▷ Links to chemistry sites on the Web

Site	URL
Carnegie Library	http://www.carnegielibrary.org/subject/homework
Discovery Schools	http://school.discovery.com
Frostburg State	http://antoine.frostburg.edu/chem/senese/101
Yahoo	http://dir.yahoo.com/Science/chemistry
Los Alamos	http://pearl1.lanl.gov/periodic
Visual Elements	http://www.chemsoc.org/viselements

To link to these Web pages, you specify each URL as the href attribute value for the appropriate <a> tag as follows:

```
<a href="http://school.discovery.com">Discovery Schools</a>
```

Use the information that Stephen has given you to create links to all six of the Web sites listed in Figure 2-30.

To add links to the Chemistry Links page:

▶ 1. If necessary, use your text editor to reopen the **links.htm** file from the tutorial.02/tutorial folder.

▶ 2. Locate the text "Carnegie Library" and insert the following link:

```
<a href="http://www.carnegielibrary.org/subject/homework">
   Carnegie Library
</a>
```

▶ 3. Locate "Discovery Schools" and insert the link:

```
<a href="http://school.discovery.com ">
   Discovery Schools
</a>
```

▶ 4. Locate "Frostburg State" and insert the link:

```
<a href="http://antoine.frostburg.edu/chem/senese/101">
   Frostburg State
</a>
```

▶ 5. Locate "Yahoo" and insert the link:

```
<a href="http://dir.yahoo.com/Science/chemistry">
   Yahoo
</a>
```

▶ 6. Locate "Los Alamos" and insert the link:

```
<a href="http://pearl1.lanl.gov/periodic">
   Los Alamos
</a>
```

▶ 7. Locate "Visual Elements" and insert the link:

```
<a href="http://www.chemsoc.org/viselements">
   Visual Elements
</a>
```

Figure 2-31 shows the revised code.

```
<blockquote><p>
<b><a href="http://www.carnegielibrary.org/subject/homework">Carnegie Library</a></b>:
Homework resources from the Carnegie Library of Pittsburgh.</p></blockquote>

<blockquote><p>
<b><a href="http://school.discovery.com">Discovery Schools</a></b>:
Get homework help from the school sponsored by the Discovery Channel.</p></blockquote>

<h2>Chemistry Resources</h2>

<blockquote><p>
<b><a href="http://antoine.frostburg.edu/chem/senese/101">Frostburg State</a></b>:
View articles, tutorials, and online quizzes from the chemistry
department at Frostburg State University in Maryland.</p></blockquote>

<blockquote><p>
<b><a href="http://dir.yahoo.com/Science/chemistry">Yahoo</a></b>:
Yahoo's list of chemistry resources on the web.</p></blockquote>

<h2>The Periodic Table</h2>

<blockquote><p>
<b><a href="http://pearl1.lanl.gov/periodic">Los Alamos</a></b>:
An interactive periodic table of the elements presented by the
National Laboratory's Chemistry Division at Los Alamos.</p></blockquote>

<blockquote><p>
<b><a href="http://www.chemsoc.org/viselements">Visual Elements</a></b>:
A stunning visual representation of the periodic table by the
RSC's chemical science network.</p></blockquote>
```

► **8.** Save your changes to the file.

► **9.** Reload **links.htm** in your Web browser. Figure 2-32 shows the revised appearance of the page. Click each of the links in the page and verify that the appropriate Web site opens.

MR. DUBÉ'S CHEMISTRY CLASSES AT ROBERT SERVICE HIGH SCHOOL

Home Page · Contact Info · Classes · Grading · Appointments · Safety

Helpful Links

Homework Aids

Carnegie Library: Homework resources from the Carnegie Library of Pittsburgh.

Discovery Schools: Get homework help from the school sponsored by the Discovery Channel.

Chemistry Resources

Frostburg State: View articles, tutorials, and online quizzes from the chemistry department at Frostburg State University in Maryland.

Yahoo: Yahoo's list of chemistry resources on the Web.

The Periodic Table

Los Alamos: An interactive periodic table of the elements presented by the National Laboratory's Chemistry Division at Los Alamos.

Visual Elements: A stunning visual representation of the periodic table by the RSC's chemical science network.

1

Trouble? To open these sites you must be connected to the Internet. If you are still having problems, compare your code to the URLs listed in Figure 2-30 to confirm that you have not made a typing error. Also keep in mind that because the Web is constantly changing, the URLs for some of these links may have changed, or a site may have disappeared entirely since this book was printed.

Web pages are only one type of resource that you can link to. Before continuing work on the chemistry Web site, let's explore how to access some of these other resources.

Linking to FTP Servers

FTP servers are one of the main resources for storing files on the Internet. FTP servers transfer information using a communications protocol called **File Transfer Protocol**, or **FTP** for short. The URL for a file stored on an FTP server follows the general format:

```
ftp://server/path/filename
```

where `server` is the name of the FTP server, `path` is the folder path on the server, and `filename` is the name of the file you want to retrieve. If you omit the path and filename information, your Web browser will likely display the folders contained on the FTP server, which you can then navigate to download the file or files of interest (see Figure 2-33). Note that different browsers can display the contents of an FTP site in different ways. Figure 2-33 shows what a site might look like in Internet Explorer.

| Figure 2-33 | An FTP site as it appears in Internet Explorer |

An FTP server requires each user to enter a password and a username to access its files. The standard username is "anonymous", which requires no password. Your browser supplies this information for you automatically, so in most situations you don't have to worry about passwords and usernames. However, some FTP servers do not allow anonymous access. In these cases, either your browser prompts you for the username and the password, or you can supply a username and password within the URL using the following format:

```
ftp://username:password@hostname/path/filename
```

where *username* and *password* are a username and password that the FTP server recognizes. It is generally *not* a good idea, however, to include usernames and passwords in URLs, as it can allow others to view your sensitive login information. It's better to let the browser send this information, or use a special program called an **FTP client**, because those programs can encrypt or hide this information during transmission.

Linking to Usenet News

Usenet is a collection of discussion forums called **newsgroups** that let users publicly exchange messages with each other on a wide variety of topics. The URL for a Usenet newsgroup has the form:

```
news:newsgroup
```

where *newsgroup* is the name of the group you want to access. For example, to access the surfing newsgroup alt.surfing, you would use the URL news:alt.surfing. When you click a link to a newsgroup, your computer opens a program for reading newsgroups, known as a **newsreader**, displaying the latest messages from the newsgroup. Figure 2-34 shows the contents of the alt.surfing newsgroup as displayed by the Outlook Express newsreader.

A sample newsreader ◄ **Figure 2-34**

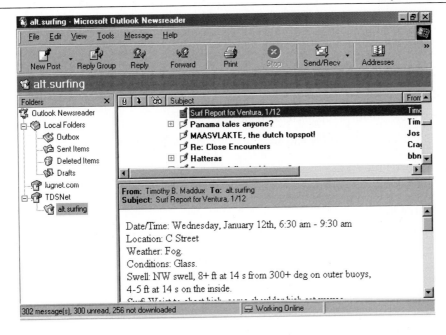

Linking to a Local File

On occasion, you may see the URL for a file stored locally on your computer or local area network. The form of this URL is:

```
file://server/path/filename
```

where *server* is the name of the local server, *path* is the path on that server to the file, and *filename* is the name of the file. This form is rarely used in Web pages, but it might appear in the address toolbar of your browser if you attempt to load a page off of your computer or LAN. If you're accessing a file from your own computer, the server name might be omitted and replaced by an extra slash (/). Thus, a file from the documents/chemistry folder might have the URL:

```
file:///documents/chemistry/chem.htm
```

If the file is on a different disk within your computer, the hard drive letter would be included in the URL as follows:

```
file://D:/documents/chemistry/chem.htm
```

Unlike the other URLs we've examined, the "file" scheme in this URL does not imply any particular communication protocol; instead, the browser retrieves the document using whatever method is the local standard for the type of file specified in the URL.

Linking to E-mail

Many Web sites use e-mail to allow users to communicate with a site's owner, or with the staff of the organization that runs the site. You can turn an e-mail address into a link, so that when a user clicks an address, the browser starts an e-mail program and automatically inserts the address into the "To" field of a new outgoing message. The URL for an e-mail address follows the form:

```
mailto:address
```

where *address* is the e-mail address. While the mailto: protocol is not technically an approved communication protocol, it is so widely supported that you should have no problem using it.

Stephen wants you to add to a link to his e-mail address on the chemistry Web site. Students and their parents can use this link to quickly send him messages about his classes. Format the e-mail address on Stephen's Contact page as a link.

To add an e-mail link to Stephen's Contact page:

1. Using your text editor, open **contacts.htm**.
2. Go to the bottom of the file and add the following link to the e-mail address, as shown in Figure 2-35.

   ```
   <a href="mailto:sdube@eps.edmonton.ab.ca">sdube@eps.edmonton.ab.ca</a>.
   ```

Figure 2-35	Creating an e-mail link

```
<h2>E-mail</h2>
<p>E-mail is a great way to reach me. I answer e-mails from students
and parents within one school day of receiving the e-mail.
My address is :</p>

<blockquote><p>
<a href="mailto:sdube@eps.edmonton.ab.ca">sdube@eps.edmonton.ab.ca</a>.
</p></blockquote>
```

3. Save your changes to the file.
4. Using your Web browser, open **contacts.htm**.
5. Scroll to the bottom of the page and verify that the e-mail address is now displayed as a link (see Figure 2-36).

Figure 2-36	E-mail link in the Contact page

E-mail

E-mail is a great way to reach me. I answer e-mails from students and parents within one school day of receiving the e-mail. My address is :

e-mail link → sdube@eps.edmonton.ab.ca

Trouble? Some browsers do not support the mailto: URL. If you use a browser other than Netscape Navigator or Internet Explorer, check to see if it supports this feature.

6. Click the e-mail address and verify that an e-mail message window, similar to the one in Figure 2-37, opens.

Testing the e-mail link   **Figure 2-37**

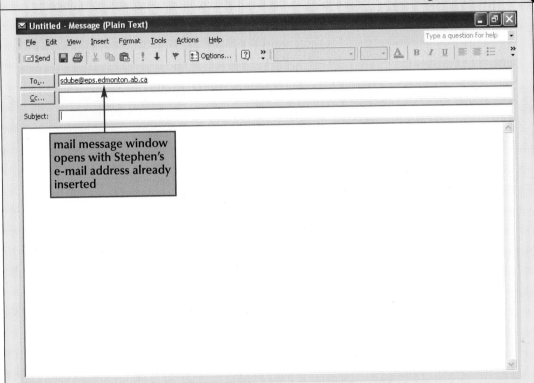

mail message window
opens with Stephen's
e-mail address already
inserted

Trouble? Your e-mail window may look different, depending on the mail program you are using.

7. Cancel the mail message by clicking the window's Close button. This e-mail address is a fictional one for illustration purposes only.

You should be aware that there are problems with placing an e-mail link in a Web page. A user may not know how to use an e-mail client, or a user's browser may open the wrong e-mail client when the user clicks the link.

Of more concern is the effect of e-mail links on increasing spam. **Spam** is unsolicited junk e-mail sent to large numbers of people, promoting products, services and in some cases, pornographic Web sites. Spammers create their e-mail lists through scanning Usenet postings, stealing Internet mailing lists, and using programs called **e-mail harvesters** that scan HTML code on the Web looking for the e-mail addresses contained in mailto URLs. Many Web developers are removing e-mail links from their Web sites in order to foil these harvesters, replacing the links with Web forms that submit e-mail requests to a secure server. If you need to include an e-mail address in your Web page, you can take a few steps to reduce problems with spam:

- Replace all e-mail addresses in your page text with inline images of those addresses.
- Write a program in a language like JavaScript to scramble any e-mail addresses in the HTML code. Users can then run the program to unscramble those addresses.

- Replace the characters of the e-mail address with character codes. You can replace the "@" symbol with the code @ replace blank spaces with the code   and so forth.
- Replace characters with words in your Web page's text—for example, replace the "@" symbol with the word "at".

There is no quick and easy solution to this problem. Fighting spammers is an ongoing battle and they have proved very resourceful in overcoming some of the traps people have written for e-mail harvesters. As you develop your Web site, you should carefully consider how you wish to handle e-mail and review the most current methods for safeguarding that information.

Reference Window	**Linking to Different Resources**

- The URL for a Web page has the form:
    ```
    http://server/path/filename#id
    ```
  where *server* is the name of the Web server, *path* is the path to a file on that the server, *filename* is the name of the file, and if necessary, *id* is the name of an id or anchor within the file.
- The URL for a FTP site has the form:
    ```
    ftp://server/path/filename
    ```
  where *server* is the name of the FTP server, *path* is the folder path, and *filename* is the name of the file.
- The URL for a Usenet newsgroup has the form:
    ```
    news:newsgroup
    ```
  where *newsgroup* is the name of the Usenet group.
- The URL for an e-mail address has the form:
    ```
    mailto:address
    ```
  where *address* is the e-mail address.
- The URL to reference a local file on your computer is:
    ```
    file://server/path/filename
    ```
  where *server* is the name of the local server or computer, *path* is the path to the file on that server, and *filename* is the name of the file. If you are accessing a file on your own computer, the server name would be replaced by another slash (/).

Working with Hypertext Attributes

HTML provides several attributes to control the behavior and appearance of your links. Let's study a few of these to see whether they would be effective in Stephen's Web site.

Opening a Secondary Window

By default, each new page you open replaces the contents of the previous page in the browser window. This means that when Stephen's students click on the six external links listed on the links page, they leave the chemistry Web site. To return to the chemistry Web site, a student would have to click their browser's Back button.

Stephen would prefer that the contents of his Web site stay open in the original browser window, and that any links to external Web sites be displayed in a second window. This arrangement would allow students and parents continued access to his chemistry Web site, even as they're browsing other sites.

To force a document to appear in a new window, you add the target attribute to the `<a>` tag. The general syntax is:

```
<a href="url" target="window">content</a>
```

where *window* is a name assigned to the new browser window. The value you use for the target attribute doesn't affect the appearance or content of the window; it's simply used by the browser to identify the different browser windows currently open. You can choose any name you wish for the target. If several links have the same target name, they all open in the same window, replacing the window's previous content. HTML also supports several special target names, described in Figure 2-38.

Target names for browser windows ◀ **Figure 2-38**

Target Name	Description
"*target*"	Opens the link in a new window named *target*
"_blank"	Opens the link in a new, unnamed, window
"_self"	Opens the link in the current browser window

Stephen suggests that all of the external links be opened in a browser window identified with the name "new".

To specify a target window for a link:

1. Return to the **links.htm** file in your text editor.

2. Locate the six links you created earlier that point to external sites. Within each of the six links, add the attribute **target="new"** as shown in Figure 2-39.

Adding a target to a link ◀ **Figure 2-39**

```
<blockquote><p>
<b><a href="http://www.carnegielibrary.org/subject/homework" target="new">Carnegie Library</a></b>:
Homework resources from the Carnegie Library of Pittsburgh. </p></blockquote>

<blockquote><p>
<b><a href="http://school.discovery.com" target="new">Discovery Schools</a></b>:
Get homework help from the school sponsored by the Discovery Channel. </p></blockquote>

<h2>Chemistry Resources</h2>

<blockquote><p>
<b><a href="http://antoine.frostburg.edu/chem/senese/101" target="new">Frostburg State</a></b>:
View articles, tutorials, and online quizzes from the chemistry
department at Frostburg State University in Maryland. </p></blockquote>

<blockquote><p>
<b><a href="http://dir.yahoo.com/Science/chemistry" target="new">Yahoo</a></b>:
Yahoo's list of chemistry resources on the web. </p></blockquote>

<h2>The Periodic Table</h2>

<blockquote><p>
<b><a href="http://pearl1.lanl.gov/periodic" target="new">Los Alamos</a></b>:
An interactive periodic table of the elements presented by the
National Laboratory's Chemistry Division at Los Alamos. </p></blockquote>

<blockquote><p>
<b><a href="http://www.chemsoc.org/viselements" target="new">Visual Elements</a></b>:
A stunning visual representation of the periodic table by the
RSC's chemical science network. </p></blockquote>
```

3. Save your changes to the file.

4. Reopen **links.htm** in your Web browser. Click each of the six external links and verify that the external sites all open within the same secondary window.

If you want all of the links in your document to point to a new window, you can add the target attribute to the <base /> tag in the document's header. The target name you specify will be applied to all of the Web page's links. You should use the target attribute sparingly in your Web site. Creating secondary windows can clog up the user's desktop and because the page is placed in a new window, users cannot use the Back button to return to the previous page in that window. This may confuse some users and annoy others. Note that the target attribute is not supported in strict XHTML-compliant code.

Creating a Popup Title

If you want to provide additional information to your users, you can add a popup title to your links. A **popup title** is descriptive text that appears whenever a user positions the mouse pointer over a link. Figure 2-40 shows an example of a popup title applied to one of the links in the chemistry Web site.

Figure 2-40 | Adding a popup title to a link

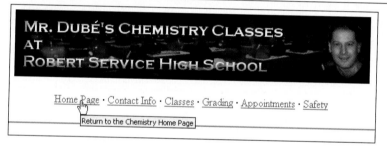

To create the popup title, add the title attribute to the <a> tag as follows:

```
<a href="url" title="text">Element</a>
```

where *text* is the text that appears in the popup title. To create the popup title shown in Figure 2-40, you would enter the HTML code:

```
<a href="chem.htm" title="Return to the Chemistry Home Page">
   Home Page
</a>
```

Note that since only some browsers support this feature, you should not place crucial information in the popup title.

Creating an Access Key

So far we've assumed that you click a link to activate it. Another way to activate a link is to assign a keyboard key, called an **access key**, to the link. The syntax for creating an access key is:

```
<a href="url" accesskey="char">Element</a>
```

where *char* is a single keyboard character. To use an access key you hold down an **accelerator key** (usually the Alt key in Windows or the Ctrl key on a Macintosh) and then press the specified access key. For example, if you modify the chem.htm link as follows:

```
<a href="chem.htm" accesskey="i">Home Page</a>
```

you can activate this link by pressing Alt+i (in Windows) or Ctrl+i (on a Macintosh). Access keys sound like a good idea, but they've proved to be impractical in most situations. One problem is that most access keys are already reserved by the browser. For example you can't use the "f" key because the browser uses it to access the File menu. In addition, it is difficult to indicate to the user which access key to press in order to activate a given link. The usual practice is to underline the access key in the Web page; however, by convention, underlining is reserved for indicating links.

Creating a Semantic Link

Two attributes, rel and rev, allow you to specify the relationship between a link and its destination. The rel attribute describes the contents of the destination document. For example, if Stephen wanted to link to a glossary of chemistry terms, he could insert the following link into his Web page:

```
<a href="terms.htm" rel="glossary">Chemistry Glossary</a>
```

The rev attribute complements the rel attribute: rev describes the contents of the source document as viewed from the destination document's perspective. For example, to go from the chemistry home page to the glossary, we might include the following rev attribute to describe where the user is coming from:

```
<a href="terms.htm" rel="glossary" rev="home">Chemistry Glossary</a>
```

Links containing the rel and rev attributes are called **semantic links** because the tag contains information about the relationship between the link and its destination. This information is not designed for the user, but rather for the browser. A browser can use the information that these attributes provide in many ways—for example, to build a custom toolbar containing a list of links specific to the page being viewed. Few browsers currently take advantage of these attributes, but future browsers may do so.

While rel and rev are not limited to a fixed set of attribute values, the specifications for HTML and XHTML include a proposed list of rel and rev names. Figure 2-41 shows some of these proposed relationship values.

Link types ◀ **Figure 2-41**

Link Types	Description
alternate	References a substitute version of the current document, perhaps in a different language or in a different medium
stylesheet	References an external style sheet
start	References the first document in a collection of documents
next	References the next document in a linear sequence of documents
prev	References the previous document in a linear sequence of documents
contents	References a table of contents
index	References an index
glossary	References a glossary
appendix	References an appendix
copyright	References a copyright statement
chapter	References a document serving as a chapter in a collection of documents
section	References a document serving as a section in a collection of documents
subsection	References a document serving as a subsection in a collection of documents
help	References a Help document
bookmark	References a bookmark

Using the Link Element

Another way to add a link to your document is to add a link element to the document's head. Link elements are created using the one-sided tag

```
<link href="url" rel="text" rev="text" target="window" />
```

where the href, rel, rev, and target attributes serve the same purpose as in the <a> tag. Link elements are intended only for the browser's use. Because they are placed within a document's head, they do not appear in the browser window. A document head can contain several link elements.

Link elements have primarily been used to connect to style sheets. Browsers have only recently started using them for other purposes. For example, the Opera browser uses link elements to generate custom toolbars containing links based on the document's relationships. Figure 2-42 shows how Opera interprets some <link /> tags to create such a toolbar.

Figure 2-42	Using link elements

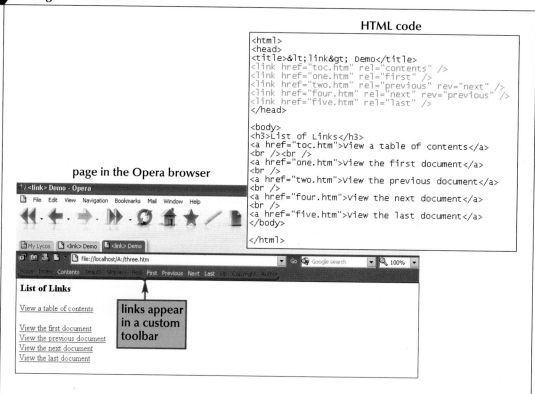

HTML code

```
<html>
<head>
<title>&lt;link&gt; Demo</title>
<link href="toc.htm" rel="contents" />
<link href="one.htm" rel="first" />
<link href="two.htm" rel="previous" rev="next" />
<link href="four.htm" rel="next" rev="previous" />
<link href="five.htm" rel="last" />
</head>

<body>
<h3>List of Links</h3>
<a href="toc.htm">View a table of contents</a>
<br /><br />
<a href="one.htm">View the first document</a>
<br />
<a href="two.htm">View the previous document</a>
<br />
<a href="four.htm">View the next document</a>
<br />
<a href="five.htm">View the last document</a>
</body>

</html>
```

page in the Opera browser

links appear in a custom toolbar

Because no single list of relationship names is widely accepted, you must check with each browser's documentation to find out what relationship names it supports. Until this use of link elements becomes widely embraced, you should not place important links in a link element unless you duplicate that information elsewhere in the page.

Reference Window

Creating a Link Element

- To create a link element, add the following tag to the document head:
  ```
  <link href="url" rel="text" rev="text" target="window" />
  ```
  where the href, rel, rev, and target attributes all serve the same purpose that they do in the <a> tag.

You show Stephen the final versions of the three Web pages you have been collaborating on. He's pleased with the results. You explain to him that the next step is to contact the school's Information Technology Department to place his site on the school's Web server. When that's done, Stephen's Web site will be available online to anyone with Internet access. You can now close any open files or editors.

Tips for Creating Effective Links

- Storyboard your Web site before you create it.
- Make sure that users can easily navigate your site by linking each page to the site's home page and a page containing a site index.
- Avoid using text like "click here" in your links. Make sure your linked text describes what the destination contains.
- Never place two links immediately adjacent to one another; separate them with text or extra spaces or a symbol.
- Avoid long pages; instead break up each page into a sequence of linked pages.
- If you do create a long page, create links to different sections of the page. Include links throughout the page that users can click to jump to the top of the page.
- Use only lowercase filenames for all of your documents.
- Use anchors if you need your internal document links to work with older browsers.
- Use care when inserting an e-mail link or address into a Web page. Research the latest tools and traps to thwart e-mail harvesters and spammers.

Review

Session 2.3 Quick Check

1. What are the five parts of a URL?
2. What tag would you enter to link the text "White House" to the URL http://www.whitehouse.gov, with the destination document displayed in a new unnamed browser window?
3. What tag would you enter to link the text "Washington" to the FTP server at ftp.uwash.edu?
4. What tag would you enter to link the text "Boxing" to the newsgroup rec.sports.boxing.pro?
5. What tag would you enter to link the text "President" to the e-mail address president@whitehouse.gov?
6. What attribute would you add to display the popup title, "Glossary of chemistry terms"?
7. What attribute would you add to a link specifying that the destination is the next page in a linear sequence of documents?
8. What tag would you add to a document's head to create a link to the file "toc.htm"? Include information telling the browser that the current document is a chapter document and the link's destination is a table of contents.

Review

Tutorial Summary

In this tutorial, you learned how to create and use links. You first saw how to create links within a single document. You learned two ways of marking a location within a document: using ids and using anchors. In the second session, you practiced creating links between documents within a Web site. The session also discussed how to build effective Web site structures and emphasized the importance of storyboarding. You also learned how to reference files in different folders using relative and absolute paths. The third session showed how to connect to different resources on the Internet, including Web pages, FTP servers, newsgroups, and e-mail addresses. The session also discussed how to use HTML attributes to open links in new windows, display popup titles, create access keys, and specify link relationships. The tutorial concluded with a presentation of the link element.

Key Terms

absolute path	FTP server	protocol
accelerator key	hierarchical structure	relative path
access key	HTTP	semantic link
anchor element	Hypertext Transfer Protocol	sibling folder
augmented linear structure	linear structure	site index
destination	link	spam
e-mail harvester	newsgroup	storyboard
File Transfer Protocol	newsreader	Uniform Resource Locator
FTP	path	URL
FTP client	popup title	Usenet

Practice

Practice the skills you learned in the tutorial using the same case scenario.

Review Assignments

Data files needed for this Review Assignment: chemtxt.htm, conttxt.htm, glosstxt.htm, linkstxt.htm, logo.jpg

Stephen has had some more work done on the chemistry Web site, including the following modifications:

- The contacts page includes a new contact for the lab assistant, Karen Cole.
- The links page contains two new Internet resources for students to explore.
- The site includes a new page, which contains a glossary of chemistry terms.

The new glossary page is very long, so Stephen wants to add a linked list of the letters of the alphabet at the top of the page so that users can click a letter to jump to the entries starting with that letter. Because of the page's length, Stephen also wants to add links that students can click to jump back to the top of the page. Figure 2-43 shows a preview of part of the completed glossary page.

Figure 2-43

MR. DUBÉ'S CHEMISTRY CLASSES
AT
ROBERT SERVICE HIGH SCHOOL

Home · Contacts · Resources · Classes · Grading · Appointments · Safety

Glossary of Chemical Terms

[A] [B] [C] [D] [E] [F] [G] [H] [I] [J] [K] [L] [M] [N] [O] [P] [Q] [R] [S] [T] [U] [V] [W] [X] [Y] [Z]

A

acid
Compound that gives off H^+ ions in solution.
acidic
Describes a solution with a high concentration of H^+ ions.
anion
Ions with a negative charge
anode
The electrode where electrons are lost (oxidized) in redox reactions.
atmospheres
Common units for measuring pressure.
atom
The smallest object that retains properties of an element. Composed of electrons and a nucleus (containing protons and neutrons).
atomic number
Number of protons in an element.
Avagadro's number
Number representing the number of molecules in one (1) mole: $6.023 * 10^{23}$.

Return to Top

B

base
Substance which gives off hydroxide ions (OH^-) in solution.

To complete these changes:

1. Use your text editor to open **chemtxt.htm** located in the tutorial.02/review folder. Save the file as **chem.htm** to the same folder. Insert *your name* and *the date* in the comment tag at the top of the file.

2. After the Safety link at the top of the page, insert the text, "Glossary", linked to the file glossary.htm. Be sure to separate this link from the Safety link using a middle dot. Close the **chem.htm** file, saving your changes.

3. Open **conttxt.htm** in your text editor, saving it as **contacts.htm**. Enter *your name* and *the date* in the comment tag at the top of the file.

4. As you did in the chem.htm file, insert a link to the glossary.htm file after the Safety link at the top of the page.

5. Change Karen Cole's e-mail address into a link.

6. Close **contacts.htm**, saving your changes.

7. Open **linkstxt.htm** in your text editor, saving it as **links.htm**. Enter *your name* and *the date* in the comment tag.

8. Insert a link to the glossary.htm file after the Safety link at the top of the page.

9. At the bottom of the file, change the text "collegeboard.com" into a link pointing to the URL **www.collegeboard.com/student/testing/ap/subjects.html** and opening in a window named "new".

10. Close **links.htm**, saving your changes.

11. Open **glosstxt.htm** in your text editor, saving it as **glossary.htm**. Enter *your name* and *the date* in the comment tag.

12. Change the entries in the topic list at the top of the page into links pointing to the appropriate documents and document sections in the chemistry Web site. (*Hint:* Use the other files in this Web site as examples.)

13. Assign the first paragraph on this page (the one containing the inline image) the id name "top".

14. Locate the h2 headings containing the letters of the alphabet. Assign each heading a lowercase id name equal to the letter. For example the "A" heading should have an id name of "a" and so forth.

15. Locate the occurrences of the text, "Return to Top". Change this text to a link pointing to the element with the id name, "top".

16. Go to the letter list at the top of the page. Change each letter to a link pointing to the heading containing the appropriate id element in the document. Note that some letters do not have corresponding headings in the document. You do not have to change these letters into links.

17. Close **glossary.htm**, saving your changes.

18. Open **chem.htm** in your Web browser. Verify that you can navigate the entire Web site by clicking the appropriate list. Verify that you can move up and down the sections of the glossary page by clicking the letter links and the "Return to Top" links.

19. Submit the completed Web site to your instructor.

Apply

Use the skills you have learned to create a Web page listing government Web sites.

Case Problem 1

Data files needed for this Case Problem: links.txt, mpllogo.jpg, mpltxt.htm

Monroe Public Library You've recently been hired by the Monroe Public Library of Monroe, Iowa. The MPL is currently setting up Internet kiosks with computers linked to the World Wide Web. Monica Vinson, who is in charge of this project, has asked you to work on developing some Web pages for the kiosks. Your first task is to create a Web page containing links to various government Web sites. Monica has given you a text file containing the URLs of 19 executive, legislative, and judicial sites. She's also created the Web page, but without the links. Monica wants you to add the links to the page. She would like the links to open in a secondary browser window, so that the MPL Web page remains available to users in the original window. Figure 2-44 shows a preview of the finished page.

Figure 2-44

Government Sites on the Web

Executive Branch   Legislative Branch   Judicial Branch

Executive Branch

The White House
Department of Agriculture
Department of Commerce
Department of Defense
Department of Education
Department of Energy
Department of Health and Human Services
Department of Housing and Urban Development
Department of the Interior
Department of Justice
Department of Labor
Department of State
Department of the Treasury

Legislative Branch

House Web
Senate Web
Congressional Quarterly

Judicial Branch

U.S. Courts
U.S. Supreme Court
U.S. Courts of Appeals
U.S. District Courts

Monroe Public Library · 2005 Main Street · Monroe, IA 68915 · (814) 555-3487

To complete this task:

1. Use your text editor open the file **mpltxt.htm** from the tutorial.02/case1 folder. Save the file as **mpl.htm**. Enter *your name* and *the date* in the comment tag at the top of the file.

2. Open the **links.txt** file in your text editor.

3. Convert each of the government sites listed in the mpl.htm file to a link using the URLs listed in the links.txt file. (*Hint*: Use the copy and paste feature of your text editor to copy the URLs from the list.txt file into the mpl.htm file).

Explore

4. Add a <base /> tag to the head of the mpl.htm file, specifying that all links in this page will, by default, open in a secondary window with the target name, "window2".

5. Add the id names "eb", "lb", and "jb" to the h2 headings Executive Branch, Legislative Branch, and Judicial Branch, respectively.

6. Link the list of branches at the top of the page to the headings.

Explore

7. For each of the three linked branches listed at the top of the page, change the target to "_self" so that these links open in the same browser window rather than in a secondary window.

8. Save your changes to **mpl.htm**.

9. Open **mpl.htm** in your Web browser. Test each of the links, verifying that each of the government sites opens in the same window (*Hint*: Change the size of the main browser window and the secondary window so that you can view each on your desktop at the same time). Verify that the links to the different sections of the document display those sections in the main browser window.

10. Submit the completed Web site to your instructor.

Explore

Broaden your knowledge and test your skills by exploring how to use inline images as links in a music history Web site.

Case Problem 2

Data files needed for this Case Problem: b9m1.jpg, b9m2.jpg, b9m3.jpg, b9m4.jpg, blank.jpg, hometxt.htm, glosstxt.htm, left.jpg, lvb.jpg, m1txt.htm, m2txt.htm, m3txt.htm, m4txt.htm, right.jpg

Western College for the Arts You're a graduate assistant in the Department of Music at Western College for the Arts. Professor Lysander Coe has asked your help in developing a Web site for his course on sonata forms. He is working on a presentation of Beethoven's Ninth Symphony and needs assistance in creating the links between the various pages in the site. The site will contain six pages: a home page, a glossary, and four pages describing each of the four movements of the Ninth Symphony. Professor Coe would like students to be able to navigate forward and backward through the movement pages, and to be able to jump to the site's home page and glossary at any time. He is also interested in using inline images as links to enhance the visual appearance of the site. Finally, the university is looking toward using more semantic links in their Web pages, so Professor Coe would like you to add semantic links to his Web site. Figure 2-45 shows a preview of one of the completed pages in the site you'll create.

Figure 2-45

Beethoven's Ninth Symphony

Home Page   Glossary

III. Third Movement

Adagio molto e cantabile (Very slow and singing)

A. A-Section
B. B-Section
C. A-Section varied
D. B-Section
E. Interlude
F. A-Section varied
G. Coda

Overview

The third movement represents a departure from the struggles of the first two movements; but it does not cancel the need to resolve the conflicts presented so far. However, there are the first hints of the resolution to come in the fourth movement.

Beethoven begins this movement with a variation on the Devotion theme, which will prove to be increasingly important as the symphony continues. In introducing the Devotion theme, Beethoven employs a technique known as *diminution* in which each melody note is replaced by several notes in smaller values. Beethoven unexpectedly fragments the theme in an interlude started by a clarinet and then imitated by the horn.

To complete the Web site:

1. Use your text editor to open the **hometxt.htm**, **glosstxt.htm**, **m1txt.htm**, **m2txt.htm**, **m3txt.htm**, and **m4txt.htm** files from the tutorial.02/case2 folder. Enter *your name* and *the date* in the comment tag at the top of each file. Save these files as: **b9home.htm**, **b9gloss.htm**, **b9m1.htm**, **b9m2.htm**, **b9m3.htm**, and **b9m4.htm** respectively.

2. Within the **b9home.htm** file, link the list entries First Movement, Second Movement, Third Movement, and Fourth Movement to the b9m1.htm, b9m2.htm, b9m3.htm, and b9m4.htm files. Link "Glossary" to the b9gloss.htm file.

Explore

3. Within the head element, add a link element pointing to the file b9gloss.htm. Add the rel attribute to the link with a value indicating that b9gloss.htm is a glossary.

4. Go to the file **b9gloss.htm**, and change the text "Home Page" to a link pointing to b9home.htm. Add a link element to the document's head referencing the home page. Use the rel attribute to specify that this link points to a chapter document.

5. Go to the file **b9m1.htm**. This file contains information about the symphony's first movement. Change the entries "Home Page" and "Glossary" into links pointing to the files b9home.htm and b9gloss.htm. Also add semantic link information to the document heading. Use the rel attribute to indicate that these links point to a chapter and a glossary page, respectively. Create two additional link elements: "next" pointing to b9m2.htm (the second movement) and "last" pointing to b9m4.htm (the last movement).

Explore

6. Locate the code for the inline image right.jpg. Link this image to the file b9m2.htm. Because browsers surround linked images with a blue or purple border by default, add the attribute style="border-width:0" to the <img /> tag to remove the border.

7. Within the file **b9m2.htm**, change "Home Page" and "Glossary" into links. Add link elements to the document head that point to the home and glossary pages, as well as the first movement in the symphony, the last movement, the previous movement, and the next movement. Add rel attributes to all of these link elements. Link the inline image left.jpg to the file b9m1.htm. Link right.jpg to the file b9m3.htm. Be sure to use the border-width style to hide the borders around these images.

8. Within the file **b9m3.htm**, change "Home Page" and "Glossary" into links. Add link elements to the document head that point to the home page, glossary, first movement, last movement, previous movement, and next movement. Link the image left.jpg to b9m2.htm. Link the image right.jpg to b9m4.htm.

9. Within the file **b9m4.htm**, change "Home Page" and "Glossary" into links. Add link elements to the document head pointing to the home page, glossary, first movement, and previous movement. Link the image left.jpg to the b9m3.htm file.

10. Save your changes to all six files.

11. Open **b9home.htm** in your Web browser. Verify that you can use the links and the linked inline images to navigate through the contents of this site.

Explore

12. Draw a storyboard of the Web site you created. Show all of the pages and the links between them. Do not include the link elements in this storyboard.

Explore

13. Using a browser that supports semantic links, such as Opera, open the Web site and test whether you can use the semantic links in the browser-built toolbar.

14. Submit the completed site to your instructor.

Explore

Broaden your knowledge and test your skills by exploring how to use anchors and popup titles in a health club Web site.

Case Problem 3

Data files needed for this Case Problem: classtxt.htm, indextxt.htm, memtxt.htm, logo.jpg

Diamond Health Club, Inc. You work for Diamond Health Club, a family-oriented health club in Seattle, Washington that has been serving active families for 25 years. The director, Karen Padilla, has asked you to help create a Web site for the club containing three pages:: the home page describing the club, a page listing classes offered, and a page describing the various membership options. You need to add links within the main page and add other links connecting the pages. Because this Web site will need to support older browsers, you will have to use anchors to mark specific locations in the three documents. Karen would also like you to create popup titles for some of the links in the site. Figure 2-46 shows a preview of the completed home page.

Figure 2-46

Home Page · Facilities · Classes · Memberships · Staff · Hours

Welcome

At Diamond Health Club, you can stay healthy year-round and have fun doing it! We offer something for everyone. Our state-of-the-art facilities can challenge the most seasoned athlete, while remaining friendly to our first-time users. Be sure to check out our great classes for everyone from children and teens to adults and seniors. No matter who you are, DHC offers a class for you.

DHC also provides several different membership options. You can register as an individual or a family. We also provide special couples plans. Planning to visit Seattle a few days, weeks, or a month? Our great temporary plans are tailored to meet the needs of any visitor. Temporary memberships also make great Christmas gifts.

Facilities

- 2 workout rooms
- Olympic size pool with at least 3 lanes always open
- Warm, 3-foot deep therapeutic pool
- 2 gymnasiums with full size basketball courts
- Five exercise rooms for private and class instruction
- Climbing gym
- 3 racquetball courts
- On-site child care

Hours

Mon. - Fri. : 5 a.m. to 11 p.m.
Sat. : 7 a.m. to 8 p.m.
Sun. : 8 a.m. to 5 p.m.

For More Information, E-mail our Staff

Ty Stoven, General Manager
Yosef Dolen, Assistant Manager
Sue Myafin, Child Care
James Michel, Health Services
Ron Chi, Membership
Marcia Lopez, Classes

Diamond Health Club · 4317 Alvin Way · Seattle, WA 98102 · (877) 555-4398
Your Year-Round Source for Fun Family Health

To complete this task:

1. Use your text editor to open the **indextxt.htm**, **classtxt.htm** and **memtxt.htm** files from the tutorial.02/case3 folder. Enter *your name* and *the date* in the comment tag at the top of each file. Save these files as: **index.htm**, **classes.htm**, and **members.htm** respectively.

Explore

2. Within the file **index.htm**, add the anchor names fac, hours, and staff to the h3 headings: "Facilities", "Hours", and "For More Information, E-mail our Staff" respectively.

Explore

3. Within the file **members.htm**, add anchor names to the h3 headings: "Individual memberships", "Family memberships", and "Temporary Memberships". Name these anchors: ind, fam, and temp.

Explore

4. Within the file **classes.htm**, add anchor names to the h3 headings: "Senior Classes", "Adult Classes", "Teen Classes", and "Children's Classes". Name these anchors: senior, adult, teen, and child.

5. Return to the **index.htm** file. In the list at the top of the page, change the text, "Home Page" into a link pointing to index.htm. Change "Facilities" into a link that points to the fac anchor within index.htm. Change "Classes" into a link pointing to classes.htm. Change "Membership" into a link pointing to members.htm. Change "Staff" into a link that points to the staff anchor within index.htm. Change "Hours" into a link that points to the hours anchor with index.htm.

Explore

6. Add the popup title "Return to the DHC Home Page" to the Home link. Add the popup title "Learn more about our facilities" to the Facilities link. Add the popup title "View our class list" to the Classes link. Add the popup title "Choose a membership plan" to the Membership link. Add the popup "Meet the DHC staff" to the Staff link. Add the popup title "View the DHC hours of operation" to the Hours link.

7. Repeat steps 5 and 6 for the entries listed at the top of **members.htm** and **classes.htm**.

8. Return to **index.htm**. Go to the staff list at the bottom of the page. Format each name as a link that points to the individual's e-mail address. The e-mail addresses are:

Ty Stoven:	tstoven@dmond-health.com
Yosef Dolen:	ydolen@dmond-health.com
Sue Myafin:	smyafin@dmond-health.com
James Michel:	jmichel@dmond-health.com
Ron Chi:	rchi@dmond-health.com
Marcia Lopez:	mlopez@dmond-health.com

9. Within the first paragraph of index.htm, link the word "children" to the child anchor in the classes.htm file. Link the word "teens" to the teen anchor in the classes.htm file. Link the word "adults" to the adult anchor in classes.htm. Finally, link "seniors" to the senior anchor in classes.htm.

10. Within the second paragraph of index.htm, link the word "individual" to the ind anchor in the members.htm file. Link the word "family" to the fam anchor in members.htm. Finally, link the first occurrence of the word "temporary" to the temp anchor in members.htm.

11. Go to the **classes.htm** file. Format the phrase, "e-mail Marcia Lopez" in the first paragraph as a link pointing to Marcia Lopez's e-mail address.

12. Go to the **members.htm** file. Format the phrase, "e-mail Ron Chi" in the first paragraph as a link pointing to Ron Chi's e-mail address.

13. Save your changes to the **index.htm**, **classes.htm**, and **members.htm** files.

14. Open **index.htm** in your Web browser. Verify that all of your links work correctly, including the links that point to sections within documents. Verify that popup titles appear as you move your mouse pointer over the six links at the top of each page.

15. Submit the completed site to your instructor.

Create

Test your knowledge of HTML by creating a Web site for Body Systems.

Case Problem 4

Data files needed for this Case Problem: about.txt, bench.jpg, bench.txt, cable.jpg, cable.txt, contact.txt, logo.jpg, lpress.jpg, lpress.txt, products.txt, smith.jpg, smith.txt, whybuy.txt

Body Systems You've been working for a few weeks as a Web site developer with Body Systems, one of the leading manufacturers of home exercise equipment. You've been asked to put together a sample Web site highlighting several Body System products. You've been given several text files containing descriptions of these products, as well as contact information for the company, and a file describing the company's history and philosophy. In addition, you've been given several image files of the products, along with an image file of the company logo. You are free to supplement these files with any other resources available to you. Your job is to use this information to create an effective Web site describing the products and the company for interested consumers.

To complete this task:

1. Locate the text files and image files in the tutorial.02/case4 folder of your Data Disk. Review the content of the text files and view the image files. Note that the files cover four products: the Linear Smith machine, the Cable Crossover machine, the Free Weight bench, and the Leg/Press Squat machine. Information about these products is stored in the smith.txt, cable.txt, bench.txt, and lpress.txt files, respectively.

Explore

2. Use one of the search sites on the Web to locate Web pages on strength training tips and advice.

3. Once you become familiar with all of the material available for your Web site, create a storyboard for the site. In the storyboard include all of the filenames of the Web pages and indicate any links between the pages. The Web site should contain at least one example of each of the following:

   - A link within a single document pointing to another section of the same document
   - A link between the documents in the Web site
   - A link to a section of another document
   - A link to an e-mail address

Explore

   - A link to at least one Web site on strength training tips and advice. Be sure to include explanatory text about the link or links you decide to include.

   Make sure that your site is easy to navigate.

4. Create the site you outlined in your storyboard. The design of the Web pages is up to you, but your code should follow correct HTML syntax rules and should be easy for others to read and interpret.

5. Within each file, include comments that document the page's content and purpose. Include your name and the current date in your comments.

6. Submit the completed site to your instructor.

Review

Quick Check Answers

Session 2.1

1. `<h2 id="csu">Colorado State University</h2>`
2. `<a href="#csu">Universities</a>`
3. Anchor tags should be placed within other tags such as the `<h3>` heading tag.
4. `<a name="photo"><img src="photo.jpg" /></a>`
5. `<a href="#links"><img src="button.jpg" /></a>`
6. Anchors should be used to support older browsers that do not recognize the id attribute.

Session 2.2

1. Storyboarding is the process of diagramming a series of related Web pages, taking care to identify all links between the various pages. Storyboarding is an important tool in creating Web sites that are easy to navigate and understand.

2. A linear structure is one in which Web pages are linked from one to another in a direct chain. Users can go to the previous page or the next page in the chain, but not to a page in a different section of the chain. A hierarchical structure is one in which Web pages are linked from general to specific topics. Users can move up and down the hierarchy tree.

3. `<a href="sports.htm">Sports Info</a>`

4. `<a href="sports.htm#bball">Basketball news</a>`

5. An absolute path indicates the location of the file based on its placement with the computer. A relative path indicates the location of the file relative to the location of the current document.

6. ../index.htm
   bio.htm
   ../dube/bio.htm
   ../dube/class/chem.htm
   ../dube/class/contacts.htm
   ../duble/class/links.htm

7. The `<base />` tag is designed to specify the location from which the browser should resolve all relative paths.

Session 2.3

1. The protocol, the hostname, the folder name, the filename, and the anchor name or id.

2. `<a href="http://www.whitehouse.gov" target="_blank">White House</a>`

3. `<a href="ftp://ftp.uwash.edu">Washington</a>`

4. `<a href="news:rec.sports.boxing.pro">Boxing</a>`

5. `<a href="mailto:president@whitehouse.gov">President</a>`

6. `title="Glossary of Chemistry Terms"`

7. `rel="next"`

8. `<link href="toc.htm" rel="contents" rev="chapter" />`

New Perspectives on
HTML and XHTML

Read This Before You Begin: Tutorials 3–5

To the Student

Data Files

To complete the Level II HTML Tutorials (Tutorials 3–5), you need the starting student Data Files. Your instructor will either provide you with these Data Files or ask you to obtain them yourself.

The Level II HTML tutorials require the folders shown to complete the Tutorials, Review Assignments, and Case Problems. You will need to copy these folders from a file server, a standalone computer, or the Web to the drive and folder where you will be storing your Data Files. Your instructor will tell you which computer, drive letter, and folder(s) contain the files you need. You can also download the files by going to www.course.com; see the inside back or front cover for more information on downloading the files, or ask your instructor or technical support person for assistance.

▼ **HTML**
    Tutorial.03
    Tutorial.04
    Tutorial.05

Student Online Companion

The Student Online Companion can be found by going to www.course.com and searching for this title. It contains additional information to supplement what you are learning in the text, as well as links to downloads, shareware, and other tools.

To the Instructor

The Data Files are available on the Instructor Resources CD for this title. Follow the instructions in the Help file on the CD to install the programs to your network or standalone computer. See the "To the Student" section above for information on how to set up the Data Files that accompany this text.

You are granted a license to copy the Data Files to any computer or computer network used by students who have purchased this book.

System Requirements

If you are going to work through this book using your own computer, you need:

- **System Requirements** An Internet connection, a text editor and a Web browser that supports HTML 4.0 and XHTML 1.1 (for example, version 6.0 or higher of either Netscape or Internet Explorer). You may wish to run an older browser version to highlight compatibility issues, but the code in this book is not designed to support those browsers.

- **Data Files** You will not be able to complete the tutorials or exercises in this book using your own computer until you have the necessary starting Data Files.

Objectives

Session 3.1
- Learn how HTML handles colors, and how to use colors effectively
- Create foreground and background colors using styles
- Select different font styles and designs using styles
- Align text with surrounding content using styles
- Control spacing between letters, words, and lines using styles

Session 3.2
- Learn about the different graphic formats supported on the Web and how to use them effectively
- Understand how to use transparent images and animated graphics
- Apply a background image to an element
- Float an image on the right or left page margin
- Set the margin size around an element

Session 3.3
- Understand image maps and how to use them
- Create image map hotspots and link them to destination documents
- Apply an image map to an inline image
- Remove the border from a linked image

Designing a Web Page

Working with Fonts, Colors, and Graphics

Case

Arcadium Amusement Park

Arcadium is a new amusement park located in northern Georgia. The park contains a wealth of rides, including roller coasters, water rides, go-kart racetracks, and gentler rides more appropriate for young children. Tom Calloway is the director of advertising for the park. In addition to radio, newspaper, and television spots, Tom is also overseeing the development of the park's Web site. He has asked you to join his Web site development team.

The team has already determined the site's content and structure. Tom wants you to concentrate on the site's design. He wants the design to convey a sense of fun and excitement to the reader. The Web pages you create should be colorful and should include a variety of images, along with animation, if possible. Tom has provided some of the graphic files you'll need to complete the site's design.

Student Data Files

▼ **Tutorial.03**

▽ **Tutorial folder**

abouttxt.htm
indextxt.htm
kartstxt.htm
maptxt.htm
ridestxt.htm
watertxt.htm
+ 3 demo pages
+ 10 graphic files

▽ **Case2 folder**

kingtxt.htm
+ 7 graphic files

▽ **Review folder**

abouttxt.htm
indextxt.htm
kartstxt.htm
maptxt.htm
ridestxt.htm
toddtxt.htm
watertxt.htm
+ 10 graphic files

▽ **Case3 folder**

crypttxt.htm
+ 5 graphic files

▽ **Case1 folder**

dc100txt.htm
dc250txt.htm
dc500txt.htm
indextxt.htm
pixaltxt.htm
+ 7 graphic files

▽ **Case4 folder**

midwest.txt
+ 9 graphic files

Session 3.1

Working with Color in HTML

The start of another tourist season is approaching and Tom has called you to discuss the appearance of the park's Web site. Other Web site developers have already worked on the site's structure and the content of the pages. Figure 3-1 shows the structure of the Arcadium Web site.

Figure 3-1 Structure of the Arcadium Web site

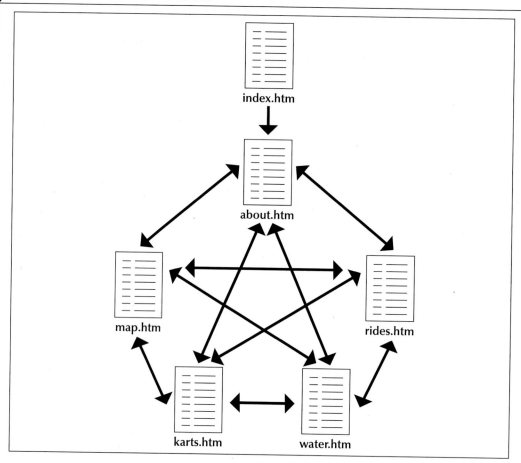

The site contains six Web pages. The index.htm page contains an introduction to Arcadium. This page acts as a **splash screen**, displaying the park logo and an interesting animated graphic, but no substantial content. The splash screen links users to the About page, which contains information about the park. The Karts, Water, and Rides pages all describe specific attractions at Arcadium. The Map page contains a map of the park. Aside from the splash screen page, the Web pages are all linked to one another, allowing users to roam freely around the site. In this case, you'll work only with the index.htm, about.htm, and map.htm files. The other files are provided to complete the Web site for you. The first page you'll work on is the About page.

To open the about.htm file:

1. Use your text editor to open **abouttxt.htm** from the tutorial.03/tutorial folder in your Data Files. Save the file as **about.htm**.

2. Enter *your name* and *the date* in the comment tag at the top of the file.

3. Save your changes to the file, but leave your text editor open.

4. Start your Web browser and open **about.htm**. Figure 3-2 shows the current format of the page.

The About Web page | **Figure 3-2**

About Arcadium   Park Map   Water Rides   Go Karts   Roller Coasters

Welcome

Exciting adventures await you at Arcadium, your affordable family fun center. The park is located 5 miles northwest of Derby - close to many of Georgia's scenic wonders. Arcadium offers over 50 rides, including some of the state's most exciting roller coasters and water rides. There's also plenty of fun for the younger kids, including two separate kiddie pools and special rides for the kids.

Arcadium is open seven days a week:

- April 1 up to Memorial Day weekend: 10am to 5pm
- Memorial Day weekend through Labor Day: 9am to 11pm
- The day after Labor Day through October 31: 10am to 5pm
- November 1 through March 31: closed

Arcadium is easy on your budget. Compare our low daily rates to the big chain parks. You can choose to purchase a gold ticket for any twenty rides, a platinum ticket for thirty rides, or for best value, a full-day pass to ride as many times as you want, wherever you want. Special off-season and large group rates are available.

Arcadium • Hwy 12, Exit 491 • Derby, GA 20010 • 1 (800) 555-5431

Tom is satisfied with the page's content, but he wants you to work on the appearance. He wants to see more color and the use of different fonts in the page. He also wants you to add photographs of people enjoying themselves at the park. Tom wants a visually pleasing page that will draw users into the site and give a good impression of the park.

You decide to start this project by creating an overall color scheme for the page. The first step is to learn how HTML handles colors. If you've worked with graphics software, you've probably made your color choices without much difficulty due to the interfaces that those applications employ. These interfaces, known as WYSIWYG (what you see is what you get), allow you to select colors visually. Selecting color with HTML is somewhat less intuitive, because HTML is a text-based language and requires you to define your colors in textual terms. This can be done in two ways: by specifying either a color value or a color name. Let's start by looking at color values.

Using Color Values

A **color value** is a numerical expression that precisely describes a color. To better understand how numbers can represent colors, it helps to review some of the basic principles of color theory and how they relate to the colors that your monitor displays.

White light is made up of three primary colors (red, green, and blue) mixed at equal intensities. By adding only two of the three primary colors we can generate a trio of complementary colors: yellow, magenta, and cyan (see Figure 3-3). To generate a wider range of colors, we simply vary the intensity of the red, green, and blue light. For example, orange is created from a high intensity of red light, a moderate intensity of green light, and an absence of blue light.

Figure 3-3 ▷ **Primary color model for light**

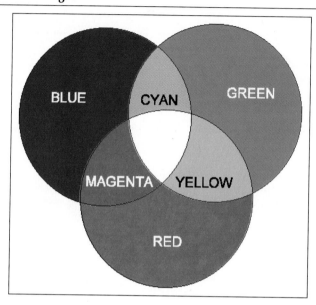

Your computer monitor generates colors by emitting red, green, and blue light at different intensities. Software programs, such as your Web browser, instruct your monitor to create colors mathematically. Each color is represented by a triplet of numbers called an **RGB triplet**, whose values are based on the strength of its red, green, and blue components. This triplet has the form

```
rgb(red, green, blue)
```

where red, green, and blue are the intensity values of the red, green, and blue components. The intensity values range from 0 (absence of color) to 255 (highest intensity). For example, the RGB triplet for white is (255, 255, 255), indicating that red, green, and blue are equally mixed at the highest intensity. Orange has the triplet (255, 165, 0) because it results from a mixture of high-intensity red, moderate-intensity green, and no blue. You can also enter each component value as a percentage, with 100% representing the highest intensity. In this form, you would specify the color orange with rgb (100%, 65%, 0%). The percentage form is less commonly used than RGB values. RGB triplets can specify 256^3 (16.7 million) possible colors, which is more colors than the human eye can distinguish.

In most software programs, you make your color choices using visual clues, sometimes without being aware of underlying RGB triplets. Figure 3-4 shows a typical color dialog box in which users make color selections based on a color's appearance, with the RGB values appearing alongside the color selection.

A typical colors dialog box ◄ **Figure 3-4**

Originally, HTML required that color values be entered using the hexadecimal system. A **hexadecimal** is a number expressed in base 16 rather than in the base 10 form we use every day. In base 10 counting, you use combinations of 10 characters (0 through 9) to represent numerical values. The hexadecimal system includes six extra characters: A (for 10), B (for 11), C (for 12), D (for 13), E (for 14), and F (for 15). For values above 15, you use a combination of those 16 characters. To represent a number in hexadecimal terms, you convert the value to multiples of 16, plus a remainder. For example, 16 is equal to $(16 \times 1) + 0$, so its hexadecimal representation is "10." A value of 21 is equal to $(16 \times 1) + 5$, for a hexadecimal representation of 15. The number 255 is equal to $(16 \times 15) + 15$, or FF in hexadecimal format (remember that F = 15 in hexadecimal). In the case of the number 255, the first F represents the number of times 16 goes into 255 (which is 15), and the second F represents the remainder of 15. A color value represented as a hexadecimal number has the form

`#redgreenblue`

where `red`, `green`, and `blue` are the hexadecimal values of the red, green, and blue components. Thus, the color yellow could be represented either by the RGB triplet (255,255,0) or in the hexadecimal form #FFFF00.

At this point you might be wondering if you have to become a math major before you can start adding color to your Web pages. Fortunately, this is not the case. You can specify most colors in your Web pages with styles that use RGB triplets rather than the hexadecimal form. However, you may see HTML code that sets a color value to something like #FFA500, and now you know what that means, even if you can't tell at a glance that it represents the color orange.

While RGB triplets can distinguish over 16.7 million colors, the number of colors that a browser actually displays depends on the user's monitor. Some monitors are capable of displaying only 256 different colors, and thus browsers on these computers are limited to a smaller **palette**, or selection, of colors. When a browser encounters a color not in its palette, it attempts to render the color using a process called **dithering**, in which the browser combines similar colors from its palette to approximate the original color's appearance. Dithering can result in an image in which individual pixels stand out, and which appears fuzzy when compared to the original (see Figure 3-5).

Figure 3-5 > Color dithering

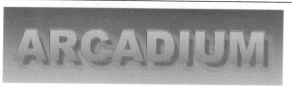

original image

dithered image

One way to avoid this problem is to stick to colors from the **safety palette**—a palette of 216 colors known as **Web-safe colors**, which are guaranteed not to be dithered by any Web browser. Intensities in the safety palette are limited to the values 0, 51, 102, 153, 204, and 255 (or 00, 33, 66, 99, CC, and FF in hexadecimal). Thus, a color value such as (51,153,255) would be part of the safety palette, while a color value such as (192,0,225) would not. You can view the color values that are part of the Safety palette by opening a demo page from your Data Files.

To view the colors of the safety palette:

▶ **1.** Use your browser to open **demo_safety_palette.htm** from the tutorial.03/tutorial folder in your Data Files.

▶ **2.** Study the tables at the bottom of the page, shown in Figure 3-6, to verify that no colors show any dithering.

Figure 3-6 > The colors of the Safety palette

▶ **3.** Close the page when you are finished.

By limiting your color selections to the colors of the safety palette, you can be assured that your images will appear the same to all users regardless of monitor resolution. However, because monitors now commonly support higher color resolutions, the need for the safety palette is not as great as it once was.

Using Color Names

If you don't want to use color values, you can also specify colors by name. HTML and XHTML support the 16 color names displayed in Figure 3-7. You've already used some of these color names in previous tutorials to insert colored lines into your pages.

The 16 basic color names ◀ **Figure 3-7**

Color Name	RGB Triplet	Hexadecimal	Color Name	RGB Triplet	Hexadecimal
Aqua	(0,255,255)	00FFFF	Navy	(0,0,128)	000080
Black	(0,0,0)	000000	Olive	(128,128,0)	808000
Blue	(0,0,255)	0000FF	Purple	(128,0,128)	800080
Fuchsia	(255,0,255)	FF00FF	Red	(255,0,0)	FF0000
Gray	(128,128,128)	808080	Silver	(192,192,192)	C0C0C0
Green	(0,128,0)	008000	Teal	(0,128,128)	008080
Lime	(0,255,0)	00FF00	White	(255,255,255)	FFFFFF
Maroon	(128,0,0)	800000	Yellow	(255,255,0)	FFFF00

Sixteen colors are not a lot, so most browsers support an extended list of 140 color names, including such colors as crimson, khaki, and peachpuff. While this extended color list is not part of the specification for either HTML or XHTML, you can feel confident that your users' browsers will support it.

To view the extended color list:

1. Use your browser to open **demo_color_names.htm** from the tutorial.03/tutorial folder in your Data Files.

2. The tables display the list of 140 extended color names, along with their color values expressed both as RGB triplets and in hexadecimal form (see Figure 3-8). The 16 color names supported by HTML and XHTML are highlighted in the table. Web-safe colors are displayed in boldface.

Figure 3-8 ▶ **A partial list of extended color names**

Sample	Name	RGB	Hexadecimal
	aliceblue	(240,248,255)	#F0F8FF
	antiquewhite	(250,235,215)	#FAEBD7
	aqua	**(0,255,255)**	**#00FFFF**
	aquamarine	(127,255,212)	#7FFFD4
	azure	(240,255,255)	#F0FFFF
	beige	(245,245,220)	#F5F5DC
	bisque	(255,228,196)	#FFE4C4
	black	**(0,0,0)**	**#000000**
	blanchedalmond	(255,235,205)	#FFEBCD
	blue	**(0,0,255)**	**#0000FF**
	blueviolet	(138,43,226)	#8A2BE2
	brown	(165,42,42)	#A52A2A
	burlywood	(222,184,135)	#DEB887

> **3.** Close the page when you are finished.

Depending on the design requirements of your site, you may sometimes need to use color values to get exactly the right color; however if you know the general color that you need, you can usually enter the color name without having to look up its RGB value.

Defining Foreground and Background Colors

With HTML you can define the foreground and background color for each element on your page. The foreground color is usually the color of the text in an element, although in the case of horizontal lines, it defines part of a line's color. The style to define the foreground color is

```
color: color
```

where *color* is either the color value or the color name. The style to define the background color is

```
background-color: color
```

If you do not define an element's color, it takes the color of the element that contains it. For example, if you specify red text on a gray background for the Web page body, all elements within the page inherit that color combination unless you specify different styles for specific elements.

Tom suggests that you change the text color in the About page from the default black to a shade of brown. You decide to use the Web-safe color value (153,102,102). You'll also set the background color of the page to white. While most browsers assume a white background color by default, it's a good idea to make this explicit in case some users have different settings. Because you're applying the color change to the entire page, you'll add the inline style to the body element.

To set the page's foreground and background colors:

> **1.** Return to the **about.htm** file in your text editor.

> **2.** Locate the <body> tag and insert the inline style:

```
<body style="color: rgb(153,102,102); background-color: white">
```

See Figure 3-9.

Setting page foreground and background colors ◄ **Figure 3-9**

foreground color   background color

```
<body style="color: rgb(153,102,102); background-color: white">
<p style="text-align: center">
    <img src="logo.gif" alt="ARCADIUM" />
    <br />
    <a href="about.htm">About Arcadium</a>    
    <a href="map.htm">Park Map</a>    
    <a href="water.htm">Water Rides</a>    
    <a href="karts.htm">Go Karts</a>    
    <a href="rides.htm">Roller Coasters</a>
</p>
```

▶ **3.** Save your changes to the file.

▶ **4.** Reload or refresh **about.htm** in your Web browser and verify that the text color has changed to a medium brown.

You can apply foreground and background colors to any page element. Tom suggests that the "Welcome" title might look better if it was formatted as white text on a medium brown background. The brown background would then act as a divider between the Arcadium logo and the main page body. To change the color, you add an inline style to the h1 element containing the text.

To change the color scheme for the h1 heading:

▶ **1.** Return to **about.htm** in your text editor.

▶ **2.** Locate the <h1> tag and insert the following inline style as shown in Figure 3-10.

```
<h1 style="color: white; background-color: rgb(153,102,102)">
```

Setting the colors for an h1 heading ◄ **Figure 3-10**

foreground color   background color

```
<h1 style="color: white; background-color: rgb(153,102,102)">
    welcome
</h1>
```

Tom would also like you to change the color of the horizontal line at the bottom of the page to match the page's new color scheme.

▶ **3.** Locate the <hr /> tag at the bottom of the file and insert the inline style shown below:

```
<hr style="color: rgb(153,102,102); background-color:
rgb(153,102,102)" />
```

▶ **4.** Save your changes to the file.

▶ **5.** Refresh **about.htm** in your Web browser and verify that the color scheme for the h1 heading and the horizontal line has changed (see Figure 3-11).

Figure 3-11 ▶ Setting foreground and background colors

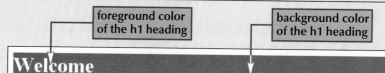

Several deprecated approaches exist for applying color to Web pages. If you want to define the background color for an entire page, you can add the bgcolor attribute to the <body> tag. To define the text color for the entire page, you would use the text attribute. Both attributes require you to enter either the hexadecimal color value or a recognized color name. For example, the following code changes the page background to yellow and the page's text color to the hexadecimal value 99CCFF:

```
<body bgcolor="yellow" text="#99CCFF">
```

If you need to color a section of text on your page, you can enclose the text within the two-sided <font> tag. The <font> tag is a deprecated element that supports several design attributes. Among those supported is the color attribute, which you can use to specify a color name or a hexadecimal color value. See the reference window for more details on these deprecated techniques, which you may still need to use for older browsers.

Reference Window

Setting Foreground and Background Colors

- To set an element's foreground color, use the style
     color: color
  where color is either a color name or a color value.
- To set an element's background color, use the style
     background-color: color

Deprecated

- To set the background color for a Web page, use the attribute
     <body bgcolor="color">
  where color is either a color name or a hexadecimal color value.
- To set a page's text color, use the attribute
     <body text="color">
  where color is either a color name or a hexadecimal color value.
- To apply color to a section of text, use the code
     <font color="color">text</font>
  where color is either a color name or a hexadecimal color value, and text is the text to which you want to apply the color.

Working with Fonts and Text Styles

Tom has reviewed your progress. He's pleased with the color scheme you've created for the Web page, but would like you to work with the appearance of the text on the page. He's concerned that all of the text on the page is displayed in the same typeface. He would also like to see more variety in the page fonts.

Choosing a Font

By default, browsers display Web page text in a single font, usually Times New Roman. You can specify a different font for any page element using the style

```
font-family: fonts
```

where *fonts* is a comma-separated list of fonts that the browser can use in the element. Font names can be either specific or generic. A **specific font** is a font such as Times New Roman, Arial, or Garamond, which is actually installed on a user's computer. A **generic font** is a name for the general description of a font's appearance. Browsers recognize five generic fonts: serif, sans-serif, monospace, cursive, and fantasy. Figure 3-12 shows examples of each. Note that each generic font can represent a wide range of designs.

Generic fonts ◀ **Figure 3-12**

Font Samples

serif	defg	defg	defg
sans-serif	defg	defg	defg
monospace	defg	defg	defg
cursive	defg	defg	defg
fantasy	defg	defg	DEFG

One issue with generic fonts is that you cannot be sure which font a given user's browser will use. For this reason, HTML and XHTML allow you to specify a list of fonts. You list the specific fonts you want the browser to try first, in order of preference, and then end the list with the generic font. If the browser cannot find any of the specific fonts you list, it substitutes the generic font. For example, to specify a sans-serif font, you could enter the following style:

```
font-family: Arial, Helvetica, sans-serif
```

This style tells the browser to first look for the Arial font; if Arial is not available, it tells the browser to look for Helvetica; if neither of those fonts is available, it tells the browser to use the generic sans-serif font defined by the user's system.

To see how the generic fonts appear on your browser, a demo page on text styles has been prepared for you.

To view your browser's generic fonts:

1. Use your browser to open the **demo_text_styles.htm** file from the tutorial.03/tutorial folder of your Data Files.

   This demo page contains a collection of the styles you'll be learning about in this session. Initially, the Preview box displays the sample text in the default text style of your Web browser. You can specify different sample text by selecting the default text and editing it. You can select different style values using the input boxes and drop-down list boxes on the left side of the page. Entering or selecting "default" in an input or drop-down list box causes the page to use the default style. Pressing the tab key activates a style change. The code for the new style appears in the page's lower-right corner.

2. In the upper-right corner box, insert the text **Arcadium**, press the **Enter** key, and then type **Amusement Park**. Press the **Tab** key.

3. Enter the rgb value **255**, **255**, **255** into the three color input boxes and **153**, **102**, **102** into the three background-color input boxes. Press the **Tab** key.

4. Select **fantasy** from the font-family drop-down list box. Figure 3-13 shows the formatted sample text with the style code (your formatted text may look different).

| Figure 3-13 | Viewing the fantasy font |

We'll work with this demo page throughout the rest of the session. You may want to keep the page open as you explore other styles.

Trouble? This demo page may look slightly different depending on your browser.

It's generally good practice not to use more than two different font faces within a single page, unless you're trying to create an interesting and striking visual effect. Serif fonts are best read in large blocks of text like paragraphs. Sans-serif fonts can work well either as paragraph text or as headings and subheads. You'll apply this principle to the About page by changing the font for the h1 heading and the list of links to a serif font.

To change the fonts for the heading and list of links:

1. Return to **about.htm** in your text editor.

2. Locate the first <p> tag in the file and insert the following inline style:

```
font-family: Arial, Helvetica, sans-serif
```

Be sure to use a semicolon to separate this new style from the text-align style already entered.

3. Go to the <h1> tag, and add the following style:

```
font-family: Arial, Helvetica, sans-serif
```

Be sure to use a semicolon to separate this style from the previous styles you entered. You may want to insert this style on a separate line to make your code more readable. Figure 3-14 shows the revised code.

Choosing fonts   **Figure 3-14**

```
<body style="color: rgb(153,102,102); background-color: white">
<p style="text-align: center; font-family: Arial, Helvetica, sans-serif">
    <img src="logo.gif" alt="ARCADIUM" />
    <br />
    <a href="about.htm">About Arcadium</a>    
    <a href="map.htm">Park Map</a>    
    <a href="water.htm">Water Rides</a>    
    <a href="karts.htm">Go Karts</a>    
    <a href="rides.htm">Roller Coasters</a>
</p>

<h1 style="color: white; background-color: rgb(153,102,102);
        font-family: Arial, Helvetica, sans-serif">
    Welcome
</h1>
```

specific fonts   generic font

4. Save your changes and then refresh **about.htm** in your Web browser, verifying that the font for the list of links and the h1 heading has changed (see Figure 3-15).

Applying a sans-serif font   **Figure 3-15**

sans-serif font

You can also use the deprecated <font> tag to change the font of a section of text. See the reference window for details.

Choosing a Font   Reference Window

- To choose a font for an element's text, use the style
    font-family: fonts
    where fonts is a comma-separated list of font names, starting with the most specific and desirable fonts, and ending with a generic font name.

Deprecated

- To apply a font to a section of text, use the code
    <font face="fonts">text</font>
    where fonts is a comma-separated list of font names and text is the text to which you want to apply the font.

Setting the Font Size

Tom likes the font change, but feels that the sizes of the Welcome heading and the list of links are too large. He would like you to reduce the font sizes of these elements. The style to change the font size of the text within an element is

```
font-size: length
```

where *length* is a length measurement. Lengths can be specified in four different ways:

- with a unit of measurement
- with a keyword description
- as a percentage of the size of the containing element
- with a keyword expressing the size relative to the size of the containing element

If you choose to specify lengths using measurement units, you can use absolute units or relative units. Because absolute and relative units come up a lot with styles, it's worthwhile to spend some time understanding them. **Absolute units** define a font size using one of five standard units of measurement: mm (millimeters), cm (centimeters), in (inches), pt (points), and pc (picas). The points and picas measurements may not be as familiar to you as inches, millimeters, and centimeters. For comparison, there are 72 points in an inch, 12 points in a pica, and 6 picas in an inch. Size values for any of these measurements can be whole numbers (0, 1, 2 ...) or decimals (0.5, 1.6, 3.9 ...). For example, if you want your text to be 1/2 inch in size, you can use any of the following styles (note that you should not insert a space between the size value and the unit abbreviation):

```
font-size: 0.5in
font-size: 36pt
font-size: 3pc
```

These measurement units are most useful when you know the physical properties of the output device. Of course this may not be the case with a Web page that could be displayed on a variety of monitor sizes and resolutions or even sent to a printer. This is a fundamental difference from desktop publishing, in which you usually know on what device your creation is being rendered.

One approach to retaining the consistency of Web page text is to instead use **relative units**, which express font size relative to the size of a standard character on the output device (whatever that may be). The two common typesetting standards are referred to as "em" and "ex." The **em unit** is equal to the width of the capital letter "M". The **ex unit** is equal to the height of a lowercase letter "x"(see Figure 3-16.)

| Figure 3-16 | The em and ex units |

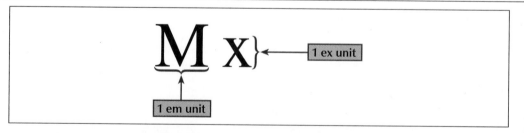

In a Web page containing several font sizes, a browser uses two different methods to determine the size of the em unit. Within an element, the value of the em unit is based on the font size of the text within that element. For example, if an element contains 12pt text, a length of 2em equals 24pts. Alternately, if you want use the em unit to define the font size itself, then the browser bases the size of the em unit on the font size used in the containing element. If the page body is set to a 10pt font, for example, a paragraph within the page set to a font size of 0.8em appears as 8pt font. The ultimate containing element is the browser itself, which has its own default font size for body text. Setting the body text to 0.8em reduces the font size to 80% of the browser's default font size.

You can use relative units to make your page **scalable**, which allows the page to be rendered the same way no matter how a user's output device is configured. For example, one user may have a large monitor with the default font size for body text set to 18pt. Another user may have a smaller monitor and a default font size of 12pt. You want your heading text to be about 50% larger than the body text for either user. Although you can't predict the default font size for a given user's output device, using a value of 1.5em for the heading ensures that it is sized appropriately on either monitor. Note that you can achieve the same effect by expressing a font size as a percentage of an element's default font size. For example, the style

```
font-size: 150%
```

causes the heading to appear 50% larger than the default size. Even though point size is the most commonly used unit in desktop publishing, the benefits of scalability often lead Web designers to opt for the em unit over points or other absolute units.

The final unit of measurement we'll examine is the **pixel**, which represents a single dot on the output device. Because the pixel is the most fundamental unit, for most length measurements, the browser assumes that a value is expressed in pixels if no unit is specified. Thus, to set the font size to 20 pixels, you could use either of the following styles:

```
font-size: 20px
font-size: 20
```

Be aware that the exact size of a pixel depends on the output device. Different devices have different resolutions, which are typically expressed in terms of **dots per inch** or **dpi**. For example, a 600dpi printer has six times more pixels per inch than a typical computer monitor. While you might assume that this would cause a 100 pixel length to appear shorter when you print a page, browsers adjust pixel sizes to ensure that a printout matches the computer screen image. Thus, not all pixels are equal!

Finally, you can express font sizes using seven descriptive keywords: xx-small, x-small, small, medium, large, x-large, or xx-large. Each browser is configured to display text at a particular size for each of these keywords, which enables you to achieve some uniformity across browsers. You can also use the relative keywords "larger" and "smaller" to make a font one size larger or smaller. For example, if a browser had been configured to display an element's text in the small size, you could move it to the medium size by using either of the following styles:

```
font-size: medium
font-size: larger
```

Armed with an almost dizzying array of possible font size values, you're ready to apply your knowledge to the list of links and the h1 heading. Recall that Tom wanted the text in these elements to be smaller. You decide to set the font size of the list of links to 0.8em (80% the size of the body text) and the font size of the h1 heading to 1.5em (50% larger than body text).

To change the font size for the heading and list of links:

▶ **1.** Return to **about.htm** in your text editor.

▶ **2.** Add the following style to the first <p> tag. Be sure to separate this new style from the previous ones with a semicolon.

```
font-size: 0.8em
```

3. Go to the `<h1>` tag, and add the following style:

```
font-size: 1.5em
```

Figure 3-17 shows the revised code.

Figure 3-17 ▸ **Setting the font sizes**

font size will be 80% of normal body text

```
<body style="color: rgb(153,102,102); background-color: white">
<p style="text-align: center; font-family: Arial, Helvetica, sans-serif;
        font-size: 0.8em">
    <img src="logo.gif" alt="ARCADIUM" />
    <br />
    <a href="about.htm">About Arcadium</a>    
    <a href="map.htm">Park Map</a>    
    <a href="water.htm">Water Rides</a>    
    <a href="karts.htm">Go Karts</a>    
    <a href="rides.htm">Roller Coasters</a>
</p>

<h1 style="color: white; background-color: rgb(153,102,102);
        font-family: Arial, Helvetica, sans-serif;font-size: 1.5em">
    Welcome
</h1>
```

font size will be 1.5 x normal body text

4. Save your changes and then refresh **about.htm** in your Web browser, verifying that the font sizes have changed. Compare Figure 3-18 with Figure 3-15.

Figure 3-18 ▸ **Resized list of links and heading**

About Arcadium   Park Map   Water Rides   Go Karts   Roller Coasters

Welcome

You can also use the deprecated `<font>` tag to set the font size for a section of text. See the reference window for details.

Reference Window | **Setting the Font Size**

- To set the font size, use the style
  ```
  font-size: value
  ```
  where *value* is either a unit of length (specified in mm, cm, in, pt, pc, em, or ex units), a keyword (xx-small, x-small, small, medium, large, x-large, or xx-large), a percentage of the default font size, or a keyword describing the size relative to the size of the containing element (smaller or larger). The default font size unit is the pixel (px).

Deprecated

- To set the font size for a section of text, use the code:
  ```
  <font size="value">text</font>
  ```
  where *value* is a number from 1 (smallest) to 7 (largest) and *text* is the text you want to size.

Controlling Spacing and Indentation

Tom feels that the text for the Welcome heading looks too crowded on the medium brown background. He would like you to spread it out more across the width of the page. He also would like to see more space between the first letter, "W," and the left edge of the brown background.

HTML and XHTML support styles that allow you to perform some basic typographic tasks, such as kerning and tracking. The amount of space between pairs of letters is referred to as the **kerning**, while the amount of space between words and phrases is called **tracking**. The styles to control an element's kerning and tracking are

```
letter-spacing: value
word-spacing: value
```

where `value` is the size of space between individual letters or words. You specify these sizes with the same units that you use for font sizing. As with font sizes, the default unit of length for kerning and tracking is the pixel (px). The default value for both kerning and tracking is 0 pixels. A positive value increases the letter and word spacing. A negative value reduces the space between letters and words.

To see how modifying these values can affect the appearance of your text, return to the text styles demo page.

To view kerning and tracking in action:

1. Return to the **demo_text_styles.htm** file in your Web browser.

2. Click the **Reset Styles** button and then change the text in the upper-right box to **Family Fun Park** and press the **Tab** key.

3. Select **sans-serif** from the font-family drop-down list box.

4. Change the value in the font-size box to **32**, the letter-spacing value to **6**, and the word-spacing value to **32**.

   Figure 3-19 shows the revised view of the sample text.

Changing the kerning and tracking ◄ **Figure 3-19**

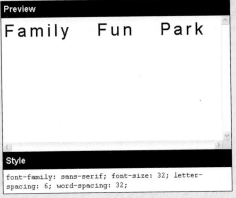

Another typographic feature that you can set is **leading**, which is the space between lines of text. The style to set the leading for the text within an element is

```
line-height: length
```

where *length* is a specific length, or a percentage of the font size of the text on those lines. If no unit is specified, a browser interprets the number to represent the ratio of the line height to the font size. The standard ratio is 1.2:1, which means that the line height is 1.2 times the font size. If Tom wanted his text to be double-spaced, you could apply the following style to the text:

```
line-height: 2
```

A common technique is to create multi-line titles with large fonts and small line heights in order to give title text more impact. Let's use the demo page to see how this works.

To view kerning and tracking in action:

1. Click the **Reset Styles** button, delete the text in the text Input box, type **Arcadium**, press **Enter**, type **Amusement Park**, and press **Tab**.

2. Select **sans-serif** from the font-family drop-down list box and choose **center** from the text-align drop-down list box.

3. Enter **32** in the font-size input box and select **px** from the font-size unit drop-down list box.

4. Enter **24** in the line-height input box and select **px** from the line-height unit drop-down list box.

Figure 3-20 shows how modifying the line height affects the impact of the title.

Figure 3-20 **Changing the line height**

An additional way to control text spacing is to set the indentation for the first line of a text block. The style is

```
text-indent: value
```

where *value* is either a length expressed in absolute or relative units, or a percentage of the width of the text block. For example, an indentation value of 5% indents the first line by 5% of the width of the block. The indentation value can also be negative, extending the first line to the left of the text block to create a **hanging indent**. Note that this technique is not well supported by many browsers.

Now you can use what you've learned about spacing to make the changes that Tom has suggested. You'll increase the kerning of the Welcome heading to 1em. This has the effect of putting one blank space between each letter. You'll also set the indentation to 1em, moving the text of the Welcome heading one space to the left.

To change the spacing of the heading:

1. Return to **about.htm** in your text editor.

2. Add the following style to the h1 heading (don't forget to include a semicolon to separate these new styles from the previous styles). You may wish to place the new styles on a separate line to make your code easier to read. See Figure 3-21.

```
letter-spacing: 1em; text-indent: 1em
```

| Setting the kerning and indentation | Figure 3-21 |

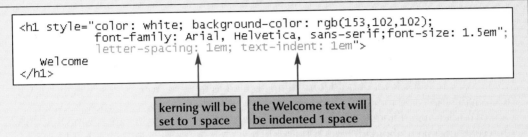

```
<h1 style="color: white; background-color: rgb(153,102,102);
        font-family: Arial, Helvetica, sans-serif;font-size: 1.5em";
        letter-spacing: 1em; text-indent: 1em">
  welcome
</h1>
```

| kerning will be set to 1 space | the Welcome text will be indented 1 space |

3. Save your changes and refresh the About page in your Web browser. Verify that the spacing of the Welcome heading has changed (see Figure 3-22).

| Revised spacing in the heading | Figure 3-22 |

Setting Text Spaces

- To set the space between letters (kerning), use the style
    ```
    letter-spacing: value
    ```
  where *value* is the space between individual letters. The default is 0 pixels.
- To set the space between words (tracking), use the style
    ```
    word-spacing: value
    ```
  where *value* is the space between individual words. The default is 0 pixels.
- To set the vertical space between lines of text (leading), use the style
    ```
    line-height: length
    ```
  where *length* is either the length between the lines, a percentage of the font size, or the ratio of the line height to the font size. The default is a ratio of 1.2.
- To set the indentation of the first line, use the style
    ```
    text-indent: value
    ```
  where *value* is the length of the indentation expressed either as a length or as a percentage of the width of the text block. The default is 0 pixels.

Setting Font Styles, Weights, and other Decorative Features

As you saw in the first tutorial, browsers often apply default font styles to particular types of elements. Text marked with an <address> tag, for example, usually appears in italics. You can specify font styles yourself using the style

```
font-style: type
```

where *type* is normal, italic, or oblique. The italic and oblique styles are similar in appearance, but may differ subtly depending on the font in use.

You have also seen that browsers render certain elements in heavier fonts. For example, most browsers render headings in a boldfaced font. You can control the font weight for any page element using the style

```
font-weight: weight
```

where *weight* is the level of bold formatting applied to the text. You express weights as values ranging from 100 to 900, in increments of 100. In practice, however, most browsers cannot render nine different font weights. For practical purposes, you can assume that 400 represents normal (unbolded) text, 700 is bold text, and 900 represents extra-bold text. You can also use the keywords "normal" or "bold" in place of a weight value, or you can express the font weight relative to the containing element, using the keywords "bolder" or "lighter".

Another style you can use to change the appearance of your text is

```
text-decoration: type
```

where *type* is none (for no decorative changes), underline, overline, line-through, or blink. You can apply several decorative features to the same element. For example, the style

```
text-decoration: underline overline
```

places a line under and over the text in the element. Note that the text-decoration style cannot be applied to non-textual elements, such as inline images.

To control the case of the text within in an element, use the style

```
text-transform: type
```

where *type* is capitalize, uppercase, lowercase, or none (to make no changes to the text case). For example, if you want to capitalize the first letter of each word in the element, you could use the style

```
text-transform: capitalize
```

To display each letter in lowercase, you can use the text-transform value "lowercase". Similarly, the setting "uppercase" displays each letter in uppercase.

Finally, you can display text in uppercase letters and a small font using the style

```
font-variant: type
```

where *type* is normal (the default) or small caps (small capital letters). Small caps are often used in legal documents, such as software agreements, in which the capital letters indicate the importance of a phrase or point, but the text is made small so as to not detract from other elements in the document.

To see the impact of these different styles, you can use the demo page.

To view the different font styles:

1. Return to the **demo_text_styles.htm** page in your Web browser and click the **Reset Styles** button.

2. Enter **32** in the font-size input box.

3. Select **italic** from the font-style drop-down list box and select **bold** from the font-weight drop-down list box.

4. Select **underline** from the text-decoration drop-down list box and **small-caps** from the font-variant drop-down list box.

   Figure 3-23 shows the impact of these style changes on the text.

Changing font styles ◄ **Figure 3-23**

Preview
Arcadium Amusement Park

Style
`font-size: 32;`

Preview
ARCADIUM *AMUSEMENT PARK*

Style
`font-style: italic; font-weight: bold; font-size: 32;` `text-decoration: underline; font-variant: small-caps;`

5. We're finished working with this demo page. You can close it now or continue to work with it if you wish to further explore the impact of these styles.

Setting Font Styles

Reference Window

- To set your font's appearance, use the style
    `font-style: type`
  where *type* is either normal, italic, or oblique.
- To set the font's weight, use
    `font-weight: value`
  where *weight* is either a value from 100 to 900 in increments of 100, or the keyword normal or bold. To increase the weight of the font relative to its containing element, use the keywords bolder or lighter.
- To decorate your text, use the style
    `text-decoration: type`
  where *type* equals underline, overline, line-through, blink, or none.
- To change the case of the text in an element, use the style
    `text-transform: type`
  where *type* equals capitalize, lowercase, uppercase, or none.
- To display a variant of the current font, use the style
    `font-variant: type`
  where *type* equals none or small-caps.

Aligning Text Vertically

One of the first styles you learned in Tutorial 1 was the text-align style, which you use to align text horizontally within a block-level element. You can also vertically align inline elements with the surrounding block. The style for setting vertical alignment is

```
vertical-align: type
```

where *type* is one of the keywords described in Figure 3-24.

Figure 3-24 | **Values of the vertical-alignment style**

Vertical Alignment	Description
baseline	Aligns the element with the bottom of lowercase letters in surrounding text. (the default)
bottom	Aligns the bottom of the element with the bottom of the lowest element in surrounding content.
middle	Aligns the middle of the element with the middle of the surrounding content.
sub	Subscripts the element.
super	Superscripts the element.
text-bottom	Aligns the bottom of the element with the bottom of the font of the surrounding content.
text-top	Aligns the top of the element with the top of the font of the surrounding content.
top	Aligns the top of the element with the top of the tallest object in the surrounding content.

Instead of using keywords, you can specify a length or a percentage for the element to be aligned relative to the surrounding content. A positive value moves the element up and a negative value lowers the element. For example, the style

```
vertical-align: 50%
```

raises the element by half of the line height of the surrounding content, while the style

```
vertical-align: -100%
```

drops the element an entire line height below the baseline of the current line.

Combining all Text Formatting in a Single Style

We've covered a lot of different text and font styles. You can combine most of them into a single style declaration, using the form

```
font: font-style font-variant font-weight font-size/line-height
font-family
```

where *font-style* is the font's style, *font-variant* is the font variant, *font-weight* is the weight of the font, *font-size* is the size of the font, *line-height* is the height of each line, and *font-family* is the font face. For example, the style

```
font: italic small-caps bold 16pt/24pt Arial, sans-serif
```

displays the text of the element in an italic, bold, and Arial or sans-serif font. The font size is 16pt, and the space between the lines is 24pt. The text will appear in small capital letters. You do not have to include all of the properties of the font style; the only required properties are size and font-family. A browser assumes the default value for any omitted property. However, you must place any properties that you do include in the order indicated above. For example, the following would be a correct style declaration to specify a 16pt, bold, monospace font:

```
font: bold 16pt monospace
```

However, it would *not* be correct to switch the order, placing the font-family property before the style and weight properties:

```
font: monospace bold 16pt
```

Tom feels that the size of the address text at the bottom of the page is too large, and he feels that it would look better in a normal sans-serif font rather than in italics. Make these changes now using the font style.

To change the style of the address element:

1. Return to **about.htm** in your text editor.

2. Add the following style to the address element at the bottom of the file (be sure to separate all style declarations with a semicolon). See Figure 3-25.

   ```
   font: normal 8pt Arial, Helvetica, sans-serif
   ```

Using the font style ◄ **Figure 3-25**

> the font style will be normal, not italic

> the font size will be 8pt

```
<address style="text-align: center; font: normal 8pt Arial, Helvetica, sans-serif">
Arcadium  &#149; 
Hwy 12, Exit 491  &#149; 
Derby, GA 20010  &#149; 
1 (800) 555-5431
</address>

</body>
</html>
```

> the text will be in Arial, Helvetica, or another sans-serif font

3. Save your changes and then refresh **about.htm** in your Web browser. Verify that the appearance of the address element has changed. See Figure 3-26.

Formatted address ◄ **Figure 3-26**

Arcadium is easy on your budget. Compare our low daily rates to the big chain parks. You can choose to purchase a gold ticket for any twenty rides, a platinum ticket for thirty rides, or for best value, a full-day pass to ride as many times as you want, wherever you want. Special off-season and large group rates are available.

Arcadium • Hwy 12, Exit 491 • Derby, GA 20010 • 1 (800) 555-5431

> address

- To combine all font properties in a single declaration, use the style

  ```
  font: font-style font-variant font-weight font-size/line-height
    font-family
  ```

  where *font-style* is the style, *font-variant* is the variant, *font-weight* is the weight, *font-size* is size, *line-height* is the height of the lines, and *font-family* is the font face. You may omit any of the properties except for font-size and font-family, but they must be entered in this order.

Using the Span Element

Tom wants to make one more change to the font styles on the page. He would like the word "Arcadium" in the first paragraph to be prominently displayed in bold and perhaps in Arial or Helvetica font, setting it off from the rest of the text in paragraph. To make this change, you first need a way of marking that single word within the paragraph. You can do that with the span element. The syntax is

```
<span>content</span>
```

where *content* is the content to be marked. The span element is just a marker; browsers do not format the content unless you also add a style to the element. For example, to display the word "Arcadium" in Arial or Helvetica, you would enter the code

```
<span style="font-family: Arial, Helvetica, sans-serif">
Arcadium</span>
```

The span element is an inline element and must be placed within a block-level element, such as a paragraph or a heading. HTML supports another marker, the div element, which is a generic block-level element. We will talk about the uses of the div element in a later tutorial.

To insert and format a span element:

1. Return to **about.htm** in your text editor.

2. Locate the first occurrence of the word Arcadium in the paragraph below the Welcome heading and enclose the text in the following span element (see Figure 3-27). You might want to place the code on its own separate line for readability.

   ```
   <span style="font-weight: bold; font-family: Arial, Helvetica,
   sans-serif">Arcadium</span>
   ```

Figure 3-27	Creating a span element

```
<p style="text-align: justify">
Exciting adventures await you at
<span style="font-weight: bold; font-family: Arial, Helvetica, sans-serif">Arcadium</span>,
your affordable family fun center. The park is located 5 miles northwest of
Derby - close to many of Georgia's scenic wonders. Arcadium offers over 50 rides,
including some of the state's most exciting roller coasters and water rides,
There's also plenty of fun for the younger kids, including two separate
kiddie pools and special rides for the kids.</p>
```

3. Save your changes. You may close the text editor if you plan on taking a break before going on to Session 3.2.

4. Reload **about.htm** in your Web browser. Figure 3-28 shows the format applied to the word Arcadium in the first paragraph.

Formatted text in the About page ◀ **Figure 3-28**

span element

Welcome

Exciting adventures await you at **Arcadium**, your affordable family fun center. The park is located 5 miles northwest of Derby - close to many of Georgia's scenic wonders. Arcadium offers over 50 rides, including some of the state's most exciting roller coasters and water rides. There's also plenty of fun for the younger kids, including two separate kiddie pools and special rides for the kids.

▶ **5.** Close your Web browser if you intend to take a break before starting Session 3.2.

Reference Window

Using the span element

- To create a generic inline element, use the HTML code
    `<span>content</span>`
    where *content* is the content of the inline element.

You've completed your work with colors and text in the About page. Tom is pleased with your work. He now wants you to examine how you can use graphics to improve the site's appearance. You'll tackle this task in the next session.

Session 3.1 Quick Check

Review

1. What style settings would you use to change the font color to yellow and the background color to the value (51,102,51)?
2. What are Web-safe colors and why would you use them in your Web pages?
3. What style setting would you use to display text in Courier New font, or in any monospace font if that specific font is not available?
4. What style setting would you use to set the font size to 16 points?
5. What is the em unit, and why would you want to use it with your Web page text?
6. What is kerning, and what style setting would you use to set an element's kerning to 2em?
7. What style would you use to make text double spaced?
8. What style settings would you use to create bold italic text?
9. What is the span element?

Session 3.2

Choosing an Image Format

Now that you've finished working with the Arcadium Web site's colors and fonts, Tom wants you to start working on the site's graphics. Most Web browsers support two image file formats: GIF and JPEG. Choosing the appropriate image format is an important part of Web page design. You must balance the goal of creating an interesting and attractive page against the need to keep the size of your page and its supporting files small and easy to retrieve. Each file format has its advantages and disadvantages, and you will probably use a combination of both formats in your Web page designs. First, let's look at the advantages and disadvantages of using GIF image files.

Working with GIF Images

GIF (Graphics Interchange Format), the most commonly used image format on the Web, is compatible with virtually all browsers. GIF files are limited to displaying 256 colors, so they are most often used for graphics requiring fewer colors, such as clip art images, line art, logos, and icons. Images that require more color depth, such as photographs, can appear grainy when saved as GIF files. There are actually two GIF file formats: GIF87 and GIF89a. The **GIF89a** format supports more features such as interlacing, transparent colors, and animation.

Interlacing refers to the way that graphics software saves a GIF file. In a **noninterlaced GIF**, which is the most common format, the image is saved one line at a time, starting from the top of the graphic and moving downward. Figure 3-29 shows the progress of a noninterlaced GIF as it opens in a Web browser. If a graphic is large, it might take a long time for the entire image to appear, which can frustrate visitors to your Web page.

Figure 3-29 ▶ **Noninterlaced GIF**

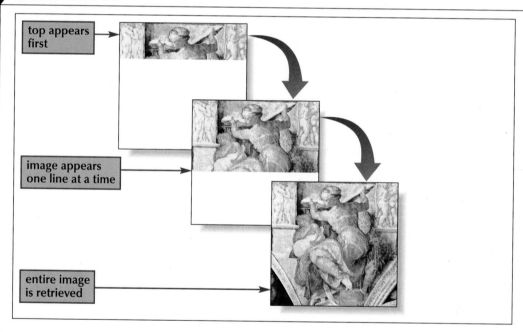

top appears first

image appears one line at a time

entire image is retrieved

An **interlaced GIF**, by contrast, is saved and retrieved in stages. For example, every fifth line of the image might appear first, followed by every sixth line, and so forth through the remaining rows. As Figure 3-30 shows, an interlaced image starts out as a blurry representation of its final appearance, then gradually comes into focus. By contrast, a noninterlaced image is always a sharp image as it's being retrieved, but it is incomplete until it is fully loaded.

Interlaced GIF | **Figure 3-30**

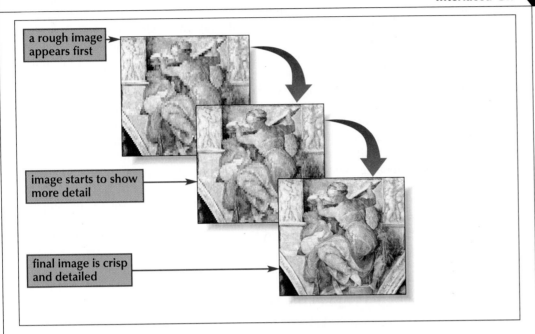

a rough image appears first

image starts to show more detail

final image is crisp and detailed

An interlaced GIF is an effective format for a large graphic that you want users to be able to see as it loads. Users with slower connections get an immediate idea of what the image looks like and can decide whether to wait for it to come into focus. On the down side, interlacing increases the size of a GIF file by anywhere from 3 to 20 kilobytes, depending on the image.

GIF image files can be large. One way to reduce the size of a GIF is to reduce the number of colors in its color palette. For example, if an image contains only 32 different colors, you can use an image editing program to reduce the palette to those 32 colors, resulting in a smaller image file that loads faster.

Working with Transparent Colors

Another feature of the GIF89a format is the ability to use transparent colors. A **transparent color** is a color that is not displayed when the image is viewed in an application. In place of the transparent color, a browser displays whatever is on the page background.

The process by which you create a transparent color depends on the graphics software you are using. Many applications include the option to designate a transparent color when saving an image, while other packages include a transparent color tool, which you use to select the color that you want to treat as transparent.

In the past, Web page designers used transparent GIFs as layout tools to help them place elements on a Web page. To accomplish this, a designer would create a GIF one pixel square in size, with the color of the pixel specified as transparent. This type of image was sometimes referred to as a **spacer**. A Web designer could then size the spacer in order to position objects in specific locations on the page. Because the spacer was transparent, users would see only the positioned object. With the advent of styles, there is little need for spacers anymore, but you may still see them in the code for older pages.

Using Animated GIFs

GIFs are also commonly used to create animated images. An **animated GIF** is composed of several images that are displayed one after the other. Some files play the frames in rapid succession, creating the illusion of motion, while other animated GIFs simply cycle slowly through multiple images or messages. You can easily find animated GIFs on the Web in online collections. You can also create your own by installing animated GIF software. Most animated GIF software allows you to control the rate at which an animation plays (as measured by frames per second) and to determine the number of times the animation repeats before stopping (or set it to repeat without stopping). You can also combine individual GIF files into a single animated file and create special transitions between images.

Animated GIFs are a mixed blessing. Because an animated GIF file is typically larger than a static GIF image file, using animated GIFs can greatly increase the size of a Web page. You should also be careful not to overwhelm users with animated images. Animated GIFs can quickly irritate users once the novelty wears off, especially because there is no way for users to turn them off! Like other GIF files, animated GIFs are limited to 256 colors. This makes them ideal for small icons and line art, but not for photographic images.

Recall that one of the pages in the Arcadium Web site is a splash screen. Tom wants to include some interesting visual effects on this page in order to draw users into the site. You decide to investigate whether this would be a good place for an animated GIF. One of the graphic designers at Arcadium has created an animated GIF of the company logo. You'll try adding that to the splash screen.

To insert the animated logo in the Web page:

1. Use your text editor to open the **indextxt.htm** file from the tutorial.03/tutorial folder of your Data Files. Enter *your name* and *the date* in the comments at the top of the file and save it as **index.htm**.

2. Replace the text "ARCADIUM" with the following tag, as shown in Figure 3-31.

   ```
   <img src="logoanim.gif" alt="ARCADIUM" />
   ```

Figure 3-31	Inserting the animated logo

```
<body style="font-family: Arial, Helvetica, sans-serif">
<p style="text-align: center">
    <img src="logoanim.gif" alt="ARCADIUM" />
    <br />
    <span style="color: red; font-size: 18pt; font-weight: bold">
    Affordable Family Fun
    </span>
    <br /><br />
    <a href="about.htm">Enter Arcadium</a>
</p>
</body>
</html>
```

3. Save your changes to the file.

4. Open **index.htm** in your Web browser. Verify that the logo displays an animated set of cars racing down the track. See Figure 3-32

Figure 3-32	Animated logo

train cars are animated

Affordable Family Fun

Enter Arcadium

Working with JPEG Images

The other main image file format is the JPEG format. **JPEG** stands for **Joint Photographic Experts Group**. JPEGs differ from GIFs in several ways. In the JPEG format you can create images that use the full 16.7 million colors available in the color palette. Because of this, JPEG files are most often used for photographs and images that cover a wide spectrum of color.

In addition, the image compression algorithm used by JPEG files yields image files that are usually (though not always) smaller than their GIF counterparts. In some situations, though, the GIF format creates a smaller and better-looking image—for example, when an image contains large sections covered with a single color. As a general rule, you should use JPEGs for photos and GIFs for illustrations that involve only a few colors.

You can control the size of a JPEG by controlling the degree of image compression applied to the file. Increasing the compression reduces the file size, though often at the expense of image quality. Figure 3-33 shows the effect of compression on a JPEG file. As you can see, the increased compression cuts the file size to a fraction of the original, but the resulting image is more poorly defined than the image with low compression.

The effects of compression on JPEG quality and file size ◄ **Figure 3-33**

| no compression (75 KB) | moderate compression (10 KB) | heavy compression (4 KB) |

By testing different compression levels with image editing software, you can reduce the size of a JPEG file while maintaining an attractive image. Note that a smaller file size does not always mean that a Web page will load faster. Because a browser has to decompress a JPEG image when it retrieves it, opening a heavily compressed image can actually take more time than retrieving and displaying a less compressed file.

JPEGs do not support animation or transparent colors. However, a format called **progressive JPEG** does create an effect similar to interlacing, in which the JPEG image fades in from a low resolution to a high resolution. Like interlaced GIFs, progressive JPEG image files are larger than nonprogressive JPEGs.

Working with PNG Images

A third graphic format that is starting to gain wide acceptance is the **Portable Network Graphics** or **PNG** format. PNG files include most of the same features as GIFs (such as animation, interlacing, and transparency) but also provide the file compression available with JPEGs. In addition, like the JPEG format, PNG supports the full 16.7 million colors of the color palette. You can also designate several transparent colors in a PNG file, rather than the single color that GIFs support. The only problem with the PNG format is that older browsers do not support it. This is becoming less of a problem as time goes by, so you may find that using the PNG format is an acceptable choice for your Web site. Figure 3-34 summarizes the features of the three major graphics formats on the Web.

Figure 3-34 ▶ **Comparison of image formats**

Feature	GIF	JPEG	PNG
Color Resolution	256	16.7 million	16.7 million
Useful for line art	Yes	No	Yes
Useful for photographs	No	Yes	Yes
Interlacing/Progressive Encoding	Yes	Yes	Yes
Compressible	Yes	Yes	Yes
Transparent colors	Yes (1)	No	Yes (multiple)
Supported by older browsers	Yes	Yes	No

Other Image Formats

Other image formats are available for your Web pages as well. The World Wide Web Consortium (W3C) is currently promoting the **Scalable Vector Graphics (SVG)** specification, which is a graphic format written with XML that you can use to create line art composed of straight lines and curves. The **Flash** software program from **Macromedia** is another popular way to add animated graphics to a Web site. You can use Flash to create interactive animations, scalable graphics, animated logos, and navigation controls for a Web site. To view a Flash animation, users must have the Flash player installed on their computers. Users can download and install the player for free, and are generally prompted to do this the first time they open a Web page that uses Flash.

Tom wants you to add a photo to the About page. The image has been saved as a JPEG file and you'll place the image in the first paragraph on the page.

To insert the photo in the About page:

▶ 1. Reopen the **about.htm** file in your text editor.

▶ 2. Directly above the line "Exciting adventures await you at", insert the following tag as shown in Figure 3-35.

```
<img src="about.jpg" alt="" />
```

Figure 3-35 ▶ **Inserting the about photo**

```
<p style="text-align: justify">
<img src="about.jpg" alt="" />
Exciting adventures await you at
<span style="font-weight: bold; font-family: Arial, Helvetica, sans-serif">Arcadium</span>,
your affordable family fun center. The park is located 5 miles northwest of
Derby - close to many of Georgia's scenic wonders. Arcadium offers over 50 rides,
including some of the state's most exciting roller coasters and water rides.
There's also plenty of fun for the younger kids, including two separate
kiddie pools and special rides for the kids.</p>
```

▶ 3. Save your changes to the file and reopen **about.htm** in your Web browser. The image appears inline with the rest of the paragraph text (see Figure 3-36).

Welcome

Exciting adventures await you at **Arcadium**, your affordable family fun center. The park is located 5 miles northwest of Derby - close to many of Georgia's scenic wonders. Arcadium offers over 50 rides, including some of the state's most exciting roller coasters and water rides. There's also plenty of fun for the younger kids, including two separate kiddie pools and special rides for the kids.

Aligning an Image

You show Tom the progress you've made on the Web page. Although he's pleased with the image of the kids, he doesn't like how the image is positioned on the page. The current layout includes a large blank space between the Welcome heading and the first paragraph. Tom wants you to wrap the paragraph text around the image.

Floating an Element

One way to achieve this is with the float style. The syntax of the float style is

```
float: position
```

where *position* is none (the default), left, or right. As shown in Figure 3-37, when a browser encounters the float style, it places the element on the specified margin and then wraps the subsequent content around the element.

Figure 3-37 The float style

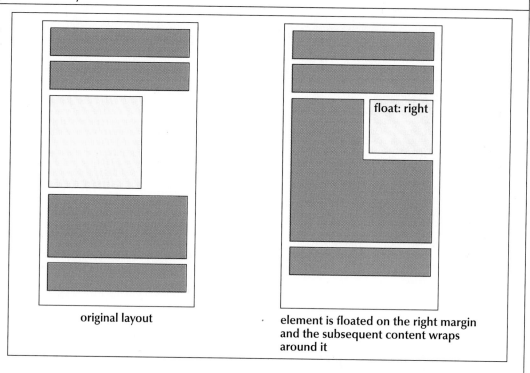

original layout

· element is floated on the right margin and the subsequent content wraps around it

In addition to images, you can use the float style with any block-level element to create interesting layout effects, such as sidebars. We'll explore this layout technique in a future tutorial.

Clearing an Element

You can use the clear style to prevent other content from wrapping around a floating element. The clear style uses the syntax

```
clear: position
```

where *position* is none (the default), left, or right. For example, setting the clear value to "right" prevents an element from being displayed until the right margin is clear of floating elements (see Figure 3-38). You use the clear style when you want to ensure that an element, such as a page footer, is not moved up and wrapped around another element.

The clear style ◀ **Figure 3-38**

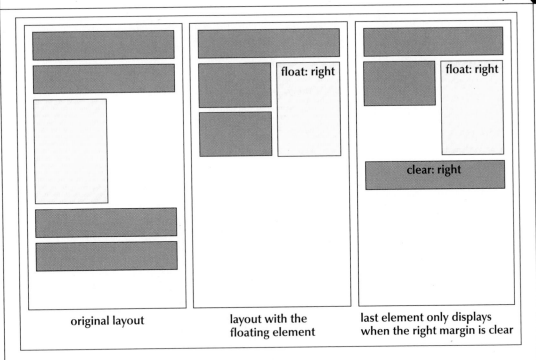

original layout   layout with the floating element   last element only displays when the right margin is clear

Using what you know about the float style, place the photo on the About page at the right margin and use the clear style to ensure that the horizontal line at the bottom of the page does not move up and wrap around the image.

To float the photo:

1. Return to the **about.htm** file in your text editor.

2. Insert the following attribute into the <img /> tag for the about photo:

   ```
   style="float: right"
   ```

3. Insert the following style into the <hr /> tag (be sure to separate this style from the other styles with a semicolon).

   ```
   clear: right
   ```

   Figure 3-39 shows the revised code.

Figure 3-39 | **Inserting the float and clear styles**

image floats at
the right margin

```
<p style="text-align: justify">
<img src="about.jpg" alt="" style="float: right" />
Exciting adventures await you at
<span style="font-weight: bold; font-family: Arial, Helvetica, sans-serif">Arcadium</span>,
your affordable family fun center. The park is located 5 miles northwest of
Derby - close to many of Georgia's scenic wonders. Arcadium offers over 50 rides,
including some of the state's most exciting roller coasters and water rides.
There's also plenty of fun for the younger kids, including two separate
kiddie pools and special rides for the kids.</p>

<p>Arcadium is open seven days a week:</p>
<ul>
    <li>April 1 up to Memorial Day weekend: 10am to 5pm</li>
    <li>Memorial Day weekend through Labor Day: 9am to 11pm</li>
    <li>The day after Labor Day through October 31: 10am to 5pm</li>
    <li>November 1 through March 31: closed</li>
</ul>

<p style="text-align: justify">Arcadium is easy on your budget. Compare our low
daily rates to the big chain parks. You can choose to purchase a gold ticket for
any twenty rides, a platinum ticket for thirty rides, or for best value, a
full-day pass to ride as many times as you want, wherever you want. Special off-season
and large group rates are available.</p>

<hr style="color: rgb(153,102,102); background-color: rgb(153,102,102); clear: right" />
```

line will not be
displayed until the
right margin is clear

4. Save your changes and reopen **about.htm** in your Web browser. Figure 3-40 shows the revised layout of the page.

Figure 3-40 | **Floating the image element**

W e l c o m e

Exciting adventures await you at **Arcadium**, your affordable family fun center. The park is located 5 miles northwest of Derby - close to many of Georgia's scenic wonders. Arcadium offers over 50 rides, including some of the state's most exciting roller coasters and water rides. There's also plenty of fun for the younger kids, including two separate kiddie pools and special rides for the kids.

Arcadium is open seven days a week:

- April 1 up to Memorial Day weekend: 10am to 5pm
- Memorial Day weekend through Labor Day: 9am to 11pm
- The day after Labor Day through October 31: 10am to 5pm
- November 1 through March 31: closed

Arcadium is easy on your budget. Compare our low daily rates to the big chain parks. You can choose to purchase a gold ticket for any twenty rides, a platinum ticket for thirty rides, or for best value, a full-day pass to ride as many times as you want, wherever you want. Special off-season and large group rates are available.

Arcadium • Hwy 12, Exit 491 • Derby, GA 20010 • 1 (800) 555-5431

Using the Align Attribute

For some older browsers, you may need to use the align attribute, which is now deprecated, to fulfill some of the same needs as the float style. The syntax of the align attribute is

```
<img align="position" />
```

where *position* indicates how you want the image aligned with the surrounding content. If you want the image placed on the left or right margin, use align values of "left" or "right". Figure 3-41 shows the other values of the align attribute.

Values of the align attribute

Figure 3-41

align=	Description
absbottom	Aligns the bottom of the object with the absolute bottom of the surrounding text. The absolute bottom is equal to the baseline of the text minus the height of the largest descender in the text.
absmiddle	Aligns the middle of the object with the middle of the surrounding text. The absolute middle is the midpoint between the absolute bottom and text top of the surrounding text.
baseline	Aligns the bottom of the object with the baseline of the surrounding text.
bottom	Aligns the bottom of the object with the bottom of the surrounding text. The bottom is equal to the baseline minus the standard height of a descender in the text.
left	Aligns the object to the left of the surrounding text. All preceding and subsequent text flows to the right of the object.
middle	Aligns the middle of the object with the surrounding text.
right	Aligns the object to the right of the surrounding text. All subsequent text flows to the left of the object.
texttop	Aligns the top of the object with the absolute top of the surrounding text. The absolute top is the baseline plus the height of the largest ascender in the text.
top	Aligns the object to the right of the surrounding text. All subsequent text flows to the left of the object.

Note that you can duplicate the align values with styles. You can recreate the effects of the left and right values using the float style. You can duplicate the rest of the align values using the vertical-align style discussed in the previous session.

There is no general attribute to prevent an element from being displayed until a margin is clear. If you need to perform this task for older browsers, you can place the tag `<br clear="position" />` before the element you want cleared, where *position* is either "left" or "right", "all", or "none". This tag creates a line break only after the specified margin is clear. Note that like the align attribute, this attribute has been deprecated.

Floating and Clearing an Element

Reference Window

- To float an element on the left or right margin, use the style
    `float: position`
  where *position* is none (the default), left, or right.
- To display an element in the first available space where the specified margin is clear of floating elements, use the style
    `clear: position`

Deprecated

- To align an inline image with the left or right page margin, add the following attribute to the <img /> tag:
    `align="position"`
  where *position* is either left or right.
- To display an element in the first available space where the specified margin is clear of other elements, enter the following tag before the element:
    `<br clear="position" />`
  where *position* is left, right, all, or none.

Setting Margins

Wrapping the content around the image has solved the problem of the large white space in the middle of the About page. However, Tom feels that the text crowds the photo too much, and would like you to slightly increase the margin between the photo and the text. Four styles control the size of an element's top, right, bottom, and left margins:

```
margin-top: length
margin-right: length
margin-bottom: length
margin-left: length
```

where *length* is one of the units of length discussed in the previous session or a percentage of the width of the containing element. You can also use the keyword "auto", which enables the browser to determine the margin size. As with font sizes, the default unit is the pixel. To create a 2-pixel margin to the left and right of an element, and a 1-pixel margin above and below, you would use the style

```
margin-top: 1; margin-right: 2; margin-bottom: 1; margin-left: 2
```

A margin value can also be negative. Web page designers can use negative margins to create interesting overlay effects by forcing the browser to render one element on top of another. Note that some browsers do not support negative margins and using them may lead to unpredictable results.

The four margin styles can be combined into a single style using the format

```
margin: top right bottom left
```

where *top*, *right*, *bottom*, and *left* are the sizes of the top, right, bottom, and left margins. (If you have trouble remembering this order, just think of moving clockwise around the element, starting with the top margin.) If you include only three values in the margin style, they are applied to the top, right, and bottom margins. If you specify only two values, a browser applies the first value to both the top and bottom margins, and the second value to both the left and right margins. If you specify only a single value, a browser applies it to all four margins.

Tom suggests that you set the size of the left margin to 15 pixels and the size of the bottom margin to 5 pixels. The top and right margins can be set to 0 pixels.

To set the image margins:

1. Return to the **about.htm** file in your text editor.

2. Add the following style to the <img /> tag for the about photo (see Figure 3-42):

   `margin: 0 0 5 15`

   Be sure to separate this style from the other styles with a semicolon.

Figure 3-42 | **Setting the margin size**

```
<p style="text-align: justify">
<img src="about.jpg" alt="" style="float: right; margin: 0 0 5 15" />
Exciting adventures await you at
<span style="font-weight: bold; font-family: Arial, Helvetica, sans-serif">Arcadium</span>,
your affordable family fun center. The park is located 5 miles northwest of
Derby - close to many of Georgia's scenic wonders. Arcadium offers over 50 rides,
including some of the state's most exciting roller coasters and water rides.
There's also plenty of fun for the younger kids, including two separate
kiddie pools and special rides for the kids.</p>
```

3. Save your changes to the file and reopen **about.htm** in your Web browser. Verify that there is now more space separating the photo from the surrounding content.

You can also set margins for elements other than inline images. You can use the margin styles to set margins for your entire Web page. Tom has looked at the splash screen and suggests that the animated logo might look better if it was further down the page. You can accomplish this by increasing the page's top margin.

To set the page margin:

1. Go to the **index.htm** file in your text editor.

2. Within the <body> tag at the top of the file, insert the following style, as shown In Figure 3-43:

   ```
   margin-top: 100
   ```

   Be sure to insert a semicolon, separating this style from the other style declarations.

Setting the top page margin for index.htm ◄ **Figure 3-43**

```
<body style="font-family: Arial, Helvetica, sans-serif; margin-top: 100">
<p style="text-align: center">
    <img src="logoanim.gif" alt="ARCADIUM" />
    <br />
    <span style="color: red; font-size: 18pt; font-weight: bold">
    Affordable Family Fun
    </span>
    <br /><br />
    <a href="about.htm">Enter Arcadium</a>
</p>
</body>
</html>
```

3. Save your changes to the file and reopen **index.htm** in your Web browser. Verify that the contents have been shifted down the page.

For older browsers you can use the deprecated attributes vspace and hspace. The vspace attribute sets the vertical space above and below the inline image. The hspace attribute sets the horizontal space to the left and right of the image. There are no presentational attributes that allow you to specify the size of individual margins.

Setting the Margin Size

Reference Window

- To set the size of the margins around an element, use the styles
    ```
    margin-top: length
    margin-right: length
    margin-bottom: length
    margin-left: length
    ```
  where *length* is a unit of length, a percentage of the width of the containing element, or the keyword "auto" (the default), which enables the browser to set the margin size.
- To combine all margin styles in a single style, use
    ```
    margin: top right bottom left
    ```
  where *top*, *right*, *bottom*, and *left* are the margins of the top, right, bottom, and left edges. If you include only three values, the margins are applied to the top, right, and bottom. If you specify only two values, the first value is applied to the top and bottom edges, and the second value to the right and left edges. If you specify only one value, it is applied to all four edges.

Deprecated

- To set the margin around an inline image, add the following attributes to the <img /> tag:
    ```
    vspace="length" hspace="length"
    ```
  where the vspace attribute sets the margin size above and below the image, and the hspace attribute sets the margin size to the left and right of the image. All *length* values are measured in pixels.

Setting the Image Size

By default, browsers display an image at its saved size. You can specify a different size by adding the following attributes to the <img /> tag:

```
width="value" height="value"
```

where the width and height values represent the dimensions of the image in pixels.

Changing an image's dimensions within the browser does not affect the file size. If you want to decrease the size of an image, you should do so using an image editing application so that the image's file size is reduced in addition to its dimensions. Because of the way that browsers work with inline images, it is a good idea to specify the height and width of an image even if you're not trying to change its dimensions. When a browser encounters an inline image, it calculates the image size and then uses this information to lay out the page. If you include the dimensions of the image, the browser does not have to perform that calculation, reducing the time required to render the page. You can obtain the height and width of an image as measured in pixels using an image editing application such as Adobe Photoshop, or with Windows Explorer.

The logo images logo.gif and logoanim.gif are 517 pixels wide by 119 pixels high, and the photo about.jpg is 210 pixels wide by 280 pixels high. Add this information to each of the <img /> tags in the about.htm and index.htm files.

To set the image dimensions:

1. Return to the **about.htm** file in your text editor.

2. Within the <img /> tag for the logo.gif graphic, insert the attributes **width="517" height="119"**.

3. Within the <img /> tag for the about.jpg graphic, insert the attributes **width="210" height="280"**. You may want to place these attributes on a separate line to make your code more readable. Figure 3-44 shows the revised code.

Figure 3-44	Setting the image size

```
<body style="color: rgb(153,102,102); background-color: white">
<p style="text-align: center; font-family: Arial, Helvetica, sans-serif;
        font-size: 0.8em">
    <img src="logo.gif" alt="ARCADIUM" width="517" height="119" />
    <br />
    <a href="about.htm">About Arcadium</a>    
    <a href="map.htm">Park Map</a>    
    <a href="water.htm">Water Rides</a>    
    <a href="karts.htm">Go Karts</a>    
    <a href="rides.htm">Roller Coasters</a>
</p>

<h1 style="color: white; background-color: rgb(153,102,102);
        font-family: Arial, Helvetica, sans-serif; 1.5em;
        letter-spacing: 1em; text-indent: 1em">
    welcome
</h1>

<p style="text-align: justify">
<img src="about.jpg" alt="" style="float: right; margin: 0 0 5 15"
        width="210" height="280" />
```

4. Save your changes to the file and reopen **about.htm** in your Web browser. The page should appear as before.

5. Return to the **index.htm** file in your text editor.

6. Within the <img /> for the logoanim.gif graphic, insert the attributes **width="517" height="119"**.

7. Save your changes and reopen **index.htm** in your Web browser. Once again, you should not see a change in the page layout.

Setting the Image Size

- To set the size of an inline image, add the following attributes to the <img /> tag:
  height="*length*" width="*length*"
  where *length* is the height and width of the image in pixels.

Inserting a Background Image

Tom has one more suggestion for the splash screen page. The art design department has created the image file displayed in Figure 3-45, which contains images of people enjoying themselves at Arcadium. He wants you to use this image file as a background for the splash screen page.

The background image file | **Figure 3-45**

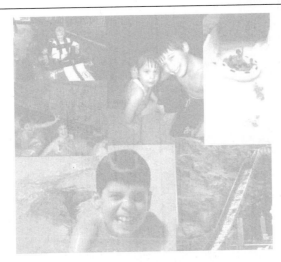

You can set a background image for any element. The style to apply a background image is

```
background-image: url(url)
```

where *url* is the name and location of the image file. When a browser loads the background image, it repeats the image in both the vertical and horizontal directions until the background of the entire element is filled with the image. This process is known as **tiling**, because of its similarity to the process of filling up a floor or other surface with tiles. Let's see how Tom's background image looks in the splash screen page. The image is stored in the paper.jpg file.

To insert a background image:

1. Return to the **index.htm** file in your text editor.
2. Add the following style to the <body> tag. Be sure to use a semicolon to separate this new style from the previous styles. You might want to place this style on a new line to make your code more readable. See Figure 3-46.

```
background-image: url(paper.jpg)
```

Figure 3-46 | Specifying a background image for the splash screen

```
<body style="font-family: Arial, Helvetica, sans-serif; margin-top: 100;
             background-image: url(paper.jpg)">
<p style="text-align: center">
    <img src="logoanim.gif" alt="ARCADIUM" width="517" height="119" />
    <br />
    <span style="color: red; font-size: 18pt; font-weight: bold">
    Affordable Family Fun
    </span>
    <br /><br />
    <a href="about.htm">Enter Arcadium</a>
</p>
</body>
</html>
```

3. Save your changes to the file. You're finished editing this file, so you may close the **index.htm** file now.

4. Reopen **index.htm** in your Web browser. Figure 3-47 shows the final version of the splash screen.

Figure 3-47 | The completed splash screen page

Note that the animated GIF that you've been using has a transparent color for its background. This allows you to see the tiled Image behind the logo.

Background Image Options

You can use other styles to control how browsers tile an image across an element's background. To specify the direction in which the tiling should take place, use the style

```
background-repeat: type
```

where *type* is repeat (the default), repeat-x, repeat-y, or no-repeat. Figure 3-48 describes each of the repeat types, and Figure 3-49 shows examples of the style values.

Background-Repeat	Description
repeat	The image is tiled both horizontally and vertically until the entire background of the element is covered.
repeat-x	The image is tiled only horizontally across the width of the element.
repeat-y	The image is tiled only vertically across the height of the element.
no-repeat	The image is not repeated at all.

Examples of the background-repeat style ◄ **Figure 3-49**

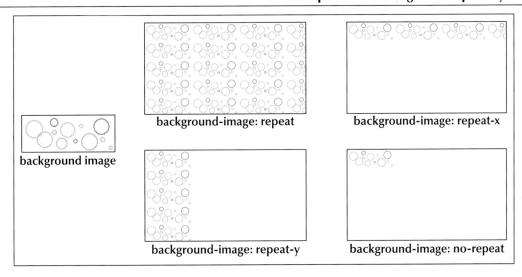

background image

background-image: repeat

background-image: repeat-x

background-image: repeat-y

background-image: no-repeat

Browsers initially place a background image in an element's upper-left corner, and then repeat the image from there if the code specifies tiling. You can change the initial position of a background image using the style

```
background-position: horizontal vertical
```

where *horizontal* is the horizontal position of the image and *vertical* is its vertical position. You can specify a position as the distance from the top-left corner of the element, a percentage of the element's width or height, or by using a keyword. Keyword options are top, center, or bottom for vertical position, and left, center, or right for horizontal placement. For example, the style

```
background-position: 10% 20%
```

specifies an initial position for the background image 10% to the right and 20% down from the upper-left corner of the element. The style

```
background-position: right bottom
```

places the background image at the bottom-right corner of the element. If you include only one position value, the browser applies that value to the horizontal position and vertically centers the image. Thus the style

```
background-position: 30px
```

places the background image 30 pixels to the right of the element's left margin and centers it vertically.

By default, a background image moves along with its element as a user scrolls through a page. You can change this using the style

```
background-attachment: type
```

where *type* is either scroll or fixed. "Scroll" (the default) scrolls the image along with the element. "Fixed" places the image in a fixed place in the browser's display window, preventing it from moving even if the user scrolls down through the Web page. Fixed background images are often used to create the effect of a **watermark**, which is a translucent graphic impressed into the very fabric of paper, often found in specialized stationery.

The Background Style

Like the font style discussed in the last session, you can combine the various background styles into the style

```
background: color image repeat attachment position
```

where *color*, *image*, and so on, are the values for the various background attributes. For example, the style

```
background: yellow url(logo.gif) no-repeat fixed center center
```

creates a yellow background on which the image file logo.gif is displayed . The image file is not tiled across the background, but is instead fixed in the horizontal and vertical center. As with the font style, you do not have to enter all of the values of the background style. However, those values that you do specify should follow the order indicated by the syntax in order to avoid unpredictable results in some browsers.

Standard procedure in the Web design team at Arcadium includes placing a watermark containing the word, "DRAFT" on any Web page that is still in the design stage. Because the About page is still undergoing review, Tom has asked you to change the background image to display the word "DRAFT". He supplies you with the appropriate image file for the watermark.

To insert the background image:

1. Return to the **about.htm** file in your text editor.
2. Replace the background-color style with the following style declaration. Be sure to use a semicolon to separate this style from the color style. See Figure 3-50.

   ```
   background: white url(draft.jpg) no-repeat fixed center center
   ```

Setting the background styles ◀ **Figure 3-50**

```
<body style="color: rgb(153,102,102);
              background: white url(draft.jpg) no-repeat fixed center center">
<p style="text-align: center; font-family: Arial, Helvetica, sans-serif;
          font-size: 0.8em">
    <img src="logo.gif" alt="ARCADIUM" width="517" height="119" />
    <br />
    <a href="about.htm">About Arcadium</a>    
    <a href="map.htm">Park Map</a>    
    <a href="water.htm">Water Rides</a>    
    <a href="karts.htm">Go Karts</a>    
    <a href="rides.htm">Roller Coasters</a>
</p>
```

3. Close the file, saving your changes.

4. Reopen **about.htm** in your Web browser. Figure 3-51 shows the completed page. Note that as you scroll through the page, the watermark remains in the center of the browser window.

The completed About page ◀ **Figure 3-51**

5. If you plan on taking a break before going to the next session, you may close your browser.

In general, older browsers do not support background images for any page element. You can add the deprecated attribute background to the <body> tag to create a background for the entire page. No attributes are available to control the tiling or placement of the background image.

Inserting a Background Image

- To insert a background image behind an element, use the style
  ```
  background-image: url(url)
  ```
  where *url* is the filename and the location of the image file.
- To control the tiling of the background image, use the style
  ```
  background-repeat: type
  ```
  where *type* is repeat (the default), repeat-x, repeat-y, or no-repeat.
- To place the background image in a specific position behind the element, use the style
  ```
  background-position: horizontal vertical
  ```
  where *horizontal* is the horizontal position of the image, and *vertical* is the vertical position. You can specify a position as the distance from the top-left corner of the element, a percentage of the element's width and height, or by using a keyword. Keyword options are top, center, or bottom for vertical position, and left, center, or right for horizontal placement.
- To control whether the background image scrolls, use the style
  ```
  background-attachment: type
  ```
  where *type* is scroll (the default) or fixed.
- To place all of the background options in a single declaration, use the style
  ```
  background: color image repeat attachment position
  ```
  where *color* is the background color, *image* is the image file, *repeat* is the method of tiling the image, *attachment* defines whether the image scrolls or is fixed, and *position* defines the position of the image within the element.

Deprecated

- To specify a background image for the page body, add the following attribute to the <body> tag:
  ```
  background="url"
  ```
  where *url* is the filename and location of the image file.

You're finished working with the inline images on your Web page. You've learned about the different image formats supported by most browsers, and their advantages and disadvantages. You've also seen how to control the appearance and placement of images on your Web page. In the next session, you'll learn how to create image maps.

Session 3.2 Quick Check

1. List three reasons for using the GIF image format instead of the JPEG format.
2. List three reasons for using the JPEG image format instead of the GIF format.
3. What style floats an element on the left margin? What style prevents an element from being displayed until that margin is clear?
4. What style sets a 10-pixel margin above and below an element, and a 15-pixel margin to the left and right of the element?
5. What attributes would you add to the <img /> tag to set the dimensions of the image to 200 pixels wide by 300 pixels high?
6. What style places the image file mark.jpg in an element's background, fixed at the top center with no tiling?
7. If you need to support older browsers, what code would you enter to use the paper.jpg image file for the page background?

Session 3.3

Understanding Image Maps

Tom has reviewed your Web site and is pleased with the progress you're making. His last task for you involves working with the park map on the Maps page. Tom wants the map to be interactive, so that when a user clicks on an area of the park, the browser opens a Web page describing the features of that area. Recall that the site includes three pages describing the different parts of the park: water.htm for the water rides, rides.htm for the roller coaster rides, and karts.htm for the go-karts. Figure 3-52 shows the relationships between the pages that Tom wants you to create.

Image map pointing to multiple pages ◄ **Figure 3-52**

To link a single image to multiple destinations, you must set up hotspots within the image. A **hotspot** is a specific area of an image formatted with its own link. Any time a user clicks a hotspot, the user's browser opens the link target.

You define hotspots for an image by creating an **image map**, which lists the boundaries of all hotspots within a particular image. As a Web designer, you can use two types of image maps: server-side image maps and client-side image maps.

Server-Side Image Maps

In a **server-side image map**, the image map is stored on the Web server (see Figure 3-53). When a user clicks a hotspot, the coordinates where the user clicked are sent to a program running on the server. The program uses the coordinates to determine which hotspot was clicked and then activates the corresponding link.

Figure 3-53 Server-side image map

user clicks a
hotspot on the
image map

the server consults
the image map and
accesses the link
indicated on the map

the server sends the
destination document
back to the user

The server-side image map was the original standard for image maps, and most graphical browsers still support server-side image maps. However, using them comes with some limitations. Because a program on the server must process the image map, you cannot test your HTML code using local files. Additionally, server-side image maps can be slow to operate, since every time a user clicks the image, the request is sent to the server for processing. With most Web browsers, the target of a link is indicated in the browser's status bar, providing valuable feedback to the user. However, this is not the case with hotspots in a server-side image map. Because the server handles the hotspots rather than the Web browser, users receive no feedback regarding hotspot locations and targets.

Client-Side Image Maps

Because of the limitations of server-side image maps, most maps are now handled by the client. To set up a **client-side image map**, you insert the image map into the same HTML file that contains the image, and the Web browser processes the image map. Because all of the processing is done locally, rather than on the Web server, you can easily test your Web pages using the HTML files stored on your computer. In addition, client-side image maps tend to respond to user interaction more quickly than server-side maps, because map coordinates and link information do not have to be sent over a network or Internet connection. Finally, when a user moves the pointer over a hotspot in a client-side image map, the browser's status bar displays the target URL. For the purposes of this tutorial, you'll concentrate solely on client-side image maps.

You create a client-side image map using the map element. The syntax of the map element is

```
<map name="map" id="map">
  hotspots
</map>
```

where *map* is the name of the map and *hotspots* are the locations of the hotspots within the map. If you need to create XHTML-compliant code, you should include both the name and id attributes within the map element, setting them to the same value; otherwise you can use only the name attribute. You can place a map element anywhere within the body of an HTML file, because the browser uses it for reference and does not actually render it. For the park map, we'll create an image map named "parkmap" directly below the inline image.

To create the map element:

1. Use your text editor to open the **maptxt.htm** file from the tutorial.03/tutorial folder of your Data Files. Enter *your name* and *the date* in the comment section at the top of the file. Save the file as **map.htm**.

2. Locate the <img /> tag for the parkmap.gif file, and directly below it, insert the following code (see Figure 3-54):

```
<map name="parkmap" id="parkmap">
</map>
```

Creating a map element   **Figure 3-54**

```
<h1 style="color:white; font-family: Arial, Helvetica, sans-serif;
        font-size: 1.5em; background-color:black; letter-spacing: 1em;
        text-indent: 1em">
    Maps
</h1>

<p style="text-align: center">
    <img src="parkmap.gif" alt="Park Map" width="610" height="395" />
    <map name="parkmap" id="parkmap">
    </map>
</p>
```

3. Save your changes to the file.

   Next, create the three Web pages that this map will be linked to.

4. Use your text editor to open the **watertxt.htm**, **kartstxt.htm**, and **ridestxt.htm** files from the tutorial.03/tutorial folder. Enter *your name* and *the date* in the comment section of each file. Save the files as **water.htm**, **karts.htm**, and **rides.htm** respectively. You will not be editing these files, so you can close them.

   Next, we'll enter the hotspots of the map.

Creating a Client-Side Image Map

Reference Window

- To create an image map, insert the code:
    ```
    <map name="map" id="map">
    hotspots
    </map>
    ```
    where *map* is the name of the image map and *hotspots* are the locations of the hotspots within the map.
- To access an image map, add the following attribute to the <img /> tag
    ```
    usemap="#map"
    ```

Defining Image Map Hotspots

You define a hotspot using two properties: its location in the image and its shape. The syntax of the hotspot element is:

```
<area shape="shape" coords="coordinates" href="url" alt="text" />
```

where *shape* is the shape of the hotspot, *coordinates* are the coordinates of the hotspot on the image, expressed in pixels, *url* is the URL of the link, and the alt attribute provides alternate text for nongraphical browsers. Note that the alt attribute is required for XHTML-compliant code.

If you want to test your coordinates but do not have a destination document ready, you can substitute the attribute "nohref" for the href attribute. The image map will then include the hotspot without a link. You can also include any of the attributes that you use with the <a> tag. Especially useful attributes for a hotspot include the target attribute, which allows you to open the destination document in a secondary browser window, and the title attribute, which creates a pop-up title describing the destination of the hotspot that appears as a user hovers the mouse pointer over the hotspot location.

One method of determining the locations and shapes of the hotspots is to open the image in an image editing application and record the coordinates of the points corresponding to the hotspot boundaries. However, this can be a time-consuming procedure if the image includes several hotspots. To make this process easier, Web designers instead often use image map software that allows you to specify hotspots by drawing over the image. Using your selections, the software generates <area /> tags that you can paste into your Web page. In this case, we'll assume that a colleague in the design department at Arcadium has given us the coordinates.

The shape attribute has three possible values: "rect" for a rectangular hotspot, "circle" for a circular hotspot, and "poly" for a polygon or an irregularly shaped hotspot. The values of the coords attribute depend on which shape you choose. You express the coordinates in terms of the distance of the top-left corner of the image. For example, the coordinate (123, 45) refers to a point that is 123 pixels from the left edge and 45 pixels down from the top.

There is no limit to the number of hotspots you can place on an image. An image's hotspots can also overlap. If this happens and a user clicks within the overlap, the browser opens the link of the first hotspot defined in the map. Thus, order can be important in entering the area elements.

Tom wants the image map to include three hotspots: a polygonal hotspot for the roller coaster rides, a circular hotspot for the go-kart track, and rectangular hotspot for the water park. You'll start with the water park hotspot.

Creating a Rectangular Hotspot

Two points define a rectangular hotspot: the upper-left corner and the lower-right corner. The syntax for entering the coordinate values is

```
shape="rect" coords="x1, y1, x2, y2"
```

where *x1* and *y1* are (x, y) coordinates for the upper-left corner and *x2*, *y2* are the coordinates of the lower-right corner. These points for the waterpark hotspot are located at (350, 38) and (582, 200). Thus the values for the shape and coords attributes are

```
shape="rect" coords="350, 38, 582, 200"
```

Add this hotspot to the parkmap image map. You'll link the hotspot to the water.htm file. The alternate text for this hotspot will be "Water Park".

To create the rectangular hotspot:

1. Return to the **map.htm** file in your text editor and below the opening <map> tag you just added, insert the following area element (you can place this tag on two lines to make your code more readable):

```
<area shape="rect" coords="350,38,582,200" href="water.htm"
      alt="Water Park" />
```

2. Save your changes to the file.

Creating a Circular Hotspot

A circular hotspot is defined by the location of its center and the size of the circle's radius. The attributes for creating a circular hotspot are

```
shape="circle" coords="x, y, r"
```

where x, y are the coordinates of the circle's center and r is the size of the radius in pixels. In the park map, the hotspot for the go-kart racetracks has the hotspot attributes

```
shape="circle" coords="255,133,74"
```

You'll link this hotspot to the water.htm file.

To create the circular hotspot:

1. Below the area element you just created, insert the following tag:

```
<area shape="circle" coords="255,133,74" href="karts.htm"
      alt="Go-Karts" />
```

2. Save your changes.

The final hotspot you need to define is for the roller coaster rides. Because of its irregular shape, you need to create a polygonal hotspot.

Creating a Polygonal Hotspot

The attributes for creating a polygonal hotspot are

```
shape="poly" coords="x1, y1, x2, y2, x3, y3, ..."
```

where $(x1, y1)$, $(x2, y2)$, $(x3, y3)$, and so on are the coordinates of each vertex in the shape. Figure 3-55 shows the coordinates for the vertices of the roller coaster hotspot.

Figure 3-55 ▷ **Coordinates for the roller coaster hotspot**

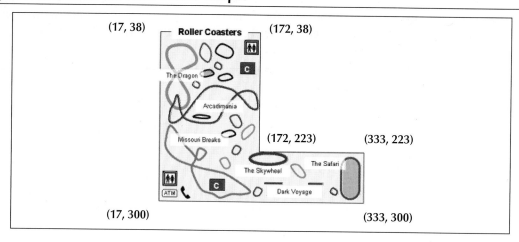

To enter these coordinates into the area element, you follow the outline clockwise around the polygonal image, and add the x and y coordinates for each point as you come to it. The attributes for the roller coaster hotspot are

```
shape="poly" coords="17,38,172,38,172,223,333,223,333,300,17,300"
```

Enter this hotspot in the parkmap image map, linking the hotspot to the rides.htm file.

To create the polygonal hotspot:

▷ **1.** Below the circular hotspot, insert the following tag:

```
<area shape="poly" coords="17,38,172,38,172,223,333,223,333,300,17,300"
      href="rides.htm" alt="Roller Coasters" />
```

Figure 3-56 shows the completed text for all three hotspots.

Figure 3-56 ▷ **Image map hotspots**

```
<p style="text-align: center">
   <img src="parkmap.gif" alt="Park Map" width="610" height="395" />
   <map name="parkmap" id="parkmap">
      <area shape="rect" coords="350,38,582,200" href="water.htm"
         alt="Water Park" />
      <area shape="circle" coords="255,133,74" href="karts.htm"
         alt="Go-Karts" />
      <area shape="poly" coords="17,38,172,38,172,223,333,223,333,300,17,300"
         href="rides.htm" alt="Roller Coasters" />
   </map>
</p>
```

▷ **2.** Save your changes.

With all of the area elements in place, you're finished defining the image map. Your next task is to instruct the browser to use the parkmap image map with the inline image. Then you'll test the map to confirm that the links work properly.

Creating Image Map Hotspots

- To create a rectangular hotspot, use the tag
  ```
  <area shape="rect" coords="x1, y1, x2, y2" href="url" alt="text"/>
  ```
  where the coordinates represent the upper-left and lower-right corners of the rectangle and *url* is the destination of the hotspot link.
- To create a circular hotspot, use the tag
  ```
  <area shape="circle" coords="x, y, r" href="url" alt="text"/>
  ```
  where *x* and *y* indicate the coordinates of the center of the circle and *r* specifies the radius of the circle, in pixels.
- To create a polygonal hotspot, use the tag
  ```
  <area shape="poly" coords="x1, y1, x2, y2, x3, y3, ..." href="url" alt="text"/>
  ```
  where the coordinates indicate the vertices of the polygon.

Using an Image Map

To apply an image map to an inline image you insert the following attribute into the <img /> tag:

```
usemap="#map"
```

where *map* is the name or id of the image map. Note the similarity between the attribute and the href attribute used in the last tutorial to create links to locations within documents. Like those links, you can place your image map in a separate file, in which case the attribute has the form

```
usemap="file#map"
```

where *file* is the name of the HTML file containing the image map coordinates. You might see this format in a group project, for example, in which one employee is responsible for the creation and maintenance of graphics, including image maps, and others access the image maps for their own pages. Be aware, however, that this feature is not well supported in most browsers.

To assign the park map image map to the image:

1. Within the <img /> tag for the parkmap graphic, insert the following attribute (see Figure 3-57):

   ```
   usemap="#parkmap"
   ```

Applying an image map to an inline image | Figure 3-57

```
<p style="text-align: center">
    <img src="parkmap.gif" alt="Park Map" width="610" height="395" usemap="#parkmap" />
    <map name="parkmap" id="parkmap">
        <area shape="rect" coords="350,38,582,200" href="water.htm"
            alt="Water Park" />
        <area shape="circle" coords="255,133,74" href="karts.htm"
            alt="Go-Karts" />
        <area shape="poly" coords="17,38,172,38,172,223,333,223,333,300,17,300"
            href="rides.htm" alt="Roller Coasters" />
    </map>
</p>
```

2. Save your changes to the file and open **map.htm** in your Web browser.
3. Click each hotspot to verify that it opens the correct page in the Arcadium Web site.

You may notice that the image map is surrounded by a colored border. Just as a browser underlines text links, it formats a linked image with a similarly colored border. In some cases, this border is distracting and can ruin the visual appearance of the image. You can remove the border by using the border-width style to set the width of the border to 0 pixels.

To remove the border from the image map:

1. Return to **map.htm** in your text editor.
2. Add the following style to the parkmap graphic, as shown in Figure 3-58:

   ```
   style="border-width: 0"
   ```

Figure 3-58 ▸ **Removing the border around a linked image**

```
<p style="text-align: center">
    <img src="parkmap.gif" alt="Park Map" width="610" height="395" usemap="#parkmap"
        style="border-width: 0" />
    <map name="parkmap" id="parkmap">
        <area shape="rect" coords="350,38,582,200" href="water.htm"
            alt="Water Park" />
        <area shape="circle" coords="255,133,74" href="karts.htm"
            alt="Go-Karts" />
        <area shape="poly" coords="17,38,172,38,172,223,333,223,333,300,17,300"
            href="rides.htm" alt="Roller Coasters" />
    </map>
</p>
```

3. Close the file, saving your changes.
4. Reopen **map.htm** in your Web browser and verify that no colored border appears around the image map. Figure 3-59 shows part of the completed page.

Figure 3-59 ▸ **The completed Map page**

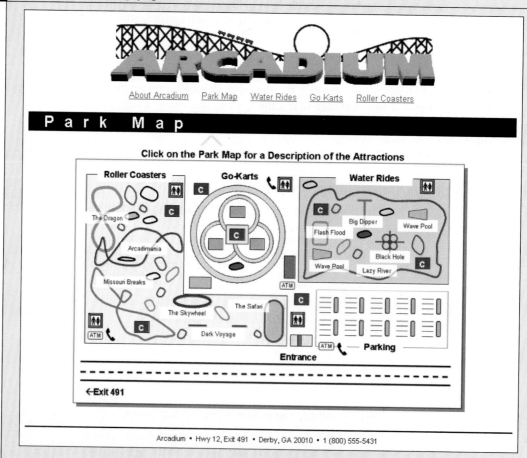

5. Close your Web browser.

The border-width style is only one of the many styles that you can use to create and format borders around page elements. We'll explore the various border styles in greater detail in a future tutorial. Note that you can also add the attribute

```
border="0"
```

to the <img /> tag to achieve the same effect. However the border attribute has been deprecated in favor of styles.

Reference Window

Removing the Colored Border from a Linked Image

- To remove a border from linked image, apply the following style to the image:
  ```
  border-width: 0
  ```

Deprecated

- To remove the border, add the following attribute to the <img /> tag:
  ```
  border="0"
  ```

As you can see, an image map can be a useful addition to a Web page. However, you should always provide textual links in addition to an image map, so that users without graphical browsers can still navigate your site. You've done this in the Map page by providing the list of links at the top of the page.

Tips for Web Page Design

- View your color and images under different color resolutions. Use Web-safe colors to prevent dithering on browsers with 256-color palettes.
- Use foreground colors that contrast well with the background.
- When specifying a font face, list the specific and most desirable faces first, and conclude with the generic font.
- Keep your font choices simple. Too many font styles within a single page can distract users. In general, you should not use more than two font faces. Large blocks of bold or italicized text can be difficult to read. Keep your fonts to about 3 or 4 basic sizes.
- Use relative units (such as the em unit) when you want your fonts to be scalable under different monitor sizes and resolutions.
- Make your code easier to read and more compact by combining the various font styles into a single style.
- Use GIFs for illustrations and line art that involve a few basic colors. Use JPEGs for photographs and illustrations that involve more than 256 colors.
- Do not overload a Web page with images. The more images you include, the longer a page takes to load. Generally a Web page should contain no more than 40 to 50 kilobytes of inline images.
- Once a browser downloads an image, it keeps a copy of it on the user's computer; therefore, you can make a Web site load faster by reusing images whenever possible throughout the site. Use a single background image or logo on every page in order to give your Web site a consistent look and feel.
- Include the width and height attributes for each of your inline images to make the page load more quickly.

- Use miniature versions of images (known as thumbnails) to let users preview large image files. Link each thumbnail to the corresponding larger image so that interested users can view the image in greater detail. You should create thumbnails in a separate graphics program, rather than simply reducing the full-size image using the width and height attributes. Changing the width and height attributes decreases an image's dimensions, but not the file size.
- View your Web page in a browser without graphical capability (or with the graphic support turned off) to verify that users with non-graphical browsers can still effectively use your site.
- Avoid large areas of white space surrounded by page content. Use the float and margin styles to move white space to the outside margins of the page.
- If you use an image map, provide text link alternatives for users with non-graphical browsers.

Review

Session 3.3 Quick Check

1. What is a hotspot? What is an image map?
2. What are the two types of image maps?
3. What HTML tag would you use to define a rectangular hotspot with the upper-left edge of the rectangle at the point (5,20) and the lower-right edge located at (85,100) and with oregon.htm displayed when the hotspot is activated?
4. What HTML tag would you use for a circular hotspot centered at (44,81) with a radius of 23 pixels to be linked to la.htm?
5. What HTML tag would you use for a hotspot that connects the points (5,10), (5,35), (25,35), (30,20), and (15,10) and that you want linked to hawaii.htm?
6. What HTML tag would you use to assign an image map named States to westcoast.gif?

Review

Tutorial Summary

In this tutorial, you learned about the styles and HTML attributes available to modify the appearance of a Web site. You first learned how HTML handles color, and how to use color to format the foreground and background of your page elements. You then learned about the different styles for formatting the appearance of Web page text. You used these styles to specify different fonts, font sizes, weights, and spacing. In the second session, you learned about the different types of image formats supported by HTML and how to apply them. You saw how to wrap content around an element like an inline image, and you learned how to set margins around your elements. The session also showed how to create and format background images. The last session discussed the different types of image maps available to a Web designer, and showed how to create and use hotspots within an image map. The session concluded with a brief discussion of borders and how to remove them from linked images.

Key Terms

absolute unit	dithering	Flash
animated GIF	dpi	generic font
client-side image map	em unit	GIF
color value	ex unit	GIF89a

Graphics Interchange Format	leading	Scalable Vector Graphics
hanging indent	Macromedia	server-side image map
hexadecimal	noninterlaced GIF	spacer
hotspot	palette	specific font
image map	pixel	splash screen
interlaced GIF	PNG	SVG
interlacing	Portable Network Graphics	tiling
Joint Photographic Experts Group	progressive JPEG	tracking
	relative unit	transparent color
JPEG	RGB triplet	watermark
kerning	safety palette	Web-safe colors
	scalable	

Practice

Practice the skills you learned in the tutorial using the same case scenario.

Review Assignments

Data files needed for this Review Assignment: about.jpg, abouttxt.htm, indextxt.htm, karts.jpg, kartstxt.htm, logo.gif, logoanim.gif, maptxt.htm, paper.jpg, parkmap.gif, review.jpg, rides.jpg, ridestxt.htm, toddler.jpg, toddtxt.htm, water.jpg, watertxt.htm

Tom has asked you to make some more changes and additions to the Arcadium Web site. The park has a new area called the Toddler Park, which is specifically designed for very young children. Tom needs you to revise the park map hotspots to accommodate the new park map, and he needs you to design a Web page for the toddler park. Figure 3-60 shows a preview of the toddler page you'll create.

Figure 3-60

About Arcadium   Park Map   Water Rides   Go Karts   Roller Coasters   Toddler Park

F o r   K i d s

Arcadium provides attractions for all ages. Opening this summer for families with young children, we present the **toddler park**, with safe, age specific, rides. At this section of Arcadium, your youngsters can:

- Ride the Arcadium Camp Bus and tour the sites of the park
- Watch the Howard Hog review, our popular show with fun characters and songs
- Play in the world's largest ball pit
- Enjoy Arcadium minature water park and kiddie pool
- Play at our 36-hole minature golf course

All toddler areas are supervised by our experienced and friendly staff.

Arcadium ▪ Hwy 12, Exit 491 ▪ Derby, GA 20010 ▪ 1 (800) 555-5431

To complete this task:

1. Use your text editor to open the files **indextxt.htm**, **abouttxt.htm**, **maptxt.htm**, **kartstxt.htm**, **ridestxt.htm**, **toddtxt.htm**, and **watertxt.htm** from the tutorial.03/review folder of your Data Files. Enter *your name* and *the date* in the comment section of each file. Save the files as **index.htm**, **about.htm**, **map.htm**, **karts.htm**, **rides.htm**, **toddler.htm**, and **water.htm**, respectively.

2. Go to the **index.htm** file in your text editor. In the body section, enclose the text "Affordable Family Fun" in a span element and display the text in a blue 22pt bold font. Enclose the text, "Enter Arcadium" in another span element. Display this text in a 14pt italicized font. Close the file, saving your changes.

3. Go to the **toddler.htm** file in your text editor and make the following changes to the page:
   - Set the text color to the rgb color value (204, 102, 0).
   - Set the background color to white.
   - Display the review.jpg file as the background image, placed in the horizontal and vertical center of the page, without scrolling, and without tiling.

4. Locate the paragraph containing the list of links and set the font size of the paragraph to 0.7em and display the text in an Arial, Helvetica, or sans-serif font.

5. Locate the h1 heading containing the text, "For Kids" and make the following changes to the heading:
   - Set the text color to white.
   - Set the background color to the color value (204, 102, 0).
   - Display the text in an Arial, Helvetica, or sans-serif font.
   - Set the font size to 1.5 em.
   - Set the kerning value to 1.5em.
   - Set the indentation to 1em.

6. Locate the inline image for the toddler.jpg file. Add the following attributes to the inline image:
   - Set the image's width and height to 250 pixels by 239 pixels.
   - Float the image on the right margin of the paragraph.
   - Set the image's left margin to 15 pixels. Set the other three margin sizes to 0 pixels.

7. Locate the horizontal line and set the page to not display this line until the right margin is clear.

8. Locate the address element and make the following changes to it:
   - Display the address in a 8pt font.
   - Display the text in a normal (non-italic) font.
   - Display the text in an Arial, Helvetica, or sans-serif font.

9. Close the file, saving your changes.

10. Go to **map.htm** in your text editor. Directly below the parkmap.gif image, insert a map element with the name and id "park". Insert the following hotspots into the map:
    - A rectangular hotspot with the corners located at (350, 48) and (582, 293). Link the hotspot to the water.htm file. Insert the alternate text "Water Park".
    - A circular hotspot centered at the coordinate (256, 216) with a radius of 81 pixels. Link the hotspot to the karts.htm file. Insert the alternate text "Go-Karts".
    - A polygonal hotspot with the vertices (18, 48), (170, 48), (170, 293), (333, 293), (333, 383), and (18, 383). Link the hotspot to the rides.htm file. Insert the alternate text "Roller Coasters".
    - A polygonal hotspot with the vertices (176, 30), (345, 30), (345, 71), (259, 116), and (176, 72). Link the hotspot to the toddler.htm. Insert the alternate text "Toddler Park".

11. Apply the park image map to the parkmap.gif inline image.
12. Set the width of the border around the parkmap.gif inline image to 0 pixels.
14. Close the file, saving your changes.
15. Open the **index.htm** file in your Web browser. View the contents of the Arcadium Web site, verifying that all of the links work correctly and that the image map in the Map page is correctly linked to the attractions at the park. Verify that the layout of the Toddler page matches Figure 3-60 (there may be slight differences depending on your browser).
16. Submit the completed Web site to your instructor.

Apply

Use the skills you've learned in this tutorial to design a Web site for a digital camera company.

Case Problem 1

Data files needed for this Case Problem: back.gif, dc100.jpg, dc100txt.htm, dc250.jpg, dc250txt.htm, dc500.jpg, dc500txt.htm, indextxt.htm, logo.jpg, logoanim.gif, menu.gif, pixaltxt.htm

Pixal Digital Products, Inc. PDP, Inc. is a new local manufacturer and distributor of digital cameras. The Web site manager, Maria Sanchez, has hired you to work on the company's Web site. Someone has already created the basic text for the Web site, which encompasses five pages: a splash screen introduction, a home page, and three pages describing the features of individual cameras. Your task is to develop a design for those pages. Figure 3-61 shows a preview of one of the pages you'll create. The box of links along the left margin of the page is an inline image. To link the text entries in that box to their targets, you will have to create an image map.

Figure 3-61

To complete this task:

1. Use your text editor to open the **indextxt.htm, pixaltxt.htm, dc100txt.htm, dc250txt.htm,** and **dc500txt.htm** files from the tutorial.03/case1 folder of your Data Files. Within each file, enter *your name* and *the date* in the comment section. Save the files as **index.htm, pixal.htm, dc100.htm, dc250.htm,** and **dc500.htm,** respectively.

2. Go to the **index.htm** file. Change the background color of the page to ivory and set the size of the top margin to 100 pixels. Locate the logoanim.gif inline image and set the dimensions of this image to 281 pixels wide by 140 pixels high. Set the border width of this inline image to 0 pixels. Save your changes to the file.

3. Go to the **pixal.htm** file. Make the following style changes to the page:
   - Set the background color to ivory and display the background image file back.gif. The image file should be tiled only in the y-direction and should scroll with the Web page.
   - Set the size of the left margin to 185 pixels.

4. Directly after the <body> tag, insert a paragraph containing the inline image menu.gif. This is the image that contains the list of links that will be displayed along the left margin of the page. Apply the following styles to this image:
   - Float the image on the left margin.
   - Set the border width to 0 pixels.
   - Set the size of the left margin to -185 pixels; this will have the effect of shifting the image to the left margin.
   - Set the dimensions of the image to 173 pixels wide by 295 pixels high.
   - Set the value of the alt attribute to an empty string, "".

5. Set the dimensions of the logo.jpg inline image to 281 pixels wide by 96 pixels high.

6. Change the color of the two horizontal lines in this page to red.

7. Apply the following style changes to the address element:
   - Display the address text in an Arial, Helvetica, or sans-serif font.
   - Set the font color to blue.
   - Set the font size to 0.7em.
   - Change the font style to normal.

8. Apply the following style changes to the paragraph containing the list of links (located below the address element):
   - Display the address text in an Arial, Helvetica, or sans-serif font.
   - Set the font size to 0.7em.

9. At the bottom of the file, above the closing </body> tag, insert an image map named "dcpages" containing the following hotspots:
   - A rectangular hotspot pointing to the pixal.htm file with coordinates (1, 1) and (81, 15). The alternate text is "Home".
   - A rectangular hotspot for the dc100.htm file with the coordinates (23, 50) and (64, 62). The alternate text is "DC100".
   - A rectangular hotspot for the dc250.htm file with the coordinates (23, 64) and (64, 79). The alternate text is "DC250".
   - A rectangular hotspot for the dc500.htm file with the coordinates (23, 81) and (64, 95). The alternate text is "DC500".

10. Apply the dcpages image map to the menu.gif inline image, located at the top of the page.

11. Save your changes to the file.

12. Go to the **dc100.htm** file and repeat Steps 3 through 11 above (you can use your text editor's copy and paste feature to transfer the code). Also, display the h1 heading,

"DC100" in a blue Arial, Helvetica, or sans-serif font. Align the inline image dc100.jpg with the page's right margin. Save your changes to the file.

13. Go to the **dc250.htm** file and apply the same style changes that you applied to the dc100.htm file. Save your changes.

14. Go to the **dc500.htm** file and match the style changes you made to the dc100.htm and dc250.htm files. Save your changes.

15. Open the **index.htm** file in your Web browser and then navigate through the Web site. Verify that the image maps work correctly in the three camera pages and in pixal.htm. Also verify that the design used in the three camera pages and in pixal.htm match.

16. Submit the completed Web site to your instructor.

Case Problem 2

Data files needed for this Case Problem: back.jpg, king1.gif - king6.gif, kingtxt.htm

Midwest University Center for Diversity Stewart Findlay is the project coordinator for the Midwest University Center for Diversity. He is currently working on a Web site titled "The Voices of Civil Rights," containing Web pages with extended quotes from civil rights leaders of the past and present. He has asked you to help develop a design for the pages in the series. He has given you the text for one of the pages, which is about Martin Luther King, Jr.

Stewart has supplied a photo of Dr. King that he would like you to include in the page. He has seen how text can be made to wrap irregularly around a photo in graphic design software, and wonders if you can do the same thing in a Web page. While you cannot use this same technique with page elements, which are always a rectangular shape, you can break a single image into a series of rectangles of different sizes. When the text wraps around these stacked rectangles, they provide the appearance of a single image with an irregular line wrap. Stewart asks you to try this with his Dr. King photo. Figure 3-62 shows a preview of the page you'll create. Note how the right margin of the text seems to wrap around Dr. King's image along a diagonal line, rather than a vertical one.

Explore

Broaden your knowledge of the float style and inline images to create a page containing an irregular text wrap.

Figure 3-62

To complete this task:

1. Use your text editor to open the **kingtxt.htm** file from the tutorial.03/case2 folder of your Data Files. Enter *your name* and *the date* in the comment section of the file. Save the file as **king.htm**.

2. Make the following style changes to the entire page:
   - Set the foreground color to black.
   - Use a single style to set the background color to the value (204, 204, 153) and fix the background image, back.jpg, in the lower-left corner of the page. Make the image scrollable.
   - Set the default font size of the text on the page to 0.9em.
   - Set the left margin of the page to 60 pixels.

3. Go to the h1 heading and add the following styles:
   - Set the foreground color to the color value (204, 204, 153) and the background color to the value (102, 102, 204).
   - Display the text in an Arial, Helvetica, or sans-serif font.
   - Center the text of the heading.

4. Stewart wants to have a drop letter starting the quote from Dr. King. To create the drop letter:
   - Enclose the first word in Dr. King's speech, "I", in a span element.
   - Float the span element on the left margin of the paragraph.
   - Display the text in a bold font that is 3em in size. Set the font color to the value (102, 102, 204).
   - Set the line height of the span element to 1em.
   - Set the right margin of the element to 5 pixels. Set the size of the three other margins to 0 pixels.

5. To create an irregular line wrap around the image, you have to break the image into several files and then stack them on the left or right margin, displaying an image only when the margin is clear of the previous image. To remove the seams between the images, you have to set the top and bottom margins to 0. The Martin Luther King, Jr. graphic has been broken into six files for you. To stack them:
   - At the very end of the first paragraph (directly before the closing </p> tag), insert the king1.gif image, aligned with the right margin of the page. Set the left margin to 5 pixels and the other three margins to 0 pixels. For nongraphical browsers display an empty text string ("").
   - Below the king1.gif image, insert the king2.gif image, aligned with the right margin. Format this element to display only when the right margin is clear. As before, set the left margin to 5 pixels and set the other three margin sizes to 0 pixels. Set the alternate text string to the empty string, "".
   - Below the king2.gif, insert the king3.gif through king6.gif images, formatted in the same way you formatted the king2.gif image. Be sure to display each of these images only when the right margin is clear or they will not stack properly.

6. Enclose the phrase, "Free at last! Free at last! Thank God Almighty, we are free at last!" in a span element and make the following style changes:
   - Change the text color to the value (102, 102, 204).
   - Change the text to boldface.
   - Set the font size to 1.2em.

7. Change the color of the horizontal line at the bottom of the page to the value (102, 102, 204). Display the line only when the right margin is clear.

8. Make the following style changes to the address text at the bottom of the page:
   - Display the text in a normal font (not italic).
   - Set the font size to 0.7em and the font color to (102, 102, 204).
   - Display the text in an Arial, Helvetica, or sans-serif font.
   - Transform the text to uppercase letters using a style.

9. Save your changes to the file.

10. Open the **king.htm** file in your Web browser and verify that the layout matches that shown in Figure 3-62 (there may be small style differences depending on your browser).

11. Submit the completed Web page to your instructor.

Broaden your knowledge of Web page design by creating a Web page for the International Cryptographic Institute.

Case Problem 3

Data files needed for this Case Problem: back1.gif, back2.gif, crypttxt.htm, locks.jpg, logo.gif, scytale.gif

International Cryptographic Institute Sela Dawes is the media representative for the ICI, the International Cryptographic Institute. The ICI is an organization of cryptographers who study the science and mathematics of secret codes, encrypted messages, and code breaking. Part of the ICI's mission is to inform the public about cryptography and data security. Sela has asked you to work on a Web site containing information about cryptography for use by high school science and math teachers. She wants the design to be visually interesting in order to help draw students into the material. Figure 3-63 shows a preview of your design.

Figure 3-63

To complete this task:

1. Use your text editor to open the **crypttxt.htm** file from the tutorial.03/case3 folder in your Data Files. Enter *your name* and *the date* in the comment section of the file. Save the file as **crypt.htm**.
2. Make the following style changes to the entire page:
   - Set the background color to black.
   - Set the text color to white.
   - Set the right margin to 10 pixels; set the left margin to 100 pixels.
   - Display the back1.gif image in the page background. Tile this image in the y-direction.
3. Locate the logo.gif element and set the following styles and attributes:
   - Set the width and height of the image to 95 pixels wide by 78 pixels high.
   - Float the image on the left page margin.
   - Set the left margin of the image to -100 pixels (moving the image to the left).
4. Go to the h1 heading and make the following style changes:
   - Change the text to a Courier New or a monospace font.
   - Change the font size to 1.8em, the kerning to 0.3em, and the leading to 0.7em.
   - Display the text in a bold yellow font.
   - Add the back2.gif image to the background of the heading.

Explore

Explore

5. Display the h2 heading in an Arial, Helvetica, or sans-serif font.
6. Indent the first and second paragraphs to 2em.
7. Go to the scytale.gif element and make the following style and attribute changes:
   - Set the width and height of the image to 250 pixels by 69 pixels.
   - Float the image on the right margin of the page.
8. Change the color of the horizontal line after the second paragraph to yellow.
9. Go to the locks.jpg element and set the width and height of the image to 510 by 110 pixels.
10. Directly below the inline image locks.jpg, insert an image map with the name and id "locks". Insert the following hotspots (note that the targets of these links are not available):
    - A circular hotspot linked to history.htm centered at the coordinate (52, 52) with a radius of 43 pixels. The alternate text is "History".
    - A circular hotspot with a radius of 43 pixels located at the coordinate (155, 52). Link the hotspot to enigma.htm. The alternate text is "Enigma".
    - A circular hotspot with a radius of 43 pixels located at the coordinate (255, 52). Link the hotspot to algo.htm. The alternate text is "Algorithms".
    - A circular hotspot with a radius of 43 pixels located at the coordinate (355, 52). Link the hotspot to single.htm. The alternate text is "Single Key".
    - A circular hotspot with a radius of 43 pixels located at the coordinate (455, 52). Link the hotspot to public.htm. The alternate text is "Public Key".
11. Apply the locks image map to the locks.jpg inline image. Set the border width for this image to 0 pixels.
12. Save your changes to the file.
13. Open **crypt.htm** in your Web browser and verify that the design matches the page shown in Figure 3-63.
14. Submit your completed Web site to your instructor.

Case Problem 4

Data files needed for this Case Problem: back.gif, logo.gif, logo.jpg, midwest,txt, r317081.jpg, r317082.jpg, r317083.jpg, r317084.jpg, thumb1.jpg, thumb2.jpg

Midwest Homes You've been hired by Midwest Homes to assist in developing their Web site. Dawn Upham, the site manager, has asked you to begin work on the new listings section. She's given you a text file containing information about Midwest Homes and the four new listings for the day. She's also provided you with two versions of the company logo (one in JPEG format, and one in GIF format with a transparent background), a background image, image files for the four new properties, and two image files containing thumbnail images of the four new properties—one oriented horizontally, and the other vertically. You are free to supplement this material with any additional resources available to you. Your job is to use this information to design a visually interesting Web site for the new listings.

To complete this task:

1. Locate the text files and image files in the tutorial.03/case4 folder of your Data Files. Review the content of the text files and view the image files. Note that there are four new properties with listing numbers: r317081, r317082, r317083, and r317084. The image files match up with the property descriptions in the midwest.txt file.

2. Once you become familiar with the contents of this proposed site, start designing the site. There should be five pages: a page introducing the new listings, and one page with details on each of the new homes. The name of the intro page should be new.htm, the names of the four listings pages should be r317081.htm, r317082.htm, r317083.htm, and r317084.htm. In your preparations for the site, create a storyboard of the site's contents and links. Make sure that you make your site easy to navigate.

3. Within each page, insert comments that include your name, the date, and a description of the page's content.

4. The design and layout of the site is up to you, but your pages should include at least one example of the following design elements:
   - A style that sets the foreground and background color for a page and an element within the page.
   - A style that sets a background image for either the entire page or an element within the page.
   - A style that changes the font family for at least one element.
   - A style that sets the font size for at least one element.
   - A style that sets the font weight and font style for at least one element.
   - An inline image that floats along the right or left border of its containing element.
   - A style that sets the margin size for an element or for the entire page.

5. Use one of the supplied thumbnail images to create an image map linking the introduction page to each of the pages describing the new listings. Use a graphics program to determine the coordinates of the hotspots in the image map.

6. Submit the completed Web site to your instructor.

Review

Quick Check Answers

Session 3.1

1. color: yellow; background-color: rgb(51,102,51)
2. Web-safe colors are colors that will not be dithered by a Web browser limited to a 256-color palette. You would use them when you want to ensure that your colors appear correctly without browser modification on monitors that display only 256 colors.
3. font-family: Courier New, monospace
4. font-size: 16pt
5. The em unit is a relative unit of length equal to the width of the capital letter "M" in the browser's default font. Because the size is expressed relative to the default font size, text that is sized with the em unit is scalable and will appear correct relative to other text, no matter what font size has been set on the user's browser.
6. Kerning refers to the amount of space between letters. To set the kerning to 2em, use the style letter-spacing: 2em.
7. line-height: 2
8. font-weight: bold; font-style: italic
9. The span element is a generic inline element used to contain or mark an inline content.

Session 3.2

1. Use GIF when you want to use a transparent color, when you want to create an animated image, and when your image is an illustration of 256 colors or less.
2. Use JPEG for photographic images, for images that contain more than 256 colors, or when you need to reduce the file size through compression.

3. float: left
   clear: left
4. margin: 10px 15px
5. width="200" height="300"
6. background: url(mark.jpg) no-repeat fixed center top
7. <body background="paper.jpg">

Session 3.3

1. A hotspot is a defined area of an image that acts as a link. An image map lists the coordinates of the hotspots within the image.
2. Server-side and client-side
3. <area shape="rect" coords="5,20,85,100" href="oregon.htm" />
4. <area shape="circle" coords="44,81,23" href="la.htm" />
5. <area shape="poly" coords="5,10,5,35,25,35,30,20,15,10" href="hawaii.htm" />
6. <img src="westcoast.gif" usemap="#States" />

Objectives

Designing a Web Page with Tables

Creating a News Page

Case

The *Park City Gazette*

Park City, Colorado, is a rural mountain community located near a popular national park. Visitors from around the world come to Park City to enjoy its natural beauty, hike and climb in the national park, and ski at the many area resorts. During the busy tourist season, the population of Park City can triple in size.

Kevin Webber is the editor of the weekly *Park City Gazette*. Kevin knows that the newspaper is a valuable source of information for tourists as well as year-round residents, and he would like to publish a Web edition.

He has approached you about designing a Web site for the paper. He would like the Web site to have the same look and feel as the printed *Gazette*, which has been published for over 100 years and maintains its classic, traditional design. The paper has a large and loyal readership.

In order to implement the design that Kevin is looking for, you'll need to learn how to use HTML to create and format tables.

Student Data Files

▼Tutorial.04

▽ **Tutorial folder**

artcltxt.htm
page1txt.htm
racetxt1.htm
racetxt2.htm
+ 4 HTML files
+ 5 graphic files

▽ **Review folder**

art2txt.htm
page2txt.htm
sighttxt.htm
+ 1 HTML file
+ 5 graphic files

▽ **Case1 folder**

dhometxt.htm
introtxt.htm
+ 4 HTML files
+ 7 graphic files

▽ **Case2 folder**

dunsttxt.htm
welctxt.htm
+ 4 HTML files
+ 3 graphic files

▽ **Case3 folder**

febtxt.htm
+ 2 graphic files

▽ **Case4 folder**

luxair.txt
photo.txt
toronto.txt
twlinks.htm
twlinks2.htm
yosemite.txt
+ 4 graphic files

Session 4.1

Tables on the World Wide Web

The annual Front Range Marathon in Boulder has just been run, and a local woman, Laura Blake, won the women's open division. As your first assignment, Kevin wants you to place the marathon story on the Web. With the story, he would also like to see a table that lists the top three male and female finishers. Kevin presents you with a table of the race results, which is shown in Figure 4-1.

Figure 4-1	Marathon results

Group	Runner	Time	Origin
Men	1. Peter Teagan	2:12:34	San Antonio, Texas
Men	2. Kyle Wills	2:13:05	Billings, Montana
Men	3. Jason Wu	2:14:28	Cutler, Colorado
Women	1. Laura Blake	2:28:21	Park City, Colorado
Women	2. Kathy Lasker	2:30:11	Chicago, Illinois
Women	3. Lisa Peterson	2:31:14	Seattle, Washington

A table can be coded in HTML in either a text or a graphical format. A **text table**, like the one shown in Figure 4-2, contains only text, which is evenly spaced on the Web page to create rows and columns. Because text tables use only standard word processing characters, cell borders and lines must be created using characters such as hyphens or equal signs.

Figure 4-2	A text table

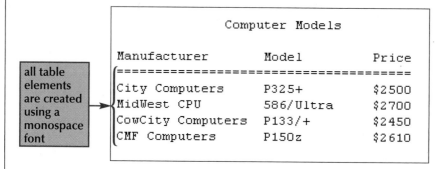

A **graphical table**, as shown in Figure 4-3, is rendered using graphical elements to distinguish the table components. In a graphical table, you can include design elements such as background colors and shaded borders. You can also control the size of individual table cells in a graphical table, and you can align text within those cells. A graphical table even allows you to create cells that span several rows or columns.

A graphical table | **Figure 4-3**

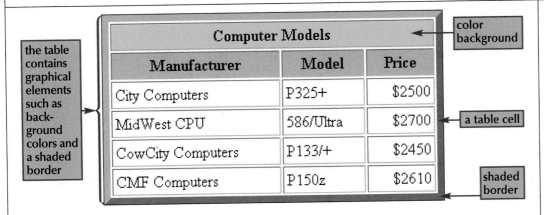

Although graphical tables are more flexible and attractive than text tables, it is quicker and easier to create a text table. You'll start on Kevin's project by creating a Web page that contains a text table; after finishing that page, you'll start working on a graphical version of the same table.

Creating a Text Table

The race results page has been created for you and is stored in your Data Files as racetxt1.htm. You will add a text table containing the race results to this page. To begin, you'll open this text file and save it with a new name.

To open racetxt1.htm and save it with a new name:

1. Using your text editor, open **racetxt1.htm** from the tutorial.04/tutorial folder. Enter **your name** and **the date** in the comment section of the file.

2. Save the file as **race1.htm** in the same folder.

   Figure 4-4 shows a preview of the page as it is displayed in a browser.

The race1 page | **Figure 4-4**

Local Woman Wins Marathon

Park City native, **Laura Blake**, won the 27th Front Range Marathon over an elite field of the best long distance runners in the country. Laura's time of 2 hr. 28 min. 21 sec. was only 2 minutes off the women's course record set last year by Sarah Rawlings. Kathy Lasker and Lisa Peterson finished second and third, respectively. Laura's victory came on the heels of her performance at the NCAA Track and Field Championships, in which she placed second running for Colorado State.

In an exciting race, **Peter Teagan** of San Antonio, Texas, used a finishing kick to win the men's marathon for the second straight year, in a time of 2 hr. 12 min. 34 sec. Ahead for much of the race, Kyle Wills of Billings, Montana, finished second, when he could not match Teagan's finishing pace. Jason Wu of Cutler, Colorado, placed third in a very competitive field.

This year's race through downtown Boulder boasted the largest field in the marathon's history, with over 9500 men and 6700 women competing. Race conditions were perfect with low humidity and temperatures that never exceeded 85°.

The page consists of an article that Kevin has written about the marathon. You'll place the race results table between the first and second paragraphs.

Using Fixed-Width Fonts

A text table relies on the widths of the characters and spaces in each row to ensure that the column boundaries for different rows are aligned. For this reason, choosing the correct font is important when you create a text table. You can ensure that the column contents align properly by using a fixed-width font and including the same number of characters in each row. In a **fixed-width font**—also known as a **monospace font**—each character takes up the same amount of space.

Most typeset documents, including the one you're reading now, use proportional fonts. **Proportional fonts** assign a different amount of space for each character depending on the width of that character. For example, since the character "m" is wider than the character "I," a proportional font assigns it more space. Because of the variable spacing, proportional fonts are more visually attractive, and typically easier to read, than fixed-width fonts. However, proportional fonts are less suitable for text tables.

The distinction between fixed-width and proportional fonts is important. If you use a proportional font in a text table, the varying width of the characters and the spaces between characters can cause errors when the page is rendered in the user's browser. Figure 4-5 shows how a text table that uses a proportional font loses alignment when the font size is increased or decreased.

Figure 4-5 ▶ **Alignment with proportional fonts**

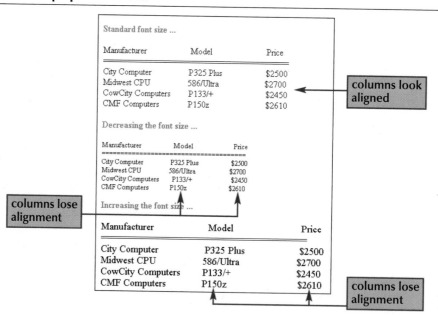

By contrast, the table shown in Figure 4-6 uses fixed-width fonts. Note that the columns remain aligned regardless of font size.

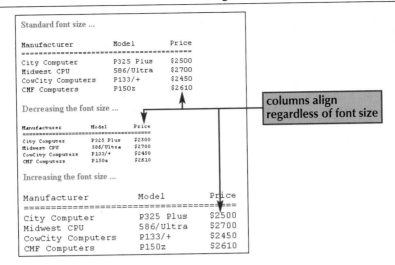

Different browsers and operating systems may use different font sizes to display your page's text, so you should always use a fixed-width font to ensure that the columns in your text tables remain in alignment.

Using Preformatted Text

To control the appearance of a text table, you need to insert extra spaces and other characters for alignment. However, HTML ignores extra occurrences of white space. One way to solve this problem is to mark the text as **preformatted text,** which retains the extra white space and causes the text to appear in the Web page as it appears in the HTML code. Preformatted text is created using the following syntax:

```
<pre>content</pre>
```

where *content* is text that will appear as preformatted text. Preformatted text is displayed by default in a monospace font, making it ideal for building text tables.

You'll use the <pre> tag to enter the table data from Figure 4-1 into race1.htm.

To create a text table using the <pre> tag:

1. Place the insertion point in the blank line located between the first and second paragraphs of Kevin's article.

2. Type **<pre>** and press **Enter** to create a blank line.

3. Type **Group** and press the spacebar **4** times.

4. Type **Runner** and press the spacebar **15** times.

5. Type **Time** and press the spacebar **10** times.

6. Type **Origin** and press the **Enter** key to create a blank line.

7. Underline each heading (Group, Runner, Time, Origin) using the equal sign symbol (see Figure 4-7) and press **Enter**.

8. Complete the table by entering the information from Figure 4-1 about the runners, their times, and their places of origin. Place a blank line between the men's and women's results, and align each entry with the left edge of the column headings.

▶ **9.** Below the women's results, type **</pre>** to turn off the preformatted text tag. Figure 4-7 shows the complete preformatted text as it appears in the file.

Figure 4-7 ▶ **Inserting preformatted text**

```
<p>Park City native, <b>Laura Blake</b>, won the 27<sup>th</sup> Front Range Marathon
over an elite field of the best long distance runners in the country. Laura's
time of 2 hr. 28 min. 21 sec. was only 2 minutes off the women's course record
set last year by Sarah Rawlings. Kathy Lasker and Lisa Peterson finished second
and third, respectively. Laura's victory came on the heels of her performance at
the NCAA Track and Field Championships, in which she placed second running for
Colorado State.</p>
<pre>
Group      Runner                  Time          Origin
=====      ======                  ====          ======
Men        1. Peter Teagan         2:12:34       San Antonio, Texas
Men        2. Kyle Wills           2:13:05       Billings, Montana
Men        3. Jason Wu             2:14:28       Cutler, Colorado

Women      1. Laura Blake          2:28:21       Park City, Colorado
Women      2. Kathy Lasker         2:30:11       Chicago, Illinois
Women      3. Lisa Peterson        2:31:14       Seattle, Washington
</pre>
<p>In an exciting race, <b>Peter Teagan</b> of San Antonio, Texas, used a finishing
kick to win the men's marathon for the second straight year, in a time of
2 hr. 12 min. 34 sec. Ahead for much of the race, Kyle Wills of Billings, Montana,
finished second, when he could not match Teagan's finishing pace. Jason Wu of
Cutler, Colorado, placed third in a very competitive field.</p>
```

table text will appear in the browser as it appears here

▶ **10.** Save your changes to **race1.htm** and close the file.

▶ **11.** Using your Web browser, open **race1.htm**. Figure 4-8 displays the page as it appears in the browser.

Figure 4-8 ▶ **A text table in the race1 page**

Local Woman Wins Marathon

Park City native, **Laura Blake**, won the 27th Front Range Marathon over an elite field of the best long distance runners in the country. Laura's time of 2 hr. 28 min. 21 sec. was only 2 minutes off the women's course record set last year by Sarah Rawlings. Kathy Lasker and Lisa Peterson finished second and third, respectively. Laura's victory came on the heels of her performance at the NCAA Track and Field Championships, in which she placed second running for Colorado State.

```
Group      Runner                  Time          Origin
=====      ======                  ====          ======
Men        1. Peter Teagan         2:12:34       San Antonio, Texas
Men        2. Kyle Wills           2:13:05       Billings, Montana
Men        3. Jason Wu             2:14:28       Cutler, Colorado

Women      1. Laura Blake          2:28:21       Park City, Colorado
Women      2. Kathy Lasker         2:30:11       Chicago, Illinois
Women      3. Lisa Peterson        2:31:14       Seattle, Washington
```

In an exciting race, **Peter Teagan** of San Antonio, Texas, used a finishing kick to win the men's marathon for the second straight year, in a time of 2 hr. 12 min. 34 sec. Ahead for much of the race, Kyle Wills of Billings, Montana, finished second, when he could not match Teagan's finishing pace. Jason Wu of Cutler, Colorado, placed third in a very competitive field.

This year's race through downtown Boulder boasted the largest field in the marathon's history, with over 9500 men and 6700 women competing. Race conditions were perfect with low humidity and temperatures that never exceeded 85°.

By using preformatted text, you've created a text table that can be displayed by all browsers, and you've ensured that the columns will retain their alignment in any font size.

You show the completed table to Kevin. He's pleased with your work and would like you to create a similar page using a graphical table. Before creating the new table, you'll study how HTML defines table structures.

Creating Preformatted Text

- To create preformatted text, which retains any white space in the HTML file, use the tag
    ```
    <pre>content</pre>
    ```
    where *content* is the text you want displayed as preformatted text.

Defining a Table Structure

The first step in creating a graphical table is to specify the table structure, which includes the number of rows and columns, the locations of column headings, and the placement of a table caption. Once the table structure is in place, you can start entering data into the table.

The page that will contain the graphical table has been created for you and stored in the file racetxt2.htm in your Data Files. Open the file using your text editor and save it with a new name.

To open racetxt2.htm and save it with a new name:

1. Using your text editor, open **racetxt2.htm** from the tutorial.04/tutorial folder. Enter *your name* and *the date* in the comment section of the file.

2. Save the file as **race2.htm**.

Figure 4-9 shows a preview of the page as it appears in the browser.

The race2 page   **Figure 4-9**

Local Woman Wins Marathon

Park City native, **Laura Blake**, won the 27th Front Range Marathon over an elite field of the best long distance runners in the country. Laura's time of 2 hr. 28 min. 21 sec. was only 2 minutes off the women's course record set last year by Sarah Rawlings. Kathy Lasker and Lisa Peterson finished second and third, respectively. Laura's victory came on the heels of her performance at the NCAA Track and Field Championships, in which she placed second running for Colorado State.

In an exciting race, **Peter Teagan** of San Antonio, Texas, used a finishing kick to win the men's marathon for the second straight year, in a time of 2 hr. 12 min. 34 sec. Ahead for much of the race, Kyle Wills of Billings, Montana, finished second, when he could not match Teagan's finishing pace. Jason Wu of Cutler, Colorado, placed third in a very competitive field.

This year's race through downtown Boulder boasted the largest field in the marathon's history, with over 9500 men and 6700 women competing. Race conditions were perfect with low humidity and temperatures that never exceeded 85°.

Marking a table, table row, and table cell

Tables are marked with a two-sided <table> tag that identifies the start and end of the table structure. Each row in a table is marked using a two-sided <tr> (for table row) tag. Finally, within each table row, the two-sided <td> (for table data) tag marks the content of individual table cells. The general syntax of a graphical table is therefore

```
<table>
   <tr>
      <td>First Cell</td>
      <td>Second Cell</td>
   </tr>
   <tr>
```

```
      <td>Third Cell</td>
      <td>Fourth Cell</td>
   </tr>
</table>
```

This example creates a table with two rows and two columns. Figure 4-10 shows the layout of a table with this HTML code.

Figure 4-10 ▶ **A simple table**

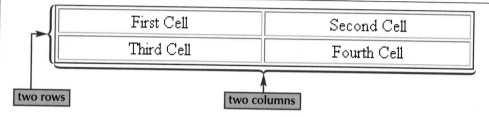

HTML includes no tag for table columns because the number of columns is determined by the number of cells within a row. For example, if each table row includes four td elements, then the table has four columns.

The table that Kevin outlined in Figure 4-1 requires seven rows and four columns. The first row contains column headings, and the remaining six rows display the table's data. HTML provides a special tag for headings, which you'll learn about shortly. For now, you'll create the table structure for the table data.

To create the structure for the race results table:

▶ 1. Place the insertion point in the blank line between the first and second paragraphs of Kevin's article.

▶ 2. Type **<table>** to identify the beginning of the table structure, and then press the **Enter** key.

▶ 3. Type the entries for the first row of the table as follows:

```
<tr>
    <td></td>
    <td></td>
    <td></td>
    <td></td>
</tr>
```

Note that you do not need to indent the <tr> or <td> tags or place them on separate lines, but you may find it easier to interpret your code if you do so.

▶ 4. Press the **Enter** key and then repeat Step 3 five times to create the six rows of the table. You might want to use the copy and paste function of your text editor to save time.

▶ 5. Press the **Enter** key and then type **</table>** to complete the code for the table structure. See Figure 4-11.

```
<p><img src="blake.jpg" alt="" width="75" height="101" style="margin: 5; float: left" />
Park City native, <b>Laura Blake</b>, won the 27<sup>th</sup> Front Range Marathon
over an elite field of the best long distance runners in the country. Laura's
time of 2 hr. 28 min. 21 sec. was only 2 minutes off the women's course record
set last year by Sarah Rawlings. Kathy Lasker and Lisa Peterson finished second
and third, respectively. Laura's victory came on the heels of her performance at
the NCAA Track and Field Championships, in which she placed second running for
Colorado State.</p>

<table>
   <tr>
      <td></td>
      <td></td>
      <td></td>
      <td></td>
   </tr>
   <tr>
      <td></td>
      <td></td>
      <td></td>
      <td></td>
   </tr>
   <tr>
      <td></td>
      <td></td>
      <td></td>
      <td></td>
   </tr>
   <tr>
      <td></td>
      <td></td>
      <td></td>
      <td></td>
   </tr>
   <tr>
      <td></td>
      <td></td>
      <td></td>
      <td></td>
   </tr>
   <tr>
      <td></td>
      <td></td>
      <td></td>
      <td></td>
   </tr>
</table>
```

With the table structure in place, you're ready to add the text for each cell.

To insert the table text:

1. Locate the first <td> tag in the table structure and type **Men** between the opening and closing <td> tags.

2. Within the next three <td> tags, type the remaining entries for the first row of the table as follows:

   ```
   <td>1. Peter Teagan</td>
   <td>2:12:34</td>
   <td>San Antonio, Texas</td>
   ```

3. Continue entering the text for the cells for the remaining five rows of the table. Figure 4-12 shows the completed text for the body of the table.

Figure 4-12   Data for the table cells

```
<table>
    <tr>
        <td>Men</td>
        <td>1. Peter Teagan</td>
        <td>2:12:34</td>
        <td>San Antonio, Texas</td>
    </tr>
    <tr>
        <td>Men</td>
        <td>2. Kyle Wills</td>
        <td>2:13:05</td>
        <td>Billings, Montana</td>
    </tr>
    <tr>
        <td>Men</td>
        <td>3. Jason Wu</td>
        <td>2:14:28</td>
        <td>Cutler, Colorado</td>
    </tr>
    <tr>
        <td>Women</td>
        <td>1. Laura Blake</td>
        <td>2:28:21</td>
        <td>Park City, Colorado</td>
    </tr>
    <tr>
        <td>Women</td>
        <td>2. Kathy Lasker</td>
        <td>2:30:11</td>
        <td>Chicago, Illinois</td>
    </tr>
    <tr>
        <td>Women</td>
        <td>3. Lisa Peterson</td>
        <td>2:31:14</td>
        <td>Seattle, Washington</td>
    </tr>
</table>
```

With the text for the body of the table entered, the next step is to add the column headings.

Creating Table Headings

Table headings are marked with the <th> tag. Table headings are like table cells, except that content marked with the <th> tag is centered within the cell and displayed in a bold-face font. The <th> tag is most often used for column headings.

In the race results table, Kevin has specified a single row of table headings. You'll mark this text using the <th> tag.

To insert the table headings:

1. Place the insertion point after the <table> tag and press the **Enter** key to create a blank line.

2. Type the following HTML code and content:

```
<tr>
    <th>Group</th>
    <th>Runner</th>
    <th>Time</th>
    <th>Origin</th>
</tr>
```

Figure 4-13 shows the code for the table headings as they appear in the file.

Inserting table headings ◄ **Figure 4-13**

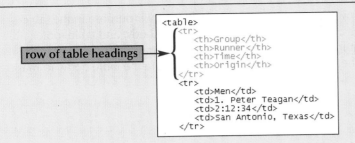

```
<table>
  <tr>
      <th>Group</th>
      <th>Runner</th>
      <th>Time</th>
      <th>Origin</th>
  </tr>
  <tr>
      <td>Men</td>
      <td>1. Peter Teagan</td>
      <td>2:12:34</td>
      <td>San Antonio, Texas</td>
  </tr>
```

row of table headings →

3. Save your changes to the file.
4. Using your Web browser, open **race2.htm**. The table is shown in Figure 4-14.

Race results table data ◄ **Figure 4-14**

Local Woman Wins Marathon

Park City native, **Laura Blake**, won the 27th Front Range Marathon over an elite field of the best long distance runners in the country. Laura's time of 2 hr. 28 min. 21 sec. was only 2 minutes off the women's course record set last year by Sarah Rawlings. Kathy Lasker and Lisa Peterson finished second and third, respectively. Laura's victory came on the heels of her performance at the NCAA Track and Field Championships, in which she placed second running for Colorado State.

headings appear bold and centered

Group	Runner	Time	Origin
Men	1. Peter Teagan	2:12:34	San Antonio, Texas
Men	2. Kyle Wills	2:13:05	Billings, Montana
Men	3. Jason Wu	2:14:28	Cutler, Colorado
Women	1. Laura Blake	2:28:21	Park City, Colorado
Women	2. Kathy Lasker	2:30:11	Chicago, Illinois
Women	3. Lisa Peterson	2:31:14	Seattle, Washington

Note that the text marked as a table heading is displayed in bold and centered above each table column.

Reference Window

Defining a Table Structure

- To mark a table, use the tag
  ```
  <table>content</table>
  ```
  where *content* includes the table's rows, headings, and cells.
- To create a table row, use the tag
  ```
  <tr>content</tr>
  ```
  where *content* includes the table's cells and headings.
- To create a table cell that contains a row or column heading, use the tag
  ```
  <th>content</th>
  ```
  where *content* is the content of the heading. Table headings are usually displayed in a centered bold font.
- To create a table cell that contains table data, use the tag
  ```
  <td>content</td>
  ```
  where *content* is the cell content.

Creating Row Groups

You can classify a table's rows into **row groups** that indicate their purpose in the table. HTML supports three types of row groups: table header, table body, and table footer. Because order is important in an HTML file, the table header must be listed before the table footer, and both the header and footer must appear before the table body. To mark the header rows of a table, use the syntax

```
<thead>
    table rows
</thead>
```

A table can contain only one set of table header rows. To mark the rows of the table footer, use the syntax

```
<tfoot>
    table rows
</tfoot>
```

A table can contain only one footer. Finally, to mark the rows of the table body, use the syntax:

```
<tbody>
    table rows
</tbody>
```

A table can contain multiple table body sections.

Row groups are sometimes used for tables that draw their data from external sources such as databases or XML documents. In those cases, programs can be written in which the contents of a table body span across several different Web pages, with the contents of the table header and footer repeated on each page. Not all browsers support this capability, however.

Although creating row groups does not affect a table's appearance, you can apply different styles to table groups in order to make them appear differently. We'll explore this more in the next session. For now, we'll mark the table's header and body; this table contains no footer.

To mark the row groups:

1. Locate the row containing the table headings. Enclose this row within a two-sided <thead> tag as shown in Figure 4-15.

2. Enclose the six rows containing the race results within a two-sided <tbody> tag as shown in Figure 4-15.

header row

body rows

```
<table>
  <thead>
  <tr>
    <th>Group</th>
    <th>Runner</th>
    <th>Time</th>
    <th>Origin</th>
  </tr>
  </thead>
  <tbody>
  <tr>
    <td>Men</td>
    <td>1. Peter Teagan</td>
    <td>2:12:34</td>
    <td>San Antonio, Texas</td>
  </tr>
  <tr>
    <td>Men</td>
    <td>2. Kyle Wills</td>
    <td>2:13:05</td>
    <td>Billings, Montana</td>
  </tr>
  <tr>
    <td>Men</td>
    <td>3. Jason Wu</td>
    <td>2:14:28</td>
    <td>Cutler, Colorado</td>
  </tr>
  <tr>
    <td>Women</td>
    <td>1. Laura Blake</td>
    <td>2:28:21</td>
    <td>Park City, Colorado</td>
  </tr>
  <tr>
    <td>Women</td>
    <td>2. Kathy Lasker</td>
    <td>2:30:11</td>
    <td>Chicago, Illinois</td>
  </tr>
  <tr>
    <td>Women</td>
    <td>3. Lisa Peterson</td>
    <td>2:31:14</td>
    <td>Seattle, Washington</td>
  </tr>
  </tbody>
</table>
```

3. Save your changes to the file.

Creating a Table Caption

You can add a caption to a table in order to provide descriptive information about the table's contents. The syntax for creating a caption is

```
<caption>content</caption>
```

where *content* is the content of the caption. The <caption> tag must appear directly after the opening <table> tag. By default, the caption appears centered above a table. However, you can change the placement of a caption using the align attribute:

```
<caption align="position">content</caption>
```

where *position* equals one of the following:

- "bottom" to place the caption centered below the table
- "top" to place the caption centered above the table
- "left" to place the caption above the table, aligned with the left table margin
- "right" to place the caption above the table, aligned with the right table margin

Internet Explorer also supports a value of "center" for the caption, which centers the caption above the table. Because HTML 3.2 specified only the "top" and "bottom" alignment options, older browsers support only those options. Note that the align attribute has been deprecated, and thus might not be supported in future browser versions. Captions are rendered as normal text without special formatting, but you can format and align captions using the styles discussed in the previous tutorial.

Reference Window	**Creating a Table Caption**

- To create a table caption, insert the following tag directly after the opening <table> tag:
  `<caption>content</caption>`
  where content is the content of the caption.

Deprecated

- To align a caption, add the following attribute to the <caption> tag:
  `align="position"`
  where position is either top (the default), bottom, left, or right. Internet Explorer also supports a position value of "center".

Kevin asks you to add the caption "Race Results" to the table in a boldface font. By default, the caption will be centered above the table.

To add the caption to the race results table:

1. Return to **race2.htm** in your text editor.

2. Insert the following code below the <table> tag (see Figure 4-16):

   `<caption style="font-weight: bold">Race Results</caption>`

Figure 4-16	Inserting the table caption

```
<table>
   <caption style="font-weight: bold">Race Results</caption>
   <thead>
   <tr>
      <th>Group</th>
      <th>Runner</th>
      <th>Time</th>
      <th>Origin</th>
   </tr>
   </thead>
```

3. Save your changes to the file.

4. Using your Web browser, reload or refresh **race2.htm**. Figure 4-17 shows the table with the newly added caption.

Figure 4-17	Viewing the table caption

```
caption ──────────► Race Results
```

Group	Runner	Time	Origin
Men	1. Peter Teagan	2:12:34	San Antonio, Texas
Men	2. Kyle Wills	2:13:05	Billings, Montana
Men	3. Jason Wu	2:14:28	Cutler, Colorado
Women	1. Laura Blake	2:28:21	Park City, Colorado
Women	2. Kathy Lasker	2:30:11	Chicago, Illinois
Women	3. Lisa Peterson	2:31:14	Seattle, Washington

Adding a Table Summary

For non-visual browsers (such as aural browsers that may be used by blind or visually impaired people) it is useful to include a summary of a table's contents. While a caption and the surrounding page text usually provide descriptive information about the table and its contents, you can use the summary attribute if you need to include a more detailed description. The syntax of the summary attribute is

```
<table summary="description"> ... </table>
```

where *description* is a description of the table's purpose and contents. For example, to summarize the race results table, you could add the following code to the HTML file:

```
<table summary="This table lists the top three male and female runners
in the recent Front Range Marathon, providing the name, time, and origin
of the runners.">
…
</table>
```

The information in the summary attribute does not affect a table's appearance in visual browsers.

You've completed your work with the initial structure of the race results table. Kevin is pleased with your progress, but he would like you to make some improvements in the table's appearance. In the next session, you'll learn how to format the table.

Session 4.1 Quick Check

Review

1. What are the two kinds of tables you can place in a Web page?
2. What is the difference between a proportional font and a fixed-width font? Which should you use in a text table, and why?
3. Which HTML tag would you use to create preformatted text?
4. Define the purpose of the following HTML tags in defining the structure of a table:

   ```
   <tr> ... </tr>
   <td> ... </td>
   <th> ... </th>
   ```

5. How do you specify the number of rows in a graphical table? How do you specify the number of columns?
6. What are three row groups and how do you create them?
7. What HTML code would you use to place the caption "Product Catalog" below a table? Where must this HTML code be placed in relation to the opening <table> tag?

Session 4.2

Working with the Table Border

After viewing the race results table in a browser, Kevin notes that the text is displayed with properly aligned columns, but the lack of gridlines and borders makes the table difficult to read. Kevin asks you to enhance the table's design by adding borders, gridlines, and a background color. He also wants you to control the placement and size of the table. HTML provides tags and attributes to do all of these things. You'll begin enhancing the race results table by adding a table border.

Adding a Table Border

By default, browsers display tables without table borders. You can create a table border by adding the border attribute to the <table> tag. The syntax for creating a table border is

```
<table border="value"> ... </table>
```

where *value* is the width of the border in pixels. Figure 4-18 shows the effect of different border sizes on a table's appearance. Note that unless you set the border size to 0 pixels, the size of the internal gridlines is not affected by the border attribute. You'll see how to change the size and appearance of these gridlines later in this session.

| Figure 4-18 | Tables with different border sizes |

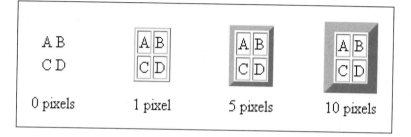

Kevin wants a wide border around the race results table, so you'll format the table with a 5-pixel-wide border.

To insert a table border:

1. Using your text editor, open **race2.htm**, if it is not currently open.
2. Locate the opening <table> tag, and within the tag, insert the attribute **border="5"**. See Figure 4-19.

| Figure 4-19 | Inserting the border size |

```
<table border="5">
    <caption style="font-weight: bold">Race Results</caption>
    <thead>
    <tr>
        <th>Group</th>
        <th>Runner</th>
        <th>Time</th>
        <th>Origin</th>
    </tr>
    </thead>
```

3. Save your changes to the file.
4. Using your Web browser, reload or refresh **race2.htm**. Figure 4-20 shows the new border.

Table with 5-pixel wide border ◄ **Figure 4-20**

Race Results

Group	Runner	Time	Origin
Men	1. Peter Teagan	2:12:34	San Antonio, Texas
Men	2. Kyle Wills	2:13:05	Billings, Montana
Men	3. Jason Wu	2:14:28	Cutler, Colorado
Women	1. Laura Blake	2:28:21	Park City, Colorado
Women	2. Kathy Lasker	2:30:11	Chicago, Illinois
Women	3. Lisa Peterson	2:31:14	Seattle, Washington

By default, table borders are displayed in two shades of gray that create a three-dimensional effect. You can change these colors by using the bordercolor attribute as follows:

```
<table bordercolor="color"> ... </table>
```

where *color* is an HTML color name or hexadecimal color value. The bordercolor attribute has been deprecated, but is still widely supported. However, it is not supported by Opera, and Internet Explorer and Netscape apply this attribute differently. As shown in Figure 4-21, while Internet Explorer applies the specified color to all parts of the border, Netscape preserves the 3-D effect.

Using the bordercolor attribute ◄ **Figure 4-21**

To work around this discrepancy, you can use two additional attributes supported by Internet Explorer: bordercolorlight and bordercolordark. These attributes allow you to specify the light and dark colors for a 3-D border. Figure 4-22 shows an example of the use of the bordercolor and bordercolorlight attributes to create a 3-D colored border in Internet Explorer. Note that Netscape does not support these attributes.

Using the bordercolorlight attribute ◄ **Figure 4-22**

<table border="10" bordercolor="blue" bordercolorlight="#b2b2ff">

A	B	C
D	E	F
G	H	I

Internet Explorer

Another way to solve this problem is to use styles that create and format the border. The applicable styles will be explored in a future tutorial. For now, you'll use the bordercolor attribute to change the border color to brown. In order to maintain the 3-D border effect for Internet Explorer users, you'll also set the bordercolorlight attribute value to tan.

Reference Window	**Creating a Table Border**

- To create a table border, add the following attribute to the table element:
  border="*value*"
  where *value* is the width of the border in pixels.

Deprecated

- To change the border color, add the following attribute to the table element:
  bordercolor="*color*"
  where *color* is either a recognized color name or a hexadecimal color value.

Internet Explorer Only

- To break the border into separate dark and light bands, add the following attributes to the table element:
  bordercolorlight="*color*" bordercolordark="*color*"
  where *color* is either a recognized color name or a hexadecimal color value.

To change the color of the table border:

1. Return to **race2.htm** in your text editor.

2. Insert the attributes **bordercolor="brown"** and **bordercolorlight="tan"** within the
   <table> tag as shown in Figure 4-23.

Figure 4-23	Changing the border color

```
<table border="5" bordercolor="brown" bordercolorlight="tan">
   <caption style="font-weight: bold">Race Results</caption>
   <thead>
   <tr>
      <th>Group</th>
      <th>Runner</th>
      <th>Time</th>
      <th>Origin</th>
   </tr>
   </thead>
```

3. Save your changes to the file and reload it in your Web browser. Figure 4-24 shows the revised appearance of the table.

Figure 4-24	Race results table with brown/tan border color

Race Results

Group	Runner	Time	Origin
Men	1. Peter Teagan	2:12:34	San Antonio, Texas
Men	2. Kyle Wills	2:13:05	Billings, Montana
Men	3. Jason Wu	2:14:28	Cutler, Colorado
Women	1. Laura Blake	2:28:21	Park City, Colorado
Women	2. Kathy Lasker	2:30:11	Chicago, Illinois
Women	3. Lisa Peterson	2:31:14	Seattle, Washington

Trouble? Depending on your browser and browser version, your table border colors might not match the ones shown in Figure 4-24.

Creating Frames and Rules

By default a table border surrounds the entire table and each of the cells within the table. You can modify this by using the frame and rules attributes of the table element.

The frame attribute allows you to determine which sides of a table will have borders. The syntax is

```
<table frame="type"> ... </table>
```

where *type* is "box" (the default), "above", "border", "below", "hsides", "vsides", "lhs", "rhs", or "void". Figure 4-25 describes each of these options.

Values of the frame attribute ◄ **Figure 4-25**

Frame Value	Border Appearance
above	only above the table
below	only below the table
border	around all four sides of the table
box	around all four sides of the table
hsides	on the top and bottom sides of the table (the horizontal sides)
lhs	only on the left-hand side
rhs	only on the right-hand side
void	no border is drawn around the table
vsides	on the left and right sides of the table (the vertical sides)

Figure 4-26 shows the effect of each of these values on a table grid. The frame attribute was introduced in HTML 4.01 and thus might not be supported in older browsers.

Frame examples ◄ **Figure 4-26**

The rules attribute lets you control how gridlines are drawn within the table. The syntax of this attribute is

```
<table rules="type"> ... </table>
```

where *type* is "all" (the default), "cols", "groups", or "none". Figure 4-27 describes each of these attribute values.

| Figure 4-27 | Values of the rules attribute |

Rules Value	Description of Rules
all	around cells
cols	around columns
groups	around row groups
none	no rules
rows	around rows

Figure 4-28 shows the effect of each of the attribute values on a table.

| Figure 4-28 | Rules examples |

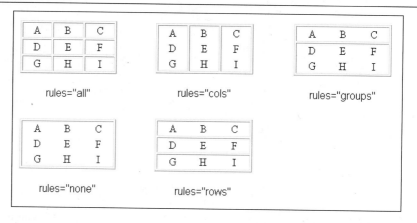

As with the frame attribute, the rules attribute was introduced in the specifications for HTML 4.01, and thus might not be supported in older browsers.

You're pleased with the current appearance of the table's border and gridlines, so you decide against making any changes to the frame or rules values.

| Reference Window | **Creating Frames and Rules** |

- To change the frame style of a table border, add the following attribute to the table element:
    ```
    frame="type"
    ```
    where *type* is "box" (the default), "above", "border", "below", "hsides", "vsides", "lhs", "rhs", or "void".
- To change the rules style of the internal gridlines, add the following attribute to the table element:
    ```
    rules="type"
    ```
    where *type* is "all" (the default), "cols", "groups", or "none".

Sizing a Table

While Kevin likes what you've done with the borders, he feels that the table still looks too crowded. He would like to see smaller internal borders, more space between the text and the borders, and would like the table to be slightly wider. Tables are sized automatically by the browser in order to create the smallest table that fits the largest amount of text into each column with the least amount of line wrapping. For the race results table, this results in cell borders that crowd the cell text. However, there are several attributes that you can use to override the size choices made by the browser.

Setting Cell Spacing

The first attribute we'll consider controls the amount of space between table cells, which is known as the **cell spacing**. By default, browsers set the cell spacing to 2 pixels. To set a different cell spacing value, use the cellspacing attribute as follows:

```
<table cellspacing="value"> ... </table>
```

where *value* is the size of the cell spacing in pixels. If you have applied a border to your table, changing this value also impacts the size of the interior borders. Figure 4-29 shows how different cell spacing values affect the appearance of these gridlines.

Different cell spacing values ◀ **Figure 4-29**

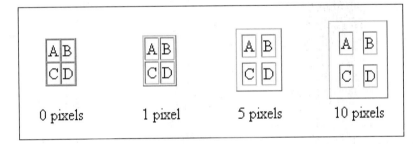

Kevin has decided that he wants the width of the gridlines to be as small as possible, so you'll decrease the cell spacing to 0 pixels. Because the interior border includes a drop shadow, even setting cell spacing to 0 will not remove the gridlines. However, this setting will reduce the gridlines to a minimal size.

To change the cell spacing:

▶ 1. Return to **race2.htm** in your text editor.

▶ 2. Insert the attribute **cellspacing="0"** within the <table> tag, as shown in Figure 4-30.

Setting the cell spacing ◀ **Figure 4-30**

```
<table border="5" bordercolor="brown" bordercolorlight="tan" cellspacing="0">
    <caption style="font-weight: bold">Race Results</caption>
    <thead>
    <tr>
        <th>Group</th>
        <th>Runner</th>
        <th>Time</th>
        <th>Origin</th>
    </tr>
    </thead>
```

▶ 3. Save your changes to the file.

> **4.** Using your Web browser, reload or refresh **race2.htm**. Figure 4-31 shows the new cell spacing. Note that the line that separates the cells has been reduced, but not eliminated. Compare Figure 4-31 with Figure 4-24.

Figure 4-31	Table with a cell spacing of 0 pixels

Race Results

Group	Runner	Time	Origin
Men	1. Peter Teagan	2:12:34	San Antonio, Texas
Men	2. Kyle Wills	2:13:05	Billings, Montana
Men	3. Jason Wu	2:14:28	Cutler, Colorado
Women	1. Laura Blake	2:28:21	Park City, Colorado
Women	2. Kathy Lasker	2:30:11	Chicago, Illinois
Women	3. Lisa Peterson	2:31:14	Seattle, Washington

Setting Cell Padding

Next, we want to set the space between the cell text and the cell border. This distance is known as the **cell padding**. The default cell padding value is 1 pixel, which to Kevin's eyes is too little. To set a different cell padding value, use the following attribute:

```
<table cellpadding="value"> ... </table>
```

where `value` is the size of the cell padding in pixels. Figure 4-32 shows how different cell padding values affect the appearance of the text within a table.

Figure 4-32	Different cell padding values

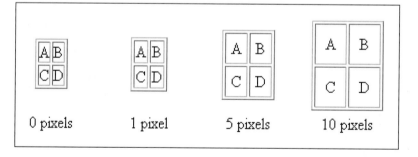

You decide to increase the cell padding of the race results table to 4 pixels in order to satisfy Kevin's request.

To increase the amount of cell padding:

> **1.** Return to **race2.htm** in your text editor.

> **2.** Insert the attribute **cellpadding="4"** within the <table> tag (you may want to place this attribute on a separate line to make your code easier to read). See Figure 4-33.

Setting the cell padding ◄ **Figure 4-33**

```
<table border="5" bordercolor="brown" bordercolorlight="tan" cellspacing="0"
        cellpadding="4">
    <caption style="font-weight: bold">Race Results</caption>
    <thead>
    <tr>
        <th>Group</th>
        <th>Runner</th>
        <th>Time</th>
        <th>Origin</th>
    </tr>
    </thead>
```

▶ **3.** Save your changes to the file, and then reload **race2.htm** in your Web browser. Figure 4-34 shows the table with the increased amount of cell padding.

Table with a cell padding of 4 pixels ◄ **Figure 4-34**

Group	Runner	Time	Origin
Men	1. Peter Teagan	2:12:34	San Antonio, Texas
Men	2. Kyle Wills	2:13:05	Billings, Montana
Men	3. Jason Wu	2:14:28	Cutler, Colorado
Women	1. Laura Blake	2:28:21	Park City, Colorado
Women	2. Kathy Lasker	2:30:11	Chicago, Illinois
Women	3. Lisa Peterson	2:31:14	Seattle, Washington

Race Results

Setting the Table Width

Kevin likes the extra cell padding, but still feels that the table would look better if it was larger. Recall that the overall size of the table is largely determined by its content. The table expands in width to match the contents of the cells. If you want to specify the overall width, use the following attribute:

```
<table width="value"> ... </table>
```

where *value* is the width in either pixels or as a percentage of the width of the containing element. If the containing element is the page itself, you can set the table to fill the entire page width by specifying a width value of "100%". You can also set the table width to a fixed value—for example, you can specify a width of 600 pixels, by changing the width value to "600". If you specify an absolute size, the table size remains constant, regardless of a user's monitor size. On the other hand, specifying a percentage allows your table to match each monitor's dimensions. For example, a table that is 600 pixels wide fills a monitor at 640 × 480 resolution, but leaves a lot of blank space if the monitor size is 1280 × 760. We'll explore this issue more in the next session as we look at tables as tools for layout. Note that a browser will never display a table with a width smaller than that required to display the content. If table content requires a width of 100 pixels, for example, then a browser ignores a width value of 50 pixels.

Many browsers, including Internet Explorer and Netscape, support the attribute

```
<table height="value"> ... </table>
```

where *value* is the height of the table either in pixels or as a percentage of the height of the containing element. However, the height attribute is not part of the HTML specifications and is not supported by XHTML. Like the width attribute, the height attribute only indicates the minimum height of the table, assuming that the content fits. If the table content cannot fit into the specified height, the table height increases to match the contents.

Kevin suggests that you set the width of the table to 70% of the page width.

To set the width of the race results table:

1. Return to **race2.htm** in your text editor.

2. Insert the attribute, **width="70%"** within the <table> tag, as shown in Figure 4-35.

Figure 4-35	Setting the table width

```
<table border="5" bordercolor="brown" bordercolorlight="tan" cellspacing="0"
       cellpadding="4" width="70%">
   <caption style="font-weight: bold">Race Results</caption>
   <thead>
   <tr>
      <th>Group</th>
      <th>Runner</th>
      <th>Time</th>
      <th>Origin</th>
   </tr>
   </thead>
```

3. Save your changes to the file and then reload it in your Web browser. Figure 4-36 shows the revised page with the table width set to 70% of the page width.

Figure 4-36	Table with a width of 70% of the page width

Local Woman Wins Marathon

Park City native, **Laura Blake**, won the 27th Front Range Marathon over an elite field of the best long distance runners in the country. Laura's time of 2 hr. 28 min. 21 sec. was only 2 minutes off the women's course record set last year by Sarah Rawlings. Kathy Lasker and Lisa Peterson finished second and third, respectively. Laura's victory came on the heels of her performance at the NCAA Track and Field Championships, in which she placed second running for Colorado State.

Race Results

Group	Runner	Time	Origin
Men	1. Peter Teagan	2:12:34	San Antonio, Texas
Men	2. Kyle Wills	2:13:05	Billings, Montana
Men	3. Jason Wu	2:14:28	Cutler, Colorado
Women	1. Laura Blake	2:28:21	Park City, Colorado
Women	2. Kathy Lasker	2:30:11	Chicago, Illinois
Women	3. Lisa Peterson	2:31:14	Seattle, Washington

Trouble? Depending on your browser and browser version, your page might appear differently from the one shown in Figure 4-36.

Setting Cell and Column Width

The width attribute can also be applied to individual cells within the table, using the form

```
<td width="value"> … </td>
```

or

```
<th width="value"> ... </th>
```

where *value* is the cell's width either in pixels or as a percentage of the width of the entire table. You can set the width of a column by setting the width of the first cell in the column; the remaining cells in the column will adopt that width. If the content of one of the other cells exceeds that width, however, the browser expands the size of all cells in the column to match the width required to display that content. If you set different widths for two cells in the same column, a browser applies the larger value to the column.

You can also set the height of a cell using the attribute

```
<td height="value"> ... </td>
```

or

```
<th height="value"> ... </th>
```

where *value* is the height either in pixels or as a percentage of the height of the table. The height attribute has been deprecated and might not be supported in future browsers.

Reference Window

Sizing a Table

- To set the size of a table, add the following attributes to the table element:
    `width="value" height="value"`
  where *value* is the size either in pixels or as a percentage of the containing element.
- To set cell spacing, add the following attribute to the table element:
    `cellspacing="value"`
  where *value* is the gap between adjacent cells in pixels. The default spacing is 2 pixels.
- To set cell padding, add the following attribute to the table element:
    `cellpadding="value"`
  where *value* is the size of the gap between the cell content and the cell border. The default padding is 1 pixel.

Deprecated

- To set the size of a table cell, add the following attributes to the td or th element:
    `width="value" height="value"`
  or
    `width="value" height="value"`
  where *value* is the size either in pixels or as a percentage of the table's width or height.

Preventing Line Wrap

If you change the widths of the table and the table cells, you might want to ensure that the contents of certain cells do not wrap. For example, if a cell contains a date or name, you might want to ensure that the name always appears on a single line. To prevent line wrapping, add the following attribute to the appropriate cell:

```
<td nowrap="nowrap"> ... </td>
```

or

```
<th nowrap="nowrap"> ... </th>
```

Some browsers also accept the nowrap attribute with no attribute value; however this form is not supported in XHTML since XHTML requires values for all attributes.

Kevin is pleased with the width and height that the browser has chosen for the cells in the race results table, so you do not need to modify these attributes.

Spanning Rows and Columns

Kevin has reviewed your table and would like to make a few more changes. He feels that repeating the group information for each row in the table is redundant and wonders if you can merge several cells into a single cell. He draws a proposed layout for the table, which is displayed in Figure 4-37.

Figure 4-37	Kevin's proposed table layout

	Runner	Time	Origin
Men	1. Peter Teagan	2:12:34	San Antonio, Texas
	2. Kyle Wills	2:13:05	Billings, Montana
	3. Jason Wu	2:14:28	Cutler, Colorado
Women	1. Laura Blake	2:28:21	Park City, Colorado
	2. Kathy Lasker	2:30:11	Chicago, Illinois
	3. Lisa Peterson	2:31:14	Seattle, Washington

To merge several cells into one, you need to create a **spanning cell**, which is a cell that occupies more than one row or column in a table. Figure 4-38 shows a table of opinion poll data in which some of the cells span several rows and/or columns.

Figure 4-38	Spanning cells

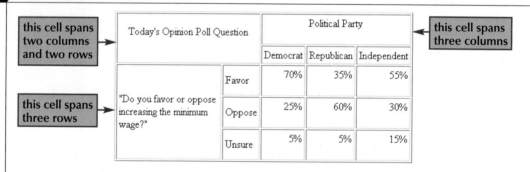

Spanning cells are created by inserting the rowspan attribute, the colspan attribute, or both attributes in a <td> or <th> tag. The syntax for these attributes is:

```
<td rowspan="value" colspan="value"> ... </td>
```

or

```
<th rowspan="value" colspan="value"> ... </th>
```

where *value* is the number of rows or columns that the cell spans in the table. The direction of the spanning is downward and to the right of the cell containing the rowspan and colspan attributes. For example, to create a cell that spans two columns in the table, you enter the <td> tag as

```
<td colspan="2"> ... </td>
```

For a cell that spans two rows, the tag is

```
<td rowspan="2"> ... </td>
```

and to span two rows and two columns at the same time, the tag is

```
<td rowspan="2" colspan="2"> ... </td>
```

It's important to remember that when a table includes a cell that spans multiple rows or columns, you must adjust the number of cell tags used in one or more table rows. For example, if a row contains five columns, but one of the cells in the row spans three columns, you only need three <td> tags within the row: two <td> tags for each of the cells that occupy a single column, and a third for the cell spanning three rows.

When a cell spans several rows, you need to adjust the number of cell tags in the rows below the spanning cell. Consider the table shown in Figure 4-39, which contains three rows and four columns. The first cell in the first row is a spanning cell that spans three rows. You need four <td> tags for the first row, but only three <td> tags for rows two and three. This is because the spanning cell from row one occupies the cells that would normally appear in those rows.

A row-spanning cell ◀ **Figure 4-39**

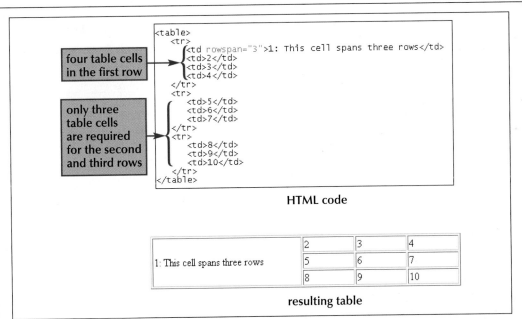

```
<table>
    <tr>
        <td rowspan="3">1: This cell spans three rows</td>
        <td>2</td>
        <td>3</td>
        <td>4</td>
    </tr>
    <tr>
        <td>5</td>
        <td>6</td>
        <td>7</td>
    </tr>
    <tr>
        <td>8</td>
        <td>9</td>
        <td>10</td>
    </tr>
</table>
```

four table cells in the first row

only three table cells are required for the second and third rows

HTML code

1: This cell spans three rows	2	3	4
	5	6	7
	8	9	10

resulting table

Creating a Spanning Cell

Reference Window

- To create a column spanning cell, add the following attribute to the td or th element:
    ```
    colspan="value"
    ```
    where *value* is the number of columns to be spanned.
- To create a row spanning cell, add the following attribute to the td or th element:
    ```
    rowspan="value"
    ```
    where *value* is the number of rows to be spanned.

To make the changes that Kevin has requested, start by deleting the table heading for the Group column, and then spanning the Runner table heading across two columns.

To create a cell that spans two columns:

1. Return to **race2.htm** in your text editor.
2. Delete the Group table heading, including both the opening and closing <th> tags.
3. Insert the attribute **colspan="2"** within the opening <th> tag for the Runner table heading.

Next, you'll delete the second and third occurrences of the "Men" and "Women" cells in the table, keeping only the first occurrences. You'll also span those two cells over three rows of the table.

To span two cells over three rows:

1. Insert the attribute **rowspan="3"** in the first <td> tag that contains the text "Men".
2. Delete the next two <td> tags that contain the text "Men".
3. Insert the attribute **rowspan="3"** in the first <td> tag that contains the text "Women".
4. Delete the next two <td> tags that contain the text "Women". Figure 4-40 shows the revised table code.

Figure 4-40 ▶ **Adding spanning cells to the race results table**

this cell spans two columns

these cells span three rows

```
<table border="5" bordercolor="brown" bordercolorlight="tan" cellspacing="0"
       cellpadding="4" width="70%">
   <caption style="font-weight: bold">Race Results</caption>
   <thead>
   <tr>
      <th colspan="2">Runner</th>
      <th>Time</th>
      <th>Origin</th>
   </tr>
   </thead>
   <tbody>
   <tr>
      <td rowspan="3">Men</td>
      <td>1. Peter Teagan</td>
      <td>2:12:34</td>
      <td>San Antonio, Texas</td>
   </tr>
   <tr>
      <td>2. Kyle Wills</td>
      <td>2:13:05</td>
      <td>Billings, Montana</td>
   </tr>
   <tr>
      <td>3. Jason Wu</td>
      <td>2:14:28</td>
      <td>Cutler, Colorado</td>
   </tr>
   <tr>
      <td rowspan="3">Women</td>
      <td>1. Laura Blake</td>
      <td>2:28:21</td>
      <td>Park City, Colorado</td>
   </tr>
   <tr>
      <td>2. Kathy Lasker</td>
      <td>2:30:11</td>
      <td>Chicago, Illinois</td>
   </tr>
   <tr>
      <td>3. Lisa Peterson</td>
      <td>2:31:14</td>
      <td>Seattle, Washington</td>
   </tr>
   </tbody>
</table>
```

5. Save your changes to **race2.htm** and reload it in your Web browser. Figure 4-41 shows the revised table.

Table with spanning cells | **Figure 4-41**

Race Results

	Runner	Time	Origin
Men	1. Peter Teagan	2:12:34	San Antonio, Texas
	2. Kyle Wills	2:13:05	Billings, Montana
	3. Jason Wu	2:14:28	Cutler, Colorado
Women	1. Laura Blake	2:28:21	Park City, Colorado
	2. Kathy Lasker	2:30:11	Chicago, Illinois
	3. Lisa Peterson	2:31:14	Seattle, Washington

Formatting Table Contents

Kevin has a few final suggestions for the appearance of the table content. He would like the group names, Men and Women, aligned with the tops of their cells and he wants to see the race times right-aligned within the Time column. He would like the table text displayed in a sans-serif font on a colored background in order to stand out better on the page. Finally, he wants the table aligned with the page's right margin, with the article text flowing around it.

Aligning the Contents of a Cell

By default, cell text is placed in the middle of a cell, aligned with the cell's left edge. You can specify a different horizontal alignment for a td or th element using the attribute

```
align="position"
```

where *position* is either left (the default for a td element), center (the default for a th element), right, justify, or char. You may recall the align attribute from the first tutorial, when it was introduced as a deprecated attribute for aligning the text of headings and paragraphs. This align attribute is similar, except that it is not deprecated. However, you can use the text-align style here as well if you wish to use styles for all of your formatting tasks.

A value of "char" for the align attribute tells the browser to align the values in a cell based on the position of a particular character, such as a decimal point. This value is primarily used for columns containing currency data or other numeric values. The default character is assumed to be a decimal point, which is determined by the language of the browser. In English this would be a period ("."), while in French it would be a comma (","). You can specify a different character using the char attribute. Thus to align the value within a cell based on the position of the comma character, you would use the following attributes:

```
<td align="char" char=","> ... </td>
```

The char attribute value and char attributes are not currently well supported by browsers. To specify a different vertical alignment of cell content, use the attribute

```
valign="position"
```

where *position* is top, middle (the default), bottom, or baseline. Figure 4-42 shows how different combinations of the align and valign attributes can affect the position of cell content in relation to cell borders.

Figure 4-42 ▶ **Values of the align and valign attributes**

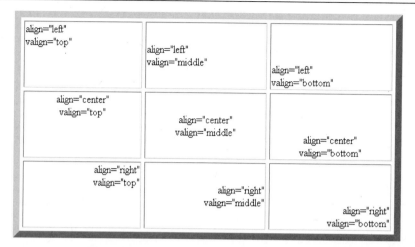

Reference Window ▶ **Aligning Cell Contents**

- To horizontally align the contents of a cell, use the following attribute for a td or th element:
      align="*position*"
  where *position* is left (the default for the td element), center (the default for the th element), right, or char.
- To vertically align the contents of a cell, use the following attribute for a td or th element:
      valign="*position*"
  where *position* is top, middle (the default), bottom, or baseline.

Kevin wants you to right-align each time value in the race results table, and align the group names with the tops of their cells.

To align the time and group values:

▶ 1. Return to **race2.htm** in your text editor.

▶ 2. Insert the attribute **align="right"** within each <td> tag in the Time column.

▶ 3. Locate the <td> tag containing the Men group name and insert the attribute **valign="top"**.

▶ 4. Locate the <td> tag containing the Women group name and insert the attribute **valign="top"**. Figure 4-43 shows the revised HTML code for the table.

Figure 4-43

```
<table border="5" bordercolor="brown" bordercolorlight="tan" cellspacing="0"
       cellpadding="4" width="70%">
  <caption style="font-weight: bold">Race Results</caption>
  <thead>
  <tr>
      <th colspan="2">Runner</th>
      <th>Time</th>
      <th>Origin</th>
  </tr>
  </thead>
  <tbody>
  <tr>
      <td rowspan="3" valign="top">Men</td>
      <td>1. Peter Teagan</td>
      <td align="right">2:12:34</td>
      <td>San Antonio, Texas</td>
  </tr>
  <tr>
      <td>2. Kyle Wills</td>
      <td align="right">2:13:05</td>
      <td>Billings, Montana</td>
  </tr>
  <tr>
      <td>3. Jason Wu</td>
      <td align="right">2:14:28</td>
      <td>Cutler, Colorado</td>
  </tr>
  <tr>
      <td rowspan="3" valign="top">Women</td>
      <td>1. Laura Blake</td>
      <td align="right">2:28:21</td>
      <td>Park City, Colorado</td>
  </tr>
  <tr>
      <td>2. Kathy Lasker</td>
      <td align="right">2:30:11</td>
      <td>Chicago, Illinois</td>
  </tr>
  <tr>
      <td>3. Lisa Peterson</td>
      <td align="right">2:31:14</td>
      <td>Seattle, Washington</td>
  </tr>
  </tbody>
</table>
```

5. Save your changes to the file and reload it in your Web browser. Figure 4-44 shows the revised alignment of the table contents.

Revised alignment in the race results table   **Figure 4-44**

Race Results			
	Runner	Time	Origin
Men	1. Peter Teagan	2:12:34	San Antonio, Texas
	2. Kyle Wills	2:13:05	Billings, Montana
	3. Jason Wu	2:14:28	Cutler, Colorado
Women	1. Laura Blake	2:28:21	Park City, Colorado
	2. Kathy Lasker	2:30:11	Chicago, Illinois
	3. Lisa Peterson	2:31:14	Seattle, Washington

Formatting Table Text

You can apply the same text and font styles that were introduced in the last tutorial to table text. The styles cascade down through the table structure, from the table element, through the row groups and table rows, and down to individual cells. For example, if you want to change the font style of all of the text in a table, you can apply a style to the table element; to change the font style of the table body, apply the style to the tbody element.

Kevin suggests that you display all of the table text in a sans-serif font. He wants the default font size for the table text to be 1em, but he wants the body text to be 80% of that size. You'll make these changes by applying the font-family and font-size styles to the table and tbody elements.

To format the table text:

1. Return to **race2.htm** in your text editor.

2. Insert the attribute **style="font-family: Arial, Helvetica, sans-serif; font-size: 1em"** in the <table> tag (you may want to insert this attribute on a separate line to make your code easier to read).

3. Insert the attribute **style="font-size: 80%"** in the <tbody> tag. This sets the table body text to 80% of the font size of the rest of the table text. Figure 4-45 shows the revised HTML code.

Figure 4-45	Setting font styles in the table

```
<table border="5" bordercolor="brown" bordercolorlight="tan" cellspacing="0"
       cellpadding="4" width="70%"
       style="font-family: Arial, Helvetica, sans-serif; font-size: 1em">
<caption style="font-weight: bold">Race Results</caption>
<thead>
<tr>
    <th colspan="2">Runner</th>
    <th>Time</th>
    <th>Origin</th>
</tr>
</thead>
<tbody style="font-size: 80%">
<tr>
    <td rowspan="3" valign="top">Men</td>
    <td>1. Peter Teagan</td>
    <td align="right">2:12:34</td>
    <td>San Antonio, Texas</td>
</tr>
```

4. Save your changes to the file and reload it in your Web browser. Figure 4-46 shows the revised table text format.

Figure 4-46	Revised font styles in the race results table

4. Save your changes to the file and reload it in your Web browser. Figure 4-46 shows the revised table text format.

If you need to support older browsers that don't recognize styles, you must enclose the content of each cell within a <font> tag in order to format the cell text.

Setting the Background Color

Table elements support the same background-color style that you used in the last tutorial. As with font styles, color styles cascade down through the table structure from the table itself down to individual cells. Kevin would like the header row to be displayed with a yellow background, the group names with backgrounds of light blue and light green, and the rest of the table with a white background.

To set the background color:

1. Return to **race2.htm** in your text editor.

2. Add the style **background-color: white** to the inline style of the table element (be sure to insert a semicolon to separate this style from the other style declarations).

3. Insert the attribute **style="background-color: yellow"** in the <tr> tag for the heading row.

4. Insert the attribute **style="background-color: lightblue"** in the <td> tag for the cell containing the Men group name.

5. Insert the attribute **style="background-color: lightgreen"** in the <td> tag for the cell containing the Women group name. Figure 4-47 shows the revised HTML code.

Setting background colors in the table ◄ **Figure 4-47**

```
<table border="5" bordercolor="brown" bordercolorlight="tan" cellspacing="0"
       cellpadding="4" width="70%"
       style="font-family: Arial, Helvetica, sans-serif; font-size: 1em;
              background-color: white">
  <caption style="font-weight: bold">Race Results</caption>
  <thead>
  <tr style="background-color: yellow">
     <th colspan="2">Runner</th>
     <th>Time</th>
     <th>Origin</th>
  </tr>
  </thead>
  <tbody style="font-size: 80%">
  <tr>
     <td rowspan="3" valign="top" style="background-color: lightblue">Men</td>
     <td>1. Peter Teagan</td>
     <td align="right">2:12:34</td>
     <td>San Antonio, Texas</td>
  </tr>
  <tr>
     <td>2. Kyle Wills</td>
     <td align="right">2:13:05</td>
     <td>Billings, Montana</td>
  </tr>
  <tr>
     <td>3. Jason Wu</td>
     <td align="right">2:14:28</td>
     <td>Cutler, Colorado</td>
  </tr>
  <tr>
     <td rowspan="3" valign="top" style="background-color: lightgreen">Women</td>
     <td>1. Laura Blake</td>
     <td align="right">2:28:21</td>
     <td>Park City, Colorado</td>
  </tr>
```

6. Save your changes to the file and reload it in your Web browser. Figure 4-48 shows the new color scheme for the race results table.

Revised color scheme in the race results table ◄ **Figure 4-48**

Race Results

	Runner	Time	Origin
Men	1. Peter Teagan	2:12:34	San Antonio, Texas
	2. Kyle Wills	2:13:05	Billings, Montana
	3. Jason Wu	2:14:28	Cutler, Colorado
Women	1. Laura Blake	2:28:21	Park City, Colorado
	2. Kathy Lasker	2:30:11	Chicago, Illinois
	3. Lisa Peterson	2:31:14	Seattle, Washington

For older browsers that don't recognize styles, you can use the deprecated bgcolor attribute. The syntax of this attribute is

```
bgcolor="color"
```

where *color* is either a recognized color name or a hexadecimal color value. The bgcolor attribute can be applied to <table>, <tr>, <th>, and <td> tags.

Setting the Background Image

Though not needed for the race results table, you can add a background image to a table using the same background-image style you learned about in the last tutorial. A background can be applied to the entire table, to a row group, a row, or an individual cell. For older browsers that don't recognize styles, you can use the deprecated background attribute, which uses the syntax

```
background="url"
```

where *url* is the name and location of the graphic image file. This attribute can be added to the <table>, <tr>, <th>, and <td> tags.

Reference Window | **Formatting the Table Background**

- To change the background color of any table element, apply the following style:
    ```
    background-color: color
    ```
  where *color* is a color name or color value.
- To change the background image of any table element, apply the following style:
    ```
    background-image: url(url)
    ```
  where *url* is the URL of the graphic image file.

Deprecated

- To change the background color of any table element, add the following attribute to the tag:
    ```
    bgcolor="color"
    ```
  where *color* is either a color name or a hexadecimal color value. This attribute can be applied to <table>, <tr>, <th>, and <td> tags.
- To change the background image of any table element, add the following attribute to the tag:
    ```
    background="file"
    ```
  where *file* is the filename of the graphic image file. This attribute can be added to <table>, <tr>, <th>, and <td> tags.

Aligning a Table on a Web Page

Kevin's final task for you is to align the table with the right margin of the page, with the rest of the article text wrapping around the table. You can align the entire table using the same style used to float an inline image on a page. To float the table, you would use the following style for the table element:

```
float: position
```

where *position* is either left or right. As with inline images, you can use the margin style to set the margin space around the floating table. Kevin would like a 5pixel space on the top, left, and bottom of the table and a 0 pixel margin on the table's right margin.

To float the race results table:

1. Return to **race2.htm** in your text editor.
2. Add the styles **float: right; margin: 5 0 5 5** to the table element (be sure to separate these styles from the other declarations with a semicolon). Figure 4-49 shows the revised HTML code.

Floating the race results table ◄ **Figure 4-49**

```
<table border="5" bordercolor="brown" bordercolorlight="tan" cellspacing="0"
       cellpadding="4" width="70%"
       style="font-family: Arial, Helvetica, sans-serif; font-size: 1em;
              background-color: white; float: right; margin: 5 0 5 5">
<caption style="font-weight: bold">Race Results</caption>
<thead>
<tr style="background-color: yellow">
   <th colspan="2">Runner</th>
   <th>Time</th>
   <th>Origin</th>
</tr>
</thead>
```

3. Save your changes to the file, then close it.
4. Reopen **race2.htm** in your Web browser. Figure 4-50 shows the final appearance of the page.

Final race2 page ◄ **Figure 4-50**

Local Woman Wins Marathon

Park City native, **Laura Blake**, won the 27th Front Range Marathon over an elite field of the best long distance runners in the country. Laura's time of 2 hr. 28 min. 21 sec. was only 2 minutes off the women's course record set last year by Sarah Rawlings. Kathy Lasker and Lisa Peterson finished second and third, respectively. Laura's victory came on the heels of her performance at the NCAA Track and Field Championships, in which she placed second running for Colorado State.

In an exciting race, **Peter Teagan** of San Antonio, Texas, used a finishing kick to win the men's marathon for the second straight year, in a time of 2 hr. 12 min. 34 sec. Ahead for much of the race, Kyle Wills of Billings, Montana, finished second, when he could not match Teagan's finishing pace. Jason Wu of Cutler, Colorado, placed third in a very competitive field.

Race Results

Runner		Time	Origin
Men	1. Peter Teagan	2:12:34	San Antonio, Texas
	2. Kyle Wills	2:13:05	Billings, Montana
	3. Jason Wu	2:14:28	Cutler, Colorado
Women	1. Laura Blake	2:28:21	Park City, Colorado
	2. Kathy Lasker	2:30:11	Chicago, Illinois
	3. Lisa Peterson	2:31:14	Seattle, Washington

This year's race through downtown Boulder boasted the largest field in the marathon's history, with over 9500 men and 6700 women competing. Race conditions were perfect with low humidity and temperatures that never exceeded 85°.

If you need to support older browsers that do not recognize styles, you can use the deprecated align attribute

```
align="position"
```

where *position* equals "left" (the default), "right", or "center". As with the float style, using left or right alignment places the table on the margin of the Web page and wraps surrounding text to the side. Center alignment places the table in the horizontal center of the page, but does not allow text to wrap around it.

| **Floating a Table**

- To float the entire table, apply the following style to the table element:
  ```
  float: position
  ```
  where *position* is none (the default), left, or right.

Deprecated

- To align the table on the margins of the containing element, add the following attribute to the <table> tag:
  ```
  align="position"
  ```
  where *position* equals "left" (the default), "right", or "center".

Working with Column Groups

In this session, you've formatted the content of the table columns by modifying the attributes of individual cells within a column. You can also organize the columns into **column groups** and format one or more entire columns with a single style declaration or attribute. To define a column group, insert the following element into the table structure:

```
<colgroup span="value" />
```

where *value* is the number of columns in the group. The colgroup element should be placed directly after the opening <table> tag. However, for a table that includes a caption, it should be placed directly after the <caption> tag. For example, a table with five columns could be organized into two groups: one group for the first three columns and a second group for the last two:

```
<colgroup span="3" />
<colgroup span="2" />
```

If you want to display the first three columns with a white background and the last two columns with a yellow background, the HTML code would be:

```
<colgroup span="4" style="background-color: white" />
<colgroup span="2" style="background-color: yellow" />
```

The colgroup element can also be expressed as a two-sided element, using the syntax:

```
<colgroup>
      columns
</colgroup>
```

where *columns* are elements that define the properties for individual columns within the group. To define a single column within the group, use the one-sided col element. The col element is useful when individual columns within a group need to have slightly different formats. For example, if you want to define a different text color for each column, you might use the following HTML code:

```
<colgroup span="3" style="background-color: white">
      <col style="color: black" />
      <col style="color: red" />
      <col style="color: blue" />
</colgroup>
```

In this case, each column in the group has a white background; however the first column has a black font, the second column has a red font, and the third column has a blue font. The col element can also be used along with the span attribute to format several columns within a group, as in the following example:

```
<colgroup span="5" style="background-color: white">
     <col style="color: black" span="2" />
     <col style="color: red" />
     <col style="color: blue" span="2" />
</colgroup>
```

In this case the column group consists of five columns: the first two columns contain black text on a white background, the middle column contains red text on a white background, and the last two columns contain blue text on a white background.

Currently, browser support for the colgroup and col elements is uneven. Thus, you may still have to format individual cells within a column if you want your table to be supported across all browsers.

You've completed your work on the race results table and the story that Kevin wanted you to work on. In the next session, you'll use tables to create a layout for this story and other features of the *Park City Gazette*.

Session 4.2 Quick Check

1. What attributes would you use to create a table with a 5-pixel-wide outside border, a 3-pixel-wide space between table cells, and 4 pixels of padding between the cell content and the cell border?
2. What attributes would you use to vertically align a cell's contents with the top of the cell?
3. What attribute would you add to center the contents of a table cell?
4. What HTML code would you use to size a table to half the width of the browser window area, regardless of the resolution of a user's monitor?
5. Under what conditions will a table cell exceed the size specified by the width attribute?
6. What attribute creates a cell that spans three rows and two columns?
7. What HTML code would you enter to create a column group spanning three columns that sets the background color of the columns to yellow?

Session 4.3

Using Tables for Layout

The table element was originally introduced simply to display tabular data, such as the race results table. However, table cells can contain any page element including inline images, headings, paragraphs, lists, and other tables. It became immediately obvious to Web designers that tables could also be used for page layout by enclosing the entire contents of a page within a collection of table cells and nested tables. Let's examine some of the classic layouts that can be achieved through the use of tables.

Layout Designs

One of the most basic layouts, which is shown in Figure 4-51, consists of placing the entire contents of the page within a table that is centered on the page. By specifying different backgrounds for the page and the table, this layout gives the effect of a printed page displayed against a colored background.

Figure 4-51 ▶ **Pseudo page**

table grid

In another popular layout, the **columnar layout**, the page content is placed in columns. Figure 4-52 shows a layout consisting of two columns. The page heading is placed in a separate table cell, spanning the two columns. This type of layout is popularly used to create a vertical column of links on the left margin of the page, while another column contains the main text of the page. Note that the text does not flow from one column to another as it would in a desktop publishing program. Instead, you have to specify the text for each column. If you want the lengths of the text in the columns to match, you have to work with the column widths or the amount of text in each column. The layout in Figure 4-52 achieves an approximate balance between the two columns by making the first column slightly narrower than the second. Also, for a columnar layout you have to vertically align the text in each column with the top of the table cell.

Figure 4-52 ▶ **Two column layout**

table grid

In a **sectional layout**, such as the one shown in Figure 4-53, you break the page content into sections, placing each section in its own table cell. You can label the sections in an accompanying table cell. Notice that in this example, the section names in the first column are right-aligned in order to better line up with the content in the second column.

Sectional layout ◄ **Figure 4-53**

Local Woman Wins Marathon

Blake Wins Women's Park City native, **Laura Blake**, won the 27th Front Range Marathon over an elite field of the best long distance runners in the country. Laura's time of 2 hr. 28 min. 21 sec. was only 2 minutes off the women's course record set last year by Sarah Rawlings. Kathy Lasker and Lisa Peterson finished second and third, respectively. Laura's victory came on the heels of her performance at the NCAA Track and Field Championships, in which she placed second running for Colorado State.

Teagan wins Men's In an exciting race, **Peter Teagan** of San Antonio, Texas, used a finishing kick to win the men's marathon for the second straight year, in a time of 2 hr. 12 min. 34 sec. Ahead for much of the race, Kyle Wills of Billings, Montana, finished second, when he could not match Teagan's finishing pace. Jason Wu of Cutler, Colorado, placed third in a very competitive field.

Race Conditions This year's race through downtown Boulder boasted the largest field in the marathon's history, with over 9500 men and 6700 women competing. Race conditions were perfect with low humidity and temperatures that never exceeded 85°.

table grid

By breaking up page content into separate pieces, you can create almost any type of layout. This technique is sometimes referred to as a **jigsaw table** or **jigsaw layout**, because the page is broken up into a number of pieces that are meticulously assembled to create the layout. Figure 4-54 shows an example of a jigsaw layout in which layout is broken into fourteen table cells, including an image file that has been sliced into nine distinct pieces. Page content can be placed within those cells and the pieces can be reassembled into the complete table. After removing the borders, it appears that the page content flows naturally alongside and within the graphic images or other features of the page.

Figure 4-54 ▶ **Jigsaw layout**

table grid

To create a jigsaw layout containing an image, you first have to cut your background image into the appropriately sized slices, saving each slice as a separate image file. Several graphics packages are available that will perform this task automatically for you. Each slice can act as either a background image in a table cell (if you intend to display text in front of the image) or as the complete cell content. To ensure that the table cells are the correct size, you should define the width and height of each cell (usually in pixels) and set the border, cellspacing, and cellpadding values to 0 pixels. You must also ensure that the cell content fits within the specified dimensions; if the content is too large, browsers increase the cell size, potentially ruining the layout. Empty cells can be another source of trouble. Some browsers reduce the size of an empty cell, even if you've specified the cell's width and height. To avoid this, all cells should have some content—either an inline image sized to match the cell's dimensions, or a nonbreaking space (which you create with the   character entity). Because jigsaw layouts often need to be precisely measured and browsers can differ in how they render tables, you should definitely test such a layout on a variety of browsers.

Fixed-width and Fluid Layouts

Table layouts generally fall into two classes: fixed-width and fluid. In a **fixed-width layout**, the Web designer defines the exact size of every table element in absolute units such as pixels. This layout has the advantage of giving the Web designer precise control over the appearance of the page. One drawback to a fixed-width layout is that it does not take into account the size of the browser window. This can result in unused blank areas for users whose browser windows are wider than the defined table width. Figure 4-55 shows a layout that has been sized for a width of 610 pixels. As the size of the browser window increases, the table width remains the same size, resulting in larger areas of unused space. This problem can be alleviated somewhat either by centering the table to cut the blank areas into two sections, or by providing background images or effects that make the unused areas more interesting.

640 x 480

800 x 600

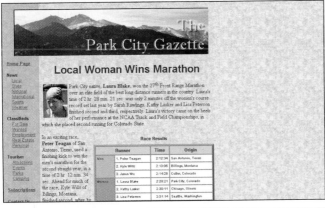

1024 x 768

Determining the correct width is another problem with fixed-width layouts. Although larger screens are being constantly introduced, screen resolutions usually vary from 640 × 480 pixels up to 1600 × 1200, with 800 × 600 being perhaps the most common. However, if you choose a width of 770 pixels for your page, users with smaller monitors may need to scroll horizontally as well as vertically through your page, which can be a source of irritation for those users.

In a **fluid layout**, one or more of the table elements is sized as a percentage of the page width. This enables the page content to flow into those blank areas as the size of the browser window increases (see Figure 4-56). One drawback of a fluid layout is that it can result in long lines of text, which can be difficult to view since the reader needs to use the muscles of the eye or neck to track from the end of one line to the beginning of the next. Fluid layouts can also be difficult to design. A layout that looks fine at a smaller resolution may not look as good as the content flows into a larger browser window.

Figure 4-56 | **Fluid Layout**

640 x 480

800 x 600

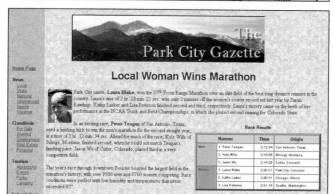

1024 x 768

Many page layouts contain combinations of fluid and fixed-width elements. For example, a column of links placed on the left margin of the page can be fixed, while the content of the page can be fluid. As with all layouts, the best approach is to examine your page under a variety of conditions, incorporating several browsers and window sizes to verify that the page always conveys a positive impression.

Challenges of Table Layouts

Not all Web designers support using tables for layout. Many now prefer to use styles to perform various layout tasks previously reserved for tables, arguing that tables should be reserved for strictly tabular information (such as the data in the race results table). Some of the challenges often associated with tables include:

- **Tables can slow down page rendering.** Unless the size of every element in the table is specified, the browser needs to first load the table content, then run an algorithm to determine how to size each element of the table. This can be time consuming for a large, complex table that involves several cells and nested elements.
- **Tables can be inflexible.** If you try to speed up page rendering by specifying the size of each table element, you're essentially creating a fixed-width layout, which may not be the best way to display your page for all users.
- **Tables can be code-heavy.** To create a visually striking table layout may require several table cells, rows, and columns, and some nested tables. This is particularly true if you create a jigsaw layout. Thus, the ratio of HTML code to actual page content becomes more heavily weighted toward the HTML code, resulting in a longer file that takes longer to load and can be difficult to interpret for people who need to edit the underlying code.
- **Tables can be inaccessible.** People with disabilities who access a table layout with an aural or Braille browser can experience difficulty with tables. The problem is that screen readers and speech output browsers read the HTML source code line-by-line in a linear direction, but a table can sometimes convey information in a non-linear direction. Figure 4-57 shows how a table whose content is quite clear visually could become jumbled when presented aurally. While this example shows the problems associated with a simple 2 × 2 table, a truly complex table layout could present even more severe difficulties.

Aural browsers and tables   **Figure 4-57**

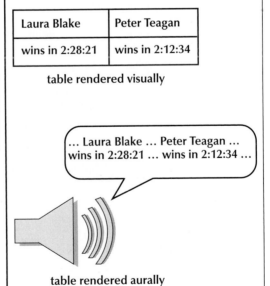

```
<table>
    <tr>
        <td>Laura Blake</td>
        <td>Peter Teagan</td>
    </tr>
    <tr>
        <td>wins in 2:28:21</td>
        <td>wins in 2:12:34</td>
    </tr>
</table>
```
HTML code

Laura Blake	Peter Teagan
wins in 2:28:21	wins in 2:12:34

table rendered visually

… Laura Blake … Peter Teagan … wins in 2:28:21 … wins in 2:12:34 …

table rendered aurally

Despite these challenges, most Web page layout is still done using tables. In the future, many of the layout tasks currently done with tables will be done using styles (and we'll explore how that is done in a later tutorial). For now, however, the layout techniques that are best suited to the widest variety of browsers and operating environments involve tables.

Creating a Newspaper-Style Layout

Kevin is satisfied with your work on the results of the Front Range Marathon. He now wants you to use that article as part of a newspaper-style Web page for the entire *Gazette*. The Web page will contain the *Gazette* logo, a list of links to other pages, and a few articles, one of which is the race results article you've been working on. Figure 4-58 displays the page layout that Kevin has in mind.

Figure 4-58 | **Design sketch for the *Gazette* home page**

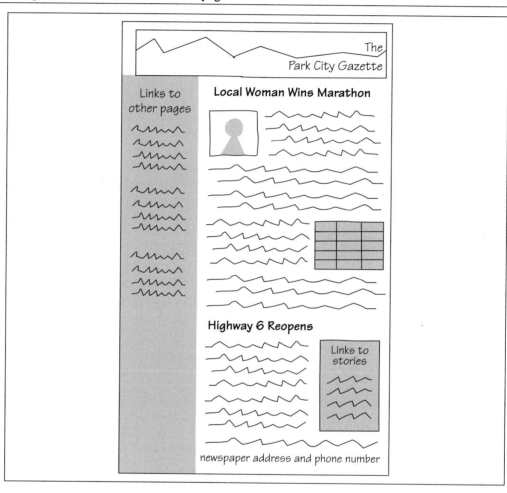

One way to lay out the page specified in Kevin's sketch is to create two tables, one nested inside the other. The outer table, shown in Figure 4-59, consists of four cells that are contained in two columns and three rows. The first cell, containing the *Gazette* logo, occupies the first row of the table and spans two columns. The second cell, displaying the list of links, occupies one column and spans the remaining two rows. The articles and newspaper address are placed in the remaining two cells, each occupying a single row and column.

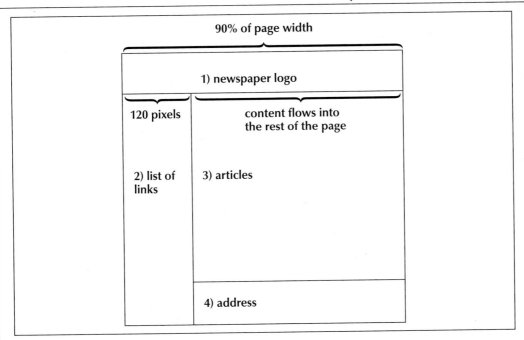

You'll use a combination of fluid and fixed-width elements in this layout. The entire layout will occupy 90% of the width of the browser window. Kevin has chosen this value in order to reduce the amount of unused space for large monitors, without making the lines too long to read comfortably. The first column, containing the list of links, will be set to 120 pixels wide, and the second column, containing the articles and the paper's address, will flow into the rest of the page.

Creating the Outer Table

Kevin has created the initial part of the file for the front page, setting the page background and text color. Your first job is to create the table structure displayed in Figure 4-59. As you add more text to this file, it will become long and unwieldy. To make it easier to navigate the code, you'll insert comments describing the different sections.

To create the outer table and comments:

1. Use your text editor to open **page1txt.htm** located in the tutorial.04/tutorial folder. Insert *your name* and *the date* in the comment section at the top of the file. Save the file as **page1.htm**.

▶ **2.** Enter the following code within the body element. In order to save space, we won't indent the various levels of the table structure code. Figure 4-60 shows the revised code.

```
<table width="90%" cellpadding="5">
<tr>
<!-- Newspaper logo -->
<td colspan="2" align="center">
</td>
</tr>


<tr>
<!-- List of links -->
<td width="120" rowspan="2" valign="top">
</td>
<!-- Articles -->
<td valign="top">
</td>
</tr>


<tr>
<!-- Address -->
<td valign="top" align="center">
</td>
</tr>
</table>
```

Figure 4-60 ▶ **Inserting the table structure for page1.htm**

```
<body style="color: rgb(82,64,32); background: white url(parch2.jpg) repeat-y">
<table width="90%" cellpadding="5">
<tr>
<!-- Newspaper logo -->
<td colspan="2" align="center">
</td>
</tr>

<tr>
<!-- List of links -->
<td width="120" rowspan="2" valign="top">
</td>
<!-- Articles -->
<td valign="top">
</td>
</tr>

<tr>
<!-- Address -->
<td valign="top" align="center">
</td>
</tr>
</table>
</body>
```

Note that in three of the cells of this outer table, you've set the vertical alignment to top, rather than using the default value of middle. This is because the cells in this table act as a framework for newspaper columns. The tables in this layout don't display any borders.

Now you place the *Gazette* logo, pcglogo.jpg, in the Web page.

To insert the logo in a table cell:

1. Within the first table cell insert the following img element:

   ```
   <img src="pcglogo.jpg" alt="The Park City Gazette" width="600"
   height="140" />
   ```

2. Save your changes to **page1.htm** and open the file in your Web browser. Your page should appear as shown in Figure 4-61.

Initial view of Page1 | **Figure 4-61**

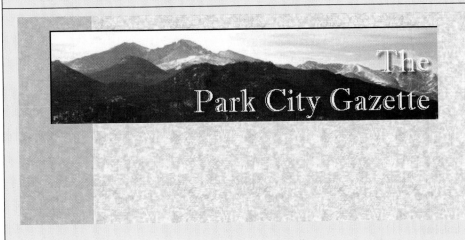

Next, you'll add the list of links to the second table cell. The contents of this cell have been created for you and stored in a file named links.htm. You'll copy the information from that document and paste it into the table cell. If you don't know how to copy and paste with your text editor, ask your instructor or technical support person for assistance.

To insert the contents of the links.htm file:

1. Using your text editor, open **links.htm** from the tutorial.04/tutorial folder.

2. Copy the HTML code within the <body> tags of links.htm, but do not include the opening and closing <body> tags.

3. Close the file and return to **page1.htm** in your text editor.

4. Paste the HTML code you copied from links.htm with the table cell for the list of links as shown in Figure 4-62.

Figure 4-62 | **Inserting the list of links**

```
<!-- List of links -->
<td width="120" rowspan="2" valign="top">
    <h5 style="font-family: sans-serif"><a href="#">Home Page</a></h5>
    <h5 style="margin-bottom: 0; font-family: sans-serif">News</h5>
        <p style="margin: 0 0 0 15; font-size: 0.8em">
        <a href="#">Local</a><br />
        <a href="#">State</a><br />
        <a href="#">National</a><br />
        <a href="#">International</a><br />
        <a href="#">Sports</a><br />
        <a href="#">Weather</a>
        </p>
    <h5 style="margin-bottom: 0; font-family: sans-serif">Classifieds</h5>
        <p style="margin: 0 0 0 15; font-size: 0.8em">
        <a href="#">For Sale</a><br />
        <a href="#">Wanted</a><br />
        <a href="#">Employment</a><br />
        <a href="#">Real Estate</a><br />
        <a href="#">Personal</a>
        </p>
    <h5 style="margin-bottom: 0; font-family: sans-serif">Tourism</h5>
        <p style="margin: 0 0 0 15; font-size: 0.8em">
        <a href="#">Attractions</a><br />
        <a href="#">Events</a><br />
        <a href="#">Parks</a><br />
        <a href="#">Camping</a>
        </p>
    <h5 style="font-family: sans-serif"><a href="#">Subscriptions</a></h5>
    <h5 style="font-family: sans-serif"><a href="#">Contact Us</a></h5>
</td>
```

insert list of links here

5. Save your changes to the file and reload **page1.htm** in your Web browser. Figure 4-63 shows the current state of the home page of the *Park City Gazette*.

Figure 4-63 | **Page1 with link list**

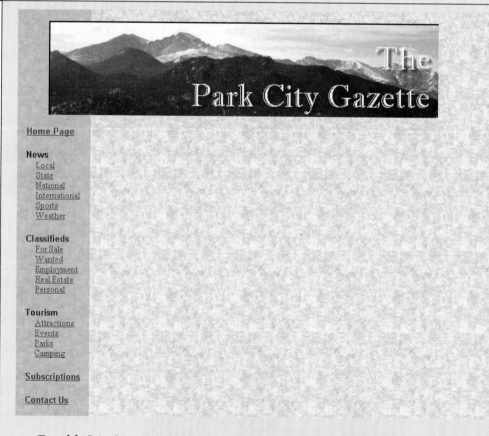

Trouble? At this point, the links on this page point to page1.htm and are acting as placeholders. Kevin will add the actual links as more work is done on the *Gazette*'s Web site.

The next part of the outer table that you'll add is the newspaper address and phone number, which will be located at the bottom of the page. The content for this cell has been created for you and saved in the file address.htm.

To insert the contents of address.htm into a table:

1. Using your text editor, open **address.htm** from the tutorial.04/tutorial folder.

2. Copy the HTML code within the <body> tags of address.htm, not including the opening and closing <body> tags.

3. Close the file and return to page1.htm in your text editor.

4. Paste the HTML code you copied from address.htm directly within the fourth table cell as shown in Figure 4-64.

Inserting the address   **Figure 4-64**

insert address here

```
<!-- Address -->
<td valign="top" align="center">
   <hr style="color: tan; background-color: tan; width: 90%" />
   <address style="font-style: normal; font-size: 0.7em; font-family: sans-serif">
      Park City Gazette &#183;
      801 Elkhart Avenue &#183;
      Park City, CO  80511 &#183;
      1 (800) 555-2918
   </address>
</td>
```

5. Save your changes to **page1.htm**.

At this point, you've populated all of the table cells with information except for the articles cell. The articles cell is the only cell with content that changes on a weekly basis. When Kevin wants to update this Web page, he only needs to edit the contents of a single cell.

Creating a Nested Table

Kevin has decided on the stories he wants you to use for the current front-page articles. The main story is the results of the marathon, and another story concerns the reopening of Highway 6 (one of Park City's main roads over the Continental Divide). He also wants the Web page to include a sidebar with links to some of the other current important stories and features. Figure 4-65 shows a layout that Kevin has sketched to assist you with the design of the Web page.

Figure 4-65 ▶ **Design sketch for the articles section**

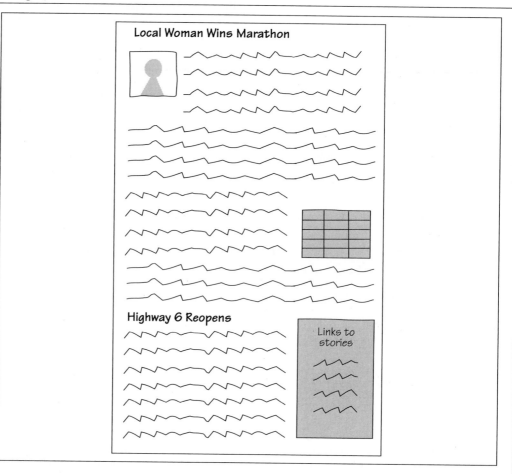

This material is best organized in a second table, an outline of which is shown in Figure 4-66. The first cell contains the marathon story and spans two columns. The second cell, 60% of the width of the table, contains the Highway 6 story. The third cell contains a list of links to other stories and occupies the remaining 40% of the table's width. For this third cell, you'll use the parch3.jpg graphic for a background image.

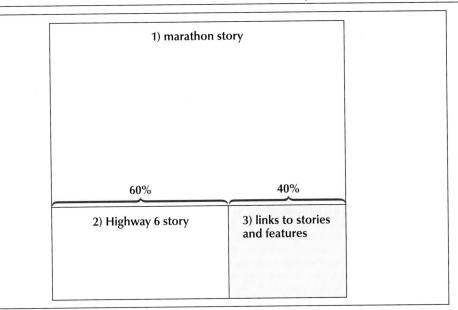

Kevin has begun creating the Web page for this table in the file artcltxt.htm, which you'll open now.

To create the outer table and comments:

▶ **1.** Using your text editor, open **artcltxt.htm** located in the tutorial.04/tutorial folder. Enter *your name* and *the date* into the comment section of the file. Save the file as **articles.htm**.

▶ **2.** Insert the following table structure within the body element:

```
<table cellpadding="5" cellspacing="5">
<tr>
   <!-- Marathon story -->
   <td colspan="2" valign="top">
   </td>
</tr>

<tr>
   <!-- Highway story -->
   <td width="60%" valign="top">
   </td>

   <!-- Features -->
   <td width="40%" valign="top"
   style="background-image: url(parch3.jpg)">
   </td>
</tr>
</table>
```

Figure 4-67 displays the revised HTML code.

Figure 4-67   **Inserting the table structure for the articles section**

```
<body>
<table cellpadding="5" cellspacing="5">
<tr>
   <!-- Marathon story -->
   <td colspan="2" valign="top">
   </td>
</tr>

<tr>
   <!-- Highway story -->
   <td width="60%" valign="top">
   </td>

   <!-- Features -->
   <td width="40%" valign="top" style="background-image: url(parch3.jpg)">
   </td>
</tr>
</table>
</body>
```

3. Save your changes to the file.

The next step is to copy the code for the marathon article that you created in race2.htm and paste it in the first cell of the table. You will also have to edit some of the contents of this material to fit the size of the cell.

To insert the contents of race2.htm into the first cell:

1. Using your text editor, open **race2.htm** from the tutorial.04/tutorial folder.

2. Copy the HTML code within the <body> tags of race2.htm, but do not include the <body> tags themselves.

3. Close the file and return to **articles.htm** in your text editor.

4. Paste the HTML code you copied from race2.htm within the first table cell.

One problem with the race results table is that when we're finished with the front page, it will be placed within a smaller area than it originally occupied in the race2.htm file. To make the text in the race results table look better, we'll reduce the font size of the text in that table.

5. Locate the inline style for the race results table and change the value of the font-size style from 1em to **0.8em**. Figure 4-68 shows part of the revised code for the articles.htm file.

Inserting the contents of race2.htm ◄ Figure 4-68

paste the contents
copied from race2.htm here

```
<body>
<table cellpadding="5" cellspacing="5">
<tr>
   <!-- Marathon story -->
   <td colspan="2" valign="top">
<h1 style="text-align: center; font-family: Arial, Helvetica, sans-serif">
  Local woman wins Marathon
</h1>

<p><img src="blake.jpg" alt="" width="75" height="101" style="margin: 5; float: left" />
Park City native, <b>Laura Blake</b>, won the 27<sup>th</sup> Front Range Marathon
over an elite field of the best long distance runners in the country. Laura's
time of 2 hr. 28 min. 21 sec. was only 2 minutes off the women's course record
set last year by Sarah Rawlings. Kathy Lasker and Lisa Peterson finished second
and third, respectively. Laura's victory came on the heels of her performance at
the NCAA Track and Field Championships, in which she placed second running for
Colorado State.</p>

<table border="5" bordercolor="brown" bordercolorlight="tan" cellspacing="0"
       cellpadding="4" width="70%"
       style="font-family: Arial, Helvetica, sans-serif; font-size: 0.8em;
           background-color: white; float: right; margin: 5 0 5 5">
```

change the font-size
value from 1em to 0.8em

6. Save your changes to the file.

Next, you need to insert the article about the reopening of Highway 6 in the second table cell. The text for this file has been created for you and stored in the highway.htm file.

To insert the contents of highway.htm in the second table cell:

1. Open **highway.htm** from the tutorial.04/tutorial folder in your text editor.

2. Copy the HTML code contained between the <body> tags of highway.htm.

3. Close the file and open **articles.htm** with your text editor if it is not currently open.

4. Paste the copied HTML code into articles.htm within the second table cell as shown in Figure 4-69.

Inserting the contents of highway.htm ◄ Figure 4-69

```
<!-- Highway story -->
<td width="60%" valign="top">
<h3 style="text-align: center; font-family: sans-serif">Highway 6 Reopens</h3>

<p>Highway 6 will reopen this Friday, May 3<sup>rd</sup>, after a final safety
inspection. A late blizzard delayed road crews, marking this as one of the
latest dates for the highway's reopening on record.</p>

<p>Rising to an elevation of 12,351 feet at Grace Pass, Highway 6 is a main link
between Park City and Lake Elton. The reopening of the road is one of the annual signs
that summer is near and the tourist season will soon be upon us!</p>
</td>

<!-- Features -->
<td width="40%" valign="top" style="background-image: url(parch3.jpg)">
</td>
```

5. Save your changes to **articles.htm** and open it in your Web browser (see Figure 4-70).

Figure 4-70 ▷ **Articles page with the highway story**

Local Woman Wins Marathon

 Park City native, **Laura Blake**, won the 27th Front Range Marathon over an elite field of the best long distance runners in the country. Laura's time of 2 hr. 28 min. 21 sec. was only 2 minutes off the women's course record set last year by Sarah Rawlings. Kathy Lasker and Lisa Peterson finished second and third, respectively. Laura's victory came on the heels of her performance at the NCAA Track and Field Championships, in which she placed second running for Colorado State.

In an exciting race, **Peter Teagan** of San Antonio, Texas, used a finishing kick to win the men's marathon for the second straight year, in a time of 2 hr. 12 min. 34 sec. Ahead for much of the race, Kyle Wills of Billings, Montana, finished second, when he could not match Teagan's finishing pace. Jason Wu of Cutler, Colorado, placed third in a very competitive field.

Race Results

	Runner	Time	Origin
Men	1. Peter Teagan	2:12:34	San Antonio, Texas
	2. Kyle Wills	2:13:05	Billings, Montana
	3. Jason Wu	2:14:28	Cutler, Colorado
Women	1. Laura Blake	2:28:21	Park City, Colorado
	2. Kathy Lasker	2:30:11	Chicago, Illinois
	3. Lisa Peterson	2:31:14	Seattle, Washington

This year's race through downtown Boulder boasted the largest field in the marathon's history, with over 9500 men and 6700 women competing. Race conditions were perfect with low humidity and temperatures that never exceeded 85°.

Highway 6 Reopens

Highway 6 will reopen this Friday, May 3rd, after a final safety inspection. A late blizzard delayed road crews, marking this as one of the latest dates for the highway's reopening on record.

Rising to an elevation of 12,351 feet at Grace Pass, Highway 6 is a main link between Park City and Lake Elton. The reopening of the road is one of the annual signs that summer is near and the tourist season will soon be upon us!

The final piece you'll add to articles.htm is the code for the links to stories and features. The code for this cell is stored in the features.htm file.

To insert the contents of features.htm in a table cell:

▷ 1. Using your text editor, open **features.htm** from the tutorial.04/tutorial folder.

▷ 2. Copy the HTML code located between the <body> tags of the file.

▷ 3. Close the file and return to **articles.htm** in your text editor.

▷ 4. Paste the copied HTML code within the third table cell as shown in Figure 4-71.

```
<!-- Features -->
<td width="40%" valign="top" style="background-image: url(parch3.jpg)">
<h3 style="text-align: center; font-family: sans-serif;
          color: ivory; background-color: rgb(82,64,32)">
   Stories Inside
</h3>
<ul style="font-family: sans-serif; font-size: 0.75em; list-style-type: square">
   <li><a href="#">Complete Marathon Results</a></li>
   <li><a href="#">National Park Acquires Land</a></li>
   <li><a href="#">School Board Election Results</a></li>
   <li><a href="#">Spending Referendum Defeated</a></li>
   <li><a href="#">Graduation Awards</a></li>
   <li><a href="#">New Highway Proposed</a></li>
   <li><a href="#">Camping Tips</a></li>
   <li><a href="#">Cougar Sightings Increase</a></li>
   <li><a href="#">Editorials</a></li>
   <li><a href="#">Park City Profile</a></li>
</ul>
</td>
```

▶ **5.** Save your changes to **articles.htm** and reload the file in your Web browser. The completed page appears in Figure 4-72.

Local Woman Wins Marathon

Park City native, **Laura Blake**, won the 27th Front Range Marathon over an elite field of the best long distance runners in the country. Laura's time of 2 hr. 28 min. 21 sec. was only 2 minutes off the women's course record set last year by Sarah Rawlings. Kathy Lasker and Lisa Peterson finished second and third, respectively. Laura's victory came on the heels of her performance at the NCAA Track and Field Championships, in which she placed second running for Colorado State.

In an exciting race, **Peter Teagan** of San Antonio, Texas, used a finishing kick to win the men's marathon for the second straight year, in a time of 2 hr. 12 min. 34 sec. Ahead for much of the race, Kyle Wills of Billings, Montana, finished second, when he could not match Teagan's finishing pace. Jason Wu of Cutler, Colorado, placed third in a very competitive field.

Race Results

	Runner	Time	Origin
Men	1. Peter Teagan	2:12:34	San Antonio, Texas
	2. Kyle Wills	2:13:05	Billings, Montana
	3. Jason Wu	2:14:28	Cutler, Colorado
Women	1. Laura Blake	2:28:21	Park City, Colorado
	2. Kathy Lasker	2:30:11	Chicago, Illinois
	3. Lisa Peterson	2:31:14	Seattle, Washington

This year's race through downtown Boulder boasted the largest field in the marathon's history, with over 9500 men and 6700 women competing. Race conditions were perfect with low humidity and temperatures that never exceeded 85°.

Highway 6 Reopens

Highway 6 will reopen this Friday, May 3rd, after a final safety inspection. A late blizzard delayed road crews, marking this as one of the latest dates for the highway's reopening on record.

Rising to an elevation of 12,351 feet at Grace Pass, Highway 6 is a main link between Park City and Lake Elton. The reopening of the road is one of the annual signs that summer is near and the tourist season will soon be upon us!

Stories Inside

- Complete Marathon Results
- National Park Acquires Land
- School Board Election Results
- Spending Referendum Defeated
- Graduation Awards
- New Highway Proposed
- Camping Tips
- Cougar Sightings Increase
- Editorials
- Park City Profile

Combining the Outer and Inner Tables

It's now time to place the code from articles.htm into page1.htm. You'll use the same copy and paste techniques that you've used to populate the other table cells.

To insert the contents of articles.htm in page1.htm:

1. Return to **articles.htm** in your text editor.

2. Copy the HTML code between the <body> tags.

3. Close the file and reopen **page1.htm** using your text editor if it is not currently open.

4. Paste the copied HTML code from Step 2 within the third table cell as shown in Figure 4-73.

Figure 4-73 | **Inserting the contents of articles.htm**

paste the contents of articles.htm here

```
<!-- Articles -->
<td valign="top">
<table cellpadding="5" cellspacing="5">
<tr>
    <!-- Marathon story -->
    <td colspan="2" valign="top">
<h1 style="text-align: center; font-family: Arial, Helvetica, sans-serif">
  Local Woman Wins Marathon
</h1>

<p><img src="blake.jpg" alt="" width="75" height="101" style="margin: 5; float: left" />
Park City native, <b>Laura Blake</b>, won the 27<sup>th</sup> Front Range Marathon
over an elite field of the best long distance runners in the country. Laura's
time of 2 hr. 28 min. 21 sec. was only 2 minutes off the women's course record
set last year by Sarah Rawlings. Kathy Lasker and Lisa Peterson finished second
and third, respectively. Laura's victory came on the heels of her performance at
the NCAA Track and Field Championships, in which she placed second running for
Colorado State.</p>
```

5. Save your changes to the file and reload it in your Web browser. Figure 4-74 shows the final appearance of the front page of the *Park City Gazette*.

Local Woman Wins Marathon

Home Page

News
Local
State
National
International
Sports
Weather

Classifieds
For Sale
Wanted
Employment
Real Estate
Personal

Tourism
Attractions
Events
Parks
Camping

Subscriptions

Contact Us

Park City native, **Laura Blake**, won the 27th Front Range Marathon over an elite field of the best long distance runners in the country. Laura's time of 2 hr. 28 min. 21 sec. was only 2 minutes off the women's course record set last year by Sarah Rawlings. Kathy Lasker and Lisa Peterson finished second and third, respectively. Laura's victory came on the heels of her performance at the NCAA Track and Field Championships, in which she placed second running for Colorado State.

In an exciting race, **Peter Teagan** of San Antonio, Texas, used a finishing kick to win the men's marathon for the second straight year, in a time of 2 hr. 12 min. 34 sec. Ahead for much of the race, Kyle Wills of Billings, Montana, finished second, when he could not match Teagan's finishing pace. Jason Wu of Cutler, Colorado, placed third in a very competitive field.

Race Results

	Runner	Time	Origin
Men	1 Peter Teagan	2:12:34	San Antonio, Texas
	2. Kyle Wills	2:13:05	Billings, Montana
	3. Jason Wu	2:14:28	Cutler, Colorado
Women	1. Laura Blake	2:28:21	Park City, Colorado
	2. Kathy Lasker	2:30:11	Chicago, Illinois
	3. Lisa Peterson	2:31:14	Seattle, Washington

This year's race through downtown Boulder boasted the largest field in the marathon's history, with over 9500 men and 6700 women competing. Race conditions were perfect with low humidity and temperatures that never exceeded 85°.

Highway 6 Reopens

Highway 6 will reopen this Friday, May 3rd, after a final safety inspection. A late blizzard delayed road crews, marking this as one of the latest dates for the highway's reopening on record.

Rising to an elevation of 12,351 feet at Grace Pass, Highway 6 is a main link between Park City and Lake Elton. The reopening of the road is one of the annual signs that summer is near and the tourist season will soon be upon us!

Stories Inside

- Complete Marathon Results
- National Park Acquires Land
- School Board Election Results
- Spending Referendum Defeated
- Graduation Awards
- New Highway Proposed
- Camping Tips
- Cougar Sightings Increase
- Editorials
- Park City Profile

Park City Gazette · 801 Elkhart Avenue · Park City, CO 80511 · 1 (800) 555-2918

6. Close your text editor and browser.

You show the final version of the Web page to Kevin. He's pleased that you were able to create a Web page that closely resembles his original design sketch, and decides to use this layout for future issues of the *Gazette*. As he compiles new articles, he may look for your help in providing design assistance.

Tips for Effective Use of Tables

- Diagram the table layout before you start writing your HTML code.
- First create a table structure with minimal content. Once the layout appears correct, start formatting the content within the table cells and add more content.
- Insert comment tags throughout the table layout to document each section.
- Indent the code for the various levels of nested tables to make your code easier to interpret.
- Enter opening and closing table tags at the same time in order to avoid the error of either omitting or misplacing the closing tag.
- Test and preview your layout as you proceed in order to catch errors early in the design process.
- Limit the number and extent of nested tables, since they can increase the amount of time required to render a page and cause accessibility problems for non-visual browsers.
- Use cell padding and cell spacing to keep the table content from appearing too crowded.
- Use row spanning to vary the size and starting point of articles within a columnar layout. Side-by-side articles that start and end at the same location are often visually boring and can be difficult to read.
- Avoid using more than three columns of text. Too many columns can result in column widths that are too narrow.
- Use fluid elements to reduce the amount of unused space in the browser window. Use fixed-width elements when you need to precisely place elements on the page.

Review

Session 4.3 Quick Check

1. What is a columnar layout? Can text flow from one column to another in such a layout?
2. What is a jigsaw layout? What cell spacing value should you use in this layout?
3. What is a fixed-width layout?
4. What is a fluid layout?
5. Why can tables be difficult for aural (non-visual) browsers?
6. What HTML code would you use to create a 2 × 2 table nested inside the upper-left cell of another 2 × 2 table?

Review

Tutorial Summary

In this tutorial, you learned how to create and use tables, both to display tabular data and as a layout tool. You first learned how to create simple text tables using preformatted text. Then you learned how to create similar tables using HTML's table elements. You learned about the different parts of a table, including table rows, table cells, and the table heading, body, and footer. You also learned how to create a table caption. In the second session, you learned how to format a table's appearance by modifying the table size, alignment, and background colors. You also learned how to create row and column spanning cells, and how to work with column groups. The third session discussed the different types of page layouts that can be created using tables. In this session, you employed some of those techniques to create a newspaper-style columnar layout.

Key Terms

cell padding	fluid layout	proportional font
cell spacing	graphical table	row group
column group	jigsaw layout	sectional layout
columnar layout	jigsaw table	spanning cell
fixed-width font	monospace font	text table
fixed-width layout	preformatted text	

Practice

Practice the skills you learned in the tutorial using the same case scenario.

Review Assignments

Data files needed for this Review Assignment: art2txt.htm, cougar.jpg, page2txt.htm, parch2.jpg, parch3.jpg, parch.jpg, pcglogo.jpg, sighttxt.htm, tips.htm

Kevin would like to place another page of the *Park City Gazette* on the Web site. Cougar sightings have recently increased in the Park City area, causing great concern for both local residents and tourists. Kevin has written an article describing the sightings and providing safety tips for effectively handling a cougar encounter. Kevin has also created a table, shown in Figure 4-75, that lists local cougar sightings for the last six months. Kevin would like you to include this table with his article.

Figure 4-75

Location	April	May	June	July	August	Total
Park City	0	2	1	3	4	10
Riley	2	1	1	3	2	9
Dixon	0	2	3	1	4	10
TOTAL	2	5	5	7	10	29

The articles should employ the same layout you designed for the paper's front page. Figure 4-76 shows a preview of the Web page you'll create for Kevin.

Figure 4-76

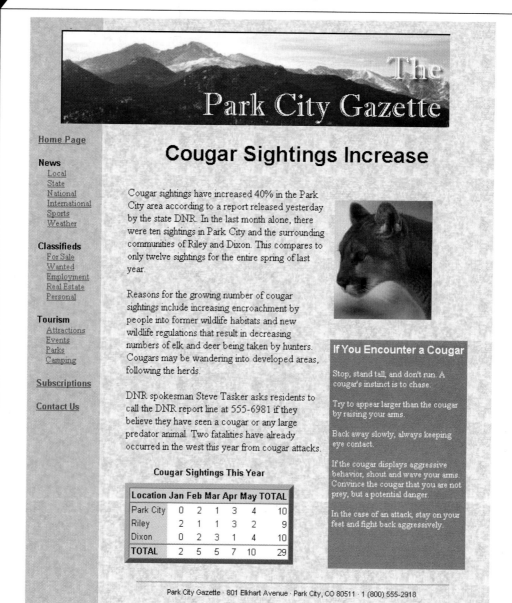

To complete this task:

1. Use your text editor to open the files **sightxt.htm**, **art2txt.htm**, and **page2txt.htm** from the tutorial.04/review folder. Enter *your name* and *the date* in the comment section of each file. Save the files as **sighting.htm**, **article2.htm**, and **page2.htm** respectively.

2. Go to the **sighting.htm** file in your text editor. Below the last paragraph in the story, insert a table with the following features:
   - The table should contain row groups for the header, table body, and footer.
   - The table should have a 7-pixel-wide brown border. The light border color should be tan.
   - Table rules should be set to "groups".
   - The default font for the table text should be sans-serif with a font size of 0.8em.
   - The cell spacing should be set to 0 pixels. The cell padding should be set to 2 pixels.

3. Insert the caption "Cougar Sightings This Year" in a bold font above the table.

4. Insert the table entries shown in Figure 4-75. The first row should be placed in the header row group and marked as table headings. Set the background color of this row to pink.

5. Below the table heading row group, insert the table footer row group. This row contains the total cougar sightings from all of the communities for each month and for the year so far. The first cell should have a pink background and the text should be displayed in a bold font. Right-align the numeric values in the row. (Note that even though this is a table footer and will appear as the last row in the rendered table, it precedes the table body in the HTML code.)

6. The next three rows should be placed in the table body group. The table body row group contains the cougar sightings for each city. Change the background color of the first cells in each row to pink and right align the numeric values in each row.

7. Save your changes to **sighting.htm**.

8. Go to the **article2.htm** file in your text editor.

9. In the body section, create a table with a cell spacing value of 3 and a cell padding value of 5.

10. Create a cell in the first row of the table that spans two columns, and identify this cell with the comment "Cougar headline". Within this cell, insert a centered h1 heading that contains the text "Cougar Sightings Increase". Display the headline in a sans-serif font.

11. In the second row of the table, insert a cell that is 60% wide and spans two rows. Vertically align the text of this cell with the cell's top border. Identify this cell with the comment "Cougar story". Insert the page contents of the **sighting.htm** file (excluding the <body> tags) into this cell.

12. Also in the table's second row, insert a cell that is 40% wide. Identify this cell with the comment "Cougar photo". Display the image, **cougar.jpg**, with an empty text string for the alternate text. The size of the photo is 150 pixels wide by 178 pixels high.

13. In the table's third row, insert a cell that is 40% wide, has a red background, and align the cell text with the cell's top border. Insert the comment "Cougar tips" for this cell. Insert the contents of the **tips.htm** file (excluding the <body> tags) into this cell.

14. Save your changes to **article2.htm**.

15. Go to the **page2.htm** file in your text editor.

16. Locate the Articles cell in the main table of this file (it will be the third cell). Insert the page contents of **article2.htm**. Save your changes to the file and view its contents with your Web browser.

17. Submit your completed Web site to your instructor.

Case Problem 1

Apply

Use the skills you've learned in this tutorial to design a Web page for a company that creates geodesic domes for businesses and homes.

Data files needed for this Case Problem: address.htm, back.jpg-back5.jpg, dhome.jpg, dhometxt.htm, footer.htm, introtxt.htm, links.jpg, textbox.htm, uses.htm

dHome, Inc. dHome is one of the nation's leading manufacturers of geodesic dome houses. Olivia Moore, the director of advertising for dHome, has hired you to work on the company's Web site. She has provided you with all of the text you need for the Web page, and your job is to design the page's layout. Olivia would like each page in the Web site to display the company logo, a column of links, a footer displaying additional links, and another footer displaying the company's address and phone number. She would like you to place the appropriate text for the topic of each Web page in the center. Olivia wants you to use a fixed-width layout. Figure 4-77 shows a preview of the completed Web page.

Figure 4-77

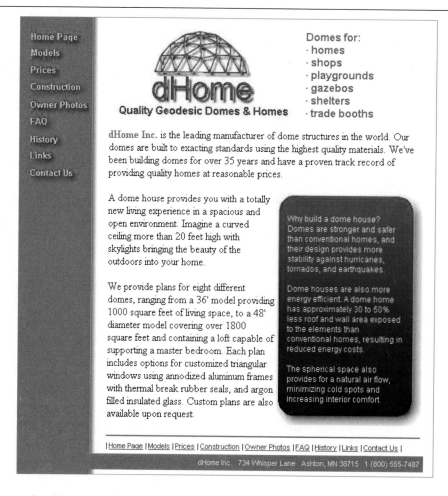

To create the dHome Web page:

1. Open **introtxt.htm** and **dhometxt.htm** from the tutorial.04/case1 folder. Enter *your name* and *the date* in the comment section of each file. Save the files as **intro.htm** and **dhome.htm** respectively.

2. Go to **intro.htm** in your text editor. Between the first and second paragraphs, create a table 224 pixels wide and 348 pixels high. Set the border, cell padding, and cell spacing values to zero. Float the table with the right margin of the Web page.

3. The table should have a single row with three columns. The first cell should be 20 pixels wide, using the **back3.jpg** file for its background. There is no content for this cell, so insert a non-breaking space into the cell.

4. The second cell should be 200 pixels wide, using the **back4.jpg** file as a background. Insert the contents of the **uses.htm** file into this cell.

5. The third cell should be 30 pixels wide and use the **back5.jpg** file as its background. There is no content for this cell, so insert a non-breaking space.

6. Save your changes to **intro.htm**.

7. Return to the file **dhome.htm** in your text editor.

8. Within the body section, create a table 620 pixels wide with a cell padding of 5 and a cell spacing of 0.

9. The first row of the table should contain three cells. The first cell should be 120 pixels wide and span three rows. Within this cell, insert the **links.jpg** image, aligning it with

the cell's top border. Set the alternate text for this image to an empty text string. The size of the image is 94 pixels wide by 232 pixels high. Identify this cell with the comment tag "List of links".

10. The second cell should be 300 pixels wide. Within this cell, insert the company's logo, found in the **dhome.jpg** file. Align the logo with the cell's top border. For non-graphical browsers, provide the alternate text "dHome Quality Geodesic Domes & Homes". The size of the inline image is 270 pixels wide by 134 pixels high. Identify this cell with the comment tag "Company logo".

11. The third cell should be 200 pixels wide. Insert the contents of the **textbox.htm** file into this cell. Align the text of the cell with the cell's top border. Change the text color of the cell content to the color value (182,29,23) and display the text in bold sans-serif font. Identify the cell with the comment "Text box".

12. In the table's second row, create a single cell 500 pixels wide that spans two columns. Insert the contents of the **intro.htm** file into this cell. Align the text with the top of the cell. Identify the cell with the comment "Intro text".

13. In the table's third row, create another cell 500 pixels wide that spans two columns. Within this cell, insert the contents of the **footer.htm** file, aligning the contents with the top of the cell. The text of this cell should be displayed in a sans-serif font that is 0.7em in size. Identify the contents of this cell with the comment "Footer".

14. In the fourth and last row of the table, create a cell 620 pixels wide and 15 pixels high, that spans three columns. Use **back2.jpg** as the background image for the cell. Insert the contents of the **address.htm** file into the cell, aligned with the cell's right border. The cell content should be displayed in yellow sans-serif font with a size of 0.7em. Identify the cell with the comment "Address".

15. Save your changes to the file.

16. Submit the completed Web site to your instructor.

Case Problem 2

Apply

Use the skills you've learned in this tutorial to design a Web page for a retreat center.

Data files needed for this Case Problem: adams.jpg, address.htm, back.jpg, dlogo.jpg, dunsttxt.htm, events.htm, letter.htm, next.htm, welctxt.htm

Dunston Retreat Center   The Dunston Retreat Center, located in northern Wisconsin, offers weekends of quiet and solitude for all who visit. The center, started by a group of Trappist monks, has grown in popularity over the last few years as more people have become aware of its services. The director of the center, Benjamin Adams, wants to advertise the center on the Internet and has asked you to create a Web site for the center. He wants the Web site to include a welcome message from him, a list of upcoming events, a letter from one of the center's guests, and a description of the current week's events. The Web page you'll create is shown in Figure 4-78.

Figure 4-78

To create the Dunston Retreat Center Web page:

1. Use your text editor to open **welctxt.htm** and **dunsttxt.htm** from the tutorial.04/case2 folder. Enter *your name* and *the date* in the comment sections. Save the files as **welcome.htm** and **dunston.htm** respectively.

2. Go to the **welcome.htm** file in your text editor. Between the second and third paragraphs, insert a table with the following attributes:
   - The table floats on the right page margin.
   - The table should have a 1-pixel-wide border and a cell padding value of 5 pixels. The table should be 40% of the page width.
   - The border color should be white. The table background should be equal to the color value (125,178,116).

3. Within the table insert a single cell containing the body contents of the **letter.htm** file. The content should be aligned with the top of the cell, and the text should appear in a white sans-serif font with a font size of 0.8em.

4. Save your changes to **welcome.htm**.

5. Go to the **dunston.htm** file in your text editor.

6. Create a table that is 90% of the width of the page with cell spacing and padding equal to 5 pixels.

7. In the first row of the table, insert a single cell two columns wide containing the image **dlogo.jpg**. The alternate text for this image is "The Dunston Retreat Center". The size of the image is 626 pixels wide by 148 pixels high. Align the contents with the left edge of the table.

8. The second row of the table should contain two cells. The first cell should be 100 pixels wide, spanning three rows. It should contain the contents of the **events.htm** file, aligned with the cell's top border. Display the contents of this cell in a sans-serif font.

9. The second cell should contain the contents of **welcome.htm**, aligned with the top border of the cell.

10. In the third row of the table, insert a single cell containing the contents of **next.htm**, aligned with the top of the cell.

11. The table's fourth row contains a single cell containing the contents of **address.htm**, centered horizontally within the cell.

12. Save your changes to the file. Open the file in your Web browser and verify that the layout displays correctly.

13. Submit the completed Web site to your instructor.

Case Problem 3

Data files needed for this Case Problem: back.jpg, ccc.gif, febtxt.htm

Chamberlain Civic Center The Chamberlain Civic Center of Chamberlain, Iowa, is in the process of designing a Web page to advertise its events and activities. Stacy Dawes, the director of publicity, has asked you to create a Web page describing the events in February, which are shown in the following list. Ticket prices are provided in parentheses.

- Every Sunday, the Carson Quartet plays at 1 p.m. ($8)
- February 1, 8 p.m.: Taiwan Acrobats ($16/$24/$36)
- February 5, 8 p.m.: Joey Gallway ($16/$24/$36)
- February 7-8, 7 p.m.: West Side Story ($24/$36/$64)
- February 10, 8 p.m.: Jazz Masters ($18/$24/$32)
- February 13, 8 p.m.: Harlem Choir ($18/$24/$32)
- February 14, 8 p.m.: Chamberlain Symphony ($18/$24/$32)
- February 15, 8 p.m.: Edwin Drood ($24/$36/$44)
- February 19, 8 p.m.: The Yearling ($8/$14/$18)
- February 21, 8 p.m.: An Ellington Tribute ($24/$32/$48)
- February 22, 8 p.m.: Othello ($18/$28/$42)
- February 25, 8 p.m.: Madtown Jugglers ($12/$16/$20)
- February 28, 8 p.m.: Robin Williams ($32/$48/$64)

Figure 4-79 shows a preview of the Web page you'll create for Stacy.

Explore

Broaden your knowledge of table design by creating a calendar table for a civic center.

Figure 4-79

the Chamberlain Civic Center

Home Page   Tickets   Events   Facilities

February will be another banner month at the Chamberlain Civic Center with a two day performance of the Tony Award winning musical, *West Side Story* by the Broadway Touring Company. Tickets are going fast, so order yours today.

Celebrate Valentine's Day with the Chamberlain Symphony and their special selection of classical music for lovers. The next day, exercise your mind by attending the Charles Dickens mystery, *Edwin Drood*.

Jazz lovers have a lot to celebrate in February with a visit from *The Jazz Masters* on February 10th, and then on February 21st, enjoy the music of The Duke with *An Ellington Tribute* performed by the Jazz Company of Kansas City.

Pins, bottles, plates, and chairs are flying at the Chamberlain Civic Center in February. The *Taiwan Acrobats* return with another

Events in February						
Sun	**Mon**	**Tue**	**Wed**	**Thu**	**Fri**	**Sat**
26	27	28	29	30	31	1 Taiwan Acrobats 8 p.m. $16/$24/$36
2 Carson Quartet 1 p.m. $8	3	4	5 Joey Gallway 8 p.m. $16/$24/$36	6	7 West Side Story 7 p.m. $24/$36/$64	8 West Side Story 7 p.m. $24/$36/$64
9 Carson Quartet 1 p.m. $8	10 Jazz Masters 8 p.m. $18/$24/$32	11	12	13 Harlem Choir 8 p.m. $18/$24/$32	14 Chamberlain Symphony 8 p.m. $18/$24/$32	15 Edwin Drood 8 p.m. $24/$36/$44
16 Carson Quartet 1 p.m. $8	17	18	19 The Yearling 7 p.m. $8/$14/$18	20	21 An Ellington Tribute 8 p.m. $24/$32/$48	22 Othello 8 p.m. $18/$28/$42
23 Carson Quartet 1 p.m. $8	24	25 Madtown Jugglers 8 p.m. $12/$16/$20	26	27	28 Robin Williams 8 p.m. $32/$48/$64	1

amazing performance. Then, on February 25th, the *Madtown Jugglers* get into the act with their unique blend of comedy, juggling, and madness.

Enjoy a classical brunch every Sunday in February with music provided by the Carson Quartet. Seating is limited, so please order your table in advance.

To create the CCC calendar:

1. Using your text editor, open **febtxt.htm** from the tutorial.04/case3 folder. Enter *your name* and *the date* in the comment section of the file. Save the file as **feb.htm**.
2. At the top of the page, create a table with the following attributes:
   - The border size should be 5 pixels with a width of 100% of the page and a cell padding value of 10 pixels. The table should have a red border.
   - The rules value should be set to "none" and the frame value to "below".
   - The content of this table should be displayed in a red sans-serif font with a font size of 18 pixels. The bottom margin size of the table should be set to 20 pixels. (Note: Some browsers may not support the rules or frame attributes).
3. The first table cell should contain the inline image **ccc.gif**. The alternate text for this image should be "The Chamberlain Civic Center". The size of the image is 322 pixels wide by 144 pixels high.
4. The next four cells in the row should contain the text strings, "Home Page", "Tickets", "Events", and "Facilities". Vertically align the contents of these cells with the bottom border of the cell. Horizontally align the contents with the cell's right border.
5. Below the table you just created, insert another table with the following attributes:
   - The table should float on the right margin of the Web page with a left margin of 5 pixels.

Explore

- The table border should be 5 pixels wide. The color of the table border should be red and pink. The cell padding value should be set to 3 pixels. The cell spacing value should be set to 0 pixels.
- The contents of the table should be displayed in a sans-serif font at a font size of 0.7em on a white background.

Explore ▶ 6. Within the table, create a column group spanning seven columns. These columns represent the seven days of the week in the calendar table. Set the width of the columns to 60 pixels and align the text in the column group with the top of each cell. (*Hint:* To set the width for each column in a column group, add the width attribute to the <colgroup> tag.)

Explore ▶ 7. Within the column group, assign the first column a background color of pink. Assign a background color of white to the next four columns, and assign a background color of pink to the last two columns.

8. In the table's first row, create a heading that spans seven columns. Insert the text "Events in February" centered horizontally within the cell.

9. In the table's second row, insert the following table headings: "Sun", "Mon", "Tue", "Wed", "Thu", "Fri", and "Sat".

10. Enclose the first two rows of the table in a table head row group. Change the background color of this row group to black and the font color to white.

11. The next five rows contain the individual days from the calendar, each placed in a separate table cell. Format the dates as follows:
    - Display the day of the month on its own line, formatted with a boldface font.
    - If there is an event for that date, display the name of the event on one line, the time the event takes place on the second line, and the ticket price on a third line. Separate one line from another using the <br /> tag.
    - If the date is not in the month of February, use the **back.jpg** image as the cell's background.

12. Save your changes to the file. Using your Web browser, verify that the table displays correctly. Note that some browsers do not support column groups, so the page rendered by those browsers may not resemble the one in Figure 4-79.

13. Submit your completed Web page to your instructor.

Create

Test your knowledge of HTML by creating a Web site for the TravelWeb E-Zine.

Case Problem 4

Data files needed for this Case Problem: luxair.txt, photo.txt, ppoint2.jpg, ppoint.jpg, toronto.txt, twlinks2.htm, twlinks.htm, twlogo.jpg, yosemite.jpg, yosemite.txt

TravelWeb E-Zine Magazine   You have joined the staff of TravelWeb, which provides travel information and tips to online subscribers. You have been asked to work on the layout for the E-Zine Magazine Web page. Figure 4-80 describes the files that you have been given to use in creating the page.

Figure 4-80

File	Description
luxair.txt	Article about LuxAir reducing airfares to Europe
photo.txt	Article about the Photo of the Week
ppoint.jpg	Large version of the Photo of the Week (320 x 228)
ppoint2.jpg	Small version of the Photo of the Week (180 x 128)
toronto.txt	Article about traveling to Toronto
twlinks.htm	Links to other TravelWeb pages (list version)
twlinks2.htm	Links to other TravelWeb pages (table version)
twlogo.jpg	Image file of the TravelWeb logo (425 x 105)
yosemite.txt	Article about limiting access to Yosemite National Park
yosemite.jpg	Image file of Yosemite National Park (112 x 158)

To create a Web page for TravelWeb:

1. Use the files listed in Figure 4-80 to create a newspaper-style page. All of these files are stored in the tutorial.04/case4 folder. The page should include several columns, but the number, size, and layout of the columns is up to you.
2. Use all of the files on the page, with the following exceptions: use only one of the two files **twlinks.htm** or **twlinks2.htm**, and use only one of the two image files **ppoint.jpg** or **ppoint2.jpg**. Note that not all of the links in the content files point to existing files.
3. Use background colors to give the Web page an attractive and interesting appearance.
4. Include comment tags to describe the different parts of your page layout.
5. Save your page as tw.htm in the tutorial.04/case4 folder.
6. Submit the completed Web page to your instructor.

Review

Quick Check Answers

Session 4.1

1. Text tables and graphical tables. Text tables are supported by all browsers and are easier to create. The graphical table is more difficult to create but provides the user with a wealth of formatting options.
2. A proportional font assigns a different amount of space to each character depending on each character's width. A fixed-width font assigns the same space to each character regardless of width. You should use a fixed-width font in a text table in order to keep columns aligned under all font sizes.
3. The <pre> tag
4. The <tr> tag identifies a table row. The <td> tag identifies individual table cells, and the <th> tag identifies table cells that act as table headings.
5. The number of rows in a table is determined by the number of <tr> tags. The number of columns is equal to the largest number of <td> and <th> tags within a single table row.
6. The three row groups are the table head, created by enclosing tables within the <thead> tag, the table body created with the <tbody> tag, and the table footer, created with the <tfoot> tag.
7. <caption align="bottom">Product Catalog</caption>
   This caption must be placed directly after the opening <table> tag.

Session 4.2

1. `<table border="5" cellspacing="3" cellpadding="4"> ... </table>`
2. `<td valign="top"> ... </td>`

   or

   `<th valign="top"> ... </th>`
3. `<td align="center"> ... </td>`

   or

   `<th align="center"> ... </th>`
4. `<table width="50%">`
5. When the contents of the table do not fit within the cell dimensions or when another cell in the same column has been set to a larger width.
6. `<td rowspan="3" colspan="2"> ... </td>`

   or

   `<th rowspan="3" colspan="2"> ... </th>`
7. `<colgroup span="3" style="background-color: yellow" />`

Session 4.3

1. A columnar layout is a layout in which the page content has been laid out in columns. Text cannot flow from one column to another.
2. A jigsaw layout breaks the page into separate pieces like the pieces of a jigsaw puzzle. The cell spacing value should be set to 0 pixels.
3. A fixed-width layout sets the absolute size of the page elements, regardless of the size of the browser window.
4. In a fluid layout, one or more of the table elements is sized as a percentage of the page width. The effect of a fluid layout is to set the sizes of page elements based on the size of the browser window.
5. Aural browsers often render the content of the table in the order in which the content appears in the HTML code. If the content is not intelligible when reproduced in that order, the table will be difficult to interpret.
6.

```
<table>
   <tr>
      <td>
      <table><tr><td></td><td></td></tr>
             <tr><td></td><td></td></tr>
      </table>
      </td>
      <td></td>
   </tr>
   <tr>
      <td></td>
      <td></td>
   </tr>
</table>
```

Objectives

Session 5.1
- Describe the uses of frames in a Web site
- Lay out frames within a browser window
- Display a document within a frame
- Format the appearance of frames by setting the margin widths, removing scrollbars, and specifying whether users can resize frames

Session 5.2
- Direct a link target to a specific frame
- Direct a link target outside of a frame layout
- Add page content for browsers that don't support frames
- Format the color and size of frame borders
- Incorporate an inline frame in a page

Designing a Web Site with Frames

Using Frames to Display Multiple Web Pages

Case

The Yale Climbing School

One of the most popular climbing schools and touring agencies in Colorado is the Yale Climbing School (YCS). Located in Vale Park, outside Rocky Mountain National Park, YCS specializes in teaching beginning and advanced climbing techniques. The school also sponsors several tours, leading individuals on some of the most exciting, challenging, and picturesque climbs in North America. The school has been in business for 15 years, and in that time it has helped thousands of people experience the mountains in ways they never thought possible.

Yale Climbing School has a lot of competition from other climbing schools and touring groups in the area. Debbie Chen is the owner of the school and is always looking for ways to market her programs and improve the visibility of the school. Early on, she decided to use the Internet and the World Wide Web as a means of promoting the school, and she has already created many Web pages.

Debbie has seen other Web sites use frames to display several Web pages in a single browser window. She feels that frames would allow the school to more effectively present its offerings to potential students. She asks you to help develop a frame-based Web site for YCS.

Student Data Files

▼**Tutorial.05**

▽ **Tutorial folder**

    linkstxt.htm
    tourstxt.htm
    yaletxt.htm
    + 22 HTML files
    + 24 graphic files

▽ **Review folder**

    headtxt.htm
    slisttxt.htm
    sltxt.htm
    stafftxt.htm
    tlisttxt.htm
    tltxt.htm
    tourstxt.htm
    yale2txt.htm
    + 16 HTML files
    + 24 graphic files

▽ **Case1 folder**

    dcctxt.htm
    headtxt.htm
    maptxt.htm
    + 5 HTML files
    + 6 graphic files

▽ **Case2 folder**

listtxt.htm
+ 17 graphic files

▽ **Case3 folder**

messtxt.htm
mxxtxt.htm
+ 9 HTML files
+ 15 graphic files

▽ **Case4 folder**

drive15l.htm
drive15l.jpg
drive20m.htm
drive20m.jpg
drive33m.htm
drive33m.jpg
drive60s.htm
drive60s.jpg
tape800.htm
tape800.jpg
tape3200.htm
tape3200.jpg
tape9600.htm
tape9600.jpg
wlogo.gif
wlogo.htm

Session 5.1

Introducing Frames

Typically, as a Web site grows in size and complexity, each page is dedicated to a particular topic or group of topics. One page might contain a list of links, another page might display contact information for the company or organization, and another page might describe the business philosophy. As more pages are added to the site, the designer might wish for a way to display information from several pages at the same time.

One solution is to duplicate that information across the Web site, but this strategy presents problems. It requires a great deal of time and effort to repeat (or copy and paste) the same information over and over again. Also, each time a change is required, you need to repeat your edit for each page in the site—a process that could easily result in errors.

Such considerations contributed to the creation of frames. A **frame** is a section of the browser window capable of displaying the contents of an entire Web page. Figure 5-1 shows an example of a browser window containing two frames. The frame on the left displays the contents of a Web page containing a list of links. The frame on the right displays an old version of the NEC Web site that utilized frames.

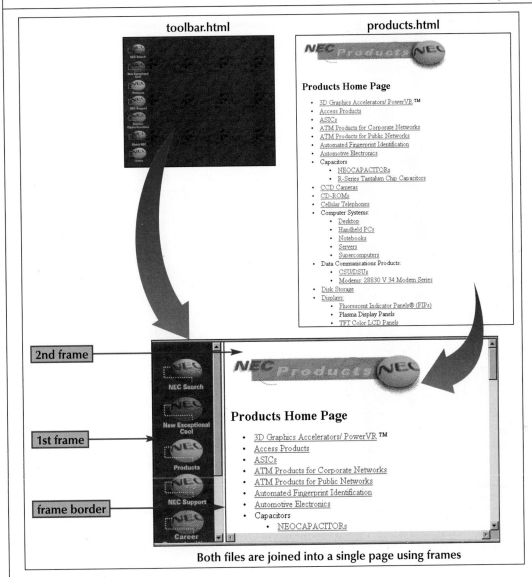

Frame examples Figure 5-1

Both files are joined into a single page using frames

This example illustrates a common use of frames: displaying a table of contents in one frame, while showing individual pages from the site in another. Figure 5-2 illustrates how a list of links can remain on the screen while the user navigates through the contents of the site. Using this layout, a designer can easily update the list of links because it is stored on only one page.

Figure 5-2 **Activating a link within a frame**

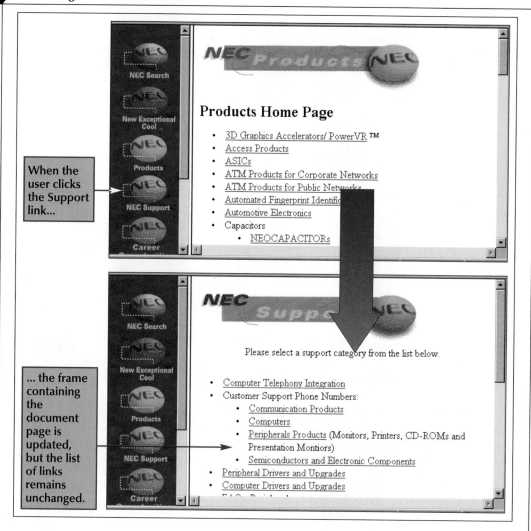

Frame-based Web sites also have their drawbacks. For example, when opening a page that uses frames, a browser has to load multiple HTML files before a user can view the contents of the site. This can result in increased waiting time for potential customers. It is also very difficult for users to bookmark pages within a Web site that uses frames. In addition, Internet search engines that create content-based catalogs can have problems adding framed pages to their listings—meaning that if you want your content to be easily found by the world, it's wise not to use frames. Some browsers also have difficulty printing the pages within individual frames, though this is less of a problem than it once was. Finally, some users simply prefer Web page designs in which the entire browser window is devoted to a single page. For these reasons, many Web designers suggest that if you still want to use frames, you should create both framed and non-framed versions for a Web site and give users the option of which one to use.

Planning Your Frames

Before you start creating your frames, it is a good idea to plan their appearance and determine how you want to use them. There are several issues to consider:

- What information will be displayed in each frame?
- How do you want the frames placed on the Web page? What is the size of each frame?
- Which frames will be static—that is, always showing the same content?
- Which frames will change in response to links being clicked?
- What Web pages will users first see when they access the site?
- Should users be permitted to resize the frames to suit their needs?

As you progress with your design for the Web site for the Yale Climbing School, you'll consider each of these questions. Debbie has already created the Web pages for the YCS Web site. Figure 5-3 describes the different Web pages you'll work with in this project.

Documents at the YCS Web site ◄ **Figure 5-3**

Topic	Filename	Content
Biographies	staff.htm	Links to biographical pages of the YCS staff
Home page	home.htm	The YCS home page
Lessons	lessons.htm	Climbing lessons offered by the YCS
Logo	head.htm	A page containing the company logo
Philosophy	philosoph.htm	Statement of the YCS's business philosophy
Table of contents	links.htm	Links to the YCS pages
Tours	diamond.htm	Description of the Diamond climbing tour
Tours	eldorado.htm	Description of the Eldorado Canyon tour
Tours	grepon.htm	Description of the Petit Grepon climbing tour
Tours	kieners.htm	Description of the Kiener's Route climbing tour
Tours	lumpy.htm	Description of the Lumpy Ridge climbing tour
Tours	nface.htm	Description of the North Face climbing tour

Debbie has organized the pages by topic, such as tour descriptions, climbing lessons, and company philosophy. Two of the files, links.htm and staff.htm, do not focus on a particular topic, but contain links to other YCS Web pages.

Debbie has carefully considered how this material should be organized on the Web site, and what information the user should see first. She has sketched a layout that illustrates how she would like the frames to be organized. See Figure 5-4.

Figure 5-4 | **Design sketch for the frames at the YCS Web site**

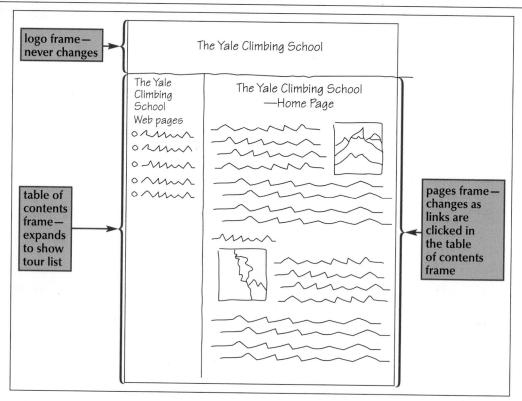

She would like you to create three frames. The top frame displays the school's logo and address. The frame on the left displays a list of the Web pages at the YCS Web site. Finally, the frame on the lower right displays the contents of those pages.

Your first task is to enter the HTML code for the frame layout that Debbie has described.

Creating a Frameset

Two elements are involved in creating frames. The **frameset** element describes how the frames are organized and displayed within the browser window. The **frame** element defines which document is displayed within a frame. The general syntax for using the frameset element is

```
<html>
<head>
<title>title</title>
</head>
<frameset>
    frames
</frameset>
</html>
```

where *frames* are the individual frames within the frameset. We'll explore how to create these frames shortly.

Note that the frameset element replaces the body element in this HTML document. Because this HTML file displays the contents of other Web pages, it is not technically a Web page and thus does not include a page body. Later in the tutorial, we'll explore situations in which you would include a body element in order to support browsers that do not display frames. For now, we'll concentrate on defining the appearance and content of the frames.

Specifying Frame Size and Orientation

Frames are placed within a frameset in either rows or columns, but not both. Figure 5-5 shows two framesets, one in which the frames are laid out in three columns, and the other in which they are placed in three rows.

Frame layouts in rows and columns ◄ **Figure 5-5**

Frames laid out in columns

| The first frame | The second frame | The third frame |

Frames laid out in rows

The first frame

The second frame

The third frame

The syntax for creating a row or column frame layout is:

```
<frameset rows="row1,row2,row3,…"> … </frameset>
```

or

```
<frameset cols="column1,column2,column3,…"> … </frameset>
```

where *row1*, *row2*, *row3*, and so on is the height of each frame row, and *column1*, *column2*, *column3*, and so forth is the width of each frame column. There is no limit to the number of rows or columns you can specify for a frameset.

Row and column sizes can be specified in three ways: in pixels, as a percentage of the total size of the frameset, or by an asterisk (*). The asterisk instructs the browser to allocate any unclaimed space in the frameset to the given row or column. For example, the tag <frameset rows="160,*"> creates two rows of frames. The first row has a height of 160 pixels, and the height of the second row is equal to whatever space remains in the display area. You can combine the three methods. The tag <frameset cols="160,25%,*"> lays out the frames in the columns shown in Figure 5-6. The first column is 160 pixels wide, the second column is 25% of the width of the display area, and the third column covers whatever space is left.

Figure 5-6	Sizing frames

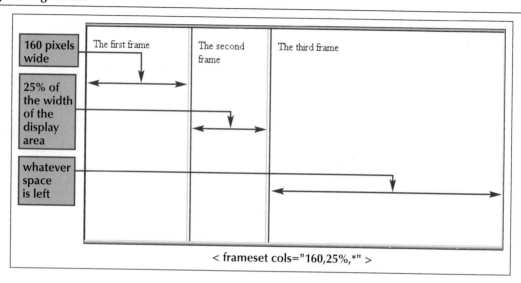

< frameset cols="160,25%,*" >

It is a good idea to specify at least one of the rows or columns of your frameset with an asterisk, in order to ensure that the frames fill up the screen regardless of a user's monitor settings. You can also use multiple asterisks. In that case, the browser divides the remaining display space equally among the frames designated with asterisks. For example, the tag <frameset rows="*,*,*"> creates three rows of frames with equal heights.

Reference Window	**Creating a Frameset**

To create frames laid out in rows, enter the following tags:
```
<frameset rows="row1,row2,row3,…">
     frames
</frameset>
```
where *row1*, *row2*, *row3*, etc. are the heights of the frame rows, and *frames* defines the frames within the frameset.

To create frames laid out in columns, enter the following tags:
```
<frameset cols="column1,column2,column3,…">
     frames
</frameset>
```
where *column1*, *column2*, *column3*, etc. are the widths of the frame columns.

The first frameset you'll create for the Yale Climbing School page has two rows. The top row is used for the company logo, and the second row is used for the remaining content of the Web page. A frame that is 85 pixels high should provide enough space to display the logo. The second row will occupy the rest of the display area.

To create the first set of frames:

1. Use your text editor to open **yaletxt.htm** from the tutorial.05/tutorial folder. Enter **your name** and **the date** in the comment section of the file. Save the file as **yale.htm**.

2. Insert the following HTML code after the closing </head> tag:

```
<frameset rows="85,*">
</frameset>
```

This code specifies a height of 85 pixels for the top row and allocates the remaining space to the second row. Figure 5-7 shows the revised yale.htm file.

Creating the initial frameset | **Figure 5-7**

frameset contains two rows: the first row is 85 pixels high, and the second row occupies the remaining space

```
<title>Yale Climbing School</title>
</head>
<frameset rows="85,*">
</frameset>
</html>
```

The initial frame layout is now defined, and you'll add to this design later to include the third frame that Debbie specified in her layout. For now, you need to specify the source for the two frame rows that you have created.

Specifying a Frame Source

To create a frame element, you use the tag

```
<frame src="url" />
```

where *url* is the URL of the document you want displayed within the frame. Frame elements must be placed within the frameset.

Creating a Frame

Reference Window

- To create a frame element, use the following HTML tag:
  ```
  <frame src="url" />
  ```
  where *url* is the URL of the document you wish to display within the frame.

The page containing the company logo and address has been saved as head.htm. You'll place this document in the first frame of the frameset as shown in Figure 5-8.

Figure 5-8 | **Placing the head.htm file**

To display the head page in the first frame:

1. After the opening <frameset> tag, insert the following code, as shown in Figure 5-9:

```
<!-- Company Logo -->
<frame src="head.htm" />
```

Figure 5-9 | **Inserting a frame for head.htm**

```
<frameset rows="85,*">
  <!-- Company Logo -->
  <frame src="head.htm" />
</frameset>
```

frame source

It is not necessary to indent the code as shown in the figure, but it makes the code easier to read and interpret.

2. Save your changes to the file.

Note that using the comment tag and indenting the <frame> tag a few spaces helps make your HTML code easier to follow and interpret.

You have successfully specified the source for the first row. Looking at Debbie's sketch in Figure 5-4, you notice that the second row contains two frames, laid out in columns. In order to lay out the second row as Debbie designed it, you need to create another set of frames.

Nesting Framesets

Because a frameset places frames in either rows or columns, but not both, in order to create a layout containing frames in rows *and* columns, you must nest one frameset within another. When you use this technique, the interpretation of the rows and cols attributes changes slightly. For example, a row height of 25% does not mean 25% of the display area, but rather 25% of the height of the frame in which that row is located.

Debbie wants the second row of the current frame layout to contain two columns: the first column will display a table of contents, and the second column will display a variety of YCS documents. You'll specify a width of 140 pixels for the first column, and whatever remains in the display area will be allotted to the second column.

To create the second set of frames:

1. Add a blank line immediately below the <frame> tag line that you just inserted.

2. Insert the following HTML code:

```
<!-- Nested Frames -->
<frameset cols="140,*">
</frameset>
```

Your file should appear as shown in Figure 5-10.

Creating a nested frameset　◄　**Figure 5-10**

```
<frameset rows="85,*">
    <!-- Company Logo -->
    <frame src="head.htm" />
    <!-- Nested Frames -->
    <frameset cols="140,*">
    </frameset>
</frameset>
```

nested frameset of two frame columns →

Next, you'll specify the sources for the two frames in the frameset. The frame in the first column displays the contents of links.htm. The Yale Climbing School home page, home.htm, is displayed in the second frame. Figure 5-11 shows the contents of these two pages and their locations in the frameset.

Placing links.htm and home.htm　◄　**Figure 5-11**

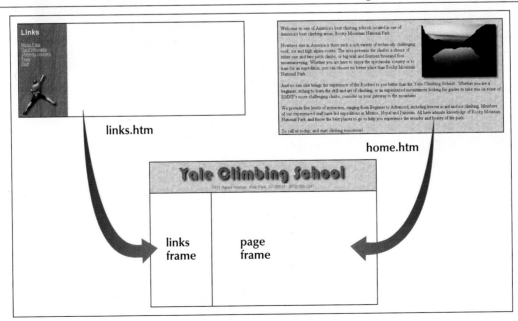

links.htm

home.htm

Yale Climbing School

links frame

page frame

To insert the sources for the two frames:

1. Add a blank line immediately below the nested <frameset> tag you just inserted.

2. Type the following HTML code:

```
<!-- List of Links -->
<frame src="links.htm" />
<!-- YCS Home Page -->
<frame src="home.htm" />
```

Figure 5-12 shows the code for the two new frames.

Figure 5-12	Inserting frame columns

```
<frameset rows="85,*">
    <!-- Company Logo -->
    <frame src="head.htm" />
    <!-- Nested Frames -->
    <frameset cols="140,*">
        <!-- List of Links -->
        <frame src="links.htm" />
        <!-- YCS Home Page -->
        <frame src="home.htm" />
    </frameset>
</frameset>
```

3. Save your changes to the file.

4. Using your Web browser, open **yale.htm**. Figure 5-13 shows the Web page at this point.

Figure 5-13	YCS Web site with frames

Trouble? Depending on the font size used by your browser, your Web page may look slightly different.

The browser window displays three Web pages from the YCS Web site. However, the design of the frame layout could use some refinement. At some screen sizes, such as the one shown in Figure 5-13, the address information is cut off in the logo frame. Because not all of the contents of the page fit into this frame, a scroll bar has been added to the frame. Scroll bars do not appear in the links frame, because the entire list of links is visible.

Debbie doesn't mind the appearance of a scroll bar for the school's home page—she realizes that the entire page won't necessarily fit into the frame—but she doesn't want a scroll bar for the frame containing the school's logo and address.

Formatting a Frame

You can control three attributes of a frame: the appearance of scroll bars, the size of the margin between the source document and the frame border, and whether or not users are allowed to change the frame size.

Reference Window

Formatting a Frame

- To control whether a frame contains a scroll bar, add the following attribute to the frame element:
  ```
  scrolling="type"
  ```
  where *type* is either "yes" (scroll bar) or "no" (no scroll bar). If you do not specify the scrolling attribute, a scroll bar appears only when the content of the frame source cannot fit within the boundaries of the frame.
- To control the amount of space between the frame source and the frame boundary, add the following attribute to the frame element:
  ```
  marginwidth="value" marginheight="value"
  ```
  where the width and height values are expressed in pixels. The margin width is the space to the left and right of the frame source. The margin height is the space above and below the frame source. If you do not specify a margin height or width, the browser assigns dimensions based on the content of the frame source.
- To keep users from resizing frames, add the following attribute to the frame element:
  ```
  noresize="noresize"
  ```

The first attribute you'll work with is the scrolling attribute.

Hiding and Displaying Scroll Bars

By default, a scroll bar is displayed when the content of the source page does not fit within a frame. You can override this setting using the scrolling attribute. The syntax for this attribute is

```
scrolling="type"
```

where *type* can be either "yes" (to always display a scroll bar) or "no" (to never display a scroll bar). If you don't specify a setting for the scrolling attribute, the browser displays a scroll bar when necessary.

Debbie feels that a scroll bar is inappropriate for the logo frame, and she wants to ensure that a scroll bar is never displayed for that frame. Therefore, you need to add the scrolling="no" attribute to the frame element. However, Debbie does want scroll bars for the other two frames, as needed, so the default value for those frames is sufficient. Note that for some browsers you need to close and then open the file for changes to the frames to take effect. If you simply reload the page, your changes may not be displayed. With other browsers, however, reloading the page does allow you to view changes to the page.

To remove the scroll bar from the logo frame:

▶ 1. Return to **yale.htm** in your text editor.

▶ 2. Within the frame element for the logo frame, insert the attribute **scrolling="no"**, as shown in Figure 5-14.

| Figure 5-14 | ▶ | Removing the scroll bars from the logo frame |

```
<frameset rows="85,*">
    <!-- Company Logo -->
    <frame src="head.htm" scrolling="no" />
    <!-- Nested Frames -->
    <frameset cols="140,*">
        <!-- List of Links -->
        <frame src="links.htm" />
        <!-- YCS Home Page -->
        <frame src="home.htm" />
    </frameset>
</frameset>
```

▶ 3. Save your changes to the file and reload it in your Web browser. Note that for some browsers you might have to close and then open yale.htm for the changes to take effect.

Although the scroll bar for the logo frame has been removed, depending on your screen size you may still not be able to see all of the text contained in head.htm. You can correct this problem by modifying the frame margins.

When working with frames, keep in mind that you should remove scroll bars from a frame only when you are convinced that the entire Web page will be visible in the frame. To do this, you should view your Web page using several different monitor settings. Few things are more irritating to Web site visitors than to discover that some content is missing from a frame with no scroll bars available to reveal the missing content.

With that in mind, your next task is to solve the problem of the missing text from the logo frame. To do so, you need to modify the internal margins of the frame.

Setting Frame Margins

When your browser retrieves a frame's Web page, it determines the amount of space between the content of the page and the frame border. Occasionally, the browser sets the margin between the border and the content too large. Generally, you want the margin to be big enough to keep the source's text or images from running into the frame's borders. However, you do not want the margin to take up too much space, because you typically want to display as much of the source as possible.

You've already noted that the margin height for the logo frame is too large, and this has shifted some of the text beyond the border of the frame. To fix this problem, you need to specify a smaller margin for the frame so that the logo can move up and allow all of the text to be displayed in the frame.

The attribute for specifying margin sizes for a frame is

```
marginheight="value" marginwidth="value"
```

where the marginheight value specifies the amount of space, in pixels, above and below the frame source, and the marginwidth value specifies the amount of space to the left and right of the frame source. You do not have to specify both the margin height and width. However, if you specify only one, the browser assumes that you want to use the same value for both. Setting margin values is a process of trial and error as you determine what combination of margin sizes looks best.

To correct the problem with the logo frame, you'll decrease its margin size to 0 pixels. This setting will allow the entire page to be displayed within the frame. Also, to keep the home page from running into the borders of its frame, you'll set the frame's margin width to 10 pixels. Debbie also wants you to decrease the margin height to 0 pixels. The links frame margin does not require any changes.

To set the margin sizes for the frames:

1. Return to the **yale.htm** file in your text editor.

2. Within the frame element for the logo frame, insert the attribute **marginheight="0"**. This sets both the margin height and the margin width to 0 by default.

3. Within the frame element for the home page frame, insert the attributes **marginheight="0" marginwidth="10"**.

   Figure 5-15 shows the revised HTML code for yale.htm.

Setting the frame margin sizes ◄ **Figure 5-15**

```
<frameset rows="85,*">
    <!-- Company Logo -->
    <frame src="head.htm" scrolling="no" marginheight="0" />
    <!-- Nested Frames -->
    <frameset cols="140,*">
        <!-- List of Links -->
        <frame src="links.htm" />
        <!-- YCS Home Page -->
        <frame src="home.htm" marginheight="0" marginwidth="10" />
    </frameset>
</frameset>
```

4. Save your changes to the file and reload or refresh it in your Web browser. The revised frames are shown in Figure 5-16.

YCS Web site with resized frame margins ◄ **Figure 5-16**

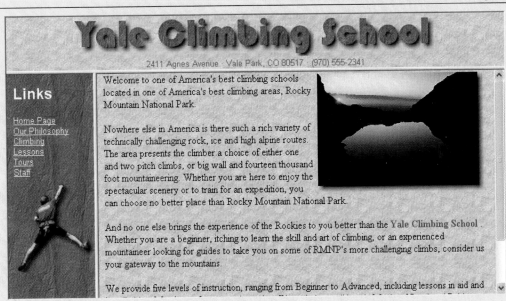

Debbie is satisfied with the changes you've made to the Web page. Your next task is to lock in the sizes and margins for each frame on the page to prevent users from resizing the frames.

Controlling Frame Resizing

By default, users can resize frame borders in the browser by simply dragging a frame border. However, some Web designers prefer to freeze, or lock, frames so that users cannot resize them. This insures that the Web site displays as the designer intended. Debbie would like you to do this for the YCS Web site. The attribute for controlling frame resizing is

```
noresize="noresize"
```

HTML also allows you to insert this attribute as

```
noresize
```

without an attribute value. However this form is not supported by XHTML, because XHTML requires all attributes to have attribute values. We'll follow this principle in the code we create for Debbie's Web site.

To prevent the frames in the YCS Web site from being resized:

▶ 1. Return to **yale.htm** in your text editor.

▶ 2. Within each of the three <frame> tags in the file, add the attribute **noresize="noresize"**

▶ 3. Save your changes to the file and reload it in your Web browser.

▶ 4. Try to drag one of the frame borders to verify that the frames are now "locked in" and cannot be resized by the user.

You're ready to take a break from working on the YCS Web site. Debbie is pleased with the progress you've made on the site. She still wants you to accomplish a few more things before your work is complete, such as specifying where the targets of the site's links should be displayed. You'll deal with this question and others in the next session.

Review

Session 5.1 Quick Check

1. What are frames, and why are they useful in displaying and designing a Web site?
2. Why is the <body> tag unnecessary for pages that contain frames?
3. What HTML code do you use to create three rows of frames with the height of the first row set to 200 pixels, the height of the second row set to 50% of the display area, and the height of the third row set to occupy the remaining space?
4. What HTML code do you use to specify home.htm as a source for a frame?
5. What HTML code do you use to remove the scroll bars from the frame for home.htm?
6. What HTML code do you use to set the size of the margin above and below the contents of the home.htm frame to 3 pixels?
7. What is the size of the margins to the right and left of the frame in Question 6?
8. What code would you use to prevent users from moving the frame borders in home.htm?

Session 5.2

Working with Frames and Links

Now that you've created frames for the Yale Climbing School Web site, you're ready to work on formatting the links for the Web page. The links page contains five links (see Figure 5-17):

- The Home Page link points to home.htm
- The Our Philosophy link points to philosph.htm
- The Climbing Lessons link points to lessons.htm
- The Tours link points to tours.htm
- The Staff link points to staff.htm

Links in the links.htm file | **Figure 5-17**

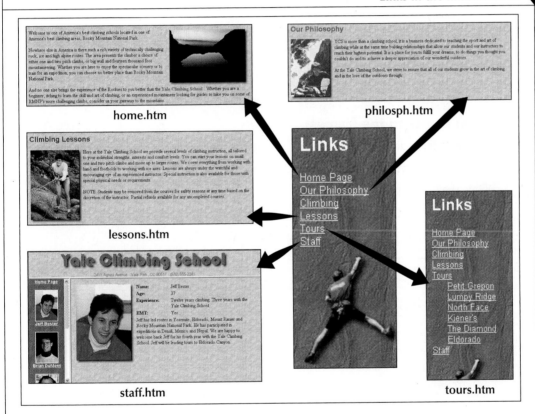

By default, clicking a link within a frame opens the linked file inside the same frame. However, this is not the way Debbie wants each of the links to work. She wants the links to work as follows:

- The Home, Our Philosophy, and Climbing Lessons pages should display in the bottom-right frame
- The Tours page should display in the table of contents frame
- The Staff page should occupy the entire browser window

Controlling the behavior of links in a framed page requires two steps: you need to give each frame on the page a name, and then point each link to one of the named frames.

Directing a Link to a Frame

- To assign a name to a frame, insert the following attribute:
  `<frame name="name" />`
  where name is of the frame.
- To point the target of a link to a named frame, use the target attribute:
  `target="name"`
  where name is the name you assigned to the frame.
- To use the same target for all links, add the target attribute to the base element in the document head.

Assigning a Name to a Frame

To assign a name to a frame, add the name attribute to the frame tag. The syntax for this attribute is

`<frame src="url" name="name" />`

where name is the name assigned to the frame. Case is important in assigning names: "information" is considered a different name than "INFORMATION". Frame names cannot include spaces.

You'll name the three frames in the YCS Web site "logo," "links," and "pages."

To assign names to the frames:

1. Using your text editor, open **yale.htm** if it is not currently open.
2. Within the tag for the logo frame, enter the attribute **name="logo"**.
3. Within the tag for the links frame, enter the attribute **name="links"**.
4. Within the tag for the home page frame, enter the attribute **name="pages"**.

   Figure 5-18 shows the revised code for the file.

Figure 5-18 ▶ Setting the frame names

```
<frameset rows="85,*">
   <!-- Company Logo -->
   <frame src="head.htm" scrolling="no" marginheight="0" name="logo" />
   <!-- Nested Frames -->
   <frameset cols="140,*">
      <!-- List of Links -->
      <frame src="links.htm" name="links" />
      <!-- YCS Home Page -->
      <frame src="home.htm" marginheight="0" marginwidth="10" name="pages" />
   </frameset>
</frameset>
```

5. Save your changes to the file.

Now that you've named the frames, the next task is to specify the "pages" frame as the target for the Home Page, Our Philosophy, and Climbing Lessons links, so that clicking each of these links opens the corresponding file in the home page frame.

Specifying a Link Target

Previously, you may have used the target attribute to open a linked document in a new browser window. You can also use the target attribute to open a linked target in a frame. To point the link to a specific frame, add the following attribute to the link:

```
target="name"
```

where *name* is the name you've assigned to a frame in your Web page. In this case, the target name for the frame you need to specify is "pages". To change the targets for the links, edit the <a> tags in links.htm. You'll start by editing only the <a> tags pointing to the Home Page, Our Philosophy, and Climbing Lessons pages. These are the links to be displayed in the "pages" frame of yale.htm. You'll work with the other links later.

To specify the targets for the links:

▶ 1. Using your text editor, open **links.htm** from the tutorial.05/tutorial folder. Enter **your name** and **the date** in the comment section of the file.

▶ 2. Within the <a> tags for the Home Page, Our Philosophy, and Climbing Lessons links, enter the attribute **target="pages"**. The revised code is shown in Figure 5-19.

Assigning a target to a link ◀ **Figure 5-19**

```
<h2>Links</h2>
<p style="font-size: 0.8em">
<a href="home.htm" target="pages">Home Page</a><br />
<a href="philosph.htm" target="pages">Our Philosophy</a><br />
<a href="lessons.htm" target="pages">Climbing Lessons</a><br />
<a href="tours.htm">Tours</a><br />
<a href="staff.htm">Staff</a>
</p>
```

▶ 3. Save your changes to the file.

Trouble? If you need to return to the original version of the file, you can open linkstxt.htm in the tutorial.05/tutorial folder in your Data Files.

Now test the first three links in the list.

▶ 4. Using your Web browser, open **yale.htm**.

▶ 5. Click the **Our Philosophy** link in the Links frame. The Our Philosophy Web page should display in the lower-right frame. See Figure 5-20.

Figure 5-20 | **Viewing the philosophy page**

Links

Home Page
Our Philosophy
Climbing
Lessons
Tours
Staff

Our Philosophy

YCS is more than a climbing school, it is a business dedicated to teaching the sport and art of climbing while at the same time building relationships that allow our students and our instructors to reach their highest potential. It is a place for you to fulfill your dreams, to do things you thought you couldn't do and to achieve a deeper appreciation of our wonderful outdoors.

At the Yale Climbing School, we strive to ensure that all of our students grow in the art of climbing and in the love of the outdoors through:

- Individual attention
- Customized climbs tailored to each student's strengths and interests
- Uncompromised safety
- Professional guides and support staff

Trouble? If the Our Philosophy page displays in the left frame instead, you may need to close and open yale.htm for your changes to take effect.

6. Click the **Home Page** and **Climbing Lessons** links, and verify that the links are working properly and the pages are displaying in the "pages" frame.

Sometimes pages can contains dozens of links that should all open in the same frame. Instead of repetitively inserting target attributes for each link, you can instead specify the target in the base element within the document head. See Tutorial 2 for a discussion of the base element. Note that the target attribute is not supported in strictly compliant XHTML code.

Using Reserved Target Names

The remaining two tags in the list of links point to a list of the tours offered by the Yale Climbing School (tours.htm) and to a staff information page (staff.htm), respectively. The tours.htm file does not contain information about individual tours; instead, it is an expanded table of contents of YCS Web pages, some of which are devoted to individual tours. Each tour has its own Web page, as shown in Figure 5-21.

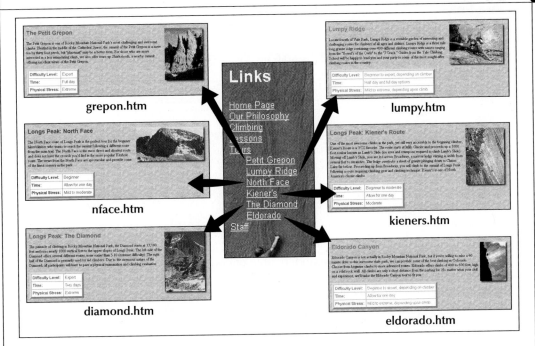

grepon.htm

lumpy.htm

nface.htm

kieners.htm

diamond.htm

eldorado.htm

Debbie wants tours.htm to display in the links frame in order to give the effect of expanding the table of contents whenever a user clicks the Tours link. You can specify "links" (the name of the frame) as the target. However, you can also do this using reserved target names.

Reserved target names are special names that can be used in place of a frame name as targets. They are useful in situations where the name of the frame is unavailable, when you want the page to appear in a new window, or when you want the page to replace the current browser window. Figure 5-22 describes the reserved target names.

Reserved Target Name	Function in a frameset
_blank	Loads the target document into a new browser window
_self	Loads the target document into the frame containing the link
_parent	Loads the target document into the parent of the frame containing the link
_top	Loads the document into the full display area, replacing the current frame layout

All reserved target names begin with the underscore character (_) to distinguish them from other target names. Note that reserved target names are case-sensitive, so you must enter them in lowercase.

Because Debbie wants the contents of tours.htm to display in the links frame, you can use the reserved target name, _self, which overrides the target specified in the <base> tag and instructs the browser to open the page in the same frame that contains the link.

To use the reserved target name to specify the target for the Tours link:

1. Return to **links.htm** in your text editor.

2. Enter the attribute **target="_self "** within the <a> tag for the Tours link. See Figure 5-23.

Figure 5-23	Using the _self target

```
<h2>Links</h2>
<p style="font-size: 0.8em">
<a href="home.htm" target="pages">Home Page</a><br />
<a href="philosph.htm" target="pages">Our Philosophy</a><br />
<a href="lessons.htm" target="pages">Climbing Lessons</a><br />
<a href="tours.htm" target="_self">Tours</a><br />
<a href="staff.htm">Staff</a>
</p>
```

3. Save your changes to **links.htm**.

The tours.htm Web page is an expanded table of contents for Web pages containing information about specific tours. Debbie wants each of these pages to display in the "pages" frame. To do this, specify the "pages" frame as the default link target in tours.htm. The tours.htm file also contains a link that takes the user back to links.htm. You should specify _self as the target for this link.

To modify tours.htm as you did links.htm:

1. Using your text editor, open **tours.htm** from the tutorial.05/tutorial folder. Enter **your name** and **the date** in the comment section of the file.

2. Insert the tag **<base target="pages" />** directly above the </head> tag. This code displays the individual tour pages in the "pages" frame when a user clicks any of the tour links.

3. Enter the attribute **target="_self"** within the <a> tag that points to links.htm. This will cause the original table of contents, links.htm, to display in the "links" frame. See Figure 5-24.

Figure 5-24	Adding targets to the tours page

```
<title>List of links</title>
<base target="pages" />
</head>

<body style="background-image: url(wall3.jpg); background-repeat: repeat-y;
          font-family: sans-serif; color: white" link="white" alink="white" vlink="white">
<h2>Links</h2>
<p style="font-size: 0.8em">
<a href="home.htm">Home Page</a><br />
<a href="philosph.htm">Our Philosophy</a><br />
<a href="lessons.htm">Climbing Lessons</a><br />
<a href="links.htm" target="_self">Tours</a><br />
      <a href="grepon.htm">Petit Grepon</a><br />
      <a href="lumpy.htm">Lumpy Ridge</a><br />
      <a href="nface.htm">North Face</a><br />
      <a href="kieners.htm">Kiener's</a><br />
      <a href="diamond.htm">The Diamond</a><br />
      <a href="eldorado.htm">Eldorado</a><br />
<a href="staff.htm">Staff</a>
</p>
```

4. Save your changes to the file.

   Trouble? If you need to revert back to the original version of tours.htm for any reason, it is saved in the tutorial.05/tutorial folder as tourstxt.htm

5. Reload **yale.htm** in your Web browser.

6. Verify that the Tours link works as you intended. As you click on the link, the table of contents list should alternately collapse and expand. In addition, click on the links to the individual tour pages to verify that they display correctly in the "pages" frame. See Figure 5-25.

Viewing a tour page | Figure 5-25

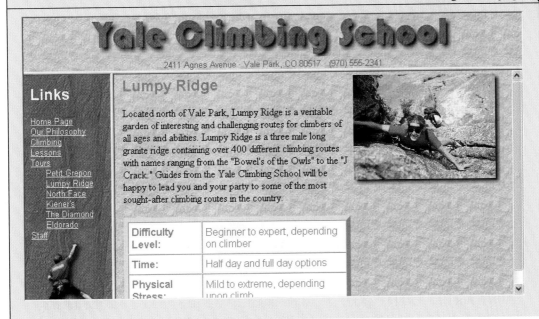

The technique employed here is commonly used for tables of contents that double as links. Clicking the Tours link gives the effect that the list is expanding and contracting, but in reality, one table of contents file is simply being replaced by another.

The final link you need to create points to a Web page of staff biographies. Debbie asked another employee to produce the contents of this Web page, and the results are shown in Figure 5-26.

Staff Web page | Figure 5-26

As you can see, this Web page also uses frames. If you specify the "pages" frame as the target, the result is a series of nested frame images, as shown in Figure 5-27.

Figure 5-27 | **Nested frame layout**

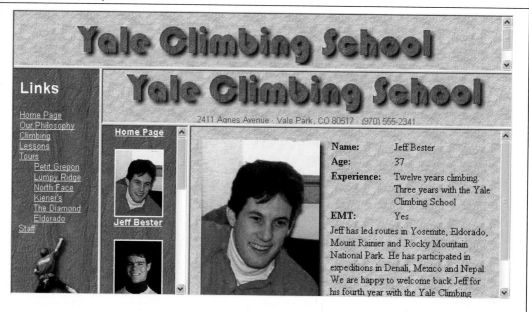

This is not what Debbie wants. She wants the Staff Web page to load into the full display area, replacing the frame layout with its own layout. To target a link to the full display area, you use the _top reserved target name. The _top target is often used when one framed page is accessed from another. It's also used when you are linking to pages that lie outside your Web site altogether.

For example, a link to the Colorado Tourism Board Web site should not display within a frame on the YCS Web site for two reasons. First, once you go outside your Web site, you lose control of the frame layout, and you could easily end up with nested frame images. The second reason is that such a design could easily confuse users, making it appear as if the Colorado Tourism Board is a component of the Yale Climbing School.

To specify the target for the Staff link:

1. Return to **links.htm** in your text editor.

2. Enter the attribute **target="_top"** within the <a> tag for the Staff link. See Figure 5-28.

Figure 5-28 | **Revised links.htm**

```
<h2>Links</h2>
<p style="font-size: 0.8em">
<a href="home.htm" target="pages">Home Page</a><br />
<a href="philosph.htm" target="pages">Our Philosophy</a><br />
<a href="lessons.htm" target="pages">Climbing Lessons</a><br />
<a href="tours.htm" target="_self">Tours</a><br />
<a href="staff.htm" target="_top">Staff</a>
</p>
```

3. Save your changes to the file.

Because tours.htm also acts as a detailed table of contents, you should edit the link to the Staff page in that file. That way, a user can click the Staff link from either the table of contents with the expanded list of tours, or the original table of contents.

To edit tours.htm:

1. Return to **tours.htm** in your text editor.

2. Enter the attribute **target="_top"** within the <a> tag for the Staff link.

3. Save your changes to the file.

4. Using your Web browser, reload **yale.htm**. Verify that the Staff link now opens the Staff page and replaces the existing frame layout with its own. Be sure to test the Staff link from both the original table of contents and the table of contents with the expanded list of tours.

   Trouble? If the Staff link does not work properly, verify that you used lowercase letters for the reserved target name.

Debbie has viewed all the links on the YCS Web site and is quite satisfied with the results. However, she wonders what would happen if a user with an older browser encountered the page. If possible, she wants to be able to accommodate browsers that don't support frames.

Using the noframes Element

You can use the noframes element to make your Web site viewable with browsers that do not support frames (known as frame-blind browsers) as well as by those that do. The noframes element marks a section of your HTML file as code that browsers incapable of displaying frames can use. The noframes element is nested within the frameset element and uses the following syntax:

```
<html>
<head>
<title>title</title>
</head>
<frameset>
    frames
    <noframes>
        <body>
            page content
        </body>
    </noframes>
</frameset>
</html>
```

where *page content* is the content that you want the browser to display in place of the frames. There can be only one noframes element in the document. When a browser that supports frames processes this code, it ignores everything within the <noframes> tag and concentrates solely on the code to create the frames. When a browser that doesn't support frames processes this HTML code, however, it doesn't know what to do with the <frameset> and <noframes> tags, so it ignores them. It does know how to render whatever appears within the <body> tags, though. Using this setup, both types of browsers are supported within a single HTML file. Note that when you use the <noframes> tag, you must include <body> tags to specify the extent of the page content.

Reference Window	**Supporting Frame-Blind Browsers**

- Create a version of your page that does not use frames.
- In the frames document, insert the following tags within the frameset element:
  ```
  <noframes>
       <body>
        page content
       </body>
  </noframes>
  ```
  where *page content* is the content of the page you want displayed in place of the frames.

The Yale Climbing School has been using the nonframed Web site displayed in Figure 5-29 for several years.

Figure 5-29	▶	**Frameless version of the YCS home page**

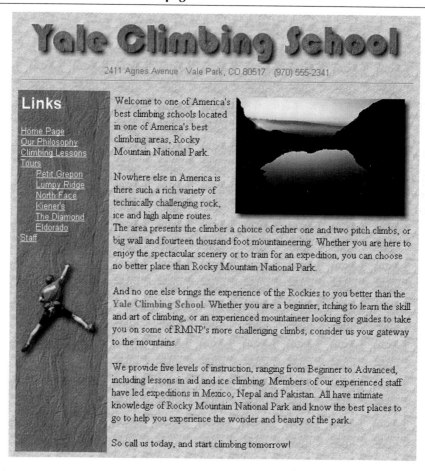

If you want this Web page to display for frame-blind browsers, while still making your framed version available as the default, copy the HTML code, including the <body> tags, from the source code of the nonframed Web page and place it within a pair of <noframes> tags in the framed Web document yale.htm.

To insert support for frame-blind browsers:

1. Using your text editor, return to **yale.htm**.

2. Create a blank line immediately above the </html> tag.

3. Enter the following HTML code directly before the closing </frameset> tag at the bottom of the file:

   ```
   <!-- Noframes version of this page -->
   <noframes>
   </noframes>
   ```

4. Save your changes to the file.

   Next, copy the code from the noframe page into **yale.htm**.

5. Using your text editor, open **noframes.htm** from the tutorial.05/tutorial folder.

6. Copy the HTML code for the page content. Be sure to include both the opening and closing <body> tags in your copy selection.

7. Return to **yale.htm** in your text editor.

8. Create a blank line immediately below the <noframes> tag.

9. Paste the text you copied from noframes.htm in the blank line you created below the <noframes> tag. Figure 5-30 shows the beginning and end of the revised code.

Inserting the noframes page version ◀ **Figure 5-30**

```
<frameset rows="85,*">
   <!-- Company Logo -->
   <frame src="head.htm" scrolling="no" marginheight="0" name="logo" />
   <!-- Nested Frames -->
   <frameset cols="140,*">
      <!-- List of Links -->
      <frame src="links.htm" name="links" />
      <!-- YCS Home Page -->
      <frame src="home.htm" marginheight="0" marginwidth="10" name="pages" />
   </frameset>

<!-- Noframes version of this page -->
<noframes>
<body style="background-image: url(wall.jpg)" link="white" vlink="white" alink="white">
<table width="620" cellpadding="5">
<tr>
```

```
      <p>We provide five levels of instruction, ranging from Beginner to
      Advanced, including lessons in aid and ice climbing. Members of our
      experienced staff have led expeditions in Mexico, Nepal and Pakistan.
      All have intimate knowledge of Rocky Mountain National Park and know the
      best places to go to help you experience the wonder and beauty of the
      park.</p>
      <p>So call us today, and start climbing tomorrow!</p>
   </td>
</tr>
</table>
</body>
</noframes>

</frameset>
</html>
```

10. Save your changes to **yale.htm**.

Another way of supporting browsers that do not display frames is to create a Web page that contains links to the framed and nonframed versions of your Web site. A user with an older browser can thereby avoid the frames. This technique also provides users with the option of not viewing frames, even though their browsers have the ability to. Some people just don't like frames.

Working with Frame Borders

Some browsers support additional attributes that you can use to change border size and appearance. For example, you can remove borders from your frames to free up more space for text and images, or you can change the color of the frame borders so that they match or complement the color scheme for your Web site.

Modifying Frame Borders

- To specify whether a frame border is displayed, insert the following attribute:
  ```
  <frame frameborder="value" />
  ```
  where a value of "0" hides the border, and a value of "1" displays it.

Internet Explorer and Netscape

- To define the width of frame borders, add the following attribute to the frameset element:
  ```
  <frameset border="value"> … <frameset>
  ```
  where *value* is the size of the border in pixels. Adding this attribute to a frameset applies the border width to all frames in the frameset. Note that you can also change border width in Internet Explorer using the framespacing attribute.
- To define a color for your frame borders, add the following attribute to either the frameset or frame element:
  ```
  bordercolor="color"
  ```
  where *color* is a color name or a hexadecimal color value.

Setting the Frame Border Color

To change the color of a frame's border, both Internet Explorer and Netscape support the bordercolor attribute. The attribute can be applied either to an entire set of frames, using the <frameset> tag, or to individual frames, using the <frame> tag. The syntax for this attribute is

```
bordercolor="color"
```

where *color* is either a color name or a hexadecimal color value. Applying the bordercolor attribute to the <frameset> tag affects all of the frames and nested frames within the set. If you apply the bordercolor attribute to a single <frame> tag, the border color for that particular frame changes in Internet Explorer, but in Netscape, all of the frame borders change. It is important to remember that when you apply these types of tags and attributes to your Web page, you should always view the page using different browsers and, if possible, browser versions. Note that this attribute is not part of the official specifications for HTML, nor is it supported by XHTML.

Debbie asks you to test the bordercolor attribute on the YCS Web site by changing the color of the frame borders to brown.

To change the frame border color:

1. Return to **yale.htm** in your text editor.
2. Enter the attribute **bordercolor="brown"** within the opening <frameset> tag.
3. Save your changes to the file, and then reload it in your Web browser. Figure 5-31 shows the frames with a brown border.

Setting the Frame Border Width

You can also remove the frame borders entirely. The attribute for specifying whether a frame border appears is

```
<frame frameborder="value" />
```

where a frameborder value of "0" removes the frame border and a value of "1" displays the border. Different browsers respond in different ways to this attribute, and some browsers do not support the attribute at all. Internet Explorer and Netscape also support the border attribute, which has the syntax:

```
<frameset border="value"> … </frame>
```

where value is the size of the border in pixels. Note that the border attribute is applied to the frameset element, while the frameborder attribute is applied only the frame element. Like bordercolor, the border attribute is not part of the specifications for HTML, and is not supported by XHTML.

Debbie has asked you to remove the frame borders from the document. In order to ensure capability with the greatest number of browsers, you'll use both the frameborder and the border attributes in your HTML code.

To change the size of the frame borders:

1. Return to **yale.htm** in your text editor.

2. Delete the bordercolor attribute that you entered in the previous set of steps. You don't need this attribute because you're going to remove the frame borders entirely.

3. Insert the attribute **border="0"** within the <frameset> tag.

4. Insert the attribute **frameborder="0"** within each of the <frame> tags. Figure 5-32 shows the revised code.

Figure 5-32	Removing the frame borders

```
<frameset rows="85,*" border="0">
   <!-- Company Logo -->
   <frame src="head.htm" scrolling="no" marginheight="0" name="logo"
          frameborder="0" />
   <!-- Nested Frames -->
   <frameset cols="140,*">
      <!-- List of Links -->
      <frame src="links.htm" name="links" frameborder="0" />
      <!-- YCS Home Page -->
      <frame src="home.htm" marginheight="0" marginwidth="10" name="pages"
             frameborder="0" />
   </frameset>
</frameset>
```

▶ **5.** Save your changes to **yale.htm** and close the file.

▶ **6.** Reload **yale.htm** in your Web browser. As shown in Figure 5-33, the frame borders are removed from the page.

Figure 5-33	The YCS Web site without frame borders

▶ **7.** Close any YCS files that may still be open.

By removing the borders, you've created more space for the text and images in each of the Web pages. You've also created the impression of a "seamless" Web page. Some Web designers prefer not to show frame borders in order to give the illusion of a single Web page rather than three separate ones. However, other Web designers believe that hiding frame borders can confuse users as they navigate the Web site.

Creating Inline Frames

Another way of using frames is to create a floating frame. Introduced by Internet Explorer 3.0 and added to the HTML 4.0 specifications, a **floating frame**, or **inline frame**, is displayed as a separate box or window within a Web page. The frame can be placed within a Web page in much the same way as an inline image. The syntax for a floating frame is

```
<iframe src="url">
    alternate content
</iframe>
```

where `url` is the URL of the document you want displayed in the inline frame and `alternate content` is the content you want displayed by browsers that don't support inline frames. For example, the following code displays the contents of the jobs.htm file within an inline frame; for browsers that don't support inline frames, it displays a paragraph containing a link to the file:

```
<iframe src="jobs.htm">
    <p>
    View the online <a href="jobs.htm">jobs listing</a>
    </p>
</iframe>
```

Inline frames support many of the same features as inline images. You can resize them, float them on the page margins, and specify the size of the margin around the frame. You can also use many of the attributes associated with frame elements. Figure 5-34 summarizes some of the attributes associated with inline frames. Note that the iframe element is not supported in strictly compliant XHTML code.

Attributes of inline frames ◄ **Figure 5-34**

Attribute	Description
align="*position*"	Places the frame in relationship to the surrounding content. **Deprecated**
border="*value*"	The size of the border around the frame, in pixels. **Deprecated**
frameborder="*value*"	Specifies whether to display a frame border (1) or not (0)
height="*value*" width="*value*"	The height and width of the frame, in pixels
hspace="*value*" vspace="*value*"	The horizontal and vertical space around the frame, in pixels. **Deprecated**
marginheight="*value*" marginwidth="*value*	The size of the internal margins of the frame, in pixels
name="*text*"	The name of the frame
scrolling="*type*"	Specifies whether the frame can be scrolled ("yes") or not ("no")
src="*url*"	The URL of the document displayed in the inline frame
style="*styles*"	Styles applied to the inline frame

Debbie is interested in working with inline frames, and she would like you to create a staff page that employs this feature.

To create an inline frame:

1. Using your text editor, open **iftxt.htm** from the tutorial.05/tutorial folder. Enter *your name* and *the date* in the comment section of the file. Save the document as **iframe.htm**.

2. Immediately following the horizontal line, insert the following HTML code. See Figure 5-35.

```
<p>
<iframe src="bios.htm" width="400" height="250"
style="float: right; margin: 0 0 0 5">
   Frames not supported.<br />
   Click to view detailed <a href="bios.htm">biographies</a>
of our staff.
</iframe>
</p>
```

Figure 5-35	Inserting an inline frame

```
<hr />
<p>
<iframe src="bios.htm" width="400" height="250" style="float: right; margin: 0 0 0 5">
   Frames not supported.<br />
   Click to view detailed <a href="bios.htm">biographies</a> of our staff.
</iframe>
</p>
<h1 style="color: brown; font-family: sans-serif">Staff</h1>
<p>The staff at the Yale Climbing School is here to help with all of your climbing needs.
All of our instructors are fully qualified with years of climbing and teaching experience.
Scroll through the biographies at the right for more information.</p>
```

3. Save your changes to **iframe.htm** and close the file.

4. Open **iframe.htm** in your Web browser. Figure 5-36 shows the resulting Web page.

   Trouble? If you're running Netscape version 4.7 or earlier, you will not see the floating frame displayed in Figure 5-36.

Figure 5-36	Viewing an inline frame

5. Use the scroll bars in the floating frame to view the entire list of staff biographies.

6. Close your Web browser.

You've completed your work for Debbie and the Yale Climbing School. Using frames, you've created an interesting presentation that is both attractive and easy to navigate. Debbie is pleased and will get back to you if she needs any additional work done.

Tips for Using Frames

- Create framed and frameless versions of your Web site to accommodate different browsers and to offer a choice to users who don't like frames.
- Do not turn off vertical and horizontal scrolling unless you are certain that the page content will fit within the specified frame size.
- Assign names to all frames, in order to make your code easier to read and interpret and to direct links to the correct target.
- Simplify your HTML code by using the base element when most of the links in your frame document point to the same target.
- NEVER display pages that lie outside of your Web site within your frames. Use the "_top" target to open external sites in the full browser window.

Session 5.2 Quick Check

Review

1. When you click a link inside a frame, in what frame does the target Web page appear by default?
2. What attribute would you use to assign the name "Address" to a frame?
3. What attribute would you add to a link to direct it to a frame named "News"?
4. What attribute would you use to point a link to the document "sales.htm" with the result that the sales.htm file is displayed in the entire browser window?
5. What tag would you use to direct all links in a document to the "News" target?
6. Describe what you would do to make your Web page readable by browsers that support frames and by those that do not.
7. What attribute would you use to set the frame border color of every frame on the page to red?
8. How would you set the frame border width to 5 pixels?

Tutorial Summary

Review

In this tutorial, you learned how to create and use frames. In the first session, you learned how to create a frameset and arrange the frames in rows or columns within a set. You also learned how to specify which document appears within each frame. The first session concluded with a discussion of some of the frame attributes used to control the frame's appearance. The second session explored how to direct a link's target to a specific frame. In addition, you learned some of the other attributes that can be used to format the frame's appearance. The session also showed how to support browsers that don't recognize frames. The tutorial concluded by demonstrating how to create inline frames.

Key Terms

floating frame	frameset	reserved target name
frame	inline frame	

Practice

Practice the skills you learned in the tutorial using the same case scenario.

Review Assignments

Data files needed for this Review Assignment: headtxt.htm, slisttxt.htm, sltxt.htm, stafftxt.htm, tlisttxt.htm, tltxt.htm, tourstxt.htm, yale2txt.htm, + 16 HTML files, + 24 JPEG files

Debbie has asked you to revise the layout for the YCS Web site. She would like links for all of the Web pages to display in separate frames so that users can always click a link for a specific page or collection of pages no matter where they are in the Web site. Figure 5-37 shows a preview of the frames you'll create for the Yale Climbing School Web site.

Figure 5-37

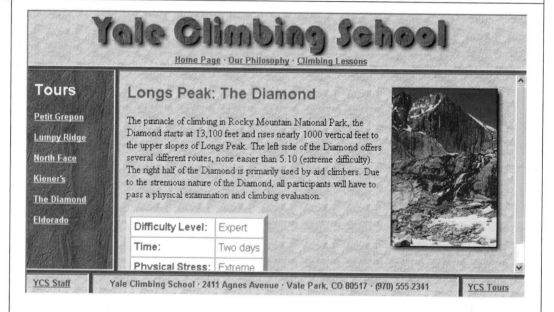

This is a large Web site containing 48 files; however you'll only have to create the following files in order to complete the site:

- tlist.htm—contains a list of links to the tour pages (data file: tlisttxt.htm)
- slist.htm—contains a list of links to staff bios (data file: slisttxt.htm)
- tours2.htm—a frame layout displaying YCS tours (data file: tourstxt.htm)

- staff2.htm—a frame layout displaying YCS staff bios (data file: stafftxt.htm)
- tourlink.htm—a Web page containing a link to tours2.htm (data file: tltxt.htm)
- staflink.htm—a Web page containing a link to staff2.htm (data file: sltxt.htm)
- head2.htm—a Web page containing the company logo and links to three pages (data file: headtxt.htm)
- yale2.htm—a frame layout displaying all of the YCS Web pages (data file: yale2txt.htm)

To create the YCS Web site:

1. Using your text editor, open the **tlisttxt.htm**, **slisttxt.htm**, **tourstxt.htm**, **stafftxt.htm**, **tltxt.htm**, **sltxt.htm**, **headtxt.htm**, and **yale2txt.htm** files from the tutorial.05/review folder. Enter *your name* and *the date* in each file. Save the files as **tlist.htm**, **slist.htm**, **tours2.htm**, **staff2.htm**, **tourlink.htm**, **staflink.htm**, **head2.htm**, and **yale2.htm**, respectively.

2. Go to the **tlist.htm** file in your text editor. This file contains a list of links to the tours pages. Define "Tours" as the default target for links in this file and close the file, saving your changes.

3. Go to the **slist.htm** file in your text editor. This file contains a list of links to the staff bios. Set "Bios" as the default target for links on this page. Save your changes and close the file.

4. Go to the **tours2.htm** file in your text editor. This file will display a frame layout showing the list of tour links and the individual tour pages. To complete this document, do the following:
   - Create a frameset consisting of two columns of frames. The first frame should be 140 pixels wide; the second frame should occupy the remaining space.
   - Make the frame borders 5 pixels wide and brown in color.
   - The source for the first frame should be the **tlist.htm** file.
   - The source for the second frame should be the **grepon.htm** file. Assign the frame the name "Tours".
   - Do not allow users to resize either frame in the frameset.

5. Save your changes and close the file.

6. Open the **staff2.htm** in your text editor. This file will display a frame layout showing the list of staff links and the individual staff bio pages. To complete the frame layout, do the following:
   - Create a frameset containing two columns. Make the first frame 140 pixels wide; the second frame should occupy the remaining space.
   - Make the frame borders 5 pixels wide and brown in color.

- The first frame should have a margin height of 1 pixel and a margin width of 10 pixels. The source for this frame should be the **slist.htm** file.

- Display the contents of the **bester.htm** file in the second frame. Name the frame "Bios". You do not have to specify a margin height or width.

- Do not allow users to resize either frame.

7. Save your changes and close the file.

8. Open **tourlink.htm** in your text editor. This page contains a link to the frameset in the tours2.htm file. To complete this page, set the target of the link in this file to the name "docs". Save your changes and close the file.

9. Open **staflink.htm** in your text editor. This page contains a link to the frameset in the staff2.htm file. To complete this page, set the target of the link in this file to the name "docs". Close the file, saving your changes.

10. Open **head2.htm** in your text editor. This file contains links for the home, philosophy, and lessons pages. Once again, point the target of these links to the name "docs". Close the file, saving your changes.

11. Open **yale2.htm** in your text editor. This document contains the frameset for the entire Web site. To complete the frameset, do the following:

- Create a frameset containing three rows of frames. The first frame should be 85 pixels high, the third frame should be 30 pixels high, and the middle frame should occupy the remaining space. The first frame will contain the Web site header, the second frame will contain informational documents, and the third frame will contain the Web site footer. Note that the second frame will either display the Web pages stored in the home.htm, philosph.htm, and lessons.htm files, or it will display the frame layouts stored in the staff2.htm and tours2.htm files.

- Make the frame borders brown, 5 pixels in width. Do not allow users to resize the frames.

- Display **head2.htm** in the first frame. Set the margin height to 0 pixels and remove the scrollbars.

- Display the contents of the **home.htm** file in the second frame and name the frame "docs". Set the second frame's margin height to 0 pixels and the margin width to 10 pixels.

- Insert a frameset containing three columns into the third frame. The first and third columns of the nested frameset should be 100 pixels wide; the second column should occupy the remaining space. Use **staflink.htm** as the source for the first frame, **footer.htm** as the source for the second frame, and **tourlink.htm** as the source for the third frame. Set the margin width and height of each frame to 5 pixels. Make the frame borders brown and 5 pixels wide. Do not allow users to resize the frames and remove the scrollbars from these three frames.

12. For browsers that don't support frames, insert the contents of **noframes.htm** into **yale2.htm** within a noframes element just before the closing </frameset> tag.

13. Save your changes and close the file.

14. Open **yale2.htm** in your Web browser, and verify that you can view all of the Web pages in the YCS Web site in the appropriate frames.

15. Submit the completed Web site to your instructor.

Case Problem 1

Data files needed for this Case Problem: **dcclogo.jpg, dccmw.htm, dccne.htm, dccs.htm, dcctxt.htm, dccw.htm, headtxt.htm, map.jpg, maptxt.htm, mwchart.jpg, nechart.jpg, report.htm, schart.jpg, wchart.jpg**

Doc-Centric Copiers Located in Salt Lake City, Doc-Centric is one of the nation's leading manufacturers of personal and business copiers. The annual shareholders' convention in Chicago is approaching, and the general manager, David Edgars, wants you to create an online report for the convention participants. The report will be posted on the company Web site before the convention so that shareholders can review the company's financial data. Most of the Web pages have been created for you. Your job is to display that information using frames. A preview of the layout you'll create is shown in Figure 5-38.

Figure 5-38

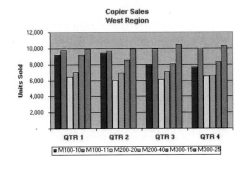

To create the Doc-Centric Copiers sales presentation:

1. Use your text editor to open the **dcctxt.htm**, **headtxt.htm**, and **maptxt.htm** files from the tutorial.05/case1 folder. Enter *your name* and *the date* in the comment section of each file. Save the files as **dcc.htm**, **head.htm**, and **map.htm**, respectively.

2. Go to the **dcc.htm** file in your text editor. This documents the frameset for the entire Web site. To complete this document, do the following:

   - Create a frameset containing two columns with a blue frame border, 10 pixels in width. The first frame should be 240 pixels wide. The second frame should occupy the remaining space in the design window.

   - Create two rows of nested frames in the first frame. The first row should be 75 pixels high; the second row should fill up the remaining space. Display the contents of the **head.htm** file in the first row. Display the contents of the **map.htm** file in the second row. Name the first frame "logo", the second frame "usmap".

   - In the second frame, display the contents of the **report.htm** file. Name the frame "reports".

3. Save your changes to the file.

4. Go to the **map.htm** file in your text editor. This page contains an image map of the sales regions. Direct each link in the map.htm file to the reports target, so that the pages will appear in the reports frame. Save your changes and close the file.

5. Go to the **head.htm** file in your text editor. This page contains the company logo, formatted as a link to the title page. Direct this link to the reports target. Close the file, saving your changes.

6. Use your Web browser to view dcc.htm. Think about what improvements could be made to the page, and what should be removed.

7. Return to **dcc.htm** in your text editor and reduce the margin for the logo frame to 1 pixel. Reduce the margin width for the usmap frame to 1 pixel, and change that frame's margin height to 30 pixels.

8. Remove scroll bars from both the logo and usmap frames.

9. View the Web page again to verify that the problems you identified in Step 6 have been resolved.

10. Return to **dcc.htm** in your text editor, and lock the size of the frames to prevent users from changing the frame sizes.

11. Using your Web browser, reload **dcc.htm** and test the image map in the usmap frame. Verify that each of the four sales reports is correctly displayed in the reports frame. Click the company logo in the upper-left frame and verify that it redisplays the opening page in the reports frame.

12. Submit the completed Web site to your instructor.

Explore

Broaden your knowledge of inline frames by creating an inline frame that shows different photos of a real estate property.

Case Problem 2

Data files needed for this Case Problem: back.jpg, brlogo.jpg, img01.jpg–img13.jpg, l20481.jpg, listtxt.htm, pback.jpg

Browyer Realty Linda Browyer is the owner of Browyer Realty, a real estate company in Minnesota. She's asked you to help her design a Web page for her current listings. Linda envisions a Web page that displays basic information about a listing, including the owner's description. She would like to have several photos of the listing on the page, but rather than cluttering up the layout with several images, she would like users to be able to view different images by clicking a link on the page. Linda wants the images to open within the listing page, not in a separate Web page. Figure 5-39 shows a preview of the page you'll create for Linda.

Figure 5-39

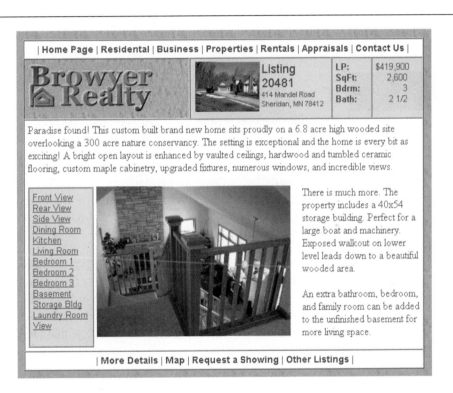

To create the Browyer Realty listing:

1. Using your text editor, open **listtxt.htm** from the tutorial.05/case2 folder. Enter *your name* and *the date* in the comment section and save the file as **listing.htm**.

Explore

2. Locate the inline image for the img01.jpg file (it's floated off the left side of the second paragraph). Use this image as the alternate content for an inline frame, enclosing the image within an inline frame with the following attributes:

   • The source of the frame is the **img01.jpg** file.
   • The name of the frame is "images".

- The frame is 310 pixels wide and 240 pixels high.
- The width of the frame border is 0.
- The frame's internal margin width and height are 0 pixels.
- The frame is floated on the left.
- The margin size around the frame is 5 pixels to the left and right and 0 pixels to the top and bottom.

3. Insert a comment above the floating frame indicating its purpose in the Web page.

4. Change each of the 13 entries in the list of photos to a link. Direct the first entry to **img01.jpg**, the second entry to **img02.jpg**, and so forth.

5. Direct the 13 links you created in the previous step to the "images" floating frame.

6. Save your changes to the file.

7. Using your Web browser, open listing.htm. Verify that each link displays a different photo in the Web page and that the rest of the page remains unchanged.

8. Submit the completed Web site to your instructor.

Explore

Expand your skill with inline frames by using nested frames to create an interactive slide show.

Case Problem 3

Data files needed for this Case Problem: messtxt.htm, mxxtxt.htm, + 9 HTML files, + 15 JPEG files

SkyWeb Astronomy   Dr. Andrew Weiss of Central Ohio University maintains an astronomy page called SkyWeb for his students. On his Web site he discusses many aspects of astronomy and observing. One of the pages he wants your help with involves the Messier catalog, which is a list of deep sky objects of particular interest to astronomers and amateur observers.

Dr. Weiss wants his page to contain a slide show of various Messier objects, displaying both a photo of the object and a text box describing the object's history and features. He wants his users to be able to click a forward or backward button to move through the slide show, and wants the rest of the Web page to remain unchanged as users view the presentation. Figure 5-40 shows a preview of the page that Dr. Weiss wants to create.

Figure 5-40

SkyWeb

The Messier Objects

 Messier objects are stellar objects, classified by astronomer **Charles Messier** in the 18th century, ranging from distant galaxies to star clusters to stellar nebula. The catalog was a major milestone in the history of astronomy, as it was the first comprehensive list of deep sky objects. Ironically, Charles Messier wasn't all that interested in the objects in his list. He made the catalog in order to *avoid* mistaking those objects for comets, which were his true passion.

Messier objects are identified by **Messier Numbers**. The first object in Messier's catalog, the Crab Nebula, is labelled **M1**. The last object, **M110** is a satellite galaxy located in the constellation Andromeda. There is no systematic ordering in the Messier Catalog. Messier entered objects into the list as he found them. Sometimes he made mistakes and once he entered the same stellar object twice. The catalog has undergone some slight revisions since Messier's time, correcting the mistakes in the original.

One of the great pursuits for amateur astronomers is to do a **Messier Marathon**, trying to view all of the objects in Messier's catalog in one night. Unfortunately, if you want to see all of them, you have to start looking right after sunset and continue until just before sunrise — hence the term, "marathon." March is the only month in the year in which an astronomer can run the complete marathon.

Use the buttons to view some of the more popular objects in Messier's catalog.

M16: The Eagle Nebula

M16, better known as the Eagle Nebula, is located in the distant constellation, Serpens. The source of light for M16 is the high-energy radiation of the massive young stars being formed in its core. By studying M16, astronomers hope to learn more about the early years

| Home Page | The Night Sky | The Moon | The Planets | The Messier Objects | Stars |

To create a presentation like this, you can nest one inline frame inside of another. Dr. Weiss has created the text you need for the Web site. Your job is to create the frames needed to complete the Web page.

To create the SkyWeb Web page:

1. Using your text editor, open **mxxtxt.htm** from the tutorial.05/case3 folder. This file will act as a model for pages that display descriptions and images of the Messier objects. You'll start by using this file to create the page for Messier object, M01. Enter *your name* and *the date* in the comment section of this file and save the file as **m01.htm**.

2. Replace the text of the page title and the first table cell with the text, "M1: The Crab Nebula".

3. Replace the inline image mxx.jpg with the image **m01.jpg**.

Explore

4. Replace the inline image mxxdesc.jpg with an inline frame of the same dimensions and attributes, displaying the contents of the file **m01desc.htm**. Copy the page content of the **m01desc.htm** file (excluding the <body> tags) and paste that content within the inline frame to provide alternate text for browsers that don't support inline frames.

5. Target the link for the Previous button located at the bottom of the page to the file **m57.htm**. Note that you'll create this file later.

6. Direct the link for the Next button to the file **m13.htm**—another file you'll create shortly.

7. Save your changes to **m01.htm**.

8. With your work on m01.htm as a guide, use your text editor with the **mxxtxt.htm** file to create similar Web pages for the other eight Messier objects. Save the files as **m13.htm**, **m16.htm**, **m20.htm**, **m27.htm**, **m31.htm**, **m42.htm**, **m51.htm**, and **m57.htm**. Be sure to enter *your name* and *the date* in the comment section of each file. The titles for these pages are:

   - M13: Hercules Globular Cluster
   - M16: The Eagle Nebula
   - M20: The Trifid Nebula
   - M27: The Dumbbell Nebula
   - M31: The Andromeda Galaxy
   - M42: The Orion Nebula
   - M51: The Whirlpool Galaxy
   - M57: The Ring Nebula

   The inline frame for each page should point to the file containing descriptive text on the Messier object. For example, the floating frame for the m13.htm file should display the m13desc.htm file, and so forth.

   The Previous and Next buttons in each page should point to the previous and next Messier object files. For example, the buttons in m27.htm should point to m20.htm and m31.htm. The Next button for m57.htm should point to m01.htm. Save your changes to all the files, and then close them.

9. Using your text editor, open **messtxt.htm** and save it as **messier.htm**.

Explore

10. At the beginning of the fourth paragraph, insert an inline frame with the following properties:

   - Make the source of the floating frame **m01.htm**.
   - Make the frame 460 pixels wide by 240 pixels high.
   - Make the internal margin width and height 0 pixels.
   - There should be no border around the frame.
   - Float the frame on the right margin of the page.
   - Make a 5-pixel margin around the frame.
   - For browsers that don't support inline frames, display a text message that contains a link to the **m01.htm** file.

11. Save your changes to **messier.htm** and close the file.

12. Open **messier.htm** in your Web browser. Click the Previous and Next buttons and verify that you can navigate through the list of Messier objects without disturbing the rest of the Web page. Verify that you can use the scroll bars around the description box to view descriptions of each object.

13. Submit the completed Web site to your instructor.

Create

Test your knowledge of frames by creating a frameset for a computer supply store.

Case Problem 4

Data files needed for this Case Problem: drive15l.htm, drive15l.jpg, drive20m.htm, drive20m.jpg, drive33m.htm, drive33m.jpg, drive60s.htm, drive60s.jpg, tape800.htm, tape800.jpg, tape3200.htm, tape3200.jpg, tape9600.htm, tape9600.jpg, wlogo.gif, wlogo.htm

Warner Peripherals, Inc. Warner Peripherals, a company located in Tucson, Arizona, makes high-quality peripherals for computers. The company is an industry leader and has been delivering innovative technical solutions to consumers for more than 20 years. Part of its line of legacy products directed toward older computer systems are the SureSave line of tape drives and the SureRite line of disk drives. You've been asked to consolidate several Web pages describing these products into a single Web presentation using frames. The files shown in Figure 5-41 are available for your use. You are free to supplement this material with any other resources available to you.

Figure 5-41

File	Contents
drive15l.htm	Description of the 15L SureRite hard drive
drive20m.htm	Description of the 20M SureRite hard drive
drive33m.htm	Description of the 33M SureRite hard drive
drive60s.htm	Description of the 60S SureRite hard drive
tape800.htm	Description of the 800 SureSave tape backup drive
tape3200.htm	Description of the 3200 SureSave tape backup drive
tape9600.htm	Description of the 9600 SureSave tape backup drive
wlogo.htm	Warner Peripherals logo

To create the Warner Peripherals Web site:

1. Create a table of contents page that includes links to the files listed in Figure 5-41. The design of this Web page is up to you. Save this page as **wtoc.htm** in the tutorial.05/case4 folder.

2. In the same folder, create a file named **warner.htm** that consolidates the logo page, table of contents page, and product description pages into a single page, using frames. Include comment tags in the file describing each element of the page.

3. Test your Web page and verify that each link works properly and appears in the correct frame.

4. Submit your completed Web site to your instructor.

Review

Quick Check Answers

Session 5.1

1. A frame is a section of a browser window capable of displaying the contents of an entire Web page. Frames do not require the same information (such as a list of links) to be repeated on multiple pages of a Web site. They also allow a Web designer to update content in one place in order to affect an entire Web site.

2. Because there is no page body in a frame document. The frame document displays the content of other pages.

3. `<frameset rows="200,50%,*"> … </frameset>`

4. `<frame src="home.htm" />`

5. `<frame src="home.htm" scrolling="no" />`

6. `<frame src="home.htm" marginheight="3" />`

7. 3 pixels

8. `<frame src="home.htm" noresize="noresize" />`

Session 5.2

1. The frame containing the link

2. `name="Address"`

3. `target="News"`

4. `target="_top"`

5. Place the tag `<base target="News" />` in the head element of the document.

6. Create a section starting with the `<noframes>` tag. After the `<noframes>` tag enter a `<body>` tag to identify the text and images you want frame-blind browsers to display. Complete this section with a `</body>` tag followed by a `</noframes>` tag.

7. `<frameset bordercolor="red">`

8. `<frameset border="5">`

New Perspectives on

HTML and XHTML

Read This Before You Begin: Tutorials 6–10

To the Student

Data Files

To complete the Level III HTML Tutorials (Tutorials 6–10), you need the starting student Data Files. Your instructor will either provide you with these Data Files or ask you to obtain them yourself.

The Level III HTML tutorials require the folders shown to complete the Tutorials, Review Assignments, and Case Problems. You will need to copy these folders from a file server, a standalone computer, or the Web to the drive and folder where you will be storing your Data Files.

Your instructor will tell you which computer, drive letter, and folder(s) contain the files you need. You can also download the files by going to http://www.course.com; see the inside back or front cover for more information

on downloading the files, or ask your instructor or technical support person for assistance.

▼ HTML

    Tutorial.06
    Tutorial.07
    Tutorial.08
    Tutorial.09
    Tutorial.10

▼ Student Online Companion

The Student Online Companion can be found at http://www.course.com/np/html. It contains additional information to supplement what you are learning in the text, as well as links to downloads, shareware, and other tools.

To the Instructor

The Data Files are available on the Instructor Resources CD for this title. Follow the instructions in the Help file on the CD to install the programs to your network or standalone computer. See the "To the Student" section above for information on how to set up the Data Files that accompany this text.

You are granted a license to copy the Data Files to any computer or computer network used by students who have purchased this book.

System Requirements

If you are going to work through this book using your own computer, you need:

• **System Requirements** An Internet connection, a text editor and a Web browser that supports HTML 4.0 and XHTML 1.1 (for example, version 6.0 or higher of either Netscape or Internet Explorer). You may wish to

run an older browser version to highlight compatibility issues, but the code in this book is not designed to support those browsers.

• **Data Files** You will not be able to complete the tutorials or exercises in this book using your own computer until you have the necessary starting Data Files.

Objectives

Session 6.1
- Describe how Web forms can interact with a server-based program
- Insert a form into a Web page
- Create and format an input box for simple text data
- Add a form label and link it to a control element

Session 6.2
- Set up a selection list for a predefined list of data values
- Create option buttons for a list of possible field values
- Add checkboxes for fields that have two possible values
- Organize fields into field sets
- Insert a text area box for multiple lines of text data

Session 6.3
- Generate form buttons to submit or reset a form
- Describe how data is sent from a Web form to a server
- Understand how to create image fields, hidden fields, and file buttons
- Apply tab indices and access keys to control elements

Creating Web Page Forms

Designing a Product Registration Form

Case

Creating a Registration Form for LanGear

LanGear, located in Farley, South Dakota, is a leading manufacturer of network hardware and software. The company has already established a presence on the World Wide Web with a Web site describing the company's products and its corporate philosophy. Now LanGear would like to build on that presence by creating interactive pages that allow customers to give feedback online.

Susan Gorski, customer support director for LanGear, would like the site to include a Web page for customer registration. She's aware that fewer than 10% of the registration cards included with the product packaging are returned to the company, and she feels that the company could improve this low response rate with a Web registration system. Susan has asked you to help her create this type of registration Web page. To do so, you'll need to learn how to create HTML forms and how to use them to record information for the company.

Student Data Files

▼**Tutorial.06**

▽ **Tutorial folder**

    regtxt.htm

    + 1 graphic file

▽ **Review folder**

    suptxt.htm

    + 3 graphic files

▽ **Case 1 folder**

    subtxt.htm

    + 2 graphic files

▽ **Case 2 folder**

    ordertxt.htm

    + 2 graphic files

▽ **Case 3 folder**

    dltxt.htm

    + 1 graphic file

▽ **Case 4 folder**

    none

Session 6.1

Introducing Web Forms

Susan has been planning the appearance of a product registration form that will allow the company to record customer information. Susan decides to model the form on the registration cards already packaged with LanGear's products. Because a long form would discourage customers from completing it, Susan wants the form to be brief and focused on the information the company is most interested in. She has provided you with a sketch of her idea, shown in Figure 6-1.

Figure 6-1	The proposed registration form

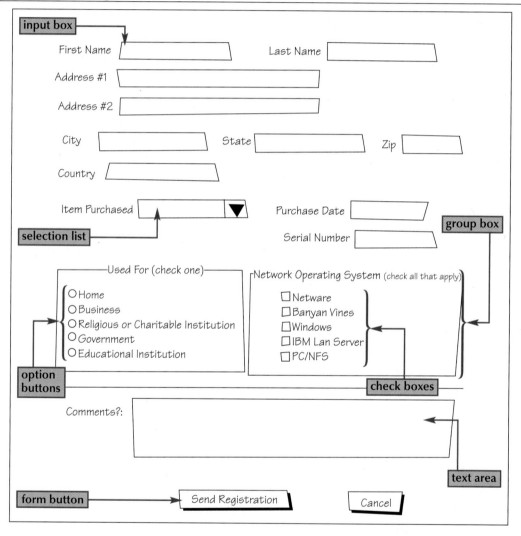

Parts of a Web Form

This form collects contact information for each customer, including information on which product the customer purchased and when, what network operating system the customer uses, and how the customer uses the product. There is also a place for customers to enter comments. The different parts of the form, which are called **control elements**, include the following:

- **input boxes** for text and numerical entries
- **selection lists** for long lists of options, usually appearing in a **drop-down list box**
- **option buttons**, also called **radio buttons**, for selecting a single option from a predefined list
- **check boxes** for specifying an item as either present or absent
- **group boxes** for organizing form elements
- **text areas** for extended entries that can include several lines of text
- **form buttons** that users can click to start processing the form

Each control element in which the user can enter information is called a **field**. Information entered into a field is called the **field value**, or simply the **value**. In some fields, users are free to enter anything they choose. Other fields, such as selection lists, limit the user to a predefined list of options.

Forms and Server-Based Programs

Before you start work on Susan's Web form, you should understand how forms are interpreted and processed on the Web. Although HTML supports tags that allow you to create forms like the one shown in Figure 6-1, the language does not include tools to process that information. One way of processing this information is through a program running on the Web server. As shown in Figure 6-2, a Web form can send information to a program running on the Web server for processing.

The interaction between a Web form and a server ◄ **Figure 6-2**

The pairing of server-based programs and Web forms represented a dramatic shift in how the Web was perceived and used. By giving users access to programs that react to user input, the Web became a more dynamic environment where companies and users could interact. Server-based programs have made many things possible, including:

- online databases containing customer information
- online catalogues for ordering and purchasing merchandise
- dynamic Web sites with content that is constantly modified and updated
- message boards for hosting online discussion forums

Because these programs run on Web servers, rather than locally, you might not have permission to create or edit them. In some cases, a programmer maintains the scripts offered by a Web server, providing Web designers with script specifications—such as what input the scripts expect and what output they generate. Internet service providers (ISPs) and universities often provide server-based programs that their customers and students can use on their Web sites, but that they cannot directly access or modify.

There are several reasons to restrict direct access to these programs. The primary reason is that when you run a server-based program, you are interacting directly with the server environment. Mindful of the security risks that computer hackers present and the drain on system resources caused by large numbers of programs running simultaneously, system administrators are understandably careful to maintain strict control over their servers and systems.

Server-based programs are written in a variety of languages. The earliest and most common of these are **Common Gateway Interface (CGI) scripts**, written in a language called **perl**. Other popular languages widely used today include

- AppleScript
- ASP
- ColdFusion
- C/C++
- PHP
- TCL
- the UNIX shell
- Visual Basic

Which language your server programs are written in depends on your Web server. Check with your ISP or system administrator to find out what programs are available and what rights and privileges you have in working with them.

The programmers at LanGear have created a script to receive the data from the registration form and e-mail it to one of Susan's assistants. The information can then be extracted from the e-mail message and entered into the company's registration database. You will not have access to the e-mail program on the Web server, so you'll just work with the Web document portion of this process. After Susan uploads the page to the company's Web server, others will test the page to verify that the information is being processed correctly.

Creating the Form Element

Now that you're familiar with the background of server-based programs and Web forms, you can begin to work on the registration form that Susan wants you to create. Forms are created using the form element, which has the structure

```
<form attributes>
        elements
</form>
```

where *attributes* are the attributes that control how the form is processed, and *elements* are elements placed within the form. Forms typically will contain many of the control elements that were discussed earlier, but can also contain page elements such as tables, paragraphs, inline images, and headings.

Form attributes usually tell the browser the location of the server-based program to be applied to the form's data, how that data is to be transferred to the script, and so forth. In addition to not needing these attributes when first designing the form, it's also useful to omit them at first. This prevents you from accidentally running the program on an unfinished form, causing the program to process incomplete information. After you've finalized the form's appearance, you can add the final features required by the server program.

You should always specify an id or name for the form. This is useful in situations where a page contains multiple forms and you need to differentiate one form from another, but it is also often required for the programs that retrieve values from the form. Two attributes are available to identify the form: the id attribute and the name attribute. The syntax of these attributes are

```
<form name="name" id="id"> . . . </form>
```

where *name* is the name of the form, and *id* is the id of the form. While these two attributes may appear to do much the same thing, each has its own history and role. The name attribute represents the older standard for form identification, and thus is often required for older browsers and older server programs. The id attribute, on the other hand, represents the current standard for HTML and XHTML. For maximum compatibility, the form element should include both attributes.

Susan has already started work on the product registration Web page. She has inserted the company logo and created a table that you'll use in this tutorial to align the form's different control elements. Your first task will be to add a form element named "reg" to the page.

To create the form element:

1. Use your text editor to open **regtxt.htm** from the tutorial.06/tutorial folder. Enter *your name* and *the date* in the comment section and save the file as **register. htm**.

2. Directly after the opening <body> tag, insert the following line:

   ```
   <form name="reg" id="reg">
   ```

3. Scroll to the bottom of the file and before the closing </body> tag, insert the closing tag:

   ```
   </form>
   ```

4. Figure 6-3 shows the revised HTML code.

Figure 6-3 ▶ **Making the Web form**

```
<body style="color: rgb(133,0,0); margin: 0">
<form name="reg" id="reg">
<table border="0" cellspacing="0" cellpadding="5" width="620"
       style="background-color: yellow">
<!-- Page Heading -->




<!-- Address -->
<tr style="background-color: white">
   <td colspan="2" align="center" valign="bottom">
      <address style="font-family: sans-serif; font-size: 0.6em; font-style: normal">
      LanGear Inc. &#183; 414 Wittlow Way &#183; Farley, SD 85312 &#183; 1 (800) 555-2377
      </address>
   </td>
</tr>
</table>

</form>
</body>
```

In order to make it easier to work with the layout, Susan has divided the form into five sections: contact information, product information, usage information, comments, and buttons. As shown in Figure 6-4, these sections are separated from each other with horizontal lines. Presenting a form in this fashion can make it easier for users to identify the sections of the form and enter data.

Figure 6-4 ▶ **Layout of the registration form**

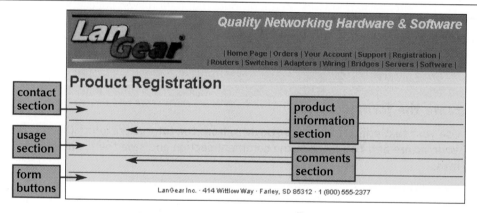

The first part of the form will contain input boxes in which LanGear customers will enter their contract information.

Creating Input Boxes

Most of the control elements in which users are asked to type input or choose a value are marked as input elements. The general syntax of this element is

```
<input type="type" name="name" id="id" />
```

where *type* specifies the type of input field, and the name and id attributes provide the field's name and id. HTML supports 10 different input types, which are described in Figure 6-5.

Type	Description	
type="button"	Display a button that can be clicked to perform an action from a script	button
type="checkbox"	Display a check box	☑
type="file"	Display a browse button to locate and select a file	Browse...
type="hidden"	Create a hidden field, not viewable on the form	
type="image"	Display an inline image that can be clicked to perform an action from a script	👤
type="password"	Display an input box that hides text entered by the user	•••••••••
type="radio"	Display an option button	◉
type="reset"	Display a button that resets the form when clicked	reset
type="submit"	Display a button that submits the form when clicked	submit
type="text"	Display an input box that displays text entered by the user	LanGear

To create an input box, set the value of the type attribute to "text":

```
<input type="text" />
```

If you omit the type attribute, the browser creates an input box by default.

Older browsers support the name attribute, while the id attribute represents the current standard. As with the form element, it's best to include both and set them to the same value. When form data is sent to the server, the server program receives the data in **name/value pairs**, in which the name or id of each field is paired with whatever value the user entered in the field. The script then processes the data according to each name/value pair.

Note that the value you enter for an element's name attribute does not necessarily need to match the label displayed next to the element in the Web document. In Figure 6-6, for example, the value for the name attribute of the first address line is "address1," while the label displayed next to the input box is "Address #1". The latter is what users see in their Web browsers, while the former is sent to the server. The two can be the same, but they don't have to be.

Figure 6-6 ▶ **Input types**

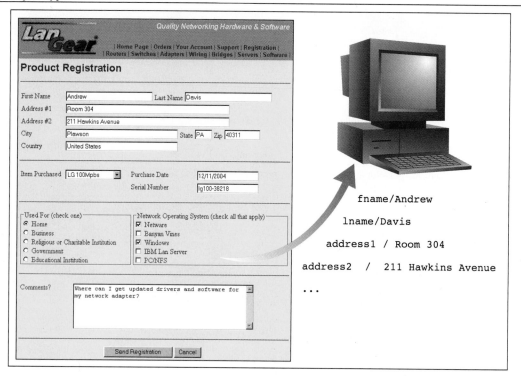

Some server-based programs require a particular field or group of fields. For example, a CGI script whose purpose is to e-mail form values to another user probably requires the e-mail address of the recipient labeled with a specific name, such as "email". Before using a server-based program, you should check the documentation for any requirements and then design your form accordingly.

Finally, be aware that case is important in field names. A program might not interpret a field named "email" in the same way as a field named "EMAIL."

The first part of Susan's registration form relates to customer contact information. Each field in this section is an input box. Because input boxes are blank and do not contain any accompanying text, you need to insert a text description, such as "First Name", adjacent to each box so that users know what to enter. You'll arrange these fields using table cells so that each field name lines up with its input box, making the form easier to read.

To insert the input boxes on the form:

▶ 1. Type the following code within the <td> tags immediately following the "Contact Information" comment tag, as shown in Figure 6-7.

```
<table>
<tr>
   <td width="100">First Name</td>
   <td><input type="text" name="fname" id="fname" />
       Last Name
       <input type="text" name="lname" id="lname" />
   </td>
</tr>
<tr>
   <td>Address #1</td>
```

```
            <td><input type="text" name="address1" id="address1" /></td>
    </tr>
    <tr>
        <td>Address #2</td>
        <td><input type="text" name="address2" id="address2" /></td>
    </tr>
    <tr>
        <td>City</td>
        <td><input type="text" name="city" id="city" />
            State
            <input type="text" name="state" id="state" />
            ZIP
            <input type="text" name="zip" id="zip" />
        </td>
    </tr>
    <tr>
        <td>Country</td>
        <td><input type="text" name="country" id="country" /></td>
    </tr>
    </table>
```

Inserting input boxes   **Figure 6-7**

```
<!-- Contact Information -->
<tr>
    <td valign="top" colspan="2">

    <table>
    <tr>
        <td width="100">First Name</td>
        <td><input type="text" name="fname" id="fname" />
            Last Name
            <input type="text" name="lname" id="lname" />
        </td>
    </tr>
    <tr>
        <td>Address #1</td>
        <td><input type="text" name="address1" id="address1" /></td>
    </tr>
    <tr>
        <td>Address #2</td>
        <td><input type="text" name="address2" id="address2" /></td>
    </tr>
    <tr>
        <td>City</td>
        <td><input type="text" name="city" id="city" />
            State
            <input type="text" name="state" id="state" />
            ZIP
            <input type="text" name="zip" id="zip" />
        </td>
    </tr>
    <tr>
        <td>Country</td>
        <td><input type="text" name="country" id="country" /></td>
    </tr>
    </table>

    </td>
</tr>
```

2. Save your changes to the file.

3. Using your Web browser, open **register.htm** (see Figure 6-8). Note that by using a table, you've created a uniform appearance for the registration form by vertically aligning the leftmost input boxes in each row.

Figure 6-8   Input boxes in the registration form

Product Registration

First Name [   ] Last Name [   ]
Address #1 [   ]
Address #2 [   ]
City [   ] State [   ] ZIP [   ]
Country [   ]

LanGear Inc. · 414 Wittlow Way · Farley, SD 85312 · 1 (800) 555-2377

Trouble? Depending on your Web browser and browser version, your Web page may look different from the one shown in Figure 6-8.

Setting the Size of an Input Box

By default, an input box displays 20 characters of text (although the actual amount of text entered into the box may be longer). This may be an appropriate length for first and last name fields, but it's too long for fields such as zip code or state abbreviation. Data entry is easier if input boxes are sized appropriately for their content. To change the width of an input box, use the size attribute:

```
<input size="value" />
```

where `value` is the size of the input box in characters.

After reviewing the form, Susan decides that the width of both the fname field and the lname field should be increased to 30 characters in order to allow the form to display longer names. Similarly, the widths of the address1 and address2 input boxes should be increased to 60 characters each to allow for street numbers and street names. The width of the state input box can be reduced to a size of three characters, and the width of the zip code input box can be reduced to 10 characters. Finally, the city and country input boxes can be set to a width of 40 characters each.

To specify the size of the input boxes:

1. Return to **register.htm** in your text editor.

2. Insert the attribute **size="30"** in the fname and lname fields.

3. Insert the attribute **size="60"** in the address1 and address2 <input> tags.

4. Add the attribute **size="3"** to the state <input> tag.

5. Add the attribute **size="10"** to the zip <input> tag.

6. Add the attribute **size="40"** to the city and country <input> tags.

Figure 6-9 shows the revised code.

Setting the width of input boxes ◄ **Figure 6-9**

```
<table>
<tr>
    <td width="100">First Name</td>
    <td><input type="text" name="fname" id="fname" size="30" />
        Last Name
        <input type="text" name="lname" id="lname" size="30" />
    </td>
</tr>
<tr>
    <td>Address #1</td>
    <td><input type="text" name="address1" id="address1" size="60" /></td>
</tr>
<tr>
    <td>Address #2</td>
    <td><input type="text" name="address2" id="address2" size="60" /></td>
</tr>
<tr>
    <td>City</td>
    <td><input type="text" name="city" id="city" size="40" />
        State
        <input type="text" name="state" id="state" size="3" />
        ZIP
        <input type="text" name="zip" id="zip" size="10" />
    </td>
</tr>
<tr>
    <td>Country</td>
    <td><input type="text" name="country" id="country" size="40" /></td>
</tr>
</table>
```

7. Save your changes to the file, and then reload it in your browser. Figure 6-10 shows the form's revised appearance. Note that Netscape users may have to close and open register.htm for the changes to the Web form to take effect.

Viewing resized input boxes ◄ **Figure 6-10**

Setting the Maximum Length of an Input Box

Setting the width of an input box does not limit the number of characters the box can hold. If a user tries to enter text longer than a box's width, the text scrolls to the left. While a user would not be able to see the entire text in such a case, all of it would still be sent to the server for processing.

There are times when you want to limit the number of characters a user can enter in order to reduce the chance of erroneous data entry. For example, if you have a Social Security Number field, you know that only nine characters are required and that any attempt to enter more than nine characters would be a mistake. The syntax for setting the maximum length for field input is

```
<input maxlength="value" />
```

where value is the maximum number of characters that can be stored in the field.

For the registration form, Susan wants to limit the width of the zip code field to ten characters, allowing users to enter a nine-digit zip code that incorporates a hyphen.

To specify the maximum length for the zip field:

1. Return to **register.htm** in your text editor.

2. Type the attribute **maxlength="10"** within the <input> tag for the zip field. See Figure 6-11.

Figure 6-11 ▶ Setting an input box's maximum length

```
<td>City</td>
<td><input type="text" name="city" id="city" size="40" />
    State
    <input type="text" name="state" id="state" size="3" />
    ZIP
    <input type="text" name="zip" id="zip" size="10" maxlength="10" />
</td>
```

no more than 10 characters can be entered into the zip field

3. Save your changes to register.htm and then reload it in your Web browser.

4. Click the input box for the Zip code, and try to type more than 10 characters in the box. Note that the browser ignores entries beyond the tenth character.

Setting a Default Value for a Field

If most people enter the same value into a field, it may make sense to define a default value for that field. Default values can save time and increase accuracy for users of your Web site. To define a default value, use the syntax

```
<input value="value" />
```

where value is the default text or number that is displayed in the field. In the case of an input box, the default value appears in the input box when the form is initially opened.

Because domestic sales account for over 80% of LanGear's income, Susan wants the country field on the registration form to have a default value of "United States".

To set the default value for the country field:

1. Return to **register.htm** in your text editor.

2. Type **value="United States"** in the country field as shown in Figure 6-12.

Setting the default field value | Figure 6-12

```
<tr>
   <td>Country</td>
   <td><input type="text" name="country" id="country" size="40" value="United States" /></td>
</tr>
</table>
```

default value for
the country field

3. Save your changes to the file and then reload it in your Web browser. Verify that the text "United States" is displayed in the Country input box.

If customers from countries other than the United States use this Web form, they can remove the default value by selecting the text and pressing the Delete key.

Creating an input box | Reference Window

- To create an input box, use the following HTML code:
  ```
  <input name="name" id="id" value="value" size="value"
  maxlength="value" />
  ```
  where the *name* and *id* attributes identify the field, the *value* attribute assigns the field's default value, the *size* attribute defines the width of the input box in characters, and the *maxlength* attribute specifies the maximum number of characters that a user can enter into the field.

Creating a Password Field

In some instances users won't want information that they enter into an input box to be displayed. For example, one part of your form might prompt a user to enter a password that allows them to enter a Web site containing sensitive or private information. In this case, you want to prevent that password from being displayed on the computer monitor, as a security measure. You can accomplish this with a password field. A **password field** is an input box in which the characters typed by the user are displayed as bullets or asterisks. The syntax for creating a Password field is:

```
<input type="password" />
```

Using a password field should not be confused with having a secure connection between the Web client and the Web server. The password itself is not encrypted, so it is still possible for someone to intercept the information as it is being sent from your Web browser to the Web server. The password field only acts as a mask for the field entry as it is entered. Susan does not need you to specify any password fields for the registration form.

Working with Form Labels

So far, you've entered text alongside the input boxes to indicate the purpose of the input box to the user. For example, the LanGear form displays the text "Last Name" next to the text field where the user should type his or her last name. HTML also allows you to expressly link a label with an associated text element for scripting purposes. The syntax for creating a form label is:

```
<label for="id">label text</label>
```

where *id* is the value of the id attribute for a field on the form, and *label text* is the text of the label. Note that if the field's name and id attributes are different, the label's id value must match the id attribute of the field, rather than its name attribute.

Labels can simplify the data entry process by allowing a user to click on either the control element or the element's label to enter data. Labels have the added advantage that users can write scripts to modify their content for interactive forms. While the label element is part of the HTML 4.0 and XHTML specifications, it might not be supported by some older browsers. Those browsers will ignore the label element but still display the label text.

To add labels to the registration form:

1. Return to **register.htm** in your text editor.

2. Locate the field name "First Name" and enclose the text **"First Name"** within a set of opening and closing <label> tags.

3. Type the attribute **for="fname"** within the opening label tag (see Figure 6-13).

Figure 6-13 **Creating the label for the fname field**

label is attached to the fname field

```
<tr>
    <td width="100"><label for="fname">First Name</label></td>
    <td><input type="text" name="fname" id="fname" size="30" />
        Last Name
        <input type="text" name="lname" id="lname" size="30" />
    </td>
</tr>
```

4. Enclose the rest of the field names in <label> tags, with the **for** attribute in each <label> tag pointing to the value of the corresponding control element's id attribute. Figure 6-14 shows the revised code.

Figure 6-14 **Creating fields for the registration input boxes**

```
<table>
<tr>
    <td width="100"><label for="fname">First Name</label></td>
    <td><input type="text" name="fname" id="fname" size="30" />
        <label for="lname">Last Name</label>
        <input type="text" name="lname" id="lname" size="30" />
    </td>
</tr>
<tr>
    <td><label for="address1">Address #1</label></td>
    <td><input type="text" name="address1" id="address1" size="60" /></td>
</tr>
<tr>
    <td><label for="address2">Address #2</label></td>
    <td><input type="text" name="address2" id="address2" size="60" /></td>
</tr>
<tr>
    <td><label for="city">City</label></td>
    <td><input type="text" name="city" id="city" size="40" />
        <label for="state">State</label>
        <input type="text" name="state" id="state" size="3" />
        <label for="zip">ZIP</label>
        <input type="text" name="zip" id="zip" size="10" maxlength="10" />
    </td>
</tr>
<tr>
    <td><label for="country">Country</label></td>
    <td><input type="text" name="country" id="country" size="40" value="United States" /></td>
</tr>
</table>
```

5. Save your changes to **register.htm**. If you wish to take a break before continuing on to the next session, you may close your text editor now.

Before going on to other tasks, you'll test the registration form by entering some test values in it. You can press the Tab key to move between input boxes. To move to the previous input box, you can press the Tab key while holding down the Shift key. Typically, pressing the Enter key submits the form, but because you have not created a submit button for the form yet, pressing the Enter key will have no effect at this point.

To test your form:

▶ 1. Reload **register.htm** in your Web browser.

▶ 2. Enter sample text in the form fields, pressing **Tab** to move from one input box to the next.

▶ 3. Test the operation of the field labels by clicking them. Clicking a label in Internet Explorer places the cursor in the input box associated with the label.

▶ 4. After you have tested the form, close your Web browser if you don't plan on going to the next session immediately.

You've completed working on the first part of the registration form. You've learned how forms and servers work together to allow Web designers to collect information from users. You've also learned how to create simple input boxes using the <input> tag, and how to create field labels associated with those input boxes. In the next session, you'll learn other uses for the <input> tag by adding new fields to the form, including a selection list, option buttons, and check boxes.

Session 6.1 Quick Check

1. What is a CGI script?
2. How do you create a form element with the id name, "order_form"?
3. What HTML code would you use to create an input box with the name "Phone"?
4. What HTML attribute would you use to create a Phone input box that is 10 characters in length?
5. What HTML attribute would you use to limit entry to the Phone input box to no more than 10 characters?
6. What HTML code would you use to create an input box named "Subscribe" with a default value of "yes"?
7. How would you prevent the contents of an input box from being displayed on the user's computer screen?
8. What HTML code would you use to insert the text "Date of Birth" as a field label associated with the control element id "dob"?

Session 6.2

Creating a Selection List

The next section of the registration form focuses on collecting information about the product that a customer has purchased and how the customer intends to use it. The first field you'll create in this section records the product name. Figure 6-15 displays the products that Susan wants you to include in the registration form.

Figure 6-15 | **LanGear Products**

Item Group	Item
Routers	LanPass 115
	LanPass 125
	LanPass 250
Switches	FastSwitch 200
	FastSwitch 400
Adapters	LG 10Mpbs
	LG 10Mpbs/w
	LG 100Mpbs
	LG 100Mpbs/w

Because the products constitute a predefined list of values for the product name, Susan wants this information displayed with a selection list. A **selection list** is a list box from which a user selects a particular value or set of values. Selection lists are a good idea when there is a fixed set of possible responses; they help prevent spelling mistakes and erroneous entries.

Defining the Selection Options

You create a selection list using the <select> tag, and you specify each individual selection item with the <option> tag. The general syntax for the select and option elements is

```
<select name="name" id="id">
   <option>item1</option>
   <option>item2</option>
   .
   .
   .
</select>
```

where the *name* and *id* attributes identify the selection field, and each option element represents an individual item in the selection list. Users see the text *item1*, *item2*, and so forth as the options in the selection list.

To add the list of LanGear products to the form as a selection list:

1. If necessary, use your text editor to reopen **register.htm**.

2. Enter the following HTML code within the <td> tag located immediately following the "Product Information" comment tag:

```
<table>
<tr>
   <td width="100" valign="top" rowspan="2">
   <label for="item">Item Purchased</label>
   </td>
   <td valign="top" rowspan="2">
   <select name="item" id="item">
      <option>LanPass 115</option>
      <option>LanPass 125</option>
      <option>LanPass 250</option>
```

```
<option>FastSwitch 200</option>
<option>FastSwitch 400</option>
<option>LG 10Mpbs</option>
<option>LG 10Mpbs/w</option>
<option>LG 100Mpbs</option>
<option>LG 100Mpbs/w</option>
</select>
</td>
```

Figure 6-16 shows the revised HTML code.

Creating a selection list ◀ **Figure 6-16**

```
<!-- Product Information -->
<tr>
  <td valign="top" colspan="2">

  <table>
  <tr>
    <td width="100" valign="top" rowspan="2">
    <label for="item">Item Purchased</label>
    </td>
    <td valign="top" rowspan="2">
    <select name="item" id="item">
      <option>LanPass 115</option>
      <option>LanPass 125</option>
      <option>LanPass 250</option>
      <option>FastSwitch 200</option>
      <option>FastSwitch 400</option>
      <option>LG 10Mpbs</option>
      <option>LG 10Mpbs/w</option>
      <option>LG 100Mpbs</option>
      <option>LG 100Mpbs/w</option>
    </select>
    </td>

  </td>
</tr>
```

3. Next, add input boxes for two other fields that record the date of purchase and the serial number for the product. Add the following code below the code you just inserted. See Figure 6-17.

```
<td valign="top" align="right">
<label for="date">Purchase Date</label>
</td>
<td valign="top">
<input type="text" name="date" id="date" size="20" />
</td>
</tr>
<tr>
    <td width="150" valign="top" align="right">
    <label for="snumber">Serial Number</label>
    </td>
    <td valign="top">
    <input type="text" name="snumber" id="snumber" size="20" />
    </td>
</tr>
</table>
```

Figure 6-17 ▶ **Adding input boxes for date of purchase and serial number**

```
<!-- Product Information -->
<tr>
    <td valign="top" colspan="2">

    <table>
    <tr>
        <td width="100" valign="top" rowspan="2">
        <label for="item">Item Purchased</label>
        </td>
        <td valign="top" rowspan="2">
        <select name="item" id="item">
            <option>LanPass 115</option>
            <option>LanPass 125</option>
            <option>LanPass 250</option>
            <option>FastSwitch 200</option>
            <option>FastSwitch 400</option>
            <option>LG 10Mpbs</option>
            <option>LG 10Mpbs/w</option>
            <option>LG 100Mpbs</option>
            <option>LG 100Mpbs/w</option>
        </select>
        </td>
        <td valign="top" align="right">
        <label for="date">Purchase Date</label>
        </td>
        <td valign="top">
        <input type="text" name="date" id="date" size="20" />
        </td>
    </tr>
    <tr>
        <td width="150" valign="top" align="right">
        <label for="snumber">Serial Number</label>
        </td>
        <td valign="top">
        <input type="text" name="snumber" id="snumber" size="20" />
        </td>
    </tr>
    </table>

    </td>
</tr>
```

▶ **4.** Save your changes to register.htm and reload the file in your browser. The form now contains the selection list. Note that the first item in the list, LanPass 115, is displayed in the selection list box.

▶ **5.** Click the **Item Purchased** list arrow to verify that the products you entered with the <option> tags are displayed. See Figure 6-18.

Figure 6-18 ▶ **Item Purchased selection list**

Trouble? Your selection list might look slightly different depending on your browser and browser version.

Modifying the Appearance of a Selection List

HTML provides several attributes you can use to modify the appearance and behavior of selection lists and selection options. By default, a select element displays one option from the selection list, along with a list arrow to view additional selection options. You can change the number of options displayed by modifying the size attribute. The syntax of the size attribute is

```
<select size="value"> . . . </select>
```

where *value* is the number of items that the selection list displays in the form. By specifying a value greater than 1, you change the selection list from a drop-down list box to a list box with a scroll bar that allows a user to scroll through the selection options. If you set the size attribute to be equal to the number of options in the selection list, the scroll bar is either not displayed or is dimmed. See Figure 6-19.

Size values of the selection list | **Figure 6-19**

Susan likes the product selection list as it is, so you don't have to specify a different value for the size attribute.

Making Multiple Selections

Users are not limited to a single selection from a selection list. Adding the multiple attribute to the select element enables multiple selections from a list. The syntax for this attribute is

```
<select multiple="multiple"> . . . </select>
```

Note that many browsers accept the minimized version of this attribute, removing the attribute value

```
<select multiple> . . . </select>
```

However, this is not correct HTML or XHTML syntax, and thus you should use the "multiple" attribute value. To make multiple selections from a selection list, a user must hold down an access key while making selections. The Windows operating system offers two different access keys:

- For noncontiguous selections, press and hold the Ctrl key (or the Command key on a Macintosh) while you make your selections.

- For a contiguous selection, select the first item, press and hold the Shift key, and then select the last item in the range. This selects the two items, as well as all the items between them.

If you decide to use a multiple selection list in a form, be aware that the form sends a name/value pair to the server for each option the user selects from the list. This requires the server-based program to be able to handle a single field with multiple values. Check and verify that your server-based programs are designed to handle this before using a multiple selection list. In most cases, you are better served using checkboxes rather selection lists with multiple values. We'll examine checkboxes shortly.

Working with Option Values

By default, a form sends the value displayed in the list for each selected item to the server. In your form, if the user selects the first option from the selection list, the text string "LanPass 115" is sent to the server. Sometimes, however, you may want to send an abbreviation or code to the server instead of the entire text string. For example, you may display descriptive text for each option in the selection list to help users make an informed choice, but only an abbreviated version is required for your records. You can specify the value that is sent to the server with the value attribute. The syntax is

```
<option value="value">item</option>
```

where value is the value associated with the selection item. In the following HTML code, the form sends the value "1" to the server if the LanPass 115 is selected, the value "2" if the LanPass 125 is selected, and so forth:

```
<option value="1">LanPass 115</option>
<option value="2">LanPass 125</option>
<option value="3">LanPass 250</option>
<option value="4">FastSwitch 200</option>
```

. . .

You can also specify which item in the selection list is selected, or highlighted, when the form is initially displayed. The first option in the list is highlighted by default, but you can specify a different value using following attribute:

```
<option selected="selected">item</option>
```

where the selected attribute indicates that item is the default item in the selection list. Many browsers also accept the form:

```
<option selected>item</option>
```

but this is not appropriate syntax for either HTML or XHTML since it does not pair an attribute value with an attribute. In the following HTML code, the LanPass 250 option is initially selected when the user first encounters the selection list field on the form, even though it is not the first item in the list:

```
<option>LanPass 115</option>
<option>LanPass 125</option>
<option selected="selected">LanPass 250</option>
<option>FastSwitch 200</option>
. . .
```

Susan doesn't need to change the default selection in the form.

Creating a Selection List

- To create a selection list, use the following set of HTML code:
    ```
    <select name="name" id="id">
        <option>item1</option>
        <option>item2</option>
        .
        .
        .
    </select>
    ```
    where the name and id attributes identify the selection field.
- To set the size of the selection list, use the size attribute:
    ```
    <select size="value"> . . . </select>
    ```
    where the *value* is the number of items to display in the selection list at any one time. The default is "1".
- To allow multiple selections from the list, use the attribute
    ```
    <select multiple="multiple"> . . . </select>
    ```
    Many browsers also accept the syntax
    ```
    <select multiple> . . . </select>
    ```
    but this is not correct syntax in either HTML or XHTML.
- To associate a value with a selection option, use the value attribute:
    ```
    <option value="value">item</option>
    ```
    where *value* is the value associated with the selection item.
- To define the default selected item, use the attribute
    ```
    <option selected="selected">item</option>
    ```
    Many browsers also accept the syntax
    ```
    <option selected>item</option>
    ```
    but this is not correct syntax in either HTML or XHTML.

Working with Option Groups

In their current state, the item names are grouped together in a single list. Susan feels that it would be easier for customers to locate a specific item if they were grouped by item type. This will be increasingly useful as she adds more items to the list.

HTML allows you to organize selection lists into distinct groups called **option groups**. The syntax for creating an option group is

```
<select attributes>
<optgroup label="label1">
    <option>itema1</option>
    <option>itema2</option>
...
</optgroup>
<optgroup label="label2">
    <option>itemb1</option>
    <option>itemb2</option>
...
</optgroup>
...
</select>
```

where *label1*, *label2*, and so forth are the labels for the different groups of options. The text for the label appears in the selection list above each group of items, but is not a selectable item from the list.

Susan would like you to create three option groups for this selection list, labeled "Routers", "Switches", and "Adapters".

To create option groups for the selection list:

1. Return to **register.htm** in your text editor.

2. Type the code: **<optgroup label="Routers">** immediately above the <option> tag for LanPass 115.

3. Type the following code immediately following the option item, "LanPass 250":

   ```
   </optgroup>
   <optgroup label="Switches">
   ```

4. Type the following two lines immediately following the option item "FastSwitch 400":

   ```
   </optgroup>
   <optgroup label="Adapters">
   ```

5. Type the following code immediately following the option item "LG 100Mpbs/w":

   ```
   </optgroup>
   ```

   Figure 6-20 shows the revised code.

Figure 6-20 | **Creating option groups**

```
<select name="item" id="item">
<optgroup label="Routers">
    <option>LanPass 115</option>
    <option>LanPass 125</option>
    <option>LanPass 250</option>
</optgroup>
<optgroup label="Switches">
    <option>FastSwitch 200</option>
    <option>FastSwitch 400</option>
</optgroup>
<optgroup label="Adapters">
    <option>LG 10Mpbs</option>
    <option>LG 10Mpbs/w</option>
    <option>LG 100Mpbs</option>
    <option>LG 100Mpbs/w</option>
</optgroup>
</select>
```

6. Save your changes to the file and then reload it in your Web browser. As show in Figure 6-21, the selection list items are now grouped by type.

Figure 6-21 | **Options groups in the selection list**

Note that older browser versions will display the selection list without the group labels.

Creating Option buttons

Option buttons, or **radio buttons**, are similar to selection lists, allowing users to make a selection from a list of choices. Unlike selection list items, however, a user can select only one option button at a time from a group. The syntax to create an option button is

```
<input type="radio" name="name" id="id" value="value" />
```

where `name` identifies the field containing the collection of option buttons, `id` identifies the specific option, and the `value` attribute indicates the value sent to the server when a user selects this particular option. Note that in the case of option buttons, the name and id attributes are not redundant as they are with the input boxes you created in the last session. In fact, the id attribute is only required if you intend to use a field label with the option button.

On the other hand, you *must* include the name attribute because it groups distinct option buttons together. Within a group, selecting one option button automatically deselects all of the others. Because there is no text attribute for an option button, you must insert descriptive text next to it in order for users to understand its purpose. If you enclose that descriptive text within a label tag, users can select an option button by clicking either the button or the label.

Figure 6-22 shows an example of HTML code that creates option buttons for party affiliations.

Creating option buttons ◄ Figure 6-22

Note that in this sample code, the value sent to the server does not match the field label. For example, if a user selects the Republican option button, the value "gop" is sent to the server paired with the field name "party".

By default, no option buttons are selected. If you wish that an option button be selected when a form opens, add the checked attribute to the <input> tag:

```
<input type="radio" checked="checked" />
```

Many browsers also accept the abbreviated form

```
<input type="radio" checked />
```

However, this syntax is not supported in the official specifications for HTML and XHTML.

Creating an Option button

- To create an option button, use the following HTML tag:

```
<input type="radio" name="name" id="id" value="value" />
```
where `name` identifies the field containing the option button, `id` identifies the specific option value, and `value` specifies the value sent to the server when the option button is selected. The id attribute is not required unless you intend to use a field label with the option button. The value attribute is required.

- To make a particular option button the default option, use the attribute

```
<input type="radio" checked="checked" />
```
Most browsers also accept the syntax

```
<input type="radio" checked />
```
though this does not follow the syntax guidelines of HTML or XHTML.

Susan would like you to create option buttons for product usage on the registration form. The name of the field is "use", and it has five possible options that describe how the consumer uses the product (id values are indicated in the parenthesis):

- home (home)
- business (bus)
- religious or charitable institution (char)
- government (gov)
- educational institution (edu)

Susan would like the business option button to be selected by default.

To create option buttons for the use field:

1. Return to **register.htm** in your text editor.

2. Type the following code within the opening and closing <td> tags below the Usage Information comment, as shown in Figure 6-23:

```
<table><tr>
  <td valign="top">
  <input type="radio" name="use" id="home" value="home" />
  <label for="home">Home</label><br />
  <input type="radio" name="use" id="bus" value="bus"
  checked="checked" />
  <label for="bus">Business</label><br />
  <input type="radio" name="use" id="char" value="char" />
  <label for="char">Religious or Charitable Institution
  </label><br />
  <input type="radio" name="use" id="gov" value="gov" />
  <label for="gov">Government</label><br />
  <input type="radio" name="use" id="edu" value="edu" />
  <label for="edu">Educational Institution</label>
  </td>
</tr></table>
```

Creating option buttons in the registration form ◄ Figure 6-23

```
<!-- Usage Information -->
<tr>
    <td valign="top" colspan="2">

    <table><tr>
        <td valign="top">
        <input type="radio" name="use" id="home" value="home" />
        <label for="home">Home</label><br />
        <input type="radio" name="use" id="bus" value="bus" checked="checked" />
        <label for="bus">Business</label><br />
        <input type="radio" name="use" id="char" value="char" />
        <label for="char">Religious or Charitable Institution</label><br />
        <input type="radio" name="use" id="gov" value="gov" />
        <label for="gov">Government</label><br />
        <input type="radio" name="use" id="edu" value="edu" />
        <label for="edu">Educational Institution</label>
        </td>
    </tr></table>

    </td>
</tr>
```

3. Save your changes to register.htm and then reload it in your Web browser. See Figure 6-24.

Option buttons in the registration form ◄ Figure 6-24

○ Home
◉ Business
○ Religious or Charitable Institution
○ Government
○ Educational Institution

4. Click each option button. Note that as you click one button, the previously selected button is deselected.

5. If you are using a browser that supports labels, click the button labels to verify that this has the same effect as clicking the buttons themselves.

Trouble? If clicking one option button fails to deselect another, check the names you've assigned to each button and verify that they are identical and that the cases (uppercase and lowercase) match.

When should you use option buttons, and when should you use a selection list? Generally, if you have a long list of options, you should use a selection list. If you want to allow users to select more than one option, you should use a selection list with the multiple attribute. If you have a short list of options, and only one option is allowed at a time, you should use option buttons.

Creating a Field Set

Susan notices that there is no label for the entire collection of option buttons. While you could insert a text string into the form for this purpose, HTML and XHTML provide another way to do this: you can organize the option buttons into a group of fields called a **field set**. Most browsers place a box, known as a **group box**, around a field set to indicate that the fields belong to a common group. The syntax for creating a field set is:

```
<fieldset>
    fields
</fieldset>
```

where *fields* are the individual fields within the set. To add a caption to a group box, you include a legend element within the field set. The syntax of the legend element is:

```
<legend>text</legend>
```

where *text* is the text of the legend. By default, the legend text is placed in the top-left corner of the group box; however you can define the location of the legend text using the align attribute:

```
<legend align="position">text</legend>
```

where *position* is either left, center, or right. Some browsers, such as Internet Explorer, will also support a value of "bottom" to place the legend caption on the bottom of the group box. The align attribute has been deprecated in favor of styles, and thus might not be supported by many browsers. However, at the moment, most browsers still support the align attribute.

Susan suggests that you create a group box for the usage option buttons. Add a legend indicating that users can only pick one of the usage options.

To create a group box:

1. Return to **register.htm** in your text editor.

2. Type the following code immediately above the <input> tag for the "home" option button:

   ```
   <fieldset>
   <legend>Used For (check one)</legend>
   ```

3. Type the following code after the Educational Institution label:

   ```
   </fieldset>
   ```

   See Figure 6-25.

Figure 6-25	Creating a field set

```
<table><tr>
  <td valign="top">
  <fieldset>
  <legend>Used For (check one)</legend>
  <input type="radio" name="use" id="home" value="home" />
  <label for="home">Home</label><br />
  <input type="radio" name="use" id="bus" value="bus" checked="checked" />
  <label for="bus">Business</label><br />
  <input type="radio" name="use" id="char" value="char" />
  <label for="char">Religious or Charitable Institution</label><br />
  <input type="radio" name="use" id="gov" value="gov" />
  <label for="gov">Government</label><br />
  <input type="radio" name="use" id="edu" value="edu" />
  <label for="edu">Educational Institution</label>
  </fieldset>
  </td>
</tr></table>
```

4. Save your changes to the file and then reload it in your Web browser. See Figure 6-26.

Figure 6-26	Option buttons in the registration form

legend → Used For (check one)
- ○ Home
- ⊙ Business
- ○ Religious or Charitable Institution
- ○ Government
group box → ○ Educational Institution

There is no attribute to control the size of the group box. The box's height is always large enough to accommodate the fields and labels in the field set. If you wish to set the width to a specific value, you can place the group box in a table cell and then set the width of the cell.

An important point to remember about field sets is that some browsers do not allow them to extend across table cells. To ensure predictable results, therefore, you should place all of the fields in a field set within a single cell.

Reference Window

Creating a Field Set

- To create a field set, enclose the fields in the following tags:

  ```
  <fieldset>
      fields
  </fieldset>
  ```
  where *fields* are the form fields in the field set. Field sets are usually displayed in a group box.
- To add a caption to a field set, add the following tag after the opening <fieldset> tag:

  ```
  <legend>text</legend>
  ```
  where *text* is the text of the field set caption.

Deprecated

- To align the legend, add the following attribute to the <legend> tag:

  ```
  align="position"
  ```
  where *position* is either top (the default), left, or right. Some browsers also accept an align value of "bottom".

Creating Check Boxes

The next type of input field you'll create in the registration form is a check box. The syntax to create a check box is

```
<input type="checkbox" name="name" id="id" value="value" />
```

where the *name* and *id* attributes identify the check box, and the *value* attribute specifies the value that is sent to the server if the check box is selected. Unlike the input boxes that you worked with in the last session, the value attribute is required with every check box. As with input boxes, the name and id attributes should both be included even though they usually contain the same information. For example, the following code assigns the value "democrat" to the party field if the check box is selected:

```
<input type="checkbox" name="party" id="party" value="democrat" />
```

As with input boxes and option buttons, check boxes do not display any text. You add text or a label next to the check box using a separate tag.

By default, a check box is not selected. To have a check box selected by default, use the checked attribute as follows:

```
<input type="checkbox" checked="checked" />
```

Most browsers also accept the minimized version without the attribute value:

```
<input type="checkbox" checked />
```

Creating a Check Box

- To create a check box, use the following HTML tag:
  ```
  <input type="checkbox" name="name" id="id" value="value" />
  ```
  where the *name* and *id* attributes identify the check box field and the value attribute specifies the value sent to the server if the check box is selected.
- To specify that a check box be selected by default, use the checked attribute as follows:
  ```
  <input type="checkbox" checked="checked" />
  ```
  Most browsers also accept the syntax:
  ```
  <input type="checkbox" checked />
  ```
  However, this does not follow the syntax guidelines of HTML or XHTML.

Susan wants you to add a total of five check boxes to the form, to allow users to indicate which network operating systems they are running with their LanGear product. Susan is tracking five network operating systems: Netware, Banyan Vines, Windows, IBM Lan Server, and PC/NFS. Even though you'll arrange these check boxes together on the form, each one is associated with a different field. Note that this is different than the option buttons you just created, which were all associated with one field.

To add check boxes to your form:

1. Return to **register.htm** in your text editor.

2. Type the following code immediately following the closing </td> tag for the option buttons (see Figure 6-27):

```
<td valign="top">
<input type="checkbox" name="nw" id="nw" value="yes" />
<label for="nw">Netware</label><br />
<input type="checkbox" name="bv" id="bv" value="yes" />
<label for="bv">Banyan Vines</label><br />
<input type="checkbox" name="win" id="win" value="yes" />
<label for="win">Windows</label><br />
<input type="checkbox" name="ibm" id="ibm" value="yes" />
<label for="ibm">IBM Lan Server</label><br />
<input type="checkbox" name="pcnfs" id="pcnfs" value="yes" />
<label for="pcnfs">PC/NFS</label>
</td>
```

Creating a collection of check boxes   **Figure 6-27**

```
            <input type="radio" name="use" id="edu" value="edu" />
            <label for="edu">Educational Institution</label>
            </fieldset>
            </td>

            <td valign="top">
            <input type="checkbox" name="nw" id="nw" value="yes" />
            <label for="nw">Netware</label><br />
            <input type="checkbox" name="bv" id="bv" value="yes" />
            <label for="bv">Banyan Vines</label><br />
            <input type="checkbox" name="win" id="win" value="yes" />
            <label for="win">Windows</label><br />
            <input type="checkbox" name="ibm" id="ibm" value="yes" />
            <label for="ibm">IBM Lan Server</label><br />
            <input type="checkbox" name="pcnfs" id="pcnfs" value="yes" />
            <label for="pcnfs">PC/NFS</label>
            </td>
        </tr></table>

        </td>
    </tr>
```

3. Save your changes to register.htm and then reload it in your Web browser.

4. Click the different check boxes in the form. Note that you can click either the check box or the label associated with the check box to select and deselect the field. See Figure 6-28.

Check boxes on the registration form   **Figure 6-28**

☐ Netware
☐ Banyan Vines
☐ Windows
☐ IBM Lan Server
☐ PC/NFS

Susan likes the check boxes, but she would like you to enclose the check boxes within a field set, with a legend that tells users to check any box that applies to their system.

To enclose the check boxes in a group box:

1. Return to **register.htm** in your text editor.

2. Type the following code immediately above the <input> tag for the Netware check box:

```
<fieldset>
<legend>Network Operating System (check all that apply)</legend>
```

3. Type the closing tag **</fieldset>** below the <label> tag for the PC/NFS label (see Figure 6-29).

Figure 6-29 | **Grouping the check boxes in a field set**

```
<td valign="top">
<fieldset>
<legend>Network Operating System (check all that apply)</legend>
<input type="checkbox" name="nw" id="nw" value="yes" />
<label for="nw">Netware</label><br />
<input type="checkbox" name="bv" id="bv" value="yes" />
<label for="bv">Banyan Vines</label><br />
<input type="checkbox" name="win" id="win" value="yes" />
<label for="win">Windows</label><br />
<input type="checkbox" name="ibm" id="ibm" value="yes" />
<label for="ibm">IBM Lan Server</label><br />
<input type="checkbox" name="pcnfs" id="pcnfs" value="yes" />
<label for="pcnfs">PC/NFS</label>
</fieldset>
</td>
```

4. Save your changes to the file and then reload it in your Web browser. See Figure 6-30.

Figure 6-30 | **Check boxes grouped in a field set**

Creating a Text Area Box

The next section of the registration form allows users to enter comments about the products they've purchased. Because these comments may contain several lines of text, an input box would be too small. To create a larger text area for the input box, use the textarea element:

```
<textarea name="name" id="id" rows="value" cols="value">
default text
</textarea>
```

where the rows and cols attributes define the dimensions of the input box. The rows attribute indicates the number of lines in the input box—though some early browser versions show more lines than indicated by the rows attribute—and the cols attribute specifies the number of characters in each line. Though not required, you can specify default text that appears in the input box when the form is initially displayed. Figure 6-31 shows an example of a text area with default text.

Figure 6-31 | **Creating a text area**

```
<label for="comments">Comments?</label> <br />

<textarea name="comments" id="comments" rows="5" cols="50">
Enter comments here.
</textarea>
```

Note that unlike an input element, a text area employs a two-sided tag—it has both an opening tag, <textarea>, and a closing tag, </textarea>. You need to include the </textarea> tag even if you don't specify default text.

The text you enter in a text area wraps to the next line when it exceeds the width of the box. Internet Explorer and Netscape both support the wrap attribute, which allows you to control how a user's browser handles text wrapping within the text area. The syntax of the wrap attribute is

```
<textarea wrap="type"> . . .</textarea>
```

where *type* is one of the values described in Figure 6-32.

Wrap values | **Figure 6-32**

Wrap Value	Description
wrap="off"	All the text is displayed on a single line, scrolling to the left if the text extends past the width of the box. Text goes to the next row in the box only if the Enter key is pressed. The text is sent to the CGI script in a single line.
wrap="soft"	Text wraps automatically to the next row when it extends beyond the width of the input box. The text is still sent to the CGI script in a single line without any information about how the text was wrapped within the input box.
wrap="hard"	Text wraps automatically to the next row when it extends beyond the width of the input box. When the text is sent to the CGI script, the line-wrapping information is included, allowing the CGI script to work with the text exactly as it appears in the input box.

The wrap attribute is not part of the specifications for HTML 4.01 or XHTML. There is also some difference in how browsers support this attribute. For example, Netscape 4 also uses wrap values of "virtual" for "soft" and "physical" for "hard". In addition, while the default wrap value for Netscape 4 is "off", for most other browsers the default behavior is to treat text wrap as "soft"—that is, the text wraps within the text area box, but this information is not sent to the server. Thus, if you need to support Netscape 4 users and want to ensure text wrapping within the text area box, you should set the wrap value to "soft" or "hard". You may also need to review the documentation for your server-based program to determine whether the program needs the text wrap information, or whether the text can be sent in one long string.

Creating a Text Area Box

- To create a text area for extended text entry, use the following tag:

  ```
  <textarea name="name" id="id" rows="value" cols="value">default
  text</textarea>
  ```
  where *default text* is the text that is displayed in the text area (optional), and the rows and cols attributes specify the number of lines in the text area and the number of characters in each line, respectively.

Internet Explorer and Netscape

- To control how text wraps in a text area, use the attribute:

  ```
  <textarea wrap="type">. . .</textarea>
  ```
  where *type* is "off" to turn off text wrapping, "soft" to wrap the text without sending the text wrap information to the server-based program, or "hard" to wrap the text and send the text wrap information to the server.

In the registration form, you'll place the product comments in a text area that is 6 lines high and 50 characters wide. You won't specify a value for the wrap attribute.

To add a text area to the registration form:

1. Return to **register.htm** in your text editor.

2. Type the following code within the opening and closing <td> tags immediately below the "Comments" comment tag (see Figure 6-33):

```
<table><tr>
   <td width="100" valign="top">
   <label for="comments">Comments?</label>
   </td>
   <td valign="top">
   <textarea name="comments" id="comments" rows="6" cols="50">
   </textarea>
   </td>
</tr></table>
```

Figure 6-33　Creating a text area

```
<!-- Comments -->
<tr>
    <td valign="top" colspan="2">

    <table><tr>
        <td width="100" valign="top">
        <label for="comments">Comments?</label>
        </td>
        <td valign="top">
        <textarea name="comments" id="comments" rows="6" cols="50"></textarea>
        </td>
    </tr></table>

    </td>
</tr>
```

3. Save your changes to register.htm and reload it in your Web browser.

4. Test the text-wrapping feature by typing the following text in the comments field (see Figure 6-34):

   I'm very pleased with my purchase of the LG 100Mpbs/w wireless network adapter. How do I obtain updates to the driver and software?

Note that the input box includes a vertical scroll bar so that a user can scroll to see the hidden text if needed.

Comments text area with sample text | **Figure 6-34**

Comments? | I'm very pleased with my purchase of the LG 100Mpbs/w wireless network adapter. How do I obtain updates to the driver and software?

Trouble? Depending on your Web browser, your Comments input box may look slightly different from the one shown in Figure 6-34.

You've created the last input field for the registration form. Using HTML you've added input boxes, a selection list, option buttons, check boxes, and a text area to your form. In the next session, you'll learn how to set up your form to work with a server-based program.

Session 6.2 Quick Check

Review

1. What HTML tag would you use to create a selection list with a field named State and with the options California, Nevada, Oregon, and Washington?
2. How would you modify the HTML tag in Question 1 to allow more than one state to be selected from the list?
3. What HTML tag would make Oregon the default selection in Question 1?
4. What HTML code would you use to place the options from Question 1 in an option group named "West Coast"?
5. What HTML tag would you use to create a series of option buttons for a field named State with the options California, Nevada, Oregon, and Washington? Place the option buttons in a group box with the legend "West Coast".
6. How would you modify the HTML tag in Question 5 to send the number 1 to the server if the user selects California, 2 for Nevada, 3 for Oregon, and 4 for Washington?
7. What HTML tag would you use to create a check box field named California?
8. What HTML tag would you use to create a text area field named Memo that is 5 rows high and 30 columns wide and has the default text "Enter notes here."?
9. What attribute would you add to the HTML tag in Question 8 to cause the Memo text to wrap to the next row and send the text-wrapping information to the server?

Session 6.3

Working with Form Buttons

Up to now, all of your control elements have been input fields of some kind. Another type of control element is one that performs an action. In forms, this is usually done with a button. Buttons can be clicked to run programs, submit forms, or reset the form to its original state.

Creating a Command button

One type of button, called a **command button**, is created using the <input> tag as follows:

```
<input type="button" value="text" />
```

where `text` is the text that appears on the button. By itself, a command button performs no actions on a Web page. To create an action for a command button, you have to write a script or program that runs automatically when the button is clicked. This can be done using a programming language such as JavaScript. Since that is beyond the scope of this tutorial, we won't examine how to use command buttons here.

Creating Submit and Reset Buttons

Two other kinds of buttons are submit and reset buttons. A **submit button** submits a form to the server for processing when clicked. Clicking the **reset button** resets a form to its original (default) values. The syntax for creating these two buttons is:

```
<input type="submit" value="text" />
<input type="reset" value="text" />
```

where the `value` attribute defines the text that appears on the button.

You can also specify name and id attributes for push, submit, and reset buttons, although these attributes are not required. You would use these attributes when a form contains multiple buttons and a program that processes the form needs to distinguish one button from the others. For example, a Web page advertising a downloadable software program might include three buttons: one used to download the program from the company's Web site, another used to retrieve additional information about the product, and a third to erase the form.

Susan wants the registration form to include both a submit button and a reset button. The submit button, labeled "Send Registration," will send the form data to the server for processing when clicked. The reset button, labeled "Cancel," will erase the user's input and reset the fields to their default values.

To add the Submit and Reset buttons to the registration form:

▶ **1.** Using your text editor, open **register.htm**.

▶ **2.** Type the following lines of code within the opening and closing <td> tags located immediately below the Buttons comment tag (see Figure 6-35):

```
<input type="submit" value="Send Registration" />
<input type="reset" value="Cancel" />
```

Creating form buttons | Figure 6-35

```
<!-- Buttons -->
<tr>
   <td valign="top" colspan="2" align="center">
   <input type="submit" value="Send Registration" />
   <input type="reset" value="Cancel" />
   </td>
</tr>
```

3. Save your changes to register.htm and then reload it in your Web browser. Figure 6-36 shows the completed registration form, including the two buttons you just created.

Completed registration form | Figure 6-36

Trouble? Depending on which browser you're using, your registration form may appear slightly different from the one shown in Figure 6-36.

4. Test the Cancel button by entering test values into the form and then clicking the Cancel button. The form should return to its initial state.

Trouble? If the Cancel button doesn't work, check the HTML code for the button and verify that you've entered the code correctly. The Send Registration button does not perform a function yet, because you have not identified a server-based program to receive the form data.

Designing a Custom Button

Buttons created with the input element do not allow Web page designers to control their appearance, other than specifying the text for the button label. For greater artistic control over the appearance of the button, you can use the button element, which has the syntax:

```
<button name="name" id="id" value="value" type="type">
   content
</button>
```

where the `name` and `value` attributes specify the name of the button and the value sent to a server-based program, the *id* attribute specifies the button's id, the *type* attribute specifies the button type (submit, reset, or button), and `content` is page content displayed within the button. The page content can include formatted text, inline images, and other design elements supported by HTML. Figure 6-37 shows an example of a button that contains both formatted text and an inline image.

| Figure 6-37 | Creating a custom button |

HTML code

```
<button name="back" type="button">
   <img src="back.gif" alt="" style="margin: 4; vertical-align: middle" />
   <span style="color: blue; font-weight: bold; font-style: italic">
      Home Page
   </span>
</button>
```

◀ Home Page

rendered button

Creating Form Buttons

- To create a button to submit form input to a program, use the following tag:
  ```
  <input type="submit" name="name" id="id" value="text" />
  ```
  where the `value` attribute defines the text that appears on the button, and is also sent to the program to indicate which button on the form has been clicked.
- To create a button that cancels or resets a form, change the value of the type attribute to "reset":
  ```
  <input type="reset" name="name" id="id" value="text" />
  ```
- To create a generic button to perform an action within the Web page, set the value of the type attribute to "button":
  ```
  <input type="button" name="name" id="id" value="text" />
  ```
- To create a button that can contain other page elements use the code
  ```
  <button name="name" id="id" value="value">content</button>
  ```
  where the `value` attribute provides an initial value for the button, and `content` consists of the page elements you want displayed in the button.

Creating File Buttons

Another type of button supported by HTML is the file button, which is used to select files so that their contents can be submitted for processing to a program. Rather than displaying a file's contents, the Web page displays only the file's location. The program can then use that information to retrieve the file for processing. Figure 6-38 shows an example of using the file button to return the location of a file named "report.doc."

Using a file button | Figure 6-38

Note that the input box and the Browse button are created for you. You cannot change the label for the browse button, but you can increase the size of the input box by using the size attribute in the <input> tag. You do not need to create a file button for the registration form.

Creating Image Fields

Another control element you can use in your Web form is the inline image. Inline images can act like submit buttons, allowing a user to click an image to submit a form. The syntax for this type of control element is

```
<input type="image" src="url" name="text" value="text" />
```

where url is the filename and location of the inline image, the $name$ attribute assigns a name to the field, and the $value$ attribute assigns a value to the image. When the form is submitted to a server-based program, the coordinates of where the user clicked within the image are attached to the image's name and value in the format

```
name.x, value.y
```

where $name$ is the name of the image, $value$ is the image's value, x is the x-coordinate of the mouse click, and y is the y-coordinate of the mouse click. For example, suppose your Web page contains the following inline image form element:

```
<input type="image" src="usamap.gif" name="usa" value="state" />
```

If a user clicks the inline image at the coordinates (15, 30), the Web form sends the text string "usa.15, state30" to the server. Once the server-based program receives this data, it can perform an action based on where the user clicked within the image. See Figure 6-39.

Figure 6-39 ▶ **Using an image control with a server-based program**

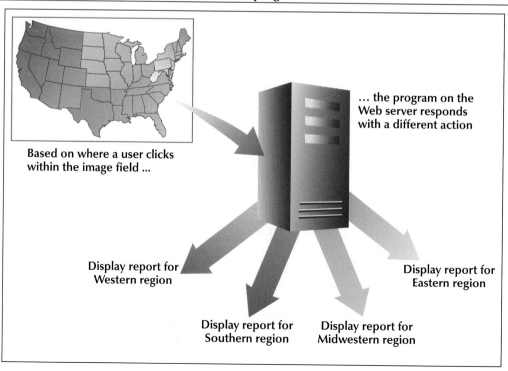

Based on where a user clicks within the image field ...

... the program on the Web server responds with a different action

Display report for Western region

Display report for Eastern region

Display report for Southern region

Display report for Midwestern region

You are not required to include any inline image controls or file buttons in your Web page form for this project.

Working with Hidden Fields

Susan is pleased with the final appearance of the registration form. She shows the code for the form to Warren Kaughman, one of the programmers at LanGear and the person responsible for the CGI script that you'll be using. Warren notices only one thing missing from the code: the e-mail address of Susan's assistant, who is to receive the registration forms via e-mail. Warren's CGI script requires that the form include the e-mail address of the recipient.

Unlike the other fields you've created so far, this field has a predefined value that users of the Web form should not be able to change. In fact, the e-mail address of Susan's assistant should not even be displayed on the form. To accomplish this, you can use a **hidden field**, which is added to the form but not displayed in the Web page. The syntax for creating a hidden field is:

```
<input type="hidden" name="name" id="id" value="value" />
```

You've learned from Warren that the name of the e-mail field should be "email", and you know from Susan that the e-mail address of her assistant is adavis@langear.com (note that this is a fictional address used for the purposes of this tutorial). Now that you know both the field name and the field value, you can add the hidden field to the registration form.

Because the field is hidden, you can place it anywhere within the form element. A common practice is to place all hidden fields in one location, usually at the beginning of the form, to make it easier to read and interpret your HTML code. You should also include a comment describing the purpose of the field.

To add the hidden field to the registration form:

1. Return to **register.htm** in your text editor.

2. Type the following code directly below the <form> tag (see Figure 6-40):

```
<!-- e-mail address of the recipient -->
<p>
<input type="hidden" name="email" id="email"
value="adavis@langear.com" />
</p>
```

Creating a hidden field ◄ **Figure 6-40**

```
<body style="color: rgb(133,0,0); margin: 0">
<form name="reg" id="reg" action="http://www.langear.com/cgi/mailer"
    method="post">
<!-- e-mail address of the recipient -->
<p><input type="hidden" name="email" id="email" value="adavis@langear.com" /></p>
<table border="0" cellspacing="0" cellpadding="5" width="620"
    style="background-color: yellow">
<!-- Page Heading -->
```

3. Save your changes to the file.

With the e-mail field now included in the registration form, you'll return to the first tag you entered into this document, the <form> tag, and insert the attributes needed for it to interact with the LanGear CGI script.

Working with Form Attributes

You've added all the elements needed for the form. Your final task is to specify where to send the form data and how to send it. You do this by adding the following attributes to the form element:

```
<form action="url" method="type" enctype="type"> . . . </form>
```

where *url* specifies the filename and location of the program that processes the form, the *method* attribute specifies how your Web browser sends data to the server, and the *enctype* attribute specifies the format of the data stored in the form's field. Let's examine the method and enctype attributes in more detail.

There are two possible values for the method attribute: "get" or "post". The **get** method is the default, and appends the form data to the end of the URL specified in the action attribute. The **post** method, on the other hand, sends form data in a separate data stream, allowing the Web server to receive the data through what is called "standard input." Because it is more flexible, most Web designers prefer the post method for sending data to a server. Because some Web servers limit the size of a URL, the post method is also safer, avoiding the possibility of data being truncated; this can happen using the get method if a long string is appended to a URL.

Don't be concerned if you don't completely understand the difference between get and post. Your Internet service provider can supply the necessary information about which of the two methods you should use when accessing a server-based program with your Web form.

The enctype attribute determines how the form data should be encoded as it is sent to the server. Figure 6-41 describes the three most common encoding types.

Figure 6-41 ▷ **Values of the enctype attribute**

enctype Values	Description
application/x-www-form-urlencoded	The default format. In this format, form data is transferred as a long text string in which spaces are replaced with the "+" character and non-text characters (such as tabs and line breaks) are replaced with their hexadecimal code values. Field names are separated from their field values with a "=" symbol.
multipart/form-data	Used when sending files to a server. In this format, spaces and non-text characters are preserved, and data elements are separated using delimiter lines. The action type of the form element must be set to "post" for this format.
text/plain	Form data is transferred as plain text with no encoding of spaces or non-text characters. This format is most often used when the action type of the form element is set to "mailto".

Finally, another attribute you might use with the form element is the target attribute, used to send form data to a different browser window or frame. This is not a concern with Susan's registration form.

Now that you've been introduced to the issues involved in sending form data to a server-based program, you are ready to make some final modifications to the register.htm file. Warren tells you that a CGI script that processes the form is located at the URL *http://www.langear.com/cgi/mailer* (a fictional address) and uses the "post" method. You do not have to specify a value for the enctype attribute.

To add the attributes to the form element:

▶ **1.** Using your text editor, type the following attributes within the <form> tag in **register.htm** (see Figure 6-42):

```
action="http://www.langear.com/cgi/mailer" method="post"
```

Setting form attributes ◀ Figure 6-42

```
<body style="color: rgb(133,0,0); margin: 0">
<form name="reg" id="reg" action="http://www.langear.com/cgi/mailer"
      method="post">
<!-- e-mail address of the recipient -->
<input type="hidden" name="email" id="email" value="adavis@langear.com" />
<table border="0" cellspacing="0" cellpadding="5" width="620"
       style="background-color: yellow">
<!-- Page Heading -->
```

▶ **2.** Save your changes to **register.htm** and close the file and your text editor.

You've finished the registration form, and Warren places a copy of register.htm in a folder on the company's Web server. From there it can be fully tested to verify that the CGI script and the form work properly, and that the form data is e-mailed to Susan's assistant.

Using the mailto Action

So far, in working with Susan's registration file, you have built a form to use Warren's e-mail CGI script. There is, however, a way to send form information via e-mail without using a server-based program: you can use the "mailto" action. This action accesses the user's own e-mail program and uses it to mail form information to a specified e-mail address, bypassing the need for using server-based programs. The syntax of the "mailto" action is

```
<form action="mailto:e-mail_address" method="post"
enctype="text/plain"> ... </form>
```

where $e\text{-}mail\_address$ is the e-mail address of the recipient of the form. Because the "mailto" action does not require a server-based program, you can avoid some of the problems associated with coordinating your page with a program running on the Web server. However there are several disadvantages with the mailto action. One is that not all browsers support it. For example, versions of Internet Explorer earlier than 4.0 and Netscape Navigator 3.0 do not. Another concern is that using the mailto action requires a user to have an e-mail client program installed on their computer and have that program configured to work with a POP mail account. Finally, you should note that messages sent via the "mailto" action are not encrypted for privacy and by inserting the e-mail address into the HTML code, you open your Web page to address harvesters used by spammers (for a discussion of address harvesters, see Tutorial 2). For these reasons, you should carefully consider all of the ramifications of the mailto action before using it in one of your forms.

When you click the submit button on a form using the "mailto" action, your mail program receives the content for the mail message from your Web browser. Depending on how your system is configured, either you will have a chance to edit the mail message further, or it will be automatically sent to the e-mail address specified by the creator of the form without allowing you to intervene.

Figure 6-43 shows an e-mail message that would be generated if you used the "mailto" action with the registration form you completed in this tutorial. The format of the mail message may look different depending on a user's browser and e-mail software.

Figure 6-43 ▷ **Mail message from the mailto action**

```
From: Andrew Davis [adavis@langear.com]
Sent: Tuesday, March 30, 2006 at 21:03:54
To: adavis@langear.com
Subject: Form posted from Microsoft Internet Explorer.

email=adavis@langear.com
fname=Andrew
lname=Davis
address1=Room 634
address2=211 Hawkins Avenue
city=Lawrence
state=WI
zip=53701
country=United States
item=FastSwitch 400
date= 4/1/2006
snumber=3983493
use=edu
nw=yes
win=yes
comments=How do I access the internal settings of the router?
```

Note that if you don't specify the "text/plain" value for the enctype attribute when using the "mailto" action, the resulting mail message is sent using the default encoding, which requires a special program to decode into plain text.

Specifying the Tab Order

Typically, users navigate through a Web form using the Tab key, which moves the cursor from one field to another in the order that the field tags are entered into the HTML file.

You can specify an alternate tab order by adding the tabindex attribute to any control element in your form. When each element is assigned a tab index number, the cursor moves through the fields from the lowest index number to the highest. For example, to assign the tab index number "1" to the fname field from the registration form, you would enter the code

```
<input name="fname" tabindex="1" />
```

Fields with zero or negative tab indexes are omitted from the tab order entirely.

Web page designers can use tab index numbers in their forms without worrying about older browsers that do not support this new standard. Such browsers simply ignore the tabindex attribute and continue to tab to the fields in the order that they appear in the HTML file.

Specifying an Access Key

Another way of accessing elements in a form is with an access key. An **access key** is a single key on the keyboard that you type in conjunction with the Alt key for Windows users or the Control key for Macintosh users, in order to jump to one of the control elements in the form. You can create an access key by adding the accesskey attribute to any of the control elements discussed in this tutorial. For example, to create an access key for the lname field, enter the following code:

```
<input name="lname" accesskey="l" />
```

If a user types Alt+l (or Command+l for Macintosh users), the control element for the lname field is selected. Note that you must use letters that are not reserved by your browser. For example, Alt+f is used by Internet Explorer to access the File menu. If you do use an access key, you should provide some visual clues about the key's existence. The accepted method is to underline the character corresponding to the access key. For example, in the previous code, you might display the lname label as "*L*ast Name".

Susan does not need you to work with the tabbing order for this form or to create any access keys. You'll have a chance to work with these attributes in the case problems at the end of the tutorial.

You're now finished working with forms and form attributes. The page you created for Susan has been stored on the company's Web server. She is reviewing the Web page with her assistant and will inform you if you need to make any changes to your work.

Tips for Creating Effective Forms

- Label all control elements clearly and concisely.
- Use horizontal lines, tables, and line breaks to separate topical groups from one another.
- Use field sets to organize common groups of fields, especially option buttons.
- Specify the tab order to ensure that users will move correctly from one field to another.
- Use option buttons, check boxes, and selection lists whenever possible to limit a user's choice of entries, thus reducing the chance of an erroneous data value. Use input boxes only when the field has no predefined list of values.
- Use selection lists for items with several possible options. Use option buttons for items with few options. Use a check box for each item with only two possible values.
- Let users know the correct format for input box text by inserting default text in the appropriate format (for example, insert the text string, "mm/dd/yyyy" in a Date input box to indicate the format for inserting date values).
- Use password fields for sensitive or confidential information (such as passwords).
- Because form elements differ between browsers, view your form on different browsers and different browser versions to ensure that the form displays correctly in all situations.

Session 6.3 Quick Check

Review

1. What tag would you use to create a submit button with the label "Send Form"?
2. What HTML tag would you use to create a reset button with the label "Cancel Form"?
3. What HTML code would you use to create an image field named Sites for sites.gif with the value attribute GotoPage?
4. What HTML tag would you use to create a hidden field named Subject with the field value "Form Responses"?
5. You need your form to work with a CGI script located at *http://www.j_davis.com/cgi-bin/post-query*. The Web server uses the "get" method. What is the correct <form> tag?
6. You want to use the "mailto" action to send your form to the e-mail address walker@j_davis.com. What is the appropriate <form> tag to accomplish this?
7. What HTML code would you use to assign the access key n to the FirstName field?

Review

Tutorial Summary

In this tutorial, you learned how to create and use Web forms. The first session dealt with the fundamentals of Web forms, discussing how Web forms interact with the Web server to submit information to programs running on the server. You learned how to create and format simple input boxes and how to work with form labels. The second session examined other types of control elements, including selection lists, option buttons, and check boxes. This session also showed how to create text area boxes for extended text entry, and how to organize fields in field sets. The last session showed how to create form buttons for resetting a form or submitting it to a program for processing. This session also examined some special input fields that can be used to create server-side image maps and file input boxes. The session concluded with a discussion of tab indices and access keys.

Key Terms

access key	field value	perl
CGI script	form button	post
check box	get	radio button
Common Gateway Inter-	group box	reset button
face script	hidden field	selection list
command button	input box	submit button
control element	name/value pair	text area
drop-down list box	option button	value
field	option group	
field set	password field	

Practice

Practice the skills you learned in the tutorial using the same case scenario.

Review Assignments

Data files needed for this Review Assignment: cancel.gif, lglogo.jpg, mail.gif, suptxt.htm

Susan and her assistant are pleased with the work you've done on the registration form, and they would like you to create a new form for users who experience technical support problems. To receive support, a user needs to provide their e-mail address, the product they're working with, information about their computing environment, and a statement describing the trouble they're having with their equipment. Some customers have support contracts with LanGear that entitle them to particular support services. Susan would like the form to have a check box to indicate whether the customer has such a contract. The form also needs an input box in which the customer can enter a service contract number.

Susan has created the layout for the page and much of the text. She needs you to enter the various control elements for the form. Figure 6-44 shows a preview of the form you'll create for Susan.

Figure 6-44

To create the tech support form:

1. Using your text editor, open **suptxt.htm** from the tutorial.06/review folder. Enter *your name* and *the date* in the head section and save the file as **support.htm**.

2. Insert a <form> tag directly after the <body> tag and name the form "support_form". Assign the fictional URL "http://www.langear.com/cgi/mailer" to the form's action. Form data is submitted using the "post" method and is encoded as "text/plain". Insert a closing </form> tag directly before the closing </body> tag.

3. When the form is completed, it should be sent to the support department. To do this, Susan needs you to insert a hidden field named "recipient" with a value of "techsupport@langear.com". Place this field directly after the opening <form> tag within a paragraph element.

4. In the second table cell below the Customer Name comment, create an input box with the name and id set to "cust_name". Set the size of the input box to 50 characters. Make the text "Your name:" a label that is connected to the cust_name field.

5. Similarly, create input boxes 50 characters wide for the Customer Phone Number and Customer E-mail sections of the document. Assign "cust_phone" as the name and id for the customer phone number input box, and assign "cust_mail" as the name and id for the customer e-mail input box. Connect the text "Your phone #:" and "Your E-mail address:" to their respective fields.

6. In the table cell below the "Check for Support Contract" comment, create a checkbox that has "contract" for its name and id before the existing text in the cell. Assign the value "yes" to this field if it is clicked by the user. Change the text, "Yes, I have a support contract" to a label linked to the checkbox.

7. In the table row with the "Support Contract" comment tag, create an input box 50 characters wide in the second cell. Assign the input box the name and id "cid". Change the text "Contract ID:" to a label that is connected to the cid field.

8. In the second cell of the row located below the "Product" comment, create a selection list with the products and option groups you created for register.htm. Assign this selection list the name and id "item". Change the text "Product:" from the preceding table cell into a label connected to the item field.

9. In the second cell of the table row containing the "Operating System" comment, create another selection list with the field name "os". The os field should contain the following entries:
   - Windows 98
   - Windows 2000
   - Windows XP
   - Windows NT
   - Macintosh
   - UNIX
   - Linux
   - OS/2

   Create two option groups for the os selection list. The first, named "Windows", contains the four Windows operating systems; the second, named "Others", contains the remaining four operating systems. Change the text "Your operating system:" to a label that is connected to the os field.

10. Locate the table row containing the "Memory Options" comment tag. In the second cell below this comment, create a group box that contains three option buttons. These option buttons allow users to specify the amount of memory on their computer.

11. Each option button should belong to a field named "memory". The first option button should have the id "mem1" and the value "1". Insert the label text "0-64MB" to the right of the option button. Insert a line break and create the second option button with the id "mem2" and the value "2". To the right of this option button, insert the label text "65-256MB". Insert another line break and create the third option button with the id "mem3" and the value "3". The text label for this option button is "257+ MB". Make sure each option button label is connected to its option button.

12. Locate the table row containing the comment tag "Message." In the second cell below this comment tag, create a text area box that is 8 rows high and 40 columns wide. The field has the name and id "message." The text area box contains the default text "Enter your tech support question here." Change the text "Message to Tech Support:" to a label that is connected to the message field.

13. In the table cell below the "Submit Button" comment, create a Submit button that contains the image **mail.gif**. The button should contain the text "Submit Your Question" in a blue, bold font that is vertically aligned with the middle of the image mail.gif. Set the margin around the image to 5 pixels.

14. Create a reset button in the table cell below the comment "Reset Button." This button contains the **cancel.gif** image and is aligned with the middle of this image. Set the margin around the image to 5 pixels. The button displays the text "Reset the Form" in a red, bold font.

15. Save your changes to **support.htm** and close the file.

16. Using your Web browser, open **support.htm** and verify that all control elements and labels work correctly. You do not have to submit the form, but verify that the reset button works correctly.

17. Submit the completed Web page to your instructor.

Case Problem 1

Data files needed for this Case Problem: parch2.jpg, pcglogo.jpg, subtxt.htm

Park City Gazette   Kevin Webber, the editor of the Park City Gazette of Park City, Colorado, has asked for your help in developing a subscription page for his Web site. The page includes a form where customers can enter the length of the subscription they want to purchase, their mailing address, and credit card information. Kevin has already created much of the layout and text for the form. Your job is to add the fields and control elements for the form. A preview of the subscription Web page you'll create for Kevin is shown in Figure 6-45.

Figure 6-45

To test the form before it gets put on the Web server in its final form, Kevin would like the results of the form mailed to the e-mail address of the Gazette business manager: *pcg_business@parkcitygazette.com*. You'll use a plain text format for the mail message.

To create the subscription Web page:

1. Using your text editor, open **subtxt.htm** located in the tutorial.06/case1 folder. Enter *your name* and *the date* in the head section. Save the file as **subscrib.htm**.

2. Create a form named "subscription" directly below the <body> tag. The form uses the "mailto" action pointing to the e-mail address *pcg_business@parkcitygazette. com*. The text of the mail message is encoded using text/plain. Note that your instructor may provide you with a different e-mail address, since this is a fictional address and cannot be tested.

3. Type the closing form tag directly before the closing </body> tag.

4. Scroll through the document to locate the "Subscription Plan Option buttons" comment tag. Insert the following four option buttons directly below this comment tag:
   - 6 mo./$24
   - 12 mo./$45
   - 18 mo./$64
   - 24 mo./$80 (best value)

   The field name for the four option buttons is "splan", and the button values are "6", "12", "18", and "24", respectively. Enclose the option buttons in a group box, but do not specify a legend for the group box. You do not need to include an id attribute for these fields.

5. Below the "Name Field" comment tag, insert an input box 50 characters wide. The name and id of the field is "name". Change the text of the preceding table cell "Name:" to a label that is connected to the "name" field.

6. Create a text area box 6 rows high and 40 columns wide below the "Address Field" comment tag. The name and id of the control element is "address". Change the text of the preceding cell "Mailing Address:" to a label connected to the "address" field.

7. Create a check box with a name and id of "cardcb" below the "Card Checkbox" comment tag. The purpose of this check box is to verify that customers wish to pay for the subscription online. Make the check box selected by default, and change the text that follows the check box to a label connected to the "cardcb" field.

8. Create a selection list with the following options: American Express, Discover Card, MasterCard, and Visa below the "Credit Card List Box" comment tag. Assign this selection list the field name "ccard", and make the values of the four options "ae", "dis", "mc", and "vis", respectively. Set the size of the list box to "4".

9. Create an input box for the cardname field with a width of 50 characters below the "cardname field" comment tag. Change the text of the preceding cell "Name on Card:" to a field label.

10. Create an input box for users to enter their credit card numbers, and name the field "cardnum". Set the width of the field to 50 characters. It is important that users' credit card numbers are not displayed on the screen as they are entered. Change the text of the preceding cell "Card Number:" to a label for the cardnum field.

11. Create a list for the months and years of the expiration dates below the "expmonth list box" and "expyear list box" comment tags. Name the two fields "expmonth" and "expyear". The selection lists should display the values "01" though "12" and "2006" through "2012", respectively.

12. Create submit and reset buttons below the comment tag "form buttons". The submit button should display the text "Subscribe". The reset button should display the text "Cancel".

13. Save your changes to the file.

14. Open subscrib.htm in your Web browser and verify that all of the controls are working properly. If you were provided with a real e-mail address to use, complete the form and submit the form to the address.

15. Submit your completed Web page to your instructor.

Explore

Broaden your knowledge of forms by creating an online form with tab index values and access keys.

Case Problem 2

Data files needed for this Case Problem: back.jpg, fflogo.jpg, ordertxt.htm

The Fitness Factory   The Fitness Factory is a new online store that specializes in exercise equipment. Carl Evans is the sales director for the company, and he has asked for your help in developing a customer order form that has the following elements:

- billing address
- shipping address
- credit card information

Carl wants you to include a check box that allows customers to choose to have their order mailed to the billing address, which is what most customers want. He also wants the form to have three buttons: one to return the customer to a page listing the items in their shopping cart, another to submit their order, and a third to reset the order form. You are not responsible for programming any of these buttons; Carl has assigned that job to a Web page programmer who will write the CGI scripts for you.

Carl also wants you to control how the tab key navigates through the form. He would like the shipping address field to be skipped initially in the tabbing order, so that users will go from the billing address fields directly to the payment information fields.

The layout and most of the text for the Web page have been created for you. Your job is to create the required control elements and fields.

A preview of the page you'll create for Carl is shown in Figure 6-46.

Figure 6-46

To create the order form:

1. Using your text editor, open **ordertxt.htm** located in the tutorial.06/case2 folder. Enter *your name* and *the date* in the head section of the document and save the file as **order.htm**.

2. Directly after the <body> tag, create a form with the name "order_form". You do not need to specify any actions or methods for this form. Insert the closing form tag directly before the closing </body> tag located at the bottom of the file.

Explore

3. Locate the "Billing Address Fields" comment and insert tags below this comment to create a group box with the legend "Billing Address". Align the legend with the right side of the group box. The group box extends to the comment "End of Billing Address Fields" located further down in the file.

Explore

4. After the "bname field" comment, insert an input box that has 40 characters. Name the text "bname" and assign it a tabindex value of "1".

5. Insert a text area box named "bstreet" after the "bstreet field" comment tag. The text area box has 3 rows and 40 columns. Give the field a tabindex value of "2".

6. Insert an input box named "bcity" after the "bcity field" comment tag. Set the size of the input box to 40 characters and give it a tabindex value of "3".

7. Insert input boxes named "bstate" and "bzip" after the appropriate comment tags in the document. Set the size of the input boxes to 30 and 10 characters, respectively, and assign the input boxes tabindex values of "4" and "5". Add a 40-character-wide input box named "bcountry" after the "bcountry field" comment. Set the default value of the bcountry field to "United States". Give this element a tabindex value of "6".

8. Insert a check box with the name "shipcb" after the "shipcb field" comment tag. Set the value of the field to "yes" and the tabindex value to "7". Add the text, "Ship to Billing Address" to the right of the check box.

9. Apply the same layout to the shipping address fields that you did for the billing address fields, except do not specify any tabindex values for these fields, and modify the field names to match the comments tags. The legend text of the group box surrounding these fields is "Shipping Address Fields" and is aligned with the right side of the group box.

10. Directly below the "Payment Information Fields" comment tag, create a group box with the legend "Payment Information" aligned with the right edge of the box. The group box extends to the comment tag "End of Payment Information Fields".

Explore

11. Create four option buttons on separate lines for the ccard field directly below the "ccard field" comment tag. The value of the first option button is "ae" and is accompanied by the text "American Express" with the letter "A" underlined. The option button has the tabindex value "8" and uses the accesskey "a". The remaining three option buttons have values of "dis", "mc", and "vis" accompanied by the text "Discover", "MasterCard", and "Visa". The tabindex values for the three option buttons range from "9" to "11". The access keys for the three option buttons are "d", "m", and "v".

12. Create an input box 40 characters wide named "cname" directly below the comment tag "cname field". Set the tabindex to "12".

Explore

13. Create a password field named "cnumber" that is 20 characters wide directly below the comment tag "cnumber field". Set the tabindex value to "13". This field contains the user's credit card number, and Carl wants to ensure that that information is not displayed on the monitor as it is entered.

14. Create a selection list named "expmonth" that contains the range of numbers from "01" to "12" directly below the "expmonth field" comment tag. This selection list is used by Carl to obtain expiration date information. The tab index for this field is set to "14".

15. Create a selection list for the year the user's credit card expires directly below the "expyear field" comment tag. The values for the expyear field range from "2006" to "2012". Set the tabindex value to "15".

16. Create three form buttons directly below the comment tag "form buttons". The first button is a simple command button with the value "Return to Shopping Cart". The second button is a submit button with the value "Submit Order". The third button is a reset button with the value "Reset Order". The tabindex values for the three buttons are 16 through 18.

17. Save your changes to the file.

Explore

18. Using your Web browser, open order.htm. Test the tabbing order in the form. Verify that the shipping address fields are skipped over when you tab. Test the operation of the access keys by pressing Alt+a, Alt+d, Alt+m, and Alt+v to select the American Express, Discover, MasterCard, and Visa option buttons, respectively. Note that Macintosh users need to use the command key instead of the Alt key. (Note that some browsers do not support access keys).

19. Submit the completed Web page to your instructor.

Explore

Design a form using styles for a travel expense report.

Case Problem 3

Data files needed for this Case Problem: delong.jpg, dltxt.htm

DeLong Enterprises, Inc. DeLong Enterprises, a manufacturer of computer components, is establishing a corporate intranet to put news and information online for their employees. One item that Dolores Crandall, a payroll manager, would like to put online is a travel expense form. Dolores has asked you for help with this project.

The travel expense form requires a DeLong employee to provide information about a business trip, and to itemize various travel deductions. A preview of the form you'll create is shown in Figure 6-47.

Figure 6-47

To create the travel expense form:

1. Using your text editor, open **dltxt.htm** from the tutorial.06/case3 folder. Enter *your name* and *the date* in the head section of the document and save the file as **delong. htm**.

2. Enclose the entire contents of the page within a form element named "travel".

3. Insert input boxes for the first and last name of employees in item 1 of the form. Assign these fields the names "first" and "last". Set the size of both input boxes to 15 characters.

4. Create a password input box for the Social Security number in item 2 of the form. Set the width and maximum length of the input box to 9 characters and name the field "ssnum".

Explore

5. Create a list box for the list of departments in item 3. Insert the following options into the list box:
   - Accounting
   - Advertising
   - Consumer Relations
   - Sales
   - Management
   - Payroll
   - Quality Control
   - R&D

   Set "dept" as the field name for the list box, and display four items in the list box at a time.

6. Create a text area field for the trip description in item 4. The text area field is 4 rows high and 50 columns wide. Set "desc" as the field name. Define "Enter description here (required)." as the default text.

7. In item 5, add four new rows to the table, with each containing the following fields and attributes:
   - In the row's first column, insert an input box with the field name "date" and a size of 10 characters. Specify "mm/dd/yyyy" as the default text.
   - In the row's second column, insert an input box 40 characters long with the field name "description".
   - In the row's third column, insert a selection list with the field name "category" and include the following options in the list: Meals, Miscellaneous, Registration, and Transportation.
   - In the row's fourth column, insert an input box named "amount" 6 characters wide.

8. Create a pair of option buttons for item #6. Name both fields "receipt". Assign the first option button the value "yes" and the second button the value "no". Insert the text "YES" next to the first option button and the text "NO" next to the second button.

9. Below item #6, insert two form buttons. The first button is a submit button with the value "Submit travel expenses." The second button is a reset button with the default value "Reset".

Explore

10. Add inline styles to each control element (except the two form buttons) to display the content of those elements in a white font on a background color of (255, 142, 0).

Explore

11. Design the form so that it sends a plain text e-mail message to the e-mail address "dcrandall@delongent.com". Note that your instructor may provide you with a different e-mail address, since this is a fictional address.

12. Save your changes to the file.

13. Submit your completed Web page to your instructor.

Create

Test your knowledge of forms by creating an order form for an online computer store.

Case Problem 4

Data files needed for this Case Problem: none

Millennium Computers   You are employed at Millennium Computers, a discount mail-order company specializing in computers and computer components. You've been asked by your supervisor, Sandy Walton, to create an order form Web page so that customers can purchase products online. Your order form is for computer purchases only. There are several options for customers to consider when purchasing computers from Millennium:

- Processor speed: 2.5 GHz, 3.3 GHz, 4.0 GHz, or 5.5 GHz
- Memory: 128 MB, 256 MB, 512 MB, or 1024 MB
- Drive size: 60 GB, 80 GB, or 120 GB
- Monitor size: 15-inch, 17-inch, 19-inch, or 21-inch
- CD-ROM: 24x, 32x, 48x, 64x, or 72x
- DVD player: yes/no
- CD burner: yes/no
- DVD burner: yes/no
- LAN card: yes/no
- Internal 56K modem: yes/no

Create Sandy's order form using the following guidelines. The design of the Web page is up to you:

1. Create input boxes for the customer's first and last name, phone number, credit card number, and credit card expiration date. Make sure the credit card information does not display on the screen.

2. Using selection boxes or option buttons, create fields in the form for the different component options.

3. Insert a check box allowing the customer to choose to be placed on the Millennium Computers mailing list.

4. Place three buttons on the form: a Submit button to send the order, a Reset button to reset the page, and a second Submit button to request that a Millennium Computers representative call the customer. Use the values "Send", "Cancel", and "Call Me" for the three buttons.

5. Name the form "c_order", submit the form using the "post" method, and set up the form to use the CGI script located at *http://www.mill_computers.com/cgmailer.cgi*. Note that this is a fictional URL.

6. Save your changes and save the file as **computer.htm** in the tutorial.06/case4 folder.

7. Submit the completed Web page to your instructor.

Quick Check Answers

Session 6.1

1. A CGI script is a program running on a Web server that receives data from a form and uses it to perform a series of tasks.

2. `<form id="order_form" name="order_form">` . . . `</form>`

3. `<input name="Phone" id="Phone" />`

4. `<input name="Phone" id="Phone" size="10" />`

5. `<input name="Phone" id="Phone" size="10" maxlength="10" />`

6. `<input name="Subscribe" id="Subscribe" value="yes" />`

7. Set the value of the type attribute to "password".

8. `<label for="dob">Date of Birth</label>`

Session 6.2

1.
```
<select name="State" id="State">
      <option>California</option>
      <option>Nevada</option>
      <option>Oregon</option>
      <option>Washington</option>
</select>
```

2. Add the attribute multiple="multiple" to the select element.

3. `<option selected="selected">Oregon</option>`

4. Place the options within a two-sided optgroup element with the label attribute value "West Coast".

5.
```
<fieldset>
      <legend>West Coast</legend>
      <input type="radio" name="State" value="California"
/>California
      <input type="radio" name="State" value="Nevada" />Nevada
      <input type="radio" name="State" value="Oregon" />Oregon
      <input type="radio" name="State" value="Washington"
/>Washington
</fieldset>
```

6.
```
<input type="radio" name="State" value="1" />California
<input type="radio" name="State" value="2" />Nevada
<input type="radio" name="State" value="3" />Oregon
<input type="radio" name="State" value="4" />Washington
```

7. `<input type="checkbox" name="California" id="California" />`

8. `<textarea rows="5" cols="30" name="Memo" id="Memo">Enter notes here.</textarea>`

9. wrap="hard"

Session 6.3

1. `<input type="submit" value="Send Form" />`

2. `<input type="reset" value="Cancel Form" />`

3. `<input type="img" name="Sites" src="sites.gif" value="GotoPage" />`

4. `<input type="hidden" name="Subject" id="Subject" value="Form Responses" />`

5. `<form method="get" action="http://www.j_davis.com/cgi-bin/post-query">` . . . `</form>`

6. `<form method="post" action="mailto:walker@j_davis.com" enctype="text/plain">` . . . `</form>`

7. accesskey="n"

Objectives

Session 7.1
- Learn the history and theory of cascading style sheets
- Create inline, embedded, and external styles
- Understand style precedence and inheritance
- Work with style selectors

Session 7.2
- Work with element ids and classes
- Work with the properties of block-level elements
- Float a block-level element
- Set a display style
- Work with margins, padding, and border styles
- Use pseudo-elements and pseudo-classes
- Apply a style to a Web site

Session 7.3
- Work with positioning styles
- Manage content overflow
- Create style sheets for different media
- Work with print styles

Working with Cascading Style Sheets

Creating a Style for Online Scrapbooks

Case

Online Scrapbooks

Scrapbooking is the popular hobby of creating albums containing photos, memorabilia, writing, and other embellishments. The primary purpose of scrapbooking is to preserve memories in visually pleasing designs and layouts. This hobby has become a multimillion-dollar industry with companies that specialize in scrapbooking supplies and support. One of these companies is Online Scrapbooks.

Kathy Pridham leads the Web development team at Online Scrapbooks. She has asked you to design a new style for the company's Web site. You'll start by laying out the page for new hobbyists, which describes how to get started in scrapbooking. Because the Web site will eventually contain a large number of pages, Kathy wants to be able to easily adapt your design to the entire site. For this reason, she wants you to use cascading style sheets to implement the design.

Student Data Files

▼**Tutorial.07**

  ▽ **Tutorial folder**

    starttxt.htm
    glosstxt.htm
    samptxt.htm
    +1 demo page
    + 3 graphic files

  ▽ **Review folder**

    galltxt.htm
    + 5 graphic files

  ▽ **Case1 folder**

    h01txt.htm–h18txt.htm
    + 22 graphic files

Student Data Files	▼Tutorial.07 (continued)		
	▽ Case2 folder	▽ Case3 folder	▽ Case4 folder
	jantxt.htm febtxt.htm martxt.htm + 2 graphic files	longstxt.htm + 11 graphic files	bizet.jpg, bizetbio.txt, bizetlist.txt, mozart.jpg, mozartbio.txt, mozartlist.txt, puccini.jpg, puccinibio.txt, puccinilist.txt, verdi.jpg, verdibio.txt, verdilist.txt, wagner.jpg wagnerbio.txt, wagnerlist.txt

Session 7.1

Introducing Cascading Style Sheets

This tutorial explores how to format the appearance of a Web page. Four factors determine how an HTML or XHTML document is rendered for an end user. The first factor is the output media. While it's easy to think of HTML and XHTML in terms of Web pages displayed on computer screens, those same pages must be compatible with a wide variety of media, from computer screens and printers to aural and Braille devices. Thus, a text-based browser, a graphical browser, and an aural device would each render a given HTML or XHTML document differently.

The second factor is the browser itself. Each browser has default settings for rendering different page elements. Thus, Netscape Navigator or Internet Explorer or Opera can display the same page with some subtle and not-so-subtle differences. A user's operating system itself can also influence the appearance of a document. For example, a sans-serif font on a Windows machine might look very different from the same font rendered on a Macintosh.

The user is the third factor in determining how a document is displayed. Most browsers allow individuals to override the browser's default settings, inserting their own settings for various page elements. This feature is especially beneficial for users with visual disabilities because it allows them, for example, to apply a larger font size to page text, or to apply greater contrast between the text and background colors.

The final factor in determining how a page is displayed is the code of the document itself. Because XHTML and HTML were primarily designed for structuring documents, many Web designers believe that these languages should contain no elements that define how documents should be rendered, and that this task should instead be left to other languages. Separating document content from document display is more easily said than done, however. In the early years of HTML, presentational features were added to the language to allow Web page authors to define how to render pages for users. Although this aspect of HTML and XHTML made it easier for Web authors to create visually pleasing documents, it also changed the nature of HTML from a language that simply described document structure and content. As noted in Tutorial 1, the latest HTML and XHTML standards are deprecating these presentational features and replacing them with style sheets.

The History of CSS

A **style sheet** is a file or form that describes the layout and appearance of a document. Web designers have advocated style sheets for HTML and XHTML because they separate document presentation from document content. Several style sheet languages exist, but the most commonly used on the Web by far is the **Cascading Style Sheets** language, also known as **CSS**. You've been using CSS since the first tutorial, when you were introduced to the style attribute. While the style attribute is part of the specifications for HTML and XHTML, the text of the attribute value is written in the CSS language.

Like HTML and XHTML, the specifications for CSS are maintained by the World Wide Web Consortium (W3C), and like those languages, several versions of CSS exist with varying levels of browser support. The first version of CSS, called **CSS1**, was introduced in 1996, but was not fully implemented by any browser for another three years. CSS1 introduced styles for the following document features:

- **Fonts**: Setting font size, type, and other properties
- **Text**: Controlling text alignment and applying decorative elements such as underlining, italics, and capitalization to text
- **Color**: Specifying background and foreground colors of different page elements
- **Backgrounds**: Setting and tiling background images for any element
- **Block-level Elements**: Controlling margins and borders around blocks, setting the padding space within a block, and floating block-level elements on a page like inline images

You've already worked with the font, text, color, and background styles in the previous tutorials. You'll learn how to use CSS to work with block-level elements later in this tutorial.

The second version of CSS, **CSS2**, was introduced in 1998. It expanded the language to support styles for:

- **Positioning**: Placing elements at specific coordinates on a page
- **Visual Formatting**: Clipping and hiding element content
- **Media Types**: Creating styles for different output devices, including printed media and aural devices
- **Interfaces**: Controlling the appearance and behavior of system features such as scrollbars and mouse cursors

Currently, browser support for CSS2 is mixed. Most of the styles for positioning and visual formatting are supported, but many of the other CSS2 styles are not. An update to CSS2, **CSS2.1**, was introduced by the W3C in April 2002. Although the update did not add any new features to the language, it cleaned up some minor errors that were introduced in the original specification.

Even though browsers are still trying to catch up to all of the features of CSS2, the W3C has pressed forward to the next version, **CSS3**. Still in development as of this writing, CSS3 is being designed in individual modules. This approach should make it easier for Web browser developers to create products that support only those parts of CSS that are relevant to their products. For example, an aural browser might not need to support the CSS styles associated with printed media, so the browser's developers would need to concentrate only on the CSS3 modules that deal with aural properties. This CSS revision promises to make browser development easier, and the resulting browser products more efficient and compact in size. CSS3 will also expand the range of styles supported by the language, adding styles for

- **User Interfaces**: Adding dynamic and interactive features
- **Accessibility**: Supporting users with disabilities and other special needs
- **Columnar layout**: Giving Web authors more page layout options
- **International Features**: Providing support for a wide variety of languages and typefaces
- **Mobile Devices**: Supporting the device requirements of PDAs and cell phones
- **Scalable Vector Graphics**: Making it easier for Web authors to add graphic elements to their Web pages

As with HTML and XHTML, the usefulness of these features depends on the support of the browser community. Because CSS2 is still not completely supported, it is unclear how long it will take after the W3C releases the final specification for CSS3 styles to be adopted. In addition, individual browsers have introduced their own extensions to CSS. For example, Internet Explorer has introduced styles to format inline images and to add slideshow effects to Web pages. Thus, a Web page designer needs to be aware of compatibility issues not just between different versions of CSS, but also among different versions of each browser.

Applying a Style Sheet

There are three ways of applying a style to an HTML or XHTML document:

- **Inline Styles**: A style is applied to a specific element through the use of the style attribute in the element's tag.
- **Embedded Styles**: A style sheet is placed in a document's head, setting the style definitions for the document's elements.
- **External Styles**: A style sheet is saved in a separate document and is applied to a group of pages in a Web site.

Each approach has its own advantages and disadvantages, and you'll probably use some combination of all three in developing your Web sites.

Using Inline Styles

Because you've already been using inline styles since Tutorial 1, we'll just briefly recap the topic here. An inline style is applied to an element using the following syntax in the element's markup tag:

```
<element style="style1: value1; style2: value2; style3: value3; ...">
```

where *element* is the name of the element, *style1*, *style2*, *style3*, and so forth are the names of the styles, and *value1*, *value2*, *value3*, and so on are the values associated with each style. If we want browsers to display an h1 heading in a sans-serif font, for example, we could use the following inline style:

```
<h1 style="font-family: sans-serif">Online Scrapbooks</h1>
```

Inline styles are easy to use and interpret because they are applied directly to the elements they affect. However there are also some problems with their use. First, an inline style applies only to the specific element that it modifies. Using inline styles, if you wanted all of your headings to be rendered in a sans-serif font, you would have to locate all of the h1 through h6 tags in the Web site and apply the same font-family style to them. This would be no small task in a large Web site containing hundreds of headings spread out among dozens of Web pages.

In addition, some developers don't feel that inline styles are consistent with the goal of separating content from style. After all, there is arguably little difference between using the inline style

```
<h1 style="text-align: right"> ... </h1>
```

and the deprecated attribute

```
<h1 align="right"> ... </h1>
```

One goal of style sheets is to separate the development of a document's style from the development of its content, to the point where one Web team could work on content and another on design. Inline styles, however, are arguably too interwoven with content for this separation to occur.

Using Embedded Styles

The power of style sheets becomes evident when you move style definitions away from document content. One way of doing this is to embed style definitions in the document head using the form

```
<style>
   style declarations
</style>
```

where *style declarations* are the declarations of the different styles to be applied to the document. Each style declaration has the syntax

selector {*style1*: *value1*; *style2*: *value2*; *style3*; *value3*; ...}

where *selector* identifies an element or elements within the document, and the *style*: *value* pairs follow the same syntax that you've been using to apply inline styles to elements. For example, to render h1 headings in the document in a sans-serif font, you could insert the following style declaration in the document's head:

```
<style>
   h1 {font-family: sans-serif}
</style>
```

In this case every h1 element in the document will be displayed in a sans-serif font, making it unnecessary to insert a separate inline style for each heading.

Style Attributes

The style element supports several attributes, which use the following syntax:

```
<style type="mime_type" media="media_type" title="text" id="text">
   style declarations
</style>
```

The type attribute specifies the MIME type of the style sheet language, the media attribute specifies the device used to render the document, and the title and id attributes provide a label for the style sheet that can be used in programming. MIME types are a system for indicating document formats. For CSS, the MIME type is "text/css". The media, title, and id attributes are all optional. If you don't specify a value for the media attribute, the style sheet is applied to all output media. So long as you are not directing your page to a specific type of output device, you do not need to include the media attribute. We'll look at media values and explore how to create styles for specific media in the third session of this tutorial.

Creating an Embedded Style Sheet

- To create an embedded style sheet, enter the following tags within the document's head element:

```
<style type="mime_type" media="media_type" title="text" id="text">
    style declarations
</style>
```

where the type attribute specifies the MIME type of the style sheet language, the media attribute specifies the output type, the title and id attributes provide labels for the style sheet, and `style declarations` are the individual style declarations applied to elements in the document. For CSS style sheets, use a type value of "text/css". The default media value is "all", which applies the style sheet to all output media.

Applying an Embedded Style

Now that we've looked at how to create an embedded style, we'll create one for a page from the Online Scrapbooks Web site. Kathy has created the content for the Getting Started page shown in Figure 7-1.

Figure 7-1 | **Initial Getting Started page**

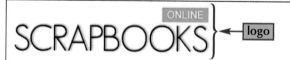

- The company logo
- A list of links
- The main text of the page
- The company address

The logo, list of links, and address will be repeated on each page of the Web site. The main text will vary from page to page. At this point Kathy has intentionally not applied any styles to the page. The page contains only content, which you'll format by adding styles. You'll start by creating an embedded style to display the h1 heading in an orange sans-serif font.

To create the embedded style:

1. Use your text editor to open **starttxt.htm** from the tutorial.07/tutorial folder. Enter *your name* and *the date* in the comment section and save the file as **start.htm**.

2. Directly before the closing </head> tag insert the following code as shown in Figure 7-2:

```
<style type="text/css">
    h1 {font-family: sans-serif; color: orange}
</style>
```

Creating an embedded style ◄ **Figure 7-2**

```
<title>Getting Started</title>
<style type="text/css">
    h1 {font-family: sans-serif; color: orange}
</style>
</head>
```

3. Save your changes to the file.

4. Open **start.htm** in your Web browser. Figure 7-3 shows the current appearance of the file. Note that the Getting Started heading is displayed in an orange sans-serif font.

H1 heading in an orange sans-serif font ◄ **Figure 7-3**

SCRAPBOOKS ONLINE

Home Getting Started Scrapbooking Tips Supply List Glossary Online Classes Sample Pages Online Store Shopping Cart Checkout Your Account Order Status Wish List Customer Service About Us Newsletter FAQ Contact Us

Getting Started

Scrapbooking is the practice of combining photos, memorabilia and stories in an album, preserving memories for future generations. In recent years scrapbooking has become a $300 million dollar industry as the public has discovered the joys of creating albums for families and friends. **Online Scrapbooks** is there to help you with all of the your scrapbooking needs.

Trouble? Depending on your browser and operating system, the sans-serif font may look different from that shown in Figure 7-3.

Using an External Style Sheet

The embedded style sheet you created only applies to the content of the start.htm file. If you want all h1 headings in the Web site to appear in an orange sans-serif font, you can place the style declaration in an external style sheet. An external style sheet is a simple text file, like an HTML or XHTML document, that contains style declarations. The file can then be linked to any page in the Web site, allowing the same style declaration to be applied to the entire site. The filename extension indicates the language of the style sheet. The extension for CSS style sheets is .css.

Create an external style sheet for the Online Scrapbooks Web site, storing the style declarations in a file named scraps.css. You'll use the same style declaration you placed in the embedded style sheet to display h1 headings in an orange sans-serif font, and you'll add a new style that formats the appearance of address text.

To create the scraps.css external style sheet:

1. Use your text editor to create a new document.

2. Insert the following lines into the file (see Figure 7-4):

   ```
   h1 {font-family: sans-serif; color: orange}
   address {color: orange; font-style: normal; font-variant: small-
           caps; text-align: center}
   ```

Figure 7-4	Creating an external style sheet

```
h1 {font-family: sans-serif; color: orange}
address {color: orange; font-style: normal; font-variant: small-caps;
        text-align: center}
```

3. Save the file as **scraps.css** in the tutorial.07/tutorial folder. Note that you must save the file as a text file.

Adding Style Comments

As you develop an external style sheet, you may want to add comments that describe the purpose and use of the sheet. This is particularly useful in Web sites that contain several style sheet files. You create comments in style sheets using the syntax

```
/* comment */
```

where *comment* is the text of the comment. Next you will add a comment to the scraps.css file that you just created.

To create a style sheet comment:

1. Insert the following text as a new line at the top of the scraps.css file (see Figure 7-5):

   ```
   /* Online Scrapbooks screen styles */
   ```

Adding a style comment ◄ **Figure 7-5**

```
/* online Scrapbooks screen styles */
h1 {font-family: sans-serif; color: orange}
address {color: orange; font-style: normal; font-variant: small-caps;
        text-align: center}
```

2. Save your changes to the file.

Note that style comments can also be added to embedded styles. Comment lines must be placed between the opening and closing <style> tags.

Linking to an External Style Sheet

To link a Web page to an external style sheet, you use the link element. Recall that the link element was first introduced in Tutorial 2 as a way of specifying general links for a Web page. The link element is most often used to link to style sheets, however. To create a link to an external style sheet, add the following tag to the head element on of the Web document:

```
<link href="url" rel="stylesheet" type="mime_type" media="media type"
id="text"title="text" />
```

where `url` is the URL of the external style sheet, and the remaining attributes have the same meanings as they did for an embedded style sheet. For example, to link a Web page to style sheet named "styles.css" written in the CSS style sheet language, you would enter the following tag:

```
<link href="styles.css" rel="stylesheet" type="text/css" />
```

Add a link element to the start.htm file that links to the scraps.css style sheet.

To link to the scraps.css style sheet:

1. Return to the **start.htm** file in your text editor.

2. Delete the style declaration between the opening and closing <style> tags. Do not remove the opening and closing <style> tags, however, because you'll be using them later.

3. Directly before the opening <style> tag, insert the following link element (see Figure 7-6):

   ```
   <link href="scraps.css" rel="stylesheet" type="text/css" />
   ```

Figure 7-6

Linking to an external style sheet

```
<title>Getting Started</title>
<link href="scraps.css" rel="stylesheet" type="text/css" />
<style type="text/css">
</style>
</head>
```

previous declarations removed from the embedded style sheet

4. Save your changes to the file.

5. Reload **start.htm** in your browser and verify that the heading still appears in an orange sans-serif font and that the address text at the bottom of the page has been formatted as shown in Figure 7-7.

Figure 7-7

Formatted company address

Your albums should contain page protectors to shield the pages from smudges, oil, and dirt that can be transferred from your hands. You should never use albums that use sticky magnetic pages. The sticky substance will be transferred to the photo and backing paper causing deterioration. Never crop Polaroid® photos (they will curl and fall apart). Mount all memorabilia on acid-free cardstock paper and photocopy all newspaper clippings on acid-free paper.

ONLINE SCRAPBOOKS • 212 SUNSET DRIVE • CUTLER, KY 83215 • 1 (800) 555-8100

Importing a Style Sheet

Another way to access an external style sheet is to import the content of one style sheet into another. To import a style sheet, add the following statement to either an embedded or an external style sheet:

```
@import url(url);
```

where url is the URL of the external stylesheet file. For example, the following embedded style sheet imports the content of the scraps.css file into the document.

```
<style type="text/css">
   @import(scraps.css);
</style>
```

The @import statement must always come before any other style declarations in the embedded or external style sheet. There is no limit to the number of @import statements that can be added to the style sheet. Although @import and the link element do basically the same thing, the link element is recommended because it is better supported by browsers.

Linking to an External Style Sheet

- To link to an external style sheet, enter the following element in the head element of the document:
  ```
  <link href="url" rel="stylesheet" type="mime-type" media="media
  type" id="text" title="text" />
  ```
  where *url* is the URL of the external style sheet, the type attribute specifies the MIME type of the style sheet language used in the file, the media attribute specifies the output media, and the id and title attributes provide a label for the style sheet (used in programming). The media, id, and title attributes are optional. If no media attribute is provided, the style sheet is applied to all output media.
  or
- Add the following statement to the embedded or external style sheet:
  ```
  @import url(url);
  ```
  where *url* is the URL of the external style sheet.

Understanding Cascading Order

Using the link element or the @import statement, you can link a single style sheet to multiple documents in your Web site. This technique allows you to apply a common look and feel to all of a site's documents (see Figure 7-8).

Applying a single style sheet to multiple documents **Figure 7-8**

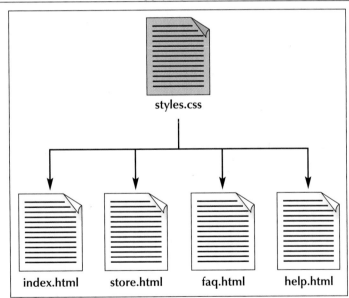

The reverse is also true: you can link a single document to several different style sheets, each containing a different collection of styles to meet specific needs. Figure 7-9 illustrates an example in which one style sheet contains general styles that apply to all pages in the Web site, another style sheet applies to Web documents for a particular department, and a more specific style sheet contains styles for a section within the document. In addition, the document itself can contain its own collection of embedded and inline styles.

Figure 7-9	Applying multiple sheets to a single document

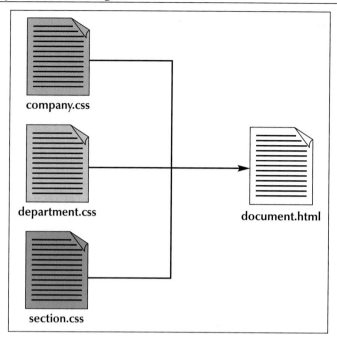

Style Precedence

With so many potential sources of styles for a single document, how does a browser determine what takes precedence when styles conflict? When styles come from several sources, they are weighted as follows (in order of increasing weight):

1. External style sheet
2. Embedded styles
3. Inline styles

Thus, an inline style takes precedence over an embedded style, which has precedence over an external style sheet. If two styles have the same weight, the one declared last has precedence. For example, in the following embedded style:

```
<style type="text/css">
   h1 {color: orange; font-family: sans-serif}
   h1 {color: blue; font-family: serif}
</style>
```

the blue serif style will be applied to the h1 heading because it is declared last, overriding the orange sans-serif style.

You can override the precedence rules by adding the !important property to a style declaration. The style sheet

```
<style type="text/css">
   h1 {color: orange !important; font-family: sans-serif}
   h1 {color: blue; font-family: serif}
</style>
```

would result in h1 headings being rendered in a orange serif font, because the orange style is given a higher weight than the blue style and the serif style appears after the sans-serif style. The !important property is useful in situations where you want to ensure that a particular style is always enforced no matter what its location in the order of precedence.

Note that any styles you specify can still be overridden by users who set up their own style sheets for use with their browsers. For example, the Accessibility dialog box in Internet Explorer (shown in Figure 7-10) is often used by people with disabilities to set up style sheets that meet specific needs (such as text being displayed in large fonts with highly contrasting colors). The styles in these sheets take precedence over a browser's default styles, as well as over the styles specified by a Web page author. Thus, you should make sure that your Web pages are still readable even when your style sheets are not adopted by the user. The ability to view your page's content should not depend on the ability to access your style sheet.

Accessibility dialog box in Internet Explorer ◀ **Figure 7-10**

user's style sheet overrides the Web author's styles

Style Inheritance

If a style is not specified for an element, it inherits the style of its parent element. This effect, known as **style inheritance**, causes style declarations to cascade down through a document's hierarchy. For example, if you want to set the text color of every element on a page to blue, you could use the declaration

```
body {color: blue}
```

Every element within the body element (which is to say every element on the page) would inherit this style. To override style inheritance, you specify an alternate style for one of the descendant elements of the parent. The styles

```
body {color: blue}
p {color: red}
```

would change the text color to blue for every element on the page except for paragraphs and for any element contained within a paragraph. You can also override style inheritance by using the !important property as you do for style precedence.

Working with Selectors

So far we've discussed only styles in which the selector is a single element in the document. However, CSS also allows you to work with a wide variety of selectors to match different combinations of elements. For example, if you want to apply the same style to a collection of elements, you can group them by entering the elements in a comma-separated list. This feature allows you to replace a set of repetitive declarations, such as

```
h1 {font-family: sans-serif}
h2 {font-family: sans-serif}
h3 {font-family: sans-serif}
h4 {font-family: sans-serif}
h5 {font-family: sans-serif}
h6 {font-family: sans-serif}
```

with a single declaration:

```
h1, h2, h3, h4, h5, h6 {font-family: sans-serif}
```

You can also combine grouped and ungrouped selectors. In the following example, the h1 headings are displayed in a red sans-serif font, while the h2 headings are displayed in a blue sans-serif font:

```
h1, h2 {font-family: sans-serif}
h1 {color: red}
h2 {color: blue}
```

Placing common styles in a single declaration is useful for simplifying your style sheet.

Contextual Selectors

The following style causes all boldfaced text to appear in a blue font:

```
b {color: blue}
```

However, if you only wanted to apply this style to boldfaced text within lists, you would need a way of applying a style based on the context in which an element is used. This is the purpose of **contextual selectors**. For example, to apply a style to an element only when it is contained in, or *descended from*, another element, you would use the form

```
parent descendant {styles}
```

where *parent* is the parent element, *descendant* is a descendant of the parent, and *styles* are the styles to be applied to the descendant element. Thus, to apply a blue color only to boldfaced text found in lists, you would use the style

```
li b {color: blue}
```

In this case, li is the parent element and b is the descendant element. Any boldfaced text not contained in a list item is not affected by this style. Note that the descendant element does not have to be a direct child of the parent element. In the code

```
<li><span><b>Special</b> Orders</span> this month!</li>
```

the boldfaced text is a descendant of the list item, but it is a direct child of the span element.

Contextual selectors can also be grouped with other selectors. For example, the following style applies a blue font to h2 headings and to boldfaced list items, but nowhere else:

```
li b, h2 {color: blue}
```

The parent/descendant form is only one example of a contextual selector. Figure 7-11 shows some of the other contextual forms supported by CSS.

Simple and contextual selectors   **Figure 7-11**

Selector	Matches
*	Any element in the hierarchy
e	The specified element in the hierarchy, where e is the specified element
e1, e2, e3, ...	The group of elements e1, e2, e3, ...
e f	The element f when it is a descendant of the element e
e > f	The element f when it is a direct child of the element e
e + f	The element f when it is immediately preceded by the sibling element e

To illustrate just how versatile these patterns can be, Figure 7-12 shows six selector patterns applied to the same document tree. Selected elements are highlighted in red for each pattern. Remember that because of style inheritance, any style applied to an element is passed down the document tree.

Examples of selector patterns   **Figure 7-12**

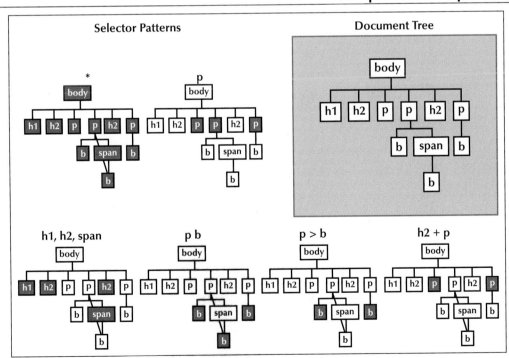

Although the contextual selectors listed in Figure 7-11 are part of the specifications for CSS2, they may not be well supported by many browsers. In particular, the e > f and e+f contextual selectors should be used with caution.

Attribute Selectors

On occasion you might also need to select elements based on their attribute values. For example, if you want to display link text in a blue font, you might use the following declaration:

```
a {color: blue}
```

However, this declaration makes no distinction between <a> tags used to mark links and <a> tags used to mark document anchors (for a discussion of anchors, see Tutorial 2). HTML makes this distinction based on the presence or absence of the href attribute. To select an element based on the element's attributes you can create an **attribute selector**, which has the form

```
element[att] {styles}
```

This declaration selects all elements named `element` that contain an attribute named `att` and applies the `styles` in the list to them. Thus, to apply a blue font to link text, you could use the declaration

```
a[href] {color: blue}
```

Any <a> tag used to mark anchors would not contain the href attribute, and thus would not be affected by this style. Figure 7-13 describes some of the other attribute selectors supported by CSS.

Figure 7-13 **Attribute selectors**

Selector	Description	Example	Matches
[att]	The element contains the *att* attribute	a[href]	a elements containing the href attribute
[att="val"]	The element's *att* attribute equals *val*	a[href="gloss.htm"]	a elements whose href attribute equals "gloss.htm"
[att~="val"]	The element's *att* attribute value is a space-separated list of words, one of which matches *val* exactly	a[rel~="glossary"]	a elements whose rel attribute contains the word "glossary"
[att|="val"]	The element's *att* attribute value is a hyphen-separated list of words beginning with *val*	p[id|="first"]	paragraphs whose id attribute starts with the word "first" in a hyphen-separated list of words
[att^="val"]	The element's *att* attribute begins with *val* (CSS3)	a[rel^="prev"]	a elements whose rel attribute begins with "prev"
[att$="val"]	The element's *att* attribute ends with *val* (CSS3)	a[href$="org"]	a elements whose href attribute ends with "org"
[att*="val"]	The element's *att* attribute contains the value *val* (CSS3)	a[href*="faq"]	a elements whose href attribute contains the text string "faq"

As with contextual selectors, browser support for attribute selectors is mixed. For this reason, you should use attribute selectors with caution. Note that some of the attribute selectors listed in Figure 7-13 are part of the proposed specifications for CSS3 and have very little browser support at the present time.

Applying a Selector Pattern

Now that you've seen how selector patterns can be used to apply styles to a variety of element collections, Kathy suggests that you change the body text color to brown and apply the orange sans-serif font style to all headings in the Online Scrapbooks Web site. You'll add these styles to the scraps.css file.

To create a style for all headings:

1. Return to the **scraps.css** file in your text editor.

2. Insert the following style below the comment line:

   `body {color: brown}`

3. Change the second style to

   `h1, h2, h3, h4, h5, h6 {font-family: sans-serif; color: orange}`

   See Figure 7-14.

Grouping selectors | Figure 7-14

```
/* Online Scrapbooks screen styles */
body {color: brown}
h1, h2, h3, h4, h5, h6 {font-family: sans-serif; color: orange}
address {color: orange; font-style: normal; font-variant: small-caps;
         text-align: center}
```

4. Save your changes to your file.

5. Reload **start.htm** in your browser and verify that all headings are now displayed in an orange sans-serif font and the body text is brown (see Figure 7-15).

| Figure 7-15 | **Headings rendered in an orange sans-serif font** |

Getting Started

Scrapbooking is the practice of combining photos, memorabilia and stories in an album, preserving memories for future generations. In recent years scrapbooking has become a $300 million dollar industry as the public has discovered the joys of creating albums for families and friends. **Online Scrapbooks** is there to help you with all of the your scrapbooking needs.

Basic Materials

- Acid-free paper, card stock, and stickers
- Acid-free pen, markers, and adhesive
- Acid-free emory book album
- Straight and pattern edge scissors
- Photos and photo corners
- Paper punches
- Journalling templates
- Decorative embellishments

Preserving Your Memories

Scrapbook albums have existed since the beginning of photography. However the sad fact is that photographs and most printed material are not permanent and will fade and yellow with age. Scrapbookers of today are aware of these problems and the industry is providing remedies that will allow scrapbook albums that suffer from minimal deterioration. The most important thing is to avoid using materials with high acid content which can cause photos and paper to deteriorate. Another thing to avoid is lignin, a material that is the bonding element in wood fibers. Over time, paper with lignin will become yellow and brittle and thus you should only use lignin-free products.

6. If you intend to take a break before continuing to the next session, you may close your open files.

You've finished adding the first few styles to the Online Scrapbooks Web site and you've learned about the history and theory of Cascading Style Sheets. In the next session, you'll learn other ways of applying style sheets, including how to use them with block-level elements and links.

| Review |

Session 7.1 Quick Check

1. Why are style sheets preferable to presentational attributes?

2. What are inline styles, embedded styles, and external style sheets? Which would you use to create a style for an entire Web site?

3. What attribute would you add to the style element to specify the device used to render the output?

4. What is the style to change the font size of paragraph text to 12 point?

5. What is the style to change the font size of paragraphs, list items, and address elements to 12 point?

6. What is the style to italicize all h2 headings that follow directly after h1 headings?

7. What is the style to change the background color of all checkboxes to ivory?

Session 7.2

Using IDs and Classes

You and Kathy have met to discuss how she would like the pages in the Online Scrapbooks laid out. Kathy prefers a two-column layout in which the list of links is placed in a box on the left margin of the page. Figure 7-16 shows a sketch of Kathy's proposal for the Getting Started page.

Kathy's proposed layout | Figure 7-16

In Kathy's layout the logo is aligned with the right margin of the page. The list of links is set off in a box on the page's left margin. The basic materials list is floated on the page's right margin, and the Getting Started text is displayed in a column in the middle of the page. Kathy also wants borders or dividers separating the various elements on the page.

Working with IDs

Your first step in creating this layout will be to align the Online Scrapbooks company logo with the right page margin. The logo image has been placed within a paragraph at the top of the page. Although you could format this paragraph using an inline style, Kathy wants the paragraph and logo repeated on every page in the site and doesn't want to modify the style on each page. Thus, it would be more efficient to instead add the style to the scraps.css style sheet.

Positioning the logo requires a way of distinguishing the paragraph from the other paragraphs in the document, which you can do by adding an id to the paragraph tag. For example, to identify this paragraph as "head", you could use the code

```
<p id="head"> ... </p>
```

To reference the paragraph in the style sheet, you would then use an id selector, which uses the form

```
#id {styles}
```

where *id* is the id value of an element in the document. For example, to align the content of the head paragraph with the right margin, you would use the style

```
#head {text-align: right}
```

Add this id and style to the HTML document and style sheet.

To create a style for the head paragraph:

1. Reopen the **start.htm** file, if necessary, in your text editor.

2. Add the attribute **id="head"** to the first paragraph of the page, as shown in Figure 7-17.

Figure 7-17 | **Marking a paragraph with an id**

id value

```
<body>
<p id="head"><img src="scraps.jpg" alt="Online Scrapbooks" width="314" height="75" /></p>
<p>
    <a href="index.htm">Home</a>
    <a href="start.htm">Getting Started</a>
    <a href="tips.htm">Scrapbooking Tips</a>
```

3. Save your changes to the file.

4. Reopen the **scraps.css** file, if necessary, in your text editor.

5. Add the following style declaration to the bottom of the file (see Figure 7-18):

```
#head {text-align: right}
```

```
/* online Scrapbooks screen styles */
body {color: brown}
h1, h2, h3, h4, h5, h6 {font-family: sans-serif; color: orange}
address {color: orange; font-style: normal; font-variant: small-caps;
        text-align: center}
#head {text-align: right}
```

id value

6. Save your changes to the file and reopen **start.htm** in your Web browser. Verify that the company logo is now right-aligned.

Working with Classes

Because HTML and XHTML require that each id be unique, a particular id value can be used only once in a document. However, you can mark a group of elements with a common identifier using the class attribute. The syntax of the class attribute is

```
<element class="class"> ... </element>
```

where *class* is a name that identifies the group to which the element belongs. For example, the following list uses the class attribute to indicate which items are fruits and which are vegetables:

```
<ul>
   <li class="fruit">Apples</li>
   <li class="vegetable">Carrots</li>
   <li class="fruit">Grapes</li>
   <li class="vegetable">Lettuce</li>
   <li class="fruit">Melons</li>
   <li class="vegetable">Onions</li>
</ul>
```

Combined with style sheets, classes can be used to apply a common set of styles to every element in a group. The syntax of the class selector is

```
.class {styles}
```

where *class* is the value of the class attribute for the group. As shown in Figure 7-19, you can use the class attribute to apply different colors to the fruits and vegetables in the list above.

Figure 7-19 ▶ **Applying a style to a class**

Classes can be applied to any element, not just those of the same type. In the following code, the same class value is used for both the h1 and the h2 headings:

```
<h1 class="title">Getting Started</h1>
<h2 class="title">with Scrapbooks</h2>
```

Any style applied to the title class is applied to both of these headings. If you want to apply a style to a class of elements of a particular type, include the element name along with the class value using the form

```
element.class {styles}
```

where *element* and *class* are the element and class names, respectively. Figure 7-20 demonstrates how to use the class value along with an element name to format the h1 and h2 headings described above. Note that the sans-serif font is applied to any element of the title class, but the italic font style is only applied to h2 headings in the title class.

Figure 7-20 ▶ **Applying a style to a class and element**

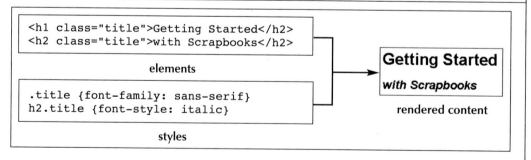

At this point you don't need to use classes in the Online Scrapbooks Web site. However, you'll have a chance to use them later in this session.

Applying Styles to ids and Classes

- To apply styles to an element with an id, use the form
  ```
  #id {styles}
  ```
  where *id* is the value of the id attribute for the element.
- To apply styles to a class of elements, use the form
  ```
  .class {styles}
  ```
  where *class* is the value of the class attribute for the elements.
- To apply styles to a class of elements of a particular type, use the form
  ```
  element.class {styles}
  ```
  where *element* is the name of the element.

Sizing Elements

The next step in designing this page is to lay out its various sections. One option for creating the two-column layout that Kathy wants would be to use tables, as you did in Tutorial 4. However, many Web designers advocate using style sheets instead of tables because style sheets are more flexible, can be applied to multiple documents, are easier to maintain, and usually result in smaller file sizes with more manageable code than tables. One drawback to using style sheets for layout is that styles are not well supported by older browsers; however, this is less of a concern than it once was. The first step in creating a columnar layout with a style sheet is to define the widths of the columns.

Setting the Element Width

Kathy wants you to place the list of links in a 150-pixel-wide column on the left edge of the page. She has already placed the links list in a paragraph element. Like all block-level elements, the default width of a paragraph is equal to the width of its parent element, which is usually the width of the browser window. To set a different width, apply the style

```
width: value
```

where `value` is the element's width expressed in one of the CSS units of measure (for a discussion of the CSS measuring units, see "Working with Fonts and Text Styles" in Tutorial 3). Place the style for the links paragraph in the scraps.css style sheet so that it can be accessed by other pages. You'll assign the paragraph the id "links".

To set the width of the links paragraph:

▶ 1. Return to the **start.htm** file in your text editor and locate the paragraph containing the list of links. Insert the attribute **id="links"** as shown in Figure 7-21.

Figure 7-21 ▶ **Entering the links id**

```
<body>
<p id="head"><img src="scraps.jpg" alt="Online Scrapbooks" width="314" height="75" /></p>
<p id="links">
    <a href="index.htm">Home</a>
    <a href="start.htm">Getting Started</a>
    <a href="tips.htm">Scrapbooking Tips</a>
    <a href="supply.htm">Supply List</a>
    <a href="gloss.htm">Glossary</a>
    <a href="classes.htm">Online Classes</a>
    <a href="samples.htm">Sample Pages</a>
    <a href="store.htm">Online Store</a>
    <a href="cart.htm">Shopping Cart</a>
    <a href="checkout.htm">Checkout</a>
    <a href="account.htm">Your Account</a>
    <a href="status.htm">Order Status</a>
    <a href="wish.htm">Wish List</a>
    <a href="service.htm">Customer Service</a>
    <a href="about.htm">About Us</a>
    <a href="news.htm">Newsletter</a>
    <a href="faq.htm">FAQ</a>
    <a href="contact.htm">Contact Us</a>
</p>
```

▶ **2.** Save your changes to the file.

▶ **3.** Return to the **scraps.css** file in your text editor.

▶ **4.** At the bottom of the file, insert the following style (see Figure 7-22):

   `#links {width: 150px}`

Figure 7-22 ▶ **Inserting the width style**

```
/* Online Scrapbooks screen styles */
body {color: brown}
h1, h2, h3, h4, h5, h6 {font-family: sans-serif; color: orange}
address {color: orange; font-style: normal; font-variant: small-caps;
        text-align: center}
#head {text-align: right}
#links {width: 150px}
```

▶ **5.** Save your changes to the file.

▶ **6.** Reload **start.htm** in your Web browser and verify that the width of the links list has been reduced to 150 pixels.

Setting the Element Height

You can also use CSS to set an element's height. By default, the height of an element is determined by its content; however, to specify a different height, use the style

`height: value`

where `value` is the height of the element. If you set the height smaller than an element's content, browsers ignore the height value by default and expand the element's height to match the content. We'll look at ways of overriding this behavior later in the tutorial. At this point you do not need to set the height of any element in the Web site.

Setting the Size of an Element

- To set the element's width, use the style
    width: *value*
  where *value* is the width of the element in one of the CSS measurement units.
- To set the element's height, use the style
    height: *value*
  where *value* is the height of the element.

Floating an Element

Next you need to float the links paragraph on the left margin of the page. The CSS style to float an element is the same one you used to float inline images in Tutorial 3:

```
float: position
```

where *position* is none, left, right, or inherit.

In addition to floating the paragraph, Kathy wants to change the format of the links within the paragraph to a white 9-point sans-serif font on a dark orange background. She also wants to set the size of the paragraph's right margin to 10 pixels, to provide additional space between the list of links and the page's main content.

To float the links paragraph and format its content:

1. Return to the **scraps.css** file in your text editor.

2. Add the following styles to the #links element.

   ```
   float: left; background-color: rgb(212, 142, 0); margin-right: 10px
   ```

3. Below the #links style declaration, add the following declaration to format the appearance of the links

   ```
   #links a {font-family: sans-serif; color: white; font-size: 9pt}
   ```

   Note that this style declaration uses contextual selector to limit the application to only those links within the paragraph. Links located elsewhere in the page will not be affected. Figure 7-23 shows the revised style sheet.

Setting the float style ◀ **Figure 7-23**

```
/* online Scrapbooks screen styles */
body {color: brown}
h1, h2, h3, h4, h5, h6 {font-family: sans-serif; color: orange}
address {color: orange; font-style: normal; font-variant: small-caps;
         text-align: center}
#head {text-align: right}
#links {width: 150px; float: left; background-color: rgb(212, 142, 0); margin-right: 10px}
#links a {font-family: sans-serif; color: white; font-size: 9pt}
```

4. Save your changes to the file.

5. Reload **start.htm** in your Web browser. Verify that the links list is floated on the page's left margin (see Figure 7-24).

Figure 7-24 | **Floating the links list**

Getting Started

Home Getting Started Scrapbooking Tips Supply List Glossary Online Classes Sample Pages Online Store Shopping Cart Checkout Your Account Order Status Wish List Customer Service About Us Newsletter FAQ Contact Us

Scrapbooking is the practice of combining photos, memorabilia and stories in an album, preserving memories for future generations. In recent years scrapbooking has become a $300 million dollar industry as the public has discovered the joys of creating albums for families and friends. **Online Scrapbooks** is there to help you with all of the your scrapbooking needs.

Basic Materials

- Acid-free paper, card stock, and stickers
- Acid-free pen, markers, and adhesive
- Acid-free emory book album

Working with the div Element

The current layout does not yet match what Kathy wants. Although the links list is floated on the left margin, the rest of the page content flows around it. Kathy wants that content in a separate column, and doesn't want the text to wrap beneath the list of links. You can do this by floating the rest of the page content against the left margin. Because the left margin is now positioned at the right edge of the links list, floating against that margin will keep the rest of the page content from wrapping farther to the left.

However, the main page content consists of several different block-level elements, which we want to treat as a single unit. HTML and XHTML support a generic block-level element called the **div element**. In the same way that the span element is used as a general inline element, the div element is used as a general block-level element. The syntax of the div element is

```
<div>
   content
</div>
```

where `content` is any page content you want to enclose. You'll enclose the main content of the page in a div element with the id "main", setting the width of the content to 70% of the page width and floating the element on the left.

To create and format the #main div element:

1. Return to **start.htm** in your text editor.

2. Directly before the h1 heading "Getting Started", insert the following line:

   ```
   <div id="main">
   ```

3. Directly before the address element at the bottom of the file, insert the closing tag

   ```
   </div>
   ```

   See Figure 7-25.

Creating a div element ◀ **Figure 7-25**

```
<div id="main">
<h1>Getting Started</h1>
<p>Scrapbooking is the practice of combining photos, memorabilia and stories in
an album, preserving memories for future generations. In recent years scrapbooking
has become a $300 million dollar industry as the public has discovered the
joys of creating albums for families and friends. <b>Online Scrapbooks</b> is there to
help you with all of the your scrapbooking needs.</p>
```

```
<p>Your albums should contain page protectors to shield the pages from smudges, oil, and
dirt that can be transferred from your hands. You should never use albums that use
sticky magnetic pages. The sticky substance will be transferred to the photo
and backing paper causing deterioration. Never crop Polaroid<sup>&reg;</sup> photos
(they will curl and fall apart). Mount all memorabilia on acid-free cardstock
paper and photocopy all newspaper clippings on acid-free paper.</p>
</div>

<address>
Online Scrapbooks &#183;
212 Sunset Drive &#183;
Cutler, KY 83215 &#183;
1 (800) 555-8100
</address>
```

4. Save your changes to the file.

5. Go to the **scraps.css** file in your text editor.

6. At the bottom of the file, insert the following style declaration:

`#main {width: 70%; float: left}`

You also want to keep the address element from being displayed until both margins are clear of floating elements.

7. Add the following style to the address element (include a semicolon separating this style from other styles in the declaration).

`clear: both`

Figure 7-26 shows the revised style sheet.

Inserting styles for the #main selector ◀ **Figure 7-26**

```
/* online Scrapbooks screen styles */
body {color: brown}
h1, h2, h3, h4, h5, h6 {font-family: sans-serif; color: orange}
address {color: orange; font-style: normal; font-variant: small-caps;
         text-align: center; clear: both}
#head {text-align: right}
#links {width: 150px; float: left; background-color: rgb(212, 142, 0); margin-right: 10px}
#links a {font-family: sans-serif; color: white; font-size: 9pt}
#main {width: 70%; float: left}
```

8. Save your changes to the file.

9. Reload **start.htm** in your Web browser. Verify that the main content now appears in a column to the right of the list of links (see Figure 7-27).

Figure 7-27 **Page layout in columns**

> ONLINE
> # SCRAPBOOKS
>
> Home Getting Started Scrapbooking Tips Supply List Glossary Online Classes Sample Pages Online Store Shopping Cart Checkout Your Account Order Status Wish List Customer Service About Us Newsletter FAQ Contact Us
>
> ## Getting Started
>
> Scrapbooking is the practice of combining photos, memorabilia and stories in an album, preserving memories for future generations. In recent years scrapbooking has become a $300 million dollar industry as the public has discovered the joys of creating albums for families and friends. **Online Scrapbooks** is there to help you with all of the your scrapbooking needs.
>
> ### Basic Materials
>
> - Acid-free paper, card stock, and stickers
> - Acid-free pen, markers, and adhesive
> - Acid-free emory book album

Kathy would also like the bulleted list of materials floated on the right margin. Because this section also contains several block-level elements, you'll enclose the entire content in a div element with the id name "box". Kathy wants the Basic Materials box to be 200 pixels wide with a 5-pixel wide margin to the top, bottom, and left. She also wants the text of the list items within the box changed to an 8-pt sans-serif font on an ivory background, and wants the h3 heading above the box to be centered.

To enter and format the #box div element:

1. Return to **start.htm** in your text editor.

2. Directly before the h3 heading "Basic Materials", insert the following line:

   ```
   <div id="box">
   ```

3. Directly after the closing </ul> tag, insert the closing tag

   ```
   </div>
   ```

   Because the Basic Materials box is a unique feature of the Getting Started page, you'll embed its styles in the start.htm file. It's best to reserve the external style sheet for those features that are common to all pages in the Web site.

4. Within the style element at the top of the file, insert the following declarations.

   ```
   #box {width: 200px; float: right; background-color: ivory;
        margin: 5px 0px 5px 5px}
   #box h3 {text-align: center}
   #box li {font-family: sans-serif; font-size: 8pt}
   ```

   Note that you are using a contextual selector to apply the text changes to h3 headings and list items only within the Basic Materials box. Figure 7-28 shows the revised code.

```
<title>Getting Started</title>
<link href="scraps.css" rel="stylesheet" type="text/css" />
<style type="text/css">
    #box {width: 200px; float: right; background-color: ivory; margin: 5px 0 5px 5px}
    #box h3 {text-align: center}
    #box li {font-family: sans-serif; font-size: 8pt}

</style>
</head>
```

```
<div id="box">
<h3>Basic Materials</h3>
<ul>
    <li>Acid-free paper, card stock, and stickers</li>
    <li>Acid-free pen, markers, and adhesive</li>
    <li>Acid-free emory book album</li>
    <li>Straight and pattern edge scissors</li>
    <li>Photos and photo corners</li>
    <li>Paper punches</li>
    <li>Journalling templates</li>
    <li>Decorative embellishments</li>
</ul>
</div>
```

5. Save your changes to the file.

6. Reopen **start.htm** in your Web browser and verify that the entire Basic Materials section is now floated on the right margin as shown in Figure 7-29.

Home Getting Started Scrapbooking Tips Supply List Glossary Online Classes Sample Pages Online Store Shopping Cart Checkout Your Account Order Status Wish List Customer Service About Us Newsletter FAQ Contact Us

Getting Started

Scrapbooking is the practice of combining photos, memorabilia and stories in an album, preserving memories for future generations. In recent years scrapbooking has become a $300 million dollar industry as the public has discovered the joys of creating albums for families and friends. **Online Scrapbooks** is there to help you with all of the your scrapbooking needs.

Preserving Your Memories

Scrapbook albums have existed since the beginning of photography. However the sad fact is that photographs and most printed material are not permanent and will fade and yellow with age. Scrapbookers of today are aware of these problems and the industry is providing remedies that will allow scrapbook albums that suffer from minimal deterioration. The most important thing is to avoid using materials with high acid content which can cause photos and paper to deteriorate. Another thing to avoid is lignin, a material that is the bonding element in wood fibers. Over time, paper with lignin will become yellow and brittle and thus you should only use lignin-free products.

Basic Materials

- Acid-free paper, card stock, and stickers
- Acid-free pen, markers, and adhesive
- Acid-free emory book album
- Straight and pattern edge scissors
- Photos and photo corners
- Paper punches
- Journalling templates
- Decorative embellishments

Setting the Display Style

Now that you've set the basic layout of the page, you'll work on improving the page's appearance. Kathy finds the list of links difficult to read and thinks it would be better if each link were on a separate line. You could fix this by enclosing each link within its own paragraph or by inserting a line break between each link; however, Kathy wants to move as much of the formatting into style sheets as she can, rather than making these changes to document content. She also may want to explore different layouts in the future—for example, placing the links list in a horizontal box at the top of the page—and doesn't want to have to remove paragraph tags or line breaks if she does that.

As we've seen, most page elements are classified as either inline elements or block-level elements. HTML and XHTML treat links as inline elements, which is why all of the entries in the links list run together on a single line. You can use CSS to change the display style applied to any element, allowing you to make inline elements appear as block-level elements and vice versa. The syntax of the display style is

```
display: type
```

where `type` is one of the CSS display types described in Figure 7-30.

Figure 7-30 | **Values of the display style**

Display	Description
block	Display as a block-level element
inline	Display as an inline element
inline-block	Display as an inline element with some of the properties of a block (much like an inline image or frame)
inherit	Inherit the display property of the element's parent
list-item	Display as a list item
none	Do not display the element
run-in	Display as either an inline or block-level element depending on the context (CSS2)
table	Display as a block-level table (CSS2)
inline-table	Display as an inline table (CSS2)
table-caption	Treat as a table caption (CSS2)
table-cell	Treat as a table cell (CSS2)
table-column	Treat as a table column (CSS2)
table-column-group	Treat as a group of table columns (CSS2)
table-footer-group	Treat as a group of table footer rows (CSS2)
table-header-group	Treat as a group of table header rows (CSS2)
table-row	Treat as a table row (CSS2)
table-row-group	Treat as a group of table rows (CSS2)

For example, to display an element as a block, you can use the style

```
display: block
```

Apply this style to the links within the links paragraph.

To change the display style of the links:

1. Return to **scraps.css** in your text editor.

2. Insert the following style in the style declaration for links within the links paragraph (see Figure 7-31):

   ```
   display: block
   ```

Inserting the display style | **Figure 7-31**

```
/* online scrapbooks screen styles */
body {color: brown}
h1, h2, h3, h4, h5, h6 {font-family: sans-serif; color: orange}
address {color: orange; font-style: normal; font-variant: small-caps;
        text-align: center; clear: both}
#head {text-align: right}
#links {width: 150px; float: left; background-color: rgb(212, 142, 0); margin-right: 10px}
#links a {display: block; font-family: sans-serif; color: white; font-size: 9pt}
#main {width: 70%; float: left}
```

3. Save your changes to the file.

4. Reload **start.htm** in your Web browser. As shown in Figure 7-32, the links in the links paragraph are displayed within a separate block.

Links displayed as block-level elements | **Figure 7-32**

each link is displayed in its own block

The Online Scrapbook Web site includes three main areas: pages that teach scrapbooking, pages that sell products, and pages that provide information about the company. Although Kathy has ordered the links by area, the sections are not separated in the rendered page. Kathy suggests that you increase the space between the groups of links. One method for doing this is to mark a class of links that represent the first link in each group, and then to increase the size of the margin above those links. You'll add this style to the style sheet now.

To enter the style for different link classes:

▶ 1. Return to **start.htm** in your text editor.

▶ 2. Locate the links for the Online Store and the About Us pages and insert the attribute **class="newgroup"** as shown in Figure 7-33.

| Figure 7-33 | Inserting the class attribute |

```
<body>
<p id="head"><img src="scraps.jpg" alt="Online Scrapbooks" width="314" height="75" /></p>
<p id="links">
    <a href="index.htm">Home</a>
    <a href="start.htm">Getting Started</a>
    <a href="tips.htm">Scrapbooking Tips</a>
    <a href="supply.htm">Supply List</a>
    <a href="gloss.htm">Glossary</a>
    <a href="classes.htm">Online Classes</a>
    <a href="samples.htm">Sample Pages</a>
    <a href="store.htm" class="newgroup">Online Store</a>
    <a href="cart.htm">Shopping Cart</a>
    <a href="checkout.htm">Checkout</a>
    <a href="account.htm">Your Account</a>
    <a href="status.htm">Order Status</a>
    <a href="wish.htm">Wish List</a>
    <a href="service.htm">Customer Service</a>
    <a href="about.htm" class="newgroup">About Us</a>
    <a href="news.htm">Newsletter</a>
    <a href="faq.htm">FAQ</a>
    <a href="contact.htm">Contact Us</a>
</p>
```

class value

▶ 3. Save your changes to the file.

▶ 4. Go to **scraps.css** in your text editor and insert the following style declaration below the #links a declaration (see Figure 7-34):

   #links a.newgroup {margin-top: 15px}

| Figure 7-34 | Formatting a class |

```
/* online Scrapbooks screen styles */
body {color: brown}
h1, h2, h3, h4, h5, h6 {font-family: sans-serif; color: orange}
address {color: orange; font-style: normal; font-variant: small-caps;
         text-align: center; clear: both}
#head {text-align: right}
#links {width: 150px; float: left; background-color: rgb(212, 142, 0); margin-right: 10px}
#links a {display: block; font-family: sans-serif; color: white; font-size: 9pt}
#links a.newgroup {margin-top: 15px}
#main {width: 70%; float: left}
```

class value

Note that we included both the element name and the group name in this style declaration to eliminate possible confusion about which elements the style is being applied to.

▶ 5. Save your changes to the style sheet and then reload **start.htm** in your Web browser. Figure 7-35 shows the list of links separated into three different groups.

Setting the Display Style

- To define the display style of an element, use the style
  ```
  display: type
  ```
  where *type* is the display. Use a *type* value of "block" to format the element as a block and "inline" to format it is an inline element.

Working with the Box Model

Although Kathy is pleased with the progress of the page layout so far, she thinks that the links list looks crowded, and would like to see more space around the link text. To make this change you can use styles to modify the space around and within the paragraph. CSS treats each element on the page using a box model. In the **box model**, an element is composed of the four sections shown in Figure 7-36:

- the **margin** between the element and other content
- the **border** of the box
- the **padding** between the element's content and the box's border
- the **content** of the element

You've already seen how to work with margins in Tutorial 3. Now we'll look at how to format the padding and border spaces.

Figure 7-36	The Box model

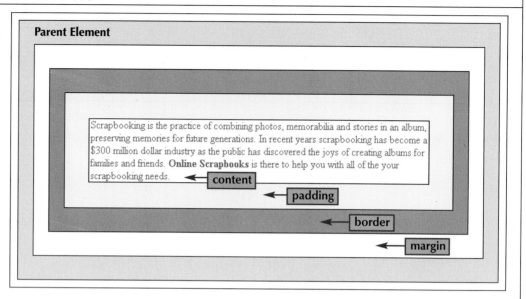

Setting the Padding Size

The styles that set the size of the padding within an element are similar to the ones you've used for setting the margin sizes around an element. Like margins, you work with each of the four sides of an element individually using the styles

```
padding-top: value
padding-right: value
padding-bottom: value
padding-left: value
```

where `value` is the size of the padding above, to the right, below, and to the left of the element in one of the CSS units of measure. You can also use the value "auto" to allow each browser to set the padding size. Similar to the margin style, you use the padding style to combine padding values into a single style:

```
padding: top right bottom left
```

where `top`, `right`, `bottom`, and `left` are the top, right, bottom and left padding sizes. If you include only three values, they are applied to the top, right, and bottom spaces and the browser assigns the left padding the same value as the right. If you include only two values, the first value is applied to the top and bottom padding spaces, and the second to the right and left. If only one value is specified, a browser will apply it to all sides equally.

Kathy suggests that you set the size of the padding within the links paragraph to 10 pixels.

To set the padding size for the links paragraph:

1. Return to **scraps.css** in your text editor.

2. Insert the following style in the declaration for the #links selector as shown in Figure 7-37 (be sure to separate the styles with semicolons):

```
padding: 10px
```

Setting the padding value of the #links selector Figure 7-37

```
/* online Scrapbooks screen styles */
body {color: brown}
h1, h2, h3, h4, h5, h6 {font-family: sans-serif; color: orange}
address {color: orange; font-style: normal; font-variant: small-caps;
        text-align: center; clear: both}
#head {text-align: right}
#links {width: 150px; float: left; background-color: rgb(212, 142, 0); margin-right: 10px;
        padding: 10px}
#links a {display: block; font-family: sans-serif; color: white; font-size: 9pt}
#links a.newgroup {margin-top: 15px}
#main {width: 70%; float: left}
```

3. Save your changes to the file and reload **start.htm** in your Web browser. Verify that the space between the links and the border of the box has increased.

Setting the Padding Size

- To set the size of the internal padding, use the style
    padding: *top right bottom left*
  where *top*, *right*, *bottom*, and *left* are the top, right, bottom and left padding sizes. To define the padding size for individual sides of an element, use the styles padding-top, padding-right, padding-bottom, and padding-left.

Kathy also feels that the bulleted items in the Basic Materials box are indented too much, resulting in a large empty space to the left of the bullets. She would like to see the bullets shifted more to the left, filling up that empty space. Although simply changing the padding or margin size around the list items seems like the most straightforward solution, this would not work for all browsers. Some browsers, such as Internet Explorer and Opera, set the indentation for list items by setting the size of the left margin, whereas other browsers, such as Netscape, set the left padding. For this reason, you need to change both of these values to shift the list items consistently in all browsers.

Internet Explorer and Opera set the size of the left margin to 40 pixels and the size of the left padding to 0. With Netscape it's just the opposite: the left margin is set to 0 pixels and the left padding is set to 40 pixels. However you modify the margin and padding size, if the sum total of the two values is less than 40 pixels, the indentation of the bulleted items will be decreased. Finding the right margin and padding combination that results in pleasing layout is a process of trial and error.

After some work, you settle on a left margin size of 20 pixels and a left padding size of 0. Kathy also wants you to change the style of the bullets to an open circle.

To set the padding size for the links paragraph:

1. Return to **start.htm** in your text editor.

▶ **2.** Insert the following line after the style declaration for the #box h3 selector (see Figure 7-38):

```
#box ul {list-style-type: circle; margin-left: 20px; padding-left: 0px}
```

Figure 7-38 ▶ **Setting the padding and margin values for an unordered list**

```
<style type="text/css">
    #box {width: 200px; float: right; background-color: ivory; margin: 5px 0 5px 5px}
    #box h3 {text-align: center}
    #box ul {list-style-type: circle; margin-left: 20px; padding-left: 0px}
    #box li {font-family: sans-serif; font-size: 8pt}
</style>
```

▶ **3.** Save your changes to the file and reload **start.htm** in your Web browser. Verify that the bullets have shifted to the left and that the marker style has changed to an open circle.

Formatting the Border

Next Kathy wants you to add borders to the different sections of the page. She feels that this will make the page more attractive and easier to read. CSS provides a wide variety of styles for setting an element's border width, border color, and border style. These styles can be applied to all four sides at once, or to individual sides. Figure 7-39 summarizes the different border styles.

Figure 7-39 ▶ **Border styles**

Border Style	Description	Notes
border-top-width: *value*	Width of the top border	Where *value* is the width of the border in absolute or relative units, or defined with the keyword "thin", "medium", or "thick"
border-right-width: *value*	Width of the right border	
border-bottom-width: *value*	Width of the bottom border	
border-left-width: *value*	Width of the left border	
border-width: *top right bottom left*	Width of any or all of the borders	
border-top-color: *color*	Color of the top border	Where *color* is a color name or color value
border-right-color: *color*	Color of the right border	
border-bottom-color: *color*	Color of the bottom border	
border-left-color: *color*	Color of the left border	
border-color: *top right bottom left*	Color of any or all of the borders	
border-top-style: *type*	Style of top border	Where *type* is one of the nine border styles: solid, dashed, dotted, double, outset, inset, groove, ridge, or none
border-right-style: *type*	Style of right border	
border-bottom-style: *type*	Style of bottom border	
border-left-style: *type*	Style of left border	
border-style: *top right bottom left*	Style of any or all of the borders	

Border widths are expressed in the standard CSS units of length, or with the keywords "thin", "medium", or "thick". Border colors can be defined using color names or color values. CSS also supports nine different border styles that can be applied to any or all of a box's borders. Figure 7-40 shows examples of each style.

Border style types ◀ **Figure 7-40**

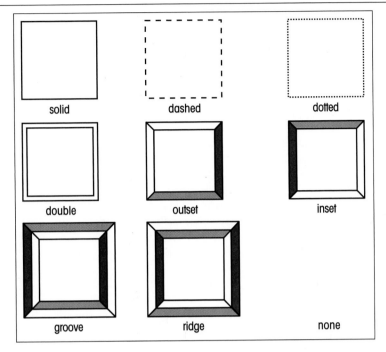

For example, to place a double border around an element, use the style

```
border-style: double
```

To place a double border only below an element, use the style

```
border-style-bottom: double
```

All of the borders can be combined into single style declarations using the following styles:

```
border-top: width style color
border-right: width style color
border-bottom: width style color
border-left: width style color
border: width style color
```

where `width` is the border width, `style` is the border style, and `color` is the border color. For example, to place a red 2-pixel-wide double border around an element, use the style

```
border: 2px double red
```

To place that border on only the top of the element, use the style

```
border-top: 2px double red
```

Kathy wants you to place a solid black 2-pixel-wide border around the links paragraph, and wants the Basic Materials box enclosed in 5-pixel-wide orange border in the outset style.

Setting the Border Style

- To set the width of an element's border, use the style
    border-width: *top right bottom left*
  where *top, right, bottom,* and *left* are the widths of the top, right, bottom, and left borders. To define the border widths for individual sides, use the styles border-top-width, border-right-width, border-bottom-width, and border-left-width.
- To set a border color, use the style
    border-color: *top right bottom left*
  where *top, right, bottom,* and *left* are the colors of the top, right, bottom, and left borders. To define the border colors for individual sides, use the styles border-top-color, border-right-color, border-bottom-color, and border-left-color.
- To set a border style, use
    border-style: *top right bottom left*
  where *top, right, bottom,* and *left* are the styles of the top, right, bottom, and left borders. Possible border style values are solid, dashed, dotted, double, outset, inset, groove, ridge, and none. To define the border styles for individual sides, use the styles border-top-style, border-right-style, border-bottom-style, and border-left-style.
- To format an entire border, use the style
    border: *width style color*
  where *width* is the border width, *style* is the border style, and *color* is the border color. To define the border appearance for individual sides, use the styles border-top, border-right, border-left, and border-bottom.

To set the border styles for the #links and #box selectors:

1. Return to **scraps.css** in your text editor.

2. Add the following style in the declaration for the #links selector as shown in Figure 7-41 (be sure to separate the styles with semicolons):

   border: 2px solid black

Figure 7-41 ▶ Setting the border style for the #links selector

```
/* Online Scrapbooks screen styles */
body {color: brown}
h1, h2, h3, h4, h5, h6 {font-family: sans-serif; color: orange}
address {color: orange; font-style: normal; font-variant: small-caps;
        text-align: center; clear: both}
#head {text-align: right}
#links {width: 150px; float: left; background-color: rgb(212, 142, 0); margin-right: 10px;
        padding: 10px; border: 2px solid black}
#links a {display: block; font-family: sans-serif; color: white; font-size: 9pt}
#links a.newgroup {margin-top: 15px}
#main {width: 70%; float: left}
```

3. Save your changes to the file and go to the **start.htm** file in your text editor.

4. Add the following style in the declaration for the #box selector as shown in Figure 7-42:

```
border: 5px outset orange
```

Setting the border style for the #box selector ◢ **Figure 7-42**

```
<style type="text/css">
   #box {width: 200px; float: right; background-color: ivory; margin: 5px 0 5px 5px;
         border: 5px outset orange}
   #box h3 {text-align: center}
   #box ul {list-style-type: circle; margin-left: 20px; padding-left: 0px}
   #box li {font-family: sans-serif; font-size: 8pt}
</style>
```

5. Save your changes and reload **start.htm** in your Web browser. See Figure 7-43.

Viewing the border styles ◢ **Figure 7-43**

Kathy also wants you to add lines separating the different sections of the document. You decide to add an orange border to the bottom of the page head, to the left of the page's main content, and above the page address.

To add lines to the different sections of the page:

1. Return to **scraps.css** in your text editor and insert the following style in the declaration for the address element:

```
border-top: 1px solid orange
```

2. Add the following style to the declaration for the #head selector:

```
border-bottom: 1px solid orange
```

3. Insert the following style in the declaration for the #main selector:

```
border-left: 1px solid orange; padding-left: 10px
```

Figure 7-44 shows the revised style declarations. Be sure you have separated the different styles with semicolons.

| Figure 7-44 | Adding additional borders to the style sheet |

```
/* Online Scrapbooks screen styles */
body {color: brown}
h1, h2, h3, h4, h5, h6 {font-family: sans-serif; color: orange}
address {color: orange; font-style: normal; font-variant: small-caps;
        text-align: center; clear: both; border-top: 1px solid orange}
#head {text-align: right; border-bottom: 1px solid orange}
#links {width: 150px; float: left; background-color: rgb(212, 142, 0); margin-right: 10px;
        padding: 10px; border: 2px solid black}
#links a {display: block; font-family: sans-serif; color: white; font-size: 9pt}
#links a.newgroup {margin-top: 15px}
#main {width: 70%; float: left; border-left: 1px solid orange; padding-left: 10px}
```

4. Save your changes to the file and reload **start.htm** in your browser. Figure 7-45 displays the revised layout including the divider lines.

| Figure 7-45 | Adding more borders to the style sheet |

ONLINE

SCRAPBOOKS

Home
Getting Started
Scrapbooking Tips
Supply List
Glossary
Online Classes
Sample Pages

Online Store
Shopping Cart
Checkout
Your Account
Order Status
Wish List
Customer Service

About Us
Newsletter
FAQ
Contact Us

Getting Started

Scrapbooking is the practice of combining photos, memorabilia and stories in an album, preserving memories for future generations. In recent years scrapbooking has become a $300 million dollar industry as the public has discovered the joys of creating albums for families and friends. **Online Scrapbooks** is there to help you with all of the your scrapbooking needs.

Preserving Your Memories

Scrapbook albums have existed since the beginning of photography. However the sad fact is that photographs and most printed material are not permanent and will fade and yellow with age. Scrapbookers of today are aware of these problems and the industry is providing remedies that will allow scrapbook albums that suffer from minimal deterioration. The most important thing is to avoid using materials with high acid content which can cause photos and paper to deteriorate. Another thing to avoid is lignin, a material that is the bonding element in wood fibers. Over time, paper with lignin will become yellow and brittle and thus you should only use lignin-free products.

Basic Materials

○ Acid-free paper, card stock, and stickers
○ Acid-free pen, markers, and adhesive
○ Acid-free emory book album
○ Straight and pattern edge scissors
○ Photos and photo corners
○ Paper punches
○ Journalling templates
○ Decorative embellishments

Your albums should contain page protectors to shield the pages from smudges, oil, and dirt that can be transferred from your hands. You should never use albums that use sticky magnetic pages. The sticky substance will be transferred to the photo and backing paper causing deterioration. Never crop Polaroid® photos (they will curl and fall apart). Mount all memorabilia on acid-free cardstock paper and photocopy all newspaper clippings on acid-free paper.

ONLINE SCRAPBOOKS · 212 SUNSET DRIVE · CUTLER, KY 83215 · 1 (800) 555-8100

Using Pseudo-Classes and Pseudo-Elements

Kathy likes the layout of the page. Now she wants to focus on some design elements to enhance the page's appearance. She doesn't like all of the text underlining in the links list. Although HTML and XHTML underline linked text by default, Kathy thinks that a large block of underlined text is difficult to read. She's seen sites in which links are underlined only when the mouse hovers over the linked text. This type of effect is called a **rollover effect** because it is applied only when a user rolls the mouse pointer over an element. She would like you to make underlining a rollover effect for the list of links.

Creating a Link Rollover

Rollover effects for links can be created using pseudo-classes. A **pseudo-class** is a classification of an element based on its status, position, or current use in the document. For example, one pseudo-class indicates whether a link has been previously visited by the user. Another pseudo-class indicates whether a link is currently being activated or clicked. To create a style for a pseudo-class use the style

```
selector:pseudo-class {styles}
```

where `selector` is an element or group of elements within a document, `pseudo-class` is the name of a pseudo-class, and `styles` are the styles you want to apply. Figure 7-46 lists some of the pseudo-classes supported by CSS.

Pseudo-classes ◁ | Figure 7-46

Pseudo-class	Description	Example
link	The link has not yet been visited by the user	a:link {color: red}
visited	The link has been visited by the user	a:visited {color: green}
active	The link is in the process of being activated by the user	a:active {color: yellow}
hover	The mouse cursor is hovering over the link (CSS2)	a:hover {color: blue}
focus	The element has received the focus of the keyboard or mouse cursor (CSS2)	input.focus {background-color: yellow}
first-child	The element is the first child of its parent (CSS2)	p:first-child {text-indent: 0}
lang	The element is in the specified language (CSS2)	q:lang(FR) {quotes: '<<' '>>'}

If you want to change the font color of all previously visited links to red, you could use the style declaration

```
a:visited {color: red}
```

In some cases, two or more pseudo-classes can apply to the same element—for example, a link can be both previously visited and hovered over. In such situations, the standard cascading rules apply: the style that is more heavily weighted or declared last will be applied to the element.

Kathy wants all of the links to display by default without underlining. If the mouse pointer is hovering over a link, however, she wants the link text to appear in a black font and underlined. The style declarations to create this rollover effect are

```
#links a:link {text-decoration: none}
#links a:visited {text-decoration: none}
#links a:hover {color: black; text-decoration: underline}
#links a:active {text-decoration: none}
```

Because of the cascading rules, order is important. The hover pseudo-class will be used only if it is listed *after* the link and visited pseudo-classes. Similarly, the active pseudo-class should be listed last in preference to the link, visited, and hover pseudo-classes. Add these styles now to the scraps.css style sheet.

To create a rollover effect for the Online Scrapbooks Web site:

1. Return to **scraps.css** in your text editor and insert the following style declarations after the declaration for the #links a selector (see Figure 7-47):

```
#links a:link {text-decoration: none}
#links a:visited {text-decoration: none}
#links a:hover {color: black; text-decoration: underline}
#links a:active {text-decoration: none}
```

Figure 7-47	Using pseudo-classes in a style

```
/* Online Scrapbooks screen styles */
body {color: brown}
h1, h2, h3, h4, h5, h6 {font-family: sans-serif; color: orange}
address {color: orange; font-style: normal; font-variant: small-caps;
        text-align: center; clear: both; border-top: 1px solid orange}
#head {text-align: right; border-bottom: 1px solid orange}
#links {width: 150px; float: left; background-color: rgb(212, 142, 0); margin-right: 10px;
        padding: 10px; border: 2px solid black}
#links a {display: block; font-family: sans-serif; color: white; font-size: 9pt}
#links a:link {text-decoration: none}
#links a:visited {text-decoration: none}
#links a:hover {color: black; text-decoration: underline}
#links a:active {text-decoration: none}
#links a.newgroup {margin-top: 15px}
#main {width: 70%; float: left; border-left: 1px solid orange; padding-left: 10px}
```

2. Save your changes and close the **scraps.css** file. Reload **start.htm** in your Web browser.

3. Verify that the links in the links box are no longer underlined, and that when you hover your mouse pointer over a link it appears in black and underlined as shown in Figure 7-48:

Figure 7-48	Viewing a rollover effect

Working with Pseudo-Classes and Pseudo-Elements

- To create a style for pseudo-class, use the style
    `selector:pseudo-class {styles}`
  where `selector` is an element or group of elements within a document, `pseudo-class` is the name of a pseudo-class, and `styles` are the styles you want to apply to the selector. Useful pseudo-classes include the link, visited, hover, and active pseudo-classes which are applied to the element to format linked, visited, hovered, and active hyperlinks.
- To create a style for pseudo-element, use the style
    `selector:pseudo-element {styles}`
  where `selector` is an element or group of elements within a document, `pseudo-element` is the name of a pseudo-element, and `styles` are the styles you want to apply to the pseudo-element. Useful pseudo-elements include the first-line and first-letter pseudo-elements, which represent the first line or first letter of an element's content.

HTML and XHTML do not support attributes to create hover effects, making these settings incompatible with older browsers. However, you can add the following presentational attributes to the body element to change the font colors of active, visited, and unvisited links:

`<body link="color" vlink="color" alink="color">`

where the link attribute specifies the color of unvisited links, the vlink attribute specifies the color of visited links, and the alink attribute specifies the color of active links. Colors must be entered either as a supported color name or as a hexadecimal color value. Note that the link, vlink, and alink attributes have been deprecated and are not supported by strictly compliant XHTML code.

Creating a Drop-Cap

You have one more formatting change to make to the Getting Started page to implement Kathy's design request. She wants you to add the following effects to the first paragraph on the page:

- The first line should be displayed in a small caps style
- The first letter should be increased in size and displayed as a drop cap

Thus far all of our selectors have been based on elements that exist somewhere in the document hierarchy. We can also define selectors that are not part of the document tree, but instead are abstracted from what we know of an element's content, use, or position. For example, a paragraph element is part of the document tree, but the first letter of that paragraph is not (there is no "first letter" element). We can still work with selectors that are not part of the hierarchy, though, by creating **pseudo-elements**, which are based on information about an element's content, use, or position.

CSS supports a wide variety of pseudo-elements, including those that select the first letter or first line of an element's content. The syntax for creating a style declaration for a pseudo-element is similar to what we used for a pseudo-class:

`selector:pseudo-element {styles}`

where `selector` is an element or group of elements within the document, `pseudo-element` is an abstract element based on the selector, and `styles` are the styles that you want to apply to the pseudo-element. Figure 7-49 lists some of the pseudo-elements supported by CSS.

Figure 7-49 ▶ **Pseudo-elements**

Pseudo-element	Description	Example
first-letter	The first letter of the element text	p:first-letter {font-size: 14pt}
first-line	The first line of the element text	p:first-line {text-transform: uppercase}
before	Content to be placed directly before the element (CSS2)	p:before {content: "Special!"}
after	Content to be placed directly after the element (CSS2)	p:after {content: "eof"}

For example, to display the first letter of every paragraph in a gold fantasy font, you could use the declaration

```
p:first-letter {font-family: fantasy; color: gold}
```

To create a drop cap, you increase the font size of an element's first letter and float it on the left margin. Drop caps also generally look better if you decrease the line height of the first letter, enabling the surrounding content to better wrap around the letter. Finding the best combination of font size and line height is a matter of trial and error, and unfortunately what may look best in one browser might not look as good in another. After trying out several combinations, you settle on a drop cap for the first paragraph that is 400% the size of the surrounding text, with a line height of 0.8. Per Kathy's request, you will also display the text of the paragraph's first line in small caps. Add these styles to the embedded style sheet in the start.htm file.

To create a drop-cap:

1. Return to **start.htm** in your text editor.

   Before inserting the styles, you must add an id to the first paragraph in the page's main section.

2. Insert the attribute **id="firstp"** in the <p> tag directly after the h1 heading.

3. Scroll up to the top of the file and insert the following style declarations after the opening <style> tag:

   ```
   #firstp:first-line {font-variant: small-caps}
   #firstp:first-letter {float: left; font-size: 400%; line-height:
   0.8}
   ```

   Figure 7-50 shows the revised code for the file.

Formatting the first line and first letter pseudo-elements | Figure 7-50

```
<style type="text/css">
    #firstp:first-line {font-variant: small-caps}
    #firstp:first-letter {float: left; font-size: 400%; line-height: 0.8}
    #box {width: 200px; float: right; background-color: ivory; margin: 5px 0 5px 5px;
        border: 5px outset orange}
    #box h3 {text-align: center}
    #box ul {list-style-type: circle; margin-left: 20px; padding-left: 0px}
    #box li {font-family: sans-serif; font-size: 8pt}
</style>
```

```
<div id="main">
<h1>Getting Started</h1>
<p id="firstp">Scrapbooking is the practice of combining photos, memorabilia and stories in
an album, preserving memories for future generations. In recent years scrapbooking
has become a $300 million dollar industry as the public has discovered the
joys of creating albums for families and friends. <b>Online Scrapbooks</b> is there to
help you with all of the your scrapbooking needs.</p>
```

4. Save your changes and close the file. You're finished working on the start.htm file.

5. Reload **start.htm** in your Web browser. Figure 7-51 shows the final appearance of the Getting Started page.

Final Getting Started page | Figure 7-51

ONLINE
SCRAPBOOKS

Getting Started

Home
Getting Started
Scrapbooking Tips
Supply List
Glossary
Online Classes
Sample Pages

Online Store
Shopping Cart
Checkout
Your Account
Order Status
Wish List
Customer Service

About Us
Newsletter
FAQ
Contact Us

SCRAPBOOKING IS THE PRACTICE OF COMBINING PHOTOS, MEMORABILIA AND stories in an album, preserving memories for future generations. In recent years scrapbooking has become a $300 million dollar industry as the public has discovered the joys of creating albums for families and friends. **Online Scrapbooks** is there to help you with all of the your scrapbooking needs.

Preserving Your Memories

Scrapbook albums have existed since the beginning of photography. However the sad fact is that photographs and most printed material are not permanent and will fade and yellow with age. Scrapbookers of today are aware of these problems and the industry is providing remedies that will allow scrapbook albums that suffer from minimal deterioration. The most important thing is to avoid using materials with high acid content which can cause photos and paper to deteriorate. Another thing to avoid is lignin, a material that is the bonding element in wood fibers. Over time, paper with lignin will become yellow and brittle and thus you should only use lignin-free products.

Basic Materials

○ Acid-free paper, card stock, and stickers
○ Acid-free pen, markers, and adhesive
○ Acid-free emory book album
○ Straight and pattern edge scissors
○ Photos and photo corners
○ Paper punches
○ Journalling templates
○ Decorative embellishments

Your albums should contain page protectors to shield the pages from smudges, oil, and dirt that can be transferred from your hands. You should never use albums that use sticky magnetic pages. The sticky substance will be transferred to the photo and backing paper causing deterioration. Never crop Polaroid® photos (they will curl and fall apart). Mount all memorabilia on acid-free cardstock paper and photocopy all newspaper clippings on acid-free paper.

ONLINE SCRAPBOOKS · 212 SUNSET DRIVE · CUTLER, KY 83215 · 1 (800) 555-8100

Trouble? Depending on your browser, your Web page may look different than the one shown in Figure 7-51.

Applying a Style to a Web Site

The power of style sheets lies in the ability to apply a common design to an entire Web site. Now that you've completed the design for the Getting Started page, let's apply this design to a different page in the Online Scrapbooks Web site. Kathy has provided you with another Web page containing a glossary of scrapbooking terms. The current design of the page is shown in Figure 7-52.

| Figure 7-52 | **Initial Glossary page** |

SCRAPBOOKS ONLINE

Home Getting Started Scrapbooking Tips Supply List Glossary Online Classes Sample Pages Online Store Shopping Cart Checkout Your Account Order Status Wish List Customer Service About Us Newsletter FAQ Contact Us

Glossary

Acid	Substance that can weaken cellulose in paper causing it to become brittle.
Acid-free	Materials that have a pH of 7.0 or higher.
Buffered Paper	Paper that has had alkaline substances added to absorb acids.
Crop	Trimming the photo to highlight a certain area or cut out unwanted activity.
Dauber	A round miniature stamp pad which can be dabbed onto a stamp to apply ink.
Embossing	Decorating using raised edges.
Encapsulation	Sealing a memory between two sheets of transparent polyester film.
Eylette	A round metal embellishment added by punching a hole and hammering down the back.

Kathy wants you to link this page to the scraps.css style sheet and add the appropriate ids, classes, and div elements to take advantage of the styles you've defined. In addition, the glossary terms and definitions have been placed in a table, and Kathy wants you to vertically align the content of each table cell with the cell's top and apply a 1-pixel-wide solid black border to the bottom of each table cell.

To apply a style to the Glossary page:

1. Use your text editor to open **glosstxt.htm** from the tutorial.07/tutorial folder. Enter **your name** and **the date** in the comment section and save the file as **gloss. htm**.

2. Directly before the closing </head> tag, insert the following link to the scraps.css style sheet:

```
<link href="scraps.css" rel="stylesheet" type="text/css" />
```

3. After the link element, insert the following embedded style sheet:

```
<style type="text/css">
    td {vertical-align: top; border-bottom: 1px solid black}
</style>
```

4. Add the id attribute **"head"** to the first paragraph element, and the id attribute **"links"** to the second paragraph element.

5. Add the class attribute **"newgroup"** to the Online Store and About Us links.

6. Enclose the h1 heading and the table in a div element with the id **"main"**. Figure 7-53 shows the new and revised code for the gloss.htm file.

Adding styles to the Glossary page | Figure 7-53

```
<link href="scraps.css" rel="stylesheet" type="text/css" />
<style type="text/css">
    td {vertical-align: top; border-bottom: 1px solid black}
</style>
</head>

<body>
<p id="head"><img src="scraps.jpg" alt="Online Scrapbooks" width="314" height="75" /></p>
<p id="links">
    <a href="index.htm">Home</a>
    <a href="start.htm">Getting Started</a>
    <a href="tips.htm">Scrapbooking Tips</a>
    <a href="supply.htm">Supply List</a>
    <a href="gloss.htm">Glossary</a>
    <a href="classes.htm">Online Classes</a>
    <a href="samples.htm">Sample Pages</a>
    <a href="store.htm" class="newgroup">Online Store</a>
    <a href="cart.htm">Shopping Cart</a>
    <a href="checkout.htm">Checkout</a>
    <a href="account.htm">Your Account</a>
    <a href="status.htm">Order Status</a>
    <a href="wish.htm">Wish List</a>
    <a href="service.htm">Customer Service</a>
    <a href="about.htm" class="newgroup">About Us</a>
    <a href="news.htm">Newsletter</a>
    <a href="faq.htm">FAQ</a>
    <a href="contact.htm">Contact Us</a>
</p>

<div id="main">
<h1>Glossary</h1>
<table>
```

```
    <tr><td>Xyron</td>
        <td>A machine that creates stickers, magnets, or laminations without
            the hazards of lamination.</td></tr>
</table>
</div>
```

7. Close the file, saving your changes, and open **gloss.htm** in your Web browser. Figure 7-54 shows the new appearance of the page using the current style sheet.

Figure 7-54 ▶ **Final Glossary page**

8. If you intend to take a break before the next session, you may close any open files now.

You can use the same process to apply the scraps.css style sheet to other pages in the Web site. If Kathy wanted you to modify the site's design in the future, you could easily modify the style sheet, thereby applying the changes to all of the site's pages at once.

In the next session, you'll learn how to use CSS to position and stack objects on the page, and you'll learn how to create styles for different media types.

Review

Session 7.2 Quick Check

1. What is the style to set the font size of an element with the id "intro" to 14 point?

2. What is the style to set the width of address elements with the class name "footer" to 500 pixels?

3. What is the style to prevent the display of paragraphs with a class name of "private"?

4. What is the style to set the padding within all h1 headings to 15 pixels?

5. What is the style to add a double 5-pixel-wide red border to the bottom of all h1 headings?

6. What is the style to display a yellow background on links whenever the mouse pointer passes over them?

7. What is the style to display the first line of all block quotes in uppercase letters?

Positioning Objects with CSS

One of the purposes of the Online Scrapbooks Web site is to teach new scrapbookers how to create beautiful and interesting pages. Every month Kathy wants to highlight a scrapbook page that displays some noteworthy features. Figure 7-55 shows the current Samples page. Note that the page uses the same layout as the other pages in the Web site. The scrapbooking sample is displayed in the main section of the document.

Initial Samples page ◀ **Figure 7-55**

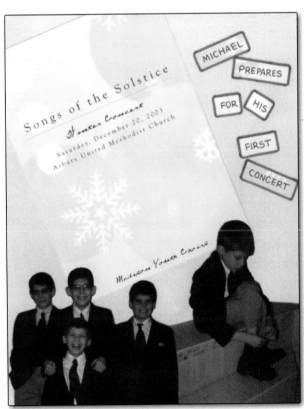

Kathy wants to augment the page by inserting callouts that highlight certain portions of the scrapbooking sample for the reader. She wants each callout to be placed in close proximity to the feature that it highlights. Kathy has drawn in the locations of the three callouts that she wants to add in the sketch shown in Figure 7-56.

Figure 7-56 ▶ **Sketch of Kathy's callouts proposal**

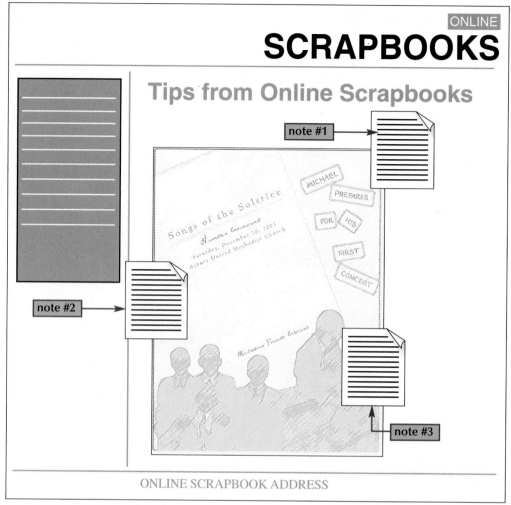

The text of the three callouts is:

note #1 Paste cut-out letters and words in your scrapbook to create a 3-D effect. Online Scrapbooks sells professionally designed cut-out letters, words, and phrases for all occasions.

note #2 Clippings, flyers, programs, and other memorabilia are valuable sources of information that can enhance your scrapbook pages. Make sure that any material is copied to acid-free paper. Newspaper clippings are especially susceptible to deterioration.

note #3 Photographic cut-outs and textured backgrounds can add visual interest to your pages. See the online store for our wide variety of textured and embossed papers.

You'll insert each of these notes in div elements placed within the main section of the page. You'll set the id values of the three elements to note1, note2, and note3 respectively, and you'll add the class value "notes" to each element so that you can apply a common set of styles to the notes.

To insert the notes text:

1. Use your text editor to open **samptxt.htm** from the tutorial.07/tutorial folder. Enter *your name* and *the date* in the comment section and save the file as **samples.htm**.

2. Directly after the h1 heading "Tips from Online Scrapbooks", insert the following paragraphs:

```
<div id="note1" class="notes">
Paste cut-out letters and words in your scrapbook to create a 3-
D effect. Online Scrapbooks sells professionally designed cut-
out letters, words, and phrases for all occasions.
</div>
<div id="note2" class="notes">
Clippings, flyers, programs, and other memorabilia are valuable
sources of information that can enhance your scrapbook pages.
Make sure that any material is copied to acid-free paper.
Newspaper clippings are especially susceptible to deterioration.
</div>
<div id="note3" class="notes">
Photographic cut-outs and textured backgrounds can add visual
interest to your pages. See the online store for our wide
variety of textured and embossed papers.
</div>
```

Next, you'll insert an embedded style sheet to format the appearance of the notes. Kathy wants the notes to appear in a brown 8-point sans-serif font on an ivory background. She wants the notes boxes to be displayed with a 2-pixel white inset border. The notes should be 130 pixels wide with a padding space of 5 pixels.

3. After the link element, insert the following embedded style sheet:

```
<style type="text/css">
   .notes {font-family: sans-serif; font-size: 8pt; color: brown;
           background-color: ivory; border: 2px inset white;
           padding: 5px; width: 130px}
</style>
```

Figure 7-57 shows the revised code of the samples.htm file.

Figure 7-57 ▶ **Enter the notes text and styles**

```
<title>Sample Scrapbook Page</title>
<link href="scraps.css" rel="stylesheet" type="text/css" />
<style type="text/css">
    .notes {font-family: sans-serif; font-size: 8pt; color: brown;
            background-color: ivory; border: 2px inset white;
            padding: 5px; width: 130px}
</style>
</head>
```

```
<h1>Tips from Online Scrapbooks</h1>
<div id="note1" class="notes">
    Paste cut-out letters and words in your scrapbook to create a 3-D effect.
    Online Scrapbooks sells professionally designed cut-out letters, words, and
    phrases for all occasions.
</div>
<div id="note2" class="notes">
    Clippings, flyers, programs, and other memorabilia are valuable sources of
    information that can enhance your scrapbook pages. Make sure that any material
    is copied to acid-free paper. Newspaper clippings are especially susceptible
    to deterioration.
</div>
<div id="note3" class="notes">
    Photographic cut-outs and textured backgrounds can add visual interest to your
    pages. See the online store for our wide variety of textured and embossed papers.
</div>
<p><img src="sample.jpg" alt="sample page" width="474" height="616" /></p>
</div>
```

▶ **4.** Save your changes to the file.

▶ **5.** Open **samples.htm** in your Web browser. Figure 7-58 shows the formatted appearance of the three notes boxes. Note that although the boxes are placed side-by-side in this figure to make them easier to read, they should appear stacked on top of one another on your page.

Figure 7-58 ▶ **Formatted notes boxes**

note 1

Paste cut-out letters and words in your scrapbook to create a 3-D effect. Online Scrapbooks sells professionally designed cut-out letters, words, and phrases for all occasions.

note 2

Clippings, flyers, programs, and other memorabilia are valuable sources of information that can enhance your scrapbook pages. Make sure that any material is copied to acid-free paper. Newspaper clippings are especially susceptible to deterioration.

note 3

Photographic cut-outs and textured backgrounds can add visual interest to your pages. See the online store for our wide variety of textured and embossed papers.

Now that you've entered the text and the formatting styles for the three callout notes, your next task is to place them at appropriate locations on the Web page.

The Position Style

Positioning was one of the first enhancements to the original CSS1 specifications. Collectively, the different positioning styles were known as **CSS-Positioning,** or more commonly, **CSS-P**. CSS-P became part of the specification for CSS2, and positioning styles were some of the first CSS2 styles to be adopted by browsers.

To place an element at a specific position on the page, use the following styles:

```
position: type; top: value; right: value; bottom: value; left: value;
```

where `type` indicates the type of positioning applied to the element, and the top, right, bottom, and left styles indicate the coordinates of the top, right, bottom, and left edges of the element. In practice, only the top and left coordinates are used, because the bottom and right coordinates can be inferred given the element's height and width. Coordinates can be expressed in the usual CSS measuring units.

The position style has five possible values: static, absolute, relative, fixed, and inherit. Let's consider each of these types in turn. The default position is static, which allows browsers to place an element based on where it flows in the document. This is essentially the same as not using any CSS positioning at all. Any values specified for the top or left styles with a static position are ignored by the browser.

Positioning an Object with CSS

Reference Window

- To place an object at a specific location, use the styles
  ```
  position: type; top: value; right: value; bottom: value; left: value
  ```
  where `type` indicates the type of positioning applied to the element (absolute, relative, static, fixed, or inherit), and the top, right, bottom, and left styles indicate the coordinates of the top, right, bottom, and left edges of the element.

Absolute Positioning

More often used than static positioning is absolute positioning, which enables you to place an element at specific coordinates either on a page or within a containing element. For example, the declaration

```
position: absolute; left: 100px; top: 50px
```

places an element at the coordinates (100, 50), or 100 pixels to the right and 50 pixels down from upper-left corner of the page or the containing element. The containing element is only used as a reference point if it too has been placed on the page using CSS positioning; otherwise, the top/left values refer to page coordinates. Absolute positioning takes an element out of the normal flow of a document, and any subsequent content flows into the space previously occupied by the element. To see how absolute positioning affects page layout, open the supplied demo page.

To work with absolute positioning:

1. Use your Web browser to open **demo_css_positioning.htm** from the tutorial.07/ tutorial folder.

The demo page contains two colored boxes that you can move by changing the values of the positioning styles in the input fields on the right edge of the page. The boxes are initially set in their default positions, as shown in Figure 7-59.

Figure 7-59 ▷ **CSS positioning demo page**

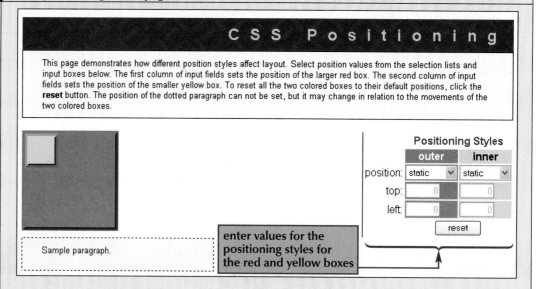

2. Select **absolute** from the drop-down list box for the outer box, enter **200** for the top value, and **250** for the left value and press the **Tab** key.

   The red box moves to the page coordinates (250, 200)—that is, 250 pixels to the right and 200 pixels down from the upper-left corner of the browser window. The yellow box retains its position with the red box, and the sample paragraph moves up into the space previously occupied by the red box.

3. Select **absolute** from the drop-down list box for the inner box, enter **50** for the top value, and **120** for the left value and press the **Tab** key.

   Because the yellow box is contained within an element that has been already positioned on the page, its coordinates are expressed in reference to the red box and thus the yellow box is moved 50 pixels down and 120 pixels to the right of the red box's upper-left corner (see Figure 7-60).

Applying absolute positioning

Figure 7-60

If you change the position of the red box to static, it is no longer being positioned using the CSS styles. In such a case, the absolute position of the yellow box is expressed in reference to the page rather than in reference to its container.

4. Select **static** from the drop-down list box for the outer box. The red box is now placed back at its original position in the document flow and the yellow box is moved 50 pixels down and 120 pixels to the right of the upper-left corner of the page (see Figure 7-61).

Applying absolute positioning to a nested element

Figure 7-61

Trouble? If you are using a Macintosh, this demo may not appear as shown or function as described.

5. Continue to experiment with different combinations of top and left values. Note that if you enter a negative value for the top and left coordinates, the element moves up and to the left.

Relative Positioning

Relative positioning is used to move an element relative to its default position on the page. An element's default position is where the browser would have placed it if no positioning style was applied to it. For example, the style

```
position: relative; left: 100px; top: 50px
```

places an element 100 pixels to the right and 50 pixels down from its normal placement in a browser window. Relative positioning does not affect the position of other elements on a page, which retain their original positions as if the element had never been moved.

To work with relative positioning:

1. Click the **reset** button on the CSS Positioning demo page to return the two colored boxes to their default positions.

2. Select **relative** from the drop-down list box for the outer box, then enter **50** for the top value and **140** for the left value and press the **Tab** key.

    The red box is placed 50 pixels down and 140 pixels to right of its default position. Note that the sample paragraph does not flow into the space previously occupied by the colored boxes. The layout of the rest of the page is unaffected when relative positioning is applied. See Figure 7-62.

Figure 7-62	Applying relative positioning

3. Explore other combinations of relative and absolute positioning to see their effects on the boxes.

Fixed and Inherited Positioning

An element placed with absolute or relative positioning scrolls with the rest of the document. Alternately, you can fix an element at a specific spot in the document window while the rest of the page scrolls by setting the value of the position style to "fixed". You can also assign an element the inherit position style so that it to inherits the position value of its parent element.

To work with fixed and inherited positioning:

1. Click the **reset** button on the CSS positioning demo page to return to the default layout.

2. Select **fixed** from the drop-down list box for the outer box, then enter **50** for the top and left values.

   The red box is placed at the page coordinates (50, 50). The sample paragraph flows into the space previously occupied by the box.

   Trouble? Depending on your browser, the fixed positioning style might not be supported; in this case, you will not see the red box move to the new position.

3. Select **inherit** from the drop-down list box for the inner box, then enter **200** for the top and left values.

   The yellow box inherits the position style of its parent. In this case it uses a fixed position value.

   Trouble? If your browser does not support inherited positioning, the position values will be grayed out and you will not be able to set the inherited position of the inner box.

4. Resize the browser window to display vertical scrollbars. Scroll through the document and verify that the two colored boxes remain fixed at the same location within the browser window.

5. Continue to experiment with different combinations of coordinates and position types. Close the Web page when finished.

Placing the Callout Notes

Now that you've seen how to work with the different positioning styles of CSS, you can apply your knowledge to position the three callout notes. After trying different values you settle on the following coordinates using absolute positioning:

- note1: (600, 150)
- note2: (170, 400)
- note3: (570, 550)

   Add styles for these positions to the embedded style sheet in the samples.htm file.

To place the three notes:

1. Return to the **samples.htm** file in your text editor.

2. Add the following declarations to the embedded style sheet (as shown in Figure 7-63):

```
#note1 {position: absolute; left: 600px; top: 150px}
#note2 {position: absolute; left: 170px; top: 400px}
#note3 {position: absolute; left: 570px; top: 550px}
```

| Figure 7-63 | Setting the position of the three notes |

```
<style type="text/css">
 .notes {font-family: sans-serif; font-size: 8pt; color: brown; background-color: ivory;
         border: 2px inset white; padding: 5px; width: 130px; margin-bottom: 5px}
 #note1 {position: absolute; left: 600px; top: 150px}
 #note2 {position: absolute; left: 170px; top: 400px}
 #note3 {position: absolute; left: 570px; top: 550px}
</style>
</head>
```

3. Save your changes to the file and reload **samples.htm** in your browser. Figure 7-64 shows the placement of the three notes.

| Figure 7-64 | Notes placed with absolute positioning |

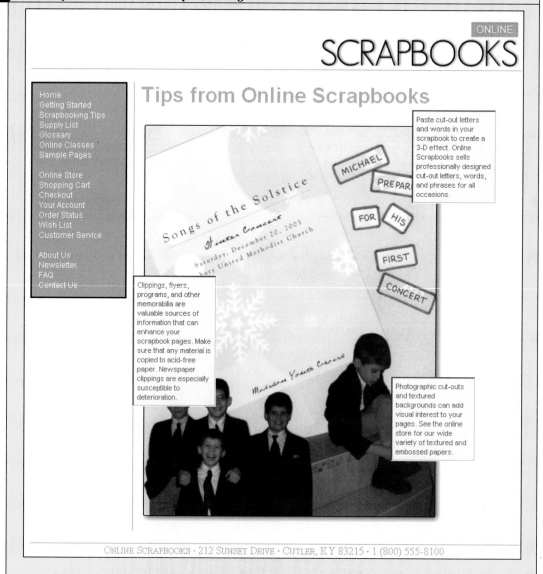

You show Kathy the revised page. She likes the position of the notes, but feels that they are too big and hide too much of the scrapbooking sample. Kathy would like you to investigate ways of making the notes less intrusive.

Working with Overflow and Clipping

Reducing the height of each note by lowering the value of its height style may seem like an easy solution to Kathy's first request; unfortunately, though, this would not meet her needs, because the height of each note still expands to accommodate its content. If you want to force an element into a specified height and width, you have to set the element's overflow property. The syntax of the overflow property is

```
overflow: type
```

where `type` is visible (the default), hidden, scroll, or auto. A value of "visible" instructs browsers to increase the height of an element to fit the overflow content. The "hidden" value keeps an element at the specified height and width, but cuts off the overflow. The "scroll" value keeps an element at the specified dimensions, but adds horizontal and vertical scrollbars to allow users to scroll through the overflow. Finally, the "auto" value keeps an element at the specified size, but adds scrollbars only if they are needed. Figure 7-65 shows examples of each overflow value.

Values of the overflow style ◄ **Figure 7-65**

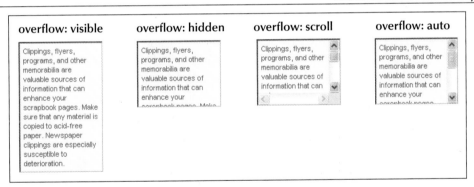

You decide to limit the height of each callout note to 100 pixels, and to allow users to view the overflow content using a scrollbar.

To define the overflow style:

► 1. Return to the **samples.htm** file in your text editor.

► 2. Add the following styles to the declaration for the notes class selector (see Figure 7-66):

```
height: 100px; overflow: auto
```

Figure 7-66 | **Setting the overflow style of the three notes**

```
<title>Sample Scrapbook Page</title>
<link href="scraps.css" rel="stylesheet" type="text/css" media="screen" />

<style type="text/css">
    .notes {font-family: sans-serif; font-size: 8pt; color: brown; background-color: ivory;
            border: 2px inset white; padding: 5px; width: 130px; height: 100px;
            overflow: auto}
    #note1 {position: absolute; left: 600px; top: 150px}
    #note2 {position: absolute; left: 170px; top: 400px}
    #note3 {position: absolute; left: 570px; top: 550px}
</style>
</head>
```

▶ **3.** Save your changes and reload **samples.htm** in your browser. Figure 7-67 shows the appearance of the notes with scrollbars.

Figure 7-67 | **Notes with scrollbars**

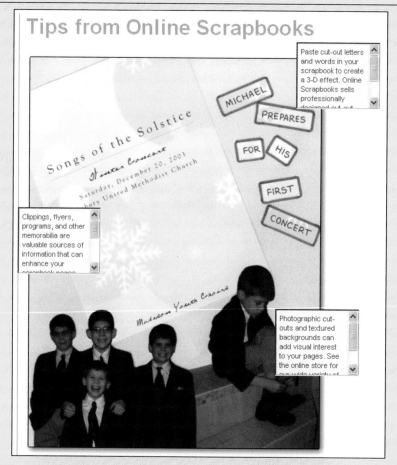

▶ **4.** Use the scrollbars to verify that the entire content of each note is still available to users.

Closely related to the overflow style is the clip style. The clip style allows you to define a rectangular region through which the element's content can be viewed. Anything that lies outside the boundary of the rectangle is hidden. The syntax of the clip style is

```
clip: rect(top, right, bottom, left)
```

where *top*, *right*, *bottom*, and *left* define the coordinates of the clipping rectangle. For example, a clip value of rect(10, 175, 125, 75) defines a clip region whose top and bottom edges are 10 and 125 pixels from the top of the element, and whose right and left edges are 175 and 75 pixels from the left side of the element (see Figure 7-68).

Clipping an element ◀ **Figure 7-68**

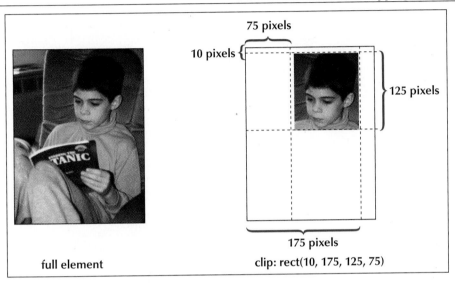

| full element | clip: rect(10, 175, 125, 75) |

The *top*, *right*, *bottom*, and *left* values can also be set to "auto", which matches the specified edge of the clipping region to the edge of the parent element. For example, a clip value of rect(10, auto, 125, 75) creates a clipping rectangle whose right edge matches the right edge of the parent element.

Stacking Elements

The ability to move elements to different page locations can lead to overlapping objects. By default, elements that are formatted later in an HTML or XHTML document are stacked on top of earlier elements. In addition, elements placed using CSS positioning are stacked on top of elements that are not. To specify a different stacking order, use the style

```
z-index: value
```

where *value* is a positive or negative integer, or the keyword "auto". As shown in Figure 7-69, objects are stacked based on their z-index values, with the highest z-index values placed on top. A value of "auto" allows the browser to determine stacking order using the default rules.

Figure 7-69 ▶ Using the z-index style

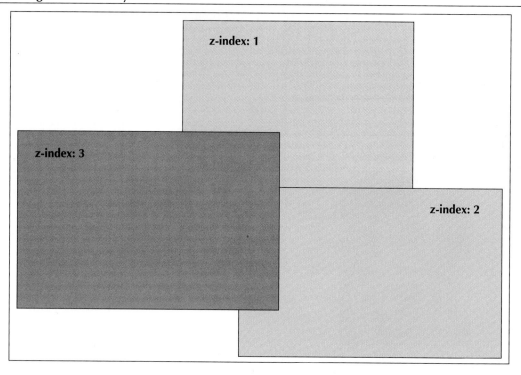

The z-index style only works for elements that are placed with absolute positioning. Also, an element's z-index value determines its position relative only to other elements that share a common parent; the style has no impact when applied to elements with different parents.

You don't need to use the clip or z-index styles, so you can move on to Kathy's next set of tasks for you.

Reference Window | **Working with Content Overflow, Clipping, and Stacking**

- To change how the browser handles content that overflows the size of an element, use the style
    `overflow: type`
  where `type` is visible (the default, which expands the element height to match the content), hidden (to hide content overflow), scroll (to always display horizontal and vertical scrollbars), or auto (to display scrollbars only when needed).
- To clip an element's content, use the style
    `clip: rect(top, right, bottom, left}`
  where `top`, `right`, `bottom`, and `left` define the coordinates of the clipping rectangle.
- To determine how positioned objects should be stacked, use the style
    `z-index: value`
  where `value` is a positive or negative integer or "auto" (to use the default stacking order). Objects with higher z-index values are stacked on top of elements with lower z-index values.

Working with Different Media

Kathy is satisfied with the final layouts for the pages in the Online Scrapbooks Web site. The pages look fine on the computer screen, but Kathy is aware that her pages might be viewed using media other than computer screens. She would like you to examine how to create style sheets that work with other devices.

Media Types

By default, a style sheet is applied to all devices, and each device must determine how best to match the styles to its own requirements. For example, when you print a Web page, the Web browser and its built-in styles prepare the document for the printer. The user also has some control over that process—for example, determining the size of the page margins or the content of the printout's header or footer.

CSS2 and subsequent versions have given more control to Web page authors to specify output styles for particular devices. You specify an output device in the media attribute of the link and style elements. Figure 7-70 lists the values of the media attribute that are defined for CSS2.

Values of the media attribute ◄ **Figure 7-70**

Media Value	Used For
all	All output devices (the default)
aural	Speech and sound synthesizers
braille	Braille tactile feedback devices
embossed	Paged Braille printers
handheld	Small or handheld devices with small screens, monochrome graphics, and limited bandwidth
print	Printers
projection	Projectors
screen	Computer screens
tty	Fixed-width devices like teletype machines and terminals
tv	Television-type devices with low resolution, color, and limited scrollability

For example, to specify that an external style sheet named "sounds.css" should be used for aural browsers, you would enter the following link element in your HTML or XHTML document:

```
<link href="sounds.css" type="text/css" media="aural" />
```

In the same way, you would use the media attribute in an embedded style sheet to indicate that its styles are intended for aural devices:

```
<style type="text/css" media="aural">
...
</style>
```

The media attribute can also contain a comma-separated list of media types. The following link element links to a style sheet designed for both print and screen media:

```
<link href="output.css" type="text/css" media="print, screen" />
```

Style sheets cascade through different media types in the same way they cascade through a document tree. A style sheet in which the output device is not specified is applied to all devices, unless it is superseded by a style designed for a particular device. In the following set of embedded style sheets, h1 headings are displayed in a sans-serif font for all devices; however text color is red for computer screens and black for printed pages:

```
<style type="text/css">
   h1 {font-family: sans-serif}
</style>
<style type="text/css" media="screen">
   h1 {color: red}
</style>
<style type="text/css" media="print">
   h1 {color: black}
</style>
```

The @media Rule

You can also specify the output media within a style sheet using the following rule:

```
@media type {style declarations}
```

where *media* is one of the supported media types and *style declarations* are the styles associated with that media type. For example, the following declarations set the font size of body text and h1 headings for a variety of different output media:

```
@media screen {body {font-size: 1em} h1 {font-size: 2em}}
@media print {body {font-size: 12pt} h1 {font-size: 16pt}}
@media handheld {body {font-size: 8pt} h1 {font-size: 12pt}}
@media tv {body {font-size: 16pt} h1 {font-size: 24pt}}
```

In this style sheet, the font size is smallest for a handheld device (which presumably has a limited screen area), and largest for a television (which is usually viewed from a greater distance). Similar to the media attribute, the @media rule also allows you to place media types in a comma-separated list:

```
@media screen, print, handheld, tv {h1 {font-family: sans-serif}}
```

Both the media attribute and the @media rule come with their own benefits and disadvantages. The @media rule allows you to consolidate all of your styles within a single style sheet; however this consolidation can result in larger and complicated files. The alternative, placing media styles in different sheets, can make those sheets easier to maintain; however, if you change the design of your site, you may have to duplicate your changes across several style sheets.

Creating Styles for Different Media

- To create a style sheet for specific media, add the following attribute to either the link element or the style element:
    ```
    media="type"
    ```
  where *type* is one or more of the following: aural, braille, embossed, handheld, print, projection, screen, tty, tv, or all. If you don't specify a value for the media attribute, the style sheet is applied to all media. Multiple types should be entered in a comma-separated list.
- To create style declarations for a specific medium within a style sheet, use the form
    ```
    @media type {style declarations}
    ```

Supporting Older Browsers

Many older browsers do not support the media attribute, the @media rule, or many CSS2 styles. For these older browsers, the most common practice for formatting output for different media is to link each page to a **printer-friendly version** of the document, which is formatted specifically for printing. The disadvantage of this approach is that it forces you to create and maintain duplicate copies of your pages. However, it ensures that all users have a choice of printed styles—they can print from the page as it appears on the computer screen, or use the specially formatted print style that you design.

Media Groups

All output media can be described based on some common properties. CSS2 uses the concept of **media groups** to describe basic facets of the output for different media, and to differentiate between different types of media based on the ways they render content. The four media groups describe content that can be

- continuous or paged
- visual, aural, or tactile
- grid (for character grid devices) or bitmap
- interactive (for devices that allow user interaction) or static (for devices that allow no interaction)

Figure 7-71 shows how all output media are categorized based on the four media groups. For example, a printout is paged (because the output comes in discrete units or pages), visual, bitmap, and static (you can't interact with it). A computer screen, on the other hand, is continuous, visual, bitmap, and can be either static or interactive.

Media groups | Figure 7-71

| Media Types | Media Groups | | | |
	continuous/paged	visual/aural/tactile	grid/bitmap	interactive/static
aural	continuous	aural	N/A	both
braille	continuous	tactile	grid	both
embossed	paged	tactile	grid	both
handheld	both	visual	both	both
print	paged	visual	bitmap	static
projection	paged	visual	bitmap	static
screen	continuous	visual	bitmap	both
tty	continuous	visual	grid	both
tv	both	visual, aural	bitmap	both

Media groups are important because the CSS2 specifications indicate which media *group* a particular style belongs to, rather than the specific media *device*. For example, the font-size style belongs to the visual media group, meaning that you should be able to use it with handheld, print, projection, screen, tty, and tv media. The pitch style, used to define the pitch or frequency of a speaking voice, belongs to the aural media group, which means that it should be supported by aural and tv devices. By studying the media groups, you can choose the styles that apply to a given output device.

Many users of the Online Scrapbooks Web site have reported to Kathy that they enjoy the monthly sample pages so much that they print the samples and store them in albums for future reference. However, these users often find that the pages don't print well. Most users would prefer to print only the scrapbook sample, without Online Scrapbooks header, links list, and footer, and would like the callout notes to appear on a separate page, perhaps in a bulleted list. Kathy has sketched a proposed design for printed scrapbook sample pages, which is shown in Figure 7-72.

Figure 7-72 ▷ **Sketch of Kathy's proposed print layout**

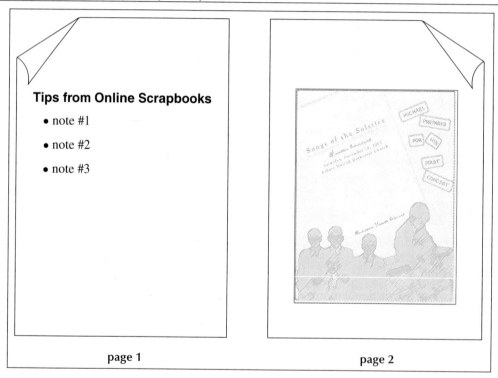

Your first task in making this proposal a reality is to hide the elements that Kathy doesn't want printed.

Hiding Elements

Two different styles allow you to hide an element: the display style and the visibility style. As you've already seen, the display style supports the value "none", which causes the element to not be rendered by the output device. Alternately, you can use the visibility style, which has the syntax

```
visibility: type
```

where *type* is visible, hidden, collapse, or inherit (the default). A value of "visible" makes an element visible; the "hidden" value hides the element; a value of "collapse" is used with the tables to prevent a row or column from being displayed; and the "inherit" value causes an element to inherit the visibility style from its parent. Unlike the display style, the visibility style hides an element, but does not remove it from the flow of elements in the page. As shown in Figure 7-73, setting the display style to "none" not only hides an element, but also removes it from the page flow.

Comparing the visibility and display styles ◄ **Figure 7-73**

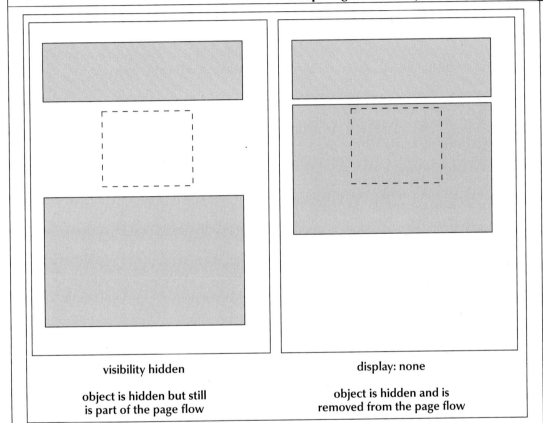

visibility hidden

object is hidden but still
is part of the page flow

display: none

object is hidden and is
removed from the page flow

The display: none style is more appropriate for hiding elements in most cases. Use of the visibility: hidden style is usually reserved for scripts in which an element is alternatively hidden and made visible to create an animated effect.

Kathy asks you to hide the address, #links, and #head elements on the Samples page for printed output. You'll add the styles to do this to an external style sheet named print. css.

To create the print.css external style sheet:

1. Use your text editor to create a new document.

2. Insert the following lines in the file (see Figure 7-74):

```
/* Online Scrapbooks print styles */
h1, h2, h3, h4, h5, h6 {font-family: sans-serif}
address, #head, #links {display: none}
```

Figure 7-74 ▶ **The print.css style sheet**

```
/* Online Scrapbooks print styles */
h1, h2, h3, h4, h5, h6 {font-family: sans-serif}
address, #head, #links {display: none}
```

▶ **3.** Save the file as **print.css** in the tutorial.07/tutorial folder, then close the file.

Kathy wants you to use the print.css style sheet for any paged visual media, which includes both printed media and projected media. You should use the scraps.css style sheet for continuous visual media, which includes computer screens, television monitors, and ttys. In the samples.htm file, add a link to the print.css style sheet and insert the media attribute to indicate which style sheets to use for which output devices.

To link to the print.css style sheet:

▶ **1.** Return to the **samples.htm** file in your text editor.

▶ **2.** Before the link element that points to the scraps.css file, insert the following link:

```
<link href="print.css" rel="stylesheet" type="text/css"
      media="print, projection" />
```

▶ **3.** Add the following attribute to the link element for the scraps.css style sheet:

```
media="screen, tv, tty"
```

Figure 7-75 shows the revised code of the samples.htm file.

Figure 7-75 ▶ **Linking to the print.css style sheet**

```
<title>Sample Scrapbook Page</title>
<link href="print.css" rel="stylesheet" type="text/css" media="print, projection" />
<link href="scraps.css" rel="stylesheet" type="text/css" media="screen, tv, tty" />
```

Next you need to modify the style for the callout notes. Rather than positioning each note in a scrollable box, you'll change their display style to list items in a 12-point sans-serif font. To display the bullet markers, you'll also have to set the margin size to 20 pixels. As you did with the external style sheets, you'll use the media attribute to match each embedded style sheet with the appropriate output device.

To create a print style for the callout notes:

▶ **1.** Before the current embedded style sheet, insert the following code:

```
<style type="text/css" media="print, projection">
   .notes {font-family: sans-serif; font-size: 12pt;
           display: list-item; margin: 20px}
</style>
```

▶ **2.** Add the following attribute to the next embedded style sheet:

```
media="screen, tv, tty"
```

Figure 7-76 shows the embedded style sheets.

Creating an embedded style sheet for paged media ◄ **Figure 7-76**

```
<style type="text/css" media="print, projection">
   .notes {font-family: sans-serif; font-size: 12pt; display: list-item; margin: 20px}
</style>
<style type="text/css" media="screen, tv, tty">
   .notes {font-family: sans-serif; font-size: 8pt; color: brown; background-color: ivory;
           border: 2px inset white; padding: 5px; width: 130px; height: 100px;
           overflow: auto}
   #note1 {position: absolute; left: 600px; top: 150px}
   #note2 {position: absolute; left: 170px; top: 400px}
   #note3 {position: absolute; left: 570px; top: 550px}
</style>
```

► **3.** Save your changes to the file.

► **4.** Reopen **samples.htm** in your Web browser and verify that the appearance of the page in your computer screen has not changed.

► **5.** Either print the Web page from within your browser, or use your browser's Print Preview command to preview the printed output. Figure 7-77 shows a preview of the printed Samples page.

Preview of the printed Samples page ◄ **Figure 7-77**

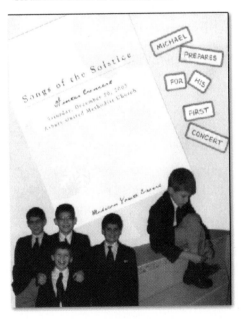

Sample Scrapbook Page   Page 1 of 1

Tips from Online Scrapbooks

- Paste cut-out letters and words in your scrapbook to create a 3-D effect. Online Scrapbooks sells professionally designed cut-out letters, words, and phrases for all occasions.

- Clippings, flyers, programs, and other memorabilia are valuable sources of information that can enhance your scrapbook pages. Make sure that any material is copied to acid-free paper. Newspaper clippings are especially susceptible to deterioration.

- Photographic cut-outs and textured backgrounds can add visual interest to your pages. See the online store for our wide variety of textured and embossed papers.

Kathy likes the printout you created; however, she still wants the notes to appear on a separate sheet. To do this, you'll have to place a page break in the middle of the document. CSS2 supports several styles specifically designed for paged media like print-outs and projection slides. Although many of the W3C specifications have yet to be adopted by the browser market, page breaks are one of the styles you can reliably use to enhance the appearance of your printed output.

Using Print Styles

CSS2 defines printed pages by extending the box model described earlier to incorporate the entire page in a **page box**. As with other objects in the box model, you can specify the size of a page, the page margins, the internal padding, and other elements. Whereas a page box specifies how a document should be rendered within the rectangular area of the page, it is the browser's responsibility to transfer that model to the printed sheet. The general rule to create and define a page box is

```
@page {styles}
```

where *styles* are the styles you want applied to the page. For example, the following embedded style sets the page margin for the printed output to 5 inches and displays the page's body text in a 12-point serif font.

```
<style type="text/css" media="print">
   @page {margin: 5in}
   body {font-size: 12pt; font-family: serif}
</style>
```

A page box does not support all of the measurement units you've used with the other elements. For example, pages do not support the em or ex measurement units.

Page Pseudo-Classes and Named Pages

In some cases you may need to define multiple page styles within the same document. You can do this through pseudo-classes or page names. The syntax to apply a pseudo-class to a page is

```
@page:pseudo-class {styles}
```

where *pseudo-class* is one of the three following supported types:

- **first** for the first page of the printout
- **left** for pages that appear on the left in double-sided printouts
- **right** for pages that appear on the right in double-sided printouts

For example, if you are doing two-sided printing, you may wish to mirror the margins of the left and right pages of the printout. The following styles result in pages in which the inner margin is set to 5 centimeters and outer margin is set to 2 centimeters.

```
@page:left {margin: 3cm 5cm 3cm 2cm}
@page:right {margin: 3cm 2cm 3cm 5cm}
```

To format specific pages other than the first, left, or right pages, you can create a named label for a page style and then apply that page to particular elements in your document. The syntax to create a page name is

```
@page name {styles}
```

where *name* is the label assigned to the page style. To access a named page, use the page style in a style declaration as follows:

```
selector {page: name}
```

For example, the following styles define a page named "large_margins" and then indicate that this page should be used for every instance of a table in a document:

```
@page large_margins {margin: 10cm}
table {page: large_margins}
```

Note that named pages can be applied only to block-level elements, meaning that you cannot apply them to inline elements. If two consecutive block-level elements are assigned different page names, browsers automatically insert a page break between the elements.

Setting the Page Size

The size of the output page can be defined using the size style. With this style, Web authors can define the dimensions of the printed page as well as whether the pages should be printed in portrait or landscape orientation. The syntax of the size style is

```
size: width height orientation
```

where *width* and *height* are the width and height of the page, and *orientation* is the orientation of the page (portrait or landscape). If you don't specify the orientation, browsers assume a portrait orientation. To format a page as a standard-size page in landscape orientation with a one-inch margin, you could use the style

```
@page {size: 8.5in 11in landscape; margin: 1in}
```

If you remove the orientation value, as in the style

```
@page {size: 8.5in 11in; margin: 1in}
```

browsers print the output in portrait by default. You can also replace the width, height, and orientation values with the keyword auto (to let the browser determine the page dimensions) or inherit (to inherit the page size from the parent element). If a page does not fit into the dimensions specified by the style, browsers either rotate the page box 90 degrees or scale the page box to fit the sheet size.

Displaying Crop Marks

In high-quality printing, crop marks are used to define where a page should be trimmed before binding. CSS2 supports the marks property, which adds crop marks to a printed sheet. The syntax of the marks style is

```
marks: type
```

where *type* is crop, cross, inherit, or none. Figure 7-78 shows examples of the crop and cross values.

Figure 7-78 | **Displaying crop marks**

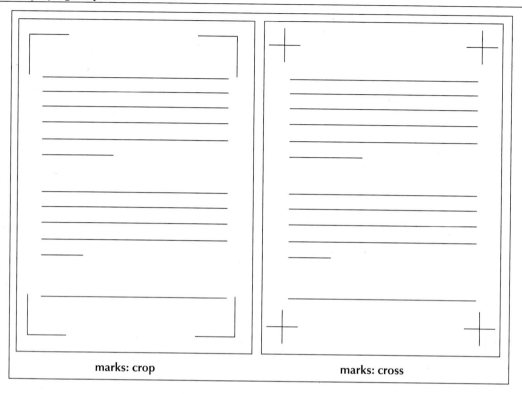

marks: crop　　　　　　　marks: cross

The size, style, and position of the crop marks depend on the browser.

Working with Page Breaks

CSS supports three styles that determine where page breaks should be placed in relation to the elements in a page. The page-break-before and page-break-after styles are used to place page breaks before or after a given element. The syntax of the page-break-before and page-break-after styles is

```
page-break-before: type
page-break-after: type
```

where *type* is always (to always place a page break), avoid (to never place a page break), left (to force a page break where the succeeding page will be a left page), right (to force a page break where the succeeding page will be a right page), auto (to allow the browser to determine whether or not to insert a page break), or inherit (to inherit the page break style of the parent element). For example, if you want tables always to appear on their own pages, you can place a page break before and after each table using the following style:

```
table {page-break-before: always; page-break-after: always}
```

You can also prevent the insertion of a page break using the page-break-inside style with the following syntax:

```
page-break-inside: type
```

where *type* is auto, inherit, or avoid. If you want to avoid placing a page break inside of a table, you would use the following style:

```
table {page-break-inside: avoid}
```

Note that the avoid type does not guarantee that there will not be a page break within the element. If the content of an element exceeds the dimensions of the sheet, the browser may be forced to insert a page break.

You can combine the various page styles to provide greater control over the printed output. For example, if your document contains several wide tables, you can place the tables on separate pages in landscape orientation using the following style declarations:

```
@page table_page {8.5in 11in landscape}
table {page: table_page; page-break-before: always; page-break-inside:
       avoid; page-break-after: always}
```

Finally, you can use CSS2 to control the sizes of the widows and orphans that appear when a page break is inserted within an element. A **widow** refers to the final few lines of an element's text when they appear at the top of a page, while most of the element's text appears on the previous page. The term **orphan** describes the first few lines of an element's text when they appear at the bottom of a page, with the bulk of the element's text appearing on the next page. The styles to control widows and orphans are

```
widow: value
orphan: value
```

where *value* is the number of lines that must appear within the element before a page break is inserted. The default value is 2, which means that widows and orphans must both contain at least 2 lines of text. If you want to increase the size of widows and orphans to three lines for the paragraphs of your document, you could use the following style declaration:

```
p {widow: 3; orphan: 3}
```

It's important to note that the widow and orphan values might not always be followed. Browsers attempt to use page breaks that obey the following guidelines:

- Insert all of the manual page breaks as indicated by the page-break-before, page-break-after styles, and page-break-inside styles.
- Avoid inserting page breaks where indicated in the style sheet.
- Break the pages as few times as possible.
- Make all pages that don't have a forced page break appear to have the same height.
- Avoid page breaking inside of a block-level element that has a border.
- Avoid breaking inside of a table.
- Avoid breaking inside of a floating element.

Only after attempting to satisfy these constraints are the recommendations of the widow and orphan styles applied.

Working with Print Styles

- To define a page box for a printout that indicates the page size, margins, and orientation, use the declaration

      @page {styles}

  where *styles* are the styles that define the page.
- To apply a style to a particular page, use the declaration

      @page:pseudo-class {styles}

  where *pseudo-class* is first (for the first page), left (for left-hand pages), or right (for right-hand pages).
- To set the page size and orientation, use the style

      size: width height orientation

  where *width* and *height* are the width and height of the page, and *orientation* is the orientation of the page (portrait or landscape).
- To display crop marks, use the style

      marks: type

  where *type* is crop, cross, inherit, or none.
- To format the page break before an element, use the style

      page-break-before: type

  where *type* is always (to always place a page break), avoid (to never place a page break), left (to force a page break where the succeeding page will be a left page), right (to force a page break where the succeeding page will be a right page), auto (to allow the browser to determine whether or not to insert a page break), or inherit (to inherit the page break style of the parent element).
- To format the page break after an element, use the style

      page-break-after: type

  where *type* has the same values as the page-break-before style.
- To apply a page break inside an element, use the style

      page-break-inside: type

  where *type* is auto, inherit, or avoid.

Now that you've seen how to insert line breaks into printed output, you are ready to insert a line break into the printed version of the Samples page. Recall that Kathy wants the list of notes to appear on one page and the scrapbooking sample to appear on another. To do this, you can either place a page break after the third callout note or place a page break before the inline image of the scrapbooking sample. You decide to place a page break before the image. This will allow you to insert additional callout notes later without having to revise the page break structure.

To insert a page break before the inline image:

1. Return to the **samples.htm** file in your text editor.

2. Add the following style declaration to the embedded style sheet for printers and projection devices (see Figure 7-79):

   #main p img {page-break-before: always}

Figure 7-79

Inserting a page break

```
<style type="text/css" media="print, projection">
   .notes {font-family: sans-serif; font-size: 12pt; display: list-item; margin: 20px}
   #main p img {page-break-before: always}
</style>
```

3. Close the file, saving your changes.

4. Reopen **samples.htm** in your Web browser and verify that the appearance of the page on your computer screen has not changed.

5. Either print or preview the printed Web page from your browser to verify that the list of notes is placed on one page and the scrapbooking sample is placed on another. See Figure 7-80.

Two-page printout ◄ **Figure 7-80**

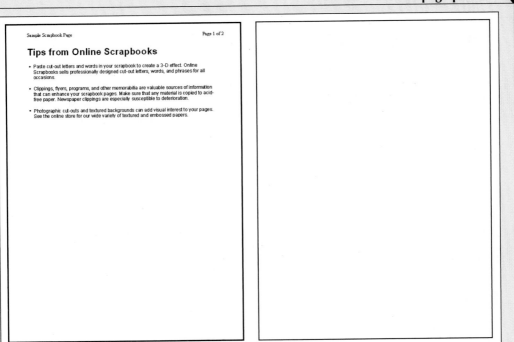

Trouble? Depending on your browser, you might not see the page breaks shown in Figure 7-80.

6. Close your Web browser and any other open files from this tutorial.

You've completed your work on the Samples page for the Online Scrapbooks Web site, and you'll be able to apply what you've learned about print styles to the other pages in the site. At the moment, most browsers support few of the page styles other than page breaking. This is sure to change in the future, however, as Web pages expand beyond the limitations of the computer screen into new media. Kathy finds this an exciting prospect, providing the opportunity to advertise the company to a whole new set of potential customers.

Session 7.3 Quick Check

Review

1. What is the style to place the element with the id "Logo" at the page coordinates: (50, 100)?

2. What is the style to move span elements with the class name "Up", up 10 pixels from their default position?

3. What is the difference between the style display: none and the style visibility: hidden?

4. Within a style sheet, how would you define a print style for the h1 element?

5. What media types belong to the continuous visual group?

6. What is the style to set the page size to 11 inches wide by 14 inches high with a landscape orientation?

7. What is the style to place a page break before every h1 heading?

Review

Tutorial Summary

In this tutorial, you learned how to use Cascading Style Sheets to create interesting and flexible layouts and designs. The first session introduced CSS, showing how to create embedded and external style sheets and discussing the advantages of these style sheets over inline styles. The first session also showed how styles cascade down through the document tree and through different levels of styles. You also learned how to apply styles to an element based on its location in the document tree or the values of its attributes. In the second session you learned how to apply styles to elements based on their id or class values. You also learned how to use CSS for page layout by floating and sizing elements, and how to add interesting visual effects such as rollovers and drop caps to your Web page. The third session introduced the wide variety of CSS positioning styles. In the third session, you also learned how to use absolute and relative positioning, as well as how to work with content overflow. The session concluded with a discussion of applying styles to media other than the computer screen with an in-depth look at CSS print styles.

Key Terms

absolute positioning	CSS2.1	page box
attribute selector	CSS3	printer friendly version
box model	CSS-P	pseudo-class
Cascading Style Sheets	div element	pseudo-element
contextual selector	embedded styles	relative positioning
CSS	external styles	rollover effect
CSS Positioning	inline styles	style sheet
CSS1	media group	widow
CSS2	orphan	

Practice

Practice the skills you've learned in the tutorial using the same case scenario.

Review Assignments

Data files needed for this Review Assignment: galltxt.htm, sample1.jpg, sample2.jpg, sample3.jpg, sample4.jpg, scraps.jpg

Kathy has stopped by to ask your help in designing a new page, which will contain scrapbooking samples sent in by users. She envisions placing thumbnail versions of the samples in a scrollable box on a Gallery Web page, while the printed versions of the same page will show the full-size versions of the samples. She also would like you to implement a new design for the page head, link list, and address. Figure 7-81 shows a preview of the page you'll create.

Figure 7-81

ONLINE
SCRAPBOOKS

May Gallery

Every month Online Scrapbooks presents the best scrapbooking samples from our customers. Scroll through the list of images to view this month's submissions. Click the image to view a full-size version of the sample page.

Interested in showcasing your work? Contact kathy_pridham@onlinescraps.com to receive a copy of our submission guidlines. Please one submission per person.

- April Gallery
- March Gallery
- February Gallery

Online Scrapbooks · 212 Sunset Drive · Cutler, KY 83215 · 1 (800) 555-8100

To create the Gallery Web page:

1. Using your text editor, open **galltxt.htm** from the tutorial.07/review folder. Enter **your name** and **the date** in the head section and save the file as **gallery.htm**. Take some time to review to content of the file, paying particular attention to the id names and document structure because those will be used in the style sheets you'll create for the page.

2. Use your text editor to create a file named **screen.css** in the tutorial.07/review folder. Enter CSS comment lines containing **your name** and **the date** at the top of the file.

3. In the **screen.css** file, enter the following styles and then close the file, saving your changes.
   - Set the margin size of the page body to 0 pixels.
   - Display all headings (h1 through h6) in a purple sans-serif font.
   - Set the left margin of the #head, #main, and address selectors to 120 pixels.
   - Add a 1-pixel solid purple border to the bottom of the #head selector.
   - Display the address text in a normal 8-point purple font, horizontally centered. Add a 1-pixel solid purple border to the top of the element. Prevent the address element from being displayed until both margins are clear.
   - Use absolute positioning to place the #links selector at the screen coordinates (0,0). Set the width of the selector to 100 pixels, and set the top margin to 0 pixels. Display the text of the #links selector to an 8-point font.
   - Display links within the #links selector as block-level elements. Change the font of the link text to a white sans-serif font on a purple background. Set the text decoration to normal, removing any underlining from the link text. Set the padding of the link element to 2 pixels and the margin size to 0 pixels. Place a 5-pixel solid purple border around the link elements.
   - For links within the #links selector, place a 5-pixel outset purple border around the link elements when the mouse hovers over the link. Also, change the font color of the link text in that situation to yellow.
   - For links within the #links selector, place a 5-pixel inset purple border around the link elements when user activates the link. Change the font color of the link text in that situation to yellow.

4. Return to the **gallery.htm** file and add a link element to the head section, linking to the screen.css style sheet. Specify that this style sheet should be used for screen, tv, and tty media.

5. Add an embedded style sheet to the gallery.htm file for use with screen, tv, and tty media. The embedded style sheet should contain the following styles:
   - Float the #gallery selector on the right margin. Set the width of the #gallery selector to 150 pixels with height of 200 pixels and a margin of 5 pixels.
   - Add a 1-pixel solid purple border around the #gallery selector.
   - Display scrollbars for overflow content in the #gallery selector, if necessary.
   - Set the width of inline images within the #gallery selector to 120 pixels and the height to 155 pixels. Add a 5-pixel margin to the images and set the border width to 0 pixels.

6. Use your text editor to create a file named **print.css** in the tutorial.07/review folder. Enter CSS comment lines containing *your name* and *the date* at the top of the file.

7. In the **print.css** file, insert styles to display all headings in a sans-serif font, and prohibit the display of the #head and #links selectors as well as the address element. Close the file, saving your changes.

8. Return to the **gallery.htm** file and add a link element to the head section, linking to the print.css style sheet. Specify that this style sheet should be used for print and projection media.

9. Add an embedded style sheet to the gallery.htm file for use with print and projection media. The embedded style sheet should contain the following styles:
   - Ensure that there are always page breaks before and after inline images within the #gallery selector. Set the dimensions of these inline images to 500 pixels wide by 650 pixels high. Set the width of the border around these images to 0 pixels.
   - Prohibit the display of list items within the #gallery selector.

10. Save your changes to **gallery.htm**.

11. Open **gallery.htm** in your browser and verify that the appearance matches the page shown in Figure 7-81. Also verify that a rollover effect is applied to the links in the links list.

12. Print or use Print Preview on the **gallery.htm** file and verify that the scrapbook samples appear on separate sheets and that the head, address, and links list are not printed.

13. Submit your completed Web site to your instructor.

Case Problem 1

Data files needed for this Case Problem: h01txt.htm through h18txt.htm, hole01.jpg through hole18.jpg, next.jpg, prev.jpg, space.gif, willet.jpg

Willet Creek Golf Course Willet Creek is a popular public golf course in central Idaho. You've been asked to work on the design of the course's Web site by Michael Carpenter, the head of promotion for the course. A portion of the Web site is a preview of each of the 18 holes of the course, complete with yardages and shot recommendations. Each hole has been given its own Web page. To apply the same style to each page, you decide to use an external style sheet. Many golfers now use handheld devices on the course, so you've also been asked to design a style sheet for use with that medium. Figure 7-82 shows a preview of the screen version of the Web site for one of the holes.

Figure 7-82

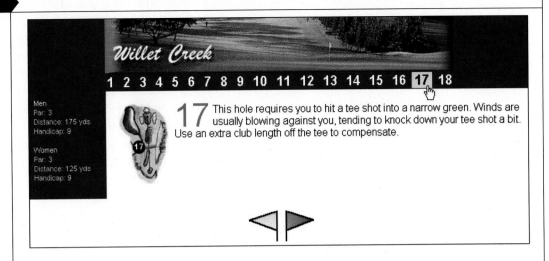

To complete this task:

1. Using your text editor, open **h01txt.htm** through **h18txt.htm** from the tutorial.07/ case1 folder. Enter *your name* and *the date* in the head section of each file and save the files as **h01.htm** through **h18.htm**. Take some time to review the content and document structure of each file, paying close attention to the use of the id attribute to identify the different sections of each document.

2. Use your text editor to create a file named **willet.css** in the tutorial.07/case1 folder. Enter CSS comment lines containing *your name* and *the date* at the top of the file.

3. In the **willet.css** file, enter the following styles and then close the file, saving your changes.

   - Set the margin and padding of the page body to 0 pixels. Set the page background color to white and the default font face to sans serif.
   - Remove underlining from all links
   - For an element with the id "head", set the bottom margin to 0 pixels, set the background color to the value (53, 43, 48), and horizontally center the element's content.
   - For an element with id, "holelist", set the margin to 0 pixels, the padding to 1 pixel, the background color to the value (53, 43, 48) and horizontally center the element's content.
   - For links within the #holelist selector, enter the following styles: set the font size to 1.25 em, the font weight to bold, the font color to white, and the padding to 0 pixels above and below the links and 5 pixels to the left and right.
   - When users hover over links within the #holelist selector, change the background color to yellow and the font color to black.
   - For an element with the id, "holestats", set the width to 120 pixels, the right margin to 10 pixels, the padding to 10 pixels except for the bottom padding which you should set to 25 pixels, the background color to the value (53, 43, 48), the font color to white, the font size to 0.7em. Float the element on the left margin.
   - Display text marked with the strong element within the #holestats selector in yellow with a normal font weight.
   - For inline images within the #holesummary selector, apply the following styles: set the left and right margins to 10 pixels, and float the image on the left margin.

- For span elements within the #holesummary selector, apply the following styles: float the element on the left margin, set the padding on the right to 2 pixels, the font color to green, the font size to 300% of normal, and the line height to 0.75.
- For the #flags selector, apply the following styles: do not display the element until both margins are clear and horizontally center the element's contents.
- For inline images within the #flags selector, set the border width to 0 pixels, the top and bottom padding to 0 pixels, and the left and right padding to 10 pixels.

4. Use your text editor to create the file **handheld.css** in the tutorial.07/case1 folder. Enter CSS comments at the top of the file containing *your name* and *the date*. Enter the following styles, saving your changes and closing the file when finished:
   - Set the font size of the body text to 8 point and the default font face to sans serif.
   - Prohibit the display of the #head and #holelist selectors.
   - Float the #holestats selector on the left margin and set the right margin to 10 pixels.
   - Float the inline image within the #holesummary selector on the left margin.
   - Float the span element within the #holesummary selector on the left margin, and set to font size to 300% of normal, the font color to green, and the line height to 0.7.
   - Center the contents of the #flags selector, and don't display the contents until both margins are clear.
   - For inline images within the #flags selector, set the border width to 0 pixels, the top and bottom padding to 0 pixels, and the left and right padding to 10 pixels.

5. Use your text editor to create the file **print.css** in the tutorial.07/case1 folder. Enter CSS comments at the top of the file containing *your name* and *the date*. Enter the following styles, saving your changes and closing the file when finished:
   - Set the page size to 8.5 inches wide by 11 inches high. Set the page orientation to landscape.
   - Do not display the #head , #holelist, or #flag selectors.
   - Apply the following styles to the #holestats selector: float the element on the left margin, change the right margin to 10 pixels, and apply a 1-pixel solid black line to the right border.
   - Float inline images within the #holesummary selector on the left margin.
   - Float span elements within the #holesummary selector on the left margin, and set the font size to 300% of normal and the line height to 0.7.

6. Return to the **h01.htm** through **h18.htm** files in your text editor and add link elements to the three style sheets you just created. The **willet.css** style sheet should be used with screen, tv, and tty media; the **handheld.css** style sheet should be used with handheld media; and the **print.css** style sheet should be used with print and projection media.

7. Open **h01.htm** in your Web browser and then navigate through the Web site. Verify that the layout matches the one shown in Figure 7-82 and that the list of holes at the top of the page displays a rollover effect.

8. Print or use Print Preview to view the print styles for the first hole. Verify that the hole stats and hole summary are the only sections displayed, and that the page is displayed in a landscape orientation (Note: This will not be true for browsers that do not support the orientation style.)

9. Submit the completed Web site to your instructor.

Apply

Use the skills you've earned in this tutorial to design a Web site for the Chamberlain Civic Center.

Case Problem 2

Data files needed for this Case Problem: back.jpg, ccc.gif, febtxt.htm, jantxt.htm, martxt.htm

The Chamberlain Civic Center Stacey Dawes, the director of publicity for the Chamberlain Civic Center, has asked you to work on the styles of several event calendar Web pages for the center. The document content has been created, but not the styles. Each event calendar page contains a table of that month's events, along with some paragraphs describing the events. Each event listed in the calendar is also linked to a page that provides more detail. Figure 7-83 shows a preview of the completed page for the month of January. Stacey would like you to include rollover effects for this page so that the links at the top of the page appear in white on a black background, and each event in the calendar appears underlined, when the mouse hovers over them. For this project, you'll work on pages for January, February, and March.

Figure 7-83

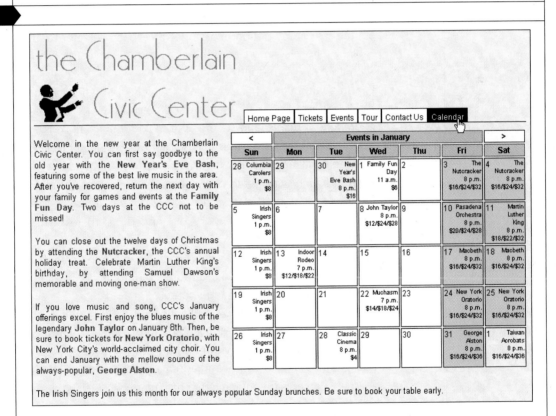

To complete this task:

1. Using your text editor, open **jantxt.htm**, **febtxt.htm**, and **martxt.htm** from the tutorial.07/case2 folder. Enter *your name* and *the date* in the head section of each file and save the files as **jan.htm**, **feb.htm**, and **mar.htm**, respectively.

2. Within each of the three HTML files you just created, do the following:
   - Enclose the CCC logo and list of links within a div element with the id name "head".
   - Add the id name "calendar" to the table element for the calendar table.
   - Add the first table heading in the first table row to the class "prev". Add the third table heading to the class "next".

- Enclose the day of month values in each table cell in a span element with the class name "date".
- If a table cell contains a date from the previous month, place that table cell in the class "prev"; if a table cell contains a date from the next month, place that table cell in the class "next"; and if a table cell contains a weekend date (Friday or Saturday), place that cell in the class "weekend".

3. Save your changes for all of the files.

4. Use your text editor to create a file named **calendar.css** in the tutorial.07/case2 folder. Insert the following styles:
   - Display the page body with the background image back.jpg. Set the default font for the page to 10-point sans-serif.
   - Display the paragraph text using full justification, and display boldfaced text within paragraphs in a blue font.
   - Remove the underlining from all links on the page, and display linked text in black.
   - Set the size of the bottom margin for the #head selector to 10 pixels, and add a 1-pixel solid black border to the bottom of the selector. Display text within this section in a 9-point font.
   - For links within the #head selector, apply the following styles: add a 1-pixel solid black border, change the background color to white, set the top, right, and left padding to 5 pixels, and set the bottom padding to 0 pixels.
   - When users hover over the links in the #head selector, change the background color to black and the font color to white.
   - Float the table with the id name "calendar" on the right margin and set the left margin to 15 pixels. Change the font size of the table text to 7 point.
   - For all links within the calendar table, underline link text when a user hovers the mouse pointer over it.
   - Apply the following styles to heading cells within the calendar table: set the font size to 9 point, change the background color to light blue, and surround the table headings in a 1-pixel solid blue border.
   - Apply the following styles to data cells within the calendar table: vertically align the table text with the top of each cell, horizontally align the text with the right side of each cell, set the width and height of the cells to 60 pixels, change the background color to white, and add a 1-pixel-wide solid black border.
   - Float all elements belonging to the date class on the left margin, and set their font size to 9 point.
   - For a calendar table, heading cells belong to the prev and next classes, set the background color to white and apply a 1-pixel solid black border.
   - Display the background image back.jpg in calendar table data cells that belong to the prev and next classes.
   - Change the background color of calendar data table cells belonging to the weekend class to pink.

Explore ▶ 5. Apply the styles you entered in the previous step to all media. (Hint: Use the @media rule.)

Explore ▶ 6. For print media only, add the following styles to the style sheet:
   - Do not display the #head selector.
   - Allow the browser to automatically set the width and height of data cells in the calendar table.

- Do not float the calendar table, and set the width of the calendar table to 95% of the page width.
7. Save your changes to the **calendar.css** file.
8. Link the **jan.htm**, **feb.htm**, and **mar.htm** files to the **calendar.css** style sheet. Do not specify a media type for the external style sheet.
9. Open **jan.htm** in your Web browser, and then navigate through to the two other monthly event pages. Verify that the layout matches the one shown in Figure 7-83.
10. Print or use Print Preview to view the print styles for the three Web pages. Verify that the head section is not displayed in the printed version of the page, and that the table calendar is not floated, but rather occupies the full width of the page.
11. Submit the completed Web site to your instructor.

Case Problem 3

Explore how to use rollover effects and positioning to create an interactive map for a National Park Web page.

Data files needed for this Case Problem: image0.jpg through image9.jpg, longstxt.htm, lpmap.jpg

Longs Peak Interactive Map Longs Peak is one of the most popular attractions of Rocky Mountain National Park (RMNP). Each year during the months of July, August, and September, thousands of people climb the Keyhole Route to reach the 14,255-foot summit. Ron Bartlett, the head of the RMNP Web site team has asked your help in creating an interactive map of the Keyhole Route for the electronic kiosks in the park's visitors center. Ron envisions a map with 10 numbered waypoints along the Keyhole Route, displaying photos and text descriptions of each waypoint when a mouse pointer hovers over its corresponding numbered point. He also expects to place this electronic map on the park's Web site, and would like the photos and text descriptions to print out nicely. However, he would like the page heading in the printout to change from "Longs Peak Online Trail Map" to simply "Longs Peak Trail Map". Figure 7-84 shows a preview of the online map with the first waypoint highlighted by the user.

Figure 7-84

Move your mouse pointer over the numbered landmarks in the map to preview the hike.

Longs Peak Online Trail Map

At 14,255 feet, Longs Peak towers above all other summits in Rocky Mountain National Park. The summer is the only season in which the peak can be climbed by a non-technical route. Early mornings break calm, clouds build in the afternoon sky, often exploding in storms of brief, heavy rain, thunder and dangerous lightning. Begin your hike early, way before dawn, to be back below timberline before the weather turns for the worse.

The Keyhole Route, Longs Peak's only non-technical hiking pathway, is a 16 mile round trip with an elevation gain of 4,850 feet. Though non-technical, the Keyhole Route is still challenging and is not recommended for those who are afraid of heights or exposed ledges. Hikers should be properly outfitted with clothing, food and water. Use caution when ascending or descending steep areas. Don't be afraid to back down when bad weather threatens.

To create this type of effect, you place the photos and text for each waypoint within a link. Because the links themselves will not actually point to another Web page, you'll set the href attribute of those links to the value "#". This setting means that if a user clicks the photo or text description, the browser simply redisplays the interactive map.

To complete this task:

1. Using your text editor, open **longstxt.htm** from the tutorial.07/case3 folder. Enter *your name* and *the date* in the head section of the file, and save the file as **longs. htm**.

2. Examine the current structure of the document. The file contains several div elements that you should review. The summary element contains an h2 heading and two paragraphs describing the route. The online_map elements contains 12 div elements for the map (lpmap), a description of how to use the map (instruction), and 10 waypoints (labeled point0 through point9), each containing an inline image and a description paragraph. For each of the 10 waypoints, perform the following:

   - Insert a class attribute to the div element, making each a member of the notes class.

   - Enclose the waypoint's inline image and paragraph within a link with the href attribute set to "#".

   - Each waypoint paragraph starts with the time at which hikers should reach the waypoint; enclose the time value within a span element.

3. Locate the h2 heading within the summary div element at the top of the document. Enclose the text "Online" in the heading within a span element with the id name "hideprint".

4. Below the title element in the head section, insert an embedded style sheet for screen, tv, and tty media and insert the following styles:
   - Display the body text in a sans-serif font.
   - Remove text decoration from any links in the document.
   - Set the border width of all inline images in the document to 0.
   - Place the summary element 350 pixels down from the top of the page and set its width to 600 pixels.
   - Place the outline_map element at the page coordinates (5,5) using absolute positioning.

Explore

   - Place the lpmap element at coordinates (0, 0) using absolute positioning, setting its width to 600 pixels and its height to 294 pixels. Set the z-index value for this element to 1.

Explore

   - Move the instruction element 300 pixels down from its default position and set its width to 600 pixels.
   - Set the margin of paragraphs within elements belonging to the notes class to 5 pixels, and set the font size of those paragraphs to 8 point.
   - Set the font color of span elements within notes paragraphs to yellow.

Explore

   - For links within notes elements, apply the following styles: the background color should be blue, the font color should be white, the width and height should be 20 pixels, any overflow content should be hidden, and the z-index value should be set to 2.

Explore

   - When the mouse pointer hovers over links within notes elements, the following styles should be applied: the width should increase to 150 pixels, the height should increase to 170 pixels, any overflow content should become visible, and the z-index value should increase to 3.

Explore

   - Place the waypoint elements at the following absolute coordinates within the online map: point0 (560, 60), point1 (277, 90), point2 (175, 0), point3 (110, 115), point4 (55, 165), point5 (5, 180), point6 (15, 222), point7 (50, 245), point8 (100, 245), and point9 (90, 220).

5. Below the style sheet you just created, create the following embedded style sheet for use with print media:
   - Body text should be displayed in a sans-serif font.
   - Linked text should have no text decoration.
   - All inline images should have a border width of 0.
   - The color of all linked and visited text should be black.
   - Elements with the id names "hideprint" and "instruction" should not be displayed.
   - A page break should be placed after the div element with the id "lpmap".

Explore

   - Page breaks should be avoided inside any element belonging to the notes class, and the margins around those elements should be set to 30 pixels.

6. Save your changes to the file.

7. Open **longs.htm** in your Web browser. Verify that the 10 waypoints are placed in the appropriate locations on the map, as shown in Figure 7-84. Also verify that only the waypoint numbers are displayed unless you hover the mouse over a waypoint, and that both the waypoint image and the waypoint description display when you hover the mouse over a waypoint (note that the waypoint at the start of the hike has no corresponding image).

8. Print or use Print Preview to view the printed version of the page. Verify that the online map and summary are placed on one page, and that the waypoint descriptions are placed on one or more separate pages. Also verify that the heading for the summary changes from "Longs Peak Online Trail Map" to "Longs Peak Trail Map".

9. Submit the completed Web site to your instructor.

Create

Test your knowledge of CSS by creating a style sheet for the university music department.

Case Problem 4

Data files needed for this Case Problem: bizet.jpg, bizetbio.text, bizetlist.txt, mozart.jpg, mozartbio.txt, mozartlist.txt, puccini.jpg, puccinibio.txt, puccinilist.txt, verdi.jpg, verdibio.txt, verdilist.txt, wagner.jpg, wagnerbio.txt, wagnerlist.txt

Midwest University Music Department You've been hired by the music department at Midwest University to create a Web site for a new course on the history of opera. The instructor of the course, Faye Dawson, has provided you with information on five different composers: Bizet, Mozart, Puccini, Verdi, and Wagner. For each composer, Prof. Dawson has given you a file containing the composer's image, a text file listing the composer's works, and a text file containing a biographical sketch. Use this information to design your Web site. You may supplement these files with any other material you feel will enhance your site's design; however the final design must display the following features:

- An embedded style sheet
- An external style sheet
- One style sheet designed for screen media and another designed for print media
- At least one style that is applied to the entire page body
- At least one style that applies to an id or to a class of elements
- At least one style involving pseudo-classes or pseudo-elements
- At least one style declaration involving a contextual selector
- At least one style declaration involving the use of padding, margins, and box styles
- At least one style that uses positioning or floating to place an element on the page
- Documentation of all style sheets and HTML files using comments

Quick Check Answers

Session 7.1

1. Style sheets separate document content from document presentation and thus make it easier to modify one without affecting the other. You can also render the same content in different output media by using applying different style sheets.

2. Inline styles are styles applied directly to an element through the use of the style attribute in the element's tag. Embedded styles are styles placed in the head section of a document and apply to elements within that document. External style sheets are placed in files separate from the document and can be applied to any document in a Web site. External style sheets are preferable for setting the styles of an entire Web site.

3. the media attribute

4. `p {font-size: 12pt}`

5. `p, li, address {font-size: 12pt}`

6. `h1+h2 {font-style: italic}`

7. `input[type="checkbox"] {background-color: ivory}`

Session 7.2

1. `#intro {font-size: 14pt}`
2. `address.footer {width: 500px}`
3. `p.private {display: none}`
4. `h1 {padding: 15px}`
5. `h1 {border-bottom: 5px double red}`
6. `a:hover {background-color: yellow}`
7. `blockquote:first-line {text-transform: uppercase}`

Session 7.3

1. `#Logo {position: absolute; left: 100px; top: 50px}`
2. `span.Up {top: -10px}`
3. The display:none style hides the element and removes it from the document flow. The visibility:hidden style hides the element, but does not remove it from the document flow.
4. `@media print {h1 {styles}}`
5. screen, handheld, tv, tty
6. `@page {size: 11in 14in landscape}`
7. `h1 {page-break-before: always}`

Objectives

Session 8.1
- Define external and embedded media
- List the different file formats for digital sound
- Link and embed a sound clip
- Create a background sound

Session 8.2
- Define the different file formats for digital video
- Link and embed a video clip
- Describe how to support browsers that don't recognize embedded media
- Work with the dynsrc attribute

Session 8.3
- Describe the history and use of Java applets
- Insert a Java applet into a Web page
- Modify applet parameters
- Understand the Internet Explorer marquee element
- Define the object element and understand how to apply it to a variety of embedded objects

Using Multimedia on the Web

Enhancing a Web Site with Sound, Video, and Applets

Case

The Mount Rainier Newsletter

Mount Rainier dominates the skyline for much of the state of Washington, and Mount Rainier National Park is a popular vacation spot for travelers from all over the world. The park publishes a monthly newsletter, Mount Rainier News, which is distributed to visitors at each park entrance. The newsletter contains information on upcoming events, tips on park trails and enjoying nature, and information on campsites and lodging. In recent years, the newsletter has also been published on the World Wide Web so that travelers can conveniently obtain park news before they arrive. The Web page contains all the information available in the printed version, as well as links to other sites on the Web about Mount Rainier and the surrounding communities of Sunrise, Longmire, and Paradise.

Tom Bennett, the editor of Mount Rainier News, has been looking at other newsletter sites on the Web and has noticed how multimedia elements such as sound, video, and animation are being used to add interest and information to those pages. Tom has asked you to add multimedia elements to the Mount Rainier News Web page in an effort to make it more eye catching. The current Web page features stories on an upcoming folk festival and a new attraction at the Paradise visitors' center. Tom would like you to locate sound and video clips to enhance those stories.

Student Data Files

▼**Tutorial.08**

▽ tutorial folder

    raintxt.htm
    CreditRoll.class
    + 4 graphic files
    + 3 audio files
    + 2 video files

▽ review folder

    raintxt2.htm
    CreditRoll.class
    credit.txt
    + 4 graphic files
    + 6 audio files
    + 2 video files

▽ case1 folder

    lmnhtxt.htm
    + 8 graphic files
    + 2 audio sound files
    + 2 video files

Student Data Files	▼ **Tutorial.08 (continued)**		
	▽ **case2 folder**	▽ **case3 folder**	▽ **case4 folder**
	rftxt.htm	fractxt.htm	concert.rm
	PopBtn.class	Cmplx.class	CreditRoll.class
	PopMenu.class	Controls.class	folksong.mp3
	+ 7 graphic files	FracPanel.class	mbc.jpg
	+ 6 audio files	Mandel.class	mbcinfo.txt
		+ 2 graphic files	mbclogo.jpg
		+ 2 video files	schedule.txt

Session 8.1

Working with Multimedia

One of the most popular and useful features of the World Wide Web is the ability to transfer information through the use of sound and video. When creating Web pages that include these elements, one of the most important factors that you need to consider is the issue of bandwidth. **Bandwidth** is a measure of the amount of data that can be sent through a communication pipeline each second. Bandwidth values range from slow connections—such as phone lines, which can transfer data at a maximum rate of 58.6 kilobits per second—to high-speed direct network connections capable of transferring data at several megabytes per second. Large sound and video files cause the most trouble for users with low-bandwidth connections because these types of files require a long time to retrieve at slower speeds. Thus, a primary goal in creating a media clip for the Web is to make it small and compact without sacrificing quality.

As shown in Figure 8-1, multimedia can be added to a Web page two different ways: as external media or inline media. With **external media**, a sound or video file is accessed through a link. An advantage of using an external file is that users are not required to retrieve a multimedia clip, but do so only if they want to. This is useful in situations where a user has a low-bandwidth connection and wants the choice of whether or not to spend time downloading a large multimedia file. An **inline media** clip, on the other hand, is placed within a Web page as an embedded object, similar to an inline image. An inline media clip can be played within a Web page itself. Because an inline clip appears within a Web page, you can supplement it with other material on the page, such as text that describes the clip's content and purpose. A downside of using inline media is that the user is forced to wait for at least part of the clip to be retrieved by the browser. If the user has a low-bandwidth connection, this can be a major inconvenience.

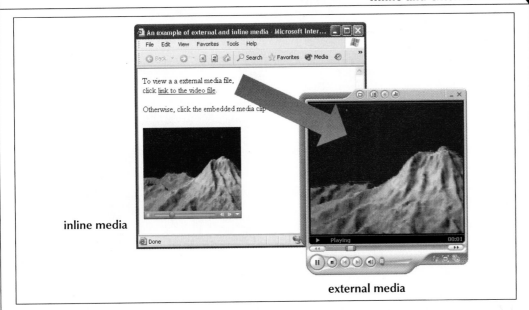

inline media

external media

You ask Tom whether he wants to use inline or external media with the Mount Rainier News Web page. He directs you to create two versions of the page: one using inline media and the other using external media. You'll target one page, which will use external media, for users with low-bandwidth Internet connections, such as phone lines; you'll name this page rainier.htm. You'll use inline media in the second page, rainier2.htm, which will be available to users at the park headquarters who can access the Web page via the park's high-speed connection.

The version of the newsletter you'll work with is shown in Figure 8-2. In addition to a table of links to other Web sites, the page contains three news features. One is the current weather forecast, located at the top of the page. The second is an article about the upcoming folk festival at Sunrise. The third feature describes MRIM, the Mount Rainier Interactive Map, recently installed at the Paradise visitors' center.

Mount Rainier News

WEATHER FORECAST
TODAY ...Partly sunny
TONIGHT...Showers with sleet

Click to view the Weather Site

— weather forecast

About the Park

Mt. Rainier Nat'n'l Park
Mt. Rainier Associates
Visitor Centers
Campgrounds
Picnic Areas
Food & Lodging
Climbing Information
Winter Recreation

Visitor Centers

Longmire
Paradise
Ohanapecosh
Sunrise
Mowich Lake

Current News

Weather Forecast
Road Conditions
Trail Conditions

Autumn Folk Festival

From September 10th - 12th, come to Sunrise for the annual autumn folk festival. The Sunrise Festival is quickly becoming one of the Northwest's top folk events, with intimate performances from world-famous troubadours. Camping spots are still available at Sunrise campground, but they're going fast.

In addition to song sharing in the campground every evening during the festival, there'll be workshops, great food and craft vendors. Call Maria Thompson at 555-9011 for camping information. Call Ted Cashman (555-8122) to sign up for one of the workshops.

Listen to music from last year's festival

— folk festival article

Visitors Prepare to Meet MRIM

Preview a clip from MRIM

Want to see what it's like to hover over Columbia Crest at 14,400 feet, or ski down the Ingraham Glacier without fear of falling? Then visit **MRIM**, the Mount Rainier Interactive Map now available at the Paradise visitors' center.

— MRIM article

MRIM uses state-of-the-art computer animation combined with data from geological satellites to help you explore places you might never visit on foot. The results of your journey are displayed on a large screen monitor - perfect for group presentations or individual explorations. Contact Doug LeCourt at Paradise for more information.

Your first task is to enhance the article on the Sunrise Folk Festival with a sound clip from the previous year's festival. Before you can do that, though, you need to learn a little more about sound file formats.

Working with Audio

To work with sound clips, it is helpful to understand some of the issues involved in converting a sound from the analog form we hear to the digital form stored on sound files and compact discs. Every sound wave is composed of two components: amplitude and frequency. Figure 8-3 shows a basic sound wave. The **amplitude** is the height of the wave, and it relates to the sound's volume—the higher the amplitude, the louder the sound. The **frequency** is the speed at which the sound wave moves, and it relates to the sound pitch. Sounds with higher frequencies have higher pitches.

A simple sound wave ▶ Figure 8-3

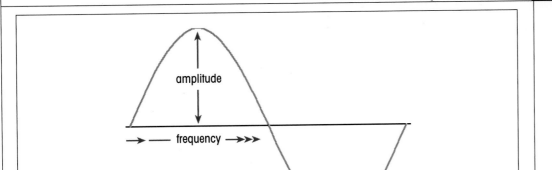

Sampling Rate, Sample Resolution, and Channels

A sound wave is an **analog** function because it represents a continuously varying signal; however, in order to store this information in a sound file, that continuous information must be converted into discrete pieces of information. A **digital** recording takes measurements of the sound's amplitude at discrete moments in time. Each measurement is called a **sample**. The number of samples taken per second is called the **sampling rate**. The sampling rate is measured in kilohertz (KHz). The most commonly used sampling rates are 11 KHz, 22 KHz, and 44 KHz. As shown in Figure 8-4, a higher sampling rate means that more samples are taken per second, resulting in a digital recording that more closely matches the analog signal. Higher quality comes with a tradeoff, however: an increased sampling rate also increases the size of a sound file.

Figure 8-4 ▸ **Different sampling rates**

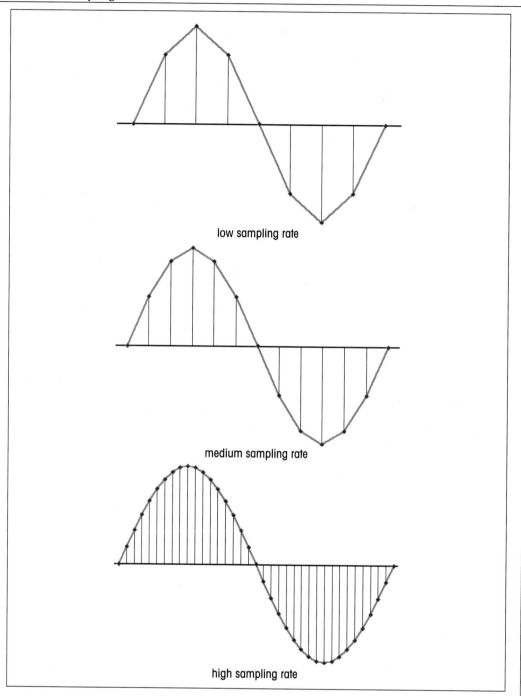

low sampling rate

medium sampling rate

high sampling rate

A second factor in converting an analog signal to a digital form is the sample resolution. **Sample resolution** indicates the precision in measuring the sound within each sample. The three most commonly used sample resolution values are 8 bit, 16 bit, and 32 bit. As shown in Figure 8-5, increasing the sample resolution creates a digital sound file that represents the analog signal more accurately but, once again, results in a larger file. For most applications, saving sound files at the 16-bit resolution provides a good balance between sound quality and file size.

Different sample resolutions Figure 8-5

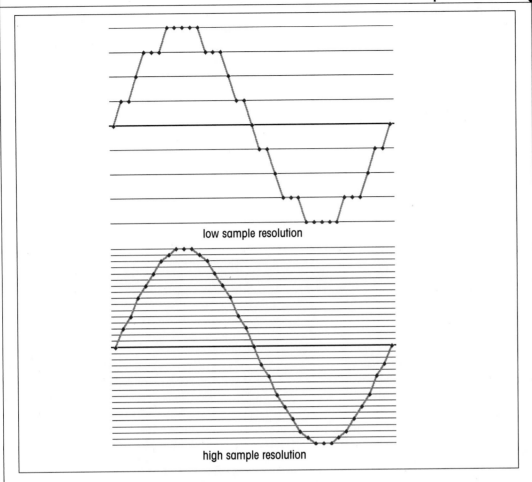

low sample resolution

high sample resolution

A final choice in working with audio is the number of channels to use. Typically, the choice is between stereo or monaural (mono) sound, although in some situations you may want to add extra channels. Stereo provides a richer sound than mono, but with the tradeoff of approximately doubling the size of the sound file.

Figure 8-6 shows how sampling rate, sample resolution, and channel size relate to sound quality in terms of everyday objects. Your telephone provides the poorest sound quality, and this is a reflection of the low sampling rate and sample resolution as well as the monaural sound. A CD player provides much higher sound quality at a higher sampling rate and sample resolution. CD players also support stereo sound and, in some cases, additional sound channels.

Sampling rate and sample resolution as related to sound quality ⟩ Figure 8-6

Sampling Rate and Sample Resolution	Sound Quality
8 KHz, 8-bit, mono	Telephone
22 KHz, 16-bit, stereo	Radio
44 KHz, 16-bit, stereo	CD
48 KHz, 16-bit, stereo	Digital Audio Tape (DAT)

To create a sound file on your computer, you need a sound card, speakers, sound-editing software, and a microphone or direct line to a sound source (such as a stereo or television). Several sound editors are available on the Web. In addition to modifying the sampling rate, sample resolution, and number of channels, these sound editors allow you to add sound effects, remove noise, and copy and paste sounds from one sound file to another.

Sound File Formats

Several different sound formats are in use on the Web. The various formats are used by different operating systems and provide varying levels of sound quality and **sound compression**, which is the ability to reduce the size of the digital sound file. Figure 8-7 lists some of the common sound file formats that you might consider using for the Sunrise Folk Festival sound clip.

Figure 8-7 ▸ **Sound file formats**

Format	Description
AIFF/AIFC	Audio Interchange File Format. Sound files with this format usually have an .aiff or an .aif filename extension. AIFF was developed by Apple for use on the Macintosh operating system. AIFF sound files can be either 8 bit or 16 bit, can be mono or stereo, and can be recorded at several different sampling rates.
AU	Also called mlaw (mu-law) format. Sound files with this format usually have an .au filename extension. One of the oldest sound formats, it is primarily used on UNIX workstations. AU sound files have 8-bit sample resolutions, use a sampling rate of 8 KHz, and are recorded in mono.
MIDI	Musical Instrument Digital Interface. MIDI files cannot be used for general sound recording like other sound formats but are limited to synthesizers and music files. The MIDI format represents sound by recording each note's pitch, length, and volume. MIDI files tend to be much smaller in size than other sound formats.
MPEG	Moving Pictures Expert Group. A format primarily used for video clips, though occasionally MPEGs are used for audio files. MPEG files are usually small due to the MPEG file compression algorithm. Because of their small size, MPEGs are most often used for transferring whole music recordings. The most recent MPEG standard is MP3.
RealAudio	Another popular sound format on the Web, RealAudio files are designed for real-time playing over low- to high-bandwidth connections. RealAudio files tend to be much smaller than AU or WAV files, but the sound quality is usually not as good.
SND	The SND format is used primarily on the Macintosh operating system for creating system sounds. This format is not widely supported on the Web.
WAV	WAV sound files were developed for the Windows operating system and are one of the most common sound formats on the Web. WAV files can be recorded in 8-bit or 16-bit sample resolutions, in stereo or mono, and under a wide range of sampling rates. WAV sound files usually have the .wav filename extension

WAV is one of the most common sound formats on the Web. Support for this format is built in to the Microsoft Windows operating system and all of the leading browsers. If your users work primarily on Macintosh systems, you should consider using either AIFF or SND files instead. Web sites designed primarily for UNIX workstations often use the AU sound format.

However, the most common sound file format on the Web today is undoubtedly **MP3**, a version of the MPEG format, which compresses audio files with minor impact on sound quality. Its popularity is due in part to the fact that it is an open standard, allowing for greater innovation from developers creating MP3-related software. For larger sound files, such as recordings of complete songs or even concerts, MP3 is the preferred sound format because of its ability to greatly compress the size of a sound file. Since its introduction, MP3 has expanded past the confines of the Web and is also used in portable music players and car stereos. Users can also convert MP3 files into WAV format files and burn them onto standard CDs. One controversy around the MP3 format involves copyrighted material that has been copied as MP3 without the permission of the artist or producers. It is especially important for Web designers to be aware of and follow copyright laws when either downloading or posting MP3 recordings.

Sound formats are generally classified into two types: nonstreaming and streaming. **Nonstreaming media** must be completely downloaded by users before being played. This requirement can create lengthy delays because users must download whole files before listening to them. When multimedia elements were first added to the Web, all media was nonstreaming. In response to the desire to be able to listen to sound without a time lag, however, RealAudio was the first to introduce streaming media. Using **streaming media**, media clips, including both sound and video, are processed in a steady and continuous stream as they are downloaded by the browser. Rather than waiting to hear a sound file, users of streaming media can listen to the sound almost immediately. This makes streaming media ideal for broadcasting up-to-the-minute news and sporting events. The success of streaming media depends in part on the speed and quality of the connection. A low-bandwidth connection can result in audio playback with frequent breaks or a decrease in quality when the connection cannot keep up with the speed of the sound clip. In addition to RealAudio, MP3, WAV, and most other sound formats can now be streamed.

Another popular sound format is the MIDI format. **MIDI**, or **Musical Instrument Digital Interface**, is a standard for synthesizers and sound cards. This format converts an analog signal to a series of functions describing the pitch, length, and volume of each note. Because MIDI is a widely supported standard, sounds created on one synthesizer can be played and manipulated on another synthesizer. Sound-editing software can also be used to manipulate the MIDI files, creating new sounds and sound effects. An additional advantage of MIDI files is their much smaller size compared with sound formats. A MIDI composition that lasts several minutes is less than 20 KB in size. A similar file in WAV format would be several megabytes in size. However, the MIDI format is limited to instrumental music and cannot be used for general sounds, such as speech.

If you don't want to create your own sound clips, many sites on the Web maintain archives of sound clips that you can download. Be aware, however, that some sound clips have copyright restrictions and that in some cases Web sites will illegally post copyrighted material.

Tom has created three sound files from last year's Folk Festival in the WAV, AU, and MP3 formats and saved them as mountain.wav, mountain.au, and mountain.mp3, respectively. The files range in size from 211 KB for the WAV and AU files to 342 KB for the MP3 file. Tom doesn't want the sound files to be much larger than this so that users can easily retrieve them. The files are stored in your Data Files.

Linking to an Audio Clip

Now that you have the sound clips, you're ready to start creating the Web pages that Tom requested. The first one you'll create, rainier.htm, will be accessed by users with low-bandwidth connections and uses links to access media files. Because media clips tend to be large, it's a good idea to include information about their formats and sizes in your Web pages. This information gives users an idea of how long it would take to retrieve a clip before deciding whether to initiate a download.

To create a link to Folk Festival sound files:

1. Use your text editor to open **raintxt.htm** from the tutorial.08/tutorial folder. Enter *your name* and *the date* in the comment section and save the file as **rainier.htm**.

2. Insert the following code in the audio div element as shown in Figure 8-8:

```
<a href="mountain.mp3">Wild Mountain Thyme Full Version (342K -
MP3)</a><br />
<a href="mountain.wav">Wild Mountain Thyme Partial Version (211K -
WAV)</a><br />
<a href="mountain.au">Wild Mountain Thyme Partial Version (211K -
AU)</a>
```

Figure 8-8	Inserting links to the sound clips

```
<div id="articles">
    <h2 id="article1">Autumn Folk Festival</h2>
    <div id="audio">
        <img src="guitar.jpg" alt="" /><br />
        Listen to music from last year's festival <br /><br />
        <a href="mountain.mp3">Wild Mountain Thyme Full Version (342K - MP3)</a><br />
        <a href="mountain.wav">Wild Mountain Thyme Partial Version (211K - WAV)</a><br />
        <a href="mountain.au">Wild Mountain Thyme Partial Version (211K - AU)</a>
    </div>

    <p class="firstp">From September 10th - 12th, come to Sunrise for the annual
    autumn folk festival. The Sunrise Festival is quickly becoming one of the
    Northwest's top folk events, with intimate performances from
    world-famous troubadours. Camping spots are still available at Sunrise
    campground, but they're going fast.</p>
    <p>In addition to song sharing in the campground every
    evening during the festival, there'll be workshops, great food and
    craft vendors. Call Maria Thompson at 555-9011 for camping information.
    Call Ted Cashman (555-8122) to sign up for one of the workshops.</p>
```

3. Save your changes to the file.

Now that you've inserted links to the sound clips, you can test the links. What happens when you activate a link to a media clip depends on how your system and browser have been configured. When your browser encounters a link to an external file, like a sound file, it checks to see if a program is installed on your system that's designed to handle that file type. Such programs are called **helper applications** because they help browsers interpret and present files. Different users have different helper applications installed on their systems. Just as there are many different sound editors, many different sound players are also available. In the latest versions of Netscape and Internet Explorer, you may be prompted to play sound clips from within the browser. If a browser does not find a helper application and cannot play the sound clip itself, the browser might display an error message and prompt you to download a player from the Web.

In the following steps, you'll test one of your newly created links. These steps assume that you have an application installed on your system that is capable of playing MP3 files. If necessary, check with your instructor or technical support person to determine which player is installed on your system. If no player has been installed, you'll need to download a player to hear the sound clip.

To test the link to mountain.mp3:

1. Open **rainier.htm** in your Web browser.

2. Click the link **Wild Mountain Thyme Full Version (342K - MP3)** located on the Web page. As shown in Figure 8-9, the browser opens a separate application to play the sound file. Note that you may need to click a play button to play the sound clip.

Trouble? If you are asked to choose whether to open the file or save it, choose to open the sound file. If you are asked to play the sound clip in its own window or frame, you may do that as well.

Playing the sound clip ◄ Figure 8-9

Autumn Folk Festival

From September 10th - 12th, come to Sunrise for the annual autumn folk festival. The Sunrise Festival is quickly becoming one of the Northwest's top folk events, with intimate performances from world-famous troubadours. Camping spots are still available at Sunrise campground, but they're going fast.

In addition to song sharing in the campground every evening during the festival, there'll be workshops, great food and craft vendors. Call Maria Thompson at 555-9011 for camping information. Call Ted Cashman (555-8122) to sign up for one of the workshops.

Listen to music from last year's festival

Wild Mountain Thyme Full Version (342K - MP3)
Wild Mountain Thyme Partial Version (211K - WAV)
Wild Mountain Thyme Partial Version (211K - AU)

mountain.mp3

File Edit Movie Favorites Window Help

00:00:02

► **3.** After listening to the sound file, close the media player playing the sound clip.

Now that you've created links to the mountain sound clips, you'll repeat this process to create a second version of the page. This time, instead of using links, you'll embed the sound clips in the Web page itself.

Embedding an Audio Clip

A sound clip placed directly into a Web page is one example of an embedded object. An **embedded object** is any media clip, file, program, or other object that can be run or viewed from within a Web page. To use embedded objects, a browser must support them and must have access to the appropriate plug-in applications. **Plug-ins** are programs that enable browsers to work with embedded objects. When a browser encounters an embedded object, it loads the appropriate plug-in, along with any controls needed to manipulate the object. For example, a sound file plug-in might place controls on a Web page that enable the user to play the sound clip, pause it, rewind it, or change the volume. Because the object is embedded, these controls are displayed as part of the Web page.

One problem with plug-ins is that they require users to download and install additional software before being able to view a Web page. When presented with this choice, many users choose not to view a given Web page rather than take the time to do this.

Many plug-ins are available for embedded sound clips. Netscape provides LiveAudio and the Winamp media player. Internet Explorer provides the ActiveMovie media player and the Windows Media Player. You can also use third-party plug-ins, such as RealPlayer. Because sound has become such a widespread feature on the World Wide Web, your Web browser probably supports one or more of these plug-ins.

Creating an Embedded Object

There are two different elements you can use to embed a media clip: embed and object. The embed element was originally introduced in Netscape version 2.0 and is supported by almost all browsers; however, it is not part of any W3C specification for either HTML or XHTML. Those specifications recommend instead using the object element to embed media clips. However, the object element is still not well supported in popular browsers. Thus, the browser market and the official specifications are in conflict. Until the browser market catches up with the W3C specifications, Web designers have to continue using the embed element rather than the object element. You'll use the embed element in your rainier2.htm Web page. Later in this tutorial, we'll examine how to use the object element as well.

The syntax of the embed element is

```
<embed src="url" width="value" height="value" autostart="type" />
```

where `url` is the URL of the file containing the media clip; the width and height attributes define the width and the height of the element in pixels; and the autostart value defines whether the browser should automatically start the media clip ("true") or allow the user to manually start it ("false"). The default autostart behavior for playing an embedded clip varies among browsers—some browsers play the clip automatically by default, whereas others do not. For this reason, you should include the autostart attribute to ensure that a clip is played the way you intend. You can also apply a style to the embed element to define its size and location on the page as well as other display attributes.

Reference Window

Embedding a Media Clip

Internet Explorer and Netscape
- To embed a sound or video clip, use the embed element:
  ```
  <embed src="url" width="value" height="value" autostart="type" />
  ```
  where `url` is the location of the object, the width and height attributes specify the width and the height of the object in pixels, and `type` is either true (to start the clip automatically when the page loads) or false (to start the clip manually).

Now that you know how to create an embedded object, you'll create the rainier2.htm file. Because users will access rainier2.htm at the visitors' center through a high-speed connection, Tom feels comfortable with embedding a media clip directly into the Web page. For this page, you'll embed the mountain.mp3 file. If your browser or operating system does not support the MP3 format, you can substitute either the mountain.wav or the mountain.au file in the steps that follow.

To embed a sound clip:

1. Return to **raintxt.htm** in your text editor, enter **your name** and **the date** in the head section of the document, and save it as **rainier2.htm**.

2. Insert the following code directly before the closing </div> tag in the audio div element, as shown in Figure 8-10 (substitute mountain.wav or mountain.au as appropriate if your system does not supports the mp3 format):

```
<embed src="mountain.mp3" width="145" height="60" autostart=
   "false" />
```

See Figure 8-10.

Inserting an embedded sound clip   **Figure 8-10**

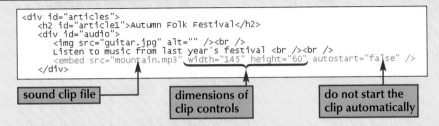

Note that when inserting an embedded sound clip it's not important to specify the clip's size, as you did earlier when inserting a link to a clip. This is because when users open a page containing an embedded sound clip, the audio file is downloaded automatically, whether the user wants it or not. The height and width values in the code you inserted were picked to give enough space to show the controls of the embedded player. When you embed your own media clips, you'll probably need to test various height and width values to find a size that looks right. Also, you set the autostart value to "false" in this case to allow users to play the clip when they choose.

3. Save your changes to the file and then close your text editor.

4. Open **rainier2.htm** in your Web browser. As shown in Figure 8-11, the page loads with the controls for the embedded sound clip placed directly on the page.

Trouble? If you do not see any controls for the sound clip on your Web page, your browser may not support embedded objects, or you might have mistyped the name of the sound file. Return to your text editor and verify that your code matches the code shown in Figure 8-10. If you are still having trouble, talk to your instructor.

Figure 8-11 ▷ **Playing an embedded sound clip**

Autumn Folk Festival

From September 10th - 12th, come to Sunrise for the annual autumn folk festival. The Sunrise Festival is quickly becoming one of the Northwest's top folk events, with intimate performances from world-famous troubadours. Camping spots are still available at Sunrise campground, but they're going fast.

In addition to song sharing in the campground every evening during the festival, there'll be workshops, great food and craft vendors. Call Maria Thompson at 555-9011 for camping information. Call Ted Cashman (555-8122) to sign up for one of the workshops.

Listen to music from last year's festival

sound clip controls
(yours may differ)

5. Click the play button on the embedded object to start playing the sound clip.

Trouble? If necessary, consult the documentation for your browser or plug-in to learn how to work with the sound clip, or ask your instructor or technical support person for assistance in working with your browser's plug-in. (The examples in this tutorial were tested on Internet Explorer, Netscape Navigator, and Opera with the QuickTime plug-in for Windows installed.)

Trouble? If you are running Netscape and have QuickTime installed, you have to set up the QuickTime plug-in to run the embedded media clip type. You might also find better success working with the MOV video clip rather than the AVI clip.

Playing Background Sounds

With version 3.0, Internet Explorer introduced an element for playing background sounds on Web pages. The syntax of the element is

```
<bgsound src="url" balance="value" loop="value" volume="value" />
```

where `url` is the URL of the sound file, the balance attribute defines how the sound should be balanced between the left and right speakers, the loop attribute defines how many times the sound clip is played in the background, and the volume attribute indicates the volume of the background sound. The value of the balance attribute can range from −10,000 to 10,000. Similarly, the value of the volume attribute ranges from 0 (muted) to 10,000 (the loudest). The loop attribute can be either an integer (1, 2, 3, ...) that specifies how many times the sound should repeat, or "infinite" if you want the sound clip to be played continuously. The default loop value is 1.

For example, to set mountain.mp3 to play once in the background when rainier2.htm is loaded, you would insert the following tag anywhere in the file:

```
<bgsound src="mountain.mp3" loop="1" />
```

Because this is a background sound, no control or object is displayed on the Web page; therefore, a user cannot stop the sound from playing, pause it, or rewind it. Because the user has no control, background sounds should be used with caution. You should also set the loop value to "1" or a small number because playing the sound clip over and over again can irritate users.

The bgsound element is not widely supported by browsers other than Internet Explorer, but you can create a similar effect by inserting an embedded sound clip on your Web page, setting its width and height attributes to 0, and specifying that the clip should start automatically when the page is loaded. For example, to insert a background sound clip that is supported by many browsers, you can use the following code:

```
<embed src="mountain.mp3" width="0" height="0" autostart="true" />
```

The sound clip will start automatically, but because it is 0 pixels wide and 0 pixels high, it does not appear on the Web page.

Reference Window

Creating a Background Sound

Internet Explorer
- To create a background sound, use the element:
    ```
    <bgsound src="url" balance="value" loop="value" volume="value" />
    ```
    where url is the URL of the sound file, the balance attribute defines how the sound should be balanced between the computer's left and right speakers, the loop attribute defines how many times the sound clip should be played in the background, and the volume attribute indicates the volume of the background sound. To play a background sound continuously, set the value of the loop attribute to "infinite".

Deprecated

- To create a background sound, use the following embed element:
    ```
    <embed src="url" width="0" height="0" autostart="true" />
    ```
    where url is the URL of the sound file.

You've finished adding sound to the Mount Rainier newsletter page. You show your work to Tom, and he approves of both files you've created. In the next session, you'll learn about various video file formats and how to insert them into your Web pages.

Session 8.1 Quick Check

Review

1. Describe two ways of adding sound to your Web page.
2. Define the following terms: bandwidth, sampling rate, and sample resolution.
3. What sound file formats would you use on an intranet composed exclusively of Macintosh computers?
4. What code would you enter to allow users to access music.mp3 as an external sound clip?
5. What is an embedded object? What two things must a browser have to use an embedded object?
6. What code would you enter to allow users to access the sound file music.mp3 as an embedded object?
7. What element does Internet Explorer support to play background sounds?

Working with Video

Tom's next task for you on this Web page is to add a video clip taken from the Mount Rainier Interactive Map, which was recently installed at the Paradise visitors' center. This video clip shows a simulated flyby of Mount Rainier.

Displaying video is one of the most popular uses of the Web. Video files can add an exciting visual element to a Web page, in addition to providing lots of information. At the same time, video files can be very large and difficult to work with. Depending on the format, a single video clip, no more than 30 seconds in length, can be as large as 10 MB.

You can create video files by using a video capture board installed on your computer to record images from a camcorder, television, or VCR. You can also create video clips using computer animation software. In either case, creating a video file can be a time-consuming process of balancing the desire to create an interesting and visually attractive clip against the need to create a compact file.

Frame Rates and Codecs

Like a film shown in a movie theater, a video file is composed of a series of single images, known as **frames**. When a video file is played, the frames are rapidly shown in sequence, giving the illusion of motion. The number of frames shown in a given amount of time is called the **frame rate**; this measurement is commonly expressed in frames per second (fps). Working with the frame rate is one way to control the size and quality of a video file: reducing the frame rate reduces the size of the file. When you reduce the frame rate, you're not slowing down the video; instead, you're reducing the number of frames shown each second, thereby reducing the total number of frames in the file. A video file with a high frame rate shows a smooth picture during playback but at the expense of consuming a lot of disk space. VHS videotape renders video at 30 fps, and video files that match this frame rate are usually quite large. Instead of using 30 frames in one second of video, you might choose instead to use only 15. The overall duration of the video clip would remain the same, but the size of the file would be reduced.

Another way of controlling the size of a video file is to compress each frame in the clip. When such a video is played, each frame is decompressed as it is displayed. You compress and decompress video frames using a **codec** (short for *compression/decompression*). Many different codecs are available, each with its own advantages and disadvantages. Some codecs create smaller video files but at the expense of choppier playback. Your video editor usually allows you to choose the codec for your video file, but you may need to experiment to determine which codec provides the best file compression without sacrificing video quality.

You can also reduce the size of your video files by simply reducing the size of the video frames. A frame size of 160 pixels wide by 120 pixels high is considered standard on the Web, but you can reduce this size if you find that your video file is too large. Reducing the number of colors in the color palette used by the video can also reduce the size of the file. Finally, if your video clip contains a sound track, you can reduce the sampling rate, the sample resolution, or the number of channels to further reduce the size of the video file. Each of these techniques is available in most video-editing software.

Video File Formats

Video on the Web appears in a wide variety of formats, including both streaming and non-streaming media. Figure 8-12 describes some of the major video formats you'll encounter.

Video file formats ◄ Figure 8-12

Format	Filename Extensions	Type	Description
AVI	.avi	Nonstreaming	Audio/Video Interleaved. AVI is a common video file format developed by Microsoft. Video quality can be very good at smaller resolutions, but files tend to be rather large. AVI files can be played by most media players and plug-ins.
MPEG	.mpg, .mpeg, .mp3	Nonstreaming	Moving Pictures Group. The MPEG format allows for high compression of the video file, resulting in smaller file size. MPEG has become a standard for video and audio file transfer on the Internet. MPEG-1 is the low-resolution format currently used on the World Wide Web for short animated files. MPEG-2 is the much higher resolution used for digital television and DVDs.
QuickTime	.mov	Streaming	A video format developed by Apple Computer for Windows and Apple computers. Like MPEG, QuickTime employs a compression algorithm that can result in smaller file sizes. Viewing QuickTime files on the Web requires the downloading and installation of the QuickTime plug-in from the Apple Computer Web site.
RealVideo	.rm, .ram	Streaming	A video format developed by RealNetworks for transmitting live video over the Internet at both low and high bandwidths. RealVideo uses a variety of data compression techniques and requires the installation of the RealPlayer media player.
Windows Media	.wmv	Streaming	Developed by Microsoft, Windows Media is a popular streaming video format. Windows Media files offer good compression and quality. Windows Media files are often smaller than other streaming video formats.

Which format should you use for your Web page? The answer depends on several factors. Do you want to have your users download the clip before playing, or do you want the clip to be streamed? If quality is an important issue, you will probably want to use a downloaded clip in either the AVI or the MPEG format. If speed, small file size, and quick access to video is important, you will probably want to use a streaming video format such as QuickTime, RealVideo, or Windows Media. You also have to take into account support for the different formats. AVI and Windows Media files were developed by Microsoft and thus enjoy built-in support by the Windows operating system. They can also be played on other operating systems but require their own software to be installed. The QuickTime format was developed for Macintosh users, but QuickTime players exist for other operating systems, such as QuickTime for Windows. RealVideo is another streaming format with broad support on many operating systems. To ensure that your video clips can reach the maximum audience, many developers recommend that you make the video clip available in several different formats and allow your users to choose the format that best fits their needs.

Tom has created a three-second video clip from the Mount Rainier Interactive Map that simulates a flyby of the summit at 14,400 feet. Using video-editing software, you and Tom have saved the video clip in the AVI format under a variety of sizes and frame rate settings, as shown in Figure 8-13.

Figure 8-13 ▶ File sizes of the MRIM video clip

| Frame Rate | Frame Size (in pixels) | |
	200 x 167	400 x 334
5 fps	222 KB	595 KB
10 fps	371 KB	719 KB
15 fps	671 KB	745 KB
20 fps	890 KB	974 KB
25 fps	917 KB	969 KB

The size of this video clip in the different files ranges from 222 KB to just under 1 MB. As you can see from the figure, there is no easy way of predicting the size of the video clip under different conditions. Instead, you must experiment to find the best setting for your needs. After viewing the different clips, you and Tom decide to use the smallest video clip (222 KB). Tom saves the clip as mrim.avi. Tom also uses his video editor to convert this file to QuickTime format and saves the file as mrim.mov. The size of this file is 212 KB. Tom gives you both of these clips, which are in your Data Files, and asks you to add links to rainier.htm that point to these files.

Linking to a Video Clip

You follow the same procedure to link to a video clip as you did to link to a sound clip. Once again, you should include information about the size of each video file so that users can determine whether they want to retrieve the clip. You'll place the links to the video clip files at the bottom of rainier.htm.

To create links to mrim.avi and mrim.mov:

1. Using your text editor, reopen **rainier.htm**.

2. Locate the div element "video", which contains the inline image from the MRIM, and enter the following code (see Figure 8-14):

```
<a href="mrim.avi">Summit Flyby (224K - AVI)</a><br />
<a href="mrim.mov">Summit Flyby (212K - MOV)</a>
```

Figure 8-14 ▶ Inserting links to the video clips

```
<h2 id="article2">Visitors Prepare to Meet MRIM</h2>
<div id="video">
    <img src="mrim.jpg" alt="" /><br />
    Preview a clip from MRIM<br /><br />
    <a href="mrim.avi">Summit Flyby (224K - AVI)</a><br />
    <a href="mrim.mov">Summit Flyby (212K - MOV)</a>
</div>

<p>Want to see what it's like to hover over Columbia Crest at 14,400 feet,
or ski down the Ingraham Glacier without fear of falling? Then visit
<b>MRIM</b>, the Mount Rainier Interactive Map now available at the
Paradise visitors' center.</p>
<p>MRIM uses state-of-the-art computer animation combined with
data from geological satellites to help you explore places you might
never visit on foot. The results of your journey are displayed on a
large screen monitor - perfect for group presentations or individual
explorations. Contact Doug LeCourt at Paradise for more information.</p>
</div>
```

3. Save your changes to the file.

As with sound files, different browsers respond in different ways to links to video clips. Both Internet Explorer and Netscape are capable of displaying AVI and MOV files directly within the browser without the use of plug-ins. In these browsers, when a user clicks a link for a video file, the clip is shown in its own Web page. The user can start the clip either by clicking a control that appears with the clip or by clicking the image if no controls appear. If no controls appear, the user can also right-click the image to view a shortcut list of commands, such as Pause, Stop, and Rewind.

In other browsers, a plug-in is activated when a user clicks a link to a video file, making the video clip play in a separate window. With this in mind, you'll test the links you created to learn if your browser supports video files and, if so, how.

To test your video file links:

1. Open **rainier.htm** with your Web browser.

2. Click the links to the AVI and MOV files you just created. Depending on their configurations, your computer and browser might be able to display only one of the video files. If so, verify that the video clip works. Figure 8-15 shows a sample of how one user might access the mrim.avi video clip.

Playing the video clip | Figure 8-15

Visitors Prepare to Meet MRIM

Want to see what it's like to hover over Columbia Crest at 14,400 feet, or ski down the Ingraham Glacier without fear of falling? Then visit **MRIM**, the Mount Rainier Interactive Map now available at the Paradise visitors' center.

MRIM uses state-of-the-art computer animation combined with data from geological satellites to help you explore places you might never visit on foot. The results of your journey are displayed on a large screen monitor - perfect for group presentations or individual explorations. Contact Doug LeCourt at Paradise for more information.

Preview a clip from MRIM

Summit Flyby (224K - AVI)
Summit Flyby (212K - M(

mrim.avi

File Edit Movie Favorites Window Help

00:00:01

Trouble? It's possible that your browser has not been set up to handle video. You might see a dialog box informing you of this fact when you click the AVI or MOV link. The dialog box may also give you the option of downloading the necessary software from the Internet. If you are working on a computer on a campus network, you should talk to your instructor or technical support person before installing any software from the Web.

Trouble? If you are asked to choose whether to open the video file or save it, select the option to open it.

3. After viewing the video, close the media player displaying the video clip.

Now that you've created a link to the video clips, your next task is to modify the rainier2 Web page by placing the video clip within the page itself.

Embedding a Video Clip

To embed a video file, you can use the same embed element you used in the previous session for embedding the sound clip. You must specify a source for an embedded video clip with the src attribute and a size for the clip using the height and width attributes. The object's height and width should be large enough to display any controls needed to operate the clip, as well. Typically, you decide on the size of a clip by trial and error. In addition to these attributes, you can use the autostart attribute to specify whether you want a clip to start when the page is loaded.

In this example, you'll embed the mrim.avi video clip in the rainier2.htm file. If your browser supports only QuickTime files, you can substitute the mrim.mov file. The size of this clip is 200 pixels wide by 167 pixels high. You'll increase the value of the height attribute to 200 to accommodate the embedded object's video clip controls. Additionally, Tom does not want the clip to start automatically, so you'll set the value of the autostart attribute to "false."

To embed the mrim video clip:

1. Using your text editor, open **rainier2.htm**.

2. Locate the inline image element for the mrim.jpg file and replace the <img> tag with the following embed element (see Figure 8-16):

```
<embed src="mrim.avi" width="200" height="200" autostart="false" />
```

Figure 8-16 | **Inserting an embedded video clip**

```
<h2 id="article2">Visitors Prepare to Meet MRIM</h2>
<div id="video">
    <embed src="mrim.avi" width="200" height="200" autostart="false" /><br />
    Preview a clip from MRIM<br /><br />
</div>
```

3. Save your changes to the file.

4. Open **rainier2.htm** in your Web browser. As shown in Figure 8-17, the inline image is now replaced with an embedded video clip along with controls for operating the clip.

Visitors Prepare to Meet MRIM

Want to see what it's like to hover over Columbia Crest at 14,400 feet, or ski down the Ingraham Glacier without fear of falling? Then visit **MRIM**, the Mount Rainier Interactive Map now available at the Paradise visitors' center.

MRIM uses state-of-the-art computer animation combined with data from geological satellites to help you explore places you might never visit on foot. The results of your journey are displayed on a large screen monitor - perfect for group presentations or individual explorations. Contact Doug LeCourt at Paradise for more information.

Preview a clip from MRIM

**video clip controls
(yours may differ)**

Trouble? Depending on your browser and its configuration, your Web page may look different from the one shown in Figure 8-17. The size of the embedded clip may display differently, or it may have different controls than the ones shown in the figure.

▶ **5.** Start the video clip by either clicking the play button or clicking the video clip itself. See the documentation for your plug-in or browser for more details on how to start the clip.

Using a Dynamic Source

If you're creating a Web page for which users will be running Internet Explorer version 3.0 and above, you can take advantage of some additional attributes that this browser provides for inline images to turn them into dynamic video clips. The syntax of the Internet Explorer attributes is

```
<img src="url" dynsrc="url" start="type" loop="value" control="control" />
```

where the dynsrc attribute specifies the URL of a dynamic (video) version of the inline image. The start attribute tells the browser when to start the video clip and has two possible values: "fileopen" to start playing the clip when the browser opens the file, and "mouseover" to start the clip when the user hovers the mouse over the inline image. The loop attribute specifies the number of times to play the clip and can be either an integer or the keyword "infinite". The control attribute specifies whether Internet Explorer should display player controls below the inline image to start and stop the video clip. If you omit the control attribute, no player controls are displayed. For example, the following tag displays the mrim.jpg inline image unless the user hovers the mouse over the image, in which case the browser runs the video clip once. No player controls are displayed in the Web page.

```
<img src="mrim.jpg" dynsrc="mrim.avi" start="mouseover" loop="1" />
<br />
```

Because only Internet Explorer supports the dynsrc attribute and its associated attributes, if you use them it's generally a good idea to supplement your HTML code with the embedded element to allow other browsers to use the embedded video clip.

Supporting Non-Embedded Elements

Older browsers don't support embedded objects such as the MRIM video clip. If you want to support older browsers, you can add the noembed element. The noembed element works like the noframe element for frames, providing a way to support older browsers that don't recognize embedded objects. The general syntax is:

```
<embed attributes />
<noembed>
   page content
</noembed>
```

A browser that recognizes the <embed> tag embeds the object on the Web page listed in the first line of code. It recognizes the <noembed> tags and ignores any content within them. An older browser, on the other hand, ignores the <embed> and <noembed> tags because it doesn't recognize them, but it displays any content between the opening and closing <noembed> tags. For example, the following code displays the embedded video clip for browsers that support embedded objects, but otherwise displays links to the two versions of the same clip.

```
<embed src="mrim.avi" width="200" height="200" autostart="false" />
<noembed>
   <a href="mrim.avi">Summit Flyby (187K - AVI)</a><br />
   <a href="mrim.mov">Summit Flyby (215K - MOV)</a>
</noembed>
```

Reference Window

Using Non-Embedded Content

- To provide alternate content for browsers that don't support embedded objects, use the code
  ```
  <embed attributes />
  <noembed>
     alternate content
  </noembed>
  ```
  where `alternate content` is the content displayed by browsers that don't support embedded objects.

Because Tom is already providing two different Web pages for embedded and non-embedded media, he does not ask you to use the <noembed> tag in the pages. This concludes your work with external and embedded video clips. In the next session, you'll supplement the rainier2 page by adding a Java applet to display a scrolling window of current news and reports.

Review

Session 8.2 Quick Check

1. Define the following terms: frame, frame rate, and codec.

2. Name three ways of reducing the size of a video file.

3. What code would you enter to allow users to access the movie.mov video clip as an external video clip?

4. What code would you enter to allow users to access the movie.mov video clip as an embedded object?

5. What code would you enter to instruct older browsers to run the tag you created in Question 3 and newer browsers to run the tag you created in Question 4?

6. If your users are running Internet Explorer, how would you modify the tag `<img src="movie.jpg">` to run the video file "movie.mov" once whenever a user hovers the mouse pointer over the inline image?

7. What are the limitations of the tag you created in Question 6?

Session 8.3

Introducing Java

Tom has reviewed your work with sound and video and has only one more task for you. The top of the Mount Rainier News Web page contains a table that shows the current weather forecast for the area. Tom would like to expand the forecast to include two-day predictions. Doing so presents a challenge because including more text in the box pushes the articles farther down the page. Tom would like to avoid this because he wants users to see as much of the newsletter as possible without scrolling. An effective solution would be to retain the current box size and have the text automatically scroll, as it does in theater marquees. Tom has seen scrolling text in other Web pages using Java applets and would like you to use it on the rainier2 Web page. Before you can add the applet to the page, you need to understand what a Java applet is and how it can be used.

A Brief History of Java

As with many computing innovations, Java came from some unexpected sources. In the early 1990s, programmers at Sun Microsystems envisioned a day when common appliances and devices, such as refrigerators, toasters, and garage door openers, would be networked and controllable using a single operating system. Such an operating system would need to be portable because it would obviously need to be able to work with a wide variety of devices. The programmers began development on such an operating system and based it on a language called **Oak**. The project did not succeed at that point (perhaps the world was not ready for toasters and refrigerators to communicate), but Oak worked so well that Sun Microsystems saw its potential for use on the Internet. Oak was modified in 1995 and renamed **Java**.

Sun Microsystems also developed a product called **HotJava**, which ran programs written in the Java language. HotJava was a **Java interpreter**, meaning that it could understand and run Java programs. The idea was that Java programs would run inside Java interpreters; and because Java interpreters could be created for different operating systems, users could run Java on any operating system, including UNIX, Windows, DOS, and Macintosh. Just as Web pages were designed at the beginning to be platform-independent, so was Java.

The advantages of Java were immediately apparent, and success soon followed. Netscape incorporated a Java interpreter into Netscape Navigator version 2.0, making HotJava unnecessary for Netscape users. Microsoft wasted little time in including its own Java interpreter with Internet Explorer version 3.0. Java programs that run within a Web browser are called **applets** because they are not stand-alone applications but rely on the browser to run.

A Java applet is downloaded along with a Web page from a Web server, but the applet itself runs on the user's computer. This frees up the Web server for other purposes (see Figure 8-18).

Figure 8-18 **Applets and Java interpreters**

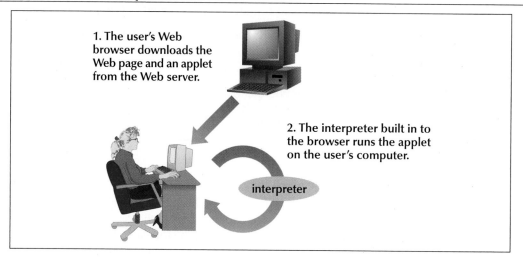

Understanding Applets and .class Files

An applet is displayed as an embedded object on a Web page in an **applet window**. You can use styles to define the location and the size of an applet window. Some applets, however, can appear outside of your browser, in separate windows that can be resized, minimized, and placed on the desktop. Several libraries of Java applets are available on the Web. Some applets are free to download and use for non-commercial purposes. In other cases, authors charge a fee to use applets. You can find Java applets for stock market tickers, games, animations, and other utilities.

To write your own Java applet, you need a Java Developer's Kit (JDK). You can download a free copy of the Java Developer's Kit from the Sun Microsystems Java Web site at *http://java.sun.com*. Commercial JDKs are also available, providing easy-to-use graphical tools and menus to help you create your Java applets quickly and easily. Once you have a JDK, be prepared to hit the books to learn the Java computing language.

After you write the code for a Java program, you save the source code as a file with the four-letter extension .java. In a process called **compiling**, the JDK changes the file into an executable file that can run by itself without the JDK. The executable filename has the four-letter extension .class and is called a **class file**. Some Java applets may require several .class files. Class files are different from the other program files you have on your computer, however. Unlike .exe or .com files, which are run by your operating system, a class file can be run only from within a Java interpreter. In most cases, the Java interpreter is your Web browser. This feature allows the same Java applet to run under a variety of operating systems, so long as a browser is available that supports Java.

Working with Applets

Once you've located a Java applet or written one of your own, you can insert the applet into a Web page using either the applet element or the object element. The applet element has been deprecated in the latest specifications for HTML and XHTML; however, because the object element has not gained wide acceptance in the browser community, we'll still use the applet element. The syntax of the applet element is

```
<applet code="file">
   parameters
</applet>
```

where *file* is the filename of the Java applet and *parameters* is a list of parameters that may be required for the applet. We'll look at parameters shortly. Some of the other attributes supported by the applet element are shown in Figure 8-19.

Attributes of the applet element ◀ **Figure 8-19**

Attribute	Description
alt="*text*"	An alternate text description of the applet for browsers that do not support applets
codebase="*url*"	A URL providing the location of the .class file, if different from the location of the Web page
code="*file*"	The filename of the .class file
height="*value*"	The height of the embedded applet in pixels
name="*text*"	The name of the applet
width="*value*"	The width of the embedded applet in pixels

One useful attribute is codebase, which enables you to run an applet placed in a different location than your Web page. Placing your applets in a central location allows you to maintain only one copy of each applet, rather than copies for each Web page. This makes it easier for you to manage your collection of applets. The codebase attribute also allows you to run someone else's Java applet from that person's Web server. However, this practice is discouraged and, in some cases, is a violation of copyright laws. If you want to use someone else's Java applet in your own Web page, you should first obtain permission and then retrieve the .class file and place it on your Web server.

Working with Applet Parameters

Many applets require Web designers to enter parameter values to control their behavior. Documentation supplied with each applet should tell what parameters, if any, are required. The syntax of the parameter element is

```
<param name="text" value="value" />
```

where the name attribute identifies the name of the parameter required by the applet, and *value* is the value you assign to the parameter. For example, the following code inserts an applet named "Button.class" in the Web page with the value of the Text parameter set to "Click to Enter":

```
<applet code="Button.class">
   <param name="Text" value="Click to Enter" />
</applet>
```

There is no limit to the number of parameters that can be associated with a particular applet.

Inserting a Java Applet

- To insert a Java applet, use the code

```
<applet code="file">
    <param name="text" value="value" />
    <param name="text" value="value" />
    . . .
</applet>
```

where *file* is the name of the Java class file, *text* is the name of an applet parameter, and *value* is the parameter's value.

In addition to param elements, you can insert other HTML elements within the applet. This can be helpful for accommodating older browsers that don't support Java applets (or new browsers that don't have support for Java installed). These browsers ignore the <applet> and <param> tags and instead display the elements you specify within the applet element. Browsers that do support Java ignore this alternate content. For example, if you use the following structure in your HTML file:

```
<applet>
    <param>
    <param>
    . . .
    <h3>To fully enjoy this page, upgrade your browser to support Java
</h3>
</applet>
```

a user's browser either runs the applet or displays the h3 heading with the message to upgrade.

Using a Java Applet

Tom has located a Java applet for you to use in rainier2.htm. The applet allows you to specify several lines of text to scroll vertically through a window, similar to the way that credits roll after a movie. The .class file for this applet, CreditRoll.class, is provided in your Data Files. Tom has already read through the documentation that accompanied the applet and determined that the CreditRoll.class file uses the parameters shown in Figure 8-20.

Parameters of the CreditRoll.class applet ◄ **Figure 8-20**

Parameter	Description
BGCOLOR	The background color of the applet window, expressed as a hexadecimal color value
FADEZONE	The text in the applet window fades in and out as it scrolls. This parameter sets the size of the area in which the text fades (in pixels).
TEXTCOLOR	The color value of the text in the applet window
FONT	The font used for the scrolling text in the applet window
TEXTx	Each line of text in the applet window requires a separate TEXTx parameter, where x is the line number. For example, the parameter TEXT1 sets the text for the first line in the applet window, TEXT2 sets the text for the second line in the applet window, and so forth.
URL	If the applet window is clicked, it opens the Web page specified in the URL parameter.
REPEAT	Specifies whether the text in the applet window is repeated. Setting this parameter's value to "yes" causes the text to scroll continuously.
SPEED	The speed at which the text scrolls, expressed in milliseconds between each movement
VSPACE	The space between each line of text, in pixels
FONTSIZE	The point size of the text in the applet window

After considering how he wants the weather information to appear, Tom asks you to use the parameter values shown in Figure 8-21. These values create a marquee box with dark purple text on a white background. The box includes eight lines of text, including two blank lines, which provide a two-day weather forecast. The text is set to scroll continuously at the speed of one pixel per second. When a user clicks the applet, the browser will open a Web page at the URL http://www.nps.gov/mora/current/weather.htm.

Parameter values of the CreditRoll.class applet ◄ **Figure 8-21**

Parameter	Value
BGCOLOR	F0F0F0
FADEZONE	20
TEXTCOLOR	8080FF
FONT	Times New Roman
TEXTx	WEATHER FORECAST TODAY. . .Partly sunny TONIGHT. . .Showers with sleet TUE. . .Rain heavy at times. Snow likely WED. . .Clearing Click to view the Weather Site
URL	http://www.nps.gov/mora/current/weather.htm
REPEAT	yes
SPEED	100
VSPACE	3
FONTSIZE	10

Now that you know the value of the parameters, you are ready to replace the static box containing the weather information with a window containing the CreditRoll applet. You'll set the size of the applet window to 200 pixels wide by 70 pixels high.

To insert the CreditRoll applet:

1. Using your text editor, reopen **rainier2.htm**.

2. At the top of the page, locate the div element with the id name "weather" and delete the content between the opening and closing <div> tags.

3. Within the weather div element, insert the following new code:

```
<applet code="CreditRoll.class" width="200" height="70">
    <param name="BGCOLOR" value="F0F0F0" />
    <param name="TEXTCOLOR" value="8080FF" />
    <param name="FADEZONE" value="20" />
    <param name="FONT" value="TIMES NEW ROMAN" />
    <param name="TEXT1" value="WEATHER FORECAST" />
    <param name="TEXT2" value=" " />
    <param name="TEXT3" value="TODAY...Partly sunny" />
    <param name="TEXT4" value="TONIGHT...Showers with sleet" />
    <param name="TEXT5" value="TUE...Rain heavy at times. Snow
likely" />
    <param name="TEXT6" value="WED...Clearing" />
    <param name="TEXT7" value=" " />
    <param name="TEXT8" value="Click to view the Weather Site" />
    <param name="URL" value="http://www.nps.gov/mora/current/
weather.htm" />
    <param name="REPEAT" value="yes" />
    <param name="SPEED" value="100" />
    <param name="VSPACE" value="3" />
    <param name="FONTSIZE" value="10" />
</applet>
```

The revised code in rainier2.htm should appear as shown in Figure 8-22. Take some time to study the HTML code you just inserted. Note that blank lines are indicated in the values for the TEXT2 and TEXT7 parameters by the empty space allotted to those values.

| Figure 8-22 | Inserting an applet window |

4. Close the **rainier2.htm** file, saving your changes.

5. Open **rainier2.htm** in your Web browser. With the large number of embedded objects and the Java applet, this Web page may take a while to load. After the page loads, you should see the weather forecast scrolling in the window at the top of the Web page. Figure 8-23 shows the CreditRoll applet as it is displayed on the Web page.

Running the Java applet | **Figure 8-23**

text scrolls vertically, fading as it leaves the applet window

TODAY...Partly sunny
TONIGHT...Showers with sleet

About the Park

Mt. Rainier Natn'l Park
Mt. Rainier Associates
Visitor Centers
Campgrounds
Picnic Areas
Food & Lodging
Climbing Information
Winter Recreation

Visitor Centers

Longmire
Paradise
Ohanapecosh
Sunrise
Mowich Lake

Autumn Folk Festival

From September 10th - 12th, come to Sunrise for the annual autumn folk festival. The Sunrise Festival is quickly becoming one of the Northwest's top folk events, with intimate performances from world-famous troubadours. Camping spots are still available at Sunrise campground, but they're going fast.

In addition to song sharing in the campground every evening during the festival, there'll be workshops, great food and craft vendors. Call Maria Thompson at 555-9011 for camping information. Call Ted

Listen to music from last year's festival

Trouble? If your browser has trouble accessing the CreditRoll applet, check the <applet> and <param /> tags for any errors or misspellings. If you are running an early version of Netscape, you may have to exit from your browser, restart Netscape, and then reopen rainier2.htm for the applet to run properly.

6. You're done working with the rainier2 Web page. You can close your browser now if you wish.

Creating a Marquee with Internet Explorer

As an alternative to using an applet to create a box with scrolling text, if you know that users accessing your Web page will be using Internet Explorer 3.0 or above, you can take advantage of the Internet Explorer's marquee element to create a theater-style marquee. The general syntax of the marquee element is

```
<marquee attributes>content</marquee>
```

where `attributes` is one or more of the attributes listed in Figure 8-24, and `content` is the page content that appears in the marquee box. Browsers that do not support the marquee element simply display the entire marquee text without any scrolling.

Figure 8-24 **Attributes of the marquee element**

Attribute	Description
begin="*value*"	The time (in seconds) before beginning the marquee. The default is "0".
behavior="*type*"	How the text behaves within the container. The default value of "scroll" causes the text to scroll across the container; "alternate" causes the text to reverse its direction when it reaches the container's edge; and "slide" stops the text once it reaches the end of the container.
direction="*type*"	The direction of the text movement (options are "left", "right", "down", or "up"). The default is "left".
end="*value*"	The time (in seconds) before ending the marquee
height="*value*"	The height of the marquee container, in pixels
width="*value*"	The width of the marquee container, in pixels
loop="*value*"	The number of times the marquee will play. A value of "0" or "−1" causes the marquee to play without stopping. The default is "−1".
scrollamount="*value*"	The distance, in pixels, that the text moves each time the marquee is redrawn. The default is "6".
scrolldelay="*value*"	The delay, in milliseconds, between subsequent redrawings of the marquee. The default is "85".

For example, to approximate the behavior of the CreditRoll applet, you could use the following marquee element:

```
<marquee scrolldelay="10" scrollamount="1" direction="up" width="200"
height="70">
<div style="background-color: #F0F0F0; color: #8080FF; font-family:
Times New Roman; font-size: 10pt">
    WEATHER FORECAST<br /><br />
    TODAY...Partly sunny<br />
    TONIGHT...Showers with sleet<br />
    TUE...Rain heavy at times. Snow likely<br />
    WED...Clearing<br /><br />
    <a href="http://www.nps.gov/mora/currentweather.htm">
       Click to view the Weather Site
    </a>
</div>
</marquee>
```

You should show restraint in using the marquee element. Like animated GIFs, marquees can distract your users from other elements on your Web page if used too often. As you can imagine, a continuous marquee can quickly become a nuisance.

Creating a Scrolling Marquee

Internet Explorer
- To create a marquee for Internet Explorer browsers, use the following element:

  `<marquee>`*content*`</marquee>`

  where *content* is the content that will scroll through the box.
- To control the behavior of text within the marquee, use the attributes

  `behavior="`*type*`" direction="`*type*`" loop="`*value*`"`

  where *behavior* is either "scroll" (to scroll the text across the box), "slide" (to slide the text across the box and stop), or "alternate" (to bounce the text back and forth across the box). The direction attribute, defining the direction the text moves, is "left" (the default), "right", "down", or "up". The loop attribute determines how often the text moves across the box and is either an integer or "infinite".
- To control the speed of the text within a marquee, use the attributes

  `scrollamount="`*value*`" scrolldelay="`*value*`"`

  where *scrollamount* is the amount of space, in pixels, that the text moves each time it advances across the page, and *scrolldelay* is the amount of time, in milliseconds, between text advances.

Working with the Object Element

As we've noted before, both the embed and applet elements represent the older standard for inserting media clips and applets into a Web page. The current specifications for HTML and XHTML call for these approaches to be replaced by the object element, which is a generic element for any object whose content is stored in a file separate from the current Web page. This can include:

- inline images
- sound clips
- video clips
- program applets
- other HTML documents

When it is fully supported, the object element takes over many of the tasks carried out by existing elements, as shown in Figure 8-25.

Specific and generic elements   **Figure 8-25**

Object	Specific Element	Generic Element
Applet	applet (**deprecated**)	object
Audio clip	embed (**not supported by the W3C**)	object
HTML document	iframe	object
Inline image	img	object
Video clip	embed (**not supported by the W3C**)	object

The syntax of the object element is

```
<object attributes>
   parameters and alternate page content
</object>
```

where *attributes* is the list of attributes associated with the object. If the object element is used for an applet, you can include a list of parameter values between the opening and closing tags using the param element. You can also insert page content in the same place to support browsers that don't recognize the object element. A list of some of the attributes associated with the object element is shown in Figure 8-26.

Figure 8-26 ▶ **Attributes of the object element**

Attribute	Description
archive="*list*"	A space-separated list of URLs for archives containing resources relevant to the object
classid="*url*"	The URL of the implementation of the object. The actual syntax of the URL depends on the object being embedded. It may be used either along with or as an alternative to the data attribute.
codebase="*url*"	The base path used to resolve relative URLs specified by the classid, data, and archive attributes
codetype="*type*"	The MIME type for the object's code
data="*url*"	The URL of the data used by the object
declare="*declare*"	Declares the object without loading it into the Web page
standby="*text*"	A text message to be displayed by the browser as it loads the object
type="*type*"	The MIME type of the object's data

Because the object element can support a wide variety of data types, you commonly indicate the type of data using the type attribute. Types are expressed using **MIME (Multipurpose Internet Mail Extension)** names. MIME was developed to allow e-mail messages to include nontext objects such as sound and video files. Later, MIME was adapted for use on the World Wide Web. Each MIME data type has a name associated with it. Figure 8-27 lists the MIME names for some of the objects you'll embed in your Web pages.

Figure 8-27 ▶ **MIME types**

Audio		Text	
Object	**MIME Type**	**Object**	**MIME Type**
aiff	audio/aiff	HTML file	text/html
au	audio/basic	Plain text file	text/plain
midi	audio/mid		
mp3	audio/mpeg		
wav	audio/wav		

Image		Video	
Object	**MIME Type**	**Object**	**MIME Type**
gif	image/gif	asf	video/x-ms-af
jpg	image/jpeg	avi	video/x-msvideo
png	image/png	mpeg	video/mpeg
		quicktime	video/quicktime

If you don't specify a value for the type attribute, users' Web browsers may have difficulty rendering the Web page.

Inserting an Inline Image

In general, to insert an object into a Web page, use the syntax

```
<object data="url" type="mime-type">
   page content
</object>
```

where *url* specifies the URL of the object file and *mime-type* is one of the MIME types associated with object. For example, the img element

```
<img src="logo.jpg" alt="Mt. Rainier News" />
```

can be replaced with the object element:

```
<object data="logo.jpg" type="image/jpeg">
   <h2>Mt. Rainier News</h2>
</object>
```

Note that the object element allows you to apply an h2 heading to the alternate text. This is an advantage of using the object element over the img element, where the alternate text cannot be formatted. The object element also supports most of the attributes associated with the img element. For example, you can insert the usemap attribute into an object element to associate an image with an image map. The main drawback of using the object element for an image is that the object element is not well supported, whereas the img element works with any browser.

Displaying an HTML file

To display an HTML file within another Web page, you can use either the iframe element

```
<iframe src="home.htm">
   View the home page.
</iframe>
```

or the object element

```
<object data="home.htm" type="text/html">
   View the home page.
</object>
```

You can use style sheets to define the size of the window displaying the HTML file. In both cases, a browser will display scrollbars to allow users to scroll through the attached document.

Displaying a Multimedia Clip

To display an audio or video clip within an object element, you can simply replace the src attribute of the embed element with the data and type attributes of the object element. You can insert content within the object element that you want displayed for browsers that do not support the embedded object. For example, you can replace the code

```
<embed src="mrim.avi" />
<noembed>
   MRIM video clip
</noembed>
```

with the object

```
<object data="mrim.avi" type="video/x-msvideo">
   MRIM video clip
</object>
```

To set the size of the object window, you can either use a style sheet or apply the width and height attributes directly to the object element.

Displaying a Java Applet

The classid attribute provides information to browsers on how an object is to be implemented on the Web page. For inline images, multimedia clips, and HTML documents, you don't need to specify a value for the classid attribute. However, for applets the classid attribute takes the place of the data attribute. To display a Java applet as an object, use the syntax

```
<object classid="java:file" width="value" height="value">
   <param name="text" value="value" />
   <param name="text" value="value" />
...
</object>
```

where *file* is the filename of the Java class file used with the applet. For example, to insert the CreditRoll.class applet, you could use the following code:

```
<object classid="java:CreditRoll.class" width="200" height="70">
   <param name="BGCOLOR" value="F0F0F0" />
...
</object>
```

Displaying an ActiveX Control

ActiveX is technology from Microsoft that attaches desktop applications to Web pages. Using ActiveX tools, Web authors can add interactive content to their Web pages, including features such as animation, spreadsheet calculations, and financial transactions. ActiveX objects are referred to as **ActiveX controls** and are roughly equivalent to Java applets—ActiveX was actually born as Microsoft's response to Java. Each ActiveX control has a unique class id, which distinguishes it from other controls. The form of the class id is CLSID: *class-identifier*, where *class-identifier* is a complex text string. For example, the class id for the Flash player is

D27CDB6E-AE6D-11cf-96B8-444553540000

To embed an ActiveX control into your Web page, use the object element as follows:

```
<object classid="clsid:class_identifier">
   parameters and page content
</object>
```

where *class_identifier* is the ActiveX control's class identifier.

There are some important differences between ActiveX and Java. ActiveX is a proprietary standard and is closely related to the various versions of Microsoft Windows. ActiveX controls can also be shared among different Microsoft applications. For example, an ActiveX calendar control used by Microsoft's e-mail program, Outlook, can also be used in Web pages viewed by Internet Explorer. By contrast, Java is not coupled with any particular operating system or group of applications. In addition, security concerns have arisen over the use of ActiveX controls. Because they have full access to a user's operating system, ActiveX controls have the potential to cause serious damage to the operating system. One way of addressing this problem is to attach authentication certificates to each ActiveX control, indicating who wrote the control; users then approve the certification before running a control.

Using the Object Element

Reference Window

- To display an inline image, use
  ```
  <object data="url" type="type">
     content
  </object>
  ```
  where *url* is the URL of the image file; *type* is image/gif, image/png, or image/jpeg; and *content* is alternate content to be displayed by the browser.
- To display an HTML file, use
  ```
  <object data="url" type="text/html">
     content
  </object>
  ```
  where *url* is the URL of the HTML file.
- To display a multimedia clip, use
  ```
  <object data="url" type="type">
     content
  </object>
  ```
  where *url* is the URL of the media file and *type* is one of the MIME types for multimedia files.
- To display a Java applet, use
  ```
  <object classid="java:file">
     <param name="text" value="value" />
     <param name="text" value="value" />
     . . .
     content
  </object>
  ```
  where *file* is the name of the Java class file, *text* is the name of the applet parameter, and *value* is the parameter's value.
- To display an ActiveX control, use
  ```
  <object classid="clsid:class_identifier">
     parameters and page content
  </object>
  ```
  where *class_identifier* is the class id of the ActiveX control.

Nesting Objects

One additional advantage of the object element is that you can nest one object inside another. This is useful in situations where you want to provide browsers with alternatives for displaying an embedded object. For example, if you have multiple versions of the MRIM video file, the following code provides the browser with four options for playing the video clip:

```
<object data="mrim.mpg" type="video/mpeg">
     <object data="mrim.mov" type="video/quicktime">
          <object data="mrim.avi" type="video/x-msvideo">
                <img src="mrim.jpg" alt="MRIM video clip" />
          </object>
     </object>
</object>
```

In this example, the browser first tries to display the MPEG version. If it can't support that video format, it tries the QuickTime version and then the AVI format. If the browser can't display any of these video formats, it displays an inline still image.

The object element shows great promise for expanding the capability of HTML in handling embedded objects. However, before using it in your Web pages, you will probably have to wait for browser support to catch up with the element's potential or at least provide workarounds for users with older browsers.

Satisfied with the condition of both the rainier.htm and the rainer2.htm pages, you present them to Tom for his approval. He is impressed with your use of sound and video in the newsletter and is happy with how the CreditRoll applet allows him to enter an almost unlimited amount of weather information without altering the layout of the page. He wants to examine the Web pages more closely and will contact you later with any requests for changes.

Tips for Using Multimedia

- When linking to multimedia, provide a variety of media formats to ensure that all users have access to formats they can use.
- Include the file size in links to large multimedia files to notify users with low-bandwidth connections.
- Do not embed multimedia clips in your Web pages unless you are sure that users will be accessing the pages through a high-speed connection.
- Do not insert media clips unless you provide a method for users to turn off the clips; if a clip plays automatically, allow it to play only once.
- Use the embed and applet elements in preference to the object element because of the broader browser support.

Review

Session 8.3 Quick Check

1. What is compiling?

2. How does a .class file differ from other executable files you might find on your computer?

3. What tag would you use to insert the Java applet StockTicker.class into your Web page?

4. What tag would you use to remotely access the applet StockTicker.class if it is located at the URL *http://www.wstreet.com*?

5. The StockTicker.class applet has two parameters. The URL parameter identifies the URL of a Web resource containing stock data, and the TIME parameter specifies the time lag, in seconds, between stock market updates. If URL="http://www.stockinfo.com" and TIME=60, what HTML tags would you add to use these values?

6. In Internet Explorer, what tags would you use to create a scrolling marquee containing the text "Stock Information" in white letters on a black background?

7. What attribute or attributes would you add to the tag in Question 6 to instruct the text to scroll once from the left side of the marquee to the right and then stop?

8. What object element would you use to insert into your Web page a video file named "rainier.mov" with a width of 150 pixels and a height of 100 pixels? What is a limitation of embedding the video file in this way?

Tutorial Summary

In this tutorial, you learned how to use multimedia elements in your Web site. You saw how to create links to sound and video clips and how to embed those clips within your Web pages. You also learned about some of issues surrounding audio and video formats. The tutorial also discussed the history and use of Java applets. You learned how to insert a Java applet into a Web page and how to set the parameter values for an applet. You also learned how to create a text marquee using Internet Explorer's proprietary marquee element. Finally, you learned about the object element and its future promise as a general element for all embedded objects.

Key Terms

ActiveX	frame	Musical Instrument Digital
ActiveX control	frame rate	Interface
amplitude	frequency	nonstreaming media
analog	helper application	Oak
applet	HotJava	plug-in
applet window	inline media	sample
bandwidth	Java	sample resolution
class file	Java interpreter	sampling rate
codec	MIDI	sound compression
compiling	MIME	streaming media
digital	MP3	WAV
embedded object	Multipurpose Internet Mail	
external media	Extension	

Review Assignments

Data files needed for this Review Assignment: raintxt2.htm, credit.txt, CreditRoll.class, mrim2.avi, mrim2.mov, song.au, song.mp3, song.wav, welcome.au, welcome.mp3, welcome.wav, + 4 graphic files

Tom has come back to you with two additional multimedia clips that he would like you to use in the Mount Rainier News Web page. One is a sound clip that includes samples of performers from the previous year's Sunrise Folk Festival, which has been saved in MP3, WAV, and AU formats. The second is a new video excerpt from the Mount Rainier Interactive Map in AVI and MOV formats. You'll create two versions of the newsletter: one with links to external files and the other with embedded media clips. Tom also wants you to add a background sound to the Web page with embedded media clips. The background sound is based on a short sound file that welcomes users to Mount Rainier.

Tom would also like you to modify the behavior of the CreditRoll applet. He thinks that the text scrolls too slowly, and he would like you to increase the scrolling speed. He wants the fadezone area set to "1" and, he has changed the text of the marquee. Figure 8-28 shows a preview of the completed Web page containing the embedded media clips.

Figure 8-28

TONIGHT
Showers with sleet
TUESDAY
Rain/Snow heavy at times
WEDNESDAY

About the Park
Mt. Rainier Natn'l Park
Mt. Rainier Associates
Visitor Centers
Campgrounds
Picnic Areas
Food & Lodging
Climbing Information
Winter Recreation

Visitor Centers
Longmire
Paradise
Ohanapecosh
Sunrise
Mowich Lake

Current News
Weather Forecast
Road Conditions
Trail Conditions

Autumn Folk Festival

From September 10th - 12th, come to Sunrise for the annual autumn folk festival. The Sunrise Festival is quickly becoming one of the Northwest's top folk events, with intimate performances from world-famous troubadours. Camping spots are still available at Sunrise campground, but they're going fast.

In addition to song sharing in the campground every evening during the festival, there'll be workshops, great food and craft vendors. Call Maria Thompson at 555-9011 for camping information. Call Ted Cashman (555-8122) to sign up for one of the workshops.

Visitors Prepare to Meet MRIM

Want to see what it's like to hover over Columbia Crest at 14,400 feet, or ski down the Ingraham Glacier without fear of falling? Then visit **MRIM**, the Mount Rainier Interactive Map now available at the Paradise visitors' center.

MRIM uses state-of-the-art computer animation combined with data from geological satellites to help you explore places you might never visit on foot. The results of your journey are displayed on a large screen monitor - perfect for group presentations or individual explorations. Contact Doug LeCourt at Paradise for more information.

Media Clips

Listen to last year's festival

Preview a clip from MRIM

To create the revised versions of the Mount Rainier News Web page:

1. Use your text editor to open **raintxt2.htm** from the tutorial.08/review folder. Enter *your name* and *the date* in the comment section of the file and save the file as **rainier3.htm**.

2. Locate the media1 div element near the bottom of the page and below the text "Listen to last year's festival" and insert links to the song.au, song.mp3, and song.wav files, each on a separate line. Be sure to include the name of the piece, A la Claire Fontaine, the file format, and the size of the sound file, in kilobytes.

3. Locate the media2 div element at the bottom of the page and below the text "Preview a clip from MRIM" and insert links to the mrim2.avi and mrim2.mov video files. The text of the link should be "Mount Rainier Flyby - East Ridge" followed by the size of the video file in kilobytes and the video format.

4. Save your changes to the **rainier3.htm** file and then open it in your Web browser. Verify that all of the links work correctly.

5. Use your text editor to open **raintxt2.htm** again. Enter *your name* and *the date* in the comment section of the file and save the file as **rainier4.htm**.

6. In the same place where you placed the links to the sound clips in the rainier3.htm file, place instead an embedded sound clip for the song.au, song.mp3, or song.wav file (depending on which format your system supports). Set the size of the embedded clip to 145 pixels wide by 60 pixels high and specify that the clip should not start automatically.

7. Replace the mrim2.jpg inline image with either the mrim2.avi or the mrim2.mov embedded video clip (depending on what your system supports). Set the size of the embedded video clip to 200 by 200 pixels and set the autostart value to "false".

8. Embed the audio file welcome.mp3, welcome.wav, or welcome.au at the bottom of the document, with a width and a height of 0 pixels and set the autostart value to "true".

9. Replace the weather forecast information at the top of the page with a scrolling marquee created with the CreditRoll applet. The text of the marquee is stored in the credit.txt file in the tutorial.08/review folder. Set the other parameters of the applet as follows:

   - Set the BGCOLOR parameter to the hexadecimal color value CECECE.
   - Set the TEXTCOLOR parameter to the hexadecimal color value 8080FF.
   - Set the FADEZONE value to 1.
   - Set the FONT value to Times New Roman.
   - Set the URL parameter to *http://www.nps.gov/mora/current/weather.htm*.
   - Set the REPEAT parameter to "yes".
   - Set the value of the SPEED parameter to 120.
   - Set the value of the VSPACE parameter to 1.
   - Set the FONTSIZE parameter to 10.
   - Set the TEXT*x* values to the text lines from the credit.txt file—be sure to include blank lines.

10. Save your changes to the file.

11. Using your Web browser, open **rainier4.htm** and verify that the embedded links and the Java applet work correctly. Also verify that the background sound file plays correctly.

12. Submit your completed Web site to your instructor.

Case Problem 1

Data files needed for this Case Problem: lmnhtxt.htm, dino.au, dino.avi, dino.mov, dino.wav, + 8 graphic files

Lincoln Museum of Natural History   Maria Kalski is the director of public relations for the Lincoln Museum of Natural History located in Lincoln, Iowa. Maria wants to overcome the idea that museums are boring, stuffy places, so she has asked you to help liven up the museum's Web page. You've accomplished this by adding some fun graphics and fonts. Maria likes the revised page, but she would also like you to add some video and sound clips. She provides you with some multimedia files that she wants added to the Web site. She wants you to create a link to the video file, which shows a clip of a dinosaur coming to life in a museum, and she wants the sound file to be added to the background of the Web page and played once each time the Web page is loaded by the browser. The final version of the Web page is shown in Figure 8-29.

Apply

Use the skills you've earned in this tutorial o create a multimedia Neb site for a museum.

Figure 8-29

The Lincoln Museum of Natural History

Located at 12 Bromhead Avenue in Lincoln, Iowa, the Lincoln Museum of Natural History is a fascinating and fun place to visit for the whole family. There's a lot going on at LMNH, and we invite you to experience the excitement. From replicas of early Native American villages, to the ice floes of the Arctic, to the mysterious world of the Amazon Rainforest, the Lincoln Museum of Natural History has something to offer everyone.

Dinosaurs Dinosaurs Dinosaurs

If dinosaurs are your bag, we have 'em in abundance. We're just down the road from some of the world's biggest dinosaur digs, and the local paleontologists pop in from time to time to give talks and demonstrations. They'll even bring samples for you to investigate. We also have several "hands-on" displays where your kids can pretend to be dinosaur hunters. Or you can become "dinosaur hunted" by trying to outrun Coelophysis in our *Slow Dinosaurs?-Not!* exhibit. When you're not busy trying to avoid becoming dino-food, enjoy our full-scale dinosaur models, including an Apatosaurus, Iguanodon, and the ever-popular Tyrannosaurus Rex.

For More Information

As you explore our Web site you will find more detailed information about our collections, exhibits, special events, educational programs, and scientific departments. Click one of the links listed at the bottom of this page. If you have further questions about any of the museum's programs, please call us at (311) 555-2311. LMNH is open every day except Thanksgiving, Christmas, and New Year's Day, from 10 a.m. to 5 p.m.

Just For Fun

We guarantee that all of our exhibits are perfectly safe. However, our dinosaur replicas appear *so* real that some of our patrons have seen some pretty strange sights. View the movie (474K - AVI) to see what we mean.

To create the home page for the Lincoln Museum of Natural History:

1. Use your text editor to open **lmnhtxt.htm** from the tutorial.08/case1 folder. Enter *your name* and *the date* in the comment section of the file and save the file as **lmnh.htm**.

2. Locate the word "movie" in the final paragraph of the page and change this text to a link that points to either dino.avi or dino.mov, depending on which video format your system supports. Specify the video format and the video file size in the text of the link.

3. At the top of the page below the inline image for the lincoln.jpg image file, insert an embedded sound clip for either the dino.wav or the dino.au sound file (depending on which format your system supports).

4. Set the width and the height of the embedded sound clip to 0 pixels.

5. Set the clip to start automatically when the page opens.

6. Save your changes to the file and close your text editor.

7. Open **lmnh.htm** in your Web browser and verify that the link displays the video clip and that the sound clip plays automatically when the Web page loads.

8. Submit the completed Web page to your instructor.

Case Problem 2

Data files needed for this Case Problem: button0.gif, button1.gif, button2.gif, button3.gif, devotion.au, devotion.mp3, devotion.wav, fireice.au, fireice.mp3, fireice.wav, PopBtn.class, PopMenu.class, rflogo.gif, rftxt.htm, sound.gif, tan.jpg

Madison State College   Professor Debra Li of the Madison State College English Department has asked you to help her create a Web page devoted to the works of the poet Robert Frost. With your help, she has created a Web page that contains a short biography of the poet and the complete text of two of his works. Professor Li would like to add sound clips of the two poems to the page so that her students can listen to Frost's poetry as well as read it.

She also wants you to create links to other Frost pages on the Web. She's located a Java applet that creates a set of graphical buttons that act as links. Professor Li thinks this applet would also make her page more interesting. The Java applet uses the PopMenu.class file with the parameters shown in Figure 8-30.

Figure 8-30

Parameter	Defines
labelpos="*type*"	The default label position for all of the buttons on the menu, where *type* is either "right" or "below"
labelpos*n*="*type*"	The label position for the *n*th button, starting with labelpos0, labelpos1, etc.
text*n*="*text*"	The text for the *n*th button, starting with text0, text1, etc.
src*n*="*url*"	The URL of the image file to be displayed in the *n*th button, starting with src0, src1, etc.
href*n*="*url*"	The URL to be opened when the *n*th button is clicked, starting with href0, href1, etc.
frame="*target*"	The target of the links when the applet is used in a frame. The default is "_top".

A preview of the page you'll create for Professor Li is shown in Figure 8-31.

Figure 8-31

To create the Robert Frost Web page:

1. Use your text editor to open **rftxt.htm** from the tutorial.08/case2 folder. Enter *your name* and *the date* in the comment section of the file and save the file as **rf.htm**.

2. Insert the inline image sound.gif directly after the title of the Fire and Ice poem, within the h4 heading located near the bottom of the page.

3. Change the Sound image to a link pointing to the fireice.mp3, fireice.wav, or fireice.au sound file, depending on which format your browser supports.

4. Repeat Steps 2 and 3 for the h4 heading for the Devotion poem. Link the Sound image to the devotion.mp3, devotion.wav, or devotion.au sound file.

5. Indicate the size of the two sound files in a paragraph before the poems.

Explore

6. Replace the four links in the links div element at the top of the page with the PopMenu.class applet. Use the text and link URLs for the text*n* and href*n* parameters (note that the first button uses the parameters text0 and href0). For the button image, use the inline image files button0.gif through button3.gif. Set the default label position to "right".

Explore

7. Add a style to the embedded style sheet that sets the width of the applet within the #links selector to 100% of the page width and the height to 30 pixels.

8. View the page in your Web browser and test the four links to the other Frost pages as well as the links to the two sound clips.

9. Submit the completed Web page to your instructor.

Case Problem 3

Data files needed for this Case Problem: Cmplx.class, Controls.class, flogo.jpg, FracPanel.class, fracttxt.htm, mandel.avi, Mandel.class, mandel.jpg, mandel.mov

Franklin High School Fractals are geometric objects discovered by mathematicians that closely model the sometimes chaotic world of nature. Doug Hefstadt, a mathematics teacher at Franklin High School in Monroe, Illinois, has just begun a unit on fractals for his senior math class. He's used the topic of fractals to construct a Web page to be placed on the school network, and he needs your help to complete the Web page. He has a video clip of a fractal that he wants placed on the Web page, along with a Java applet that allows students to interactively explore the Mandelbrot Set, a type of fractal object. He wants your assistance in putting these two objects on his Web page. A preview of the page you'll create is shown in Figure 8-32.

Create

Extend the skills you've earned in this tutorial to create a page on fractals, using a fractal movie and a fractal applet.

Figure 8-32

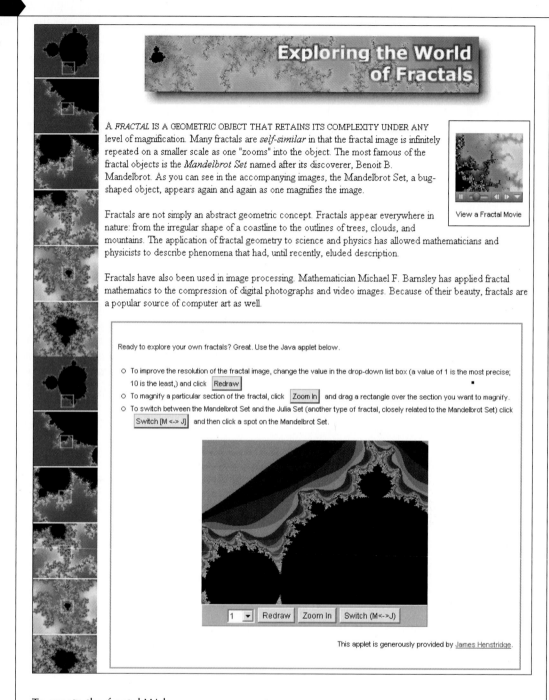

To create the fractal Web page:

1. Use your text editor to open **fracttxt.htm** from the tutorial.08/case3 folder. Enter *your name* and *the date* in the comment section of the file and save the file as **fractal.htm**.

2. Locate the div element with the id "movie" and insert the embedded movie clip mandel.avi (or mandel.mov if your system supports that video type).

3. Set the size of the video clip to 104 pixels wide by 120 pixels high. The clip should not start automatically.

Explore

4. For browsers that do not support embedded media clips, display a link to the mandel.avi and mandel.mov files. Be sure to indicate the size of the video file as well as the format.
5. Locate the div element with the id "applet" and insert a Java applet for the Mandel.class file.
6. Set the size of the applet to 350 pixels wide by 280 pixels high.
7. For browsers that do not support Java applets, display the text "Your browser does not support Java applets."
8. Save your changes to the file.

Explore

9. Open the Web page in your Web browser and verify that the video plays correctly. Test the fractal applet.
10. Submit your completed Web page to your instructor.

Create

Test your knowledge of frames by creating a multimedia Web page for a boy choir.

Case Problem 4

Data files needed for this Case Problem: concert.rm, CreditRoll.class, folksong.mp3, mbc.jpg, mbcinfo.txt, mbclogo.jpg, schedule.txt

Madison Boy Choir The Madison Boy Choir is one of the premier boy choirs in the United States. Rachel Dawes, the choir director, has asked you to help create a Web site that contains a sound clip and a video clip of the choir. You need to create two Web pages for Rachel: one that contains links to the media clips and another in which the clips are embedded in the page. She also wants the page with the embedded clips to contain a scrolling marquee that displays upcoming events for the choir.

The design of the Web site is up to you, but you can use the following files in creating the page:
- **concert.rm** A RealMedia video clip of the choir
- **CreditRoll.class** The scrolling marquee applet
- **folksong.mp3** An MP3 clip of the boy choir
- **mbc.jpg** A photo of the choir
- **mbcinfo.txt** General information about the choir
- **mbclogo.jpg** The Madison Boy Choir logo
- **schedule.txt** The choir's schedule of upcoming events

To complete this assignment:
1. Create a file named **mbc1.htm** in the tutorial.08/case4 folder in the location where your Data Files are stored. Include a comment section with *your name* and *the date*.
2. The mbc1.htm file should contain information about the choir, the choir logo, a photo, and the schedule of upcoming events.
3. Include links to the concert.rm and folksong.mp3 media clips.
4. View the contents of mbc1.htm in your Web browser. Verify that it works properly.
5. Create a file named **mbc2.htm** in the tutorial.08/case4 folder of your Data Files.
6. Along with the other choir information, embed the concert.rm and the folksong.mp3 media clips. Ensure that your Web page provides access to the media files for those users running browsers that do not support embedded clips.
7. Display the schedule of upcoming events in a scrolling marquee using the CreditRoll.class applet.

8. Using your Web browser, open mbc2.htm and verify that the embedded clips work properly.
9. Submit your completed Web site to your instructor.

Quick Check Answers

Session 8.1

1. You can add sound by either embedding a sound clip into the Web page or providing a link to a sound file.

2. Bandwidth is a measure of the amount of data that can be sent through a communication pipeline each second. The number of samples taken per second from a sound source is called the sampling rate. Sample resolution indicates the precision in measuring the sound within each sample.

3. MP3, AIFF, or SND

4. <a href="music.mp3">music.mp3</a>

5. An embedded object is any media clip, file, program, or other object that can be run or viewed from within the Web page. A browser must support the <embed> tag, and it must have a plug-in or an add-on installed to work with the object.

6. <embed src="music.mp3" />

7. The bgsound element

Session 8.2

1. A frame is an individual image in a video file. A video file is composed of a series of single images, known as frames. The number of frames shown in a given amount of time is called the frame rate. You compress and decompress video frames using a codec (short for *compression/decompression*).

2. Reducing the size of each frame, reducing the frame rate, compressing the file via the codec, reducing the size of the sound track by changing the sample size or the sampling rate, or reducing the color depth of the images in the video file

3. <a href="movie.mov">movie.mov</a>

4. <embed src="movie.mov" />

5. <embed src="movie.mov" /><noembed> <a href="movie.mov">movie.mov</a></noembed>

6. <img src="movie.jpg" dynsrc="movie.mov" start="mouseover" loop="1" />

7. It may not be supported by browsers other than Internet Explorer.

Session 8.3

1. Compiling is the process by which a JDK changes a .java file into an executable file that can run by itself without the JDK.

2. It must be run within a Java interpreter, such as your Web browser.

3. <applet code="StockTicker.class">

4. <applet code="StockTicker.class" codebase="http://www.wstreet.com">

5. <param name="URL" value="http://www.stockinfo.com" /><param name="TIME" value="60" />

6. <marquee behavior="scroll" style="color: white; background-color: black">Stock Information</marquee>

7. direction="right" loop="1"

8. <object data="rainier.mov" height="100" width="150" type="video/quicktime"> </object>

This tag is not supported by some browsers.

Objectives

Session 9.1
- Describe the history and theory of XHTML
- Describe the three XHTML DTDs and the differences between XHTML versions
- List the syntax rules for well-formed XHTML documents
- Understand the rules for creating valid XHTML documents under each of the three XHTML DTDs

Session 9.2
- Create a structured XHTML document
- Apply a DTD to an XHTML document
- Understand how to apply a namespace
- Combine different XML language elements into a single document
- Test an XHTML document for well-formedness and validity
- Describe how to create a CDATA section for an embedded style sheet

Working with XHTML

Creating a Well-Formed Valid Document

Case

Wizard Works Fireworks

Wizard Works is one of the largest sellers of brand-name and customized fireworks in the U.S. One of their biggest sources of sales comes from their Web site. Tom Blaska is the head of the advertising for Wizard Works and is also intimately involved with the company's Web site. Because the Web site has been around for many years, some of the code dates back to earlier versions of HTML. Tom would like the Web site code to be updated to reflect current standards and practices. Specifically, he wants you to look into rewriting the Web site code in XHTML rather than HTML. He also would like you to find ways to ensure that the code used by Wizard Works meets the standards specified for XHTML.

Student Data Files

▼tutorial.09

▽ **tutorial folder**

    workstxt.htm
    dtd_list.txt
    + 3 graphic files

▽ **review folder**

    founttxt.htm
    dtd_list.txt
    + 2 graphic files

▽ **case1 folder**

    breaktxt.htm
    dinnrtxt.htm
    lunchtxt.htm
    dtd_list.txt
    + 4 graphic files

Student Data Files	▼**tutorial.09 (continued)**		
	▽ **case2 folder**	▽ **case3 folder**	▽ **case4 folder**
	gargtxt.htm	cast.htm	address.txt
	dtd_list.txt	casttxt.htm	astro.txt
	+ 5 graphic files	hebd.htm	chem.txt
		hebdtxt.htm	elect.txt
		high.htm	eng.txt
		hightxt.htm	physics.txt
		lake.htm	dtd_list.txt
		laketxt.htm	+ 2 graphic files
		scotttxt.htm	
		dtd_list.txt	
		+ 6 graphic files	

Session 9.1

Introducing XHTML

Before you can create your first XHTML document, it's useful to review some of the history of the language. We'll start at the very beginning, with SGML.

SGML

Introduced in the 1980s, Standard Generalized Markup Language, or SGML, is a meta-language used to create markup languages. SGML is device-independent and system-independent, which means that it can be used with almost any type of document stored in almost any format. SGML has been widely used to create documents in businesses and government organizations of all sizes. For example, think of the daunting task of documenting all of the parts used in manufacturing the space shuttle, while at the same time creating a structure that shuttle engineers can use to quickly retrieve and edit that information. SGML provides tools to manage documentation projects of this magnitude.

While powerful, SGML is also quite complex. Thus, SGML is limited to those organizations that can afford the cost and overhead of maintaining large SGML environments. SGML is most useful for creating applications, based on the SGML architecture, that apply to specific types of documents. The most famous of these applications is HTML.

HTML

The success of the World Wide Web is due in no small part to HTML, which has allowed Web authors to easily create documents that can be displayed across different operating systems. Creating Web sites with HTML is a straightforward process that does not require a programming background.

One problem with HTML, however, was that various Web browsers developed their own unique flavors of HTML to provide customers with new and useful features not available with other browsers. Netscape saw a need for frames, so its Communicator browser introduced a version of HTML that included the frameset and frame elements, both of which were not part of standard HTML at that time. Microsoft saw a need for internal frames and introduced the iframe element into its browser, Internet Explorer—an innovation that also represented a departure from standard HTML. While these extensions were later adopted into the official HTML specifications by the W3C, many other extensions were not adopted—for example, Internet Explorer's marquee element.

The result was a confusing mixture of competing HTML standards—one for not just each browser, but for each browser version. Although the innovations offered by Netscape, Microsoft, and others certainly increased the scope and power of HTML, they did so at the expense of clarity. Web designers could no longer easily create Web sites without taking into account the cross-browser compatibility of the Web page code.

A second problem with HTML is that it can be applied inconsistently. For example, the following code does not follow HTML specifications because the h1 element has not been closed with an ending </h1> tag:

```
<body>
   <h1>Web Page Title
</body>
```

Although this code does not follow the correct syntax, most browsers would still render it correctly. Likewise, the following code would likely be interpreted correctly even though the colspan attribute value is not enclosed in quotation marks:

```
<td colspan=2>Heading</td>
```

Although browsers that do not enforce standards are very forgiving of new Web page authors, this courtesy affects the browser design. By making allowances for inconsistently applied HTML code, the source code for the browser must be larger and more complex to deal with all contingencies. In addition to creating a headache for browsers developers, this is also a problem for consumers. As the Web has branched out in recent years it has grown to include smaller, handheld devices, which limit the size of the software that can be run on them. The idea of a cleaner, more systematized version of HTML promised an easier job for developers creating new browsers for the Web.

Due in part to these very reasons, the need evolved for a language that could be easily customized, but at the same time be consistent and rigid enough for developers to create applications for it. One language created to meet these needs was XML.

XML

Extensible Markup Language, or XML, was designed to be a minor version of SGML, without SGML's complexity and overhead. Like SGML, XML can be used to design markup languages for different types of structured documents. Thus, an XML author can create a collection of elements and attributes for special types of data. XML has been used to create several markup languages, including MathML for mathematical content and CML for documenting chemical structures. Because MathML and CML were created using XML, documents written in these languages are also XML documents. Individual users can also create their own XML documents tailored for specific needs. For example, a business might design an XML document that contains elements for recording inventory and pricing data.

XML documents must be evaluated with an **XML parser**, a program that checks the document for errors in syntax and content (see Figure 9-1). An XML document that employs the correct syntax is known as a **well-formed** document. Unlike HTML, in which browsers usually accept documents that violate HTML syntax (so long as the violation is not too severe), an XML parser rejects any XML document that is not well formed.

Figure 9-1 ▶ **Testing a well-formed document**

The parser checks for syntax errors in the XML document.

If the document is well formed, it is passed by the parser and its content is displayed by the browser or other XML application.

The document author writes the code of the XML document.

A well-formed XML document that also contains the correct content and structure is known as a **valid** document. To specify what the correct content and structure for a document should be, the document developers create a collection of rules called the **document type definition** or **DTD**. As shown in Figure 9-2, the parser tests the content of the document against the rules in the DTD, and rejects the document if it does not conform to those rules.

Figure 9-2 ▶ **Testing a valid document**

The parser checks for syntax errors in the XML document and compares the document content with the rules specified in the DTD.

If the document is well formed, and valid, it is passed by the parser and displayed by the browser or other XML application.

The document author writes the code of the XML document.

DTD

For example, an XML document for a business might contain elements that store the names of each product in inventory. The DTD for that document could require that each product name element be accompanied by an id attribute value, and that no products share the same name or id. An XML parser would reject any XML document for that business that didn't satisfy those rules, even if the document was well formed. In this way, XML differs from HTML, in which browsers can ignore other browsers' proprietary extensions without causing an entire document to be rejected, thus making HTML more like XML is a way to make the language more rigid.

XHTML

This takes us to XHTML, which is a reformulation of HTML written in the XML language. As with HTML and XML, the W3C maintains the specifications and standards for XHTML. Figure 9-3 describes the different versions of the language released by the W3C or in progress.

Versions of XHTML　　**Figure 9-3**

Version	Date Released	Description
XHTML 1.0	January 26, 2000	Duplicates much of the content and structure of HTML 4.01, reformulated in XML. There are three DTDs for this version: strict, transitional, and frameset.
XHTML Basic	December 19, 2000	A reduced version of XHTML 1.1 geared toward mobile applications.
XHTML 1.1	May 31, 2001	A modularized language based on the strict version of XHTML 1.0. Each module covers a different group of page elements.
XHTML 2.0	In progress	The next version of XHTML expected to remain similar to XHTML 1.1; however, the markup language may be altered to conform to the requirements of related XML standards such as XML Linking and XML Schema.

The most widely supported version of XHTML is XHTML 1.0. The specifications for XHTML 1.0 most closely match those for HTML 4.01, with the added requirement that XHTML 1.0 documents must be both well formed and valid. Three DTDs are associated with XHTML 1.0:

- **transitional.** The transitional DTD supports many of the presentational features of HTML, including the deprecated elements and attributes. It is best used for older documents that contain deprecated features.
- **frameset.** The frameset DTD is used for documents containing frames, and also supports deprecated elements and attributes.
- **strict.** The strict DTD does not allow any presentational features or deprecated HTML elements and attributes, and does not support frames or inline frames. It is best used for documents that need to strictly conform to the latest standards.

XHTML 1.1 is a restructuring of XHTML 1.0 in which different elements are placed within modules. This allows browsers to support only those portions of the entire language that are relevant to their needs. Each module has its own corresponding DTD. Figure 9-4 describes some of the different modules in XHTML 1.1.

Figure 9-4 ▶ **XHTML 1.1 modules**

Module	Use	Supported Elements and Attributes
Structure	Used to define the basic structure of the document	body, head, html, title
Metainformation	Used to add meta-information to the document	meta
Text	Used for text content	abbr, acronym, address, blockquote, br, cite, code, dfn, div, em, h1, h2, h3, h4, h5, h6, kbd, p, pre, q, samp, span, strong, var
Presentation	Used for presentational elements	b, big, hr, i, small, sub, sup, tt
List	Used for list content	dl, dt, dd, ol, ul, li
Object	Used for embedded objects	object, param
Image	Used for inline images	img
Client-side Image Map	Used for client-side image maps	area, map
Hypertext	Used for links	a
Frames	Used for frames	frameset, frame, noframes
Iframe	Used for inline frames	iframe
Forms	Used for Web forms	button, fieldset, form, input, label, legend, select, optgroup, option, textarea
Table	Used for Web tables	caption, col, colgroup, table, tbody, td, tfoot, th, thead, tr
Scripting	Used for adding scripts to the document	noscript, script
Style Sheet	Used for accessing style sheets	style
Style Attribute	Used for adding the style attribute to individual elements	attribute: style attribute (deprecated)
Legacy	Used for deprecated elements and attributes	basefont, center, dir, font, isindex, menu, s, strike, u attributes: align, alink, background, bgcolor, color, face, link, size, text, type, vlink

For example, a browser designed for a handheld device that displays only text might support only those modules that deal with text content, and not the modules that deal with images or embedded objects. This enables browser developers to reduce the sizes of their applications to fit the requirements of specific devices. Browser developers can also use XHTML Basic, a version of XHTML 1.1 that limits the modules to those of use with handheld devices.

XHTML 2.0 is still in draft form, and thus is not supported in the Web community. When completed, this version is expected to represent a great departure from previous versions of XHTML and HTML. In fact, it is quite possible that documents written in XHTML 2.0 will not be backward-compatible with earlier versions—a point that concerns many developers. The development of XHTML 2.0 will likely require the development of new XHTML modules, or revisions to existing XHTML modules.

Creating a Well-Formed Document

Because all XHTML documents must be well formed, it's important to be familiar with all of the rules of proper syntax. You should already be familiar with most of these rules because you've been working with well-formed HTML from the first tutorial; however, if you examine older Web pages you may find document code that violates basic syntax, but which most browsers can nonetheless support. Figure 9-5 lists seven syntax requirements of XHTML, which some older HTML documents may violate.

Rules for well-formed XHTML documents ◄ **Figure 9-5**

Rule	Incorrect	Correct
Element names must be lowercase	`<P>This is a paragraph.</P>`	`<p>This is a paragraph.</p>`
Elements must be properly nested	`<p>This text is <b>bold.</p></b>`	`<p>This text is <b>bold.</b></p>`

All elements must be closed	`<p>This is the first paragraph.`
	`<p>This is the second paragraph.`
		`<p>This is the first paragraph.`
		`</p><p>This is the second`
		`paragraph.</p>`

Empty elements must be terminated	`This is a line break `	`This is a line break `
Attribute names must be lowercase	`<td ALIGN="right">`	`<td align="right">`
Attribute values must be quoted	`<table width=620>`	`<table width="620">`
Attributes must have values	`<option selected>`	`<option selected="selected">`

In addition to the rules specified in Figure 9-5, all XML documents must also include a single root element that contains all other elements. For XHTML, that root element is the html element.

In some older HTML documents, you may find cases of **attribute minimization**, a situation in which some attributes lack attribute values. XHTML does not allow attribute minimization. Figure 9-6 lists the minimized attributes that you may see in some HTML documents, along with their XHTML-compliant versions.

Attribute minimization in HTML and XHTML ◄ **Figure 9-6**

HTML	XHTML
compact	compact="compact"
checked	checked="checked"
declare	declare="declare"
readonly	readonly="readonly"
disabled	disabled="disabled"
selected	selected="selected"
defer	defer="defer"
ismap	ismap="ismap"
nohref	nohref="nohref"
noshade	noshade="noshade"
nowrap	nowrap="nowrap"
multiple	multiple="multiple"
noresize	noresize="noresize"

For example, in earlier versions of HTML the following code was used to indicate that a radio box should be selected by default:

```
<input type="radio" checked>
```

In XHTML, this code would be rewritten as

```
<input type="radio" checked="checked" />
```

The common rule is that a minimized attribute should be updated to XHTML by using the name of the attribute as the attribute's value.

Creating a Valid Document

To create a valid XHTML document we need to know the rules for the document content and structure. As noted earlier, XHTML 1.0 supports three DTDs: transitional, frameset, and strict. Which one you use for a given document depends on the content of the document and the needs of your users.

The Valid Use of Elements

If you need to support older browsers, you should use the transitional DTD, which recognizes deprecated elements and attributes like the font element and the bgcolor attribute. If you need to support older browsers in a framed Web site, you should use the frameset DTD. If you only need to support more current browsers and want to weed out any use of deprecated features, and have no need to support frames, then you should use the strict DTD.

In addition to browser-specific elements (like Internet Explorer's marquee element) the following elements are not allowed under the strict DTD:

- applet
- basefont
- center
- dir
- font
- iframe
- isindex
- menu
- s
- strike
- u

These elements are allowed in the transitional DTD, however. The frameset DTD supports these elements plus the frame, frameset, and noframes elements. Thus, the code

```
<font color="red">Wizard Works</font>
```

would be considered valid code under the transitional or frameset DTDs, but not under the strict one.

In addition to prohibiting the use of certain elements, the strict DTD also prohibits certain elements from being used as children within other elements. For example, you cannot place a block-level element within an inline element. In this case, the DTD is enforcing a particular structure on the document's content. Figure 9-7 lists the prohibited child elements under the strict DTD.

Child elements prohibited in the strict DTD ◀ **Figure 9-7**

Element	Prohibited Children
inline element	block-level elements
body	a, abbr, acronym, b, bdo, big, br, button, cite, code, dfn, em, i, img, input, kbd, label, map, object, q, samp, select, small, span, strong, sub, sup, textarea, tt, var
button	button, form, fieldset, iframe, input, isindex, label, select, textarea
blockquote	a, abbr, acronym, b, bdo, big, br, button, cite, code, dfn, em, i, img, input, kbd, label, map, object, q, samp, select, small, span, strong, sub, sup, textarea, tt, var
form	a, abbr, acronym, b, bdo, big, br, cite, code, dfn, em, form, i, img, kbd, map, object, q, samp, small, span, strong, sub, sup, tt, var
label	label
pre	big, img, object, small, sub, sup
all other page elements	big, small

For example, the following code would be disallowed under the strict DTD because it places an inline image as a child of the body element:

```
<body>
   <img src="logo.jpg" alt="Wizard Works" />
</body>
```

However, you could make this code compliant with the strict DTD by placing the inline image within its own paragraph:

```
<body>
   <p><img src="logo.jpg" alt="Wizard Works" /></p>
</body>
```

The goal of this rule is to enforce the inline nature of the img element. Because an inline image is displayed inline within a block element such as a paragraph, it should not be found outside of that context. For the same reason, form elements like the input or select elements should be found only within a form, not outside of one.

Finally, all three DTDs require that the following elements be present in every valid XHTML document:

- html
- head
- title
- body

While the html, head, and body elements are generally expected under HTML, XHTML requires that every valid document include the title element as well. Any XML document that omits the title element is rejected.

The Valid Use of Attributes

DTDs also include different rules for attributes and their use. Under the strict DTD, deprecated attributes are not allowed. A list of these prohibited attributes with their corresponding elements is displayed in Figure 9-8.

Figure 9-8	**Attributes prohibited in the strict DTD**

Element	Prohibited Attributes
a	target
area	target
base	target
body	alink, bgcolor, link, text, vlink,
br	clear
caption	align
div	align
dl	compact
form	name, target
h*n*	align
hr	align, noshade, size, width
img	align, border, hspace, name, vspace
input	align
li	type, value
link	target
map	name
object	align, border, hspace, vspace
ol	compact, start
p	align
pre	width
script	language
table	align, bgcolor
td	bgcolor, height, nowrap, width
th	bgcolor, height, nowrap, width
tr	bgcolor
ul	type, compact

These attributes are supported in the transitional and frameset DTDs, however. Thus the code

```
<img src="logo.jpg" alt="Wizard Works" align="left" />
```

would not be valid under the strict DTD because it includes the align attribute; this code would be valid under the transitional and frameset DTDs, however. To make this code valid under all three DTDs, you could replace the align attribute with an inline style that employs the float style:

```
<img src="logo.jpg" alt="Wizard Works" style="float: left" />
```

You may also find that you have to make changes to older HTML code in the use of the name attribute. The strict DTD requires the use of the id attribute in place of the name attribute. Thus, the tags

```
<a name="top">
<form name="order">
<img name="logo" />
<map name="parkmap">
```

would be written in strict XHTML as

```
<a id="top">
<form id="order">
<img id="logo" />
<map id="parkmap">
```

The transitional and frameset DTDs also require the use of the id attribute, but do not reject documents that contain both the name and id attributes. For those DTDs, it's best to include both if you want to make your code backward-compatible.

Finally, unlike the transitional and frameset DTDs, the strict DTD does not support the target attribute. This means that you cannot open links in secondary browser windows if you want your code to be strictly compliant with XHTML. This decision was not greeted with enthusiasm by many developers, so the target attribute was reintroduced in XHTML 1.1 as part of the Target module. If your users' browsers support XHTML 1.1 and the Target module, you can use the target attribute in all of your links.

Whereas some attributes are prohibited, others are required. A list of the required attributes and the elements they're associated with is shown in Figure 9-9.

Required XHTML attributes   Figure 9-9

Element	Required Attributes
applet	height, width (transitional and frameset only)
area	alt
base	href
basefont	size (transitional and frameset only)
bdo	dir
form	action
img	alt, src
map	id
meta	content
optgroup	label
param	name (transitional and frameset only)
script	type
style	type
textarea	cols, rows

For example, an inline image is valid only if it contains both the src and alt attributes, and a form element is valid only if it contains an action attribute.

Although the list of rules for well-formed and valid documents may seem long and onerous, they simply reflect good coding practice. You would not, for example, want to create a Web page without a page title, or an inline image without alternate text. In addition to being required for valid well-formed code, there are many advantages to using a DTD. Perhaps their most significant advantage is the help DTDs provide in troubleshooting documents. If you create or edit your XHTML code by hand, you can easily make mistakes in syntax, content, or structure. Using a DTD allows you to test your document and correct any mistakes. In the next session, we'll look at some of the tools available for testing, and you'll use them to test an XHTML document created for the Wizard Works Web site.

Session 9.1 Quick Check

1. What is a well-formed document? What is a valid document?

2. Describe the three DTDs used with XHTML.

3. Why is the following element not well formed? How would you correct it?
   ```
   <img src="logo.jpg" alt="Wizard Works">
   ```

4. Why is the following element not well formed? How would you correct it?
   ```
   <input type="radio" disabled />
   ```

5. Why is the following code sample not valid under the strict XHTML?
   ```
   <blockquote>
   For more information go to the <a href="faq.htm">FAQ page</a>
   </blockquote>
   ```

6. Why is the following element not valid under strict XHTML? Suggest a correction to the problem.
   ```
   <img src="logo.jpg" alt="Wizard Works" align="right" />
   ```

7. Why is the following tag not valid under the transitional DTD? Suggest a correction to the problem. Make your new code backward-compatible.
   ```
   <map name="parkmap">
   ```

Session 9.2

Creating an XHTML Document

Now that you've learned about the history and issues surrounding XHTML, you can start updating the code for the Wizard Works home page so that it complies with the standards of XHTML.

To open the Wizard Works home page:

▶ 1. Use your text editor to open **workstxt.htm** from the tutorial.09/tutorial folder. Enter *your name* and *the date* in the comment section and save the file as **works.htm**.

▶ 2. Open **works.htm** in your Web browser. Figure 9-10 shows the layout and design of the page.

The Wizard Works home page | Figure 9-10

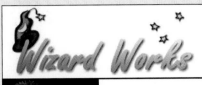

The XML Declaration

Because all XHTML documents are also XML documents, the first line of an XHTML document should contain a declaration indicating that the document adheres to the syntax and rules of XML. The syntax of the XML declaration is

```
<?xml version="value" encoding="type" standalone="type" ?>
```

where the version attribute indicates the XML version of the document, the encoding attribute specifies character encoding, and the standalone attribute indicates whether the document contains references to an external DTD. Although the xml declaration is not required, you should always include it in any XML or XHTML document. It provides useful information about the content and coding of the document, freeing XML parsers and browsers from having to guess about those properties.

At present the only versions of XML approved by the W3C are versions 1.0 and 1.1. Version 1.1 makes some changes in the requirements for well-formed code and in character encoding, but it is essentially the same specification as version 1.0. For XHTML documents you should use "1.0" as the xml version number.

The encoding attribute tells the parser or browser how to read the document. Each XML document (and thus every XHTML document) is based on a **character set**, which is a set of abstract symbols matched to code numbers. For example the character "A" is matched to the code number "65" in the ASCII character set. Because the ASCII character set is not sufficiently large for the thousands of characters used in languages throughout the world, many documents use the more complete **Universal Character Set** (**UCS**) or **Unicode** standard. When a document is sent over the Internet, each character is encoded as a sequence of bytes. The process by which those bytes are translated back into a character set (and vice versa) is known as the **character encoding**. The most common encodings are UTF-8 and UTF-16, which transmit Unicode characters as a sequence of 8-bit and 16-bit values, respectively. All XML parsers and browsers must support these two encodings, and parsers assume UTF-8 or UTF-16 by default if no encoding is specified. For our XHTML document we'll specify the UTF-8 encoding.

The standalone attribute should be set to "no" for XHTML documents, because these documents rely on the external strict, transitional, or frameset DTDs supplied by the W3C for validation. You would only set the standalone attribute value to "yes" for XML documents in which the DTD is either not present, or placed within the XML document itself.

To add an xml declaration to the document:

1. Return to the **works.htm** file in your text editor.

2. At the top of the file, insert the following line as shown in Figure 9-11.

   ```
   <?xml version="1.0" encoding="UTF-8" standalone="no" ?>
   ```

Figure 9-11 | **Inserting the xml declaration**

```
<?xml version="1.0" encoding="UTF-8" standalone="no" ?>
<html>
<head>
```

3. Save your changes to the file.

Reference Window | **Adding an xml Declaration**

- To declare that a document is written in XML, enter the following as the first line of the file:

  ```
  <?xml version="value" encoding="type" standalone="type" ?>
  ```
  where the version attribute indicates the XML version of the document, the encoding attribute specifies the character encoding, and the standalone attribute indicates whether the document contains references to an external DTD.
- For XHTML documents, use the declaration

  ```
  <?xml version="1.0" encoding="UTF-8" standalone="no" ?>
  ```

Note that you can also indicate the character set and encoding employed by your HTML document in the meta element. The syntax is for doing this is

```
<meta http-equiv="Content-Type" content="mime-type; charset=character_
set"/>
```

where *mime-type* is the MIME type of the document content and *character_set* is the character set in use. For example, to specify the character set and encoding for an HTML document, you can enter the following meta element:

```
<meta http-equiv="Content-Type" content="text/html; charset=utf-8" />
```

Other possible values for the charset include us-ascii and iso-8859-1.

The DOCTYPE Declaration

The next element to add to an XHTML document is the DOCTYPE declaration, which tells XML parsers what DTD is associated with the document. The syntax of the DOCTYPE declaration for a general XML document is

```
<!DOCTYPE root type "id" "url">
```

where *root* is the name of the root element of the document, *type* identifies the type of DTD, *id* is a recognized public identifier of the DTD, and *url* is the location of the external DTD file.

For XHTML documents the *root* is always "html" and the *type* is "PUBLIC". The *id* and *url* values depend on the DTD being used. If the parser recognizes the public identifier, it translates that id into a URL for the external DTD. If the parser doesn't recognize the id, however, it uses the URL specified in the DOCTYPE declaration to locate the DTD.

Figure 9-12 lists the complete DOCTYPE declarations for different languages. Note that you can validate a document not only against different versions of XHTML 1.0, but also against different versions of HTML, even down to the W3C's specifications for HTML 2.0. You can access the most recent versions of these DTDs on the W3C Web site.

DOCTYPE declarations for different languages | **Figure 9-12**

DTD	DOCTYPE
HTML 2.0	<!DOCTYPE html PUBLIC "-//IETF//DTD HTML 2.0//EN">
HTML 3.2	<!DOCTYPE HTML PUBLIC "-//W3C//DTD HTML 3.2 Final//EN">
HTML 4.01 strict	<!DOCTYPE HTML PUBLIC "-//W3C//DTD HTML 4.01//EN" "http://www.w3.org/TR/html4/strict.dtd">
HTML 4.01 transitional	<!DOCTYPE HTML PUBLIC "-//W3C//DTD HTML 4.01 Transitional//EN" "http://www.w3.org/TR/html4/loose.dtd">
HTML 4.01 frameset	<!DOCTYPE HTML PUBLIC "-//W3C//DTD HTML 4.01 Frameset//EN" "http://www.w3.org/TR/html4/frameset.dtd">
XHTML 1.0 strict	<!DOCTYPE html PUBLIC "-//W3C//DTD XHTML 1.0 Strict//EN" "http://www.w3.org/TR/xhtml1/DTD/xhtml1-strict.dtd">
XHTML 1.0 transitional	<!DOCTYPE html PUBLIC "-//W3C//DTD XHTML 1.0 Transitional//EN" "http://www.w3.org/TR/xhtml1/DTD/xhtml1-transitional.dtd">
XHTML 1.0 frameset	<!DOCTYPE html PUBLIC "-//W3C//DTD XHTML 1.0 Frameset//EN" "http://www.w3.org/TR/xhtml1/DTD/xhtml1-frameset.dtd">
XHTML 1.1	<!DOCTYPE html PUBLIC "-//W3C//DTD XHTML 1.1//EN" "http://www.w3.org/TR/xhtml11/DTD/xhtml11.dtd">

Tom would like you to validate the Wizard Works home page against the transitional DTD for XHTML 1.0, so you'll add the DOCTYPE declaration for this DTD to the file. Because the code for the DOCTYPE declaration can be long and complicated, a text file with the declarations from Figure 9-12 has been created for you to copy from.

To add a DOCTYPE declaration to the document:

▶ **1.** Open the **dtd_list.txt** file in your text editor.

▶ **2.** Copy the DOCTYPE declaration for the XHTML 1.0 transitional DTD.

> **3.** Close the file.
>
> **4.** Return to the **works.htm** file in your text editor.
>
> **5.** Directly below the xml declaration, paste the DOCTYPE declaration you copied from the dtd_list.txt file. Figure 9-13 shows the revised code for your file.

Figure 9-13	Inserting the DOCTYPE declaration

```
<?xml version="1.0" encoding="UTF-8" standalone="no" ?>
<!DOCTYPE html PUBLIC "-//W3C//DTD XHTML 1.0 Transitional//EN"
   "http://www.w3.org/TR/xhtml1/DTD/xhtml1-transitional.dtd">
<html>
<head>
```

> **6.** Save your changes to the file.

Reference Window | Setting the Document DTD

- To apply the XHTML 1.0 strict DTD, add the following line after the xml declaration:
  ```
  <!DOCTYPE html PUBLIC "-//W3C//DTD XHTML 1.0 Strict//EN"
     "http://www.w3.org/TR/xhtml1/DTD/xhtml1-strict.dtd">
  ```
- To apply the XHTML 1.0 transitional DTD, use
  ```
  <!DOCTYPE html PUBLIC "-//W3C//DTD XHTML 1.0 Transitional//EN"
     "http://www.w3.org/TR/xhtml1/DTD/xhtml1-transitional.dtd">
  ```
- To apply the XHTML 1.0 frameset DTD, use
  ```
  <!DOCTYPE html PUBLIC "-//W3C//DTD XHTML 1.0 Frameset//EN"
     "http://www.w3.org/TR/xhtml1/DTD/xhtml1-frameset.dtd">
  ```

The xml Namespace

The last modification we'll make to the works.htm file is to add a namespace declaration to the html element. Understanding the concept of a namespace requires looking a little more into the nuts and bolts of XML. As we noted in the previous session, XHTML is not the only XML-based language. Another XML language, MathML, is used for documents containing mathematical content, symbols, equations, and operations. For a math professor interested in creating a Web site, MathML provides many elements and attributes not available with HTML or XHTML. For the professor it would be useful to have a document language that combined features from both XHTML and MathML. Recall from the history of HTML that browser developers dealt with the issue of needing new features in their documents by adding extensions to the HTML language. XML (and through it, XHTML) deals with this problem by allowing elements and attributes from several different document types to be combined within a single document. Thus, our math professor could combine the elements of XHTML and MathML in his document without having to invent a new language or modify the specifications of an old one.

The problem is that you need a way of distinguishing the elements from the different languages. This is done by using namespaces. A **namespace** is a unique identifier for the elements and attributes originating from a particular document type, such as XHTML or MathML. There are two types of namespaces: default and local. A **default namespace** is the namespace applied to the root element and any element within it—which includes, by default, any element within the document. To declare a default namespace, you use the syntax

```
<root xmlns="namespace">
```

where *root* is the name of the root element and *namespace* is the namespace id. For example, if you wish to declare that the elements in your document belong to the XHTML namespace by default, you would add the following attribute to the opening <html> tag:

```
<html xmlns="http://www.w3.org/1999/xhtml">
```

The namespace id for XHTML looks like a URL, but it's not treated as one. The id can actually be any string of characters so long as it uniquely identifies the document namespace. For XHTML, it was decided to use "http://www.w3.org/1999/xhtml" as the unique identifier.

Setting the XHTML Namespace

- To set XHTML as the default namespace for a document, add the xmlns attribute to the html element with the following value:
  ```
  <html xmlns="http://www.w3.org/1999/xhtml">
  ```

To define a namespace for specific parts of a document, you use a **local namespace**, which applies only to select elements. Each of the elements in the local namespace is marked by a prefix attached to the element name. To create a local namespace, you add the following attribute to a document's root element:

```
xmlns:prefix="namespace"
```

where *prefix* is the prefix you'll use to mark elements in this local namespace and *namespace* is the namespace id. You should identify any element belonging to that namespace by modifying the element name in the tag as follows:

```
prefix:element
```

where *prefix* is the local namespace prefix and *element* is the element name.

Figure 9-14 shows an example of a document that combines elements from both XHTML and MathML, and indicates how this page would appear in an application that supports both markup languages.

Figure 9-14 — **A combined document**

```
<?xml version="1.0"?>
<html xmlns="http://www.w3.org/1999/xhtml"
      xmlns:ml="http://www.w3.org/1998/Math/MathML">
<head>
   <title>MathML with XHTML</title>
</head>
<body>
<h1>A MathML Equation</h1>
<hr />
<ml:math mode="display">
   <ml:mrow>
      <ml:mi>x</ml:mi>
      <ml:mo>+</ml:mo>
      <ml:mn>1</ml:mn>
   </ml:mrow>
</ml:math>
<hr />
</body>
</html>
```

MathML Equation
———————
$x + 1$

Combined document   **Display document**

Note that in this figure, each element that belongs to the MathML namespace has the "ml" prefix in the element name. Any element without this prefix belongs to the default namespace, which in this example is XHTML. In this way, elements from two different languages can coexist in the same document. Though not shown here, this document could also be tested for well-formedness and validity by attaching DOCTYPE declarations for both the XHTML and MathML DTDs. Browser support for combining languages like MathML and XHTML in a single document is currently limited, but this will certainly change in coming years.

If you don't intend to combine different document types within the same document, it's still a good idea to add a namespace to an XHTML file. In practical terms, an XHTML document is still interpretable by most browsers without a namespace. However, the W3C requires that the XHTML namespace be added to the html element to avoid any possible confusion in the future when mixed documents become more prevalent.

To add the XHTML namespace:

1. In your text editor, locate the html element in the **works.htm** file.
2. Insert the attribute **xmlns="http://www.w3.org/1999/xhtml"** as shown in Figure 9-15.

Inserting the XHTML namespace   Figure 9-15

```
<?xml version="1.0" encoding="UTF-8" standalone="no" ?>
<!DOCTYPE html PUBLIC "-//W3C//DTD XHTML 1.0 Transitional//EN"
  "http://www.w3.org/TR/xhtml1/DTD/xhtml1-transitional.dtd">
<html xmlns="http://www.w3.org/1999/xhtml">
<head>
```

3. Save your changes to the file.

You've completed converting the works.htm file from an HTML document into an XHTML document. Now you can test whether the document is both well formed and valid.

Testing an XHTML Document

To test your document you need to send the file to an XML parser or an XHTML validator. Several validators are available on the Web. We'll use the one hosted on the W3C Web site.

To access the W3C validation page:

1. Use your browser to open the Web page at **http://validator.w3.org**
2. Click the **Browse, Choose,** or **Choose File** button in the Validate by File Upload section.
3. Locate and select the **works.htm** file in the tutorial.09/tutorial data folder.
4. Click the **Check** button on the W3C validation page. Figure 9-16 shows the first five error statements of the validation check.

Figure 9-16 **Results of the first validation test**

THIS PAGE IS **NOT** VALID XHTML 1.0 TRANSITIONAL!

Below are the results of attempting to parse this document with an SGML parser.

1. *Line 46, column 55*: **end tag for "img" omitted, but OMITTAG NO was specified**

```
<img src="logo.jpg" alt="Wizard Works" align="left">
```

You may have neglected to close a tag, or perhaps you meant to "self-close" a tag; that is, ending it with "/>" instead of ">".

2. *Line 46, column 3*: **start tag was here**

```
<img src="logo.jpg" alt="Wizard Works" align="left">
```

3. *Line 70, column 40*: **required attribute "alt" not specified**

```
<img src="firework.gif" align="right">
```

The attribute given above is required for an element that you've used, but you have omitted it. For instance, in most HTML and XHTML document types the "type" attribute is required on the "script" element and the "alt" attribute is required for the "img" element.

Typical values for type *are* type="text/css" *for* <style> *and* type="text/javascript" *for* <script>.

4. *Line 70, column 41*: **end tag for "img" omitted, but OMITTAG NO was specified**

```
<img src="firework.gif" align="right">
```

5. *Line 70, column 3*: **start tag was here**

```
<img src="firework.gif" align="right">
```

Trouble? Depending on your browser or validator, your report might look slightly different.

A total of 14 errors were reported by the validator. This doesn't mean that there are 14 separate mistakes in the file, though. In some cases, the same mistake results in several errors being noted in the report, and fixing one mistake can result in several of the errors reported by the validator being resolved. In the case of a large error list, it's unlikely that you can fix everything at once. It's best to fix the most obvious mistakes first to reduce the size of the list, leaving the more subtle errors to be fixed last. Let's examine the error list in more detail. The first error reported was

1. *Line 46, column 55*: **end tag for "img" omitted, but OMITTAG NO was specified**

```
<img src="logo.jpg" alt="Wizard Works" align="left">
```

When the validator reports that the end tag for an element is missing, it means that either a two-sided tag is missing an end tag or a one-sided tag was improperly entered. This is a syntax error and indicates that the document is not well formed. If you examine the code for the logo.jpg inline image, you'll notice that the img element was not written as a one-sided tag. This is a common problem with older HTML code, in which tags for empty elements use the same form as the opening tags of two-sided tags. Note that even though the tag was improperly entered, we still saw the page rendered correctly by the browser earlier in the tutorial.

Let's look at another error in the list. The third error reported by the browser indicates a problem with the document's validity:

3. *Line 70, column 40*: **required attribute "alt" not specified**

```
<img src="firework.gif" align="right">
```

Here we have an inline image without the alt attribute. Because the alt attribute is required for all inline images, omitting it results in an error. This inline image was also not inserted using a one-sided tag, resulting in a syntax error as well. Let's fix these errors and resubmit the file for testing.

To fix and resubmit the file:

1. Return to the **works.htm** file in your text editor.

2. Locate the img element for the logo.jpg file and change it to a one-sided tag using the proper syntax.

3. Locate the img element for the firework.gif image, add the attribute, **alt=""**, and change the tag to a one-sided tag. Figure 9-17 shows the revised code in the file.

Fixing the errors in the img elements　　**Figure 9-17**

```
<body bgcolor="white">
<div id="head">
    <img src="logo.jpg" alt="Wizard Works" align="left" />
    <a href="#" target="new">Review Cart</a>
    <a href="#" target="new">Check Out</a>
</div>

<div id="linklist">
    <a href="#">Home</a>
    <a href="#" class="newgroup">Assortments</a>
    <a href="#">Firecrackers</a>
    <a href="#">Fountains</a>
    <a href="#">Cones</a>
    <a href="#">Rockets</a>
    <a href="#">Sparklers</a>
    <a href="#" class="newgroup">Online Store</a>
    <a href="#">Shopping Cart</a>
    <a href="#">Your Account</a>
    <a href="#" class="newgroup">Safety</a>
    <a href="#">Tech Support</a>
    <a href="#">Customer Service</a>
    <a href="#">About Us</a>
    <a href="#" class="newgroup">Contact Us</a>
</div>

<div id="main">
    <img src="firework.gif" align="right" alt="" />
    <p class="firstp">
        Welcome to Wizard Works, your one-stop shopping source for discount
        fireworks on the Web! We maintain a select variety of consumer fireworks
        on our web site year round. You'll find the fireworks you want with the
        speed and convenience of the Internet, and you'll always have the best
        show in the neighborhood when you shop at Wizard Works.
```

4. Save your changes, return to the browser window displaying the validation report, and click the **Refresh** or **Reload** button to resubmit the validation check. You may be queried whether or not to resend the previous information. Click the **Retry** or **OK** button to resend the previous information.

   Trouble? If clicking the Refresh or Reload button does not resubmit the page for testing, you can click the Back button on your browser to return to the opening validation page and reselect the page for testing.

By fixing these two errors, we reduced the size of the list from 14 errors to nine. Let's try to trim that down even more. The first error in the latest list states:

1. *Line 78, column 5*: **document type does not allow element "p" here; missing one of "object", "applet", "map", "iframe", "button", "ins", "del" start-tag**

```
<p>
```

which may indicate that an element has been improperly nested within the p element—but let's read on. The fourth error states:

4. *Line 97, column 5*: end **tag for "p" omitted, but OMITTAG NO was specified**

```
</div>
```

which indicates that the paragraph element was not properly closed with the closing </p> tag. In this case the same mistake has caused both errors. By not closing the paragraph element, it appears that other elements have been improperly placed inside of it. By adding the closing tag, both errors should be corrected.

To fix the paragraphs:

1. Return to the **works.htm** file in your text editor.

2. Locate the three paragraph elements in the main section and add closing **</p>** tags to each paragraph as shown in Figure 9-18.

Figure 9-18	Fixing the errors in the paragraph elements

```
<div id="main">
    <img src="firework.gif" align="right" alt="" />
    <p class="firstp">
    Welcome to Wizard Works, your one-stop shopping source for discount
    fireworks on the web! We maintain a select variety of consumer fireworks
    on our web site year round. You'll find the fireworks you want with the
    speed and convenience of the Internet, and you'll always have the best
    show in the neighborhood when you shop at Wizard Works. </p>
    <p>
    We supply quality fireworks to buy online at wholesale prices. Our
    professional firework display team are available to design and organize
    your display, or if you want to organize your own firework party, our
    experienced fireworks designers have selected the best fireworks for the
    occasion. We've made it easy for you to buy on-line for delivery direct
    to your home. </p>
    <p>
    We also create customized fireworks and displays for special needs. Please
    contact one of our design engineers to see if we can create a display for
    your special event. Be sure to order special event fireworks early to ensure
    on-time delivery. </p>
```

3. Save your changes and return to the validation page. Click the **Refresh** or **Reload** button in your browser to redo the validation check. As shown in Figure 9-19, the page should now pass the validation check for XHTML 1.0 transitional.

Report showing a successful validation under XHTML 1.0 transitional ◄ Figure 9-19

THIS PAGE IS VALID XHTML 1.0 TRANSITIONAL!

TIP OF THE DAY: Use international date format

NOTE: The HTTP Content-Type header sent by your web browser (unknown) did not contain a "charset" parameter, but the Content-Type was one of the XML text/* sub-types (text/xml). The relevant specification (RFC 3023) specifies a strong default of "us-ascii" for such documents so we will use this value regardless of any encoding you may have indicated elsewhere. If you would like to use a different encoding, you should arrange to have your browser send this new encoding information.

NOTE: The Validator XML support has some limitations.

The uploaded file was checked and found to be valid XHTML 1.0 Transitional. This means that the resource in question identified itself as "XHTML 1.0 Transitional" and that we successfully performed a formal validation using an SGML or XML Parser (depending on the markup language used).

W3C XHTML 1.0 ✔ To show your readers that you have taken the care to create an interoperable Web page, you may display this icon on any page that validates. Here is the HTML you should use to add this icon to your Web page:

```
<p>
  <a href="http://validator.w3.org/check?uri=referer"><img
      src="http://www.w3.org/Icons/valid-xhtml10"
      alt="Valid XHTML 1.0!" height="31" width="88" /></a>
</p>
```

Thanks to this code, you will be able to re-validate your Web page by following the link (click on the image), and we encourage you to do so every time you modify your document.

Now that we've passed the validation check for XHTML 1.0 transitional, Tom wants the page tested under XHTML 1.0 strict. To perform this test we'll first have to change the DOCTYPE declaration to use the strict XHTML 1.0 DTD.

To change the DOCTYPE declaration and resubmit the file for testing:

► **1.** Reopen the **dtd_list.txt** file in your text editor, copy the DOCTYPE declaration for the XHTML 1.0 strict, then close the file.

► **2.** Return to the **works.htm** file in your text editor.

► **3.** Paste the copied DOCTYPE declaration into the file, replacing the old DOCTYPE declaration. Figure 9-20 shows the revised file.

| Figure 9-20 | Changing the DOCTYPE declaration to XHTML 1.0 strict |

```
<?xml version="1.0" encoding="UTF-8" standalone="no" ?>
<!DOCTYPE html PUBLIC "-//W3C//DTD XHTML 1.0 Strict//EN"
   "http://www.w3.org/TR/xhtml1/DTD/xhtml1-strict.dtd">
<html xmlns="http://www.w3.org/1999/xhtml">
<head>
```

4. Save your changes and return to the validation page. Click the **Refresh** or **Reload** button in your browser to redo the validation check. Because the DOCTYPLE declaration has been changed, the test should now be done based on the strict DTD. As shown in Figure 9-21, the page fails XHTML 1.0 strict with five errors.

| Figure 9-21 | Results of the XHTML 1.0 strict validation test |

THIS PAGE IS **NOT** VALID   STRICT!

Below are the results of attempting to parse this document with an SGML parser.

1.   *Line 45, column 14:* **there is no attribute "bgcolor"**

```
<body bgcolor="white">
```

2.   *Line 47, column 48:* **there is no attribute "align"**

```
<img src="logo.jpg" alt="Wizard Works" align="left" />
```

3.   *Line 48, column 22:* **there is no attribute "target"**

```
<a href="#" target="new">Review Cart</a>
```

4.   *Line 92, column 18:* **there is no attribute "color"**

```
<font color="blue">Wizard Works</font> &#183;
```

5.   *Line 92, column 24:* **element "font" undefined**

```
<font color="blue">Wizard Works</font> &#183;
```

Because all of the syntax errors have been fixed through the validation test using the XHTML 1.0 transitional DTD, these errors involve the use of elements and attributes not supported in the strict DTD. The first error occurs because of the use of the deprecated bgcolor attribute to set the page's background color. The second error occurs because of the use of the deprecated align attribute to position the inline image on the page. The third error is due to the use of the target attribute in a hyperlink. The fourth and fifth errors occur because of the use of the font element and an attribute within that deprecated element.

We can correct most of these errors by using style sheets to format the page's appearance rather than deprecated elements and attributes. For the error involving the target attribute, we have no choice but to remove the attribute from the element.

To modify the document:

1. Return to the **works.htm** file in your text editor.

2. Add the style **background-color: white** to the declaration for the body element in the embedded style sheet and then delete the attribute **bgcolor="white"** from the <body> tag.

3. Add the following style declaration to the embedded style sheet:

   ```
   #head img {float: left}
   ```

4. Delete the attribute **align="left"** from logo.jpg inline image located within the head div element.

5. Delete the attribute **target="new"** from the a elements for the Review Cart and Check Out links located within the head div element.

6. Add the following style declaration to the embedded style sheet:

   ```
   #main img {float: right}
   ```

7. Delete the attribute **align="right"** from firework.gif inline image located within the main div element.

8. Go to the address element at the bottom of the file and replace <font color="blue">Wizard Works</font> with the following:

   ```
   <span>Wizard Works</span>
   ```

9. Add the following style declaration to the embedded style sheet:

   ```
   address span {color: blue}
   ```

   Figure 9-22 shows the revised code for the document.

Figure 9-22 ▶ **The revised works.htm file**

```
<title>wizard works</title>
<style type="text/css">
    body {background-image: url(back.jpg); background-repeat: repeat-y;
        font-size: 12pt; margin-right: 20px; background-color: white}
    #head {position: absolute; top: 0px; left: 0px; width: 100%; font-size: 14pt;
        font-family: sans-serif; background-color: white; text-align: right;
        border-bottom: 2px solid black}
    #head img {float: left}
    #head a {color: white; background-color: blue; font-size: 8pt; font-weight: bold;
        text-decoration: none; text-align: center; border: 5px outset white;
        width: 100px; padding: 2px; margin-left: 20px}
    #head a:hover {color: black; background-color: yellow; border: 5px inset white}

    #linklist {position: absolute; top: 125px; left: 0px; font-size: 10pt;
        font-weight: bold; font-family: sans-serif; width: 140px; padding: 10px}
    #linklist a {color: rgb(247,233,64); text-decoration: none; display: block}
    #linklist a:hover {color: white; text-decoration: underline}
    #linklist .newgroup {margin-top: 10px}

    #main {position: absolute; top: 125px; left: 160px}
    #main img {float: right}
    .firstp:first-letter {font-size: 300%; line-height: 0.8; float: left}

    address {border-top: 2px solid black; font-style: normal; font-size: 8pt;
        font-family: sans-serif; text-align: center}
    address span {color: blue}
</style>
</head>

<body>
<div id="head">
    <img src="logo.jpg" alt="wizard works" />
    <a href="#">Review Cart</a>
    <a href="#">Check Out</a>
</div>

<div id="linklist">
    <a href="#">Home</a>
    <a href="#" class="newgroup">Assortments</a>
    <a href="#">Firecrackers</a>
    <a href="#">Fountains</a>
    <a href="#">Cones</a>
    <a href="#">Rockets</a>
    <a href="#">Sparklers</a>
    <a href="#" class="newgroup">Online Store</a>
    <a href="#">Shopping Cart</a>
    <a href="#">Your Account</a>
    <a href="#" class="newgroup">Safety</a>
    <a href="#">Tech Support</a>
    <a href="#">Customer Service</a>
    <a href="#">About Us</a>
    <a href="#" class="newgroup">Contact Us</a>
</div>

<div id="main">
    <img src="firework.gif" alt="" />
    <p class="firstp">
    Welcome to wizard works, your one-stop shopping source for discount
    fireworks on the web! We maintain a select variety of consumer fireworks
    on our web site year round. You'll find the fireworks you want with the
    speed and convenience of the Internet, and you'll always have the best
    show in the neighborhood when you shop at wizard works. </p>
    <p>
    We supply quality fireworks to buy online at wholesale prices. Our
    professional firework display team are available to design and organize
    your display, or if you want to organize your own firework party, our
    experienced fireworks designers have selected the best fireworks for the
    occasion. We've made it easy for you to buy on-line for delivery direct
    to your home. </p>
    <p>
    We also create customized fireworks and displays for special needs. Please
    contact one of our design engineers to see if we can create a display for
    your special event. Be sure to order special event fireworks early to ensure
    on-time delivery. </p>

    <address>
        <span>wizard works</span> &#183;
        4311 Tower Street &#183;
        Avondale, KY 75481 &#183;
        (812) 555-3188
    </address>
```

▶ **10.** Save your changes to the file.

11. Return to the validation page and click the **Reload** or **Refresh** button. As shown in Figure 9-23, the document should now be validated under XHTML 1.0 strict.

Report showing a successful validation under XHTML 1.0 strict ◄ **Figure 9-23**

THIS PAGE IS VALID XHTML 1.0 STRICT!

TIP OF THE DAY: Use `class` with semantics in mind

NOTE: The HTTP Content-Type header sent by your web browser (unknown) did not contain a "charset" parameter, but the Content-Type was one of the XML text/* sub-types (`text/xml`). The relevant specification (RFC 3023) specifies a strong default of "us-ascii" for such documents so we will use this value regardless of any encoding you may have indicated elsewhere. If you would like to use a different encoding, you should arrange to have your browser send this new encoding information.

NOTE: The Validator XML support has some limitations.

The uploaded file was checked and found to be valid XHTML 1.0 Strict. This means that the resource in question identified itself as "XHTML 1.0 Strict" and that we successfully performed a formal validation using an SGML or XML Parser (depending on the markup language used).

W3C XHTML 1.0 ✔ To show your readers that you have taken the care to create an interoperable Web page, you may display this icon on any page that validates. Here is the HTML you should use to add this icon to your Web page:

```
<p>
  <a href="http://validator.w3.org/check?uri=referer"><img
     src="http://www.w3.org/Icons/valid-xhtml10"
     alt="Valid XHTML 1.0!" height="31" width="88" /></a>
</p>
```

Thanks to this code, you will be able to re-validate your Web page by following the link (click on the image), and we encourage you to do so every time you modify your document.

Once you have a document that passes the validation test, you may want to make a note of this on your Web page. The W3C provides code that you can paste into your document to advertise this fact. Tom suggests that you add this code to the works Web page.

To insert the W3C code:

1. Select the code sample near the bottom of the validation page, click **Edit** from your browser menu, and then click **Copy**.

2. Return to the **works.htm** file in your text editor. Below the closing </address> tag, past the following code as shown in Figure 9-24.

```
<p>
<a href="http://validator.w3.org/check?uri=referer"><img
     src="http://www.w3.org/Icons/valid-xhtml10"
     alt="Valid XHTML 1.0!" height="31" width="88" /></a>
</p>
```

Figure 9-24 ▶ **Inserting the W3C code into the Web page**

```
<p>
  <a href="http://validator.w3.org/check?uri=referer"><img
      src="http://www.w3.org/Icons/valid-xhtml10"
      alt="Valid XHTML 1.0!" height="31" width="88" /></a>
</p>

</div>

</body>
</html>
```

▶ **3.** Save your changes to the file and close your text editor.

▶ **4.** Reopen **works.htm** in your Web browser. Figure 9-25 shows the final version of the page.

Figure 9-25 ▶ **Final works page**

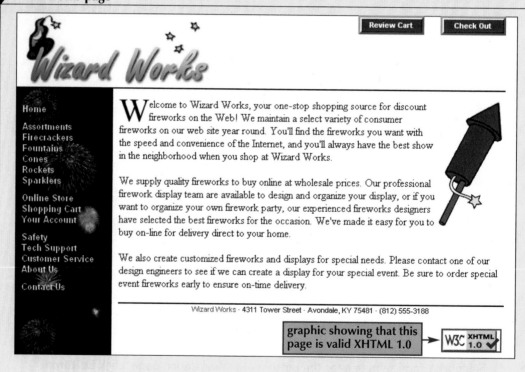

You show the completed Web page to Tom. He's pleased with your work in updating the file to meet the specifications for XHTML. He feels that these changes will help the Web site in the future as the company tries to stay current with the latest developments in XHTML.

Using Style Sheets and XHTML

Although XHTML and HTML files are simple text documents, not all text is the same. Browsers and parsers distinguish between two types of text: parsed character data and unparsed character data. **Parsed character data**, or **PCDATA**, is text that is processed (parsed) by a browser or parser. The following code is an example of PCDATA:

```
<title>Wizard Works</title>
```

When a browser encounters this string of characters, it processes it and uses that information to change the text of the browser's title bar. In PCDATA, you cannot enter character symbols like "<", ">", or "&" directly into a document as text because they are used to process information. The "<" and ">" symbols are used to mark the beginning and end of element tags. The "&" symbol is used to indicate a special character. If you want to display a "<" symbol in your document, for example, you have to use the special character symbol <.

Unparsed character data, or **CDATA**, is text that is not processed by the browser or parser. In CDATA, you can use any character you like without worrying about it being misinterpreted—browsers and parsers essentially ignore it.

The DTDs for XML and XHTML specify whether an element contains CDATA or PCDATA. Most elements contain PCDATA. This prevents document authors from putting symbols like "<" into the element content.

However, this also has an impact on embedded style sheets. The content of an embedded style sheet is treated as PCDATA, meaning that a parser attempts to process the information contained in the style sheet's characters. This can cause problems if the style sheet contains a character that could be processed by the parser. For example, the following embedded style sheet contains the ">" character, which a parser would interpret as the end of an element tag:

```
<style type="text/css">
   p > img {float: left}
</style>
```

A parser encountering this code would be confused and would probably invalidate the document (assuming that the code didn't crash the page entirely). This problem also occurs with scripts (a topic we'll cover in the next tutorial), in which the "<", ">", and "&" symbols are frequently used.

One way of dealing with this problem is to use a special construct called a **CDATA section**, which marks a block of text as CDATA so that parsers ignore any text within it. The syntax of the CDATA section is

```
<![CDATA[
text
]]>
```

where *text* is the content that you want treated as CDATA. To apply this to our style sheet, we could place the CDATA section within the style element as follows:

```
<style type="text/css">
<![CDATA[
   p > img {float: left}
]]>
</style>
```

The problem with this solution is that many browsers do not understand or recognize CDATA sections and this may cause problems in displaying your page. In the end, the best solution may be to replace all embedded style sheets in XHTML documents with external style sheets. This has the added advantage that it completely removes style from content, because they are placed in separate files. Note that this is not an issue if the embedded style sheet does not contain any characters that could be processed by the parser, as in the works.htm file.

Tips for Converting old HTML Code to XHTML

- Include an xml declaration in the first line of your file so that your document can be accessed by XML parsers.
- Add a DOCTYPE declaration for one of the XHTML DTDs and check your document for well-formedness and validity whenever you make a change to the code.
- Add the XHTML default namespace to the html element of your document.
- Make sure that all element and attribute names are in lowercase letters and that all attribute values are placed in quotes.
- Make sure that all empty elements are entered as one-sided tags. Look especially for improper syntax in the img, hr, and br elements.
- Make sure that all two-sided tags are properly closed. Old HTML code often does not have closing tags for the p element.
- Make sure that all inline images contain the alt attribute.
- Look for deprecated attributes such as align, bgcolor, and background, and replace them with the float (or text-align), background-color, and background-image styles.
- Replace the name attribute with the id attribute.
- Fix all instances of attribute minimization.
- Replace the use of the font element with either the span element or with a style that applies the same formatting specified by the font element.
- Replace the use of the width attribute in the td or th element with the width style.

Review

Session 9.2 Quick Check

1. What line would you add to the start of your XHTML file to declare it as an xml document?

2. What is character encoding? What are the two default encodings supported by all browsers?

3. What declaration would you add to your XHTML document to associate it with the XHTML 1.0 transitional DTD?

4. What attribute would you add to the html element to place your document in the XHTML namespace?

5. The Chemical Markup Language, CML, is an XML-based language used to document chemical structures. The namespace for CML is: http://www.xml-cml.org/dtd/cml1_0_1.dtd. For an XHTML document that contains CML elements, what attribute would you add to the html element to create a local namespace for CML? (Assume that all CML element names will have the prefix "cml").

6. An XHTML transitional validation test reports the following error:

   Line 51, column 3: **end tag for "br" omitted, but OMITTAG NO was specified**

   ```
   <br>
   ```
   Suggest a possible cause of the error and how you would correct it.

7. A validation test under XHTML 1.0 strict reports the following error:

   Line 22, column 1: **there is no attribute "name"**

   ```
   <form name="orders">
   ```
   Suggest how you could modify this code to make it valid under XHTML 1.0 strict.

8. What is a CDATA section? Why would you want to place the embedded style sheet of an XHTML document within a CDATA section?

Review

Tutorial Summary

In this tutorial, you learned about how to create and work with XHTML documents. The first session reviewed the history of XHTML and its development from XML. You learned about well-formed and valid documents, and the different DTDs associated with XHTML. The tutorial then discussed how certain coding practices in HTML documents would lead to syntax errors in XHTML. The first session concluded with a look at how to make valid XHTML documents, and which elements and attributes are prohibited in XHTML. In the second session, you learned how to create an XHTML document. The session covered the xml and DOCTYPE declarations, as well as issues around specifying the XHTML namespace. The session also showed how XHTML can be used with other XML elements to create combined documents. You then learned how to use an online validator to test a document for well-formedness and validity. The tutorial concluded with a discussion of the syntax issues surrounding embedded styles sheets.

Key Terms

attribute minimization	DTD	transitional DTD
CDATA	frameset DTD	UCS
CDATA section	local namespace	Unicode
character encoding	namespace	Universal Character Set
character set	parser	unparsed character data
default namespace	parsed character data	valid
document type	PCDATA	well formed
definition	strict DTD	XML parser

Practice

Practice the skills you learned in the tutorial using the same case scenario.

Review Assignments

Data files needed for this Review Assignment: back.jpg, dtd_list.txt, founttxt.htm, logo.jpg

Tom has another file that he wants you to update to XHTML. This page contains an order form for some of the fountains sold by Wizard Works. The file may have some older HTML elements and syntax in it, so he wants you to confirm that the file is well formed and valid after you've updated for XHTML. Figure 9-26 shows a preview of the completed Web page.

Figure 9-26

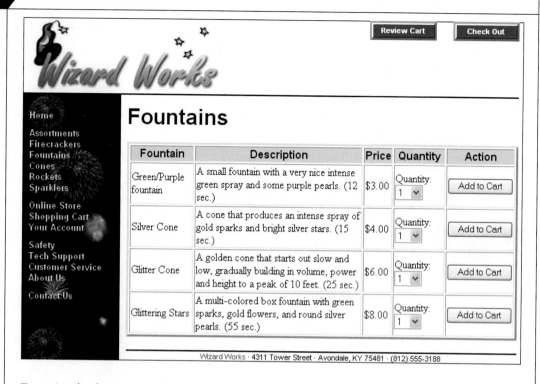

To revise the fountains Web page:

1. Use your text editor to open **founttxt.htm** from the tutorial.09/review folder. Enter ***your name*** and ***the date*** in the comment section of the file and save the file as **fountain.htm**.

2. Insert an xml declaration at the top of the file, setting the version number to 1.0, the character encoding to UTF-8, and the standalone to "no".

3. Below the xml declaration, insert a DOCTYPE declaration indicating that this document conforms to the XHTML 1.0 strict DTD (you can copy the code for this declaration from the dtd_list.txt file).

4. Set the default namespace for the document to the XHTML namespace.

5. Use a validator to test whether the document is well formed and valid under the XHTML 1.0 strict DTD. If any deprecated presentational attributes are found, replace them with the equivalent inline style. Note that when this form is run, it should use the CGI script at http://wizardworks.com/cgi/cart.

6. After the document passes XHTML 1.0 strict, save your changes and submit the completed Web page to your instructor.

Apply

Use the skills you've learned in this tutorial to convert an online menu to an XHTML document.

Case Problem 1

Data files needed for this Case Problem: breakfst.jpg, breaktxt.htm, dinner.jpg, dinnrtxt.htm, dtd_list.txt, lunch.jpg, lunchtxt.htm, tan.jpg

Kelsey's Diner   You've been asked to update the Web pages for Kelsey's Diner, a well-established restaurant in Worcester, Massachusetts. Cindy Towser, the manager of the diner, would like the pages that display breakfast, lunch, and dinner menus updated so that they comply with XHTML standards. A preview of one of the menu pages is shown in Figure 9-27.

Figure 9-27

To revise the menu pages:

1. Use your text editor to open **breaktxt.htm**, **lunchtxt.htm**, and **dinnrtxt.htm** from the tutorial.09/case1 folder. Enter ***your name*** and ***the date*** in the comment section of each file and save the files as **breakfst.htm**, **lunch.htm**, and **dinner.htm**, respectively.

2. Go to the **breakfst.htm** file in your text editor and insert an xml declaration at the top of the file. Use the default values for the version, encoding, and standalone attributes.

3. After the xml declaration, insert a DOCTYPE declaration for the XHTML 1.0 strict DTD (you may copy the entry from the dtd_list.txt file in the tutorial.09/case1 folder for the code of this declaration).

4. Set the default namespace of the document to the XHTML namespace.

5. Test the file on the validator and make a note of the errors reported. Here are some possible ways of fixing the errors:

   - Convert any deprecated presentational attribute to an embedded style.
   - Correct any syntax errors for one-sided tags.
   - Replace any prohibited attributes (such as the name attribute) with an equivalent valid attribute.
   - Replace the formatting done with the b and font elements with a span element and an embedded style.

6. Save your changes to **breakfst.htm** and continue to test the file until it passes the XHTML 1.0 strict validation test.

7. Repeat Steps 2 through 6 for the **lunch.htm** and **dinner.htm** files.

8. Test the completed Web site on your browser and verify that you can move between the pages by clicking the image map links in the logo at the top of the page.

9. Submit the completed Web site to your instructor.

Apply

Use the skills you've learned in this tutorial to update an old product page.

Case Problem 2

Data files needed for this Case Problem: cassini.jpg, dtd_list.txt, gargtxt.htm, gbar.jpg, glogo.jpg, maa.jpg, oneil.jpg

Middle Age Arts   Middle Age Arts (MAA) is a company that creates and sells replicas of historical European works of art for home and garden use. Nicole Swanson is the head of the Web site team at MAA. She has recently started a project to update the old HTML code in the site's many pages. She's asked you to update the page describing the company's collection of decorative gargoyles. She wants the page to comply with XHTML 1.0 strict standards. Figure 9-28 shows a preview of the completed Web page.

Figure 9-28

Middle Age Arts

Middle Age Arts

Home Page
View the catalog
Place an order

About Gargoyles

Gargoyle Products

Other Collections

The Vatican Collection
The Rodin Collection
Renaissance Masters

From the President

This month Middle Age Arts introduces the Gargoyle Collection. I'm really excited about this new set of classical figures.

The collection contains faithful reproductions of gargoyles from some of the famous cathedrals of Europe, including Notre Dame, Rheims and Warwick Castle. All reproductions are done to exacting and loving detail.

The collection also contains original works by noted artists such as Susan Bedford and Antonio Salvari. Our expert artisans have produced some wonderful and whimsical works, perfectly suited for home or garden use.

Don't delay, order your gargoyle today.

Irene O'Neil
President

What can you do with a gargoyle?

Don't think you need a gargoyle? Think again. Gargoyles are useful as:

- Bird baths
- Bookends
- Paperweights
- Pen holders
- Wind chimes

Go to our catalog for more ideas!

Profile of the Artist

This month's artist is Michael Cassini. Michael has been a professional sculptor for ten years. He has won numerous awards, including the prestigious *Reichsman Cup* and an Award of Merit at the 1997 Tuscany Arts Competition.

Michael specializes in recreations of gargoyles from European cathedrals. You'll usually find Michael staring intently at the church walls in northern France. His work is represented by the *Turin Gargoyle*, a great entry to our Gargoyle Collection.

To revise the gargoyle page:

1. Use your text editor to open **gargtxt.htm** from the tutorial.09/case2 folder. Enter *your name* and *the date* in the comment section and save the file as **gargoyle.htm**.
2. Insert an xml declaration at the top of the file. Use the standard attribute defaults for an XHTML file.

3. After the xml declaration, insert a DOCTYPE declaration for the XHTML 1.0 strict DTD.

4. Set the default namespace of the document to the XHTML namespace.

5. Test the file on the validator. Fix the errors as follows:
   - Convert the attributes for the body element into styles in an embedded style sheet. (HINT: The link, alink, and vlink attributes are used to set the colors of hyperlinks, active links, and visited links in the Web page.)
   - Use proper syntax for any empty element.
   - Set the color and text alignment of an h4 element using an inline style.
   - Ensure that all two-sided tags are properly closed.
   - Use the float style to align all inline images.
   - Use an inline style to set a table cell's width and background color.
   - Remove all deprecated elements and attributes.

6. Save your final version of the file once it passes the validation test for XHTML 1.0 strict.

7. Submit the completed Web page to your instructor.

Create

Explore how to use XHTML with frames.

Case Problem 3

Data files needed for this Case Problem: cast.htm, castles.jpg, casttxt.htm, dtd_list.txt, hebd.htm, hebdtxt.htm, hebrides.jpg, high.htm, highland.jpg, hightxt.htm, lake.htm, lake.jpg, laketxt.htm, scottxt.htm, tourlist.gif, tslogo.gif

Travel Scotland! Travel Scotland! is an online Web site that books tours of Scotland and the British Isles. You've recently been hired by Travel Scotland! to update their Web site. Fiona Findlay, the head of advertising for the company, has given you a set of pages in a framed Web site that describe four of the company's tours. She would like you to update the code so that it complies with XHTML standards for the transitional and frameset DTDs. A preview of the completed Web site is shown in Figure 9-29.

Figure 9-29

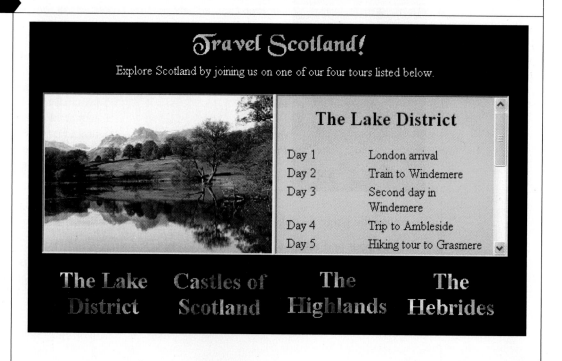

To revise the tours pages:

1. Use your text editor to open the files **casttxt.htm**, **hebdtxt.htm**, **hightxt.htm**, **laketxt.htm**, and **scottxt.htm** from the tutorial.09/case3 folder. Enter *your name* and *the date* in the comment section of each file and then save the files as **casttour.htm**, **hebdtour.htm**, **hightour.htm**, **laketour.htm**, and **scotland.htm** respectively.

2. Go to the **scotland.htm** file in your text editor and insert an xml declaration at the top of the file.

3. Below the xml declaration, insert a DOCTYPE declaration that indicates that this file conforms to the standards for XHTML 1.0 transitional.

4. Set the default namespace to the XHTML namespace.

5. Save your changes and submit the page for validation. Correct any errors reported by the validator. (HINT: If alternate text is required for the image map hotspots, use the text displayed in the tourlist.gif graphic.)

6. Go to the **casttour.htm** file in your text editor and insert an xml declaration at the top of the file.

Explore

7. Specify that the document uses the XHTML 1.0 frameset DTD and the XHTML namespace.

8. Save your changes and submit the page for validation. Correct any errors in syntax or validity.

9. Repeat Steps 6 through 8 for the **hebdtour.htm**, **hightour.htm**, and **laketour.htm** files.

10. Test the Web site in your browser to verify that the inline frames and the framed pages work correctly.

11. Submit the completed Web site to your instructor.

Case Problem 4

Create

Test your knowledge of XHTML by creating a well-formed valid document for an educational site.

Data files needed for this Case Problem: address.txt, apple.jpg, astro.txt, chem.txt, dtd_list.txt, elect.txt, eng.txt, mwslogo.gif, physics.txt

Maxwell Scientific   Maxwell Scientific is a online Web site that sells science kits and educational products to schools and educators. Chris Todd, the head of the Web site development team, is leading an effort to update the company's Web site. He has given you some text files and graphic images. You may supplement this material with any additional files and resources at your disposal. Your job will be to develop this material into a Web site that is compliant with XHTML 1.0 strict standards. To ensure that the completed Web page is both well formed and valid, he wants you to test it on a validator before submitting it to him.

The design of the Web site and each individual page is up to you, but it should include the following features:

1. The Web site should include six files, with the names **astro.htm**, **chem.htm**, **elect.htm**, **eng.htm**, **physics.htm**, and **Maxwell.htm** (the home page). Include *your name* and *the date* in a comment section for each file, along with a description of the purpose of the page.

2. Include appropriate links between the pages.

3. Each page should be designed as an XHTML 1.0 strict document. Include all necessary declarations and namespaces.

4. Test each page against a validator for compliance with XHTML 1.0 strict. Correct any errors in syntax or validity.

5. Submit the completed Web site to your instructor.

Review

Quick Check Answers

Session 9.1

1. An XML document that employs the correct syntax is known as well formed. A well formed XML document that also contains the correct content is known as a valid document.

2. The transitional DTD supports deprecated elements and attributes and is designed as a bridge between older HTML code and new standards. The frameset DTD is similar to the transitional DTD and also supports frames. The strict DTD does not support deprecated features and is designed for browsers that support the current standards.

3. The img element is not correctly entered as a one-sided tag. The correct form is:

   ```
   <img src="logo.jpg" alt="Wizard Works" />
   ```

4. The disabled attribute has no value. The correct form is:

   ```
   <input type="radio" disabled="disabled" />
   ```

5. The block quote element cannot contain the a element.

6. The align attribute is not a support attribute in the strict DTD. You can correct this as follows:

   ```
   <img src="logo.jpg" alt="Wizard Works" style="float: right" />
   ```

7. The map element requires the id attribute to be valid. The following is a valid form:

   ```
   <map name="parkmap" id="parkmap">
   ```

Session 9.2

1. ```
   <?xml version="1.0" encoding="UTF-8" standalone="no" ?>
   ```

2. Character encoding is the process by which a character set is translated into bytes (and vice versa) for transfer over the Internet. UTF-8 and UTF-16 are the two default codings.

3. ```
   <!DOCTYPE html PUBLIC "-//W3C//DTD XHTML 1.0 Transitional//EN"
   "http://www.w3.org/TR/xhtml1/DTD/xhtml1-transitional.dtd">
   ```

4. ```
   <html xmlns="http://www.w3.org/1999/xhtml">
   ```

5. ```
   <html xmlns:cml=" http://www.xml-cml.org/dtd/cml1_0_1.dtd">
   ```

6. The br element should be created with an empty tag as

   ```
   <br />
   ```

7. Replace the name attribute with the id attribute as follows:

   ```
   <form id="orders">
   ```

8. A CDATA section identifies the enclosed text as unparsed character data. Any text entered into the CDATA section is not be processed by parsers. This avoids the possibility of a parser erroneously trying to process a style sheet symbol.

Objectives

Working with JavaScript

Creating a Programmable Web Page for North Pole Novelties

Case

North Pole Novelties

North Pole Novelties (NPN), located in Seton Grove, Minnesota, is a gift shop specializing in toys, decorations, and other items for the Christmas holiday season. Founded in 1968 by David Watkins, NPN is one of the largest holiday supply stores in the country, with over 300 employees serving customers from around the world.

Because NPN's business is focused around December 25, the store is always aware of the number of shopping days remaining until Christmas and wants its customers to be aware of this, too. In this spirit, Andrew Savatini, director of marketing, wants to display the number of days remaining until Christmas on the company's home page. To accomplish this, the Web page must be updated daily to reflect the correct number of days left until the big day. Although the company could assign someone the task of manually changing the Web page each morning, it would be more efficient and reliable if the update could be performed automatically by a program running on the Web page itself.

Andrew has asked you to create such a program. To do this, you'll learn how to write and run programs in JavaScript, a programming language specifically designed for Web pages.

Student Data Files

▼Tutorial.10

▽ **tutorial folder**

  npntxt.htm
  styles.css
  + 3 graphic files

▽ **review folder**

  npn2txt.htm
  lib2txt.js
  styles2.css
  + 3 graphic files

▽ **case1 folder**

  mwutxt.htm
  spamtxt.js
  mwstyles.css
  mwu.jpg

▽ **case2 folder**

  twaintxt.htm
  randtxt.js
  mtstyles.css
  + 4 graphic files

▽ **case3 folder**

  bcctxt.htm
  caltxt.js
  bcc.css
  calendar.css
  + 2 graphic files

▽ **case4 folder**

  chartxt.htm
  wd.jpg

Session 10.1

Introduction to JavaScript

In your work with HTML and XHTML so far, you've created static Web pages whose content and layout did not change. Beginning with this tutorial, you'll work with scripts to modify the appearance and content of your Web pages.

Server-side and Client-side Programs

In Tutorial 6, you learned how to access scripts that run on a Web server. While this is one approach to creating a Web page that responds to user input, it comes with several disadvantages: a user must be connected to the Web server in order to run the script; only a programmer can create or alter the script; and the Web server's system administrator can place limitations on access to the script. A server-side approach also poses problems for the system administrator, who has to be concerned about users continually accessing the server and potentially overloading the system.

Issues like these led to the development of programs and scripts that could be run on the client side in a Web browser, as illustrated in Figure 10-1.

Figure 10-1	Server-side and client-side programming

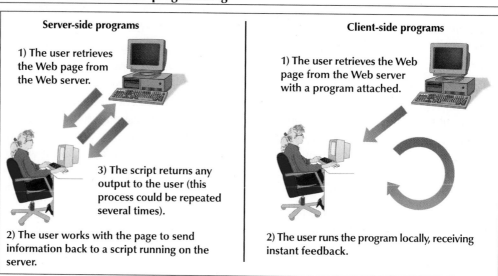

Client-side programs solve many of the problems associated with server-side scripts. Computing is distributed over the Web so that no one server is overloaded with programming requests. A client-side program can be tested locally without first uploading it to a Web server. Client-side programs are also likely to be more responsive to users, because users do not have to wait for data to be sent over the Internet to the Web server. However, client-side programs can never completely replace server-side scripts. Jobs such as running a search form or processing a purchase order must be run from a central server, because only the server contains the database needed to complete those types of operations.

The Development of JavaScript

As you learned in Tutorial 8, one client-side programming language that has gained popular support is Java. When Java came out, however, nonprogrammers found it difficult to learn and use. The language also required users to have access to the Java Developer's Kit (JDK) in order to create an executable Java applet.

To address these obstacles, a team of developers created a programming language called JavaScript. There are several important differences between Java and JavaScript. Java is an example of a **compiled language**, meaning that the program code has to be submitted to a compiler, which translates the code into a language that a computer can understand. For Java, this compiled code is the Java applet. Thus, to run a program written in a compiled language, you need both the compiler and an application or operating system that can run the compiled code.

On the other hand, JavaScript is an **interpreted language**, in which the program code is converted into an executable application each time it is run. There is no need for a compiler to create the executable file; the browser must simply be able to interpret and run the JavaScript code. Unlike Java, JavaScript code can be inserted directly into an HTML or XHTML file or placed in a separate text file that is linked to a Web page. This means that you or other users can easily read any JavaScript code that you write. JavaScript is not as powerful a computing language as Java, but it is simpler to use and it meets the needs of most users who want to create programmable Web pages.

Figure 10-2 highlights some of the key differences between Java and JavaScript.

Comparing Java and JavaScript ◄ **Figure 10-2**

Java	JavaScript
A compiled language	An interpreted language
Requires the JDK (Java Developer's Kit) to create the applet	Requires a text editor
Requires a Java virtual machine or interpreter to run the applet	Requires a browser that can interpret JavaScript code
Applet files are distinct from the HTML and XHTML code	JavaScript programs are integrated and can be placed within HTML and XHTML code
Source code is hidden from the user	Source code is made accessible to the user
Powerful, requires programming knowledge and experience	Simpler, requiring less programming knowledge and experience
Secure: programs cannot write content to the hard disk	Secure: programs cannot write content to the hard disk, but there are more security holes than in Java
Programs run on the client side	Programs run on the client side

Through the years, JavaScript has undergone several revisions. Internet Explorer actually supports a slightly different version of JavaScript called **JScript**. Essentially, JScript is identical to JavaScript, but some JavaScript commands are not supported in JScript, and vice versa. For this reason, you should test your JavaScript programs on a variety of Web browsers. Although it may be tempting to use commands available in the latest JavaScript or JScript versions, remember that your programs might not run on older browsers.

Because of all these competing versions and revisions, the responsibility for the development of a scripting standard has been transferred to an international body called the **European Computer Manufacturers Association (ECMA)**. Although the standard developed by the ECMA is called **ECMAScript**, browsers still generally refer to it as JavaScript.

Figure 10-3 lists the versions of JavaScript and JScript and their corresponding browser support.

Figure 10-3 ▶ **Versions of JavaScript and JScript**

Version	Browser	Year
JavaScript 1.0	Netscape Navigator 2.0	1995
JScript 1.0	Internet Explorer 3.0	1996
JavaScript 1.1	Netscape Navigator 3.0	1996
JavaScript 1.2	Netscape Navigator 4.0	1997
JScript 3.0	Internet Explorer 4.0	1997
JavaScript 1.3	Netscape Navigator 4.5	1998
JScript 5.0	Internet Explorer 5.0	1999
JavaScript 1.5	Netscape Navigator 6.0	2001

Other client-side programming languages are also available to Web page designers, such as the Internet Explorer scripting language, **VBScript**. However, because of the nearly universal support for JavaScript, you'll use this language for your work with North Pole Novelties.

Inserting JavaScript into a Web Page File

Your task is to use JavaScript to create a Web page that displays the days remaining until Christmas on the company's home page. Figure 10-4 shows the layout of the home page.

Figure 10-4 ▶ **Initial North Pole Novelties Web page**

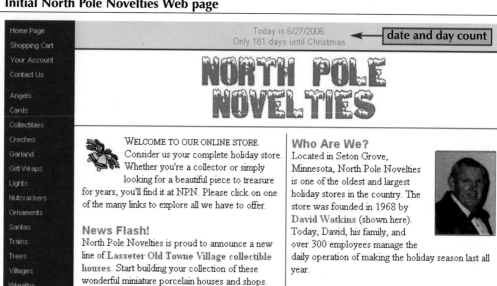

The information shown in Figure 10-4 has been explicitly entered into the HTML file, and therefore is correct only on June 27, 2006. Andrew wants a program that automatically displays the current date. Furthermore, if the current date falls between December 25 and December 31, he wants the page to display the text "Happy Holidays from North Pole Novelties" instead of the day count.

Before you begin writing a program, it's a good idea to outline the main tasks you want the program to perform. In this case, the tasks are as follows:

> ☐ 1) Learn how to display text on a Web page using JavaScript
> ☐ 2) Display date values on a Web page
> ☐ 3) Calculate the number of days between the test date and December 25th
> ☐ 4) If the date is December 25th or later (through December 31st), display a
>   greeting message; otherwise, display the number of days remaining until Christmas

Your first task is to create and test a JavaScript program that sends output to your Web page. JavaScript code is interpreted and run by a browser either as it encounters the code within the file, or in response to a user-initiated event such as clicking a button on a Web form. In the case of North Pole Novelties, your JavaScript program will run automatically when a browser loads the Web page.

A JavaScript program can be either placed directly in a Web page file or saved in an external text file. Placing the code in a Web page file means that users need only retrieve one file from the server. In addition, because the code and the page content it affects are both within the same file, it may be easier to locate and fix programming errors. If you place the code in a separate file, the different pages in your Web site can use the programs you write in the same way that an entire site can use an external style sheet. In this tutorial, you'll enter your code both directly in the page and in an external file.

Using the Script Element

You insert a client-side script in a Web page using the script element. A script can be either embedded in the page or referenced as an external file. The syntax to embed a script is

```
<script type="mime-type">
      script commands and comments
</script>
```

where `mime-type` is the MIME type of the language in which the program is written. The type attribute is required in XHTML documents and should be used in HTML documents as well. The MIME type for JavaScript programs is "text/javascript". Other client-side scripting languages have different MIME types. For example, if you use Microsoft's VBScript, the MIME type is "text/vbscript".

The type attribute replaces the now-deprecated language attribute, which was used to indicate the script language. The default language value is "JavaScript". Note that you cannot use the language attribute under the strict DTD for XHTML 1.0.

To reference a script placed in an external file, the command is similar:

```
<script src="url" type="mime-type"></script>
```

where `url` is the location of the external script file.

Reference Window

Accessing a Client-Side Script

- To embed a client-side script in a Web page, use the element
  ```
  <script type="mime-type">
      script commands and comments
  </script>
  ```
  where *mime-type* is the MIME type of the script language. To create a script element for JavaScript, set *mime-type* to "text/javascript".
- To access an external script, use the syntax
  ```
  <script src="url" type="mime-type"></script>
  ```
  where *url* is the location of the external file containing the script.

Deprecated

- To specify the language of the script, add the following attribute to the style element:
  ```
  language="text"
  ```
  where *text* is the name of the script language. Use the name "JavaScript" for JavaScript program code.

The script elements can be placed anywhere within the HTML file. Many programmers favor placing their programs within the head element to separate the programming code from the Web page content and layout, whereas others prefer placing programs within the body of the Web page at the location where the program output is generated and displayed. If you are referencing an external script, you should place the script element in the head section; this allows the browser to load all of the external script commands before processing the body of the page.

Adding Comments

JavaScript supports comments that you can use to document the features of your program. Comments can be either single-line or multi-line. The syntax of a single-line comment is

```
// comment text
```

whereas the syntax of a multi-line comment is

```
/*
    comment text covering several lines
*/
```

Comments are also useful if you need to hide your script from older browsers.

Hiding the Script from Older Browsers

Older browsers that do not support JavaScript can present a problem for Web designers. If such a browser encounters JavaScript commands, it may display the program code as part of the Web page body. To avoid this problem, you can hide the script from these browsers using a combination of HTML and JavaScript comment lines. The syntax for doing this is

```
<script type="text/javascript">
<!-- Hide from non-JavaScript browsers
    JavaScript commands
// Stop hiding from older browsers -->
</script>
```

When a Web browser that doesn't support scripts encounters this code, it ignores the <script> tag, as it does any tag it doesn't recognize. The next line it sees is the start of the HTML comment tag, which doesn't close until the --> symbol in the second-to-last line. These comment tags result in the browser ignoring everything in the JavaScript program. The final </script> tag is similarly ignored by the older browser.

A browser that supports JavaScript recognizes the <script> tag and ignores any HTML tags found between the <script> and </script> tags. Therefore, in this example, it bypasses the comment tag in the second line and processes the JavaScript program as written. The JavaScript comment (starting with the // symbol) in the second-to-last line helps other users understand and interpret your code.

Specifying a Script Alternative

For browsers that don't support scripts (or have their script support disabled), you can specify alternative content using the noscript element. The syntax of the noscript element is

```
<noscript>
    alternative content
</noscript>
```

where *alternative content* is the content the browser should display in place of accessing and running the script. For example, the following code displays a text message indicating that the page requires the use of JavaScript:

```
<noscript>
    <p>This page requires JavaScript. Please turn on JavaScript if
your browser supports it and reload the page.</p>
</noscript>
```

Browsers that support client-side scripts and have that support enabled ignore the content of the noscript element.

Using JavaScript and XHTML

XML parsers treat the content of a JavaScript program as PCDATA (for a discussion of PCDATA, see "Using Style Sheets and XHTML" in Tutorial 9). Because character symbols such as "<", ">", and "&" are often used in JavaScript programs, this can lead to the page being rejected by an XHTML validator. To avoid this problem, you can either place the JavaScript code within comments as described above for older browsers, or within a CDATA section as follows:

```
<script type="text/javascript">
<![cdata[
    JavaScript code and comments
]]>
</script>
```

Unfortunately, the CDATA section is not well supported by current browsers. A third alternative is not to embed your scripts within the Web page file at all, and instead always place them in external files. This has the added advantage of separating program code from page content. If you need to create valid XHTML documents, this option is probably the best solution.

Embedding a Script

Having seen the basic structure of a JavaScript program, you're ready to embed the necessary code into the North Pole Novelties home page. Your first task will be to delete the HTML tags that contain the 6/27/2006 date information so that you can replace them with a program that works for any date.

To embed the script element:

1. Use your text editor to open **npntxt.htm** from the tutorial.10/tutorial folder. Enter **your name** and **the date** in the comment section and save the file as **npn.htm**.

2. Scroll through the file until you locate the HTML comment tag, "<-- Days until Christmas -->".

3. Delete the following code:

   ```
   Today is 6/27/2006<br />
   Only 181 days until Christmas
   ```

4. Insert the following code in place of the code you just deleted (it's a good idea to indent the new code to make it easier to interpret):

   ```
   <script type="text/javascript">
      <!-- Hide from non-JavaScript browsers
      // Stop hiding -->
   </script>
   ```

   Your file should appear as shown in Figure 10-5. Because you have entered only comment tags at this point, no date information would display on the Web page if you opened it with a browser.

Figure 10-5	Inserting the script element

```
<!-- Days until Christmas -->
<td id="daycell">
<script type="text/javascript">
   <!-- Hide from non-JavaScript browsers
   // Stop hiding -->
</script>
</td>
</tr>

<tr>
<!-- Company Logo -->
<td id="logo">
   <img src="logo.jpg" alt="North Pole Novelties" />
</td>
</tr>
```

5. Save your changes to the file.

With the script element in place, your next task is to write a JavaScript program that sends output to the Web page. Because you haven't yet learned how to determine the current date or calculate the number of days between the current date and December 25, you'll start by entering a program limited to displaying a predetermined text string.

Writing Output to the Web Page

JavaScript provides two methods to write text to a Web page: the document.write() and document.writeln() method. The syntax for these commands is

```
document.write("text");
document.writeln("text");
```

where *text* is a string of characters for display in the Web page. For example, the following command adds the text "Only 45 days until Christmas" to a Web page:

```
document.write("Only 45 days until Christmas");
```

The document.write() and document.writeln() methods reflect the object-oriented nature of the JavaScript language. An **object-oriented** programming language accomplishes the task by manipulating objects. With JavaScript, an object can be any item associated with a Web page or Web browser, including a document itself, headings or list items within the document, inline images, frames, applets, the browser window, or even the browser itself. In the document.write() command, for example, the object being manipulated is the Web document itself.

One way of manipulating an object is to perform an action on it. An action that you perform on an object is called a **method**. For example, if you thought of a car as an object, one action you could perform on it would be to drive it. One action that can be applied to the document object is to write content to it; thus we refer to this action as the write method.

Most of the time, you will use the document.write() method instead of the document.writeln() method. The document.writeln() method is used when you want to preserve the line breaks within the text string. This becomes relevant only when the text string is formatted with the pre element, in which browsers recognize the existence of line breaks.

Reference Window

Writing Output to the Web Page

- To write text to a Web page, use the following JavaScript commands:
    ```
    document.write("text");
    ```
    or
    ```
    document.writeln("text");
    ```
    where *text* is the content to be written to the page. The document.write() and document.writeln() methods are identical, except that the document.writeln() method preserves any line breaks in the text string.

You're not limited to displaying text with these commands—you can also include HTML tags in the text string to format the text and to insert images. For example, the following command displays the text "News Flash!" formatted as an h3 heading:

```
document.write("<h3>News Flash!</h3>");
```

The text string specified by the document.write() method can be enclosed within either double or single quotation marks. This flexibility allows you to include quotation marks as characters within your text strings, which is particularly important when you need to write elements that contain attribute values. For example, the JavaScript command

```
document.write('<td class="calendar_head" colspan="7">');
```

writes the table cell tag

```
<td class="calendar_head" colspan="7">
```

to the Web page. In this example, the single quotes are used to mark the beginning and ending of the text string, and the double quotes are simply treated as characters within that string. Alternately, if your text string contains single quotes, you have to enclose the string with double quotation marks.

You should be aware of some syntax issues that you may encounter with JavaScript. Most JavaScript commands and names are case-sensitive. This means that, for example, you could not replace the command "document.write()" with "Document.Write()" without JavaScript generating an error message.

Note also that each JavaScript command line ends with a semicolon to separate it from the next command line in the program. Although the semicolon is optional in some situations, it is a good idea to use it consistently to make your code easier to follow and interpret.

Now that you've learned the basics for the document.write() method, you'll use it to write date and day values to the Web page, along with the number of days until Christmas, assuming a date of December 15, 2006.

To write text to your Web page with JavaScript:

▶ 1. Insert the following two commands directly below the line "<!--- Hide from non-JavaScript browsers":

```
document.write("Today is 12/15/2006<br />");
document.write("Only 10 days until Christmas");
```

Note that the text you're sending to the Web page includes the br element, to place a line break between the first line and the second. Figure 10-6 shows the revised file.

| Figure 10-6 | Inserting document.write() methods |

```
<!-- Days until Christmas -->
<td id="daycell">
<script type="text/javascript">
   <!-- Hide from non-JavaScript browsers
   document.write("Today is 12/15/2006<br />");
   document.write("only 10 days until Christmas");
   // Stop hiding -->
</script>
</td>
</tr>
```

▶ 2. Save your changes to **npn.htm** and then open it in your Web browser. As the browser loads the page, it encounters the two document.write() commands you inserted and processes them, placing the specified text at the top of the page, in the same location as the old text appeared.

Trouble? If you receive a JavaScript error message, close the Error Message dialog box and return to your text editor. Compare the code you entered to the code shown in the steps. Minor errors, such as omitting a quotation mark, can cause your program to fail.

You've completed your first JavaScript program! Although the program does little more than display text you could have entered directly with HTML, you'll build on it over the next two sessions to complete the more sophisticated task of calculating and displaying the number of days until Christmas.

Review

Session 10.1 Quick Check

1. What are the disadvantages of using server-side programs? In what situations would you use a server-side program over a client-side program?
2. Describe two differences between Java and JavaScript.
3. Within what element should be placed your JavaScript code?
4. Why should you place your JavaScript commands within an HTML comment tag?

5. Why would you enclose an embedded script within a CDATA section? What is a problem with this approach?

6. What JavaScript command writes the text "Avalon Books" marked as an h1 heading to your Web page?

Session 10.2

Working with Variables and Data

In the previous session, you learned how to write page content to a Web page using the document.write() method. Because you specified the content explicitly, though, the program did little more than what you could have accomplished by entering that content using basic HTML. The next task on your list for the North Pole Novelties home page, however, is to modify your program to determine the current date and then write that information to the Web page.

1) Learn how to display text on a Web page using JavaScript

2) Display date values on a Web page

3) Calculate the number of days between the test date and December 25th

4) If the date is December 25th or later (through December 31st), display a greeting message; otherwise, display the number of days remaining until Christmas

To do this, you need to create a JavaScript variable. A **variable** is a named item in a program that stores information. Variables are useful because they can store information created in one part of your program and allow you to use that information in another. For example, you can use the following JavaScript command to create a variable named "Year" that stores the value of the current year:

```
Year=2006;
```

With the Year variable assigned a value, you can use the document.write() method to display this value on the Web page, as follows:

```
document.write(Year);
```

This code writes the value "2006" to the Web page. You can also combine text with the variable value by using a plus symbol (+), as shown in the following example:

```
document.write("The year is " + Year);
```

This command writes the text "The year is 2006" to the Web page. Note that variables are distinguished from text strings by the absence of quotation marks. If JavaScript encounters a text string missing quotation marks, it attempts to interpret the text as a JavaScript command, object, or variable name.

In the program you're creating for Andrew, you won't explicitly enter the date information. Instead, your program will determine the current date and year for you and store that information in a variable so that you can use it later in the program. For now, you'll learn about variables by entering a fixed value.

The following restrictions apply to variable names:

- The first character must be either a letter or an underscore character (_).
- The remaining characters can be letters, numbers, or underscore characters.

- Variable names cannot contain spaces.
- You cannot use words that JavaScript has reserved for other purposes. For example, you cannot name a variable "document.write".

Variable names are case-sensitive. A variable named "Year" is different from a variable named "YEAR". If you create a JavaScript program that doesn't work properly, it may be because you did not match the uppercase and lowercase letters.

Variable Types

JavaScript supports four different variable types:

- numeric variables
- string variables
- Boolean variables
- null variables

A **numeric variable** can be any number, such as 13, 22.5, or -3.14159. Numbers also can be expressed in scientific notation, such as 5.1E2 for the value 5.1×10^2, or 510. A **string variable** is any group of text characters, such as "Hello" or "Happy Holidays!" Strings must be enclosed within either double or single quotation marks, but not both; the string value 'Hello' is acceptable, but the string value "Hello' is not. **Boolean variables** accept only the values true and false. They are most often used in programs that have to act differently based on different conditions. For example, you could create a Boolean variable to determine whether the user is running the Netscape browser or not. When the value of this Boolean variable was true, you could have the program optimize its behavior for Netscape users. Finally, a **null variable** is a variable that has no value at all. This happens when you create a variable in a program, but do not immediately assign it a value. Once a value has been assigned to a null variable, it falls into one of the three previous variable types.

Declaring a Variable

Before you can use a variable in your program, you need to create, or **declare**, it. You declare a variable in JavaScript either by using the "var" command or by assigning a value to the variable. Any of the following commands is a legitimate way of creating a variable named "Month":

```
var Month;
var Month = "December";
Month = "December";
```

The first command creates the variable without assigning it a value, while the second and third commands both create the variable and assign it a value.

It's considered good programming style to include the var command whenever you create a variable. Doing so helps you keep track of the variables a program uses and also makes it easier for others to read and interpret your code. Many Web designers place all of their variable declarations at the beginning of a program along with comments describing the purpose of each variable in the program.

Declaring a JavaScript Variable

- You can declare variables with any of the following JavaScript commands:

```
var variable;
var variable = value;
variable = value;
```

where `variable` is the name of the variable and `value` is the initial value of the variable. The first command creates the variable without assigning it a value; the second and third commands both create the variable and assign it a value.

You need to create the following variables for your JavaScript program:

- **Today** — containing information about the current date and time
- **ThisDay** — storing the current day of the month
- **ThisMonth** — storing a number indicating the current month
- **ThisYear** — storing a number indicating the current year
- **DaysLeft** — storing the number of days until December 25

To add variables to the JavaScript program:

1. If necessary, use your text editor to open **npn.htm**.

2. Insert the following JavaScript code directly below the "<!-- Hide from non-JavaScript browsers" line (see Figure 10-7):

```
var Today;
var ThisDay;
var ThisMonth;
var ThisYear;
var DaysLeft;
```

Declaring JavaScript variables ◄ Figure 10-7

```
<!-- Days until Christmas -->
<td id="daycell">
<script type="text/javascript">
    <!-- Hide from non-JavaScript browsers
    var Today;
    var ThisDay;
    var ThisMonth;
    var ThisYear;
    var DaysLeft;
    document.write("Today is 12/15/2006<br />");
    document.write("Only 10 days until Christmas");
    // Stop hiding -->
</script>
</td>
</tr>
```

Now that you've declared the variables, you need to use the JavaScript date methods to calculate the variable values.

Working with Dates

In your program for North Pole Novelties, you'll be working with dates as you calculate the number of days remaining until December 25. To store date information, you must create a **date object**, which is an object containing date information. There are two ways to create a date object:

```
variable = new Date("month day, year, hours:minutes:seconds")
```
or
```
variable = new Date(year, month, day, hours, minutes, seconds)
```

where *variable* is the name of the variable that contains the date information, and *month, day, year, hours, minutes,* and *seconds* indicate the date and time. In the previous example, the keyword "new" indicates that you're creating a new object. Note that in the first command form you specify the date using a text string, and in the second command form you use values. Both of the following commands create a variable named "SomeDay" corresponding to a date of June 15, 2006, and a time of 2:35 p.m.:

```
SomeDay = new Date("June 15, 2006, 14:35:00");
SomeDay = new Date(2006, 5, 15, 14, 35, 0);
```

In this example, you can observe a couple of interesting aspects of how JavaScript handles dates. First, when you specify the month with values rather than a text string, you must subtract 1 from the month number. This is because JavaScript numbers the months 0 for January through 11 for December. So, in the second command, the date for June 15 is expressed as (2006, 5, 15 ...) and not as (2006, 6, 15 ...) as you might otherwise expect. Also note that hours are expressed in military (24-hour) time (14:35 rather than 2:35 p.m.).

If you omit the hours, minutes, and seconds values, JavaScript assumes that the time is 0 hours, 0 minutes, and 0 seconds. If you omit both the date and time information, JavaScript returns the current date and time, which it gets from the system clock on the user's computer. For example, the following command creates a variable named "Today" containing the current date and time:

```
var Today = new Date();
```

This is the command that you'll eventually want to use in your program.

Now that you've seen how to store date and time information in a variable, you can add that feature to the JavaScript program. Eventually, you'll want to set the Today variable to whatever the current date is. For now, use the date October 15, 2006, so that the date on your Web page matches the one shown throughout this tutorial.

To enter a value for the Today variable:

1. Return to **npn.htm** in your text editor.

2. Change the line that declares the Today variable from "var Today;" to:

   ```
   var Today=new Date("October 15, 2006");
   ```

   Note that you do not need to include spaces between the = symbol and the other characters in the expression. See Figure 10-8.

Setting a date for the Today variable ◀ **Figure 10-8**

date object ──▶

test date

```
<script type="text/javascript">
<!-- Hide from non-JavaScript browsers
var Today=new Date("October 15, 2006");
var ThisDay;
var ThisMonth;
var ThisYear;
var DaysLeft;
document.write("Today is 12/15/2006<br />");
document.write("Only 10 days until Christmas");
// Stop hiding -->
</script>
```

3. Save your changes to the file.

Retrieving the Day Value

The Today variable contains all of the date and time information that you need, but unfortunately it's not in a form that is very useful to you. The problem is that JavaScript stores dates and times as the number of milliseconds since 6 p.m. on December 31, 1969. All of the JavaScript date and time functions are numerical calculations of these hidden numbers. Fortunately, you don't have to do the calculations that translate those numbers into dates. You can instead use some of the built-in JavaScript date methods to do the calculations for you. For each part of the date that you want displayed in your Web page or used in a calculation, you need to use a date method to retrieve its value.

For example, you want the ThisDay variable to store the day of the month. To get that information, you apply the getDate() method to your date variable. The general syntax of this method is

```
DayValue = DateObject.getDate()
```

where *DayValue* is the name of a variable that contains the day of the month and *DateObject* is a date object or a date variable that contains the complete date and time information. To apply this method to the Today variable, you would modify your variable declaration to read

```
ThisDay = Today.getDate();
```

The day of the month would then be stored in the ThisDay variable. If the current date were October 15, 2006, then the ThisDay variable would have the value "15".

Retrieving the Month Value

A similar method exists for extracting the value of the current month. This method is named getMonth(). Note that because JavaScript starts counting the months with 0 for January, you may want to add 1 to the month number returned by the getMonth() method. The following JavaScript code extracts the current month number, increases it by 1, and stores it in a variable named ThisMonth:

```
ThisMonth = Today.getMonth()+1;
```

Thus, for a date of October 15, the ThisMonth variable would have a value of "10".

Retrieving the Year Value

The final date method you'll be using in your program is the getFullYear() method. As the name suggests, the getFullYear() method extracts the year value from the date variable. The following code shows how you could store the value of the current year in a variable named ThisYear:

```
ThisYear = Today.getFullYear();
```

If the date stored in the Today variable was October 15, 2006, the value of the getFullYear variable would be "2006".

This method is named getFullYear() to distinguish it from the getYear() method, which returns only the last two digits of the year for years prior to 2000. For example, instead of 1999, getYear() would return a date of 99. As shown in Figure 10-9, you can run into difficulty using this method for years after 1999.

| Figure 10-9 | Values of the getYear() method from 1998 to 2001 |

Year	GetYear() Value
1998	98
1999	99
2000	2000
2001	2001

The getYear() date method returns a value of 2000 for year 2000, so if you use it to calculate the number of years between 1998 and 2000, you would come up with an answer of 1902 years! This is a classic example of the Y2K bug that caused so much concern in the late 1990s with the new millennium approaching. The getFullYear() date method was introduced in JavaScript 1.3 to correct this problem, and it is supported by Netscape 4.5 and Internet Explorer 4.0 and above. So even though there is a getYear() date method, you should not use it if your program is calculating a difference in dates before and after the year 2000. In this program, we'll use the getFullYear() date method.

Most of the date methods you can use with JavaScript are shown in Figure 10-10.

| Figure 10-10 | Date Methods |

Method	Description	Value
In the following examples, assume that the variable Today stores the date object: Date("April, 8, 2006, 12:25:28")		
Today.getSeconds()	Retrieves the seconds from the date	28
Today.getMinutes()	Retrieves the minutes from the date	25
Today.getHours()	Retrieves the hour from the date	12
Today.getDate()	Retrieves the day of the month from the date	8
Today.getDay()	Retrieves the day of the week from the date (0=Sunday, 1=Monday, 2=Tuesday, 3=Wednesday, 4=Thursday, 5=Friday, 6=Saturday)	6
Today.getMonth()	Retrieves the month from the date (0=January, 1=February, ...)	3
Today.getFullYear()	Retrieves the four-digit year number from the date	2006
Today.getTime()	Retrieves the time value, as expressed in milliseconds since December 31, 1969, 6 P.M.	1,144,520,728,000

Retrieving Date and Time Values

- To retrieve the four-digit year value from a date object, use the command
  Year = DateObject.getFullYear();
- To retrieve the month value from a date and time variable named *DateObject*, use the command
  Month = DateObject.getMonth();
- To retrieve the day of the month value from a date and time variable named *DateObject*, use the command
  Day = DateObject.getDate();
- To retrieve the day of the week value from a date and time variable named *DateObject*, use the command
  DayofWeek = DateObject.getDay();

Now that you've learned how to extract date information, you are ready to modify your JavaScript program to work with the Today variable. Remember that you'll eventually set up the program to use whatever the current date is, but for now you'll use October 15, 2006 to test the program.

To extract the day, month, and year values:

▶ 1. Return to **npn.htm** in your text editor.

▶ 2. Modify the variable declarations for the ThisDay, ThisMonth, and ThisYear variables, so they read as follows:

```
var ThisDay=Today.getDate();
var ThisMonth=Today.getMonth()+1;
var ThisYear=Today.getFullYear();
```

See Figure 10-11.

Extracting the day, month, and year values ◀ **Figure 10-11**

```
<script type="text/javascript">
  <!-- Hide from non-JavaScript browsers
  var Today=new Date("October 15, 2006");
  var ThisDay=Today.getDate();
  var ThisMonth=Today.getMonth()+1;
  var ThisYear=Today.getFullYear();
  var DaysLeft;
  document.write("Today is 12/15/2006<br />");
  document.write("Only 10 days until Christmas");
  // Stop hiding -->
</script>
```

day of month
month number
year number

To display this date information in your Web page, you can use the command

```
document.write("Today is "+ThisMonth+"/"+ThisDay+"/"+ThisYear+"
<br />");
```

If the current date is October 15, 2006, JavaScript returns the following text:

```
Today is 10/15/2006
```

You haven't calculated the value of the DaysLeft variable yet. At this point, you'll set this value equal to "999". You'll learn how to calculate the true value shortly.

To display the day, month, and year values:

▶ **1.** Modify the variable declaration for the DaysLeft variable to read

```
var DaysLeft=999;
```

▶ **2.** Replace the first document.write() command with

```
document.write("Today is "+ThisMonth+"/"+ThisDay+"/"+ThisYear+"
<br />");
```

▶ **3.** Replace the second document.write() command with:

```
document.write("Only "+DaysLeft+" days until Christmas");
```

When entering this code, be sure to carefully note the placement of the double quotation marks and uppercase and lowercase letters. Your complete code should appear as shown in Figure 10-12.

| Figure 10-12 | Displaying date information |

```
<script type="text/javascript">
   <!-- Hide from non-JavaScript browsers
   var Today=new Date("October 15, 2006");
   var ThisDay=Today.getDate();
   var ThisMonth=Today.getMonth()+1;
   var ThisYear=Today.getFullYear();
   var DaysLeft=999;
   document.write("Today is "+ThisMonth+"/"+ThisDay+"/"+ThisYear+"<br />");
   document.write("Only "+DaysLeft+" days until Christmas");
   // Stop hiding -->
</script>
```

▶ **4.** Save your changes to the file, and then open npn.htm in your Web browser. The revised page should appear as shown in Figure 10-13.

| Figure 10-13 | Generated date value |

Today is 10/15/2006
Only 999 days until Christmas

Home Page
Shopping Cart
Your Account
Contact Us
Angels
Cards

NORTH POLE NOVELTIES

Trouble? If you receive an error message when you try to open this page, or if the page looks incorrect, you might not have inserted all of the double quotation marks required in the code. Return to your text editor and compare your code with the code shown in Figure 10-12. Make any necessary corrections, save your file, and then reload or refresh it in your Web browser.

You've completed the second item on your task list, displaying date information on the Web page.

● 1) Learn how to display text on a Web page using JavaScript
● 2) Display date values on a Web page
○ 3) Calculate the number of days between the test date and December 25th
○ 4) If the date is December 25th or later (through December 31st), display a greeting message; otherwise, display the number of days remaining until Christmas

Your next step is to use those date values to calculate the days remaining until December 25. To do this, you need to learn how to work with expressions, operators, and functions.

Working with Expressions and Operators

Expressions are JavaScript commands that assign values to variables. You've already worked with several expressions in your JavaScript program. For example, you used the expression DaysLeft=999 to assign the value 999 to the DaysLeft variable. You create expressions using variables, values, and **operators,** which are elements that perform actions within expressions. One of the most commonly used operators is the + operator, which performs the action of adding or combining two elements. You used the plus operator in your program with the command

```
var ThisMonth = Today.getMonth()+1;
```

to increase the value returned by the getMonth() method by 1. You also used the + operator to combine text strings:

```
document.write("Only " + DaysLeft + " days until Christmas");
```

In both of these examples, the plus operator combines two or more values or elements to create a single value or element.

Arithmetic Operators

The + operator belongs to a group of operators called **arithmetic operators**, which perform simple mathematical calculations. Figure 10-14 lists some of the arithmetic operators and gives examples of how they work.

Arithmetic operators — Figure 10-14

Operator	Description	Example

+	Adds two values together	var Men = 20;
		var Women = 25;
		var TotalPeople = Men + Women;

–	Subtracts one value from another	var Price = 1000;
		var Expense = 750;
		var Profit = Price - Expense;

*	Multiplies two values together	var Width = 50;
		var Length = 25;
		var Area = Width*Length;

/	Divides one value by another	var People = 50;
		var TotalCost = 200;
		var CostperPerson = TotalCost/People;

%	Shows the remainder after dividing one value by another	var TotalEggs = 64;
		var CartonSize = 12;
		var EggsLeft = TotalEggs % CartonSize;

++	Increases a value by 1 (unary operator)	var Eggs = 12; var BakersDozen = Eggs++;
- -	Decreases a value by 1 (unary operator)	var Eggs = 12; var EggsIfOneIsBroken = Eggs- -;
–	Changes the sign of a value (unary operator)	var MyGain = 50; var YourLoss = – MyGain;

Some of the arithmetic operators in Figure 10-14 are also known as **binary operators** because they work on two elements in an expression. There are also **unary operators**, which work on only one variable. Unary operators include the increment (++), decrement (--), and negation (-) operators. The **increment operator** can be used to increase the value of a variable by 1. In the following code, an increment operator is used to increase the value of the *x* variable by one:

```
x = 100;
x++;
```

After both commands are run, the value of the *x* variable would be 101.

The decrement operator has the opposite effect, reducing the value of a variable by 1. The following JavaScript code assigns the value 99 to the *x* variable:

```
x = 100;
x--;
```

Finally, the negation operator changes the sign of a variable, as in the following example:

```
x = -100;
y = -x;
```

In this example, the value of the *x* variable is -100, and the value of the *y* variable is opposite that, or 100.

Assignment Operators

Expressions assign values using **assignment operators**. The most common assignment operator is the equals sign (=). JavaScript provides additional assignment operators that both manipulate elements in an expression and assign values in a single operation. One of these is the += operator. In JavaScript, the following two expressions create the same result:

```
x = x + y;
x += y
```

In both expressions, the value of the *x* variable is added to the value of the *y* variable and then the new value is assigned to the *x* variable.

An assignment operator also can be used with numbers to increase a variable by a specific amount. For example, to increase the value of the *x* variable by 2, you can use either of the following two expressions:

```
x = x + 2;
x += 2
```

A common use of the += operator is to create extended text strings. In this case, the operator appends one text string to another. For example, you may find it difficult to store a text string that covers several lines in a variable using a single command. However, you can do so in the following manner:

```
quote = "To be or not to be. ";
quote +="That is the question. ";
quote +="Whether tis nobler of the mind to suffer the slings and arrows
of outrageous fortune, ";
quote +="Or to take arm against a sea of troubles";
quote +="And by opposing end them. ";
...
```

Continuing in this fashion, the quote variable eventually contains the complete text of Hamlet's soliloquy, but it does so using a series of short, simple expressions rather than one long and cumbersome expression. This technique is often used to store long text strings. You could create the code for an entire Web page in this fashion. Other assignment operators are discussed in Figure 10-15.

Assignment operators ◄ **Figure 10-15**

Operator	Description
=	Assigns the value of the variable on the right to the variable on the left (x = y)
+=	Adds the two variables and assigns the result to the variable on the left (equivalent to x = x + y)
−=	Subtracts the variable on the right from the variable on the left and assigns the result to the variable on the left (equivalent to x = x − y)
*=	Multiplies the two variables together and assigns the result to the variable on the left (equivalent to x = x*y)
/=	Divides the variable on the left by the variable on the right and assigns the result to the variable on the left (equivalent to x = x/y)
%=	Divides the variable on the left by the variable on the right and assigns the remainder to the variable on the left (equivalent to x = x % y)

As you can see, once you master the syntax, assignment operators allow you to create expressions that are both efficient and compact. As you start learning JavaScript, you might prefer using the longer form for such expressions. However, if you study the code of other JavaScript programmers, you will certainly encounter programs that make substantial use of assignment operators to reduce program size.

The Math Object and Math Methods

For calculations other than simple addition, subtraction, multiplication, or division, JavaScript uses an object called the **Math object**. The Math object supports a collection of mathematical operations that you can apply to your program's variables and values. Each of these operations is accessed using the syntax

```
value = Math.method(variable);
```

where `method` is the mathematical operation you want to apply to a variable, and `value` is the value returned by the operation. For example, to calculate the absolute value of a variable named NumVar, you would apply the "abs" method to the Math object:

```
AbsValue = Math.abs(NumVar);
```

If NumVar had the value "-4", this operation would store the value "4" in the AbsValue variable. Figure 10-16 lists some of the other math methods supported by the Math object.

Figure 10-16	Math methods

Math Method	Description
Math.abs(*number*)	Returns the absolute value of *number*
Math.sin(*number*)	Calculates the sine of *number*, where *number* is an angle expressed in radians
Math.cos(*number*)	Calculates the cosine of *number*, where *number* is an angle expressed in radians
Math.round(*number*)	Rounds *number* to the closet integer
Math.ceil(*number*)	Rounds *number* up to the next-highest integer
Math.floor(*number*)	Rounds *number* down to the next-lowest integer
Math.random()	Returns a random number between 0 and 1

As with the other JavaScript commands and objects discussed earlier, the Math object is case-sensitive. You must type "Math" (with an uppercase M) instead of "math" when using this object.

Creating JavaScript Functions

You can use all of the JavaScript expressions and operators to create your own customized functions. A **function** is a series of commands that performs an action or calculates a value. A function consists of the **function name**, which identifies it; **parameters**, which are values used by the function; and a set of commands that are run when the function is used. Not all functions require parameters. The general syntax of a JavaScript function is

```
function function_name(parameters){
    JavaScript commands
}
```

where `function_name` is the name of the function, `parameters` are the values sent to the function, and `JavaScript commands` are the actual commands and expressions used by the function. Note that curly braces { } are used to mark the beginning and end of the commands in the function. The group of commands set off by the curly braces is called a **command block**; as you'll see, command blocks exist for other JavaScript structures in addition to functions.

Function names, like variable names, are case-sensitive. XMASDAYS and XmasDays are different function names. The function name must begin with a letter or underscore (_) and cannot contain any spaces.

There is no limit to the number of function parameters that a function may contain. The parameters must be placed within parentheses, following the function name, and the parameters must be separated by commas.

Creating and Using a JavaScript Function

- To create a user-defined function, use the following syntax:
  ```
  function function_name(parameters) {
    JavaScript commands
  }
  ```
  where *function_name* is the name of the function, *parameters* are the parameters of the function, separated by commas, and the opening and closing braces enclose the *JavaScript commands* used by the function.
- To run a user-defined function, use the following command:
  ```
  function_name(values);
  ```
  where *function_name* is the name of the function, and *values* are the values substituted for each of the function parameters.

Performing an Action with a Function

To see how a function works, consider the following function, which displays a message containing the current date:

```
function ShowDate(date) {
   document.write("Today is " + date + "<br />");
}
```

In this example, the function name is ShowDate, and it has one parameter: date. The function's command block contains one line, which displays the current date along with a text string. To run, or **call**, a function, you insert a JavaScript command containing the function name and any parameters it requires. To call the ShowDate function, you would enter the following commands:

```
var Today = "3/25/2006";
ShowDate(Today);
```

In this example, the first command creates a variable named "Today" and assigns it the text string "3/25/2006". The second command runs the ShowDate function, using the value of the Today variable as a parameter. Calling the ShowDate function results in the following sentence being displayed on the Web page:

Today is 3/25/2006

Returning a Value from a Function

You can also use a function to calculate a value. This is achieved by placing a return command at the end of the function command block, along with a variable or value. Consider the following Area function:

```
function Area(Width, Length) {
   var Size = Width*Length;
   return Size;
}
```

Here, the Area function calculates the area of a rectangular region and places the value in a variable named "Size". The value of the Size variable is returned by the function. A simple JavaScript program that uses this function might appear as follows:

```
var x = 8;
var y = 6;
var z = Area(x,y);
```

The first two commands assign the values 8 and 6 to the x and y variables, respectively. The values of both of these variables are then sent to the Area function, corresponding to the Width and Length parameters. The Area function uses these values to calculate the area, which it then returns, assigning that value to the z variable. As a result of these commands, 48 is assigned to the value of the z variable.

Placing a Function in an HTML File

Where you place a function in the HTML file is important. The function definition must be placed before the command that calls the function. If you try to call a function before it is defined, you might receive an error message from the browser. Although not a requirement, one programming convention is to place all of the function definitions used in the Web page either within the head section of the document or in an external file. This ensures that each function definition has been read and interpreted before being called by the JavaScript commands in the body of the Web page. When the browser loads the HTML file containing a function, the browser bypasses the function without executing it. The function is executed only when called by another JavaScript command.

One of the advantages of placing a custom function in an external file is that it can be accessed by other documents in your Web site. It's common practice for JavaScript programmers to create libraries of functions located in external files to be easily accessible to an entire Web site.

Creating the XmasDays Function

You now have all of the information you need to create your own customized function: the XmasDays function. The function has only one parameter, CheckDay, which contains a date object. The function returns one value: the number of days between the date stored in CheckDay and December 25 of the current year. The function has three variables:

- **XYear**: The year of the CheckDay date object
- **XDay**: The date of Christmas. The initial value of this variable is the date "December 25, 2006."
- **DayCount**: The number of days between current date and December 25. This is the value that is returned by the function.

The initial command block of the XmasDays function looks as follows:

```
function XmasDays(CheckDay) {
   var XYear=CheckDay.getFullYear();
   var XDay=new Date("December, 25, 2006");
}
```

These commands set the initial values of the XYear and XDay variables. However, the function needs to change the value of the XDay variable from December, 25, 2006 to December 25 of the year specified in the CheckDay parameter. After all, it might not be 2006! This is done using the JavaScript setFullYear() method. The command looks as follows:

XDay.setFullYear(XYear);

If the year specified in the CheckDay parameter is actually 2007, the date stored in the XDay variable changes from "December 25, 2006" to "December 25, 2007". Figure 10-17 shows other JavaScript functions that allow you to set or change the values of date objects.

Method	Description
DateObject.setSeconds(*seconds*)	Set the seconds value of the *DateObject* to seconds
DateObject.setMinutes(*minutes*)	Set the minutes value of the *DateObject* to minutes
DateObject.setHours(*hours*)	Set the hours value of the *DateObject* to hours
DateObject.setDate(*date*)	Set the day of the month value of the *DateObject* to date
DateObject.setMonth(*month*)	Set the month value of the *DateObject* to month
DateObject.setFullYear(*year*)	Set the full year (four digit) value of the *DateObject* to year
DateObject.setTime(*time*)	Set the time of the DateObject to *time*, which is the number of milliseconds since December 31, 1969 at 6 p.m.

Next, the function needs to calculate the time difference between December 25 and the current date. This can be calculated using the following expression:

```
var DayCount=XDay - CheckDay;
```

However, recall that JavaScript stores date information in milliseconds. Thus, taking the difference between these two dates calculates the number of milliseconds before Christmas. This is hardly the information that you want to display on the Web page. To make it a more meaningful measure, you must convert this value into days by dividing the difference by the number of milliseconds in one day. This calculation would be

```
var DayCount=(XDay - CheckDay)/(1000*60*60*24);
```

because there are 1000 milliseconds in a second, 60 seconds in a minute, 60 minutes in an hour, and 24 hours in one day.

There is one more issue. When a user displays the Web page, it's unlikely that the number of days before Christmas will be precisely a whole number. It's more likely that it will be a number of days, plus a fraction of a day before Christmas. Andrew doesn't want that fractional part displayed. You'll remove the fractional part by rounding the value of DayCount to the nearest day using the round Math method. The command is

```
DayCount = Math.round(DayCount);
```

Thus, the complete XmasDays function will look as follows:

```
function XmasDays(CheckDay) {
   var XYear=CheckDay.getFullYear();
   var XDay=new Date("December, 25, 2006");
   XDay.setFullYear(XYear);
   var DayCount=(XDay-CheckDay)/(1000*60*60*24);
   DayCount=Math.round(DayCount);
   return DayCount;
}
```

The XmasDays function is pretty valuable to a store like North Pole Novelties, and Andrew figures that they could use it on other pages in their Web site too. For this reason, you'll store the function in an external file named library.js. Note that the names of external JavaScript files end with the ".js" filename extension to distinguish them from other file types. When you insert the function you should also include a few comment lines that describe the function, its purpose, parameters, and variables.

To create the XmasDays() function:

▸ 1. Use your text editor to create a file named **library.js** in the tutorial.10/tutorial folder.

▸ 2. Insert the following lines of code into the file:

```
/* Function XmasDays()
    Purpose: Calculate the number of days between Christmas and a
given date


    Variables
    CheckDay: A date object containing the given date
    XYear: The 4-digit year value of the given date
    XDay: December 25 in the year of the given date
    DayCount: The number of days between Christmas and the
given date
*/


function XmasDays(CheckDay) {
    var XYear=CheckDay.getFullYear();
    var XDay=new Date("December, 25, 2006");
    XDay.setFullYear(XYear);
    var DayCount=(XDay-CheckDay)/(1000*60*60*24);
    DayCount=Math.round(DayCount);
    return DayCount;
}
```

Figure 10-18 shows the complete function and comment lines.

Figure 10-18	The complete XmasDays function

```
/* Function XmasDays()
    Purpose: Calculate the number of days between Christmas and a given date

    Variables
    CheckDay: A date object containing the given date
    XYear: The 4-digit year value of the given date
    XDay: December 25 in the year of the given date
    DayCount: The number of days between Christmas and the given date
*/

function XmasDays(CheckDay) {
    var XYear=CheckDay.getFullYear();
    var XDay=new Date("December, 25, 2006");
    XDay.setFullYear(XYear);
    var DayCount=(XDay-CheckDay)/(1000*60*60*24);
    DayCount=Math.round(DayCount);
    return DayCount;
}
```

▸ 3. Save your changes and close the **library.js** file.

Next, you'll create a link to the library.js file and then insert a command to run the XmasDays function. Recall that you previously set the value of the DaysLeft variable to 999 to act as a placeholder. You'll replace that command with one that calls the XmasDay function, using the Today variable as the date object referenced in the CheckDay parameter. The DaysLeft variable will then be set to whatever value is returned by the XmasDays function.

To call the XmasDays function:

▸ 1. Return to the **npn.htm** file in your text editor.

▸ 2. Directly above the closing </head> tag, insert the following line:

```
<script src="library.js" type="text/javascript"></script>
```

By placing the script element here, you are loading the contents of the library.js file into the page. Any commands or functions in that external file are then available to the rest of the page, including commands within other script elements on the page. This means that you can use the XmasDays() function later on in the document.

3. Go down to the JavaScript commands and replace the line "var DaysLeft=999" with

```
var DaysLeft=XmasDays(Today);
```

Figure 10-19 shows the revised code.

Accessing the XmasDays function ◄ **Figure 10-19**

```
<title>North Pole Novelties</title>
<link href="styles.css" rel="stylesheet" type="text/css" />
<script src="library.js" type="text/javascript"></script>
</head>
```

```
<script type="text/javascript">
  <!-- Hide from non-JavaScript browsers
  var Today=new Date("October 15, 2006");
  var ThisDay=Today.getDate();
  var ThisMonth=Today.getMonth()+1;
  var ThisYear=Today.getFullYear();
  var DaysLeft=XmasDays(Today);
  document.write("Today is "+ThisMonth+"/"+ThisDay+"/"+ThisYear+"<br />");
  document.write("Only "+DaysLeft+" days until Christmas");
  // Stop hiding -->
</script>
```

4. Save your changes to **npn.htm** and close it if you are not continuing on to the next session.

5. Reload **npn.htm** in your Web browser. As shown in Figure 10-20, the Web page now shows that there are 71 days between the test date of October 15 and December 25.

Days between October 15 and December 25 ◄ **Figure 10-20**

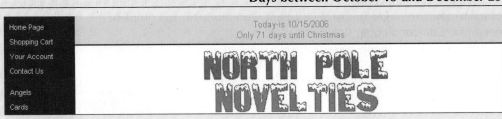

Trouble? If you receive a JavaScript error message or if your Web page shows an incorrect value, check your use of uppercase and lowercase letters, and verify that each JavaScript command ends with a semicolon.

You've completed the XmasDays function. Andrew plans to test the Web page you've created and get back to you with any suggestions or changes he wants you to make.

Session 10.2 Quick Check

1. What are the four variable types supported by JavaScript?
2. What JavaScript command stores the current date in a variable named "Now"?
3. What JavaScript command extracts the current day of the month from the Now variable, storing it in a variable named "Tdate"?
4. If the current month is September, what value would be returned by the getMonth() method?
5. Define the following terms: expression, operator, binary operator, and unary operator.
6. Provide the general syntax of a JavaScript function.
7. What JavaScript command calls the function, "calcMort" using the variables: loan, interest, and period as the parameter values and storing the resulting value in a variable named "mortgage"?

Session 10.3

Working with Conditional Statements

Now that you've created a function that calculates the number of days between a given date and December 25, you and Andrew review your progress through the list of tasks that he's given you.

1) Learn how to display text on a Web page using JavaScript
2) Display date values on a Web page
3) Calculate the number of days between the test date and December 25th
4) If the date is December 25th or later (through December 31st), display a greeting message; otherwise, display the number of days remaining until Christmas

The only task remaining is to have the Web page display a greeting message in place of a day count from December 25 through December 31. To complete this task, you need to create conditional statements.

Conditional statements are commands that run only when specific conditions are met. Each conditional statement requires a **Boolean expression**, which is an expression that can be evaluated as either true or false. Let's first examine how to create a Boolean expression.

Comparison, Logical, and Conditional Operators

To create a Boolean expression, you need one of three types of operators: a comparison operator, a logical operator, or a conditional operator. A **comparison operator** is an operator that compares the value of one item to another. The following are two examples of Boolean expressions created using comparison operators:

```
x < 100;
y == 20;
```

In the first example, if x is less than 100, this expression returns the Boolean value *true*; however if x is 100 or greater, the expression returns *false*. In the second example, the expression is true only if y is equal to 20. Note that this comparison operator uses a double equals sign (==) rather than a single equals sign (=). The single equals sign is an assignment operator and should be used for making comparisons (a very easy mistake to make!). Figure 8-21 lists some of the other comparison operators that JavaScript supports.

Comparison operators ◄ **Figure 10-21**

Operator	Description
==	Returns true if variables are equal (x = y)
!=	Returns true if variables are not equal (x != y)
>	Returns true if the variable on the left is greater than the variable on the right (x > y)
<	Returns true if the variable on the left is less than the variable on the right (x < y)
>=	Returns true if the variable on the left is greater than or equal to the variable on the right (x >= y)
<=	Returns true if the variable on the left is less than or equal to the variable on the right (x <= y)

A **logical operator** connects two or more Boolean expressions. One such operator is the && operator, which returns a value of true only if all of the Boolean expressions are true. For example, the following expression is true only if x is less than 100 and y is equal to 20:

```
(x < 100) && (y == 20);
```

Figure 10-22 lists some of the logical operators used by JavaScript.

Logical operators ◄ **Figure 10-22**

Operator	Description	Example
In the following examples, assume that x = 20 y = 25		
&&	Returns true when both expressions are true.	(x == 20) && (y == 25) returns true (x == 20) && (y == 20) returns false
||	Returns true when either expression is true.	(x == 20) || (y == 20) returns true (x == 25) || (y == 20) returns false
!	Returns true if the expression is false and false if the expression is true.	! (x == 20) returns false ! (x == 25) returns true

Finally, a **conditional operator** tests whether a condition is true, and returns values that you specify depending on whether the condition is true or false. The syntax of the conditional operator is

```
(condition) ? value1: value2
```

where `condition` is the condition being tested, `value1` is the value returned by the operator if the condition is true, and `value2` is the value if the condition is false. For example, the statement

```
message = (mail == "Yes") ? "You have mail": "No mail";
```

tests whether the mail variable is equal to the value "Yes". If it is, the statement assigns the message variable the value "You have mail"; otherwise it assigns the message variable the value "No mail".

Using an If Statement

One of the conditional statements supported by JavaScript is the If statement, which has the syntax

```
if (condition) {
    conditional JavaScript commands
}
```

where `condition` is a Boolean expression, and `conditional JavaScript commands` is the command block that is run if the Boolean expression is true. The following is an example of an If statement that controls what text is sent to the Web page:

```
if (Day=="Friday") {
    document.write("The weekend is almost here!");
}
```

In this example, if the Day variable is equal to "Friday", the text string "The weekend is almost here!" is sent to the Web page. If the Day variable is not equal to "Friday", no action is taken.

Using an If...Else Statement

The If statement runs a command block if the condition is true, but it does nothing if the condition is false. On some occasions, though, you might want an If statement to run for one set of commands if the condition is true, and another set of commands if the condition is false. This is done using an If...Else statement. The syntax is

```
if (condition) {
    JavaScript commands if true
} else {
    JavaScript commands if false
}
```

where `condition` is the Boolean expression, the first set of commands is run if the expression is true, and the second set of commands is run if the expression is false. The following is an example of an If...Else statement:

```
if (Day=="Friday") {
    document.write("The weekend is almost here!");
} else {
    document.write("It's not Friday yet");
}
```

In this example, the text "The weekend is almost here!" is generated if Day equals "Friday"; otherwise, the text "It's not Friday yet" appears.

If...Else structures can also be nested within one another. Here is an example of a nested structure:

```
if (Day=="Friday") {
    document.write("The weekend is almost here!");
} else {
    if(Day=="Monday") {
        document.write("Time for another work week");
    } else {
        document.write("Hello");
    }
}
```

In this example, the text "The weekend is almost here!" appears if the day is Friday. If the day is Monday, the text "Time for another work week" appears. On days other than Friday and Monday, the text "Hello" is generated.

Applying an If Statement

- To create a command block that runs only if a certain condition is met, use the syntax
  ```
  if (condition) {
      commands if condition is true
  }
  ```
  where `condition` is Boolean expression. If `condition` is true, the command block is run. If `condition` is false, the command block is skipped.
- To choose between two command blocks, use the syntax
  ```
  if(condition) {
      commands if condition is true
  } else {
      commands if condition is false
  }
  ```

Using a Switch Statement

When there are several possible conditions, nesting if statements inside of one another can be tedious and prone to error. A simpler structure is the switch statement, otherwise known as the case statement. The syntax of the switch statement is

```
switch (expression) {
    case label1: commands1
    break;
    case label2: commands2
    break;
    case label3: commands3
    break;
...
    default: default commands
}
```

where `expression` is a JavaScript expression that evaluates to a value (not a Boolean expression), `label1`, `label2`, etc. are possible values of that expression, `commands1`, `commands2`, etc. are commands to run if corresponding labels match, and `default commands` are the commands to run if no label matches. The previous if...else statement rewritten as a switch statement would look like this:

```
switch (Day) {
    case "Friday": document.write("The weekend is almost here!");
    break;
    case "Saturday": document.write("It's the weekend!");
    break;
    case "Sunday": document.write("The weekend is almost over");
    break;
    case "Monday": document.write("Time for another work week");
    break;
    default: document.write("It's not Friday yet");
}
```

As the JavaScript interpreter moves through the different case values, it executes any command in which the expression matches the case label. The break statement is optional and is used to halt the execution of a conditional statement. If you remove the break statements, then any and all commands corresponding to case labels matching the expression are executed. If you include the break statements, only the first matching case is used, and the remaining cases are ignored.

Reference Window

Applying a Switch Statement

- To run commands for a wide collection of cases, use the conditional statement

```
switch (expression) {
    case label1: commands1
    break;
    case label2: commands2
    break;
    case label3: commands3
    break;
    ...
    default: default commands
}
```

where *expression* is a JavaScript expression that evaluates to a value, *label1*, *label2*, etc. are possible values of that expression, *commands1*, *commands2*, etc. are commands to run if corresponding labels match, and *default commands* are the commands to run if no label matches.

Applying an If Statement to the NPN Page

You can use a conditional statement to complete your final task in the code for the North Pole Novelties page. If the current date is before December 25, Andrew wants the page to display the number of days until Christmas as calculated by the XmasDays function; if the date is between December 25 and December 31, he wants it to display a holiday greeting instead.

You can distinguish between the two situations by creating an If...Else statement that looks at the value returned by the XmasDays function. If that value is positive, then the current date is before December 25, and the page displays the number of days left in the holiday season. On the other hand, if the value is zero or negative, then the current date is December 25 or later in the year, and a holiday message is displayed. The code to perform this is

```
if (DaysLeft > 0) {
    document.write("Only " + DaysLeft + " days until Christmas");
} else {
    document.write("Happy Holidays from North Pole Novelties");
}
```

You need to insert these statements into the Web page, replacing the previous document.write() method you used to display the number of days until Christmas.

To create an If...Else structure:

1. Using your text editor, open **npn.htm**, if necessary.

2. Replace the line 'document.write("Only " + DaysLeft + " days until Christmas");'
with the following code:

```
if (DaysLeft > 0) {
   document.write("Only "+DaysLeft+" days until Christmas");
} else {
   document.write("Happy Holidays from North Pole Novelties");
}
```

Indent the various lines of your program to make it easier to read. The revised code should appear as shown in Figure 10-23.

Inserting an if..else conditional statement | **Figure 10-23**

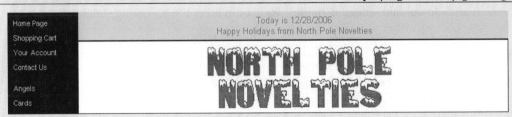

```
<script type="text/javascript">
   <!-- Hide from non-JavaScript browsers
   var Today=new Date("October 15, 2006");
   var ThisDay=Today.getDate();
   var ThisMonth=Today.getMonth()+1;
   var ThisYear=Today.getFullYear();
   var DaysLeft=XmasDays(Today);
   document.write("Today is "+ThisMonth+"/"+ThisDay+"/"+ThisYear+"<br />");
   if (DaysLeft > 0) {
      document.write("Only "+DaysLeft+" days until Christmas");
   } else {
      document.write("Happy Holidays from North Pole Novelties");
   }
   // Stop hiding -->
</script>
```

command run for days before December 25

command run for days from December 25 to December 31

3. Save your changes to the file and then open it in your Web browser. The page displays the text "Only 71 days until Christmas" because the date specified in the Today variable is still October 15, 2006 and this date falls before December 25.

4. Return to **npn.htm** in your text editor.

5. Change the date of the Today variable to **"December 28, 2006"**.

6. Save your changes to the file and reload it in your Web browser. As shown in Figure 10-24, the page now displays the Happy Holidays greeting.

Displaying a holiday greeting | **Figure 10-24**

Home Page
Shopping Cart
Your Account
Contact Us
Angels
Cards

Today is 12/28/2006
Happy Holidays from North Pole Novelties

NORTH POLE
NOVELTIES

You've completed all of the tasks on your list.

1) Learn how to display text on a Web page using JavaScript
2) Display date values on a Web page
3) Calculate the number of days between the test date and December 25th
4) If the date is December 25th or later (through December 31st), display a
   greeting message; otherwise, display the number of days remaining until Christmas

Next you need to turn your attention to some of the things Andrew wants you to change.

Using Arrays

Andrew has received feedback on your Web page. Although everyone likes the Christmas Day countdown feature, many users would prefer a date format that's easier to read.
Instead of displaying
Today is 10/15/2006
The reviewers would rather see:
Today is October 15, 2006
Although there are no built-in JavaScript methods to display dates in this format, you can create your own. One approach would be to create a series of conditional statements based on the value of the ThisMonth variable, and display a different text string for each month. This would require either 12 nested If...Else statements or a long switch statement. Fortunately, you can use arrays to display the desired text more easily.

An **array** is an ordered collection of values referenced by a single variable name. The syntax for creating an array variable is

```
var variable = new Array(size);
```

where `variable` is the name of the array variable and `size` is the number of elements in the array. Specifying a size for an array is optional. If you don't specify a size, JavaScript increases the size of the array as you add more elements. For example to create an array to contain weekday names, you could enter the following statement:

```
var weekdays = new Array();
```

Once you create an array, you then create values for each individual element in the array. To populate the weekdays array with the abbreviated names of the weekdays, you would enter the following code:

```
weekdays[0]  =  "Sun";
weekdays[1]  =  "Mon";
weekdays[2]  =  "Tue";
weekdays[3]  =  "Wed"
weekdays[4]  =  "Thu";
weekdays[5]  =  "Fri";
weekdays[6]  =  "Sat";
```

These commands create 7 new elements within the weekdays array. Each element is identified by its index, which is an integer displayed between brackets. For example, the value "Fri" has an index value of 5 in the weekdays array. Note that the first element in any array has an index value of 0, the second item has an index value of 1, and so on. You can use a variable in place of an index number. For example, if the variable "i" has the value 3, then weekdays[i]

is equal to the value of weekdays[3], which is "Wed".

You can combine the statements that create and populate the array into a single statement called a **dense array**. A dense array has the form

```
var variable = new Array(values);
```

where *values* is the comma-separated list of values to be placed into the array. To create the weekdays array as a dense array you would use the statement

```
var weekdays = new Array("Sun", "Mon", "Tue", "Wed", "Thu", "Fri",
"Sat");
```

Creating and Populating an Array

Reference Window

- To create an array variable, use the command
    ```
    var variable = new Array(size);
    ```
  where *variable* is the name of the array variable and *size* is the number of items in the array. The *size* value is optional. If you don't include a *size* value, the array expands to match the number of items you specify.
- To populate the array with values, use the command
    ```
    variable[i]=value;
    ```
  where *variable* is the name of the array, *i* is the ith item of the array (1st, 2nd, etc.), and *value* is the value of the ith element. The first array item has an index value of 0, the second has an index value of 1, and so forth.
- To create a dense array, which both creates and populates the array in a single statement, use the command
    ```
    var variable = new Array(values);
    ```
  where *values* is a comma-separated list of array values.

You decide to create an array named "MonthTxt" that contains the name of each month. The statement to create the MonthTxt array is

```
var MonthTxt = new Array("", "January", "February", "March", "April",
"May", "June", "July", "August", "September", "October",
"November", "December");
```

Note that the first value in the MonthTxt array is the empty text string " ". This was done to match the index numbers of the array with the month numbers. Thus "January" will have an index value of "1" rather than "0". With the MonthTxt array in place, we will be able to retrieve the name of each month using the expression

```
MonthTxt[ThisMonth]
```

Recall that ThisMonth is the variable we created in the previous session to store the month number of the current date.

To use the MonthTxt array in the NPN Web page:

► **1.** Return to **npn.htm** in your text editor.

► **2.** Insert the following code directly above the first document.write() statement:

```
var MonthTxt = new Array("", "January", "February", "March",
"April", "May",
```

```
                "June", "July", "August", "September", "October", "November",
          "December");
```

3. Change the document.write() statement that displays the current date to

```
document.write("Today is "+MonthTxt[ThisMonth]+" "+ThisDay+
", "+ThisYear+" <br />");
```

See Figure 10-25.

Figure 10-25	Creating and applying the MonthTxt array

```
<script type="text/javascript">
  <!-- Hide from non-JavaScript browsers          populating the
  var Today=new Date("December 28, 2006");         MonthTxt array
  var ThisDay=Today.getDate();
  var ThisMonth=Today.getMonth()+1;
  var ThisYear=Today.getFullYear();
  var DaysLeft=xmasDays(Today);
  var MonthTxt = new Array("", "January", "February", "March", "April", "May",
        "June", "July", "August", "September", "October", "November", "December");
  document.write("Today is "+MonthTxt[ThisMonth]+" "+ThisDay+", "+ThisYear+"<br />");
  if (DaysLeft > 0) {
    document.write("only "+DaysLeft+" days until Christmas");
  } else {
    document.write("Happy Holidays from North Pole Novelties");
  }
  // Stop hiding -->
</script>
```

referencing the MonthTxt array

4. Save your changes to the file.

5. Reload **npn.htm** in your Web browser. As shown in Figure 10-26, the date text should now be in the easier-to-read format.

Figure 10-26	Web page with formatted date

Home Page
Shopping Cart
Your Account
Contact Us

Angels
Cards
Collectibles
Creches
Garland
Gift Wraps
Lights
Nutcrackers
Ornaments
Santas
Trains
Trees
Villages
Wreaths

Today is December 28, 2006.
Happy Holidays from North Pole Novelties

NORTH POLE
NOVELTIES

WELCOME TO OUR ONLINE STORE. Consider us your complete holiday store. Whether you're a collector or simply looking for a beautiful piece to treasure for years, you'll find it at NPN. Please click on one of the many links to explore all we have to offer.

News Flash!
North Pole Novelties is proud to announce a new line of Lasseter Old Towne Village collectible houses. Start building your collection of these wonderful miniature porcelain houses and shops.

Each model has accessories to enhance the collection. Be sure to order extra trees, fences, street lights and signs to bring activity and a festive atmosphere to your miniature town.

Who Are We?
Located in Seton Grove, Minnesota, North Pole Novelties is one of the oldest and largest holiday stores in the country. The store was founded in 1968 by David Watkins (shown here). Today, David, his family, and over 300 employees manage the daily operation of making the holiday season last all year.

The store itself is the size of two football fields and attracts visitors from around the world. If you can't pay us a visit, order our catalogue. We will deliver to any spot in the United States and overseas. In a rush? We can deliver your order overnight! We also gift wrap.

North Pole Novelties | 25 Oakdale Avenue | Seton Grove, MN 53112 | (404) 555-1225

Trouble? If the code fails, look for errors in the creation of the MonthTxt array. Possible errors include not closing all double quotes around the array values and failing to separate one item value from another with a comma.

Before showing the Web page to Andrew for his final approval, you need to remove the test date and allow the page to use the current date (whatever that might be). Remember that if you don't specify a date value, the script uses the current date and time.

To use the current date in the North Pole Novelties Web page:

1. Return to **npn.htm** in your text editor.

2. Change the line 'var Today=new Date("December, 28, 2006")' to:

   ```
   var Today=new Date();
   ```

   You've completed your work with the JavaScript program. Figure 10-27 shows the final version of the code.

Completed code | Figure 10-27

```
<script type="text/javascript">
  <!-- Hide from non-JavaScript browsers
  var Today=new Date();
  var ThisDay=Today.getDate();
  var ThisMonth=Today.getMonth()+1;
  var ThisYear=Today.getFullYear();
  var DaysLeft=XmasDays(Today);
  var MonthTxt = new Array("", "January", "February", "March", "April", "May",
       "June", "July", "August", "September", "October","November", "December");
  document.write("Today is "+MonthTxt[ThisMonth]+" "+ThisDay+", "+ThisYear+"<br />");
  if (DaysLeft > 0) {
     document.write("Only "+DaysLeft+" days until Christmas");
  } else {
     document.write("Happy Holidays from North Pole Novelties");
  }
  // Stop hiding -->
</script>
```

3. Save your changes to the file and then close your text editor.

4. Reload **npn.htm** in your browser, and verify that it shows the correct date and number of days until December 25.

5. Close your Web browser.

Working with Program Loops

In the future, Andrew may have additional JavaScript programs he wants you to run. He suggests that you learn about the other types of programs you can create. He notes that the JavaScript code you created for North Pole Novelties is designed to run once every time the Web page is either opened or refreshed with a browser. However, programming often involves code that does not run just once, but is repeated until a particular condition has been fulfilled.

To provide a program with this capability you use a **program loop**, which is a set of instructions that is executed repeatedly. There are two types of loops: those that repeat a set number of times before quitting, and those that repeat as long as a certain condition is met. You create the first type of loop using a For statement.

The For Loop

The For loop allows you to configure a group of commands to be executed a set number of times. The loop uses a **counter** to track the number of times the command block has been run. You set an initial value for the counter, and each time the command block is executed, the counter changes in value. When the counter reaches a value above or below a certain stopping value, the loop ends. The general syntax of a For loop is

```
for (start; condition; update) {
    JavaScript commands
}
```

where *start* is the starting value of the counter, *condition* is a Boolean expression that must be true for the loop to continue, and *update* specifies how the counter changes in value each time the command block is executed. As in a function, the command block in the For loop is set off by curly braces { }. Figure 10-28 shows an example of a For loop used to write a row of table cells.

Figure 10-28	Creating a For loop

```
<table border="2">
<tr>
<script type="text/javascript">
    for (num = 1; num <=4; num++) {
        document.write("<td>"+num+"</td>");
    }
</script>
</tr>
</table>
```

For loop

1 2 3 4

resulting table

The num variable is the counter in this example, starting with an initial value of 1. So long as the value of num is less than or equal to 4, the condition for running the loop is met; when num exceeds 4, the loop stops. Finally, the expression "num++" indicates that each time the command block is run, the value of the num variable increases by 1. As you learned earlier in the discussion of arithmetic operators, this is an example of an incremental operator. As the loop is run, then, the num variable has the values 1, 2, 3, and finally, 4.

For loops can be nested inside one another. Figure 10-29 shows code used to write a table containing three rows and four columns. This example includes two counter variables: rownum and colnum. The rownum variable loops through the values 1, 2, and 3. For each value of rownum, the colnum variable takes on the values 1, 2, 3, and 4. For each value of the colnum variable, a table cell is written. For each value of the rownum variable, a table row is written.

Nesting a For loop   **Figure 10-29**

```
<table border="2">
<script type="text/javascript">
for (rownum = 1; rownum <=3; rownum++) {
    document.write("<tr>");
    for (colnum = 1; colnum <=4; colnum++) {
        document.write("<td>" + rownum + "," + colnum + "</td>");
    }
    document.write("</tr>");
}
</script>
</table>
```

nested For loop

1,1	1,2	1,3	1,4
2,1	2,2	2,3	2,4
3,1	3,2	3,3	3,4

resulting table

The For loop is not limited to incrementing the value of the counter by 1. Figure 10-30 shows examples of other ways of incrementing the counter in a For loop.

Specifying counter values in a For loop   **Figure 10-30**

For Loop	Counter Values
for (i = 1; i <= 5; i++)	i = 1, 2, 3, 4, 5
for (i = 5; i > 0; i--)	i = 5, 4, 3, 2, 1
for (i = 0; i <= 360; i += 60)	i = 0, 60, 120, 180, 240, 300, 360
for (i = 2; i <= 64; i *= 2)	i = 2, 4, 8, 16, 32, 64

The While Loop

Similar to the For loop, the While loop runs a command group so long as a specific condition is met. However, the While loop does not employ any counters. The general syntax of the While loop is

```
while (condition) {
    JavaScript Commands
}
```

where *condition* is a Boolean expression that can be either true or false. So long as the condition is true, the commands in the command block are executed. Figure 10-31 shows how you can create a set of table cells using a While loop.

Figure 10-31	Creating a While loop

```
<table border="2">
<tr>
<script type="text/javascript">
   var num = 1;
   while (num <= 4) {
      document.write("<td>"+num+"</td>");
      num++;
   }
</script>
</tr>
</table>
```

While loop

resulting table

Note that this particular While loop produces the same results as does the sample For loop discussed earlier. The num variable starts with a value of 1 and is increased by 1 each time the command block is run. The loop ends when the condition—that num should be less than or equal to 4—is no longer true.

As with For loops, While loops can be nested inside one another (see Figure 10-32).

Figure 10-32	Nesting a While loop

```
<table border="2">
<script type="text/javascript">
var rownum = 1;
var colnum = 1;
while (rownum <=3) {
   document.write("<tr>");
   while (colnum <=4) {
      document.write("<td>" + rownum + "," + colnum + "</td>");
      colnum++;
   }
   document.write("</tr>");
   colnum = 1;
   rownum++;
}
</script>
</table>
```

nested While loop

1,1	1,2	1,3	1,4
2,1	2,2	2,3	2,4
3,1	3,2	3,3	3,4

resulting table

For loops and While loops share many of the same characteristics, and the loop type that you choose for a particular application is often a matter of personal preference. Generally, a While loop is used for conditions that don't yield themselves to using counter variables.

Creating Program Loops

- To create a For loop, use the syntax

```
for (start; condition; update) {
   JavaScript Commands
}
```

where *start* is an expression defining the starting value of the For loop's counter, *condition* is a Boolean expression that must be true for the loop to continue, and update is an *expression* defining how the counter changes as the For loop progresses.
- To create a While loop, use the syntax

```
while (condition) {
   JavaScript Commands
}
```

where *condition* is a Boolean expression that halts the While loop when its value becomes false.

You've completed your study of JavaScript. Andrew has received the final version of your Web page and the JavaScript programs you created. He has viewed the page with his Web browser and is happy that it works so well. He'll review the Web page with his colleagues and get back to you with any final modifications that they might suggest.

Debugging Your JavaScript Programs

As you work with JavaScript you will inevitably encounter scripts that fail to work or report an error. There are three types of errors: load-time errors, run-time errors, and logical errors. A **load-time error** occurs when a script is first loaded by the JavaScript interpreter and the script entirely fails to execute. For example, the following simple JavaScript program would result in an error because the document.write() method is not properly closed:

```
<script type="text/javascript">
   document.write("North Pole Novelties");
</script>
```

When a JavaScript interpreter uncovers a load-time error, it halts loading the script. Depending on the browser, an error message then appears. Figure 10-33 shows the message generated by the above error. The error message typically displays the line number and character number in the script where the interpreter encountered the error. This does not mean that the error occurred at this location in the document, however—the source of the trouble could be much earlier in the script. The information in the error message simply indicates the location at which the JavaScript interpreter was forced to cancel loading the script.

Load-time error | Figure 10-33

A second type of error, a **run-time error**, occurs after a script has been successfully loaded and is being executed. When a JavaScript interpreter catches a run-time error, it displays an error message, halting execution of the script and indicating the location where it was forced to quit.

Finally, **logical errors** are free from syntax and structural mistakes, but result in incorrect results. A logical error is often the hardest to fix and may require you to meticulously trace every step of your code to detect the mistake.

Common Mistakes

To fix a script problem, you have to **debug** your program, meaning that you must search the code to locate the source of the trouble. Following are some common errors that may creep into your scripts:

- **Misspelling a variable name.** For example if you name a variable "ListPrice", misspellings such as "listprice", "ListPrices", or "list_price" would result in the program failing to run correctly.
- **Mismatched parentheses or braces**. The following code would result in an error because the second command block lacks the opening brace:
  ```
  if (DaysLeft > 0) {
     document.write("Only " + DaysLeft + " days until Christmas");
  } else
     document.write("Happy Holidays from North Pole Novelties");
  }
  ```
- **Mismatched quotes**. If you neglect the closing quotes around a text string, JavaScript treats the text string as an object or variable, resulting in an error. The following code would result in an error because the closing quote is missing from the first variable:
  ```
  var firstname="Andrew;
  var lastname="Savatini";
  document.write(firstname+" "+lastname);
  ```
- **Missing quotes**. When you combine several text strings using the "+" symbol, you may neglect to quote all text strings. For example, the following code is incorrect because of the missing quotes around the <br /> tag:
  ```
  document.write("Welcome to North Pole Novelties"+<br />);
  ```
- **Using (instead of [**. Array indices and index values must be placed within square brackets. If you use parenthesis around an index value, for example, a JavaScript interpreter would interpret the code as a function call. The following code suffers from this error:
  ```
  document.write("This month is "+MonthTxt(ThisMonth));
  ```
- **Using = in place of ==**. To compare values in a Boolean expression you need to use the == symbol rather than the = symbol. The = symbol is used only to assign values to an item. Thus, the following if statement is erroneous:
  ```
  if (Day="Friday") {
     document.write("The weekend is almost here!");
  }
  ```

Debugging Tools and Techniques

There are several techniques you can employ both to avoid making mistakes and to quickly locate the mistakes you do make. One is to write **modular code**, meaning that you break up the different tasks of your program into smaller, more manageable chunks. In the NPN page, we implemented modularization by placing the code to calculate the number of days until December 25 in its own function rather than placing all of the code within a single script. Modular code can also be easily reused for different purposes.

If you encounter a logical error in which a browser displays incorrect results, you can monitor the changing values of your variables using an alert dialog box. The command

```
alert(DaysLeft);
```

displays the value of the DaysLeft variable in a dialog box. You can insert alert dialog boxes throughout your code in an attempt to locate the section in which the logical error occurs. Alert dialog boxes are also useful for locating exactly where a syntax error occurs. If an alert dialog box is displayed, you can be assured that there are no run-time errors up to that point in the code.

You can also use different programs as tools for debugging. Microsoft offers the **Microsoft Script Debugger** for use with its Internet Explorer browser. Using the debugger you can easily create and debug your JavaScript programs. The Microsoft Script Debugger is available for free from the Microsoft Web site and is also included with Microsoft's Office suite.

Netscape also provides its own debugger called the **Netscape JavaScript Console**. When you open a document in the console, it displays a list of all script errors generated by the document. You can open the console by typing **javascript:** in the Netscape address bar. Figure 10-34 shows the console listing an error in the script from the current Web page.

Error message in the Netscape JavaScript Console ◄ **Figure 10-34**

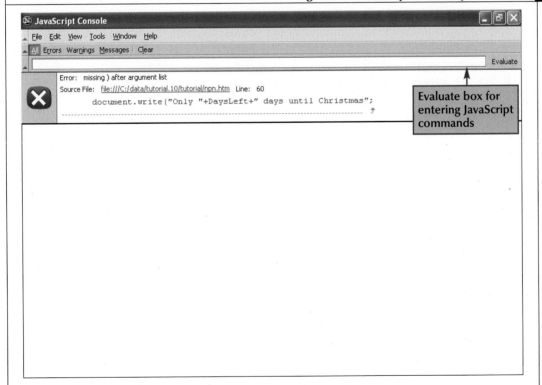

The console also includes an Evaluate box in which you can insert JavaScript code commands to evaluate your code and variable values. You can learn more about the Netscape JavaScript Console by using Netscape's online help.

Tips for Writing Good JavaScript Code

- Use good layout to make your code more readable. Indent command blocks to make them easier to read and to set them off from other code.
- Use descriptive variable names to indicate the purpose of your variables.
- Be careful how you use uppercase and lowercase letters in your code, because JavaScript commands and names are case-sensitive.
- Add comments to your code to document the purpose of each script.
- Initialize all variables at the top of your script and insert comments describing the purpose and nature of your variables.
- Create customized functions that can be reused in different scripts. Place your customized functions in external files to make them available to your entire Web site.

Review

Session 10.3 Quick Check

1. What JavaScript code displays the text "Welcome back to school!" if the value of the MonthName variable is "September"?
2. What JavaScript code displays the text "Welcome back to school!" if MonthName equals "September," or the text "Today's Headlines" if the month is not September?
3. What JavaScript code displays the text "Welcome back to school!" if MonthName equals September, "Summer's here!" if the MonthName equals June, or "Today's headlines" for other months?
4. What is an array? What command would you use to create an array named Colors?
5. What JavaScript command would you enter to place the values "Red", "Green", "Blue", "Black", and "White" into an array named "Colors"?
6. What is a program loop? Name the two types of program loops supported by JavaScript.
7. What code would you use to run the command document.write("News Flash!
"); five times?
8. What values will the counter variable *i* take in the following For loop?

```
for (i=5; i<=25; i+=5)
```

Review

Tutorial Summary

In this tutorial, you learned how to create and run Web page programs written in the JavaScript language. In the first session, you learned about the history of JavaScript and how it compares to Java. You then studied how to create a script element and to send text to a Web page. In the second session, you learned about the structure of JavaScript and how to create and use variables. You learned about different data types and how to work with date objects. The second session, also covered operators, expressions, and customized functions. Using this information you created a customized function. The third session covered conditional statements, Boolean expressions, program loops, and arrays. You used this information to better format the output from your JavaScript program. The tutorial concluded with a discussion of common scripting errors, and an overview of some of the tools and techniques you can use to make your code error-free.

Key Terms

arithmetic operator
array
assignment operator
binary operators
Boolean expression
Boolean variable
call
command block
comparison operator
compiled language
conditional operator
conditional statement
counter
date object
debug
declare

dense array
ECMA
ECMAScript
European Computer Manu-
    facturers Association
expression
function
function name
increment operator
interpreted language
JavaScript
JScript
load-time error
logical error
logical operator
Math object

method
Microsoft Script Debugger
modular code
Netscape JavaScript Console
null variable
numeric variable
object-oriented
operator
parameter
program loop
run-time error
string variable
unary operator
variable
VBScript

Review Assignments

Data files needed for this Review Assignment: bells.jpg, lib2txt.js, logo.jpg, npn2txt.htm, styles2.css, watkins.jpg

Andrew has already reviewed and tested your Web page and shown it to other employees at North Pole Novelties. A few changes have been made to the NPN home page and they would like you to do the following:

- Create a custom function named showDate() that displays the date from a date object in the form *weekday, month day, year,* where *weekday* is the day of the week, *month* is the complete month name, *day* is the day of the month, and *year* is the four-digit year.
- At the top of the NPN home page include the day of the week in the date information. In other words, instead of displaying, "October 15, 2006", display "Monday, October 15, 2006".
- Change the message for December 24 so that it reads "Last day for Christmas shopping." Keep the other messages the same.

Figure 10-35 shows a preview of the completed page for the date of December 24, 2006.

Figure 10-35

North Pole Novelties home page figure

To complete this Web page:

1. Using your text editor, open **npn2txt.htm** from the tutorial.10/review folder. Enter *your name* and *the date* in the head section and save the file as **npn2.htm**. Use your text editor to open the **lib2txt.js** file from the same folder. Enter *your name* and *the date* in the comments at the top of the file and save the file as **library2.js**.

2. Go to the **library2.js** file in your text editor and create a new function named showDate(). The function has a single parameter named thisDate. The thisDate parameter will store a date object. Within the showDate() function, add the following commands:

   a. Declare a variable named thisWDay that is equal to weekday number of the thisDate variable. (HINT: Use the getDay() date method to extract the weekday number.)

   b. Declare a variable named thisDay that is equal to the day of the month value from the thisDate variable.

   c. Declare a variable named thisMonth that is equal to the month number value from the thisDate variable.

   d. Declare a variable named thisYear which is equal to the four-digit year value from the thisDate variable.

   e. Create a dense array named monthName that contains the names of all twelve months starting with "January". (HINT: Set up the array so that monthName[0]="January".)

   f. Create a dense array named wdayName that contains the names of all seven weekdays starting with "Sunday". (HINT: Set up the array so that wdayName[0]="Sunday".)

   g. Create a variable named dateString which is equal to the following text string:
      weekday, month day, year
      where weekday is the name of the weekday, month is the name of the month, day is the day of the month, and year is the four-digit year value. (HINT: Use the wdayName array using thisWDay variable as the index value to display the

weekday name, the monthName array along with the thisMonth variable to display the month name, the thisDay variable to display the day of the month value, and the thisYear variable to display the year value.)

  h. Return the value of the dateString variable from the function.

3. Close the **library2.js** file, saving your changes.

4. Go to the **npn2.htm** file in your text editor.

5. Within the head section of the file, directly below the link element that links the page to the styles2.css style sheet, insert a script element linking to the library2.js script file.

6. Scroll down the file and locate the table cell with the id "daycell". Within this table cell insert an embedded script element. Add the appropriate comments to hide the contents of the script element from older browsers that do not support JavaScript.

7. Within the embedded script add create the following variables:

  a. Declare a date object variable named "today". Set the initial value of the today variable to December 24 of the current year.

  b. Declare a variable named "niceDate" and set the value equal to the text string returned by the showDate() function you created using the today variable as the parameter value.

  c. Declare a variable named "daysLeft" and set it equal to the value returned by the XmasDays() function using the today variable as the parameter value.

8. Write the value of the niceDate variable to the Web page, followed by a <br /> tag.

9. Create nested set of if...else conditional statements that contain the following:

  a. If daysLeft > 1, write the text string, "Only *daysLeft* days until Christmas" where *daysLeft* is the value of the daysLeft variable.

  b. If daysLeft = 1, write the text string, "Last day for Christmas shopping". (HINT: Be sure to use == and not = as your comparison operator.)

  c. Otherwise, write the text string, "Happy Holidays from North Pole Novelties".

10. Save your changes to the file.

11. Test your script using each of the following dates. Print a copy of the resulting Web page.

  • August 12, 2006
  • December 24, 2006
  • December 31, 2006

12. Return to the **npn2.htm** file in your text editor and set the final value of the today variable to display the current date.

13. Submit the completed Web site to your instructor.

Case Problem 1

Data files needed for this Case Problem: mwu.jpg, mwutxt.htm, spamtxt.js, mwstyles.css

Department of Astronomy   The Midwest University's Department of Astronomy is putting its faculty directory online. The directory includes links to the e-mail address of each professor. Assistant Professor Kate Howard is responsible for the design of the department's Web site. She is concerned that putting the faculty's e-mail addresses in the Web page will cause her and her colleagues to be subjected to spam as their addresses are collected by address harvesters (for a discussion of spam and address harvesters, see Tutorial 2). She's heard that JavaScript can be used to hide e-mail address and has asked you to set up some scripts to do this for the faculty page.

Apply

Use the skills you learned in this tutorial to write a script to hide email addresses from address harvesters.

Each entry in the faculty list includes an e-mail address link using the following format:

```
<a href="mailto:name@server">name@server</a>
```

where *name* is the professor's username and *server* is the e-mail server. Kate wants you to create a function named emLink() that writes this code using the text strings of the username and server names entered in reverse order as parameter values. The command to call the function would look as follows:

```
emLink("eman","revres")
```

Kate feels that this will do a good job of hiding the actual e-mail addresses from the harvesters. A function to reverse the order of the characters in a text string has already been provided for you. Your job is to write the emLink() function and then apply that function to the entries in the faculty list. A preview of the page you'll create is shown in Figure 10-36.

Figure 10-36

To complete this Web page:

1. Using your text editor, open **mwutxt.htm** from the tutorial.10/case1 folder. Enter *your name* and *the date* in the head section and save the file as **mwu.htm**. Use your text editor to open the **spamtxt.js** file from the same folder. Enter *your name* and *the date* in the comments at the top of the file and save the file as **spam.js**.

2. Go to the **spam.js** file in your text editor and create a new function named emLink(). The function will have two parameters: name and server. Add the following commands to the function:

   a. Declare a variable named "rname" and set it equal to the value of the name parameter but in reverse order. (HINT: Call the stringReverse() function with name as the parameter value to reverse the order of the characters.)

   b. Declare a variable named "rserver" equal to the value of the server parameter in reverse order.
   c. Declare a variable named "email" and set it equal to the text string, *rname@rserver*, where *rname* is the rname variable and *rserver* is the rserver variable.
   d. Create a variable named "mailText" equal to the text string:
       <a href="mailto:*email*">*email*</a>
       where *email* is the email variable.
       (HINT: To create a text string that contains double quotes, you have to use single quotes to enclose the entire text string. You may also find it easier to create this text string in several lines of code, as in the example creating the extended quote from Hamlet in the Assignment Operators section of this tutorial.)
   e. Write the value of the mailText variable to the Web page.
3. Close the **spam.js** file, saving your changes.
4. Return to the **mwu.htm** file in your text editor.
5. Within the head section of the file, directly below the link element that links the page to the mwstyles.css style sheet, insert a script element linking the file to the spam.js script file.
6. Scroll down the file to the first table cell containing an e-mail address link. Replace the link with a script element. Within the script element call the emLink() function using the professor's username and server as parameter values in reverse order. Be sure to enclose the reversed username and server name in quotes.
7. Repeat Step 6 for the remaining entries in the faculty list.
8. Save your changes to the file and then open **mwu.htm** in your Web browser. Verify that each entry in the faculty directory table shows the correct e-mail address and that as you hover your mouse pointer over the e-mail link, the browser's status bar shows the correct link target.
9. Submit your completed Web site to your instructor.

Apply

Use the skills you learned in this tutorial to create a page that displays a random quote from an American author.

Case Problem 2

Data files needed for this Case Problem: button.gif, logo.gif, mtstyles.css, paper.gif, randtxt.js, twain.gif, twaintxt.htm

Madison State College Professor Stewart Templeton of the Humanities Department at Madison State College has created a Web site devoted to the works of Mark Twain. One of the Web pages in the site is dedicated to Mark Twain's quotations. Stewart would like you to help him with the Web page by creating a JavaScript program to display random quotes from the legendary author and humorist. He has provided you with a Web page and a list of five quotes to work with. You must use these components to create a function, MQuote, to display one of the quotes on the Web page.

JavaScript includes a Math method for generating random numbers, but it only can create a random number between 0 and 1. You can convert the random number it generates to an integer from 1 to *n*, where *n* is the upper range of the integers, using the JavaScript command

```
Rnum = Math.ceil(Math.random()*n)
```

In this function, the random number is multiplied by *n* and then, using the Math.ceil method, that value is rounded up to the next highest integer. Rnum is therefore restricted to integer values from 1 to *n*.

You'll use this command with *n* set to 5, to select which one of the five quotes to be shown on the Web page. The Mark Twain quotes Stewart wants you to use are:

- "I smoke in moderation, only one cigar at a time."
- "Be careful of reading health books, you might die of a misprint."
- "Man is the only animal that blushes or needs to."
- "Clothes make the man. Naked people have little or no influence on society."
- "One of the most striking differences between a cat and a lie is that a cat has only nine lives."

A preview of the Web page you'll create is shown in Figure 10-37.

Figure 10-37

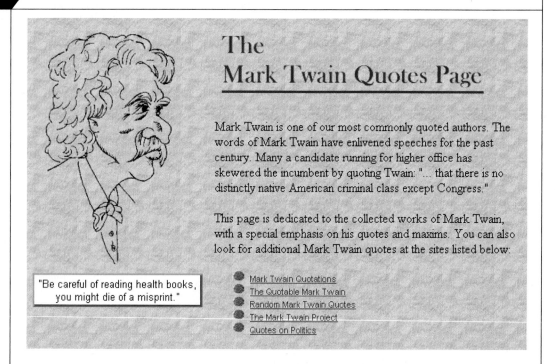

To complete this Web page:

1. Using your text editor, open **twaintxt.htm** from the tutorial.10/case2 folder. Enter *your name* and *the date* in the head section and save the file as **twain.htm**. Use your text editor to open the **randtxt.js** file from the same folder. Enter *your name* and *the date* in the comments at the top of the file and save the file as **random.js**.
2. Go to the **random.js** file in your text editor and create a new function named randInt(). The function will have only one parameter named "size". Add the following commands to the function:
   a. Declare a variable named "rNum" which is equal to a random integer between 1 and the value of the size variable.
   b. Return the value of the rNum variable from the function.
3. Close the **random.js** file, saving your changes.
4. Return to the **twain.htm** file in your text editor.
5. Within the head section of the file, directly below the link element that links the page to the mtstyles.css style sheet, insert a script element linking the file to the random.js script file.

6. Below that script element, insert an embedded script containing the getQuote() function. The getQuote() function will have only a single parameter named "qNum". The function should do the following:

   a. Create an array named mtQuotes that contains the five Mark Twain quotes listed above. The first quote should have an array index value of "1", the second quote should have an index value of "2", and so forth. There should be no quotes for the array index, "0".

   b. Return the value of the mtQuotes array for the qNum index.

7. Scroll down the file to the div element with the id "quotes". Within this div element, insert another embedded script element. The script element should contain the following commands:

   a. Declare a variable named "randValue" which is equal to a random integer between 1 and 5. (HINT: Use the randInt() function you created earlier with a size parameter value of 5.)

   b. Declare a variable named "quoteText" containing the Mark Twain quote whose array index value is equal to randValue. (HINT: Use the getQuote() function you created to extract the correct quote from the array.)

   c. Write the value of quoteText to the Web page.

8. Save your changes to the file and open **twain.htm** in your Web browser. Verify that the Mark Twain quote changes as you continually reload or refresh the Web page.

9. Submit the completed Web site to your instructor.

Case Problem 3

Data files needed for this Case Problem: bcc.css, bcc.jpg, bcctxt.htm, calendar.css, caltxt.js, paper.jpg

Butler Community Center   Beth Heurtzel is the director of the Butler Community Center in Butler, Utah. One of her jobs is to organize the calendar of events for the center and to publish that information on the center's Web site. Beth would like the ability to place a monthly calendar on the Web page along with a list of events for that month.

To do this, you'll create a JavaScript function named "calendar" that creates a table displaying a monthly calendar with a specified date highlighted. For example, if the user inserts the function

```
calendar("February 8, 2006")
```

into the HTML code, the browser displays the monthly calendar for February 2006 with the date, February 8, highlighted. Furthermore, Beth would like the option to replace the date with the text "today" as follows:

```
calendar("today")
```

which instructs the browser to display the calendar for the current month and to highlight today's date.

You'll save this function in a separate JavaScript file so that Beth can use it for other Web pages as well. The format of the table is determined from a Cascading Style Sheet (CSS). The calendar table has five elements you can modify with the style sheet:

- The calendar table, identified with the id name "calendar_table"
- The calendar heading, where the month and year are displayed, identified with the id name "calendar_head"

- The calendar headings, which display the names of the seven weekdays, identified with the class name "calendar_weekdays"
- The individual table cells, which display the days of the month, identified with the class name "calendar_dates"
- The highlighted date in the calendar, identified with the id name "calendar_today"

Beth has already created a style sheet that formats these elements and has stored it in the file calendar.css. She has also created the Web page that she wants the calendar to appear in. Your job is to create the calendar() function, save it in a file, and apply it to Beth's Web page. A preview of the completed Web page with the calendar highlighting the date, April 8, 2006, is shown in Figure 10-38.

Figure 10-38

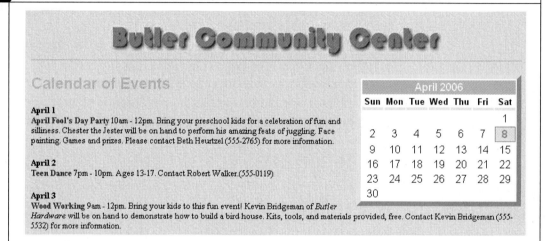

To create the calendar() function:

1. Using your text editor, open **bcctxt.htm** from the tutorial.10/case3 folder. Enter *your name* and *the date* in the head section and save the file as **bcc.htm**. Use your text editor to open the **caltxt.js** file from the same folder. Enter *your name* and *the date* in the comments at the top of the file and save the file as **calendar.js**.

2. Go to the **calendar.js** file in your text editor. To create the calendar() function, we'll first create several smaller functions that will create particular parts of the calendar table. We'll start with a function named writeCalTitle() that writes the code for the first row of the table. The first table row contains a single cell that spans seven columns displaying the name of month and the year. To create the writeCalTitle() function, do the following:

   a. Create the writeCalTitle() function with a single parameter named "calendarDay". The calendarDay parameter represents a date object containing the highlighted date for the calendar table.

   b. Create an array named "monthName" to contain the names of the months. The value of monthName[0] should "January", monthName[1] should be "February" and so forth.

   c. Extract the month value from the calendarDay parameter and store the value in a variable named "thisMonth".

   d. Extract the four-digit year value from calendarDay and store it in a variable named "thisYear".

e. Write the following code to the Web page:

```
<tr><th id="calendar_head" colspan="7">month year</th></tr>
```

where *month* is name of the month and *year* is the four-digit year value.

Explore

3. Next, create a function named writeDayTitle(). This function has no parameters and is used to write the table row containing the abbreviated names of the seven weekdays, starting with "Sun". To create the writeDayTitle() do the following:

a. Create an array named wdName containing the following text strings: "Sun", "Mon", "Tue", "Wed", "Thu", "Fri", and "Sat".

b. Write the tag, "<tr>" to the Web page.

c. Create a for loop in which the counter value, i, goes from 0 to 6. Each time through the loop write the following code to the Web page:

```
<th class="calendar_weekdays">weekday</th>
```

where *weekday* is the abbreviated weekday name. (HINT: Use the wdName array with the index value set to the value of the counter, i.)

d. Write the closing "</tr>" tag to the Web page.

Explore

4. The next function named writeCalDays() writes the actual calendar dates into the table. The function has a single parameter named "calendarDay" which we'll use to track the days of the month as we proceed through the calendar table. This function has two distinct parts. The first part of the function is used to determine on which day of the week the month starts. Any weekdays before that day should have no date values displayed in them. Thus we need to create a set of blank table cells up to the first day of the month. To create these empty cells, insert the following commands into the writeCalDays() function:

a. Extract the day of the month value from the calendarDay parameter and store it in a variable named "thisDay". We'll use this variable to record the day that should be highlighted in the calendar.

b. Use the setDate() method to set the calendarDay parameter to the first day of the month. (HINT: Use setDate(1).)

c. Extract the day of the week from the calendarDay parameter and store the value in a variable named "weekDayNum". This value is the number of weekday in which the calendar month starts. A value of 0 means that the month starts on a Sunday, a value of 1 means the month starts on a Monday and so forth.

d. Write the tag "<tr>" to the Web page.

e. Create a For loop with a counter that ranges from the value 0 to less than the value of the weekDayNum variable, increasing by 1 with each loop. Within each loop, write the following code to the Web page:

```
<td></td>
```

This loop creates the blank table cells up to the first day of the month.

Explore

5. In the next part of the writeCalDays() function we write the actual calendar dates into the table. Each table row starts on a Sunday and ends on a Saturday. When we reach the day of the month that matches the date specified by the user, we want to highlight that day, distinguishing it from the others.

We also need a trick to tell us when to stop adding dates to the table. To do this we'll create two variables: cellCount and dayCount. The cellCount variable counts the number of table cells starting with the first day of the month. The dayCount variable calculates the day of the month based on the date stored in the calendarDay variable. As we proceed through the month, the cellCount and dayCount variables will increase together. The variables will continue to be equal (one table cell for each calendar day) until the cellCount value exceeds the total days of the month. At that point the two variables will be unequal because dayCount will drop back down to 1, representing the first day of the next month and we'll know that we've reached the end of the month and that we can stop adding table cells. To complete the writeCalDays() function, add the following commands:

a. Declare the cellCount and dayCount variables, setting their initial values to 1.

b. Create a While loop that will run only when cellCount is equal to dayCount. Within the while loop, do the following in order:

- If the value of the weekDayNum variable is equal to 0, write the "<tr>" tag to the Web page to start a new table row.
- If the value of the dayCount variable equals the value of the thisDay variable, then write the following code to the Web page:
  ```
  <td class="calendar_dates" id="calendar_today">dayCount</td>
  ```
  otherwise, write the following code:
  ```
  <td class="calendar_dates">dayCount</td>
  ```
- If the value of the weekDayNum variable is equal to 6, write the "</tr>" tag to the Web page to end the table row.
- Increase the value of cellCount by 1. This will lead to the next cell of the table.
- Use the setDate() method to change the day of the month of the calendarDay variable to cellCount. (HINT: Use setDate(cellCount).) Note that when the value of cellCount becomes greater than the total number of days in the month, the calendarDay variable will shift to the next month of the calendar. For example, the 31st day of November will be represented as the 1st day of December.
- Use the getDate() method to extract the day of the month from the calendarDay variable and store the value in the dayCount variable.
- Use the getDay() method to extract the day of the week from the calendarDay variable and store the value in the weekDayNum variable.

Explore

6. Finally, we create the calendar() function. The calendar() function has a single parameter named "thisDate", which is the date specified by the user to highlight in the calendar table. Add the following commands to the calendar() function:

a. If the value of thisDate is equal to the text string "today", create a date object named calDate to store the current date and time; otherwise create a date object named calDate with the date and time equal to value of the thisDate parameter.

b. Write the following tag to the Web page:
```
<table id="calendar_table">
```

c. Call the writeCalTitle() function, using calDate as the parameter value. This creates the first table row of the calendar, displaying the month and year.

d. Call the writeDayTitle() function. This creates the second table row of the calendar, displaying the weekday names.

e. Call the writeCalDays() function, using calDate as the parameter value. This writes the table rows containing the dates.

f. Write the following tag to the Web page to close the calendar table:
```
</tr></table>
```

7. Close the **calendar.js** file, saving your changes.

8. Return to the **bcc.htm** file in your text editor.

9. Within the head section of the file, directly below the link element that links the page to the bcc.css style sheet, insert a script element linking the file to the calendar.js script file.

10. Scroll down the file and locate the div element with the id "main". Directly above this element insert a script that calls the calendar() function using "April 8, 2006" as the parameter value. Be sure to enclose the date in quotes.

11. Save your changes to the file and open **bcc.htm** in your Web browser. Verify that it shows the monthly calendar for April, 2006 and that the 8th day of the month is highlighted. If the function doesn't work or an error is reported, check your code. Common sources of trouble are:

    - Using different uppercase and lowercase letters for variable names or misspelling a variable or function name.
    - Forgetting the opening or closing curly braces {} around the if, for, and while command blocks.
    - Forgetting the opening or closing quotes with the document.write() method.
    - Using the = symbol rather than the == symbol when comparing variable values in an if, for, or while statement.

12. Return to **bcc.htm** in your text editor and change the date value in the calendar() function from "April 8, 2006" to "today". Save your changes and reload the page in your browser to verify that it shows the calendar for the current month and that the current day is highlighted.

13. Submit your completed Web site to your instructor.

Case Problem 4

Create

Test your knowledge of JavaScript by creating a table of HTML character entities for a Web design page.

Data files needed for this Case Problem: chartxt.htm, wd.jpg

Web Design Chloe MacDonald runs a Web site that contains information on Web page design. She often finds it necessary to look up the character entity numbers for the Web pages that she designs. Chloe would like to have this information placed in an easy-to-use table for herself and for her readers. Rather than entering all 256 character entities into a table, she would like to use JavaScript to generate the table automatically for her. She's asked for your help in writing a JavaScript program to create a 16-by-16 table that displays the first 256 character entities with the entity number and corresponding symbol for each. The design and layout of the page is up to you. One possible solution is displayed in Figure 10-39.

Figure 10-39

Web Design

The following table lists the extended character set for HTML, also known as the ISO Latin-1 Character set. Characters can be entered into your HTML code using the form: &#*num*; where *num* is a number listed at the top of each cell in the adjacent table. For example to display the symbol ®, enter ® into your HTML code.

HTML Character Entities

1	2	3	4	5	6	7	8	9	10	11	12	13	14	15	16
□	□	□	□	□	□	□	□						□	□	□

17	18	19	20	21	22	23	24	25	26	27	28	29	30	31	32
□	□	□	□	□	□	□	□	□	□	□	□	□	□	□	

33	34	35	36	37	38	39	40	41	42	43	44	45	46	47	48
!	"	#	$	%	&	'	(	)	*	+	,	-	.	/	0

49	50	51	52	53	54	55	56	57	58	59	60	61	62	63	64
1	2	3	4	5	6	7	8	9	:	;	<	=	>	?	@

65	66	67	68	69	70	71	72	73	74	75	76	77	78	79	80
A	B	C	D	E	F	G	H	I	J	K	L	M	N	O	P

81	82	83	84	85	86	87	88	89	90	91	92	93	94	95	96
Q	R	S	T	U	V	W	X	Y	Z	[	\	]	^	_	`

97	98	99	100	101	102	103	104	105	106	107	108	109	110	111	112
a	b	c	d	e	f	g	h	i	j	k	l	m	n	o	p

113	114	115	116	117	118	119	120	121	122	123	124	125	126	127	128
q	r	s	t	u	v	w	x	y	z	{	|	}	~	□	€

129	130	131	132	133	134	135	136	137	138	139	140	141	142	143	144
□	‚	ƒ	„	…	†	‡	^	‰	Š	‹	Œ	□	Ž	□	□

145	146	147	148	149	150	151	152	153	154	155	156	157	158	159	160
`	'	"	"	•	–	—	~	™	š	›	œ	□	ž	Ÿ	

161	162	163	164	165	166	167	168	169	170	171	172	173	174	175	176
¡	¢	£	¤	¥	¦	§	¨	©	ª	«	¬		®	¯	°

177	178	179	180	181	182	183	184	185	186	187	188	189	190	191	192
±	²	³	´	µ	¶	·	¸	¹	º	»	¼	½	¾	¿	À

193	194	195	196	197	198	199	200	201	202	203	204	205	206	207	208
Á	Â	Ã	Ä	Å	Æ	Ç	È	É	Ê	Ë	Ì	Í	Î	Ï	Ð

209	210	211	212	213	214	215	216	217	218	219	220	221	222	223	224
Ñ	Ò	Ó	Ô	Õ	Ö	×	Ø	Ù	Ú	Û	Ü	Ý	Þ	ß	à

225	226	227	228	229	230	231	232	233	234	235	236	237	238	239	240
á	â	ã	ä	å	æ	ç	è	é	ê	ë	ì	í	î	ï	ð

241	242	243	244	245	246	247	248	249	250	251	252	253	254	255	256
ñ	ò	ó	ô	õ	ö	÷	ø	ù	ú	û	ü	ý	þ	ÿ	Ā

To create this Web page:

1. Using your text editor, open **chartxt.htm** from the tutorial.10/case4 folder. Enter *your name* and *the date* in the head section and save the file as **char.htm**.
2. Within the file, create a JavaScript program to generate the entity table. One way is to use a set of nested For loops using the following structure to increment the value of the k variable from 1 to 256.

```
k=1;
for (i = 1; i <= 16; i++) {
   for (j = 1; j <= 16; j++) {
      k++
   }
}
```

   - Within the inner For loop, write the individual table cells, sending the following code to the Web page:
   ```
   <td> k <br /> &#k; </td>
   ```
   where *k* is the value of the k variable in the structure defined above.

- Within the outer for loop, write tags to start and end each table row as follows:

```
for (i = 1; i <= 16; i++) {
    document.write("<tr>");
    for (j = 1; j <= 16; j++) {
        table cells
    }
    document.write("</tr>");
}
```

- Finally, outside the loops, write tags to start and close the table:

```
document.write("<table>");
for (i = 1; i <= 16; i++) {
    document.write("<tr>");
    for (j = 1; j <= 16; j++) {
        table cells
    }
    document.write("</tr>");
}
document.write("</table>");
```

3. Add whatever styles you wish to make the table more attractive or easier to read.
4. Include comments to document your finished code.
5. Submit the completed Web page to your instructor

Review

Quick Check Answers

Session 10.1

1. Disadvantages of using server-side programs include the following: a user must be connected to the Web server to run the script; only a programmer can create or alter the script; and the Web server's system administrator can place limitations on access to the script; and a server-side approach poses problems for the system administrator, who has to be concerned about users continually accessing the server and potentially overloading the system. Jobs such as running a search form or processing a purchase order must be run from a central server, because only the server contains the database needed to complete those types of operations.

2. Java is a compiled language; JavaScript is an interpreted language. Java requires a development kit to create executable applets; JavaScript does not. Java requires a Java virtual machine or interpreter to run the applet; JavaScript requires a browser that can interpret JavaScript code. Java source code is hidden from users; JavaScript source code is made accessible to users. Java is the more powerful of the two languages and requires programming knowledge and experience; JavaScript is simpler and requires less programming knowledge and experience. Java is more secure than JavaScript.

3. script

4. To prevent older browsers that do not support JavaScript from displaying the JavaScript commands on the Web page.

5. Character symbols such as "<", ">" and "&" are often used in JavaScript programs, which can lead to a page being rejected by an XHTML validator. However, because many browsers do not support CDATA sections, it is best to use only external scripts if this is a concern.

6. document.write("<h1>Avalon Books</h1>");

Session 10.2

1. numbers, strings, Boolean, and null values
2. var Now = new Date();
3. var Tdate = Now.getDate();
4. 8
5. Expressions are JavaScript commands that assign values to variables. Operators are elements that perform actions within expressions. Binary operators work on two elements in an expression. Unary operators work on only one variable.
6. function *function_name(parameters)* {

   ```
   JavaScript commands
   ```
   }

7. ```
var mortgage=calcMort(loan, interest, period);
```

### Session 10.3

1. ```
if (MonthName == "September") {
    document.write("Welcome back to school!");
}
```

2. ```
if (MonthName == "September") {
     document.write("Welcome back to school!");
} else {
   document.write("Today's Headlines");
}
```

3. ```
if (MonthName == "September")
     document.write("Welcome back to school!");
} else {
   if(MonthName == "June") {
      document.write("Summer's here!")
   } else {
      document.write("Today's headlines");
   }
}
```

   OR

   ```
switch (MonthName) {
  case "September": document.write("Welcome back to school!");
  break;
  case "June": document.write("Summer's here!");
  break;
  default: document.write("Today's headlines");
}
```

4. An array is an ordered collection of values referenced by a single variable name.

   ```
var Colors = new Array();
```

5. var Colors = new Array("Red", "Green", "Blue", "Black", "White");
6. A program loop is a set of instructions that is executed repeatedly. There are two types of loops: loops that repeat a set number of times before quitting (For loops) and loops that repeat until a certain condition is met (While loops.)
7. ```
for (i=1; i<=5; i++) {
     document.write("News Flash!
");
}
```

8. 5, 10, 15, 20, 25
```

Objectives

- Apply a common style to a Web site
- Work with embedded, inline, and external style sheets
- Transfer text content into a Web page
- Work with table and form elements

Creating a Company Web Site

Case

FrostiWear Winter Clothes

FrostiWear is a company that specializes in winter clothing and gear. About 20% of the company's sales come from its Web site. Susan Crawford, the director of the company's Web development team, has asked you to make some changes to the company's Web site. She would like you to work on the site's main page and also some of the pages that describe FrostiWear's gloves and other handwear. She's provided you with a list of popular products that she would like you to add to the company's Web site. Later, after she approves your work, she'll ask you to add the complete company line, which includes more than 35 styles of gloves and mittens.

Apply

Use the skills you've learned in this book to create a company Web site.

Additional Case 1

Data files needed for this Case Problem: arcticb.jpg, fless.jpg, flogo.jpg, form.txt, frosttxt.htm, glomitt.jpg, gloves.jpg, glovetxt.htm, gordtxt.htm, gprodtxt.htm, gsummary.txt, polyflce.jpg, products.txt, sweaters.jpg

FrostiWear Susan gives you some of the data files used in FrostiWear's Web site. The first page you'll work on is the site's main page. The file she's given you contains the main content, but little formatting. She wants you to design a style sheet for the page's content. The style sheet will then be used for other pages in the site as well. Figure AC1-1 shows a preview of the main page you'll create for Susan.

Figure AC1-1

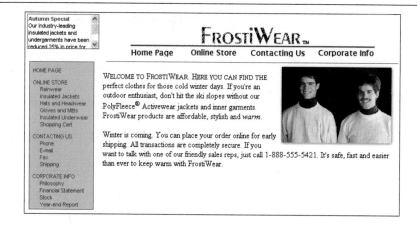

To complete this assignment:

1. Using your text editor, open **frosttxt.htm** from the tutorial.add/case1 folder. Enter *your name* and *the date* in the head section and save the file as **frosti.htm**.

2. Below the flogo.jpg inline image, insert an image map named "logo" with the following hotspots:
   - A rectangular hotspot with coordinates (0, 55) (100, 76) linked to the frosti.htm file. Use the alternate text "Home Page" for the hotspot.
   - A rectangular hotspot with coordinates (124, 55) (226, 76) linked to the store.htm file. Use the alternate text "Online Store" for the hotspot.
   - A rectangular hotspot with coordinates (247, 55) (366, 76) linked to the contact.htm file. Use the alternate text "Contacting Us" for the hotspot.
   - A rectangular hotspot with coordinates (386, 55) (508, 76) linked to the info.htm file. Use the alternate text "Corporate Info" for the hotspot.

3. Apply the logo image map to the flogo.jpg inline image.

4. Within the links div element, place the following links in the "mainlink" class: frosti.htm, store.htm, contact.htm, and info.htm. Put the rest of the links in the "sublink" class.

5. In the main div element, use an inline style to float the sweaters.jpg image on the right margin. Set the size of the margin around the image to 5 pixels.

6. Locate the word "PolyFleece" in the first paragraph of the main div element and after that word insert the registered trademark symbol ®, displayed as a superscript.

7. Within the special div element, place the text "Autumn Special" within a span element.

8. Save your changes to the **frosti.htm** file and then use your text editor to create a file named **frosti.css** in the tutorial.add/case1 folder. At the top of the file, insert *your name* and *the date* as CSS comments.

9. Within the **frosti.css** external style sheet, insert the following styles:
   - Set the body background color to white.
   - Display all headings in a blue Arial, Helvetica, or sans-serif font.
   - Float the element with the links id on the page's left margin. Set the width to 135 pixels and the padding to 2 pixels. Set the background color to the value (192, 192, 255). Add a 1-pixel-wide solid border with the color value (0, 0, 153).
   - Any linked text within the links div element should be displayed as a block element in an 8-point Arial, Helvetica, or sans-serif font. There should be no text decoration. Set the size of the left margin for the linked text to 5 pixels. The color of the linked text should be the value (0, 0, 153) in all cases. When the mouse hovers over that linked text, the background color should change to white. Linked text that belongs to the mainlink class should be displayed in uppercase letters with a top margin of 10 pixels. Linked text belonging to the sublink class should be indented 15 pixels.
   - The content of the head div element font should be horizontally centered. The size of the left margin should be set to 160 pixels. Add a solid 1-pixel-wide border to the bottom of the section with the color value (0, 0, 153).
   - Set the border width of the inline image within the head div element to 0 pixels.
   - Set the size of the left margin of the main div element to 150 pixels.
   - Display the first line of the paragraph with the id "firstp" in small caps.
   - Use absolute positioning to place the special div element at the page coordinates (5, 5). Set the dimensions of the element to 150 pixels wide by 70 pixels high. Set the padding to 2 pixels. Add a solid blue 1-pixel-wide border to the element. Have scrollbars displayed automatically if the element's content exceeds its size. Display the text of the element in an 8-point Arial, Helvetica, or sans-serif font.
   - Display the content of the span element nested within the special div element in a blue bold font.

10. Save your changes to **frosti.css** and then return to the **frosti.htm** file in your text editor. Insert a link to the frosti.css style sheet and then save your changes. Open **frosti.htm** in your Web browser and verify that it closely resembles the page shown in Figure AC1-1 (there may be slight differences depending on the browser).

11. Using your text editor, open **glovetxt.htm** from the tutorial.add/case1 folder. Enter *your name* and *the date* in the head section and save the file as **gloves.htm**. Figure AC1-2 shows a preview of the completed gloves page.

12. To complete the gloves page, copy the code for the head, links, main, and special div elements from the **frosti.htm** page into **gloves.htm**. Create a link to the **frosti.css** style sheet. Replace the content of the main div element with the text in the gsummary.txt file and then add the following markup elements to the content of the main div element:

   - Mark the heading "Gloves and Mitts" as an h1 heading.
   - Directly above the h1 heading, insert the gloves.jpg inline image, floated on the page's right margin with a margin width of 5 pixels.
   - Mark the three paragraphs of the text in the main div element.
   - In the second paragraph, change the text "Fingerless Gloves" into a link pointing to the FLess anchor in the gproduct.htm file. Change the text "PolyFleece mitts" into a link pointing to the PolyF anchor in the gproduct.htm file. Change "Glomitt" into a link pointing to the Glomitt anchor in the gproduct.htm file. Finally, change the text "ArcticBlast Gore-Tex mitts" into a link pointing to the ArcticBlast anchor within the gproduct.htm file.
   - In the second paragraph, change the text "online order form" into a link pointing to the gorder.htm file.

13. Change the text of the special div element to: "Glove Special Enjoy savings of 10% on all Glomitts - this week only at FrostiWear". Place the text "Glove Special" in a span element and insert a line break between "Glove Special" and the remaining text.

14. Save your changes to the file and open **gloves.htm** in your Web browser. Verify that the content and layout resemble that shown in Figure AC1-2.

15. Using your text editor, open **gprodtxt.htm** from the tutorial.add/case1 folder. Enter *your name* and *the date* in the head section and save the file as **gproduct.htm**. Copy the structure of the head, links, main, and div elements from the **frosti.htm** file. Use the same content for the special div element as you did in the **gloves.htm** file. Figure AC1-3 shows a preview of the completed page of glove products.

Figure AC1-3

Member's Discount
Become a FrostiWear member and receive a 5% discount on all merchandise!

FROSTIWEAR ™

Home Page   Online Store   Contacting Us   Corporate Info

HOME PAGE

ONLINE STORE
   Rainwear
   Insulated Jackets
   Hats and Headwear
   Gloves and Mitts
   Insulated Underwear
   Shopping Cart

CONTACTING US
   Phone
   E-mail
   Fax
   Shipping

CORPORATE INFO
   Philosophy
   Financial Statement
   Stock
   Year-end Report

Fingerless Gloves

Our Fingerless Glove design keeps your hands warm, while at the same time allowing greater dexterity in performing outdoor tasks. The gloves are made of lightweight, warm, and quick-drying PolyFleece. As with all of our products, the glove features inline cross-stitching for improved durability. Order online.

Specification	Description
Product ID	G725
Color	Burgundy, Red, Black, Gray
Size	Small, Medium, Large, XLarge
Price	$28.00

PolyFleece Mitts

Our PolyFleece is perfect for hiking, snowshoeing, or winter walks. Made with quick-drying PolyFleece, these gloves will keep your hands warm even when wet. The long cuff made of PolyFleece adds an extra layer of warmth and protection. Order online.

Specification	Description
Product ID	G726
Color	Burgundy, Red, Black, Gray
Size	Small, Medium, Large, XLarge
Price	$38.00

Glomitts

Our Glomitts represent the best of both worlds. The mitts fold back to allow you to work with your fingers for maximum dexterity. After your work is through, slip the mitt hood back over your fingers for warmth and comfort. The Glomitt is made from a blend of 75% wool and 25% synthetic fabric for extra comfort, warmth, and durability. Order online.

Specification	Description
Product ID	G727
Color	Burgundy, Red, Black, Gray
Size	Small, Medium, Large, XLarge
Price	$18.00

ArticBlast Gore-Tex Mitts

For the serious outdoor enthusiast, the ArticBlast Gore-Tex mitt provides maximum protection against the frigid cold. The ArticBlast provides PolyFleece mitt inserts for comfort and added protection, eliminating the uncomfortable feel of traditional high performance gloves. The outer shell provides tough palm grips, great for grasping ski poles or ice axes in severe weather conditions. Order online.

Specification	Description
Product ID	G728
Color	Burgundy, Red, Black, Gray
Size	Small, Medium, Large, XLarge
Price	$98.00

16. Copy the text from the **products.txt** file into the content of the main div element. Add the following markup to the content:
    - Mark the four headings as h3 headings with the following ids: FLess, PolyF, Glomitt, and ArcticBlast.
    - Mark each product description as a paragraph.
    - Within each paragraph, change the text "Order Online" to a link pointing to the gorder.htm file.
17. Below each paragraph, insert a table describing the product ids, colors, sizes, and prices of each model. Figure AC1-4 lists the content of the table for each product.

Figure AC1-4

Models	Specifications	Descriptions
Fingerless Gloves	Product ID	G725
	Color	Burgundy, Red, Black, Gray
	Size	Small, Medium, Large, XLarge
	Price	$28.00
PolyFleece Mitts	Product ID	G726
	Color	Burgundy, Red, Black, Gray
	Size	Small, Medium, Large, XLarge
	Price	$38.00
Glomitts	Product ID	G727
	Color	Burgundy, Red, Black, Gray
	Size	Small, Medium, Large, XLarge
	Price	$18.00
ArcticBlast Gore-Text Mitts	Product ID	G728
	Color	Burgundy, Red, Black, Gray
	Size	Small, Medium, Large, XLarge
	Price	$98.00

The tables should be marked up as follows:
- Each table should have a 2-pixel-wide border and belong to the class, "ptable."
- The first cell of the first row should contain an inline image of the glove product. The image files are fless.jpg, polyflce.jpg, glomitt.jpg, and arcticb.jpg. Set the alternate text for the inline images to an empty text string. The table cell should span five rows.
- The next two cells of the first row should contain table headings. The first table heading should contain the text "Specification" and belong to the class "spec". The second table heading should contain the text "Description" and belong to the class "desc".
- Add four additional rows to each table containing the product id, color, size, and price data shown in Figure AC1-4.

18. Add links to the file, accessing the style sheets **frosti.css** and **ptables.css** (you'll create this style sheet file next). Close the file, saving your changes.

19. Use your text editor to create a file named **ptables.css** in the tutorial.add/case1 folder. At the top of the file, insert *your name* and *the date* as CSS comments.

20. Within the **ptables.css** external style sheet, insert the following styles:
    - Set the font size of text in tables belonging to the ptable class to 8 point.
    - Display the text of any table heading within a ptable class table in a blue Arial, Helvetica, or sans-serif font.
    - Set the width of any table heading belonging to the spec class within a ptable class table to 100 pixels.
    - Set the width of any table heading belonging to the desc class within a ptable class table to 300 pixels.

21. Close the **ptables.css** file, saving your changes, and then open **gproduct.htm** in your Web browser, verifying that the layout and content of the page resemble that shown in Figure AC1-3.

22. Using your text editor, open **gordtxt.htm** from the tutorial.add/case1 folder. Enter *your name* and *the date* in the head section and save the file as **gorder.htm**. Copy the structure of the head, links, main, and div elements from the **frosti.htm** file. Link the file to the **frosti.css** style sheet. Figure AC1-5 shows a preview of the completed glove order form.

Figure AC1-5

23. Replace the content of the main div element with the following:
    - Add an h1 heading "Gloves and Mitts Order Form".
    - Below the h1 heading, insert the paragraph: "Go to the Gloves and Mitts page to learn more about our products and styles." Change the text "Gloves and Mitts" to a link pointing to the **gloves.htm** file.

24. Below that paragraph, insert a form element using the design shown in Figure AC1-5 and the form text stored in the **form.txt** file. The form should contain the following markup:
    - The form id is "order". When the form is submitted, it should access the cgi script at *http://www.frostiwear.com/cgi/cart*.
    - Each of the five numbered items and the pair of form buttons should be placed within a separate paragraph.
    - The first input element is a checkbox with the id name "club_yn". Set the text, "I am a FrostiWear Club Member" as the label for this checkbox.
    - The second input element is the input box with the id name "clubid". The size of the input box should be set to 10 characters and the default text should be "FC-######". Set the text "Club ID:" as the label for this input box.
    - The third input element is a selection list containing the four brand names and prices. The id of the selection list is "brand" and the label is the text string "Brand:".
    - The fourth and fifth input elements are option buttons that belong to the gender field. The id of the first option button is "male" and the second is "female". Define the text strings "Male" and "Female" as labels for their respective option buttons.
    - The sixth input element is a selection list containing the four glove sizes. The id of the selection list is "size" and the label is the text string "Size: ".
    - The seventh input element is a selection list containing the four glove colors. The id of the selection list is "color" and the label is the text string "Color: ".
    - The form contains two buttons: a submit button displaying the text "Add to Shopping Cart" and a reset button with the text "Reset Form".

25. Add an embedded style sheet at the top of the file containing the following styles:
    - The form element should be displayed on an ivory background with a 1-pixel-wide solid blue border.
    - The padding within the form element should be set to 5 pixels.
    - The font color of input elements and select elements should be blue.

26. Change the text of the special div element to "Member's Discount Become a FrostiWear member and receive a 5% discount on all merchandise!". Place the text "Member's Discount" in a span element and insert a line break between "Member's Discount" and the remaining text.

27. Save your changes to the **gorder.htm** file and then open it in your Web browser, verifying that the layout and content resemble the page shown in Figure AC1-5.

28. Reopen the **gloves.htm** file in your Web browser and verify that the links between the different pages work correctly. (Most of the links in the navigation bars on the top and left of the page will not work because the pages they link to do not yet exist.)

29. Submit the completed Web site to your instructor.

Objectives

- Apply a common style to a Web site
- Work with embedded, inline, and external style sheets
- Transfer text content into a Web page

Designing a Style for a Web Site

Case

Mayer Photography

Mayer Photography is a family-owned photography studio founded by Ted and Jane Mayer in 1972. They've created a successful business in Elmridge, New Hampshire, and the neighboring communities. Ted recently approached you to create a Web site for his studio. Ted envisions four Web pages for his Web site: a home page that describes the company and provides contact information for customers, a page describing the company's wedding services, a page devoted to the company's portrait services, and a final page that will describe monthly specials offered by the company. You'll design the site using some material supplied by Ted.

Additional Case 2

Data files needed for this Case Problem: address.txt, comment1.jpg, comment1.txt, comment2.jpg, comment2.txt, comment3.jpg, comment3.txt, comment4.jpg, comment4.txt, couple.jpg, family.jpg, guitar.jpg, mayer.txt, mayertxt.htm, portraits.txt, porttxt.htm, slides.gif, specials.txt, spectxt.htm, wedding.avi, wedding.jpg, wedding.mov, weddings.txt, weddtxt.htm

Mayer Photography   Ted Mayer wants you to create four Web pages, named mayer.htm, weddings.htm, portraits.htm, and specials.htm. He has collected four recommendations from Mayer Photography customers that he would like to include on each of the four pages. He has also provided text files containing the general text that he wants you to place on the Web site. In addition, Ted has given you image files containing samples of his company's work. Because Mayer Photography has lately been involved in providing video services for weddings, he has also provided a video clip (in AVI and QuickTime formats) that he would like you to add to the Web page describing the company's wedding services. You'll start by creating the mayer.htm page, and then you'll apply the design used in that page to the remaining three pages. Figure AC2-1 shows a preview of the completed home page for Mayer Photography.

Figure AC2-1

To complete this assignment:

1. Using your text editor, open **mayertxt.htm** from the tutorial.add/case2 folder. Enter *your name* and *the date* in the head section and save the file as **mayer.htm**.
2. At the top of the page body, insert a div element with the id "header" containing the inline image "mlogo.jpg". The alternate text for the image should be "Mayer Photography". Insert an inline style that sets the border width of the image to 0 pixels.
3. Below the inline image (but still within the header div element) create an image map named "MSites" containing the following polygonal hotspots:
   - A hotspot with coordinates (3, 83)(20, 69)(40, 66)(60, 69)(81, 83)(60, 97)(40, 100)(20, 97) linked to the mayer.htm file with the alternate text, "Home".

- A hotspot with coordinates (103, 83)(120, 69)(140, 66)(160, 69)(181, 83)(160, 97)(140, 100)(120, 97) linked to the weddings.htm file with the alternate text, "Weddings".
- A hotspot with coordinates (203, 83)(220, 69)(240, 66)(260, 69)(281, 83)(260, 97)(240, 100)(220, 97) linked to the portraits.htm file with the alternate text, "Portraits".
- A hotspot with coordinates (303, 83)(320, 69)(340, 66)(360, 69)(381, 83)(360, 97)(340, 100)(320, 97) linked to the specials.htm file with the alternate text, "Specials".

4. Apply the image map to the mlogo.jpg inline image.

5. Below the image map (but still within the header div element) insert a second inline image for the slides.gif image file. Specify an empty text string for the alternate text.

6. Below the header div element, insert a table with the id "linktable". The table should have a 1-pixel-wide border. The table frame should be set to "above", and the table rules should be set to "cols". The table should have one row containing four table header cells. Within each cell, insert links to the four Mayer Photography Web pages with the link text: "Home", "Weddings", "Portraits", and "Specials".

7. Below the table, insert a div element with the class name "comments". The comments div element should contain the following three paragraphs:
   - The first paragraph should contain the inline image "comment1.jpg". The alternate text for this image should be an empty text string.
   - The second paragraph should contain the tribute from the comment1.txt file.
   - The third paragraph should contain the byline of the author of the comment in the comment1.txt file.

8. Below the comments div element, insert the content of the mayer.txt file. The headings in the file should be marked as h2 headings. Mark the other text as paragraphs.

9. At the start of the first paragraph, insert the guitar.jpg inline image. Use an inline style to float the image on the right page margin and set the size of the top, right, bottom, and left image margins to 5, 0, 5, and 5 pixels.

10. Within the first paragraph, link the text "portraits" to the portraits.htm file, and the text "weddings" to the weddings.htm file.

11. Below the second paragraph, insert an address element containing the text from the address.txt file. Insert a line break between "Mayer Photography" and the rest of the address information. Insert a middle dot character between the street address and the city, and between the postal code and the phone number.

12. Within the head element, insert an embedded style sheet with the following styles:
    - Display linked text in a brown font.
    - Set the background color of elements with the class named "comments" to brown.
    - Display all headings in a brown font.

13. Above the embedded style sheet, insert a link to the mayer.css style sheet (you'll create this file next). Save your changes and close the file.

14. Use your text editor to create the **mayer.css** file in the tutorial.add/case2 folder. Insert CSS comments at the top of the file containing *your name* and *the date*. Within the file, insert the following styles:

    - Set the body background color to white, the font color to black, and the page margin to 2 pixels.
    - Horizontally center the content of the header div element.
    - Set the width of the linktable table to 100% of the page width. Set the font size of the text in the table to 10 point. Set the size of the top and bottom margins to 5 pixels.
    - Set the width of table headers within the linktable table to 25% of the table width.
    - Remove the underlining from links within the linktable table, set their color to black and their width to 100% of their parent element.
    - When a mouse hovers over links in the linktable table, change the background color to yellow.
    - Display headings, the content of the elements belonging to the comments class, and the content of the linktable table in an Arial, Helvetica, or sans-serif font.
    - Float elements belong to the comments class on the page's left margin; set the width of the element to 180 pixels, the padding to 5 pixels, the text color to white, and the font size to 8 point.
    - Display addresses in an 8-point Arial, Helvetica, or sans-serif font. Add a 1-pixel, solid black border. Horizontally center the address text. Display the address only when the left margin is clear.

15. Save your changes to **mayer.css**. Open **mayer.htm** in your Web browser and verify that the layout and content of the page resemble that shown in Figure AC2-1.

16. Use your text editor to open **weddtxt.htm** from the tutorial.add/case2 folder. Enter *your name* and *the date* in the head section and save the file as **weddings.htm**. Figure AC2-2 shows a preview of the completed Web page.

Figure AC2-2

17. Use the same layout for this page as you did for the mayer.htm file. Use the text from the **weddings.txt** and **comment2.txt** files for the page content. Use the **comment2.jpg** inline image for the comments image and **wedding.jpg** for the inline image displayed in the page's first paragraph. Link the page to the **mayer.css** style sheet.

18. Italicize the words "Draybeck Video Services" in the page's second paragraph.

19. Just above the address, insert a centered embedded video clip using either the wedding.avi or wedding.mov file (depending on which video format your browser supports). Set the dimensions of the clip to 120 pixels wide by 120 pixels high.

20. If a customer's browser does not support embedded media, have the page instead display a link to the wedding.avi and wedding.mov files. Include information on the size and format of each video clip.

21. Change the color scheme of the embedded style from brown to the color value (153, 102, 255).

22. Save your changes to the file and open it in your Web browser. Verify that the layout and content resemble that shown in Figure AC2-2.

23. Use your text editor to open **porttxt.htm** from the tutorial.add/case2 folder. Enter *your name* and *the date* in the head section and save the file as **portraits.htm**. Figure AC2-3 shows a preview of the completed Web page.

Figure AC2-3

24. Use the same layout for this page as you did for the earlier files. Use the text from the **portraits.txt** and **comment3.txt** files for the page content. Use the **comment3.jpg** inline image for the comments image and **family.jpg** for the inline image displayed in the page's first paragraph. Link the page to the **mayer.css** style sheet.

25. Change the color scheme in the embedded style to the color value (0, 102, 153).

26. Save your changes to the file and open it in your Web browser. Verify that the layout and content resemble that shown in Figure AC2-3.

27. Use your text editor to open **spectxt.htm** from the tutorial.add/case2 folder. Enter *your name* and *the date* in the head section and save the file as **specials.htm**. Figure AC2-4 shows a preview of the completed Web page.

Figure AC2-4

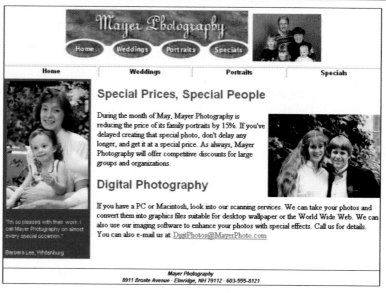

28. Use the same layout for this page as you did with the other three pages. Use the text from the **specials.txt** and **comment4.txt** files for the page content. Use the **comment4.jpg** inline image for the comments image and **couple.jpg** for the inline image displayed in the page's first paragraph. Link the page to the **mayer.css** style sheet.

29. Change the color scheme in the embedded style to the color value (0, 102, 0).

30. Change the e-mail address in the second paragraph to a link.

31. Save your changes to the file and open it in your Web browser. Verify that the layout and content resemble that shown in Figure AC2-4. Also verify that the links in the linktable table and the image map correctly open the different pages in the Web site.

32. Submit the completed Web site to your instructor.

Objectives

- Design and create an online newsletter Web site
- Format the newsletter using tables, styles, special fonts, and other layout features
- Create an image map containing a hotspot for each page in the Web site
- Create a JavaScript program that displays the current date
- Insert a scrolling banner Java applet that displays a list of events
- Create an online survey form containing several form elements

Creating an Online Newsletter

Case

Twin Life Magazine

Twin Life is a magazine created for parents of twins, triplets, and other multiple-birth children. Recently the company has decided to go online and publish parts of its monthly magazine on the Web. Elise Howard, the magazine's editor, has asked you to create a Web site for the content of *Twin Life*. You've been given a disk containing text files of the articles she wants you to add and image files she wants placed on the site.

Create

Use the skills you've learned in this book to create a Web site for an online newsletter.

Additional Case 3

Data files needed for this Case Problem: calendar.txt, chicago.txt, CreditRoll.class, deliver.jpg, deliver.txt, editor.txt, howard.jpg, kerkman.jpg, kuhlman.jpg, lasker.jpg, lawson.jpg, mbirths.txt, rates.txt, recipe.txt, roles.txt, staff.txt, survey.txt, talk.txt, twinlogo.gif, twins.jpg, twintips.txt

Twin Life You and Elise meet to discuss the design and content of the Web site. Elise envisions a total of five Web pages for the site: a front page, a news page, a monthly features page, a page of special articles, and a customer survey page. Figure AC3-1 lists the files that you should use for each page of the Web site. You are free to supplement these files with any other appropriate material.

Figure AC3-1 ▶ **Files for the *Twin Life* Web site**

Web Page	File(s)	File Description
Front page		
	twinlogo.gif	The magazine logo
	twins.jpg	An image of twins to be used on the front page
	editor.txt	A message from the editor
	howard.jpg	An image of the editor
	staff.txt	A list of the magazine's staff
	calendar.txt	A list of upcoming events (to be displayed as scrolling text via a Java applet)
News		
	chicago.txt	An article on a convention in Chicago of mothers of multiple births
	lasker.jpg	An image of the author of the Chicago article
	rates.txt	An article on twin birth rates
	mbirths.txt	An article on the increase in multiple-birth pregnancies
Features		
	twintips.txt	Twin Tips question and answer forum
	lawson.jpg	An image of the author of Twin Tips
	deliver.jpg	Image of the month
	deliver.txt	Text to accompany the photo of the month
	recipe.txt	The recipe of the month
Articles		
	roles.txt	An article on the roles that twins play
	kerkman.jpg	An image of the author of the Roles article
	talk.txt	An article on how twins acquire speech
	kuhlman.jpg	An image of the author of the Talk article
Survey	survey.txt	The text of the online survey form

The actual design of the pages in the Web site is up to you, but it should incorporate the following features:

- The completed Web site should be written to the standards of transitional XHTML. You must validate each file in the Web site.
- The files of the Web site you create should be named twinlife.htm, news.htm, feature.htm, articles.htm, and survey.htm.

- Each Web page should have a title, and you need to specify a style for the colors of the background, text, and linked text.
- The front page should display a message containing the current date—for example, "Today is 11/4/2006."
- The magazine's logo (twinlogo.gif) should include an image map linking to the five Web pages in the Web site. You will have to determine the coordinates for each hotspot using either your image-editing software or an image map editor.
- The pages should use tables or styles to format the layout of the different articles in the newsletter. There should be at least one example of an article that has a different background color from the rest.
- The list of upcoming events (found in the calendar.txt file) should be displayed in a scrolling window, using the CreditRoll.class Java applet. You need to determine the values of each parameter in the applet, aside from the TEXTx parameters.
- Any text in an article that refers to the content of another article should be changed to a link pointing to that article.
- A Submit button and a Reset button should be included with the online survey form. The form should be submitted to a CGI script at *http://www.twinlifemag.com/cgi/survey*.

New Perspectives on

HTML, XHTML, and DHTML

Read This Before You Begin: Tutorials 11–16

To the Student

Data Files

To complete the Level IV DHTML Tutorials (Tutorials 11–16), you need the starting student Data Files. Your instructor will either provide you with these Data Files or ask you to obtain them yourself.

The Level IV DHTML Tutorials require the folders shown to complete the Tutorials, Review Assignments, and Case Problems. You will need to copy these folders from a file server, a standalone computer, or the Web to the drive and folder where you will be storing your Data Files.

Your instructor will tell you which computer, drive letter, and folder(s) contain the files you need. You can also download the files by going to www.course.com; see the inside back or front cover for more information on

downloading the files, or ask your instructor or technical support person for assistance.

▼**DHTML**

Tutorial.11
Tutorial.12
Tutorial.13
Tutorial.14
Tutorial.15
Tutorial.16

▼**Student Online Companion**

The Student Online Companion can be found at *www.course.com/carey*. It contains additional information to supplement what you are learning in the text, as well as links to downloads and other tools.

To the Instructor

The Data Files are available on the Instructor Resources CD for this title. Follow the instructions in the Help file on the CD to install the programs to your network or standalone computer. See the "To the Student" section above for information on how to set up the Data Files that accompany this text.

You are granted a license to copy the Data Files to any computer or computer network used by students who have purchased this book.

System Requirements

If you are going to work through this book using your own computer, you need:

• **System Requirements** A text editor, and a Web browser that supports the current standards for HTML and either the W3C or Internet Explorer Document Object Model. Browsers meeting these requirements include the 6.0 (and higher) versions of Internet Explorer, Netscape, and Opera, and the 1.0 (and higher) versions of Safari for Macintosh and Firefox.

We do not recommend use of a Netscape 4 level browser or Internet Explorer 5.2 for the Macintosh, as both browsers have compatibility issues with current standards. Users who wish to understand how to write code for Netscape 4 level browsers can review the material in Appendix J.

• **Data Files** You will not be able to complete the tutorials or exercises in this book using your own computer until you have the necessary starting Data Files.

Objectives

Session 11.1
- Define DHTML and describe its uses
- Understand objects, properties, methods, and the document object model
- Distinguish between different object models
- Work with object references and object collections
- Modify an object's properties
- Apply a method to an object
- Create a cross-browser Web site using object detection

Session 11.2
- Work with the style object to change the styles associated with an object
- Write functions to apply positioning styles to an object

Session 11.3
- Insert event handlers to run a script in response to an event
- Place a JavaScript command in a link
- Run timed-delay and timed-interval commands
- Work with the properties of the display window
- Describe the techniques of linear and path animation

Working with Objects

Creating an Animated Web Page

Case

Avalon Books

Avalon Books is a popular bookstore chain, with several stores scattered throughout the western United States and Canada. In recent years, Avalon Books has begun to make its products available online. You've been hired as part of the Web site development team.

Your supervisor, Terry Schuler, wants you to create the opening screen for the company's Web site. The page should be visually interesting, with eye-catching motion and graphics. Some of this can be done with animated GIFs and Java applets, but Terry doesn't want too many of these kinds of elements because they take longer to load. If the browser doesn't promptly display the page, potential customers might be unlikely to wait, and will do their shopping elsewhere. Terry doesn't want the total size of the page and associated elements to be more than 40 KB.

You can add animation to a page without the overhead of extra applets or large graphics by using JavaScript to move, hide, and re-display the objects in the page. You decide to investigate how to use JavaScript to create these effects.

Student Data Files

▼tutorial.11

▽ tutorial folder	▽ review folder	▽ case1 folder
abtxt.htm	abtxt2.htm	golftxt.htm
scripttxt.js	indextxt.htm	golftxt.js
styles.css	script2txt.js	ballpath.txt
+1 demo file	styles2.css	styles.css
+4 graphic files	+ 5 graphic files	+ 3 graphic files

Session 11.1

Introduction to DHTML

Early in the development of HTML, Web page authors were limited to creating completely static Web pages—pages whose content and layout were fixed after being downloaded from their Web servers. As the Web became an increasingly important vehicle for sharing information, Web page authors and Web browser developers began to look for ways to create dynamic pages—pages whose content and style could be modified after being loaded, in response to events such as a reader's actions. Some early attempts involved the use of applets that the Web browser would retrieve and install along with the Web page.

The 4.0 and later versions of Netscape and Internet Explorer allowed for a new approach, in which the HTML code itself supported dynamic elements. Unlike applets, no additional software was needed to create and display dynamic Web pages—only browsers capable of working with JavaScript. These enhancements were known collectively as **dynamic HTML**, or **DHTML**. DHTML involves the interaction of three aspects of Web design:

- A page's HTML/XHTML code
- A style sheet that defines the styles used in the page
- A script, usually written in either JavaScript or VBScript, to control the behavior of elements on the page

DHTML is not a separate language. Instead, it can be thought of as a collection of programming techniques that use the scripting language to modify a Web page's contents or styles after the page is initially rendered by the browser. In this way, the Web page author can create documents that dynamically interact with users. Some uses for DHTML that you may have seen include:

- Animated text that moves and changes in response to user action
- Pop-up menus that provide users with quick access to other pages in a Web site without devoting valuable screen space to a long, complicated list of links
- Rollovers in which images and text change in response to mouse pointer movement
- Web pages that retrieve their content from external data sources, giving Web page authors more freedom in the types of materials they can display in their pages
- Elements that can be dragged from one location on the page and dropped at another

In the following tutorials, you'll examine how to create these effects and more. In the current tutorial, you'll study how to use DHTML to add animated effects to the Avalon Books Web site. Let's first look at the opening page of the Avalon Books Web site.

To open the Web page:

1. Use your text editor to open **abtxt.htm** from the tutorial.11/tutorial folder. Enter *your name* and *the date* in the comment section and save the file as **avalon.htm**.

2. Scroll through the contents of the file and familiarize yourself with the page's elements.

3. Open **avalon.htm** in your Web browser. Figure 11-1 shows the current appearance of the page.

The Avalon Books opening page | **Figure 11-1**

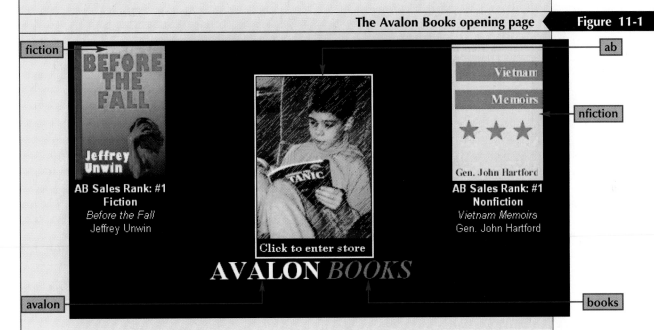

The page contains five different items placed in separate div elements. These items and their id values are:

- An image of Avalon Books' best-selling fiction book (id="fiction")
- An image of Avalon Books' best-selling nonfiction book (id="nfiction")
- An image of a person reading a book, which contains a link to the rest of Avalon Books' Web site (id="ab")
- The text string "Avalon" (id="avalon")
- The text string "Books" (id="books")

The position of each item on the page is set using absolute positioning with an external style sheet. Terry wants you to change this page from a static layout to a dynamic one by adding the following animated effects (see Figure 11-2):

- The word "Avalon" should appear near the top of the document window and then drop vertically down the page.
- After "Avalon" has dropped down the page, the word "Books" should appear from behind it moving from left to right.
- After the word "Books" has finished moving, the other three items should appear on the screen in sequence.

Figure 11-2 ▶ Terry's plan for animating the Avalon Books' opening page

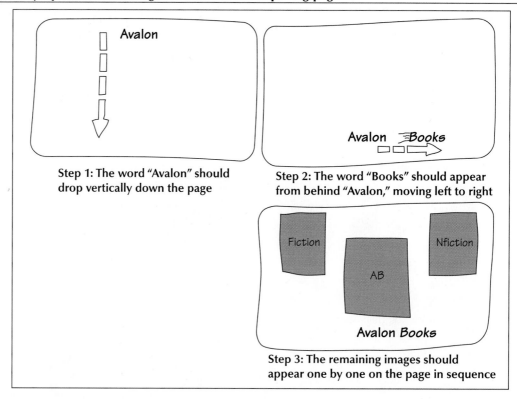

Step 1: The word "Avalon" should drop vertically down the page

Step 2: The word "Books" should appear from behind "Avalon," moving left to right

Step 3: The remaining images should appear one by one on the page in sequence

To create these effects, you first need to know how to use JavaScript to work with different page objects. Let's start by examining what we mean by the term "object."

Understanding JavaScript Objects

JavaScript is an **object-based language,** which means that it is based on manipulating objects by modifying their properties or by applying methods to them. That definition might sound complex, but the concept is simple. An **object** is any item associated with a Web page or Web browser. Each object has **properties** that describe its appearance, purpose, or behavior. Each object also has **methods,** which are actions that can be performed with the object or to it.

JavaScript objects are similar to most everyday objects you come into contact with. Take an oven as an example. It has certain properties, such as model name, age, size, and temperature. There are certain methods you can perform with the oven, such as turning on the grill or the self-cleaner. Some of these methods change the properties of the oven, such as the oven's temperature when you're preheating it.

Similarly, your Web browser has its own set of objects, properties, and methods. The Web browser itself is an object, and the page you're viewing is also an object. If the page contains frames, each frame is an object, and if the page contains a form, the form and any fields it contains are objects. A paragraph is also an object, and the text within that paragraph can be considered its own object.

Each of these objects has its own set of properties. The browser object has a property that indicates its type, such as Netscape or Internet Explorer, and another that indicates its version. A form object has a name or id property that distinguishes it from other forms. An object that has been placed on a page has properties for its page coordinates. Most objects also have methods. You apply a method to the browser when you open it, close it, reload its contents, or move back and forth in its history list. You apply a method to a Web form when you submit it to a program on a Web server for processing.

We can create a program in JavaScript to alter object properties or apply methods to an object. Thus, we could use a program to apply methods to reload a Web page or to submit a Web form. For the Avalon Books page, we can create an animation by altering the position properties of the various elements. We'll learn more about properties and methods later in this session. First, though, we'll examine the different objects available to us.

Exploring the Document Object Model

All of the objects within documents and browsers need to be organized in a systematic way in order for programming languages like JavaScript to be able to work with them. The organized structure of objects and events is called the **document object model**, or **DOM**. In theory, every object related to documents or to browsers should be part of the document object model and thus accessible to a scripting language like JavaScript or VBScript. However, in practice, browsers—and sometimes even different versions of the same browser—differ in the objects that their document object models support. Some DOMs only support a few Web page or browser objects. In other cases, every single item is part of the DOM, including individual lines of text. The fact that we can encounter different DOMs depending on which browser a user is running makes it difficult to write code that satisfies all browsers and browser versions. In order to appreciate the complexity of the different document object models, we need to briefly review the history of their development.

Development of a Common DOM

The first document object model for the Web was introduced in Netscape Navigator 2.0. This is often referred to as the **basic model**, or in some cases, the **DOM Level 0**. The basic model supported the common objects used in many JavaScript programs, such as the browser window, the Web document, and the browser itself. Using the basic model, a programmer could reference these objects in the scripting language, but in most cases could not modify their properties once the page was loaded by the browser. Only form elements could be modified after the page was loaded; the rest of the page was static and could not be changed. Internet Explorer 3.0 was the first version of Internet Explorer to support the basic model.

However, like the development of HTML, the development of a more comprehensive DOM followed two paths: one adopted by Netscape and the other adopted by Internet Explorer. Unfortunately, differences between the two browsers' DOMs have proved more difficult to reconcile than their differences in introducing HTML.

The next objects to be added to the DOM were inline images. Netscape 3.0 introduced the ability to create image rollovers, in which the source of an inline image could be switched in response to a mouse pointer hovering over the image. This effect made Web pages more interesting and dynamic; however, since earlier browser versions did not support rollovers, programmers who wanted to avoid error messages from other browsers had to write scripts that would detect which browser was in use before attempting to implement a rollover effect. Internet Explorer eventually supported rollovers in version 4.0.

Netscape 4 further expanded the scope of its document object model by adding the ability to capture mouse and keyboard events occurring within the browser. Thus, a script could be run in response to a user pressing a particular key, clicking a mouse button, or dragging the mouse pointer across the document window. Netscape 4 also introduced the concept of layers, allowing page content to be isolated in containers whose properties could be manipulated almost as if they were separate documents. While layers were a great innovation, they were not supported by Internet Explorer; the layer concept is no longer being developed by Netscape, and support for layers was dropped by later Netscape versions.

Internet Explorer 4.0 introduced perhaps the most sweeping extension to the document object model. In Internet Explorer 4.0, all Web page elements were added to the DOM. CSS attributes also became part of the DOM. This meant you could write a program that could modify objects such as the text of a heading, a page's background image, text color, and even the font face used by a browser. Moreover, because all of the elements became dynamic, they could be modified even after a page was loaded by the browser. The Internet Explorer DOM also provided a technique for responding to—or **capturing**—events occurring within the browser. Unfortunately, the approach adopted by Internet Explorer was incompatible with the approach of Netscape 4.

Thus, the browser wars had reached a stage at which two fundamentally incompatible document object models were in use, and programmers who wanted to create dynamic Web pages had major headaches trying to reconcile the differences. At this point, the World Wide Web Consortium (W3C) stepped in—much like it did with HTML—to develop specifications for a common document object model.

The first specification, **DOM Level 1**, was released in October 1998 and provided support for all elements contained within HTML and XML documents. An update to this specification was released in September 2000 and fixed some errors from the earlier release. DOM Level 1 enjoys nearly universal support in current browser versions.

The second specification, **DOM Level 2**, was released in November 2000. This specification enhanced the document object model by providing an event model in which programs could be written to capture and respond to events occurring within a browser. DOM Level 2 also added a style model to work with CSS style sheets, and a range model to allow programmers to manipulate sections of text within a document. The DOM Level 2 specifications were also placed within six different modules, allowing browser developers to support those sections of the DOM of importance to them. Current browsers support many, but not all, of the features of DOM Level 2.

The most recent specification is **DOM Level 3**, released in April 2004. DOM Level 3 provides a framework for working with document loading and saving, as well as for working with DTDs and document validation. Few browsers support the DOM Level 3 specifications at the time of this writing.

Figure 11-3 summarizes the different DOMs and indicates their support in different versions of Internet Explorer, Netscape, and Opera.

Document Object Models ◄ Figure 11-3

DOM	Description	Netscape	Internet Explorer	Opera
DOM Level 0 (Basic Model)	The basic DOM that supported few page and browser objects and allowed dynamic content only for form elements	NS2, NS3, NS4, NS6, NS7	IE3, IE4, IE5, IE6	OP3, OP4, OP5, OP6, OP7
DOM Level 0 + Images	The basic DOM with added support for image rollovers	NS3, NS4, NS6, NS7	IE3 (Macintosh), IE4, IE5, IE6	OP3, OP4, OP5, OP6, OP7
Netscape 4 (layers)	The basic DOM with support for the Netscape 4 layer element and the ability to capture events within the browser	NS4		
Internet Explorer 4	An expanded DOM allowing dynamic content for most page elements		IE4, IE5, IE6	OP6, OP7
Internet Explorer 5	The IE 4 DOM with additional refinements and enhancements		IE5, IE6	OP6, OP7
W3C DOM Level 1	The first DOM specification by the W3C, which supported all page and browser elements and handled all events occurring within the browser	NS6, NS7	IE5, IE6	OP6, OP7
W3C DOM Level 2	The second DOM specification, allowing for the capture of events, manipulation of CSS styles, working with element text, and document subsets	NS6, NS7	IE6	OP6, OP7
W3C DOM Level 3	The third DOM specification provides a framework for working with document loading and saving, as well as working with DTDs and document validation			

Be aware that within each DOM, particular features may not be supported by every browser. With so many DOMs, writing a dynamic Web page that accommodates all browsers, all browser versions, and all operating systems is not a simple task, and the conscientious programmer should be ready to do a lot of testing. Generally if you want to ensure the widest compatibility across browsers, your code should be compatible with the following DOMs:

- Netscape 4
- Internet Explorer 5
- W3C DOM Level 1 and 2

The Netscape 4 DOM refers to the document object model used in the fourth-generation Netscape browsers (4.0 and 4.7). You may be tempted to think that you could use the Netscape 4 DOM for all subsequent versions of Netscape, but this is not the case. The DOM supported by Netscape version 6 and above is not backward-compatible with the Netscape 4 DOM. For the purposes of creating dynamic Web pages, you should treat Netscape 4 and Netscape 6 as totally different browsers instead of different versions of the same browser. The number of users running Netscape 4 has dwindled considerably in recent years, so supporting the Netscape 4 DOM is not as essential as it once was. For more information about the Netscape 4 DOM and how to write code for it, see Appendix J.

For the Avalon Books Web page, we'll concentrate on Level 1 and Level 2 of the W3C DOM; however we'll also examine the features of the Internet Explorer 5 DOM when circumstances warrant. In the text that follows, you should assume that any code samples refer to the Level 1 and Level 2 W3C DOMs unless otherwise noted.

The Document Tree

Each DOM organizes objects into a hierarchy known as a document tree. Figure 11-4 shows part of this hierarchy.

Figure 11-4 | **The object hierarchy**

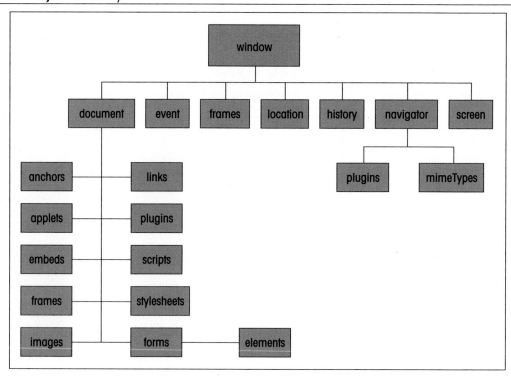

The topmost object in the hierarchy is the window object, which represents the browser window. Within the browser window are objects for the Web page document, each frame, the history of Web pages visited, and even the browser itself. Those objects can themselves contain yet another level of objects. For example, the document object contains objects for Web forms, images, applets, inline frames, and links. Obviously as document object models encompass more objects, the tree structure itself became more elaborate, including more of the objects within the window, browser, and document. The object hierarchy for the W3C Level 1 and Level 2 DOMs even includes a structure for individual tags, tag attributes, and text strings within an HTML file.

Referencing Objects

A DOM defines how the objects and events for browsers and documents are organized; it can be used by any scripting language including JavaScript and Java. Thus, once you understand how to work with a document object model, you can often apply the lessons you learn to several programming languages. In this case we'll look at how to work with a DOM using JavaScript. We'll start by examining how to reference particular elements or groups of elements within a document object model.

Object Names

In JavaScript each object is identified by an **object name**. Figure 11-5 lists the object names for some of the objects at the top of the hierarchy.

Object names · Figure 11-5

Object Name	Description
window	The browser window
document	The Web document displayed in the window
document.body	The body of the Web document displayed in the browser window
event	Events or actions occurring within the browser window
history	The list of previously visited Web sites within the browser window
location	The URL of the document currently displayed in the browser window
navigator	The browser itself
screen	The screen displaying the document

In the previous tutorial you used the document object when writing content to the Web page. To indicate the location of an object within the hierarchy, you separate different levels using a dot. The general form is

```
object1.object2.object3. ...
```

where `object1` is at the top of the hierarchy, `object2` is a child of `object1`, `object3` is a child of `object2`, and so forth. Thus, to reference the history of Web pages visited within the browser window, you would use the form

```
window.history
```

However, in some cases you do not have to indicate an object's location in the hierarchy. For example, when you simply use the object name "document", JavaScript automatically assumes that it is located within the browser window. Thus, if you wanted to work with the body part of a document (that is, the part of the document displayed in the browser window), you could use the object reference

```
document.body
```

Working with Object Collections

When more than one of the same type of object exists, these objects are organized into arrays called **object collections**. This occurs chiefly within Web page documents that include several objects of the same type. To reference a particular collection within the document, JavaScript uses the form

```
document.collection
```

where `collection` is the name of the object collection. Figure 11-6 displays a list of the different object collections along with the browser support information for each. Not all collections are supported by all browsers or browser versions. In addition, the Netscape 4 DOM has its own object collections, which are discussed in Appendix J.

| Figure 11-6 | ▶ **Object collections** |

Object Collection	Description	Netscape	Internet Explorer	Opera
document.all	All elements		IE4, IE5, IE6	OP6, OP7
document.anchors	All anchors	NS2, NS3, NS4, NS6	IE3, IE4, IE5, IE6	OP4, OP5, OP6, OP7
document.applets	All applets	NS3, NS4, NS6, NS7	IE4, IE5, IE6	OP4, OP5, OP6, OP7
document.embeds	All embed elements	NS3, NS4, NS6, NS7	IE4, IE5, IE6	OP4, OP5, OP6, OP7
document.forms	All Web forms	NS2, NS3, NS4, NS6, NS7	IE3, IE4, IE5, IE6	OP4, OP5, OP6, OP7
document.*form*.elements	All elements within a specific *form*	NS3, NS4, NS6, NS7	IE4, IE5, IE6	OP5, OP6, OP7
document.frames	All inline frames		IE4, IE5, IE6	OP4, OP5, OP6, OP7
document.images	All inline images	NS3, NS4, NS6, NS7	IE4, IE5, IE6	OP4, OP5, OP6, OP7
document.links	All links	NS2, NS3, NS4, NS6, NS7	IE3, IE4, IE5, IE6	OP4, OP5, OP6, OP7
document.namespaces	All namespaces defined in the document		IE6	
document.plugins	All plug-ins in the document	NS4, NS6, NS7	IE5, IE6	OP5, OP6, OP7
document.scripts	All script elements		IE4, IE5, IE6	OP6, OP7
document.styleSheets	All style sheet elements	NS6, NS7	IE4, IE5, IE6	
document.all.tags	All tags defined in the document		IE4, IE5, IE6	OP6, OP7
navigator.plugins	All plug-ins supported by the browser	NS4, NS6, NS7	IE5, IE6	OP5, OP6, OP7
navigator.mimeTypes	All mime-types supported by the browser	NS6, NS7	IE5, IE6	OP6, OP7
window.frames	All frames within the browser window	NS4, NS6, NS7	IE4, IE5, IE6	OP4, OP5, OP6, OP7

To reference a specific object within a collection, you can use either of the following forms:

```
document.collection["idref"]
document.collection.idref
```

where `idref` is either an index number representing the position of the object in the array or the value of the id or name attribute assigned to that element. As with other arrays, the first object in the collection has an index number of 0. For example, if the first form element in the HTML file is

```
<form id="Survey"> ... </form>
```

you can reference the form using any of the following expressions:

```
document.forms[0]
document.forms["Survey"]
document.forms.Survey
```

Using document.all and document.getElementById

Not all elements are associated with an object collection. For example, in Terry's HTML file, she has placed much of the content within div elements. Although JavaScript does not support a div collection, she can reference these objects using their id values. The

Internet Explorer and W3C DOMs provide different methods for doing this. In the Internet Explorer DOM, you can use the document.all collection to reference all elements in a document. Thus, to reference a specific element by its id, you can use either of the following forms:

```
document.all["id"]
document.all.id
```

where *id* is the id value of the element. Alternatively, you can omit "document.all" from the reference and simply use

```
id
```

as the object reference. Using the Internet Explorer DOM, any of the following could be used to reference an element whose id value is "Greetings":

```
document.all["Greetings"]
document.all.Greetings
Greetings
```

In the W3C DOMs, you use the getElementById method to reference a specific element. The syntax is

```
document.getElementById("id")
```

Thus, the reference for an element with an id of "Greetings" would be

```
document.getElementById("Greetings")
```

Case is important when using the getElementById method. A common mistake is to enter the code as getElementByID; however, because the final letter is incorrectly capitalized, this code would result in an error. Internet Explorer also supports the getElementById method.

Referencing Tags

You can also create object collections based on HTML tag names. In the Internet Explorer DOM, you would use the form

```
document.all.tags(tag)
```

where *tag* is the name of the HTML tag. For example the reference

```
document.all.tags(p)
```

returns an object collection of all of the paragraph tags in the document. To reference the first paragraph, you would use the expression

```
document.all.tags(p)[0]
```

In the W3C DOMs, you reference tags using the getElementsByTagName method. The syntax is

```
document.getElementsByTagName("tag")
```

Thus, the expression to access a document's first paragraph would be

```
document.getElementsByTagName("p")[0]
```

We'll explore other methods for accessing specific elements and objects within an HTML document in a later tutorial.

Reference Window **Referencing Objects**

- To reference an object as part of the collection in a document, use the syntax
    document.*collection*[*idref*]
  where *idref* is either an index number representing the position of the object in the collection or the value of the id or name attribute assigned to that element.
- To reference a document object based on its id, use
    document.getElementById(*id*)
- To reference a document object based on its element tag, use
    document.getElementsByTagName(*tag*)
  where *tag* is the name of the element tag. Note that this returns a collection of elements with that tag name rather than a single item.

Working with Object Properties

Each object in JavaScript has properties associated with it. The number of properties depends on the type of object: some objects have only a few properties, while others have many. The syntax for setting the value of an object property is

object.*property* = *expression*

where *object* is the JavaScript name of the object you want to manipulate, *property* is a property of that object, and *expression* is a JavaScript expression that assigns a value to the property. For example, one of the properties of a document is the document title. If you want to set the document title using JavaScript instead of using the HTML title element, you could run the following command:

document.title = "Avalon Books"

The text "Avalon Books" would then appear in the title bar of a Web browser displaying the document. Figure 11-7 presents other examples of setting object properties using JavaScript. To make it easier to separate the object names, properties, and expressions, the object names are displayed in red, the properties are displayed in blue, and the values of the expressions are displayed in green.

Figure 11-7 ▶ **Setting object property values**

Expression	Description
document.bgColor="black"	Sets the background color of the document to black
document.fgColor="white"	Sets the foreground color of the document to white
document.links[0].href="http://www.avalon.com"	Sets the URL of the document's first link to "http://www.avalon.com"
document.images[2].src="avalon.gif"	Sets the source of the document's third inline image to "avalon.gif"
document.getElementById("books").style.fontWeight="bold"	Sets the font weight of the element with the id "books" to bold
document.getElementsByTagName("p")[0].style.fontSize="16pt"	Sets the font size of the document's first paragraph to 16pt
document.forms[1].action="http://www.avalon.com/mailer"	Sets the action of the second Web form to "http://www.avalon.com/mailer"
location.href="http://www.avalon.com"	Sets the page displayed by the browser to the URL "http://www.avalon.com"
window.status="Page Loaded"	Displays the text "Page Loaded" in the browser window's status bar

We'll explore additional objects and their properties throughout the next four tutorials; you can review the list of these objects and properties in Appendix G. Figure 11-7 gives you an idea of the scope of what you can do by modifying the property values of objects in your document and browser.

Not all properties can be changed. Some properties are **read-only**, meaning that you can read the property value, but you cannot modify it. One such property is the appVersion property of the navigator object, which identifies the version of the user's Web browser. Although it could come in handy to be able to upgrade a user's browser by running a simple JavaScript command, this value is not changeable. Figure 11-8 describes some of the other properties that provide information about your browser and its operating environment.

Browser properties | Figure 11-8

Browser Property	Description
navigator.appName	The name of the browser
navigator.appVersion	The major version number of the browser (may also include a compatibility value and the name of the operating system)
navigator.appMinorVersion	The minor version number of the browser
navigator.appCodeName	The name of the browser's code
navigator.userAgent	The name of the browser associated user agent
navigator.platform	The operating system under which the browser is running
navigator.cpuClass	The type of CPU in use with the browser
navigator.systemLanguage	The language used by the browser
navigator.cookieEnabled	A Boolean value indicating whether cookies are enabled

Storing a Property in a Variable

Although you cannot change the value of read-only properties, you can assign a value to a variable in a JavaScript program. The syntax for assigning a property value to a variable is

```
variable = object.property
```

where *variable* is the variable name, *object* is the name of the object, and *property* is the name of the property. For example, to store the name of a user's browser in a variable, you could use the command

```
BrowserName = navigator.appName
```

Using Properties in Conditional Expressions

Sometimes you need to work with properties in conditional statements, which change how a Web page behaves based on the value of certain object properties. The following JavaScript code shows how you can incorporate object properties into a simple conditional expression:

```
if(document.bgColor=="black") {
   document.fgColor="white";
} else {
   document.fgColor="black";
}
```

In this example, JavaScript first checks the background color of the Web page. If the background color is black, JavaScript changes the color of the text on the page to white, using the page's fgColor property. If the background color is not black, then the text color is changed to black. As you can see, using objects, properties, and conditional statements provides you with a great deal of control over the appearance of your Web pages.

Working with Object Properties

- To set the value of object property, use
    object.property = expression
  where object is the object reference, property is the object property, and expression is the value you want to assign to the property.
- To store an object property value, use
    variable = object.property
  where variable is the variable that will store the property value.

Working with Object Methods

You can also manipulate objects by applying methods to them. The syntax for applying a method is

object.method(parameters)

where object is the name of the object, method is the method to be applied, and parameters is a comma-separated list of parameter values used with the method. In the previous tutorial you applied the "write" method to a document in order to write content to the page. In that case, the parameter value was the text of the content to be written. Figure 11-9 lists some other examples of applying methods to objects. In the figure, object names are highlighted in red, methods are displayed in blue, and parameter values are displayed in green. Not every method requires parameter values.

Figure 11-9 **Browser methods**

Expression	Action
location.reload()	Reload the current page in the browser
document.forms[0].reset()	Reset the first form in the Web page
document.forms[0].submit()	Submit the first form in the Web page
document.write("Avalon Books")	Write "Avalon Books" to the Web page
history.back()	Go back to the previous page in the browser's history list
thisDay.getFullYear()	Return the four digit year value from the thisDay date object
Math.rand()	Return a random value using the Math object
navigator.javaEnabled()	Return a Boolean value indicating whether Java is enabled in the browser
window.close()	Close the browser window
window.print()	Print the contents of the browser window
window.scroll(x, y)	Scroll the browser window to the (x, y) coordinate

Working with Object Methods

- To apply a method to an object, use
    `object.method(parameters)`
  where `object` is the object reference, `method` is the method to be applied, and `parameters` is a comma-separated list of parameter values used by the method.

Creating a Cross-Browser Web Site

As you learned earlier, different browsers can support different document object models. Current browsers all do a good job of supporting Level 1 and Level 2 of the W3C DOM. However, if you need to support older browsers your code must be able to accommodate different DOMs. You can create this kind of code, known as **cross-browser** code, using two different approaches: browser detection or object detection.

Using Browser Detection

Using **browser detection**, your code determines which browser (and browser version) a user is running. In some cases, the code may even have to establish which operating system a browser is running under. After collecting this information, the program then runs code tailored for the user's system. Successfully using browser detection requires that you do your homework and map out the requirements of each browser, browser version, and perhaps even operating system. This is no small task!

Recall that information about a browser is stored in the navigator object. To retrieve a browser's name, you use the property

`navigator.appName`

For Netscape, this expression returns the value "Netscape." For Internet Explorer, the value would be "Microsoft Internet Explorer." However, for Opera, the value of the app-Name property is often listed as "Microsoft Internet Explorer". This is because Opera supports many of the features of the Internet Explorer DOM. If you need to determine whether a user is running the Opera browser, you can test whether the browser supports the window.opera property. We'll examine how to perform object detection in the next section.

No property returns the browser version in an easy-to-read text string. The expression navigator.appVersion returns both the version number and additional text that describes features of the version. Unfortunately, this text is usually not reliable in determining the version number. For example, the following values of the appVersion property correspond to the listed versions of Netscape, Internet Explorer, and Opera:

- Netscape 7.1 for Windows: 5.0 (Windows; en-US)
- Internet Explorer 6.0 for Windows: 4.0 (compatible; MSIE 6.0; Windows NT 5.1)
- Opera 7.51 for Windows: 4.0 (compatible; MSIE 6.0; Windows NT 5.1)

Additional information about the browser is stored in the navigator.userAgent property, and most browser detection scripts—commonly known as **browser sniffers**—use this property to extract information about the version number. Because these programs can be long and complicated, we won't go into the details here. However, you can find a number of browser detection scripts of varying degrees of sophistication through a simple Web search. In summary, while it is relatively easy to determine which browser a user is running, it is not so easy to extract detailed information about the browser version.

Using Object Detection

Most Web page developers recommend bypassing browser detection entirely, and relying instead on object detection. With **object detection**, you determine which document object model a browser supports by testing which object references it recognizes. For example, only the Netscape 4 DOM recognizes the document.layers object collection, only the Internet Explorer DOM uses the document.all reference, and only the W3C DOM recognizes the document.getElementById object reference.

We can use this information to construct three Boolean variables whose values are true if a user's browser supports the Netscape 4, Internet Explorer, or W3C document object models, respectively. The code is:

```
var NS4DOM = document.layers ? true:false;
var IEDOM = document.all ? true:false;
var W3CDOM = document.getElementById ? true:false;
```

This code uses the comparison operator to test whether the browser recognizes each object reference. If a browser understands a given object reference, then we can assume that the browser supports the document object model associated with that object reference. For example, if the browser recognizes the document.all reference, the IEDOM variable returns a value of true, indicating that the browser supports the Internet Explorer DOM; otherwise the IEDOM variable returns a value of false.

One advantage of the object detection approach is that it can work for any object and any browser. You can also use it to test for support of earlier versions of the document object model. For example, the expression

```
var BasicDOM = document.forms ? true:false;
var ImagesDOM = document.images ? true:false;
```

creates two variables that we can use to test whether the browser supports DOM Level 0 or DOM Level 0 plus image rollovers. To demonstrate these concepts, a demo page has been prepared for you to display the properties of your browser and the objects that it supports. Open this page now.

To view supported objects and browser properties:

1. Use your browser to open **demo_browser.htm** from the tutorial.11/tutorial folder.

2. Study the tables on the page to learn about the properties of your browser and the supported objects.

   You can also enter your own object name to test whether it is supported by your browser. Try this now to see whether your browser supports the document.all object reference (necessary for browsers that support the Internet Explorer DOM).

3. Type **document.all** in the Enter an object name text box at the bottom of the page and click the **test** button.

   Figure 11-10 shows the content of the page for the Internet Explorer 6.0 browser for Windows.

Browser properties and supported objects | Figure 11-10

Navigator Object Properties

navigator.appName	Microsoft Internet Explorer
navigator.appVersion	4.0 (compatible; MSIE 6.0; Windows NT 5.1)
navigator.appMinorVersion	;SP1;Q822925;Q330994;Q824145;Q832894;Q837009;Q831167;
navigator.appCodeName	Mozilla
navigator.userAgent	Mozilla/4.0 (compatible; MSIE 6.0; Windows NT 5.1)
navigator.platform	Win32
navigator.cpuClass	x86
navigator.systemLanguage	en-us
navigator.cookieEnabled	true

Supported Objects

document.all	yes	document.images	yes
document.anchors	yes	document.layers	no
document.applets	yes	document.links	yes
document.childNodes	yes	document.namespaces	yes
document.classes	no	document.plugins	yes
document.embeds	yes	document.scripts	yes
document.forms	yes	document.styleSheets	yes
document.frames	yes	document.tags	no
document.getElementById	yes	navigator.plugins	yes
document.getElementsByName	yes	navigator.mimeTypes	yes
document.getElementsByTagName	yes	window.frames	yes
document.ids	no		

Enter an object name: document.all   [test] yes

4. Close the page and any other files you've opened in this session.

Employing Cross-Browser Strategies

Once you settle on a mechanism to determine the capabilities of your users' browsers (by either browser or object detection), your next task is to choose a cross-browser strategy for your Web site. One strategy, called **page branching**, creates separate pages for each browser (and, if you need to get really detailed, for each browser version) along with an initial page. When a user opens the initial page, a script determines the capabilities of the user's browser and automatically loads the appropriate page. See Figure 11-11. The initial page itself can be used for browsers that don't support a scripting language or any of the document object models.

Figure 11-11 | **Page branching**

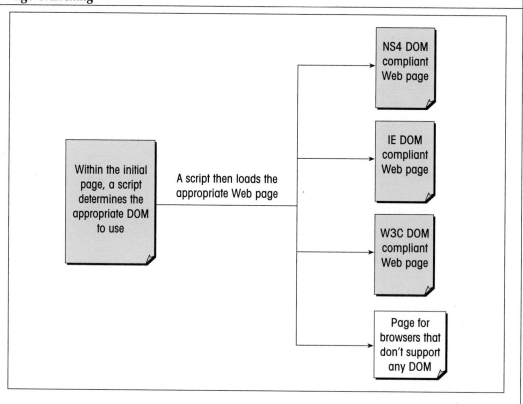

To automatically load a page into a browser based on the type of browser detected, use the command

```
location.href=url;
```

where *url* is the URL of the new page to be loaded. The page branching commands should be placed in the header section of the HTML file to ensure that the script is run before the initial page is loaded.

The following example shows code for a page that loads the page_ns4.htm page if the user's browser works with the Netscape 4 DOM. If the browser doesn't support that model, the code then tests for support of the Internet Explorer DOM and loads the page_ie.htm page if appropriate. Finally, if the browser doesn't support either of those DOMs, the code tests for support of the W3C DOM, loading the page_w3c.htm file if it is supported. If none of these DOMs are supported, the browser continues to open the current file.

```
<html>
   <head>
   <title>Avalon Books</title>
   <script language="JavaScript">
      if (document.layers) location.href="page_ns4.htm"
      else if (document.all) location.href="page_ie.htm"
      else if (document.getElementById) location.href= "page_w3c.htm"
   </script>
   </head>
   <body>
   <h1>Welcome to Avalon Books!</h1>
   </body>
</html>
```

Page branching requires you to maintain several versions of the same page. In a Web site containing many pages, this means a lot of extra work keeping all of the pages consistent.

A second cross-browser strategy is to use internal branching, in which each piece of DHTML code is enclosed in an if...else statement. The general syntax is:

```
if (document.layers) {
   JavaScript commands for the Netscape 4 DOM;
   } else if (document.all) {
   JavaScript commands for the Internet Explorer DOM;
   } else if (document.getElementById) {
   JavaScript commands for the W3C DOM;
   }
}
```

This construction would have to be repeated every time you run a set of DHTML commands. Internal branching works well for pages that do not employ a lot of DHTML code. Pages that contain a lot of DHTML code quickly become unwieldy and prone to errors if you use internal branching, however.

Many Web developers apply a third cross-browser strategy: they create an application programming interface. An **application programming interface** or **API** is an external text file that contains custom commands and functions. These customized functions are written to resolve any cross-browser differences. When you create a Web page, you link it to the API and use commands from the API file in your Web page (see Figure 11-12) rather than placing the code within the HTML file on your page.

Using an API file ◄ Figure 11-12

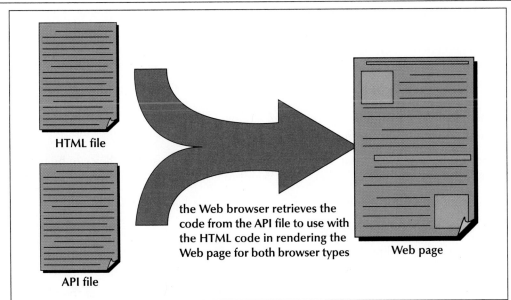

HTML file

API file

the Web browser retrieves the code from the API file to use with the HTML code in rendering the Web page for both browser types

Web page

You've completed your work reviewing the concepts behind objects, properties, methods, and the document object model. In the next session, you'll put what you've learned to work in creating an animated page for the Avalon Books Web site.

Session 11.1 Quick Check

1. What is the document object model? What are three DOMs that you should write code for if you wish to support the widest range of browsers and browser versions?
2. What object would you use to write a program to access the pages previously visited in a user's browser?
3. What object collection would you use to access a Web form?
4. How do the IE DOM and the W3C DOMs differ in referencing objects by their id value?
5. What command could you run to change the source of the first inline image in a document to the file logo.jpg?
6. What object and property should you use to retrieve the name of the browser in use?
7. What object and method would you use to print the contents of the browser window?
8. What is object detection and how could you use it to determine which DOM a user's browser supports?

Session 11.2

Creating Custom Functions for Avalon Books

You and Terry determine that you'll need the following functions to create the animation for the Avalon Books Web page:

- A function that returns an object's left coordinate
- A function that returns an object's top coordinate
- A function to place an object at specific coordinates on the page
- A function to move an object a certain distance from its current location
- A function to hide an object
- A function to unhide an object

You'll put these functions in a separate file named scripts.js so that they can be used again by other pages in the Avalon Books Web site if Terry chooses.

To create the scripts.js file:

1. Use your text editor to open the **scripttxt.js** file from the tutorial.11/tutorial folder. Save the file as **scripts.js**.

2. Enter **your name** and **the date** in the comment section at the top of the file.

Working with the Style Object

To create the animation effect that Terry wants, you have to be able to place each of the five div elements from the avalon.htm file at specific locations on the page. Positioning is done using CSS positioning styles, so you have to apply one of those styles to each of the elements. JavaScript treats the styles associated with an element as an object. The syntax for applying a style is:

```
object.style.attribute = value
```

where *object* is a reference to an object in the Web document, *attribute* is one of the CSS styles that apply to that object, and *value* is the value of the style. The style attribute is converted to a JavaScript style value by removing any dashes in the style name and capitalizing the first letter following each removed dash. For example, the CSS style

```
background-image
```

becomes

```
backgroundImage
```

in JavaScript. Thus, to change the font size of the first paragraph in a document to 16 points, you could use the following JavaScript command:

```
document.getElementsByTagName("p")[0].style.fontSize="16pt"
```

Figure 11-13 lists some other applications of the style object.

Using the style object ◄ **Figure 11-13**

Expression	Description
document.getElementById("logo").style.color="black"	Sets the foreground color of the logo element to black
document.getElementById("logo").style.fontWeight="bold"	Displays the text in the logo element in a boldfaced font
document.getElementById("logo").style.fontStyle="italic"	Displays the text in the logo element in italics
document.getElementById("logo").style.margin="10px"	Sets the margin around the logo element to 10 pixels
document.getElementById("logo").style.fontFamily ="Arial"	Sets the font of the logo element to Arial
document.getElementById("logo").style.width="100px"	Sets the width of the logo element to 100 pixels
document.getElementById("logo").style.textAlign="center"	Horizontally centers the contents of the logo element
document.getElementById("logo").style.backgroundImage= "url(paper.gif)"	Sets the background image of the logo element to paper.gif

Reference Window

Setting an Object's Style Attribute

- To change the value of a style associated with an object, use
    `object.style.attribute = value`
  where *object* is the object reference, *attribute* is one of the style attributes associated with the object, and *value* is the value assigned to the style attribute.

Setting an Element's Position

JavaScript uses the same positioning style values as CSS. Thus, you can set an element's top and left coordinates, specify its z-index value (for stacked elements), and hide or re-display it using the display or visibility styles. Figure 11-14 describes the positioning styles we'll use in the Avalon Books Web page.

Figure 11-14 **Positioning properties**

Positioning Property	Sets
object.style.position="*value*"	the position type of the *object*, where *value* is absolute, relative, fixed, static, or auto
object.style.left="*value*"	the left coordinate of the *object*
object.style.top="*value*"	the top coordinate of the *object*
object.style.right="*value*"	the right coordinate of the *object*
object.style.bottom="*value*"	the bottom coordinate of the *object*
object.style.zIndex="*value*"	the z-index value of the *object*
object.style.visibility="*type*"	the visibility of the *object* where *type* is either "hidden" or "visible"
object.style.width="*value*"	the width of the *object*
object.style.height="*value*"	the height of the *object*
object.style.overflow="*type*"	the type of overflow applied to the *object* where *type* is "auto", "visible", "hidden", or "scroll"
object.style.clip="*value*"	the size of the clipping rectangle where *value* is a text string containing the clipping rectangle values

For example, if you wanted to set the left coordinate of an object with the id "avalon" to 100 pixels you would enter the following JavaScript command:

```
document.getElementById("avalon").style.left="100px"
```

Note that coordinate values also contain the unit of length. If you need to add to or subtract from a coordinate (in order to move an object on the page), you have to first extract the numeric value. This can be done using the parseInt() method, which extracts a numeric value from a text string. For example, the expression

```
leftpos=parseInt("100px")
```

stores the numeric value 100 in the leftpos variable. At that point you could apply any mathematical operation to change the position value, and then store the new coordinate in the left style object for the element. The following code moves the avalon object 5 pixels to the left:

```
leftpos=parseInt(document.getElementById("avalon").style.left);
leftpos=leftpos+5;
document.getElementById("avalon").style.left=leftpos+"px";
```

Note that when the code updates the left position of the object it also appends the unit "px" to indicate to the browser that the unit of length is pixels.

Positioning Properties in the IE DOM

The Internet Explorer DOM supports the style object described above, as well as some additional properties that can be used to position objects on the Web page. Figure 11-15 describes the Internet Explorer DOM positioning properties.

Figure 11-15 **IE DOM positioning properties**

Positioning Property	Sets
object.style.pixelLeft="*value*"	The position of the left edge of the *object* in pixels
object.style.pixelTop="*value*"	The position of the top edge of the *object* in pixels
object.style.posLeft="*value*"	The position of the left edge of the *object* in the specified unit of length
object.style.posTop="*value*"	The position of the top edge of the *object* in the specified unit of length

The posLeft and posTop properties are equivalent to the left and top properties in the W3C DOM. The pixelLeft and pixelTop properties assume that the unit of length is the pixel and thus use only numeric values with no length unit. Thus the expressions

```
parseInt(object.style.left)
parseInt(object.style.posLeft)
object.style.pixelLeft
```

return the same value in a browser supporting the IE DOM when pixels are the unit of the length.

Creating the Positioning Functions for Avalon Books

Now that you've reviewed some of the issues associated with positioning objects with JavaScript, you're ready to create the functions for the Avalon Books Web site. Each function will take as an input value the id of an object in the Web page, and will then set the positioning property values for the object. When the animation runs, the code will need the current location of the objects on the page, so the first two functions we'll create will return the values of the left and top coordinates. The code for the first two functions is

```
function xCoord(id) {
    object=document.getElementById(id);
    xc=parseInt(object.style.left);
    return xc;
}
function yCoord(id) {
    object=document.getElementById(id);
    yc=parseInt(object.style.top);
    return yc;
}
```

The xCoord() function returns the position of the object's left edge. Note that the parseInt() method is used to return only the numeric value and not the unit. For this project we'll assume that all coordinates are expressed in pixels. The yCoord() function returns the position of the object's top edge.

To insert the xCoord() and yCoord() functions:

1. Return to the **scripts.js** file in your text editor.

2. Below the comment section, insert the following code:

```
function xCoord(id) {
    object=document.getElementById(id);
    xc=parseInt(object.style.left);
    return xc;
}


function yCoord(id) {
    object=document.getElementById(id);
    yc=parseInt(object.style.top);
    return yc;
}
```

The next function places an object at specific coordinates on the page. The full text of the function is

```
function placeIt(id, x, y) {
   object=document.getElementById(id);
   object.style.left=x+"px";
   object.style.top=y+"px";
}
```

The placeIt() function takes three parameters: the id name of the object, and (x, y) coordinates at which we want to place it. The function first uses the id value to create a reference to the appropriate object in the document, and then places the object by modifying the values of the left and top style properties. For example, if we call the function using the command

```
placeIt("avalon", 100, 50)
```

the browser places the avalon object at the coordinates (100, 50).

To insert the placeIt() function:

1. Below the yCoord() function insert the following code:

   ```
   function placeIt(id, x, y) {
      object=document.getElementById(id);
      object.style.left=x+"px";
      object.style.top=y+"px";
   }
   ```

Next, we need a function that moves an object a specified distance in the x and y directions from its current location. We will use this function when we create the animation that moves the words "Avalon" and "Books" across the Web page. This function, which we will call shiftIt(), will have three parameters, named id, dx, and dy. The id parameter contains the id value of the object. The dx and dy parameters contain the distance, in pixels, to move the object to the right and down. The code for the complete shiftIt() function is

```
function shiftIt(id, dx, dy) {
   object=document.getElementById(id);
   object.style.left=xCoord(id)+dx+"px";
   object.style.top=yCoord(id)+dy+"px";
}
```

In this function we use the xCoord() and yCoord() functions we created earlier to retrieve the current coordinates of the object. The shiftIt function then adds the value of the dx and dy parameters to those coordinates and appends these values with the "px" text string to indicate that coordinate values are in pixels.

To insert the shiftIt() function:

1. Below the placeIt() function insert the following code:

   ```
   function shiftIt(id, dx, dy) {
      object=document.getElementById(id);
      object.style.left=xCoord(id)+dx+"px";
      object.style.top=yCoord(id)+dy+"px";
   }
   ```

In the final part of Terry's proposed animation, images will appear to "pop up" on the Web page. To achieve that effect, we need to create functions to both hide objects, and to unhide previously hidden objects. The functions are

```
function hideIt(id) {
    object=document.getElementById(id);
    object.style.visibility="hidden";
}
function showIt(id) {
    object=document.getElementById(id);
    object.style.visibility="visible";
}
```

To add the hideIt() and showIt() functions:

1. Below the shiftIt() function insert the following code:

   ```
   function hideIt(id) {
       object=document.getElementById(id);
       object.style.visibility="hidden";
   }


   function showIt(id) {
       object=document.getElementById(id);
       object.style.visibility="visible";
   }
   ```

2. Figure 11-16 shows the completed functions for the script.js file. You should check the code you entered against this figure. Make sure that the text matches exactly, including the use of uppercase and lowercase letters and quotation marks.

Functions in the scripts.js file ◀ **Figure 11-16**

```
function xCoord(id) {
    object=document.getElementById(id);
    xc=parseInt(object.style.left);
    return xc;
}

function yCoord(id) {
    object=document.getElementById(id);
    yc=parseInt(object.style.top);
    return yc;
}

function placeIt(id, x, y) {
    object=document.getElementById(id);
    object.style.left=x+"px";
    object.style.top=y+"px";
}

function shiftIt(id, dx, dy) {
    object=document.getElementById(id);
    object.style.left=xCoord(id)+dx+"px";
    object.style.top=yCoord(id)+dy+"px";
}

function hideIt(id) {
    object=document.getElementById(id);
    object.style.visibility="hidden";
}

function showIt(id) {
    object=document.getElementById(id);
    object.style.visibility="visible";
}
```

3. Close **scripts.js**, saving your changes.

You've completed inserting the functions in the scripts.js file. In the next session, you'll create a link to this file and use the functions you created to animate the Avalon Books Web page.

Session 11.2 Quick Check

1. What JavaScript command increases the z-index value of the Logo object by 1?
2. What JavaScript commands would place the Logo object at the coordinates (150, 350)? Assume that the unit of measure is pixels.
3. What JavaScript command would you use to hide the Logo object?
4. What JavaScript command would you use to set the width of the Logo object to 100 pixels?
5. What JavaScript command would you use to set the size of the clipping rectangle around the Logo object to (10, 210, 150, 10)?
6. What JavaScript command would you use to display scrollbars if the contents of the Logo object overflow its boundaries?
7. If you were supporting the IE DOM, what JavaScript command would you enter to place the Logo object at the coordinates (150, 350). Assume that the unit of measure is pixels.

Session 11.3

Working with Event Handlers

You can now use the functions that you entered to animate the contents of Terry's Web page. Recall from Figure 11-12 that Terry first wants the single word "Avalon" to appear near the top of the page and then drop vertically down the page. At a certain point, "Avalon" should stop dropping, and the word "Books" should appear, moving to the right from behind the word "Avalon." After that, the three other images should appear on the screen in sequence.

To create this animation, you'll place the words "Avalon" and "Books" near the top of the page, with "Avalon" stacked on top of "Books" to hide it. You'll also place the three images in the appropriate locations on the page, but hidden. While some of these tasks (such as placing the objects on the page) can be performed with CSS style attributes, you can use this opportunity to test the functions you created by performing the tasks with JavaScript instead.

First you'll set the initial places for the five objects. The coordinates for the ab, fiction, and nfiction objects should remain unchanged, but the avalon and books objects should be placed at new coordinates: 175 pixels to the left and 10 pixels down from the upper-left corner of the window. Because the avalon object has a higher z-index value than the books object, it will appear on top of the books object. The coordinates for the five objects are therefore

- "avalon": (175, 10)
- "books": (175, 10)
- "ab": (230, 40)—as before
- "fiction": (5, 5)—as before
- "nfiction": (475, 5)—as before

You'll also hide the ab, fiction, and nfiction objects. You'll place all of these actions within a single file named placeObjects(), which you'll add to the avalon.htm file. The initial code for the placeObjects() function is

```
function placeObjects() {
    placeIt("avalon", 175,10);
    placeIt("books",175,10);
    placeIt("ab",230,40);
    placeIt("fiction",5,5);
    placeIt("nfiction",475,5);
    hideIt("ab");
    hideIt("fiction");
    hideIt("nfiction");
}
```

Because the placeObjects() function calls the functions we added to the scripts.js file, we also need to add a link to that file. Revise the avalon.htm file now.

To edit the avalon.htm file:

1. Reopen **avalon.htm** in your text editor.

2. Directly above the </head> tag insert the following line:

   ```
   <script src="scripts.js" type="text/javascript"></script>
   ```

3. Below this link insert the following script element:

   ```
   <script type="text/javascript">
   function placeObjects() {
       placeIt("avalon",175,10);
       placeIt("books",175,10);
       placeIt("ab",230,40);
       placeIt("fiction",5,5);
       placeIt("nfiction",475,5);
       hideIt("ab");
       hideIt("fiction");
       hideIt("nfiction");
   }
   </script>
   ```

4. Figure 11-17 shows the newly added code.

Inserting the placeObjects() function   Figure 11-17

```
<title>Avalon Books</title>
<link href="styles.css" rel="stylesheet" type="text/css" />
<script src="scripts.js" type="text/javascript"></script>
<script type="text/javascript">
function placeObjects() {
    placeIt("avalon", 175,10);
    placeIt("books",175,10);
    placeIt("ab",230,40);
    placeIt("fiction",5,5);
    placeIt("nfiction",475,5);
    hideIt("ab");
    hideIt("fiction");
    hideIt("nfiction");
}
</script>
</head>
```

Next you need a way of triggering this function when the page is initially loaded by a browser. You can do this using an **event handler**, which is an attribute added to an element that specifies a program to be run in response to an event. The general syntax of an event handler attribute is

`onevent="script"`

where `event` is the name of an event and `script` is a command or collection of commands to be run in response to the event. For example, a standard form button supports the "click" event that occurs when a user clicks the button. Figure 11-18 shows a sample implementation of the onclick event handler using a collection of option buttons. When a user clicks an option button, the click event is initiated and the onclick event handler triggers the browser to run a JavaScript command that changes the background color of the Web page. Note that a JavaScript command invoked with an event handler does not require a <script> tag, but must be placed within a pair of single or double quotation marks within the relevant tag. You can enter several commands in the same tag using this method, separating one command line from another with a semicolon. However, when you need to run several JavaScript commands, the standard practice is to place them in a function, which can be called using a single command line.

| Figure 11-18 | Using the onclick event handler |

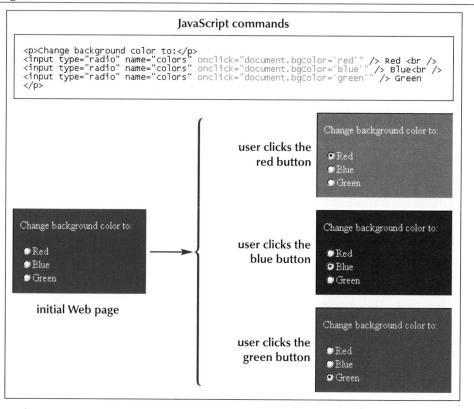

Figure 11-19 lists some other event handlers you can use on your Web sites. You can also view an extended list of event handlers in Appendix G.

Category	Event Handler	Description
Window and Document event handlers	onload	The browser has completed loading the document
	onunload	The browser has completed unloading the document
	onerror	An error has occurred in the JavaScript program
	onmove	The user has moved the browser window
	onresize	The user has resized the browser window
	onscroll	The user has moved the scrollbar within the browser window
Form event handlers	onfocus	The user has entered an input field
	onblur	The user has exited an input field
	onchange	The content of an input field has changed
	onselect	The user has selected text within an input or text area field
	onsubmit	The user has submitted the Web form
	onreset	The user has reset the Web form
Mouse and keyboard event handlers	onkeydown	The user has pressed a key
	onkeypress	The user has pressed and released a key
	onclick	The user has clicked the mouse button
	ondblclick	The user has double-clicked the mouse button
	onmousedown	The user has pressed down the mouse button
	onmouseup	The user has released the mouse button
	onmousemove	The user has moved the mouse pointer over the element
	onmouseout	The user has moved the mouse pointer off of the element

Running JavaScript Commands as Links

You can easily run a command in response to the click event by creating a link around the object to be clicked. The syntax for doing this is

```
<a href="javascript:script">content</a>
```

where *script* is the command you want to run when a user clicks the link. For example, the following code changes the Web page's background color to red when a user clicks the text "Change background to red":

```
<a href="javascript:document.bgcolor='red'">
   Change background color to red
</a>
```

One advantage of this technique is that you can apply it to objects that might not support the onclick event handler in all browsers or browser versions.

Running a Script in Response to an Event

- To run a script in response to an event, add an event handler to the object's HTML tag using the syntax

    `onevent = "script"`

    where `event` is the name of an event associated with the object and `script` is a command or collection of commands to be run in response to the event.
- To run a script as a link use

    `<a href="javascript:script">content</a>`

    where `script` is the command or collection of commands run when a user clicks the link.

Using the onload Event Handler

Now that you've learned how to work with event handlers, you can add an event handler to the Avalon Books Web page to run the placeObjects() function when a browser loads the page. In this case you will add the onload event handler to the document's body element.

To add the onload event handler:

1. Within the <body> tag, insert the attribute **onload="placeObjects()"** as shown in Figure 11-20.

Figure 11-20 | **Inserting the onload event handler**

```
<script type="text/javascript">
function placeObjects() {
    placeIt("avalon", 175,10);
    placeIt("books",175,10);
    placeIt("ab",230,40);
    placeIt("fiction",5,5);
    placeIt("nfiction",475,5);
    hideIt("ab");
    hideIt("fiction");
    hideIt("nfiction");
}
</script>
</head>

<body onload="placeObjects()">
```

2. Save your changes to the file and then load **avalon.htm** in your Web browser.

3. The page opens as shown in Figure 11-21. Since the three images are hidden, they do not appear in the page. In addition, the word "Books" is hidden behind the word "Avalon."

Trouble? If you receive an error message when loading the page, check the code in the scripts.js file. Some common programming errors include mismatching uppercase and lowercase letters, misspellings of variable names, forgetting to close up double-quote-marked text, and forgetting to enclose command blocks and functions within curly braces.

Animating an Object

The first piece of animation you'll add to the Avalon Web page will be the word "Avalon" dropping down the page. The initial position of the word is at the coordinates (175, 10). Terry suggests dropping it down to the coordinates (175, 270). This means that while moving the object, the function will need to monitor the value of the y-coordinate and stop moving the word when that value exceeds 260 (note that the x-coordinate does not change). Once the function stops moving the word "Avalon," the browser should then run a function that moves the word "Books" to the right. The initial form of the moveAvalon() function will appear as follows:

```
function moveAvalon() {
   var y=yCoord("avalon");
   if (y <=260) {
      shiftIt("avalon",0,10);
      shiftIt("books",0,10);
      moveAvalon();
   } else {
      // run moveBooks function;
   }
}
```

There are a couple of important things to notice about this function. First, it retrieves the current y-coordinate from the yCoord() function you entered into the API. Second, it uses the shiftIt() function you created in the last session to move both the word "Avalon" and the word "Books" down 10 pixels at a time. Remember, you want the word "Books" to remain behind "Avalon" as it moves down the page. Once it has moved those two words, the function calls itself to start the moving process all over again. Finally, when the y-coordinate exceeds 260, the function then runs the moveBooks function (which you haven't written yet) to begin moving the word "Books" out from behind "Avalon." For now we'll mark that spot with a comment.

The only thing missing from the function is a way to control the timing. Because a Web browser will run this function in a millisecond, from the viewpoint of a user the word "Avalon" will jump down the page in a blink of an eye. We need some way to slow down this process a bit.

Working with Time-Delayed Commands

Unlike some other programming languages, JavaScript does not provide a pause command to temporarily halt the execution of program code. Instead, you can specify that a JavaScript command be executed after a given time delay. You can do this using the setTimeout command, as follows:

```
setTimeout("command", delay);
```

where *command* is a JavaScript command or expression, which must be placed within quotes, and *delay* is the delay time in milliseconds. For example, to set a five-millisecond delay before the browser runs the moveAvalon() function, you would use the command

```
setTimeout("moveAvalon()", 5);
```

There is no limit to the number of time-delayed commands a browser can process. Therefore, if you wanted to be able to access a time-delayed command in progress—for example, to cancel it before it is actually run—you would need some way of specifying which time-delayed command you wanted to work with. You can do this using the unique id that browsers assign to each command. You store the value of this id in a variable using the command

```
timeID = setTimeout("command",delay);
```

Storing the id value of the time-delayed command is only necessary if you want to interact with the command later in the program. The method to cancel a time-delayed command is

```
clearTimeout(timeID);
```

where *timeID* is the id of the command. If only a single time-delayed command is in progress, however, you don't need the id; you can use the command

```
clearTimeout();
```

to cancel the only time-delayed command that the browser is running.

Running Commands at Specified Intervals

You can also time commands by instructing users' browsers to repeatedly run the same command at specified intervals. For example, a function that displays the current time on a page might run every second. The method to run a command repeatedly at specified intervals is

```
timeID=setInterval("command",interval);
```

where *timeID* is an id value that identifies the timed-interval command, *command* is the JavaScript command that is to be run repeatedly, and *interval* is the interval, in milliseconds, before the command is run again. The id variable is not necessary unless you need to cancel the command at some point. If you don't need the id, or you only have one time-interval command running, use the simpler form

```
setInterval("command",interval);
```

To cancel the command, use the clearInterval() method with the syntax

```
clearInterval(timeID);
```

or, if you have only a single time-interval command, with no id variable needed

```
clearInterval();
```

After a browser processes a request to run a command at a later time using the setTimeout() or setInterval() commands, it proceeds without stopping to the next command in the script and continues processing the function. Thus, if you use the following structure to try to run three functions at 50-millisecond intervals, your browser will run all three functions almost simultaneously 50 milliseconds later:

```
setTimeout("function1()",50);
setTimeout("function2()",50);
setTimeout("function3()",50);
```

To run the functions with a separation of about 50 milliseconds between one function and the next, you need to use three different delay times, as follows:

```
setTimeout("function1()",50);
setTimeout("function2()",100);
setTimeout("function3()",150);
```

In this case, a browser runs the first function after 50 milliseconds, the second function 50 milliseconds after that, and the third function after an additional 50 milliseconds has passed.

Running Timed Commands

Reference Window

- To run a command after a delay, use the method
    timeID = setTimeout("*command*", *delay*)
  where *command* is the command to be run, *delay* is the delay time in milliseconds, and *timeID* is a variable that stores the id associated with the time-delayed command.
- To repeat a command at set intervals, use the method
    timeID = setInterval("*command*", *interval*)
  where *interval* is the interval, in milliseconds, before the command is run again.
- To cancel a time-delayed command use
    clearTimeout(*timeID*)
  where *timeID* is the id of the time-delayed command. To clear all time-delayed commands, use the method clearTimeout().
- To cancel a repeated command, use
    clearInterval(*timeID*)
  where *timeID* is the id of the repeated command. To clear all repeated commands, use the method clearInterval().

Animating the Avalon Books Web page

Using the knowledge you have gained about controlling the timing of your commands, you can adjust the moveAvalon() function as follows:

```
function moveAvalon() {
   var y=yCoord("avalon");
   if (y <= 260) {
      shiftIt("avalon",0,10);
      shiftIt("books",0,10);
      setTimeout("moveAvalon()",30);
   } else {
      // run moveBooks function;
   }
}
```

The function now moves the words "Avalon" and "Books" down 10 pixels every 30 milliseconds until the avalon object is 260 pixels from the top of the page. Generally, when you do animation, you have to experiment with several different movement and time-delay values before you arrive at a combination that creates a smooth motion. The value of 30 milliseconds was chosen after some experimentation.

To insert the moveAvalon() function:

1. Return to the **avalon.htm** file in your text editor.

2. After the placeObjects() function, insert the following code:

```
function moveAvalon() {
   var y=yCoord("avalon");
   if (y <= 260) {
      shiftIt("avalon",0,10);
      shiftIt("books",0,10);
      setTimeout("moveAvalon()",30);
   } else {
      // run moveBooks function;
   }
}
```

You also need to call the moveAvalon() function from within the placeObjects() function.

3. At the end of the placeObjects() function, directly after the command to hide the nfiction object, insert the command

```
moveAvalon();
```

Your script should resemble the code shown in Figure 11-22.

The moveAvalon() function ◄ **Figure 11-22**

```
<script type="text/javascript">
function placeobjects() {
    placeIt("avalon", 175,10);
    placeIt("books",175,10);
    placeIt("ab",230,40);
    placeIt("fiction",5,5);
    placeIt("nfiction",475,5);
    hideIt("ab");
    hideIt("fiction");
    hideIt("nfiction");
    moveAvalon();
}

function moveAvalon() {
    var y=yCoord("avalon");
    if (y <= 260) {
        shiftIt("avalon",0,10);
        shiftIt("books",0,10);
        setTimeout("moveAvalon()",30);
    } else {
        // run moveBooks function;
    }
}
</script>
```

run moveAvalon() after placing the objects

4. Save your changes and reopen or refresh the **avalon.htm** file in your Web browser.

   The text "Avalon" should now move down the page once, and "Books" should move with it, hidden behind it.

Next, your script needs to move the books object out from behind the avalon object. The moveBooks() function will resemble the moveAvalon() function, except that it will move only the books object and will move it from the left to the right. Terry used trial and error to determine that you should move "Books" from the coordinates (175, 270) to (330, 270). Once the text is in this location, the script should unhide the remaining figures; for now you'll just add a comment to the script indicating this. Following is the moveBooks() function that you'll use:

```
function moveBooks() {
    var x=xCoord("books");
    if (x <= 320) {
        shiftIt("books",10,0);
        setTimeout("moveBooks()",50);
    } else {
    // display the hidden images;
    }
}
```

Instead of using the yCoord() function from the API, moveBooks() uses the xCoord() function to track the object as it moves in the horizontal direction. Also, the second and third parameters of the shiftIt() function are switched so that the books object moves 10 pixels to the right every 50 milliseconds.

To insert the moveBooks() function:

1. Return to the **avalon.htm** file in your text editor.

2. After the moveAvalon() function, insert the following code:

```
function moveBooks() {
   var x=xCoord("books");
   if (x <= 320) {
      shiftIt("books",10,0);
      setTimeout("moveBooks()",50);
   } else {
   // display the hidden images;
   }
}
```

Next you need to revise the moveAvalon() function so that it calls moveBooks() when it finishes.

3. Scroll up to the moveAvalon() function and replace the comment text "// run move-Books function;" with

```
moveBooks();
```

Figure 11-23 shows the revised text.

Figure 11-23 ▶ **The moveBooks() function**

```
function moveAvalon() {
   var y=yCoord("avalon");
   if (y <= 260) {
      shiftIt("avalon",0,10);
      shiftIt("books",0,10);
      setTimeout("moveAvalon()",30);
   } else {
      moveBooks();
   }
}

function moveBooks() {
   var x=xCoord("books");
   if (x <= 320) {
      shiftIt("books",10,0);
      setTimeout("moveBooks()",50);
   } else {
   // display the hidden images;
   }
}
</script>
```

run moveBooks() after moving the avalon object

4. Save your changes to the file and then reload or refresh **avalon.htm** in your Web browser.

The text "Avalon" should move down the page and after it stops the text "Books" should move from behind it.

The last step in the animation is to unhide the three images: ab, fiction, and nfiction. You decide to unhide each image at half-second intervals. The function to do this is

```
function showObjects() {
   setTimeout("showIt('ab')",500);
   setTimeout("showIt('fiction')",1000);
   setTimeout("showIt('nfiction')",1500);
}
```

Notice that you insert the object names in single quotes rather than double quotes, because you have to enclose the entire command in double quotes. Also notice that in order to unhide the images at half-second intervals, you specify 500 milliseconds, then 1000 milliseconds, and finally 1500 milliseconds for the delay times.

To insert the showObjects() function:

1. Return to the **avalon.htm** file in your text editor.

2. After the moveBooks() function, insert the following code:

```
function showObjects() {
    setTimeout("showIt('ab')",500);
    setTimeout("showIt('fiction')",1000);
    setTimeout("showIt('nfiction')",1500);
}
```

3. Replace the comment in the moveBooks() function with:

```
showObjects();
```

Figure 11-24 shows the revised code.

The showObjects() function ◀ **Figure 11-24**

```
function moveBooks() {
    var x=xCoord("books");
    if (x <= 320) {
        shiftIt("books",10,0);
        setTimeout("moveBooks()",50);
    } else {
        showObjects();
    }
}

function showObjects() {
    setTimeout("showIt('ab')",500);
    setTimeout("showIt('fiction')",1000);
    setTimeout("showIt('nfiction')",1500);
}
</script>
```

run showObjects() after moving the books object

4. Save your changes to the file and then reload or refresh **avalon.htm** in your Web browser.

You should see the complete animation, ending with the three images appearing in sequence.

You may have noticed that in creating this animation, each function called the next one in sequence after it was finished. This is a common technique when creating animation in DHTML. By calling the next function only after the current function is finished, you ensure that your effects are presented in the proper order. In this example, this technique ensures that the "Books" text doesn't come out from behind the "Avalon" text until after they are both at the correct location near the bottom of the screen, and that the three images don't appear until the "Books" text has moved out from behind the "Avalon" text.

Controlling Layout for Different Monitor Resolutions

Terry is pleased with the opening screen you've designed. She notices, however, that you've created the page based on a monitor resolution of 640 x 480 pixels. What happens, she wonders, when users view the page at other resolutions? After experimenting, she shows you your page viewed at three different, but commonly used, resolutions (see Figure 11-25).

Figure 11-25 **The Avalon Books Web page at different monitor resolutions**

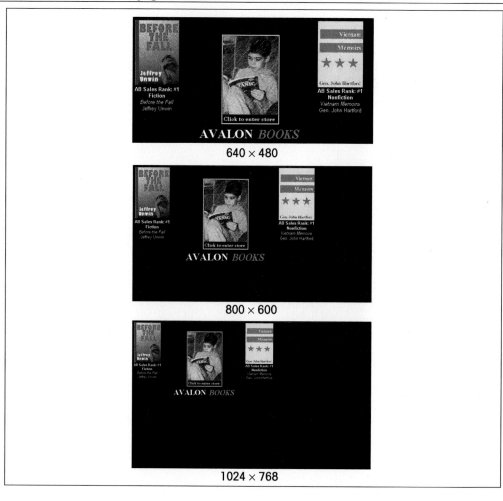

At sizes larger than 640 x 480, the images and text move progressively toward the upper-left corner of the display window. Terry would like to see the images remain in the center of the display window, both horizontally and vertically. Rather than create a different page for each monitor resolution, Terry suggests that you think of the objects as existing on a canvas that is 620 pixels wide by 300 pixels high. Every object would then be offset from the left and top edges of the window by a distance equal to the size of the border around this imaginary canvas. For example, if the dimensions of the display window are 760 x 560 pixels, the border width would be (760 − 620)/2 or 70 pixels, and the border height would be (560 − 300)/2 or 80 pixels (see Figure 11-26).

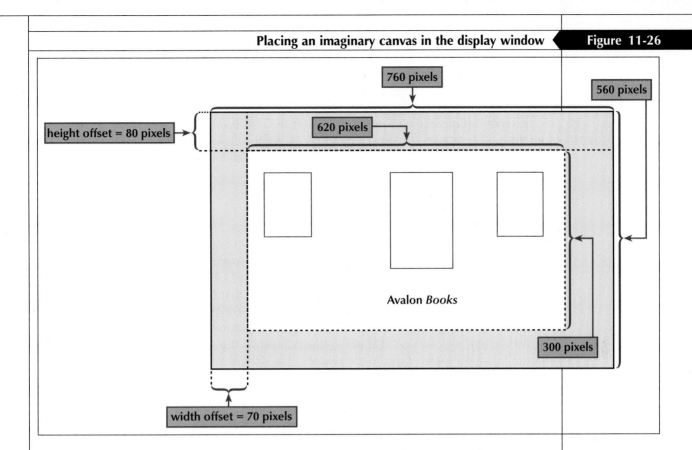

Placing an imaginary canvas in the display window ◄ **Figure 11-26**

Under Terry's proposal, if the width of the display window is W, then the space in the horizontal direction would be (W – 620)/2. If the height of the window is H, the space in the vertical direction would be (H – 300)/2. By adding these spaces to the current coordinates of each object, the display would be centered at any monitor resolution. However, to use this calculation, you first need to determine the width (W) and height (H) of the user's display window.

Calculating the Size of the Display Window

For the Level 1 and Level 2 W3C DOMs, the width and height of the browser window are stored in the properties

```
window.outerWidth
window.outerHeight
```

These values include the display window and the browser's toolbars, menus, and status bars. For our calculations, we want to exclude those elements. To determine the size of only the display window, without any other browser features, we can use the properties

```
window.innerWidth
window.innerHeight
```

However, no version of Internet Explorer supports these properties. For Internet Explorer 4.0 or Internet Explorer 5.0, the closest approximation is

```
document.body.clientWidth
document.body.clientHeight
```

The document.body reference is used in Internet Explorer 4.0 and 5.0 to refer to the size of the Web page body. In this case, the clientWidth and clientHeight properties return the document's width and height in pixels. However, the document.body reference is no longer supported in Internet Explorer 6.0 and has been replaced by the object reference document.documentElement.

Internet Explorer 6.0 also does not support the clientWidth and clientHeight properties for this object. With the Internet Explorer 6 DOM, the approximation of the document window size that gives the most reasonable answer and doesn't cause an error message in other browsers comes from the properties

```
document.documentElement.offsetWidth
document.documentElement.offsetHeight
```

In general, the values returned by the innerWidth/innerHeight properties in Netscape and the values returned by the offsetWidth/offsetHeight properties do not agree, although they are close. Currently, this is one of the headaches of DHTML for which there is no easy way of resolving the conflicts. The bottom line is that if you need to do precise work involving the dimensions of your document window, you must create a complicated script that accounts for cross-browser differences and quirks.

Fortunately, we don't need anything that precise for our page. Terry simply wants the layout to appear more or less in the center of the document window, and she's willing to accept layouts that differ by a few pixels in one direction or the other. With this in mind, you and Terry decide to add functions to the scripts.js file named winWidth() and win-Height() that calculate the size of the document window using the following approach:

1. If the window.innerWidth and window.innerHeight properties are supported, return those values.
2. Otherwise, if the browser supports the document.documentElement object, return the value of the document.documentElement.offsetWidth and document.documentElement.offsetHeight properties.
3. Otherwise, use the document.body.clientWidth and document.body.clientHeight properties, if they are supported.

You can be confident that this approach will return an acceptable answer in all browsers. The functions to calculate the window's width and height are therefore

```
function winWidth() {
   if (window.innerWidth) return window.innerWidth;
   else if (document.documentElement) return document.documentElement.
offsetWidth;
   else if (document.body.clientWidth) return document. body.
clientWidth;
}

function winHeight() {
   if (window.innerHeight) return window.innerHeight;
   else if (document.documentElement) return document.documentElement.
offsetHeight;
   else if (document.body.clientHeight) return document.body.
clientHeight;
}
```

Add these functions to the scripts.js file now.

To insert the winWidth() and winHeight() functions:

1. Open **scripts.js** in your text editor.

2. At the bottom of the file insert the following code (see Figure 11-27):

```
function winWidth() {
    if (window.innerWidth) return window.innerWidth;
    else if (document.documentElement) return document.
 documentElement.offsetWidth;
    else if (document.body.clientWidth) return document. body.
clientWidth;
}


function winHeight() {
    if (window.innerHeight) return window.innerHeight;
    else if (document.documentElement) return document.
documentElement.offsetHeight;
    else if (document.body.clientHeight) return document.body.
clientHeight;
}
```

Trouble? Make sure that each else if statement is on a single line.

Inserting the winWidth() and winHeight() functions ◄ **Figure 11-27**

```
function winwidth() {
    if (window.innerwidth) return window.innerwidth;
    else if (document.documentElement) return document.documentElement.offsetwidth;
    else if (document.body.clientwidth) return document.body.clientwidth;
}
function winHeight() {
    if (window.innerHeight) return window.innerHeight;
    else if (document.documentElement) return document.documentElement.offsetHeight;
    else if (document.body.clientHeight) return document.body.clientHeight;
}
```

3. Close the file, saving your changes.

Now you'll be able to use the winWidth() and winHeight() functions in your avalon. htm file. To calculate the value of the W and H variables, use the following code:

```
W=(winWidth()-620)/2;
H=(winHeight()-300)/2;
```

You need to put this code within the <script> tags at the top of the file, so that the W and H variables are made available to all functions within the file.

To modify the avalon.htm file:

1. Return to **avalon.htm** in your text editor.

2. Directly above the placeObjects() function, insert the following code (see Figure 11-28):

```
W=(winWidth()-620)/2;
H=(winHeight()-300)/2;
```

Figure 11-28 | **Creating the W and H variables**

```
<script type="text/javascript">
W=(winWidth()-620)/2;
H=(winHeight()-300)/2;

function placeobjects() {
    placeIt("avalon", 175,10);
    placeIt("books",175,10);
    placeIt("ab",230,40);
    placeIt("fiction",5,5);
    placeIt("nfiction",475,5);
    hideIt("ab");
    hideIt("fiction");
    hideIt("nfiction");
    moveAvalon();
}
```

Next you have to add the W and H values to each coordinate in the placeObjects() function so that objects are placed in appropriate locations for all display windows.

To modify the coordinate values in the placeObjects() function:

1. In the placeObjects() function directly below the code you just entered, change the coordinates from (175, 10) to **(W+175, H+10)** for the avalon and books objects.

2. Change the coordinates for the ab object to **(W+230, H+40)**.

3. Change the coordinates for the fiction object to **(W+5, H+5)**.

4. Change the coordinates for the nfiction object to **(W+475, H+5)**.

Figure 11-29 shows the revised placeObjects() function.

Figure 11-29 | **Final placeObjects() function**

```
function placeobjects() {
    placeIt("avalon", W+175,H+10);
    placeIt("books",W+175,H+10);
    placeIt("ab",230,H+40);
    placeIt("fiction",W+5,H+5);
    placeIt("nfiction",W+475,H+5);
    hideIt("ab");
    hideIt("fiction");
    hideIt("nfiction");
    moveAvalon();
}
```

You also need to change the value of the coordinates used to determine where to stop moving the Avalon and Books text.

To modify the moveAvalon() and moveBooks() functions:

1. Scroll down to the moveAvalon() function.

2. Change the text, "y <= 260" to **y <= H+260**.

3. Scroll down to the moveBooks() function.

4. Change the text, "x <= 320" to **x <= W+320**.

Figure 11-30 shows the revised code in these functions.

Final moveAvalon() and moveBooks() functions ◄ Figure 11-30

```
function moveAvalon() {
    var y=yCoord("avalon");
    if (y <= H+260) {
        shiftIt("avalon",0,10);
        shiftIt("books",0,10);
        setTimeout("moveAvalon()",30);
    } else {
        moveBooks();
    }
}

function moveBooks() {
    var x=xCoord("books");
    if (x <= W+320) {
        shiftIt("books",10,0);
        setTimeout("moveBooks()",50);
    } else {
        showObjects();
    }
}
```

5. Close **avalon.htm** saving your changes and then reload the file in your browser and verify that the animation still works correctly.

6. If you have the capability of changing the resolution of your monitor, view the page under different screen sizes and verify that the page objects appear approximately in the center of the page each time. If you are using a large or high-resolution monitor, you can simply reduce the size of the browser window and reload the page to verify that the page contents recenter themselves.

Using Path Animation

The animation you created for the Avalon Books page is an example of **linear animation**, meaning that the animation takes place over a straight line, going from one point to the next (either down or to the right). Another type of animation is **path animation**, in which each set of coordinates in the path is entered into an array, and the animation moves from point to point. The path can be any shape, as shown in Figure 11-31.

Linear and path animations ◄ Figure 11-31

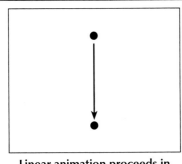

Linear animation proceeds in a straight line

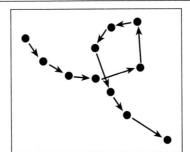

Path animation can jump to any coordinate on the page

To use path animation, you store the x- and y-coordinate values in arrays. This means you need to do the work of calculating all of the coordinate positions in your path. Once you enter the values into two arrays, you can retrieve the coordinates from the arrays, one coordinate at a time, until both arrays have been entirely read. The following sample shows code for a path animation:

```
x=new Array(0,40,80,120,200,300,400,300,150);
y=new Array(0,20,40,120,120,80,60,30,0);
index = 0;

function moveObject() {
    if (index <= x.length-1) {
        shiftIt("path_object", x[index], y[index]);
        index++;
        setTimeout("moveObject()", 10);
    }
}
```

In this example, an object named "path object" is moved from point to point following the x- and y-coordinate values in the x and y arrays. The index value is initially set to 0, to point to the first item in each array. Each time the object moves to a new location, the index value is increased by one using the increment operator (++). When the value of the index exceeds the length of the array minus one, as indicated by the property x.length-1, the path animation stops.

Why use the length of the array minus one, rather than the length of the array? Recall that the first array element has an index value of zero; therefore for an array with a length of n, the last array element has the array value n − 1.

For more interesting path animations, you can add a third array containing the delay times between each movement, rather than using the same delay time throughout.

You've completed your work on the Avalon Books opening Web page. Terry is going to have some other people in the design team review your work. She'll get back to you with any changes she wants you to make. You can close any open files now.

Tips for working with JavaScript Objects and DHTML

- If your code reuses the same object reference, store the object in a variable.
- Place your customized functions in external files so that they can be reused throughout your Web site.
- Use object detection to test the capabilities of browsers running your code. Provide workarounds for browsers that do not support your objects.
- Use path animation and create interesting visual effects by varying the path coordinates and delay times.
- Break up your animated effects into separate functions that call one another, preserving the sequence.

Review

Session 11.3 Quick Check

1. What command would you enter to run the function moveGraphic() after a tenth-of-a-second delay?
2. What command would you enter to run the function moveGraphic() every tenth of a second, saving the time id for the command in a variable named "mg"?
3. What command would you enter to stop running the function you started in Question 2?
4. What W3C object property returns the height of the entire browser window?
5. What W3C object property returns the height of the browser window excluding the toolbars, menus, and status bars?
6. What is the difference between linear animation and path animation?

Tutorial Summary

In this tutorial you were introduced to the principles of DHTML and the document object model. The first session covered the history of the document object model and discussed the different types of DOMs supported by the browser market. The session then examined how objects are organized within the DOM and you can use JavaScript to access those objects. The session also examined how to work with object properties and object methods and showed how they can be used in a JavaScript program to apply different effects to a Web page and a user's browser. The second session introduced the style object and showed how you can apply CSS styles using JavaScript. The session then showed how to use this information to create simple functions for applying positioning styles to the objects on a Web page. In the third session these functions were used to add a simple animation to a Web page. The session also covered how to work with event handlers and discussed the different types of event handlers available to programmers. In creating the animation, you learned how to work with timed-interval and time-delay commands, and you learned how to work with the width and height properties of the browser display window. The session concluded with a discussion of linear and path animation.

Key Terms

API	document object model	object
application	DOM	object-based language
programming	DOM Level 0	object collection
interface	DOM Level 1	object detection
basic model	DOM Level 2	object name
browser detection	DOM Level 3	page branching
browser sniffer	dynamic HTML	path animation
capture	event handler	property
cross-browser	linear animation	read-only
DHTML	method	

Review Assignments

Data files needed for this Review Assignment: ab.gif, ablogo.gif, abtxt2.htm, fiction.jpg, indextxt.htm, kids.jpg, nfiction.jpg, script2txt.js, styles2.css

Terry's design team has reviewed your page and recommended the following changes:

- Add a page, named index.htm, that supports older browsers. If a browser that doesn't support the W3C DOM is detected, this page should be loaded.
- Replace the animation on the Avalon Books page with one that moves the title "Avalon Books" from the left edge of the page to the center when the page opens. Also, the text "Books" should appear in a red italic font below and overlapping the text "Avalon," rather than appearing from behind.
- After moving the title, display the three image files kids.jpg, fiction.jpg, and nfiction.jpg in rotation below the title. The images should be stacked on top of each other, and every two seconds the top image in the stack should be moved to the bottom, and the other images should be moved up in the stack. This causes the images to appear to rotate, allowing viewers to see one at a time.

Figure 11-32 shows a preview of the page you'll create for Terry.

Figure 11-32

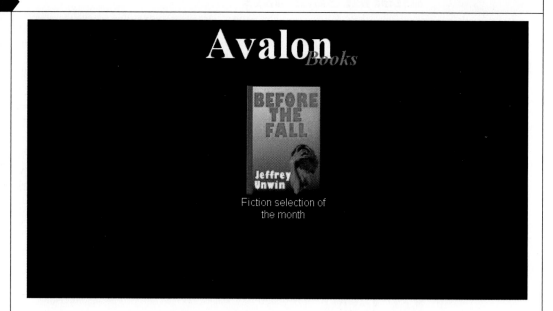

To create the new opening page for Avalon Books:

1. Use your text editor to open the **indextxt.htm** file from the tutorial.11/review folder. Enter *your name* and *the date* in the comment section and save the file as **index.htm**. Open the **script2txt.js** file from the same folder and enter *your name* and *the date* in the comment section. Save the file as **scripts2.js**. Open the **abtxt2.htm** file and enter *your name* and *the date* in the comment section. Save the file as **avalon2.htm**.

2. Go to the **index.htm** file. Below the title element insert an embedded script that uses an if statement to test whether the browser supports the W3C DOM. (*Hint*: Use object detection with the document.getElementById object.) If the browser does support the DOM, have the browser load the avalon2.htm file using the href property of the location object.

3. Save your changes and close the file.

4. Go to the **scripts2.js** file and create a new function named setZ(). The function should have two parameters: id and z. The function should use the value of the id parameter to select the object in the document with that id value. It should then set the z-index of the object to the value of the z parameter.

5. Create a new function named swapIt(). The purpose of the swapIt() function is to swap the order of three overlapping objects on the page, moving the object on top to the bottom of the stack and then moving the other two objects up. The function should be created as follows:

   • The function should have three parameters named id1, id2, and id3 that contain the id values of the three objects.

   • Use the getObject() function to create three variables named object1, object2, and object3 that reference objects with id values of id1, id2, and id3.

   • Create three variables named z1, z2, and z3, setting these variables equal to the z-index values of object1, object2, and object3.

   • Change the z-index value of object1 to z3 (thus moving it to the bottom of the stack). Change the z-index value of object2 to z1 (moving it the top of the stack) and finally change the z-index value of object3 to z2 (moving it to the middle of the stack).

6. Save your changes to the file and close it.

7. Go to the **avalon2.htm** file in your text editor and directly below the link to the styles2.css stylesheet, place a link to the **scripts2.js** file.

8. Below the link to the scripts2.js file, insert an embedded script.

9. Within the embedded script insert a function named placeObjects(). The purpose of this function is to set the initial placement of the objects on the page. Have the function do the following:
   - Declare a variable named "W" that is equal to half of the value returned by the winWidth() function.
   - Use the placeIt() function to place the "avalon" object at the coordinates (0, 0).
   - Place the "kids", "fiction", and "nfiction" objects at the coordinates (W-75, 100).
   - Use the setZ() function to set the z-index value of the "kids" object to 3.
   - Set the z-index value of the "fiction" object to 2.
   - Set the z-index value of the "nfiction" object to 1.
   - Call the moveAvalon() function. (You'll create this function in the next step.)

10. Below the placeObjects() function, insert the moveAvalon() function. The purpose of the moveAvalon() function is to move the text "Avalon Books" across the page. Create the function as follows:
    - Create a variable named "x" that is equal to the x-coordinate of the "avalon" object. (*Hint*: Use the xCoord() function from the scripts2.js file.)
    - If x is less than or equal to the value of W minus 125, then do the following: (a) use the shiftIt() function from the scripts2.js file to move the "avalon" object 10 pixels to the right, and (b) call the moveAvalon() function again after a delay of 50 milliseconds.
    - If x is greater than W – 125, then run the swapImages() function. (You'll create this function next.)

11. Below the moveAvalon() function, insert the swapImages() function. The purpose of the swapImages() function is to change the stacking order of the three image objects. The function should do the following:
    - Use the showIt() function to unhide the "kids", "fiction", and "nfiction" objects.
    - Every two seconds, have the browser run the swapIt() function from the scripts2.js file to change the stacking order of the "kids", "fiction", and "nfiction" objects.

12. Add an onload event handler to the body element to run the placeObjects() function when the page is loaded.

13. Save your changes to **avalon2.htm**.

14. Load the **index.htm** file in your Web browser. Verify that the following occurs:
    - The page automatically loads the avalon2.htm file.
    - The avalon2.htm file starts with the text "Avalon Books" on the left edge of the page.
    - The text "Avalon Books" moves to the center of the page.
    - After "Avalon Books" reaches the center, the image file kids.jpg appears along with its caption.
    - Every two seconds thereafter, the image file is swapped with the next image file in the stack.

15. If you can, test the layout of your page at various monitor resolutions. Verify that the content appears horizontally centered at each resolution.

16. Submit the completed Web site to your instructor.

Apply

*Use the skills you
learned to create a Web
page employing path
animation*

Case Problem 1

**Data files needed for this Case Problem: ball.gif, ballpath.txt, clouds.jpg, golfer.gif,
golftxt.htm, golftxt.js, styles.css**

The Golf Page Mark Reim, the owner of an online golf store called "The Golf Page,"
has asked you to create an animated opening screen for his Web site. Mark envisions a
golf ball flying across the screen, from the top left down to the bottom of the screen,
bouncing once, and then landing in the middle of the company name, taking the place
of the letter "o" in "Golf."

Mark also wants the text "Your Online Source of Golf Equipment" to appear after the ball
has landed. The text should appear with a font size of 0 points and then increase up to
20 points.

Functions that you can use in this Web page are stored in the golf.js file. One of the
functions is named placeIt() and is used to place an object at a specified page
coordinate. A second function named showIt() unhides a hidden object. Another text file
available to you is the ballpath.txt file, which contains the coordinates of the flying ball
relative to its final location on the page. Figure 11-33 shows a preview of the page you'll
work with.

Figure 11-33

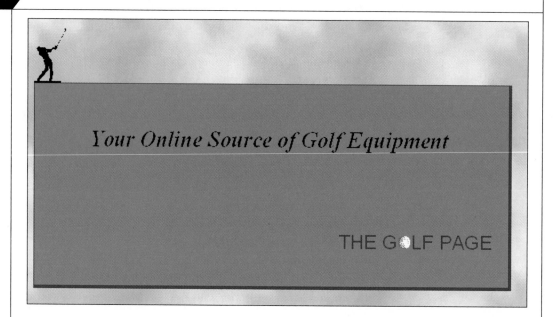

To create the animation for The Golf Page:

1. Use your text editor to open the **golftxt.htm** file from the tutorial.11/case1 folder.
   Enter ***your name*** and ***the date*** in the comment section and save the file as **golfpage.
   htm**. Take some time to study the contents of the file to become familiar with the
   objects and id values. Note that the company's slogan is located in a span element
   with the id name "slogan" and the image of the golf ball is located in a span element with the id name "Ball". Next, open the **golftxt.js** file from the same folder and
   enter ***your name*** and ***the date*** in the comment section. Save the file as **golf.js**.

2. Go to the **golf.js** file in your text editor. At the bottom of the file create a function named getFontSize(). The function should only have one parameter named "id" which represents the id value of an object in the document. Within the function create a variable named object that represents the object with the specified id value; then, return the font size of the text in that object. Use the style object to retrieve the font size and use the parseInt() function to extract the numeric value of the font size only.

3. Below the getFontSize() function insert another function named setFontSize(). The purpose of this function is to set the font size for an object. We'll assume that all font sizes are expressed in points. The function should have two parameters: id (for the id value of the object) and fs (for the font size you want to apply to the object). In the first step of the function, create a variable named object that represents the object with the specified id value. In the second step of the function, set the font size of the object to the value of fs appended by the text string "pt" (to represent points).

4. Below the setFontSize() function insert a third function named changeFontSize(). The purpose of this function is to increase the font size by a specified amount. There are two parameters for this function: id and dfs. The id parameter contains the object's id value and the dfs parameter contains the amount by which the font size should be increased. In the function's first step, use the id parameter to call the getFontSize() function and retrieve the current font size of the object. Store the value in a variable named "fs". In the second step, use the id parameter again to call the setFontSize() function and set the new font size of the object to the value, fs+dfs.

5. Close **golf.js**, saving your changes.

6. Go to the **golfpage.htm** file in your text editor. Directly below the link to the styles. css style sheet, create a link to the golf.js file.

7. Below the link to the golf.js script, insert an embedded script. Within the embedded script, paste the code found in the ballpath.txt file. The x array contains the x-coordinates of the flying ball. The y array contains the y-coordinates.

8. Below the array declaration, create a variable named "index", setting the initial value of the index to 0.

9. Below the index variable, create a function named "moveBall()". The purpose of the moveBall() function is to move the golf ball across the page until it stops at the location of the letter "o" in the word "golf." The moveBall() function should do the following:

   - Create an if statement to test whether the value of the index variable is less than or equal to the length of the x array minus 1. (*Hint*: The length of the x array can be determined using the expression: x.length.)
   - If condition of the if statement is met, then: (a) use the placeIt() function from the golf.js file to place the "Ball" object at the coordinates (x[index], y[index]), (b) increase the value of the index variable by 1, and (c) run the moveBall() function again after a five-millisecond delay.
   - Otherwise do the following: (a) Use the setFontSize() function to set the font size of the "slogan" object to 0, (b) use the showIt() function to display the "slogan" object, and (c) run the growText() function. (You'll create this function next.)

10. Below the moveBall() function, insert the growText() function. The purpose of this function is to grow the text in the "slogan" object from 0 points up to 21 points. The function should contain the following steps:

   - Call the getFontSize() function using "slogan" as the parameter value to retrieve the current font size of the "slogan" object. Store the value in a variable named "fs".
   - Create an if statement that tests whether the value of the fs variable is less than or equal to 20.
   - If the condition is met, then: (a) call the changeFontSize() function to increase the font size of the "slogan" object by 1, and (b) rerun the growText() function after a delay of 20 milliseconds.

11. Add an event handler to the body element to run the moveBall() function when the page is loaded.

12. Save your changes to the file.

13. Open the **golfpage.htm** file in your Web browser and verify that the ball flies across the page, landing in the title, appearing as the letter "o". Also verify that the slogan "Your Online Source of Golf Equipment" appears after the golf ball has landed and steadily grows in size.

14. Submit the completed Web site to your instructor.

Apply

Use the skills you learned to create a scrolling marquee

Case Problem 2

Data files needed for this Case Problem: back.jpg, ccc.gif, ccctxt.htm, ccctxt.js, styles.css

The Chamberlain Civic Center Laura Bromquist, the director of the Chamberlain Civic Center, has asked you to design a page listing the upcoming events at the center. Laura would like the page to display a marquee in which event names automatically scroll for the user. She would also like to give the user the ability to start and stop the marquee. A preview of the page you'll create is shown in Figure 11-34.

Figure 11-34

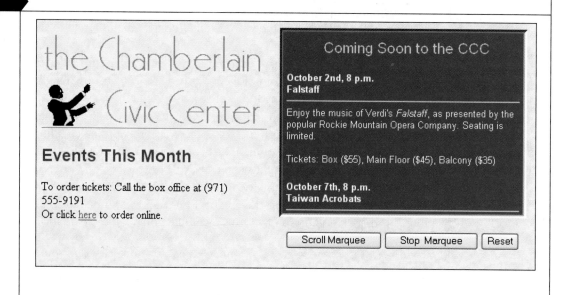

Much of the work in setting up the page has already been done for you. Your remaining task is to program the movements of the marquee.

To create the scrolling marquee:

1. Use your text editor to open the **ccctxt.js** file from the tutorial.11/case2 folder. Enter *your name* and *the date* in the comment section and save the file as **ccc.js**. Also open the **ccctxt.htm** with your text editor. Enter *your name* and *the date* in the comment section and save the file as **ccc.htm**.

   Take some time to study the contents of the ccc.htm file to become familiar with the objects and id values. Note that the text of the marquee has been stored in a div element with the id "BOX" and that the marquee text is divided into six separate div elements with ids from "Text1" through "Text6". Each of the six div Text elements is positioned using absolute positioning and has a different value for the top coordinate. You'll change this value to create the marquee effect.

2. Go to the **ccc.js** file in your text editor. Create the following functions: placeIt() to place objects at a specified coordinate given the object's id, and values for the x and y coordinate (assume coordinates are measured in pixels); shiftIt() to shift an object a specified distance given the object's id and the distance to be shifted in the x and y direction; and yCoord() to return the numeric value of an object's top coordinate given the object's id (assume that coordinate is measured in pixels).

3. Close the file, saving your changes.

4. Go to the **ccc.htm** file in your text editor and insert a link to the ccc.js file directly below the link to the styles.css style sheet.

5. Below the link to the ccc.js file, insert an embedded script. Within the embedded script create a function named moveIt(). The purpose of this function is to move an object vertically within the marquee. The moveIt() function should have a single parameter named "id" that indicates the id value of the object to be moved. Write the moveIt() function as follows:

   - Use the yCoord() function from the ccc.js file to retrieve the current y-coordinate of the id object. Store this coordinate value in a variable named "y".
   - If the value of y is less than −100, use the placeIt() function from the ccc.js file to place the id object at the page coordinate (5, 750). This has the effect of dropping the id object back down to the beginning of the marquee.
   - If the value of y is greater than or equal to −100, use the shiftIt() function from the ccc.js file to move the id object up 5 pixels. This has the effect of moving the object back up the marquee.

6. Above the moveIt(id) function, create a function named "Marquee()". This function will be used to start the marquee text moving for all six text objects. The Marquee() function should do the following:

   - Run the moveIt() function every 130 milliseconds with the value of the id parameter set to "Text1". This has the effect of continuously moving the text contained in the Text1 object. Store the time id for this command in a variable named "t1".
   - Also run the moveIt() function every 130 milliseconds for the objects "Text2" through "Text6". Store the value of the time ids for these commands in variables named "t2" through "t6".

7. Below the Marquee() function, create a function named Stop(). This function should halt the marquee text by clearing the time interval commands for the time ids t1 through t6.

8. Locate the button labeled Scroll Marquee and add an onclick event handler to run the Marquee() function when the button is clicked.

9. Locate the button labeled Stop Marquee and add an onclick event handler to run the Stop() function when it's clicked.

10. Locate the reset button and add an onclick event handler to reload the current page when the button is clicked. (*Hint*: Use the reload() method of the location object.)

11. Save your changes to the file and open the page in your Web browser. Verify that when you click the Scroll Marquee button, the marquee starts scrolling vertically from bottom to top, when you click the Stop Marquee button, the movement stops, and when you click the Reset button, the scrolling stops and the listings return to their original position.

12. Submit the completed Web site to your instructor.

Challenge

Explore how to create an animated trail map using object properties and methods

Case Problem 3

Data files needed for this Case Problem: button.gif, path.txt, photo2.jpg-photo8.jpg, redball.gif, text1.gif-text9.gif, trail.css, trail.gif, trail.js, trailtxt.htm

Chiricahua National Monument   Located in southeastern Arizona, the Chiricahua National Monument is a wilderness area containing the remnants of volcanic mountains rising between 5000 and 8000 feet above the surrounding grasslands. The park's unusual rock formations and beautiful spires make it a favorite spot of hikers and birders. The rangers at the Chiricahua National Monument have asked you to help them create an animated trail map that will highlight some of the most striking features of the area. They hope that by creating an animated map, more people will be encouraged to visit and enjoy the trails at Chiricahua. When completed, the map will be made available on the Web and at kiosks in the visitors' center. Figure 11-35 shows a preview of the map that you'll work on.

Figure 11-35

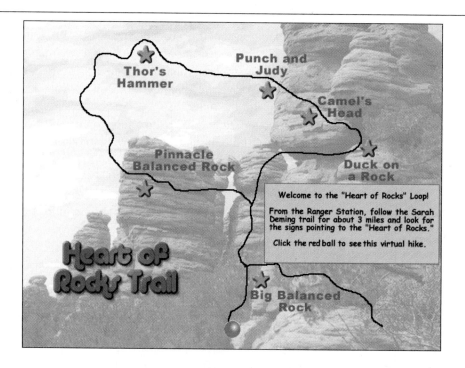

Much of the design work on the map has already been done. Another employee at Chiricahua has created all of the graphic images required for the map, including image files that display text descriptions of nine landmarks along the trail. For six of these landmarks, the employee has also scanned a photo of a rock formation or spire. The text descriptions are stored in graphic files named "text1.gif" through "text9.gif." The corresponding photo images are stored in files named "photo2.jpg" through "photo8.jpg" (there are no photos for the first and ninth landmarks).

For the animated map, the rangers would like a red ball to move along the Heart of Rocks Trail, stopping at each of the nine landmarks. At each landmark, the browser should display the corresponding text description and, if one exists for that landmark, the corresponding photo. Clicking the red ball should cause it to start moving again to the next landmark. After the red ball has reached the last landmark, the page should reload back to its original conditions after a delay of seven seconds.

A script file has already been created for you that contains functions for moving and placing an object on the Web page. The coordinates of the trail have been stored in two arrays in a text file. Your job is to write the program code that uses the functions and these coordinates to create the red ball animation.

To create the animated trail map:

1. Use your text editor to open the **trailtxt.htm** file from the tutorial.11/case3 folder. Enter *your name* and *the date* in the comment section and save the file as **trail.htm**. Take some time to study the contents of the file. There are nine landmarks on the trail with each trail description and photo located in a separate div element. Figure 11-36 lists the div elements for the photos, along with the text description of each landmark. Note that some landmarks contain only text descriptions and not photos. Also take some time to study the contents of the trail.js file. Note that it includes three functions: placeIt(), showIt(), and hideIt(). You should now be familiar with the purpose of these functions.

Figure 11-36

Landmark	Text	div Elements
1	A Welcome Message	text1
2	The Big Balanced Rock	text2, photo2
3	Duck on a Rock	text3, photo3
4	The Camel's Head	text4, photo4
5	Punch and Judy	text5, photo5
6	Thor's Hammer	text6, photo6
7	The Pinnacle Balanced Rock	text7, photo7
8	The Big Balanced Rock	text8, photo8
9	An Exit Message	text9

2. Below the link to the trail.css style sheet, insert a link to the trail.js script file.
3. Below the link to the trail.js script file, insert an embedded script element. Copy and paste the arrays in the path.txt file into this script element. The xArray contains the x coordinates of the trail path and the yArray contains the y coordinates. Each array contains a total of 270 values, marking out 270 distinct points along the trail.

4. Directly below the yArray variable declare a variable named "index". The index variable will be used to track the position of the red ball as it moves through the trail. Set the initial value of the index variable to 1.

5. Directly below the statement that declares the index variable, create the hideAll() function. The hideAll() function will ensure that all text and photo objects on the screen are hidden as the red ball travels around the trail. To create this effect, have the function hide each of the div elements with ids text1 through text9 and photo2 through photo8. (*Hint*: Use the hideIt() function from the trail.js file.)

Explore

6. Below the hideAll() function, create the describeIt() function, which will display the text description and photo for a given landmark. The describeIt() function should have two parameters, named text and photo, containing the id values of the text and photo to be displayed. Use the showIt() function from the trail.js file to display the text object. Since not every landmark has a photo, use object detection to determine whether a div element with the value of the photo parameter exists and if it does call the showIt() function to display the photo.

Explore

7. Below the describeIt() function, create the runPath() function. The runPath() function will move the red ball along the hiking trail, stopping if the red ball encounters one of the nine landmarks. The runPath() function should do the following:

   • Call the hideAll() function to ensure that all text and photos are hidden on the page.

   • Increase the value of the index variable by 1.

   • Use the placeIt() function to place the "redBall" object at the (xArray[index], yArray[index]) coordinate.

   • Use a switch statement to test the different values of the index variable. If the index variable equals 0, call the describeIt() function with the text parameter equal to "text1". This causes the red ball to stop and display the text description for the first landmark. You do not have to supply a value for the photo parameter. Be sure to include a break statement so that the program stops after running this command. If the index variable equals 16, call the describeIt() function with the text parameter equal to "text2" and the photo parameter equal to "photo2".

   • Continue adding case statements for the remaining landmarks. The third landmark should be displayed when the index variable equals 68. The fourth landmark corresponds to an index value of 82. The fifth landmark matches an index value of 97. The sixth landmark corresponds to an index value of 130. The seventh landmark appears when the index value equals 188. The eighth landmark is displayed when the index value equals 231. Make sure that you include a break statement after each case statement.

   • If the index variable equals 269, do the following in the case statement: (a) call the describeIt() function with "text9" as the parameter value, (b) set the value of the index variable to 0, and (c) reload the Web page after a seven-second delay. Be sure to place a break at the end of this case statement.

   • If the value of the index variable matches none of the case statements, the default behavior is to call the runPath() function again after a tenth-of-a-second delay. This will have the effect of continuing the red ball's trip through the hiking trail until it reaches one of the nine landmarks.

Explore

8. Locate the div element for the red ball. Mark the redball.gif inline image as a link and set the href attribute of the link to run the runPath() function when the ball is clicked.

9. Save your changes to the file.

10. Open the Web page in your browser and click on the red ball image. The red ball should move to the Big Balanced Rock landmark and display a text description and photo of the formation. There should be no descriptions or photos displayed as the red ball moves. To move to the next landmark on the trail, click the red ball again. Verify that the red ball traverses the entire trail, displaying photos and descriptions at each landmark. When you reach the end of the trail, the page should reload after a delay of seven seconds.

11. Submit the completed Web site to your instructor.

Create

Test your knowledge of objects and animation by creating an animated Web page

Case Problem 4

Data files needed for this Case Problem: bug.jpg, bug.txt, bugdead.jpg, shoe.jpg

The Exterminators   The Exterminators is a pest control company that specializes in the removal of insects, rodents, and small animals from urban homes and offices. Bruce Feinman has asked you to create a Web site for his company. He would like to have an opening screen in which a small bug flies around the page, only to be squashed. After the opening animation, he would like information about the company to appear on the page. Bruce provides you with the following files:

- bug.jpg — a clip art image of a bug
- bugdead.jpg — a clip art image of a squashed bug
- shoe.jpg — a clip art image of a giant shoe print
- bug.txt — a text file describing Bruce's company

You may supplement these files with any additional materials available to you. The final design of the Web site is up to you, but it must include the following features:

1. If a viewer's browser doesn't support DHTML, an index.htm file should appear that is static but informative.

2. If a customer's browser supports DHTML, use page branching to send the user from the index.htm file to an animated page named bug.htm.

3. Integrate at least one example of each of the following techniques into the bug.htm file:
   - Positioning with JavaScript
   - Linear animation
   - Path animation
   - Unhiding objects
   - The setTimeout or the setInterval method

4. Submit the completed Web site to your instructor.

Quick Check Answers

Session 11.1

1. The document object model is the organized structure of objects and events within a document. The three main DOMs used by the browser market are the W3C DOMs, the Internet Explorer DOM, and the Netscape 4 DOM.
2. the history object
3. document.forms
4. The IE DOM uses the document.all.*id* object and the W3C DOMs use document.getElementById("*id*") where *id* is the id value.
5. document.images[0].src="logo.jpg"
6. navigator.appName
7. window.print()
8. Object detection tests whether the browser supports a particular object. If the browser supports the object reference, then it most likely supports the DOM. You can test for support of the Netscape 4 DOM using the document.layers object reference. To test for support of the IE DOM use document.all. To test for support of the W3C DOMs use document.getElementById.

Session 11.2

1. getElementById("Logo").style.zIndex = getElementById("Logo").style.zIndex+1;
2. getElementById("Logo").style.left = "150px";
3. getElementById("Logo").style.top = "350px";
4. getElementById("Logo").style.visibility = "hidden";
5. getElementById("Logo").style.width = "100px";
6. getElementById("Logo").style.clip = "rect(10 210 150 10)";
7. getElementById("Logo").style.overflow = "auto";
8. document.all("Logo").style.pixelLeft=150;
9. document.all("Logo").style.pixelTop=350;

Session 11.3

1. setTimeout("moveGraphic()", 100);
2. mg = setInterval("moveGraphic()", 100);
3. clearInterval(mg);
4. window.outerHeight
5. window.innerHeight
6. In linear animation, you add or subtract a fixed value to change the coordinates of the object. In path animation, the coordinates are retrieved from an array of coordinate values.

Objectives

Session 12.1
- Understand how to work with the JavaScript document. images collection
- Create image objects and image object arrays
- Set the properties of image objects
- Create image rollovers with image objects and the document.images collection
- Understand how to create text rollovers

Session 12.2
- Understand how to work with pop-up and pull-down menus
- Hide and unhide objects in a Web page

Session 12.3
- Understand and implement Internet Explorer's filter styles
- Understand and apply Internet Explorer's transition styles
- Create an interpage transition using the meta element

Working with Special Effects

Creating Rollovers, Menus, Filters, and Transitions

Case

The World of Shakespeare

Clare Daynes is a professor of English literature at MidWest University. One of Clare's areas of research is the writings of William Shakespeare. In conjunction with her work, Clare is creating a site on the World Wide Web containing the complete works of Shakespeare. The site will include several tools of interest to researchers, including a search engine to locate particular words or phrases from Shakespeare's plays.

Clare has asked for your help in designing the Web site. She wants the site to have a user-friendly interface, and also some visual impact. She has seen sites on the Web that employ special effects such as rollovers and pop-up menus to aid in navigation. She would like to see these elements added to her site. She also wonders whether there are other special effects that can be added to her site.

Clare wants the page to load quickly, so she doesn't want any large multimedia files or applets attached to the site. Thus, she hopes you can create an interesting site using only DHTML.

Student Data Files

▼tutorial.12

  ▽ **tutorial folder**

    playstxt.htm
    wstxt.htm
    scripts.js
    styles1.css
    styles2.css
    + 2 demo files
    + 17 graphic files

  ▽ **review folder**

    temptxt.htm
    linktest.htm
    scripts.js
    plays.css
    + 14 graphic files

  ▽ **case1 folder**

    housetxt.htm
    premier.css
    + 18 graphic files

Student Data Files	▼tutorial.12 continued		
	▽ **case2 folder**	▽ **case3 folder**	▽ **case4 folder**
	tilestxt.htm	scavtxt.htm	lp.txt
	tiles.js	start.htm	ps.txt
	games.css	styles.css	sm.txt
	+ 10 graphic file	const.gif	+ 7 graphic files

Session 12.1

Working with Image Objects

You and Clare sit down to discuss the current state of her Web site. She shows you the opening page, shown in Figure 12-1. This page contains graphical links to five different pages, covering the following topics: Shakespeare's plays, his sonnets, his biography, the Globe Theatre, and the town of Stratford-upon-Avon. Open this page now.

To open the Shakespeare Web page:

1. Use your text editor to open **wstxt.htm** from the tutorial.12/tutorial folder. Enter **your name** and **the date** in the comment section and save the file as **ws.htm**.

2. Scroll through the document to familiarize yourself with its layout and its HTML code.

3. Open **ws.htm** in your Web browser. Figure 12-1 shows the current appearance of the page.

Figure 12-1	The World of Shakespeare opening page

The first addition that Clare would like you to create is a rollover effect, so that as users move the pointer over each of the five links, the graphic image changes. Clare suggests that you add a red drop shadow to each graphic image as the pointer moves over the link (see Figure 12-2). She feels that the addition of this effect will give the page visual interest, as well as give a tangible clue that the pointer is currently over a link.

as the pointer moves over the image, the image changes to one containing a colored drop shadow

To create a rollover effect for Clare's page, you first have to study how JavaScript can be used to create and manage images.

Referencing an Inline Image

Support for images is one of the oldest technologies in JavaScript, incorporated in the Level 0 document object model. (For a discussion of the different DOMs, see Tutorial 11.) Each inline image is part of an array of images in the document called the **image collection**. The image collection follows the same reference syntax used for other object collections. To reference a particular image in the document you can use either of the following forms:

```
document.images[idref]
document.images.idref
```

where *idref* is either an index number representing the position of the image in the array of all images in the document, or the text of the id or name attribute assigned to the image. As with arrays, the first image in the document has an index number of 0. For example, if the first inline image is

```
<img name="logo" id="logo" src="logo.jpg" alt="WS Page" />
```

you can reference this image using any of the following:

```
document.images[0]
document.images["logo"]
document.images.logo
```

Note that the id or name attribute must be placed in quotes. You can also bypass the document.images collection entirely and rely solely on the id attribute using the getElementById() method, which was discussed in the previous tutorial. In that case you could reference this image using the form

```
document.getElementById("logo")
```

Finally, many browsers also recognize the form

```
document.name
```

where *name* is the value of the name attribute for the inline image. However, since the name attribute has been deprecated in favor of the id attribute, it's generally safer to use the document.images object collection.

While the id and name attributes may seem to serve the same function of providing a unique identifier for an image, you should still use both of them in your HTML code (with their attribute values set to the same value). This is to provide backward-compatibility with earlier browser versions, which may not recognize the id attribute, but will recognize the name attribute. If you're writing code to be compliant with strict XHTML, you should use only the id attribute.

Reference Window	**Referencing an Inline Image**

- To reference an inline image, use the object collection
  ```
  document.images[idref]
  ```
  where *idref* is either the index number of the image object, or the text of its id or name attribute (enclosed in quotes). Note that the first inline image in the document has an index number of 0.
- You can also reference an inline image using the form
  ```
  document.getElementById(id)
  ```
  where *id* is the value of the id attribute for the inline image.
- Other browsers also support the reference form
  ```
  document.name
  ```
  where *name* is the value of the name attribute for the inline image.

Figure 12-3 shows the object references for the five inline images on the Shakespeare page. You'll be using this image collection to refer to individual images when you create the image rollovers later, so you'll need to keep this information in mind. Background images are not part of the images collection because they are not treated as inline images in the document. Also note that the index numbers refer to the order in which the <img> tags appear in an HTML file, not how the images are presented on the rendered Web page.

Figure 12-3	**Images in the Shakespeare page**

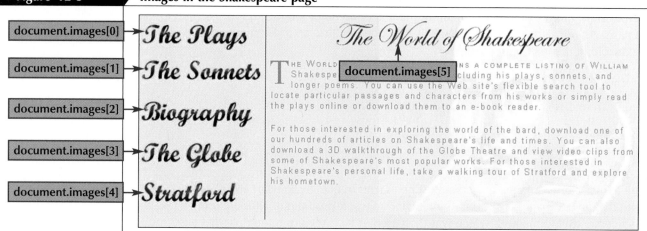

Creating an Image Object

JavaScript treats all inline images as objects known as **image objects**. You can also use JavaScript to create new image objects that are not part of a document but can be stored in the browser memory for use in your program. The syntax to create a new image object is

```
image = new Image(width, height);
```

where *image* is the variable that you'll use to store in the image object, and *width* and *height* are optional values specifying the width and height of the image in pixels. If you don't specify a width and height, the image object is sized to match the dimensions of whatever graphic file is stored in the image. Notice that the image object does not support a parameter for specifying the source of the image object. To provide this information you need to modify the properties of the image object itself.

Creating an Image Object

Reference Window

- To create an image object, use the syntax
    ```
    image = new Image(width, height);
    ```
    where *image* is the variable name you give the image object, and *width* and *height* are optional values specifying the width and height of the image in pixels. If you don't specify a width and height, the image object is sized to match the dimensions of the graphic file.
- To specify the source for an image object, use the property
    ```
    image.src = "url";
    ```
    where *image* is the image object and *url* is the URL of the image's graphic file.

Properties of Image Objects

Like all objects, image objects have properties that determine how they appear and how they are used by the browser. Most of these properties will be very familiar to you since they are derived from the attributes associated with inline images in HTML. Figure 12-4 summarizes some of the properties of image objects.

| Figure 12-4 | Properties of the image object |

Property	Description	Example
alt	Alternate text displayed by non-graphical browsers	document.images[5].alt = "The World of Shakespeare";
border	The size of the image border in pixels	document.images.[0].border = 0;

complete	A Boolean value indicating whether the image has been completely loaded by the browser	if (document.images[0].complete) {
		   commands to run
		}

height	The height of the image in pixels	document.images[0].height = 50;
hspace	The horizontal space around the image in pixels	document.images[0].hspace = 10;
id	The id of the image object	document.images[5].id = "logo";
lowsrc	The URL of a low resolution version of the image	document.images[5].lowsrc = "logo_small.jpg";
name	The name of the image object	document.images[5].name = "logo";
src	The URL of the graphic image to be displayed in the image object	document.images[5].src = "logo.jpg";
vspace	The vertical space around the image in pixels	document.images[0].vspace = 10;
width	The width of the image in pixels	document.images[0].width = 100;

For example, to create an image object and then define its source, you would use the src property, as in the following set of commands:

```
var newImage = new Image();
newImage.src = "logo.jpg";
```

When run, these commands create the newImage image object and then store the source file, logo.jpg, as part of its definition. In addition to the properties listed in Figure 12-4, you can also use the style property discussed in Tutorial 11 to modify the appearance of an image object as it appears in your Web browser. Thus, if you wanted to set the border size around the image to 5 pixels, you could use either of the following JavaScript commands:

```
newImage.border = "5px";
newImage.style.borderWidth = "5px";
```

Because the border property is derived from HTML's deprecated border attribute, you may wish to use the style property to keep your code consistent with current HTML and XHTML standards.

Note that older browsers such as Netscape 4 do not allow you to modify the appearance of an inline image once your browser has loaded it. For example, you cannot change the dimensions of an image by modifying its height and width properties. Netscape 4 allows you to do this only before the page has been loaded. Current browsers, on the other hand, make all of the attributes of an inline image available to you to modify at any time. Thus, if you're writing a script in which the appearance of an inline image is to be modified by the users' browsers, you should be aware that your code might not work correctly for users of older browser versions.

Detecting Image Objects

It is possible (though not likely) that your users will be running a very early browser version that does not support JavaScript's treatment of image objects. If this is a concern, you can use object detection to determine each user's level of browser support. The following structure tests for support of the document.images object and then runs a command block if that support is detected:

```
if (document.images) {
    Command block to create and modify images
}
```

If a user is running an older browser that doesn't support the images object collection, the value of document.images is false, and the command block that follows is skipped. Such users will still be able to use the Web site, but they won't see the image rollovers. Browsers that do support the document.images object collection will run the command block.

Creating an Image Rollover

An **image rollover** is created when you change the source of an inline image from one graphic file to another, usually in response to the mouse pointer hovering over and then leaving the image. Clare shows you a collection of images and alternate images to be used in the Web page, as shown in Figure 12-5. When the user hovers the mouse pointer over an image, the browser should load the corresponding image from the right column in Figure 12-5. When the mouse pointer moves off the image, the corresponding image from the left column in Figure 12-5 should be redisplayed.

Rollover images | **Figure 12-5**

image	rollover image
The Plays	*The Plays*
plays_out.jpg	plays_over.jpg
The Sonnets	*The Sonnets*
son_out.jpg	son_over.jpg
Biography	*Biography*
bio_out.jpg	bio_over.jpg
The Globe	*The Globe*
globe_out.jpg	globe_over.jpg
Stratford	*Stratford*
strat_out.jpg	strat_over.jpg

Preloading the Images

Performance is an important consideration when creating a rollover effect. You do not want users to have to wait while their browsers download the new images. To avoid this problem, you can preload all of the image objects a user may need, storing the images in the browser's memory. When the browser invokes the rollover effect, the new image file is then quickly retrieved from memory rather than going through a process of loading the graphic file. Thus, all of the loading of image objects is done when the document is initially loaded by the browser.

In cases where you apply rollover effects to several images on a page, it is often more efficient to store your image objects in arrays. The following is a typical example:

```
var ImgOver = new Array();
ImgOver[0] = new Image();
ImgOver[1] = new Image();
ImgOver[2] = new Image();
```

With the image objects in arrays, you can reference them in your program using their array index numbers rather than with distinct variable names. In Clare's page, you need to create five pairs of image objects. Place these images in two image object arrays, named ImgOver and ImgOut. In addition, add an object test to ensure that the browser supports the document.images object collection.

To create the ImgOver and ImgOut image arrays:

1. Above the closing </head> tag, insert the following embedded script (see Figure 12-6):

```
<script type="text/javascript">
if (document.images) {
    var ImgOver = new Array();
    ImgOver[0] = new Image();
    ImgOver[1] = new Image();
    ImgOver[2] = new Image();
    ImgOver[3] = new Image();
    ImgOver[4] = new Image();


    var ImgOut = new Array();
    ImgOut[0] = new Image();
    ImgOut[1] = new Image();
    ImgOut[2] = new Image();
    ImgOut[3] = new Image();
    ImgOut[4] = new Image();
}
</script>
```

Creating the ImgOver and ImgOut arrays ◄ **Figure 12-6**

```
<link href="styles1.css" rel="stylesheet" type="text/css" />
<script type="text/javascript">
if (document.images) {
    var ImgOver = new Array();
    ImgOver[0] = new Image();
    ImgOver[1] = new Image();
    ImgOver[2] = new Image();
    ImgOver[3] = new Image();
    ImgOver[4] = new Image();

    var ImgOut = new Array();
    ImgOut[0] = new Image();
    ImgOut[1] = new Image();
    ImgOut[2] = new Image();
    ImgOut[3] = new Image();
    ImgOut[4] = new Image();
}
</script>
</head>
```

▶ **2.** Save your changes to the file.

Next, you have to specify the graphic file for each of these image objects. For the objects in the ImgOver array you'll use the graphic files specified in the right column of Figure 12-5. For objects in the ImgOut array, you'll use the graphic files from the left column in Figure 12-5.

To populate the ImgOver and ImgOut arrays:

▶ **1.** Before the command to create the ImgOut array, insert the following commands to specify the source for the ImgOver objects:

```
ImgOver[0].src = "plays_over.jpg";
ImgOver[1].src = "son_over.jpg";
ImgOver[2].src = "bio_over.jpg";
ImgOver[3].src = "globe_over.jpg";
ImgOver[4].src = "strat_over.jpg";
```

▶ **2.** Before the closing curly brace, insert the source for the ImgOut objects (you can use the copy and paste features of your editor, changing just "Over" to "Out" twice in each line, to reduce the amount of typing required).

```
ImgOut[0].src = "plays_out.jpg";
ImgOut[1].src = "son_out.jpg";
ImgOut[2].src = "bio_out.jpg";
ImgOut[3].src = "globe_out.jpg";
ImgOut[4].src = "strat_out.jpg";
```

Figure 12-7 shows the revised ws.htm file.

Figure 12-7 ▶ **Specifying sources for the ImgOut and ImgOver arrays**

```
if (document.images) {
   var ImgOver = new Array();
   ImgOver[0] = new Image();
   ImgOver[1] = new Image();
   ImgOver[2] = new Image();
   ImgOver[3] = new Image();
   ImgOver[4] = new Image();
   ImgOver[0].src = "plays_over.jpg";
   ImgOver[1].src = "son_over.jpg";
   ImgOver[2].src = "bio_over.jpg";
   ImgOver[3].src = "globe_over.jpg";
   ImgOver[4].src = "strat_over.jpg";

   var ImgOut = new Array();
   ImgOut[0] = new Image();
   ImgOut[1] = new Image();
   ImgOut[2] = new Image();
   ImgOut[3] = new Image();
   ImgOut[4] = new Image();
   ImgOut[0].src = "plays_out.jpg";
   ImgOut[1].src = "son_out.jpg";
   ImgOut[2].src = "bio_out.jpg";
   ImgOut[3].src = "globe_out.jpg";
   ImgOut[4].src = "strat_out.jpg";
}
```

Swapping Image Objects

Once the images are preloaded, you can use JavaScript to swap the source for one image with the source for another. When you place image objects in arrays, you can match the array of image objects with the array of inline images in the document.images collection. For example, the command

```
document.images[0].src = ImgOver[0].src
```

replaces the source of the first inline image in the document with the source of the first image object in the ImgOver array. A more general function to do this would be

```
function RollOver(i) {
   if (document.images) document.images[i].src = ImgOver[i].src;
}
```

where the i parameter indicates which objects in the two arrays should be swapped. Note that we use object detection again to verify that the browser supports image objects before attempting to do the swap. A similar function would swap the images in the document.images collection with the images in the ImgOut array:

```
function RollOut(i) {
   if (document.images) document.images[i].src = ImgOut[i].src;
}
```

Add these two functions to the embedded script element in Clare's Web page.

To add the RollOver() and RollOut() functions to the file:

1. Before the closing </script> tag, enter the following commands (see Figure 12-8):

```
function RollOver(i) {
   if (document.images) document.images[i].src = ImgOver[i].src;
}
function RollOut(i) {
   if (document.images) document.images[i].src = ImgOut[i].src;
}
```

The RollOver() and RollOut() functions | Figure 12-8

```
function RollOver(i) {
    if (document.images) document.images[i].src = ImgOver[i].src;
}

function RollOut(i) {
    if (document.images) document.images[i].src = ImgOut[i].src;
}
</script>
</head>
```

▶ **2.** Save your changes to the file.

Running the Image Rollover

To run the two functions we just created we'll use event handlers. Recall from Tutorial 11 that event handlers specify the commands that should be run in response to an event occurring within an element. In this case, we'll use two event handlers: onmouseover and onmouseout. When the mouse pointer hovers over the image, the onmouseover event handler is used to run the RollOver() function. When the mouse pointer moves off of the image, the onmouseout event handler is used to run the RollOut() function. We'll attach these two event handlers to each of the five images in the list of links on the Shakespeare home page. The parameter values for the RollOver() and RollOut() functions will be based on the image being rolled over. For example, because the image displaying the "The Plays" graphic is the first inline image in the document, we'll add the following event handlers to that image:

```
onmouseover = "RollOver(0)" onmouseout = "RollOut(0)"
```

Remember that the DOM numbers elements starting from 0 rather than 1. Thus, because this is the first inline image, the index number sent to the RollOver() and RollOut() functions is "0". The other images will have index values of 1, 2, 3, and 4, corresponding to the locations of those images in both the document.images collection and the image object arrays.

To call the RollOver() and RollOut() functions:

▶ **1.** Scroll down the file until you locate the inline image element for the plays_out.jpg graphic image.

▶ **2.** Add the following attributes the <img /> tag for that inline image:

```
onmouseover="RollOver(0)" onmouseout="RollOut(0)"
```

Now add the onmouseover and onmouseout event handlers for the rest of the inline images in the list of links (again, you can use the copy and paste features of your text editor to make this task easier).

▶ **3.** Locate the inline image for the son_out.jpg graphic and insert the event handlers:

```
onmouseover="RollOver(1)" onmouseout="RollOut(1)"
```

▶ **4.** Within the <img /> tag for the bio_out.jpg graphic insert:

```
onmouseover="RollOver(2)" onmouseout="RollOut(2)"
```

▶ **5.** Insert the following within the <img /> tag for the globe_out.jpg graphic:

```
onmouseover="RollOver(3)" onmouseout="RollOut(3)"
```

6. Finally, locate the inline image for the strat_out.jpg graphic and insert the event handlers:

```
onmouseover="RollOver(4)" onmouseout="RollOut(4)"
```

Your revised code should match that shown in Figure 12-9.

| Figure 12-9 | Running the image rollover functions |

```
<div id="links">
<a href="plays.htm">
   <img src="plays_out.jpg" alt="The Plays" onmouseover="Rollover(0)" onmouseout="Rollout(0)" />
</a>

<a href="sonnets.htm">
   <img src="son_out.jpg" alt="The Sonnets" onmouseover="Rollover(1)" onmouseout="Rollout(1)" />
</a>

<a href="bio.htm">
   <img src="bio_out.jpg" alt="Biography" onmouseover="Rollover(2)" onmouseout="Rollout(2)" />
</a>

<a href="globe.htm">
   <img src="globe_out.jpg" alt="The Globe" onmouseover="Rollover(3)" onmouseout="Rollout(3)" />
</a>

<a href="stratford.htm">
   <img src="strat_out.jpg" alt="Stratford" onmouseover="Rollover(4)" onmouseout="Rollout(4)" />
</a>
</div>
```

Note that you also could have produced the same rollover effect by adding these event handlers to the <a> tags that surround the inline images. You can now test the page to see the effects of the rollover functions.

To test the rollovers:

1. Save your changes to the **ws.htm** file and close your text editor.

2. Reopen or refresh **ws.htm** in your Web browser.

3. Move your mouse cursor over each of the five linked images and verify that a red drop shadow appears as a rollover image is swapped with the original image. (Note that Clare hasn't created the other five Web pages yet, so if you test the links you will get an error message from your browser.)

Trouble? If the rollover effect does not work, check your code against the code shown in Figures 12-6 to 12-9. Pay close attention to the use of uppercase and lowercase letters.

4. Close your Web browser.

Creating a Text Rollover

While the Shakespeare page employs rollovers only of graphical images, the rollover effect can also be applied directly to text. This is usually done with linked text, but can also be applied to other elements in a Web document. Note that older browsers such as Netscape 4.7 or earlier and versions of Internet Explorer prior to 5.0 do not support text rollovers.

Using the Hover Pseudo-Class

If you are creating a rollover effect for linked text, the simplest approach is to use a style declaration for the <a> tag that employs the hover pseudo-class. The general syntax is

```
a:hover {styles}
```

where *styles* are the styles you want applied to the linked text when the mouse hovers over the link. For example, to change your links to a bold red font in response to the hover event, apply the style

```
a:hover {color:red; font-weight:bold}
```

This approach allows you to create a rollover effect without writing JavaScript code.

General Text Rollovers

A more general approach is to modify the style properties of an element in response to the rollover event. The following code shows how you would change the appearance of a bulleted list item:

```
<script type="text/javascript">
function RollOver() {
   this.style.color="red";
   this.style.fontWeight = "bold";
}
function RollOut() {
   this.style.color = "black";
   this.style.fontWeight = "normal";
}
</script>
<ul>
   <li onmouseover="RollOver()" onmouseout="RollOut()">
      The Globe
   </li>
</ul>
```

As the mouse pointer passes over the list item, the font color of the text "The Globe" changes to a boldfaced red, and then changes to a normal black when the pointer moves off of the item. Note that to apply the style to the list item, the RollOver() and RollOut() functions use the "this" keyword, which is an object name that refers to whatever the current object is. When the RollOver() and RollOut() functions are called in response to the onmouseover and onmouseout events, the current object is the list item containing the text "The Globe".

You've completed your work with rollovers for Clare. She's pleased with the visual interest it adds to her page. She now has some other work she wants you to do on her Web site. In the next session, you'll learn how to use DHTML to create a menu system for a page listing Shakespeare's plays.

Session 12.1 Quick Check

Review

1. The second inline image on your Web page has the name "Links". What are two ways of referencing this image in JavaScript?
2. What code would you enter to change the dimensions of an inline image named "Links" to 150 pixels wide by 200 pixels high?
3. What code would you enter to change the source of the Links image to "links2.jpg"?
4. What code would you use to create an image object named "LinksOver" that is 75 pixels wide and 100 pixels high?

5. What code would you enter to create an array of image objects named LinksArray, containing image objects pointing to graphic files image1.jpg, image2.jpg, and image3.jpg?
6. What "if" condition must you use to determine whether a browser supports the image collection?

Session 12.2

Working with Menus

Clare is pleased with your modifications to the opening page. She wants you to work next on a page that contains links to all of Shakespeare's plays. Shakespeare wrote almost 40 plays, and Clare is concerned that a page with so many links will be cumbersome. Ideally, she would like all of the links to fit within the space of a single screen.

Clare wonders whether you can create a series of menus containing links to each of the plays. She envisions four menus, one for each of the four types of Shakespeare's plays: comedies, histories, tragedies, and romances. Clare sketches out her idea for you, as shown in Figure 12-10.

Figure 12-10 ▶ **Menus for the Plays page**

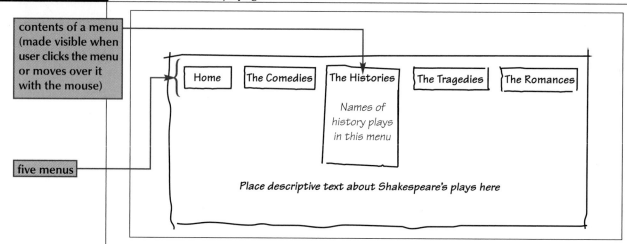

contents of a menu (made visible when user clicks the menu or moves over it with the mouse)

Home | The Comedies | The Histories | The Tragedies | The Romances

Names of history plays in this menu

five menus

Place descriptive text about Shakespeare's plays here

Clare suggests placing five headers at the top of the page: one for each of the four types of plays, and a fifth box that is linked to the opening page. When a user moves the mouse pointer over one of the four play type headers, a menu box should appear, listing all of Shakespeare's plays of that type. The user can then click one of the plays from the list to go to a Web page containing the text of that play. If the user moves the mouse pointer off of the list, the list of plays should disappear, leaving just the five headers at the top of the page.

Creating a Pop-Up Menu

Menus fall into two general classes: pop-ups and pull-downs. In a **pop-up menu**, a user clicks an object on the page and the menu appears, sometimes elsewhere on the page. To close a pop-up menu, a user clicks either the menu itself or another item on the page.

One common way to create a pop-up menu for the Web is to place the menu contents within a set of <div> container tags, hidden on the page using the visibility style attribute. When a user clicks an object on the page, a JavaScript program is run that unhides the menu (see Figure 12-11). To rehide the menu, a second JavaScript program is run that changes the menu's visibility property back to hidden.

Creating a pop-up menu | **Figure 12-11**

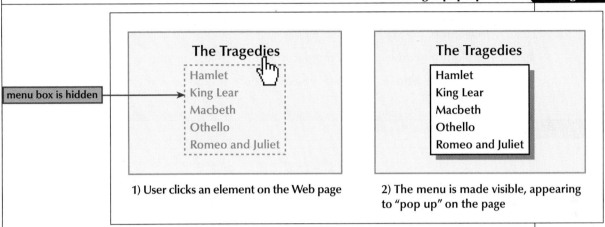

1) User clicks an element on the Web page

2) The menu is made visible, appearing to "pop up" on the page

Creating a Pull-Down Menu

In a **pull-down menu**, part of the menu—usually a header for the title—is visible. When a user clicks the visible part (or moves the mouse pointer over it), the rest of the menu is revealed. This creates the illusion that the rest of the menu is being "pulled down" from the visible part.

To create a pull-down menu, you again place the contents within a set of <div> tags, but this time you use the clip style attribute to "cut off" part of the menu. The part of the menu that is still visible usually contains a title describing the menu's contents. When a user either clicks the title or moves the mouse pointer over it, a JavaScript command is run that displays the hidden section (see Figure 12-12). Clicking another title on the page or moving the pointer off of the title pulls the menu back up. To change the size of the clipping rectangle, you modify the value of the clip property.

Creating a pull-down menu | **Figure 12-12**

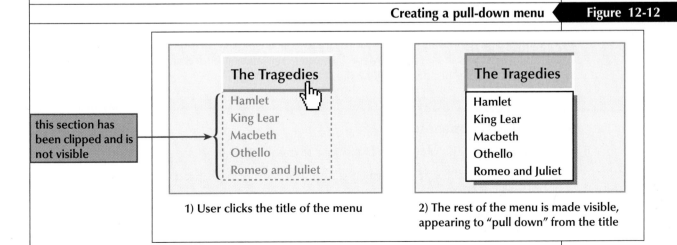

1) User clicks the title of the menu

2) The rest of the menu is made visible, appearing to "pull down" from the title

Clare decides to use a pop-up rather than a pull-down menu. Most of the work of setting up the contents of the menus and their positions on the page has already been done for you. The Plays page is in the playstxt.htm file. Open this file now.

To open the Plays Web page:

1. Use your text editor to open **playstxt.htm** from the tutorial.12/tutorial folder. Enter **your name** and **the date** in the comment section and save the file as **plays.htm**.

2. Scroll through the code for the document to familiarize yourself with its content.

3. Open **plays.htm** in your Web browser. Figure 12-13 shows the current appearance of the page.

Figure 12-13 | **The menus for the Plays page**

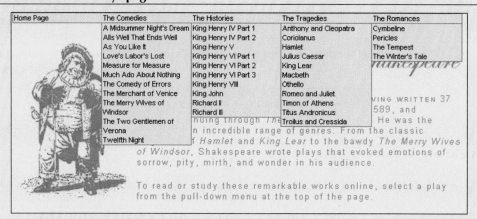

Trouble? Different browsers might display the Web page slightly differently. Figure 12-13 shows how the page appears in the Internet Explorer 6.0 browser for Windows.

The menu contains five submenu titles, created using <div> tags and given the id values "Home," "Comedy," "History," "Tragedy," and "Romance." The contents of the Comedy, History, Tragedy, and Romance menus are placed in their own div elements with the ids "ComedyMenu," "HistoryMenu," "TragedyMenu," and "RomanceMenu." Within each menu box is a list of all the plays of that genre, linked to individual pages for each play. The rest of the page is contained in a div element named "main".

As the page stands, the menu boxes hide most of the page, so we'll start editing Clare's page by hiding the menus using the visibility style. The menus all belong to the same class, which is named "Menu", so we'll add an embedded style sheet to the plays. htm file to hide this class of elements.

To hide the menus:

1. Return to the **plays.htm** file in your text editor.

2. Add the following embedded style above the closing </head> tag as shown in Figure 12-14:

```
<style type="text/css">
   .Menu {visibility: hidden}
</style>
```

Hiding the menus | **Figure 12-14**

```
<title>Shakespeare's Plays</title>
<link href="styles2.css" rel="stylesheet" type="text/css" />
<style type="text/css">
    .Menu {visibility: hidden}
</style>

</head>
```

3. Save your changes to the file.

4. Refresh or reopen **plays.htm** in your Web browser. As shown in Figure 12-15 the menus should now be hidden.

The Plays page with hidden menus | **Figure 12-15**

| Home Page | The Comedies | The Histories | The Tragedies | The Romances |

Creating Pop-Up Menu Functions

You discuss with Clare exactly how she wants the menus to work. Clare outlines the following behaviors:

• The contents of only one pop-up menu should be displayed at a time.
• If a user clicks a menu title, the corresponding menu should be displayed, and any other menu should be hidden.
• If a user clicks the page content that appears below the menus, any active menu should be hidden.

To perform these tasks, you need some functions to hide and unhide elements on the page. Two functions named hideIt() and showIt() have already been created for you and stored in the scripts.js file. Figure 12-16 shows the code for these two functions.

The functions in the scripts.js file | **Figure 12-16**

```
function hideIt(object) {
    object.style.visibility="hidden";
}

function showIt(object) {
    object.style.visibility="visible";
}
```

Both functions have a single parameter named "object" which represents an object on the page that you want to either hide or show. Add a link to this file's functions in the plays.htm file.

To link to the scripts.js file:

1. Return to the **plays.htm** file in your text editor.

2. Add the following external script element directly above the closing </head> tag:

```
<script src="scripts.js" type="text/javascript"></script>
```

3. Save your changes to the file.

To create Clare's pop-up menus, you need a way to track which menu, if any, is currently visible. We'll do this by creating a global variable named "ActiveMenu" that stores an object representing the current menu. The initial value of this variable will be null, because no menus are visible when a browser initially loads the page.

To create the ActiveMenu variable:

1. Above the external script element you just inserted, add the following embedded script element as shown in Figure 12-17:

```
<script type="text/javascript">
   var ActiveMenu = null;
</script>
```

Figure 12-17 **Creating the ActiveMenu variable**

```
<script type="text/javascript">
     var ActiveMenu = null;
</script>
<script src="scripts.js" type="text/javascript"></script>
</head>
```

2. Save your changes to the file.

Displaying Menu Contents

Next, you need to create two functions: one to display one of the hidden menus, and the other to hide the visible menu. The first function you'll create will hide the currently active menu. The code for the hideActive() function is

```
function hideActive() {
if (ActiveMenu !== null) {
   hideIt(ActiveMenu);
   ActiveMenu = null;
}
}
```

The function first has to test whether there is an active menu to hide (to avoid generating an error message if there is not). It does this by testing whether the value of the ActiveMenu variable has been set to null. If the variable is not null, the function calls the hideIt() function from the scripts.js file to hide the active menu, and then resets the value of the ActiveMenu variable to null to indicate that no menu is now actively displayed on the Web page.

To insert the hideActive() function:

▶ **1.** Insert the following code below the declaration that creates the ActiveMenu variable as shown in Figure 12-18:

```
function hideActive() {
if (ActiveMenu !== null) {
   hideIt(ActiveMenu);
   ActiveMenu = null;
}
}
```

Inserting the hideActive() function ◀ | **Figure 12-18**

```
<script type="text/javascript">
    var ActiveMenu = null;

    function hideActive() {
    if (ActiveMenu !== null) {
        hideIt(ActiveMenu);
        ActiveMenu = null;
    }
    }
</script>
```

▶ **2.** Save your changes to the file.

Next you'll create a function named popMenu() to display a menu. This function will perform three actions:

1. Hide the active menu.
2. Set the menu selected by the user as the new active menu.
3. Display the menu selected by the user.

The code for the popMenu() function is

```
function popMenu(M) {
   hideActive();
   ActiveMenu = document.getElementById(M);
   showIt(ActiveMenu);
}
```

The popMenu() function has one parameter, M, which is the id of the menu that will be displayed on the page. The first line of the function calls the hideActive() function to hide the previous menu. The second line sets the ActiveMenu variable to the menu selected by the user. The third line of the function uses the showIt() function from the scripts.js file to display the newly selected menu. For example, to display the contents of the Comedy menu, you would use the command

```
popMenu("ComedyMenu");
```

and the browser would hide the active menu (if one exists), and then display the Comedy menu, making it the new active menu. Add the popMenu() function to the plays.htm file now.

To insert the popMenu() function:

1. Insert the following code below the hideActive() function as shown in Figure 12-19:

```
function popMenu(M) {
    hideActive();
    ActiveMenu = document.getElementById(M);
    showIt(ActiveMenu);
}
```

| Figure 12-19 | Inserting the popMenu() function |

```
<script type="text/javascript">
    var ActiveMenu = null;

    function hideActive() {
    if (ActiveMenu !== null) {
        hideIt(ActiveMenu);
        ActiveMenu = null;
    }
    }

    function popMenu(M) {
        hideActive();
        ActiveMenu = document.getElementById(M);
        showIt(ActiveMenu);
    }
</script>
```

2. Save your changes to the file.

Calling the Menu Functions

You want to run the popMenu() function when the user clicks one of the menu titles. Each of the menu titles is enclosed within <a> tags. For example, the code for the Comedy Menu title is

```
<div id="Comedy" class="MenuTitle">
    <a href="#">The Comedies</a>
</div>
```

The link currently points to "#", which causes the page to reload. However, you want to change this so that the menu title runs the popMenu() function when clicked. You can do this by changing the target of the link to the JavaScript function. The revised HTML code is

```
<div id="Comedy" class="MenuTitle">
    <a href="JavaScript:popMenu('ComedyMenu')">The Comedies</a>
</div>
```

When a user clicks the Comedy menu title, the contents of the Comedy menu are displayed. Make this change for the Comedy menu title and the other menu titles on Clare's page.

To call the popMenu() function:

1. Scroll down the plays.htm file and locate the <div> tag for the Comedy element.

2. Change the target of the link from "#" to **"JavaScript: popMenu('ComedyMenu')"**.

3. Change the target of the History link from "#" to **"JavaScript: popMenu('HistoryMenu')"**.

4. Change the target of the Tragedy link from "#" to **"JavaScript: popMenu('TragedyMenu')"**.

5. Change the target of the Romance link from "#" to **"JavaScript: popMenu('RomanceMenu')"**.

Figure 12-20 shows revised HTML code for the menu titles.

Calling the popMenu() functions ◄ **Figure 12-20**

```
<div id="Home" class="MenuTitle">
    <a href="ws.htm">Home Page</a>
</div>
<div id="Comedy" class="MenuTitle">
    <a href="JavaScript:popMenu('ComedyMenu')">The Comedies</a>
</div>
<div id="History" class="MenuTitle">
    <a href="JavaScript:popMenu('HistoryMenu')">The Histories</a>
</div>
<div id="Tragedy" class="MenuTitle">
    <a href="JavaScript:popMenu('TragedyMenu')">The Tragedies</a>
</div>
<div id="Romance" class="MenuTitle">
    <a href="JavaScript:popMenu('RomanceMenu')">The Romances</a>
</div>
```

If a user clicks in the main body of the Web page you want to hide the active menu. You can do this by adding an onclick event handler to the div element for the main page content, running the hideActive() function in response.

To call the hideActive() function:

1. Scroll down the file and locate the <div> tag for the main element.

2. Add the event handler **onclick="hideActive()"** to the <div> tag as shown in Figure 12-21.

Calling the hideActive() function ◄ **Figure 12-21**

```
<div id="main" onclick="hideActive()">
    <p id="falstaff"><img src="falstaff.jpg" alt="" /></p>
    <p id="title"><img src="theplays.jpg" alt="The Plays of Shakespeare" /></p>
    <p id="firstp">
    William Shakespeare is credited with having written 37 plays,
    starting with <i>Henry VI, Part 1</i> in 1589, and continuing through
    <i>The Tempest</i> in 1611. He was the master of an incredible range of
    genres. From the classic tragedies of <i>Hamlet</i> and <i>King Lear</i>
    to the bawdy <i>The Merry Wives of Windsor</i>, Shakespeare wrote plays
    that evoked emotions of sorrow, pity, mirth, and wonder in his audience. </p>
    <p>To read or study these remarkable works online, select a play
    from the pull-down menu at the top of the page. </p>
</div>
```

3. Close the file, saving your changes.

4. Reload or refresh **plays.htm** in your Web browser. Verify that as you click the menu titles, the menu contents appear on the page and that when you click the rest of the page contents the active menu is hidden. Figure 12-22 shows the pop-up menu in action.

Figure 12-22 | The pop-up menu for the Plays Web page

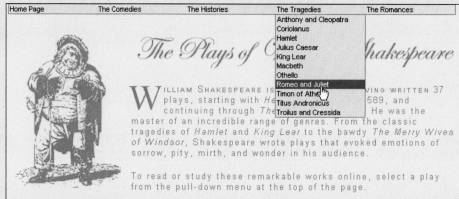

Trouble? At this point, the Web pages for the individual plays have not been created, so you will receive an error message if you click the links in the pop-up menus.

Trouble? If you click a blank area of the document window outside of the page content, the pop-up menu will not close.

5. After you are finished viewing the Web page, close your Web browser.

Clare is pleased with the Web page. She feels that the pop-up menus you created will give her users quick access to the rest of her Web site, while leaving the page simple and easy to use. She has a few other features that she wants you to add to the page. You'll discuss those changes in the next session.

Review

Session 12.2 Quick Check

1. What is a pop-up menu?
2. What is a pull-down menu?
3. What JavaScript command would you use to hide an object with the id "main"?
4. What JavaScript command would you use to unhide an object with the id "main"?

Session 12.3

Working with Internet Explorer Filters

You've employed two special effects for Clare's Web site: an image rollover and a pop-up menu. Clare would like you to investigate another type of special effect supported by Internet Explorer, called a filter. A **filter** is an effect that is applied to an object or page to change its appearance. Using Internet Explorer filters, you can make text or images appear partially transparent, add a drop shadow, or make an object appear to glow. Filters were introduced in Internet Explorer version 4.0 and are not supported by other browsers, so you have to use them with caution.

Filters cannot be applied to every element on a page. In Internet Explorer 4.0, filters can be applied only to the following elements:

- div and span elements with a defined height, width, or absolute position
- inline images and marquees
- form buttons, input fields, and text area fields
- table headings, rows, and cells

If you want to apply a filter to a div or span element in Internet Explorer 4.0, you must define an absolute position for the element, or set its height or its width; otherwise, Internet Explorer will generate an error message. In Internet Explorer 5.5 and above, any element that has a defined height and width can be filtered.

A filter is applied either by adding a filter style to the Web page's style sheet or by running a JavaScript command that applies a filter to an object in the document. Let's first look at how to create a filter using styles.

Applying Filters by Using Styles

The syntax that Internet Explorer uses to employ the filter style differs between browser versions. In version 4.0, the filter style is expressed as

```
filter: filter_name(params)
```

where `filter_name` is the name of one of the many Internet Explorer 4.0 filters, and `params` are the parameter values (if any) that apply to the filter. The syntax for filter styles employed in Internet Explorer 5.5 and above is

```
filter: progid:DXImageTransform.Microsoft.filter_name(params)
```

Besides the syntactical differences between the two versions, there are some differences in how different versions of Internet Explorer apply the filter style. In Internet Explorer 4.0, the filter effect is clipped when it is set too close to an object's boundary; with Internet Explorer 5.5 and above, the filter effect extends beyond an object's boundary.

Figure 12-23 lists some of the filter names and parameters supported by Internet Explorer 5.5 and above.

Figure 12-23 ▶ **Internet Explorer 5.5 filters**

Filter Name	Parameters	Description
Alpha	style=0, 1, 2, 3 opacity=1–100 finishOpacity=1–100 startX=1–100 finishX=1–100 startY=1–100 finishY=1–100	Applies a transparency filter. A low opacity value makes the object transparent, while a high value makes the object opaque. The style parameter is used to indicate the direction of the transparency effect. The rest of the parameters control where in the element the transparency is applied
BasicImage	rotation=0, 1, 2, 3 opacity=0–1 mirror=0, 1 invert=0, 1 xRay=0, 1 grayscale=0,1	Modifies the appearance of the object. The rotation parameter rotates the object (0=0 deg., 1=90 deg., 2=180 deg., 3=270 deg.). The opacity parameter sets the opacity of the object. The remaining parameters, if their values are set to "1," create a mirror image, invert the object, apply an "x-ray" effect, or display the object in grayscale
Blur	pixelRadius=*value* makeShadow=true, false shadowOpacity=0–1	Blurs the object. The pixelRadius parameter determines the amount of the blurring. The makeShadow and shadowOpacity parameters apply shadowing to the blur effect
Chroma	color=#*rrggbb*	Makes a specified color in the object transparent
DropShadow	color=#*rrggbb* offX=*value* offY=*value*	Creates a drop shadow of the specified color with a length offX in the x-direction and offY in the y-direction
Emboss		Applies an embossing effect to the object
Engrave		Applies an engraving effect to the object
Glow	color=#*rrggbb* strength=1–255	Applies a glowing border around the object with the size of the glow determined by the strength parameter and the glow's color determined by the color parameter
Gradient	gradientType=0, 1 startColorStr=#*rrggbb* endColorStr=#*rrggbb*	Applies a color gradient to the object. The gradientType parameter determines the direction of the gradient, either vertical (0) or horizontal (1). The startColorStr and endColorStr parameters indicate the starting and ending colors. Intermediate colors are supplied by the filter
MotionBlur	direction=*angle* strength=1–255	Applies a motion blur effect. The direction parameter provides the angle of the motion, and the strength parameter indicates the length of the motion lines
Pixelate	maxSquare=*value*	Pixelates the object, where maxSquare is the size of the pixel
Shadow	direction=*angle* color=#*rrggbb* strength=1–255	Applies a simple drop shadow to the object with the angle of the shadow specified by the direction parameter, the color by the color parameter, and the size of the shadow determined by the strength parameter
Wave	freq=*value* lightStrength=*value* phase=*value* strength=*value*	Applies a sine-wave distortion to the object; the appearance of the wave is determined by the four parameters

For example, to apply a drop shadow filter in Internet Explorer 5.5 or above, you would add the following filter style to the element:

```
filter: progid:DXImageTransform.Microsoft.
dropShadow(color=#FF0000, offX=5, offY=10)
```

With this filter style, the element will appear with a red drop shadow (since #FF0000 is the hexadecimal color value for red), offset 5 pixels to the right and 10 pixels down.

Internet Explorer 5.5 supports a wider range of filter effects than version 4.0. Figure 12-24 describes how some of the version 4.0 filters are matched with their 5.5 forms.

IE 4.0 Filter	IE 5.5 Filter
Alpha	progid:DXImageTransform.Microsoft.Alpha
Blur	progid:DXImageTransform.Microsoft.MotionBlur
Chroma	progid:DXImageTransform.Microsoft.Chroma
DropShadow	progid:DXImageTransform.Microsoft.dropShadow
FlipH	progid:DXImageTransform.Microsoft.BasicImage(rotation=2, mirror=1)
FlipV	progid:DXImageTransform.Microsoft.BasicImage(mirror=1)
Glow	progid:DXImageTransform.Microsoft.Glow
Gray	progid:DXImageTransform.Microsoft.BasicImage(grayscale=1)
Invert	progid:DXImageTransform.Microsoft.BasicImage(invert=1)
Light	progid:DXImageTransform.Microsoft.Light
Mask	progid:DXImageTransform.Microsoft.MaskFilter
Shadow	progid:DXImageTransform.Microsoft.Shadow
Wave	progid:DXImageTransform.Microsoft.Wave
Xray	progid:DXImageTransform.Microsoft.BasicImage(xray=1)

The Internet Explorer 4.0 filters are supported in version 5.5, so you may prefer to use them for greater compatibility. If compatibility is not an issue, however, you should take advantage of the greater power and flexibility offered by the 5.5 filters. Filters are difficult to understand and appreciate without actually working with them. To better understand how filters work, a demonstration page has been created for you. Open it now.

To view the filters demo:

► **1.** Open the **demo_filter.htm** file from the tutorial.12/tutorial folder in your Internet Explorer browser.

► **2.** Select a filter type from the **Filter Type** drop-down list box.

► **3.** If the filter uses parameters, select values for each of the parameters.

As you select the filter and parameter values, the object on the right side of the page is modified. The code for filter style is shown at the bottom of the page (see Figure 12-25). Note that the filter is applied to the entire object, which consists of an inline image and text all contained within a <div> tag.

Figure 12-25 | **Running the filter demo**

Filter Parameters

Filter Type: Wave

Freq: 3

LightStrength: 40

Phase: 50

Strength: 25

Sample Image

```
filter: progid:DXImageTransform.Microsoft.Wave(freq=3, lightStrength=40, phase=50,
strength=25)
```

Trouble? If you're not running Internet Explorer 4.0 or above, you will not be able to see any of these filter effects.

4. Continue going through the list of filters and parameter values and close the Web page when finished.

Reference Window | **Creating a Filter Style**

- To create a filter style in Internet Explorer 4.0, use the style attribute
    ```
    filter: filter_name(params)
    ```
  where *filter_name* is the name of one of the Internet Explorer 4.0 filters, and *params* are the parameter values (if any) that apply to the filter.
- To create a filter style in Internet Explorer 5.5 and above, use the style attribute
    ```
    filter: progid:DXImageTransform.Microsoft.filter_name(params)
    ```

Filters can also be combined to create interesting visual effects. The effects are added in the order in which they are entered into the style declaration. To combine the alpha filter with a drop shadow, for example, you would enter the following set of filters:

```
filter: progid:DXImageTransform.Microsoft.Shadow(direction=135,
color=#0000FF strength=5)
progid:DXImageTransform.Microsoft.Alpha(style=0, opacity=30)
```

This code applies a drop shadow to the object and then changes the opacity value to 30. If you switch the order of the filters, the drop shadow is added after the object is made transparent, meaning that the shadow itself is not made transparent (see Figure 12-26). You can also apply the same filter several times. For example, you can add two drop shadows to the same object by applying two shadow filters.

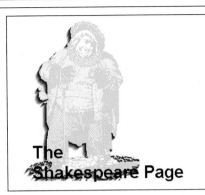

Shadow filter applied first and then the Opacity filter

Opacity filter applied first and then the Shadow filter

Most browsers do not support the Internet Explorer filter styles, and they are not part of the official specifications for CSS. When other browsers encounter a style sheet that employs the filter style, they usually ignore those particular styles while processing the other styles in the sheet. One exception is Netscape 4. If Netscape 4 encounters an unknown style attribute, such as the filter style, it can cause the browser to ignore *all* of the style declarations for that object. One way to avoid this problem is to place the filter styles in a separate declaration, away from the other, more standard, style attributes. Another option is to apply the filter style using a JavaScript program instead of a style sheet.

Running Filters with JavaScript

As with other style attributes, the filter style can be applied in JavaScript using the style property. The syntax for applying a filter style is

```
object.style.filter = "filter text";
```

where `object` is an object in the Web page, and `filter text` is the text of the filters applied to the object. As in a style sheet, the text string can contain multiple filters separated by spaces. For example, to apply the alpha filter to the first inline image in a document, you could use the following JavaScript command:

```
document.images[0].style.filter = "progid:DXImageTransform.Microsoft.
Alpha(style=0, opacity=30)";
```

Internet Explorer's version of JavaScript also recognizes the **filter collection**, which is the collection of all filters associated with a particular object. The reference syntax of the filter collection is

```
object.filters[idref]
```

where `object` is an object that has some filters applied to it, and `idref` is either the index number or the name of a filter within that collection. As with other arrays, the index numbering starts at 0. For example, the expression

```
document.images[0].filters[1]
```

references the second filter associated with the first inline image in the document. If you want to reference the filter by its name, you would use a reference like the following:

```
document.images[0].filters["DXImageTransform.Microsoft.Alpha"]
```

where Internet Explorer's Alpha filter is one of the filters applied to the first inline image in the document. One of the purposes of using JavaScript to work with filter styles is to modify the parameter values. You can reference specific parameters within each filter using the syntax

```
filter.param
```

where *filter* is a specific filter in an object's filters collection, and *param* is the name of a parameter associated with the filter. For example, to change the opacity value of the Alpha filter for the first inline image, you could run the expression

```
document.images[0].filters["DXImageTransform.Microsoft.Alpha"].
opacity=25;
```

Note that this command only works if the Alpha filter has already been defined for the inline image.

Reference Window

Working with Filters in JavaScript

- To apply a filter to an object, use the JavaScript expression
    object.style.filter = "*filter text*";
  where *object* is an object in the Web document, and *filter text* is the filter name (or names) and the filter parameters.
- To access a particular filter associated with an object, use the reference
    object.filters[*idref*]
  where *object* is an object that has a set of filters defined for it and *idref* is either the index number or name of a filter in the collection.
- To access a parameter associated with a filter, use the syntax
    filter.param
  where *filter* is a filter in the object's filter collection and *param* is one of the parameters associated with the filter.

If your users' browsers support them, you can use filters to create the same kind of rollover effects you worked with in the last session. Rather than creating two versions of the same image, you can use JavaScript to apply a filter effect in response to the onmouseover event, and then remove that filter in response to the onmouseout event. The following functions show how the RollOut() and RollOver() functions might look if you wanted to apply a drop shadow to an inline image in a document:

```
function RollOver(i) {
document.images[i].style.filter=
"progid:DXImageTransform.Microsoft.DropShadow(Color=#DDDDDD, offX=10,
offY=10)";
}

function RollOut(i) {
document.images[i].style.filter="";
}
```

Adding a Filter Effect to the Plays Page

You discuss the Internet Explorer filters capability with Clare. She's intrigued by the idea and suggests that you add a filter to the Plays page. Clare suggests you add a drop shadow to the menus. To add the drop shadow, you'll insert another style declaration in the embedded style sheet. Since all of the menus belong to the Menu class, you can apply the drop shadow style using the declaration

```
.Menu {filter: progid:DXImageTransform.Microsoft.DropShadow
(Color=#999999, offX=3, offY=3)}
```

This drop shadow will appear in a medium shade of gray offset 3 pixels to the right and below each of the menus. Add this filter style to Clare's page.

To add the drop shadow filter style to the menu items:

1. Open the **plays.htm** file in your text editor.

2. Within the embedded style sheet, insert the following style declaration (see Figure 12-27):

   ```
   .Menu {filter:progid:DXImageTransform.Microsoft.DropShadow
   (Color=#999999, offX=3, offY=3)}
   ```

Adding the drop shadow filter style | Figure 12-27

```
<style type="text/css">
   .Menu {visibility: hidden}
   .Menu {filter:progid:DXImageTransform.Microsoft.DropShadow(Color=#999999, offX=3, offY=3)}
</style>
```

3. Save your changes to the file.

4. Open **plays.htm** in your Internet Explorer browser. Access the menus and verify that the menus now appear with a gray drop shadow located to the right and below the menu box. (See Figure 12-28.)

Viewing the drop shadow filter | Figure 12-28

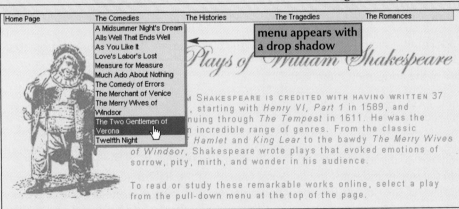

Trouble? If you're running a browser other than Internet Explorer 4.0 or later, you will not see any drop shadow effect, but the page should still be rendered correctly.

Using a Light Filter

Another popular filter that can add visual interest to your Web pages is the Light filter, which creates the illusion of a light (or multiple lights) illuminating an object. Much like the drop shadow, adding a light source can give your page elements a dynamic 3D effect. The style to create a light filter in Internet Explorer 4.0 is:

```
filter: Light()
```

In Internet Explorer 5.5 and above, the style is:

```
filter: progid:DXImageTransform.Microsoft.Light()
```

Once you've created the light filter, the next step is to define a light source for the object. This is done not with a style declaration, but with a JavaScript command. There are three methods for creating a light source: addAmbient(), addPoint(), and addCone(). The addAmbient() method applies an overall or ambient light on the object. The syntax of the method is

```
object.filters.Light.addAmbient(red, green, blue, strength)
```

where *object* is the object being illuminated, *red*, *green*, and *blue* are the RGB color values of the light, and *strength* is the strength of the light source, expressed as a number from 0 to 100. For example, the following statement adds a red light source at highest intensity on the document's first inline image:

```
document.images[0].filters.Light.addAmbient(255,0,0,100)
```

The addAmbient() method doesn't assume a specific location for the light source. To specify a location for the light you can use the addPoint() method which creates a point light source hovering above the object. The syntax to add a point light source to the light filter is

```
object.filters.Light.addPoint(x, y, z, red, green, blue, strength)
```

where *x* and *y* are the horizontal and vertical coordinates of the light source, and *z* is the height, in pixels, of the light source above the object. For example, to create a high-intensity red light source 50 pixels above the object at the (x,y) coordinates (50, 75) you would use the following expression:

```
document.images[0].filters.Light.addPoint(50,75,50,255,0,0,100)
```

The addPoint() method assumes that the light is shone directly down on the object. If you want the light source to shine at an angle, you need to use the addCone() method. The syntax of the addCone() method is

```
object.filters.Light.addCone(x, y, z, x2, y2, red, green, blue,
strength, spread)
```

where *x*, *y*, *z* are once again the coordinates of the light source and *x2*, *y2* are the coordinates of the focus of the light—where the light actually "hits" the object. The spread parameter indicates the angle (or spread) of the light between the light source and the surface of the object. The spread parameter varies from 0 to 90 degrees. The other parameters have the same meanings as those used with the addAmbient() and addPoint() methods. If all this seems confusing to you, you can explore the parameter values of the Light filter in more detail using the Filter Demo Web page.

You can create up to 10 light sources for a particular object. Internet Explorer assigns each light source a number. The first light source you define has a light number of 0; the second light source has a value of 1, and so forth. Once a light source has been created, Internet Explorer provides several methods to manipulate it. You can move the light source to a new location, change its color, change its intensity, or remove the light altogether. To move the light source to another location, use the method

```
object.filters.Light.moveLight(light, x, y, z, absolute)
```

where *light* is the light source's light number, *x*, *y*, and *z* are the new coordinates of the light source, and *absolute* is a Boolean value that has the value true when the new coordinates are expressed in absolute terms, and has the value false when the coordinates are expressed relative to the present coordinates of the light source.

To change the color of the light, use the method

```
object.filters.Light.changeColor(light, red, green, blue, absolute)
```

where *red*, *green*, and *blue* are the new RGB color values of the light source, and *absolute* is a Boolean value that is true when the color values are expressed as absolute values, and false when the color values are to be added to the light source's current color values. You can use negative color values if the absolute parameter is set to false.

To change the intensity of the light source, use the method

```
object.filters.Light.changeStrength(light, strength, absolute)
```

where *strength* is the new strength of the light source, and *absolute* is a Boolean value that is set to true if the strength parameter is expressed in absolute terms, and false if the value of the strength parameter is to be added to the light source's current strength. Once again, the strength parameter can be negative if the value of the absolute parameter is set to false.

As you create light sources, you can remove the effect of a particular light source by setting its strength parameter back to 0. You can remove all of the light sources applied to a particular object by using the method

```
object.filters.Light.clear()
```

Internet Explorer does not provide a method of removing a specific light source while keeping all of the others. Clare does not need to use the light filter in her Web page. However, you will get a chance to apply this interesting filter in the third Case Problem at the end of the tutorial.

Working with Transitions

A second type of special effect supported by Internet Explorer is the transition. A **transition** is a visual effect that is applied to an object over an interval of time. For example, instead of having a pop-up menu disappear instantaneously, you can apply a transition that makes the pop-up menu appear to gradually blend into the background until it disappears.

Applying Transition Styles

As with the filter style, the transition you use depends on the version of Internet Explorer you're trying to support. Internet Explorer 4.0 supports two kinds of transitions: blend and reveal. A **blend transition** is a transition in which one object is blended into another. The style to create a blend transition is

```
filter: blendTrans(duration = value)
```

where *value* is the amount of time, in seconds, for the blending transition to take place. Two separate objects need not be used. You can apply a blend transition on a single object by initially making the object invisible (using the visibility style) and then applying the blendTrans() filter to move it to a visible state.

A **reveal transition** is a more general transition in which a visual effect is applied as one object is changed into another. The style for the reveal transition is

```
filter: revealTrans(duration = value, transition = type)
```

where *type* is a number from 0 to 23, specifying the transition effect. The various transition effects and their numeric values are listed in Figure 12-29.

Figure 12-29 ⟩ **Internet Explorer 4.0 revealTrans types**

Transition	Numeric Code	Transition	Numeric Code
Box In	0	Random Dissolve	12
Box Out	1	Split Vertical In	13
Circle In	2	Split Vertical Out	14
Circle Out	3	Split Horizontal In	15
Wipe Up	4	Split Horizontal Out	16
Wipe Down	5	Strips Left Down	17
Wipe Right	6	Strips Left Up	18
Wipe Left	7	Strips Right Down	19
Vertical Blinds	8	Strips Right Up	20
Horizontal Blinds	9	Random Bars Horizontal	21
Checkerboard Across	10	Random Bars Vertical	22
Checkerboard Down	11	Random	23

In Internet Explorer 5.5, the blendTrans() and revealTrans() transitions were replaced by a whole library of transition effects. The style is similar to the syntax Internet Explorer 5.5 uses for applying filters

```
filter: progid:DXImageTransform.Microsoft.transition(param)
```

where *transition* is the name of the transition, and *param* is parameters of the transition that define how the transition operates. Figure 12-30 describes some of the Internet Explorer 5.5 transitions and their parameters. In addition to the parameters listed in Figure 12-30, each transition also supports the duration parameter, which indicates how many seconds the transition lasts.

Internet Explorer 5.5 transitions | Figure 12-30

Transition Name	Parameters	Description
Barn	motion=out, in orientation=horizontal, vertical	Applies a "barn door" transition
Blinds	bands=value direction=up, down, left, right	Applies a "window blinds" effect
Checkboard	direction=up, down, left, right squaresX=value squaresY=value	Creates a checkboard transition. The size of the checkboard is determined by the squaresX and squaresY parameters
Fade	overlap=0–1	Fades one object into another. The overlap parameter controls the degree of overlap as the fade occurs
GradientWipe	gradientSize=0–1 wipeStyle=0, 1 motion=forward, reverse	Wipes one object into another. The gradientSize parameter controls the blurring effect. The wipeStyle parameter indicates whether to wipe left to right (0) or up to down (1)
Inset		Applies an inset transition
Iris	irisStyle=multiple motion=out, in	Applies an iris-opening transition effect. The style of the iris is determined by the irisStyle parameter
Pixelate	maxSquare=value	Applies a pixelate transition, where maxSquare is the size of the pixel
RadialWipe	wipeStyle=clock, wedge, radial	Applies a radial wipe transition
RandomBars	orientation=horizontal, vertical	Applies a random bars transition
RandomDissolve	duration=value	Dissolves one object into another. The duration parameter indicates the dissolve time in seconds
Slide	slideStyle=hide, push, swap bands=value	Slides one object over or into another
Spiral	gridSizeX=value gridSizeY=value	Spirals one object into another
Stretch	stretchStyle=hide, push, spin	Stretches one object into another
Strips	motion=left-up, left-down, right-up, right-down	Wipes one object over another in a diagonal direction
Wheel	spokes=value	Applies a wheel transition
ZigZag	gridSizeX=value gridSizeY=value	Applies a zig-zag transition

| **Creating Transition Styles**

- To create a blend transition in Internet Explorer 4.0, use the style
  ```
  filter: blendTrans(duration = value)
  ```
  where *value* is the amount of time, in seconds, for the blending process to take place.
- To create a reveal transition in Internet Explorer 4.0, use the style
  ```
  filter: revealTrans(duration = value, transition = type)
  ```
  where *type* is a number from 0 to 23, specifying the transition effect.
- To create a transition in Internet Explorer 5.5 and above, use the style
  ```
  filter: progid:DXImageTransform.Microsoft.transition(param)
  ```
  where *transition* is the name of the transition, and *param* is parameters used with that transition.

Figure 12-31 shows how some of the version 4.0 transitions are translated into their 5.5 forms.

Figure 12-31 | **Comparison of Internet Explorer 4.0 and 5.5 transitions**

IE 4.0 Transition	IE 5.5 Transition
blendTrans()	DXImageTransform.Microsoft.Fade()
revealTrans(0)	DXImageTransform.Microsoft.Iris(irisStyle="square", motion="in")
revealTrans(1)	DXImageTransform.Microsoft.Iris(irisStyle="square", motion="out")
revealTrans(2)	DXImageTransform.Microsoft.Iris(irisStyle="circle", motion="in")
revealTrans(3)	DXImageTransform.Microsoft.Iris(irisStyle="circle", motion="out")
revealTrans(4)	DXImageTransform.Microsoft.Blinds(direction="up", bands="1")
revealTrans(5)	DXImageTransform.Microsoft.Blinds(direction="down", bands="1")
revealTrans(6)	DXImageTransform.Microsoft.Blinds(direction="right", bands="1")
revealTrans(7)	DXImageTransform.Microsoft.Blinds(direction="left", bands="1")
revealTrans(8)	DXImageTransform.Microsoft.Blinds(direction="right")
revealTrans(9)	DXImageTransform.Microsoft.Blinds(direction="down")
revealTrans(10)	DXImageTransform.Microsoft.Checkerboard(direction="right")
revealTrans(11)	DXImageTransform.Microsoft.Checkerboard(direction="down")
revealTrans(12)	DXImageTransform.Microsoft.RandomDissolve()
revealTrans(13)	DXImageTransform.Microsoft.Barn(orientation="vertical", motion="in")
revealTrans(14)	DXImageTransform.Microsoft.Barn(orientation="vertical", motion="out")
revealTrans(15)	DXImageTransform.Microsoft.Barn(orientation="horizontal", motion="in")
revealTrans(16)	DXImageTransform.Microsoft.Barn(orientation="horizontal", motion="out")
revealTrans(17)	DXImageTransform.Microsoft.Strips(motion="leftdown")
revealTrans(18)	DXImageTransform.Microsoft.Strips(motion="leftup")
revealTrans(19)	DXImageTransform.Microsoft.Strips(motion="rightdown")
revealTrans(20)	DXImageTransform.Microsoft.Strips(motion="rightup")
revealTrans(21)	DXImageTransform.Microsoft.RandomBars(orientation="horizontal")
revealTrans(22)	DXImageTransform.Microsoft.RandomBars(orientation="vertical")

To better understand these various transition effects, a demo of transition effects has been prepared for you. Open it now.

To view the transitions demo:

1. Open the **demo_transitions.htm** file from the tutorial.12/tutorial folder in your Internet Explorer browser.

2. Select a filter type from the **Transition Type** drop-down list box.

3. Select a duration value from the **Duration** drop-down list box.

4. Select parameter values for the selected transition.

   As you change the transition type, duration, and transition parameter values, the object on the right displays the transition effect for the parameters you've entered. The style for the selected transition is shown in the box at the bottom of the page. See Figure 12-32.

Running the transition demo   Figure 12-32

Transition Parameters

Transition Type: Strips

Duration (seconds):   2.0

Motion: Right-down

Second Sample Image

```
filter:progid:DXImageTransform.Microsoft.Strips(Motion=rightdown)
```

Trouble? If you're not running Internet Explorer 4.0 or above, you will not be able to see any of these transition effects.

5. Continue going through the list of transition effects and parameter values.

6. Close the Web page when finished.

Scripting Transitions

The code for scripting a transition follows the same syntax you used earlier for filters. For example, the code to apply the RadialWipe transition with a WipeStyle value of "clock" to an object is:

```
object.style.filter =
"progId:DXImageTransform.Microsoft.RadialWipe(WipeStyle=clock)"
```

You can also use the filters collection to modify the parameter value of a selected transition:

```
object.filters["DXImageTransform.Microsoft.RadialWipe"].
WipeStyle="clock";
```

Once again, if you use a filters collection, you must define a filter style in the style sheet for the object.

Running a Transition

If you want to see the effect of a transition style on your object, you have to run it using a series of JavaScript commands. Running a transition involves four steps:

1. Setting the initial state of the object
2. Applying a transition to the object
3. Specifying the final state of the object
4. Playing the transition

The initial state of the object is the status of the object before the transition. This includes such things as the visibility property of the object, the source of the inline image, or the HTML code applied to the object. Once the initial state of the object has been determined, you apply the transition by using the apply() method as follows

```
object.filters[idref].apply();
```

where *object* is the object that you want to apply the transition to and *idref* is either the index number or the text of the transition name. Applying the transition does not actually run the transition, because the final state of the object has not been determined yet. At this point, it simply "freezes" the object in its initial state. Once the transition has been applied, you can write code to modify the appearance of the object, but since the object is frozen, these changes will not appear in the Web page.

After you've defined the final state of the object, you use the play() method to "unfreeze" the object and run the transition effect, moving the object from its initial state to its final state. The syntax for playing a transition is

```
object.filters[idref].play(duration);
```

where *duration* is the time, in seconds, for the transition to run. Note that for IE 4.0 transitions, the duration of the transition is entered as a parameter of the transition. The following code demonstrates how to create a transition between two sources for an inline image:

```
<style type="text/css">
#Img1 {filter: progid:DXImageTransform.Microsoft.
Slide(slideStyle=push,Bands=1)}
</style>
<script type="text/javascript">
function newSlide() {
    document.getElementById("Img1").filters[0].apply();
    document.getElementById("Img1").src = "slide2.jpg";
    document.getElementById("Img1").filters[0].play(2);
}
</script>
<img id="Img1" src="slide1.jpg" onclick="newSlide()" alt="" />
```

The object in this case is an inline image named "Img1." Initially, the image uses the slide1.jpg source file. When a user clicks the inline image, the newSlide() function is called. The apply() method applies the Slide transition to the image and freezes it. The source of the inline image is changed to a new file. The play() method is then invoked, running the Slide transition for two seconds. After the transition is complete, the Img1 object is left displaying a new inline image.

To create a Fade-in or Fade-out transition you use the same basic structure, except that the initial and final states are based on the object's visibility. The following is an example of a transition that is applied to the text "The Rest is Silence":

```
<style type="text/css">
#Hamlet {visibility: visible}
#Hamlet {filter: progid:DXImageTransform.Microsoft.Fade(overlap=1)}
</style>
<script type="text/javascript">
function fadeOut() {
   Hamlet.filters[0].apply();
   Hamlet.style.visibility="hidden";
   Hamlet.filters[0].play();
}
</script>
<div id="Hamlet" onclick="fadeOut()">
   <h1>The Rest is Silence</h1>
</div>
```

In this example, the text string will fade out when the user clicks on it, changing its state from visible to hidden. We also could have used the blendTrans() method from Internet Explorer 4.0 if we wanted to ensure compatibility across browsers. Because this is a div element, we have to define an absolute position before the transition can be applied. The span element has a similar requirement.

Running a Transition

- To play a transition, first set the initial state of the object.
- Next, apply the transition effect to the object using the syntax
     `object.filters[idref].apply();`
  where `object` is the object that the transition is applied to, and `idref` is either the index number or name of a transition defined in the object's style sheet.
- Then specify the final state of the object after the transition.
- Finally, play the transition, using the syntax
     `object.filters[idref].play(duration);`
  where `duration` is the duration of the transition in seconds.

Adding a Transition to the Plays Page

You discuss the use of transition effects in Internet Explorer with Clare. Clare wonders whether you can use a Wipe Down transition when the user selects a menu from the page. Clare's idea is that when the menu is displayed, the transition will be invoked, giving the illusion of a menu unwrapping. Figure 12-33 demonstrates Clare's idea. Users of other browsers won't be able to see this effect, but they will still be able to use the menus as before.

Figure 12-33 ▶ **Applying a transition to a menu**

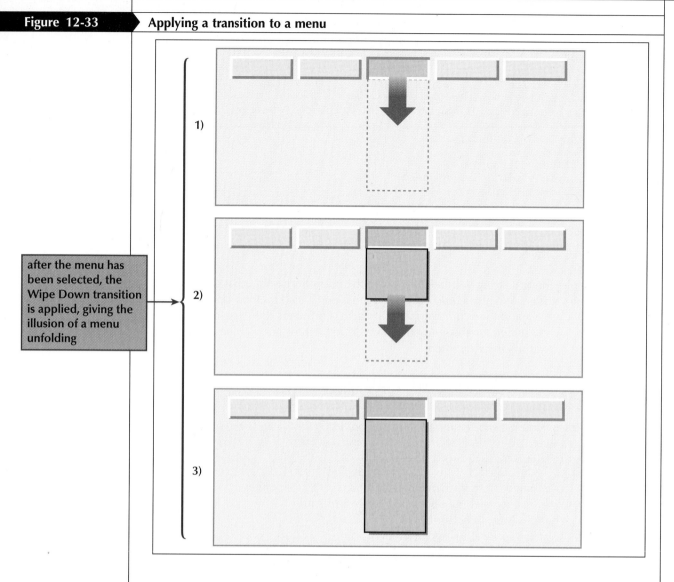

after the menu has been selected, the Wipe Down transition is applied, giving the illusion of a menu unfolding

To create this effect, you can use either the Internet Explorer 4.0 transition

`revealTrans(transition=5)`

or the Internet Explorer 5.5 transition

`progId:DXImageTransform.Microsoft.Blinds(direction=down,bands=1)`

Clare asks you to use the Internet Explorer 5.5 transition. Add this style to the style declaration for the menus in Clare's Web page.

To add the transition filter:

▶ **1.** Return to the **plays.htm** file in your text editor.

▶ **2.** Add the following style to the style declaration for the Menu class (see Figure 12-34):

```
progid:DXImageTransform.Microsoft.Blinds(direction=down, bands=1)
```

Adding the transition filter style | **Figure 12-34**

```
<style type="text/css">
   .Menu {visibility: hidden}
   .Menu {filter:progid:DXImageTransform.Microsoft.DropShadow(Color=#999999, offX=3, offY=3)
              progid:DXImageTransform.Microsoft.Blinds(direction=down, bands=1)}
</style>
```

Next you have to run the transition on the active menu. Since the transition style is supported only by Internet Explorer, you have to include object detection to determine whether the browser supports transitions before attempting to run it. We'll add the transition commands to the popMenu() function. The revised popMenu() function looks as follows:

```
function PopMenu(M) {
   hideActive();
   ActiveMenu = document.getElementById(M);
   if (ActiveMenu.filters) ActiveMenu.filters[1].apply();
   showIt(ActiveMenu);
   if (ActiveMenu.filters) ActiveMenu.filters[1].play(0.5);
}
```

In the revised function after the ActiveMenu variable is set to the new menu, we apply the transition filter to it. Note that we first verify that the browser supports the ActiveMenu.filters object before attempting to apply the transition. In the next step we use the showIt() function to show the contents of the active menu; however since we've applied the transition filter to this object, the active menu is not shown until the transition is run. In the next step we run the transition with a duration of 0.5 seconds. Revise the popMenu() function now.

To revise the popMenu() function:

▶ **1.** Go to the popMenu() function and add the following statement after the second step in the function:

   `if (ActiveMenu.filters) ActiveMenu.filters[1].apply();`

▶ **2.** Add the following statement as the last line in the popMenu() function:

   `if (ActiveMenu.filters) ActiveMenu.filters[1].play(0.5);`

   Figure 12-35 shows the revised popMenu() function.

Revising the popMenu() function | **Figure 12-35**

```
function popMenu(M) {
   hideActive();
   ActiveMenu = document.getElementById(M);
   if (ActiveMenu.filters) ActiveMenu.filters[1].apply();
   showIt(ActiveMenu);
   if (ActiveMenu.filters) ActiveMenu.filters[1].play(0.5);
}
```

▶ **3.** Close the **plays.htm** file, saving your changes.

▶ **4.** Reopen or refresh the **plays.htm** file in your Web browser.

▶ **5.** Click the menus and verify that they appear using the unfolding transition effect.

   Trouble? If you are using a browser other than Internet Explorer, you will not see any Wipe Down effect in the menus.

Using Interpage Transitions

You can also create transitions between one Web page and another. These transitions, known as **interpage transitions**, involve effects applied to a page when a browser either enters or exits the page. Interpage transitions are created using the meta element within the head section of the HTML file. The meta element specifies the type of transition, the duration, and whether it's applied on entering or exiting the page. There are four types of transitions, which are run when a user initially enters the Web page, exits the page, enters the Web site, or exits the site, respectively. The syntax for each of the four different interpage transitions is

```
<meta http-equiv = "Page-Enter" content = "type" />
<meta http-equiv = "Page-Exit" content = "type" />
<meta http-equiv = "Site-Enter" content = "type" />
<meta http-equiv = "Site-Exit" content = "type" />
```

where *type* is one of the transitions supported by Internet Explorer and the `http-equiv` attribute specifies when the transition should be applied. The syntax for the transition type is the same for interpage transitions as it is for an object within a page. These transitions appear only when you go from one page to another or from one Web site to another. A user does not see a Page-Enter transition if the page is the first file the user opens when starting a Web browser.

Reference Window	**Creating an Interpage Transition**

- To create an interpage transition when either entering or exiting a Web page, add one or more of the following meta elements to the document head:
    ```
    <meta http-equiv = "Page-Enter" content = "type" />
    <meta http-equiv = "Page-Exit" content = "type" />
    <meta http-equiv = "Site-Enter" content = "type" />
    <meta http-equiv = "Site-Exit" content = "type" />
    ```
    where *type* is one of the transitions supported by Internet Explorer.

For example, to display an inset transition with a duration of 3 seconds when a user enters the page, you would apply the following meta element:

```
<meta http-equiv="Page-Enter" content="progid:DXImageTransform.
Microsoft.Inset(duration=3)" />
```

To apply a 2-second Wheel transition upon exiting the page, you would use the meta element:

```
<meta http-equiv="Page-Exit" content=" progid:DXImageTransform.
Microsoft.Wheel(Spokes=8, duration=2)" />
```

Clare suggests that you modify the ws.htm file so that it runs a 3-second Wipe Up transition whenever the user exits the page. You'll use the Internet Explorer 4.0 form of this transition.

To insert the Wipe Up interpage transition:

1. Reopen the **ws.htm** file in your text editor.

2. After the title element, insert the following meta element, as shown in Figure 12-36:

```
<meta http-equiv="Page-
Exit" content="revealTrans(duration=3, transition=4)" />
```

Creating an interpage transition | Figure 12-36

run the transition when the browser exits the page

```
<title>The World of Shakespeare</title>
<meta http-equiv="Page-Exit"
      content="revealTrans(duration=3, transition=4)" />
<link href="styles1.css" rel="stylesheet" type="text/css" />
```

the transition runs over a 3-second interval

run the Wipe Up transition

3. Close the file, saving your changes.

4. Reopen **ws.htm** in your Web browser.

5. Click the **The Plays** link and verify that as the browser exits the home page, the Wipe Up transition is played (see Figure 12-37).

Running an interpage transition | Figure 12-37

The Plays

The Sonnets

Biography

The World of Shakespeare

The WORLD OF SHAKESPEARE CONTAINS A COMPLETE LISTING OF WILLIAM Shakespeare's published works including his plays, sonnets, and longer poems. You can use the Web site's flexible search tool to locate particular passages and characters from his works or simply read the plays online or download them to an e-book reader.

For those interested in exploring the world of the bard, download one of our hundreds of articles on Shakespeare's life and times. You can also ... tragedies of Hamlet and King Lear to the bawdy The Merry Wives of Windsor, Shakespeare wrote plays that evoked emotions of sorrow, pity, mirth, and wonder in his audience.

To read or study these remarkable works online, select a play from the pull-down menu at the top of the page.

Trouble? If you are using a browser other than Internet Explorer, you will not see the interpage transition effect.

6. Close your Web browser.

You've completed your work on Clare's Web site for now. Clare is pleased with the special effects that you've created for her. She feels that they add a lot of visual interest to the page. As she adds more pages to her Web site, she'll get back to you for further assistance.

Tips for Working with Special Effects

- Preload all images used in image rollovers to speed up the rollover effect
- Place rollover images in image arrays to make it easier to write programs that swap the images

- Place long lists of links into pop-up or pull-down menus to save screen space
- Place filter styles in separate style declarations to avoid problems with older browsers
- If you use filter or transition styles, test your Web site on non-Internet Explorer browsers to ensure that their use does not cause problems for those browsers

Review

Session 12.3 Quick Check

1. What style would you use to flip an inline image in the vertical direction? Give the answer for both Internet Explorer 4.0 and Internet Explorer 5.5.
2. What JavaScript command would you enter to apply the emboss filter to an object named "Logo"? Give the answer for Internet Explorer 5.5.
3. What JavaScript command would you enter to store the opacity level of an object named "Logo" in a variable named "OpLevel"? Assume that the filter is the first and only filter applied to the object.
4. Describe the two types of transitions supported by Internet Explorer 4.0.
5. What transition would you use in Internet Explorer 5.5 to duplicate the effect of the blendTrans() method?
6. What JavaScript command would you use to store the duration of the Logo object's first transition in a variable named "DLevel"?
7. What HTML tag would you enter to create a Random transition effect lasting 2 seconds, whenever the HTML file is opened by the browser?

Review

Tutorial Summary

In this tutorial you learned how to add special visual effects to a Web site. The first session explored how to create image rollovers by working with image objects and the document.images collection. In this session you learned how to preload images and how to place those images in an image array. The session concluded with a brief discussion of text rollovers and uses of the hover class. The second session looked at techniques to create pop-up and pull-down menus. In this session you learned how to use the visibility style to alternately hide and unhide an object on the page. The third session focused on styles supported by Internet Explorer to add visual effects to a Web page. You learned how to use the filter style to modify the appearance of objects in a Web document and you saw how to create a transition effect from one object to another. The session concluded with a discussion of interpage transitions that run when a browser switches from one page to another.

Key Terms

blend transition	image object	pull-down menu
filter	image rollover	reveal transition
filter collection	interpage transition	transition
image collection	pop-up menu	

Review Assignments

Data files needed for this Review Assignment: bio_out.jpg, bio_over.jpg, caliban.gif, globe_out.jpg, globe_over.jpg, linktest.htm, menu1.jpg, menu2.jpg, plays.css, plays_out. jpg, plays_over.jpg, scripts.js, son_out.jpg, son_over.jpg, strat_out.jpg, strat_over.jpg, tempest.jpg, temptxt.htm

Clare is pleased with the work you did on the two Shakespeare pages. She now wants you to work on the design for the opening screen for a page on Shakespeare's play *The Tempest*. In this page, you'll employ some of the features you used in the ws.htm and plays.htm files.

Your job will include the following tasks:
- Create a rollover effect for a list of graphic links at the top of the page, so that when a user passes the mouse pointer over one of the five links, a drop shadow appears.
- Add a drop shadow to the graphic image of Caliban, located on the right side of the page.
- Create separate pop-up menus that appear when a user clicks the graphic images "The Play" or "Dramatis Personae." Have the pop-up menus disappear when the user clicks anywhere within the description of the play.
- Add a Wipe Right transition effect that plays when the pop-up menu is displayed on the page.
- Add a Box Out interpage transition, to be run when the user initially enters the page.

A preview of the page you'll create is shown in Figure 12-38.

Figure 12-38

Much of the work in setting up the page has been done for you. Text for the two pop-up menus is located within <div> tags with the id names "ThePlay" and "Dramatis". You'll use these id names to identify which pop-up menu to display. The HTML file also contains a link to an external JavaScript file named scripts.js. This file contains the functions hideIt() and showIt(), which can be used to hide and show the pop-up menus.

To create the Web page for *The Tempest*:

1. Use your text editor to open the **temptxt.htm** file from the tutorial.12/review folder. Enter *your name* and *the date* in the comment section and save the file as **tempest.htm**.

2. Add an embedded script element to the head section of the document. Within the embedded script, create two image arrays named ImgOver and ImgOut. Populate the ImgOver array with the following images: plays_over.jpg, son_over.jpg, bio_over.jpg, globe_over.jpg, and strat_over.jpg. Populate the ImgOut array with the image files: plays_out.jpg, son_out.jpg, bio_out.jpg, globe_out.jpg, and strat_out.jpg. Use the arrays created in the first session of this tutorial as your model.

3. Create a function named RollOver() with a single parameter named "i". Have the function test whether the user's browser supports the document.images() collection, and if so, swap the image whose index value is i between the document.images collection and the ImgOver array. Create a similar function named RollOut(), that swaps images between the document.images() collection and the ImgOut array.

4. Add onmouseover and onmouseout event handlers to the <a> tags for the plays_out.jpg, son_out.jpg, bio_out.jpg, globe_out.jpg, and strat_out.jpg inline images. When the user passes the mouse over these images, run the RollOver() function, using the image's index number from the document.images() collection. Similarly, when the user's mouse cursor leaves each image, run the RollOut() function, with the appropriate index number.

5. The two pop-up menus belong to the Menu class. Add an embedded style sheet to the document's head section and within the style sheet, create a style for objects belonging to the Menu class, setting their visibility style to "hidden".

6. Within your embedded script element, create a variable named ActiveMenu that will contain the active pop-up menu object. Set the initial value of ActiveMenu to null.

7. Create a function named HideMenu(), whose purpose is to hide the active menu. Have the function test whether the ActiveMenu variable is not equal to null. If that is the case, hide the active menu (using the hideIt() function from the scripts.js file), and set the value of the ActiveMenu variable to null. (*Hint*: Use the hideActive() function from this tutorial as a model for your function.)

8. Add another style declaration to your embedded style sheet for objects in the Menu class. Have all Menu class objects employ the Internet Explorer 4.0 revealTrans filter with a duration of 0.5 seconds and a transition type of 6 (the Wipe Right transition).

9. Create a function named PopMenu() with a single parameter variable, M. The M parameter will contain the name of a pop-up menu to be displayed. Using the popMenu() function from the tutorial as a model, have the PopMenu() function do the following:
   a. Hide the active menu by calling the HideMenu() function you just created.
   b. If the user's browser supports transition filters, apply the first transition filter for the ActiveMenu object.
   c. Call the showIt() function from the scripts.js file to show the contents of the ActiveMenu object.
   d. If the user's browser supports filters, play the first transition filter for the ActiveMenu object.

10. Change the href attributes of the links around the menu1.jpg and menu2.jpg inline images so that the browser runs the PopMenu() function when the user clicks the images. For the menu1.jpg image, use the parameter value "ThePlay" for the value of the M parameter. For the menu2.jpg image, use the parameter value "Dramatis."

11. Add an event handler to the div element with the id "main" that runs the Hide-Menu() function when a user clicks within this object.

12. Add an Internet Explorer 5.5 glow filter style to the caliban.gif graphic. Set the color parameter to #40853D and the strength parameter to 15.

13. Add an interpage transition to the Web page, running the Internet Explorer 5.5 Slide transition over an interval of 2 seconds whenever a user enters the page. Set the slideStyle parameter to "push" and the bands parameter to 1.

14. Close the file, saving your changes.

15. Open the **linktest.htm** file in your Web browser. Click the Tempest link and verify that the browser runs the Slide transition (for users of Internet Explorer 5.5 and above). In the tempest.htm page, verify that as you pass the mouse pointer over the list of links at the top of the page, a red drop shadow appears behind the link names. Also test that as you click the graphic images "The Play" and "Dramatis Personae," menus pop up with links for the individual scenes and characters from the play. Verify that these pop-up menus disappear whenever you click the description of the play.

16. If you are running Internet Explorer, verify that a green glow effect appears behind the inline image of Caliban, located at the right edge of the page. Test whether the Wipe Right transition is run when you open the pop-up menus.

17. Submit the completed Web site to your instructor.

Case Problem 1

Data files needed for this Case Problem: housetxt.htm, ldown.gif, lup.gif, pback.jpg, pr.gif, premier.css, rdown.gif, rup.gif, slide00.jpg – slide11.jpg

Premier Realty Connie Peres of Premier Realty in Vale Park, Colorado, has asked you to help her with the design of Web pages detailing the company's listings. Each listing will have its own page with a brief introductory paragraph, a table of specific information, and a collection of photos of the property.

Connie would like to see the photos organized in a slide show. Potential buyers would click buttons to move forward and backward through the slide show. If you could add some transitional effects to the slide show to increase the visual impact, Connie thinks that would be great. A preview of the page you'll create is shown in Figure 12-39.

Figure 12-39

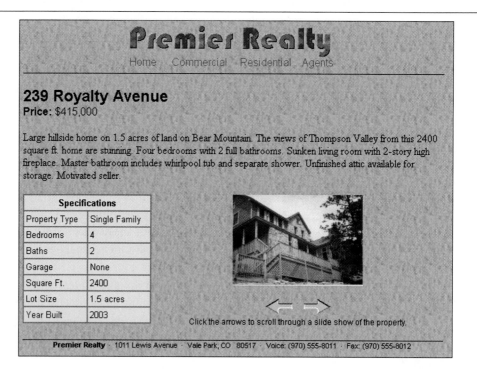

The photos for the slide show are stored in 12 JPEG files, named in consecutive order, starting with slide00.jpg and finishing with slide11.jpg. The initial photo displayed in the page is slide00.jpg. The name assigned to the inline image in the HTML file is "Photo."

In addition, graphic images for the left and right arrow buttons are provided. The graphic files ldown.gif and lup.gif display the left arrow button when it is pressed down and released back up. Similarly, the down and up positions of the right arrow button are stored in the rdown.gif and rup.gif files. The names of these two inline images in the HTML file are LeftArrow and RightArrow.

When a user clicks the left arrow in the slide show, the page should display the previous graphic image in the list. For example, if the user is viewing slide05.jpg, clicking the left arrow should open slide04.jpg. When the beginning of the list is reached, the slide show should jump to the end of the list. Clicking the right arrow moves the user up in the list of images. When the user reaches the end of the slide show, the first slide should be displayed.

When Internet Explorer users click the left or right arrow buttons, an Internet Explorer 5.5 GradientWipe transition should be played as the page swaps the image files. Users of other browsers will not see these transition effects.

To create the slide show:

1. Use your text editor to open the **housetxt.htm** file from the tutorial.12/case1 folder. Enter **your name** and **the date** in the comment section and save the file as **house.htm**.

2. Add an embedded script element to the head section of the document. Within the script element create four image objects named RUp, RDown, LUp, and LDown. Set the source of these four image objects to the graphic files rup.gif, rdown.gif, lup.gif, and ldown.gif respectively.

3. Create four functions named LIn(), LOut(), RIn(), and ROut(). The purpose of these functions is to change the images used for the left and right arrows. The functions should do the following:
   a. The LIn() function should set the source of the LeftArrow inline image to the source of the LDown image object.
   b. The LOut() function should set the source of the LeftArrow inline image to the source of the LUp image object.
   c. The RIn() function should set the source of the RightArrow inline image to the source of the RDown image object.
   d. The ROut() function should set the source of the RightArrow inline image to the source of the RUp image object.

4. Add event handlers to the <a> tag that surrounds the LeftArrow inline image. Run the LIn() function when the user presses the mouse button down. Run the LOut() function when the user releases the mouse button. Make similar changes to the <a> tag that surrounds the RightArrow inline image.

5. Save your changes to the file, and open the page in your browser. Verify that the left and right arrows change appearance briefly when you click them.

Explore ▶ 6. Return to the **house.htm** file in your text editor. Add an embedded style sheet to the head section of the document. Within the style sheet apply the Internet Explorer 5.5 GradientWipe transition filter to the Photo image. (*Hint*: The Photo image has an id value of "Photo".) Set the gradientSize parameter to 0.5, the wipeStyle parameter to 0, and the motion parameter to forward.

7. Within the embedded script element create an image array named "Slides" that contains image objects for each of the 12 slide graphic files. Start your array with an index value of 0, and continue up through an index value of 11.

8. Create a variable named SlideNum. The purpose of the SlideNum variable is to store the number of the currently displayed slide. Set the initial value of SlideNum to 0.

Explore ▶ 9. Create a function named SlideShow(). The function has a single parameter named direction, which will be used to indicate the direction of the slide show (either "forward" or "reverse"). The purpose of this function is to move the house image slide show either forward or backward by swapping in the correct image from the list of slide show images. Add the following commands to the SlideShow() function:
   a. Set the value of the SlideNum variable by creating a conditional structure that tests whether the value of the direction parameter is equal to "forward" or "reverse". If the value of the direction parameter is "forward", use a conditional operator that tests whether the current value of the SlideNum variable is equal to 11 (the last slide in the list). If SlideNum is equal to 11, set its new value to 0 (bringing it back to the first slide in the list); otherwise increase the value of SlideNum by 1. If the value of the direction parameter is "reverse", use a conditional operator that tests whether SlideNum is equal to 0 (the first slide), in which case set the new value of SlideNum to 11 (the last slide); otherwise decrease the value of the SlideNum variable by 1.

    b.   Determine whether to apply an Internet Explorer transition to the slide show by creating a conditional structure to test whether the user's browser supports transitions. (*Hint*: Use object detection with the object document. images["Photo"].filters as the object in the conditional statement.) If a user's browser doesn't support transitions, set the source of the Photo inline image to the image in the Slides image array with the index value equal to SlideNum. If the user's browser does support transitions run a function named TransSlide() with the direction variable as the parameter value. You'll create this function next.

10. Create a function named TransSlide(). The purpose of this function is to run the slide show for Internet Explorer users with a gradient wipe transition applied to the moving images. The function has a single parameter named direction, which indicates the direction of the gradient wipe. Add the following commands to the TransSlide() function:

    a.   Set the value of the motion parameter for the Photo image's filter to the value of the direction parameter. (*Hint*: Use the object document.images["Photo"]. filters[0].motion to reference to the motion parameter.)

    b.   Apply the transition to the Photo inline image.

    c.   Change the source of the Photo inline image to the image in the Slides image array with the index value equal to SlideNum.

    d.   Play the transition for the Photo inline image over a duration of 2 seconds.

11. Add event handlers to run the slide show functions you just created. Go to the <a> tag for the LeftArrow image, and change the href attribute so that it runs the SlideShow() function when clicked. Set the parameter value of the SlideShow() function to "reverse".

12. Go to the <a> tag for the RightArrow image, and change the href attribute so that it also runs the SlideShow() function when clicked. Use a parameter value of "forward".

13. Save your changes to the file.

14. Reopen **house.htm** in your Web browser and verify that when you click the left arrow button under the house image, the browser scrolls back through the slide show. Also verify that when you click the right arrow button, the browser moves forward through the slide show.

15. If you are running Internet Explorer 5.5 or later, verify that when you move forward and backward through the slide show, the GradientWipe transition is applied to the photos.

16. Submit the completed Web site to your instructor.

Case Problem 2

Data files needed for this Case Problem: games.css, image1.jpg – image8.jpg, logo.jpg, tile.jpg, tiles.js, tilestxt.htm

Games, Etc. Games, Etc. is a company that specializes in games and puzzles. Part of the company's Web site includes online games for customers to enjoy while shopping around. Pete Burdette, the supervisor of the Web site development team, has asked you to help create a Concentration game. In Concentration, images are turned over on a table, and the object is to turn over matched pairs of images, until all of the images have been turned over. Pete has set up a board with eight pairs of images laid out in a four-by-four grid. The eight images for the game are stored in JPEG files with the names image1. jpg through image8.jpg. An additional image file, tile.jpg, represents the tile when an image is hidden. A preview of this page is shown in Figure 12-40.

Figure 12-40

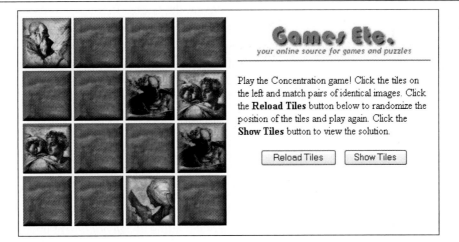

Pete wants you to program part of this page. Some of the programming has already been done for you and is stored in the file tiles.js. The tiles.js file contains code that creates an image array named Tiles containing 16 image objects, representing the 16 possible tile images. The first image object in the array is Tiles[0], which stores the image hidden under the tile located in the first row and first column of the game board. The last image object is Tiles[15], which stores the image for the tile in the last row and column. The source for each of the 16 image objects is randomly assigned, and will change each time the page is reopened.

Your job is to program the action of the game. The rules are as follows:
- A tile is turned over by clicking the tile image with the mouse.
- If a player turns over two tiles with the same image, the tiles remain face up on the board.
- If the player turns over tiles with different images, the tiles are flipped over after 8/10 of a second.
- A player can view the complete solution to the puzzle at any time by clicking the Show All button on the page.
- A player can reload the page, and thus scramble the tiles, by clicking the Reload Tiles button.

To create the Concentration game:

1. Use your text editor to open the **tilestxt.htm** file from the tutorial.12/case2 folder. Enter **your name** and **the date** in the comment section and save the file as **tiles.htm**.
2. Within the head section of the HTML file, create an external script element pointing to the **tiles.js** file. This provides access to the code that creates and populates the Tiles image array.
3. Below the external script element insert an embedded script. In the embedded script create three global variables named FlipCount, Tile1, and Tile2. The FlipCount variable will be used to count the number of tiles that have been previously flipped in the current turn (either 0 or 1). Set the initial value of the FlipCount variable to zero. The Tile1 variable will be used to store the board location of the first tile flipped during the current turn. The Tile2 variable records the location of the second tile flipped. Board locations are represented by index numbers from 0 to 15. Do not set initial values for the Tile1 and Tile2 variables.

4. Create a function named ShowAll(). The purpose of the ShowAll() function is to display all of the hidden tiles on the board. There are no parameters for this function. To complete this function add a For loop with an index number, i, that runs from 0 to 15. The value of the i variable represents each of the 16 images in the document. images collection and the Tiles image array. For each value of i, swap the source of the image in the document.images collection whose index value is i with the source of the corresponding image object in the Tiles image array.

5. Create a function named FlipBack() used to rehide the images of the two flipped tiles. The FlipBack() function will be run whenever a player flips two tiles containing different images. There are no parameters for the FlipBack() function. Add the following commands to the function:

   a. Set the source of the inline image document.images[Tile1] to the tile.jpg file. This has the effect of hiding the image under the tile.

   b. Also set the source of the inline image document.images[Tile2] to the tile.jpg file.

   c. Change the value of the FlipCount variable to 0, indicating that a new turn is about to begin.

6. Create a function named CheckTiles(). The purpose of the CheckTiles() function is to check whether the images of the two flipped tiles is the same. There are no parameters for this function. Add the following commands to the function:

   a. Insert an if condition that tests whether the source of the document.images[Tile1] inline image is different from the source for the document.images[Tile2] image.

   b. If the images are different then run the FlipBack() function after an interval of 0.8 seconds. (*Hint*: Use the setTimeout() method discussed in the previous tutorial.)

   c. If the images are the same, set the value of the FlipCount variable back to 0. This has the effect of leaving the matching tiles flipped and prepares the board for the user's next turn.

7. Create a function named Flip(). The purpose of the Flip() function is to flip a single tile, displaying the image underneath and then checking whether the user has flipped a matching tile. The Flip() function has a single parameter "i" representing the location of the tile to be flipped. Add the following commands to the Flip() function:

   a. Set the source of the ith image in the document.images collection to the source of the ith image in the Tiles image array (thus displaying the hidden image under the tile).

   b. Create an if condition that tests whether the current value of the FlipCount variable is 0. This test indicates whether the first tile or the second tile in the current turn has been flipped.

   c. If FlipCount equals 0 (meaning that the first tile has been flipped), then: 1) Set the value of the Tile1 variable to i (storing the location of the first flipped tile), and 2) Set the value of the FlipCount variable to 1 (indicating that 1 tile has been flipped in the current turn).

   d. Otherwise: 1) Set the value of the Tile2 variable to i (storing the location of the second flipped tile), and 2) Run the CheckTiles() function you created earlier to test whether the two flipped tiles have the same image.

8. Locate the 16 inline images for the Concentration board. For each <a> tag surrounding those inline images, change the href attribute so that the browser runs the Flip() function whenever the user clicks the tile. The Flip() function should have a single parameter value—the index number of the tile image in the document.images collection. (*Hint*: The first tile will have a parameter value of 0, the second will have a parameter value of 1, and so forth.)

9. Locate the Reload Tiles button at the bottom of the HTML file. When this button is clicked, have the browser reload the page. (Run the location.reload() method.)

10. Locate the Show All button. When this button is clicked, have the browser run the ShowAll() function.

11. Close the file, saving your changes.

12. Open **tiles.htm** in your Web browser. Play the game and test whether pairs of unlike tiles are automatically flipped after a brief interval. Verify that pairs of like tiles remain face up. Click the Show Tiles button and confirm that it displays the location of all of the tiles. Click the Reload Tiles button and verify that it randomizes the order of the tiles on the game board.

13. Submit the completed Web site to your instructor.

Case Problem 3

Data files needed for this Case Problem: const.gif, scavtxt.htm, start.htm, styles.css

Scavenger   Scavenger is a Web site that provides users with state-of-the-art search tools and utilities. Scavenger specializes in unusual and hard-to-find merchandise that other sites ignore. Lori Vandzandt, who works on Scavenger's Web site development team, has approached you about designing an opening splash screen for the site. She envisions a "searchlight" moving across the opening page, illuminating the company's logo and the list of links. When a user clicks a link, a new page should open using an interpage transition that displays a circle rapidly opening a view into the new page. Figure 12-41 shows a preview of the opening page.

This assignment can be completed only by users of the Internet Explorer browser.

To create the Scavenger splash screen:

1. Use your text editor to open the **scavtxt.htm** file from the tutorial.12/case3 folder. Enter *your name* and *the date* in the comment section and save the file as **scav.htm**.

(Left margin:)

Challenge

xplore how to use the ight filter in a splash creen

Figure 12-41

Explore

2. Insert an embedded style sheet in the head section of the document. In the style sheet add the Internet Explorer 4.0 filter style for the Light style for the object with the id value of "Main".

3. In the head section insert an embedded script element. Within the script element create a global variable named count. The count variable will be used to keep track of the animated searchlight as it moves across the page. Set the initial value of the count variable to 0.

Explore

4. Below the count variable, create a function named "init()". The purpose of the init() function is to start the searchlight animation over the Main object. Have the function do the following:

   a. Use the addPoint() method to create a point light source for the Main object located at the x-y coordinates (35, 100) and placed 70 pixels above the object in the z-direction. Set the RGB color value of the light to (0, 255, 0). Set the strength of the light source to 70.

   b. Call a function named moveRight(). There are no parameter values for this function. You'll create this function next.

Explore

5. Below the init() function, insert the moveRight() function. The purpose of this function is to move a light source to the right above the Main object. Have the function do the following:

   a. Use the MoveLight() method of the Light filter object to move the Main object's light filter 10 pixels in the y-direction. Specify a value of 0 for the x, z, and *strength* parameters and set the *absolute* parameter to "false". (*Hint*: Reference the Main object's light filter using the object reference: document.getElementById("Main").filters[0].)

   b. Increase the value of the count variable by 1.

   c. If the value of the count variable is less than or equal to 40, run the moveRight() function again after a delay of 125 milliseconds; otherwise, a) reset the value of the count variable to 0, and b) call the moveLeft() function.

6. Below the moveRight() function insert the moveLeft() function. The purpose of this function is to move the light source to the left. Have the function do the following:

   a. Use the MoveLight() method to move the Main object's light filter 10 pixels to the left. (*Hint*: Use a value of –10 for the value of the *y* parameter in this method.)

   b. Increase the value of the count variable by 1.

   c. If the value of the count variable is less than or equal to 15, run the moveLeft() function again after a delay of 125 milliseconds, otherwise: a) reset the value of the count variable to 0; and b) run the moveUp() function.

7. Below the moveLeft() function insert the moveUp() function. The purpose of this function is to move the light source up above the object in the z-direction. Have the function do the following:

   a. Use the MoveLight() method to move the Main object's light filter 10 pixels up in the z-direction. The value of the x, y, and *strength* parameters should be 0 and the value of the *absolute* parameter should be "false".

   b. Increase the value of the count variable by 1.

   c. If the value of the count variable is less than or equal to 15, run the moveUp() function again after a delay of 125 milliseconds, otherwise run the endAnim() function after a delay of 300 milliseconds.

8. Below the moveUp() function insert the endAnim() function. The purpose of this function is to illuminate the four links on the page, completing the searchlight animation. The function should do the following:
    a. Use the addPoint() method of the Light filter object to add a second light source to the Main object located at the x-y coordinates (100, 120) and placed 50 pixels above the object in the z-direction. Set the RGB color value of the light to (255, 0, 0). Set the strength of the light source to 100.
    b. Use the addPoint() method to add a third light source at the x-y coordinates (230, 120) placed 50 pixels above the Main object. Set the RGB color of the light to (0, 0, 255) with a strength of 100.
    c. Add a fourth light source at the x-y-z coordinates (380, 120, 50) with a color value of (0, 0, 255) and a strength of 100.
    d. Add a fifth light source at the x-y-z coordinates (520, 120, 50) with a color value of (255, 0, 0) and a strength of 100.
9. Add an event handler to the <body> tag to run the init() function when the page is loaded.

Explore

10. In the head section of the document, insert an interpage transition that runs the Internet Explorer 5.5 Iris transition when the user exits the page. Set the style of the iris to display a circle. Set the motion of the iris to "out". Make the duration of the transition 5 seconds.
11. Close the file, saving your changes.
12. Open **scav.htm** in your Internet Explorer Web browser, and verify that the searchlight appears to move right and then left and then high above the page. Also verify that four additional light sources appear above the four links in the file and that when you click any one of the links the iris interpage transition is played.
13. Submit the completed Web site to your instructor.

Create

Test your knowledge of special effects by adding them to a Web page

Case Problem 4

Data files needed for this Case Problem: jackson.jpg, lp1.gif, lp2.gif, lp.txt, ps1.gif, ps2. gif, ps.txt, sm1.gif, sm2.gif, sm.txt

Jackson Electronics   You work for Paul Reichtman of Jackson Electronics, a company specializing in printers and scanners. Paul has asked you to update some Web pages that describe three of the company's products: the ScanMaster, the LaserPrint 5000, and the Print/Scan 150. Information on these three products can be found in the files sm.txt, lp.txt, and ps.txt respectively.

Paul would like you to insert graphical links between these three pages. He's supplied you with three graphic files named sm1.gif, lp1.gif, and ps1.gif. He's also supplied "rollover" versions of these files, named sm2.gif, lp2.gif, and ps2.gif.

To create the Web site for Jackson Electronics:

1. Create three files named **scanner.htm**, **printer.htm**, and **ps150.htm**, containing the information on the ScanMaster, the LaserPrint 5000, and the Print/Scan 150. The layout and design of the pages are up to you. You may supplement the material provided with any other additional resources you think will help the Web site. Save these files in the tutorial.12/case4 folder.
2. Each page should have graphical links to the other files, with rollover effects.

3. Add an Internet Explorer 5.5 interpage transition effect to each page; display another Internet Explorer 5.5 transition whenever the user exits the site.

4. Submit the completed Web site to your instructor.

Review

Quick Check Answers

Session 12.1

1. document.images["Links"]
   document.images[1]
   document.images.Links
   document.getElementById["Links"]
   document.Links

2. document.images["Links"].width = 150;
   document.images["Links"].height = 200;

3. document.images["Links"].src = "links2.jpg";

4. LinksOver = new Image(75, 100);

5. LinksArray = new Array();
   LinksArray[0] = new Image();
   LinksArray[1] = new Image();
   LinksArray[2] = new Image();
   LinksArray[0].src = image1.jpg;
   LinksArray[1].src = image2.jpg;
   LinksArray[2].src = image3.jpg;

6. if (document.images)

Session 12.2

1. In a pop-up menu, a user clicks an object on the page and the menu appears, sometimes elsewhere on the page.

2. In a pull-down menu, part of the menu is visible. When a user either clicks the visible part or moves a mouse pointer over it, the rest of the menu is revealed.

3. document.getElementById("main").visibility="hidden";

4. document.getElementById("main").visibility="visible";

Session 12.3

1. Internet Explorer 4.0: FlipV();
   Internet Explorer 5.5: progid:DXImageTransform.Microsoft.BasicImage(mirror=1)

2. document.getElementById("Logo").style.filter =
   "progid:DXImageTransform.Microsoft.Emboss()";

3. OpLevel = document.getElementById("Logo").filters[0].opacity;

4. A blend transition is a transition in which one object is blended into another. A reveal transition is a more general transition in which a visual effect is applied as one object is changed into another.

5. DXImageTransform.Microsoft.Fade()

6. DLevel = document.getElementById("Logo").filters[0].duration;

7. <meta http-equiv = "Page-Enter"
   content = "revealTrans (Transition=23, Duration=2)" />

Objectives

Session 13.1
- Learn about the properties of the window object
- Create permanent and transient status bar messages
- Work with the properties of the location and history objects
- Apply automatic page navigation to a Web site

Session 13.2
- Use JavaScript to create a pop-up window
- Learn how to adjust your code to accommodate pop-up blockers
- Work with the properties and methods of pop-up windows
- Create alert, confirm, and prompt dialog boxes
- Understand how to write content directly into a pop-up window
- Study how to work with modal and modeless windows

Session 13.3
- Work with frame and frameset objects
- Study how to navigate between frames
- Learn how to change the content of a frame
- Study how to change a frame layout
- Block frames and force pages into framesets
- Learn how to work with inline frames

Working with Windows and Frames

Enhancing a Web Site with Interactive Windows

Case

iMusicHistory

Teresa Jenner, a professional musician and college instructor, started a music history Web site two years ago to supplement the university courses she teaches. Since she and her students found it to be so helpful, Teresa decided to expand the site further, create a new name for it, and market it as an online course. Last month Teresa bought a new domain name for the Web site, iMusicHistory, so that she can take it off her university's server. Teresa has hired you to add interactive features to her online music history course Web site.

Because this is a new site, she needs you to create scripts to redirect users automatically to the new URL from the old university one. Beyond that, Teresa wants to have more control over the interaction between users' browsers and her Web site. For example, she would like to create her own customized status bar messages. She would also like to add pop-up windows to her Web site for use in an online quiz, and add a glossary of musical terms.

Finally, because part of her Web site uses frames, she would like you to write some scripts to control their appearance and behavior. Teresa hopes that any solutions you create will be cross-browser compatible.

Student Data Files

▼**tutorial.13**

▽ **tutorial folder**

concertotxt.htm
defaulttxt.htm
indextxt.htm
lesson3txt.htm
navtxt.htm
quiztxt.htm
sonatatxt.htm
symphonytxt.htm
+ 10 HTML files
+ 2 style sheets
+ 7 graphic files
+ 1 text file

▽ **review folder**

atempotxt.htm
bottomtxt.htm
defaulttxt.htm
maintxt.htm
quiz2txt.htm
+ 11 HTML files
+2 style sheets
+ 7 graphic files

▽ **case1 folder**

covertxt.htm
cwjtxt.htm
formtxt.htm
+2 style sheets
+4 graphic files

▽ **case2 folder**

braintxt.htm
+2 style sheets
+ 1 graphic file

▽ **case3 folder**

titletxt.htm
+ 3 HTML files
+ 2 style sheets
+ 1 graphic file
+ 2 text files

▽ **case4 folder**

allentxt.htm
birdtxt.htm
boottxt.htm
corraltxt.htm
courthousetxt.htm
indextxt.htm
schieftxt.htm
+ 1 style sheet
+ 14 graphic files

Session 13.1

Working with the Window Object

At your first meeting with Teresa, she shows you the current status of her music Web site, and discusses the changes she wants you to make. You'll start by examining the work she's done already.

To open the iMusicHistory home page:

▶ 1. In your text editor, open the **defaulttxt.htm** file located in the tutorial.13/tutorial folder. Enter **your name** and **the date** in the comment section and save the file as **default.htm**.

▶ 2. Open the **default.htm** page in your Web browser (see Figure 13-1).

Music History
An Interactive Online Approach

Welcome to iMusicHistory, an interactive approach to music history.

Based on the widely used text *A History of Western Music* by Donald Jay Grout and Claude V. Palisca, this resource offers a motivating, interactive environment for exploring, reviewing, listening to, and learning about music history.

Contact us with any questions you may have about our interactive music history course. We look forward to hearing from you.

Features include:

- Study quizzes with immediate interactive responses.
- Hypertext music terms throughout the Web site with unobtrusive, convenient pop-up windows that open and close, supplementing the lessons.

  Click here for a sample: *a tempo*

- Glossary of Music Terms.

Coming Soon:

- Listening samples.
- Links to further resources.
- Public and private message boards.
- The entire Web site will be available for electronic download or via CD-ROM.

To top

iMusicHistory

Home - Lessons - Quiz - Glossary

Contact: Teresa Jenner, Ph.D., 123 March Lane, San Rafael, CA 12345

Trouble? Some of the links in the Web page will not work yet, since you haven't created the required files.

As you can see from the links on the home page, the iMusicHistory Web site has four main pages:

- A home page, describing the purpose and features of the site
- A Lessons page, containing an interactive lesson on music history
- A Quiz page, containing an online quiz for students to review
- A Glossary page, containing definitions of musical terms

The first changes that Teresa wants you to make to her Web site involve the text that appears in the Web browser's status bar. Teresa would like a status bar message welcoming visitors to the site to appear as soon as the home page of the Web site loads. She would also like a description of each navigational link to appear in the status bar whenever someone moves the mouse pointer over a navigation link.

To create the messages in the status bar that Teresa wants, you'll need to manipulate the appearance of the browser window. JavaScript considers the browser window an object, which it calls the **window object**. Thus, many features of the browser window, including the text in the status bar, are properties of the window object. Figure 13-2 lists some of the other properties of the window object.

| Figure 13-2 | Properties of the window object |

Property	Description
closed	Returns a Boolean value indicating whether the window has been closed
defaultStatus	Defines the default message displayed in the status bar
document	The document object displayed in the window
frames	The collection of frames within the window
history	The history object, containing a list of Web sites visited within that window
innerHeight	The inner height of the window excluding all toolbars, scrollbars, and other features (Netscape only)
innerWidth	The inner width of the window excluding all toolbars, scrollbars, and other features (Netscape only)
location	The location object containing the URL of the current Web document
name	The name of the window
opener	The source browser window, which opened the current window
outerHeight	The outer height of the window including all toolbars, scrollbars, and other features (Netscape only)
outerWidth	The outer width of the window including all toolbars, scrollbars, and other features (Netscape only)
scrollbars	The scrollbar object contained in the browser window
status	The temporary or transient message displayed in the status bar
statusbar	The status bar object used for displaying messages in the browser window
toolbar	A Boolean value indicating whether the window's toolbar is visible

The syntax to set a property of the window object is

```
windowObject.property = "value"
```

where *windowObject* is a browser window, *property* is a property of the window, and *value* is the value that we assign to the property. Note that you can have more than one browser window open during a session, and you can use JavaScript to work with the properties and content of those different windows. We'll discuss how to work with multiple windows later in this tutorial. If you're only working with the properties of the current browser window, you don't need to specify the browser window and can instead use the object name "window", or in some cases leave the window object reference out entirely. For example, to set the value of the inner height of the current browser window to 300 pixels, you would use the command

```
window.innerHeight = "300";
```

If the property of the window object is itself an object, you can drop the reference to the window object. Thus, the following object reference

```
window.location
```

which references the location bar, is equivalent to

```
location
```

as long as you are looking at the properties and objects of the current browser window. If you want to reference the objects and properties of another window, you then need to include the reference to that window object in the command.

Working with Status Bars

The borders of a browser window, including items such as the toolbars and scrollbars, are collectively referred to as the window's **chrome**. One part of the chrome that is common to all browsers is the **status bar**, used to display messages to the user about actions occurring within the window. These messages can be either permanent or transient. Let's look first at how to work with permanent status bar messages.

Setting the Default Status Bar Message

The **permanent status bar message** is the message that appears in the status bar by default when no actions are occurring with the browser window. The syntax for setting the permanent status bar message is

```
windowObject.defaultStatus="text"
```

where *text* is the message that will appear by default in the browser window's status bar. Note that this message is only permanent for the current document. Once the browser loads a different page, the permanent status bar message returns to either the browser default or a permanent message specified for the new page.

Teresa asks you to set the permanent message of the browser window's status bar for the iMusicHistory home page to "Welcome to iMusicHistory".

To change the default status bar message:

▶ **1.** Return to the **default.htm** file in your text editor.

▶ **2.** Add the following event handler to the body element as shown in Figure 13-3.

```
onload="window.defaultStatus='Welcome to iMusicHistory'"
```

Setting the default status bar message ◀ **Figure 13-3**

```
<title>Teresa Jenner's iMusicHistory course</title>
<link href="main.css" rel="stylesheet" type="text/css" />
</head>

<body onload="window.defaultStatus='Welcome to iMusicHistory'">
```

status bar message

▶ **3.** Save your changes.

▶ **4.** Reload **default.htm** in your Web browser and verify that the welcome message appears in the status bar (see Figure 13-4).

Figure 13-4 | **The modified status bar text**

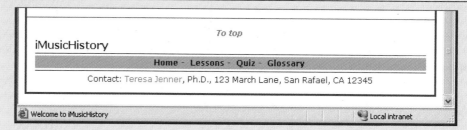

Trouble? Some browsers, such as Firefox, do not allow JavaScript to modify the status bar message by default. See your browser's documentation to learn if this feature can be enabled.

Creating a Transient Status Bar Message

The iMusicHistory home page contains several links at the bottom of the page. By default, most browsers display the URL of a link in the status bar when a user passes the pointer over the link. However, Teresa would like the message "Learn more about iMusicHistory" to appear in the status bar when users pass the pointer over the Home link. This message is an example of a **transient status bar message** because it appears only temporarily in response to an event occurring within the browser. Once the event is over the transient message should disappear, being replaced by the permanent message.

To create a transient status bar message, you need to run the following two lines of code:

```
windowObject.status="text";
return true;
```

where *text* is the text that will appear as a transient message in the status bar. The first line sets the transient message in the status bar. The second line returns the Boolean value "true" to the browser. Recall that the return keyword essentially tells a browser to stop running a process and return the indicated value. You have already used this keyword to stop a function; however, it can also apply to other types of processes. Remember that by default, a browser generates its own transient message for the action of hovering over a link: it displays the URL of the link. In this case, you need to stop that default action from happening, because you want to display your own message instead. Running the return command stops that process before it occurs, thereby keeping the browser from displaying its own transient message.

To change the transient status bar message for the Home link, you'll add the following onmouseover event handler to the link:

```
onmouseover = "window.status='Learn more about iMusicHistory';
return true"
```

When the user moves the pointer off the link, you want the status bar to become blank. However, by default transient status bar messages remain until some other event replaces them. In order to remove your message, you need to also add an onmouseout event handler that changes the transient message to an empty text string. The event handler for this action is

```
onmouseout = "window.status='';return true"
```

When the browser encounters a blank transient message, it understands that as a signal to display no message, or to redisplay the permanent status bar message if one exists.

To add a status bar message to the Home link:

▶ 1. Return to the **default.htm** file in your text editor.

▶ 2. Scroll down to the bottom of the file and locate the Home link.

▶ 3. Insert the following event handlers into the link as shown in Figure 13-5:

```
onmouseover = "window.status='Learn more about iMusicHistory';
return true"
onmouseout = "window.status='';return true"
```

Setting the transient status bar message ◀ Figure 13-5

```
<!-- Begin navigation text cell -->
<tr>
<td valign="middle" bgcolor="#99CC99" align="center" class="nav">
<a class="nav" href="default.htm"
   onmouseover="window.status='Learn more about iMusicHistory';return true"
   onmouseout="window.status='';return true">Home</a> - 
<a class="nav" href="lesson3.htm">Lessons</a> - 
<a class="nav" href="quiz.htm">Quiz</a> - 
<a class="nav" href="terms.htm">Glossary</a><br />
<img src="dotclear.gif" border="0" /></td>
</tr>
```

▶ 4. Save your changes.

▶ 5. Reload **default.htm** in your Web browser and pass the mouse pointer over the **Home** link at the bottom of the page. Verify that the text "Learn more about iMusicHistory" appears in the status bar (see Figure 13-6).

Viewing the transient status bar message ◀ Figure 13-6

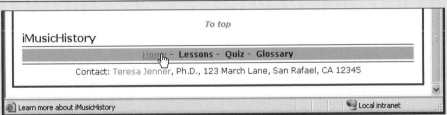

Trouble? Some browsers, such as Opera, will not override the default transient status bar message for this link, and the permanent message you entered earlier will still appear.

Setting the Status Bar Message

Reference Window

- To set the permanent message displayed in the browser window's status bar, use the JavaScript command
    ```
    windowObject.defaultStatus="text";
    ```
  where *windowObject* is the browser window and *text* is the new default message.
- To create a transient status bar message, use the commands
    ```
    windowObject.status="text";
    return true;
    ```

Recently, some browser developers have begun disabling the ability of JavaScript programs to modify permanent and transient status bar messages because of potential security issues. Modifying status bar messages can be used as part of an overall process of creating counterfeit Web sites that resemble real, legitimate sites. Counterfeit sites are sometimes created in order to trick unsuspecting users into revealing personal information such as contact information, passwords, and credit card numbers. Because it's possible that a user's browser won't display your customized status bar messages, you should never put essential information into a status bar message.

You've completed your work for now on the status bar messages. Later you'll have to apply the techniques you just learned to the other links and pages in the Web site. For now, however, Teresa wants you to work more with the main browser window.

Working with the History and Location Objects

Previously, the iMusicHistory Web site was stored on the servers at Teresa's university and the home page was located in a file named index.htm (rather than default.htm). Teresa still wants to include the index.htm page in her site since some users will still have links or bookmarks that point to it; however, she wants that page to alert users about the changes and provide a link to default.htm. Teresa would also like a link on the old home page that, when clicked, takes users back to the previous page they visited. This will make it easier for users to notify the authors of pages linked to the iMusicHistory Web site that the link should be updated. Finally, if a user does nothing, Teresa would like the browser to load the new site automatically after a brief interval.

Browsers maintain information about where users have been and the pages they're currently visiting within each window. You can access this information through the location and history objects. The **location object** contains information about the page that is currently displayed in the window. The **history object** holds a list of the sites the Web browser has displayed before reaching the current page in the window.

Moving Forward and Backward in the History List

In a browser window, you usually navigate through the history list by clicking the Back and Forward buttons on the browser toolbar. To do the same using JavaScript, you use the following methods of the history object:

```
history.back();
history.forward();
```

The back() method causes the window to load the page prior to the current page in the history list; in other words, it changes the page visible in the window to the page the user was previously viewing. If a user is at the beginning of the history list, there is no page to go back to, and the current page is not replaced. The forward() method loads the next page in the history list after the current page. If you're at the end of the history list, there is no page to go to, and the current page remains in the browser. Note that both of the above commands access the history object within the current browser window. If you want to use history objects in other browser windows, you have to specify the window object as follows:

```
windowObject.history.back();
```

where *windowObject* is a reference to the browser window. You can also navigate to a particular page in the history object using the method

```
history.go(integer)
```

where *integer* can be a positive or negative number or zero, and represents how many pages the browser should move through in the history list. For example, the command history.go(-1) moves the user back one page in the history list. The command history.go(1) moves the user to the next page in the list, and the command history.go(0) keeps the user at the current page.

A common way to implement the back() and forward() methods is as links with the following structure:

```
<a href="javascript:history.back()">Back</a>
```

and

```
<a href="javascript:history.forward()">Forward</a>
```

You'll implement this approach in Teresa's old home page. Much of the content of the revised index.htm page has been created for you and stored in the index.htm file. Your first task will be to create a link on the index.htm page that points to the page previously visited by the user.

To create a link to the previously visited page:

1. Open **indextxt.htm** from the tutorial.13/tutorial folder in your text editor. Enter *your name* and *the date* in the comment section and save the file as **index.htm**.

2. Locate the word "return" in the third paragraph in the document body and link it to the following target (see Figure 13-7).

   ```
   javascript:history.back()
   ```

Creating a link to the previously visited page ◀ **Figure 13-7**

```
<p>If a link has led you erroneously to this page, <br />
   please click <a href="javascript:history.back()">return</a>
   to go back to the previous page,<br />
   and notify the page's author of the outdated link.</p>

</body>
</html>
```

3. Save your changes to the file.

4. Return to your current browser window and use it to open the **index.htm** page shown in Figure 13-8.

   Trouble? In some browsers you have to insert the URL of the index.htm file in the browser's address bar in order to open it in the current browser window.

> # Teresa Jenner's
> # Music History Course
> # has Moved
>
> You will automatically be transported there
> in 8 seconds or less.
>
> If your browser doesn't recognize the command,
> please click iMusicHistory.com to move to the new page.
>
> If a link has led you erroneously to this page,
> please click return to go back to the previous page,
> and notify the page's author of the outdated link.

5. Verify that when you click **return** on the page, the browser reloads the previous page you opened (in this case, the default.htm file).

With the link to the previous page taken care of, your next task is to redirect users' browsers to the new Web site automatically, so that if users don't click any of the links or their Back or Forward buttons, the new default.htm file will be loaded.

Automatic Page Navigation

There are two ways to redirect the user to another Web page automatically. One way is to add a command to the <meta> tag located in the Head section of an HTML file. The other is to create a JavaScript program that runs when the page is loaded and opens the new page automatically. Since some browser versions do not support JavaScript, you'll employ both methods in the index.htm file.

The syntax to redirect a browser to a new page using the meta element is

```
<meta http-equiv="Refresh" content="sec;URL=url" />
```

where sec is the amount of time in seconds that will elapse before the new page opens, and url is the new page to be loaded. For example, to load the default.htm page automatically after 8 seconds, you would add the following tag to the index.htm file:

```
<meta http-equiv="Refresh" content="8;URL=default.htm" />
```

Setting the time value to zero causes the redirection to occur almost instantaneously, so that often users are not even aware that a redirection has taken place. However, for Teresa's site you want users to have time to read the text notifying users that they need to update their links to iMusicHistory.

The other approach to redirecting a browser to another page, using the location object, employs the following syntax:

```
windowObject.location.href = "url";
```

where url is the new page to be loaded. To redirect the current browser window to the default.htm page, you would add the following JavaScript command to the index.htm file:

```
location.href="default.htm";
```

To add a delay, you can run this command with the setTimeout() method, setting a delay time of 8000 milliseconds (8 seconds):

```
function redirect() {
    setTimeout("location.href='default.htm'",8000);
}
```

To ensure maximum compatibility with all browsers, use both techniques in the outdated home page for iMusicHistory.

To add automatic redirection to the index.htm page:

1. Return to the **index.htm** file in your text editor.

2. Add the following meta element to the head section of the document:

   ```
   <meta http-equiv="Refresh" content="8;URL=default.htm" />
   ```

3. Add the following embedded script to the head section:

   ```
   <script type="text/javascript">
   function redirect() {
       setTimeout("location.href='default.htm'",8000);
   }
   </script>
   ```

4. Add the following event handler to the body element so that the redirect() functions runs when the page is loaded:

   ```
   onLoad="redirect()"
   ```

   Figure 13-9 shows the revised code.

Adding automatic redirection to the index.htm file ◀ **Figure 13-9**

```
<title>iMusicHistory has moved</title>
<meta http-equiv="Refresh" content="8;URL=default.htm" />

<script type="text/javascript">
function redirect() {
    setTimeout("location.href='default.htm'",8000);
}
</script>

<style>
body {text-align: center; background-color: white}
h1 {color:red; font-family:Arial, Helvetica, sans-serif}
p {font-size:medium}
</style>
</head>

<body onload="redirect()">
<h1>Teresa Jenner's<br />
    Music History Course<br />
    has Moved<hr /></h1>
```

5. Close the file, saving your changes.

6. Reopen the **index.htm** file in your browser window. Verify that, after about 8 seconds, the window opens the default.htm file.

Reference Window

Automatically Redirecting Web Pages

- To redirect visitors automatically from one page to another, add the following meta element to the document's head:

  ```
  <meta http-equiv="Refresh" content="sec;URL=url" />
  ```
  where *sec* is the amount of time in seconds that will elapse before opening the new page, and *url* is the new page to be loaded.
- To redirect to a new page using JavaScript, run the command:

  ```
  setTimeout("location.href='url'",msec);
  ```
  where *msec* is the delay time in milliseconds.

Security Issues

In Netscape, the history object also supports the properties current, next, and previous, which contain the URLs of the previous, current, and next page in a user's history list. However, use of these properties is restricted to prevent Web page authors from creating scripts to record what sites their users have been visiting. Most people would consider such tracking an invasion of privacy.

Netscape (version 4.0 and above) uses signed scripts to request permission to access restricted information such as the current, next, and previous properties. The process of creating a signed script involves acquiring digital certification of your identity as a legitimate developer or organization. Digital certification can come from a variety of sources on the Web including www.thawte.com and www.verisign.com. Signed scripts are not available in Internet Explorer, however, and prior to Netscape version 4 these properties were not available at all from a script.

Another way of retrieving this information is through the document.referrer property, which records the URL of the page from which the current page was accessed. The following code uses the document.referrer property to write the name of the page from which the current page was loaded. Note that the document.referrer property works only when the current page is accessed via a link, and that some browsers disable this property for security reasons:

```
if (document.referrer) {
    document.write('You came from: ' + document.referrer);
}
```

Teresa has finished examining your work and is pleased with the messages you created for the status bar, as well as your solution to redirecting visitors from her old domain to her new one. In the next session you'll work on her online music history glossary terms, which will require creating new windows with JavaScript.

Review

Session 13.1 Quick Check

1. Explain the difference between permanent and transient status bar messages.
2. What single JavaScript command would you enter to move a user two places backward in the history list?
3. What JavaScript command(s) would you enter to change the transient status bar message to "View News page"?

4. Describe at least two methods (a JavaScript method and a non-JavaScript method) of redirecting visitors from a Web site or Web page to its new location.
5. What is the document.referrer property used for? What are two limitations of this property?

Session 13.2

Creating New Browser Windows

The iMusicHistory Web site contains a glossary of musical terms. When a user clicks a linked term, its definition on the glossary page is displayed. See Figure 13-10.

Accessing the music glossary ◄ **Figure 13-10**

clicking a music term ...   ... causes the browser to load the glossary page

Teresa is concerned that jumping from one page to another to view definitions is inconvenient and distracting. As a user goes back and forth between the two windows, it's easy to get lost. She would much rather see a smaller window containing the definition of the clicked word appear alongside the main window. A user could then quickly read the definition without losing contact with the main window. Figure 13-11 shows a preview of the system Teresa would like you to create.

Viewing a definition in a pop-up window ◄ **Figure 13-11**

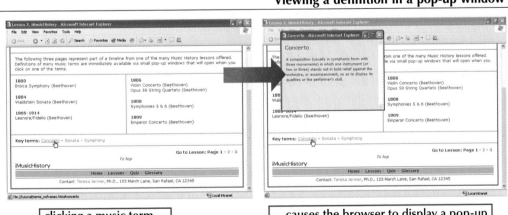

clicking a music term ...   ... causes the browser to display a pop-up window containing the definition

Windows that open in addition to the main browser window are called **secondary windows** or **pop-up windows**. Teresa wants you to add pop-up windows to her Web site.

Opening New Windows with HTML

By default, each new Web page that a user opens appears in the main browser window. As users move from one page to another, the contents of the browser window change accordingly. If you want one of your links to open the target document in a new window, you specify the window name using the target property. The general syntax is

```
<a href="url" target="name">link text</a>
```

where *url* is the URL of the target document, and *name* is the name of the secondary browser window in which the document should appear. The value of the target attribute doesn't affect the appearance or content of the new window. In fact, you need to keep track of the target attribute's value only if you intend to use the same window for other links. For example, Teresa's Web site could open a secondary window that displays biographies of the great composers. HTML tags for links to that window could appear as follows:

```
<a href="Wagner.htm" target="Composer">View Wagner's biography</a>
<a href="Mozart.htm" target="Composer">View Mozart's biography</a>
```

Clicking either link would open a secondary window with the target name "Composer". If the Composer window were already open, its contents would be replaced with the new page.

You can give a new window any name, except one that is reserved by HTML for other purposes. For example, if your Web page contains frames, you can't give the new window the name assigned to one of your frames, because the page will appear in the frame rather than in a separate window.

Opening New Windows with JavaScript

You can also use JavaScript to create new windows. JavaScript offers more control and many more options for creating new windows than the target property does. For example, you can control the contents of a window you create, the window size (height and width properties), its position on the screen, and whether the new window has toolbars (and which ones), a menu bar, and a status bar. In contrast, any new windows created using the target property draw their appearance (toolbars, menu bars, scroll bars, etc.) from the appearance of the main browser window.

The JavaScript command to create a new browser window is

```
window.open("url","name","features")
```

where *url* is the URL of the page to be displayed in the new window, *name* is the target name assigned to the window, and *features* is a comma-separated list of features that control the appearance and behavior of the window. If you don't need to specify a target name for the new window, you can specify an empty text string for the *name* value. The features list can include the size and width of the window, as well as whether the window's scroll bar, toolbar, status bar, and menu bar are to be displayed.

You can store a new window as an object in a JavaScript program. This is useful if your script will be modifying the appearance or content of the window later. To store a new window as an object, you use the syntax

```
windowObject = window.open("url","name","features")
```

where *windowObject* is the object representing the new browser window you open.

Creating a Pop-up Window

- To create a pop-up window, use the JavaScript command
  ```
  window.open("url","name","features")
  ```
  where *url* is the URL of the document to be displayed in the window, *name* is the target name assigned to the window, and *features* is a comma-separated list of the features of the window.
- To assign a pop-up window to an object, use the command
  ```
  windowObject = window.open("url","name","features")
  ```
  where *windowObject* is the name of the window object representing the pop-up window.

Before creating a window for Teresa's glossary, let's examine the features list in more detail.

Setting the Features of a Pop-up Window

The features list obeys the following syntax:

```
"feature1=value1,feature2=value2,...featureN=valueN"
```

where *feature1*, *feature2*, ... are the names of the different window features, and *value1*, *value2*, ... are the values associated with those features. Figure 13-12 describes these features and their values.

| Figure 13-12 | Feature list values |

Feature	Description	Value
alwaysLowered	Sets the window below all other windows (Netscape only)	yes/no
alwaysRaised	Sets the window above all other windows (Netscape only)	yes/no
dependent	Window is a dependent of the parent window that created it and closes when it closes (Netscape only)	yes/no
fullscreen	Displays the window in full screen mode (Internet Explorer only)	yes/no
height	Window height, in pixels	integer
hotkeys	Disables keyboard hotkeys in the window (Netscape only)	yes/no
innerHeight	Inner height of the window, in pixels (Netscape only)	integer
innerWidth	Inner width of the window, in pixels (Netscape only)	integer
left	Sets the screen coordinate of the left edge of the window, in pixels (Internet Explorer only)	integer
location	Displays the location bar in the window	yes/no
menubar	Displays the menu bar in the window	yes/no
outerHeight	Outer height of the window, in pixels (Netscape only)	integer
outerWidth	Outer width of the window, in pixels (Netscape only)	integer
resizable	Allows users to resize the window	yes/no
screenX	Sets the screen coordinate of the left edge of the window, in pixels (Netscape only)	integer
screenY	Sets the screen coordinate of the top edge of the window, in pixels (Netscape only)	integer
scrollbars	Displays scrollbars in the window	yes/no
status	Displays the status bar in the window	yes/no
top	Sets the screen coordinate of the top edge of the window, in pixels (Internet Explorer only)	
titlebar	Displays the title bar (Netscape only)	yes/no
toolbar	Displays the window's toolbar	yes/no
width	Sets the width of the window, in pixels	integer
z-lock	Prevents the window from rising above other windows (Netscape only)	yes/no

For example, to create a browser window that is resizable, but without the menu bar, location box, and toolbar, you would use the following features list:

```
"resizable=yes,menubar=no,location=no,toolbar=no"
```

You can substitute the numbers "1" for "yes" and "0" for "no" in your features list; thus, you could also enter the above features list as:

```
"resizable=1,menubar=0,location=0,toolbar=0"
```

A features list is not required. If you don't specify a features list, the new window adopts the characteristics of the browser window that created it. However, once you start applying a features list, the new window follows these rules:

- If you don't specify a width or height, the width or height of the original browser window is used.
- If you don't include a particular feature in the list, that feature will not appear in the window.

For example, if the features list appears as

```
"width=300,height=200,resizable=yes"
```

the new window will have a width of 300 pixels, a height of 200 pixels, and will be resizable; however, none of the other objects of the window (toolbars, status bar, scroll bars, etc.) will appear.

By default a pop-up window will appear in the upper-left corner of your screen; however you can specify a different location in the window.open() method. Internet Explorer and Netscape use different features for this. Internet Explorer uses features named left and top, while Netscape uses screenX and screenY (Netscape 4.0 and above also supports the left and top feature names). By default, a pop-up window appears near the upper-left corner of the screen. If you instead wanted to place a window at the screen coordinates (200, 250)—200 pixels from the left edge and 250 pixels down—you would specify the features as follows:

```
"left=200,top=250,screenX=200,screenY=250"
```

To see how JavaScript can be used to define the properties of the pop-up window, a demo page has been prepared for you.

To open the pop-up window demo:

1. Use your Web browser to open the **demo_popup.htm** file from the tutorial.13/ tutorial folder.

2. In the Web page form, enter **400** in the Left edge box.

   Note that as you change values and select check boxes from the form, a box at the bottom of the page showing the JavaScript code to create the pop-up window changes in response.

3. Enter **35** in the Top edge box.

4. Set the width and height values to **200** and **150**, respectively.

5. Click the **Display status bar** check box to select it.

6. Click the **Show pop-up window** button on the form.

   Your browser displays a pop-up window (see Figure 13-13).

Figure 13-13 ▶ **Running the pop-up demo**

Carey, P. *New Perspectives on HTML, XHTML and DHTML*, Course Technology: Boston, 2005.

Trouble? Depending on your browser, your window will look slightly different. If you are running a pop-up blocker, you may have to turn it off to run this demo.

▶ **7.** Close the pop-up window.

▶ **8.** Continue generating pop-up windows with different features.

▶ **9.** Close the demo page when finished.

Controlling Pop-up Window Features

- To define the width and height of the pop-up window, add the following to the features list in the window.open() method:

  ```
  width=x,height=y
  ```
  where x and y are the width and height of the window, in pixels.
- Internet Explorer: To set the screen position of a pop-up, add the features

  ```
  left=x,top=y
  ```
  where x is the coordinate of the left edge, in pixels, and y is the coordinate of the window's top edge.
- Netscape: To set the screen position of a pop-up, add the features

  ```
  screenX=x,screenY=y
  ```
- To display the directory buttons, location box, menu bar, scroll bar, status bar, or toolbar, add the features

  ```
  directories=value,location=value,menubar=value,
  scrollbars=value,status=value,toolbar=value
  ```
  where `value` is either "yes" (to show the feature) or "no" (to hide the feature). You can also substitute the values "1" for "yes" and "0" for "no."

Working with Pop-up Blockers

In recent years, pop-up windows have become a common and often annoying feature of the World Wide Web. In general, pop-ups come in two types: those that users open by clicking a link, and those that open automatically whether users want to see them or not. Many Web sites, eager to generate commercial revenue, have incorporated automated pop-ups to display sponsors' advertisements. On some sites, a user can be inundated with so many commercial pop-up windows that it can be difficult to view the contents of the Web site itself! In response to the proliferation of pop-ups, browsers and third-party software developers have created **pop-up blockers** that prevent pop-up windows from opening. There are a variety of pop-up blockers on the market. Some make a distinction between automated pop-ups and pop-ups opened by users, and others do not.

There's not a lot you can do to override pop-up blockers—and this is not something you should do anyway, if you wish to create a user-friendly Web site that respects each user's preferences regarding pop-ups. However, you can work to ensure that any failure to open a pop-up window is dealt with constructively by a user's browser. You can have the browser check whether the pop-up window has been opened or not. If it hasn't, you can then open the linked file in the current browser window. A function to test whether a pop-up window has failed to open has the general form

```
function popWin(url) {
 winObj = window.open("url","name","features")
 test=(winObj == null || typeof(winObj) == "undefined") ? true: false;
 return test;
}
```

The important variable in this function is *test*, which has a value of true if the pop-up fails to open and a value of false if the pop-up opens normally. You use a conditional operator to test whether the pop-up opens. You know that the pop-up did not open if either *winObj* is null (which means that it was not created) or the type of the *winObj* variable is undefined. Note that popWin uses the typeof() function to determine the variable type of the object. The popWin() function then returns the value of the *test* variable. You call the popWin() function from a link on the page using the following code:

```
<a href="url" onclick="return(popWin('url'))"> Link Text </a>
```

If the popWin() function returns the Boolean value true, then the link code processes the onclick event, thus overriding the normal action of the browser to process the href attribute in response to a mouse click. However, if the popWin() function returns the value false, it cancels the click event and the browser opens the link via the href attribute in the usual way—but not as a pop-up window. Thus, in either case, a user sees the contents of the pop-up window—in one case as a pop-up, and in the other in the current browser window. Note that the return keyword has the same purpose here as it did in creating a transient status bar message in the last session: it breaks the normal behavior of the Web browser and allows us to ensure that the linked page is available to the user.

If pop-up windows are an important part of your Web site, you should test your code against various pop-up blockers and under a variety of conditions. You need to ensure that the contents of your Web site are always accessible to your users, no matter what browser and pop-up blocker they may be using. Keep in mind that most pop-up blockers block only automated pop-ups and not those activated by a user clicking a link to a pop-up window.

Adding a Pop-up Window to the iMusicHistory Site

Teresa has begun the process of copying the musical definitions into their own separate HTML files for use as pop-up windows. She has already created three HTML files for the musical terms concerto, sonata, and symphony. The links for these three definitions are stored in the lesson3.htm file. Since you'll be modifying the contents of these files later, open and save them under different names now.

To open and view Teresa's files:

▶ 1. In your text editor, open the **concertotxt.htm**, **sonatatxt.htm**, **symphonytxt. htm**, and **lesson3txt.htm** files. Enter *your name* and *the date* in the comment section of each file. Save the files as **concerto.htm**, **sonata.htm**, **symphony.htm**, and **lesson3.htm** respectively.

▶ 2. Open **lesson3.htm** in your Web browser.

▶ 3. Go the bottom of the page and click the **Concerto**, **Sonata**, and **Symphony** links to verify that the links open the corresponding definitions on the glossary page.

Teresa would like the pop-up window for the definitions to be fairly small, perhaps containing a link or button to close it, and without any features other than the scroll bar. To avoid retyping the same commands for each definition, you'll create the following function, named popWin(), to display each Web page as a pop-up window:

```
function popWin(url) {
    defwin=window.open(url,"pop","width=330,height=220,scrollbars=yes");
    testpop=(defwin==null || typeof(defwin)=="undefined") ? true: false;
    return testpop;
}
```

In this function, the url parameter contains the URL of the document appearing in the pop-up window. Of the different features of the window, only the scroll bar will be displayed. Since the other features are not included in the list, they will not be applied to the pop-up window. As discussed earlier, this function checks if the pop-up window has been blocked and returns a value of true if the pop-up window is blocked.

To add the popWin() function to the lesson3 page:

1. Return to **lesson3.htm** in your text editor.

2. Insert an embedded script in the document's head and add the following function, as shown in Figure 13-14:

```
function popWin(url) {
    defwin=window.open(url,"pop","width=330,height=220,
    scrollbars=yes");
    testpop=(defwin==null || typeof(defwin)=="undefined") ? true:
    false;
    return testpop;
}
```

The popWin() function ◄ **Figure 13-14**

```
<title>Lesson 3, iMusicHistory</title>
<link href="main.css" rel="stylesheet" type="text/css" />
<script type="text/javascript">
function popwin(url) {
    defwin=window.open(url,"pop","width=330,height=220,scrollbars=yes");
    testpop=(defwin==null || typeof(defwin)=="undefined") ? true: false;
    return testpop;
}
</script>
</head>
```

Next you need to call the function from the three links on the lesson3 page.

To call the popWin() function:

1. Scroll to the Key Terms section of the lesson3.htm file (located near the midpoint of the file).

2. In the code for the link for the Concerto definition, add the event handler

   `onclick="return(popWin('concerto.htm'))"`

3. Add the following event handler to the sonata definition link:

   `onclick="return(popWin('sonata.htm'))"`

4. Finally add the same event handler to the symphony.htm file:

   `onclick="return(popWin('symphony.htm'))"`

   Figure 13-15 shows the revised code for the three links.

Calling the popWin() function ◄ **Figure 13-15**

```
<!--- Key Terms --->
    <tr>
    <td colspan="2" bgcolor="white" class="body">
    <p><b>Key terms:</b>
    <a href="terms_noframes.htm#concerto"
        onclick="return(popwin('concerto.htm'))">Concerto</a> -
    <a href="terms_noframes.htm#sonata"
        onclick="return(popwin('sonata.htm'))">Sonata</a> -
    <a href="terms_noframes.htm#symphony"
        onclick="return(popwin('symphony.htm'))">Symphony</a><br />
    </p>
    </td>
    </tr>
```

5. Save your changes to the file and then reopen or refresh the file in your Web browser.

6. Verify that when you click the **Concerto** link located near the bottom of the page, the Concerto pop-up window appears (see Figure 13-16).

Figure 13-16 Viewing the definition pop-up window

music definition pop-up window

user clicks the link to display the pop-up window

7. Close the Concerto definition window and verify that the two other music definition links display pop-up windows.

Window Security Issues

A browser's ability to open new windows on a user's computer raises some security issues. For example, you cannot create a new window with a width and height less than 100 pixels. This restriction is designed as a precaution to prevent the creation of windows that might be invisible or almost invisible to the visitor.

Working with Window Methods

Teresa likes the work you've done on the pop-up definitions, but she is concerned that users will not like extra windows cluttering their desktops. She wonders if there's a way the pop-up window can be automatically closed once a user is done looking at it—perhaps when the user returns to the Lesson 3 page.

You can use JavaScript to control the interaction between your various browser windows. You can specify which browser window has the focus (is active) on your desktop. You can remove the focus from one window and give it to another. You can also allow users to move windows to different locations on the screen and resize them, and you can automatically close windows that are no longer needed. Most of these features are controlled by methods applied to the window object.

Window Methods

Figure 13-17 describes some of the methods you can use to manipulate your windows once they're created.

Methods of the window object **Figure 13-17**

Method	Description
blur()	Removes the focus from the window
close()	Closes the window
focus()	Gives the window the focus
moveBy(*dx, dy*)	Moves the window *dx* pixels to the right and *dy* pixels down
moveTo(*x, y*)	Moves the top left corner of the window to the screen coordinates (*x, y*)
print()	Prints the contents of the window
resizeBy(*dx, dy*)	Resizes the window by *dx* pixels to the right and *dy* pixels down
resizeTo(*x, y*)	Resizes the window to *x* pixels wide and *y* pixels high
scrollBy(*dx, dy*)	Scrolls the document content in the window by *dx* pixels to the right and *dy* pixels down
scrollTo(*x, y*)	Scrolls the document in the window to the page coordinates (*x, y*)

Most of the time your scripts will be used to open and close browser windows or to add or remove the focus from a window. For example, you can create a window object named "PopWin" using the command

```
PopWin=window.open("pop.htm", "Demo", "width=200,height=150")
```

If you wanted to give PopWin the focus somewhere in a script, you would use the Java-Script command

```
PopWin.focus();
```

PopWin would then become the active window on your desktop. To remove the focus from PopWin, you would use the command

```
PopWin.blur();
```

Finally, if you wanted to close the window, you would run the JavaScript command

```
PopWin.close();
```

You can also use the resizeBy() and resizeTo() methods to change the dimensions of your browser windows, and the moveBy() and moveTo() methods to move windows around users' screens.

Reference Window | **Applying Methods to a Window Object**

- To give the focus to a window, use the command
  `windowObject.focus()`
  where `windowObject` is the window to receive the focus.
- To remove the focus from a window, use the command
  `windowObject.blur()`
- To close a window, use the command
  `windowObject.close()`
- To move a window, use either
  `windowObject.moveBy(dx, dy)`
  or
  `windowObject.moveTo(x, y)`
  where dx and dy are the distance in pixels to shift the window to the right and down, respectively, and x and y are the screen coordinates of the window's top-left corner.
- To resize a window, use either
  `windowObject.resizeBy(dx, dy)`
  or
  `windowObject.resizeTo(x, y)`
  where dx and dy are the number of pixels to increase the width and height of the window, respectively, and x and y are the width and height of the window in pixels.

To see how you can use these methods in your Web pages, a demo page has been prepared in which you use JavaScript to open a pop-up window on your desktop, move it and resize it, and then close it.

To run the pop-up demo:

1. In your Web browser, open **demo_popup2.htm** from the tutorial.13/tutorial folder on your Data Disk.

2. Click the **Show Pop-up Window** button to display the pop-up window.

3. Click the **Move Window** buttons to move the pop-up window around your screen.

4. Click the **Resize Window** buttons to expand and contract the width and height of the pop-up window (see Figure 13-18).

Trouble? You cannot reduce the width or height of the pop-up window to below 100 pixels.

Trouble? As the focus shifts between the main browser window and the pop-up window, you may notice a bit of sluggishness in moving the window around your desktop.

5. Click the **Close Pop-up Window** button to close the pop-up window.

6. Continue experimenting with the demo page and then close the file when finished.

The Self and Opener Keywords

If your script opens several windows, it can be confusing for users to keep track of them. There are several ways of identifying the different windows. One way is through the object name you assign to each window as you create it, as in the PopWin example above. JavaScript also provides two keywords: self and opener.

The **self keyword** refers to the current window. The self keyword is synonymous with the window keyword, but you may see it used to improve clarity when a script refers to many different windows and frames. This means that to close the current window, you can use either the command

```
self.close();
```

or

```
window.close();
```

The **opener keyword** refers to the window or frame that used the window.open() method to open the current window. For example, when a secondary window is spawned from another window, the secondary window can close the original window with the command

```
opener.close();
```

Automatically Closing the Definition Window

You now have the information to make the change to the pop-up window that Teresa requested. Recall that Teresa wants the pop-up window to close whenever it loses the focus. You can do this by adding the following onblur event handler to the body element of each pop-up definition window:

```
onblur="self.close()"
```

You have to make this change to all three of the files for the definitions.

To add the onblur event handler to the pop-up definitions:

1. If necessary, reopen **concerto.htm** in your text editor.

2. Add the following event handler to the body element, as shown in Figure 13-19.

   ```
   onblur="self.close()"
   ```

| Figure 13-19 | Adding an onblur event handler |

```
<body onblur="self.close()">
<h2>Concerto</h2>
<p>A composition (usually in symphonic form with three movements) in which
one instrument (or two or three) stands out in bold relief against the
orchestra, or accompaniment, so as to display its qualities or the
performer's skill.
</p>
</body>
```

3. Save your changes to the file and close it.

4. Return to **sonata.htm** in your text editor. Insert **onblur="self.close()"** into the <body> tag and then close the file, saving your changes.

5. Add the same onblur event handler to the <body> tag of the **symphony.htm** file, and then save and close the file.

6. Return to your Web browser and reopen the **lesson3.htm** file.

7. Click each of the definitions, and verify that when you click back anywhere on the Lesson3 page, the pop-up window closes automatically.

   Trouble? If you are using the Safari browser you may have to close the pop-up windows yourself.

Now that you have completed pop-up windows for some of the definitions, you can turn your attention to the changes Teresa wants you to make to her online quiz.

Creating Dialog Boxes

The next part of the iMusicHistory Web site that Teresa wants you to work on is a page containing a quiz about music history. The page consists of a series of multiple-choice questions in a Web form. Open this file now.

To open the Quiz page:

▶ **1.** In your text editor, open **quiztxt.htm** from the tutorial.13/tutorial folder. Enter *your name* and *the date* in the comment section of the file and save it as **quiz. htm**.

▶ **2.** Open **quiz.htm** in your Web browser. Do not attempt to answer the quiz questions yet.

There are four questions and four choices for each question. Teresa has already added event handlers to each of the radio buttons in the form to run a function named answer() when a user clicks one of the choices. For example, the HTML code for the four choices in the first question is:

```
<input type="radio" name="Q1"
   onclick="answer('Robert Minute',
false)" />
<input type="radio" name="Q1"
   onclick="answer('Johannes Brahms',
false)" />
<input type="radio" name="Q1"
   onclick="answer('Frederic Chopin',
true)" />
<input type="radio" name="Q1"
   onclick="answer('None of the above',
false)" />
```

The answer function has two parameters. The first parameter contains the text of the user's guess, and the second parameter contains a Boolean value indicating whether the guess is correct or not. Teresa wants the answer() function to display a window containing the text of the user's choice that indicates whether that choice is correct or not. Teresa has not written that function yet and has asked for your help.

A dialog box is a simple way to create a window containing customized text. Java-Script supports three types of customized dialog boxes: alert, prompt, and confirm. An **alert dialog box** displays a message along with an OK button, which can be used to close the dialog box. A **prompt dialog box** displays both a message and a text box in which a user can enter text. A **confirm dialog box** displays a message along with OK and Cancel buttons. The syntax to create each of these dialog boxes is

```
alert("message")
prompt("message","default")
confirm("message")
```

where *message* is the text that appears in the dialog box, and *default* is the default text that appears in a prompt dialog box. Figure 13-20 shows examples of each type of dialog box. Note that different browsers display their dialog boxes with slight differences, but all browsers display dialog boxes with the common features of a title bar, a default value (in the case of prompt dialog boxes), an OK button, and a Cancel button (in the case of prompt and confirm dialog boxes).

Figure 13-20 | Alert, prompt, and confirm dialog boxes

alert("Form Completed")

prompt("User Name", "Enter your name")

confirm("Continue Program?")

In addition to displaying messages, the prompt and confirm dialog boxes return a value indicating the action that the user took within the dialog box. For the prompt dialog box, the value returned is the value entered into the text box. For the confirm dialog box, the Boolean value "true" is returned if a user clicks the OK button, while the value "false" is returned if a user clicks the Cancel button.

Reference Window | **Creating Dialog Boxes**

- To create an alert box, use the window method
    alert("*message*")
  where *message* is the text that appears in the dialog box.
- To create a prompt box, use the window method
    prompt("*message*","*default*")
  where *message* is the text that appears in the dialog box, and *default* is the default text appearing in the text input box.
- To create a confirm box, use the window method
    confirm("*message*")
  where *message* is a statement that you want users to confirm or cancel.

For the Quiz page, you'll use an alert box that indicates whether a user has answered the question correctly. The text of the answer function is

```
function answer(choice, guess) {
   if (guess) {
      alert(choice + " is correct!");
   } else {
      alert(choice + " is incorrect. Try again");
   }
}
```

In this function, the guess parameter contains the Boolean value indicating whether the user responded correctly. If the guess is true, the function displays an alert box containing the text of the answer followed by "is correct!" If the guess is false, the alert box displays the text of the answer followed by "is incorrect. Try again." Add this function to the quiz. htm page and test the quiz form.

To create and run the answer() function:

1. Return to **quiz.htm** in your text editor.

2. Add the following embedded script in the head section of the document (see Figure 13-21):

   ```
   <script type="text/javascript">
   function answer(choice, guess) {
      if (guess) {
         alert(choice + " is correct!");
      } else {
         alert(choice + " is incorrect. Try again");
      }
   }
   </script>
   ```

Creating alert boxes with the answer() function ◀ **Figure 13-21**

```
<title>iMusicHistory Quiz</title>
<link href="main.css" rel="stylesheet" type="text/css" title="General" />

<script type="text/javascript">
function answer(choice, guess) {
   if (guess) {
      alert(choice + " is correct!");
   } else {
      alert(choice + " is incorrect. Try again");
   }
}
</script>

</head>
```

3. Save your changes to the file.

4. Reopen **quiz.htm** in your Web browser.

5. Click the option button for **a) Robert Minute** below the first question. Your browser should display the first alert box shown in Figure 13-22.

6. Click the **OK** button and then click **c) Frederic Chopin** below the first question. The browser should display an alert indicating that your choice is correct (see Figure 13-22).

Figure 13-22	Alert boxes from the answer() function

7. Verify that the rest of the quiz works as planned. The correct answers are: 1-c, 2-c, 3-c, and 4-b.

Working between Windows

You show the current state of the Quiz page to Teresa. While she's happy with the dialog boxes you've created, she feels that they're not visually interesting. Teresa wonders if you can add graphic images and formatted text. While it is not possible to do this with the alert() method, you can do it by creating a customized pop-up window. In order to change the message for each response, you need to either create a separate file for each possible response or write the HTML code directly into the pop-up window. You'll employ the latter method for Teresa's Web site.

Writing Content to a Window

To write content to a pop-up window, you use the document.write() method, specifying the window that will receive the new content. The syntax is

```
windowObject.document.write("Content");
windowObject.document.close();
```

where *windowObject* is the window object and *Content* is a text string containing the HTML code that will be placed in the window. The document.close() method is used to close the input stream to the window. Some browsers require you to close this input stream before they will write the window content. When you are writing the entire HTML code in the window, you usually want to break up the *Content* text string into smaller text strings. You can do this by using multiple write commands as follows:

```
windowObject.document.write("Content 1");
windowObject.document.write("Content 2");
 . . .
windowObject.document.write("Content N");
windowObject.document.close();
```

Alternatively, you can create a single variable containing part of the text string, and then use an assignment operator to add additional text strings to it.

```
textstring="String 1";
textstring+="String 2";
textstring+="String 3";
...
textstring+="String N";
windowObject.document.write(textstring);
windowObject.document.close();
```

In this case, *textstring* is a variable that contains all of the text contained in the text strings *"String 1"* to *"String N"*. Which approach you take is a matter of personal preference.

Accessing an Object within a Window

The use of the document.write() method highlights an important point about working with the content of other browser windows. Once you specify a window object, you can work with the objects contained in the window's document. For example, to access a document object based on its id value, you can use the object reference

windowObject.document.getElementById(*id*)

where *id* is the id of the document object. Thus, you can run a script in one window that manipulates objects and properties in another window. These objects can also include the variables and functions defined in other browser windows, which JavaScript treats as objects within that window. To access a variable defined in another browser window, you use the object reference

windowObject.*variable*

where *variable* is the name of the JavaScript variable. To call a function from another browser window, you use the reference

windowObject.*function*()

where *function* is the name of a function defined in the *windowObject* window. Note that a document must be open in a browser window for you to access the variables and functions contained in that document. For example, if your primary window opens a pop-up window, the pop-up window can access a variable named "logoName" from the document in the primary window using the object reference

opener.logoName

Recall that opener is a special JavaScript keyword that refers to the window or frame that opened the current window. In the same way, you can run a function named "showLogo" contained in the original browser window using the command

opener.showLogo()

Working between Windows

- To write content to a pop-up window, use the commands
    ```
    windowObject.document.write(content);
    windowObject.document.close();
    ```
    where *windowObject* is the window that you wish to write to and *content* is a text string of HTML code to be written into the window.
- To access an object within a document window, use the object reference
    ```
    windowObject.document.getElementById(id)
    ```
    where *id* is the id of the object in the document.
- To access a variable within a document window, use the object reference
    ```
    windowObject.variable
    ```
    where *variable* is the name of a variable defined in the window.
- To run a function from another window, use the reference
    ```
    windowObject.function()
    ```
    where *function* is the name of a function in the window.

Creating the Quiz Pop-up Window

You'll write the following HTML code to the answer window for Teresa's quiz:

```
<html>
<head>
   <title>iMusicHistory Quiz</title>
   <link rel="stylesheet" href="quiz.css" type="text/css" />
</head>
<body>
   <p>
   <img src="treble2.gif" alt="" />
   message
   <br />
   <input type="button" value="OK" onclick="self.close()" />
   </p>
</body>
</html>
```

where *message* is the message in the pop-up window that indicates whether a student's answer is correct or not. Figure 13-23 shows how this pop-up window will appear for incorrect and correct answers. Note that this window mimics an alert box by including a form button that uses the self.close() command to close the window.

Figure 13-23 ▶ Customized windows

To write this content to the pop-up windows, you'll use the following function:

```
function writeContent(windowObj, choice, guess) {
   content="<html><head><title>iMusicHistory Quiz</title>";
   content+="<link rel='stylesheet' href='quiz.css' type='text/css' /
   >";
   content+="</head><body><p><img src='treble2.gif' alt='' />";
   if (guess) {
      content += choice + " is correct!";
```

```
} else {
    content += choice + " is incorrect. Try again";
}
content+="<br /><input type='button' value='OK' onclick='self.
close()' />";
content+="</p></body></html>";
windowObj.document.write(content);
windowObj.document.close();
}
```

The writeContent() function has three parameters. The windowObj parameter is the window object that will receive this HTML code. The choice and guess parameters have the same purpose and values as they did for the answer() function you just created. Due to the way browsers process white space in HTML code, you can insert several HTML tags on the same line, reducing the number of statements in the function. Additionally, while the HTML code is enclosed using double quotes, any attribute values within that code are enclosed in single quotes. Because this is a complicated function and it would be easy to make a typing mistake, the function code has been provided for you to copy and paste into the Quiz document.

To create the writeContent() function:

1. Use your text editor to open the **writeContent.txt** text file from the tutorial.13/ tutorial folder.

2. Copy the text of the function and then close the text file.

3. Return to **quiz.htm** in your text editor.

4. Below the answer() function paste the code of the writeContent() function, as shown in Figure 13-24.

The writeContent() function ◄ Figure 13-24

```
<script type="text/javascript">
function answer(choice, guess) {
    if (guess) {
        alert(choice + " is correct!");
    } else {
        alert(choice + " is incorrect. Try again");
    }
}

function writeContent(windowObj, choice, guess) {
    content="<html><head><title>iMusicHistory Quiz</title>";
    content+="<link rel='stylesheet' href='quiz.css' type='text/css' />";
    content+="</head><body><p><img src='treble2.gif' alt='' />";
    if (guess) {
        content += choice + " is correct!";
    } else {
        content += choice + " is incorrect. Try again";
    }
    content+="<br /><input type='button' value='OK' onclick='self.close()' />";
    content+="</p></body></html>";
    windowObj.document.write(content);
    windowObj.document.close();
}
</script>
```

Your last task is to revise the answer() function to create the pop-up window. This involves three steps:

1. Use the window.open() method to open the pop-up window.

2. Test whether the pop-up window has been blocked or has otherwise failed to open.

3. If the pop-up window has failed to open, display alert dialog boxes as before (they are not blocked by pop-up blockers); otherwise, call the writeContent() function to display the pop-up window.

The revised code for the answer() function is as follows:

```
function answer(choice, guess) {
ansWin=window.open("","","width=250,height=100,left=250,screenX=250,
top=250, screenY=250");
popfailed = (ansWin == null || typeof(ansWin) == "undefined") ? true :
 false;
if (popfailed) {
   if (guess) {
      alert(choice + " is correct!");
   } else {
      alert(choice + " is incorrect. Try again");
   }
} else {
   writeContent(ansWin, choice, guess);
}
}
```

The answer() function first creates a window object named ansWin that is 250 pixels wide and 100 pixels high and placed 250 pixels to the right and below the upper-left corner of the screen. There is no URL or target name specified for this window because you will be writing the HTML directly into it. The next line of the function creates the popfailed variable to test whether the pop-up window opened. If the pop-up failed, you run the conditional statement you created earlier to display the appropriate alert dialog box; otherwise, the writeContent() function is run using the ansWin window as the window object and the choice and guess variables as the second and third parameter values.

To revise the answer() function and test it:

1. Revise the answer() function so that the code for the function reads as follows:

```
function answer(choice, guess) {
ansWin=window.open("","","width=250,height=100,left=250,
screenX=250,top=250,screenY=250");
popfailed = (ansWin == null || typeof(ansWin) == "undefined") ?
true : false;
if (popfailed) {
   if (guess) {
      alert(choice + " is correct!");
   } else {
      alert(choice + " is incorrect. Try again");
   }
} else {
   writeContent(ansWin, choice, guess);
}
}
```

Figure 13-25 shows the answer() function with the newly inserted code highlighted in red.

```
function answer(choice, guess) {
  answin=window.open("","","width=250,height=100,left=250,screenX=250,top=250,screenY=250");
  popfailed = (answin == null || typeof(answin) == "undefined") ? true : false;
  if (popfailed) {
    if (guess) {
      alert(choice + " is correct!");
    } else {
      alert(choice + " is incorrect. Try again");
    }
  } else {
    writeContent(answin, choice, guess);
  }
}
```

2. Close the file, saving your changes.

3. Reopen **quiz.htm** in your Web browser.

4. Click the various answers in the Web form and verify that a formatted pop-up window appears. Click the **OK** button to close each pop-up window before answering a different question from the form.

5. Close any open browser or editor windows.

Working with Modal and Modeless Windows

Dialog boxes and windows can either be modal or modeless. A **modal window** is a window that prevents users from doing work in any other window or dialog box until the window is closed. A **modeless window**, on the other hand, allows users to work in other dialog boxes and windows even as the window stays open. An alert box in a browser window is an example of a modal window, because you cannot do any other work in the browser window until you close the alert box. Pop-up windows, by contrast, are generally modeless. You can force a pop-up window to be modal, however, by adding the following event handler to the window's body element:

```
onblur = "self.focus()"
```

Starting with version 4.0, Internet Explorer introduced new methods to allow JavaScript to create modal and modeless windows. Internet Explorer 4 introduced the showModalDialog() method to create modal windows, and Internet Explorer 5 added the showModelessDialog() method for modeless windows. The syntax of the showModalDialog() method is

windowObject.showModalDialog("*url*", "*arguments*", "*features*")

where *url* is the URL of the file to display in the modal window, *arguments* is an optional parameter containing a value, variable, object, or array of values to pass to the window, and *features* is a comma-separated list of features that control the appearance of the window. The syntax to create a modeless dialog box is similar:

windowObject.showModelessDialog("*url*", "*arguments*", "*features*");

Both methods allow a dialog box to return values back to the browser window that called it. For example, you can create a modal or modeless dialog box containing a Web form, and then return values from that form to the original browser window. While both the showModalDialog() and showModelessDialog() methods are useful ways of creating specialized pop-ups and dialog boxes, they are not generally supported by browsers other than Internet Explorer.

Working with the Features List

The features list of the showModalDialog() and showModelessDialog() methods is similar to that used with the window.open() method. Figure 13-26 describes some of the features and their values.

Figure 13-26

Features of Internet Explorer modal and modeless dialog boxes

Feature	Value	Description
dialogHeight	Numeric	Sets the height of the dialog window; the default unit of measurement is "em" in Internet Explorer 4.0, and pixels in Internet Explorer 5.0
dialogLeft	Numeric	Specifies the screen coordinates of the left edge of the dialog box, in pixels
dialogTop	Numeric	Specifies the screen coordinates of the top edge of the dialog box, in pixels
dialogWidth	Numeric	Sets the width of the dialog window; the default unit of measurement is "em" in Internet Explorer 4.0, and pixels in Internet Explorer 5.0
center	yes, no	Specifies whether to center the dialog box on the desktop
dialogHide	yes, no	Specifies whether to hide the dialog box when printing or using print preview
edge	sunken, raised	Specifies the edge style of the window; the default is raised
help	yes, no	Specifies whether the window displays the context-sensitive Help icon in the title bar
resizable	yes, no	Specifies whether the window is resizable
scroll	yes, no	Specifies whether the window displays scroll bars
status	yes, no	Specifies whether the window displays a status bar
unadorned	yes, no	Specifies whether the window displays the browser chrome

For example, you could create a modal window with the following features list:

```
window.showModalDialog("name.htm","dialogHeight:150, dialogWidth:
300,edge:sunken,resizable:yes,scroll:yes,status:no,unadorned:no");
```

In this case, the name.htm file would be displayed in the modal window. The window would be 150 pixels high and 300 pixels wide. It would have sunken edges and scroll bars, but would not have a status bar or any other part of the browser chrome. The user would be able to resize the window, however. No arguments parameter is used in creating this window.

Exchanging Information between the Windows

Neither the showModalDialog() nor the showModelessDialog() methods allow direct interaction between the calling browser window and the pop-up window. Thus, you cannot use the document.write() method to write content directly to a new window created with either of these methods. If you need to send information, you must include that data in the *arguments* parameter for the method you're using. The value stored in this parameter can then be accessed within the pop-up window using the dialogArguments property of the window object. For example, if the *arguments* parameter contains an array of values, you can retrieve the first value of the array and store it in a variable using the command

```
data = window.dialogArguments[0];
```

You can then use the data variable in a program running within the pop-up. Since you also can't write information from a pop-up back to the original window, you store any information that you want returned using the following window property:

```
window.returnValue;
```

As with the *arguments* parameter, the returnValue property can store any type of information including a number, text string, array, or object. To access the returned value, simply use the showDialogModal() or showDialogModeless() methods in a statement that assigns a value. The syntax is

```
variable = windowObject.showModalDialog("url", "arguments", "features")
variable = windowObject.showModelessDialog("url", "arguments",
"features");
```

Because these methods are not well supported by browsers other than Internet Explorer, you decide against using them in the iMusicHistory Web site.

You've now completed your work on creating a variety of new windows, closing windows, and writing to a window via script-generated HTML. In the next session, you'll learn how to enhance the Glossary section of Teresa's iMusicHistory Web site with interactive frames.

Session 13.2 Quick Check

Review

1. What HTML tag would you use to create a link that opens the file home.htm as a new window with the target name "HomePage"?
2. What JavaScript command would you run to open the file home.htm as a pop-up window that is 300 pixels wide and 150 pixels high? You do not have to specify a value for the window's target name, but can instead use an empty text string.
3. What JavaScript command would you enter to include scroll bars and a status bar in the pop-up window described in the previous question?
4. What JavaScript command would you enter to write the HTML tag <body bgcolor="yellow"> to a window object named "Home"?
5. What JavaScript command would you use to create an alert box containing the text, "Script Finished"?
6. What JavaScript command would you use to create a confirm dialog box containing the text, "Proceed"?
7. What is a modal window? What is a modeless window?

Session 13.3

Working with Frames

Frames are considered one of the most powerful features of HTML. They enable the division of the browser window into multiple panes, with each frame displaying a separate document. Recall that frames are organized into framesets, using the following HTML tag structure:

```
<frameset id="frameset">
    <frame id="fname1" name="fname1" src="url1" />
    <frame id="fname2" name="fname2" src="url2" />
```

```
...
    <frame id="fnameN" name="fnameN" src="urlN" />
</frameset>
```

where each frame displays a separate URL. A single window can contain multiple framesets, and framesets can be nested inside each other. Each frame element in this example contains both an id value and a name value. The name attribute is used when creating links whose targets are designed to appear in specific frames. Thus, the syntax for linking content to a specific frame is

```
<a href="url" target="fname"> content </a>
```

where *fname* is the name of a specific frame in the browser window. However, if you want to reference a specific frame in your JavaScript code, you need to use the id attribute rather than the name attribute. The current practice, therefore, is to use both the name and id attributes, setting them to the same value as in the following frame element:

```
<frame id="top" name="top" src="home.htm" />
```

Teresa has decided to use frames in iMusicHistory's Glossary page. One of the files displayed in the frameset is nav.htm. The nav.htm file contains the iMusicHistory logo and some navigational text that you'll use in editing Teresa's page. Open this file now, and then use your Web browser to open the Glossary page.

To view the iMusicHistory glossary:

1. Use your text editor to open the **navtxt.htm** file from the tutorial.13/tutorial folder. Enter *your name* and *the date* in the comment section and save the file as **nav.htm**.

   The iMusicHistory Glossary frameset is stored in the terms.htm file. Open the glossary now.

2. Use your Web browser to open the **terms.htm** file from the tutorial.13/tutorial folder. Figure 13-27 shows the contents of the Glossary frameset.

Figure 13-27 ▶ **Customized windows**

The Glossary frameset is composed of three frames. The header frame displays the contents of the nav.htm file, providing an alphabetic list of links to the glossary terms; the main frame displays the contents of the main.htm file, listing the glossary of musical terms; and the footer frame, drawn from the footer.htm file, displays a navigation bar with links to the other pages of the iMusicHistory Web site.

The following is the HTML code for the Glossary frameset:

```
<frameset rows="160,*,64" id="Glossary" frameborder="0" border="0">
   <frame name="header" id="header" src="nav.htm" scrolling="no" />
   <frame name="main" id="main" src="main.htm" />
   <frame name="footer" id="footer" src="footer.htm" scrolling="no" />
</frameset>
```

One problem with frames is that they can take up valuable screen space. Teresa would like to give users the option of allocating more space to the list of the music terms shown in the main frame. As shown in Figure 13-28, Teresa envisions users clicking links in the header frame that alternately hide or display the footer frame, providing more screen space to the definition list.

Collapsing and expanding the footer frame | **Figure 13-28**

To create this effect, you first have to learn how JavaScript handles frames.

Working with the Frame and Frameset Objects

In the document object model, each frame in a frameset is part of the frames collection—an array of all of the frames within the browser window. The frames collection uses the following reference syntax:

```
windowObject.frames[idref]
```

where *windowObject* is the browser window containing the frames and *idref* is either the id or the index number of a frame in the collection. For example, to reference the header frame in the current browser window, you would use either of the following object references:

```
window.frames[0]
window.frames["header"]
```

There is no frameset object in JavaScript. If you need to reference the frameset element, you must provide an id for the frameset and then use the getElementById() method the reference the frameset element. For example, to reference the Glossary frameset from within the terms.htm file, you would use the object reference

```
document.getElementById("Glossary")
```

Reference Window | **Referencing Frames and Framesets**

- To reference a particular frame in a frameset, use
     `windowObject.frames[idref]`
  where `windowObject` is the browser window containing the frameset and `idref` is the id or index number of a frame in the frames collection.
- To reference a frameset element, use the reference
     `document.getElementById(id)`
  where `id` is the value of the id attribute in the <frameset> tag.

Navigating between Frames

JavaScript treats the frames in a frameset as elements in a hierarchical tree. Figure 13-29 shows a schematic diagram of the Glossary frameset. The top of the hierarchy is the browser window containing the terms.htm file and the Glossary frameset. At the second level of the tree are the nav.htm, main.htm, and footer.htm files, containing the header, main, and footer frames.

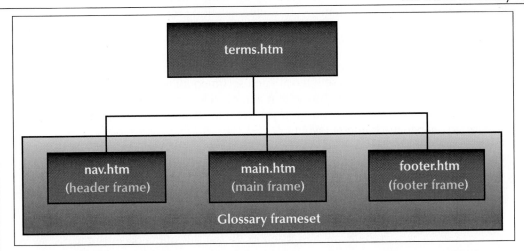

If you want to access the contents of one frame from another, you have to navigate through this hierarchy of objects. JavaScript provides two keywords to do this: parent and top. The **parent keyword** refers to any object that is placed immediately above another object in the hierarchy. The browser window containing the terms.htm file is the parent object of the three frames in the Glossary frameset. To reference one of the other frames, you first go up to the parent and then down the hierarchy. Thus, to reference the main frame from within the header frame you would use either of the following object references:

```
parent.frames[1]
parent.frames["main"]
```

If you have several levels of nested objects, you can stack parent references to go up through the different levels of the tree. The reference

```
parent.parent.parent.object
```

points to a child element of the parent object three levels up in the hierarchy.

If you want to go directly to the top of the hierarchy, you can use the **top keyword**. In the case of frames, the top keyword refers to the browser window that contains the frameset document and the frames within that frameset. When the frames are direct children of the browser window (as is the case with the Glossary frameset), the parent and top keywords are synonymous.

Note that the Glossary frameset itself is not a parent of the frames it contains. The Glossary frameset is an object within the document displayed in that window. If you need to reference the Glossary frameset directly, you have to go down the document hierarchy using the document object and the getElementById() method. The complete reference to the Glossary frameset from one of the child frames is therefore

```
parent.document.getElementById("Glossary")
```

Treating Frames as Windows

In most cases JavaScript treats a frame as a separate browser window, meaning that most of the properties and methods you've been applying to window objects can also be applied to frame objects. For example, if you want to write content into a frame, you would use the commands

```
frameObject.document.write(content)
frameObject.document.close()
```

where `frameObject` is the object reference to the frame. To change the source of the document displayed within a frame, you use the location property as follows:

`frameObject.location.href = "url"`

where `url` is the URL of the document to appear in the frame. The frame object also supports such window methods as setInterval() and setTimeout() for time-delayed commands, and alert() for displaying an alert box within a frame. However, you cannot close a frame the same way that you close a window. If you want to remove a frame from a frameset, you have to change the frameset layout.

Reference Window | Changing the Content of a Frame Document

- To change a frame's source document, use the command:
  `frameObject.location.href="url";`
  where `frameObject` is the frame object and `url` is the URL of the document to display in the frame.
- To write content into a frame, use the commands:
  `frameObject.document.write(content);`
  `frameObject.document.close();`
  where `content` is a text string of HTML code to be written into the frame.
- To reference the document displayed within a frame, use the object reference
  `frameObject.document.getElementById(id)`
  where `id` is the id of the object in the document.

Setting the Frameset Layout

Recall that a frameset is laid out in either rows or columns using the rows and cols attribute of the <frameset> tag. To do the same thing in JavaScript, you use the rows and cols properties of the frameset object. The syntax is

```
frameset.rows = "text"
frameset.cols = "text"
```

where `frameset` is an object reference to a frameset element and `text` is a text string specifying the frame layout. Currently, the value of the row attribute for the Glossary frameset is the text string "160,*,64". To change this to "180,*,64", for example, you would use the command

```
document.getElementById("Glossary").rows = "180,*,64";
```

To remove or hide a frame from a frameset, you set its height (or width) value to 0 pixels. Thus, to remove the footer frame from the Glossary frameset, you could use the command

```
document.getElementById("Glossary").rows = "160,*,0";
```

The footer frame would still be present in the frameset, but it would not be visible to users.

Collapsing and Expanding a Frame

You now have the information you need to create functions to collapse and expand the glossary's footer frame. You'll add two functions to the nav.htm file, named collapse() and expand(). The collapse() function reduces the height of the footer frame. The expand() function resets the footer frame's height to its original 64 pixels. Since you'll be running these functions from within the nav.htm file, you need to go up the object hierarchy to access the properties of the Glossary frameset. The code for the collapse() and expand() functions is

```
function collapse() {
    parent.document.getElementById("Glossary").rows = "160,*,1";
}
function expand() {
    parent.document.getElementById("Glossary").rows = "160,*,64";
}
```

Note that in the collapse() function, we set the height of the footer frame to 1 pixel rather than 0 pixels. For some browsers, like Netscape, setting the height to 0 pixels removes the frame entirely from the frameset. With the footer frame removed, you would not be able to re-display it later. To resolve this problem, you can set the height to 1 pixel, which preserves the footer frame in the layout, but essentially hides it from the user. You'll call the collapse() and expand() functions from links within the nav.htm file. Add these functions to the nav.htm file now.

To create and run the collapse() and expand() functions:

1. Return to **nav.htm** in your text editor.

2. Add the following embedded script to the head section of the document (see Figure 13-30):

```
<script type="text/javascript">
function collapse() {
    parent.document.getElementById("Glossary").rows = "160,*,1";
}
function expand() {
    parent.document.getElementById("Glossary").rows = "160,*,64";
}
</script>
```

The collapse() and expand() functions   **Figure 13-30**

```
<title>Glossary of Terms, iMusicHistory</title>
<link href="main.css" rel="stylesheet" type="text/css" title="General" />

<script type="text/javascript">
function collapse() {
    parent.document.getElementById("Glossary").rows = "160,*,1";
}
function expand() {
    parent.document.getElementById("Glossary").rows = "160,*,64";
}

</script>
</head>
```

3. Scroll down the document to the <a> tag for the text, "Hide Navigation Bar" and set the value of the href attribute to:

```
href="javascript:collapse()"
```

4. Set the value for the href attribute for the "Display Navigation Bar" link to:

`href="javascript:expand()"`

Figure 13-31 shows the revised HTML code for the two links.

Figure 13-31 ▶ **Calling the collapse() and expand() functions**

```
<!--- Place Display/Hide Navigation Bars Here -->
<tr>
<td width="100" align="left">
<p class="gloss">
<a href="javascript:collapse()">Hide Navigation Bar</a></p>
</td>

<td bgcolor="white" class="body" valign="top" align="center">
<a class="gloss" name="glossary">Glossary of Music Terms</a></td>

<td width="100" align="right">
<p align="right" class="gloss">
<a href="javascript:expand()">Display Navigation Bar</a></p>
</td>
</tr>
<!--- End of Navigation Bars --->
```

5. Save your changes to the file and reopen **terms.htm** in your Web browser.

6. Click the **Hide Navigation Bar** and **Display Navigation Bar** links and verify that they hide and redisplay the footer frame.

Next, Teresa would like you to control the interaction between the pages in her Web site and other sites on the Web. She's particularly concerned about the behavior of frames.

Controlling Frame Behavior

Many users don't like the effect that frames can have on Web sites that they view. For example, some Web site designers either aren't aware of or don't add code to prevent external Web sites from being caught inside their frames. This can confuse viewers by making it appear that an external Web site is actually part of the frameset. Additionally, a page designed to be viewed only within a frame might be mistakenly opened outside of its frameset. Without the context that the frameset provides, such a page can be meaningless or irritating to viewers.

The iMusicHistory Web site has experienced both problems in the past. Teresa has noticed that sometimes her Web site gets stuck inside another Web site's frameset, and search engines often bring visitors to the iMusicHistory site via one of the frames in the Glossary frameset. She would like you to control the behavior of her Web site's frames to prevent these two problems from happening.

Blocking an Unwanted Frame

When one of Teresa's Web pages gets stuck within another Web site's frame, her page in essence becomes a child of that browser window frameset. A demo page has been prepared for you to display this effect in action. Open the demo now.

To view the frame-blocking demo:

1. Open the **demo_frameblocker.htm** file in your Web browser.

2. Click the **default.htm** link in the left frame.

   As shown in Figure 13-32, the default.htm file appears in the right frame of the browser window.

   Trouble? This demo might not work with the Safari browser.

Frame blocking demo page ◄ **Figure 13-32**

When this happens to one of Teresa's pages, she would like the page to move out of the frame and occupy the browser window. To do this, you need to run a command testing whether the page is at the top of the window hierarchy when the browser loads the page. The condition to do this test is

```
if (top.location.href != self.location.href) {
   top.location.href = self.location.href;
}
```

In this code, JavaScript compares the URL of the document in the topmost window to the URL of the document in the current window or frame. If they're different, JavaScript changes the URL of the topmost window's document to the current window's document. As a result, the page cannot be forced into another site's frameset. It will always jump to the top of the hierarchy, occupying the browser window and replacing any frameset file. If the page is already at the top of the hierarchy, the code has no effect. Try this now by adding frame blocking to the default.htm file and then retesting the file in the demo page.

To add frame blocking to the iMusicHistory home page:

1. Reopen **default.htm** in your text editor.

2. Add the following embedded script to the document's head, as shown in Figure 13-33:

```
<script type="text/javascript">
    if (top.location.href != self.location.href) {
        top.location.href = self.location.href;
    }
</script>
```

Figure 13-33 ▶ **Blocking a page from appearing in a frame**

```
<title>Teresa Jenner's iMusicHistory course</title>
<link href="main.css" rel="stylesheet" type="text/css" />
<script type="text/javascript">
    if (top.location.href != self.location.href) {
        top.location.href = self.location.href;
    }
</script>
</head>
```

3. Close the file, saving your changes.

4. Reopen **demo_frameblocker.htm** in your Web browser.

5. Click the **default.htm** link in the left frame and verify that the document now jumps out of the frame to occupy the entire browser window.

Now Teresa can be confident that her home page won't get stuck within the frame of another Web site.

Forcing a Page into a Frameset

Teresa's second task involves the opposite problem: instead of forcing a page out of a frameset, she wants to ensure that the three files that compose the Glossary frameset (nav.htm, main.htm, and footer.htm) are always displayed within the frameset, and never as separate Web pages. This prevents visitors from inadvertently accessing one of those pages outside the context of the iMusicHistory Glossary.

Although the problem is different, the solution is similar. It involves verifying that whenever a browser opens the nav.htm, main.htm, or footer.htm files, the topmost window is always the browser window containing the terms.htm file. The code to make this happen is

```
if (top.location.href == self.location) {
    top.location.href="terms.htm";
}
```

Here, JavaScript checks whether the URL of the document in the topmost window is the same as that of the active window or frame. If this condition is true for a file like nav. htm, it means that the file is occupying the top browser window rather than a frame within that window. In that case, the script changes the URL of the top window so that it displays the frameset located in the terms.htm file. Apply this code to the nav.htm file now.

To force nav.htm to always appear in the Glossary frameset:

1. Return to **nav.htm** in your text editor.

2. Add the following commands to the embedded script element, as shown in Figure 13-34:

```
if (top.location.href == self.location.href) {
    top.location.href="terms.htm";
}
```

Forcing a file into a frameset | **Figure 13-34**

```
<script type="text/javascript">

if (top.location.href == self.location.href) {
    top.location.href = "terms.htm";
}

function collapse() {
    parent.document.getElementById("Glossary").rows = "160,*,1";
}
function expand() {
    parent.document.getElementById("Glossary").rows = "160,*,64";
}

</script>
```

3. Close the file, saving your changes.

4. Open **nav.htm** in your Web browser and verify that the browser opens the entire Glossary frameset, not just the navigation bar.

5. Close your Web browser.

Blocking and Forcing Frames

Reference Window

- To prevent a document from appearing within a frame, run the following commands when a browser loads the page:
  ```
  if (top.location.href != self.location.href) {
      top.location.href = self.location.href;
  }
  ```
- To force a document to always appear within a frameset, run the following commands when the page is loaded:
  ```
  if (top.location.href == self.location.href) {
      top.location.href = "url";
  }
  ```
  where *url* is the URL of the frameset document.

Working with Inline Frames

Another way to use frames in a Web site is by incorporating an inline frame, which appears as a separate window within the document. Recall that inline frames are created in HTML using the tag

```
<iframe src="url" id="text" name="text" width="value" height="value">
    alternate content
</iframe>
```

where *url* is the URL of the document that appears in the inline frame, the id and name attributes identify the frame, the width and height attributes specify the size of the frame in pixels, and *alternate content* is content that appears in the document window for browsers that don't support inline frames. As with other HTML elements, you should include both the name and id attributes to ensure maximum compatibility across browsers, setting those attributes to the same value.

JavaScript allows you to treat an inline frame either as an object in the current document or as a frame in the frames collection. For example, if you create the following inline frame:

```
<iframe src="logo.htm" id="logo" name="logo" width="300" height="200">
</iframe>
```

you can reference it from the current document window using the object reference

```
document.getElementById("logo")
```

or as a frame using the frames reference

```
window.frames["logo"]
```

To change the document displayed by the inline frame, you once again have two choices. You can either treat the frame as an object in the document and change the value of its src property, or you can treat it as a frame and change the value of the href property of its location object. Thus, to change the URL of the logo frame to point to the logo2.htm file, you could use either of the following commands:

```
document.getElementById("logo").src = "logo2.htm";
```

or

```
window.frames["logo"].location.href = "logo2.htm";
```

If you want to write content directly into an inline frame, you have to treat it as part of the frames collection. To write content into the logo inline frame, you would use the document.write() method as follows:

```
window.frames["logo"].document.write(content)
```

Treating inline frames as frame objects is more widely supported than treating them as document objects. Opera 6.0, for example, treats inline frames only as part of the frames collection and not as objects in the document (though this is not true of more recent releases of Opera). However, if you need to manipulate the appearance or placement of an inline frame within a document, you may find it easier to work with it as an object in the document and change its style values. For example, you could float the logo inline frame on the page's left margin by simply changing the value of the float property:

```
document.getElementById("logo").style.float = "left";
```

In the end, how you treat inline frames depends on the task you're trying to accomplish with your script. Fortunately, JavaScript and most browsers support either approach.

Since Teresa has not chosen to include inline frames in her Web site, your work on her project is finished. Teresa is excited about the progress you've made with her Web site. Later, she wants you to incorporate the work you've done on these pages into the rest of the iMusicHistory Web site.

Tips for Working with Windows and Frames

- If you use JavaScript to write a transient status bar message, be sure to properly erase the message when the action or event is finished, so that other messages your browser may wish to display are not prevented.
- Due to their unpopularity in the eyes of some users, keep the use of pop-up windows to a minimum, and forewarn your users if possible about the presence of a pop-up window.
- Include code to verify that a pop-up window has not been blocked and, if possible, provide alternative methods of displaying the same content if the pop-up is blocked.
- Include code that makes it easy for users to close your pop-up windows, in order to prevent those windows from cluttering a user's desktop.
- Allow your users to resize your pop-up windows to ensure that no content is hidden.
- If the existence of pop-up blockers poses a problem, consider using alert, prompt, and confirm dialog boxes in place of pop-up windows.
- If frames are a concern, add conditional statements to your documents to prevent them from appearing within the framesets of other Web sites.
- Add JavaScript code to your frame documents so that they always appear within the context of their framesets.

Session 13.3 Quick Check

Review

1. What reference name would you use to access a frame named "Logo" located in the topmost window of the browser window hierarchy?
2. What command would you use to change the source of the document in the Logo frame to "logo.html"?
3. What command would you use to write the text string "<html></html>" to the document in the Logo frame?
4. Assume that the Logo frame is part of a frameset with the id "Home". What command would you use to change the column widths of the frames in the Home frameset to "150,150,*"?
5. The Home frameset is saved in an HTML file named "home.htm." What JavaScript command(s) would you add to the logo.html file so that it always appears within the home.htm page?
6. A Web page contains an inline frame with the id "report". Provide two ways of changing the source of the inline frame to the document report.htm. Assume that you are running the command from within the document containing the inline frame.

Tutorial Summary

In this tutorial you learned how to use JavaScript to create and format browser windows and frames. In the first session you learned how to work with the properties of the window's status bar, location object, and history objects. You also saw how to employ automatic page navigation using both the meta element and a JavaScript program. The second session focused on techniques to create and populate new browser windows. You first learned how to use the window.open() method to create a new browser window based on a pre-existing source document. You saw how to specify the properties of that window and how to work with methods of the window object to close a pop-up window and to set the focus on it. The second session also showed how to create alert, prompt, and confirm dialog boxes. The session then showed how to write content into a pop-up window using the document.write() method and discussed how to reference variables and functions in other browser windows. The second session concluded with a discussion of specialized Internet Explorer methods to create modal and modeless dialog boxes. The third session concerned working with frames and framesets. You learned how to navigate through the object hierarchy of a frameset and how to reference the contents of one frame from another. You also saw how to modify the layout of a frameset by changing the properties of the frameset object. The third session also provided a demonstration of how to use JavaScript to block frames and to force documents to remain within framesets. The tutorial concluded with a brief discussion of inline frames, showing how they can be treated either as frames in the frames collection or as objects with a document.

Key Terms

alert dialog box	opener keyword	self keyword
chrome	parent keyword	status bar
confirm dialog box	permanent status bar	top keyword
history object	message	transient status bar
location object	pop-up blocker	message
modal window	pop-up window	window object
modeless window	prompt dialog box	

Review Assignments

Data files needed for this Review Assignment: atempotxt.htm, bottomtxt.htm, concerto. htm, defaulttxt.htm, dotclear.gif, header.gif, index.htm, lesson3.htm, lesson3a.htm, lesson3b.htm, lvb.gif, main.css, maintxt.htm, nav.htm, navy8th.gif, quiz2.css, quiz2.gif, quiz2txt.htm, quiz.htm, sonata.htm, symphony.htm, terms.htm, terms_noframes.htm, treble2.gif, treble.gif

Teresa has reviewed your work on the iMusicHistory Web site. She's happy with your progress and wants you to apply the changes you've made so far to the rest of the Web site. Here are the tasks for your next assignment:

- Add transient status bar messages to the other three links at the bottom of the iMusicHistory home page.
- Add a pop-up window to the iMusicHistory home page that displays the definition of the term "a tempo", which appears on the page.
- Create a customized pop-up window and alert box for the questions on the Quiz 2 Web page.

- Prevent the Quiz 2 Web page from appearing within a frame.
- Write code to ensure that the contents of the bottom.htm and main.htm files always appear within the context of the Glossary frameset.

Make sure that any pop-up windows you create will behave nicely if they encounter pop-up blockers. Figure 13-35 shows a preview of the pop-up window you'll create for the new quiz page.

Figure 13-35

To revise the iMusicHistory Web site:

1. Go to the tutorial.13/review folder and use your text editor to open the **defaulttxt. htm**, **atempotxt.htm**, **quiz2txt.htm**, **maintxt.htm**, and **bottomtxt.htm** files. Within each file enter *your name* and *the date* in the comment section and save the files as **default.htm**, **atempo.htm**, **quiz2.htm**, **main.htm**, and **bottom.htm**, respectively.

2. Return to the **default.htm** file in your text editor, and add the following transient status bar messages to the document:

   a. Go to the navigation cell text near the bottom of the document and locate the link to the lesson3.htm file. Add an onmouseover event handler to this link that displays the message: "Go to the Lessons page". Add an onmouseout event handler that removes the status bar message when the mouse leaves the link.

   b. Use an onmouseover event handler to change the transient status bar message for the quiz.htm link to "Go to the First Online Quiz". Be sure to remove this message using the onmouseout event handler.

   c. Repeat the process to change the transient status bar message for the terms.htm link to "View the Music Glossary".

3. In the embedded script at the top of the page, insert a function named showDef(). The purpose of this function is to display a pop-up window. The function has a single parameter named source that contains the URL of the document to be displayed. Add the following commands to the showDef() function:

   a. Use the window.open() method to open a window displaying a document with a URL equal to the value of the source parameter. Leave the target name as a blank text string. The window should be 200 pixels wide by 100 pixels high, displayed at the screen coordinates (100, 100). Store the window object in a variable named defWin.

   b. Create a variable named notPop that tests whether the defWin window object was blocked. The notPop variable should have a value of "true" if the window was blocked and "false" if otherwise.

   c. Return the value of the notPop variable.

4. Scroll down to the center of the document and locate the link for the "a tempo" term. Add an onclick event handler that returns the value of the showDef() function. (*Hint*: Use the music definitions pop-ups from the tutorial as an example.)

5. Close the **default.htm** file, saving your changes.

6. Go to the **atempo.htm** file in your text editor. Add an onblur event handler to the body element that closes the window when it loses the focus. Close the file, saving your changes.

7. Return to the **quiz2.htm** file in your text editor. Add an embedded script in the head section of the document, and within the script element insert a function named answer(). The purpose of the answer() function is to write a pop-up window telling the student whether he or she answered the quiz question correctly. The answer() function should have one parameter named "correct" used to store a Boolean value indicating whether the student's answer is correct or not. Appropriate parameter values for the answer() function have already been added to onclick event handlers for the radio buttons in the form. Complete the answer() function as follows:

   a. Use the window.open() method to create a pop-up window named popWin that is 200 pixels wide by 200 pixels high and placed at the screen coordinates (250, 250). Specify a blank text string for the window's URL and target name.

   b. Create a variable named notPop that has a value of true if the popWin window failed to open and a value of false if it opened without error.

   c. If the value of notPop is true (indicating that the pop-up window failed to open) create a conditional statement that tests whether the value of the correct parameter is true or false. If correct is true, display an alert box containing the text, "Correct!" If correct is false display an alert box with the text, "Sorry, that is incorrect".

d. If the value of notPop is false (indicating that a pop-up window was generated) write the following HTML code into the popWin window:

```
<html>
<head>
<title>Answer</title>
<link rel='stylesheet' href='quiz2.css' type='text/css' />
</head>
<body>
message
<p><input type='button' value='OK' onclick='self.close()' /></p>
</body>
</html>
```

where *message* is either the text string "<p>Correct!</p>" if the correct parameter is true or the text string "<p>Sorry, that is incorrect</p>" if the correct parameter is false.

8. Add JavaScript commands to the **quiz2.htm** file so that the page cannot be placed in a frame. Close the file, saving your changes.

9. Go to the **bottom.htm** and **main.htm** files in your text editor. Add scripts to both files that force them to be displayed only within the Glossary frameset of the terms. htm file. Close both files, saving your changes.

10. Open **default.htm** in your browser. Verify that: a) Transient status bar messages appear for the Lessons, Quizzes, and Glossary links at the bottom of the page and b) Clicking the "a tempo" definition link displays a pop-up window showing the term's definition and that this pop-up window automatically closes when it loses the focus.

11. Open **quiz2.htm** in your browser. Verify that clicking the radio buttons in the quiz form displays an appropriate pop-up window indicating whether the answer is correct or not. Also verify that clicking the OK button within the pop-up window closes it.

12. Open **bottom.htm** and **main.htm** in your Web browser and verify that both files are opened within the context of the Glossary frameset.

13. Submit your completed Web site to your instructor.

Apply

Use the skills you learned to create a subscription pop-up window

Case Problem 1

Data files needed for this Case Problem: cover.css, cover.jpg, covertxt.htm, cwj.css, cwj.jpg, cwjtxt.htm, formtxt.htm, logo.gif, parch.jpg

The Civil War Journal   Terrence Whyte is the editor of the online version of *The Civil War Journal*, a magazine for people interested in the Civil War. Terrence would like to have a small pop-up window appear when users open the home page of the online edition. The window will advertise the print version of the magazine and provide a link to a subscription form. Also, Terrence would like the status bar to display informative text for links on the page. Figure 13-36 shows a preview of the windows you'll create.

Figure 13-36

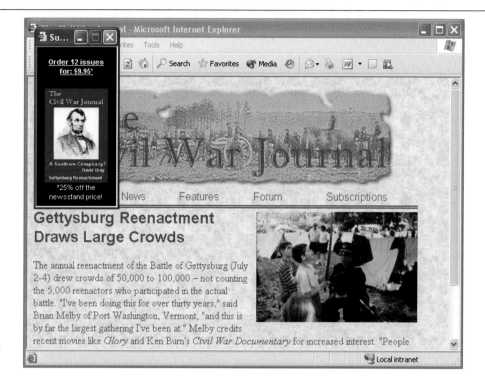

To create the pop-up windows:

1. Use your text editor to open the **cwjtxt.htm**, **covertxt.htm**, and **formtxt.htm** files from the tutorial.13/case1 folder. Enter *your name* and *the date* in each file and save them as **cwj.htm**, **cover.htm**, and **form.htm** respectively.

2. Go to the **cwj.htm** file in your text editor. Locate the five links at the top of the page and create the following transient status bar messages for them:

   - Home Page: "Go to the Home Page"
   - News: "View Current Events"
   - Features: "Go to Feature Articles"
   - Form: "Go to the Civil War Form"
   - Subscription: "Subscribe Today!"

   Configure the messages to appear in response to the onmouseover event. Make sure the messages are removed in response to the onmouseout event.

3. In the head section of the document, insert an embedded script containing a function named subscribe(). The subscribe() function should open a new browser window containing the cover.htm document. Give the pop-up window a target name of "popWin". Set the width and height of the pop-up window to 125 pixels by 240 pixels. Open the window 10 pixels down and to the right of the upper-left corner of the screen. Since this pop-up window displays only an advertisement for the magazine and not critical content, Terrence has not requested that you check for the presence of pop-up blockers.

4. Add an event handler to the body element to run the subscribe() function when the page loads.

5. Close the file, saving your changes.

Explore

6. Return to the **cover.htm** file in your text editor. Within the head section insert an embedded script containing the showForm() function. The purpose of this function is to display the contents of the form.htm file in the main browser window. Have the function do the following:

   a. Display the form.htm file in the browser window that was used to open the cover.htm file. (*Hint*: Use the "opener" keyword to reference the main browser window, and the location.href property to specify the document to be displayed in that window.)

   b. Close the current window.

7. Locate the linked text in the body of the document and change the value of the href attribute so that it runs the showForm() function when clicked.

8. Close the file, saving your changes.

9. Return to the **form.htm** file in your text editor and create the same set of transient status bar messages that you created for the cwj.htm file. Close the file, saving your changes.

10. Open **cwj.htm** in your Web browser. Verify that the status bar messages change in response to hovering the mouse pointer over the five links at the top page and verify that a subscription pop-up window appears on your screen.

11. Click the link in the subscription pop-up window. Verify that the pop-up closes and that the subscription form now appears in the original browser window.

12. Submit the completed Web site to your instructor.

Challenge

Case Problem 2

Data files needed for this Case Problem: brain.css, brain.jpg, braintxt.htm, frame.css

Explore how to write content into an inline frame

Anatomy 101   Jacob Terrell teaches Anatomy 101 at Thomas More College. He's asked for your help in creating a Web page on the brain. The page will display an inline image showing different parts of the human brain. As students move their mouse pointers over a section, he would like an inline frame to display a description of that part of the brain. Figure 13-37 shows a preview of the page he wants you to create for him.

Figure 13-37

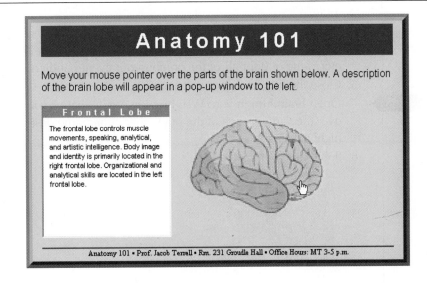

The text of the inline frame has already been entered for you and stored in two arrays. The Head array stores the names of four different brain lobes. The Summary array contains a brief description of each lobe. Your job is to insert the contents of these arrays into the inline frame.

To create Professor Terrell's Web page:

1. Use your text editor to open **braintxt.htm** from the tutorial.13/case2 folder. Enter *your name* and *the date* in the file and save it as **brain.htm**.

Explore

2. Within an embedded script element in the document's head section, create a function named writeFrame() that contains a single parameter named "i". The purpose of this function is to write the content that appears in the inline frame. The i parameter stores the index number of the entry from the Head and Summary arrays that should appear in the inline frame. The writeFrame() function should perform the following actions:

   a. Create a variable named frameWin that contains the object reference to the first frame in the current browser window.

   b. Write the following HTML code into frameWin:
   ```
   <html>
   <head>
   <title>Head</title>
   <link rel='stylesheet' href=frame.css' type='text/css' />
   </head>
   <body>
   <h2>Head</h2>
   <p>Summary</p>
   </body>
   </html>
   ```
   where *Head* is the text contained in the ith element in the Head array and *Summary* is the ith entry in the Summary array.

3. Add an onmouseover handler to the Frontal lobe <area> tag to run the writeFrame() function, with a parameter value of 1. Running this function sets the content of the inline frame to describe information about the brain's frontal lobe.

4. Add an onmouseout handler to the Frontal lobe <area> tag to run the writeFrame() function, with a parameter value of 0. Running this function removes the text content from the frame since both Head[0] and Summary[0] are empty elements in the array.

5. Repeat Steps 3 and 4 for the remaining <area> tags. Use a parameter value of 2 for the parietal lobe, 3 for the occipital lobe, and 4 for the temporal lobe. Use a parameter value of 0 for all of the onmouseout event handlers.

6. Close the file, saving your changes.

Explore

7. Open **brain.htm** in your Web browser. Verify that as you pass your mouse pointer over the various parts of the brain, the inline frame describes the part of the brain highlighted.

8. Submit the completed Web site to your instructor.

Challenge

xplore how to write
TML and CSS code
ito a frame

Case Problem 3

Data files needed for this Case Problem: code.css, css.htm, css.txt, demo.gif, demo.htm, html.htm, html.txt, title.css, titletxt.htm

Web Designers   Andrew Seaborn teaches a class in Web design. During the first few weeks of the course he teaches students the basics of HTML tags and CSS style sheets. Andrew thinks it would be useful for his students to have a demo page in which they can enter HTML and CSS code directly into one set of frames and then have that code rendered as a Web page in another frame. As one of his teaching assistants, you've been asked to create the demo page for him. Figure 13-38 shows a preview of the page you'll create.

Figure 13-38

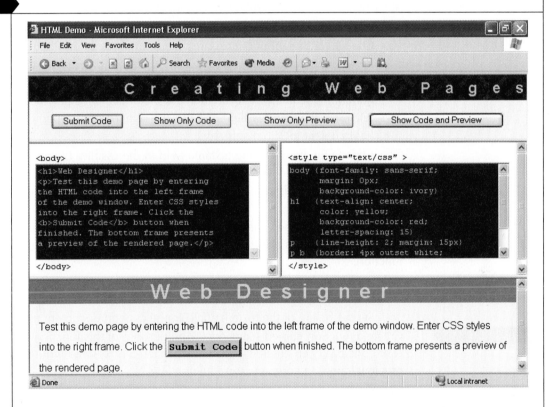

The demo is organized into four files. The demo.htm file displays a frameset named "demo" containing four frames named title, htmlcode, csscode, and preview. The title frame contains the contents of the title.htm file. You'll create the JavaScript programs in this file that you need to run the demo. The htmlcode frame contains the contents of the html.htm file. This file contains a textarea field with the id value inputhtml where you'll enter the HTML code that you want to display. The csscode frame contains the contents of the css.htm file. This file also contains a textarea field with the id value inputcss. You'll use this textarea field to enter the CSS styles that you want to apply to the elements in your HTML. The preview pane does not contain any document at all. Instead, you'll create the document content by writing the content of the two textarea boxes into the preview frame.

To create the demo page:

1. Use your text editor to open the **titletxt.htm** file from the tutorial.13/case3 folder. Enter *your name* and *the date* in the file and save it as **title.htm**.

Explore

2. Insert an embedded script element in the head section of the document. Within the script element create a function named showPreview(). The purpose of this function is to hide the htmlcode and csscode frames, providing more screen space to the preview frame. To hide those two frames, change the value of the rows attribute for the demo frameset to "100,1,*". (*Hint*: You will have to go up to the parent element of the current document to access the frameset object. Remember that the id of the frameset object is "demo".)

Explore

3. Insert a function named showCode(). The purpose of this function is to hide the preview frame and to increase the size of the textarea fields in the html.htm and css.htm documents. Add the following commands to the function:

   a. Set the value of the demo frameset's row attribute to "100,*,1".

   b. Change the height of the textarea field in the html.htm file to 300 pixels. (*Hint*: Remember that you will have to move up to the parent object and then down to the second frame in the frames collection to reference the contents of the html.htm document. You can then use the document.getElementById() method to reference the textarea field and use the style.height property to set the textarea field's height to 300 pixels.)

   c. Change the height of the textarea field in the css.htm file to 300 pixels. Use the same techniques you employed for the textarea field in the html.htm file to reference this object. The css.htm file is stored in the third frame of the frames collection.

4. Insert a function named showBoth(). The purpose of this function is to show both the code and preview frames in the demo frameset. Add the following commands to the function:

   a. Set the value of the demo frameset's row attribute to "100,210,*".

   b. Set the height of the textarea field in the html.htm document to 150 pixels.

   c. Set the height of the textarea field in the css.htm document to 150 pixels.

Explore

5. Create a function named sendCode(). The purpose of this function is to extract whatever code has been entered into the two textarea boxes and write that code to the preview frame. To complete this function:

   a. Create a variable named previewFrame that references the fourth frame in the demo frameset.

   b. Create a variable named htmlCode that is equal to the value of the textarea field in the html.htm document. (*Hint*: The value of the textarea field can be extracted using the value property in the expression *object*.value, where *object* is the object reference to the textarea field. To reference the textarea field you will once again have to navigate through the frames hierarchy and then down through the contents of the html.htm document.)

   c. Create a variable named cssCode that is equal to the value of the textarea field in the css.htm document.

   d. Write the following code to the document within the previewFrame object:

```
<html>
<head>
<title></title>
<style type='text/css'>
    styles
```

```
     </style>
   </head>
   <body>
      html code
   </body>
   </html>
```

where *styles* is the value of the cssCode variable and *html code* is the value of the htmlCode variable.

6. Add an onclick event handler to the Submit Code button to run the sendCode() function. Add similar onclick event handlers to the other three buttons in the Web form to run the appropriate function when each button is clicked.

7. Close the file, saving your changes.

8. Open the **demo.htm** file in your Web browser. Copy the html code from the **html.txt** file and paste it into the textarea box in the left frame. Copy the css code from the **css.txt** file and paste it into the textarea box in the right frame. Click the Submit Code button and verify that the preview frame displays the elements and styles from the two code frames.

9. Click the Show Only Preview button. Verify that it hides the two code frames and increases the size of the preview pane.

10. Click the Show Only Code button. Verify that it hides the preview frame and increases the height of the code frames and the textarea boxes they contain.

11. Click the Show Code and Preview button. Verify that it restores the frameset layout, displaying all four frames with the textarea boxes back to their original heights.

12. Submit your completed Web site to your instructor.

Create

Test your knowledge of pop-up windows in tourism Web site

Case Problem 4

Data files needed for this Case Problem: allen-img.jpg, allen-logo.gif, allentxt.htm, birdcage-img.jpg, birdcage-logo.gif, birdtxt.htm, boothill-img.jpg, boothill-logo.gif, boottxt.htm, corral-img.jpg, corral-logo.gif, corraltxt.htm, courthouse-img.jpg, courthouse-logo.gif, courthousetxt.htm, indextxt.htm, logo.gif, map.gif, schief-img.jpg, schief-logo.gif, schieftxt.htm, styles.css

Tombstone Chamber of Commerce   The Tombstone, Arizona Chamber of Commerce has a small office in the main tourist area of Tombstone. Tony Diaz is in charge of designing a Web site that advertises the features of interest in the town. The Web site's home page will have a map of Tombstone with hot spots linked to different tourist attractions. When a user clicks a hot spot, a page describing the attraction is displayed. Tony would like your help in making the following changes to his Web site:

- Change the transient status bar message for each hot spot to a text string that describes the tourist attraction.
- Have each hot spot open a pop-up window describing the attraction.
- If a pop-up window loses the focus, have it close automatically.
- If a user is running a pop-up blocker, have links to the area attractions appear in the main browser window and not as a pop-up.

To complete this assignment:

1. Open the **allentxt.htm**, **birdtxt.htm**, **boottxt.htm**, **corraltxt.htm**, **courthousetxt.htm**, **indextxt.htm**, and **schieftxt.htm** files using your text editor. Enter *your name* and *the date* in the comment section of each file. Save the files as **allen.htm**, **bird.htm**, **boot. htm**, **corral.htm**, **courthouse.htm**, **index.htm**, and **schief.htm** respectively.

2. Go to the **index.htm** file and create a transient status bar message for the six hot spots in the image map. The text of the status bar messages is up to you, but it should include some brief description of the tourist attraction.

3. Create a permanent status bar message for the Tombstone home page. The text of the message is up to you, but it should convey a welcome greeting to the casual tourist.

4. Create a function named tourWin() that generates a pop-up window. The features of the pop-up window are up to you. Include code that verifies that the pop-up window has been properly opened. If it hasn't, have the browser open the target document within the main browser window.

5. Apply the tourWin() function to the six links in the image map.

6. Go to the six target documents in your text editor. Add event handlers to each of them so that if they lose their focus as pop-up windows, the browser closes them automatically.

7. Open **index.htm** in your Web browser and test the hot spot links. Verify that: a) each of your links has a customized status bar message, b) the home page has a permanent status bar message conveying a greeting, c) each hot spot link opens in a customized pop-up window, and d) each pop-up window closes automatically when it loses the focus.

8. Submit your completed Web site to your instructor.

Review

Quick Check Answers

Session 13.1

1. A permanent status bar message appears by default in the status bar. A transient status bar message only appears in response to a particular action or event.

2. history.go(-2)

3. window.status="View News page"
   return true;

4. One way is with the following meta element:
   <meta http-equiv="Refresh" content="*sec*;URL=*url*" />
   where *sec* is the amount of time in seconds that will elapse before opening the new page, and *url* is the new page to be loaded.
   Another way is to use the window.location.href property along with the setTimeout method.

5. The document.referrer property records the URL of the page from which the current page was accessed. However, this property only works when the current page is accessed via a link, and some browsers disable it for security reasons.

Session 13.2

1. <a href="home.htm" target="HomePage"> *link text* </a>

2. window.open("home.htm","width=300,height=150");

3. window.open("home.htm","width=300,height=150,scrollbars=yes,status=yes");
   or
   window.open("home.htm","width=300,height=150,scrollbars=1,status=1");
4. Home.document.write("<body bgcolor='yellow'>");
5. alert("Script Finished");
6. confirm("Proceed?");
7. A modal window prevents users from doing anything outside the window until it is closed. A modeless window allows users to work in other windows while it's open.

Session 13.3

1. top.frames ["Logo"]
2. top.frames["Logo"].location.href="logo.html";
3. top.frames["Logo"].document.write("<html></html>");
4. top.document.getElementById("Home").cols="150,150,*";
5. if (top.location.href == self.location) {
   top.location.href = "home.htm";
   }
6. document.getElementById("report").src = "report.htm";
   or
   window.frames["report"].location.href = "report.htm";

Objectives

Working with Forms and Regular Expressions

Validating a Web Form with JavaScript

Case

GPS-ware

GPS-ware is a company that specializes in mapping and global positioning software and hardware. The company is in the planning stages of making its products available online. Carol Campbell is heading the development effort and has asked for your help in developing a Web form for domestic sales.

A GPS-ware employee has already created three Web forms for the Web site. The forms include fields in which users enter the details of their purchases, delivery Information, and credit card data. Carol would like the forms to automatically calculate the cost of a user's order and validate any data that the user has entered. All of this should be done before the form is submitted to the Web server for processing.

Student Data Files

Session 14.1

Working with Forms and Fields

You meet with Carol to discuss the forms she has created for online ordering. Figure 14-1 shows the three forms that you'll be working with. Customers enter order information in the first form, delivery information in the second form, and method of payment in the third form.

| Figure 14-1 | The GPS-ware forms |

You'll start working on Carol's Web site by looking at the order form. Open this form now.

To open the page containing the order form:

1. In your text editor, open the **form1txt.htm**, **form2txt.htm**, and **form3txt.htm** files located in the tutorial.14/tutorial folder. Enter *your name* and *the date* in the comment section of each and save the files as **form1.htm**, **form2.htm**, and **form3.htm** respectively.

2. Close the form2.htm and form3.htm files. You will not be working with them in this session.

3. Take some time to review the HTML code in the form1.htm file, and then open **form1.htm** in your Web browser. Figure 14-2 displays the contents of the form1 form, including the names assigned to the different form elements.

Trouble? You cannot enter data in either the date field or any of the fields that display the cost of the product, tax, or shipping. Carol has set these fields to read-only, and their values can only be set using JavaScript.

Customers use the order form to select a GPS-ware product to purchase, indicating the product name, quantity, and shipping method. Customers are given three choices for shipping: standard, which costs $4.95 and arrives in four to six business days; express, which costs $8.95 and arrives in two days; and overnight, which costs $12.95. There is also a 5% sales tax on all orders. Carol wants this form to automatically calculate the cost of the items purchased, add the cost of shipping, determine the sales tax, and then calculate the total order cost. All of these calculations should be done automatically by the browser. At the top of the form is a date field in which the current date should be displayed. Carol wants this information to be automatically entered by the Web browser as well.

Referencing a Web form

To program a Web form like this, you have to work with the properties and methods of the form object and the elements it contains. As shown in Figure 14-3, Web forms and their elements are part of the hierarchy of objects within a Web document.

| Figure 14-3 | The forms hierarchy |

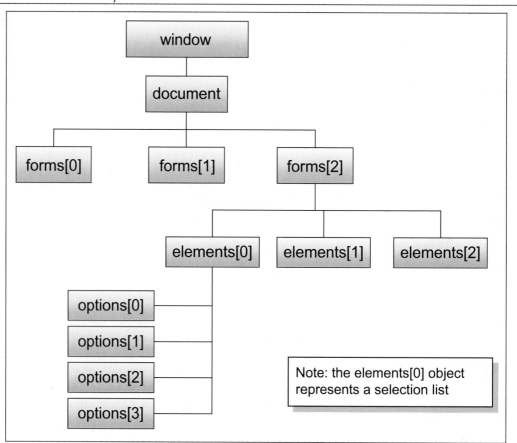

Since a Web page can contain multiple Web forms, JavaScript supports an object collection for forms. Thus, you can access a form within the current document using object reference

```
document.forms[idref]
```

where *idref* is the id or index number of the form. JavaScript also allows you to reference a form by its name attribute, using the object reference

```
document.fname
```

where *fname* is the value of the name attribute assigned to the form. In addition, you can always use the document.getElementById() method to reference a form based on the value of its id attribute. Carol has named her order form "form1", and it is the first (and only) form in the Web page. Based on this information, you can access the form using either of the following object references:

```
document.forms[0]
document.form1
```

Referencing a form element

The elements within a form, including all input fields, buttons, and labels, are organized into an elements collection. You can reference a form element either by its position in the collection or by its name or id attributes. For example, the first element in Carol's order form is the date input box. To reference this object you use either

`formObject.elements[0]`

or

`formObject.date`

where `formObject` is the reference to the order form using one of the two methods described above. If the element is a selection list, it contains its own object collection consisting of the options within the list. Likewise, option buttons belonging to the same group have a unique syntax. You'll examine how to work with both selection lists and option buttons later in this session.

Figure 14-4 lists the object references for the fields and buttons in Carol's order form. Note that the object references are drawn from the element names, which were displayed earlier in Figure 14-2.

Objects in the order form ◄ **Figure 14-4**

Object	Reference
The order form	document.form1
The date field	document.form1.date
The product selection list	document.form1.prod
The quantity selection list	document.form1.qty
The price of the product field	document.form1.price
The group of shipping options	document.form1.shipType
The shipping cost field	document.form1.ship
The subtotal field	document.form1.sub
The tax field	document.form1.tax
The total field	document.form1.tot
The cancel button	document.form1.cancelb
The next button	document.form1.nextb

Referencing Form Objects

- To access a Web form, use the object reference
    document.forms[*idref*]
  where *idref* is the id or index number of the form. You can also use
    document.*fname*
  where *fname* is the name of the form.
- To reference an element within a form, use the object reference
    formObject.elements[*idref*]
  where *formObject* is the object reference to the form and *idref* is the id or index number of the form element. You can also use:
    formObject.*ename*
  where *ename* is the name of the form element.

Working with Input Fields

The first task on Carol's list is to have the current date displayed in the Web form. To change the value of the date field you need to work with the properties and methods of input fields.

Setting the field value

To set the value contained in a field such as an input box, you use the value property. The general syntax is

```
formObject.element.value = fieldvalue;
```

where *formObject* is a reference to the Web form, *element* is the object reference to the form element, and *fieldvalue* is the value you want placed in the field. For example, to have the date field display the text string "6-23-2006" you would run the command

```
document.form1.date.value = "6-23-2006";
```

The value property is one of many properties and methods associated with input fields. Figure 14-5 shows a few of the others.

Properties and methods of the input field ◄ Figure 14-5

Property	Description
defaultvalue	The default value that is initially displayed in the field
form	References the form containing the field
maxlength	The maximum number of characters allowed in the field
name	The name of the field
size	The width of the input field in characters
type	The type of input field (button, check box, file, hidden, image, password, radio, reset, submit, text)
value	The current value of the field

Method	Description
blur()	Remove the focus from the field
focus()	Give focus to the field
select()	Select the field

Working with Fields

Reference Window

- To set the value of a form field, use the object property
  ```
  field.value = "value"
  ```
  where *field* is the reference to the form field and *value* is the value you want to assign to the field.
- To move the focus to a form field, use the method
  ```
  field.focus()
  ```

Navigating between fields

Carol also wants the product selection list to be selected automatically when the form opens, so it's ready for data entry. Like pop-up windows, form fields support the focus and blur events. The focus event occurs when a user's cursor moves to the field. The blur event occurs when the cursor moves away from the field. Thus, to place the cursor in a particular field on a form, you would use the following focus() method:

```
formObject.element.focus();
```

To remove the focus from this field, you would use the blur() method:

```
formObject.element.blur();
```

You now have enough information to write the first function to be used in the order form. Carol has created a function named todayTxt() that returns a text string with the current date in the format *mm-dd-yyyy*. She's stored this function in the external script file functions.js, which has already been linked to the files in her Web site. You'll use this function to set the value of the date field and then change the focus to the product selection list. The code appears as follows:

```
function startForm() {
    document.form1.date.value = todayTxt();
    document.form1.prod.focus();
}
```

Add the startForm() function to the form1.htm file and run it using an onload event handler applied to the document's body element.

To create and run the startForm() function:

▶ **1.** Return to the **form1.htm** file in your text editor.

▶ **2.** Insert the following embedded script element above the closing `</head>` tag in the document:

```
<script type="text/javascript">
function startForm() {
    document.form1.date.value = todayTxt();
    document.form1.prod.focus();
}
</script>
```

▶ **3.** Add the event handler **onload="startForm()"** to the body element as shown in Figure 14-6.

Figure 14-6	Creating the startForm() function

```
<title>Product Order Form 1</title>
<link href="gpsware.css" rel="stylesheet" type="text/css" />
<script type="text/javascript" src="functions.js"></script>
<script type="text/javascript">
function startForm() {
    document.form1.date.value = todayTxt();
    document.form1.prod.focus();
}
</script>
</head>

<body onload = "startForm()">
<form name="form1" id="form1" method="post" action="form2.htm">
```

▶ **4.** Save your changes to the file and then reopen or refresh the **form1.htm** file in your Web browser.

As shown in Figure 14-7, the current date should now be displayed in the date field and the product selection list should be highlighted, ready for a customer to select a product to purchase.

Figure 14-7	Displaying the current date

the product selection list is given the focus

current date

Working with Selection Lists

In the rest of the form you need to create functions to calculate the cost of a customer's order. This involves: 1) determining the price of the order (equal to the price of the product multiplied by the quantity ordered), 2) determining the cost of shipping, 3) calculating the cost of the sales tax, and 4) adding up all of these costs to arrive at the grand total. You'll start by creating a function to calculate the price of the order.

The product price and quantities have been both placed within selection lists. This is done to ensure that customers select only valid products and quantities. However, unlike an input box, there is no value property for an entire selection list only for each option within the list. For example, the product selection list contains the following options and values:

```
<select name="prod" id="prod">
    <option value="0">Products from GPS-ware</option>
    <option value="19.95">GoMap 1.0 ($19.95)</option>
    <option value="29.95">Drive Planner 2.0 ($29.95)</option>
    <option value="29.95">Hiker 1.0 ($29.95)</option>
    <option value="149.50">G-Receiver I ($149.50)</option>
    <option value="199.50">G-Receiver II ($199.50)</option>
    <option value="249.50">G-Receiver III ($249.50)</option>
</select>
```

JavaScript organizes all of the options into an options collection contained within the selection list object. The syntax to reference a particular option in the collection is

```
element.options[idref]
```

where *element* is the reference to the selection list object and *idref* is the index number or id of the option. Each option in the selection list supports text and value properties specifying the text and value associated with the option. Figure 14-8 shows the text and value properties for the different options in the product selection list.

Properties in the products selection list   **Figure 14-8**

object	object.text	object.value
document.form1.prod.options[0]	Products from GPS-ware	0
document.form1.prod.options[1]	GoMap 1.0 ($19.95)	19.95
document.form1.prod.options[2]	Drive Planner 2.0 ($29.95)	29.95
document.form1.prod.options[3]	Hiker 1.0 ($29.95)	29.95
document.form1.prod.options[4]	G-Receiver I ($149.50)	149.50
document.form1.prod.options[5]	G-Receiver II ($199.50)	199.50
document.form1.prod.options[6]	G-Receiver III ($249.50)	249.50

Figure 14-9 summarizes the properties of both selection list objects and selection list option objects.

Figure 14-9	Properties of selection list and option objects

selection list	Property	Description
	length	The number of options in the list
	name	The name of the selection list
	options	The collection of options in the list
	selectedIndex	The index number of the currently selected option in the list

selection list option	Property	Description
	defaultSelected	A Boolean value indicating whether the option is selected by default
	index	The index value of the option
	selected	A Boolean value indicating whether the option is currently selected
	text	The text associated with the option
	value	The value associated with the option

Since there is no value property for the entire selection list, you use the value or text of the selected option in any calculations you need to perform. To determine the currently selected option in a list, you use the selectedIndex property of the selection list object. The following code demonstrates how you would determine the price associated with a product selected by a customer:

```
product = document.form1.prod;
pindex = product.selectedIndex;
product_price = product.options[pindex].value;
```

In this code the product variable stores the object reference to the product selected in the form1 Web form. The pindex variable stores the index of the currently selected option (whatever that may be). Finally the product_price variable stores the value of that selected option, which is the product's price. The code to determine the quantity ordered is similar:

```
quantity = document.form1.qty;
qindex = quantity.selectedIndex;
quantity_ordered = quantity.options[qindex].value;
```

To calculate the total price for a given product, you multiply the price of the product by the quantity ordered. The following calcPrice() function performs the necessary calculation to determine the price, and then displays the value in the price field of the Web form:

```
function calcPrice() {
   product = document.form1.prod;
   pindex = product.selectedIndex;
   product_price = product.options[pindex].value;
   quantity = document.form1.qty;
   qindex = quantity.selectedIndex;
   quantity_ordered = quantity.options[qindex].value;
   document.form1.price.value = product_price*quantity_ordered;
}
```

You want to run the calcPrice() function whenever a user selects a new option from either the product or the quantity selection lists. One way of doing this is to use the onchange event handler, which runs a command whenever the selected option in the list changes. Add the calcPrice() function and the onchange event handler to Carol's Web form.

To create and run the calcPrice() function:

1. Return to the **form1.htm** file in your text editor.

2. Add the following function to the embedded script element (see Figure 14-10):

```
function calcPrice() {
    product = document.form1.prod;
    pindex = product.selectedIndex;
    product_price = product.options[pindex].value;
    quantity = document.form1.qty;
    qindex = quantity.selectedIndex;
    quantity_ordered = quantity.options[qindex].value;
    document.form1.price.value = product_price*quantity_ordered;
}
```

Creating the calcPrice() function | Figure 14-10

```
function calcPrice() {
    product = document.form1.prod;
    pindex = product.selectedIndex;
    product_price = product.options[pindex].value;
    quantity = document.form1.qty;
    qindex = quantity.selectedIndex;
    quantity_ordered = quantity.options[qindex].value;
    document.form1.price.value = product_price*quantity_ordered;
}

</script>
</head>
```

3. Scroll down the document and add the following event handler to the select element for the "prod" selection list.

```
onchange = "calcPrice()"
```

4. Add the **onchange = "calcPrice()"** event handler to the <select> tag for the "qty" field as well (see Figure 14-11).

Calling the calcPrice() function | Figure 14-11

```
<td class="inputcell">
    <select name="prod" id="prod" onchange="calcPrice()">
    <option value="0">Products from GPS-ware</option>
    <option value="19.95">GoMap 1.0 ($19.95)</option>
    <option value="29.95">Drive Planner 2.0 ($29.95)</option>
    <option value="29.95">Hiker 1.0 ($29.95)</option>
    <option value="149.50">G-Receiver I ($149.50)</option>
    <option value="199.50">G-Receiver II ($199.50)</option>
    <option value="249.50">G-Receiver III ($249.50)</option>
    </select>

    <select name="qty" id="qty" onchange="calcPrice()">
    <option value="0">Quantity</option>
    <option value="1">1</option><option value="2">2</option><option value="3">3</option>
    <option value="4">4</option><option value="5">5</option><option value="6">6</option>
    <option value="7">7</option><option value="8">8</option><option value="9">9</option>
    <option value="10">10</option>
    </select>
</td>
```

5. Save your changes to the file and then reopen **form1.htm** in your Web browser.

6. Select **Hiker 1.0 ($29.95)** from the selection list for the product list box and **2** from the quantity list box. Notice as you select these options (changing the selected options in the list) the value in the price field is updated. See Figure 14-12.

Figure 14-12 **Calculating the price of an order quantity**

7. Select other product and quantity options and verify that the price field automatically changes in response.

   Trouble? You will notice that for some product/quantity combinations the value in the price field is not displayed with a two-digit cents value. You'll learn to format the calculated output to always show the price in dollars and cents later in this session.

Some selection lists are set up to collect multiple selections. In those cases the selectedIndex property returns only the index number of the first selected item. If you wanted to determine the indices of all the selected items, you would have to create a For loop that would run through all of the options in the list, checking each to determine whether the selected property is true (indicating that the option was selected by the user). The selected options could then be added to an array from which further calculations and operations could be performed.

Reference Window | **Working with Selection Lists**

- To determine which option in a selection list has been selected, use the object property
  `field.selectedIndex`
  where *field* is the selection list object.
- To extract the text of an option in a selection list, use the object reference
  `field.options[idref].text`
  where *idref* is the index number or id of the option.
- To extract the value of an option in a selection list, use the object reference
  `field.options[idref].value`

Working with Option Buttons and Checkboxes

Your next task is to display the cost of the shipping option that a user selects. Carol has placed the shipping options within a group of option buttons using the following HTML tags:

```
<input type="radio" name="shipType" id="ship1" value="4.95" />
<input type="radio" name="shipType" id="ship2" value="8.95" />
<input type="radio" name="shipType" id="ship3" value="12.95" />
```

You need to add event handlers to each of these buttons so that the value in the ship field reflects whatever option button has been clicked.

Using option buttons

Since each option button in a group shares a common name value, JavaScript places the individual buttons within that group into an array. Individual option buttons have the reference

```
element[idref]
```

where *element* is the reference to the group of option buttons and *idref* is either the index number or id of the individual option button within that group. In Carol's form, either of the following object references could be used for the first shipType option button:

```
document.form1.shipType[0]
document.form1.shipType["ship1"]
```

You can also reference an option button using the document.getElementById() method if an id has been assigned to it. Figure 14-13 describes some of the properties associated with option buttons.

Properties of option buttons ◄ **Figure 14-13**

Property	Description
checked	A Boolean value indicating whether the option button is currently selected
defaultChecked	A Boolean value indicating whether the option button is selected by default
name	The name of the option button
value	The value associated with the option button

Thus, to extract the value of the first shipType option button, you would use the expression

```
document.form1.shipType[0].value
```

Reference Window

Working with Option Button Groups

- To reference a specific option button within a group, use the object reference
     `element[idref]`
  where *element* is the reference to the option button group, and *idref* is the id or index number of the option button.
- To determine whether an option button is currently checked, use the object property
     `element[idref].checked`
  which returns the Boolean value true if the button is checked.
- To determine which button in the option button group is checked, create a For loop that examines each option button's checked property, returning the index of the checked button.

Using the "this" keyword

To calculate the cost of shipping, you want to use the following function, which displays the cost of the selected shipping option in the ship field:

```
function calcShipping(shipOption) {
    document.form1.ship.value = shipOption.value;
}
```

In this function the shipOption parameter represents the shipping option button selected by a customer. But how do you determine which option button is selected? Unfortunately, there is no selectedIndex property for option buttons as there is for selection lists. However, other methods are available to determine which option button a customer clicked. One technique is to loop through all of the option buttons in the group and use the checked property, described in Figure 14-13, to determine which button the user clicked.

Another approach is to use the "this" keyword. The **this keyword** is a JavaScript object reference that refers to the currently selected object, whatever that may be. The keyword is particularly useful in situations when a function might be called from several different objects and you need a way to work with the object that called the function. Indeed, that is the situation you are currently in. To use the "this" keyword with the calcShipping() function, you add the following onclick event handlers to the tags for the three option buttons:

```
<input type="radio" name="shipType" id="ship1" value="4.95"
     onclick="calcShipping(this)" />
<input type="radio" name="shipType" id="ship2" value="8.95"
     onclick="calcShipping(this)" />
<input type="radio" name="shipType" id="ship3" value="12.95"
     onclick="calcShipping(this)" />
```

When a customer clicks one of the shipType option buttons, the calcShipping() function is called. The object indicated by the "this" keyword is stored in the shipOption parameter, which is then used in determining the cost of the selected shipping option.

To create and run the calcShipping() function:

1. Return to the **form1.htm** file in your text editor.

2. Add the following calcShipping() function to the embedded script element, as shown in Figure 14-14.

```
function calcShipping(shipOption) {
   document.form1.ship.value = shipOption.value;
}
```

Creating the calcShipping() function | **Figure 14-14**

```
function calcShipping(shipoption) {
    document.form1.ship.value = shipOption.value;
}

</script>
</head>
```

3. Scroll down the document and add the event handler **onclick="calcShipping(this)"** to each of the shipType option buttons. (See Figure 14-15.)

Calling the calcShipping() function | **Figure 14-15**

```
<td>
    <p><input type="radio" name="shipType" id="ship1" value="4.95"
        onclick="calcShipping(this)" />
        <label for="ship1">Standard (4-6 business days): $4.95</label>
    </p>
    <p><input type="radio" name="shipType" id="ship2" value="8.95"
        onclick="calcShipping(this)" />
        <label for="ship2">Express (2 days): $8.95</label>
    </p>
    <p><input type="radio" name="shipType" id="ship3" value="12.95"
        onclick="calcShipping(this)" />
        <label for="ship3">Next Day (1 day): $12.95</label>
    </p>
</td>
```

4. Save your changes to the file and then reload **form1.htm** in your Web browser. Verify that each time you click one of the three shipping options, the shipping cost appears in the ship field on the right edge of the form.

Working with check boxes

Carol's order form contains no check boxes, which work the same way as option buttons. Like an option button, a check box supports the checked property, indicating whether the box is checked or not. In addition, the value associated with a check box is stored in the value property of the check box object. This value is applied only when the check box is checked, however; if a check box is not checked, its field has no value assigned to it. As with option buttons, you can run a function in response to a user clicking a check box by applying the onclick event handler. However, unlike option buttons, there is only one check box for each entry field.

Creating Calculated Fields

To complete Carol's Web form, you need to calculate the form's remaining values: the subtotal (the product price plus the shipping cost), the sales tax, and the total cost of the order (the subtotal plus the sales tax). JavaScript treats the contents of input fields as text strings. This means you cannot simply add the input field values together, because JavaScript would append the text strings rather than add the values they represent. For example, if the value displayed in the price field is "39.9" and the value in the ship field is "9.95", then the expression

```
document.form1.price.value + document.form1.ship.value
```

returns the text string "39.99.95" (adding the two text strings together). If you want to treat the contents of input fields as numeric values, you must first convert them from text strings to numbers.

Converting between text strings and numeric values

One simple way to convert a text string to a number is to apply an arithmetic operator (other than the plus operator) that does not change the number's value. The following expression creates a new variable named priceVal that stores the numeric value of the price field.

```
priceVal = document.form1.price.value*1;
```

To instead convert a number to text, you can add a text string, as in the following expression:

```
priceText = priceVal + "";
```

While this approach works with most browsers, it isn't recommended because it relies on a trick that assumes the browser knows enough to convert the text string to a number and vice versa based on the values in the operation. It's more reliable to explicitly indicate that you want to convert a text string to a number, rather than doing it implicitly with a formula. One approach is the parseInt() function, which extracts the leading integer value from a text string. The syntax of the parseInt() function is

```
parseInt(text)
```

where *text* is the text string to be converted. The parseInt() function determines whether the first non-blank character in the text string is a number. If it is, the method extracts characters from the text string from left to right until it encounters the first character that is not a digit. Any characters in the string from that point on are discarded. Note that only the first integer in the string is returned, and the parseInt() function does not return decimal points or numbers to the right of a decimal. If the text string does not begin with a number, the parseInt() method returns the value NaN, indicating that the text string contains no accessible number (NaN stands for "Not a Number"). The following are some sample values returned by the parseInt() function:

```
parseInt("120 lbs")                 // returns 120
parseInt("206.58 lbs")              // returns 206
parseInt("50 lbs, 60 lbs, 70 lbs")  // returns 50
parseInt("weight equals 55 lbs")    // returns NaN
```

The other function you can use in converting a text string to a numeric value is the parseFloat() function, which has a similar syntax:

```
parseFloat(text)
```

The parseFloat() function works like the parseInt() method except that it retrieves both integers and numbers with decimals. The following are sample values returned by the parseFloat() function:

```
parseFloat("120 lbs")                 // returns 120
parseFloat("206.58 lbs")              // returns 206.58
parseFloat("50 lbs, 60 lbs, 70 lbs")  // returns 50
parseFloat("weight equals 55 lbs")    // returns NaN
```

Extracting a Number from a Text String

- To extract an integer value from a text string, use the function
      parseInt(*text*)
  where *text* is the text string. The parseInt() method returns the first integer found in the string.
- To extract a numeric value from a text string, use the function
      parseFloat(*text*)

To explicitly convert a number to a text string, you can use the String() function. The syntax of the function is

String(*value*)

where *value* is the value that you want to convert to a text string. The String() method works with different number formats, including numbers expressed in exponential fashion. For example, the expression 995e-2 is equal to 995×10^{-2} or 9.95; thus, the function

String(995e-2)

returns the text string "9.95" because this is the string representation of the number stored by the browser. If you're unsure whether JavaScript considers a particular value to be text or a number, you can use the typeof() function to find out. The expression

typeof(*value*)

returns "string" if *value* is considered a text string, and "number" if it's considered numeric.

Because the values in Carol's form involve decimal places, you'll apply the parseFloat() method to convert them to numeric values. The following set of commands uses the parseFloat() method to add the numeric values stored in the price and ship fields, storing the result in the sub field:

```
priceVal = parseFloat(document.form1.price.value);
shipVal = parseFloat(document.form1.ship.value);
document.form1.sub.value = priceVal+shipVal;
```

You'll use these commands in a function named calcTotal() that calculates the values of the subtotal, tax, and total fields. The text of the calcTotal() function is

```
function calcTotal() {
   priceVal = parseFloat(document.form1.price.value);
   shipVal = parseFloat(document.form1.ship.value);
   taxVal = 0.05*(priceVal+shipVal);
   document.form1.sub.value = priceVal+shipVal;
   document.form1.tax.value = taxVal;
   document.form1.tot.value = priceVal+shipVal+taxVal;
}
```

You want to run the calcTotal() function whenever a customer makes a selection on the form. This occurs when a product or quantity is picked from a selection list, or when a shipping option is selected. Since you've already created event handlers for each of those actions to run the calcPrice() and calcShipping() functions, you can simply add a command to the end of those functions to run calcTotal().

To create and run the calcTotal() function:

1. Return to the **form1.htm** file in your text editor.

2. Add the following calcTotal() function to the embedded script element:

```
function calcTotal() {
    priceVal = parseFloat(document.form1.price.value);
    shipVal = parseFloat(document.form1.ship.value);
    taxVal = 0.05*(priceVal+shipVal);
    document.form1.sub.value = priceVal+shipVal;
    document.form1.tax.value = taxVal;
    document.form1.tot.value = priceVal+shipVal+taxVal;
}
```

3. Go to the calcPrice() and calcShipping() functions and add a line to the end of each function calling the calcTotal() function. See Figure 14-16.

Figure 14-16	Creating the calcTotal() function

```
function calcPrice() {
    product = document.form1.prod;
    pindex = product.selectedIndex;
    product_price = product.options[pindex].value;
    quantity = document.form1.qty;
    qindex = quantity.selectedIndex;
    quantity_ordered = quantity.options[qindex].value;
    document.form1.price.value = product_price*quantity_ordered;
    calcTotal();
}

function calcShipping(shipoption) {
    document.form1.ship.value = shipoption.value;
    calcTotal();
}

function calcTotal() {
    priceVal = parseFloat(document.form1.price.value);
    shipVal = parseFloat(document.form1.ship.value);
    taxVal = 0.05*(priceVal+shipval);
    document.form1.sub.value = priceval+shipval;
    document.form1.tax.value = taxval;
    document.form1.tot.value = priceVal+shipVal+taxval;

}
</script>
</head>
```

4. Save your changes to the file and reload **form1.htm** in your Web browser.

5. Select **Drive Planner 2.0 ($29.95)** from the product selection list, **2** from the quantity selection list, and click the **Standard (4–6 business days) $4.95** option button.

6. As you select each of these options the subtotal, tax, and total values should be automatically updated in the Web form. See Figure 14-17.

Figure 14-17	Calculating the total cost of an order

Using the options you selected, the form automatically calculates the subtotal value to be $64.85, the tax value to be approximately $3.24, and the total cost of the order to be about $68.09. All of these monetary values need to be displayed in dollars and cents, rounded to two decimal places. Our next task is to round these figures to currency values.

Formatting numeric values

When your browser displays a numeric value, it displays all of the calculated digits of that value. Since JavaScript stores numbers to 16 decimal places of accuracy, some very simple formulas can result in long numeric strings. For example, the code

```
var y= 1/3;
document.write("y = " + y);
```

causes the following text string to be written to the Web page:

```
y = 0.3333333333333333
```

In most cases you don't need 16 digits of accuracy, and with currency you will only want to display results to 2 decimal places. To specify the number of digits displayed by the browser, you can apply the toFixed() method to a numeric value. The syntax of this method is

```
value.toFixed(n)
```

where `value` is the numeric value and `n` is the number of decimal places to be displayed in the output. The following code shows an example of using the toFixed() method to display the same number to different decimal places:

```
testValue = 2.835;
testValue.toFixed(0)    // displays "3"
testValue.toFixed(1)    // displays "2.8"
testValue.toFixed(2)    // displays "2.84"
testValue.toFixed(3)    // displays "2.835"
```

Note that the toFixed() method rounds rather than truncates the right-most digits in the number. You should also be aware that the toFixed() method converts any number into a text string. Thus, if you use the toFixed() method in a program, you may have to convert your formatted values back to numbers using the techniques described above. You can also use other methods to convert and format your numeric values, including displaying values in exponential form or setting the number of significant digits in the output. Figure 14-18 summarizes some of the other JavaScript functions and methods for numeric values.

| Figure 14-18 | Numeric and string functions and methods |

Method	Description
isFinite(*value*)	Returns a Boolean value indicating whether *value* is finite and a legal number
isNaN(*value*)	Returns a Boolean value indicating whether *value* is "not a number"
parseFloat(*string*)	Extracts the first numeric value from a text string
parseInt(*string*)	Extracts the first integer value from a text string
String(*object*)	Converts an *object* to a text string representing the object's value; when used with numeric values, it changes the number to a text string
value.toExponential(*n*)	Returns a text string displaying *value* in exponential notation with *n* digits to the right of the decimal point
value.toFixed(*n*)	Returns a text string displaying the *value* to *n* decimal places
value.toPrecision(*n*)	Returns a text string displaying the *value* to *n* significant digits either to the left or to the right of the decimal point

Reference Window

Formatting Numeric Values

- To set the number of decimals displayed by the browser, use the method
  ```
  value.toFixed(n)
  ```
  where `value` is the numeric value and `n` is the number of decimals to be displayed.
- To set the precision of a displayed number, use the method
  ```
  value.toPrecision(n)
  ```
  where `n` is the number of significant digits displayed either to the left or to the right of the decimal point.

You'll use the toFixed() method to display the currency values in Carol's form to two decimal places.

To apply the toFixed() method:

1. Return to the **form1.htm** file in your text editor.

2. Go to the calcPrice() function and change the statement that sets the value of the price field to the following:

   ```
   document.form1.price.value = (product_price*quantity_ordered).
   toFixed(2);
   ```

3. Go to the calcTotal() function and change the statements that set the values of the sub, tax, and tot fields to the following:

   ```
   document.form1.sub.value = (priceVal+shipVal).toFixed(2);
   document.form1.tax.value = taxVal.toFixed(2);
   document.form1.tot.value = (priceVal+shipVal+taxVal).toFixed(2);
   ```

   You do not have to make any changes to the calcShipping() function since the three shipping values are stored in the selection list already in currency format. Figure 14-19 shows the revised code in the document.

Applying the toFixed() method   Figure 14-19

```
function calcPrice() {
    product = document.form1.prod;
    pindex = product.selectedIndex;
    product_price = product.options[pindex].value;
    quantity = document.form1.qty;
    qindex = quantity.selectedIndex;
    quantity_ordered = quantity.options[qindex].value;
    document.form1.price.value = (product_price*quantity_ordered).toFixed(2);
    calcTotal();
}

function calcShipping(shipoption) {
    document.form1.ship.value = shipoption.value;
    calcTotal();
}

function calcTotal() {
    priceval = parseFloat(document.form1.price.value);
    shipval = parseFloat(document.form1.ship.value);
    taxVal = 0.05*(priceval+shipval);
    document.form1.sub.value = (priceval+shipval).toFixed(2);
    document.form1.tax.value = taxVal.toFixed(2);
    document.form1.tot.value = (priceval+shipval+taxVal).toFixed(2);
}
</script>
</head>
```

4. Save the **form1.htm** file. If you plan on taking a break before starting the next session, you may also close the file.

5. Reopen **form1.htm** in your Web browser and select **G-Receiver I ($149.50)** from the product selection list, **3** from the quantity selection list, and click the **Next Day (1 day) $12.95** shipping. Figure 14-20 shows the resulting values in the order form.

Displaying formatted currency values   Figure 14-20

Order Form

| | 6-23-2007 |

Select a Product

| Product | G-Receiver I ($149.50) ▾ | 3 ▾ | | 448.50 |

Shipping	○ Standard (4-6 business days): $4.95		12.95
	○ Express (2 days): $8.95	
	◉ Next Day (1 day): $12.95	

	Subtotal	461.45
	Tax (5%)	23.07
	TOTAL	484.52

Cancel   Next

Trouble? If you are using an older browser, it may not support the toFixed() method. In this case, you can instead use the customized function toFixed2(*value*) where *value* is the value you want formatted to two decimal places. You'll learn about the toFixed2() function shortly.

6. Continue to experiment with different order options to verify that the form works as expected. Close the Web page when you're finished.

You've completed your work on creating a Web form to perform automatic calculations and correctly format values. Carol will look over your work and get back to you with further tasks in the next session.

Working with Older Browsers

Before going on to the next session, it's important to note that the toFixed() method was introduced in JavaScript 1.5, and thus is not supported by older browsers. Specifically, it is not supported in browser versions earlier than Internet Explorer 5.5, Netscape 6.0, and Opera 6.02. If you need to support those browsers, you must format your output using a JavaScript program. Let's consider a few examples.

When you want to limit your output to a certain number of decimal places, you have to round the value to those decimal places. JavaScript does not support a generalized rounding function. The only built-in rounding functions are the Math.floor(), Math.ceil(), and Math.round() methods used to round a number to the next highest, next lowest, and closest integer, respectively. If you need to round a number to a specified number of decimals, you can use the following customized function:

```
function roundValue(value, n) {
    return Math.round(Math.pow(10,n)*value)/Math.pow(10,n);
}
```

where the `value` parameter is the number to be rounded and the `n` parameter is the number of digits the value can be rounded to. The value of the `n` parameter must be an integer, but it can be either positive or negative; a negative `n` parameter has the effect of rounding a value to the nearest ten, hundred, thousand, and so forth. The following code shows how the roundValue() function can be used to round the same number to different decimal places:

```
roundValue(45.783,2)   // returns 45.78
roundValue(45.783,1)   // returns 45.8
roundValue(45.783,0)   // returns 46
roundValue(45.783,-1)  // returns 50
```

The roundValue() function returns a numeric value, but not a text string with a value displayed to a set number of decimals as the toFixed() method does. To simulate the toFixed() method for currency values displayed with two decimal places, you can use the following function:

```
function toFixed2(value) {
    n = Math.round(value*100)/100;
    if (n == Math.round(n)) return n+".00";
    else if (n*10 == Math.round(n*10)) return n+"0";
    else return String(n);
}
```

The following are the text strings returned by this function for a set of numeric values:

```
toFixed2(45.783) // returns "45.78"
toFixed2(45.787) // returns "45.79"
toFixed2(45.8)   // returns "45.80"
toFixed(45)      // returns "45.00"
```

These two functions and a few other number formatting functions have been placed in the functions.js file for your use in your own Web site. If you are using an older browser, you can use these functions in place of the more recent JavaScript methods. At this point you've completed your work in creating calculated fields for Carol's Web form. In the next session, you'll explore how to ensure that a Web form is correctly filled out.

Session 14.1 Quick Check

1. Specify the object reference to the second Web form in a document.
2. Specify the object reference to the lastname input field found in a Web form named "register".
3. What command would change the value of the lastname field to "Carol Campbell"? What command would move the cursor to the lastname field?
4. Specify the object reference to the fourth option in the statename selection list. Assume that the name of the Web form is "register".
5. What expression would return the index number of the selected option from the statename selection list?
6. What expression would indicate whether the contactme check box field in the register Web form is selected?
7. What value is returned by the expression parseInt("2007 is the current year")? What value is returned by the expression parseInt("The current year is 2007")?
8. What expression would you use to convert the value 3.14159 to a text string displaying the value rounded to 2 decimal places? What problems might old browsers encounter in using this expression?

Session 14.2

Working with Form Validation

Carol has now had some time to work with your changes to her order form. While she appreciates the form's ability to automatically calculate the different costs associated with an order, she's concerned that the form contains nothing to prevent customers from filling it out incorrectly. She points out that users could submit an order without specifying a shipping option. Carol would like to see the form contain some checks on whether a customer has correctly filled it out.

Carol's request is an example of **form validation**, a process by which the server or a user's browser checks a form for data entry errors. On the Web, validation can occur on the client side or the server side. As shown in Figure 14-21, with **server-side validation**, a form is sent to the Web server for checking. If an error is found, the user is notified and asked to resubmit the form. In **client-side validation**, the Web browser checks the form, which is not submitted to the server until it passes inspection.

Figure 14-21 ▶ **Server-side and client-side validation**

Web server | **Web server**

Server-side validation

1) The user submits the form to the Web server.

2) The Web server validates the user's responses and, if necessary, returns the form to the user for correction.

3) After correcting any errors, the user resubmits the form to the Web server for another validation.

Client-side validation

1) The user submits the form, and validation is performed on the user's computer.

2) After correcting any errors, the user submits the form to the Web server.

In practice, server-side and client-side validation are commonly used together. Client-side validation provides immediate feedback to users and lessens the load on servers by distributing some of the validation tasks to users' computers. The server then has the task of performing a final check on submitted data before processing it. Carol is aware that GPS-ware's Web server might handle hundreds of orders per hour on a good business day, and anything that can be done to reduce the load on the server helps. Carol would like you to ensure that before her form can be submitted to the server, a customer has done the following:

1. Selected a GPS-ware product.
2. Selected a quantity of the product to order.
3. Selected a shipping option

If these conditions are not met, Carol would like the user's browser to alert the customer of the problem and refuse to submit the form to the server.

Submitting a Form

When a user completes a form and then clicks the submit button, the form initiates a submit event. By default, the browser initiates the action indicated in the form's action and method attributes. As you may have already discovered by working with the form1. htm file, submitting Carol's first order form causes a user's browser to open the second of her three Web forms. The submit button is the button labeled "Next" on the Web form.

To control this submission process, JavaScript provides the onsubmit event handler that can be added to the form element. The syntax used with the onsubmit event handler is

```
<form onsubmit="return function()"> ... </form>
```

where *function* is a function that returns the Boolean value true or false. As you saw in the previous tutorial when working with pop-up windows and transient status bar messages, you can use such a function to prevent a browser's default behavior in response to an event. In this case, if the function returns a value of false, the submit event is cancelled, while a value of true allows the submit event to continue unabated.

For the first of Carol's three Web forms, you'll create a function named checkForm1() that tests whether the selected index of the product or quantity selection lists is equal to zero (indicating that no product or quantity was selected), or if the cost of shipping is equal to "0.00" (indicating that no shipping option was selected). If the function identifies any of these problems, it means that the form has not been properly completed. In this case, the function will display an alert box specifying the problem to the user, and return a value of false. If the function does not identify any of these problems, it will return a value of true and allow the form to be submitted. The complete code of the checkForm1() function is

```
function checkForm1() {
   if (document.form1.prod.selectedIndex == 0)
      {alert("You must select a GPS-ware product");
       return false;}
   else if (document.form1.qty.selectedIndex == 0)
      {alert("You must select a quantity to order");
       return false;}
   else if (document.form1.ship.value == "0.00")
      {alert("You must select a shipping option");
       return false;}
   else return true;
}
```

Note that the return keyword ends this function when one of the conditions is met. Thus, only one alert box will be displayed at a time, even if more than one error is present in the form.

To create and apply the checkForm1() function:

1. If necessary, reopen the **form1.htm** file in your text editor.

2. Add the following function to the embedded script element in the document's head section:

```
function checkForm1() {
   if (document.form1.prod.selectedIndex == 0)
      {alert("You must select a GPS-ware product");
       return false;}
   else if (document.form1.qty.selectedIndex == 0)
      {alert("You must select a quantity to order");
       return false;}
   else if (document.form1.ship.value == "0.00")
      {alert("You must select a shipping option");
       return false;}
   else return true;
}
```

3. Scroll down the file and add the following event handler to the form element:

```
onsubmit = "return checkForm1()"
```

Figure 14-22 shows the new code in the form1.htm file.

Figure 14-22 ▶ **Creating the checkForm1() function**

```
function checkForm1() {
   if (document.form1.prod.selectedIndex == 0)
      {alert("You must select a GPS-ware product");
       return false;}
   else if (document.form1.qty.selectedIndex == 0)
      {alert("You must select a quantity to order");
       return false;}
   else if (document.form1.ship.value == "0.00")
      {alert("You must select a shipping option");
       return false;}
   else return true;
}
</script>
</head>

<body onload = "startForm()">
<form name="form1" id="form1" method="post" action="form2.htm"
      onsubmit="return checkForm1()">
```

▶ **4.** Save your changes to the file.

▶ **5.** Reopen **form1.htm** in your Web browser.

▶ **6.** Click the **Next** button without selecting any products, quantities, or shipping options from the form.

As shown in Figure 14-23, the browser displays an alert box indicating that you have not selected a product to order (the first mistake found in the form).

Figure 14-23 ▶ **Validating the Web form**

▶ **7.** Click **OK** to close the alert box and then continue to test the form by omitting one of three required pieces of information when you submit the form. Verify that the browser fails to accept the form.

▶ **8.** Correctly complete the order form and then click the **Next** button. Verify that the browser has accepted the completed form and displayed the contents of the second of Carol's three Web forms.

Resetting a Form

The other event associated with Web forms is the reset event, which occurs when a user clicks a reset button within the form. Clicking the reset button has the effect of resetting all form fields to their default values. You can control how the reset event is handled by adding an onreset event handler to the form element in the same way that you add the onsubmit event handler to manage form submission.

In Carol's order form, the Cancel button plays the role of the reset button. However, Carol wants to modify what happens when the form is reset. Recall that the first action this form takes is to insert the current date into the date field. Thus, Carol wants the reset button to both reset the fields to their default values and to rerun the startForm() function which inserts the current date into the date field. You can perform both of these actions by having the browser reload the document when the reset event is initiated. When the page is reloaded, the startForm() function runs automatically and the fields return to their default values. To reload the page, you use the reload() method of the location object.

To apply the onreset event handler:

▶ 1. Return to the **form1.htm** file in your text editor.

▶ 2. Add the following event handler to the form element as shown in Figure 14-24:

```
onreset = "location.reload()"
```

Working with the onreset event handler ◀ Figure 14-24

Note that you are not using the return keyword in this event handler. This is because you don't want to cancel the reset event, but simply to change what actions are caused by the occurrence of a form reset.

▶ 3. Close the **form1.htm** file, saving your changes.

▶ 4. Reopen **form1.htm** in your Web browser.

▶ 5. Select a product to order, a quantity, and a shipping option and then click the **Cancel** button at the bottom of the form. Verify that the page reloads, setting the fields to their default values and displaying the current date in the date field. The product selection list should be the selected field in the form.

Reference Window

Validating a Web Form

- To validate a Web form when it is submitted, add the following event handler to the form element:

  ```
  <form onsubmit="return function()"> ... </form>
  ```
  where *function* is a function that returns a Boolean value. A value of false cancels the submission of the form, while a value of true allows the form to be submitted.
- To control the resetting of a form, add the event handler

  ```
  <form onreset="function"> ... </form>
  ```
  where *function* is a function that is run when the reset event is initiated.

Working with Text Strings

You've completed your work on the first of Carol's Web forms. The second form, shown in Figure 14-25, contains fields for collecting a customer's contact and delivery information.

Figure 14-25 | **The delivery form**

Figure 14-26 lists the object references for each of the elements in the form.

Figure 14-26 | **Objects in the delivery form**

Object	Reference
The first name field	document.form2.fname
The last name field	document.form2.lname
The street text area box	document.form2.street
The city field	document.form2.city
The state selection list	document.form2.state
The zip code field	document.form2.zip
The previous button	document.form2.prevb
The next button	document.form2.nextb

While this form requires no calculations, Carol would like you to implement the following validation checks before the form is accepted by the browser:

1. A customer must specify a first name, last name, street address, and city.
2. If a ZIP code is entered, it should consist of five digits with no non-numeric characters.

Since you need to apply these validation checks to text strings, you'll now take a deeper look at the properties and methods of text strings.

The string object

JavaScript treats each text string as an object called a **string object**. The most common way to create a string object is to assign a text string to a variable. You can also create a string object using the object constructor

```
stringVariable = new String("text");
```

where *stringVariable* is a variable that stores the text string, and *text* is the text of the string. This approach has the advantage of explicitly identifying a variable as containing a text string, rather than having JavaScript implicitly create a string object based on the content of a variable.

Calculating the length of a text string

Only a few properties are associated with string objects. Of chief interest to us is the length property, which returns the number of characters in the text, including all white-space characters and nonprintable characters. The following code calculates the number of characters in the stringVar variable, storing the value 17 in the lengthValue variable:

```
stringVar = "GPS-ware Products";
lengthValue = stringVar.length;
```

The length property is commonly used for functions that process a text string character by character, and need some way of knowing when to stop. You can also use the length property to validate the entries in Carol's delivery form. Her first requirement is that customers enter a first and last name, a street address, and a city. Thus, for each of those fields the length of the text string must be greater than zero. You'll use the length property to verify this condition for each of these fields in your first set of validation checks for the delivery form, which will be stored in a function called checkForm2(). As with the earlier checkForm1() function, you'll have the browser display an appropriate alert dialog box the first time it encounters an invalid field. The initial code for the checkForm2() function is

```
function checkForm2() {
   if (document.form2.fname.value.length == 0)
      {alert("You must enter a first name");
       return false;}
   else if (document.form2.lname.value.length == 0)
      {alert("You must enter a last name");
       return false;}
   else if (document.form2.street.value.length == 0)
      {alert("You must enter a street address");
       return false;}
   else if (document.form2.city.value.length == 0)
      {alert("You must enter a city name");
       return false;}
   else return true;
}
```

Notice that since JavaScript treats field values as text strings—that is to say, string objects—you can use the length property to determine whether a customer has entered a value. You will not be checking whether those values make any sense, but simply verifying that the customer has entered something. Add this function to the form2.htm file and then call it by adding an onsubmit event handler to the form element.

To create and apply the checkForm2() function:

1. Open the **form2.htm** file in your text editor. Take some time to review its contents to understand the HTML code.

2. Directly above the closing </head> tag, insert the following embedded script element and function:

```
<script type="text/javascript">
function checkForm2() {
    if (document.form2.fname.value.length == 0)
       {alert("You must enter a first name");
        return false;}
    else if (document.form2.lname.value.length == 0)
       {alert("You must enter a last name");
        return false;}
    else if (document.form2.street.value.length == 0)
       {alert("You must enter a street address");
        return false;}
    else if (document.form2.city.value.length == 0)
       {alert("You must enter a city name");
        return false;}
    else return true;
}
</script>
```

Since this is a long piece of code, take some time to ensure that you have correctly entered the code. Make sure that you close all command blocks within curly braces {} and that you use the == symbol rather than a single = symbol in a conditional statement.

3. Scroll down the file and add the following event handler to the form element:

```
onsubmit = "return checkForm2()"
```

Figure 14-27 shows the new code in the form2.htm file.

Figure 14-27 | Adding the checkForm2() function

```
<script type="text/javascript">
function checkForm2() {
    if (document.form2.fname.value.length == 0)
       {alert("You must enter a first name");
        return false;}
    else if (document.form2.lname.value.length == 0)
       {alert("You must enter a last name");
        return false;}
    else if (document.form2.street.value.length == 0)
       {alert("You must enter a street address");
        return false;}
    else if (document.form2.city.value.length == 0)
       {alert("You must enter a city name");
        return false;}
    else return true;
}
</script>

</head>

<body>
<form name="form2" id="form2" method="post" action="form3.htm"
        onsubmit="return checkForm2()">
```

4. Save your changes to the file and open **form2.htm** in your Web browser.

As with the previous form, the Next button submits this form for processing. In this case, submitting the form will cause the browser to load the form3.htm file.

5. Click the **Next** button without entering any contact information in the first name, last name, street, or city fields.

   The browser displays an alert box indicating that you have not specified a first name.

6. Click **OK** to close the alert box, and then continue to test the form by omitting different required fields and then clicking the **Next** button. Verify that you have to type in all the required information before the browser accepts the completed form.

Working with string object methods

Carol's second validation check involves examining the digits in the ZIP field. This field should be five characters long and should consist only of numeric characters (you'll look at how to validate extended ZIP codes that include a dash and additional digits in the next session).

To validate the ZIP code, you'll create a function called checkZip(). The initial version of this function will check only the length of the ZIP code. Since a ZIP code is not required for delivery, you'll allow valid ZIP codes to contain either 0 or 5 digits; any other length will be invalid. The initial code for the checkZip() function is

```
function checkZip(zip) {
   if (zip.length != 0 && zip.length != 5) return false;
   return true;
}
```

Add this function to the form2.htm file.

To create the checkZip() function:

1. Return to the **form2.htm** file in your text editor.

2. Add the following function to the embedded script (see Figure 14-28):

   ```
   function checkZip(zip) {
      if (zip.length != 0 && zip.length != 5) return false;
      return true;
   }
   ```

The initial checkZip() function ◀ Figure 14-28

```
function checkZip(zip) {
   if (zip.length != 5 && zip.length != 0) return false;
   return true;
}
</script>
```

3. Save your changes to the file.

The checkZip() function can confirm that the ZIP code contains five characters, but does not check whether each of those characters are digits. To do that, you'll use some of the JavaScript methods associated with string objects.

JavaScript supports methods that allow you to examine the individual characters within a text string. A character is identified by its placement in the text string. Like arrays and object collections, the first character has an index value of 0, the second has an index value of 1, and so forth. If you want to reference a character with a particular index, use the method

```
string.charAt(i)
```

where *string* is the string object and *i* is the index of the character. For example, the expression

```
"GPS-ware".charAt(2)
```

returns the third character from the text string, which in this case is an uppercase "S". The charAt() method extracts only a single character. To extract longer text strings, known as **substrings**, use the slice() method:

```
string.slice(start, end)
```

where *start* is the starting index and *end* is the index at which the slicing stops. If you do not specify an *end* value, the substring is extracted to the end of the text string. For example, the statement

```
"GPS-ware Products For Sale".slice(9,17)
```

returns the substring "Products", since it starts at index number 9 and ends right before index 17. You can also extract substrings based on their length using the method

```
string.substr(start, length)
```

where *length* is the number of characters in the substring. If you do not specify a *length* value, JavaScript extracts the substring to the end of the string. Thus, to extract the word "Products" from the previous text string, you can also use

```
"GPS-ware Products For Sale".substr(9,8)
```

Both the slice() and substr() methods are limited in that they create only a single substring. In some cases, you may need to break a text string into several substrings. For example, you may need to break a long sentence into individual words. Another common use would be to break a field in which customers enter both their first and last names into two strings. Rather than run the substr() or slice() methods several times on the same text string, you can create an array of substrings in a single expression using the method

```
strArray = string.split(str)
```

where *strArray* is the array that will store the substrings and *str* is a text string that marks the break between one substring and another, which is known as a **delimiter**. For example, the command

```
words = "GPS-ware Products For Sale".split(" ")
```

splits the text string at each occurrence of a blank space, storing the substrings in the words array. The substrings stored in the words array are

```
words[0] = "GPS-ware"
words[1] = "Products"
words[2] = "For"
words[3] = "Sale"
```

Note that the characters specified in the delimiter are not placed in the substrings. This is one technique you can use to remove character strings from a large text string.

Other string object methods are used to search for the occurrence of particular substrings within larger text strings. The most often used method is

```
string.indexOf(str, start)
```

which returns the index value of the first occurrence of the substring *str* within *string*. The *start* parameter is optional, and indicates from which character to start the search. The default value of the *start* parameter is 0, indicating that the search should start with the first character. For example, the expression

```
"GPS-ware Products For Sale".indexOf("P")
```

returns the value 1 since that is the index number of the first occurrence of an uppercase "P" in the text. To locate the next occurrence of "P", you can set the *start* value to 2 so that the search starts with the third character in the string. The expression

```
"GPS-ware Products For Sale".indexOf("P",3)
```

returns the value 9. Note that if there is no occurrence of the substring, the indexOf() method returns the value −1. For this reason, the indexOf() method is often used to test whether a text string contains a particular substring.

Working with String Objects

Reference Window

- To determine the number of characters in a text string, use the object property
    ```
    string.length
    ```
  where *string* is a text string object.
- To extract a character from a text string, use the method
    ```
    string.charAt(i)
    ```
  where *i* is the index of the character. The first character in the text string has an index number of 0.
- To extract a substring from a text string, use the method
    ```
    string.slice(start, end)
    ```
  where *start* is the starting index and *end* is the index at which the substring stops. If you do not specify an *end* value, the substring is extracted to the end of the string.
- To split a string into several substrings, use the command
    ```
    strArray = string.split(str)
    ```
  where *strArray* is the array that will store the substrings and *str* is a text string that marks the break between one substring and another.
- To search a string, use the method
    ```
    string.indexOf(str, start)
    ```
  where *str* is the substring to search for within the larger string and *start* is the index of the character from which to start the search. If you do not specify a *start* value, the search starts with the first character in the string.

Figure 14-29 summarizes the different string object methods used to extract information from text strings.

Figure 14-29 ▶ **String extracting methods**

Method	Description	Example(text= "GPS-ware Products")
string.charAt(*i*)	Returns the *i*th character from *string*	text.charAt(4);// returns "w"
string.charCodeAt(*i*)	Returns the *i*th character's Unicode value from the *string*	text.charCodeAt(4);// returns 119
string.concat(*str2*, *str3*, ...)	Appends *string* with the text strings *str2*, *str3*, etc.	text.concat(" Sale"); // returns "GPS-ware Products Sale"
String.fromCharCode(*n1*, *n2*, ..)	Returns a text string consisting of characters whose Unicode values are *n1*, *n2*, etc.	String.fromCharCode(71,80,83); // returns "GPS"
string.indexOf(*str*, *start*)	Searches *string*, beginning at the *start* index number, returning the index number of the first occurrence of *str*; if no *start* value is specified, the search begins with the first character	text.indexOf("P",5);// returns 9
string.lastIndexOf(*str*,*start*)	Searches *string*, beginning at the *start* index number, returning the index number of the last occurrence of *str*; if no *start* value is specified, the search begins with the first character	text.lastIndexOf("P");// returns 9
string.slice(*start*, *end*)	Extracts a substring from *string*, between the *start* and *end* index values if no *end* value is specified, the substring extends to the end of the string	text.slice(4,8);// returns "ware"

string.split(*str*)	Splits *string* into array of string characters at each occurrence of *str*	word=text.split(" ");
		// word[0] = "GPS-ware"
		// word[1]="Products"

string.substr(*start*, *length*)	Returns a substring from *string* starting at the *start* index value and continuing for *length* characters; if no *length* value is specified, the substring continues to the end of *string*	text.substr(9,4);// returns "Prod"
string.substring(*start*, *end*)	Extracts a substring from *string*, between the *start* and *end* index values; if no *end* value is specified, the substring extends to the end of the string (identical to the slice() method)	text.substring(4,8);// returns "ware"

You'll use the charAt() and indexOf() methods to determine whether a customer has entered 5 digits in the ZIP code. First you'll create a string object named validchars that stores the digits from 0 to 9. Then you loop through the ZIP code string, extracting the character at each index using the charAt() method. For each character you'll use the indexOf() method to check whether it can be found in the validchars text string. If it can't be found in that text string, the indexOf() method will return the value –1, and you'll know that the ZIP code contains a non-numeric character. The complete code is

```
validchars = "0123456789";
for (i=0; i<5; i++) {
   zipchar=zip.charAt(i);
   if (validchars.indexOf(zipchar) == -1) return false;
}
```

You'll add these commands to the checkZip() function, running them as another condition in the structure you created earlier.

To modify the checkZip() function:

1. Return to **form2.htm** in your text editor.

2. Add the following code to the checkZip() function as shown in Figure 14-30:

```
else {
   validchars = "0123456789";
   for (i=0; i<5; i++) {
      zipchar=zip.charAt(i);
      if (validchars.indexOf(zipchar) == -1) return false;
   }
}
```

Checking for valid characters in the zip code ◄ **Figure 14-30**

```
function checkZip(zip) {
   if (zip.length != 5 && zip.length != 0) return false;
   else {
      validchars = "0123456789";
      for (i=0; i<5; i++) {
         zipchar=zip.charAt(i);
         if (validchars.indexOf(zipchar) == -1) return false;
      }
   }
   return true;
}
</script>
```

Next you'll call the checkZip() function from the checkForm2() function in order to add this validation check to the others.

3. Add the following code to the checkForm2() function as shown in Figure 14-31:

```
else if (checkZip(document.form2.zip.value) == false)
   {alert("You must enter a valid zip code");
    return false;}
```

| Figure 14-31 | Calling the checkZip() function |

```
function checkForm2() {
    if (document.form2.fname.value.length == 0)
        {alert("You must enter a first name");
        return false;}
    else if (document.form2.lname.value.length == 0)
        {alert("You must enter a last name");
        return false;}
    else if (document.form2.street.value.length == 0)
        {alert("You must enter a street address");
        return false;}
    else if (document.form2.city.value.length == 0)
        {alert("You must enter a city name");
        return false;}
    else if (checkZip(document.form2.zip.value) == false)
        {alert("You must enter a valid zip code");
        return false;}
    else return true;
}
```

▶ **4.** Save your changes to the file, then reload **form2.htm** in your browser.

▶ **5.** Enter text into the first name, last name, street, and city fields, and then click the **Next** button to submit the delivery form.

Your browser should display the contents of Carol's third Web form.

▶ **6.** Return to the **form2.htm** page. Enter the value **ZIP1** into the ZIP field and click the **Next** button. Repeat for the values **123**, **1234a**, and **12345**. Your browser should display an alert box and fail to accept the form except for the ZIP code value of 12345.

▶ **7.** If you want to take a break before starting the next session, close your browser and editor.

Formatting text strings

Another set of JavaScript methods allows you to format a text string's appearance. For example, to display a text string in all uppercase letters you would use the method

```
string.toUpperCase()
```

where *string* is the string object. Thus, to change the text "GPS-ware" to all uppercase letters you would use the JavaScript expression

```
"GPS-ware".toUpperCase()
```

Figure 14-32 lists other formatting methods for string objects along with their equivalent HTML tags. Note that running these methods does not add the HTML tags to the object, but rather achieves the same effects that you would get if you applied those formatting tags to the text string.

String formatting methods | **Figure 14-32**

Method	Description	HTML Equivalent
string.anchor(*text*)	Creates an anchor with the anchor name *text*	`<a name="text">string</a>`
string.big()	Changes the size of the *string* font to big	`<big>string</big>`
string.blink()	Changes *string* to blinking text	`<blink>string</blink>`
string.bold()	Changes the font weight of *string* to bold	`<bold>string</bold>`
string.fixed()	Changes the font of *string* to a fixed width font	`<tt>string</tt>`
string.fontcolor(*color*)	Changes the color of *string* to the hexadecimal *color* value	`<font color="color">string</font>`
string.fontsize(*value*)	Changes the font size of *string* to *value*	`<font size="value">string</font>`
string.italics()	Changes *string* to italics	`<i>string</i>`
string.link(*url*)	Changes *string* to a link pointing to *url*	`<a href="url">string</a>`
string.small()	Changes the size of the *string* font to small	`<small>string</small>`
string.strike()	Adds strikethrough characters to *string*	`<strike>string</strike>`
string.sub()	Changes *string* to a subscript	`<sub>string</sub>`
string.sup()	Changes *string* to a superscript	`<sup>string</sup>`
string.toLowerCase()	Changes *string* to lowercase letters	
string.toUpperCase()	Changes *string* to uppercase letters	

You may have noticed that many of the HTML tags shown in Figure 14-32 have been deprecated in favor of style sheets. In the same way, the string formatting methods are not often used in preference to formatting text strings using the style object. The most often used formatting methods are the toUpperCase() and toLowerCase() methods. At this point you don't have to do any text formatting for Carol's Web forms, but you'll keep these methods in mind for future tasks.

Session 14.2 Quick Check

Review

1. What is server-side validation? What is client-side validation?
2. You've written a function named testForm() that validates your Web form. What event handler should you add to the form element to run the validation before the form is submitted?
3. What expression returns the number of characters in the username string object?
4. What expression returns the first character from the username string? What expression returns the last character from the string?

5. What expression returns the first five characters from the username string?
6. E-mail addresses are usually written in the format: *username@domain*. Write code that breaks an e-mail variable into two text strings: one containing *username* and the other containing *domain*.
7. Government e-mail addresses will often end with ".gov". What expression tests whether the e-mail string object contains the ".gov" substring?
8. What expression would change the username string object to uppercase letters?

Session 14.3

Introducing Regular Expressions

Carol is finished examining your work on the delivery form. While she likes the form validation functions you created, she is concerned about the function that validates the ZIP code. Domestic ZIP codes commonly come in two forms: five digits (*nnnnn*), and five digits followed by a dash and four more digits (*nnnnn-nnnn*). In recent years, the second version has become more prevalent and Carol wants your validation functions to support either format. While you could revise the checkZip() function to accommodate the extended ZIP code format, a much quicker and easier approach is to use a regular expression.

A **regular expression** is a text string that defines a character pattern. One use of regular expressions is **pattern-matching**, in which a text string is tested to see whether it matches the pattern defined by a regular expression. In our ZIP code example, you might create a regular expression for the pattern of five digits followed by a dash and another four digits, and then verify that a customer's ZIP code matches that pattern. Pattern matching is just one use of regular expressions. They can also be used to extract substrings, insert new text, or replace old text. The greatest advantage of regular expressions is that the code is compact and powerful, so that what might take several lines of code using other methods can be done in a single line with a regular expression. However, with this power comes complexity: the syntax of regular expressions can be intimidating to new programmers, taking time and practice to master.

Creating a regular expression

You create a regular expression in JavaScript using the command

```
re = /pattern/;
```

where `pattern` is the text string of the regular expression and `re` is the object that stores the regular expression. This syntax for creating regular expressions is sometimes referred to as a **regular expression literal**. A regular expression is treated by a JavaScript interpreter as an object with a collection of properties and methods that can be applied to it. You'll explore some of those properties and methods later in this session. For now you'll work on understanding the language of regular expressions. To help you understand regular expressions, a demo page has been created in which you can enter a regular expression and apply pattern matching against a sample text string. Open this page now.

To view the Regular Expressions demo:

1. Open the **demo_regexp.htm** file from the tutorial.14/tutorial folder in your Web browser.

   The demo page contains a text box in the upper-left corner in which you enter your sample text. Below the text box you can either enter a predefined regular expression or type one of your own. To match the regular expression against the sample text, you click the Pattern Test button.

2. Type the following text into the text box in the upper-left corner of the page (see Figure 14-33):

   `GPS-ware Products Are Prepared With Care`

The Regular Expression Demo page   **Figure 14-33**

Matching a substring

The most basic regular expression consists of a substring that you want to locate in the test string. The regular expression to match the first occurrence of a substring is

`/chars/`

where *chars* is the text of the substring. Regular expressions are case sensitive, so *chars* must match the uppercase and lowercase letters of the substring you're searching for. To see how this applies to the test string you've already entered in the demo page, create regular expressions to locate the occurrences of the substrings "are" and "Are".

To match a simple substring:

1. Click the text area box for the regular expression (located directly below the drop-down list box) and type **/are/**.

2. Click the **Pattern Test** button.

   As shown in Figure 14-34, the first occurrence of the "are" substring is highlighted and the Pattern Test Result field displays the word "match", indicating that a matching pattern has been found in the test string.

Figure 14-34 | **Matching a substring**

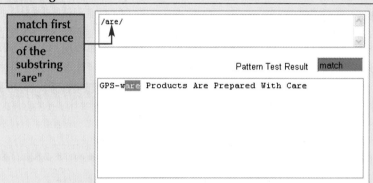

match first occurrence of the substring "are"

/are/

Pattern Test Result   match

GPS-ware Products Are Prepared With Care

3. Change the regular expression to **/Are/** and click the **Pattern Test** button.

   The pattern now matches the word "Are" occurring later in the test string.

Before continuing, it's important to note that spaces are considered characters in a regular expression pattern. While JavaScript allows some flexibility in the use of white space, regular expressions do not. The patterns / GPS / and /GPS/ are considered two totally different regular expressions: in one, the substring "GPS" is surrounded by blank spaces; in the other, it is not. While you might be tempted to insert spaces to make a regular expression more readable, adding spaces changes the regular expression.

Setting regular expression flags

By default, pattern matching stops after the first match is discovered, and the match is case sensitive. You can override both of these behaviors by adding flags to a regular expression. To make a regular expression not sensitive to case, use the regular expression literal

```
/pattern/i
```

To allow a global search for all matches in a test string, use the regular expression literal

```
/pattern/g
```

To apply both at the same time, simply apply both flags to the regular expression:

```
/pattern/ig
```

Try this now on the demo page.

To set the global and case-insensitive flags:

1. Change the regular expression to **/are/ig**.

2. Click the **Pattern Test** button. As shown in Figure 14-35, all examples of the "are" substring are highlighted, regardless of case.

Matching a substring using the g and i flags ◄ Figure 14-35

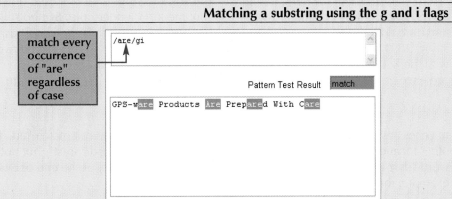

match every occurrence of "are" regardless of case

Defining character positions

So far you've only used regular expressions to match simple text strings, which is not much more than you could have accomplished using the string object methods from the last session. The true power (and complexity!) of regular expressions comes with the introduction of special characters that allow you to match text based on the type, content, and placement of the characters in the text string. The first such characters you'll consider are positioning characters. The four positioning characters are described in Figure 14-36.

Positioning characters ◄ Figure 14-36

Character	Description	Example
^	Indicates the beginning of the text string	/^GPS/ matches "GPS-ware" but not "Products from GPS-ware"
$	Indicates the end of the text string	/ware$/ matches "GPS-ware" but not "GPS-ware Products"
\b	Indicates the presence of a word boundary	/\bart/ matches "art" and "artists" but not "dart"
\B	Indicates the absence of a word boundary	/art\B/ matches "dart" but not "artist"

Regular expressions recognize the beginning and end of a text string, indicated by the ^ and $ character respectively. The following pattern uses the ^ character to mark the start of the text string:

```
/^GPS/
```

In this pattern, any text string starting with the substring "GPS" would be matched; however, the expression would not match the GPS substring occurring elsewhere in the text string. In the same way, the end of the text string is indicated with the $ character. Thus, the following expression matches any text string that ends with the characters "-ware":

```
/-ware$/
```

The ^ and $ characters are often used together to define a pattern for the complete text string. For example, the pattern

```
/^GPS-ware$/
```

would match only a string containing the text "GPS-ware" and nothing else.

The other positioning characters are used to locate words within a text string. The term "word" has a special meaning in regular expressions. Words are composed of word characters, where a **word character** is any letter, numeral, or underscore. Symbols like *, &, and - are not considered word characters, nor are spaces, periods, or tabs. Thus, the string "R2D2" is considered a single word, but "R2D2&C3PO" is considered two words, with the & symbol acting as a boundary between the words. In a regular expression, the presence of a word boundary is indicated with the \b symbol. Thus, the pattern

```
/\bart/
```

matches any word that starts with the characters "art", but does not match "art" found in other locations. For example, this pattern would match the word "artist", but not the word "dart". The \b symbol can also indicate a word boundary at the end of a word. For example, the pattern

```
/art\b/
```

matches any word that ends in "art"—such as "dart" or "heart"—but not "artist". By using the \b symbol at both the beginning and the end of a pattern, you can define a complete word. The pattern

```
/\bart\b/
```

would match only the word "art" and nothing else. In some cases, you want to match substrings only within words. In these situations you use the \B symbol, which indicates the absence of a word boundary. For example, the pattern

```
/\Bart\B/
```

matches the substring "art" only when it occurs within a word like "hearts" or "darts".

The \b and \B symbols illustrate a common element of syntax in regular expression symbols: many regular expression symbols have opposite meanings in uppercase letters. Thus, \B means the opposite of \b. You'll see this pattern in some of the other regular expression characters that you'll be examining shortly.

To view the effect of word boundaries on regular expressions:

▶ **1.** Return to the demo page and change the regular expression to **/\bare\b/gi**.

▶ **2.** Click the **Pattern Test** button. As shown in Figure 14-37, only the word "Are" is highlighted, since it is the only occurrence of the substring "are" as a complete word.

Matching a whole word ◄ **Figure 14-37**

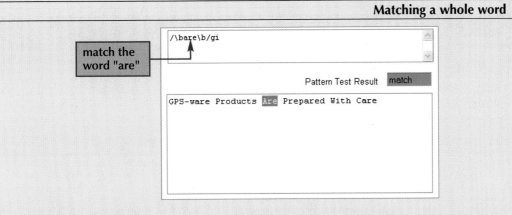

3. Change the regular expression to **/\Bare\b/gi** and click the **Pattern Test** button.

   Now the pattern matches words that end in "are", while ignoring words that start with "are" (see Figure 14-38).

Matching with mixed word boundaries ◄ **Figure 14-38**

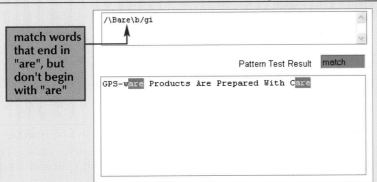

4. Change the regular expression to **/\Bare\B/gi** and click the **Pattern Test** button to locate all instances of the substring "are" that occur within a word.

   The pattern now matches only the substring "are" found within the word "Prepared".

Defining character types and character classes

Another class of regular expression characters indicates character type. There are three general types of characters: word characters, digits (numeric characters from 0 to 9), and white space characters (blank spaces, tabs, and new lines). Figure 14-39 describes the regular expression symbols for these character types.

| Figure 14-39 | **Character classes** |

Character	Description	Example
\d	A digit (from 0 to 9)	/\dth/ matches "5th" but not "ath"
\D	A non-digit	/\Ds/ matches "as" but not "5s"
\w	A word character (an upper or lower case letter, a digit, or an underscore)	/\w\w/ matches "to" or "A1" but not "$x" or " *"
\W	A non-word character	/\W/ matches "$" or "&" but not "a", "B", or "3"
\s	A white space character (a blank space, tab, new line, carriage return, or form feed)	/\s\d\s/ matches " 5 " but not "5"
\S	A non-white space character	/\S\d\S/ matches "345" or "a5b" but not "5"
.	Any character	/./ matches anything

For example, digits are represented by the \d character. To match any occurrence of a single digit, you would use the regular expression

/\d/

This would find matches in such text strings as "105", "6", or "U2", since all of these contain an instance of a single digit. If you want to match several consecutive digits, you can simply repeat the \d symbol. The regular expression

/\d\d\d/

matches the occurrence of any three consecutive digits. It would find matches in strings like "105", "1250", or "EX500". If you want to limit yourself only to words consisting of three digit numbers, you can use the \b character to mark the boundaries around the digits; thus, the pattern

/\b\d\d\d\b/

would match strings like "105" or "229", but not "1250" or "EX500".

At this point you've barely scratched the surface of regular expressions, but you already have enough information to create a regular expression for a five-digit ZIP code. The pattern is

/^\d\d\d\d\d$/

This regular expression matches only a text string that contains five digits and no other characters (recall that the ^ and $ symbols mark the beginning and end of the entire text string). Test this pattern now in the demo page.

To test the ZIP code pattern:

1. Change the text in the sample text string box to **12345**.

2. Change the regular expression in the Pattern input box to **/^\d\d\d\d\d$/** and click the **Pattern Test** button.

   The Pattern Test Result box displays the result "match".

3. Continue experimenting with the pattern, trying sample text strings of **1, 123**, and **1234a**. Verify that you receive a valid match only if you enter a five-digit value and no other characters or numbers.

You have now achieved with a single regular expression what took several lines of code to do in the previous session. This should give you some idea of the power of regular expressions in detecting character patterns.

For more general character matching you can use the \w symbol, which matches any word character, or the \s symbol, which matches any white space character. For example, the pattern

```
/\s\w\w\w\s/
```

matches any three-letter word surrounded by white space. Remember, however that a word character can be a letter, digit, or the underscore character. Thus, this pattern would match a text string like " car " as well as " 123 ". There is no character type that matches only letters. However, you can specify a collection of characters known as a **character class** to limit the regular expression to only a select group of characters. The syntax to define a character class is

```
[chars]
```

where `chars` are characters in the class. To create a negative character class that matches any character not in the class, you use the syntax

```
[^chars]
```

Note that the negative character set uses the same ^ symbol that you used to mark the beginning of a text string. While the symbol is the same, however, the meaning is very different in this context. To explore working with a character class, you'll create character classes for vowels and consonants.

To create a character class:

1. Change the sample text to **GPS Products For Sale**.

2. Change the regular expression in the Pattern input box to **/[aeiou]/gi** and click the **Pattern Test** button.

   As shown in Figure 14-40, every vowel in the sample text string is highlighted.

Matching a character set · Figure 14-40

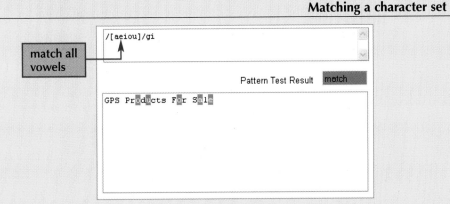

match all vowels

Next, create a character class for all of the consonants.

3. Change the regular expression in the Pattern input box to **/[^aeiou\s]/gi** and click the **Pattern Test** button again.

By including the \s symbol in your negative character class, you prevent the pattern from matching white space characters like blank spaces. Figure 14-41 shows the revised pattern match as it applies to the text string.

Figure 14-41 ▶ | **Matching a negative character set**

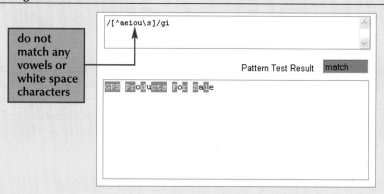

For a larger character class, you can define a range of characters by separating the starting and ending characters in the range with a dash. Since characters are arranged in sequential and alphabetical order, to create a character class for all lowercase letters you would use

`[a-z]`

For uppercase letters, you would use

`[A-Z]`

For both uppercase and lowercase letters, you would use

`[a-zA-Z]`

You can continue to add ranges of characters to a character class. The following character class matches only uppercase and lowercase letters and digits:

`[0-9a-zA-Z]`

Figure 14-42 summarizes the syntax for creating regular expression character classes.

Character classes ◄ **Figure 14-42**

Character	Description	Example
[*chars*]	Match any character in the list of characters, *chars*	/[dog]/ matches "god" and "dog"
[^*chars*]	Do not match any character in *chars*	/[^dog]/ matches neither "god" nor "dog"
[*char1-charN*]	Match characters in the range *char1* through *charN*	/[a-c]/ matches the lowercase letters a through c
[^*char1-charN*]	Do not match characters in the range *char1* through *charN*	/[^a-c]/ does not match the lowercase letters a through c
[a-z]	Match lowercase letters	/[a-z][a-z]/ matches any two consecutive lowercase letters
[A-Z]	Match uppercase letters	/[A-Z][A-Z]/ matches any two consecutive uppercase letters
[a-zA-Z]	Match letters	/[a-zA-Z][a-zA-Z]/ matches any two consecutive letters
[0-9]	Match digits	/[1][0-9]/ matches the numbers "10" through "19"
[0-9a-zA-Z]	Match digits and letters	/[0-9a-zA-Z][0-9a-zA-Z]/ matches any two consecutive letters or numbers

Repeating characters

So far our regular expression symbols have applied to single characters. Regular expressions also include symbols that indicate the number of times a particular character should be repeated. To exactly specify the number of times to repeat a character, you append the character with the symbols

$\{n\}$

where n is the number of times to repeat the character. For example, to specify that a text string contain only five digits, like a ZIP code, you could use either

/^\d\d\d\d\d$/

or the more compact form

/^\d{5}$/

If you don't know exactly how many times to repeat a character you can use the symbol * (for 0 or more repetitions), + (for 1 or more repetitions), or ? (for 0 or 1 repetition). Figure 14-43 describes these and other repetition characters supported by regular expressions.

Figure 14-43 ▶ Repetition characters

Repetition Character(s)	Description	Example
*	Repeat 0 or more times	/\s*/ matches 0 or more consecutive white space characters
?	Repeat 0 or 1 time	/colou?r/ matches "color" or "colour"
+	Repeat 1 or more times	/\s+/ matches 1 or more consecutive white space characters
{n}	Repeat exactly *n* times	/\d{9}/ matches a nine digit number
{n, }	Repeat at least *n* times	/\d{9,}/ matches a number with at least nine digits
{n,m}	Repeat at least *n* times but no more than *m* times	/\d{5,9}/ matches a number with 5 to 9 digits

Now practice using some of the repetitive symbols to create a regular expression in the demo page.

To apply a repetition pattern:

▶ **1.** Change the sample text to **To be or not to be. That is the question.**

Next you'll create a regular expression for all words that begin with the letter t followed by any number of uppercase or lowercase letters.

▶ **2.** Change the regular expression in the Pattern input box to **/\bt[a-zA-Z]*\b/gi** and click the **Pattern Test** button. As shown in Figure 14-44, words of varying length beginning with the letter t are selected.

Figure 14-44 ▶ Using repetitive characters

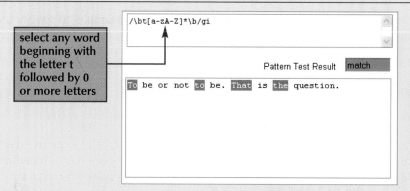

select any word beginning with the letter t followed by 0 or more letters

Next you'll revise the pattern so that it selects only three-letter words beginning with the letter t. You'll do this by limiting the number of letters after the t to two.

▶ **3.** Change the regular expression to **/\bt[a-zA-Z]{2}\b/gi** and click the **Pattern Test** button. Now only the word "the" is highlighted.

Escape sequences

Many regular expression symbols are reserved. For example, the forward slash symbol / is reserved to mark the beginning and end of a regular expression literal. The ?, +, and * symbols are used in specifying the number of times a character may be repeated. What if you need to use one of these characters in your regular expression? For example how would you create a regular expression matching the date pattern *mm/dd/yyyy* when the / symbol is already used to mark the boundaries of the regular expression?

In these cases, you use an escape sequence. An **escape sequence** is a special command inside a text string that tells the JavaScript interpreter not to interpret what follows as a character. The character that indicates an escape sequence in a regular expression is the backslash character \. You've actually been using escape sequences for several pages now—for example, you've used the characters "\d" to represent a numeric digit, while "d" simply represents the letter d. The \ character can also be applied to reserved characters to indicate their use in a regular expression. For example, the escape sequence \$ represents the $ character while the escape sequence \\ represents a single \ character. Figure 14-45 provides a list of escape sequences for other special characters.

Escape sequences   Figure 14-45

Escape Sequence	Represents	Example
\/	The / character	/\d\/\d/ matches "5/9" "3/1" but not "59" or "31"
\\	The \ character	/\d\\\d/ matches "5\9" or "3\1" but not "59" or "31"
\.	The . character	/\d\.\d\d/ matches "3.20" or "5.95" but not "320" or "595"
*	The * character	/[a-z]{4}*/ matches "help*" or "pass*"
\+	The + character	/\d\+\d/ matches "5+9" or "3+1" but not "59" or "39"
\?	The ? character	/[a-z]{4}\?/ matches "help?" or "info?"
|	The	character	/a|b/ matches "a|b"
\(\)	The (and) characters	/\(\d{3}\)/ matches "(800)" or "(555)"
\{ \}	The { and } characters	/\{[a-z]{4}\}/ matches "{pass}" or "{info}"
\^	The ^ character	/\d+\^\d/ matches "321^2" or "4^3"
\$	The $ character	/\$\d{2}\.\d{2}/ matches "$59.95" or "$19.50"
\n	A new line	/\n/ matches the occurrence of a new line in the text string
\r	A carriage return	/\r/ matches the occurrence of a carriage return in the text string
\t	A tab	/\t/ matches the occurrence of a tab in the text string

Enter an escape sequence in the demo page to create a regular expression for the date pattern.

To use an escape sequence:

1. Change the sample text to the date **5/21/2007**

   You'll create a regular expression for a text string that starts with one or two digits followed by a forward slash, then another one or two digits followed by a forward slash, followed by four digits.

2. Change the regular expression in the Pattern input box to **/^\d{1,2}\/\d{1,2}\/ \d{4}$/** and click the **Pattern Test** button. As shown in Figure 14-46 the test date you entered matches the regular expression pattern.

Figure 14-46	Using an escape sequence

match dates in the format mm/dd/yyyy

3. Test the regular expression pattern against other possible dates and verify that it matches any date in the format mm/dd/yyyy.

Note that the regular expression you used for the date format also matches some invalid date patterns such as 23/99/0007 or 0/0/0000. It does not check that the month values go from 1 to 12 or that the day values always range from 1 to 31. You can explore the date expressions available from the selection list on the demo page to learn more about writing expressions that control for these factors.

Alternate Patterns and Grouping

The final aspects of regular expression patterns that you'll examine are alternate patterns and grouping. In some regular expressions you may want to define two possible patterns for the same text string. The syntax for creating alternate patterns is to use the alternation character | with the syntax

pattern1|pattern2

where *pattern1* and *pattern2* are two distinct patterns. For example, the expression

/^\d{5}$|^$/

matches a text string that either contains only five digits or is empty. Explore how to use the alternate character in the demo page by creating a regular expression that matches the honorifics Mr., Mrs., or Miss.

To choose between alternate patterns:

1. In the regular expression demo, change the sample text to **Mr.**

2. Change the regular expression pattern to **/Mr\.|Mrs\.|Miss/** and click the **Pattern Test** button. The pattern test result shows a match.

3. Change the sample text to **Mrs.** and then to **Miss**, and verify that the text string matches the pattern in both cases.

Another useful technique in regular expressions is to group character symbols. Once you create a group, the symbols within that group can be treated as a single unit. The syntax to create a group is

`(pattern)`

where `pattern` is a regular expression pattern.

Groups are often used with the alternation character to create regular expressions that match different variations of the same text. For example, a phone number might be entered with an area code or without. The pattern for the phone number without an area code, matching such numbers as 555-1234, is

`/^\d{3}-\d{4}$/`

If an area code is included in the format 800-555-1234, the pattern is

`/^\d{3}-\d{3}-\d{4}$/`

To allow the area code to be added or not, you place it within a group and use the ? repetition character applied to the entire area code group. The regular expression is therefore:

`/^(\d{3}-)?\d{3}-\d{4}$/`

which matches either 555-1234 or 800-555-1234. Test this now in the demo page.

To create a pattern group:

1. Go back to the regular expression demo and change the text string to **555-1234**

2. Change the regular expression pattern to **/^(\d{3}-)?\d{3}-\d{4}$/** and click the **Pattern Test** button. The pattern test result shows a match (see Figure 14-47).

Creating a group | **Figure 14-47**

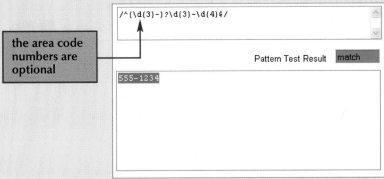

the area code numbers are optional

```
/^(\d{3}-)?\d{3}-\d{4}$/
```

Pattern Test Result match

```
555-1234
```

3. Change the phone number to **800-555-1234** and click the **Pattern Test** button again to verify that this form of the phone number also matches the regular expression.

Another benefit of grouping is that the captured groups can be referenced as distinct entities within the regular expression. This is known as creating a **back-reference**. Groups are referenced using the expression

\group

where *group* is the number of the group in the regular expression. The first group has a back-reference of \1, the second group has the back-reference \2, and so forth. For example, you could use back-referencing to create a regular expression that searches for consecutive occurrences of the same word (a common typing mistake). First you would create a regular expression to match a single word of one or more characters, placing that word within a group. The pattern would be

/(\b\w+\b)/

Next you would add a back-reference to match that group. Since you are looking for consecutive words separated by a space, you would add the space character to the pattern as well. The regular expression would be

/(\b\w+\b)\s\1/

Remember that the \1 symbol is the back-reference for the first group in the regular expression, indicating that you are looking for a repeat of the characters in the first group. Now enter this expression in the demo page to test it against consecutive occurrences of the same word.

To match multiple occurrences of the same word:

1. Go back to the regular expression demo and change the text string to **GPS-ware products for for sale**

2. Change the regular expression pattern to **/(\b\w+\b)\s\1/** and click the **Pattern Test** button. The pattern test result matches the two consecutive occurrences of the word "for" (see Figure 14-48).

Figure 14-48 | **Matching consecutive occurrences of the same word**

3. Close the demo page.

The ( ) group is only one type of group used in regular expressions. You can also create groups that do not allow for back-referencing (which reduces the process time required to run the regular expression). Figure 14-49 summarizes the character codes for grouping and performing alternate matching.

Alternation and grouping characters | Figure 14-49

Characters	Description	Example
pattern1|pattern2	Matches either pattern1 or pattern2	/color|colour/ matches either "color" or "colour"
(pattern)	Treats pattern as a single group and allows a back-reference to the captured group	/(Mr\.\s)?\w+/ matches either "Mr. Smith" or "Smith"
\n	Back-reference to group n in the regular expression	/(\s)\1/ matches consecutive occurrences of white space
(?pattern)	Treats pattern as a single group, but does not allow for back-referencing	

The regular expression object constructor

The regular expression literal that you've been using so far in this session is only one way of creating a regular expression in JavaScript. Another approach is to create a regular expression object using the following object constructor:

```
re = new RegExp(pattern, flags)
```

where re is the regular expression object, pattern is a text string of the regular expression pattern, and flags is a text string of the regular expression flags. The following two commands are equivalent as far as JavaScript is concerned:

```
var re = /GPS-ware/ig;
var re = new RegExp("GPS-ware","ig");
```

While JavaScript treats both commands the same, there are some important differences between them. For one, the regular expression literal is already compiled, which means that it is ready to perform pattern matching and other regular expression tasks. The new RegExp() object, on the other hand, must be compiled before it can be used. (You'll learn how to compile a regular expression in the next section.) The other important difference is that the new RegExp() constructor takes a text string for its parameter value. Even though they are not regular expressions, such text strings can also contain escape sequences, which may be used to insert non-textual characters like tabs or carriage returns. As a result, to avoid conflict between escape sequences designed for text strings and escape sequences designed for regular expressions, you have to insert an additional escape character \ for each regular expression escape sequence. Thus, the regular expression literal

```
/\b\w*\b\s\d{3}/
```

would appear in the new RegExp() operator as

```
new RegExp("\\b\\w*\\b\\s\\d{3}")
```

In most cases you'll use the regular expression literal form in your code. The new RegExp() operator is most often used when your script needs to retrieve the regular expression text string from another source, such as a data entry field.

Creating a Regular Expression

- The syntax to create a regular expression literal is
    ```
    re = /pattern/flags
    ```
  where *re* is the regular expression object, *pattern* is the regular expression pattern and *flags* are the flags assigned to the regular expression.
- The syntax to create a regular expression with the object constructor is
    ```
    re = new RegExp(pattern, flags)
    ```
  where *pattern* is the text string of the regular expression and *flags* is the text string of the regular expression flags.

Working with the Regular Expression Object

Now that you've looked at the syntax involved in writing a regular expression, you can use regular expressions in your JavaScript programs. As noted earlier, a regular expression is treated as an object with its own collection of properties and methods. Before implementing regular expressions for Carol's Web forms, familiarize yourself with some of the methods associated with regular expressions.

Regular Expression methods

One method associated with regular expressions is the test() method, which is used to determine whether a text string contains a substring that matches the pattern defined by a regular expression. The syntax of the test() method is

```
re.test(text)
```

where *re* is a regular expression object and *text* is the text string you want to test. The test() method returns the Boolean value true if a match is located and false otherwise. For example, the following code tests whether a given text string matches a five-digit ZIP code:

```
zipstring = "12345";
reg = /^\d{5}$/;
testvalue = reg.test(zipstring);
```

If zipstring matches the pattern of the reg regular expression, then the testvalue variable will have the Boolean value true; otherwise, it will have the value false.

Sometimes you need to know where in a text string a pattern match has been found. In such a case, you can apply the search() method, which has the syntax

```
re.search(text)
```

The search() method returns the index of the first matching substring from *text*. If no match is found, it returns the value –1, just like the indexOf() method discussed in the last session. The search() method starts with the first character in *text* and locates the first match. Unlike the indexOf() method, there is no way to start the search() method at a location other than the start of the text string.

You can also use regular expression methods that extract substrings from a text string. The match() method creates an array of substrings from a text string that match the pattern defined in a regular expression. The syntax of the match() method is

```
results = re.match(text)
```

where *results* is an array containing each matched substring. For example, the following set of commands extracts the individual words from the text string, placing each word in the words array:

```
re = /\b\w+\b/g;
words = "GPS-ware Products For Sale".split(re);
```

Note that the global flag has to be set to locate all matches in the text string. If you neglect to include the g flag, only the first match is returned. Similar to the match() method is the split() method, which splits the text string at each location where a pattern match is found. You saw how to use the split() method in the last session when it was applied to string objects. It can likewise be used with regular expressions. The following code shows how to split a text string at each word boundary followed by a white space character:

```
re = /\b\s*/g;
words = "GPS-ware Products For Sale".split(re);
```

In this example each element in the words array contains a word from the larger text string.

Besides pattern matching and extracting substrings, regular expressions can also be used to replace text. The syntax of the replace method is

```
text.replace(re,newsubstr)
```

where *text* is a text string containing text to be replaced, *re* is a regular expression defining the substring to be replaced, and *newsubstr* is the replacement substring. The following code shows how to apply the replace() method to change a text string:

```
oldtext = "<h1>GPS-ware Products</h1>";
reg = /h1/g;
newtext = oldtext.replace(reg,"h2");
```

The *newtext* variable now contains the text string "<h2>GPS-ware Products</h2>". Thus, this code replaces every occurrence of the substring "h1" with the substring "h2". A program that utilizes regular expressions can be very useful in revising HTML code. Note that if you neglect to include the "g" flag, only the first occurrence of the substring is replaced.

Working with Regular Expressions

- To test whether a text string matches a regular expression, use the method
    ```
    re.test(text)
    ```
  where *re* is the regular expression object and *text* is the text string to be tested. The test() method returns a Boolean value.
- To search a text string, use
    ```
    re.search(text)
    ```
  The search() method returns the index of the first matching substring from the text string.
- To create an array of the matching substrings from a text string, use
    ```
    results = re.match(text)
    ```
  where *results* is an array containing each matched substring.
- To split a string into substrings, use
    ```
    results = text.split(re)
    ```
  where *results* is an array containing the substrings, *text* is the original text string, and *re* is a regular expression that indicates the splitting points in the text string.
- To replace a substring with a new substring, use
    ```
    text.replace(re, newsubstr)
    ```
  where *text* is the text string containing the text to be replaced, *re* is a regular expression defining the substring to be replaced, and *newsubstr* is the replacement substring.

Figure 14-50 summarizes the methods associated with the regular expression object.

Figure 14-50 ▶ **Methods of the regular expression object**

Method	Description
re.compile(*pattern,flags*)	Compiles or recompiles a regular expression *re*, where *pattern* is the text string of new regular expression pattern and *flags* are flags applied to the *pattern*
re.exec(*text*)	Executes a search on *text* using the regular expression *re*; pattern results are returned in an array and reflected in the properties of the global RegExp object
re.match(*text*)	Performs a pattern match in *text* using the *re* regular expression; matched substrings are stored in an array
text.replace(*re, newsubstr*)	Replaces the substring defined by the regular expression *re* in the text string *text* with *newsubstr*
text.search(*re*)	Searches *text* for a substring matching the regular expression *re*; returns the index of the match, or -1 if no match is found
text.split(*re*)	Splits *text* at each point indicated by the regular expression *re*; the substrings are stored in an array
re.test(*text*)	Performs a pattern match on the text string *text* using the regular expression *re*, returning the Boolean value true if a match is found and false otherwise

Validating a ZIP code

You'll now use what you've learned of regular expressions to create a new function to validate customers' entries in the ZIP field. In the first line of the function, you'll create a regular expression that matches either a five-digit or a nine-digit ZIP code or an empty text string (since the ZIP code is not required for delivery). The regular expression is

```
/^\d{5}(-\d{4})?$|^$/
```

This regular expression matches ZIP codes in the form ddddd or ddddd-dddd, and also uses the alternation character | to allow for empty text strings. Take some time to study this regular expression so that you understand how it works. The second line of the function uses the test() method to determine whether a customer's ZIP code matches that pattern, returning the test result as a Boolean value. The complete code of the checkZip2() function is

```
function checkZip2(zip) {
   re = /^\d{5}(-\d{4})?$|^$/;
   return re.test(zip);
}
```

Compared to the checkZip() function you created in the last session, this is a more compact function that still manages to test for more variation in ZIP code patterns than the original function did. Add this function to the validation tests for Carol's delivery form now.

To create the checkZip2() function:

1. Reopen **form2.htm** in your text editor.

2. Add the following function to the embedded script in the head section of the file:

```
function checkZip2(zip) {
   re = /^\d{5}(-\d{4})?$|^$/;
   return re.test(zip);
}
```

3. Change the checkForm2() function so that it calls the **checkZip2()** function to validate the ZIP code field. Figure 14-51 shows the new and revised code in the file.

The checkZip2() function ◀ Figure 14-51

```
function checkForm2() {
   if (document.form2.fname.value.length == 0)
      {alert("You must enter a first name");
      return false;}
   else if (document.form2.lname.value.length == 0)
      {alert("You must enter a last name");
      return false;}
   else if (document.form2.street.value.length == 0)
      {alert("You must enter a street address");
      return false;}
   else if (document.form2.city.value.length == 0)
      {alert("You must enter a city name");
      return false;}
   else if (checkZip2(document.form2.zip.value) == false)
      {alert("You must enter a valid zip code");
      return false;}
   else return true;
}

function checkZip(zip) {
   if (zip.length != 5 && zip.length != 0) return false;
   else {
      validchars = "0123456789";
      for (i=0; i<5; i++) {
         zipchar=zip.charAt(i);
         if (validchars.indexOf(zipchar) == -1) return false;
      }
   }
   return true;
}

function checkZip2(zip) {
   re = /^\d{5}(-\d{4})?$|^$/;
   return re.test(zip);
}
</script>
```

4. Save your changes to **form2.htm** and close the file.

5. Reopen **form2.htm** in your Web browser. Enter some sample text in the first name, last name, street, and city fields.

6. Enter **12345-1234** in the ZIP field and click the **Next** button. Verify that your browser opens the third of Carol's Web forms, indicating that the delivery form passed the validation test.

7. Return to **form2.htm** in your Web browser and verify that the form validates only when a proper ZIP code (or no ZIP code at all) is entered in the ZIP field.

You've completed your validation checks for the delivery form. Now you'll look at the last of Carol's forms.

Validating Financial Information

The final of Carol's three forms is the payment form, in which customers enter the credit card information that indicates how they will pay for their order. Figure 14-52 shows the contents of the payment form.

Figure 14-52	The payment form

Figure 14-53 lists the object reference for each element in the form.

Figure 14-53	Objects in the payment form

Object	Reference
The American Express radio button	document.form3.ccard[0]
The Diners Club radio button	document.form3.ccard[1]
The Discover radio button	document.form3.ccard[2]
The MasterCard radio button	document.form3.ccard[3]
The Visa radio button	document.form3.ccard[4]
The credit card name field	document.form3.cname
The credit card number field	document.form3.cnumber
The credit card month selection list	document.form3.cmonth
The credit card year selection list	document.form3.cyear
The previous button	document.form3.prevb
The next button	document.form3.nextb

A user's credit card data will eventually be validated on the Web server against an online database containing valid credit card numbers and customer names; however, you can do some validation checks on the client side in order to weed out problems before they get to the server. One such validation check is to ensure that each customer selects a credit card type and enters the name and number appearing on the card. The following two functions have already been entered into the form3.htm file to perform these three validation checks:

```
function checkForm3() {
    if (selectedCard() == -1)
        {alert("You must select a credit card");
         return false;}
    else if (document.form3.cname.value.length == 0)
        {alert("You must enter the name on your credit card");
         return false;}
    else if (document.form3.cnumber.value.length == 0)
        {alert("You must enter the number on your credit card");
         return false;}
    else return true;
}
function selectedCard() {
    card=-1;
    for (i=0; i<5; i++) {
        if (document.form3.ccard[i].checked) card=i;
    }
    return card;
}
```

The first function, checkForm3(), verifies that: 1) the customer has selected a credit card, 2) the customer has entered the name on the card, and 3) the customer has entered the number on the card. While you have no way of knowing whether the name and number represent real credit card accounts, you're using the checkForm3() function to verify that each customer enters something in those fields. The checkForm3() function tests whether one of the five credit cards on the payment form has been selected by calling the selectedCard() function. The selectedCard() function goes through all of the option buttons from the ccard field and returns the index number (from 0 to 4) of the checked option button. If no option button is checked (meaning that the customer has not selected a credit card from the list), then it returns a value of −1 and the form is not validated. Verify that these functions are working correctly by attempting to submit the form without entering any of the required financial information.

To test the payment form:

1. Open **form3.htm** in your Web browser.

2. Click the **Next** button without filling in different parts of the Web form or without selecting option buttons from the form. Verify that the form is accepted by the browser only when you have entered all of the financial information.

Removing blank spaces from credit card numbers

Beyond verifying that a customer has entered something for each field, you can also check whether a user has entered a legitimate credit card number. Credit card numbers often appear on credit cards broken up by spaces in order to make it easier for cardholders to read off the card numbers. Therefore, before you examine the actual card numbers you have to remove any blank spaces that a customer may have entered into the credit card number field. You can do this by creating a regular expression that searches for any occurrence of white space in the credit card number field, and then applying the replace() method to replace each occurrence of white space with an empty text string. The regular expression to match all occurrences of white space in a text string is

```
wsre = /\s/g
```

Note that you add the "g" flag so that the regular expression searches the entire text string, instead of stopping at the first occurrence of white space. The command to remove the white space from the credit card number field is

```
cnum = document.form3.cnumber.value.replace(wsre,"");
```

Now add both of these commands to a function named checkNumber() that you'll build upon to validate your customers' credit card numbers.

To insert the checkNumber() function:

1. Open **form3.htm** in your text editor.

2. Within the embedded script element, insert the following function, as shown in Figure 14-54:

```
function checkNumber() {
    wsre = /\s/g
    cnum = document.form3.cnumber.value.replace(wsre,"");
}
```

Figure 14-54	Removing white space from the credit card numbers

```
function selectedCard() {
    card=-1;
    for (i=0; i<5; i++) {
        if (document.form3.ccard[i].checked) card=i;
    }
    return card;
}

function checkNumber() {
    wsre = /\s/g
    cnum = document.form3.cnumber.value.replace(wsre,"");
}
</script>
</head>
```

match all white space in the text string

Validating credit card number patterns

Each credit card has a certain pattern to its numbers that uniquely identifies it. GPS-ware accepts five different credit cards: American Express, Diners Club, Discover, MasterCard, and Visa. Figure 14-55 lists the number pattern for each card, along with a regular expression that matches the described pattern.

Credit Card	Number Pattern	Regular Expression
American Express	Starts with 34 or 37 followed by 13 other digits	`/^3[47]\d{13}$/`
Diners Club	Starts with 300-305 followed by 11 digits, or starts with 36 or 38 followed by 12 digits	`/^30[0-5]\d{11}$|^3[68] \d{12}$/`
Discover	Starts with 6011 followed by 12 other digits	`/^6011\d{12}$/`
MasterCard	Starts with 51, 52, 53, 54, or 55 followed by 14 other digits	`/^5[1-5]\d{14}$/`
Visa	Starts with a 4 followed by 12 or 15 other digits	`/^4(\d{12}|\d{15})$/`

To validate the credit card number entered by a customer, you can use the test() method with the regular expressions indicated in Figure 14-55. Recall from the earlier code that the selectedCard() function returns the index number of the selected option button, where 0=American Express, 1=Diners Club, 2=Discover, 3=MasterCard, and 4=Visa. The following code uses a switch statement to test each of the five card patterns based on the credit card type selected by a user in the Web form:

```
switch (selectedCard()) {
   case 0: re=/^3[47]\d{13}$/;break;
   case 1: re=/^30[0-5]\d{11}$|^3[68]\d{12}$/;break;
   case 2: re=/^6011\d{12}$/;break;
   case 3: re=/^5[1-5]\d{14}$/;break;
   case 4: re =/^4(\d{12}|\d{15})$/;break;
}
pattern = re.test(cnum);
return pattern;
```

Based on the value returned by the selectedCard() function, the switch statement applies the appropriate regular expression pattern to the card number. The results of the pattern match are placed in the pattern variable. A value of true indicates that a customer's credit card number matches the selected pattern, and a value of false means that the number does not match and is thus invalid. Add this switch statement to the checkNumber() function.

To add the credit card number patterns:

1. Add the following commands to the checkNumber() function (see Figure 14-56):

```
switch (selectedCard()) {
   case 0: re=/^3[47]\d{13}$/;break;
   case 1: re=/^30[0-5]\d{11}$|^3[68]\d{12}$/;break;
   case 2: re=/^6011\d{12}$/;break;
   case 3: re=/^5[1-5]\d{14}$/;break;
   case 4: re =/^4(\d{12}|\d{15})$/;break;}
pattern = re.test(cnum);
return pattern;
```

Figure 14-56 | **Checking credit card number patterns**

```
function checkNumber() {
    wsre = /\s/g
    cnum = document.form3.cnumber.value.replace(wsre,"");

    switch (selectedCard()) {
        case 0: re =/^3[47]\d{13}$/; break;
        case 1: re =/^30[0-5]\d{11}$|^3[68]\d{12}$/; break;
        case 2: re =/^6011\d{12}$/; break;
        case 3: re =/^5[1-5]\d{14}$/; break;
        case 4: re =/^4(\d{12}|\d{15})$/; break;
    }
    pattern = re.test(cnum);
    return pattern;
}
```

> **2.** Save your changes to the file.

Next, call this function from the checkForm3() function to add it to the list of validation checks already present in the payment form.

To check for valid credit card number patterns:

> **1.** Add the following command to the checkForm3() function as shown in Figure 14-57:

```
else if (checkNumber() == false)
    {alert("Your card number is not valid");
     return false;}
```

Figure 14-57 | **The final checkForm3() function**

```
function checkForm3() {
    if (selectedCard() == -1)
        {alert("You must select a credit card");
         return false;}
    else if (document.form3.cname.value.length == 0)
        {alert("You must enter the name on your credit card");
         return false;}
    else if (document.form3.cnumber.value.length == 0)
        {alert("You must enter the number on your credit card");
         return false;}
    else if (checkNumber() == false)
        {alert("Your card number is not valid");
         return false;}
    else return true;
}
```

> **2.** Save your changes to the file.

> **3.** Reopen **form3.htm** in your Web browser.

Now test the form to confirm that the browser accepts the completed form only when a valid credit card number is entered.

> **4.** Enter sample text in the name field so that the form is not invalidated for lack of a credit card name.

> **5.** Click each of the credit card option buttons and enter the corresponding sample credit card numbers displayed in Figure 14-58. Verify that the form accepts the valid numbers and rejects the invalid ones.

Credit Card	Valid	Invalid
American Express	34 12345 67890 123	35 12345 67890 123
Diners Club	303 12345 67890 1	310 12345 67890 1
Discover	6011 12345 67890 12	6012 12345 67890 12
MasterCard	51 12345 67890 1234	59 12345 67890 1234
Visa	4 12345 67890 12345	8 12345 67890 12345

6. Continue testing other combinations of credit card numbers to verify that only numbers that match the card patterns described in Figure 14-55 are accepted by the browser.

The Luhn Formula

There is one last test you can do on the client side to weed out mistakes that a customer might make in entering his or her credit card number. All credit card numbers must satisfy the **Luhn Formula**, or **Mod10 algorithm**, which is a formula developed by a group of mathematicians in the 1960s to provide a quick validation check on an account number by adding up the digits in the number. Almost all institutions that employ unique account or identification numbers, including credit card companies, use numbers that satisfy the Luhn Formula. The following steps are used to determine whether a particular number satisfies the Luhn Formula (see Figure 14-59):

1. Starting from the second to the last digit in the account number, separate every other digit into two groups, moving to the left.
2. Double the value of each digit in the first group (the group containing the first digit you selected).
3. Calculate the sum of the digits (not the numbers) in both groups.
4. Add the values of the two sums together.
5. If the total sum is evenly divisible by 10, then the number satisfies the Luhn Formula.

Figure 14-59 ▶ **The Luhn Formula**

A function to calculate the Luhn Formula has been created for you and is stored in the functions.js file. The code for the luhn() function is

```
function luhn(num) {
   var luhnTotal=0;
   for (i=num.length-1; i>=0; i--) {
      luhnTotal += parseInt(num.charAt(i));
      i--;
      num2 = new String(num.charAt(i)*2);
      for (j=0; j < num2.length; j++) {
         luhnTotal += parseInt(num2.charAt(j));
      }
   }
   return (luhnTotal % 10 == 0);
}
```

The luhn() function has a single parameter, num, which contains the text string of the account number to be validated. It assumes that all white space characters have already been removed from the text string. The function loops through each digit in the text string, adding up the digit sums. Each time it encounters a digit that should be doubled, it stores the doubled digit in a string object named num2, which is then summed before continuing through the larger number string. A running total of the digit sum is stored in the luhnTotal variable. After the last digit has been added, the function then uses the % operator to test whether dividing luhnTotal by 10 results in a remainder of 0. If it does, a Boolean value of true is returned by the function; otherwise, it returns a Boolean value of false. Take some time to study the code in this function. While this function may seem daunting at first, it is composed totally of string object methods and properties you learned earlier in this tutorial.

You can call the luhn() function from the checkNumber() function you just created. The checkNumber() function will then have two tests: first it will check whether the selected card number matches the number pattern of the credit agency, and then it will check whether the card number fulfills the criterion of the Luhn Formula. Add the test for the Luhn Formula to your code now.

To add the test for the Luhn Formula:

1. Return to **form3.htm** in your text editor.

2. Go to the checkNumber() function and insert the following line before the "return pattern" statement:

   ```
   luhnCheck = luhn(cnum);
   ```

3. Change the statement "return pattern;" to **return (pattern && luhnCheck);**. Figure 14-60 shows the revised code of the checkNumber() function.

The final checkNumber() function ◄ **Figure 14-60**

```
function checkNumber() {
    wsre = /\s/g
    cnum = document.form3.cnumber.value.replace(wsre,"");

    switch (selectedCard()) {
        case 0: re =/^3[47]\d{13}$/;break;
        case 1: re =/^30[0-5]\d{11}$|^3[68]\d{12}$/;break;
        case 2: re =/^6011\d{12}$/;break;
        case 3: re =/^5[1-5]\d{14}$/;break;
        case 4: re =/^4(\d{12}|\d{15})$/;break;
    }
    pattern = re.test(cnum);
    luhnCheck = luhn(cnum);
    return (pattern && luhnCheck);
}
```

Note that the checkNumber() function returns a value of true only if both the pattern and the luhnCheck variables are true. In other words, the credit card number must both match the specified pattern and fulfill the Luhn Formula.

4. Close the file, saving your changes.

5. Reopen **form3.htm** in your Web browser.

6. Click **American Express** from the list of credit cards. Enter a sample name in the Name field.

7. Enter **34 12345 67890 123** in the Number field and click the **Next** button. Your browser should alert you that the number is not valid.

8. Change the credit card number to **34 12345 67890 127** and click the **Next** button. This number is accepted and a Web page opens indicating that the order has been submitted successfully.

At this point the customer's order could be sent to the Web server for further processing and validation checks. Obviously the server would have to consult secure databases to verify that the credit card information represented a real account. By adding these validation checks on the client side, however, your program can weed out some errors that the company's server would otherwise have to deal with.

Passing Data from a Form

To simplify form validation for the GPS-ware Web site, Carol broke up the data that she wanted collected into three separate forms. When customer input is spread out over several forms, you usually need some way of passing collected data along as customers move from one form to another. One way of doing this in JavaScript is by appending a data string to a URL.

Appending data to a URL

Text strings can be appended to any URL by adding the ? character to the Web address followed by the text string. For example, the link

```
<a href="form2.htm?GPS-ware">Go to form2</a>
```

opens the form2.htm file, passing along the substring "GPS-ware" as part of the URL. When a user clicks the above linked text, form2.htm opens in the Web browser displaying the URL

```
http://server/path/form2.htm?GPS-ware
```

where *server* and *path* are the server and path names in the Web address. How do you access the data appended to the URL from within the form2.htm page? Recall that the URL of the current Web page is stored in the location object. One property of the location object is the location.search property, which contains the text of any data appended to the URL, including the ? character. Thus, running the following command from within the form2.htm file:

```
document.write("Products from " + location.search);
```

causes the following text to be written to the document window:

```
Products from ?GPS-ware
```

You can remove the ? character by running the slice() or substring() methods (see Figure 14-29), extracting all of the characters from the second character forward. The expression to display only the data part of the URL is therefore

```
document.write("Products from " + location.search.slice(1));
```

which writes the following text to the document window:

```
Products from GPS-ware
```

There are several limitations to the technique of appending data to a URL. For one, URLs are limited in their length. Internet Explorer, for example, limits the length of a URL text string to 2083 characters. Thus, you cannot append huge amounts of data to a URL. In addition, characters other than letters and numbers cannot be passed in the URL without modification. Because URLs cannot contain blank spaces, for example, a blank space is converted to the character code %20. Thus, the link

```
<a href="form2.htm?GPS-ware Products">Go to form2</a>
```

would result in the URL

```
http://server/path/form2.htm?GPS-ware%20Products
```

Character codes like %20 can be removed from a text string and replaced with the characters they represent (such as blank spaces) by running the unescape() function on the text string. The syntax of the unescape() function is

```
unescape(text)
```

where *text* is the text string containing the character codes. Thus, the command

```
unescape("GPS-ware%20Products")
```

returns the text string

```
GPS-ware Products
```

JavaScript also supports the escape() function, which inserts character codes into text strings. You use this function when you need to convert a text string into a format that can be easily passed as a single text string with no white space or other unprintable characters.

Appending and retrieving form data

You can use the technique of appending data to the URL with Web forms, too. You do this by setting a form's action attribute to the URL of the page to which you want to pass the data, and setting the method of the form to "get". For example, the form element

```
<form action="form2.htm" method="get">
```

causes the form2.htm file to be opened when the form is submitted. When the browser opens the form2.htm file, it will have the URL

```
http://server/path/form2.htm?field1=value1&field2=value2& ...
```

where *field1*, *field2*, etc. are the names of the fields in the Web form and *value1*, *value2*, etc. are the corresponding values in each of those fields. For example, if your Web form contains fields named "firstname" and "lastname" with values of "Carol" and "Campbell", then the following URL is applied to the form2.htm file when it appears in the browser:

```
http://server/path/form2.htm?firstname=Carol&lastname=Campbell
```

Because URLs cannot contain blank spaces, any blank space in a field value is converted to a + symbol. If your Web form contains a single field named "username" with a field value of "Carol Campbell", the URL for the submitted form is

```
http://server/path/form2.htm?username=Carol+Campbell
```

As before, you can use the location.search property with the slice() method to extract only the part of the URL containing the field names and field values. For example, the expression

```
location.search.slice(1)
```

returns the text string

```
field1=value1&field2=value2& ...
```

Once you have the field names and values in this format, you can extract the form information using what you've learned about string methods and regular expressions. The four steps to extracting form data from a URL are therefore:

1. Use the location.search property and the slice() method to extract only the text string of the field names and values.
2. Use the unescape() function to remove any escape sequence characters from the text string.
3. Convert each occurrence of the + symbol to a blank space.
4. Split the text string at every occurrence of a = or & character, storing the substrings into an array.

The following code shows how these steps would appear in a function:

```
function retrieveData() {
    searchString = location.search.slice(1);
    searchString = unescape(searchString);
    formString = searchString.replace(/\+/g, " ");
    data = formString.split(/[&=]/g);
}
```

Note that you use the regular expression /\+/g to match all occurrences of the + symbol in a text string, and the regular expression /[&=]/g to match all occurrences of the & or = characters. After running this function, the data array contains a separate item for each field name and field value. Thus, data[0] stores the name of the first field, data[1] stores the value of the first field, and so forth.

To see how transferring data from one form to another works in practice, a demo page has been created for you. Open this page now.

To view the demo form:

1. Open **demo_form1.htm** from the tutorial.14/tutorial folder in your Web browser.

2. Enter **your name**, **your age**, and **your city** in the appropriate fields in the form (see Figure 14-61).

Figure 14-61 | **Entering form data**

P a s s i n g   F o r m   D a t a

This demo page displays how to pass data from one form to another by appending the data to a URL. Fill out the form below and click the **Submit** button to open the second form in the demo. The values you enter in the form will be appended to the URL of the second form. A script running in the second form will extract the field names and values and display them in the page.

1) Enter your name   Carol Campbell
2) Enter your age   43
3) Enter your city of residence   Mount Vernon
Submit

3. Click the **Submit** button.

As shown in Figure 14-62, the values you entered in the first form are retrieved from the URL and displayed in the second form.

R e c e i v i n g   F o r m   D a t a

This demo page retrieves the data that you entered in the demo_form1.htm file. Form names and values are extracted from the URL for this page using the location.search property and the slice() method. The + symbol in the field values (used to represent a blank space) is replaced with a blank space. Finally, the text string is split into individual field names and values using the split() method. The following function is run when the page is loaded by the browser:

```
function retrieveData() {
    searchString = location.search.slice(1);
    searchString = unescape(searchString);
    formString = searchString.replace(/\+/g, " ");
    data = formString.split(/[&=]/g);
    document.dform2.name.value=data[1];
    document.dform2.age.value=data[3];
    document.dform2.city.value=data[5];
}
```

1) Your name is   Carol Campbell

2) Your age is   43

3) Your city of residence is   Mount Vernon

4. Close your Web browser.

Note that this script works only when all form fields are filled out. An empty field value causes the script to fail. At this point, you won't add the ability to pass form data to Carol's Web form. However, she will probably want you to add this in the future.

You've completed your work on Carol's order forms. She'll take some time to study your work and get back to you with future projects.

Tips for Validating Forms

- Use selection lists, option buttons, and check boxes to limit the ability of users to enter erroneous data.
- Indicate to users which fields are required, and if possible, indicate the format that each field value should be entered in.
- Use the maxlength attribute of the input element to limit the length of text entered into a form field.
- Format financial values using the toFixed() and toPrecision() methods. For older browsers use custom scripts to format financial data.
- Apply client-side validation checks to lessen the load of the server.
- Use regular expressions to verify that field values correspond to a required pattern.
- Use the length property of the string object to test whether the user has entered a value in a required field.
- Test credit card numbers to verify that they match the patterns specified by credit card companies.
- Test credit card numbers to verify that they fulfill the Luhn Formula.

Session 14.3 Quick Check

1. What is the regular expression to match every occurrence of the substring "GPS" in a text string, regardless of case?
2. What is the regular expression to match the first occurrence of the word "products"?
3. A social security number consists of nine digits. Write a regular expression to match this pattern.
4. Social security numbers can be entered either as ddddddddd or ddd-dd-dddd. Write a regular expression to match either pattern.
5. Write a regular expression that matches any of the substrings "street", "avenue", or "lane". Make the match case insensitive and match every occurrence of the substring in the text string.
6. What JavaScript command would you enter to test whether the text string "username" matches the pattern specified in the regular expression object reuser?
7. What JavaScript command would you enter to split the text string "date" at every occurrence of the / character?
8. What is the Luhn Formula?
9. What object property would you use to extract any data appended to the URL of the current Web document?

Tutorial Summary

This tutorial explored how JavaScript can be used to validate Web forms. In the first session you learned how to reference different elements in a Web form, including input boxes, selection lists, and option button groups. You saw how to extract values from form fields and use them to create calculated fields. You also learned about some of the difficulties in displaying numeric values in a Web form and learned some of the techniques to create nicely formatted output. The second session introduced the concept of form validation: comparing the benefits and costs of client-side and server-side validation. You learned how to validate a form before allowing it to be processed, and you also learned about the properties and methods associated with string objects. The third session introduced the language of regular expressions. You learned how to create a regular expression to match a wide variety of patterns, and you learned about the properties and methods associated with regular expression objects. In the third session you employed regular expressions to validate both ZIP code and credit card data. You also learned about the Luhn Formula and saw how it could be used to validate credit card numbers before they're submitted to a Web server. The third session concluded with a discussion of passing data from one Web page to another, with a special emphasis on passing field names and values from one Web form to another.

Key Terms

back-reference
character class
client-side validation
delimiter
escape sequence
form validation

Luhn Formula
Mod10 algorithm
pattern matching
regular expression
regular expression literal
server-side validation

string object
substring
this keyword
word character

Practice

Practice the skills you learned in the tutorial using the same case scenario.

Review Assignments

Data files needed for this Review Assignment: border.jpg, done.htm, functions.js, gps. css, gpsware.jpg, ordertxt.htm

After reviewing the first order form, Carol has a few changes she wants you to make. Rather than displaying the GPS-ware products in a selection list, Carol would like the product names to appear as separate fields. This allows customers to purchase more than one product without having to open a second form. Also, instead of displaying the quantity to order in a selection list, Carol wants the quantity value placed in an input field, so that customers can specify any quantity in their order. Figure 14-63 shows a preview of the new order form.

Figure 14-63

Carol wants the new form to include the following features:

- When a customer opens the form, the current date should appear in the date field.
- When a customer enters a new quantity in the Quantity column, the cost of the order should be automatically updated.
- Customers should be prevented from entering anything other than digits in the Quantity column. If a value other than a digit is entered, the customer should be notified of the error and the quantity value that was incorrectly entered should be reset to 0.
- When a customer selects a shipping option, the cost of the order should automatically be updated to reflect the price of shipping.
- The form should not be submitted unless a shipping option has been selected.

To complete this Web form:

1. Use your text editor to open the **ordertxt.htm** file from the tutorial.14/review folder. Enter *your name* and *the date* in the comment section and save the file as **order. htm**. Examine the contents of the file to become familiar with the order form and its elements.

2. The external script file functions.js contains a function named todayTxt() that returns the current date in the format *mm/dd/yyyy*. A link to the file has already been placed in the order.htm file. Below the script element for this external script, insert an embedded script element.

3. In the embedded script add the function setDate(). The purpose of this function is to display the current date in the date field. There are no parameters to the function. Add the following commands to the function:

   a. Change the value of the date field to the value returned by the todayTxt() function.

   b. Move the focus to the qty1 field.

   c. Use the select() method to select the contents of the qty1 field.

4. Below the setDate() function insert the productCosts() function. The purpose of the productCosts() function is to return the sum of the total costs of the six GPS-ware products in the order form. The costs of items are stored in input fields named cost1 through cost6. Have the function do the following:

   a. Create a variable named pc1 that is equal to the value of the cost1 field. Use the parseFloat() function to convert the field's value from a text string to a number.

   b. Use the same process to create variables pc2 through pc6, which are equal to the numeric values of the cost2 through cost6 fields.

   c. Return the sum of the pc1 through pc6 variables.

5. Create a function named shipExpense(). The purpose of the shipExpense() function is to return the cost of the selected shipping option. The shipping options are stored within a selection list named shipping. Have the function do the following:

   a. Create a variable named sindex equal to the selected index from the shipping selection list.

   b. Return the numeric value of the option from the shipping selection list whose index is equal to the sindex variable. Be sure to use the parseFloat() function to convert the option value from a text string to a number.

6. Create a function named calcTotal(). The purpose of the calcTotal() function is to display the cost of the sales tax and also the total cost of the order. Add the following commands to the function:

   a. Create a variable named ordercost equal to the value returned by the product-Costs() function. Create a variable named ordertax equal to 5% of the ordercost variable. Create a variable named ordership equal to the value returned by the shipExpense() function. Finally, create a variable named ordertotal equal to the sum of the ordercost, ordertax, and ordership variables.

   b. Store the value of the ordertax variable in the tax field. Display the value rounded to two decimal places. (*Hint*: Use the toFixed() method [or if you are using an older browser, the toFixed2() function] found in the function.js file).

   c. Store the value of the ordertotal variable in the total field. Also display the value rounded to two decimal places.

7. Create a function named calcShipping(). The purpose of the function is to display the cost of the selected shipping option and to update the total order costs. Add the following commands to the function:

   a. Store the value returned by the shipExpense() function in the shipcost field.

   b. Run the calcTotal() function.

8. Create a function named calcCost(). The purpose of the calcCost() function is to display the cost of the quantity of items ordered by a customer and to update the total cost of the order. This function will also test whether a customer has correctly entered an integer in one of the quantity fields. The calcCost() function has a single parameter named item. The item parameter will store an integer from 1 to 6, representing one of the six items sold by GPS-ware. The purpose of the item parameter is to indicate which item the customer has ordered. Note that the price of each item is stored in the price*item* field where *item* is the item number. The cost of each item is stored in the cost*item* field. And the quantity ordered by each item is stored in the qty*item* field. To complete the calcCost() function, add the following commands:

   a. Create a variable named price which references the price*item* field where *item* is the value of the item parameter. (*Hint:* Use the document.orders.elements collection along with the field's name to reference the price*item* field.)

   b. Create a variable named qty which references the qty*item* field.

   c. Create a variable named cost which references the cost*item* field.

   d. Create a regular expression object named reqty for a text string containing 1 or more digits and no other characters.

   e. Still within the colcCost() fucntion, test whether the value of the qty object matches the pattern defined by the reqty regular expression. If the pattern matches, then: 1) Set the value of the cost object equal to the value of the price object multiplied by the value of the qty object. Display the value of the cost object to two decimal places; 2) Run the calcTotal() function. If the pattern does not match (meaning that the customer has not entered a quantity value in integers), then: 1) Display the alert message "Please enter a digit greater than or equal to 0"; 2) Set the value of the qty object to 0; 3) Set the focus back to the qty object and use the select() method to select that object's value; 4) Rerun the calcCost() function using item as the parameter value.

9. Create a function named validateForm(). The purpose of this function is to ensure that the form has been filled out correctly before it is submitted. Add the following commands to the function:

   a. Test whether the selected index in the shipping field is equal to 0. If it is (meaning that no shipping method has been chosen by the customer), then: 1) Display the alert message "You must select a shipping option"; 2) Return the value false.

   b. Otherwise return the value true.

10. Add an event handler to the form element to run the validateForm() function whenever the form is submitted.

11. Add an event handler to the form element that reloads the Web page in response to the reset event.

12. Locate the input element for the qty1 field. Add an event handler to this element that runs the calcCost() function in response to the blur event. Use 1 as the value for the item parameter.

13. In the same fashion, run the calcCost() function in response to the blur event for the qty2 through qty6 input fields. Set the item parameter's value equal to the item number of each field.

14. Locate the shipping selection list. Add an event handler to the select element that runs the calcShipping() function whenever the value of the selected item in the list changes. (*Hint:* Use the onchange event handler.)

15. Close **order.htm**, saving your changes. Open the file in your Web browser and verify that it correctly updates the total cost of the order as you change the values in the quantity column. Also verify that the form will not accept any quantity values other than integers. Check that the cost of shipping changes to reflect the shipping method selected by the customer and that the form cannot be submitted unless a shipping method has been selected. Verify that clicking the Reset button reloads the Web page.

16. Submit the completed Web site to your instructor.

Apply

Use the skills you learned to create a select and go navigation list

Case Problem 1

Data files needed for this Case Problem: mpl.jpg, mplstyles.css, mpltxt.htm

The Monroe Public Library   Denise Kruschev works at the Monroe Public Library on the library's Web site. One of her jobs is to add content to the site that will be of interest to the library's patrons. Denise's latest assignment is to create a Web page containing links to hundreds of government Web sites. She is aware that a long list of links will fill up the page, making the page difficult to use. Instead, Denise wants to use "select and go navigation," in which the links are placed within a selection list. When a user selects a link from the list, the linked page should open automatically. Denise has set up the selection lists, but she needs your help in writing the JavaScript program. Figure 14-64 shows a preview of the Web page.

Figure 14-64

To create the select and go navigation list:

1. Open the **mpltxt.htm** file from the tutorial.14/case1 folder in your text editor. Enter *your name* and *the date* in the comment section and save the file as **mpl.htm**.

2. Insert an embedded script element in the head section of the document.

Explore

3. Each option in the selection matches the URL of a government Web site. Create a function named selectLink() whose purpose is to open the Web site specified by the option value. The selectLink() function has a single parameter named siteList which references a selection list in the Web page. Add the following commands to the function:
   a. Create a variable named sindex equal to the index number of the selected option in siteList.
   b. Use the location.href property to open the Web site indicated in the value property of the selected option in siteList.

4. Locate the select element for the first selection list. Add an event handler to run the selectLink() function whenever the selected option in the list changes. Use the this keyword as the object specified in the siteList parameter.

5. Repeat step 4 for the three remaining selection lists.

6. Save your changes to the file and then open **mpl.htm** in your Web browser. Verify that each linked Web site that you select from the selection list opens in your Web browser.

7. Submit your completed Web site to your instructor.

Apply

Use the skills you learned to create an online travel expense report

Case Problem 2

Data files needed for this Case Problem: back.jpg, done.htm, exp.css, exptxt.htm, functions.js, links.jpg, logo.jpg

DeLong Enterprises   Kay Ramirez is the payroll manager for DeLong Enterprises, a manufacturer of computer components. The company has been busy putting corporate information up on the company's intranet. Kay is heading a project to put all of the payroll-related forms and reports online. She has come to you for help in writing a program for the online travel expense form. The travel expense report form requires employees to itemize their various travel expenses for corporate trips. Kay would like scripts added to the form to ensure that all of the required data is entered in the correct format. If a required data field is left blank or if data is entered in an improper format, Kay would like the program to highlight the field in yellow and refuse submission of the form to the corporate Web server. Kay wants the form to support the following features:

- An employee must enter his or her last name, first name, social security number, an address for the reimbursement check, and a summary of the trip.

- The employee must enter the account ID number in the format ACTdddddd, the department ID number in the format DEPTdddddd, and the project ID number in the format PROJdddddd.

- For each day in which the employee has recorded an expense, the travel date must be entered.

- When the employee enters a travel, lodging, or meal expense, the subtotal of expenses for that day and the total cost of the trip should be automatically updated.

- Travel expenses must be entered as digits (either with or without the two-digit decimal place) and displayed to two digits.

A preview of the completed form (highlighting a few erroneous entries) is displayed in Figure 14-65.

Figure 14-65

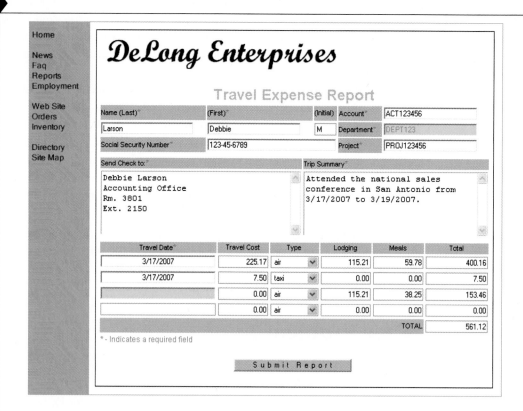

To complete this assignment:

1. Use your text editor to open the **exptxt.htm** file from the tutorial.14/case2 folder. Enter *your name* and *the date* in the comment section and save the file as **exp.htm**. Take some time to examine the contents of the file. Pay close attention to the field names and the organization of the form.

2. In the head section of the file, create an embedded script element and insert a function named testLength(). The purpose of the testLength() function is to test whether the user has entered any text in a required field. If no text has been entered, the function should highlight the field and return the value false. If any text has been entered, the function should remove any highlighting and return the value true. The function has a single parameter named "field" that represents the field object to be tested. To complete the function:

   a. Insert conditional expression that tests whether the length of the field value is equal to 0.

   b. If the length is equal to 0, then: 1) Change the background color of the field object to yellow and 2) return the Boolean value false.

   c. Otherwise: 1) Change the background color of the field object to white and 2) return the Boolean value true.

3. Create a function named testPattern(). The purpose of this function is to compare the value of a field against a regular expression pattern. If the field's value does not match the regular expression, the function should highlight the field on the form and return the Boolean value false. If the field's value does match the regular expression, the function should remove any highlighting and return the Boolean value true. The function has two parameters: the field parameter representing the field object to be tested and reg, a regular expression literal containing the pattern used for the testing. To complete the testPattern() function:

   a. Insert a conditional expression that employs the test() method to test whether the value of the field object matches the regular expression contained in the reg parameter.

   b. If the test() method returns the value false, then: 1) Change the background color of the field object to yellow; 2) Change the color of the field object to red; and 3) return the Boolean value false.

   c. Otherwise: 1) Change the background color of the field object to white; 2) Change the color of the field object to black; and 3) return the Boolean value true.

4. Create a function named testDates(). The purpose of this function is to check whether a travel date has been entered for a day in which the employee has recorded an expense. The function has no parameters. Add the following commands to the function:

   a. Create a variable named dateExists. The purpose of this function is to record whether the employee recorded a traveling expense without entering the date. Set the initial value of this variable to true.

   b. Create a For loop that loops through integer values from 1 to 4. The purpose of this loop is to examine each of the four rows in the travel expense table. If the subtotal value in the row is greater than 0, there should be a date entered in the corresponding date field. The subtotal fields in the table are named sub1 through sub4. The date fields in the table are named date1 through date4.

   c. Within the For loop, insert a conditional statement that tests whether the value of sub$i$ is not equal to "0.00", where i is the value of the counter in the For loop. (*Hint*: Use the object reference document.expform.elements["sub"+i].value) where i is the counter in the For loop.)

   d. If sub$i$ is not equal to "0.00", (indicating that an expense has been entered in that row of the travel expense table), do the following: 1) Call the testLength() function using the date$i$ field as the parameter; 2) Store the value returned by the testLength() function in a variable named rowDateExists; and 3) If the value of the rowDateExists variable is false, set the value of the dateExists value to false.

   e. After the For loop, return the value of the dateExists variable.

5. Create a function named validateForm(). The purpose of this function is to validate the form before it can be submitted to the server by calling the testPattern(), testLength(), and testDates() functions you just created. The function has no parameters. Add the following commands to the function:

   a. Create a variable named valid. The purpose of this variable is to record whether the form is valid or not. Set the initial value of the valid variable to true.

   b. Call the testLength() function with the lname field object as the parameter. (*Hint*: Use the object reference document.expform.lname.) If the value returned by the testLength() function is false, set the value of the valid variable to false. Repeat this step for the fname, address, and summary fields.

   c. Call the testPattern() function with the account field object for the field parameter. For the reg parameter insert a regular expression literal that matches a text string containing only the text "ACT" followed by 6 digits. If the value returned by the testPattern() function is false, set the value of the valid variable to false.

   d. Call the testPattern() function with the department field for the field parameter. The reg parameter should contain a regular expression literal for a text string containing only the characters "DEPT" followed by six digits. If the value of the testPattern() function is false, set the value of the valid variable to false.

   e. Repeat the previous step for the project field, using a regular expression that matches a text string containing only the characters "PROJ" followed by six digits.

   f. Call the testPattern() function for the ssn field (containing the social security number of the employee). The regular expression should match either a nine-digit number or a text string in the form ddd-dd-dddd. If the testPattern() function returns the value false, set the value of the valid variable to false.

   g. Call the testDates() function. If the function returns the value false, set the value of the valid variable to false.

   h. Insert a conditional statement that tests whether the value of the valid variable is false. If it is false then: 1) Display the following alert message: "Please fill out all required fields in the proper format."

   i. Return the value of the valid variable.

6. Locate the form element and add an event handler to run and return the value of the validateForm() function whenever the form is submitted.

7. Go back to the embedded script element and add a function named calcRow(). The purpose of this function is to return the subtotal of the expenses within a single row in the travel expense table. The function has a single parameter named row, which represents the number of the table row (from 1 to 4) to calculate from. Add the following commands to the function:

   a. Create a variable named travel equal to the numeric value of the travel*row* field, where *row* is the value of the row parameter. (*Hint*: Use the object reference document.expform.elements["travel"+row].value.) Be sure to use the parseFloat() function to convert the field value to a number. In the same fashion, create a variable named lodge equal to the numeric value of the lodge*row* field and a variable named meal equal to the numeric value of the meal*row* field.

   b. Return the sum of the travel, lodge, and row variables.

8. Create a function named calcTotal(). The purpose of this function is to return the total of all expenses in the travel expense table by calling the calcRow() function for each row in the table. The function has no parameters. Add the following commands to the function:

   a. Create a variable named totalexp and set its initial value to 0.

   b. Insert a For loop with a counter that runs from 1 to 4.

   c. Within the For loop increase the value of the totalexp variable by the value returned by the calcRow() function using the value of the counter as the value of the row parameter.

   d. Return the value of the totalexp variable.

Explore

9. Create a function named update(). The purpose of this function is to update the expense values displayed in the table and to verify that the employee has entered a valid expense amount. The function will be called whenever the employee exits from one of the 12 expense fields in the table. The function has a single parameter named expense that represents the field object that called the function. Add the following commands to the function:

   a. Create a variable named numRegExp that contains the regular expression literal /^\d*(\.\d{0,2})?$/. This pattern matches any text string that only contains a number with or without two decimal place accuracy.

   b. Insert a conditional statement that tests whether value property of the expense parameter matches the numRegExp pattern.

   c. If the condition is met (meaning that the employee has entered a valid expense amount), then run the following commands: 1) Display the value property of the expense parameter to decimal places (*Hint*: Use the toFixed() method; if your browser does not support this method, use the toFixed2() function from the functions.js file.) 2) Insert a For loop with a counter that runs from 1 to 4. Within the For loop set the value of the sub*i* field to the value returned by the calcRow() function, where *i* is the value of the For loop counter. Format the value to appear to two decimal places; and 3) Set the value of the total field equal to the value returned by the calcTotal() function. Display the total field value to two decimal places.

   d. If the condition is not met (meaning that the user has entered an invalid number), then: 1) Display the alert message "Invalid currency value"; 2) Change the value property of the expense parameter to "0.00"; and 3) Return the focus to the expense object.

10. Locate the HTML tag for the travel1 input field. Add an event handler that runs the update() function in response to the blur event. Use the this keyword for the expense object parameter. Add the same event handler to the travel2 through travel4 fields, the lodge1 through lodge4 fields, and the meal1 through meal4 fields.

11. Save your changes to the file. Open **exp.htm** in your Web browser. Test the operation of the travel expense table, verifying that it automatically updates the travel expenses as you add new values to the table.

12. Test the form validation commands by attempting to submit the form under the following conditions: 1) Without all of the required fields filled out; 2) With invalid entries for the account, department, project, and social security number fields; and 3) With travel expenses entered without corresponding dates in the travel expense table. The form should highlight the errors and alert you of the mistake.

13. Submit your completed Web site to your instructor.

Challenge

Case Problem 3

Explore how to pass data from a Web form

Data files needed for this Case Problem: back.jpg, conf.css, conftxt.htm, edge.jpg, links. jpg, logo.jpg, summary.css, sumtxt.htm

The CGIP Conference   Rajiv Rammohan is a Web site consultant for the annual conference of Computer Graphics and Image Processing. This year the conference will be putting all of its registration forms and documents online. Rajiv is working on the form in which participants will enter their registration information. Rajiv wants the form to have the following features:

- The participant must enter his or her first and last name, address, e-mail address, and phone number.
- Phone numbers must follow the pattern ddd-ddd-dddd.

- The form should calculate the total registration fee. The fee is equal to $145 plus $30 for every person attending the conference banquet. ACGIP members receive a $25 discount on the conference fee.

When a successful form is submitted, Rajiv wants the browser to display a page summarizing all of the registration information and choices made by the participant. Figure 14-66 shows a preview of both the registration form and the summary page.

Figure 14-66

 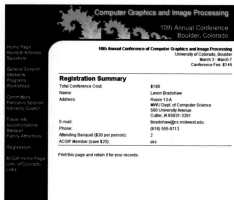

To complete this assignment:

1. Use your text editor to open the **conftxt.htm** and **sumtxt.htm** files from the tutorial. 14/case3 folder. Enter *your name* and *the date* in the comment section of each, and save the files as **conf.htm** and **summary.htm** respectively.

2. Go to the **conf.htm** file in your text editor. Examine the contents of the file and the Web form. Note that the form has a hidden field named total. In this field you'll store the total cost of the registration.

3. Insert a script element in the document head and create a function named calcCost(). The purpose of this function is to calculate the total registration fee. There are no parameters for this function. Add the following commands to the function:

   a. Create a variable named cost and set its initial value to 145, the default cost of the conference.

   b. Retrieve the value of the selected index property from the guests selection list. This value indicates the number of guests invited to the banquet. Multiply the selected index by 30 and add this to the cost variable.

   c. If the first member radio button is checked, subtract 25 from the value of the cost variable.

   d. Set the value of the total field equal to the value of the cost variable.

4. Create a function named testLength(). The purpose of the function is to test whether the user has entered any text in a required field. The function has a single parameter named field that represents the field object to be tested. To complete the function:

   a. Insert a conditional expression that tests whether the length of the field value is equal to 0.

   b. If the length is equal to 0, then: 1) Change the background color of the field object to yellow and 2) return the Boolean value false. Otherwise: 1) Change the background color of the field object to white and 2) return the Boolean value true.

5. Create a function named testPattern(). The purpose of this function is to compare the value of a field against a regular expression pattern. The function has two parameters: the field parameter representing the field object to be tested and reg, a regular expression literal containing the pattern used for the testing. To complete the testPattern() function:

   a. Insert a conditional statement that employs the test() method to test whether the value of the field object matches the regular expression contained in the reg parameter.

   b. If the test() method returns the value false, then: 1) Change the background color of the field object to yellow; 2) Change the color of the field object to red; and 3) return the Boolean value false. Otherwise: 1) Change the background color of the field object to white; 2) Change the color of the field object to black; and 3) return the Boolean value true.

6. Create a function named submitForm(). The purpose of this function is to validate the form and calculate the total registration fee. Add the following commands to the function:

   a. Create a variable named valid. Set the initial value of the variable to true.

   b. Call the testLength() function using the fname field as the parameter. If the function returns the value false, change the value of the valid variable to false. Repeat this step for the lname, address, and email fields.

   c. The phone number is divided into three fields named phone1, phone2, and phone3, representing the area code, exchange, and local number. The phone1 and phone2 fields should both contain only three digits. The phone3 field should contain only four digits. Call the testPattern() function for each field along with the appropriate regular expression literal. If the value returned by the testPattern() function is false for any of the fields, set the value of the valid variable to false.

   d. Insert a conditional statement that tests whether neither of the member radio buttons is checked. If neither has been checked then: 1) Change the background color of each member radio button to yellow, and 2) Set the value of the valid variable to false. (*Hint*: To test whether neither radio button has been checked, use the condition: ((*form*.member[0].checked || *form*.member[1].checked) == false) where *form* is the object reference to the registration form.)

   e. If the valid variable is false then display the alert message "Enter all required information in the appropriate format"; otherwise run the calcCost() function.

   f. Return the value of the valid variable.

7. Add an event handler to the form element that runs and returns the value of the submitForm() function when the form is submitted.

8. Save your changes to **conf.htm**. Open the file in your Web browser and verify that the form cannot be submitted unless all of the required fields are filled out and the phone number is entered in the appropriate format and the user has indicated whether or not he or she is a member of the ACGIP. A valid form should open the summary.htm file with a list of field names and values appended to the URL. Note that browsers differ in how they change the background color of option buttons. If you are running Internet Explorer, the background color of the option buttons changes to yellow. If you are running Netscape, the background color of the option buttons does not turn yellow. If you are running Opera, the internal color of the option buttons changes color.

Explore

9. Open the **summary.htm** file in your text editor. Add an embedded script element to the head section of the document. Add the following commands to the script element:

   a. Create a variable named searchString equal to everything but the first character of the location.search object.

   b. Use the replace() method to replace every occurrence of the + character in the searchString variable with a blank space. Store the revised text string in a variable named formString.

   c. Apply the unescape() method to the formString variable to remove any escape characters from the string. Store the revised text string in a variable named dataString.

   d. Use the split() method to split the dataString at every occurrence of a & or = character. Store the substrings in an array named data.

Explore

10. Scroll down the file. Notice that embedded script elements have already been placed in the table. Your next task is to write the field values from the data array into the appropriate places in the table. Field values are stored in data[1], data[3], data[5], and so forth. The total cost of the conference is stored in data[1]. In the first script element use the document.write() method to write the value of data[1] preceded by a $ symbol to the document. The participant's first and last name is stored in data[3] and data[5]. In the second script element write the values data[3] and data[5], separated by a blank space.

Explore

11. The next row in the table displays the participant's address. This value is stored in data[7]. However, the value came from a textarea field that could contain multiple lines of text. Each line return has to be converted into <br /> tags to preserve the appearance of the address text. To write the participant's address, do the following:

   a. Create a regular expression literal named reg that matches the occurrences of every new line character. (*Hint*: Use the \n escape sequence.)

   b. Use the replace() method with the reg regular expression object, replace every occurrence of the new line character in the data[7] text string with the substring <br />. Store the revised text string in a variable named address.

   c. Write the address variable to the document.

12. Write the remaining field values to the remaining table cells. Use data[9] for the e-mail address, data[11], data[13], and data[15] for the phone number; data[17] for the number of banquet guests, and data[19] for whether the participant is an ACGIP member.

13. Save your changes to the file.

14. Reopen **conf.htm** in your Web browser. Fill out the form correctly, including a multi-line address in the address field. Submit the form. Verify that the field values and total cost of the conference are written to the table cells in the summary page. Also verify that the summary page retains the line breaks present in the address field.

15. Submit the completed Web site to your instructor.

Create

Create an Order Form for a Commercial Web Site

Case Problem 4

Data files needed for this Case Problem: back.jpg, functions.js, info.txt, logo.jpg

Wizard Works   Wizard Works is a leading seller of customized and brand name fireworks in the United States. Roger Blaine supervises the company's Web site development team. He's asked you to work on the order form for the company's line of custom fountains. Roger wants the following elements to appear on the form:

- Data entry fields for the customer's first and last name, address, and phone number.
- Data entry fields for the customer's credit card type (Wizard Works accepts American Express, Diners Club, Discover, MasterCard, and Visa), name of the credit card, credit card number, and expiration date.
- Data entry fields from which the customer can select which item or items to order, and the quantity of each item.
- Data entry fields from which the customer can select a shipping option (standard for $4.95, express for $8.95, or next day for $12.95).

The final design of the order form is up to you. Roger has provided several files to aid you in creating the order form. You may supplement this material with material of your own. However, the order form needs to perform the following tasks:

- Automatically calculate the total cost of the order, including the cost of shipping. The cost of the order should be formatted to two decimal places.
- Confirm that the user has entered an integer quantity of items to order.
- Confirm that the customer has entered a first and last name, address, and phone number.
- Confirm that the phone number follows one of the following patterns: (ddd) ddd-dddd, ddd-ddd-dddd, or ddd ddd dddd.
- Confirm that the customer has selected a credit card type, entered a credit name, and entered a credit card number that matches both the number pattern for the selected card and fulfills the Luhn Formula.

To complete this assignment:

1. Using the material found in the tutorial.14/case4 folder, create a Web form in a file named **works.htm**. The form should contain all of the entry fields specified by Roger.
2. Design the form so that it opens a file named done.htm using the post method when it is successfully submitted to the browser. Create the done.htm file, displaying a message that the order form has been correctly filled out.
3. Add scripts to the Web page to perform all of the necessary calculations and validation tasks.
4. Use regular expressions to test whether the credit card numbers match the card patterns specified by the card company. See the info.txt file for information on the appropriate number patterns for each card.
5. Test your Web form, verifying that it performs all calculations and validation tasks correctly.
6. Submit the completed Web site to your instructor.

Quick Check Answers

Session 14.1

1. document.forms[1]
2. document.forms["register"].elements["lastname"]
   or
   document.register.lastname
3. document.register.lastname.value = "Carol Campbell";
   document.register.lastname.focus();
4. document.register.statename.option[3]
5. document.register.statename.selectedIndex
6. document.register.contactme.checked
7. 2007
   NaN
8. 3.14159.toFixed(2)
   This expression might not be supported by older browsers.

Session 14.2

1. Client-side validation is the validation of a data entry form that occurs on the user's Web browser. Server-side validation is validation that occurs on the Web server.
2. onsubmit = "return testForm()"
3. username.length
4. username.charAt(0)
   username.charAt(username.length-1)
5. username.slice(0,5)
6. words = email.split("@")
   words[0] contains the *username*; words[1] contains the *domain*
7. email.indexOf("gov")
8. username.toUpperCase()

Session 14.3

1. /GPS/gi
2. /\bproducts\b/
3. /^\d{9}$/
4. /^\d{9}$|^\d{3}-\d{2}-\d{4}$/
   or
   /^\d{3}-?\d{2}-?\d{4}$/
   Other solutions are also possible.
5. /(street|avenue|lane)/ig
6. reuser.test(username)
7. date.split(/\//g)
8. The Luhn Formula is a formula developed by a group of mathematicians in the 1960s to provide a quick validation check for a number string. It calculates the sum of digits in an account number to verify that the number is valid.
9. location.search

Objectives

Working with the Event Model

Creating a Drag-and-Drop Shopping Cart

Case

Games Etc.

Games Etc., a company that sells puzzles and games, recently decided to put its merchandise online. You have been hired to create a Web page for the company's monthly specials. Your supervisor, Pete Burdette, wants users to be able to select the specials they want to purchase from a list of items.

Because of the nature of the company, Pete also wants the page to have an interface that incorporates various elements of board games. For example, rather than clicking a check box to select an item, Pete would like to see users click and drag items into a shopping cart area, much as game pieces are moved on a game board. Thus, the elements on the page won't be fixed in one place; rather, users will be able to move them around.

To add this feature to the Games Etc. Web page, you have to work with the event models of Internet Explorer and the W3C, learning how to make the Web page respond to mouse and keyboard actions initiated by users.

Student Data Files

▼**tutorial.15**

▽ **tutorial folder**

gamestxt.htm
shoptxt.js
+ 1 style sheet
+ 3 graphic files
+ 2 demo files

▽ **review folder**

puzztxt.htm
+ 3 JavaScript files
+ 1 style sheet
+ 26 graphic files

▽ **case1 folder**

survtxt.htm
+ 1 JavaScript file
+ 1 style sheet
+ 3 graphic files

Session 15.1

Working with Events

You and Pete meet to discuss his idea for a shopping cart page. He has already designed the page layout. Open the file now to view the current page.

To open the Games Etc. Web page:

▶ 1. In your text editor, open the **gamestxt.htm** file from the tutorial.15/tutorial folder. Enter **your name** and **the date** in the comment section and save the file as **games.htm**.

▶ 2. Take some time to study the HTML code for this file, taking careful note of the div elements and their id values.

▶ 3. Open **games.htm** in your Web browser. Figure 15-1 shows the current appearance of the page.

Figure 15-1	The Games Etc. Web page

The Games Etc. page displays the four specials for the current month in separate boxes on the left side of the page. The box on the right acts as a shopping cart for prospective customers, displaying the items a user has decided to purchase. Many of the objects on the page have been stored within div elements and placed on the page using absolute positioning. In particular, each of the four monthly specials is entered as a separate div element, as is the shopping cart box. The id names for the four specials are item1, item2, item3, and item4. The id name for the shopping cart box is cartBox.

To assist you in programming this page, Pete has acquired an external JavaScript file containing several customized functions that will handle various tasks that you'll need to complete this project. Figure 15-2 describes the different functions available in the shop.js file. You'll be adding some additional functions to this file as you work on the Games Etc. page.

Functions in the shop.js file ◀ **Figure 15-2**

Function	Description
placeIt(object, x, y)	Places object at coordinates (x, y)
getXCoord(object)	Returns the x-coordinate of object
getYCoord(object)	Returns the y-coordinate of object
withinIt(x, y, object)	Returns a Boolean value indicating whether the coordinates (x, y) lie within object's boundaries (true) or not (false)
colorIt(object, color)	Changes the font color and border color of object to "color"

Open the shop.js file now to familiarize yourself with these functions.

To open the shop.js file:

▶ 1. Use your text editor to open the **shoptxt.js** file from the tutorial.15/tutorial folder. Enter **your name** and **the date** in the comment section and save the file as **shop.js**.

▶ 2. Review the contents of the file.

For scripts you'll use in this tutorial, you'll need to create the following global variables:

• dragItem: Used to store a reference to the object being dragged
• shop1 - shop4: Used to store a reference to the four shopping cart items
• cart: Used to store a reference to the shopping cart box

Add these global variables to a script in the Web page. Then set the initial values for each of these variables in a function named setUp() that you'll run when the page is loaded by the browser. The initial value of the dragItem variable should be left null since no objects are being dragged when the page is loaded by the browser.

To create the global variables and the setUp() function:

▶ 1. Return to **games.htm** in your text editor and above the closing </head> tag insert an embedded script element containing the following global variables:

```
var dragItem, shop1, shop2, shop3, shop4, cart;
```

Note that you can declare several variables in a single statement if you separate them by commas.

2. Below the global variables you just created, insert the following function to set the object references of these variables:

```
function setUp() {
    shop1 = document.getElementById("item1");
    shop2 = document.getElementById("item2");
    shop3 = document.getElementById("item3");
    shop4 = document.getElementById("item4");
    cart = document.getElementById("cartBox");
}
```

3. Add the event handler **onload = "setUp()"** to the body element. Figure 15-3 shows the new and revised code in the file.

Figure 15-3 | **Creating the setUp() function**

```
<script type="text/javascript">
var dragItem, shop1, shop2, shop3, shop4, cart;

function setUp() {
    shop1 = document.getElementById("item1");
    shop2 = document.getElementById("item2");
    shop3 = document.getElementById("item3");
    shop4 = document.getElementById("item4");
    cart = document.getElementById("cartBox");
}

</script>
</head>

<body onload="setUp()">
```

You may wonder why you were instructed to place the commands for setting up the object references in the setUp() function, rather than when you first declared the global variables. The reason is that when a browser encounters an embedded script element in the head section of a document, it has not yet processed the contents of the Web page body, and thus would not recognize references to elements in the page body. However, when the setUp() function is run in response to the onload event, the browser has already read in the complete contents of the HTML file and thus can assign those object references.

Event Handlers

Pete describes how he wants the page to operate. As shown in Figure 15-4, Pete wants to give customers the ability to drag and drop each of the four sales items into the shopping cart box. Then, when a user clicks the "Go to the checkout" link, a CGI script can be run that totals the cost of the selected items and prompts the user for additional purchase information. Your task is to program only the drag-and-drop aspect of this page. Someone else will create the rest of the shopping cart application for the company.

Dragging items into the shopping cart Figure 15-4

To complete the drag-and-drop part of this task, your script must be able to do the following:

- Select a sales item on the page when the customer depresses the mouse button on the object.
- Move the sales item along with the mouse pointer as it travels across the screen.
- Place the sales item in its new location when the customer releases the mouse button.

To create this effect, the browser needs to react to the actions of pressing the mouse button down, moving the mouse pointer, and finally releasing the mouse button. As each of these events occurs, you need to modify the page layout in response. As you've seen in previous tutorials, one common way of responding to an event is by adding an event handler attribute to an element's tag using the syntax:

```
<element onevent = "script" ...> ... </element>
```

where `element` is the document element, `event` is the name of the event, and `script` is a command or command block that the browser will run in response to the event occurring within the element. Figure 15-5 lists the event handlers associated with mouse events.

Mouse event handlers ◄ Figure 15-5

Event Handler	Description
oncontextmenu	The right (or secondary) mouse button has been clicked
onclick	A mouse button has been clicked
ondblclick	A mouse button has been double-clicked
onmousedown	A mouse button has been depressed
onmousemove	The mouse pointer has moved
onmouseout	The mouse pointer has moved off of the element
onmouseover	The mouse pointer has moved over the element
onmouseup	A mouse button has been released

For example if you wanted to run a script named moveItem() in response to the mousemove event occurring within the first sales item, you could add the onmousemove event handler to that item's HTML tag, as follows:

```
<div id="item1" onmousemove="moveItem()" ...>
```

Most current browsers can apply event handlers to any element with a Web page or browser. However, older browsers such as Netscape 4.0 or 4.7 can apply event handlers only to a specific group of elements. (For a discussion of the elements supported by Netscape 4, see Appendix J.) Thus, if you're creating a Web site that needs to support older browsers, you will have to consider those browsers' limitations when scripting for events.

Event Handlers as Object Properties

Another way to apply an event handler is to treat it as an object property. The syntax of this approach is

```
object.onevent = function;
```

where *object* is the object that the event applies to, *onevent* is the event handler, and *function* is the name of the JavaScript function that is run in response to the event. For example, to run the moveItem() function whenever the mousemove event occurs within the item1 element, you could run the following JavaScript command:

```
document.getElementById("item1").onmousemove=moveItem;
```

Note that this form uses the name of the function as the property value; it does not call the function. It would not be correct syntax to use the construction

```
document.getElementById("item1").onmousemove=moveItem();
```

Also note that the name of the event handler must be in lowercase letters. For example, you can specify "onmouseover" as an event handler, but not "onMouseOver". Using an event handler as an object property provides programmers with greater flexibility in designing their scripts. For example, the function assigned to an event can be changed at one or more points in a program. The function name can also be passed as a variable. A programmer could write a script that prompts a user for the function the user wants to run in response to specific events. Finally, in a Web page that may contain dozens of elements that require event handlers, a programmer could write a program that assigns event handlers to the appropriate objects without having to go through the process of adding event handler attributes to each of the HTML tags.

One of the main disadvantages of handling events as object properties is the inability to include a function's parameter values in a property. In addition, you can assign only one function at a time to a particular object and event—although, as you'll see later, there are ways of working around this limitation. Another important consideration in using the object property method is that you must insert the event handler *after* an object has been loaded by the browser. You can do this either by placing the JavaScript commands at the bottom of the file or by running the commands in a function after the page is loaded.

Event Handlers as Script Elements

You can also invoke event handlers as attributes of the script element. The general syntax is

```
<script type="text/javascript" for="id" event="onevent">
```

where *id* is the id of an element in the Web page and *onevent* is the event handler. For example, the code

```
<script type="text/javascript" for="item1" event="onmousemove">
   commands
</script>
```

runs the *commands* in the embedded script when the mousemove event occurs within the item1 element. Note that this syntax can only be applied to elements with a specified id.

Using Event Handlers

- To add an event handler to an element, add the following attribute to the element's tag:
     onevent="script"
  where *event* is the name of the event and *script* is the command or commands run in response to the event occurring within the element.
- To apply an event handler as a property of an object, use the JavaScript command
     object.onevent = function;
  where *object* is the object in the Web page or browser and *function* is the name of the function to assign to *event*.
- To apply an event handler to a script element, create a script element like the following:
     ```
     <script type="text/javascript" for="id" event="onevent">
        commands
     </script>
     ```
  where *id* is the id of an element in the Web page and *commands* are the commands to be run in response to the event.

Using an Event Handler to Cancel an Action

As you've seen in previous tutorials, many events have default actions associated with them. Hovering a mouse pointer over a link changes the text of the window status bar; clicking a submit button in a Web form submits the contents of the form for processing. You've also seen that you can cancel the default action for any event by assigning a function to the event handler that returns the Boolean value false. For example, in the following sample code, the disableLink() function returns the Boolean value false. This has the effect of canceling the default action of the onclick event handler for the first link in the document.

```
document.links[0].onclick=disableLink;
function disableLink() {
   return false;
}
```

To restore the default action associated with clicking the link, you could run a second function that returns the Boolean value true:

```
document.links[0].onclick=enableLink;
function enableLink() {
   return true;
}
```

Canceling the default action associated with an event is most often used when you want to substitute your own actions for those usually undertaken by the browser. You'll use this technique later in the tutorial in creating the drag-and-drop script for Pete's Web page.

Assigning an Event Handler

For the task that Pete wants you to accomplish, you need to control the movements of the mouse as applied to several different objects on the Web page. While you could write a separate event handler for each object on the page, this would be a cumbersome process. Instead, you'll use the object property method to invoke your event handlers, which gives you more flexibility in writing your script. You'll start this task by creating event handlers that run a function named grabIt() whenever a customer depresses the mouse button in one of the shopping cart items. Because you'll be creating several event handlers in this tutorial and applying them to several objects, you'll place all of your event handlers for the sales items within a general function named assignF(). This saves you the effort of writing the same code four times for each of the four sales items. The initial code of the assignF() function is

```
function assignF(object) {
    object.onmousedown=grabIt;
}
```

Here the *object* parameter represents the object that receives the onmousedown event handler. You'll call this function for each of the shopping cart items from the setUp() function you created earlier. Recall that you've placed references to those shopping cart items in four global variables named shop1 through shop4.

To create the assignF() function:

1. Within the **games.htm** file in your text editor, insert the following function below the setUp() function:

```
function assignF(object) {
    object.onmousedown=grabIt;
}
```

2. Add the following commands to the setUp() function. Figure 15-6 shows the revised code.

```
assignF(shop1);
assignF(shop2);
assignF(shop3);
assignF(shop4);
```

| Figure 15-6 | Creating the assignF() function |

```
function setUp() {
    shop1 = document.getElementById("item1");
    shop2 = document.getElementById("item2");
    shop3 = document.getElementById("item3");
    shop4 = document.getElementById("item4");
    cart = document.getElementById("cartBox");

    assignF(shop1);
    assignF(shop2);
    assignF(shop3);
    assignF(shop4);
}

function assignF(object) {
    object.onmousedown=grabIt;
}
```

3. Close the file, saving your changes.

With this new code, each of the shopping cart items will now run the grabIt() function when a customer depresses the mouse button in them. The purpose of the grabIt() function is to select the shopping cart item in preparation for dragging it across the Web page. Before you can create the grabIt() function, you need to look at how browsers handle events.

Introducing the Internet Explorer Event Model

Events, like other objects in a Web page, have their own properties and methods. The way that a browser works with events is called its **event model**. When you were creating event handlers in this and previous tutorials, you were working with an early version of an event model. Generally, this event model is considered part of the DOM Level 0 standard discussed in Tutorial 11. Since this model was created, more sophisticated event models have been developed. You'll consider two event models in this tutorial: the **Internet Explorer event model** developed for the Internet Explorer browser, and the **DOM event model** developed by the W3C for DOM Level 2. The Internet Explorer event model is supported by Internet Explorer version 5 and higher. The DOM event model is supported by Netscape 6 and 7, Firefox, and other Mozilla browsers. A third event model was developed for Netscape 4 and Netscape 4.7, but you won't consider it here. You can learn more about the Netscape 4 event model in Appendix J.

Eventually all browsers will likely support the DOM event model; however, for now you'll need to create code that accommodates both event models. The differences between the two lie in how they capture events within a Web page, how they refer to events, and the methods and properties that they associate with those events. We'll start with the Internet Explorer Event model.

Event Bubbling

The first thing you'll examine for the Internet Explorer model is how events are captured and propagated through the browser. When a user performs an action such as clicking an element on a Web page, that event originates within the given element. If an event handler has been added to the element, a function may run in response to the event. However, elements are often nested within other elements; in addition, all page elements are ultimately nested within the document element itself, and the document is nested within the browser window. In the case of nested objects, how does a browser determine which object really initiated the event?

In the Internet Explorer Event model, events are initiated at the bottom of the document tree and rise to the top of the object hierarchy in a process known as **event bubbling**. Thus the event passes through the lowest object in the tree, though every object in the path to the top of the tree has an opportunity to respond to the event (see Figure 15-7).

| Figure 15-7 | Event bubbling in the IE Event Model |

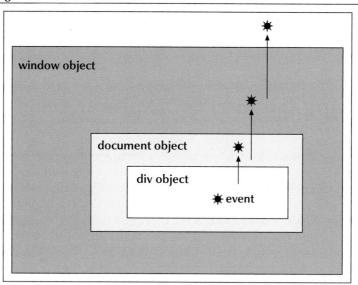

To see how event bubbling works in practice, a demo page has been prepared for you. Open this page now in a browser that supports the Internet Explorer event model.

To view the event bubbling demo:

1. With an Internet Explorer browser (or a browser such as Opera that supports the Internet Explorer event model), open the **demo_bubble.htm** file from the tutorial. 15/tutorial folder.

2. Click within the **Level 1** box on the Web page (see Figure 15-8).

| Figure 15-8 | Event bubbling |

When you click within the Level 1 box (the lowest level on the document tree in this Web page), the onclick event bubbles up through the other three boxes and into the main document object. Note that the propagation is slowed down so that you can see it happen more clearly. In actual practice, the propagation of the event occurs almost instantaneously.

One of the advantages of event bubbling is that you can set up different functions to handle the event as it propagates up the document tree. One function can be run when the event is detected within a nested object, and another function can be run when the click event bubbles to the document object itself.

Canceling Event Bubbling

In some scripts you may want to prevent an event from propagating up the document tree. This would occur if you wanted an event like the onclick event to be noticed only by a nested object, but ignored by all of the parent elements of that object. To prevent event bubbling from occurring, run the following command when the event reaches the level at which you want the propagation to stop:

```
event.cancelBubble=true;
```

To turn event bubbling back on, run the command

```
event.cancelBubble = false;
```

The following set of commands illustrates this process:

```
document.getElementById("Level 3").onclick=clickMsg;
event.cancelBubble=true;
```

The first command runs the clickMsg() function when the onclick event is encountered in the Level 3 object. The second command cancels the event, preventing it from propagating up the object hierarchy to the next level. Thus, the onclick event is essentially hidden from objects higher up on the document tree. Return to the demo page to see this effect in action.

To cancel event bubbling:

▶ 1. Click the **Level 3 option** button to cancel event bubbling starting at that level in the demo page.

▶ 2. Once again, click within the **Level 1** box on the Web page (see Figure 15-9).

Canceling event bubbling ◀ **Figure 15-9**

onclick event propagates until it reaches an event.cancelBubble command

The onclick event is recognized up to Level 3 in the demo page. After that, the event is not propagated to the upper levels in the object hierarchy, and thus no onclick event is detected.

▶ 3. Close **demo_bubble.htm**.

If you want to cancel an event at the current level as well as all levels above the object, run the command

```
event.returnValue = false;
```

This has the same effect as accessing a function that returns the Boolean value false to cancel any default actions associated with an event. Note that the returnValue property is supported only in the Internet Explorer event model.

Attaching and Detaching Events

One problem with the object.property method of attaching event handlers to objects is that you can assign only one function to a particular event. The Internet Explorer event model overcomes this limitation with the attachEvent() method. The syntax is

```
object.attachEvent(onevent, function);
```

where *object* is the object receiving the event, *onevent* is the text string of the event handler, and *function* is the function that runs in response to the event. For example, the following command runs both the Rollover() and showColor() functions when the mouse pointer is passed over the Logo object:

```
document.getElementById("Logo").attachEvent("onmouseover",Rollover);
document.getElementById("Logo").attachEvent("onmouseover",showColor);
```

If you then wanted to detach one of these functions from the mouseover event, you would use the detachEvent() method as follows:

```
document.getElementById("Logo").detachEvent("onmouseover",showColor);
```

Once a function is detached from an object, the event no longer triggers the function. Functions can be attached and detached multiple times, depending on the needs of a given program. It's important to stress that the attachEvent() and detachEvent() methods are supported only by Internet Explorer 5.0 and above, along with any other browser that supports the Internet Explorer event model.

Introducing the DOM Event Model

The DOM event model uses a different approach to propagating events through the document tree. In the DOM model, an event starts at the top and moves down the object hierarchy until it reaches the target of the event; at that point, the event bubbles back up the object hierarchy (see Figure 15-10).

Event propagation in the DOM event model ◀ **Figure 15-10**

In the DOM model, an event is split into three phases:

1. A **capture phase** as the event moves down the object hierarchy
2. A **target phase** in which the event reaches the object from which the event originated
3. A **bubbling phase** in which the event moves back up the object hierarchy

The DOM event model is particularly powerful because it allows you to run a function that responds to an event at any phase in this process. To run a function, you create an **event listener** that detects when a particular event has reached an object in the document. The syntax for creating an event listener is

```
object.addEventListener(event, function, capture);
```

where `object` is the object receiving the event, `event` is the text string describing the event, `function` is the function that runs in response to the event, and `capture` is a Boolean variable that tells the browser when to apply the event handler. If `capture` is true, the function is executed in the capture phase as the event travels down the object hierarchy. If `capture` is false, the function is executed in the bubble phase. For example, to apply the RollOver() function to the Logo object during the bubble phase, you would use the following command:

```
document.getElementById("Logo").addEventListener("mouseover",
RollOver, false);
```

The addEventListener() method is similar to Internet Explorer's attachEvent() method. Like the attachEvent() method, you can use this method to attach several functions to the same event. Note that the addEventListener() method does not identify events using the "on" form. Thus, to respond to a click event, you would use "click" rather than "onclick" as you would with the attachEvent() method in the Internet Explorer event model.

To remove an event listener, use the command

```
object.removeEventListener(event, function, capture);
```

The three parameters have the same meaning as those in the addEventListener() method. Finally, you can prevent an event from propagating through the object hierarchy using the method

```
evt.stopPropagation();
```

where *evt* is the event object in the DOM event model. You'll learn about event objects in the next session. For now, it's only important to understand that the stopPropagation() method has the same impact as the cancelBubble() method for the Internet Explorer event model except that it stops the event from further moving either down or up the object hierarchy.

To cancel an event entirely, use the method

```
evt.preventDefault();
```

where once again *evt* is the event object in the DOM event model. As with the returnValue=false approach in the Internet Explorer event model, running this method cancels default actions associated with the event on the part of the browser.

Reference Window | Working with Event Propagation

Internet Explorer Event Model

- To prevent an event from bubbling up the document tree, run the command
  ```
  event.cancelBubble = true;
  ```
- To allow an event to continue bubbling up the document tree, run
  ```
  event.cancelBubble = false;
  ```
- To attach a function to an object, run
  ```
  object.attachEvent(onevent, function);
  ```
  where *object* is the object receiving the event, *onevent* is the text string of the event handler, and *function* is the function that runs in response to the event. Multiple functions can be attached to the same event in the same object.
- To detach a function, run
  ```
  object.detachEvent(onevent, function);
  ```
- To cancel an event, run
  ```
  event.returnValue=false;
  ```

DOM Event Model

- To prevent an event from propagating through the object hierarchy, run the command
  ```
  evt.stopPropagation();
  ```
  where *evt* is the event object that is propagating through the object hierarchy.
- To run a function when an event reaches an object, use
  ```
  object.addEventListener(event, function, capture);
  ```
  where *object* is the object receiving the event, *event* is the text string describing the event, *function* is the function to run in response to the event, and *capture* equals true if the event is moving down the document tree and false if the event is bubbling up the tree.
- To stop listening for an event, run
  ```
  object.removeEventListener(event, function, capture);
  ```
- To cancel the default action associated with an event, run
  ```
  evt.preventDefault();
  ```

Creating a Cross-Browser Event Model

Since two event models exist, with different approaches and syntax, you need to determine which event model a user's browser supports and then run commands appropriate for that model. Recall from Tutorial 11 that one way of working with different models is through object detection. In object detection, you find an object, property, or method that is unique for a particular model and create a Boolean variable that indicates whether the current browser supports that object, property, or method. For the IE and DOM event models, you can use the attachEvent and addEventListener methods as parts of the object detection. The code to employ object detection in this case is

```
var IE = document.attachEvent ? true:false;
var DOM = document.addEventListener ? true: false;
```

If a user's browser supports the IE model, the IE variable has the value true; otherwise it has the value false. Similarly, browsers that support the DOM model return a value of true for the DOM variable and false otherwise. Since you'll be doing a lot of object detection in this tutorial, add these two variables as global variables to the shop.js file. You can then use them whenever you need to determine which event model is being run by a user's browser.

To create the IE and DOM variables:

1. Go to the **shop.js** file in your text editor.

2. Directly before the placeIt() function, insert the following global variables, as shown in Figure 15-11:

   ```
   var IE = document.attachEvent ? true:false;
   var DOM = document.addEventListener ? true: false;
   ```

Performing object detection **Figure 15-11**

```
var IE = document.attachEvent ? true:false;
var DOM = document.addEventListener ? true: false;

function placeIt(object, x, y) {
    object.style.left=x;
    object.style.top=y;
}
```

   Next you'll need a cross-browser function to apply an event function to an object. Since the Internet Explorer event model uses the attachEvent() method and the DOM event model uses the addEventListener() method, you'll have to use the IE and DOM variables you created to determine which method to apply. The function will look as follows:

```
function applyEventF(obj,ename,fname,capture) {
   if (IE) obj.attachEvent("on"+ename, fname);
   else if (DOM) obj.addEventListener(ename,fname,capture);
}
```

The function has four parameters: `obj` represents the object that the event is applied to, `ename` is the event name, `fname` is the name of the function associated with the event, and `capture` indicates whether the event is traveling down the hierarchy or bubbling up. For example, if you call the function using the parameters

```
applyEventF(shop1,"click",grabIt,false)
```

browsers that support the Internet Explorer event model run the command

```
shop1.attachEvent("onclick",grabIt)
```

and browsers that support the DOM event model run

```
shop1.addEventListener("click",grabIt,false)
```

The cross-browser function to remove an event function from an object is similar:

```
function removeEventF(obj,ename,fname,capture) {
   if (IE) obj.detachEvent("on"+ename, fname);
   else if (DOM) obj.removeEventListener(ename,fname,capture);
}
```

Add these two functions to the shop.js file.

To create the applyEventF() and removeEventF() functions:

1. At the end of the **shop.js** file, insert the following functions (see Figure 15-12):

```
function applyEventF(obj,ename,fname,cap) {
   if (IE) obj.attachEvent("on"+ename, fname);
   else if (DOM) obj.addEventListener(ename,fname,cap);
}
function removeEventF(obj,ename,fname,cap) {
   if (IE) obj.detachEvent("on"+ename, fname);
   else if (DOM) obj.removeEventListener(ename,fname,cap);
}
```

| Figure 15-12 | Creating two custom functions |

```
function colorIt(object, color) {
    object.style.color=color;
    object.style.borderColor=color;
}

function applyEventF(obj,ename,fname,cap) {
    if (IE) obj.attachEvent("on"+ename, fname);
    else if (DOM) obj.addEventListener(ename,fname,cap);
}

function removeEventF(obj,ename,fname,cap) {
    if (IE) obj.detachEvent("on"+ename, fname);
    else if (DOM) obj.removeEventListener(ename,fname,cap);
}
```

2. Close the file, saving your changes.

You've completed the initial work on the shopping cart Web page. In the next session you'll work on creating the functions that will enable you to drag an item across the Web and drop it on a new location.

Review

Session 15.1 Quick Check

1. What JavaScript command would you enter to run the function CalcTotal when the user presses the mouse button down while the mouse pointer is in an object with the id "Total"?
2. What script element would you enter to run a script in response to the event described in the previous question?

3. How do events propagate through the document tree under the Internet Explorer event model?

4. What command would you run under the IE model to attach the function CalcTotal to the Total object in response to the click event?

5. What command would you enter to cancel event bubbling under the Internet Explorer event model?

6. Describe how events propagate under the DOM event model.

7. What command would you run under the DOM event model to apply the function CalcTotal to the Total object in response to the click event?

8. What command would you enter to cancel event propagation under the DOM event model?

Session 15.2

Working with Event Objects

In the last session you examined how the two main document object models detect and react to events; however, this is only part of what's involved with an event model. You also need to get information about an event itself. If a user has clicked a mouse button in a document, you may need to know where the mouse pointer was located when this happened. If the user has pressed a key on the keyboard, you may want to know which key was pressed. This type of information is stored in an **event object**. The two event models provide different means of working with event objects. Start by looking at the event object under the Internet Explorer event model.

The Internet Explorer Event Object

In the Internet Explorer event model, the event object has the object reference

```
windowObject.event
```

where `windowObject` is the browser window in which the event occurred. If you are dealing with events in the current browser window, you can drop the `windowObject` reference and reference the event object as simply

```
event
```

You may recognize the event object from the last session, when it was used in the command to cancel event bubbling or the default action associated with an event. Under the Internet Explorer model, the event object can be treated as a global variable—one that is never declared by you, but is accessible in any function you write. This system works because only one event is being processed at any given time; thus, there is no need to reference multiple event objects within a given function. The Internet Explorer event model always knows which event the event object is referencing based on the function that has been attached and called by the program.

The event object supports a wide variety of properties. A partial list is displayed in Figure 15-13. You may recognize some of these from the previous session.

Figure 15-13	Properties of the IE event object

Property	Description
event.altKey event.ctrlKey event.shiftKey	Returns a Boolean value indicating whether the Alt, Ctrl, or Shift key was pressed down during the event
event.button	Returns the number of the button pressed by the user (1=left, 2=right, 4=middle)
event.cancelBubble	Set this property to true to cancel event bubbling; false to continue event bubbling
event.clientX event.clientY	Returns the x- and y-coordinates of the event within the browser window
event.fromElement	For mouseover and mouseout events, returns the object from which the mouse pointer is moving
event.keyCode	Returns the Unicode character code of the key that was struck by the user
event.offsetX event.offsetY	Returns the x and y distances of the event from the object in which the event was initiated
event.returnValue	Set this property to false to cancel the default action of the event; true to retain the default action
event.screenX event.screenY	Returns the x- and y-coordinates of the event within the computer screen
event.srcElement	Returns the object in which the event was generated
event.toElement	For mouseover and mouseout events, returns the object to which the mouse pointer is moving
event.type	Returns a text string indicating the type of event
event.X event.Y	Returns the x and y positions of the event relative to the element that initiated the event

One of the more important properties is srcElement, which returns the object that initiated the event. The srcElement property is akin to the "this" keyword discussed in the previous tutorial, allowing you to determine which of many possible objects on the page called the function that responded to the event. In the shopping cart example, you could store the object in the dragItem variable using the expression

```
dragItem = event.srcElement;
```

The other properties of immediate interest are the clientX and clientY properties, which return the (x, y) coordinates of the event within the browser window. You'll use these properties later to determine the location of the mouse pointer as it moves across the Web page.

The DOM Event Object

The DOM event model takes a different approach to referencing the event object. In the DOM event model, the event object is inserted as a parameter of whatever function responds to the event. You can give the event object any parameter name, but the standard practice is to name the parameter "e" or "evt". For example, if you wanted to run the grabIt() function when a user presses the mouse button down in a document, you could insert the JavaScript commands

```
document.onmousedown=grabIt;
function grabIt(e) {
    commands
}
```

The e parameter in the grabIt() function represents the mousedown event object, and contains information describing that event. As with the Internet Explorer event object, since functions are called by specific events, there is no confusion over which event a particular event object is referring to. Figure 15-14 lists the properties associated with the DOM event object.

Properties of the DOM event object **Figure 15-14**

Property	Description
evt.altKey evt.ctrlKey evt.shiftKey evt.metaKey	Returns a Boolean value indicating whether the Alt, Ctrl, Shift, or any meta key was pressed down during the event
evt.bubbles	Returns a Boolean value indicating whether evt can bubble
evt.button	Returns the number of the button pressed by the user (0=left, 1=middle, 2=right; in Netscape 6: 1=left, 2=middle, 3=right)
evt.cancelable	Returns a Boolean value indicating whether evt can have its default action canceled
evt.clientX evt.clientY	Returns the x- and y-coordinates of the event within the browser window
evt.currentTarget	Returns the object that is currently handling the event
evt.eventPhase	Returns the phase in the event propagation of evt (1=capture, 2=target, 3=bubbling)
evt.relatedTarget	For mouseover events, returns the object that the mouse left when it moved over the target of the event; for mouseout events, returns the object that the mouse entered when leaving the target
evt.screenX evt.screenY	Returns the x- and y-coordinates of the event within the computer screen
evt.target	Returns the object that initiated the event
evt.timeStamp	Returns the date and time that the event was initiated
evt.type	Returns a text string indicating the event type

For the DOM event model, the object currently responding to an event is returned using the currentTarget property. Thus, to set the object reference for the dragItem variable, you would use the command

```
dragItem = evt.CurrentTarget;
```

where evt is the parameter of the event function. The DOM event model also supports the target property, which returns a reference to the object that initiated the event. There is no matching property in the Internet Explorer event model. Finally, you can determine the (x, y) coordinates of an event within the browser window using the clientX and clientY properties just as you would with the Internet Explorer event model. To give you a feeling for the type of information that can be returned by the event object (under either event model), a demo page has been prepared for you.

To view the event demo page:

1. Use your Web browser to open the **demo_events.htm** file from your tutorial.15/ tutorial folder.

2. Move your mouse pointer over the page. As you move the pointer, the page displays the different event coordinates supported by the event model. In addition, the event type "mousemove" is displayed in the type field.

   Trouble? Only browsers that support the Internet Explorer event model display values for the offsetX and offsetY properties.

3. Click and hold down the left mouse button within the container element. The demo page indicates which button was clicked and provides the event coordinates within the container, on the page, and on the screen (see Figure 15-15).

Figure 15-15 | **Event object demo**

4. Close the demo page when finished.

Working with Event Objects

Internet Explorer Event Model

- To reference the event object, use the object reference
    `windowObject.event`
  where `windowObject` is the browser window in which the event occurred. For the current browser window, simply use
    `event`
- To return the object that initiated an event, use the property
    `event.srcElement`
- To return the (x,y) window coordinates that indicate where an event was initiated, use the properties
    `event.clientX`
    `event.clientY`

DOM Event Model

- To reference the event object, use
    `evt`
  where `evt` is the parameter of the function assigned to the event.
- To return the object that initiated an event, use the property
    `evt.target`
- To return the object that is currently handling an event, use the property
    `evt.currentTarget`
- To return the (x,y) window coordinates that indicate where an event was initiated, use the properties
    `evt.clientX`
    `evt.clientY`

Now that you know a little more about event objects, you are ready to create objects that users can drag and drop on the shopping cart Web page. Start with the grabIt() function.

Creating the grabIt() Function

Recall that you entered code in the last session to run the grabIt() function whenever a user depresses the mouse button while the mouse pointer lies within one of the four sales items. The purpose of this function is to prepare the sales item for being dragged across the page. To do so, the function has to perform the following tasks:

1. Identify the object that lies beneath the pointer.
2. Determine the page coordinates of the mouse pointer at the moment the user presses the mouse button down.
3. Calculate the difference between the coordinates of the mouse pointer and the coordinates of the selected object.
4. Assign functions to the object that run whenever the user moves the mouse pointer or releases the mouse button.

Determining the Event Source

Because you have two event models to accommodate, you'll create cross-browser functions that resolve the differences between the two models for each of these tasks, as you did in the last session. You can then call these functions in the grabIt() function without having to worry about which event model is supported by a customer's browser. The first function you'll create is the eventSource() function, which has the following code:

```
function eventSource(e) {
    if (IE) return event.srcElement;
    else if (DOM) return e.currentTarget;
}
```

In this function, you've named the event parameter used by the DOM event model "e". The function uses the object detection variables created in the last session to determine which event object property to return. If a user's browser supports the Internet Explorer event model, the function returns the property event.srcElement; if the browser supports the DOM event model, the function returns the e.CurrentTarget property. Add this function to the shop.js file.

To add the eventSource() function:

▶ 1. Open the **shop.js** file in your text editor.

▶ 2. At the end of the file, insert the following function (see Figure 15-16).

```
function eventSource(e) {
    if (IE) return event.srcElement;
    else if (DOM) return e.currentTarget;
}
```

Figure 15-16 ▶ **The eventSource() function**

```
function removeEventF(obj,ename,fname,cap) {
    if (IE) obj.detachEvent("on"+ename, fname);
    else if (DOM) obj.removeEventListener(ename,fname,cap);
}

function eventSource(e) {
    if (IE) return event.srcElement;
    else if (DOM) return e.currentTarget;
}
```

Determining the Event Coordinates

Next you need two cross-browser functions to determine the window coordinates of the mouse pointer when the mousedown event occurs. For this task you'll use the clientX and clientY properties of the event objects in both event models. You'll add the following two functions to the shop.js file:

```
function eventPositionX(e) {
    if (IE) return event.clientX;
    else if (DOM) return e.clientX;
}
function eventPositionY(e) {
    if (IE) return event.clientY;
    else if (DOM) return e.clientY;
}
```

Once again, you use "e" as the event parameter for the DOM event model.

To add the eventPositionX() and eventPositionY() functions:

1. At the end of the file, insert the following functions (see Figure 15-17).

```
function eventPositionX(e) {
    if (IE) return event.clientX;
    else if (DOM) return e.clientX;
}
function eventPositionY(e) {
    if (IE) return event.clientY;
    else if (DOM) return e.clientY;
}
```

The eventPosition() functions   **Figure 15-17**

```
function eventSource(e) {
    if (IE) return event.srcElement;
    else if (DOM) return e.currentTarget;
}

function eventPositionX(e) {
    if (IE) return event.clientX;
    else if (DOM) return e.clientX;
}

function eventPositionY(e) {
    if (IE) return event.clientY;
    else if (DOM) return e.clientY;
}
```

2. Save your changes to the file.

   Now you can return to the games.htm file and start using all of the cross-browser functions you've created. A script element linked to the shop.js file has already been created for you, so you don't have to add that to the file. The initial code for the grabIt() function is

```
function grabIt(e) {
   dragItem = eventSource(e);
   mouseX=eventPositionX(e);
   mouseY=eventPositionY(e);
}
```

The grabIt() function assigns the object returned by the eventSource() function to the dragItem variable you created in the last session. This should be the object in which the mousedown event was initiated. You've also stored the (x,y) coordinates of that event in the variables mouseX and mouseY. In addition, you have to include an event parameter in your functions to support the DOM event model. This allows the event object to be passed to the cross-browser functions you created in the shop.js file.

To create the grabIt() function:

1. Reopen the **games.htm** file in your text editor.

2. Below the assignF() function insert the following code, as shown in Figure 15-18.

```
function grabIt(e) {
    dragItem=eventSource(e);
    mouseX=eventPositionX(e);
    mouseY=eventPositionY(e);
}
```

Figure 15-18 ▶ **Determining the event source and coordinates**

```
function grabIt(e) {
    dragItem = eventSource(e);
    mouseX=eventPositionX(e);
    mouseY=eventPositionY(e);
}

</script>
</head>

<body onload="setup()">
```

The next piece to add to the grabIt() function is code to calculate the distance between the mouse pointer and dragItem. You'll need this information later to keep dragItem a constant distance away from the mouse as you move it across the page.

Calculating the Distance from the Pointer

The coordinates of an object are often expressed in relation to the object's upper-left corner. This means that you need to calculate the value of the variables diffX and diffY, which represent the horizontal and vertical distances between the mouse pointer and the object's upper-left corner (see Figure 15-19).

Figure 15-19 ▶ **The diffX and diffY variables**

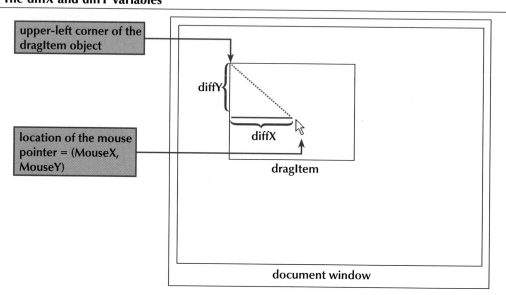

upper-left corner of the dragItem object

diffY

location of the mouse pointer = (MouseX, MouseY)

diffX

dragItem

document window

The coordinates of dragItem can be determined by using the getXCoord() and getYCoord() functions from the shop.js file. Thus, the values of diffX and diffY are

```
diffX=mouseX-getXCoord(dragItem);
diffY=mouseY-getYCoord(dragItem);
```

To create the diffX and diffY variables:

1. In the grabIt() function below the statement to create the mouseY variable, insert the following two lines:

   ```
   diffX=mouseX-getXCoord(dragItem);
   diffY=mouseY-getYCoord(dragItem);
   ```

2. Save your changes to the file.

The final task in the grabIt() function is to assign functions to dragItem that will run whenever the user moves the mouse pointer or releases the mouse button. When the mouse pointer moves, you'll run a function named moveIt() that will be used to move dragItem across the page. When the mouse button is released, you'll run the dropIt() function that drops dragItem onto the page in a new location. To call these two functions, you'll use the applyEventF() function created in the last session. The code you need to add to the grabIt() function is

```
applyEventF(dragItem,"mousemove",moveIt,false);
applyEventF(dragItem,"mouseup",dropIt,false);
```

Recall that you created applyEventF() in the last session as a cross-browser function to accommodate the attachEvent() and addEventListener() methods of the Internet Explorer and DOM event models.

To call the applyEventF() function:

1. Add the following commands to the grabIt() function (see Figure 15-20):

   ```
   applyEventF(dragItem,"mousemove",moveIt,false);
   applyEventF(dragItem,"mouseup",dropIt,false);
   ```

The grabIt() function | **Figure 15-20**

```
function grabIt(e) {
    dragItem = eventSource(e);
    mouseX=eventPositionX(e);
    mouseY=eventPositionY(e);

    diffX=mouseX-getXCoord(dragItem);
    diffY=mouseY-getYCoord(dragItem);

    applyEventF(dragItem,"mousemove",moveIt,false);
    applyEventF(dragItem,"mouseup",dropIt,false);
}
```

2. Save your changes to the file.

Now the grabIt() function is complete. Your next task is to create the moveIt() function, which will allow users to move items on the page from one location to another.

Creating the moveIt() Function

To move dragItem across the Web page, the moveIt() function needs to perform the following tasks:

1. Determine the current location of the mouse pointer.
2. Maintain dragItem at a constant distance from the mouse pointer.

By keeping an object a constant distance from the mouse pointer as it moves across the page, you create the illusion that the pointer is dragging the object (see Figure 15-21). You already know what that distance should be: it's the value of the diffX and diffY variables calculated in the dropIt() function.

| Figure 15-21 | Maintaining a constant distance from the mouse pointer |

To place dragItem at specific page coordinates, you'll use the placeIt() function from the shop.js file, subtracting the values of the diffX and diffY variables from the current position of the mouse pointer. The code for the moveIt() function is therefore

```
function moveIt(e) {
   mouseX=eventPositionX(e);
   mouseY=eventPositionY(e);
   placeIt(dragItem, mouseX-diffX, mouseY-diffY);
}
```

To create the moveIt() function:

1. Directly below the grabIt() function insert the following code (see Figure 15-22):

   ```
   function moveIt(e) {
      mouseX=eventPositionX(e);
      mouseY=eventPositionY(e);
      placeIt(dragItem, mouseX-diffX, mouseY-diffY);
   }
   ```

```
function grabIt(e) {
    dragItem = eventSource(e);
    mouseX=eventPositionX(e);
    mouseY=eventPositionY(e);

    diffX=mouseX-getXCoord(dragItem);
    diffY=mouseY-getYCoord(dragItem);

    applyEventF(dragItem,"mousemove",moveIt,false);
    applyEventF(dragItem,"mouseup",dropIt,false);
}

function moveIt(e) {
    mouseX=eventPositionX(e);
    mouseY=eventPositionY(e);
    placeIt(dragItem, mouseX-diffX, mouseY-diffY);
}
```

2. Save your changes to the file.

Creating the dropIt() Function

The next function to create for the Games Etc. drag-and-drop effect is the dropIt()
function. The dropIt() function is run whenever the user releases the mouse button, initiat-
ing the mouseup event. In response, the dropIt() function causes the browser to stop running the function assigned to the mousemove event. With the moveIt() function no longer
being called, dragItem ceases to follow the mouse pointer across the page, leaving it at
the place where it was moved. To release the function assigned to the mousemove event,
you'll use the removeEventF() function you created in the last session. The code for the
dropIt() function is therefore

```
function dropIt(e) {
    removeEventF(dragItem,"mousemove",moveIt,false);
}
```

To create and test the dropIt() function:

1. Directly below the moveIt() function insert the following code (see Figure 15-23):

```
function dropIt(e) {
    removeEventF(dragItem,"mousemove",moveIt,false);
}
```

```
function moveIt(e) {
    mouseX=eventPositionX(e);
    mouseY=eventPositionY(e);
    placeIt(dragItem, mouseX-diffX, mouseY-diffY);
}

function dropIt(e) {
    removeEventF(dragItem,"mousemove",moveIt,false);
}
```

2. Save your changes to the file.

3. Reload **games.htm** in your Web browser.

4. Move the mouse pointer over any of the four sales items, then click and hold the
left mouse button. Verify that as you move the mouse pointer, the sales item moves
across the page, following the mouse pointer, and that when you release the
mouse button the sales item is left at the new page location (see Figure 15-24).

Figure 15-24 ▶ **Dragging the first sales item**

Trouble? If you click the blue highlighted letter within a sales item box, the sales item might not move across the page. This is because these letters are objects nested within each sales item and are not set up to capture the mouse events.

Refining the Drag-and-Drop Feature

You show the games.htm page to Pete. As Pete works with the page, he notices that in some instances, the object that is being moved "disappears" behind other objects on the page (see Figure 15-25). He'd like you to make sure the dragged item is always on top.

Figure 15-25 ▶ **A dragged item hidden by another object on the page**

Keeping Dragged Items on Top

To do this, you'll create a global variable named maxZ, which stores the maximum value of the z-index style on the page. Each time you grab an item, the value of maxZ is increased by 1 and then applied to the z-index style of the grabbed item. Thus, when the grabbed item is dragged across the page, it will have the highest z-index of any object on the page and will always appear on top. Set the initial value of the maxZ variable to 1.

To create the maxZ variable:

1. Return to the **games.htm** file in your text editor.

2. Directly above the setUp() function, insert the following line:

   ```
   var maxZ=1;
   ```

3. Scroll down to the grabIt() function and insert the following two lines as shown in Figure 15-26.

   ```
   maxZ++;
   dragItem.style.zIndex=maxZ;
   ```

Keeping dragged items on top   Figure 15-26

```
function grabIt(e) {
    dragItem = eventSource(e);
    mouseX=eventPositionX(e);
    mouseY=eventPositionY(e);

    diffX=mouseX-getXCoord(dragItem);
    diffY=mouseY-getYCoord(dragItem);

    maxZ++;
    dragItem.style.zIndex=maxZ;

    applyEventF(dragItem,"mousemove",moveIt,false);
    applyEventF(dragItem,"mouseup",dropIt,false);
}
```

4. Save your changes to the file and reload **games.htm** in your Web browser. Verify that the sales items remain on top when they are dragged across the page.

Returning a Dragged Item to Its Starting Point

Another problem Pete notices is that users can drag an item from the list of specials and drop it anywhere on the page—not just in the shopping cart. He points out that the CGI script that you'll be using with the page expects that monthly specials stay either in the shopping cart box or back at their starting points on the page. Therefore, Pete wants you to add the following tasks to the dropIt() function:

1. Determine whether the dropped item lies within the boundaries of the shopping cart.
2. If the item does fall within the shopping cart's boundaries, leave it there.
3. If the item lies outside the cart's boundaries, it should snap back to its original location on the page.

To determine whether dragItem falls within the boundaries of the shopping cart, Pete suggests you use the same withinIt function that you used earlier. You'll add the following command block to the dropIt function:

```
dropPosX=getXCoord(dragItem);
dropPosY=getYCoord(dragItem);
if (!withinIt(dropPosX, dropPosY, cart)) snapBack();
```

Here dropPosX and dropPosY represent the (x, y) coordinates of the sales item as it is dropped onto the page. The "!" symbol is a negation operator and has the effect of switching the value of a Boolean variable. In this case it switches the value of the withinIt() function from false to true, and vice versa. Thus, if the expression !withinIt(dropPosX, dropPosY, cart) is true (in other words, if the coordinates are not inside the cart object), then the snapBack() function is run.

You'll create the snapBack() function shortly. For now, add the command block to the dropIt() function to determine whether dragItem is dropped in the shopping cart.

To test whether the item has been dropped into the shopping cart:

1. Return to the **games.htm** file in your text editor.

2. Add the following commands to the dropIt() function as shown in Figure 15-27:

```
dropPosX=getXCoord(dragItem);
dropPosY=getYCoord(dragItem);
if (!withinIt(dropPosX, dropPosY, cart)) snapBack();
```

Figure 15-27 ▶ **Revised dropIt() function**

```
function dropIt(e) {
    dropPosX=getXCoord(dragItem);
    dropPosY=getYCoord(dragItem);
    if (!withinIt(dropPosX, dropPosY, cart)) snapBack();
    removeEventF(dragItem,"mousemove",moveIt,false);
}
```

Finally, you need to create the snapBack() function, which should return the dragItem item to its original location. From the <div> tags in the games.htm file, you know that the original coordinates for the four monthly specials are:

- shop1 (Scribble): (10, 140)
- shop2 (Antietam): (10, 185)
- shop3 (Query): (10, 230)
- shop4 (Dragons): (10, 275)

The snapBack() function should therefore appear as follows:

```
function snapBack() {
    if (dragItem==shop1) placeIt(dragItem, 10, 140);
    else if (dragItem==shop2) placeIt(dragItem, 10, 185);
    else if (dragItem==shop3) placeIt(dragItem, 10, 230);
    else if (dragItem==shop4) placeIt(dragItem, 10, 275);
}
```

Add the above function to the games.htm file.

To create and test the snapBack() function:

1. Below the dropIt() function, insert the following code as shown in Figure 15-28:

```
function snapBack() {
    if (dragItem==shop1) placeIt(dragItem, 10, 140);
    else if (dragItem==shop2) placeIt(dragItem, 10, 185);
    else if (dragItem==shop3) placeIt(dragItem, 10, 230);
    else if (dragItem==shop4) placeIt(dragItem, 10, 275);
}
```

The snapBack() function — **Figure 15-28**

```
function dropIt(e) {
    dropPosX=getXCoord(dragItem);
    dropPosY=getYCoord(dragItem);
    if (!withinIt(dropPosX, dropPosY, cart)) snapBack();
    removeEventF(dragItem,"mousemove",moveIt,false);
}

function snapBack() {
    if (dragItem==shop1) placeIt(dragItem, 10, 140);
    else if (dragItem==shop2) placeIt(dragItem, 10, 185);
    else if (dragItem==shop3) placeIt(dragItem, 10, 230);
    else if (dragItem==shop4) placeIt(dragItem, 10, 275);
}
```

2. Save your changes to the file.

3. Reload **games.htm** in your Web browser and verify that you cannot drop any of the sales items anywhere but within the shopping cart box. If you drop an item elsewhere, it should jump back to its original location.

   Trouble? If the monthly specials all jump to the fourth spot in the list, check the code for the snapBack() function and verify that you used double equal signs (==) in the IF...THEN statement, rather than a single equals sign (=).

Canceling the selectStart Event

Pete tests the latest version of the page and notices a problem for Internet Explorer users: when the sales item snaps back, the text on the page often becomes selected (see Figure 15-29).

Content automatically selected by the snapBack() function — **Figure 15-29**

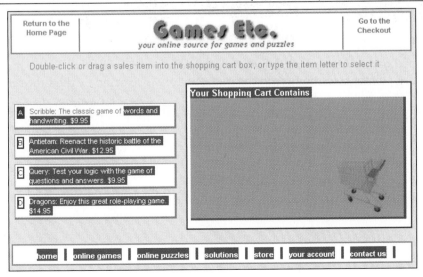

This happens because the default action of the browser is to select text on the Web page when the mouse button is held down and dragged through the page. As the sales items are snapped back, the text selection event kicks in as objects are moved across the mouse pointer.

The action of selecting text on the page is indicated in Internet Explorer by the select-Start event. If you cancel this event, then you can prevent the action of selecting text in the Web page by both the user and the browser itself. Recall from the last session that you can cancel an event by creating a function that returns the Boolean value "false." You'll do that now for this problem, inserting the following code into the document:

```
document.onselectstart=stopSelect;
function stopSelect() {
    return false;
}
```

To cancel the selectStart event:

1. Return to the **games.htm** file in your text editor.

2. At the bottom of the setUp() function, insert the following line:

   `document.onselectstart=stopSelect;`

3. Below the setUp() function insert the following function. Figure 15-30 shows the revised code.

   ```
   function stopSelect() {
       return false;
   }
   ```

Figure 15-30	Canceling text selection within the Web document

```
function setup() {
    shop1 = document.getElementById("item1");
    shop2 = document.getElementById("item2");
    shop3 = document.getElementById("item3");
    shop4 = document.getElementById("item4");
    cart = document.getElementById("cartBox");

    assignF(shop1);
    assignF(shop2);
    assignF(shop3);
    assignF(shop4);

    document.onselectstart=stopSelect;
}

function stopSelect() {
    return false;
}
```

4. Close the file, saving your changes.

5. Reload **games.htm** in your Internet Explorer browser. Verify that as you drag your mouse pointer over the text on the page, no text is selected by the browser.

   Trouble? The selectStart event is supported only in the Internet Explorer document object model. There is no comparable event handler for the Netscape 4 or W3C DOMs.

You've completed your work on enhancing the drag-and-drop features of the Games Etc. page. Pete wants you to add a few more things to the page, which you'll look at in the next session.

Session 15.2 Quick Check

1. What is the reference for the event object in Internet Explorer? What is the reference in the DOM event model?
2. What property would you use to determine the type of event associated with the event object?
3. What properties would you use to determine the screen coordinates of an event?
4. What properties would you enter to determine the window coordinates of an event?
5. What technique can you use to ensure that a dragged item will always be on top as it moves across the Web page?
6. A function associated with the click event is called "stopClick()". What line should you add to this function to cancel default action associated with the click event?

Session 15.3

Formatting a Dragged Object

Pete has looked over your Web page and would like it to provide users with more visual feedback. For example, when a user hovers the pointer over one of the movable objects, Pete would like the pointer to change shape to 🖑 to indicate that the object is clickable. When an object is being moved across the page, he wants the pointer to change to ✛ .

Setting the Cursor Style

Mouse pointers can be defined using an object's style properties. The syntax is

```
object.style.cursor=cursorType;
```

where `object` is an object in the document, and `cursorType` is a text string that identifies the type of pointer to be displayed. You can also define the pointer style in a CSS style declaration by using the syntax

```
cursor: cursorType
```

Figure 15-31 shows the different types of pointers you can display with either the JavaScript object property command or a style sheet declaration. In addition to the types listed in the figure, you can also specify a pointer type of "auto", which allows a user's browser to determine the appearance of the pointer for you. If you want to use a customized pointer, you can load one from a URL using the style `cursor: url( url )` where `url` is the location of the cursor image. Cursor images are stored in files with the file extensions .uri or .ani. Many browsers do not yet support customized cursors, so you should not rely on them if you need a Web page to be cross-browser compatible. In addition, many browsers support an extended list of cursor styles not shown in Figure 15-31.

Figure 15-31 Cursor styles

Cursor	Style	Cursor	Style
+	cursor: crosshair	↕	cursor: n-resize
↖	cursor: default	↗	cursor: ne-resize
↖?	cursor: help	↔	cursor: e-resize
⊕	cursor: move	↘	cursor: se-resize
🖑	cursor: pointer	↕	cursor: s-resize
I	cursor: text	↗	cursor: sw-resize
⌛	cursor: wait	↔	cursor: w-resize
↖	cursor: url(*url*)	↘	cursor: nw-resize

Reference Window

Setting Cursor Styles

- To change the appearance of a mouse pointer use the cursor style
  ```
  object.style.cursor = cursorType;
  ```
  where `object` is an object on the Web page and `cursorType` is a text string of one of the cursor styles supported by CSS.
- To change the pointer using CSS, add the following style to the style declaration for an object:
  ```
  cursor: cursorType
  ```

Pete wants to change the cursor style for each of the sales items to 🖑 . When a customer moves a sales item, he wants the cursor to change to ⊕ while the object is in motion. After the customer drops the sales item, the cursor style should return to ⊕ . To make this change you'll add commands to the assignF(), grabIt(), and dropIt() functions that set the cursor style when the page loads, during the mousedown event, and after the sales item is dropped during the mouseup event.

To set the cursor style:

▶ 1. Reopen the **games.htm** file in your text editor.

▶ 2. Add the following line to the end of the assignF() function:

```
object.style.cursor="pointer";
```

Remember that assignF() contains the general code that sets the style for each of the four sales items.

3. Add the following line to the grabIt() function after the command to increase the z-index value of the dragItem object:

```
dragItem.style.cursor="move";
```

4. Add the following line to the start of the dropIt() function. Figure 15-32 highlights the inserted code.

```
dragItem.style.cursor="pointer";
```

Changing the cursor style ◄ Figure 15-32

```
function assignF(object) {
    object.onmousedown=grabIt;
    object.style.cursor="pointer";
}

function grabIt(e) {
    dragItem = eventSource(e);
    mouseX=eventPositionX(e);
    mouseY=eventPositionY(e);

    diffX=mouseX-getXCoord(dragItem);
    diffY=mouseY-getYCoord(dragItem);

    maxZ++;
    dragItem.style.zIndex=maxZ;
    dragItem.style.cursor="move";

    applyEventF(dragItem,"mousemove",moveIt,false);
    applyEventF(dragItem,"mouseup",dropIt,false);
}

function moveIt(e) {
    mouseX=eventPositionX(e);
    mouseY=eventPositionY(e);
    placeIt(dragItem, mouseX-diffX, mouseY-diffY);
}

function dropIt(e) {
    dragItem.style.cursor="pointer";
    dropPosX=getXCoord(dragItem);
    dropPosY=getYCoord(dragItem);
    if (!withinIt(dropPosX, dropPosY, cart)) snapBack();
    removeEventF(dragItem,"mousemove",moveIt,false);
}
```

5. Save your changes to the file and reload **games.htm** in your Web browser. Verify that the cursor style for each of the sales items is now 🖑 and that the cursor style while dragging an object is ✛ (see Figure 15-33).

The pointer and move cursor styles ◄ Figure 15-33

Trouble? If you are running Opera you will not see the cursor style change to the "move" pointer. Internet Explorer 4 does not support the "pointer" cursor, using the cursor style, "hand" instead.

Changing the Color

The second enhancement that Pete wants you to make is to change the color of items once they've been placed into the shopping cart. Pete would like all items in the shopping cart to appear in blue, while outside the cart they should appear in red. This provides additional visual feedback to customers that sales items have been properly dropped into the shopping cart. One of the functions in the shop.js file is the colorIt function, which allows you to specify the text and border color of an object (see Figure 15-2). To change the color of the dragItem object to blue, you would use the command

```
colorIt(dragItem, "blue");
```

You'll insert the following command block into the moveIt function so that whenever a user moves an item into the shopping cart box, the item will change color:

```
if (withinIt(mouseX-diffX, mouseY-diffY, cart)) colorIt
(dragItem, "blue");
else colorIt(dragItem, "red");
```

Once again, the withinIt function determines whether the coordinates of the upper-left corner of the object fall within the shopping cart boundaries. You determine these coordinates by subtracting the values of the diffX and diffY variables from the coordinates of the current mouse position. Thus, the upper-left corner of the dragItem is located at the coordinates (MouseX-diffX, MouseY-diffY). (You can refer back to Figure 15-21 for an illustration.)

To set the color of the dragged item:

1. Return to the **games.htm** file in your text editor.

2. Locate the moveIt() function and add the following lines as shown in Figure 15-34.

```
if (withinIt(mouseX-diffX, mouseY-diffY, cart)) colorIt
(dragItem, "blue");
else colorIt(dragItem, "red");
```

Figure 15-34 Changing the object color

```
function moveIt(e) {
    mouseX=eventPositionX(e);
    mouseY=eventPositionY(e);
    placeIt(dragItem, mouseX-diffX, mouseY-diffY);
    if (withinIt(mouseX-diffX, mouseY-diffY, cart)) colorIt(dragItem, "blue");
    else colorIt(dragItem, "red");
}
```

3. Save your changes and reload **games.htm** in your Web browser. Verify that when you drag a sales item over the shopping cart box, its border color and font color change to blue.

Working with the Double-Click Event

Pete is aware that some customers do not like using drag-and-drop techniques for manipulating objects, and prefer one-step methods. Pete would like those customers to have the option of moving a sales item by double-clicking it. He suggests that you add a double-click event handler to the Web page so that if a customer double-clicks a sales item, it is placed in the sales cart; double-clicking an item in the sales cart should remove it from the cart. To complete this task, you'll create a function called snapIn(), which will be similar to the snapBack() function you created at the end of the last session. Unlike snapBack(), snapIn() will place each sales item in an appropriate spot within the shopping cart. The snapIn() function will also change the color of dragItem to blue in order to provide the visual indication that it lies within the shopping cart. The code for the function is

```
function snapIn() {
   if (dragItem==shop1) placeIt(dragItem, 300, 140);
   else if (dragItem==shop2) placeIt(dragItem, 300, 185);
   else if (dragItem==shop3) placeIt(dragItem, 300, 230);
   else if (dragItem==shop4) placeIt(dragItem, 300, 275);
   colorIt(dragItem, "blue");
}
```

Add this function to the games.htm file.

To add the snapIn() function:

1. Return to the **games.htm** file in your text editor.

2. Below the snapBack() function, insert the following function.

   ```
   function snapIn() {
       if (dragItem==shop1) placeIt(dragItem, 300, 140);
       else if (dragItem==shop2) placeIt(dragItem, 300, 185);
       else if (dragItem==shop3) placeIt(dragItem, 300, 230);
       else if (dragItem==shop4) placeIt(dragItem, 300, 275);
       colorIt(dragItem, "blue");
   }
   ```

   You also need to modify the snapBack() function so that it sets the color of an object placed back in its original location to red.

3. Add the following line to the end of the snapBack() function. Figure 15-35 shows the final code for both functions.

   ```
   colorIt(dragItem, "red");
   ```

The snapBack() and snapIn() functions ◄ Figure 15-35

```
function snapBack() {
    if (dragItem==shop1) placeIt(dragItem, 10, 140);
    else if (dragItem==shop2) placeIt(dragItem, 10, 185);
    else if (dragItem==shop3) placeIt(dragItem, 10, 230);
    else if (dragItem==shop4) placeIt(dragItem, 10, 275);
    colorIt(dragItem, "red");
}

function snapIn() {
    if (dragItem==shop1) placeIt(dragItem, 300, 140);
    else if (dragItem==shop2) placeIt(dragItem, 300, 185);
    else if (dragItem==shop3) placeIt(dragItem, 300, 230);
    else if (dragItem==shop4) placeIt(dragItem, 300, 275);
    colorIt(dragItem, "blue");
}
```

Next you'll create the jumpIt() function that determines the location of the sales item. If the item is within the shopping cart, the function calls the snapBack() function to move the item back to its original location. If the item is not within the shopping cart, the function calls the snapIn() function to put it in the cart. The code for the jumpIt() function is

```
function jumpIt() {
  dragPosX=getXCoord(dragItem);
  dragPosY=getYCoord(dragItem);
  if (withinIt(dragPosX, dragPosY, cart)) snapBack();
  else snapIn();
}
```

Add this function to the games.htm file.

To create the jumpIt() function:

1. Below the assignF() function, insert the following code:

   ```
   function jumpIt() {
     dragPosX=getXCoord(dragItem);
     dragPosY=getYCoord(dragItem);
     if (withinIt(dragPosX, dragPosY, cart)) snapBack();
     else snapIn();
   }
   ```

2. Save your changes to the file.

Finally, you need to create an event handler to respond to a double-click event within any of the four sales items. You'll add the following line to the assignF() function (recall that the assignF() function is the general function that assigns event handlers and properties to the four sales items):

```
object.ondblclick=mouseDouble;
```

The code for the mouseDouble() function called by this event handler is

```
function mouseDouble(e) {
   dragItem = eventSource(e);
   jumpIt();
}
```

Note that the mouseDouble() function calls the cross-browser function eventSource() to accommodate the differences between the event models in determining the source of the double-click event.

To complete and test the double-click event handler:

1. Add the following command to the end of the assignF() function:

   ```
   object.ondblclick=mouseDouble;
   ```

2. Below the assignF() function insert the mouseDouble() function as shown in Figure 15-36.

   ```
   function mouseDouble(e) {
      dragItem = eventSource(e);
      jumpIt();
   }
   ```

```
function assignF(object) {
    object.onmousedown=grabIt;
    object.style.cursor="pointer";
    object.ondblclick=mouseDouble;
}

function mouseDouble(e) {
    dragItem = eventSource(e);
    jumpIt();
}

function jumpIt() {
    dragPosX=getXCoord(dragItem);
    dragPosY=getYCoord(dragItem);
    if (withinIt(dragPosX, dragPosY, cart)) snapBack();
    else snapIn();
}
```

3. Save your changes to the file and reload **games.htm** in your Web browser. Verify that as you double-click each of the four sales items they are alternately moved into and out of the shopping cart.

   Trouble? Under some browsers, the double-click action may display one of the browser's shortcut menus in addition to moving the sales item. If you double-click the letter box within a sales item, the letter box will change color, but the sales item will not move.

Working with the Mouse Button

So far in this case, you've assumed that users press the left (or primary) mouse button to move items around the page; however, this is not necessarily the case. Users can also drag and drop the sales items using the right mouse button—or even the middle button, for mice that have them. If you need to determine which mouse button a user has pressed, you can use the button property, which returns a numeric value indicating the button. In the DOM event model, the button values are 0=left, 1=middle, 2=right. In the Internet Explorer event model, these values are 0=left, 2=right, 4=middle. For Netscape 6 the values are 1=left, 2=middle, 3=right. Thus any script you write that incorporates the mouse button has to adjust for these differences. You can determine which button values are assigned by your browser by using the demo_events.htm file from the previous session.

The right and middle mouse buttons usually have default actions associated with them. For example, the right mouse button usually displays a shortcut menu for the highlighted object. Thus, you may not wish to interfere with these default actions.

Working with Keyboard Events

Some users with disabilities are unable to work with mouse pointers and must interact with Web pages using solely their keyboards. Pete wants his Web site to be widely accessible, so he asks you to add a keyboard interface to the shopping cart page. He suggests allowing customers to select or deselect sales items by pressing the letter on the keyboard that corresponds to the item (see Figure 15-37).

Figure 15-37 ▶ **Creating an event handler for a keyboard event**

pressing the A key moves the first sales item into the shopping cart

pressing the A key again takes the sales item out

Capturing a Keyboard Event

Three main keyboard events are available to work with:

- **keydown**: The user has pressed a key down.
- **keyup**: The user has released a key.
- **keypress**: The user has pressed and released a key.

For this page, you'll work with the keydown event, running a function named key-Drag() to move a sale item either into or out of the shopping cart whenever the user presses the a, b, c, or d key. Since the user is not pressing the key down within any particular object, you'll add an event handler for this event to the entire document.

To create an event handler for the key down event:

▶ 1. Return to the **games.htm** file in your text editor.

▶ 2. Add the following command to the setUp() function as shown in Figure 15-38.

```
document.onkeydown=keyDrag;
```

Final setUp() function ◄ **Figure 15-38**

Final setUp() function ◄ **Figure 15-38**

```
function setUp() {
    shop1 = document.getElementById("item1");
    shop2 = document.getElementById("item2");
    shop3 = document.getElementById("item3");
    shop4 = document.getElementById("item4");
    cart = document.getElementById("cartBox");

    assignF(shop1);
    assignF(shop2);
    assignF(shop3);
    assignF(shop4);

    document.onselectstart=stopSelect;
    document.onkeydown=keyDrag;
}
```

Examining Key Codes

Now that you've created an event handler for the keydown event, your next task is to determine which key a user has pressed. Both event models use the keyCode property of the event object to return the numeric value associated with the pressed key. While no set standard yet matches a particular key code to a specific key, most of the key code values have common meanings among all browsers. Figure 15-39 lists some keyboard keys and their corresponding key code values. For example, if a user presses the letter A on the keyboard, the corresponding keycode value is 65.

Keys and keycode values ◄ **Figure 15-39**

Keys(s)	Key Code Value(s)	Keys(s)	Key Code Value(s)
[0 - 9]	48 - 57	page up	33
[a - z]	65 - 90	page down	34
backspace	8	end	35
tab	9	home	36
enter	13	left arrow	37
shift	16	up arrow	38
ctrl	17	right arrow	39
alt	18	down arrow	40
pause/break	19	insert	45
caps lock	20	delete	46
esc	23	[f1 - f12]	112 - 123
space	32		

To test whether these key code values match the key codes returned by your browser, you can reopen the demo_events.htm file that you used in the second session of this tutorial and press and hold down different keys on your keyboard. The corresponding keycode value for each key will be displayed on the Web page.

If you need to determine which keyboard letter a user has pressed, you do not need to go through all 26 of the keycode values. You can quickly return the letter character through the String method:

```
String.fromCharCode( key )
```

where `key` is the keycode value. For example, the expression

```
String.fromCharCode(65)
```

returns the character "a" because 65 is the keycode value of that character.

Because there are differences between the two event models in how they refer to event objects, you decide to create a cross-browser function named getKeyCode() to return the keycode value. Add this function to shop.js along with your other cross-browser functions.

To create the getKeyCode() function:

1. If necessary, reopen the **shop.js** file in your text editor.

2. At the bottom of the file, insert the following function (see Figure 15-40):

   ```
   function getKeyCode(e) {
       if (IE) return event.keyCode;
       else if (DOM) return e.keyCode;
   }
   ```

Figure 15-40	The getKeyCode() function

```
function eventPositionY(e) {
    if (IE) return event.clientY;
    else if (DOM) return e.clientY;
}

function getKeyCode(e) {
    if (IE) return event.keyCode;
    else if (DOM) return e.keyCode;
}
```

3. Close **shop.js**, saving your changes.

Creating the keyDrag() Function

With all of the other functions in place, you can now write the keyDrag() function. This function is similar to the mouseDouble() function you just created for the double-click event. The difference is that instead of setting the dragItem object equal to the event source, you'll use the key code values to determine which sales item to move. The code of the keyDrag() function is

```
function keyDrag(e) {
    dragItem = null;
    key=getKeyCode(e);
    if (key==65) dragItem=shop1;
    else if (key==66) dragItem=shop2;
    else if (key==67) dragItem=shop3;
    else if (key==68) dragItem=shop4;
    jumpIt();
}
```

This script starts by setting dragItem to a null value, which ensures that the function does not inherit a dragItem setting from any other event functions that have moved a sales item. Add this function to the games.htm file.

To insert the keyDrag() function:

1. Return to **games.htm** in your text editor.

2. Below the assignF() function, insert the following code (see Figure 15-41):

```
function keyDrag(e) {
    dragItem = null;
    key=getKeyCode(e);
    if (key==65) dragItem=shop1;
    else if (key==66) dragItem=shop2;
    else if (key==67) dragItem=shop3;
    else if (key==68) dragItem=shop4;
    jumpIt();
}
```

The keyDrag() function | Figure 15-41

```
function assignF(object) {
    object.onmousedown=grabIt;
    object.style.cursor="pointer";
    object.ondblclick=mouseDouble;
}

function keyDrag(e) {
    dragItem=null;
    key=getKeyCode(e);
    if (key==65) dragItem=shop1;
    else if (key==66) dragItem=shop2;
    else if (key==67) dragItem=shop3;
    else if (key==68) dragItem=shop4;
    jumpIt();
}
```

3. Close the file, saving your changes.

4. Reopen **games.htm** in your Web browser. Verify that when you press **a**, **b**, **c**, and **d** the four sales items are alternately added to and removed from the shopping cart.

   Trouble? In some browsers, the a, b, c, or d keys may be associated with browser commands.

Modifier Keys

In addition to keyboard characters, keyboards contain modifier keys. For a PC, the **modifier keys** are Ctrl, Alt, and Shift. Modifier keys pressed along with letter keys are used as keyboard shortcuts to menu commands in many programs. For example, in many browsers, holding down the Ctrl key while pressing p runs the Print command. You can create your own key combinations to run customized functions from the keyboard. However, in doing so you must be careful not to interfere with the key combinations already reserved by a user's browser; in case of a conflict, the browser might ignore your customized keyboard shortcut.

Both event models use the following properties of the event object to determine the state of the Alt, Ctrl, and Shift keys:

```
altKey;
ctrlKey;
shiftKey;
```

Each of these properties returns a Boolean value indicating whether the modifier key is being pressed. In addition, the DOM event model also supports the event object property

```
metaKey;
```

to determine whether the Meta key is being pressed. The Meta key is a key found on a UNIX workstation and is usually equivalent to the Alt key on PC keyboards or the Command key on Macintosh keyboards. You can use modifier keys along with other events occurring within a user's Web browser. For example, you could add the following conditional expression to the grabIt() function so that a customer can grab an item for dragging only when the Shift key is being pressed:

```
function grabIt(e) {
    if (event.shiftKey || e.shiftKey) {
    commands
    }
}
```

You've completed your work on the Web page, having created code for several different mouse and keyboard events in order to achieve the drag-and-drop shopping cart Pete wanted for the Games Etc. Web page. He will look over your document and get back to you with any further ideas or projects. You can close any open files in your text editor or browser.

Tips for Working with Events

- Create customized cross-browser functions that resolve the differences among the event models
- Position any objects that will be dragged and dropped using inline styles prior to running the drag-and-drop commands
- In a drag-and-drop application, provide users with additional visual feedback that an object is being moved, such as color changes and pointer changes
- Capture keyboard and mouse events to make your Web page more accessible to users with disabilities

Review

Session 15.3 Quick Check

1. What style declaration would you use to display an hourglass as the pointer? What is the equivalent JavaScript command to do this?
2. What property would you use to determine which mouse button was pressed during an event? Describe how the event models differ in their interpretations of the value returned by this property.
3. What event corresponds to a user pressing and holding down a keyboard key?
4. What event object property would you use to determine which key was pressed by a user?
5. What keycode value is generated when a user presses the spacebar?
6. What event object property would you use to determine whether the user is pressing the Alt key?

Review

Tutorial Summary

In this tutorial you learned how to work with the DOM and Internet Explorer event models to capture and respond to mouse and keyboard events. The first session examined different ways of attaching event handlers to your objects and scripts. It then explored the two main event models, examining how events are propagated through the document tree. The session concluded with the task of creating cross-browser functions to capture and release functions attached to events and objects. The second session looked at the properties of the event object and demonstrated how to determine the coordinates of an event and the object that initiated it. Using these properties, you created objects that could be dragged and dropped on the Web page. The third session displayed how to work with the double-click event and examined how to determine which mouse button was pressed by the user. The third session concluded with keyboard events. You learned how to capture a keyboard action, how to determine which key was pressed by the user, and to work with modifier keys.

Key Terms

bubbling phase	event model	keypress
capture phase	event object	keyup
DOM event model	Internet Explorer event	modifier key
event bubbling	model	target phase
event listener	keydown	

Practice

Practice the skills you learned in the tutorial using the same case scenario.

Review Assignments

Data files needed for this Review Assignment: events.js, functions.js, games.css, image1. jpg-image24.jpg, logo.jpg, makepuzzle.js, puzzle.jpg, puzztxt.htm

Pete has approved your design of the monthly specials page for the Games Etc. Web site. He now wants you to finish a Web page he's been working on that displays a sliding block puzzle. In a sliding block puzzle, the puzzle pieces are laid out in a grid with one blank space. The object of the puzzle is to use the blank space to move the pieces around in the puzzle until the puzzle image is restored. A preview of the page is shown in Figure 15-42. The puzzle is divided into a 5 × 5 grid, with each piece in the grid 60 pixels wide by 60 pixels high. Each piece is formatted as a separate div element with the image set as the tile's background. Starting at the upper left of the grid and moving right and then down, the div elements have the id names piece01, piece02, and so forth. The blank space is also a div element, with the id name "blank".

Figure 15-42

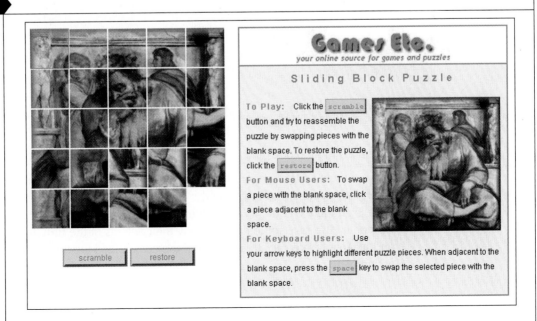

Pete wants this puzzle to work with both the mouse and the keyboard. He needs you to program the following actions:

- If a user clicks a piece to the left, right, above, or below of the blank space, that piece should swap positions with the blank space.
- Pieces adjacent to the blank space should display the pointer cursor, while all other pieces should display the default cursor.
- One piece in the puzzle is highlighted with a red border. A user can highlight different pieces by pressing the arrow keys on the keyboard.
- If the highlighted piece is adjacent to the blank space, a user can swap the highlighted piece with the blank space by pressing the spacebar on the keyboard.

Pete has also provided several JavaScript files that contain functions you'll be able to use in your Web page. The makepuzzle.js file contains functions to create and scramble the puzzle pieces. The events.js file contains several functions that resolve the differences between the event models in working with the event object. The functions.js file contains functions to work with the properties of objects on the Web page. Figure 15-43 summarizes the functions that you'll use in this problem. Some of these functions should be familiar to you from this and previous tutorials.

Figure 15-43

File	Function	Description
makepuzzle.js	setUpBoard()	Sets up the initial layout of the puzzle
	scramble()	Scrambles the board layout
	colorPiece(*object, z, color*)	Changes the border color and z-index value of a puzzle piece where *object* is the piece, *z* is the new z-index value, and *color* is the new color.
events.js	applyEventF(*obj,ename,fname,cap*)	Attaches an event handler for an event *ename* occurring in an object *obj*, attaching the function *fname* to it.
	removeEventF(*obj,ename,fname,cap*)	Removes an event handler from an object
	eventSource(*e*)	Returns the source of an event *e*
	getKeyCode(*e*)	Returns the keycode of a keyboard event *e*
functions.js	getDIV(*x,y*)	Returns the div element that contains the coordinates (*x, y*)
	swapIt(*object1, object2*)	Swaps the positions of *object1* and *object2*
	getXCoord(*object*) getYCoord(*object*)	Returns the x and y coordinate of *object*

To create the sliding block puzzle:

1. Use your text editor to open the **puzztxt.htm** file from the tutorial.15/review folder. Enter *your name* and *the date* in the comment section and save the file as **puzzle. htm**. Examine the contents of the file to become familiar with the order form and its elements. Also take some time to study the contents of the **functions.js**, **events.js**, and **makepuzzle.js** files to understand the customized functions you'll use in this assignment.

2. If necessary, return to the **puzzle.htm** file in your text editor. Within the init() function in the embedded script element, add the following commands:

    a. Create four variables named pieceLeft, pieceTop, pieceRight, and pieceBottom. These variables will reference the four pieces adjacent to the blank space. Set the initial value of the pieceLeft variable equal to the div element with the id "piece24". Set the initial value of the pieceTop variable equal to the div element with the id "piece20". Set the initial values of pieceRight and pieceBottom to null.

    b. Create a variable named blankPiece that represents the blank space in the puzzle. Set the value of the blankPiece variable equal to the div element with the id "blank".

    c. Call the watchPiece() function using pieceLeft as the parameter value. Call the watchPiece() function again using pieceTop as the parameter value.

3. Below the init() function insert the watchPiece() function. The purpose of this function is to watch one of the pieces for the click event. The function has a single parameter named object. Add the following commands to the function:

    a. Use the applyEventF() function to run the mouseSwap function when the click event occurs within the object (you'll create the mouseSwap() function shortly). Set the capture parameter to false.

    b. Change the cursor style of the object to "pointer".

4. Create another function named ignorePiece(). This function is similar to the watchPiece() function except that it detaches the click event from the piece object. Add the following commands to the function:

    a. Use the removeEventF() function to ignore the mouseSwap function when the click event occurs within the object. Set the capture parameter to false.

    b. Change the cursor style of the object to "default".

5. Add the mouseSwap() function. The purpose of this function is to swap the position of a piece clicked in the puzzle with the blank space. The mouseSwap() function has a single parameter, e, which represents the event object. Add the following commands to the function:

    a. Create a variable named pieceClicked which is equal to the source of the event. (*Hint*: Use the eventSource() function from the events.js file.)

    b. Use the swapIt() function to swap the positions of pieceClicked and blankPiece.

    c. Call the resetPieces() function.

6. Insert the resetPieces() function. The purpose of this function is to remove the event handlers from the pieces that were formerly adjacent to the blank space (now that the blank space has been moved, you will have to determine where the adjacent pieces are now located). There are no parameters for this function. Add the following commands:

    a. If pieceLeft is not equal to null, call the ignorePiece() function using pieceLeft as the parameter value. Repeat this step for the pieceTop, pieceRight, and pieceBottom variables.

    b. Call the findNewPieces() function.

7. Insert the findNewPieces() function. The purpose of this function is to determine which four pieces are now adjacent to the blank space. There are no parameters for this function. Add the following commands:

    a. Use the getXCoord() and getYCoord() functions to determine the x and y coordinates of the blankPiece. Store the values returned by these functions in variables named x and y respectively.

    b. Use the getDIV() function to locate the piece to the left of the blank space. The first parameter value is equal to x – 30. The second parameter value is equal to y + 30. Store the object returned by the getDIV() function in the pieceLeft variable.

    c. If pieceLeft is not equal to null (indicating there is a piece to the left of the blank space), call the watchPiece() function using pieceLeft as the parameter value.

    d. Repeat Steps b and c for the pieceTop, pieceRight, and pieceBottom variables. The coordinates for pieceTop should be: (x + 30, y – 30); for pieceRight the coordinates are: (x + 90, y + 30); and for pieceBottom the coordinates are: (x + 30, y + 90).

8. Save your changes to the file. Open **puzzle.htm** in your Web browser and verify: (a) that only pieces adjacent to the blank space display the pointer cursor; (b) clicking a piece adjacent to the blank space swaps the positions of the piece and the blank space.

9. Return to **puzzle.htm** in your text editor. Next you'll create the keyboard interface for the puzzle. Within the init() function add the following commands:

    a. Apply an event handler to the document that runs the function keyOnPiece() in response to a keydown event.

    b. Create a variable named keyPiece that represents the piece highlighted in the puzzle. Set the initial value to the div element with the id name "piece01".

    c. Use the colorPiece() function to set the z-index value of keyPiece to 2 and the border color to red.

10. Insert the function keyOnPiece(). The purpose of this function is to either move the highlighted piece or swap it with the blank space. The function has a single parameter, e, representing the event object. Add the following commands:

    a. Use the getKeyCode() function to return the key code value of the event. Store the value in a variable named key.

    b. If the left arrow key has been pressed, call the function moveKeyPiece() with the parameter value "left". (*Hint*: Refer to Figure 15-39 to determine the key code value for the left arrow key.)

    c. Repeat the previous step for the up, right, and down arrows. For the up arrow, call the moveKeyPiece() function with a parameter value of "up"; for the right arrow the parameter value is "right", and for the down arrow the parameter value is "down".

    d. Otherwise, if the key value indicates that the spacebar has been pressed, run the swapKeyPiece() function.

11. Insert the function moveKeyPiece(). The purpose of this function is to move the highlighting from one piece to another. The function has a single parameter named direction. Add the following commands to the function:

    a. Create a variable named nextKeyPiece. This variable represents the next piece that will be highlighted in the puzzle. Set the initial value of nextKeyPiece to null.

    b. Use the getXCoord() and getYCoord() functions to retrieve the (x,y) coordinate of keyPiece. Store these values in variables named x and y respectively.

    c. If direction equals "left", use the getDIV() function to determine the position of the next piece to be highlighted. Use parameter values of x – 30, and y + 30. Store the object returned by the getDIV() function in the nextKeyPiece variable.

d. Repeat the previous step for direction values equal to "up", "right", and "down". For "up" the coordinates of the next piece are $(x + 30, y - 30)$; for "right" the coordinates are: $(x + 90, y + 30)$; and for "down" the coordinates are: $(x + 30, y + 90)$.

e. If nextKeyPiece is not equal to null (meaning that there is a piece adjacent to the current piece in the direction indicated), then: (1) Call the colorPiece() function to change the z-index of keyPiece to 1 and the border color to "white"; (2) Call the colorPiece() function to change the z-index of nextKeyPiece to 2 and the border color to "red"; (3) Change the value of keyPiece to nextKeyPiece.

12. Insert the function swapKeyPiece(). The purpose of this function is to swap the highlighted piece with the blank space, if they are adjacent. There are no parameters for this function. Add the following commands:

a. Use the getXCoord() and getYCoord() functions to retrieve the (x,y) coordinates of keyPiece. Store these values in variables named x and y respectively.

b. Call the getDIV() function using the parameter values $x - 30$ and $y + 30$. If the object returned by this function is equal to blankPiece, then call the swapIt() function to swap the positions of keyPiece and blankPiece.

c. Repeat the previous step with the following coordinates: $(x + 30, y - 30)$, $(x + 90, y + 30)$, and $(x + 30, y + 90)$. You must put the four If statements in an If...Else conditional structure to ensure that only one swap occurs.

d. Call the resetPieces() function.

13. Save your changes to the file and reopen **puzzle.htm** in your Web browser. Verify that: (a) pressing the arrow keys moves the highlighting from one piece to another; (b) that pressing the spacebar when the highlighted piece is next to the blank space swaps the position of the two.

14. Submit your completed assignment to your instructor. You may try to scramble the puzzle and solve it, but it is not necessary to complete the assignment.

Case Problem 1

Data files needed for this Case Problem: bkgrnd.jpg, links.jpg, logo.jpg, styles.css, survey.js, survtxt.htm

Online Market Surveys   Derek Mahnaz organizes the Online Market Survey, a Web site that reports consumer preferences and opinions. Derek has asked you to create a Web page in which consumers can list their preferences for computer manufacturers. Derek envisions the Web page listing the manufacturers in separate boxes. Users would then be able to drag and drop the boxes in order of preference, with the computer manufacturers they prefer most at the top, and those least preferred at the bottom. Figure 15-44 shows a preview of Derek's page.

Figure 15-44

Each of the five computer manufacturer names has been placed in a separate div element, with id names of Store1 through Store5. Derek has also provided a file, survey.js, that includes some functions of use to you. The placeIt() function places objects that specific coordinates on the page. The getXCoord() and getYCoord() functions return the x and y coordinates of a page object. A link to this file has already been added to Derek's Web page.

To complete the Market Survey page:

1. Use your text editor to open the **survtxt.htm** file from the tutorial.15/case1 folder. Enter *your name* and *the date* in the comment section and save the file as **survey.htm**.

2. In the embedded script element, insert the following global variables:
   a. Store, startX, startY, diffX, diffY, and maxZ. Set the initial value of maxZ to 2.
   b. Add two more global variables: one that returns a Boolean value indicating whether the user's browser supports the Internet Explorer event model, and the other that returns a Boolean value indicating whether the browser supports the DOM event model.

3. Add the following five cross-browser functions that support both event models: (a) a function to determine the source of events occurring in the Web page; (b) a function to determine the x-coordinate of the event; (c) a function to determine the y-coordinate of the event; (d) a function to attach or listen for an event occurring within an object and apply a function to that event; and (e) a function to remove an attached event function from an object.

4. Create a function named setEvents(). In this function add event handlers to the Store1 through Store5 elements, running the selectStore() function when a user depresses the mouse button within each element.

5. Create the selectStore() function to grab a store element in preparation for dragging it across the Web page. The function should have a single parameter, e. Add the following commands to the function:
   a. Set the Store variable equal to the source of the event. Set startX equal to the x-coordinate of the Store object and startY equal to the y-coordinate of the Store object.

    b. Set mouseX equal to the x-coordinate of the event object and mouseY equal to the y-coordinate of the event object. Subtract startX from mouseX and store the difference in a variable named diffX. Subtract startY from mouseY and store the difference in diffY.

    c. Ensure that the dragged store is always on top by increasing the value of maxZ by 1 and changing the z-index value of the Store object to maxZ.

    d. Attach the moveStore() function to the Store object and run it in response to a mousemove event. Attach the dropStore() function to the Store object, running it in response to a mouseup event. Use event bubbling as the propagation method for both functions.

6. Create the moveStore() function to enable moving the Store object across the page alongside the mouse pointer. The function has a single parameter, e, representing the event object. Add the following commands:

    a. Store the x-coordinate of the event in the variable mouseX. Store the y-coordinate of the event in mouseY.

    b. Use the placeIt() function to place the Store object at the page coordinates (mouseX-diffX, mouseY-diffY).

7. Create the dropStore() function to enable dropping the Store object on the page. The function has a single parameter, e, for the event object. Add the following commands:

    a. Detach the moveStore() function from the Store object in the case of a mousemove event.

    b. Store the current x-coordinate of the Store object in a variable named x. Store the y-coordinate of the Store object in a variable named y.

    c. Derek wants the Store object to line up neatly within the blank boxes on the page. Thus, if x falls in the range 440–590 and y falls in the range 100–130 use the placeIt() function to place the Store object at the page coordinates (440, 100). Repeat this for the other four blank boxes. If x falls in the range 440–590 and y lies within 140–170 move Store to (440,140). If x falls in the range 440–590 and y lies within 180–210 move Store to (440, 180). If x lies within 440–590 and y lies within 220–250 move Store to (440, 220). If x lies within 440–590 and y lies within 260–290 move Store to (440, 260). Otherwise, do nothing.

8. Create a function named cancelSelect() that returns the Boolean value false. Add an event handler to the setEvents() function to run the cancelSelect() function in response to the start of text selection within the document.

9. Add an event handler to the body element, running the setEvents() function when the page is loaded.

10. For the inline styles of the Store1 through Store5 div elements, add a style to change the appearance of the cursor to "pointer".

11. Save your changes to the file and load **survey.htm** in your Web browser. Verify that you can drag and drop the five computer manufacturer boxes to the boxes in the preference list and that the manufacturer names line up within the boxes. Verify that each of the manufacturer boxes displays the pointer cursor.

12. Submit your completed Web site to your instructor.

Apply

*Use the skills you
learned to create a
horizontal scrollbar for
a slideshow*

Case Problem 2

**Data files needed for this Case Problem: back.jpg, badgtxt.htm, bar.jpg, corner.jpg,
functions.js, image0.jpg - image9.jpg, links.jpg, logo.jpg, styles.css**

Badger Aviation   Wayne Statz is the president and owner of Badger Aviation, an aviation company specializing in tours, charters, lessons, and shuttles in southern Wisconsin.
He's hired you to update the company's Web page. One of the pages you'll work with
contains a slideshow from one of Badger Aviation's tours of the area. Wayne would like
you to create a horizontal scrollbar for the slideshow that users can navigate with either
the mouse or the keyboard. Figure 15-45 shows a preview of the page you'll create for
Wayne.

Figure 15-45

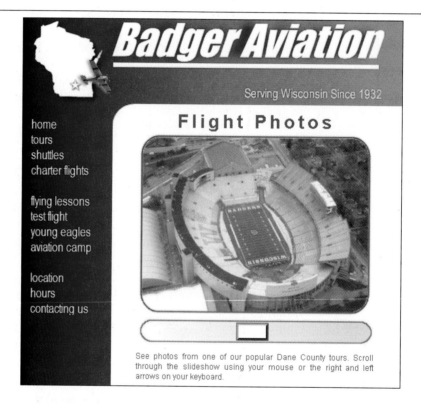

Much of the layout has been done for you. Your job is to create the array of images for
the slideshow and program the operation of the scrollbar. The scroll button in the scrollbar has been stored in the Web page as a div element with the id name "button". An
external JavaScript file named functions.js contains two functions that you can use in
completing this Web page: the placeIt() function places objects at specified coordinates
on the page and the getXCoord() function contains the x-coordinate of an object on the
page. You'll have to create any other functions that you need.

To complete the Badger Aviation slideshow:

1. Use your text editor to open the **badgtxt.htm** file from the tutorial.15/case2
   folder. Enter *your name* and *the date* in the comment section and save the file as
   badger.htm.
2. Add an embedded script element to the document head. Within the script element
   do the following:

   a. Create an image array named slide. Populate the array with the 10 image files image0.jpg through image9.jpg.

   b. Create two global variables: one that indicates whether a user's browser supports the Internet Explorer event model and another that indicates whether the browser supports the DOM event model.

3. Create the following four cross-browser event functions: (a) one to attach a function to an object when an event occurs; (b) one to remove an attached event function from an object; (c) one to return the x-coordinate of an event; and (d) one to return the key code value of a keyboard event.

4. Create a function named setup() to set up the page for the operation of the horizontal scrollbar. Add the following commands to the function:

   a. Create a variable named scrollbutton that references the element with the id "button".

   b. Apply a mousedown event handler to the scrollbutton object that runs the grabIt() function.

   c. Apply a selectstart event handler to the document object that runs the stopSelect() function.

   d. Apply a keydown event handler to the document that runs the keyShow() function.

5. Create the stopSelect() function that returns the value false.

6. Create the grabIt() function used to grab the scrollbar button. The function has a single parameter, e, the event object. Add the following commands to the function:

   a. Set the x-coordinate of the event in a variable named mouseX.

   b. Calculate the difference between the mouseX and the x-coordinate of the scrollbutton object and store the value in the diffX variable.

   c. Attach or listen for the mousemove event in the scrollbutton object, running the moveIt() function in response. Set the capture parameter to "false".

   d. Attach or listen for the mouseup event in the scrollbutton object, running the dropIt() function in response. Set the capture parameter to "false".

7. Create the moveIt() function. The function has a single parameter: the event object e. Add the following commands:

   a. Store the current x-coordinate of the event in the mouseX variable.

   b. Subtract diffX from the mouseX variable and store the difference in a variable named buttonposX. This represents the current horizontal position of the scrollbar button.

   c. The scrollbar button should be prohibited from being dragged off the scrollbar. To do this, the x-coordinate of the button should always remain between 20 and 299. If the value of buttonposX is less than 20, set its value to 20. If the value of buttonposX is greater than 299, set its value to 299.

   d. Use the placeIt() function to place the scrollbutton object. The x-coordinate should be equal to buttonposX and the y-coordinate should be equal to 6.

   e. Call the function showImage() using buttonposX as the parameter value. You'll create this function later.

8. Create the dropIt() function. The function should detach the moveIt() function from the mousemove event occurring in the scrollbutton object.

9. Create the keyShow() function. The purpose of this function is to move the scrollbar button using the left and right arrows on the keyboard. The function has a single parameter, e, equal to the event object. Add the following commands to the function:

   a. Store the key code value of the pressed keyboard button in a variable named key.

   b. Store the current x-coordinate of the scrollbutton object in the buttonposX variable.

   c. If the user has pressed the left arrow key, decrease the value of the buttonposX variable by 31. If the user has pressed the right arrow key, increase the value of buttonposX by 31.

   d. If the value of buttonposX is less than 20, set its value to 20. If the value of buttonposX is greater than 299, set its value to 299.

   e. Place the scrollbutton object at the coordinates (*buttonposX*, 6).

   f. Call the function showImage() using buttonposX as the parameter value.

10. Create the showImage() function. The purpose of this function is to determine which of the 10 images to display based on the horizontal position of the scrollbar button. The x-coordinate of the scrollbar button ranges from 20 to 299, while the index numbers of images in the slide array range from 0 to 9. One aspect of this function is to convert the x-coordinate values into a corresponding index number. The function has a single parameter named x. Add the following commands to the function:

   a. Subtract 20 from the value of x and divide that difference by 31. Round the calculated value down to the next lowest integer and store the result in a variable named i. (*Hint*: Use the Math.floor() function to round the value down.) This converts the x-coordinate range into an index number.

   b. Change the source of the "photo" image in the Web document to the source of the slide[i] image.

11. Add an event handler to the body element that runs the setup() function when the page loads.

12. Add a cursor style to the inline style for the "button" element that sets the cursor image to "pointer".

13. Save your changes to the file and open **badger.htm** in your Web browser. Verify that you can navigate through the slideshow using either your mouse button or the left/right arrows on your keyboard.

14. Submit your completed Web site to your instructor.

Challenge

Explore how to create a crossword-style puzzle

Case Problem 3

Data files needed for this Case Problem: across.gif, crosstxt.htm, down.gif, functions.js, makepuzzle.js, pcglogo.jpg, styles.css

Park City Gazette   The *Park City Gazette*, edited by Kevin Webber, is the weekly newspaper of Park City, Colorado. In addition to its print offerings, the newspaper has an online version for distribution on the Web. The paper is known for its puzzles and games, so recently Kevin decided to include a puzzle in the online edition of the *Gazette*.

Kevin would like users to be able to type their answers directly into the puzzle. They should be able to navigate the puzzle by pressing the arrow keys on their keyboard, and typing a letter should move a user to the next cell. A user should also be able to toggle whether typing is entered vertically or horizontally by pressing the spacebar on the keyboard.

The current cell in the puzzle should be displayed with a yellow background. If a user enters a correct letter into a cell, the background should be changed to light green. If an incorrect letter is entered, a light red background should be displayed. Blank puzzle cells should be displayed with a white background. Figure 15-46 shows a preview of a partially completed puzzle with some correct and incorrect answers.

Figure 15-46

Each of the 25 cells in the puzzle is stored in a separate div element with the id "gridxy", where x represents the row number and y represents the column number. The row and column numbers start with 0 and go up to the number 4. Thus, the first cell in the puzzle has the id value "grid00", the cell in the first row and second column has the id value "grid01", and so forth. The last cell in the puzzle has an id value of "grid44". You'll need to use this information to place the letters that users type in the correct cells in the puzzle.

One of Kevin's assistants has already entered the HTML code for the puzzle page and has also produced some JavaScript code to generate the puzzle grid and its solution. These functions are in an external JavaScript file named makepuzzle.js. In addition to this file, Kevin's assistant has also created an external JavaScript file named functions.js that contains a function named writeText(*object, text*), which writes a text string *text* into an *object* on the Web page. You'll use this function to insert a user's guesses into the correct puzzle cells. The correct answer to the puzzle is stored in an array named "words".

To complete the *Park City Gazette* puzzle:

1. Use your text editor to open the **crosstxt.htm** file from the tutorial.15/case3 folder. Enter *your name* and *the date* in the comment section and save the file as **cross.htm**.
2. Above the init() function, create the following global variables:
   a. An image array named handImage. Set the source of the first image in the array to the across.gif file; set the source of the second image to the file down.gif.
   b. A variable that determines whether the user's browser supports the IE event model; create another variable that determines whether the browser supports the DOM event model.
   c. A variable named currentX that indicates the current row number. Set its initial value to 0. Create a variable named currentY that indicates the current column. Set its initial value to 0 as well.

    d. A variable named currentCell that will be used to point to the currently high-lighted cell in the puzzle. Create a variable named currentColor that stores the color of the current cell. Set its initial value to "white".

    e. A Boolean variable named across that indicates the direction of the user's typing (either across or down the puzzle grid). Set its initial value to true to indicate that letters are entered in the across direction.

    f. A variable named keyNum that will be used to store the key code number of a pressed key. Do not set an initial value for this variable.

3. Within the init() function add the following commands:

    a. Set the currentCell variable equal to the element with the id "grid00". Change the background color of the currentCell object to yellow.

    b. Add an event handler to the document object that runs getKey() function when a user presses a key.

4. Add the function getKey(). The purpose of this function is to capture the key code of the pressed key and then to call the appropriate function for that key. The function has a single parameter, the event object e. Add the following commands to the function:

    a. Retrieve the key code value of the pressed key and store it in the variable keyNum.

    b. If the user pressed the spacebar, run the toggleDirection() function.

    c. If the user pressed one of the four arrow keys, run the moveCursor() function.

    d. Otherwise, run the writeGuess() function.

5. Directly below the getKey() function, create the toggleDirection() function. The purpose of this function is to allow a user to press the spacebar to toggle the typing direction from across to down and vice versa. It will also swap the pointing hand image on the page to match the typing direction. To complete this function:

    a. If the value of the across variable is true, then: (1) Change the across value to false; (2) Change the source of the second image in the document to the source of the second image in the handImage array.

    b. If the value of the across variable is false, then: (1) Change the across value to true; (2) Change the source of the second image in the document to the source of the first image in the handImage array.

6. Below the toggleDirection() function, create the following functions, which will be used to update the values of the currentX and currentY variables as the cursor moves around the puzzle grid.

    a. moveLeft(): In this function, decrease the value of the currentX variable by 1. If currentX is less than 0, change its value to 4.

    b. moveRight(): Increase the value of currentX by 1. If currentX is greater than 4, change its value to 0.

    c. moveUp(): Decrease the value of the currentY variable by 1. If currentY is less than 0, change its value to 4.

    d. moveDown(): Increase the value of currentY by 1. If currentY is greater than 4, change its value to 0.

7. Directly below these four functions, create a function named moveCursor(). The purpose of this function is to move the active cell in response to a user pressing the arrow keys on the keyboard. Add the following commands to the function:

    a. Set the background color of currentCell to the value of the currentColor variable.

b. If the value of the keyNum variable indicates that the user pressed the left arrow key, call the moveLeft() function. If the user pressed the up arrow key, call the moveUp() function. If the user pressed the right arrow key, call the moveRight() function. If the user pressed the down arrow key, call the moveDown() function.

c. Change currentCell to the element whose id is "gridxy" where x is the value of currentX and y is the value of currentY.

d. Store the current background color of currentCell in the currentColor variable.

e. Change the background color of currentCell to yellow.

8. Create a function named "writeGuess()". The purpose of this function is to write the letter typed by the user into the current cell and then to change the background color of that cell to indicate whether the user typed the correct letter. After the letter has been written, the current cell should move either to the right or down, depending on the typing direction (as indicated in the across variable). The function should, therefore, do the following:

a. Use the fromCharCode() String method to extract the letter corresponding to the value of the keyNum variable. Store the letter in a variable named outChar.

b. Use the toUpperCase() string method to change the outChar variable to an uppercase letter.

c. Use the writeText() function to write outChar to the current cell.

d. If the value of outChar is correct, change the background color of the current cell to "lightgreen". (*Hint*: To test whether the outChar letter is correct, compare outChar's value to the value of words array item words[y * 5 + x] where y is the value of the current column and x is the value of the current row.) If the value is not correct, change the background color of the current cell to pink.

e. If the value of the across variable is true, then move the location of the current cell to the right using the moveRight() function; otherwise, call the moveDown() function to move down.

f. Point the currentCell object to the element with the id "gridxy" where x is the value of the currentX variable and y is the value of the currentY variable. Store the background color of currentCell in the currentColor variable. Change the background color of currentCell to yellow.

9. Add an event handler to the body element that runs the init() function when the page is loaded.

10. Add an event handler to the reveal element that runs the showAns() function when the element is clicked. (The showAns() function is a function in the makepuzzle.js file that displays the correct answer to the puzzle.) Add an inline style to the reveal element that changes the cursor style to "pointer".

11. Save your changes to the file and load the cross.htm file in your Web browser. Verify that: (a) when you type letters on the keyboard, those letters are displayed in the puzzle grid; (b) the current cell is displayed with a yellow background; (c) correct letters are displayed with a light green background; (d) incorrect letters are displayed with a pink background; (e) pressing the arrow keys moves the current cell around the puzzle grid; (f) pressing the spacebar toggles the typing direction and swaps the pointing hand image; (g) clicking **Reveal Answer** reveals the puzzle solution.

12. Submit the completed Web site to your instructor.

Explore

Explore

Explore

Create

Create a drag-and-drop shopping cart

Case Problem 4

Data files needed for this Case Problem: *none supplied*

Produce World Produce World, a local grocery store, is making some of its products available on the World Wide Web. Customers will be able to visit the Web site and select items for purchase. Their selections will be sent to the store, where they will be gathered and packaged for pickup by the customer. Steve Adronski, a manager at Produce World, has asked for your help in creating a Web page that will feature a drag-and-drop shopping cart. The page will display the following items for purchase:

- Bananas at $1.60/bunch
- Red Delicious Apples at $2.80/bag
- Georgia Peaches at $1.90/bag
- Blueberries at $1.49/carton
- Strawberries at $2.49/carton
- Cantaloupe at $2.00/piece
- Red Seedless Grapes at $1.59/bag
- Green Seedless Grapes at $1.59/bag

The design of the shopping cart is up to you. You can add inline graphics for each of the produce items, if you would like to locate the appropriate clip art. You may also want to create a distinctive logo for Produce World.

To complete this assignment:

1. Create a file named **produce.htm** that contains the layout and content of your Web page.
2. Create an external JavaScript file named **produce.js** that contains any specialized JavaScript functions you need for your page.
3. Add drag-and-drop capability to the produce items in the produce.htm file.
4. Display a helpful mouse cursor symbol when the user selects produce to drag.
5. If a customer fails to drop a selected produce item in the shopping cart, have the item snap back to its original spot on the page.
6. Create a button named "Total" on the page that tallies up the total number of items selected and the total cost, and then displays that information in an alert dialog box when the Total button is clicked.
7. Submit the completed Web site to your instructor.

Review

Quick Check Answers
Session 15.1

1. document.getElementById("Total").onmousedown=CalcTotal;
2. <script type="text/javacript" for="Total" event="onclick"> ... </script>
3. From the bottom of the object hierarchy to the top.
4. document.getElementById("Total").attachEvent("onclick",CalcTotal);
5. event.cancelBubble = true;
6. Events are propagated from the top of the hierarchy during the capture phase, down to the event's target, and then back up the hierarchy during the bubbling phase.
7. document.getElementById("Total").addEventListener("click",CalcTotal, *capture*) where *capture* is either true (to listen for the event in the capture phase) or false (to listen for the event in the bubbling phase).

8. *evt*.stopPropagation()
   where *evt* is the event object.

Session 15.2

1. IE event model: event or *windowObject*.event
   DOM event model: the parameter of the event function
2. type
3. screenX and screenY
4. clientX and clientY
5. Increase the z-index of the object to be the maximum on the page.
6. return false;

Session 15.3

1. cursor: wait
   object.style.cursor = "wait";
2. button
   The IE event model uses 1=left, 2=middle, 4=right
   The DOM event model uses 0=left, 1=middle, 2=right
3. keydown
4. keyCode
5. 32
6. altKey

Objectives

Session 16.1
- Learn how to create dynamic content under the Internet Explorer DOM
- Understand the methods and properties of nodes and the node tree
- Learn to create element and text nodes
- Understand how to attach nodes to a Web page document

Session 16.2
- Apply node properties and styles to create dynamic content
- Work with the properties and methods of attribute nodes
- Work with element attributes

Session 16.3
- Hide and redisplay Web page objects
- Understand how to create recursive functions to navigate a node tree
- Learn to work with the properties and methods of style sheet objects

Working with Dynamic Content and Styles

Creating a Dynamic Table of Contents

Case

MidWest University Dept. of History

Norene Somerville is a professor of history at Midwest University. One of her recent projects involves putting the text of important historic documents online for her students to download and study. The Web site she's creating will support a variety of different document formats, but Professor Somerville also wants each document to be available in HTML format on a single Web page. This format makes it easier for students to print out the complete text of a document without having to navigate an entire site or install word processing or document software. However, Norene is concerned that some of the documents are very long and would be difficult to manage if placed on a single page.

She believes that a table of contents that summarizes the different sections within a document and provides links to those sections would be a great aid to students. However, Norene doesn't have the time to create such a table of contents for each of the documents in her online library. She wants a program to automatically generate these tables of contents, and she has approached you for help in developing such a utility.

Student Data Files

▼tutorial.16

▽ **tutorial folder**
  treattxt.htm
  uscontxt.htm
  toctxt.js
  + 3 style sheets
  + 3 graphic file

▽ **review folder**
  fed10txt.htm
  keytxt.js
  + 2 style sheets
  + 3 graphic files

▽ **case1 folder**
  fr5txt.htm
  engfrtxt.js
  french5.js
  + 1 style sheet

▽ **case2 folder**
  camtxt.htm
  filttxt.js
  + 1 style sheet
  + 2 graphic files

▽ **case3 folder**
  clisttxt.htm
  newtxt.js
  data.js
  + 1 style sheet
  + 1 graphic file

▽ **case4 folder**
  temptxt.htm
  scenetxt.js
  + 1 style sheet
  + 6 graphic files

Session 16.1

Introducing Dynamic Content

You and Norene meet to discuss her proposal for the table of contents utility. Her idea is to base the table of contents on the heading elements often used to break up long HTML documents into topical sections. For example, the h1 heading usually marks a primary section in a document, h2 marks a secondary heading, and so forth. Figure 16-1 shows a sketch that Norene has made of how her table of contents script would work. The utility would search the Web page for heading elements, copying the text of each heading into the TOC. The table of contents would be organized as a nested list with higher-level headings placed at the top of the list. For example, all h1 headings would be placed at the top, h2 headings would be placed within the h1 headings, and so on.

Figure 16-1   **Converting document content into a table of contents**

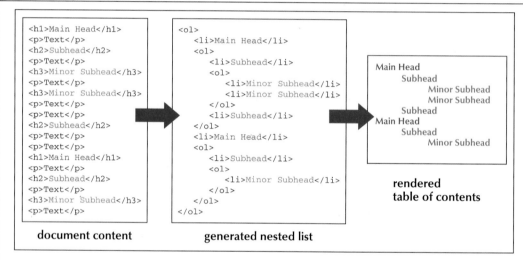

document content   generated nested list   rendered table of contents

Before starting work on the table of contents application, first examine the files that Norene has supplied for you. The sample document that she wants you to practice on is the text of the United States Constitution. This is an ideal test, since the document involves three levels of headings plus long text passages. Open this document now.

To open Norene's Web page:

1. In your text editor, open the **uscontxt.htm** file located in the tutorial.16/tutorial folder. Enter **your name** and **the date** in the comment section and save the file as **usconst.htm**.

2. Look through the HTML code for the document.

   Note that the document contains a div element named "toc" in which you'll place the table of contents. It also includes a div element named "doc" that contains the text of the document upon which the table of contents will be based.

3. Open **usconst.htm** in your Web browser. Figure 16-2 shows the current appearance of the page. The table of contents will be placed in the blue box on the page's left margin.

Historic Documents Online

Department of History
Midwest University

<< 1600 | 1600 - 1700 | 1700 - 1800 | 1800 - 1900 | 1900 - 2000 | 2000 >>

table of contents box

The Constitution of the United States

Preamble

WE THE PEOPLE OF THE UNITED STATES, IN ORDER TO FORM A MORE PERFECT UNION, establish Justice, insure domestic Tranquility, provide for the common defence, promote the general Welfare, and secure the Blessings of Liberty to ourselves and our Posterity, do ordain and establish this Constitution for the United States of America.

Articles of the Constitution

Article I - The Legislative Branch

Section 1: The Legislature

All legislative Powers herein granted shall be vested in a Congress of the United States, which shall consist of a Senate and House of Representatives.

All of the JavaScript code that generates the table of contents will be located in an external file. This will allow Norene to use the finished utility with other documents in her library. A file containing some initial code has been created for you. Open this file now.

To open the JavaScript file:

▶ **1.** In your text editor, open the **toctxt.js** file located in the tutorial.16/tutorial folder. Enter **your name** and **the date** in the comment section and save the file as **toc.js**.

The file contains a function named makeTOC() that you'll use to generate the table of contents when the Web page is loaded in a browser. At the moment, this function contains no commands. Return to the usconst.htm file and create a link to this JavaScript file along with an event handler that runs the makeTOC() function when the page loads.

▶ **2.** Return to the **usconst.htm** file in your text editor.

▶ **3.** Above the closing </head> tag insert the following external script element:

```
<script src="toc.js" type="text/javascript"></script>
```

▶ **4.** Add the following event handler to the body element: **onload="makeTOC()"**. Figure 16-3 shows the revised code.

```
<title>The Constitution of the United States</title>
<link href="history.css" rel="stylesheet" type="text/css" />
<link href="toc.css" rel="stylesheet" type="text/css" />

<script src="toc.js" type="text/javascript"></script>
</head>

<body onload="makeTOC()">
<div id="logo"><img src="hlogo.jpg" alt="Historic Documents" /></div>
<div id="logosub">Department of History<br />Midwest University</div>
<div id="doctitle"><h1>The Constitution of the United States</h1></div>
```

5. Close the file, saving your changes.

From this point on, almost all of your work will be done within the toc.js file.

Inserting HTML Content into an Element

Generating a table of contents involves working with **dynamic content**, which is content determined by the operation of a script running within the browser. Often dynamic content is determined either by users' actions or by the content of other elements on the Web page or within the Web site.

Norene wants her table of contents to display the heading "Table of Contents". While you could place an embedded script within the toc element and employ the document. write() method to insert this content, you want to create an application that is self-contained and can be applied to any document with a minimal amount of coding within each document. It would be better to add the heading to the table of contents using a function run from an external JavaScript file. One property that can be used to write content in an element is the innerHTML property. The syntax is

```
object.innerHTML = content
```

where *object* is a Web page object and *content* is a text string containing the HTML content of the object. For example, to add an h1 heading to the toc element, you would run the following commands:

```
TOC = document.getElementById("toc");
TOC.innerHTML="<h1>Table of Contents</h1>";
```

Add these commands to the makeTOC() function.

To insert a heading into the TOC:

1. Return to the **toc.js** file in your text editor.

2. Go to the makeTOC() function at the bottom of the file and insert the following commands (see Figure 16-4):

```
TOC = document.getElementById("toc");
TOC.innerHTML="<h1>Table of Contents</h1>";
```

Figure 16-4	Inserting HTML code into the toc element

```
function makeTOC() {
    TOC = document.getElementById("toc");
    TOC.innerHTML="<h1>Table of Contents</h1>";
}
```

3. Save your changes to the file.

4. Reload **usconst.htm** in your Web browser. Figure 16-5 shows the table of contents with the new heading.

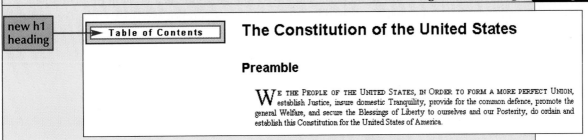

The styles for the table of contents and the document have already been created for you and stored in the toc.css and history.css style sheets. If you want to study the display styles that will appear as you create the table of contents throughout the course of this tutorial, you may review the contents of those two files.

Dynamic Content in Internet Explorer

The innerHTML property is not part of the official specifications for the W3C document object model. Instead, it is part of the DOM for Internet Explorer. However, since it has proven valuable and easy to use, it is supported by all browsers. The Internet Explorer DOM also supports other properties and methods to aid in the creation of dynamic content; however, these properties and methods are not as widely supported as the innerHTML property. You'll look at a few of them before studying how the W3C DOM handles dynamic content.

The innerHTML property defines the content within an HTML element. If you want to change both the content and the HTML element itself, you use the outerHTML property. The syntax for the two properties is similar:

```
object.outerHTML = content;
```

where *object* is once again the Web page object, but *content* is a text string of the HTML code for both the object and the content it contains. For example, if Norene's Web page contained the element

```
<h1 id="title">History Online</h1>
```

then the commands

```
title = document.getElementById("title");
title.outerHTML="<h2>Historic Documents</h2>";
```

would change the element to

```
<h2>Historic Documents</h2>
```

Be aware that changing the element tags in addition to the element's content can result in unforeseen errors. Running the above code removes the title element from the document hierarchy since the id attribute is not included in the new h2 element. Any subsequent part of the script that references the title element would result in an error. Thus, you should use caution whenever applying the outerHTML property, to ensure that you don't change more of an element's content than you wish.

Related to both the innerHTML and outerHTML properties are the innerText and outerText properties. These properties are used to change the text content of an element. Any text that you specify is treated by browsers as text and not as HTML code. For example, the command

```
title.innerHTML="<i>Historic Documents</i>";
```

results in the title element being displayed as

Historic Documents

By contrast, the command

```
title.innerText="<i>Historic Documents</i>";
```

results in the title element being displayed as

\<i>Historic Documents\</i>

In this case, the \<i> tags are treated as text, rather than HTML elements.

You can use methods in the Internet Explorer DOM to insert elements at specific locations within the document tree. The syntax of the methods is

```
object.insertAdjacentHTML(position, content);
object.insertAdjacentText(position, content);
```

where *position* is a text string specifying the position in which the new HTML code or text is to be inserted relative to *object*, and *content* is the content to be inserted. The *position* parameter has four possible values:

- **BeforeBegin** inserts the content before the object's opening tag
- **AfterBegin** inserts the content directly after the object's opening tag
- **BeforeEnd** inserts the content directly before the object's closing tag
- **AfterEnd** inserts the content after the object's closing tag

For example, to insert the word "Online" at the end of the element

```
<h1 id="title">Historic Documents</h1>
```

you could run the command

```
title.insertAdjacentHTML("BeforeEnd"," Online");
```

This would change the code of the title element to

```
<h1 id="title">Historic Documents Online</h1>
```

The various properties and methods of the Internet Explorer DOM offer quick and easy ways to insert dynamic content. However, keep in mind that only the innerHTML property is supported by other browsers.

Dynamic Content in the IE DOM

- To change the HTML content of a page object, use the property
    `object.innerHTML="content"`
  where `object` is an object on the Web page and `content` is a text string of the object's HTML content.
- To change the HTML code of the object, including the object itself, use
    `object.outerHTML="content"`
- To change the text of a page object, use the property
    `object.innerText="content"`
  where `content` is the text (not HTML content) contained within the element.
- To change the text of a page object, including the object itself, use
    `object.outerText="content"`
- To insert HTML content at a specific location relative to a page object, use the property
    `object.insertAdjacentHTML="position, content"`
  where `position` is "BeforeBegin" (to insert `content` before the opening tag of `object`), "AfterBegin" (to insert `content` directly after the opening tag of `object`), "BeforeEnd" (to insert `content` directly before the closing tag of `object`), or "AfterEnd" (to insert `content` after the closing tag of `object`).

Working with Nodes

Dynamic content in the specifications for the W3C document object model works differently than in the Internet Explorer DOM. In the W3C DOM, objects are organized into **nodes**, with each node representing an object within the Web page and Web browser. In the W3C DOM, anything in an HTML file can be treated as a node. This includes every HTML tag and all of a tag's attributes. Even the tags in a document's head section, comment tags, and the <html> tag itself can be treated as nodes. The text within an HTML tag can also be treated as a node. For example, the tag, "<h1>Table of Contents</h1>" actually consists of two nodes: one node for the h1 element and one node for the text "Table of Contents".

The Node Tree

Nodes are arranged into a hierarchal structure called a **node tree**, which indicates the relationship between each of the nodes. Figure 16-6 shows a representation of a node tree for a simple HTML document. Notice that in the node tree, not only is each element treated as a separate node, but text within each element is treated as a node as well.

| Figure 16-6 | A document node tree |

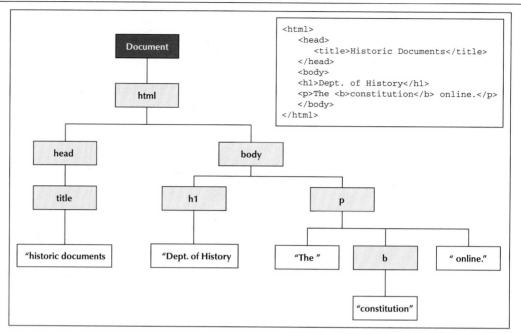

Nodes in a node tree have a familial relationship, as each node can be a parent, child, and/or sibling of other nodes. The syntax to reference a node based on its relationship with the current node is

```
node.relationship
```

where *node* is the currently selected node or object and *relationship* is the relationship of another node to the current node. For example, the expression

```
node.parentNode
```

refers to the parent of *node*. In the node tree shown in Figure 16-6, the parent of the body node is the html node, and the parent of the html node is the Document node. The parent of all nodes within a document is the **root node**. For HTML documents, the root node is the html element. A document's root node can also be referenced using the object document.documentElement. The root node is itself a child of the document node, which represents the entire document.

Each node can contain one or more child nodes. To reference the first child of the current node, use the expression

```
node.firstChild
```

In the node tree shown in Figure 16-6, the h1 node is the first child of the body node, and the text node "Dept. of History" is its first (and only) child. All of the child nodes are organized into the object collection

```
node.childNodes
```

To reference a particular object from this collection, you specify the item's index number:

```
node.childNodes[i]
```

where i is the index number of the child node. Thus, to reference the first child of the current node, you could also use the expression

```
node.childNodes[0]
```

For HTML files, the order of the child nodes matches the order of the elements in the file. To determine the total number of child nodes for a given node, you use the length property:

```
node.childNodes.length
```

The length of the childNodes collection for the paragraph element in Figure 16-6 would be 3 (the two text nodes and the bold element). Figure 16-7 summarizes the rest of the familial relationships in the node tree.

Node relationships | **Figure 16-7**

Property	Description
node.firstChild	Returns the first child of *node*
node.lastChild	Returns the last child of *node*
node.childNodes	Returns a collection containing the children of *node*
node.previousSibling	Returns the sibling prior to *node*
node.nextSibling	Returns the sibling after *node*
node.ownerDocument	Returns the root node of the document
node.parentNode	Returns the parent of *node*

Reference Window

Node Relationships

- To access the parent of a node object, use the reference
  ```
  node.parentNode
  ```
  where *node* is a node object in the node tree.
- To reference the first and last child of a node, use
  ```
  node.firstChild
  node.lastChild
  ```
- To reference the collection of all child nodes, use
  ```
  node.childNodes
  ```
- To reference the previous and next sibling, use
  ```
  node.previousSibling
  node.nextSibling
  ```

Node types, names, and values

There are some important differences between browsers in how they handle white space in an HTML file. The W3C DOM calls for occurrences of white space to be treated as text nodes. Thus, the HTML code

```
<h1>Table of Contents</h1>
<h2>U.S. Constitution</h2>
```

contains five nodes: 1 node for the h1 element, 1 node for the h2 element, 2 nodes for the text contained within those two elements, and a fifth node for the white space that separates the h1 and h2 elements. While Internet Explorer version 5.0 and higher supports nodes in its document object model, it does not treat occurrences of white space as text nodes. For Internet Explorer, the above code would contain only four nodes. Netscape, Opera, and most other browsers would see five nodes. This difference affects how you write program code that involves nodes, meaning that you often have to test whether the node that a program is currently working with represents a text node, an element node, or some other type of node. The following properties provide information about a node's type, name, and value:

- *node*.nodeType
- *node*.nodeName
- *node*.nodeValue

The nodeType property is an integer indicating whether the node refers to an element, a text string, a comment, an attribute, and so forth. The nodeName property is the name of the node within the document. For document elements, the nodeName property returns to the name of the element in uppercase letters. The nodeValue property returns the node's value. Figure 16-8 summarizes the values of the three properties for the different nodes you would typically encounter in an HTML file.

Figure 16-8			

Node types, names, and values

Node	*node*.nodeType	*node*.nodeName	*node*.nodeValue
Element	1	*ELEMENT NAME*	null
Attribute	2	*attribute name*	*attribute value*
Text	3	#text	*text string*
Comment	8	#comment	*comment text*
Document	9	#document	null

To see how these properties compare to the sample node tree you saw earlier, Figure 16-9 displays the nodeType, nodeName, and nodeValue property values for each of the nodes from Figure 16-6.

Nodes from the sample node tree | Figure 16-9

Node	*node*.nodeType	*node*.NodeName	*node*.NodeValue
Document	9	#document	null
html	1	HTML	null
head	1	HEAD	null
body	1	BODY	null
title	1	TITLE	null
"historic documents"	3	#text	historic documents
h1	1	H1	null
"Dept. of History"	3	#text	Dept. of History
p	1	P	null
"The "	3	#text	The
b	1	B	null
"constitution"	3	#text	constitution
" online"	3	#text	online

One issue you may have noticed with element nodes is that they have no value. It's tempting to think that an element node's value should be the content it contains; however, that content is already its own node. Thus, if you want to change the text contained within an element, you have to modify the value of that element's text node. For example, the title element contains the following text:

```
<h1 id="title">History Online</h1>
```

To change the text of the title to "Historic Documents Online" you could run the following code under the W3C DOM:

```
title = document.getElementById("title");
title.firstChild.nodeValue = "Historic Documents Online";
```

This code sample uses the firstChild reference since the text node is the first (and only) child of the title element.

Node Properties

- To determine the type of object a node represents, use the property
    node.nodeType
  where *node* is a node object in the node tree. The nodeType property returns the value 1 for elements, 2 for attributes, and 3 for text nodes.
- To return the value of a node, use
    node.nodeValue
  For elements, the value of the nodeValue property is null. For attributes, the value represents the attribute's value. For text nodes, the value represents the text string contained in the node.
- To return the name of a node, use
    node.nodeName
  For elements, the name of the node matches the name of the element in uppercase letters. For attributes, the node name matches the attribute name. For text nodes, the node name is #text.

Creating and Attaching Nodes

Norene is most interested in adding new content to the Web page. The W3C DOM supports several methods to create new nodes, which are listed in Figure 16-10.

Figure 16-10 | **Methods to create nodes**

Method	Descripton
document.createAttribute(*att*)	Creates an attribute node with the name *att*
document.createComment(*text*)	Creates a comment node containing the comment text string, *text*
document.createElement(*elem*)	Creates an element node with the name *elem*
document.createTextNode(*text*)	Creates a text node containing the text string, *text*
node.cloneNode(*deep*)	Creates a copy of *node*. If the Boolean parameter *deep* is true, the copy extends to all descendants of the node object, otherwise only *node* is copied.

Using these methods, you can create a wide variety of objects that can be used in a Web page document. For example, to create a text node containing the text "Historic Documents Online" you would use the following expression:

```
document.createTextNode("Historic Documents Online")
```

All of the methods described in Figure 16-10 create single nodes, with the exception of the cloneNode() method. The cloneNode() method is useful when you need to create a copy of an existing node, including any descendants of that node. The command

```
newtitle = title.cloneNode(true)
```

creates a copy of the title node, including any descendants of that node. The cloneNode() method provides a quick and easy way of creating elements and their content without having to go through the process of creating each node individually.

Creating Nodes

- To create a node for an element, use the method
    ```
    document.createElement(text)
    ```
  where *text* is the name of the element.
- To create a node for an attribute, use the method
    ```
    document.createAttribute(text)
    ```
  where *text* is the name of the attribute.
- To create a text node, use
    ```
    document.createTextNode(text)
    ```
  where *text* is the text string of the text node.
- To copy a preexisting node, use the method
    ```
    node.cloneNode(deep)
    ```
  where *node* is the preexisting node and *deep* is a Boolean value indicating whether to copy all descendants of the node (true) or only the node itself (false).

Once a node has been created, it still has to be attached to a node in the document's node tree if it is to be part of the document. Unattached nodes and node trees are known as **document fragments** and exist only in a browser's memory. You can still access document fragments and work with them in your script, but they are not displayed in a Web page document. Figure 16-11 describes several methods for attaching one node to another.

Methods to attach or remove nodes ◄ **Figure 16-11**

Method	Description
node.appendChild(*new*)	Appends a *new* child node to *node*, attaching it as the last child node.
node.insertBefore(*new*, *child*)	Inserts a *new* child node to *node*, placing it before the *child* node. If no *child* is specified the *new* child node is added as the last child node.
node.normalized()	Traverses all child nodes of *node*; any adjacent text nodes are merged into a single text node.
node.removeChild(*old*)	Removes the child node *old* from *node*.
node.replaceChild(*new*, *old*)	Replaces the child node *old* with the child node *new*.

Using the properties and methods described in Figures 16-10 and 16-11, you can elaborate node trees that consist of several different nodes. Figure 16-12 describes the process by which you would create the following code using the methods listed in Figures 16-10 and 16-11:

```
<p><i>Historic</i> Documents</p>
```

Figure 16-12 ▶ **Creating and attaching nodes**

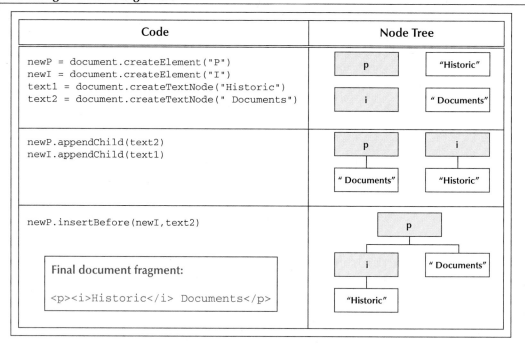

The approach shown in Figure 16-12 first uses the createElement() and createText-Node() methods to create four nodes: an element node for a paragraph, an element node for italicized text, a text node containing the text string "Historic", and a text node containing the text "Documents". The appendChild() method is then employed to attach the text nodes to the element nodes. The last line of code uses the insertBefore() method to insert the italicized text before the second text node. While at first glance this approach may seem more cumbersome than simply using the innerHTML method, the great advantage of working with nodes is that you can work with individual elements and text strings at a detail and flexibility that is not possible with other methods.

Reference Window | **Attaching and Removing Nodes**

- To append a new node as a child of a preexisting node, use the method
    node.appendChild(*new*)
  where *node* is the preexisting node and *new* is the new child. The new child node is appended to the end of the child nodes collection.
- To insert a new node at a specific location in the child nodes collection, use the method
    node.insertBefore(*new*, *child*)
  where *child* is the child node that the new node should be placed in front of.
- To remove a child node, use the method
    node.removeChild(*old*)
  where *old* is the child node to be removed.
- To replace one child node with another, use
    node.replace(*new*, *old*)

Now that you've seen how to create and attach nodes, you'll create a node for an ol (ordered list) element and attach it to the table of contents in Norene's Web page. Currently, the content of the toc element consists of the following elements:

```
<div id="toc">
   <h1>Table of Contents</h1>
</div>
```

You want to change this to

```
<div id="toc">
   <h1>Table of Contents</h1>
   <ol></ol>
</div>
```

The code to create the ol list element and attach it to the table of contents is therefore

```
TOCList = document.createElement("ol");
TOC.appendChild(TOCList);
```

Add this code to the makeTOC() function.

To append the ol element to the TOC:

1. Return to the **toc.js** file in your text editor.

2. Add the following commands to the makeTOC() function as shown in Figure 16-13:

```
TOCList = document.createElement("ol");
TOC.appendChild(TOCList);
```

Creating and attaching the ol element ◀ **Figure 16-13**

```
function makeTOC() {
    TOC = document.getElementById("toc");
    TOC.innerHTML="<h1>Table of Contents</h1>";
    TOCList = document.createElement("ol");
    TOC.appendChild(TOCList);
}
```

3. Save your changes to the file.

Creating a List of Heading Elements

The next task is to populate the ordered list with list items, where the text of each list item matches the text of a heading element in the constitution document. Your code needs to do the following:

1. Examine the child nodes of the constitution document
2. For each child node, test whether it represents a heading element
3. If it is a heading element, extract the element's text and create a list item containing that same text
4. Append the list item as a new child of the ordered list in the table of contents

For simplicity's sake, assume that each heading element is a child of the "doc" element in Norene's Web page (rather than nested within other elements), and that the heading elements contain only text and no other content. For the moment, you'll place all of the text from the section headings on the same level in the table of contents, rather than at different levels as Norene requested in her sketch (Figure 16-1). You'll explore how to create nested lists in the next session.

Looping Through the Child Node Collection

There are two ways of looping through a collection of child nodes. In one approach, you use a counter variable that starts with a value of 0 and increases by 1 for each node, up to the length of the childNodes collection. The general form of this loop is

```
for (var i=0; i < node.childNodes.length; i++) {
    commands for node.childNode[i]
}
```

In this form, the child nodes in the for loop have the object reference

```
node.childNode[i]
```

where *node* is the parent node of the child nodes collection and *i* is the value of the counter variable in the for loop.

The second approach uses familial references, starting with the first child of the parent node and then moving to each subsequent sibling until no more siblings are left. The general form of this for loop is

```
for (var n=node.firstChild; n!= null; n=n.nextSibling) {
    commands for n
}
```

In this form, the current child node in the loop has the object reference

```
n
```

Note that when no next sibling is available, the value of n is equal to null and the loop stops. While both approaches yield the same results, the use of familial references is generally preferred because it does not require a browser to calculate the total length of the child nodes collection. For large documents containing thousands of nodes, this can speed up the processing time for the program. This method also gives you the flexibility to insert new nodes into a document during the for loop without having to recalculate the length of the child nodes collection.

You'll use familial references in the following function to create the list of heading elements. The initial code for the function is

```
function createList(list) {
    for (var n=historyDoc.firstChild; n!=null; n=n.nextSibling) {
    }
}
```

This function has a single parameter named list that represents an ol list element found in the table of contents. The historyDoc variable in the for loop is the history document in Norene's Web page. Add this initial version of the function to the toc.js file.

To insert the createList() function:

1. Add the following line to the makeTOC() function:

```
historyDoc = document.getElementById("doc");
```

2. Below the makeTOC() function, insert the following code as shown in Figure 16-14:

```
function createList(list) {
    for (var n=historyDoc.firstChild; n!=null; n=n.nextSibling) {
    }
}
```

The initial createList() function ◄ **Figure 16-14**

```
                    function makeTOC() {
the history            TOC = document.getElementById("toc");
document               TOC.innerHTML="<h1>Table of Contents</h1>";
                       TOCList = document.createElement("ol");
                       TOC.appendChild(TOCList);

loop from the        historyDoc = document.getElementById("doc");
first child        }
node of the
history            function createList(list) {
document to          for (var n=historyDoc.firstChild; n!=null; n=n.nextSibling) {
the last child       }
                   }
```

Matching the Heading Elements

Next you have to determine whether the current node in the for loop matches one of the heading elements Norene wants to use as section dividers. To aid you, the following code is included in the toc.js file:

```
var sections = new Array("h1","h2","h3","h4","h5","h6");
function levelNum(node) {
    for (var i=0; i<sections.length; i++) {
        if (node.nodeName==sections[i].toUpperCase()) return i;
    }
    return -1;
}
```

The sections array and the levelNum() function are two important pieces in creating your dynamic table of contents, so it's worthwhile to take some time to understand how they work. The sections variable contains an array of the elements that Norene wants to use as section dividers. The array is ordered from the element representing the highest level in the TOC (the h1 element) to the lowest (the h6 element). In the constitution document, you will need to use only elements h1 through h3; however, including the full range of headings allows you to generalize the makeTOC() function for other documents in Norene's library.

The levelNum() function uses the nodeName property to test whether a given node matches one of the elements listed in the sections array. Since element names in the nodeName property are returned in uppercase letters, you have to use the toUpperCase() String method to convert the element names in the section array to uppercase letters as well. The function goes through each item in the sections array and if a match is found, the function returns the array index number. Thus, an h1 element returns the value 0 (indicating that it represents the highest level in the TOC), an h2 element returns the value 1, and so forth. If a node object doesn't represent a section heading, the function returns the value -1. You'll apply the levelNum() function to the createList() function by adding the following if condition:

```
nodeLevel = levelNum(n);
if (nodeLevel != -1) {
    peform actions on a element node
    representing a section heading
}
```

Add this if condition to the createList() function.

To create the nodeLevel variable:

1. Within the for loop of the createList() function, insert the following code (see Figure 16-15):

```
nodeLevel = levelNum(n);
if (nodeLevel != -1) {
}
```

Figure 16-15 **Testing whether the current node is a section heading**

if nodeLevel does not equal -1 it means that the node represents one of the section headings

```
function createList(list) {
    for (var n=historyDoc.firstChild; n!=null; n=n.nextSibling) {
        nodeLevel = levelNum(n);
        if (nodeLevel != -1) {
        }
    }
}
```

2. Save your changes to the file.

Creating the List Item Elements

The final task is to create and append a list item element, basing its content on the content of the heading element. You'll use the innerHTML property to extract the content of the heading element and apply that content to the list item. The list item then needs to be added as a new child to the list in the table of contents. The code to create and attach the new list item is

```
listItem = document.createElement("li");
listItem.innerHTML = n.innerHTML;
list.appendChild(listItem);
```

Once you add these commands, you can call createList() from the makeTOC() function using the TOCList object as the parameter value. The command to populate the list in the TOC is

```
createList(TOCList);
```

Add these commands to the toc.js file.

To create the listItem object:

1. Add the following commands to the command block of the if statement in the createList() function:

```
listItem = document.createElement("li");
listItem.innerHTML = n.innerHTML;
list.appendChild(listItem);
```

2. Add the following command to the makeTOC() function:

```
createList(TOCList);
```

Figure 16-16 highlights the new code added to the toc.js file.

Creating the list item elements | **Figure 16-16**

```
function makeTOC() {
    TOC = document.getElementById("toc");
    TOC.innerHTML="<h1>Table of Contents</h1>";

    TOCList = document.createElement("ol");
    TOC.appendChild(TOCList);

    historyDoc = document.getElementById("doc");
    createList(TOCList);
}

function createList(list) {
    for (var n=historyDoc.firstChild; n!=null; n=n.nextSibling) {
        nodeLevel = levelNum(n);
        if (nodeLevel != -1) {
            listItem = document.createElement("li");
            listItem.innerHTML = n.innerHTML;

            list.appendChild(listItem);
        }
    }
}
```

3. Save your changes. If you want to take a break before starting the next session, you may also close your file.

   Next, test the makeTOC() function to verify that it displays a list of all of the heading elements in the constitution document.

4. Reload **usconst.htm** in your Web browser. As shown in Figure 16-17 the table of contents should now be populated with the titles of the h1, h2, and h3 elements in the constitution document.

Figure 16-17 ▶ **The initial table of contents**

Trouble? The list items appear in uppercase letters because of a style set in the toc.css file, not because of any command in the makeTOC() function.

5. Close your Web browser if you want to take a break before starting the next session.

You've completed your initial work on the dynamic table of contents. In the next session you'll learn how to turn the table of contents into a nested list in which the text from different section headings appears at different levels. You'll also learn how to link the entries from the table of contents list to the section headings in the constitution document.

Review

Session 16.1 Quick Check

1. In the Internet Explorer DOM, what property is used to change the inner HTML content of an element?
2. What are nodes? What objects of an HTML file do they represent?
3. What property do you use to reference the parent of a node?
4. What object reference would you use to reference the third child node of an object?
5. For an element node representing a blockquote element, what value is returned by the nodeType, nodeName, and nodeValue properties?
6. What command would you enter to create a node containing the text string: "U.S. Constitution"? Give the text string the variable name docText. What command would you enter to create an h2 element? Give the h2 element the variable name mainTitle.
7. What command would you enter to place the text string you created in the previous question in the h2 element?
8. What is a document fragment?

Session 16.2

Creating a Nested List

Norene has had a chance to study the initial table of contents you created in the last session. She's pleased that the TOC was able to track all of the heading elements in the constitution document; now she wants you to make the TOC a nested list so that the h1 headings are on one level of the TOC, the h2 headings are on a second level, and so forth. Figure 16-18 shows the current HTML code created by the makeTOC() function alongside the code that Norene wants the function to generate.

The nested list ◄ **Figure 16-18**

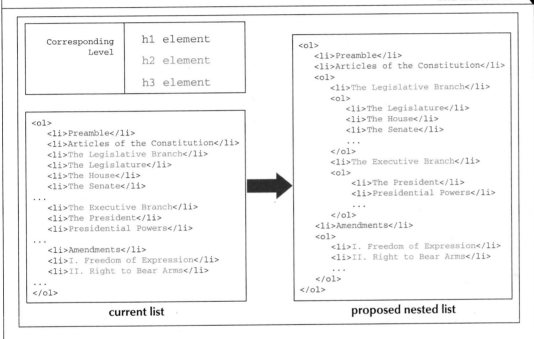

current list

proposed nested list

As you go through Norene's proposed layout for the TOC, there are three rules that you can use to determine where to place a particular list item:

1. If the level of the list item is unchanged from the level of the previous item, simply append it to the current list.
2. If the level is lower than the previous heading (such as when an h3 heading follows an h2 heading) create a new ordered list and append the list item to that.
3. If the level is above the previous heading (for example, when an h1 heading follows an h3 heading), append the list item at a level higher up in the TOC.

To keep track of the level associated with each section heading in the last session, you created the nodeLevel variable, where a nodeLevel value of 0 indicates a section heading corresponding to the highest level (h1), a value of 1 indicates the next level (h2), and so forth. In addition to the nodeLevel variable, you need to create two other variables:

- **prevLevel**   The level of the previous heading element
- **newList**   An element node for a new ol (ordered list) element

The general code for the revisions that you'll make to the createList() function appears as follows:

```
function createList(list) {
   prevLevel = 0;
   for (var n=historyDoc.firstChild; n!=null; n=n.nextSibling) {
      nodeLevel = levelNum(n);
      if (nodeLevel != -1) {
         create a list item element
         if (nodeLevel = prevLevel)
            append the list item to the list
         else if (nodeLevel > prevLevel)
            append the list item to a new list
            change the prevLevel value
         else if (nodeLevel < prevLevel)
            append the list to the list of that level
            change the prevLevel value
      }
   }
}
```

You set the initial value of the prevLevel variable to 0. Each time through the loop, the code compares the level of the current section heading with the level of the previous section heading, running different commands for each of three possibilities: the levels are equal, the level of the current heading is higher than the previous heading, or the level of the current heading is lower than the previous heading. You'll look at the specific code for each of these if conditions later; for now, add this general structure to the createList() function.

To insert if conditions into the createList() function:

1. If necessary, reopen **toc.js** in your text editor.

2. Locate the createList() function and insert the following as the first line of the function:

   ```
   var prevLevel = 0;
   ```

3. Delete the line "`list.appendChild(listItem);`" and replace it with the following commands:

   ```
   if (nodeLevel == prevLevel) {
      // append listitem to the list
   }
   else if (nodeLevel > prevLevel) {
      // append listitem to a new list
      // change the prevLevel value
   }
   else if (nodeLevel < prevLevel) {
      // append listitem to the list of that level
      // change the prevLevel value
   }
   ```

   Be sure to indent your code appropriately, to make it easier to read. Figure 16-19 shows the revised text of the createList() function.

Creating the if structure for the nested list ◄ **Figure 16-19**

```
function createList(list) {
    var prevLevel=0;
    for (var n=historyDoc.firstChild; n!=null; n=n.nextSibling) {
        nodeLevel = levelNum(n);
        if (nodeLevel != -1) {
            listItem = document.createElement("li");
            listItem.innerHTML = n.innerHTML;

            if (nodeLevel == prevLevel) {
                // append listitem to the list
            }
            else if (nodeLevel > prevLevel) {
                // append listitem to a new list
                // change the prevLevel value
            }
            else if (nodeLevel < prevLevel) {
                // append listitem to the list of that level
                // change the prevLevel value
            }
        }
    }
}
```

delete the line to append the list item →

▶ **4.** Save your changes to the file.

Next enter the code for each if condition. If nodeLevel equals prevLevel, this means that the current node is at the same level in the nested list, and you simply need to append the list item to the current list. Figure 16-20 shows how creating and appending this node compares to inserting the code in an HTML document. To simplify the node tree diagram, the text nodes are omitted from the figure; remember, though, that they are also part of the node tree.

Adding a list item to a list ◄ **Figure 16-20**

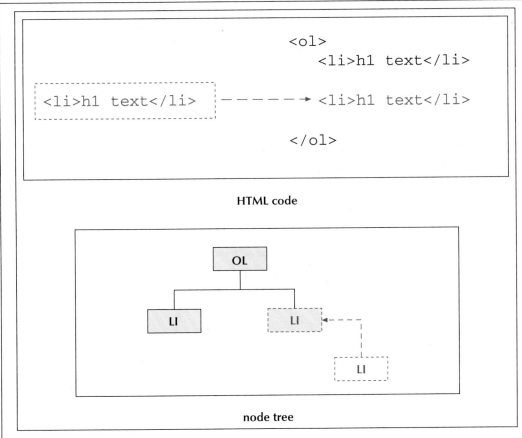

```
                    <ol>
                        <li>h1 text</li>
 <li>h1 text</li>  - - - - →  <li>h1 text</li>
                    </ol>
```

HTML code

node tree

Add the command to insert the list item to the first condition in the createList() function.

To add the appendChild() command:

1. Add the following command as shown in Figure 16-21:

   ```
   list.appendChild(listItem);
   ```

Figure 16-21 **Inserting the command for the first condition**

```
function createList(list) {
    var prevLevel=0;
    for (var n=historyDoc.firstChild; n!=null; n=n.nextSibling) {
        nodeLevel = levelNum(n);
        if (nodeLevel != -1) {
            listItem = document.createElement("li");
            listItem.innerHTML = n.innerHTML;

            if (nodeLevel == prevLevel) {
                // append listitem to the list
                list.appendChild(listItem);
            }
            else if (nodeLevel > prevLevel) {
                // append listitem to a new list
                // change the prevLevel value
            }
            else if (nodeLevel < prevLevel) {
                // append listitem to the list of that level
                // change the prevLevel value
            }
        }
    }
}
```

2. Save your changes to the file.

3. Reload **usconst.htm** in your Web browser. The table of contents should now only show the three h1 headings since they represent the headings with a level value of 0 (see Figure 16-22). No other headings are shown since the value of the prevLevel variable was set to 0 and was not changed by the code.

Figure 16-22 **Displaying only the top level headings**

Table of Contents
PREAMBLE
ARTICLES OF THE CONSTITUTION
AMENDMENTS

The Constitution of the United States

Preamble

WE THE PEOPLE OF THE UNITED STATES, IN ORDER TO FORM A MORE PERFECT UNION, establish Justice, insure domestic Tranquility, provide for the common defence, promote the general Welfare, and secure the Blessings of Liberty to ourselves and our Posterity, do ordain and establish this Constitution for the United States of America.

Articles of the Constitution

Article I - The Legislative Branch

Section 1: The Legislature

In the next if condition, you need to insert commands when the section heading is of a lower level than the previous heading (such as an h2 heading following an h1 heading). In these cases, you have to create a new ordered list and append the list item to it. The new list is then appended as a child of the current list (creating a nested list). Finally, you need to make the nested list the list object for the next time through the for loop and change the value of the prevLevel variable to the level of the current section heading. Figure 16-23 compares the HTML code with the equivalent operation in the node tree. Once again, the text nodes have been omitted to highlight the general structure of the node tree.

Appending a nested list to the node tree **Figure 16-23**

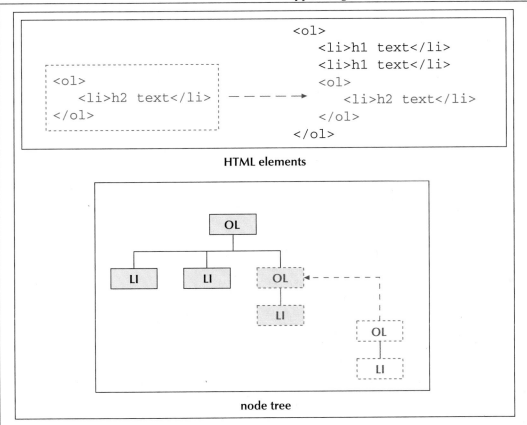

The code to change the structure of the node tree in this way is

```
newList = document.createElement("ol");
newList.appendChild(listItem);
list.appendChild(newList);
list = newList;
prevLevel = nodeLevel;
```

Add these commands to the createList() function within the second if condition.

To create the nested list:

▶ **1.** Return to **toc.js** in your text editor.

▶ **2.** Add the following commands to the second if condition in the createList() function as shown in Figure 16-24:

```
newList = document.createElement("ol");
newList.appendChild(listItem);
list.appendChild(newList);
list = newList;
prevLevel = nodeLevel;
```

Figure 16-24	Inserting the command for the second condition

```
if (nodeLevel == prevLevel) {
    // append listitem to the list
    list.appendChild(listItem);
}
else if (nodeLevel > prevLevel) {
    // append listitem to a new list
    // change the prevLevel value
    newList = document.createElement("ol");
    newList.appendChild(listItem);
    list.appendChild(newList);
    list = newList;
    prevLevel = nodeLevel;
}
else if (nodeLevel < prevLevel) {
    // append listitem to the list of that level
    // change the prevLevel value
}
```

▶ **3.** Save your changes to the file and reload **usconst.htm** in your Web browser. The table of contents should now appear as shown in Figure 16-25.

Figure 16-25	Nested table of contents

```
Table of Contents

PREAMBLE
ARTICLES OF THE CONSTITUTION
    Article I - The Legislative Branch
        Section 1: The Legislature
        Section 2: The House
        Section 3: The Senate
        Section 4: Meetings
        Section 5: Membership
        Section 6: Compensation
        Section 7: Bills
        Section 8: Congressional Powers
        Section 9: Congressional Limits
        Section 10: State Limits
        Section 1: The President
        Section 2: Presidential Powers
        Section 3: State of the Union
        Section 4: Disqualification
        Section 1: Judicial Powers
        Section 2: Trial by Jury
        Section 3: Treason
        Section 1: Interstate Relationships
        Section 2: State Citzenship
        Section 3: New States
        Section 4: State Government
        Paragraph
        Paragraph
        Paragraph
```

Trouble? The other headings are missing from the table of contents because you have not entered code to enable moving back up in the nested list. The loop can only move down at present. You'll add the commands for moving up next.

The final if condition occurs when the level of the current heading is higher than the previous heading (such as when an h1 heading follows an h3 heading). How should this occurrence be represented in the node tree? Figure 16-26 shows a nested list represented by both its HTML elements and as a node tree. Note that each ordered list element (OL) has as its parent another ordered list element, until you get to the topmost list. When you encounter a higher level section heading, such as the h1 heading, you have to append it as a child of an ordered list element higher up in the node tree.

Appending a list item to a higher level list | **Figure 16-26**

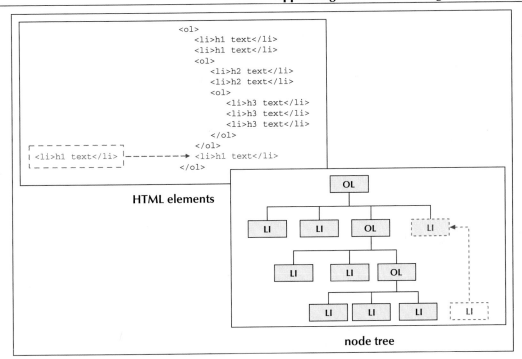

To decide which ordered list element the new list item should be appended to, you need to calculate how many levels up the node tree the item has to go. This is simply the difference between the previous level and the new level. For example, all h1 headings are on level 0 and all h3 headings are on level 2. The difference between them is 2, and thus you have to move up two levels in the TOC node tree whenever an h1 heading follows an h3 heading. To move up the node tree, you use the parentNode property to move from the list to its parent. You repeat this process for each level that you want to go up. The code for this is

```
levelUp = prevLevel - nodeLevel;
for (j=1; j<=levelUp; j++) list=list.parentNode;
```

Each time through, the for loop changes the list object to its parent. The loop stops when it has gone up the correct number of levels as indicated by the levelUp variable. Once it is at the correct level, you need to append the list item to it as a new child and change the value of the prevLevel variable so that it points to the new level in the node tree. The complete code is

```
levelUp = prevLevel - nodeLevel;
for (j=1; j<=levelUp; j++) list=list.parentNode;
list.appendChild(listItem);
prevLevel = nodeLevel;
```

Add these commands to the third if condition.

To complete the nested list:

1. Return to **toc.js** in your text editor.

2. Add the following commands to the third if condition in the createList() function as shown in Figure 16-27:

```
levelUp = prevLevel - nodeLevel;
for (j=1; j<=levelUp; j++) list=list.parentNode;
list.appendChild(listItem);
prevLevel = nodeLevel;
```

Figure 16-27 ▶ **Inserting the command for the third condition**

```
if (nodeLevel == prevLevel) {
    // append listitem to the list
    list.appendChild(listItem);
}
else if (nodeLevel > prevLevel) {
    // append listitem to a new list
    // change the prevLevel value
    newList = document.createElement("ol");
    newList.appendChild(listItem);
    list.appendChild(newList);
    list = newList;
    prevLevel = nodeLevel;
}
else if (nodeLevel < prevLevel) {
    // append listitem to the list of that level
    // change the prevLevel value
    levelUp = prevLevel - nodeLevel;
    for (j=1; j<=levelUp; j++) list=list.parentNode;
    list.appendChild(listItem);
    prevLevel = nodeLevel;
}
```

3. Save your changes to the file and reload **usconst.htm** in your Web browser. The table of contents should now show all of the headings from the constitution document in a nested list (see Figure 16-28). Note that the headings displayed in the table of contents go up and down the nested list matching the level of each heading in the constitution document.

Figure 16-28 ▶ **Table of contents as a nested list**

Working with Attributes

Norene stops by to check on your progress. She's thrilled with the table of contents your script has generated for her document. Since this is a hypertext document, she wonders whether the entries in the table of contents could contain links to the section headings they represent.

Once again, it's useful to write out the markup tags for proposed change, even if you can't view those markup tags in your document. As indicated in Figure 16-29, making this change involves two steps:

1. Adding an id attribute to each section heading (if it doesn't already have one)
2. Changing the content of each list item to a link pointing to the corresponding section heading

Linking to section headings ◀ **Figure 16-29**

table of contents links
```
<ol>
    <li><a href="#head1">Preamble</a></li>
    <li><a href="#head2">Articles of the Constitution</a></li>
    <ol>
        <li><a href="#head3">Legislative Branch</a></li>
        <ol>
            <li><a href="#head4">Section 1: The Legislature</a></li>
            <li><a href="#head5">Section 2: The House</a></li>
            <li><a href="#head6">Section 3: The Senate</a></li>
    ...
```

section headings with id values
```
<h1 id="head1">Preamble</h1>
<p> ... </p>
<h1 id="head2">Articles of the Constitution</h1>
<p> ... </p>
<h2 id="head3">Legislative Branch</h2>
<p> ... </p>
<h3 id="head4">Section 1: The Legislature</h3>
<p> ... </p>
<h3 id="head5">Section 2: The House</h3>
<p> ... </p>
<h3 id="head6">Section 3: The Senate</h3>
<p> ... </p>
...
```

To create and add the id and href attributes, you first need to understand how to work with attributes in the W3C document object model.

Attribute Nodes

Attributes and their values are considered nodes and can be attached to element nodes. Unlike element and text nodes, however, they are not part of the node tree because attribute nodes are not counted as children of element nodes as text nodes are (see Figure 16-30). Thus, attribute nodes have no familial relation with any node in the node tree.

Figure 16-30 ▶ **Attribute nodes**

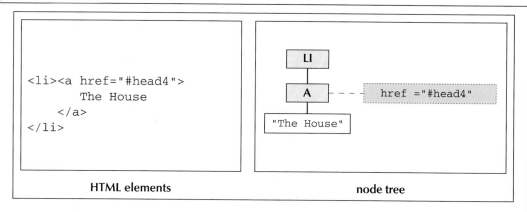

| HTML elements | node tree |

The document object model supports several methods to create, attach, and set the values of attributes. See Figure 16-31.

Figure 16-31 ▶ **Methods of attribute nodes**

Method	Description
document.createAttribute(*att*)	Create an attribute node with the name *att*.
node.getAttribute(*att*)	Returns the value of an attribute *att* from a *node* to which it has been attached.
node.hasAttribute(*att*)	Returns a Boolean value indicating whether *node* has the attribute *att*.
node.removeAttribute(*att*)	Removes the attribute *att* from *node*.
node.removeAttributeNode(*att*)	Removes an attribute node *att* from *node*.
node.setAttribute(*att*, *value*)	Creates or changes the *value* of the attribute *att* of *node*.

To create or set an attribute for an element, you use the setAttribute() method. The following code creates a list item element and then uses the setAttribute() method to set the id value of the list item to the text string "TOChead1":

```
listItem = document.createElement("li");
listItem.setAttribute("id","TOChead1");
```

The net effect of these two commands is to create the following element:

```
<li id="TOChead1"> ... </li>
```

In some cases, you need to determine whether an element has a particular attribute, such as the id attribute. In these situations, you use the hasAttribute() method, which returns the Boolean value true if the element contains the attribute. For example, the expression

```
listItem.hasAttribute("id")
```

would return the value true if the list item had an id.

Attributes as Object Properties

For element nodes in an HTML or XHTML document, the document object model also supports a shorthand way of applying attributes as properties of an element. The general syntax is

```
elem.att
```

where *elem* is an element node and *att* is an attribute of that element. To create and set the id attribute for a list item in this shorthand form, you would enter the following commands:

```
listItem = document.createElement("li");
listItem.id = "TOChead1";
```

Rather than using the hasAttribute(), you test whether an attribute exists by testing whether its value equals an empty text string. For example, to test whether the listItem node has an id attribute, you can use the following expression:

```
listItem.id != ""
```

which has the Boolean value true if the id attribute is present and false if it is an empty text string or missing. In general, it's easier and more intuitive to use this shorthand form. The attribute node methods are usually reserved for working with the attributes of nodes that are not HTML elements, as would be the case if you were writing a script for an XML document.

Setting the Section Heading Ids

Now that you've learned how to work with attributes, you'll return to the next task, which is to insert ids into all of the section headings in the constitution document. You'll name each of the section headings

```
head i
```

where *i* is a variable that equals 1 for the first section heading, two for the second heading and so forth. See Figure 16-29 for an example of how the ids of the first six section headings will be numbered. You need to be careful, however, not to overwrite any preexisting ids, since it is quite possible that Norene will have already placed ids in some of the section headings. You should first test whether an id attribute already exists for an element and only insert an id if it doesn't already have one. As you create section ids, you'll store each id in a variable named sectionId; you'll use this variable later in the code to create the hypertext references for the links. The code to insert the section heading ids is

```
headNum++;
if (n.id == "") {
   sectionId = "head"+headNum;
   n.id = sectionId;
}
else sectionId = n.id;
```

Here headNum is a counter variable that is increased each time the code encounters a section element in the constitution document. If the element has no id, an id is created for it; otherwise, the sectionId variable stores the value of the preexisting id. Add these commands to the createList() function.

To insert the section ids:

1. Return to **toc.js** in your text editor and go to the createList() function.

   First you must set the initial value of the headNum variable to 0.

2. Directly below the line "var prevLevel = 0" insert the command:

   ```
   var headNum = 0;
   ```

3. At the top of the for loop, insert the following commands, as shown in Figure 16-32:

   ```
   // insert ids for the section headings
   headNum++;
   if (n.id == "") {
      sectionId = "head"+headNum;
      n.id = sectionId;
   }
   else sectionId = n.id;
   ```

Figure 16-32   Inserting section ids

```
function createList(list) {
   var prevLevel=0;
   var headNum = 0;
   for (var n=historyDoc.firstChild; n!=null; n=n.nextSibling) {
      nodeLevel = levelNum(n);
      if (nodeLevel != -1) {

         // insert ids for the section headings
         headNum++;
         if (n.id == "") {
            sectionId = "head"+headNum;
            n.id = sectionId;
         }
         else sectionId = n.id;

         listItem = document.createElement("li");
         listItem.innerHTML=n.innerHTML;
```

4. Save your changes to the file.

Inserting Links

Now you need to revise the structure of the TOC node tree to include links. The href value for each link will be #*sectionId* where *sectionId* is the value of the sectionId variable. You'll also set the id of each list element to "TOC*sectionId*". This will allow you to easily match list items in the TOC with section headings in the document. You'll need this information for some of the tasks you'll do in the next session. Figure 16-33 shows the node structure of the list items with and without the links.

Changing a list item to a hypertext link ◄ Figure 16-33

To create the new node structure, you'll replace the old commands to create the list item with the following:

```
listItem=document.createElement("li");
listItem.id="TOC"+sectionId;
linkItem = document.createElement("a");
linkItem.innerHTML = n.innerHTML;
linkItem.href="#"+sectionId;
listItem.appendChild(linkItem);
```

Insert these commands into the createList() function and then test the links in the table of contents.

To turn the list items into links:

1. Within the createList() function, delete the line "listItem.innerHTML=n.innerHTML".

2. Replace the deleted line with the following code (see Figure 16-34):

```
listItem.id="TOC"+sectionId;
linkItem = document.createElement("a");
linkItem.innerHTML = n.innerHTML;
linkItem.href="#"+sectionId;
listItem.appendChild(linkItem);
```

Figure 16-34 | **Inserting links**

delete the line to place the heading content into the list item

```
// insert ids for the section headings
headNum++;
if (n.id == "") {
    sectionId = "head"+headNum;
    n.id = sectionId;
}
else sectionId = n.id;

listItem = document.createElement("li");
listItem.id="TOC"+sectionId;

linkItem = document.createElement("a");
linkItem.innerHTML = n.innerHTML;
linkItem.href="#"+sectionId;

listItem.appendChild(linkItem);

if (nodeLevel == prevLevel) {
    // append listitem to the list
    list.appendChild(listItem);
}
```

3. Save your changes. If you plan to take a break before starting the next session you may close the file.

4. Reopen **usconst.htm** in your Web browser.

5. As shown in Figure 16-35, the entries in the table of contents should now act as links to the different sections of the constitution document. Test different links to verify that they take you to the appropriate sections of the document.

Figure 16-35 | **Viewing the list of links**

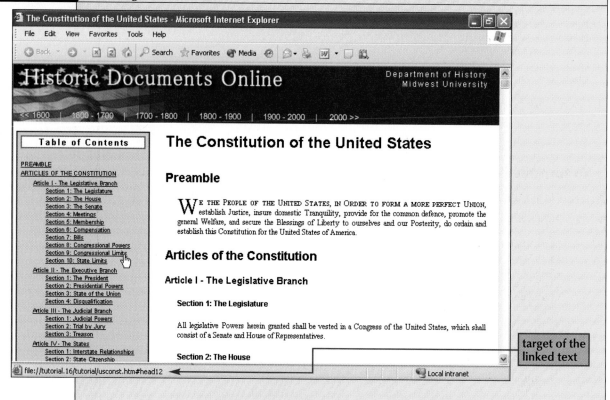

6. Close your browser if you plan to take a break before the next session.

You've completed your work in making the table of contents into a nested list of links. In the next session you'll add more features to the table of contents, including the ability to contract and expand the table of contents and the constitution document.

Session 16.2 Quick Check

1. What code would you write to create two ul list elements, one nested inside of the other? Use the variable name topList for the upper list element and the variable named bottomList for the bottom list element.
2. In the previous question, what is the node reference to the topList object from a list item found in the bottom list?
3. Why are attribute nodes not part of the document node tree?
4. What node method would you use to determine whether an element contains the type attribute?
5. What command would you use to create an input element with the variable name CBox and a type attribute value of "checkbox"? Use an attribute node method in your answer.
6. What commands would you add to the previous question if you were to create the type attribute using a property rather than an attribute node method?
7. What property would you use in the previous question to determine whether the CBox input element had a type attribute?

Session 16.3

Expanding and Collapsing a Document

You and Norene have met again to discuss your progress on the table of contents application. Norene has seen a few other lists in which the nested entries can be alternately hidden or displayed by clicking a plus/minus box. In a **plus/minus box**, when the box shows a + symbol, it indicates that there is hidden content within and clicking the + box reveals the hidden content. When the box shows a -- symbol, it indicates that all of the items are displayed, but clicking the box will hide them (see Figure 16-36).

Expanding and contracting a list with a plus/minus box | Figure 16-36

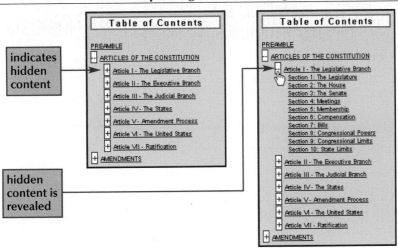

Norene asks whether you can add this feature to the table of contents so that users can expand or contract the TOC. She also wants the contents of the document to mimic the appearance of the table of contents, so that as items are hidden in the TOC they are also hidden within the document. Creating this kind of dynamic content involves several of the tools and techniques you've learned in the last few tutorials, including working with event objects and object styles.

Creating a plus/minus Box

The first things you'll add to the TOC are the plus/minus boxes. Since you want to treat each plus/minus box as a single object, you'll place the text of the plus/minus box within a span element. Initially the plus/minus box will display the text "--" since the TOC will open with all list items displayed to users. The commands to create the plus/minus box are

```
plusMinusBox = document.createElement("span");
plusMinusBox.innerHTML="--";
```

Next you have to determine where to place the plus/minus boxes in Norene's TOC. Since the boxes are designed to alternately hide or display nested lists, they should be placed directly before the ordered list elements containing those items. Figure 16-37 shows where you would place the plus/minus box if you were writing the HTML tags directly, and how it would be rendered on the Web page. Notice that the styles for the span element, including the background color and border, have already been placed in the toc.css file. This means that you don't have to worry about formatting your plus/minus boxes for the Web page, but you can focus instead on inserting the content.

Figure 16-37 ▶ **Placing the plus/minus box**

```
<li id="TOChead34">
    <span>--</span>
    <a href="#head34">
       Amendments
    </a>
</li>
<ul>
    <li id="TOChead35">
       <a href="#head35">
          I. Freedom of Expression
       </a>
    </li>
    <li id="TOChead36">
       <a href="#head36">
          II. Right to bear Arms
       </a>
    </li>
...
</ul>
```

HTML elements

Rendered elements

Figure 16-38 shows how this HTML code would appear in the node tree (attribute nodes are not shown in order to simplify the diagram). As indicated in the figure, the span element used for the plus/minus box has to be inserted as the first child of any list item that precedes a nested list.

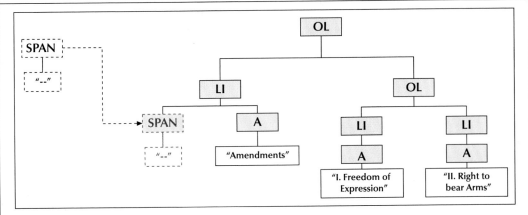

To place the box in the correct location, you create a variable for the previous list item using the previousSibling property:

```
prevListItem = list.previousSibling;
```

You then insert the plus/minus box as a child of this previous list item by using the insertBefore() method. Recall that the insertBefore() method allows you to insert new child nodes at specific locations in the child nodes collection. In this case, you want to insert the plus/minus box in front of the current first child of the previous list item. The code to insert the plus/minus box is therefore

```
prevListItem.insertBefore(plusMinusBox, prevListItem.firstChild);
```

The complete code to create and insert the plus/minus box is

```
plusMinusBox = document.createElement("span");
plusMinusBox.innerHTML="--";
prevListItem = list.previousSibling;
prevListItem.insertBefore(plusMinusBox, prevListItem.firstChild);
```

Add these commands to the createList() function in the command block in which the nested list elements are created.

To create and place the plus/minus boxes:

1. If necessary, reopen **toc.js** in your text editor.

2. Go to the createList() function and insert the following code at the end of the second if condition, as shown in Figure 16-39:

```
// create and place the plus-minus box
plusMinusBox = document.createElement("span");
plusMinusBox.innerHTML="--";
prevListItem = list.previousSibling;
prevListItem.insertBefore(plusMinusBox, prevListItem.firstChild);
```

Figure 16-39 ▶ Creating and placing the plus/minus boxes

```
if (nodeLevel == prevLevel) {
    // append listitem to the list
    list.appendChild(listItem);
}
else if (nodeLevel > prevLevel) {
    // append listitem to a new list
    // change the prevLevel value
    newList = document.createElement("ol");
    newList.appendChild(listItem);
    list.appendChild(newList);
    list = newList;
    prevLevel = nodeLevel;

    // create and place the plus-minus box
    plusMinusBox = document.createElement("span");
    plusMinusBox.innerHTML="--";
    prevListItem = list.previousSibling;
    prevListItem.insertBefore(plusMinusBox, prevListItem.firstChild);
}
else if (nodeLevel < prevLevel) {
    // append listitem to the list of that level
    // change the prevLevel value
    levelUp = prevLevel - nodeLevel;
    for (j=1; j<=levelUp; j++) list=list.parentNode;
    list.appendChild(listItem);
    prevLevel = nodeLevel;
}
```

▶ **3.** Save your changes to the file.

▶ **4.** Reopen **usconst.htm** in your Web browser. As shown in Figure 16-40, plus/minus boxes should now be placed in front of the nested items within the table of contents.

Figure 16-40 ▶ Viewing the plus/minus boxes

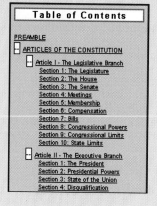

Adding Event Handlers to the plus/minus Boxes

When a plus/minus box is clicked, the browser should do the following:

1. Toggle the text of the box, changing a "+" to a "--" and vice-versa.
2. Alternately hide and display the contents of the nested list next to the plus/minus box.
3. Alternately hide and display the corresponding content in the constitution document.

You'll place these actions in a function named expandCollapse(). The first part of the function will toggle the display in the plus/minus box. The initial code for the expandCollapse() function is

```
function expandCollapse(e) {
   var plusMinusBox=eventSource(e);
   if (plusMinusBox.innerHTML=="--") plusMinusBox.innerHTML="+";
   else plusMinusBox.innerHTML="--";
}
```

The function has a single parameter: the event object e (for a review of event objects see the previous tutorial). In the first line of the function, the cross-browser eventSource() function is used to determine from which plus/minus box the click event originated. If the text of the plusMinusBox is "--", it is changed to "+"; otherwise, it is changed to "--". Add this function to the toc.js file and create an event handler for it.

To insert the expandCollapse() function:

1. Return to the **toc.js** file in your text editor.

2. At the end of the file, insert the following function:

   ```
   function expandCollapse(e) {
      var plusMinusBox=eventSource(e);
      if (plusMinusBox.innerHTML=="--") plusMinusBox.innerHTML="+";
      else plusMinusBox.innerHTML="--";
   }
   ```

   You also have to add an event handler to each plus/minus box to run the expand-Collapse function in response to the click event.

3. Go up to the createList() function and insert the following command as shown in Figure 16-41:

   ```
   plusMinusBox.onclick = expandCollapse;
   ```

Creating the expandCollapse() function ◀ **Figure 16-41**

run the expandCollapse() function
when the user clicks a plus/minus box

```
            // create and place the plus-minus box
            plusMinusBox = document.createElement("span");
            plusMinusBox.innerHTML="--";
            plusMinusBox.onclick = expandCollapse;
            prevListItem = list.previousSibling;
            prevListItem.insertBefore(plusMinusBox, prevListItem.firstChild);
         }
         else if (nodeLevel < prevLevel) {
            // append listitem to the list of that level
            // change the prevLevel value
            levelUp = prevLevel - nodeLevel;
            for (j=1; j<=levelUp; j++) list=list.parentNode;
            list.appendChild(listItem);
            prevLevel = nodeLevel;
         }
      }
   }
}

function expandCollapse(e) {
   var plusMinusBox=eventSource(e);
   if (plusMinusBox.innerHTML=="--") plusMinusBox.innerHTML="+";
   else plusMinusBox.innerHTML="--";
}
```

4. Save your changes to the file and reopen **usconst.htm** in your Web browser. Verify that each time you click a plus/minus box the content of the box changes between + and --.

Hiding and Displaying Objects

The next action of the expandCollapse() function is to alternately hide or display the nested items within the TOC. There are two different styles that you can use for hiding an object on a Web page: the visibility style and the display style. While both styles hide page elements, they differ in how other page elements are affected. With the visibility style, the hidden items still occupy their positions within the flow of a page. With the display style, the hidden items are removed from the page and the other elements flow into the space that the hidden items previously occupied (see Figure 16-42).

Figure 16-42 ▶ **Comparing the visibility and display styles**

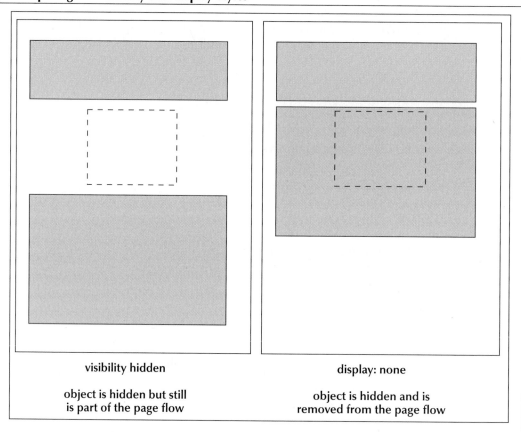

visibility hidden	display: none
object is hidden but still is part of the page flow	object is hidden and is removed from the page flow

For the table of contents, you'll use the display style since you want the TOC to collapse and expand as items are hidden and then redisplayed. To hide an object, you use the command

```
object.style.display = "none"
```

where *object* is the page object to be hidden. To redisplay the object, you set the display style to an empty text string. This removes the display style from the object, causing browsers to apply the default display style to the object. The command is

```
object.style.display = "";
```

In the table of contents, the only elements you need to hide and redisplay are the ordered list elements (ol). Since every nested object inherits the display status of its parent, hiding an ol element also hides any descendant elements such as list items and nested lists. To determine which ordered list to hide, you once again look at the position of the ol element relative to the plus/minus box; however, in this case you create a reference *from* the plus/minus box *to* the ol element. As indicated in Figure 16-43, to go from the plus/minus box to the ol element, you go up to the parent node (in this case the list item element) and then to the next sibling (the ol element).

The position of the plus/minus box relative to the nested list ◄ **Figure 16-43**

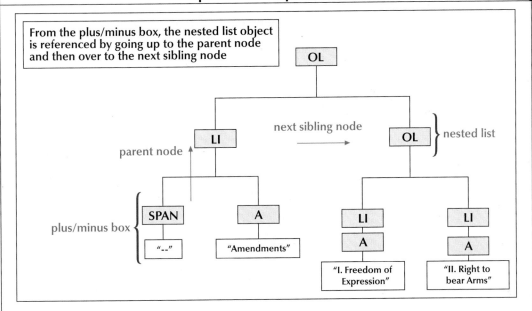

The object reference to move from the plus/minus box to a nested list is therefore

```
var nestedList = plusMinusBox.parentNode.nextSibling;
```

Next, as you did when toggling the text in a plus/minus box between + and -- , you toggle the display status of the contents of the nested list. The code is

```
if (nestedList.style.display=="") nestedList.style.display="none";
else nestedList.style.display="";
```

Add these commands to the expandCollapse() function.

To expand and collapse the nested lists in the TOC:

1. Return to the **toc.js** file in your text editor.

2. Within the expandCollapse() function, add the following code as shown in Figure 16-44:

```
var nestedList = plusMinusBox.parentNode.nextSibling;
if (nestedList.style.display=="") nestedList.style.display="none";
else nestedList.style.display="";
```

Figure 16-44 ▶ **Expanding and collapsing the nested lists**

```
function expandCollapse(e) {
   var plusMinusBox=eventSource(e);
   if (plusMinusBox.innerHTML=="--") plusMinusBox.innerHTML="+";
   else plusMinusBox.innerHTML="--";

   var nestedList = plusMinusBox.parentNode.nextSibling;
   if (nestedList.style.display=="") nestedList.style.display="none";
   else nestedList.style.display="";
}
```

▶ **3.** Save your changes to the file.

▶ **4.** Reload **usconst.htm** in your Web browser. Verify that as you click the plus/minus boxes in the table of contents, the nested lists within the TOC are alternately hidden and redisplayed. Figure 16-45 shows the table of contents with a mixture of hidden and displayed nested lists.

Figure 16-45 ▶ **Table of contents with hidden lists**

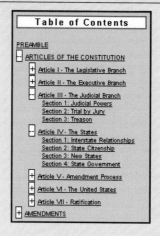

Expanding and Collapsing the Document

The final piece of the dynamic table of contents is to expand and collapse the document itself so that it mimics the appearance of the TOC. The structure of the document is fundamentally different from the structure of the TOC, however. In the TOC, different sections are nested within one another. In the document itself, by contrast, all sections are siblings, with only the section headings indicating when a section begins and ends and the element names indicating what level each section represents (see Figure 16-46). This means you have to take a fundamentally different approach in deciding which elements to hide and to display.

The structure of the TOC list and the document elements ◄ Figure 16-46

```
<ol>
    <li>Main Head</li>
    <ol>
        <li>Subhead</li>
        <ol>
            <li>Minor Subhead</li>
            <li>Minor Subhead</li>
        </ol>
        <li>Subhead</li>
    </ol>
    <li>Main Head</li>
    <ol>
        <li>Subhead</li>
        <ol>
            <li>Minor Subhead</li>
        </ol>
    </ol>
</ol>
```

nested list

```
<h1>Main Head</h1>
<p>Text</p>
<h2>Subhead</h2>
<p>Text</p>
<h3>Minor Subhead</h3>
<p>Text</p>
<h3>Minor Subhead</h3>
<p>Text</p>
<p>Text</p>
<h2>Subhead</h2>
<p>Text</p>
<p>Text</p>
<h1>Main Head</h1>
<p>Text</p>
<h2>Subhead</h2>
<p>Text</p>
<h3>Minor Subhead</h3>
<p>Text</p>
```

document elements

Our approach is to move through the document sibling by sibling. Each time you encounter a heading element, you determine whether its corresponding entry in the TOC is currently being displayed. If it's hidden in the TOC, you hide the heading element and all subsequent siblings until you encounter the next section heading; otherwise, you display the heading element and the siblings that follow until the next section heading is encountered. The general structure of the code is

```
historyDoc = document.getElementById("doc");
for (n=historyDoc.firstChild; n!=null; n=n.nextSibling) {
    nodeLevel=levelNum(n);
    if (nodeLevel != -1) {
        set the display status for the heading
    }
    if (n.nodeType==1) {
        apply the display status to the element
    }
}
```

In this code you loop through the nodes in the document using the same structure that you used in the createList() function by starting with the first child of the doc element and moving to the next sibling node until there are no siblings left. For each node you first test whether it is a heading element by using the levelNum() function. If the value returned by the levelNum() is not equal to –1 (indicating that the node represents one of the section headings) you set the display status for the heading. Then you test whether the current node is any element node (such as a paragraph) by verifying that the value of the nodeType property is equal to 1. If it is an element node, you apply the current display status to the node and then move on to the next sibling in the document.

You'll add these commands to a function named expandCollapseDoc(). Create this function now.

To insert the expandCollapseDoc():

1. Return to the **toc.js** file in your text editor.

2. At the bottom of the file, insert the following function (see Figure 16-47):

```
function expandCollapseDoc() {
    historyDoc = document.getElementById("doc");
    for (n=historyDoc.firstChild; n!=null; n=n.nextSibling) {
        nodeLevel = levelNum(n);
        if (nodeLevel != -1) {
            //set the display status for the heading
        }
        if (n.nodeType==1) {
            //apply the display status to the element
        }
    }
}
```

| Figure 16-47 | Inserting the expandCollapseDoc() function |

```
function expandCollapse(e) {
    var plusMinusBox=eventSource(e);
    if (plusMinusBox.innerHTML=="--") plusMinusBox.innerHTML="+";
    else plusMinusBox.innerHTML="--";

    var nestedList = plusMinusBox.parentNode.nextSibling;
    if (nestedList.style.display=="") nestedList.style.display="none";
    else nestedList.style.display="";
}

function expandCollapseDoc() {
    historyDoc = document.getElementById("doc");
    for (n=historyDoc.firstChild; n!=null; n=n.nextSibling) {
        nodeLevel = levelNum(n);
        if (nodeLevel != -1) {
            //set the display status for the heading
        }
        if (n.nodeType==1) {
            //apply the display status to the element
        }
    }
}
```

3. Save your changes to the file.

To set the display status, you first create a variable named displayStatus, setting its initial value to "" (indicating that the item will be displayed on the page).

```
displayStatus = "";
```

Then you match the heading element to its corresponding entry in the TOC. Recall that in the last session each list item in the TOC was given an id based on the id of a section heading. If the section heading has the id *sectionId* then the list item has the id TOC*sectionId*. You can use the getElementById() method to locate the list item for each section heading as follows:

```
TOCitem = document.getElementById("TOC"+n.id);
```

Now you need to determine whether the corresponding entry in the TOC is hidden or visible. Each list item has as its parent node an ordered list element, and the parent of that element is also an ordered list element, all the way up to the top of the TOC. If the display style of *any* of those ordered list elements is set to "none", the list item is hidden in the TOC. Thus, to determine whether the list item is hidden, you have to look at the display style of all of its parents. The following code provides a for loop that starts with the current value of the nodeLevel variable, decreasing it by one each time through the loop (as you move up to the higher levels in the TOC list); when the value of the counter is less than 0, the loop stops.

```
for (l=nodeLevel; l >= 0; l--) {
   TOCitem = TOCitem.parentNode;
   if (TOCitem.style.display == "none") {displayStatus = "none";
 break;}
}
```

Each time through the loop, you change the reference of the TOCitem variable to its parent. If the value of the display style for TOCitem is "none", you set the value of the displayStatus variable to "none" and break out of the loop (since there is no need to continue checking the higher levels in the TOC after you discover that the list item lies within a hidden list). Figure 16-48 demonstrates how this code moves up the node tree from one nested list to another.

Testing for hidden lists ◄ Figure 16-48

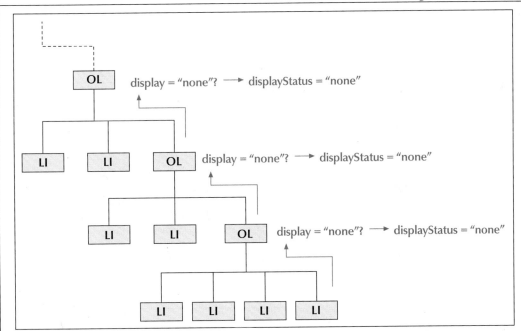

Once the value of the displayStatus variable has been determined, you apply it to the current node in the constitution document using the command

```
n.style.display = displayStatus;
```

Add these commands to the expandCollapseDoc() function.

To complete the expandCollapseDoc():

1. In the expandCollapseDoc() function below the comment "set the display status for the heading", insert the following commands:

```
displayStatus = "";
TOCitem = document.getElementById("TOC"+n.id);
for (l=nodeLevel; l >= 0; l--) {
   TOCitem = TOCitem.parentNode;
   if (TOCitem.style.display == "none") {displayStatus = "none";
break;}
}
```

2. Below the comment "apply the display status to the element", insert the command:

```
n.style.display = displayStatus;
```

Figure 16-49 shows the final code of the expandCollapseDoc() function.

Figure 16-49 — **The final expandCollapseDoc() function**

```
function expandCollapseDoc() {
   historyDoc = document.getElementById("doc");
   for (n=historyDoc.firstChild; n!=null; n=n.nextSibling) {
      nodeLevel = levelNum(n);
      if (nodeLevel != -1) {
         //set the display status for the heading
         displayStatus = "";
         TOCitem = document.getElementById("TOC"+n.id);
         for (l=nodeLevel; l >= 0; l--) {
            TOCitem = TOCitem.parentNode;
            if (TOCitem.style.display == "none") {displayStatus = "none"; break;}
         }
      }
      if (n.nodeType==1) {
         //apply the display status to the element
         n.style.display = displayStatus;
      }
   }
}
```

Next, call the expandCollapseDoc() function.

3. Insert the following command as shown in Figure 16-50:

```
expandCollapseDoc();
```

Figure 16-50 — **The final expandCollapse() function**

```
function expandCollapse(e) {
   var plusMinusBox=eventSource(e);
   if (plusMinusBox.innerHTML=="--") plusMinusBox.innerHTML="+";
   else plusMinusBox.innerHTML="--";

   var nestedList = plusMinusBox.parentNode.nextSibling
   if (nestedList.style.display=="") nestedList.style.display="none";
   else nestedList.style.display="";

   expandCollapseDoc();
}
```

4. Close the **toc.js** file, saving your changes.

5. Reopen the **usconst.htm** file in your Web browser. Click the different plus/minus boxes in the TOC and verify that the content displayed in the constitution document mimics the TOC. See Figure 16-51.

Historic Documents Online

Department of History
Midwest University

<< 1600 | 1600 - 1700 | 1700 - 1800 | 1800 - 1900 | 1900 - 2000 | 2000 >>

Table of Contents

PREAMBLE
- ARTICLES OF THE CONSTITUTION
  + Article I - The Legislative Branch
  + Article II - The Executive Branch
  + Article III - The Judicial Branch
  + Article IV - The States
  + Article V - Amendment Process
    Paragraph
  + Article VI - The United States
  + Article VII - Ratification
+ AMENDMENTS

The Constitution of the United States

Preamble

WE THE PEOPLE OF THE UNITED STATES, IN ORDER TO FORM A MORE PERFECT UNION, establish Justice, insure domestic Tranquility, provide for the common defence, promote the general Welfare, and secure the Blessings of Liberty to ourselves and our Posterity, do ordain and establish this Constitution for the United States of America.

Articles of the Constitution

Article I - The Legislative Branch

Article II - The Executive Branch

Article III - The Judicial Branch

Article IV - The States

Article V - Amendment Process

Paragraph

The Congress, whenever two thirds of both Houses shall deem it necessary, shall propose Amendments to this Constitution, or, on the Application of the Legislatures of two thirds of the several States, shall call a Convention for proposing Amendments, which, in either Case, shall be valid to all Intents and Purposes, as part of this Constitution, when ratified by the Legislatures of three fourths of the several States, or by Conventions in three fourths thereof, as the one or the other Mode of Ratification may be proposed by the Congress; Provided that no Amendment which may be made prior to the Year One thousand eight hundred and eight shall in any Manner affect the first and fourth Clauses in the Ninth Section of the first article; and that no State, without its Consent, shall be deprived of its equal Suffrage in the Senate.

Article VI - The United States

Article VII - Ratification

Amendments

Testing the Dynamic TOC

You show the completed table of contents to Norene. She's very pleased with the final product. She asks whether your work can be easily applied to other documents in her library. You decide to show her by testing it on a document containing the text of a 1790 peace treaty between the United States government and the Creek Indians.

To test the TOC application on a new document:

1. Use your text editor to open the **treattxt.htm** file from the tutorial.16/tutorial folder. Enter *your name* and *the date* in the head section of the document and save it as **treaty.htm**.

2. Above the closing </head> tag insert an external script element pointing to the toc.js file:

   ```
   <script src="toc.js" type="text/javascript"></script>
   ```

3. Add the event handler **onload="makeTOC()"** to the body element.

4. Insert the following div element below the <body> tag:

   ```
   <div id="toc"></div>
   ```

5. Enclose the content of the document within a div element by adding the following opening tag directly before the Preamble h1 element:

   ```
   <div id="doc">
   ```

6. Add a closing **</div>** directly before the closing </body> tag at the bottom of the file. Figure 16-52 shows the revised code of the treaty.htm file.

Figure 16-52 ▶ **Revising the treaty document**

```
<script  src="toc.js" type="text/javascript"></script>
</head>

<body onload="makeTOC()">
<div id="toc"></div>

<div id="logo"><img src="hlogo.jpg" alt="Historic Documents" /></div>
<div id="logosub">Department of History<br />Midwest University</div>
<div id="doctitle"><h1>Treaty with the Creek Indians: 1790</h1></div>

<div id="doc">
<h1>Preamble</h1>
<p>THE parties being desirous of establishing permanent peace and friendship
between the United States and the said Creek Nation, and the citizens and
members thereof, and to remove the causes of war by ascertaining their limits,
and making other necessary, just and friendly arrangements: The President of the
United States, by Henry Knox, Secretary for the Department of War, whom he hath
constituted with full powers for these purposes, by and with the advice and
consent of the Senate of the United States, and the Creek Nation, by the
undersigned Kings, Chiefs and Warriors, representing the said nation, have
agreed to the following articles. </p>



</div>
</body>
</html>
```

7. Close the **treaty.htm** file, saving your changes.

8. Open **treaty.htm** in your Web browser and explore the functionality of the table of contents. As shown in Figure 16-53, the dynamic table of contents should be displayed on the left margin. Clicking the plus/minus boxes should collapse and expand the document contents, and clicking the entries in the TOC should move you to the corresponding sections in the treaty.

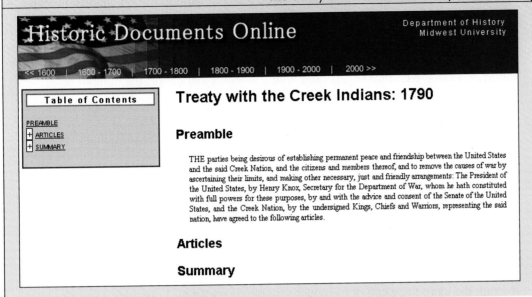

Traversing the Node Tree using Recursion

In creating the dynamic table of contents, you made several simplifying assumptions. One was that all of the section headings in each historic document would be siblings and children of the "doc" element. You did not allow for the possibility that a section heading would be further nested within another element. However, some applications that involve working with the node tree require a script to be able to traverse the entire tree, touching each node.

At first glance this may seem like a daunting task. A single node may have many child nodes, and each of those child nodes may have its own collection of child nodes, and so forth down through several levels of the tree. The path through the node tree must be able to go down each of the branches of the tree, touching each node and not touching any node more than once. To do that, scripts employ recursion. **Recursion** is a programming technique in which a function calls itself repeatedly until a stopping condition is met. Figure 16-54 shows the general form of a recursive function.

A recursive function ◀ **Figure 16-54**

```
function fname() {
    if (stopping condition not met) {
    commands;
    fname();
    }
}
```

In this code, the function *fname*() is run as long as the stopping condition is not met. One part of the if statement's command block is a command to run the *fname*() function again. Thus, you have a series of nested function calls that create a sequence of function calls. At some point, one of the nested functions fulfills the stopping condition and you move back to the previous function in the sequence and continue from that point. Eventually you move back to the beginning of the sequence and the entire process stops. The following example of recursion is used with a function that counts the number of descendant nodes within a given node:

```
function countNodes(nodeObject) {
    for (var n=nodeObject.firstChild; n!= null; n=n.nextSibling) {
        count++;
        countNodes(n);
    }
    return count;
}
```

Figure 16-55 illustrates the behavior of this function for a small node tree. The count-Nodes() function uses a for loop to examine each child node of the node object. The loop begins with the first child of the node object, moves to the next sibling each time through the loop, and halts when there are no more next siblings to go to. Each time through the loop, the value of the count variable increases by 1, keeping a running total of the number of child nodes. At the same time, each time through the loop the function applies the countNodes() function to the current child node to determine how many child nodes it contains. When the loop is finished, the final value of the count variable is retuned.

Figure 16-55	**Counting the total number of child nodes**

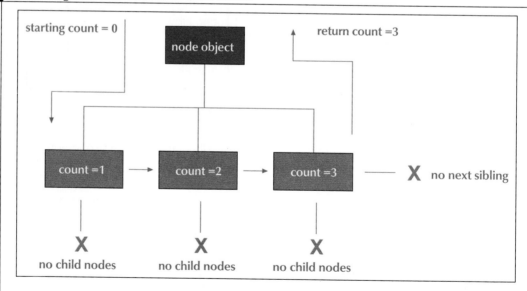

One important point to remember: the node variable, n, in this example must be entered as "var n = nodeObject.firstChild" in the for loop and not "n = nodeObject.firstChild". This is because the n variable would be treated as a global variable if it were not re-initialized with the var statement each time the recursive function is called.

Each recursive function needs a starting point, and in the case of the countNodes() function, a starting value for the count variable. The following code shows how you would call the countNodes() function using the top of the document (the html element in the case of HTML documents) as the starting node and setting the initial value of the count variable to 0:

```
function reportCount() {
    count = 0;
    return countNodes(document.documentElement);
}
```

Figure 16-56 displays the recursive action of the countNodes() function on a larger node tree. Note that the function "drills" down the node tree until it reaches the lowest node on the left-most part of tree. From there it continues to the right and up until it returns to the root node. Whenever it encounters a node it first counts the child nodes for the element before going to the next sibling. As it moves through the node tree, the value of the count variable increases by one at each node it encounters, eventually returning a count value of 10.

Recursion in the node counter | **Figure 16-56**

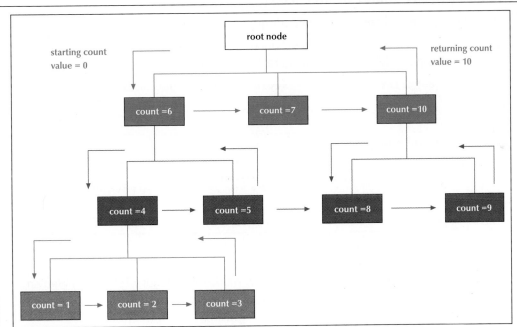

You don't need to use recursion with Norene's Web site; this technique will be useful for future projects that Norene may have for you.

Working with Style Sheets

Norene is pleased with all of the work you've done on the dynamic table of contents. She's approached you with one last problem. Norene wants to provide users with a version of each historic document that is suitable for printing. This version of the layout would contain only the historic document with none of the other features from the Web page. For example, such pages would include no table of contents box or history department logo. One way of making this revision would be to create a style sheet specifically designed for printed output (see Tutorial 7 for a discussion of print style sheets). However, Norene would rather give users the option of choosing which version of the page to print. She asks whether you can use objects on the page that students can click to switch from one style sheet to another.

Norene has provided two icons that you can have users click to switch between the Web version of the constitution page and the printer version. You'll float these two images on the right margin of the document title. Add these images to the Web page now.

To insert the Web and printer icons:

1. Reopen **usconst.htm** in your text editor.

2. Locate the div element with the id "doctitle". Directly before the h1 element insert the following code, as shown in Figure 16-57:

   ```
   <img src="print.jpg" alt="" style="float: right; cursor:
   pointer" />
   <img src="web.jpg" alt="" style="float: right; cursor: pointer" />
   ```

Figure 16-57	Inserting Web and printer icons

```
<body onload="makeTOC()">
<div id="logo"><img src="hlogo.jpg" alt="Historic Documents" /></div>
<div id="logosub">Department of History<br />Midwest University</div>
<div id="doctitle">
<img src="print.jpg" alt="" style="float: right; cursor: pointer" />
<img src="web.jpg" alt="" style="float: right; cursor: pointer" />
<h1>The Constitution of the United States</h1></div>
```

3. Save your changes to the file.

4. Reload **usconst.htm** in your Web browser. As shown in Figure 16-58, the Web and printer icons now float on the right margin of the page.

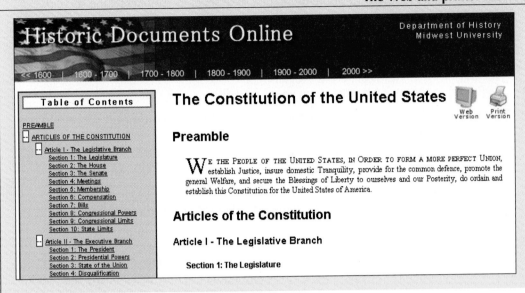

Norene has also provided an external style sheet file, print.css that defines the format of the printed version of the constitution page.

Working with the link element

So far in this tutorial you've worked only with elements found in the body of a Web page; however, elements in a document's head can be modified as well. The head of the constitution page contains a link element that loads the history.css style sheet. The code for the tag is

```
<link href="history.css" rel="stylesheet" type="text/css" />
```

You want to change this tag to

```
<link href="print.css" rel="stylesheet" type="text/css" />
```

to load the print styles for the page (and thus unload the Web version styles). You could examine the HTML code for the usconst.htm document to determine exactly where this element falls in the document node tree, but a quicker way would be to use the document.getElementsByTagName() method. Recall from Tutorial 11 that this method returns an object collection of all tags with a particular tag name. For example, to create an object collection of all the link elements in the document you would use the expression

```
document.getElementsByTagName("link")
```

The first link element, which in this case is the link element for the history.css style sheet, has the object reference

```
document.getElementsByTagName("link")[0]
```

To change the link so that it uses the print.css style sheet instead, you change the value of the href attribute to "print.css":

```
document.getElementsByTagName("link")[0].href="print.css";
```

Use this information to add two functions to the constitution page. One, named show-PrintVer(), changes the href attribute of the first style sheet to "print.css"; the second, named showWebVer(), changes the style sheet to the history.css file.

To create the showPrintVer() and showWebVer() functions:

1. Return to the **usconst.htm** file in your text editor.

2. Above the closing </head> tag, insert an embedded script element containing the following two functions:

```
function showPrintVer() {
   document.getElementsByTagName("link")[0].href="print.css";
}
function showWebVer() {
   document.getElementsByTagName("link")[0].href="history.css";
}
```

3. Locate the img element for the print.jpg image and insert the event handler **onclick="showPrintVer()"**. Insert the event handler **onclick="showWebVer()"** in the web.jpg inline image. Figure 16-59 highlights the new code for the file.

Figure 16-59 | **The showPrintVer() and showWebVer() functions**

```
<title>The Constitution of the United States</title>
<link href="history.css" rel="stylesheet" type="text/css" />
<link href="toc.css" rel="stylesheet" type="text/css" />
<script src="toc.js" type="text/javascript"></script>

<script type="text/javascript">
function showPrintVer() {
   document.getElementsByTagName("link")[0].href="print.css";
}
function showWebVer() {
   document.getElementsByTagName("link")[0].href="history.css";
}
</script>
</head>

<body onload="makeTOC()">
<div id="logo"><img src="hlogo.jpg" alt="Historic Documents" /></div>
<div id="logosub">Department of History<br />Midwest University</div>
<div id="doctitle">
<img src="print.jpg" alt="" style="float: right; cursor: pointer"
   onclick="showPrintVer()" />
<img src="web.jpg" alt="" style="float: right; cursor: pointer"
   onclick="showWebVer()" />
```

4. Close the file, saving your changes.

5. Reload **usconst.htm** in your Web browser. Verify that as you click the printer and Web icons, the layout of the page changes between the print version and the Web version. See Figure 16-60.

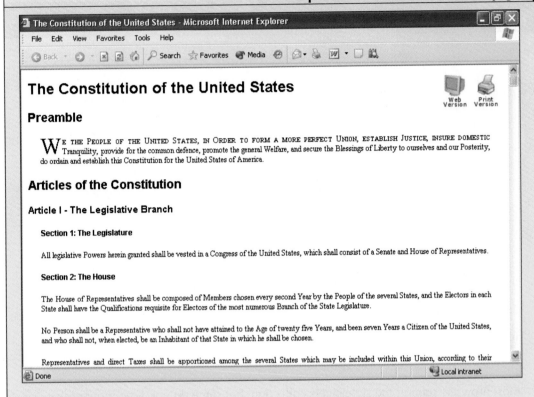

6. Close your Web browser.

The Style Sheet Collection

In addition to working with style sheets by modifying the link element, you can also work with them directly as objects in document object model. The DOM organizes style sheets into object collections using the form

```
document.styleSheets[i]
```

where i is the index number of the style sheet. The first style sheet that a browser encounters has an index value 0, the second has an index value of 1, and so forth. Figure 16-61 lists the properties of the style sheet object. Note that most of the properties are read-only, which means that they allow you to extract information about the style sheet object, but not to change, for example, the value of its href attribute.

| Figure 16-61 | Properties of style sheets |

Property	Description
styleSheet.cssText	The text of the declarations in the style sheet (Internet Explorer DOM).
styleSheet.disabled	Returns a Boolean value indicating whether the style sheet has been disabled (true) or has been enabled (false).
styletSheet.href	The url of the style sheet. For embedded style sheets, the href value is an empty text string [read-only].
styleSheet.media	A text string containing the list of media types associated with the style sheet [read-only].
styleSheet.rules	Returns the collection of rules within the style sheet (Internet Explorer DOM).
styleSheet.cssRules	Returns the collection of rules within the style sheet (W3C DOM).
styleSheet.title	The title of the style sheet [read-only].
styleSheet.type	The MIME type of the style sheet [read-only].

You can enable style sheets or disable them using the disabled property of the style sheet object. For example, to disable the first style sheet, you use the command

```
document.styleSheets[0].disabled = true;
```

To enable the style sheet, you set the disabled property to false:

```
document.styleSheets[0].disabled = false;
```

Most browsers support the styleSheets collection, but some do not. One browser that does not recognize the styleSheets collection is Opera. If you need to support these browsers, it's best to modify the attributes of the link element instead of working with the styleSheets collection. For a more general approach, however, it's better to work with the styleSheets object collection since it includes both external and embedded style sheets.

Working with Style Sheet Rules

The style sheet object also contains an object collection for each rule in a style sheet. In the W3C DOM the object reference to the rules collection is

```
styleSheet.cssRules
```

where *styleSheet* is a styleSheet object. For example, if the first style sheet in a Web page contains the declarations

```
<style type="text/css">
   h1 {color: red}
   h2 {color: blue}
</style>
```

then the object reference

```
document.styleSheets[0].cssRules[0]
```

refers to the style sheet declaration h1 {color: red}. Note that in the Internet Explorer DOM, style sheet rules are referenced using the object collection:

```
styleSheet.rules
```

Figure 16-62 lists some of the methods you can use to create and edit the rules within your style sheets. Note that the two document object models use different methods to add and remove style sheet rules.

Methods of style sheet rules ◄ **Figure 16-62**

Method	Description
styleSheet.addRule(*selector, style, index*)	Adds a new rule to the style sheet object where *selector* is the selector to receive the style, *style* is the text of style rule, and *index* specifies position where the rule should insert. The default *index* value is 0 which places the rule at the beginning of the style sheet. (Internet Explorer DOM)
styleSheet.deleteRule(*index*)	Deletes the rule with the index number *index* from the style sheet (W3C DOM)
styleSheet.insertRule(*rule, index*)	Inserts a new *rule* into the style sheet at index number *index* (W3C DOM)
styleSheet.removeRule(*index*)	Removes the rule with the index number *index* from the style sheet (Internet Explorer DOM)

Norene tells you that she doesn't require you to modify any properties of the style sheets or rules in her documents. You've completed your work on her project. She'll apply the modifications you've made to the other documents in her library and get back to you with future projects.

Tips for Working with Dynamic Content and Styles

- Use the innerHTML property as a quick and easy way of modifying the contents of element nodes. Do not use other Internet Explorer properties, since they are not well supported by other browsers.
- Use familial references rather than counter variables in for loops to increase the speed and flexibility of your program code.
- When writing scripts that modify node elements, be sure to test the active node is an element node by using the nodeType property.
- Be aware that browsers will treat white space found in HTML files differently. The Internet Explorer browser does not treat occurrences of white space as text nodes, while in the W3C DOM and in many browsers, white space is treated as a text node.
- Use attribute properties as a quick and easy way to work with the attributes of element nodes.
- Use recursive functions to navigate an entire node tree, ensuring that each node is included in the path.
- Use the getElementsByTagName() method as a quick and easy way of generating object collections for elements in your document that share a common element name.

Review

Session 16.3 Quick Check

1. What commands would you enter to create an inline image node named imgObj and then to append it as the first child of a node named listItem?
2. What command would you use to hide and remove from the page flow a page element with the id "imgObj"?
3. What is recursion?
4. What expression would you enter to create a collection of all div elements in the document? How would you reference the second div element in the collection?
5. What expression would you enter to reference the third style sheet attached to the document?
6. What expression would you enter to reference the second rule from the document's third style sheet. Provide an answer for both Internet Explorer and W3C document object models.

Review

Tutorial Summary

In this tutorial you learned how to create and manage dynamic content and styles to develop a dynamic table of contents application that could be applied to a wide variety of documents. In the first session, you were introduced to the Internet Explorer DOM's approach to dynamic content and you learned how to apply the innerHTML property to insert new content into a page element. The first session also introduced the node tree, exploring how to navigate through a node tree, create new nodes, and attach them to a Web page document. Using this information you were able to create a list of section headings from a document. In the second session, you applied what you learned about node properties and methods to create a nested list of section headings. The second session also demonstrated how to work with attribute nodes and how to work with element attributes. In the third session, you created an expandable/collapsible document by applying the display style to elements within the dynamic table of contents and within the sample document. The third session also discussed how to navigate through a node tree by using a recursive function. The session and tutorial concluded with a discussion of style sheet objects, creating a Web page in which different style sheets could be loaded and applied to a document.

Key Terms

document fragment
dynamic content
node

node tree
plus/minus box

recursion
root node

Practice

Practice the skills you earned in the tutorial using the same case cenario.

Review Assignments

Data files needed for this Review Assignment: fed10txt.htm, fedpaper.css, hlogo.jpg, keytxt.js, print.css, print.jpg, web.jpg

Norene has another application for you to add to her library of historic documents. Some documents are not broken into sections, so creating a table of contents would not be appropriate. For those documents, Norene would like the Web page to display a box containing a sorted list of important keywords and phrases found in the document. Each keyword or phrase has been marked in the documents with a dfn (definition) element. The entries in the keyword list need to search the current historic document for the presence of these dfn elements and create links between the keyword list entries and the keywords in the document. Norene also wants the page to have a Web version and a print version, and she wants users to be able to easily switch between the two.

Figure 16-63 shows a preview of the page created for the tenth Federalist paper written by James Madison in 1787 on the danger of factions to the republic.

Figure 16-63

Norene has already provided the source document and external style sheets that format the appearance of the document and the keyword list for both the Web and printer. Your job is to write the application that creates the content of the keyword list.

To create the keyword list:

1. Use your text editor to open the **fed10txt.htm** file from the tutorial.16/review folder. Enter **your name** and **the date** in the comment section and save the file as **fed10. htm**. Take some time to study the contents of the file, paying attention to the id names assigned to various elements in the document.

2. Insert an external script element that points to the **keywords.js** file. Add an event handler to the body element that runs the function makeKeyWordBox() when the page is loaded. Close the file, saving your changes.

3. Use your text editor to open the **keytxt.js** file from the tutorial.16/review folder. Enter **your name** and **the date** in the comment section and save the file as **keywords.js**.

4. Create a function named makeElemList(). The purpose of this function is to return an array containing a sorted list of the contents of elements with a common tag name. You'll use this function later to create a list of the keywords in the document. The function has a single parameter named elem that contains the text of the tag name. Add the following commands to the function:

   a. Store the collection of elements whose tag name equals the elem parameter in a variable named elemList. (*Hint*: Use the document.getElementsByTagName() method.)

   b. Create a new array named elemTextArr.

   c. Create a for loop that goes through each of the objects in the elemList object collection. For each object, change the text to lowercase letters and store the content of the element in the corresponding elemTextArr array item. (*Hint*: Use the toLowerCase() String method to change the content of the object to lowercase letters.)

   d. Sort the entries in the elemTextArr array using the *array*.sort() method where *array* is the name of the array.

   e. Return the elemTextArr array.

5. Create a function named setElemId(). The purpose of this function is to create and return id values for elements in the document that match a specific tag name and element content. You'll use this function later to insert matching id values between the items in the keyword list and the keywords found in the document. The function has two parameters: elem, which contains the text of the tag name, and elemText, which contains the text of the element content. Add the following commands to the function:

   a. Store the collection of elements whose tag name equals the elem parameter in a variable named elemList.

   b. Create a for loop that goes through each of the objects in the elemList object collection.

   c. Within the for loop, test whether content of the current elemList object, converted to lowercase letters, equals the value of the elemText parameter. If it does, test whether the id of the object is equal to an empty text string. If the id is missing, create a variable named elemId equal to the text string "keyword*i*" where *i* is the value of counter variable in the for loop and set the id of the object to the value of the elemId variable. If the id is not missing, set the value of the elemId variable to the value of the id attribute of the object.

   d. After the for loop has run, return the value of the elemId variable.

Explore

6. Create a function named makeKeyWordBox(). The purpose of this function is to create a list of keywords from the dfn elements in the historic document. There are no parameters for this function. Add the following commands:

   a. Create a variable named historyDoc that references the element with the id "doc".

   b. Create an element node named keywordBox for a div element. Set the id of the keywordBox to "keywords". Create another element node named keywordBoxTitle for an h1 element. Set the content of the h1 element to the text "Keywords" and append keywordBoxTitle to the keywordBox node as a child node. Create an element node named ulList that stores a ul element. Append ulList as a second child of the keywordBox node.

   c. Call the makeElemList() function using the text string "dfn" as the parameter value. Store the array returned by the function in a variable named keywords.

   d. Next, create and format the items in the keyword list. For the keywords array, create a for loop that does the following for each item in the array: (1) Create an element node named newListItem that contains a list item element; (2) Create an element node named newLink that contains a hyperlink element; (3) Set the content of newLink to the value of the current item in the keywords array (*Hint*: use the reference keywords[*i*] where *i* is the value of the counter variable in the for loop); (4) Create a variable named linkId whose value is equal to the value returned by the setElemId() function. The first parameter value in the setElemId() function should be the text string "dfn". The second parameter value should be the current item in the keywords array; (5) Change the href attribute of newLink to the value of the linkId variable; (6) Append newLink to newListItem and append newListItem to ulList.

   e. Append keywordBox as the first child of the historyDoc node.

   f. Call a function named createPrintWebImages().

7. Create a function named createPrintWebImages(). The purpose of this function is to insert Web and printer icons at the top of the Web page, format the appearance and content of those icons, and apply an event handler to each icon. The function has no parameters. Add the following commands:

   a. Create a variable named historyDoc that references the element with the id name "doc" in the document.

   b. Create an element node named printImg that contains an img element. Set the source of printImg to the print.jpg file. Set the value of the alt attribute for printImg to "Printer Version". Set the cursor style of printImg to "pointer". Run the showPrintVer() function when users click on the printImg node.

   c. Repeat step b to create an element node named webImg that also contains an img element. The source of this image is the web.jpg file, the value of the alt attribute should be "Web version", the cursor style should be "pointer", and the showWebVer() function should be run when the user clicks the webImg node.

   d. Insert the printImg node before the first child of the historyDoc object. Do the same for the webImg node.

8. Create a function named showPrintVer() to switch the browser to the print.css style sheet.

9. Create a function named showWebVer() to switch the browser to the fedpaper.css style sheet.

10. Close **keywords.js** and close the file, saving your changes.

11. Open **fed10.htm** in your Web browser. Verify that a keyword box containing a list of 13 keywords from Federalist Paper #10 is generated and that the entries in the keyword letter are in lowercase letters and sorted in alphabetical order. Further verify that clicking a keyword in the list moves the browser to the keyword entry in the document. Click the Web and printer icons to confirm that you can switch from a Web view to a printer view of the document.

12. Submit the completed Web site to your instructor.

Apply

Use the skills you learned to create an English to French translation page

Case Problem 1

Data files needed for this Case Problem: engfrtxt.js, fr5txt.htm, french5.js, styles.css

French 101 Professor Eve Granger teaches French 101 at a local university. She is working on a Web site containing French phrases that she wants her students to review for the weekly quiz. She's asked you to help her create the Web site. She wants a student to be able to press the mouse button down on a French phrase in the site and have the English translation appear. When the student releases the mouse button, the French phrase should reappear. Figure 16-64 shows a preview of the Web page you'll create for Professor Granger.

Figure 16-64

Professor Granger has already created an external script file named french5.js that contains two arrays. The french array contains 10 French phrases. The english array contains the 10 English translations of those phrases. You'll use these arrays to insert the French phrases and their translations into the Web page.

To complete this Web site:

1. Use your text editor to open the **fr5txt.htm** file from the tutorial.16/case1 folder. Enter *your name* and *the date* in the comment section and save the file as **french5.htm**.

2. Insert two external script elements that link to the french5.js and engfr.js files.

3. Insert an event handler into the body element that runs the function setUpTranslation() when the page loads.

4. Close the file, saving your changes.

5. Use your text editor to open the **engfrtxt.js** file from the tutorial.16/case1 folder. Enter *your name* and *the date* in the comment section and save the file as **engfr.js**.

6. Create a function named setUpTranslation(). The purpose of this function is to place the French phrases into the document and set up the event handlers for the mouse-down and mouseup events. Add the following commands:

   a. In Professor Granger's document the phrases are placed in paragraphs. The phrase number is placed within the first span element inside the paragraph. The phrase text is placed in the second span element within the paragraph. Create a variable named phrases that contains the object collection of all the paragraph elements in Professor Granger's document. (*Hint*: Use the document.getElementsBy-TagName() method.)

   b. Create a for loop that loops through each of the objects in the phrases collection. For each object in the collection do the following: (1) Change the inner content of the second child node of the object to french[*i*] where *i* is the value of the counter variable in the for loop; (2) Run the swapFE() function in response to a mouse-down event occurring within the object's second child node; (3) Run the swapEF() function in response to a mouseup event occurring within the object's second child node.

7. Create a function named swapFE(). The purpose of this function is to exchange the French phrase for the English translation. The function has a single parameter, the event object e. Add the following commands to the function:

   a. Store the source of the event in a variable named phrase. This variable represents the phrase that was clicked in the document. (*Note*: You will have to create a cross-browser function or insert code that will determine the source of the event.)

   b. There are 10 phrases in the document. Determine the phrase number by extract-ing the integer value from the previous sibling of the phrase node. (*Hint*: Use the parseInt() function applied to the inner content of the previous sibling node.) Store the phrase number in the variable phrasenum.

   c. The index values from the English and French arrays range from 0 to 9. Change the inner content of the phrase node to the value of array item english[*phrasenum* -1] where *phrasenum* is the value of the phrasenum variable.

   d. Change the font style of the phrase node to normal. Change the color of the phrase node to the color value (155, 102, 102).

8. Create a function named swapEF(). The purpose of this function is to exchange the English translation for the French phrase. Apply the same commands you used in the swapFE() function to this function, except that the phrase node should store the value of the french[*phrasenum*-1] item, the font style should be italic, and the font color should be black.

9. Close the file, saving your changes.

10. Open **french5.htm** in your Web browser. Verify that as you press the mouse button down on each phrase, the English translation appears. When you release the mouse button, the French phrase should reappear.

11. Submit the completed Web site to your instructor.

Case Problem 2

Data files needed for this Case Problem: camtxt.htm, filttxt.js, links.jpg, logo.jpg, styles.css

MicroCity   David Forrest works at MicroCity, an online store for computers and electronics. One of his jobs is to create a table listing the different digital cameras sold by MicroCity. The company carries hundreds of digital camera models and David thinks that the data table will be too long for customers to easily view. He would like to give customers the ability to filter the data table, showing only those models that match certain criteria. Customers should be able to select the criteria from a drop-down list box. Figure 16-65 shows a preview of the Web page that David wants you to help him create.

Figure 16-65

The data table contains seven columns, indicating each camera's model name, manufacturer, resolution, zoom capability, storage media, support for video, and whether it contains a microphone. The drop-down list boxes on the left contain the unique values from each of the columns in the data tables. If a customer selects a zoom value of "3.0 x" from the drop-down list box, only those cameras with that zoom feature should be displayed in the data table. Customers should be able to select more than one filter, and only those cameras satisfying all filter values should be shown. A table named "records" displays the records in the data table after filtering.

To complete this Web site:

1. Use your text editor to open the **camtxt.htm** file from the tutorial.16/case2 folder. Enter *your name* and *the date* in the comment section and save the file as **cameras.htm**.

2. In the head section, insert a script element pointing to the **filter.js** file. Add an event handler to the body element to run the function init() when the page loads. Close the file, saving your changes.

3. Use your text editor to open the **filttxt.js** file from the tutorial.16/case2 folder. Enter *your name* and *the date* in the comment section and save the file as **filter.js**.

4. Create a function named resetTable(). The purpose of this function is to reset the data table by displaying all hidden table rows. Add the following commands to the function:

   a. Use the getElementsByTagName() method to create a collection of all tr elements in the Web page. Store the object collection in the allRows variable.

   b. Create a for loop that goes through each object in the allRows collection. For each object set the display style to an empty text string (thus displaying the table row in the Web page).

5. Create the countRecords() function. The purpose of this function is to count the number of visible rows in the data table after the table headings. The total is then displayed in the table cell with the id "records". Add the following commands to the function:

   a. Create an object named headRow that points to the table row with the id "titleRow". Create a variable named rowCount, setting its initial value to 0.

   b. Create a for loop that uses familial references starting with the first sibling of headRow and moving to the next sibling until there are no siblings left. Within the for loop, test whether the node name of the current node is equal to "TR". If it is, test whether the value of its display style is equal to an empty text string. If it is (indicating that it is visible in the document) increase the value of the rowCount variable by 1.

   c. Change the inner content of the "records" table cell to the value of the rowCount variable.

6. Create the checkCell() function. The purpose of this function is to test whether a value in a cell from the data table equals the text string of a filter value. If it does not, the table row containing the table cell should be hidden. The function has two parameters: cell and filterText. The cell parameter points to the table cell object. The filterText parameter contains the text of the filter value. Add the following command to the function:

   a. Insert an if condition that tests whether the inner content of the cell object does not equal the value of the filterText parameter. If it doesn't, change the display style of the parent node of the cell object to "none".

7. Create the findCell() function. The purpose of this function is to determine in which cell in the data table row the checkCell() function should be run. The function has three parameters: row, cellNum, and filterText. The row parameter contains an object for the current table row. The cellNum contains the column number (from 1 to 7) of the cell to check for filtering. The filterText parameter contains the text string of the filter value. Add the following commands to the function:

   a. Create a variable named cellCount. Set its initial value to 0.

   b. Create a for loop that uses familial references to loop through each cell in the current table row, starting with the first child of the table row and moving to the next sibling until there are no more siblings left. Within the for loop, test whether the name of the current node is "TD". If it is, increase the value of cellCount by 1 and run the checkCell() function if cellCount equals cellNum, using the current cell node and the value of filterText as the parameter values.

8. Create the filterTable() function. The purpose of this function is to loop through each row in the data table, running the findCell() function. The function has two parameters: cellNum and filterText. Add the following commands:

   a. Create an object named headRow that points to the document object with the id "titleRow". This object represents the title row in the data table.

   b. Create a for loop that uses a familial reference to loop through each row in the data table starting with the first sibling of headRow and moving to the next sibling until there are no siblings left. If the node name of the current node equals "TR" call the findCell() function using the current node, cellNum, and filterText as the parameter values.

9. Create the filter() function. The purpose of this function is to extract the selected values from each of the selection lists in the Web page and then call the filterTable() function for each filter value. Add the following commands to the function:

   a. Call the resetTable() function to redisplay all rows in the data table.

   b. Create an object collection named allSelects containing all select elements in the document.

   c. Create a for loop that loops each object in the allSelects collection. The loop should have a counter variable that starts with the value 0 and increases by 1 as long as it is less than the length of the allSelects collection. For each select object in the collection, extract the text of the selected option and store the text in the filterText variable, and then if filterText is not equal to an empty text string, call the filterTable() function using the value of the counter variable plus 1 as the value for the cellNum parameter and filterText as the value of the filterText parameter.

   d. After the for loop, run the countRecords() function to update the value in the "records" table cell.

10. Create the init() function. The purpose of this function is to add event handlers to all of the selection lists in the document so that they run the filter() function whenever a customer changes the selected value in a list. The function should also set the initial value of the "records" cell, displaying the total number of records in the data table. Add the following commands:

    a. Create an object collection named allSelects containing all select elements in the document.

    b. For each object in the allSelects collection, add an event handler for the onchange event that runs the filter() function.

    c. Call the countRecords() function.

11. Close the file, saving your changes.

12. Open **cameras.htm** in your Web browser. Verify that when the page opens the total number of cameras in the data table (24) is displayed in the upper-left table cell. Select Kamtec from the Manufacturer drop-down list box and verify that five camera models are displayed in the data table. Continue to select filter values from the other drop-down list boxes, confirming that the data table is automatically updated to reflect the selected filter. To undo a filter, select the empty text string from the appropriate selection list.

13. Submit the completed Web site to your instructor.

Challenge

Explore how to use dynamic content to create a data entry form

Case Problem 3

Data files needed for this Case Problem: clisttxt.htm, data.js, lhouse.css, logo.jpg, newtxt.js

The Lighthouse Aaron Kitchen is the fundraising coordinator for The Lighthouse, a charitable organization located in central Kentucky. One of his responsibilities is to maintain a contact list of donors and the amount each has contributed to the organization. Aaron wants to create an interactive Web page that contains a table of contributors with the most recent contributors listed at the top. He wants the page to include tools that allow him to add new contributors to the table or delete old contributors from the list. Figure 16-66 shows a preview of the Web page.

Figure 16-66

The page includes a data entry form named "donations" in which Aaron can enter a contributor's name, address, and amount and date of contribution. By clicking the Add Contributor button, the new record should be added to the table and the total number of contributors, displayed in the upper-left corner of the page, should be updated. Each row in the contributors table contains a check box. If a user selects a check box and then clicks the Remove Checked Items button, the selected contributors should be removed from the table and the total values should be updated.

Aaron has already created several JavaScript arrays containing information about current contributors and stored them in the file data.js. There are eight arrays:

- firstName: the first name of each contributor
- lastName: the last name of each contributor
- street: each contributor's street address
- city: each contributor's city of residence

- state: each contributor's state of residence
- zip: each contributor's zip code
- amount: the amount of the contribution
- date: the date of the contribution

Currently each array contains 10 entries representing 10 different contributors. You'll use the information in these arrays to populate the rows of the contributors table. As you add or remove rows from the contributors table, you'll also add or remove entries from the array. To remove an array entry, you can use the command

```
array.splice(start, deleteCount)
```

where *array* is an array, *start* is the starting index of the array items to remove, and *deleteCount* is the number of items to remove. For example, the command

```
firstName.splice(5,1)
```

removes the sixth item from the firstName array.

To complete this Web site:

1. Use your text editor to open the **clisttxt.htm** file from the tutorial.16/case3 folder. Enter **your name** and **the date** in the comment section and save the file as **clist.htm**.
2. Insert two script elements in the head section that link to the **data.js** and **newdata.js** files.
3. Add an event handler to the body element that runs the function makeTable() when the page is loaded. Locate the input element for the Add Contributor button. Add an event handler that runs the function addRecord() when the button is clicked. Locate the input element for the Remove Check Items button. Add an event handler to run the removeRecords() function when the button is clicked.
4. Close the **clist.htm** file, saving your changes.
5. Open **newtxt.js** from the tutorial.16/case3 folder with your text editor. Enter **your name** and **the date** in the comment section and save the file as **newdata.js**.
6. Create the updateTotals() function. The purpose of this function is to display the total number of contributors and contributions in the table cells whose ids are "totalContr" and "totalAmt". Add the following commands to the function:
   a. Within the totalContr table cell display the length of the amount array.
   b. Create a variable named totalContributions and set its initial value to 0.
   c. Create a for loop that loops through each entry in the amount array. Each time through the loop increases the value of the totalContributions variable by the amount in the current entry in the amount array.
   d. Within the totalAmt table cell display the value of the totalContributions variable.

7. Create the makeTable() function. The purpose of this function is to create the contributors table by adding new table rows for each of the entries in the eight data arrays. The contributors table initially opens with an empty table row that you'll clone to create the new table rows containing contributor data. Add the following commands to the function:

   a. Create a variable named headingRow that references the table row with the id "titleRow". This row contains the titles from the contributors table. Create a second variable named blankRow that references the table row with the id "emptyRow".

   Explore
   b. Use the cloneNode() method to clone the blankRow node. Set the value of the *deep* variable to true in order to copy the entire node tree. Store this document fragment in a variable named dataRow.

   c. Create a for loop that loops through the entries in the amount array. For each entry call the addRow() function using the value of the counter variable in the for loop as the parameter value in the addRow() function.

   d. Call the updateTotals() function.

8. Create the addRow() function. The purpose of this function is to add a single row to the contributors table, extracting information from the eight data arrays. The function has a single parameter named index that is equal to the array index number from which data is to be taken. Add the following commands to the function:

   Explore
   a. Use the cloneNode() method to clone the dataRow document fragment you created in the makeTable() function. Set the value of the deep parameter to true. Store this document fragment in the variable newRow.

   b. Change the content of newRow's second child node to the value of the date array using the current index. Change the content of newRow's third child node to the text string "*lastName, firstName*" where *lastName* and *firstName* are the values of the lastName and firstName arrays using the current index. Change the content of newRow's third child node to the text string: "*street <br /> city, state zip*" where *street*, *city*, *state*, and *zip* are the current values from the street, city, state, and zip arrays. Change the content of newRow's fourth child node to the value of the amount array.

   Explore
   c. If the value of the index variable equals 0, meaning that this is the first row being added to the contributor table, then use the replaceChild() method to replace the blankRow node with newRow. (*Hint*: Apply the replaceChild() method to the blankRow.parentNode node.) If the index variable is not equal to 0, then insert the newRow node before the next sibling of the headingRow node. (*Hint*: Apply the insertBefore() method to the headingRow.parentNode node.)

9. Create the addRecord() function. The purpose of this function is to create a new contributor record based on the values entered by the user in the Web form. Add the following commands to the function:

   a. Create a variable named recordNum equal to the length of the amount array.

   b. Set the value of first[recordNum] to the value of the fname field from the donations Web form. Set the value of last[recordNum] to the value of the lname field. Set the value of the street array item to the value of the street field and the value of the city array item to the value of the city field. Determine which state option has been selected by the user and store the text of the selected option in the state array item. Set the value of the zip, amount, and date array items to the values of the zip, amount, and date fields in the donations Web form.

    c. Call the addRow() function using the value of the recordNum variable as the parameter value.

    d. Call the updateTotals() function.

10. Create the removeRecord() function. The purpose of this function is to remove a record from each of the eight data arrays. The function has a single parameter named index that indicates the array item to remove. Add the following commands to the function:

    a. Use the splice() method to remove the item from the firstName array whose index value equals the value of the index parameter. Remove only one array item.

    b. Repeat step a) for the lastName, street, city, state, zip, amount, and date arrays.

11. Create the removeNode() function. The purpose of this function is to remove a node from a node tree and then return a reference to the node's previous sibling. You'll use it later to remove rows from the contributor table. The parameter has a single parameter named node representing the node you want to remove. Add the following commands to the function:

    a. Create a variable named prevNode referencing the node's previous sibling.

Explore

    b. Use the removeChild() method to remove the node. (*Hint:* Apply the removeChild() to the nodes' parent node.)

    c. Return the prevNode variable from the function.

12. Create the removeRecords() function. The purpose of this function is to remove contributor records from the contributor table and the eight data arrays if the check box for that record has been checked in the contributor table. Add the following commands to the function:

    a. Create a variable named headerRow referencing the row with the id "titleRow".

    b. Create a variable named recordNum equal to the length of amount array.

Explore

    c. Create a for loop that uses familial references, starting with the node variable, n, equal to the first sibling of the headerRow node and proceeding to the next sibling (the next table row) until there is no next sibling. Within the for loop decrease the value of the recordNum variable by 1. Then, insert an if condition that tests whether the name of the current node is "TR" (a table row). If it is, insert a second if condition that tests whether the check box within the first table cell of the current row has been selected. (*Hint:* Reference the check box using the reference n.firstChild.firstChild.) If the check box has been checked, then: (1) Call the removeRecord() function using recordNum as the parameter value, and (2) Let the node counter, n, be equal to the value returned by the removeNode() function using the n as the parameter value.

    d. After the for loop has finished, call the updateTotals() function to update the contribution totals in the Web page.

13. Close **newdata.js**, saving your changes.

14. Open **clist.htm** in your Web browser. Verify that the page displays a list of 10 contributors totaling $1800 in contributions. Verify that you can enter a new contributor by inserting the contributor data into the Web form and clicking the Add Contributor button. Verify that you can remove contributor records from the arrays and the table by clicking check boxes in the table and clicking the Remove Check Items button. Check that the contributor totals are automatically updated for you.

15. Submit the completed Web site to your instructor.

Create

Create a JavaScript utility to filter lines from an online play

Case Problem 4

Data files needed for this Case Problem: bio_out.jpg, globe_out.jpg, plays.css, plays_out.jpg, scenetxt.js, son_out.jpg, strat_out.jpg, tempest.jpg, temptxt.htm

The World of Shakespeare Clare Daynes, the professor of English literature at MidWest University, continues to work on her Web site of Shakespeare's works. She would like to give students who are doing textual analysis of the plays the ability to display only those lines spoken by selected characters. She has asked you to create a utility that generates a drop-down list containing all of the characters from a particular scene, listed in alphabetical order. When a student selects a character from the list, only those lines spoken by that character should be displayed. Figure 16-67 shows a preview of a Web page that fulfills Professor Daynes' request.

Figure 16-67

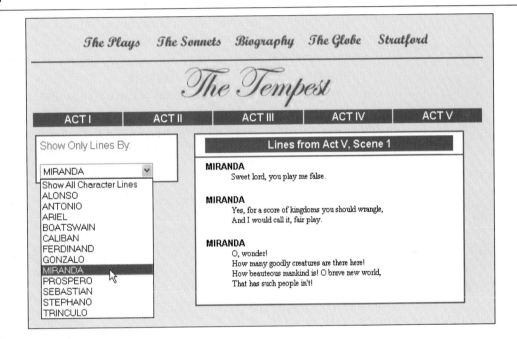

Professor Daynes has already created a Web page containing the text from the last act of *The Tempest*. The play text has been placed within a div element with the id "scenes". The character names have been placed in h3 headings within that div element with their lines following immediately after in blockquote elements. She has also created a div element with the id "characterList" in which she wants the drop-down list box to be placed. She wants the content to be automatically generated by your utility. The HTML content of the list box should be as follows:

```
<p>Show Only Lines By:</p>

<select id="cList">

    <option>Show All Character Lines</option>

    <option>Character 1</option>

    <option>Character 2</option>

...

</select>
```

where *Character 1* is the name of the first character in alphabetical order, *Character 2* is the name of the second character, and so forth. To create a list of the characters from the scene, the following function has been provided for you:

```
uniqueElemText(elemName)
```

This function returns an array containing the unique text from HTML tags whose name equals elemName, sorted in order. For example, running the command

```
characterNames = uniqueElemText("h3")
```

creates an array named characterNames containing all of the unique character names found in h3 heading elements, sorted in alphabetical order.

To complete this assignment:

1. Use your text editor to open the **temptxt.htm** file from the tutorial.16/case4 folder. Enter *your name* and *the date* in the comment section and save the file as **tempest.htm**. Create a link in the file to an external script file named scene.js.
2. Open the **scenetxt.js** file in your text editor, enter *your name* and *the date* in the comment section and save the file as **scene.js**.
3. Write a function that creates the contents of the character list box. Run the function when this page is loaded by the browser.
4. Add an event handler to the selection list you generated that runs a function to filter the contents of the scene whenever the user changes the selected character from the list.
5. Modify the function to filter the play so that it shows only the character name and succeeding lines for the selected character. All lines from other characters should be hidden. If the user selects "Show All Character Lines", the entire scene should be displayed.
6. Test your Web page in your browser. Verify that only the lines from the selected character are displayed in the Web page and that the entire scene is displayed if "Show All Character Lines" is selected.
7. Submit your completed Web site to your instructor.

Quick Check Answers

Session 16.1

1. innerHTML
2. A node is part of the document object model that represents a particular type of content. Nodes can represent any element or object, including text strings, attributes, and HTML elements placed in either the head or body section of the document.
3. parentNode
4. childNodes[2]
5. The nodeType property returns the value 1. The nodeName property returns "BLOCKQUOTE". The nodeValue property returns a null value.
6. docText = document.createTextNode("U.S. Constitution")mainTitle = document. createElement("h2");
7. mainTitle.appendChild(docText);
8. A document fragment is a collection of nodes that is not attached to the document, but instead resides in computer memory.

Session 16.2

1. topList = document.createElement("ul");bottomList = document. createElement("ul")top.List.appendChild(bottomList)
2. listItem.parentNode.parentNode;
3. Because they are not considered child nodes of the node to which the attribute has been applied.
4. hasAttribute("type")
5. CBox = document.createElement("input");CBox.setAttribute("type", "checkbox");
6. CBox.type = "checkbox";
7. CBox.type == ""

Session 16.3

1. listNode.insertBefore(imgObj, listNode.firstChild);
2. imgObj.style.display = "none";
3. Recursion is a programming technique in which a function calls itself repeatedly until a stopping condition is met.
4. document.getElementsByTagName("div");document. getElementsByTagName("div")[1]
5. document.styleSheets[2]
6. W3C DOM: document.styleSheets[2].cssRules[1]IE DOM: document.styleSheets[2]. rules[1]

Color Names and Color Values

Both HTML and XHTML allow you to define colors using either color names or color values. HTML and XHTML support a list of 16 basic color names. Most browsers also support an extended list of color names, which are listed in the following table along with their RGB and hexadecimal values. The sixteen color names supported by HTML and XHTML appear highlighted in the table. Web-safe colors appear in a bold font.

If you want to use only Web-safe colors, limit your RGB values to 0, 51, 153, 204, and 255 (or limit your hexadecimal values to 00, 33, 66, 99, CC, and FF). For example, an RGB color value of (255, 51, 204) would be Web safe, while an RGB color value of (255, 192, 128) would not.

Color Name	RGB Value	Hexadecimal Value
aliceblue	(240,248,255)	#F0F8FF
antiquewhite	(250,235,215)	#FAEBD7
aqua	**(0,255,255)**	**#00FFFF**
aquamarine	(127,255,212)	#7FFFD4
azure	(240,255,255)	#F0FFFF
beige	(245,245,220)	#F5F5DC
bisque	(255,228,196)	#FFE4C4
black	**(0,0,0)**	**#000000**
blanchedalmond	(255,235,205)	#FFEBCD
blue	**(0,0,255)**	**#0000FF**
blueviolet	(138,43,226)	#8A2BE2
brown	(165,42,42)	#A52A2A
burlywood	(222,184,135)	#DEB887
cadetblue	(95,158,160)	#5F9EA0
chartreuse	(127,255,0)	#7FFF00
chocolate	(210,105,30)	#D2691E
coral	(255,127,80)	#FF7F50
cornflowerblue	(100,149,237)	#6495ED
cornsilk	(255,248,220)	#FFF8DC
crimson	(220,20,54)	#DC1436
cyan	**(0,255,255)**	**#00FFFF**
darkblue	(0,0,139)	#00008B
darkcyan	(0,139,139)	#008B8B
darkgoldenrod	(184,134,11)	#B8860B
darkgray	(169,169,169)	#A9A9A9
darkgreen	(0,100,0)	#006400

Color Name	RGB Value	Hexadecimal Value
darkkhaki	(189,183,107)	#BDB76B
darkmagenta	(139,0,139)	#8B008B
darkolivegreen	(85,107,47)	#556B2F
darkorange	(255,140,0)	#FF8C00
darkorchid	(153,50,204)	#9932CC
darkred	(139,0,0)	#8B0000
darksalmon	(233,150,122)	#E9967A
darkseagreen	(143,188,143)	#8FBC8F
darkslateblue	(72,61,139)	#483D8B
darkslategray	(47,79,79)	#2F4F4F
darkturquoise	(0,206,209)	#00CED1
darkviolet	(148,0,211)	#9400D3
deeppink	(255,20,147)	#FF1493
deepskyblue	(0,191,255)	#00BFFF
dimgray	(105,105,105)	#696969
dodgerblue	(30,144,255)	#1E90FF
firebrick	(178,34,34)	#B22222
floralwhite	(255,250,240)	#FFFAF0
forestgreen	(34,139,34)	#228B22
fuchsia	**(255,0,255)**	**#FF00FF**
gainsboro	(220,220,220)	#DCDCDC
ghostwhite	(248,248,255)	#F8F8FF
gold	(255,215,0)	#FFD700
goldenrod	(218,165,32)	#DAA520
gray	(128,128,128)	#808080
green	(0,128,0)	#008000
greenyellow	(173,255,47)	#ADFF2F
honeydew	(240,255,240)	#F0FFF0
hotpink	(255,105,180)	#FF69B4

Color Name	RGB Value	Hexadecimal Value
indianred	(205,92,92)	#CD5C5C
indigo	(75,0,130)	#4B0082
ivory	(255,255,240)	#FFFFF0
khaki	(240,230,140)	#F0E68C
lavender	(230,230,250)	#E6E6FA
lavenderblush	(255,240,245)	#FFF0F5
lawngreen	(124,252,0)	#7CFC00
lemonchiffon	(255,250,205)	#FFFACD
lightblue	(173,216,230)	#ADD8E6
lightcoral	(240,128,128)	#F08080
lightcyan	(224,255,255)	#E0FFFF
lightgoldenrodyellow	(250,250,210)	#FAFAD2
lightgreen	(144,238,144)	#90EE90
lightgrey	(211,211,211)	#D3D3D3
lightpink	(255,182,193)	#FFB6C1
lightsalmon	(255,160,122)	#FFA07A
lightseagreen	(32,178,170)	#20B2AA
lightskyblue	(135,206,250)	#87CEFA
lightslategray	(119,136,153)	#778899
lightsteelblue	(176,196,222)	#B0C4DE
lightyellow	(255,255,224)	#FFFFE0
lime	**(0,255,0)**	**#00FF00**
limegreen	(50,205,50)	#32CD32
linen	(250,240,230)	#FAF0E6
magenta	**(255,0,255)**	**#FF00FF**
maroon	(128,0,0)	#800000
mediumaquamarine	(102,205,170)	#66CDAA
mediumblue	(0,0,205)	#0000CD
mediumorchid	(186,85,211)	#BA55D3

Color Name	RGB Value	Hexadecimal Value
mediumpurple	(147,112,219)	#9370DB
mediumseagreen	(60,179,113)	#3CB371
mediumslateblue	(123,104,238)	#7B68EE
mediumspringgreen	(0,250,154)	#00FA9A
mediumturquoise	(72,209,204)	#48D1CC
mediumvioletred	(199,21,133)	#C71585
midnightblue	(25,25,112)	#191970
mintcream	(245,255,250)	#F5FFFA
mistyrose	(255,228,225)	#FFE4E1
moccasin	(255,228,181)	#FFE4B5
navajowhite	(255,222,173)	#FFDEAD
navy	**(0,0,128)**	#000080
oldlace	(253,245,230)	#FDF5E6
olive	(128,128,0)	#808000
olivedrab	(107,142,35)	#6B8E23
orange	(255,165,0)	#FFA500
orangered	(255,69,0)	#FF4500
orchid	(218,112,214)	#DA70D6
palegoldenrod	(238,232,170)	#EEE8AA
palegreen	(152,251,152)	#98FB98
paleturquoise	(175,238,238)	#AFEEEE
palevioletred	(219,112,147)	#DB7093
papayawhip	(255,239,213)	#FFEFD5
peachpuff	(255,218,185)	#FFDAB9
peru	(205,133,63)	#CD853F
pink	(255,192,203)	#FFC0CB
plum	(221,160,221)	#DDA0DD
powderblue	(176,224,230)	#B0E0E6
purple	**(128,0,128)**	#808080

Color Name	RGB Value	Hexadecimal Value
red	**(255,0,0)**	**#FF0000**
rosybrown	(188,143,143)	#BC8F8F
royalblue	(65,105,0)	#4169E1
saddlebrown	(139,69,19)	#8B4513
salmon	(250,128,114)	#FA8072
sandybrown	(244,164,96)	#F4A460
seagreen	(46,139,87)	#2E8B57
seashell	(255,245,238)	#FFF5EE
sienna	(160,82,45)	#A0522D
silver	(192,192,192)	#C0C0C0
skyblue	(135,206,235)	#87CEEB
slateblue	(106,90,205)	#6A5ACD
slategray	(112,128,144)	#708090
snow	(255,250,250)	#FFFAFA
springgreen	(0,255,127)	#00FF7F
steelblue	(70,130,180)	#4682B4
tan	(210,180,140)	#D2B48C
teal	(0,128,128)	#008080
thistle	(216,191,216)	#D8BFD8
tomato	(255,99,71)	#FF6347
turquoise	(64,224,208)	#40E0D0
violet	(238,130,238)	#EE82EE
wheat	(245,222,179)	#F5DEB3
white	**(255,255,255)**	**#FFFFFF**
whitesmoke	(245,245,245)	#F5F5F5
yellow	**(255,255,0)**	**#FFFF00**
yellowgreen	(154,205,50)	#9ACD32

HTML Character Entities

The following table lists the extended character set for HTML, also known as the ISO Latin-1 Character Set. You can specify characters by name or by numeric value. For example, you can use either ® or ® to specify the registered trademark symbol, ®.

Not all browsers recognize all code names. Some older browsers that support only the HTML 2.0 standard do not recognize × as a code name, for instance. Code names that older browsers may not recognize are marked with an asterisk in the following table.

CHARACTER	CODE	CODE NAME	DESCRIPTION
	&#09;		Tab
	&#10;		Line feed
	&#32;		Space
!	&#33;		Exclamation mark
"	&#34;	&quot;	Double quotation mark
#	&#35;		Pound sign
$	&#36;		Dollar sign
%	&#37;		Percent sign
&	&#38;	&amp;	Ampersand
'	&#39;		Apostrophe
(	&#40;		Left parenthesis
)	&#41;		Right parenthesis
*	&#42;		Asterisk
+	&#43;		Plus sign
,	&#44;		Comma
-	&#45;		Hyphen
.	&#46;		Period
/	&#47;		Forward slash
0 - 9	0–9		Numbers 0–9
:	&#58;		Colon
;	&#59;		Semicolon
<	&#60;	&lt;	Less than sign

CHARACTER	CODE	CODE NAME	DESCRIPTION
=	&#61;		Equal sign
>	&#62;	&gt;	Greater than sign
?	&#63;		Question mark
@	&#64;		Commercial at sign
A - Z	A–Z		Letters A–Z
[	&#91;		Left square bracket
\	&#92;		Back slash
]	&#93;		Right square bracket
^	&#94;		Caret
_	&#95;		Horizontal bar (underscore)
`	&#96;		Grave accent
a - z	a–z		Letters a–z
{	&#123;		Left curly brace
|	|		Vertical bar
}	&#125;		Right curly brace
~	&#126;		Tilde
,	&#130;		Comma
ƒ	&#131;		Function sign (florin)
"	&#132;		Double quotation mark
…	&#133;		Ellipsis
†	&#134;		Dagger
‡	&#135;		Double dagger
^	&#136;		Circumflex

CHARACTER	CODE	CODE NAME	DESCRIPTION
‰	&#137;		Permil
A	&#138;		Capital S with hacek
‹	&#139;		Left single angle
Œ	&#140;		Capital OE ligature
	–		Unused
'	&#145;		Single beginning quotation mark
'	&#146;		Single ending quotation mark
"	&#147;		Double beginning quotation mark
"	&#148;		Double ending quotation mark
•	&#149;		Bullet
–	&#150;		En dash
—	&#151;		Em dash
~	&#152;		Tilde
™	&#153;	™*	Trademark symbol
B	&#154;		Small s with hacek
›	&#155;		Right single angle
œ	&#156;		Lowercase oe ligature
Ÿ	&#159;		Capital Y with umlaut
		*	Non-breaking space
¡	&#161;	¡*	Inverted exclamation mark
¢	&#162;	¢*	Cent sign
£	&#163;	£*	Pound sterling
C	&#164;	¤*	General currency symbol

CHARACTER	CODE	CODE NAME	DESCRIPTION
¥	&#165;	¥*	Yen sign
¦	&#166;	¦*	Broken vertical bar
§	&#167;	§*	Section sign
¨	&#168;	¨*	Umlaut
©	&#169;	©*	Copyright symbol
ª	&#170;	ª*	Feminine ordinal
«	&#171;	«*	Left angle quotation mark
¬	&#172;	¬*	Not sign
	&#173;	­*	Soft hyphen
®	&#174;	®*	Registered trademark
¯	&#175;	¯*	Macron
°	&#176;	°*	Degree sign
±	&#177;	±*	Plus/minus symbol
²	&#178;	²*	Superscript 2
³	&#179;	³*	Superscript 3
´	&#180;	´*	Acute accent
µ	&#181;	µ*	Micro sign
¶	&#182;	¶*	Paragraph sign
·	&#183;	·*	Middle dot
¸	&#184;	¸*	Cedilla
¹	&#185;	¹*	Superscript 1
º	&#186;	º*	Masculine ordinal
»	&#187;	»*	Right angle quotation mark

CHARACTER	CODE	CODE NAME	DESCRIPTION
¼	&#188;	¼*	Fraction one-quarter
½	&#189;	½*	Fraction one-half
¾	&#190;	¾*	Fraction three-quarters
¿	&#191;	¿*	Inverted question mark
À	&#192;	&Agrave;	Capital A, grave accent
Á	&#193;	&Aacute;	Capital A, acute accent
Â	&#194;	&Acirc;	Capital A, circumflex accent
Ã	&#195;	&Atilde;	Capital A, tilde
Ä	&#196;	&Auml;	Capital A, umlaut
Å	&#197;	&Aring;	Capital A, ring
Æ	&#198;	&Aelig;	Capital AE ligature
Ç	&#199;	&Ccedil;	Capital C, cedilla
È	&#200;	&Egrave;	Capital E, grave accent
É	&#201;	&Eacute;	Capital E, acute accent
Ê	&#202;	&Ecirc;	Capital E, circumflex accent
Ë	&#203;	&Euml;	Capital E, umlaut
Ì	&#204;	&Igrave;	Capital I, grave accent
Í	&#205;	&Iacute;	Capital I, acute accent
Î	&#206;	&Icirc;	Capital I, circumflex accent
Ï	&#207;	&Iuml;	Capital I, umlaut
Ð	&#208;	Ð*	Capital ETH, Icelandic
Ñ	&#209;	&Ntilde;	Capital N, tilde
Ò	&#210;	&Ograve;	Capital O, grave accent

CHARACTER	CODE	CODE NAME	DESCRIPTION
Ó	&#211;	&Oacute;	Capital O, acute accent
Ô	&#212;	&Ocirc;	Capital O, circumflex accent
Õ	&#213;	&Otilde;	Capital O, tilde
Ö	&#214;	&Ouml;	Capital O, umlaut
×	&#215;	×*	Multiplication sign
Ø	&#216;	&Oslash;	Capital O slash
Ù	&#217;	&Ugrave;	Capital U, grave accent
Ú	&#218;	&Uacute;	Capital U, acute accent
Û	&#219;	&Ucirc;	Capital U, circumflex accent
Ü	&#220;	&Uuml;	Capital U, umlaut
Ý	&#221;	&Yacute;	Capital Y, acute accent
Þ	&#222;	&THORN;	Capital THORN, Icelandic
ß	&#223;	&szlig;	Small sz ligature
à	&#224;	&agrave;	Small a, grave accent
á	&#225;	&aacute;	Small a, acute accent
â	&#226;	&acirc;	Small a, circumflex accent
ã	&#227;	&atilde;	Small a, tilde
ä	&#228;	&auml;	Small a, umlaut
å	&#229;	&aring;	Small a, ring
æ	&#230;	&aelig;	Small ae ligature
ç	&#231;	&ccedil;	Small c, cedilla
è	&#232;	&egrave;	Small e, grave accent
é	&#233;	&eacute;	Small e, acute accent

CHARACTER	CODE	CODE NAME	DESCRIPTION
ê	&#234;	&ecirc;	Small e, circumflex accent
ë	&#235;	&euml;	Small e, umlaut
ì	&#236;	&igrave;	Small i, grave accent
í	&#237;	&iacute;	Small i, acute accent
î	&#238;	&icirc;	Small i, circumflex accent
ï	&#239;	&iuml;	Small i, umlaut
ð	&#240;	&eth;	Small eth, Icelandic
ñ	&#241;	&ntilde;	Small n, tilde
ò	&#242;	&ograve;	Small o, grave accent
ó	&#243;	&oacute;	Small o, acute accent
ô	&#244;	&ocirc;	Small o, circumflex accent
õ	&#245;	&otilde;	Small o, tilde
ö	&#246;	&ouml;	Small o, umlaut
÷	&#247;	÷*	Division sign
ø	&#248;	&oslash;	Small o slash
ù	&#249;	&ugrave;	Small u, grave accent
ú	&#250;	&uacute;	Small u, acute accent
û	&#251;	&ucirc;	Small u, circumflex accent
ü	&#252;	&uuml;	Small u, umlaut
ý	&#253;	&yacute;	Small y, acute accent
þ	&#254;	&thorn;	Small thorn, Icelandic
ÿ	&#255;	&yuml;	Small y, umlaut

Putting a Document on the World Wide Web

Once you complete work on a Web page, you're probably ready to place it on the World Wide Web for others to see. To make a file available on the World Wide Web, it must be located on a computer connected to the Web called a **Web server**.

Your **Internet Service Provider (ISP)**—the company or institution through which you have Internet access—probably has a Web server available for your use. Because each Internet Service Provider has a different procedure for storing Web pages, you should contact your ISP to learn its policies and procedures. Generally you should be prepared to do the following:

- Extensively test your files with a variety of browsers and under different display conditions. Eliminate any errors and design problems before you place the page on the Web.
- Check the links and inline objects in each of your documents to verify that they point to the correct filenames. Verify your filename capitalization—some Web servers distinguish between a file named "Image.gif" and one named "image.gif." To be safe, use only lowercase letters in all your filenames.
- If your links use absolute pathnames, change them to relative pathnames.
- Find out from your ISP the name of the folder into which you'll be placing your HTML documents. You may also need a special user name and password to access this folder.
- Use FTP, an Internet protocol for transferring files, or e-mail to place your pages in the appropriate folder on your Internet Service Provider's Web server. This capability is built in to some Web browsers, including Internet Explorer and Netscape, allowing you to easily transfer files to your Web server.
- Decide on a name for your Web site (such as "http://www.jackson_electronics.com"). Choose a name that will be easy for customers and interested parties to remember and return to.
- If you select a special name for your Web site, you may have to register it. Registration information can be found at http://www.internic.net. Your ISP may also provide this service for a fee. Registration is necessary to ensure that any name you give to your site is unique and not already in use. Usually you will have to pay a yearly fee to use a special name for your Web site.

Once you've completed these steps, your work will be available on the World Wide Web in a form that is easy for users to access.

Making the Web More Accessible

Accessibility and the Web

Studies indicate that about 20% of the population has some type of disability. Many of these disabilities do not impact an individual's ability to interact with the World Wide Web. For example, a person who is paralyzed below the waist can generally still navigate the Web without difficulty. Likewise, a person with a heart condition can still use most of the features of the Web.

However, other disabilities can severely affect an individual's ability to participate in the Web community. For example, on a news Web site, a blind user could not see the latest headlines. A deaf user would not be able to hear a news clip embedded in the site's main page. A user with motor disabilities might not be able to move a mouse pointer to activate important links featured on the site's home page.

Disabilities that inhibit an individual's ability to use the Web fall into four main categories:

- **Visual disability:** A visual disability can include complete blindness, color-blindness, or an untreatable visual impairment.
- **Hearing disability:** A hearing disability can include complete deafness or the inability to distinguish sounds of certain frequencies.
- **Motor disability:** A motor disability can include the inability to use a mouse, to exhibit fine motor control, or to respond in a timely manner to computer prompts and queries.
- **Cognitive disability:** A cognitive disability can include a learning disability, attention deficit disorder, or the inability to focus on large amounts of information.

While the Web includes some significant obstacles to full use by disabled people, it also offers the potential for contact with a great amount of information that is not otherwise cheaply or easily accessible. For example, before the Web, in order to read a newspaper, a blind person was constrained by the expense of Braille printouts and audio tapes, as well as the limited availability of sighted people willing to read the news out loud. As a result, blind people would often only be able to read newspapers after the news was no longer new. The Web, however, makes news available in an electronic format and in real-time. A blind user can use a browser that converts electronic text into speech, known as a **screen reader**, to read a newspaper Web site. Combined with the Web, screen readers provide access to a broader array of information than was possible through Braille publications alone.

In addition to screen readers, many other programs and devices—known collectively as **assistive technology** or **adaptive technology**—are available to enable people with different disabilities to use the Web. The challenge for the Web designer, then, is to create Web pages that are accessible to everyone, including (and perhaps especially) to people with disabilities. In addition to being a design challenge, for some designers, Web accessibility is the law.

Working with Section 508 Guidelines

In 1973, Congress passed the Rehabilitation Act, which aimed to foster economic independence for people with disabilities. Congress amended the act in 1998 to reflect the latest changes in information technology. Part of the amendment, **Section 508**, requires that any electronic information developed, procured, maintained, or used by the federal government be accessible to people with disabilities. Because the Web is one of the main sources of electronic information, Section 508 has had a profound impact on how Web pages are designed and how Web code is written. Note that the standards apply to federal Web sites, but not to private sector Web sites; however, if a site is provided under contract to a federal agency, the Web site or portion covered by the contract has to comply. Required or not, though, you should follow the Section 508 guidelines not only to make your Web site more accessible, but also to make your HTML code more consistent and reliable. Thus, the Section 508 guidelines are of interest not just to Web designers who work for the federal government, but to all Web designers.

The Section 508 guidelines encompass a wide range of topics, covering several types of disabilities. The part of Section 508 that impacts Web design is sub-section 1194.22, titled

§ 1194.22   Web-based intranet and internet information and applications.

Within this section are 15 paragraphs, numbered (a) through (p), which describe how each facet of a Web site should be designed so as to maximize accessibility. Let's examine each of these paragraphs in detail.

Graphics and Images

The first paragraph in sub-section 1194.22 deals with graphic images. The standard for the use of graphic images is that

§1194.22 (a)   A text equivalent for every non-text element shall be provided (e.g., via "alt", "longdesc", or in element content).

In other words, any graphic image that contains page content needs to include a text alternative to make the page accessible to visually impaired people. One of the simplest ways to do this is to use the alt attribute with every inline image that displays page content. For example, in Figure D-1, the alt attribute provides the text of a graphical logo for users who can't see the graphic.

Figure D-1	Using the alt attribute

<img src="jkson.jpg" alt="Jackson Electronics" />

Not every graphic image requires a text alternative. For example, a decorative image such as a bullet does not need a text equivalent. In those cases, you should include the alt attribute, but set its value to an empty text string. You should never neglect to include the alt attribute. If you are writing XHTML-compliant code, use of the alt attribute is required. In other cases, screen readers and other non-visual browsers will recite the filename of a graphic imagep file if no value is specified for the alt attribute. Since the filename is usually of no interest to the end-user, this results in needless irritation.

The alt attribute is best used for short descriptions that involve five words or less. It is less effective for images that require long descriptive text. You can instead link these images to a document containing a more detailed description. One way to do this is with the longdesc attribute, which uses the syntax

```
<img src="url" longdesc="url" />
```

where *url* for the longdesc attribute points to a document containing a detailed description of the image. Figure D-2 shows an example that uses the longdesc attribute to point to a Web page containing a detailed description of a sales chart.

Using the alt attribute ◄ **Figure D-2**

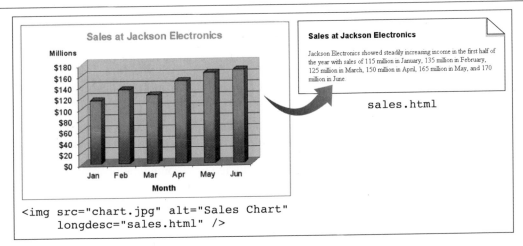

```
<img src="chart.jpg" alt="Sales Chart"
     longdesc="sales.html" />
```

In browsers that support the longdesc attribute, the attribute's value is presented as a link to the specified document. However, since many browsers do not yet support this attribute, many Web designers currently use a D-link. A **D-link** is an unobtrusive "D" placed next to the image on the page, which is linked to an external document containing a fuller description of the image. Figure D-3 shows how the sales chart data can be presented using a D-link.

Using a D-link ◄ **Figure D-3**

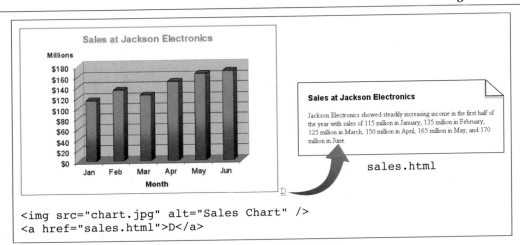

```
<img src="chart.jpg" alt="Sales Chart" />
<a href="sales.html">D</a>
```

To make your page accessible to visually-impaired users, you will probably use a combination of alternative text and linked documents.

Multimedia

Audio and video have become important ways of conveying information on the Web. However, creators of multimedia presentations should also consider the needs of deaf users and users who are hard of hearing. The standard for multimedia accessibility is

§1194.22 (b)   Equivalent alternatives for any multimedia presentation shall be synchronized with the presentation.

This means that any audio clip needs to be accompanied by a transcript of the audio's content, and any video clip needs to include closed captioning. Refer to your multimedia software's documentation on creating closed captioning and transcripts for your video and audio clips.

Color

Color is useful for emphasis and conveying information, but when color becomes an essential part of the site's content, you run the risk of shutting out people who are color blind. For this reason the third Section 508 standard states that

§1194.22 (c)   Web pages shall be designed so that all information conveyed with color is also available without color, for example from context or markup.

About 8% of men and 0.5% of women are afflicted with some type of color blindness. The most serious forms of color blindness are:

- **deuteranopia**: an absence of green sensitivity; deuteranopia is one example of red-green color blindness, in which the colors red and green cannot be easily distinguished.
- **protanopia**: an absence of red sensitivity; protanopia is another example of red-green color blindness.
- **tritanopia**: an absence of blue sensitivity. People with tritanopia have much less loss of color sensitivity than other types of color blindess.
- **achromatopsia**: absence of any color sensitivity.

The most common form of serious color blindness is red-green color blindness. Figure D-4 shows how each type of serious color blindness would affect a person's view of a basic color wheel.

Figure D-4 **Types of color blindness**

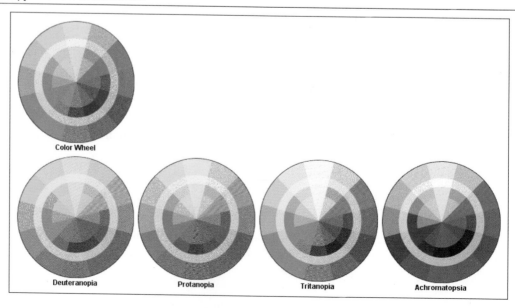

Color Wheel

Deuteranopia   Protanopia   Tritanopia   Achromatopsia

Color combinations that are easily readable for most people may be totally unreadable for users with certain types of color blindness. Figure D-5 demonstrates the accessibility problems that can occur with a graphical logo that contains green text on a red background. For people who have deuteranopia, protanopia, or achromatopsia, the logo is much more difficult to read.

The effect of color blindness on graphical content ◄ **Figure D-5**

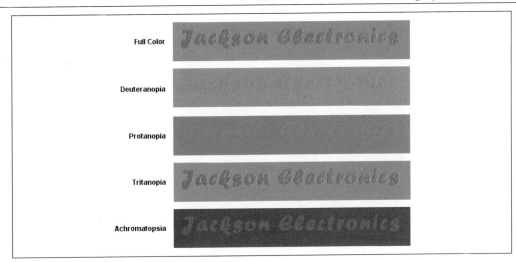

To make your page more accessible to people with color blindness, you can do the following:

- Provide non-color clues to access your page's content. For example, some Web forms indicate required entry fields by displaying the field names in a red font. You can supplement this for color blind users by marking required fields with a red font *and* with an asterisk or other special symbol.
- Avoid explicit references to color. Don't instruct your users to click a red button in a Web form when some users are unable to distinguish red from other colors.
- Avoid known areas of color difficulty. Since most color blindness involves red-green color blindness, you should avoid red and green text combinations.
- Use bright colors, which are the easiest for color blind users to distinguish.
- Provide a grayscale or black and white alternative for your color blind users, and be sure that your link to that page is easily viewable.

Several sites on the Web include tools you can use to test your Web site for color blind accessibility. You can also load color palettes into your graphics software to see how your images will appear to users with different types of color blindness.

Style Sheets

By controlling how a page is rendered in a browser, style sheets play an important role in making the Web accessible to users with disabilities. Many browsers, such as Internet Explorer, allow a user to apply their own customized style sheet in place of the style sheet specified by a Web page's designer. This is particular useful for visually impaired users who need to display text in extra large fonts with a high contrast between the text and the background color (yellow text on a black background is a common color scheme for such users). In order to make your pages accessible to those users, Section 508 guidelines state that

§1194.22 (d)   Documents shall be organized so they are readable without requiring an associated style sheet.

To test whether your site fulfills this guideline, you should view the site without the style sheet. Some browsers allow you to turn off style sheets; alternately, you can redirect a page to an empty style sheet. You should modify any page that is unreadable without its style sheet to conform with this guideline.

Image Maps

Section 508 provides two standards that pertain to image maps:

§1194.22 (e)   Redundant text links shall be provided for each active region of a server-side image map.

and

§1194.22 (f)   Client-side image maps shall be provided instead of server-side image maps except where the regions cannot be defined with an available geometric shape.

In other words, the *preferred* image map is a client-side image map, unless the map uses a shape that cannot be defined on the client side. Since client-side image maps allow for polygonal shapes, this should not be an issue; however if you must use a server-side image map, you need to provide a text alternative for each of the map's links. Because server-side image maps provide only map coordinates to the server, this text is necessary in order to provide link information that is accessible to blind or visually impaired users. Figure D-6 shows a server-side image map that satisfies the Section 508 guidelines by repeating the graphical links in the image map with text links placed below the image.

Figure D-6   Making a server-side image map accessible

Client-side image maps do not have the same limitations as server-side maps because they allow you to specify alternate text for each hotspot within the map. For example, if the image map shown in Figure D-6 were a client-side map, you could make it accessible using the following HTML code:

```
<img src="servermap.jpg" alt="Jackson Electronics"
usemap="#links" />
<map name="links">
<area shape="rect" href="home.html" alt="home"
coords="21,69,123,117" />
<area shape="rect" href="products.html" alt="products"
coords="156,69,258,117" />
<area shape="rect" href="stores.html" alt="stores"
coords="302,69,404,117" />
<area shape="rect" href="support.html" alt="support"
coords="445,69,547,117" />
</map>
```

Screen readers or other non-visual browsers use the value of the alt attribute within each <area /> tag to give users access to each area. However, because some older browsers cannot work with the alt attribute in this way, you should also include the text alternative used for server-side image maps.

Tables

Tables can present a challenge for disabled users, particular those who employ screen readers or other non-visual browsers. To render a Web page, these browsers employ a technique called **linearizing**, which processes Web page content using a few general rules:

1. Convert all images to their alternative text.
2. Present the contents of each table one cell at a time, working from left to right across each row before moving down to the next row.
3. If a cell contains a nested table, that table is linearized before proceeding to the next cell.

Figure D-7 shows how a non-visual browser might linearize a sample table.

Linearizing a table ◄ **Figure D-7**

One way of dealing with the challenge of linearizing is to structure your tables so that they are easily interpreted even when linearized. However, this is not always possible, especially for tables that have several rows and columns or may contain several levels of nested tables. The Section 508 guidelines for table creation state that

§1194.22 (g)   Row and column headers shall be identified for data tables.

and

§1194.22 (h)   Markup shall be used to associate data cells and header cells for data tables that have two or more logical levels of row or column headers.

To fulfill the 1194.22 (g) guideline, you should use the <th> tag for any table cell that contains a row or column header. By default, header text appears in a bold centered font; however, you can override this format using a style sheet. Many non-visual browsers can search for header cells. Also, as a user moves from cell to cell in a table, these browsers can announce the row and column headers associated with each cell. Thus, using the <th> tag can significantly reduce some of the problems associated with linearizing.

You can also use the scope attribute to explicitly associate a header with a row, column, row group, or column group. The syntax of the scope attribute is

```
<th scope="type"> … </th>
```

where *type* is either row, column, rowgroup, or colgroup. Figure D-8 shows how to use the scope attribute to associate the headers with the rows and columns of a table.

Figure D-8 **Using the scope attribute**

```
<table border="1" cellpadding="5">
<tr>
  <th scope="col">Model</th>
  <th scope="col">Processor</th>
  <th scope="col">Memory</th>
</tr>
<tr>
  <th scope="row">Paragon 2.4</th>
  <td>Intel 2.4GHz</td>
  <td>256MB</td>
</tr>
<tr>
  <th scope="row">Paragon 3.7</th>
  <td>Intel 3.7GHz</td>
  <td>512MB</td>
</tr>
</table>
```

HTML code

Model	Processor	Memory
Paragon 2.4 ➡	Intel 2.4GHz	256MB
Paragon 3.7 ➡	Intel 3.7GHz	512MB

table

A non-visual browser that encounters the table in Figure D-8 can indicate to users which rows and columns are associated with each data cell. For example, the browser could indicate that the cell value, "512MB" is associated with the Memory column and the Paragon 3.7 row.

For more explicit references, HTML also supports the headers attribute, which specifies the cell or cells that contain header information for a particular cell. The syntax of the headers attribute is

```
<td headers="ids"> … </td>
```

where *ids* is a list of id values associated with header cells in the table. Figure D-9 demonstrates how to use the headers attribute.

```
<table>
<tr>
  <th id="c1">Model</th>
  <th id="c2">Processor</th>
  <th id="c3">Memory</th>
</tr>
<tr>
  <th id="r1" headers="c1">Paragon 2.4</th>
  <td headers="r1 c2">Intel 2.4GHz</td>
  <td headers="r1 c3">256MB</td>
</tr>
<tr>
  <th id="r2" headers="c1">Paragon 3.7</th>
  <td headers="r2 c2">Intel 3.7GHz</td>
  <td headers="r2 c3">512MB</td>
</tr>
</table>
```

Model	Processor	Memory
Paragon 2.4	Intel 2.4GHz	256MB
Paragon 3.7	Intel 3.7GHz	512MB

HTML code   table

Note that some older browsers do not support the scope and headers attributes. For this reason, it can be useful to supplement your tables with caption and summary attributes in order to provide even more information to blind and visually impaired users. See Tutorial 4 for a more detailed discussion of these elements and attributes.

Frame Sites

When a non-visual browser opens a frame site, it can render the contents of only one frame at a time. Users are given a choice of which frame to open. Thus, it's important that the name given to a frame indicate the frame's content. For this reason, the Section 508 guideline for frames states that

§1194.22 (i)   Frames shall be titled with text that facilitates frame identification and navigation.

Frames can be identified using either the title attribute or the name attribute, and different non-visual browsers use different attributes. For example, the Lynx browser uses the name attribute, while the IBM Home Page Reader uses the title attribute. For this reason, you should use both attributes in your framed sites. If you don't include a title or name attribute in the frame element, some non-visual browsers retrieve the document specified as the frame's source and then use that page's title as the name for the frame.

The following code demonstrates how to make a frame site accessible to users with disabilities.

```
<frameset cols="25%, *">
   <frame src="title.htm" title="banner" name="banner" />
   <frameset rows="100, *">
      <frame src="links.htm" title="links" name="links" />
      <frame src="home.htm" title="documents" name="documents" />
   </frameset>
</frameset>
```

Naturally, you should make sure that any document displayed in a frame follows the Section 508 guidelines.

Animation and Scrolling Text

Animated GIFs, scrolling marquees, and other special features can be a source of irritation for any Web user; however, they can cause serious problems for certain users. For example, people with photosensitive epilepsy can experience seizures when exposed to a screen or portion of a screen that flickers or flashes within the range of 2 to 55 flashes per second (2 to 55 Hertz). For this reason, the Section 508 guidelines state that

§1194.22 (j)   Pages shall be designed to avoid causing the screen to flicker with a frequency greater than 2 Hz and lower than 55 Hz.

In addition to problems associated with photosensitive epilepsy, users with cognitive or visual disabilities may find it difficult to read moving text, and most screen readers are unable to read moving text. Thus, if you decide to use animated elements, you must ensure that each element's flickering and flashing is outside of the prohibited range, and you should not place essential page content within these elements.

Scripts, Applets and Plug-ins

Scripts, applets, and plug-ins are widely used to make Web pages more dynamic and interesting. The Section 508 guidelines for scripts state that

§1194.22 (l)   When pages utilize scripting languages to display content, or to create interface elements, the information provided by the script shall be identified with functional text that can be read by adaptive technology.

Scripts are used for a wide variety of purposes. The following list describes some of the more popular uses of scripts and how to modify them for accessibility:

- **Pull-down menus**: Many Web designers use scripts to save screen space by inserting pull-down menus containing links to other pages in the site. Pull-down menus are usually accessed with a mouse. To assist users who cannot manipulate a mouse, include keyboard shortcuts to all pull-down menus. In addition, the links in a pull-down menu should be repeated elsewhere on the page or on the site in a text format.
- **Image rollovers**: Image rollovers are used to highlight linked elements. However, since image rollovers rely on the ability to use a mouse, pages should be designed so that rollover effects are not essential for navigating a site or for understanding a page's content.
- **Dynamic content**: Scripts can be used to insert new text and page content. Because some browsers designed for users with disabilities have scripting turned off by default, you should either not include any crucial content in dynamic text, or you should provide an alternate method for users with disabilities to access that information.

Applets and plug-ins are programs external to a Web page or browser that add special features to a Web site. The Section 508 guideline for applets and plug-ins is

§1194.22 (m)   When a Web page requires that an applet, plug-in or other application be present on the client system to interpret page content, the page must provide a link to a plug-in or applet that complies with §1994.21(a) through (i).

This guideline means that any applet or plug-in used with your Web site must be compliant with sections §1994.21(a) through (i) of the Section 508 accessibility law, which deal with accessibility issues for software applications and operating systems. If the default applet or plug-in does not comply with Section 508, you need to provide a link to a version of that applet or plug-in which does. For example, a Web page containing a Real Audio clip should have a link to a source for the necessary player. This places the responsibility on the Web page designer to know that a compliant application is available before requiring the clip to work with the page.

Web Forms

The Section 508 standard for Web page forms states that

§1194.22 (n) **When electronic forms are designed to be completed on-line, the form shall allow people using assistive technology to access the information, field elements, and functionality required for completion and submission of the form, including all directions and cues.**

This is a general statement that instructs designers to make forms accessible, but it doesn't supply any specific instructions. The following techniques can help you make Web forms that comply with Section 508:

- **Push buttons** should always include value attributes. The value attribute contains the text displayed on a button, and is rendered by different types of assistive technology.
- **Image buttons** should always include alternate text that can be rendered by non-visual browsers.
- **Labels** should be associated with any input box, text area box, option button, checkbox, or selection list. The labels should be placed in close proximity to the input field and should be linked to the field using the label element.
- **Input boxes** and **text area boxes** should, when appropriate, include either default text or a prompt that indicates to the user what text to enter into the input box.
- **Interactive form elements** should be triggered by either the mouse or the keyboard.

The other parts of a Web form should comply with other Section 508 standards. For example, if you use a table to lay out the elements of a form, make sure that the form still makes sense when the table is linearized.

Links

It is common for Web designers to place links at the top, bottom, and sides of every page in their Web sites. This is generally a good idea, because those links enable users to move quickly and easily through a site. However, this technique can make it difficult to navigate a page using a screen reader, because screen readers move through a page from the top to bottom, reading each line of text. Users of screen readers may have to wait several minutes before they even get to the main body of a page, and the use of repetitive links forces such users to reread the same links on each page as they move through a site. To address this problem, the Section 508 guidelines state that

§1194.22 (o) **A method shall be provided that permits users to skip repetitive navigation links.**

One way of complying with this rule is to place a link at the very top of each page that allows users to jump to the page's main content. In order to make the link unobtrusive, it can be attached to a transparent image that is one pixel wide by one pixel high. For example, the following code lets users of screen readers jump to the main content of the page without needing to go through the content navigation links on the page; however, the image itself is invisible to other users and thus does not affect the page's layout or appearance.

```
<a href="#main">
   <img src="spacer.gif" height="1" width="1" alt="Skip to main
content" />
</a>

...

<a name="main"> </a>
page content goes here …
```

One advantage to this approach is that a template can be easily written to add this code to each page of the Web site.

Timed Responses

For security reasons, the login pages of some Web sites automatically log users out after a period of inactivity, or if users are unable to log in quickly. Because disabilities may prevent some users from being able to complete a login procedure within the prescribed time limit, the Section 508 guidelines state that

§1194.22 (p) When a timed response is required, the user shall be alerted and given sufficient time to indicate that more time is required.

The guideline does not suggest a time interval. To satisfy Section 508, your page should notify users when a process is about to time out and prompt users whether additional time is needed before proceeding.

Providing a Text-Only Equivalent

If you cannot modify a page to match the previous accessibility guidelines, as a last resort you can create a text-only page:

§1194.22 (k) A text-only page, with equivalent information or functionality, shall be provided to make a Web site comply with the provisions of this part, when compliance cannot be accomplished in any other way. The content of the text-only pages shall be updated whenever the primary page changes.

To satisfy this requirement, you should

- Provide an easily accessible link to the text-only page.
- Make sure that the text-only page satisfies the Section 508 guidelines.
- Duplicate the essential content of the original page.
- Update the alternate page when you update the original page.

By using the Section 508 guidelines, you can work towards making your Web site accessible to everyone, regardless of disabilities.

Understanding the Web Accessibility Initiative

In 1999, the World Wide Web Consortium (W3C) developed its own set of guidelines for Web accessibility called the **Web Accessibility Initiative (WAI)**. The WAI covers many of the same points as the Section 508 rules, and expands on them to cover basic Web site design issues. The overall goal of the WAI is to facilitate the creation of Web sites that are accessible to all, and to encourage designers to implement HTML in a consistent way.

The WAI sets forth 14 guidelines for Web designers. Within each guideline is a collection of checkpoints indicating how to apply the guideline to specific features of a Web site. Each checkpoint is also given a priority score that indicates how important the guideline is for proper Web design:

- **Priority 1:** A Web content developer **must** satisfy this checkpoint. Otherwise, one or more groups will find it impossible to access information in the document. Satisfying this checkpoint is a basic requirement for some groups to be able to use Web documents.
- **Priority 2:** A Web content developer **should** satisfy this checkpoint. Otherwise, one or more groups will find it difficult to access information in the document. Satisfying this checkpoint will remove significant barriers to accessing Web documents.

- **Priority 3:** A Web content developer **may** address this checkpoint. Otherwise, one or more groups will find it somewhat difficult to access information in the document. Satisfying this checkpoint will improve access to Web documents.

The following table lists WAI guidelines with each checkpoint and its corresponding priority value.

WAI Guidelines	Priority
1. Provide equivalent alternatives to auditory and visual content	
1.1 Provide a text equivalent for every non-text element (e.g., via "alt", "longdesc", or in element content). *This includes:* images, graphical representations of text (including symbols), image map regions, animations (e.g., animated GIFs), applets and programmatic objects, ascii art, frames, scripts, images used as list bullets, spacers, graphical buttons, sounds (played with or without user interaction), stand-alone audio files, audio tracks of video, and video.	1
1.2 Provide redundant text links for each active region of a server-side image map.	1
1.3 Until user agents can automatically read aloud the text equivalent of a visual track, provide an auditory description of the important information of the visual track of a multimedia presentation.	1
1.4 For any time-based multimedia presentation (e.g., a movie or animation), synchronize equivalent alternatives (e.g., captions or auditory descriptions of the visual track) with the presentation.	1
1.5 Until user agents render text equivalents for client-side image map links, provide redundant text links for each active region of a client-side image map.	3
2. Don't rely on color alone	
2.1 Ensure that all information conveyed with color is also available without color, for example from context or markup.	1
2.2 Ensure that foreground and background color combinations provide sufficient contrast when viewed by someone having color deficits or when viewed on a black and white screen. [Priority 2 for images, Priority 3 for text].	2
3. Use markup and style sheets and do so properly	
3.1 When an appropriate markup language exists, use markup rather than images to convey information.	2
3.2 Create documents that validate to published formal grammars.	2
3.3 Use style sheets to control layout and presentation.	2
3.4 Use relative rather than absolute units in markup language attribute values and style sheet property values.	2
3.5 Use header elements to convey document structure and use them according to specification.	2
3.6 Mark up lists and list items properly.	2
3.7 Mark up quotations. Do not use quotation markup for formatting effects such as indentation.	2
4. Clarify natural language usage	
4.1 Clearly identify changes in the natural language of a document's text and any text equivalents (e.g., captions).	1
4.2 Specify the expansion of each abbreviation or acronym in a document where it first occurs.	3
4.3 Identify the primary natural language of a document.	3
5. Create tables that transform gracefully	
5.1 For data tables, identify row and column headers.	1
5.2 For data tables that have two or more logical levels of row or column headers, use markup to associate data cells and header cells.	1
5.3 Do not use a table for layout unless the table makes sense when linearized. If a table does not make sense, provide an alternative equivalent (which may be a linearized version).	2
5.4 If a table is used for layout, do not use any structural markup for the purpose of visual formatting.	2

WAI Guidelines	Priority
5.5 Provide summaries for tables.	3
5.6 Provide abbreviations for header labels.	3

6. Ensure that pages featuring new technologies transform gracefully

6.1 Organize documents so they may be read without style sheets. For example, when an HTML document is rendered without associated style sheets, it must still be possible to read the document.	1
6.2 Ensure that equivalents for dynamic content are updated when the dynamic content changes.	1
6.3 Ensure that pages are usable when scripts, applets, or other programmatic objects are turned off or not supported. If this is not possible, then provide equivalent information on an alternative accessible page.	1
6.4 For scripts and applets, ensure that event handlers are input device-independent.	2
6.5 Ensure that dynamic content is accessible or provide an alternative presentation or page.	2

7. Ensure user control of time-sensitive content changes

7.1 Until user agents allow users to control flickering, avoid causing the screen to flicker.	1
7.2 Until user agents allow users to control blinking, avoid causing content to blink (i.e., change presentation at a regular rate, such as turning on and off).	2
7.3 Until user agents allow users to freeze moving content, avoid movement in pages.	2
7.4 Until user agents provide the ability to stop the refresh, do not create periodically auto-refreshing pages.	2
7.5 Until user agents provide the ability to stop auto-redirect, do not use markup to redirect pages automatically. Instead, configure the server to perform redirects.	2

8. Ensure direct accessibility of embedded user interfaces

8.1 Make programmatic elements such as scripts and applets directly accessible or compatible with assistive technologies [Priority 1 if functionality is important and not presented elsewhere, otherwise Priority 2.]	2

9. Design for device-independence

9.1 Provide client-side image maps instead of server-side image maps except where the regions cannot be defined with an available geometric shape.	1
9.2 Ensure that any element with its own interface can be operated in a device-independent manner.	2
9.3 For scripts, specify logical event handlers rather than device-dependent event handlers.	2
9.4 Create a logical tab order through links, form controls, and objects.	3
9.5 Provide keyboard shortcuts to important links (including those in client-side image maps), form controls, and groups of form controls.	3

10. Use interim solutions

10.1 Until user agents allow users to turn off spawned windows, do not cause pop-ups or other windows to appear and do not change the current window without informing the user.	2
10.2 Until user agents support explicit associations between labels and form controls, ensure that labels are properly positioned for all form controls with implicitly associated labels.	2
10.3 Until user agents (including assistive technologies) render side-by-side text correctly, provide a linear text alternative (on the current page or some other) for *all* tables that lay out text in parallel, word-wrapped columns.	3
10.4 Until user agents handle empty controls correctly, include default, place-holding characters in edit boxes and text areas.	3
10.5 Until user agents (including assistive technologies) render adjacent links distinctly, include non-link, printable characters (surrounded by spaces) between adjacent links.	3

11. Use W3C technologies and guidelines

11.1 Use W3C technologies when they are available and appropriate for a task and use the latest versions when supported.	2
11.2 Avoid deprecated features of W3C technologies.	2

WAI Guidelines	Priority
11.3 Provide information so that users may receive documents according to their preferences (e.g., language, content type, etc.)	3
11.4 If, after best efforts, you cannot create an accessible page, provide a link to an alternative page that uses W3C technologies, is accessible, has equivalent information (or functionality), and is updated as often as the inaccessible (original) page.	1
12. Provide context and orientation information	
12.1 Title each frame to facilitate frame identification and navigation.	1
12.2 Describe the purpose of frames and how frames relate to each other if this is not obvious from frame titles alone.	2
12.3 Divide large blocks of information into more manageable groups where natural and appropriate.	2
12.4 Associate labels explicitly with their controls.	2
13. Provide clear navigation mechanisms	
13.1 Clearly identify the target of each link.	2
13.2 Provide metadata to add semantic information to pages and sites.	2
13.3 Provide information about the general layout of a site (e.g., a site map or table of contents).	2
13.4 Use navigation mechanisms in a consistent manner.	2
13.5 Provide navigation bars to highlight and give access to the navigation mechanism.	3
13.6 Group related links, identify the group (for user agents), and, until user agents do so, provide a way to bypass the group.	3
13.7 If search functions are provided, enable different types of searches for different skill levels and preferences.	3
13.8 Place distinguishing information at the beginning of headings, paragraphs, lists, etc.	3
13.9 Provide information about document collections (i.e., documents comprising multiple pages.).	3
13.10 Provide a means to skip over multi-line ASCII art.	3
14. Ensure that documents are clear and simple	
14.1 Use the clearest and simplest language appropriate for a site's content.	1
14.2 Supplement text with graphic or auditory presentations where they will facilitate comprehension of the page.	3
14.3 Create a style of presentation that is consistent across pages.	3

You can learn more about the WAI guidelines and how to implement them by going to the World Wide Web Consortium Web site at http://www.w3.org.

Checking your Web Site for Accessibility

As you develop your Web site, you should periodically check it for accessibility. In addition to reviewing the Section 508 and WAI guidelines, you can do several things to verify that your site is accessible to everyone:

- Set up your browser to suppress the display of images. Does each page still convey all of the necessary information?
- Set your browser to display pages in extra large fonts and with a different color scheme. Are your pages still readable under these conditions?
- Try to navigate your pages using only your keyboard. Can you access all of the links and form elements?
- View your page in a text-only browser. (You can use the Lynx browser for this task, located at http://www.lynx.browser.org.)

- Open your page in a screen reader or other non-visual browser. (The W3C Web site contains links to several alternative browsers that you can download as freeware or on a short-term trial basis in order to evaluate your site.)
- Use tools that test your site for accessibility. (The WAI pages at the W3C Web site contains links to a wide variety of tools that report on how well your site complies with the WAI and Section 508 guidelines.)

Following the accessibility guidelines laid out by Section 508 and the WAI will result in a Web site that is not only more accessible to a wider audience, but whose design is also cleaner, easier to work with, and easier to maintain.

"The power of the Web is in its universality. Access by everyone regardless of disability is an essential aspect."
— Tim Berners-Lee, W3C Director and inventor of the World Wide Web

HTML and XHTML Elements and Attributes

This appendix provides descriptions of the major elements and attributes of HTML and XHTML. It also indicates the level of browser support for the Windows version of three major browsers: Internet Explorer (IE), Netscape (NS), and Opera (OP). Browser support is indicated in the columns on the right of each of the following tables. For example, a value of 4.0 in the Internet Explorer column indicates that the element or attribute is supported by the Windows version of Internet Explorer 4.0 and above. A version number with an asterisk indicates that the browser support is not extended to the more recent browser versions. For example, the entry "4.0*" in the Netscape column means that the feature is supported only in the 4.0 version of the Netscape browser and not in any other version (including later versions). In each of the tables that follow, values in the first column indicate the page number in the text in which the element or attribute is introduced and discussed.

Be aware that browsers are constantly being modified, so you should check a browser's documentation for the most current information. Also, the level of browser support can vary between operating systems.

The following data types are used throughout this appendix:

- *char* — A single text character
- *char code* — A character encoding
- *color* — An HTML color name or hexadecimal color value
- *date* — A date and time in the format: *yyyy-mm-dd*T*hh:mm:ss*TIMEZONE
- *integer* — An integer value
- *mime-type* — A MIME data type, such as "text/css", "audio/wav", or "video/x-msvideo"
- *mime-type list* — A comma-separated list of mime-types
- **option1**|option2| ... — The value is limited to the specified list of *options*. A default value, if it exists, is displayed in **bold**.
- *script* — A script or a reference to a script
- *styles* — A list of style declarations
- *text* — A text string
- *text list* — A comma-separated list of text strings
- *url* — The URL for a Web page or file
- *value* — A numeric value
- *value list* — A comma-separated list of numeric values

General Attributes

Several attributes are common to many page elements. Rather than repeating this information each time it occurs, the following tables summarize these attributes.

Core Attributes

The following five attributes, which are laid out in the specifications for HTML and XHTML, apply to all page elements and are supported by most browser versions.

PAGE	ATTRIBUTE	DESCRIPTION	HTML	XHTML	IE	NS	OP
367	class="*text*"	Specifies the class or group to which an element belongs	4.0	1.0	3.0	4.0	3.5
58	id="*text*"	Specifies a unique identifier to be associated with the element	4.0	1.0	3.0	4.0	3.5
18	style="*styles*"	Defines an inline style for the element	4.0	1.0	3.0	4.0	3.5
86	title="*text*"	Provides an advisory title for the element	2.0	1.0	4.0	6.0	3.0

Language Attributes

The Web is designed to be universal and has to be adaptable to languages other than English. Thus, another set of attributes provides language support. This set of attributes is not as widely supported by browsers as the core attributes are. As with the core attributes, they can be applied to most page elements.

PAGE	ATTRIBUTE	DESCRIPTION	HTML	XHTML	IE	NS	OP
	dir="**ltr** | rtl"	Indicates the text direction as related to the lang attribute. A value of ltr displays text from left to right. A value rtl displays text from right to left.	4.0	1.0	5.5	6.0	7.1
	lang="*text*"	Identifies the language used in the page content	4.0	1.0	4.0		

Form Attributes

The following attributes can be applied to most form elements or to a Web form itself, but not to other page elements.

PAGE	ATTRIBUTE	DESCRIPTION	HTML	XHTML	IE	NS	OP
332	accesskey="*char*"	Indicates the keyboard character that can be pressed along with the accelerator key to access a form element	4.0	1.0	4.0	6.0	7.0
	disabled="disabled"	Disables a form field for input	4.0	1.0	4.0	6.0	7.0
332	tabindex="*integer*"	Specifies a form element's position in a document's tabbing order	4.0	1.0	4.0	6.0	7.0

Internet Explorer Attributes

Internet Explorer supports a collection of attributes that can be applied to almost all page elements. Other browsers do not support these attributes, or support them only for a more limited collection of elements.

PAGE	ATTRIBUTE	DESCRIPTION	HTML	XHTML	IE	NS	OP
332	accesskey="*char*"	Indicates the keyboard character that can be pressed along with the accelerator key to access the page element			5.0		
	contenteditable="true | false | **inherit**"	Specifies whether the element's content can be modified online by the user			5.5		
	disabled="disabled"	Disables the page element for input			5.0		
	hidefocus="true | **false**"	Controls whether the element provides a visual indication of whether the element is in focus			5.5		
332	tabindex="*integer*"	Specifies the position of the page element in the tabbing order of the document			5.0		
	unselectable="on | **off**"	Specifies whether the element can be selected by the user			5.5		

Event Attributes

To make Web pages more dynamic, HTML and XHTML support event attributes that identify scripts to be run in response to an event occurring within an element. For example, clicking a main heading with a mouse can cause a browser to run a program that hides or expands a table of contents. Each event attribute has the form

`event = "script"`

where *event* is the name of the event attribute and *script* is the name of the script or command to be run by the browser in response to the occurrence of the event within the element.

Core Events

The general event attributes are part of the specifications for HTML and XHTML. They apply to almost all page elements.

PAGE	ATTRIBUTE	DESCRIPTION	HTML	XHTML	IE	NS	OP
	onclick	The mouse button is clicked.	4.0	1.0	3.0	2.0	3.0
	ondblclick	The mouse button is double-clicked.	4.0	1.0	4.0	6.0	7.0
	onkeydown	A key is pressed down.	4.0	1.0	4.0	4.0	5.0
	onkeypress	A key is initially pressed.	4.0	1.0	4.0	4.0	5.0
	onkeyup	A key is released.	4.0	1.0	4.0	4.0	5.0
	onmousedown	The mouse button is pressed down.	4.0	1.0	4.0	4.0	5.0
	onmousemove	The mouse pointer is moved within the element's boundaries.	4.0	1.0	4.0	6.0	5.0
	onmouseout	The mouse pointer is moved out of the element's boundaries.	4.0	1.0	4.0	3.0	3.0
	onmouseover	The mouse pointer hovers over the element.	4.0	1.0	3.0	2.0	3.0
	onmouseup	The mouse button is released.	4.0	1.0	4.0	4.0	5.0

Document Events

The following list of event attributes applies not to individual elements within the page, but to the entire document as it displayed within the browser window or frame.

PAGE	ATTRIBUTE	DESCRIPTION	HTML	XHTML	IE	NS	OP
	onafterprint	The document has finished printing.			5.0		
	onbeforeprint	The document is about to be printed.			5.0		
	onload	The page is finished being loaded.	4.0	1.0	3.0	2.0	3.0
	onunload	The page is finished unloading.	4.0	1.0	3.0	2.0	3.0

Form Events

The following list of event attributes applies either to the entire Web form or fields within the form.

PAGE	ATTRIBUTE	DESCRIPTION	HTML	XHTML	IE	NS	OP
	onblur	The form field has lost the focus.	4.0	1.0	3.0	2.0	3.0
	onchange	The value of the form field has been changed.	4.0	1.0	3.0	2.0	3.0
	onfocus	The form field has received the focus.	4.0	1.0	3.0	2.0	3.0
	onreset	The form has been reset.	4.0	1.0	4.0	3.0	3.0
	onselect	Text content has been selected in the form field.	4.0	1.0	4.0	6.0	
	onsubmit	The form has been submitted for processing.	4.0	1.0	3.0	2.0	3.0

Data Events

The following list of event attributes applies to elements within the Web page capable of data binding. Note that these events are supported only by the Internet Explorer browser.

PAGE	ATTRIBUTE	DESCRIPTION	HTML	XHTML	IE	NS	OP
	oncellchange	Data has changed in the data source.			5.0		
	ondataavailable	Data has arrived from the data source.			4.0		
	ondatasetchange	The data in the data source has changed.			4.0		
	ondatasetcomplete	All data from the data source has been loaded.			4.0		
	onrowenter	The current row in the data source has changed.			5.0		
	onrowexit	The current row is about to be changed in the data source.			5.0		
	onrowsdelete	Rows have been deleted from the data source.			5.0		
	onrowsinserted	Rows have been inserted into the data source.			5.0		

Internet Explorer Events

The Internet Explorer browser supports a wide collection of customized event attributes. Unless otherwise noted, these event attributes can be applied to any page element and are not supported by other browsers or included in the HTML or XHTML specifications.

PAGE	ATTRIBUTE	DESCRIPTION	HTML	XHTML	IE	NS	OP
	onactive	The element is set to an "active" state.			5.5		
	onafterupdate	Data has been transferred from the element to a data source.			4.0		
	onbeforeactivate	The element is about to be set to an "active" state.			6.0		
	onbeforecopy	A selection from the element is about to be copied to the clipboard.			5.0		
	onbeforecut	A selection from the element is about to be cut to the clipboard.			5.0		
	onbeforedeactivate	The element is about to be "deactivated".			5.5		
	onbeforeeditfocus	The element is about to become "active".			5.0		
	onbeforepaste	Data from the clipboard is about to be pasted into the element.			5.0		
	onbeforeunload	The page is about to be unloaded.			4.0		
	onbeforeupdate	The element's data is about to be updated.			5.0		
	onblur	The element has lost the focus.			5.0		
	oncontextmenu	The right mouse button is activated.			5.0	6.0	
	oncontrolselect	Selection using a modifier key (Ctrl for Windows, Command for Macintosh) has begun within the element.			5.5		
	oncopy	Data from the element has been copied to the clipboard.			5.0		
	oncut	Data from the element has been cut to the clipboard.			5.0		
	ondrag	The element is being dragged.			5.0		
	ondragdrop	The element has been dropped into the window or frame.			5.0		
	ondragend	The element is no longer being dragged.			5.0		

PAGE	ATTRIBUTE	DESCRIPTION	HTML	XHTML	IE	NS	OP
	ondragenter	The dragged element has entered a target area.			5.0		
	ondragleave	The dragged element has left a target area.			5.0		
	ondragover	The dragged element is over a target area.			5.0		
	ondragstart	The element has begun to be dragged.			5.0		
	ondrop	The dragged element has been dropped.			5.0		
	onerrorupdate	The data transfer to the element has been cancelled.			4.0		
	onfocus	The element has received the focus.			5.0		
	onfocusin	The element is about to receive the focus.			6.0		
	onfocusout	The form element has just lost the focus.			6.0		
	onhelp	The user has selected online help from the browser.			4.0		
	oninput	Text has just been entered into the form field.			6.0		
	onlosecapture	The element has been captured by the mouse selection.			5.0		
	onmouseenter	The mouse pointer enters the element's boundaries.			5.5		
	onmouseleave	The mouse pointer leaves the element's boundaries.			5.5		
	onmousewheel	The mouse wheel is moved.			6.0		
	onmove	The browser window or element has been moved by the user.			5.5		
	onmoveend	Movement of the element has ended.			5.5		
	onmovestart	The element has begun to move.			5.5		
	onpaste	Data has been pasted from the clipboard into the element.			5.0		
	onpropertychange	One or more of the element's properties has changed.			5.0		
	onreadystatechange	The element has changed its ready state.			4.0		
	onresize	The browser window or element has been resized by the user.			4.0		
	onscroll	The scrollbar position within the element has been changed.			4.0	7.0	7.0
	onselectstart	Selection has begun within the element.			4.0		
	onstop	The page is finished loading.			5.0		

HTML and XHTML Elements and Attributes

The following table contains an alphabetic listing of the elements and attributes supported by HTML, XHTML, and the major browsers. Some attributes are not listed in this table, but are described instead in the general attributes tables presented in the previous section of this appendix.

PAGE	ELEMENT/ATTRIBUTE	DESCRIPTION	HTML	XHTML	IE	NS	OP
10	`<!-- text -->`	Inserts a comment into the document (comments are not displayed in the rendered page)	2.0	1.0	1.0	1.0	2.1
497	`<!doctype>`	Specifies the Document Type Definition for a document	2.0	1.0	2.0	1.0	4.0
61	`<a> </a>`	Marks the beginning and end of a link	2.0	1.0	1.0	1.0	2.1
86	`accesskey="char"`	Indicates the keyboard character that can be pressed along with the accelerator key to activate the link	4.0	1.0	4.0	6.0	7.0
	`charset="text"`	Specifies the character encoding of the linked document	4.0	1.0			7.0
154	`coords="value list"`	Specifies the coordinates of a hotspot in a client-side image map; the value list depends on the shape of the hotspot: shape="rect" "left, right, top, bottom" shape="circle" "x_center, y_center, radius" shape="poly" "x1, y1, x2, y2, x3, y3, ..."	4.0	1.0		6.0	7.0
61	`href="url"`	Specifies the URL of the link	3.2	1.0	1.0	2.0	2.1
	`hreflang="text"`	Specifies the language of the linked document	4.0	1.0		6.1	
63	`name="text"`	Specifies a name for the enclosed text, allowing it to be a link target	2.0	1.0	1.0	1.0	2.1
87	`rel="text"`	Specifies the relationship between the current page and the link specified by the href attribute	2.0	1.0	3.0	6.0	7.0
87	`rev="text"`	Specifies the reverse relationship between the current page and the link specified by the href attribute	2.0	1.0	3.0	6.0	7.0
154	`shape="rect|circle|polygon"`	Specifies the shape of the hotspot	4.0	1.0		6.0	7.0
86	`title="text"`	Specifies the pop-up text for the link	2.0	1.0	4.0	6.0	3.0
84	`target="text"`	Specifies the target window or frame for the link	4.0	1.0	3.0	1.0	2.1
	`type="mime-type"`	Specifies the data type of the linked document	4.0	1.0			7.0

PAGE	ELEMENT/ATTRIBUTE	DESCRIPTION	HTML	XHTML	IE	NS	OP
32	`<abbr> </abbr>`	Marks abbreviated text	4.0	1.0		6.0	4.0
32	`<acronym> </acronym>`	Marks acronym text	3.0	1.0	4.0	6.0	4.0
31	`<address> </address>`	Marks address text	2.0	1.0	1.0	1.0	2.1
458	`<applet> </applet>`	Embeds an applet into the browser. **Deprecated**	3.2	1.0*	3.0	2.0	3.5
140	`align="absmiddle|` `absbottom|baseline|` `bottom|center` `|left|middle` `|right|texttop` `|top"`	Specifies the alignment of the applet with the surrounding text	3.2	1.0*	3.0	2.0	3.0
459	`alt="text"`	Specifies alternate text for the applet. **Deprecated**	3.2	1.0*	3.0	2.0	
	`archive="url"`	Specifies the URL of an archive containing classes and other resources to be used with the applet. **Deprecated**	4.0	1.0*	4.0	3.0	
459	`code="url"`	Specifies the URL of the applet's code/class. **Deprecated**	3.2	1.0*	3.0	2.0	3.5
459	`codebase="url"`	Specifies the URL of all class files for the applet. **Deprecated**	3.2	1.0*	3.0	2.0	
	`datafld="text"`	Specifies the data source that supplies bound data for use with the applet	4.0		4.0		
	`datasrc="text"`	Specifies the ID or URL of the applet's data source	4.0		4.0		
459	`height="integer"`	Specifies the height of the applet in pixels	3.2	1.0*	3.0	2.0	3.5
143	`hspace="integer"`	Specifies the horizontal space around the applet in pixels. **Deprecated**	3.2	1.0*	3.0	2.0	4.0
	`mayscript="mayscript"`	Permits access to the applet by programs embedded in the document				3.0*	
459	`name="text"`	Specifies the name assigned to the applet. **Deprecated**	3.2	1.0*	3.0	2.0	3.5
	`object="text"`	Specifies the name of the resource that contains a serialized representation of the applet. **Deprecated**	4.0	1.0*			
458	`src="url"`	Specifies an external URL reference to the applet			4.0		3.5
143	`vspace="integer"`	Specifies the vertical space around the applet in pixels. **Deprecated**	3.2	1.0*	3.0	2.0	4.0
459	`width="integer"`	Specifies the width of the applet in pixels. **Deprecated**	3.2	1.0*	3.0	2.0	3.5

PAGE	ELEMENT/ATTRIBUTE	DESCRIPTION	HTML	XHTML	IE	NS	OP
154	`<area />`	Marks an image map hotspot	3.2	1.0	1.0	2.0	2.1
154	`alt="text"`	Specifies alternate text for the hotspot	3.2	1.0	4.0	3.0	2.1
154	`coords="value list"`	Specifies the coordinates of the hotspot; the value list depends on the shape of the hotspot: shape="rect" "left, right, top, bottom" shape="circle" "x_center, y_center, radius" shape="poly" "x1, y1, x2, y2, x3, y3, ..."	3.2	1.0	1.0	2.0	2.1
154	`href="url"`	Specifies the URL of the document to which the hotspot points	3.2	1.0	1.0	2.0	2.1
154	`nohref="nohref"`	Specifies that the hotspot does not point to a link	3.2	1.0	1.0	2.0	2.1
154	`shape="rect|circle| polygon"`	Specifies the shape of the hotspot	3.2	1.0	1.0	2.0	2.1
84	`target="text"`	Specifies the target window or frame for the link	3.2	1.0*	1.0	2.0	2.1
32	`<b> </b>`	Marks text as bolded	2.0	1.0	1.0	1.0	2.1
76	`<base />`	Specifies global reference information for the document	2.0	1.0	1.0	1.0	2.1
76	`href="url"`	Specifies the URL from which all relative links in the document are based	2.0	1.0	1.0	1.0	2.1
85	`target="text"`	Specifies the target window or frame for links in the document	2.0	1.0*	1.0	1.0	2.1
	`<basefont />`	Specifies the font setting for the document text. **Deprecated**	3.2	1.0*	1.0	1.0	2.1
	`color="color"`	Specifies the text color. **Deprecated**	3.2	1.0*	1.0	1.0	2.1
	`face="text list"`	Specifies a list of fonts to be applied to the text. **Deprecated**	3.2	1.0*	1.0	1.0	2.1
	`size="integer"`	Specifies the size of the font range from 1 (smallest) to 7 (largest). **Deprecated**	3.2	1.0*	1.0	1.0	2.1
	`<bdo> </bdo>`	Indicates that the enclosed text should be rendered with the direction specified by the dir attribute	4.0	1.0	5.0	6.0	4.0
448	`<bgsound />`	Plays a background sound clip when the page is opened			2.0		2.1
448	`balance="integer"`	Specifies the balance of the volume between the left and right speakers where balance ranges from -10,000 to 10,000			4.0		
448	`loop="integer| infinite"`	Specifies the number of times the clip will be played (a positive integer or infinite)			2.0		2.1
448	`src="url"`	Specifies the URL of the sound clip file			2.0		2.1
448	`volume="integer"`	Specifies the volume of the sound clip, where the volume ranges from -10,000 to 0			4.0		

PAGE	ELEMENT/ATTRIBUTE	DESCRIPTION	HTML	XHTML	IE	NS	OP
32	`<big> </big>`	Increases the size of the enclosed text relative to the default font size	3.0	1.0	3.0	1.0	2.1
	`<blink> </blink>`	Blinks the enclosed text on and off			4.0	1.0	7.0
31	`<blockquote> </blockquote>`	Marks content as quoted from another source	2.0	1.0	1.0	1.0	2.1
19	`align="left|center|right"`	Specifies the horizontal alignment of the content			4.0	4.0	
	`cite="url"`	Provides the source URL of the quoted content	4.0	1.0		6.0	
141	`clear="none|left|right|all"`	Prevents content rendering until the specified margin is clear	3.0*		4.0		4.0
14	`<body> </body>`	Marks the page content to be rendered by the browser	2.0	1.0	1.0	1.0	2.1
389	`alink="color"`	Specifies the color of activated links in the document. **Deprecated**	3.2	1.0*	4.0	1.1	7.1
150	`background="url"`	Specifies the background image file used for the page. **Deprecated**	3.0	1.0*	1.0	1.1	2.1
116	`bgcolor="color"`	Specifies the background color of the page. **Deprecated**	3.2	1.0*	1.0	1.1	2.1
	`bgproperties="fixed"`	Fixes the background image in the browser window			2.0		
	`bottommargin="integer"`	Specifies the size of the bottom margin in pixels			2.0		7.0
	`leftmargin="integer"`	Specifies the size of the left margin in pixels			2.0	6.2	7.0
389	`link="color"`	Specifies the color of unvisited links. **Deprecated**	3.2	1.0*	1.0	1.1	2.1
	`marginheight="integer"`	Specifies the size of the margin above and below the page				4.0	4.0
	`marginwidth="integer"`	Specifies the size of the margin to the left and right of the page				4.0	4.0
	`nowrap="false|true"`	Specifies whether the content wraps using normal HTML line-wrapping conventions			4.0		
	`rightmargin="integer"`	Specifies the size of the right margin in pixels			4.0		
	`scroll="yes|no"`	Specifies whether to display a scrollbar			4.0		
116	`text="color"`	Specifies the color of page text. **Deprecated**	3.2	1.0*	1.0	1.1	2.1
	`topmargin="integer"`	Specifies the size of the top page margin in pixels			2.0	6.2	7.0
389	`vlink="color"`	Specifies the color of previously visited links. **Deprecated**	3.2	1.0*	1.0	1.1	2.1

PAGE	ELEMENT/ATTRIBUTE	DESCRIPTION	HTML	XHTML	IE	NS	OP
38	` `	Inserts a line break into the page	2.0	1.0	1.0	1.0	2.1
141	`clear="none|left|right|all"`	Displays the line break only when the specified margin is clear. **Deprecated**	3.2	1.0*	1.0	1.0	2.1
326	`<button> </button>`	Creates a form button	4.0	1.0	4.0	6.0	5.0
	`datafld="text"`	Specifies the column from a data source that supplies bound data for the button			4.0		
	`dataformatas="html|plaintext|text"`	Specifies the format of the data in the data source bound with the button			4.0		
	`datasrc="url"`	Specifies the URL or ID of the data source bound with the button			4.0		
326	`name="text"`	Provides the name assigned to the form button	4.0	1.0	4.0	6.0	5.0
326	`type="submit|reset|button"`	Specifies the type of form button	4.0	1.0	4.0	6.0	5.0
326	`value="text"`	Provides the value associated with the form button	4.0	1.0	4.0	6.0	5.0
185	`<caption> </caption>`	Creates a table caption	3.0	1.0	2.0	1.1	2.1
185	`align="bottom|center|left|right|top"`	Specifies the alignment of the caption. **Deprecated**	3.0	1.0*	2.0	1.1	2.1
	`valign="top|bottom"`	Specifies the vertical alignment of the caption			2.0		
31	`<center> </center>`	Centers content horizontally on the page. **Deprecated**	3.2	1.0*	1.0	1.0	2.1
32	`<cite> </cite>`	Marks citation text	2.0	1.0	1.0	1.0	2.1
32	`<code> </code>`	Marks text used for code samples	2.0	1.0	1.0	1.0	2.1
208	`<col> </col>`	Defines the settings for a column or group of columns	4.0	1.0	3.0	6.0	4.0
201	`align="left|right|center"`	Specifies the alignment of the content of the column(s)	4.0	1.0	4.0		7.0
116	`bgcolor="color"`	Specifies the background color of the column(s)			4.0		
201	`char="char"`	Specifies a character in the column used to align column values	4.0	1.0			
201	`charoff="integer"`	Specifies the offset in pixels from the alignment character specified in the char attribute	4.0	1.0			
208	`span="integer"`	Specifies the number of columns in the group	4.0	1.0	3.0	6.0	7.0
201	`valign="top|middle|bottom|baseline"`	Specifies the vertical alignment of the content in the column(s)	4.0	1.0	4.0		4.0
197	`width="integer"`	Specifies the width of the column(s) in pixels	4.0	1.0	3.0	6.0	7.0

PAGE	ELEMENT/ATTRIBUTE	DESCRIPTION	HTML	XHTML	IE	NS	OP
208	`<colgroup> </colgroup>`	Creates a container for a group of columns	4.0	1.0	3.0	6.0	4.0
201	`align="left|right center"`	Specifies the alignment of the content of the column group	4.0	1.0	4.0		7.0
116	`bgcolor="color"`	Specifies the background color of the column group			4.0		
201	`char="char"`	Specifies a character in the column used to align column group values	4.0	1.0			
201	`charoff="integer"`	Specifies the offset in pixels from the alignment character specified in the char attribute	4.0	1.0			
208	`span="integer"`	Specifies the number of columns in the group	4.0	1.0	3.0	6.0	7.0
201	`valign="top|middle |bottom|baseline"`	Specifies the vertical alignment of the content in the column group	4.0	1.0	4.0		4.0
197	`width="integer"`	Specifies the width of the columns in the group in pixels	4.0	1.0	3.0	6.0	7.0
28	`<dd> </dd>`	Marks text as a definition within a definition list	2.0	1.0	1.0	1.0	2.1
32	`<del> </del>`	Marks text as deleted from the document	3.0	1.0	4.0	6.0	4.0
	`cite="url"`	Provides the URL for the document that has additional information about the deleted text	3.0	1.0	4.0	6.1	4.0
	`datetime="date"`	Specifies the date and time of the text deletion	3.0	1.0	4.0	6.1	4.0
32	`<dfn> </dfn>`	Marks the defining instance of a term	3.0	1.0	1.0	6.0	2.1
31	`<dir> </dir>`	Contains a directory listing. **Deprecated**	2.0	1.0*	1.0	1.0	2.1
	`compact="compact"`	Permits use of compact rendering, if available. **Deprecated**	2.0	1.0*			
372	`<div> </div>`	Creates a generic block-level element	3.0	1.0	3.0	2.0	2.1
19	`align="left|center right|justify"`	Specifies the horizontal alignment of the content. **Deprecated**	3.0	1.0*	3.0	2.0	2.1
	`datafld="text"`	Indicates the column from a data source that supplies bound data for the block			4.0		
	`dataformatas="html |plaintext|text"`	Specifies the format of the data in the data source bound with the block			4.0		
	`datasrc="url"`	Provides the URL or ID of the data source bound with the block			4.0		
	`nowrap="nowrap"`	Specifies whether the content wraps using normal HTML line-wrapping conventions	3.0*		4.0		
28	`<dl> </dl>`	Encloses a definition list using the dd and dt elements	2.0	1.0	1.0	1.0	2.1
	`compact="compact"`	Permits use of compact rendering, if available. **Deprecated**	2.0	1.0*	4.0	1.0	
28	`<dt> </dt>`	Marks a definition term in a definition list	2.0	1.0	1.0	1.0	2.1
	`nowrap="nowrap"`	Specifies whether the content wraps using normal HTML line-wrapping conventions			4.0		

PAGE	ELEMENT/ATTRIBUTE	DESCRIPTION	HTML	XHTML	IE	NS	OP
32	`<em> </em>`	Marks emphasized text	2.0	1.0	1.0	1.0	2.1
446	`<embed> </embed>`	Places an embedded object into the page			3.0	1.0	3.0
140	`align="bottom|left` `|right|top"`	Specifies the alignment of the object with the surrounding content			3.0	1.0	3.5
446	`autostart="true` `|false"`	Starts the embedded object automatically when the page is loaded			3.0	1.0	3.0
446	`height="integer"`	Specifies the height of the object in pixels			3.0	1.0	3.0
	`hidden="true|false"`	Hides the object on the page			3.0	2.0	3.0
143	`hspace="integer"`	Specifies the horizontal space around the object in pixels				1.1	4.0
	`name="text"`	Provides the name of the embedded object			4.0	4.0	
	`pluginspage="url"`	Provides the URL of the page containing information on the object			3.0	2.0	3.5
	`pluginurl="url"`	Provides the URL of the page for directly installing the object				4.0	
	`src="url"`	Provides the location of the file containing the object			3.0	1.1	3.5
466	`type="mime-type"`	Specifies the mime-type of the embedded object			3.0	3.0	3.5
	`units="text"`	Specifies the measurement units of the object			4.0	3.0	
143	`vspace="integer"`	Specifies the vertical space around the object in pixels				1.1	4.0
446	`width="integer"`	Specifies the width of the object in pixels			3.0	1.1	3.0
315	`<fieldset> </fieldset>`	Places form fields in a common group	4.0	1.0	4.0	6.0	4.0
315	`align="left|center` `|right"`	Specifies the alignment of the contents of the field set			4.0		4.0
	`datafld="text"`	Indicates the column from a data source that supplies bound data for the field set			4.0		
	`dataformatas="html|` `plaintext|text"`	Specifies the format of the data in the data source bound with the field set			4.0		
	`datasrc="url"`	Provides the URL or ID of the data source bound with the field set			4.0		
116	`<font> </font>`	Formats the enclosed text. **Deprecated**	3.2	1.0*	2.0	1.0	2.1
116	`color="color"`	Specifies the color of the enclosed text. **Deprecated**	3.2	1.0*	2.0	2.0	2.1
119	`face="text list"`	Specifies the font face(s) of the enclosed text. **Deprecated**	3.2	1.0*	2.0	3.0	3.0
122	`size="integer"`	Specifies the size of the enclosed text with values ranging from 1 (smallest) to 7 (largest). A value of +*integer* increases the font size relative to the font size specified in the basefont element. **Deprecated**	3.2	1.0*	2.0	3.0	2.1

PAGE	ELEMENT/ATTRIBUTE	DESCRIPTION	HTML	XHTML	IE	NS	OP
295	`<form> </form>`	Encloses the contents of a Web form	2.0	1.0	1.0	1.0	2.1
466	`accept="mime-type list"`	Lists mime-types that the server processing the form will handle	4.0	1.0			
	`accept-charset= "char code"`	Specifies the character encoding that the server processing the form will handle	4.0	1.0			
330	`action="url"`	Provides the URL to which the form values are to be sent	2.0	1.0	1.0	1.0	2.1
	`autocomplete="on|off"`	Enables automatic insertion of information in fields in which the user has previously entered data			5.0		
330	`enctype="mime-type"`	Specifies the mime-type of the data to be sent to the server for processing; the default is "application/x-www-form-urlencoded"	2.0	1.0	1.0	1.0	2.1
330	`method="get|post"`	Specifies the method of accessing the URL specified in the action attribute	2.0	1.0	1.0	1.0	2.1
295	`name="text"`	Specifies the name of the form	2.0	1.0	1.0	1.0	2.1
84	`target="text"`	Specifies the frame or window in which output from the form should appear	4.0	1.0	3.0	2.0	2.1
251	`<frame> </frame>`	Marks a single frame within a set of frames	4.0	1.0*	3.0	2.0	2.1
270	`border="integer"`	Specifies the thickness of the frame border in pixels				4.0*	
270	`bordercolor="color"`	Specifies the color of the frame border			4.0	3.5	
270	`frameborder="1|0"`	Determines whether the frame border is visible (1) or invisible (0); Netscape also supports values of yes or no	4.0	1.0*	3.0	3.5	7.0
D3	`longdesc="url"`	Provides the URL of a document containing a long description of the frame's contents	4.0	1.0*			
255	`marginheight= "integer"`	Specifies the space above and below the frame object and the frame's borders, in pixels	4.0	1.0*	3.0	2.0	2.1
255	`marginwidth="integer"`	Specifies the space to the left and right of the frame object and the frame's borders, in pixels	4.0	1.0*	3.0	2.0	2.1
260	`name="text"`	Specifies the name of the frame	4.0	1.0*	3.0	2.0	2.1
255	`noresize="noresize"`	Prevents users from resizing the frame	4.0	1.0*	3.0	2.0	2.1
255	`scrolling="auto| yes|no"`	Specifies whether the browser will display a scrollbar with the frame	4.0	1.0*	3.0	2.0	2.1
251	`src="url"`	Provides the URL of the document to be displayed in the frame	4.0	1.0*	3.0	2.0	2.1

PAGE	ELEMENT/ATTRIBUTE	DESCRIPTION	HTML	XHTML	IE	NS	OP
248	`<frameset> </frameset>`	Creates a collection of frames	4.0	1.0*	3.0	2.0	2.1
270	`border="integer"`	Specifies the thickness of the frame borders in the frameset in pixels			4.0	3.0	2.1
270	`bordercolor="color"`	Specifies the color of the frame borders			4.0	3.0	
249	`cols="value list"`	Arranges the frames in columns with the width of each column expressed either in pixels, as a percentage, or using an asterisk (to allow the browser to choose the width)	4.0	1.0*	3.0	2.0	2.1
270	`frameborder="1|0"`	Determines whether frame borders are visible (1) or invisible (0); Netscape also supports values of yes or no			3.0	3.5	
	`framespacing="integer"`	Specifies the amount of space between frames in pixels			3.1		
249	`rows="value list"`	Arranges the frames in rows with the height of each column expressed either in pixels, as a percentage, or using an asterisk (to allow the browser to choose the height)	4.0	1.0*	3.0	2.0	2.1
17	`<hi> </hi>`	Marks the enclosed text as a heading, where i is an integer from 1 (the largest heading) to 6 (the smallest heading)	2.0	1.0	1.0	1.0	2.1
19	`align="left|center|right|justify"`	Specifies the alignment of the heading text. **Deprecated**	3.0	1.0*	1.0	1.0	2.1
14	`<head> </head>`	Encloses the document head, containing information about the document	2.0	1.0	1.0	1.0	2.1
	`profile="url"`	Provides the location of metadata about the documenta	4.0	1.0			
36	`<hr />`	Draws a horizontal line (rule) in the rendered page	2.0	1.0	1.0	1.0	2.1
37	`align="left|center|right"`	Specifies the horizontal alignment of the line. **Deprecated**	3.2	1.0*	1.0	1.0	2.1
37	`color="color"`	Specifies the color of the line			3.0		
	`noshade="noshade"`	Removes 3-D shading from the line. **Deprecated**	3.2	1.0*	1.0	1.0	2.1
37	`size="integer"`	Specifies the height of the line in pixels or as a percentage of the enclosing element's height. **Deprecated**	3.2	1.0*	1.0	1.0	2.1
37	`width="integer"`	Specifies the width of the line in pixels or as a percentage of the enclosing element's width. **Deprecated**	3.2	1.0*	1.0	1.0	2.1

PAGE	ELEMENT/ATTRIBUTE	DESCRIPTION	HTML	XHTML	IE	NS	OP
14	`<html> </html>`	Encloses the entire content of the HTML document	2.0	1.0	1.0	1.0	2.1
	`version="text"`	Specifies the version of HTML being used	2.0	1.1			
499	`xmlns="text"`	Specifies the namespace prefix for the document		1.0	5.0		
32	`<i> </i>`	Displays the enclosed text in italics	2.0	1.0	1.0	1.0	2.1
273	`<iframe> </iframe>`	Creates an inline frame in the document	4.0	1.0*	3.0	6.0	4.0
273	`align="bottom|left` `|middle|top` `|right"`	Specifies the horizontal alignment of the frame with the surrounding content. **Deprecated**	4.0	1.0*	3.0	6.0	6.0
	`datafld="text"`	Indicates the column from a data source that supplies bound data for the inline frame			4.0		
	`dataformatas="html|` `plaintext|text"`	Specifies the format of the data in the data source bound with the inline frame			4.0		
	`datasrc="url"`	Provides the URL or ID of the data source bound with the inline frame			4.0		
273	`frameborder="1|0"`	Specifies whether to display a frame border (1) or not (0)	4.0	1.0*	3.0	6.0	4.0
273	`height="integer"`	Specifies the height of the frame in pixels	4.0	1.0*	3.0	6.0	4.0
273	`hspace="integer"`	Specifies the space to the left and right of the frame in pixels	4.0	1.0*	3.0	6.0	4.0
D3	`longdesc="url"`	Indicates the document containing a long description of the frame's content	4.0	1.0*			
273	`marginheight=` `"integer"`	Specifies the space above and below the frame object and the frame's borders, in pixels	4.0	1.0*	3.0	6.0	4.0
273	`marginwidth="integer"`	Specifies the space to the left and right of the frame object and the frame's borders, in pixels	4.0	1.0*	3.0	6.0	4.0
273	`name="text"`	Specifies the name of the frame	4.0	1.0*	3.0	6.0	4.0
273	`scrolling="auto|` `yes|no"`	Determines whether the browser displays a scrollbar with the frame	4.0	1.0*	3.0	6.0	4.0
273	`src="url"`	Indicates the document displayed within the frame	4.0	1.0*	3.0	6.0	4.0
273	`vspace="integer"`	Specifies the space to the top and bottom of the frame in pixels	4.0	1.0*	3.0	6.0	4.0
273	`width="integer"`	Specifies the width of the frame in pixels	4.0	1.0*	3.0	6.0	4.0
	`<ilayer> </ilayer>`	Creates an inline layer used to display the content of external document				4.0*	
	`above="text"`	Specifies the name of the layer displayed above the current layer				4.0*	
	`background="url"`	Provides the URL of the file containing the background image				4.0*	
	`below="text"`	Specifies the name of the layer displayed below the current layer				4.0*	

PAGE	ELEMENT/ATTRIBUTE	DESCRIPTION	HTML	XHTML	IE	NS	OP
	bgcolor="color"	Specifies the layer's background color				4.0*	
	clip="top, left, bottom, right"	Specifies the coordinates of the viewable region of the layer				4.0*	
	height="integer"	Specifies the height of the layer in pixels				4.0*	
	left="integer"	Specifies the horizontal offset of the layer in pixels				4.0*	
	pagex="integer"	Specifies the horizontal position of the layer in pixels				4.0*	
	pagey="integer"	Specifies the vertical position of the layer in pixels				4.0*	
	src="url"	Provides the URL of the document displayed in the layer				4.0*	
	top="integer"	Specifies the vertical offset of the layer in pixels				4.0*	
	visibility="hide|inherit|show"	Specifies the visibility of the layer				4.0*	
	width="integer"	Specifies the width of the layer in pixels				4.0*	
	z-index="integer"	Specifies the stacking order of the layer				4.0*	
35	<img> </img>	Inserts an inline image into the document	2.0	1.0	1.0	1.0	2.1
140	align="left|right|top|texttop|middle|absmiddle|baselines|bottom|absbottom"	Specifies the alignment of the image with the surrounding content. **Deprecated**	2.0	1.0*	1.0	1.0	2.1
35	alt="text"	Specifies alternate text to be displayed in place of the image	2.0	1.0	1.0	1.0	2.1
159	border="integer"	Specifies the width of the image border. **Deprecated**	3.2	1.0*	1.0	1.0	2.1
455	controls="control"	For video images, displays a playback control below the image			2.0		
	datafld="text"	Names the column from a data source that supplies bound data for the image			4.0		
	dataformatas="html|plaintext|text"	Specifies the format of the data in the data source bound with the image			4.0		
	datasrc="url"	Provides the URL or ID of the data source bound with the image			4.0		

PAGE	ELEMENT/ATTRIBUTE	DESCRIPTION	HTML	XHTML	IE	NS	OP
455	dynsrc="*url*"	Provides the URL of a video or VRML file			2.0		2.1
144	height="*integer*"	Specifies the height of the image in pixels	3.0	1.0	1.0	1.0	2.1
143	hspace="*integer*"	Specifies the horizontal space around the image in pixels. **Deprecated**	3.0	1.0*	1.0	1.0	2.1
	ismap="ismap"	Indicates that the image can be used as a server-side image map	2.0	1.0	1.0	1.0	2.1
D3	longdesc="*url*"	Provides the URL of a document containing a long description of the image	4.0	1.0		6.1	
455	loop="*integer*"	Specifies the number of times the video will play			2.0		2.1
	lowsrc="*url*"	Provides the URL of the low-resolution version of the image			4.1	1.0	
	name="*text*"	Specifies the image name	4.0	1.0*	4.0	3.0	3.0
35	src="*url*"	Specifies the image source file	2.0	1.0	1.0	1.0	2.1
455	start="fileopen| mouseover"	Indicates when to start the video clip (either when the file is opened or when the mouse hovers over the image)			2.0		2.1
	suppress="true| **false**"	Suppresses the display of the alternate text and the placeholder icon until the image file is located				4.0*	
157	usemap="*url*"	Provides the location of a client-side image associated with the image (not well-supported when the URL points to an external file)	3.2	1.0	1.0	2.0	2.1
143	vspace="*integer*"	Specifies the vertical space around the image in pixels. **Deprecated**	3.2	1.0*	1.0	1.0	2.1
144	width="*integer*"	Specifies the width of the image in pixels	3.0	1.0	1.0	1.0	2.1
296	**<input> </input>**	Marks an input field in a Web form	2.0	1.0	1.0	1.0	2.1
140	align="left|right| top|texttop| middle|absmiddle| baseline|bottom| absbottom"	Specifies the alignment of the input field with the surrounding content. **Deprecated**	2.0	1.0*	1.0	1.0	2.1
35	alt="*text*"	Specifies alternate text for image buttons and image input fields	4.0	1.0	4.0	4.0	4.0
313	checked="checked"	Specifies that the input check box or input radio button is selected	2.0	1.0	1.0	1.0	2.1
	datafld="*text*"	Indicates the column from a data source that supplies bound data for the input field	4.0		4.0		
	dataformatas="html| plaintext|text"	Specifies the format of the data in the data source bound with the input field	4.0		4.0		
	datasrc="*url*"	Provides the URL or ID of the data source bound with the input field	4.0		4.0		

PAGE	ELEMENT/ATTRIBUTE	DESCRIPTION	HTML	XHTML	IE	NS	OP
328	height="*integer*"	Specifies the height of the image input field in pixels			4.0	1.0	4.0
328	hspace="*integer*"	Specifies the horizontal space around the image input field in pixels			5.0	4.0	4.0
328	ismap="ismap"	Enables the image input field to be used as a server-side image map	4.0	1.1		6.0	
302	maxlength="*integer*"	Specifies the maximum number of characters that can be inserted into a text input field	2.0	1.0	1.0	1.0	2.1
313	name="*text*"	Specifies the name of the input field	2.0	1.0	1.0	1.0	2.1
	readonly="readonly"	Prevents the value of the input field from being modified	2.0	1.0	1.0	1.0	2.1
300	size="*integer*"	Specifies the number of characters that can be displayed at one time in an input text field	2.0	1.0	1.0	1.0	2.1
328	src="*url*"	Indicates the source file of an input image field	2.0	1.0	1.0	1.0	2.1
296	type="button| checkbox|file| hidden|image| password|radio| reset|submit| **text**"	Specifies the type of input field	2.0	1.0	1.0	1.0	2.1
328	usemap="*url*"	Provides the location of a client-side image associated with the image input field (not well-supported when the URL points to an external file)	4.0	1.0	2.0	2.0	2.1
302	value="*text*"	Specifies the default value of the input field	2.0	1.0	2.0	2.0	2.1
143	vspace="*integer*"	Specifies the vertical space around the image input field in pixels			5.0	4.0	4.0
328	width="*integer*"	Specifies the width of an image input field in pixels			4.0	1.0	4.0
32	**<ins> </ins>**	Marks inserted text	3.0	1.0	4.0	6.0	4.0
	cite="*url*"	Provides the URL for the document that has additional information about the inserted text	3.0	1.0	4.0	6.1	4.0
	datetime="*date*"	Specifies the date and time of the text insertion	3.0	1.0	4.0	6.1	4.0
	<isindex />	Inserts an input field into the document for search queries. **Deprecated**	2.0	1.0*	1.0	1.0	2.1
	action="*url*"	Provides the URL of the script used to process the sindex data			1.0	4.0*	2.1
	prompt="*text*"	Specifies the text to be used for the input prompt. **Deprecated**	3.0	1.0*	1.0	1.0	2.1

PAGE	ELEMENT/ATTRIBUTE	DESCRIPTION	HTML	XHTML	IE	NS	OP
32	**\<kbd> \</kbd>**	Marks keyboard-style text	2.0	1.0	1.0	1.0	3.5
303	**\<label> \</label>**	Associates the enclosed content with a form field	4.0	1.0	4.0	6.0	4.0
	datafld="text"	Indicates the column from a data source that supplies bound data for the label			4.0		
	dataformatas="html|plaintext|text"	Specifies the format of the data in the data source bound with the label			4.0		
	datasrc="url"	Provides the URL or ID of the data source bound with the label			4.0		
304	for="text"	Provides the ID of the field associated with the label	4.0	1.0	4.0	6.0	7.0
	\<layer> \</layer>	Creates a layer used to display the content of external documents; unlike the ilayer element, layer elements are absolutely positioned in the page				4.0*	
	above="text"	Specifies the name of the layer displayed above the current layer				4.0*	
	background="url"	Provides the URL of the file containing the background image				4.0*	
	below="text"	Specifies the name of the layer displayed below the current layer				4.0*	
	bgcolor="color"	Specifies the layer's background color				4.0*	
	clip="top, left, bottom, right"	Specifies the coordinates of the viewable region of the layer				4.0*	
	height="integer"	Specifies the height of the layer in pixels				4.0*	
	left="integer"	Specifies the horizontal offset of the layer in pixels				4.0*	
	pagex="integer"	Specifies the horizontal position of the layer in pixels				4.0*	
	pagey="integer"	Specifies the vertical position of the layer in pixels				4.0*	
	src="url"	Provides the URL of the document displayed in the layer				4.0*	
	top="integer"	Specifies the vertical offset of the layer in pixels				4.0*	
	visibility="hide|inherit|show"	Specifies the visibility of the layer				4.0*	
	width="integer"	Specifies the width of the layer in pixels				4.0*	
	z-index="integer"	Specifies the stacking order of the layer				4.0*	

PAGE	ELEMENT/ATTRIBUTE	DESCRIPTION	HTML	XHTML	IE	NS	OP
316	`<legend> </legend>`	Marks the enclosed text as a caption for a field set	4.0	1.0	4.0	6.0	7.0
316	`align="bottom|left |top|right"`	Specifies the alignment of the legend with the field set; Internet Explorer also supports the center option. **Deprecated**	4.0	1.0*	4.0	6.0	
24	`<li> </li>`	Marks an item in an ordered (ol), unordered (ul), menu (menu), or directory (dir) list.	2.0	1.0	1.0	1.0	2.1
28	`type="A|a|I|i |1|disc|square |circle"`	Specifies the bullet type associated with the list item: a value of "1" is the default for ordered list; a value of "disc" is the default for unordered list. **Deprecated**	3.2	1.0*	1.0	1.0	2.1
	`value="integer"`	Sets the value for the current list item in an ordered list; subsequent list items are numbered from that value. **Deprecated**	3.2	1.0*	1.0	1.0	2.1
88	`<link />`	Creates an element in the document head that establishes the relationship between the current document and external documents or objects	2.0	1.0	3.0	4.0	3.5
88	`charset="char code"`	Specifies the character encoding of the external document	4.0	1.0			7.0
88	`href="url"`	Provides the URL of the external document	2.0	1.0	3.0	4.0	3.5
	`hreflang="text"`	Indicates the language of the external document	4.0	1.0			
355	`media="all|aural| braille|handheld| print|projection| screen|tty|tv"`	Indicates the media in which the external document is presented	4.0	1.0	4.0	4.0	3.5
88	`name="text"`	Specifies the name of the link			4.0		
88	`rel="text"`	Specifies the relationship between the current page and the link specified by the href attribute	2.0	1.0	3.0	4.0	3.5
88	`rev="text"`	Specifies the reverse relationship between the current page and the link specified by the href attribute	2.0	1.0	3.0	4.0	3.5
88	`target="text"`	Specifies the target window or frame for the link	4.0	1.0*	4.0	7.0	
88	`title="text"`	Specifies the title of the external document	2.0	1.0		6.0	7.0
88	`type="mime-type"`	Specifies the mime-type of the external document	4.0	1.0	3.0	4.0	3.5
152	`<map> </map>`	Creates an element that contains client-side image map hotspots	3.2	1.0	1.0	2.0	2.1
152	`name="text"`	Specifies the name of the image map	3.2	1.0*	1.0	2.0	2.1

PAGE	ELEMENT/ATTRIBUTE	DESCRIPTION	HTML	XHTML	IE	NS	OP
463	`<marquee> </marquee>`	Displays the enclosed text as a scrolling marquee			2.0	7.0	7.2
463	`behavior="alternate `|`scroll`|`slide"`	Specifies how the marquee should move			2.0	7.0	7.2
	`bgcolor="color"`	Specifies the background color of the marquee			2.0		7.2
	`datafld="text"`	Indicates the column from a data source that supplies bound data for the marquee			4.0		
	`dataformatas="html`|`plaintext`|`text"`	Indicates the format of the data in the data source bound with the marquee			4.0		
	`datasrc="url"`	Provides the URL or ID of the data source bound with the marquee			4.0		
463	`direction="down`|`left`|`right`|`up"`	Specifies the direction of the marquee			2.0	7.0	7.2
463	`height="integer"`	Specifies the height of the marquee in pixels			2.0	7.0	7.2
143	`hspace="integer"`	Specifies the horizontal space around the marquee in pixels			2.0		
463	`loop="integer`|`infinite"`	Specifies the number of times the marquee motion is repeated			2.0		7.2
463	`scrollamount="integer"`	Specifies the amount of space, in pixels, between successive draws of the marquee text			2.0	7.0	7.2
	`scrolldelay="integer"`	Specifies the amount of time, in milliseconds, between marquee actions			2.0	7.0	7.2
463	`truespeed="truespeed"`	Indicates whether the scrolldelay value should be set to its exact value; otherwise any value less than 60 milliseconds is rounded up			4.0		
143	`vspace="integer"`	Specifies the vertical space around the marquee in pixels			2.0		
463	`width="integer"`	Specifies the width of the marquee in pixels			2.0	7.0	7.2
31	`<menu> </menu>`	Contains a menu list. **Deprecated**	2.0	1.0*	1.0	1.0	2.1
	`compact="compact"`	Reduces the space between menu items. **Deprecated**	2.0	1.0*			
	`start="integer"`	Specifies the starting value of the items in the menu list			6.0	4.0	
28	`type="A`|`a`|`I`|`i`|`1`|`disc`|`square`|`circle`|`none"`	Specifies the bullet type associated with the list items	3.2	1.0*	1.0	1.0	2.1

PAGE	ELEMENT/ATTRIBUTE	DESCRIPTION	HTML	XHTML	IE	NS	OP
38	`<meta> </meta>`	Creates an element in the document's head section that contains information and special instructions for processing the document	2.0	1.0	2.0	1.0	3.0
38	`content="text"`	Provides information associated with the name or http-equiv attributes	2.0	1.0	2.0	1.0	3.0
38	`http-equiv="text"`	Provides instructions to the browser to request the server to perform different http operations	2.0	1.0	2.0	1.0	3.0
38	`name="text"`	Specifies the type of information specified in the content attribute	2.0	1.0	2.0	1.0	3.0
	`scheme="text"`	Supplies additional information about the scheme used to interpret the content attribute	4.0	1.0			
	`<nobr> </nobr>`	Disables line wrapping for the enclosed content			1.0	1.0	2.1
456	`<noembed> </noembed>`	Encloses alternate content for browsers that do not support the embed element			3.0	2.0	3.0
267	`<noframes> </noframes>`	Encloses alternate content for browsers that do not support frames	4.0	1.0*	3.0	2.0	2.1
	`<nolayer> </nolayer>`	Encloses alternate content for browsers that do not support the layer or ilayer elements				4.0*	
527	`<noscript> </noscript>`	Encloses alternate content for browsers that do not support client-side scripts	4.0	1.0	3.0	3.0	3.0
465	`<object> </object>`	Places an embedded object (image, applet, sound clip, video clip, etc.) into the page	4.0	1.0	3.0	6.0	4.0
466	`archive="url"`	Specifies the URL of an archive containing classes and other resources preloaded for use with the object	4.0	1.0		6.0	
140	`align="absbottom|absmiddle|baseline|bottom|left|middle|right|texttop|top"`	Aligns the object with the surrounding content. **Deprecated**	4.0	1.0*	3.0	6.0	
	`border="integer"`	Specifies the width of the border around the object. **Deprecated**	4.0	1.0*	6.0	6.0	7.0
466	`classid="url"`	Provides the URL of the object	4.0	1.0	3.0	6.0	4.0
466	`codebase="url"`	Specifies the base path used to resolve relative references within the embedded object	4.0	1.0	3.0	6.0	4.0
466	`codetype="mime-type"`	Indicates the mime-type of the embedded objects' code	4.0	1.0	3.0	6.0	4.0

PAGE	ELEMENT/ATTRIBUTE	DESCRIPTION	HTML	XHTML	IE	NS	OP
466	`data="url"`	Provides the URL of the object's data file	4.0	1.0	3.0	6.0	4.0
	`datafld="text"`	Identifies the column from a data source that supplies bound data for the embedded object	4.0				
	`dataformatas="html|plaintext|text"`	Specifies the format of the data in the data source bound with the embedded object	4.0				
	`datasrc="url"`	Provides the URL or ID of the data source bound with the embedded object	4.0				
466	`declare="declare"`	Declares the object without embedding it on the page	4.0	1.0			
144	`height="integer"`	Specifies the height of the object in pixels	4.0	1.0	3.0	6.0	4.0
143	`hspace="integer"`	Specifies the horizontal space around the image in pixels	4.0	1.0	3.0	6.0	4.0
	`name="text"`	Specifies the name of the embedded object	4.0	1.0	3.0	6.0	4.0
466	`standby="text"`	Specifies the message displayed by the browser while loading the embedded object	4.0	1.0			7.0
466	`type="mime-type"`	Indicates the mime-type of the embedded object	4.0	1.0	3.0	6.0	4.0
143	`vspace="integer"`	Specifies the vertical space around the embedded object	4.0	1.0	3.0	6.0	4.0
144	`width="integer"`	Specifies the width of the object in pixels	4.0	1.0	3.0	6.0	4.0
24	`<ol> </ol>`	Contains an ordered list of items	2.0	1.0	1.0	1.0	2.1
	`compact="compact"`	Reduces the space between ordered list items. **Deprecated**	2.0	1.0*			
	`start="integer"`	Specifies the starting value in the list. **Deprecated**	3.2	1.0*	1.0	1.0	2.1
28	`type="A|a|I|i|1"`	Specifies the bullet type associated with the list items. **Deprecated**	3.2	1.0*	1.0	1.0	2.1
311	`<optgroup> </optgroup>`	Contains a group of option elements in a selection field	4.0	1.0	6.0	6.0	7.0
311	`label="text"`	Specifies the label for the option group	4.0	1.0	6.0	6.0	7.0
306	`<option> </option>`	Formats an option within a selection field	2.0	1.0	1.0	1.0	2.1
	`label="text"`	Supplies the text label associated with the option	4.0	1.0			
310	`selected="selected"`	Selects the option by default	2.0	1.0	1.0	1.0	2.1
310	`value="text"`	Specifies the value associated with the option	2.0	1.0	1.0	1.0	2.1
21	`<p> </p>`	Marks the enclosed content as a paragraph	2.0	1.0	1.0	1.0	2.1
19	`align="left|center|right|justify"`	Horizontally aligns the contents of the paragraph. **Deprecated**	3.0	1.0*	1.0	1.0	2.1

PAGE	ELEMENT/ATTRIBUTE	DESCRIPTION	HTML	XHTML	IE	NS	OP
459	`<param> </param>`	Marks parameter values sent to an object element or an applet element	3.2	1.0	3.0	2.0	3.5
459	`name="text"`	Specifies the parameter name	3.2	1.0	3.0	2.0	3.5
466	`type="mime-type"`	Specifies the mime-type of the resource indicated by the value attribute	4.0	1.0	6.0		6.0
459	`value="text"`	Specifies the parameter value	3.2	1.0	3.0	2.0	3.5
	`valuetype="data|ref|object"`	Specifies the data type of the value attribute	4.0	1.0	6.0		6.0
	`<plaintext> </plaintext>`	Marks the enclosed text as plain text		1.0	1.0	1.0	2.1
172	`<pre> </pre>`	Marks the enclosed text as preformatted text, retaining white space from the document	2.0	1.0	1.0	1.0	2.1
	`width="integer"`	Specifies the width of preformatted text, in number of characters. **Deprecated**	2.0	1.0*		6.0	
32	`<q> </q>`	Marks the enclosed text as a quotation	3.0	1.0	4.0	6.0	4.0
	`cite="url"`	Provides the source URL of the quoted content	4.0	1.0		6.0	
32	`<s> </s>`	Marks the enclosed text as strikethrough text. **Deprecated**	3.0	1.0*	1.0	3.0	2.1
32	`<samp> </samp>`	Marks the enclosed text as a sequence of literal characters	2.0	1.0	1.0	1.0	2.1
525	`<script> </script>`	Encloses client-side scripts within the document; this element can be placed within the head or the body element or refer to an external script file	3.2	1.0	3.0	2.0	3.0
	`charset="char code"`	Specifies the character encoding of the script	4.0	1.0	3.0	7.0	7.0
	`defer="defer"`	Defers execution of the script	4.0	1.0	4.0		
	`event="text"`	Specifies the event that the script should be run in response to	4.0		4.0		
	`for="text"`	Indicates the name or ID of the element to which the event attribute refers to	4.0		4.0		
526	`language="text"`	Specifies the language of the script. **Deprecated**	4.0	1.0*	3.0	2.0	3.0
525	`src="url"`	Provides the URL of an external script file	4.0	1.0	3.0	3.0	3.0
525	`type="mime-type"`	Specifies the mime-type of the script	4.0	1.0	4.0	4.0	
306	`<select> </select>`	Creates a selection field (drop-down list box) in a Web form	2.0	1.0	1.0	1.0	2.1
140	`align="left|right|top|texttop|middle|absmiddle|baseline|bottom|absbottom"`	Specifies the alignment of the selection field with the surrounding content. **Deprecated**	3.0*		4.0		

PAGE	ELEMENT/ATTRIBUTE	DESCRIPTION	HTML	XHTML	IE	NS	OP
	datafld="*text*"	Identifies the column from a data source that supplies bound data for the selection field	4.0		4.0		
	dataformatas="html| plaintext|text"	Specifies the format of the data in the data source bound with the selection field	4.0		4.0		
	datasrc="*url*"	Provides the URL or ID of the data source bound with the selection field	4.0		4.0		
309	multiple="multiple"	Allows multiple sections from the field	2.0	1.0	1.0	1.0	2.1
303	name="*text*"	Specifies the selection field name	2.0	1.0	1.0	1.0	2.1
309	size="*integer*"	Specifies the number of visible items in the selection list	2.0	1.0	1.0	1.0	2.1
32	**<small> </small>**	Decreases the size of the enclosed text relative to the default font size	3.0	1.0	3.0	1.0	2.1
130	**<span> </span>**	Creates a generic inline elment	3.0	1.0	3.0	2.0	2.1
	datafld="*text*"	Identifies the column from a data source that supplies bound data for the inline element			4.0		
	dataformatas="html| plaintext|text"	Specifies the format of the data in the data source bound with the inline element			4.0		
	datasrc="*url*"	Provides the URL or ID of the data source bound with the inline element			4.0		
32	**<strike> </strike>**	Marks the enclosed text as strikethrough text. **Deprecated**	3.0	1.0*	1.0	3.5	2.1
32	**<strong> </strong>**	Marks the enclosed text as strongly emphasized text	2.0	1.0	1.0	1.0	2.1
351	**<style> </style>**	Encloses global style declarations for the document	3.0	1.0	3.0	4.0	3.5
351	media="all|aural| braille|handheld| print|projection| screen|tty|tv|"	Indicates the media of the enclosed style definitions	4.0	1.0	4.0	4.0	3.5
351	title="*text*"	Specifies the style of the style definitions	4.0	1.0			
351	*type*="*mime-type*"	Specifies the mime-type of the style definitions	4.0	1.0	3.0	4.0	
32	**<sub> </sub>**	Marks the enclosed text as subscripted text	3.0	1.0	3.0	1.1	2.1
32	**<sup> </sup>**	Marks the enclosed text as superscripted text	3.0	1.0	3.0	1.1	2.1

PAGE	ELEMENT/ATTRIBUTE	DESCRIPTION	HTML	XHTML	IE	NS	OP
179	`<table> </table>`	Encloses the contents of a Web table	3.0	1.0	2.0	1.1	2.1
207	`align="left|center |right"`	Aligns the table with the surrounding content. **Deprecated**	3.0	1.0*	2.0	2.0	2.1
206	`background="url"`	Provides the URL of the table's background image			3.0	4.0	5.0
116	`bgcolor="color"`	Specifies the background color of the table. **Deprecated**	4.0	1.0*	2.0	3.0	2.1
188	`border="integer"`	Specifies the width of the table border in pixels	3.0	1.0	2.0	1.1	2.1
189	`bordercolor="color"`	Specifies the table border color			2.0	4.0	
189	`bordercolordark= "color"`	Specifies the color of the table border's shaded edge			2.0		
189	`bordercolorlight= "color"`	Specifies the color of the table border's unshaded edge			2.0		
194	`cellpadding= "integer"`	Specifies the space between the table data and the cell borders in pixels	3.2	1.0	2.0	1.1	2.1
193	`cellspacing= "integer"`	Specifies the space between table cells in pixels	3.2	1.0	2.0	1.1	2.1
	`cols="integer"`	Specifies the number of columns in the table			3.0	4.0	
	`datafld="text"`	Indicates the column from a data source that supplies bound data for the table	4.0		4.0		
	`dataformatas="html| plaintext|text"`	Specifies the format of the data in the data source bound with the table	4.0		4.0		
	`datapagesize= "integer"`	Sets the number of records displayed within the table	4.0	1.1	4.0		
	`datasrc="url"`	Provides the URL or ID of the data source bound with the table	4.0		4.0		
191	`frame="above|below |border|box| hsides|lhs|rhs| void|vside"`	Specifies the format of the borders around the table	4.0	1.0	3.0	6.0	7.1
195	`height="integer"`	Specifies the height of the table in pixels			2.0	1.1	2.1
143	`hspace="integer"`	Specifies the horizontal space around the table in pixels				2.0	
192	`rules="all|cols| groups|none|rows"`	Specifies the format of the table's internal borders or gridlines	4.0	1.0	3.0	7.0	7.1
187	`summary="text"`	Supplies a text summary of the table's content	4.0	1.0		6.1	
143	`vspace="integer"`	Specifies the vertical space around the table in pixels				2.0	
195	`width="integer"`	Specifies the width of the table in pixels	3.0	1.0	2.0	1.1	2.1

PAGE	ELEMENT/ATTRIBUTE	DESCRIPTION	HTML	XHTML	IE	NS	OP
184	**<tbody> </tbody>**	Encloses the content of the Web table body	4.0	1.0	3.0	6.0	4.0
201	align="left|center |right|justify |char"	Specifies the alignment of the contents in the cells of the table body	4.0	1.0	4.0	6.0	4.0
116	bgcolor="*color*"	Specifies the background color of the table body			4.0	6.0	
201	char="*char*"	Specifies the character used for aligning the table body contents when the align attribute is set to "char"	4.0	1.0			
201	charoff="*integer*"	Specifies the offset in pixels from the alignment character specified in the char attribute	4.0	1.0			
201	valign="baseline| bottom|middle|top"	Specifies the vertical alignment of the contents in the cells of the table body	4.0	1.0	4.0	6.0	4.0
179	**<td> </td>**	Encloses the data of a table cell	3.0	1.0	2.0	1.1	2.1
	abbr="*text*"	Supplies an abbreviated version of the contents of the table cell	4.0	1.0			
201	align="**left**|center |right"	Specifies the horizontal alignment of the table cell data	3.0	1.0	2.0	1.1	2.1
206	background="*url*"	Provides the URL of the background image file			3.0	4.0	4.0
116	bgcolor="*color*"	Specifies the background color of the table cell. **Deprecated**	4.0	1.0*	2.0	3.0	2.1
189	bordercolor="*color*"	Specifies the color of the table cell border			2.0		
189	bordercolordark= "*color*"	Specifies the color of the table cell border's shaded edge			2.0		
189	bordercolorlight= "*color*"	Specifies the color of the table cell border's unshaded edge			2.0		
201	char="*char*"	Specifies the character used for aligning the table cell contents when the align attribute is set to "char"	4.0	1.0			
201	charoff="*integer*"	Specifies the offset in pixels from the alignment character specified in the char attribute	4.0	1.0			
108	colspan="*integer*"	Specifies the number of columns the table cell spans	3.0	1.0	2.0	1.1	2.1
D8	headers="*text*"	Supplies a space-separated list of table headers associated with the table cell	4.0	1.0			
197	height="*integer*"	Specifies the height of the table cell in pixels. **Deprecated**	3.2	1.0*	2.0	1.1	2.1
	nowrap="nowrap"	Disables line-wrapping within the table cell. **Deprecated**	3.0	1.0*	2.0	1.1	2.1
198	rowspan="*integer*"	Specifies the number of rows the table cell spans	3.0	1.0	2.0	1.1	2.1
D8	scope="col|colgroup |row|rowgroup"	Specifies the scope of the table for which the cell provides data	4.0	1.0			
201	valign="top|**middle** |bottom"	Specifies the vertical alignment of the contents of the table cell	3.0	1.0	2.0	1.1	2.1
197	width="*integer*"	Specifies the width of the cell in pixels. **Deprecated**	3.2	1.0*	2.0	1.1	2.1

PAGE	ELEMENT/ATTRIBUTE	DESCRIPTION	HTML	XHTML	IE	NS	OP
320	`<textarea> </textarea>`	Marks the enclosed text as a text area input box in a Web form	2.0	1.0	1.0	1.0	2.1
	`datafld="text"`	Specifies the column from a data source that supplies bound data for the text area box	4.0		4.0		
	`dataformatas="html|plaintext|text"`	Specifies the format of the data in the data source bound with the text area box	4.0		4.0		
	`datasrc="url"`	Provides the URL or ID of the data source bound with the text area box	4.0		4.0		
320	`cols="integer"`	Specifies the width of the text area box in characters	2.0	1.0	1.0	1.0	2.1
320	`name="text"`	Specifies the name of the text area box	2.0	1.0	1.0	1.0	2.1
	`readonly="readonly"`	Specifies the value of the text area box cannot be modified	4.0	1.0	4.0	6.0	5.0
320	`rows="integer"`	Specifies the number of visible rows in the text area box	2.0	1.0	1.0	1.0	2.1
321	`wrap="off|soft|hard"`	Specifies how text is wrapped within the text area box and how that text-wrapping information is sent to the server-side program; in earlier versions of Netscape Navigator, the default value is "off" (Netscape also accepts the values "off", "virtual", and "physical".)			4.0	4.0*	
184	`<tfoot> </tfoot>`	Encloses the content of the Web table footer	4.0	1.0	3.0	6.0	4.0
201	`align="left|center|right|justify|char"`	Specifies the alignment of the contents in the cells of the table footer	4.0	1.0	4.0	6.0	4.0
116	`bgcolor="color"`	Specifies the background color the table body			4.0	6.0	
201	`char="char"`	Specifies the character used for aligning the table footer contents when the align attribute is set to "char"	4.0	1.0			
201	`charoff="integer"`	Specifies the offset in pixels from the alignment character specified in the char attribute	4.0	1.0			
201	`valign="baseline|bottom|middle|top"`	Specifies the vertical alignment of the contents in the cells of the table footer	4.0	1.0	4.0	6.0	4.0
182	`<th> </th>`	Encloses the data of a table header cell	3.0	1.0	2.0	1.1	2.1
	`abbr="text"`	Supplies an abbreviated version of the contents of the table cell	4.0	1.0			
201	`align="left|center|right"`	Specifies the horizontal alignment of the table cell data	3.0	1.0	2.0	1.1	2.1
206	`axis="text list"`	Provides a list of table categories that can be mapped to a table hierarchy	3.0	1.0			

PAGE	ELEMENT/ATTRIBUTE	DESCRIPTION	HTML	XHTML	IE	NS	OP
206	background="*url*"	Provides the URL of the background image file			3.0	4.0	4.0
116	bgcolor="*color*"	Specifies the background color of the table cell. **Deprecated**	4.0	1.0*	2.0	3.0	2.1
189	bordercolor="*color*"	Specifies the color of the table cell border			2.0		
189	bordercolordark= "*color*"	Specifies the color of the table cell border's shaded edge			2.0		
189	bordercolorlight= "*color*"	Specifies the color of the table cell border's unshaded edge			2.0		
201	char="*char*"	Specifies the character used for aligning the table cell contents when the align attribute is set to "char"	4.0	1.0			
201	charoff="*integer*"	Specifies the offset in pixels from the alignment character specified in the char attribute	4.0	1.0			
198	colspan="*integer*"	Specifies the number of columns the table cell spans	3.0	1.0	2.0	1.1	2.1
D8	headers="*text*"	A space-separated list of table headers associated with the table cell	4.0	1.0			
197	height="*integer*"	Specifies the height of the table cell in pixels. **Deprecated**	3.2	1.0*	2.0	1.1	2.1
	nowrap="nowrap"	Disables line-wrapping within the table cell. **Deprecated**	3.0	1.0*	2.0	1.1	2.1
198	rowspan="*integer*"	Specifies the number of rows the table cell spans	3.0	1.0	2.0	1.1	2.1
D8	scope="col| colgroup|row| rowgroup"	Specifies the scope of the table for which the cell provides data	4.0	1.0			
201	valign="top|**middle** |bottom"	Specifies the vertical alignment of the contents of the table cell	3.0	1.0	2.0	1.1	2.1
197	width="*integer*"	Specifies the width of the cell in pixels. **Deprecated**	3.2	1.0*	2.0	1.1	2.1
184	**\<thead> \</thead>**	Encloses the content of the Web table header	4.0	1.0	3.0	6.0	4.0
201	align="left|center |right|justify |char"	Specifies the alignment of the contents in the cells of the table header	4.0	1.0	4.0	6.0	4.0
116	bgcolor="*color*"	Specifies the background color of the table body			4.0	6.0	
201	char="*char*"	Specifies the character used for aligning the table header contents when the align attribute is set to "char"	4.0	1.0			
201	charoff="*integer*"	Specifies the offset in pixels from the alignment character specified in the char attribute	4.0	1.0			
201	valign="baseline| bottom|middle| top"	Specifies the vertical alignment of the contents in the cells of the table header	4.0	1.0	4.0	6.0	4.0
14	**\<title> \</title>**	Specifies the title of the document, placed in the head section of the document	2.0	1.0	1.0	1.0	2.1

PAGE	ELEMENT/ATTRIBUTE	DESCRIPTION	HTML	XHTML	IE	NS	OP
179	`<tr> </tr>`	Encloses the content of a row within a Web table	3.0	1.0	2.0	1.1	2.1
201	`align="left|center |right"`	Specifies the horizontal alignment of the data in the row's cells	3.0	1.0	2.0	1.1	2.1
206	`background="url"`	Provides the URL of the background image file for the row				4.0	
116	`bgcolor="color"`	Specifies the background color of the row. **Deprecated**	4.0	1.0*	2.0	3.0	2.1
189	`bordercolor="color"`	Specifies the color of the table row border			2.0		
189	`bordercolordark= "color"`	Specifies the color of the table row border's shaded edge			2.0		
189	`bordercolorlight= "color"`	Specifies the color of the table row border's unshaded edge			2.0		
201	`char="char"`	Specifies the character used for aligning the table row contents when the align attribute is set to "char"	4.0	1.0			
201	`charoff="integer"`	Specifies the offset in pixels from the alignment character specified in the char attribute	4.0	1.0			
197	`height="integer"`	Specifies the height of the table row in pixels			5.0	6.0	4.0
201	`valign="baseline| bottom|middle|top"`	Specifies the vertical alignment of the contents of the table row	3.0	1.0	2.0	1.1	2.1
32	`<tt> </tt>`	Marks the enclosed text as teletype or monospaced text	2.0	1.0	1.0	1.0	2.1
32	`<u> </u>`	Marks the enclosed text as underlined text. **Deprecated**	3.0	1.0*	1.0	3.5	2.1
24	`<ul> </ul>`	Contains an unordered list of items	2.0	1.0	1.0	1.0	2.1
	`compact="compact"`	Reduces the space between unordered list items. **Deprecated**	2.0	1.0*			
28	`type="disc|square| circle"`	Specifies the bullet type associated with the list items. **Deprecated**	3.2	1.0*	1.0	1.0	2.1
32	`<var> </var>`	Marks the enclosed text as containing a variable name	2.0	1.0	1.0	1.0	2.1
	`<wbr />`	Forces a line-break in the rendered page			1.0	1.0	
	`<xml> </xml>`	Encloses XML content (also referred to as a "data island") or references an external XML document			5.0		
	`ns="url"`	Provides the URL of the namespace that the XML content is bound to			5.0		
	`prefix="text"`	Specifies the namespace prefix of the XML content			5.0		
	`src="url"`	Provides the URL of an external XML document			5.0		
	`<xmp> </xmp>`	Marks the enclosed text as preformatted text, preserving the white space of the source document; replaced by the pre element. **Deprecated**	2.0		1.0	1.0	2.1

Cascading Style Sheets

This appendix describes the selectors, units, and attributes supported by Cascading Style Sheets (CSS), Internet Explorer (IE), Netscape, and Opera. Version numbers indicate the lowest version that supports the given selector, unit, or attribute. Note that support might be incomplete. A particular version might not support all aspects of the CSS feature. You should always check your code against different browsers and browser versions to ensure that your page is being rendered correctly. The page column indicates the page number in which the style, unit, or attribute is discussed in the book. Additional information about CSS can be found at the World Wide Web Consortium Web site at *www.w3.org*.

Selectors

The general form of a style declaration is:

selector {attribute1:value1; attribute2:value2; ...}

where *selector* is the selection of elements within the document to which the style will be applied; *attribute1*, *attribute2*, etc. are the different style attributes; and *value1*, *value2*, etc. are values associated with those styles. The following table shows some of the different forms that a selector can take and the corresponding support from CSS, IE, Netscape, and Opera.

Page	Selectors	Matches	CSS	IE	NS	OP
361	*	All elements in the document	2.0	5.0	6.0	4.0
361	e	An element, *e*, in the document	1.0	3.0	4.0	3.5
361	e1, e2, e3, ...	A group of elements, *e1*, *e2*, *e3* in the document	1.0	3.0	4.0	3.5
361	e1 e2	An element *e2* nested within the parent element, *e1*	1.0	3.0	4.0	3.5
361	e1 > e2	A element *e2* that is a child of the parent element, *e1*	2.0		6.0	3.5
361	e1+e2	An element, *e2*, that is adjacent to element *e1*	2.0		6.0	5.0
368	e1.class	An element, *e1*, belonging to the *class* class	1.0	3.0	4.0	3.5
367	.class	Any element belonging to the *class* class	1.0	3.0	4.0	3.5
366	#id	An element with the id value *id*	1.0	3.0	4.0	3.5
362	[att]	The element contains the *att* attribute	2.0		6.0	4.0
362	[att="val"]	The element's *att* attribute equals "*val*"	2.0		6.0	4.0
362	[att~="val"]	The element's *att* attribute value is a space-separated list of "words," one of which is exactly "*val*"	2.0		6.0	4.0
362	[att|="val"]	The element's *att* attribute value is a hyphen-separated list of "words" beginning with "val"	3.0		6.0	
362	[att^="val"]	The element's *att* attribute begins with "*val*"	3.0		6.0	
362	[att$="val"]	The element's *att* attribute ends with "*val*"	3.0		6.0	
362	[att*="val"]	The element's *att* attribute contains the value "*val*"	3.0		6.0	
	[ns|att]	References all *att* attributes in the *ns* namespace	3.0		6.0	

Pseudo-Elements and Pseudo-Classes

Pseudo-elements are elements that do not exist in HTML code but whose attributes can be set with CSS. Many pseudo-elements were introduced in CSS2 and are not widely supported by browsers.

Page	Pseudo-Element	Matches	CSS	IE	NS	OP
390	`e:after {content: "text"}`	Text content, *text*, that is inserted at the end of an element, *e*	2.0		6.0	4.0
390	`e:before {content: "text"}`	Text content, *text*, that is inserted at the beginning of an element, *e*	2.0		6.0	4.0
390	`e:first-letter`	The first letter in the element, *e*	1.0	5.5	6.0	3.5
390	`e:first-line`	The first line in the element, *e*	1.0	5.5	6.0	3.5

Pseudo-classes are classes of HTML elements that define the condition or state of the element in the Web page. Many pseudo-classes were introduced in CSS2 and are not widely supported by browsers.

Page	Pseudo-Class	Matches	CSS	IE	NS	OP
	`:canvas`	The rendering canvas of the document			6.0	
416	`:first`	The first printed page of the document (used only with print styles created with the @print rule)	2.0			
416	`:last`	The last printed page of the document (used only with print styles created with the @print rule)	2.0			
416	`:left`	The left side of a two-sided printout (used only with print styles created with the @print rule)	2.0			
416	`:right`	The right side of a two-sided printout (used only with print styles created with the @print rule)	2.0			
	`:root`	The root element of the document (the html element in HTML and XHTML documents)			6.0	
	`:scrolled-content`	The content that is scrolled in the rendering viewport			6.0	
	`:viewport`	The rendering viewport of the document			6.0	
	`:viewport-scroll`	The rendering viewport of the document plus the scrollbar region			6.0	
387	`e:active`	The element, *e*, is being activated by the user (usually applies only to hyperlinks)	1.0	4.0	6.0	5.0
	`e:empty`	The element, *e*, has no content			6.0	
387	`e:first-child`	The element, *e*, which is the first child of its parent element	2.0		6.0	7.0
	`e:first-node`	The first occurrence of the element, *e*, in the document tree			6.0	
387	`e:focus`	The element, *e*, has received the focus of the cursor (usually applies only to Web form elements)	2.0	6.0	7.0	
387	`e:hover`	The mouse pointer is hovering over the element, *e* (usually applies only to hyperlinks)	2.0	4.0	6.0	4.0
	`e:lang(text)`	Sets the language, *text*, associated with the element, *e*	2.0			
387	`e:last-child`	The element, *e*, that is the last child of its parent element	2.0		6.0	7.0
	`e:last-node`	The last occurrence of the element, *e*, in the document tree			6.0	

Page	Pseudo-Class	Matches	CSS	IE	NS	OP
387	e:link	The element, *e*, has not been visited yet by the user (applies only to hyperlinks)	1.0	3.0	4.0	3.5
	e:not	Negate the selector rule for the element, *e*, applying the style to all *e* elements that do not match the selector rules			6.0	
387	e:visited	The element, *e*, has been already visited by the user (to only to hyperlinks)	1.0	3.0	4.0	3.5

@ Rules

CSS supports different "@ rules" designed to run commands within a style sheet. These commands can be used to import other styles, download font definitions, or define the format of printed output.

Page	@ Rule	Description	CSS	IE	NS	OP
	@charset "*encoding*"	Defines the character set encoding used in the style sheet (this must be the very first line in the style sheet document)	2.0	5.5	6.0	3.5
	@font-face {font-family: *e*; *font-styles*; src: url(*url*) }	Downloads a font definition from an external file, where is the name assigned to the font, *font-styles* are CSS styles to format the font's appearance, and *url* is the location of the external font file	2.0	4.0	6.0	3.5
356	@import url(*url*) *media*	Imports an external style sheet document into the current style sheet, where *url* is the location of the external style sheet and *media* is a comma-separated list of media types (optional)	1.0	4.0	6.0	3.5
410	@media *media* {*style declaration*}	Defines the media for the styles in the *style declaration* block, where *media* is a comma-separated list of media types	2.0	4.0	6.0	3.5
	@namespace *prefix* url(*url*)	Defines the namespace used by selectors in the style sheet, where *prefix* is the local namespace prefix (optional) and *url* is the unique namespace identifier; the @namespace rule must come before all CSS selectors			6.0	
416	@page *label pseudo-class* {*styles*}	Defines the properties of a printed page, where *label* is a label given to the page (optional), *pseudo-class* is one of the CSS pseudo-classes designed for printed pages, and *styles* are the styles associated with the page	2.0	5.5	6.0	4.0

Miscellaneous Syntax

The following syntax elements do not fit into the previous categories but are useful in constructing CSS style sheets.

Page	Item	Description	CSS	IE	NS	OP
358	*style* !important	Places high importance on the preceding *style*, overriding the usual rules for inheritance and cascading	1.0	4.0	6.0	3.5
354	/* *comment* */	Attaches a *comment* to the style sheet	1.0	3.0	4.0	3.5

Units

Many style attribute values use units of measurement to indicate color, length, angles, time, and frequencies. The following table describes the measuring units used in CSS.

Page	Units	Description	CSS	IE	NS	OP
	Color	**Units of color**				
113	*name*	A color name; all browsers recognize 16 base color names: aqua, black, blue, fuchsia, gray, green, lime, maroon, navy, olive, purple, red, silver, teal, white, and yellow	1.0	3.0	4.0	3.5
111	*#rrggbb*	The hexadecimal color value, where *rr* is the red value, *gg* is the green value, and *bb* is the blue value	1.0	3.0	4.0	3.5
	#rgb	A compressed hexadecimal value, where the *r*, *g*, and *b* values are doubled so that, for example, #A2F = #AA22FF	1.0	3.0	4.0	3.5
110	*rgb(red, green, blue)*	The decimal color value, where *red* is the red value, *green* is the green value, and *blue* is the blue value	1.0	3.0	4.0	3.5
110	*rgb(red%, green%, blue%)*	The color value percentage, where *red*% is the percent of maximum red, *green*% is the percent of maximum green, and *blue*% is the percent of maximum blue	1.0	3.0	4.0	3.5
	Length	**Units of length**				
120	auto	Keyword which allows the browser to automatically determine the size of the length	1.0	4.0	4.0	3.5
120	em	A relative unit indicating the width and the height of the capital "M" character for the browser's default font	1.0	4.0	4.0	3.5
120	ex	A relative unit indicating the height of the small "x" character for the browser's default font	1.0	4.0	4.0	3.5
120	px	A pixel, representing the smallest unit of length on the output device	1.0	3.0	4.0	3.5
120	in	An inch	1.0	3.0	4.0	3.5
120	cm	A centimeter	1.0	3.0	4.0	3.5
120	mm	A millimeter	1.0	3.0	4.0	3.5
120	pt	A point, approximately 1/72 inch	1.0	3.0	4.0	3.5
120	pc	A pica, approximately 1/12 inch	1.0	3.0	4.0	3.5
120	%	A percent of the width or height of the parent element	1.0	3.0	4.0	3.5
121	xx-small	Keyword representing an extremely small font size	1.0	3.0	4.0	3.5
121	x-small	Keyword representing a very small font size	1.0	3.0	4.0	3.5
121	small	Keyword representing a small font size	1.0	3.0	4.0	3.5
121	medium	Keyword representing a medium-sized font	1.0	3.0	4.0	3.5
121	large	Keyword representing a large font	1.0	3.0	4.0	3.5
121	x-large	Keyword representing a very large font	1.0	3.0	4.0	3.5
121	xx-large	Keyword representing an extremely large font	1.0	3.0	4.0	3.5
	Angle	**Units of angles**				
	deg	The angle in degrees	2.0			
	grad	The angle in gradients	2.0			
	rad	The angle in radians	2.0			

Page	Units	Description	CSS	IE	NS	OP
	Time	**Units of time**				
	ms	Time in milliseconds	2.0			
	s	Time in seconds	2.0			
	Frequency	**Units of frequency**				
	hz	The frequency in hertz	2.0			
	khz	The frequency in kilohertz				

Attributes and Values

The following table describes the attributes and values for different types of elements. The attributes are grouped into categories to help you locate the features relevant to your particular design task.

Page	Attribute	Description	CSS	IE	NS	OP
	Aural	**Styles for Aural Browsers**				
	azimuth: *location*	Defines the location of the sound, where *location* is left-side, far-left, left, center-left, center, center-right, right, far-right, right-side, leftward, rightward, or an angle value	2.0			
	cue: url(*url1*) url(*url2*)	Adds a sound to an element: if a single value is present, the sound is played before and after the element; if two values are present, the first is played before and the second is played after	2.0			
	cue-after: url(*url*)	Specifies a sound to be played immediately after an element	2.0			
	cue-before: url(*url*)	Specifies a sound to be played immediately before an element	2.0			
	elevation: *location*	Defines the vertical location of the sound, where *location* is below, level, above, lower, higher, or an angle value	2.0			
	pause: *time1 time2*	Adds a pause to an element: if a single value is present, the pause occurs before and after the element; if two values are present, the first pause occurs before and the second occurs after	2.0			
	pause-after: *time*	Adds a pause after an element	2.0			
	pause-before: *time*	Adds a pause before an element	2.0			
	pitch: *value*	Defines the pitch of a speaking voice, where *value* is x-low, low, medium, high, x-high, or a frequency value	2.0			
	pitch-range: *value*	Defines the pitch range for a speaking voice, where *value* ranges from 0 to 100; a low pitch range results in a monotone voice, whereas a high pitch range sounds very animated	2.0			
	play-during: url(*url*) mix repeat *type*	Defines a sound to be played behind an element, where *url* is the URL of the sound file; mix overlays the sound file with the sound of the parent element; repeat causes the sound to be repeated, filling up the available time; and *type* is auto to play the sound only once, none to play nothing but the sound file, or inherit	2.0			
	richness: *value*	Specifies the richness of the speaking voice, where *value* ranges from 0 to 100; a low value indicates a softer voice, whereas a high value indicates a brighter voice	2.0			
	speak: *type*	Defines how element content is to be spoken, where *type* is normal (for normal punctuation rules), spell-out (to pronounce one character at a time), none (to suppress the aural rendering), or inherit	2.0			

Page	Attribute	Description	CSS	IE	NS	OP
	`speak-numeral: type`	Defines how numeric content should be spoken, where *type* is digits (to pronounce one digit at a time), continuous (to pronounce the full number), or inherit	2.0			
	`speak-punctuation: type`	Defines how punctuation characters are spoken, where *type* is code (to speak the punctuation literally), none (to not speak the punctuation), or inherit	2.0			
	`speech-rate: value`	Defines the rate of speech, where *value* is x-slow, slow, medium, fast, x-fast, slower, faster, or a value in words per minute	2.0			
	`stress: value`	Defines the maximum pitch, where *value* ranges from 0 to 100; a value of 50 is normal stress for a speaking voice	2.0			
	`voice-family: text`	Defines the name of the speaking voice, where *text* is male, female, child, or a text string indicating a specific speaking voice	2.0			
	`volume: value`	Defines the volume of a voice, where *value* is silent, x-soft, soft, medium, loud, x-loud, or a number from 0 (lowest) to 100 (highest)	2.0			
	Backgrounds	**Styles applied to an element's background**				
148	`background: color url(url) repeat attachment position`	Defines the background of the element, where *color* is a CSS color name or value, *url* is the location of an image file, *repeat* defines how the background image should be repeated, *attachment* defines how the background image should be attached, and *position* defines the position of the background image	1.0	3.0	4.0	3.5
148	`background-attachment: type`	Specifies how the background image is attached, where *type* is inherit, scroll (move the image with the page content), or fixed (fix the image and not scroll)	1.0	4.0	4.0	3.5
114	`background-color: color`	Defines the color of the background, where *color* is a CSS color name or value; the keyword "inherit" can be used to inherit the background color of the parent element, or "transparent" can be used to allow the parent element background image to show through	1.0	4.0	4.0	3.5
145	`background-image: url(url)`	Specifies the image file used for the element's background, where *url* is the URL of the image file	1.0	4.0	4.0	3.5
147	`background-position: x y`	Sets the position of a background image, where *x* is the horizontal location in pixels, as a percentage of the width of the parent element, or the keyword "left", "center", or "right", *y* is the vertical location in pixels, as a percentage of the height and of the parent element, or the keyword, "top", "center", or "bottom"	1.0	4.0	4.0	3.5
146	`background-repeat: type`	Defines the method for repeating the background image, where *type* is no-repeat, repeat (to tile the image in both directions), repeat-x (to tile the image in the horizontal direction only), or repeat-y (to tile the image in the vertical direction only)	1.0	4.0	4.0	3.5
	Block-Level Styles	**Styles applied to block-level elements**				
382	`border: length style color`	Defines the border style of the element, where *length* is the border width, *style* is the border design, and *color* is the border color	1.0	4.0	4.0	3.5
382	`border-bottom: length style color`	Defines the border style of the bottom edge of the element	1.0	4.0	4.0*	3.5
382	`border-left: length style color`	Defines the border style of the left edge of the element	1.0	4.0	4.0	3.5
382	`border-right: length style color`	Defines the border style of the right edge of the element	1.0	4.0	4.0	3.5
382	`border-top: length style color`	Defines the border style of the top edge of the element	1.0	4.0	4.0	3.5

Page	Attribute	Description	CSS	IE	NS	OP
382	border-color: *color*	Defines the color applied to the element's border using a CSS color unit	1.0	4.0	4.0	3.5
382	border-bottom-color: *color*	Defines the color applied to the bottom edge of the element	1.0	4.0	4.0	3.5
382	border-left-color: *color*	Defines the color applied to the left edge of the element	1.0	4.0	4.0	3.5
283	border-right-color: *color*	Defines the color applied to the right edge of the element	1.0	4.0	4.0	3.5
283	border-top-color: *color*	Defines the color applied to the top edge of the element	1.0	4.0	4.0	3.5
382	border-style: *style*	Specifies the design of the element's border (dashed, dotted, double, groove, inset, none, outset, ridge, or solid)	1.0	4.0	4.0	3.5
382	border-style-bottom: *style*	Specifies the design of the element's bottom edge	1.0	4.0	4.0	3.5
382	border-style-left: *style*	Specifies the design of the element's left edge	1.0	4.0	4.0	3.5
382	border-style-right: *style*	Specifies the design of the element's right edge	1.0	4.0	4.0	3.5
382	border-style-top: *style*	Specifies the design of the element's top edge	1.0	4.0	4.0	3.5
382	border-width: *length*	Defines the width of the element's border, in a unit of measure or using the keyword "thick", "medium", or "thin".	1.0	4.0	4.0	3.5
382	border-width-bottom: *length*	Defines the width of the element's bottom edge	1.0	4.0	4.0	3.5
382	border-width-left: *length*	Defines the width of the element's left edge	1.0	4.0	4.0	3.5
382	border-width-right: *length*	Defines the width of the element's right edge	1.0	4.0	4.0	3.5
382	border-width-top: *length*	Defines the width of the element's top edge	1.0	4.0	4.0	3.5
142	margin: *top right bottom left*	Defines the size of the margins around the top, right, bottom, and left edges of the element, in one of the CSS units of length	1.0	4.0	4.0	3.5
142	margin-bottom: *length*	Defines the size of the element's bottom margin	1.0	4.0	4.0	3.5
142	margin-left: *length*	Defines the size of the element's left margin	1.0	4.0	4.0	3.5
142	margin-right: *length*	Defines the size of the element's right margin	1.0	4.0	4.0	3.5
142	margin-top: *length*	Defines the size of the element's top margin	1.0	4.0	4.0	3.5
380	padding: *top right bottom left*	Defines the size of the padding space within the top, right, bottom, and left edges of the element, in one of the CSS units of length	1.0	4.0	4.0	3.5
380	padding-bottom: *length*	Defines the size of the element's bottom padding	1.0	4.0	4.0	3.5
380	padding-left: *length*	Defines the size of the element's left padding	1.0	4.0	4.0	3.5
380	padding-right: *length*	Defines the size of the element's right padding	1.0	4.0	4.0	3.5
380	padding-top: *length*	Defines the size of the element's top padding	1.0	4.0	4.0	3.5
	Content	**Styles to attach additional content to elements**				
	content: *text*	Generates a text string to attach to the content of the element	2.0			4.0
	content: attr(*attr*)	Returns the value of the *attr* attribute from the element	2.0		6.0	4.0
	content: close-quote	Attaches a close quote using the characters specified in the quotes style	2.0		6.0	4.0
	content: counter(*text*)	Generates a counter using the text string *text* attached to the content (most often used with list items)	2.0			4.0
	content: counters(*text*)	Generates a string of counters using the comma-separated text string *text* attached to the content (most often used with list items)	2.0			4.0
	content: no-close-quote	Prevents the attachment of a close quote to an element	2.0		6.0	4.0
	content: no-open-quote	Prevents the attachment of an open quote to an element	2.0		6.0	4.0
	content: open-quote	Attaches an open quote using the characters specified in the quotes style	2.0		6.0	4.0
	content: url(*url*)	Attaches the content of an external file indicated in the *url* to the element	2.0		6.0	4.0

Page	Attribute	Description	CSS	IE	NS	OP
	counter-increment: *id integer*	Defines the element to be automatically incremented and the amount by which it is to be incremented, where *id* is an identifier of the element and *integer* defines by how much	2.0			4.0
	counter-reset: *id integer*	Defines the element whose counter is to be reset and the amount by which it is to be reset, where *id* is an identifier of the element and *integer* defines by how much	2.0			4.0
	quotes: *text1 text2*	Defines the text strings for the open quotes (*text1*) and the close quotes (*text2*)	2.0		6.0	4.0
	Display Styles	**Styles that control the display of the element's content**				
407	clip: rect(*top, right, bottom, left*)	Defines what portion of the content is displayed, where *top, right, bottom,* and *left* are distances of the top, right, bottom, and left edges from the element's top-left corner; use a value of auto to allow the browser to determine the clipping region	2.0	4.0	4.0	7.0
376	display: *type*	Specifies the display type of the element, where *type* is one of the following: block, inline, inline-block, inherit, list-item, none, run-in, table, inline-table, table-caption, table-column, table-cell, table-column-group, table-header-group, table-footer-group, table-row, or table-row-group	1.0	4.0	4.0	3.5
370	height: *length*	Specifies the height of the element in one of the CSS units of length	1.0	4.0	6.0	3.5
	min-height: *length*	Specifies the minimum height of the element	2.0		6.0	4.0
	min-width: *length*	Specifies the minimum width of the element	2.0		6.0	4.0
	max-height: *length*	Specifies the maximum height of the element	2.0		6.0	4.0
	max-width: *length*	Specifies the maximum width of the element	2.0		6.0	4.0
405	overflow: *type*	Instructs the browser on how to handle content that overflows the dimensions of the element, where *type* is auto, inherit, visible, hidden, or scroll	2.0	4.0	6.0	4.0
	overflow-x: *type*	Instructs the browser on how to handle content that overflows the element's width, where *type* is auto, inherit, visible, hidden, or scroll		5.0		
	overflow-y: *type*	Instructs the browser on how to handle content that overflows the element's height, where *type* is auto, inherit, visible, hidden, or scroll		5.0		
	text-overflow: *type*	Instructs the browser on how to handle text overflow, where *type* is clip (to hide the overflow text) or ellipsis (to display the ... text string)		6.0		
412	visibility: *type*	Defines the element's visibility, where *type* is hidden, visible, or inherit	2.0	4.0	4.0	4.0
369	width: *length*	Specifies the width of the element in one of the CSS units of length	1.0	4.0	4.0	3.5
	Fonts and Text	**Styles that format the appearance of fonts and text**				
114	color: *color*	Specifies the color of the element's foreground (usually the font color)	1.0	3.0	4.0	3.5
128	font: *style variant weight size/line-height family*	Defines the appearance of the font, where *style* is the font's style, *variant* is the font variant, *weight* is the weight of the font, *size* is the size of the font, *line-height* is the height of the lines, and *family* is the font face; the only required attributes are *size* and *family*	1.0	3.0	4.0	3.5
117	font-family: *family*	Specifies the font face used to display text, where *family* is sans-serif, serif, fantasy, monospace, cursive, or the name of an installed font	1.0	3.0	4.0	3.5

Page	Attribute	Description	CSS	IE	NS	OP
120	font-size: *value*	Specifies the size of the font in one of the CSS units of length	1.0	3.0	4.0	3.5
	font-size-adjust: *value*	Specifies the aspect *value* (which is the ratio of the font size to the font's ex height) for the font	2.0			
	font-stretch: *type*	Expands or contracts the font, where *type* is narrower, wider, ultra-condensed, extra-condensed, condensed, semi-condensed, normal, semi-expanded, extra-expanded, or ultra-expanded	2.0			
126	font-style: *type*	Specifies a style applied to the font, where *type* is normal, italic, or oblique	1.0	3.0	4.0	3.5
126	font-variant: *type*	Specifies a variant of the font, where *type* is inherit, normal, or small-caps	1.0	4.0	6.0	3.5
126	font-weight: *value*	Defines the weight of the font, where *value* is 100, 200, 300, 400, 500, 600, 700, 800, 900, normal, lighter, bolder, or bold	1.0	4.0	4.0	3.5
123	letter-spacing: *value*	Specifies the space between letters, where *value* is a unit of length or the keyword "normal"	1.0	4.0	6.0	3.5
123	line-height: *value*	Specifies the height of the lines, where *value* is a unit of length or the keyword, "normal"	1.0	3.0	4.0	3.5
19	text-align: *type*	Specifies the horizontal alignment of text within the element, where *type* is inherit, left, right, center, or justify	1.0	3.0	4.0	3.5
126	text-decoration: *type*	Specifies the decoration applied to the text, where *type* is blink, line-through, none overline, or underline	1.0	3.0	4.0	3.5
124	text-indent: *length*	Specifies the amount of indentation in the first line of the text, where *length* is a CSS unit of length	1.0	3.0	4.0	3.5
	text-shadow: *color* *x y blur*	Applies a shadow effect to the text, where *color* is the color of the shadow, *x* is the horizontal offset in pixels, *y* is the vertical offset in pixels, and *blur* is the size of the blur radius (optional); multiple shadows can be added with effect shadow effect separated by commas	2.0			
126	text-transform: *type*	Defines a transformation applied to the text, where *type* is capitalize, lowercase, none, or uppercase	1.0	4.0	4.0	3.5
128	vertical-align: *type*	Specifies how to vertically align the text with the surrounding content, where *type* is baseline, middle, top, bottom, text-top, text-bottom, super, sub, or one of the CSS units of length	1.0	4.0	4.0	3.5
	white-space: *type*	Specifies the handling of white space (blank spaces, tabs, and new lines), where *type* is inherit, normal, pre (to treat the text as preformatted text), or nowrap (to prevent line-wrapping)	1.0	5.5	6.0	4.0
123	word-spacing: *length*	Specifies the amount of space between words in the text, where *length* is either a CSS unit of length or the keyword "normal" to use normal word spacing	1.0	40.	6.0	3.5
	Layout	**Styles that define the layout of elements**				
399	bottom: *y*	Defines the vertical offset of the element's bottom edge, where *y* is either a CSS unit of length or the keyword "auto" or "inherit"	2.0	4.0	6.0	4.0
138	clear: *type*	Places the element only after the specified margin is clear of floating elements, where *type* is inherit, none, left, right, or both	1.0	4.0	4.0	3.5
137	float: *type*	Floats the element on the specified margin with subsequent content wrapping around the element, where *type* is inherit, none, left, right, or both	1.0	4.0	4.0	3.5
399	left: *x*	Defines the horizontal offset of the element's left edge, where *x* is either a CSS unit of length or the keyword "auto" or "inherit"	2.0	4.0	6.0	4.0

Page	Attribute	Description	CSS	IE	NS	OP
399	position: *type*	Defines how the element is positioned on the page, where *type* is absolute, relative, fixed, static, and inherit	1.0	4.0	4.0	3.5
399	right: *x*	Defines the horizontal offset of the element's right edge, where *x* is either a CSS unit of length or the keyword "auto" or "inherit"	2.0	4.0	6.0	4.0
399	top: *y*	Defines the vertical offset of the element's top edge, where *y* is a CSS unit of length or the keyword "auto" or "inherit"	2.0	4.0	6.0	4.0
399	z-index: *value*	Defines how overlapping elements are stacked, where *value* is either the stacking number (elements with higher stacking numbers are placed on top) or the keyword "auto" to allow the browser to determine the stacking order	2.0	5.0	4.0	4.0
	Lists	**Styles that format lists**				
27	list-style: *type image position*	Defines the appearance of a list item, where *type* is the marker type, *image* is the URL of the location of an image file used for the marker, and *position* is the position of the marker	1.0	4.0	4.0	3.5
26	list-style-image: url(*url*)	Defines image used for the list marker, where *url* is the location of the image file	1.0	4.0	6.0	3.5
26	list-style-type: *type*	Defines the marker type used in the list, where *type* is disc, circle, square, decimal, decimal-leading-zero, lower-roman, upper-roman, lower-alpha, upper-alpha, or none	1.0	4.0	4.0	3.5
27	list-style-position: *type*	Defines the location of the list marker, where *type* is inside or outside	1.0	4.0	6.0	3.5
	marker-offset: *length*	Defines the distance between the marker and the enclosing list box, where *length* is either a CSS unit of length or the keyword "auto" or "inherit"	2.0			
	Outlines	**Styles to create and format outlines**				
	outline: *color style width*	Creates an outline around the element content, where *color* is the color of the outline, *style* is the outline style, and *width* is the width of the outline	2.0			7.0
	outline-color: *color*	Defines the color of the outline	2.0			7.0
	outline-style: *type*	Defines the style of the outline, where *type* is dashed, dotted, double, groove, inset, none, outset, ridge, solid, or inherit	2.0			7.0
	outline-width: *length*	Defines the width of the outline, where *length* is expressed in a CSS unit of length	2.0			7.0
	Printing	**Styles for printed output**				
416	page: *label*	Specifies the page design to apply, where *label* is a page design created with the @page rule.	2.0			T7?
418	page-break-after: *type*	Defines how to control page breaks after the element, where *type* is avoid (to avoid page breaks), left (to insert a page break until a left page is displayed), right (to insert a page break until a right page is displayed), always (to always insert a page break), auto, or inherit	2.0	4.0	7.0	3.5
418	page-break-before: *type*	Defines how to control page breaks before the element, where *type* is avoid left, always, auto, or inherit	2.0	4.0	7.0	3.5
418	page-break-inside: *type*	Defines how to control page breaks within the element, where *type* is avoid, auto, or inherit	2.0			3.5
417	marks: *type*	Defines how to display crop marks, where *type* is crop, cross, none, or inherit	2.0			T7?
417	size: *width height orientation*	Defines the size of the page, where *width* and *height* are the width and the height of the page and *orientation* is the orientation of the page (portrait or landscape)	2.0			4.0

Page	Attribute	Description	CSS	IE	NS	OP
419	orphans: *value*	Defines how to handle orphaned text, where *value* is the number of lines that must appear within the element before a page break is inserted	2.0			3.5
419	widow: *value*	Defines how to handle widowed text, where *value* is the number of lines that must appear within the element before a page break is inserted	2.0			3.5
	Scrollbars and Cursors	**Styles to format the appearance of scrollbars and cursors**				
	cursor: *type*	Defines the cursor image used, where *type* is n-resize, ne-resize, e-resize, se-resize, s-resize, sw-resize, w-resize, nw-resize, crosshair, pointer, move, text, wait, help, auto, default, inherit, or a URL pointing to an image file; individual browsers also support dozens of other cursor types	2.0	4.0	6.0	7.0
	scrollbar-3dlight-color: *color*	Defines the *color* of the outer top and left edge of the slider		5.5		7.0
	scrollbar-arrow-color: *color*	Defines the *color* of the scrollbar directional arrows		5.5		7.0
	scrollbar-base-color: *color*	Defines the *color* of the scrollbar button face, arrow, slider, and slider tray		5.5		7.0
	scrollbar-darkshadow-color: *color*	Defines the *color* of the outer bottom and right edges of the slider		5.5		7.0
	scrollbar-face-color: *color*	Defines the *color* of the button face of the scrollbar arrow and slider		5.5		7.0
	scrollbar-highlight-color: *color*	Defines the *color* of the inner top and left edges of the slider		5.5		7.0
	scrollbar-shadow-color: *color*	Defines the *color* of the inner bottom and right edges of the slider		5.5		7.0
	Special Effects	**Styles to create special visual effects**				
	filter: *type parameters*	Applies transition and filter effects to elements, where *type* is the type of filter and *parameters* are parameter values specific to the filter		4.0		
	Tables	**Styles to format the appearance of tables**				
	border-collapse: *type*	Determines whether table cell borders are separate or collapsed into a single border, where *type* is separate, collapse, or inherit	2.0	5.0	7.0	4.0
	border-spacing: *length*	If separate borders are used for table cells, defines the distance between borders, where *length* is a CSS unit of length or inherit	2.0		6.0	4.0
	caption-side: *type*	Defines the position of the caption element, where *type* is bottom, left, right, top, or inherit	2.0		6.0	4.0
	empty-cells: *type*	If separate borders are used for table cells, defines whether to display borders for empty cells, where *type* is hide, show, or inherit	2.0		6.0	4.0
	speak-header: *type*	Defines how table headers are spoken in relation to the data cells, where *type* is always, once, or inherit	2.0			
	table-layout: *type*	Defines the algorithm used for the table layout, where *type* is auto (to define the layout once all table cells have been read), fixed (to define the layout after the first table row has been read), or inherit	2.0	5.0	6.0	7.0

JavaScript

Objects, Properties, Methods, and Event Handlers

This appendix defines some of the important JavaScript objects, properties, methods, and event handlers and their compatibility with the Internet Explorer (IE) and Netscape browsers.

JavaScript Elements	Description	IE	Netscape
Anchor	An anchor in the document (use the anchor name)	4.0	4.0
Properties			
accessKey	The hotkey that gives the element focus	4.0	6.0
charset	The character set of the linked document	6.0	6.0
coords	The coordinates of the object, used with the shape attribute	6.0	6.0
hreflang	The language code of the linked resource	6.0	6.0
name	The name of the anchor	4.0	4.0
nameProp	The string holding the filename portion of the URL in the href	5.0	
shape	The string defining the shape of the object	6.0	6.0
tabIndex	The numeric value that indicates the tab order for the object	4.0	6.0
text	The anchor text	4.0	4.0
type	Specifies the media type in the form of a MIME type for the link target	6.0	6.0
Methods			
blur( )	Removes focus from the element	4.0	6.0
handleEvent (*event*)	Causes the Event instance *event* to be processed	4.0	
focus( )	Gives the element focus	4.0	6.0
Applet	A Java applet in the document	4.0	3.0
Properties			
align	Specifies alignment, for example, "left"	4.0	6.0
alt	Specifies alternative text for the applet	6.0	
altHTML	Specifies alternative text for the applet	4.0	
archive	A list of URLs		6.0
code	The URL for the applet class file	4.0	6.0
codeBase	The base URL for the applet	4.0	6.0
height	The height of the object in pixels	4.0	6.0
hspace	The horizontal margin to the left and the right of the applet	4.0	6.0
name	The name of the applet	4.0	3.0
object	The name of the resource that contains a serialized representation of the applet		
vspace	The vertical margin above and below the applet	4.0	6.0
width	The width of the object in pixels	4.0	6.0

JavaScript Elements	Description	IE	Netscape
Area	An area defined in an image map	3.0	3.0
Properties			
accessKey	The hotkey that gives the element focus	4.0	6.0
alt	Alternative text to the graphic	4.0	6.0
cords	Defines the coordinates of the object	6.0	6.0
hash	The anchor name from the URL	3.0	3.0
host	The host and domain names from the URL	3.0	3.0
hostname	The hostname from the URL	3.0	3.0
href	The entire URL	3.0	3.0
pathname	The pathname from the URL	3.0	3.0
port	The port number from the URL	3.0	3.0
protocol	The protocol from the URL	3.0	3.0
search	The query portion from the URL	3.0	3.0
shape	The shape of the object, for example, "default", "rect", "circle", or "poly"	4.0	6.0
tabIndex	Numeric value that indicates the tab order for the object	4.0	6.0
target	The target attribute of the <area> tag	3.0	3.0
Methods			
getSelection()	Returns the value of the current selection		3.0
Event Handlers			
onDblClick()	Runs when the area is double-clicked	4.0	4.0
onMouseOut()	Runs when the mouse leaves the area	3.0	3.0
onMouseOver()	Runs when the mouse enters the area	3.0	3.0
Array	An array object	3.0	3.0
Properties			
index	For an array created by a regular expression match, the zero-based index of the match in the string	5.5	4.0
input	Reflects the original string against which the regular expression was matched	5.5	4.0
length	The next empty index at the end of the array	4.0	3.0
prototype	A mechanism to add properties to an array object	3.0	3.0
Methods			
concat(*array*)	Combines two arrays and stores the result in a third array named *array*	4.0	4.0
join(*string*)	Stores each element in a text string named *string*	3.0	3.0
pop( )	"Pops" the last element of the array and reduces the length of the array by 1	5.5	4.0
push(*arg1, arg2, ...*)	"Pushes" the elements in the list to the end of the array and returns the new length	5.5	4.0
reverse( )	Reverses the order of the elements in the array	3.0	3.0
shift( )	Removes the first element from an array, returns that element, and shifts all other elements down one index	5.5	4.0
slice(*array, begin,end*)	Extracts a portion of the array, starting at the index number *begin* and ending at the index number *end*; the elements are then stored in *array*	4.0	4.0
sort(*function*)	Sorts the array based on the function named *function*; if *function* is omitted, the sort applies dictionary order to the array	3.0	3.0
splice(*start,howMany,* [,*item1*[,*item2* [,...]]])	Removes *howMany* elements from the array, beginning at index *start* and replaces the removed elements with the *itemN* arguments (if passed); returns an array of the deleted elements	5.5	4.0
toString( )	Returns a string of the comma-separated values of the array	4.0	3.0
unshift([Item1 [,item2[,...]]])	Inserts the items to the front of an array and returns the new length of the array	5.5	4.0

JavaScript Elements	Description	IE	Netscape
Button	A push button in an HTML form (use the button's name)	3.0	3.0
Properties			
accessKey	Indicates the hotkey that gives the element focus	4.0	6.0
align	Specifies the alignment of the element, for example, "right"	4.0	6.0
disabled	A Boolean indicating whether the element is disabled	4.0	6.0
enabled	Indicates whether the button has been enabled	3.0	4.0
form	The name of the form containing the button	3.0	4.0
name	The name of the button element	3.0	2.0
size	Indicates the width of the button in pixels	4.0	6.0
tabIndex	Indicates the tab order for the object	4.0	6.0
type	The value of the type attribute for the <button> tag	4.0	3.0
value	The value of the button element	3.0	2.0
Methods			
blur()	Removes focus from the button	3.0	3.0
click()	Emulates the action of clicking the button	3.0	2.0
focus()	Gives focus to the button	4.0	4.0
Event Handlers			
onBlur	Runs when the button loses the focus	3.0	3.0
onClick	Runs when the button is clicked	3.0	2.0
onFocus	Runs when the button receives the focus	4.0	4.0
onMouseDown	Runs when the mouse button is pressed	3.0	2.0
onMouseUp	Runs when the mouse button is released	3.0	2.0
Checkbox	A check box in an HTML form	3.0	2.0
Properties			
accessKey	Indicates the hotkey that gives the element focus	4.0	6.0
align	Specifies the alignment of the element, for example, "right"	4.0	6.0
checked	Indicates whether the check box is checked	3.0	2.0
defaultChecked	Indicates whether the check box is checked by default	3.0	2.0
disabled	Boolean indicating whether the element is disabled	4.0	6.0
enabled	Indicates whether the check box is enabled	3.0	4.0
form	The name of the form containing the check box	3.0	4.0
height	The height of the checkbox in pixels	5.0	
name	The name of the check box element	3.0	2.0
size	Indicates the width of the check box in pixels	4.0	6.0
status	Boolean indicating whether the check box is currently selected	4.0	
tabIndex	Indicates the tab order for the object	4.0	6.0
type	The value of the type attribute for the <input> tag	4.0	3.0
value	The value of the check box element	3.0	2.0
width	The width of the check box in pixels	5.0	
Methods			
blur()	Removes the focus from the check box	3.0	3.0
click()	Emulates the action of clicking on the check box	3.0	2.0
focus()	Gives focus to the check box	4.0	4.0
Event Handlers			
onBlur	Runs when the check box loses the focus	4.0	3.0
onClick	Runs when the check box is clicked		
onFocus	Runs when the check box receives the focus	4.0	4.0
Date	An object containing information about a specific date or the current date; dates are expressed either in local time or in UTC (Universal Time Coordinates), otherwise known as Greenwich Mean Time	3.0	2.0

JavaScript Elements	Description	IE	Netscape
Methods			
getDate()	Returns the day of the month, from 1 to 31	3.0	2.0
getDay()	Returns the day of the week, from 0 to 6 (Sunday = 0, Monday = 1, etc.)	3.0	2.0
getFullYear()	Returns the year portion of the date in four-digit format	4.0	4.0
getHours()	Returns the hour in military time, from 0 to 23	3.0	2.0
getMilliseconds()	Returns the number of milliseconds	4.0	4.0
getMinutes()	Returns the minute, from 0 to 59	3.0	2.0
getMonth()	Returns the value of the month, from 0 to 11 (January = 0, February = 1, etc.)	3.0	2.0
getSeconds()	Returns the seconds	3.0	2.0
getTime()	Returns the date as an integer representing the number of milliseconds since December 31, 1969, at 18:00:00	3.0	2.0
getTimezoneOffset()	Returns the difference between the local time and Greenwich Mean Time in minutes	3.0	2.0
getYear()	Deprecated. Returns the number of years since 1900; for example, 1996 is represented by '96'—this value method is inconsistently applied after the year 1999	3.0	2.0
getUTCDate()	Returns the UTC getDate() value	4.0	4.0
getUTCDay()	Returns the UTC getDay() value	4.0	4.0
getUTCFullYear()	Returns the UTC getFullYear() value	4.0	4.0
getUTCHours()	Returns the UTC getHours() value	4.0	4.0
getUTCMilliseconds()	Returns the UTC getMilliseconds() value	4.0	4.0
getUTCMinutes()	Returns the UTC getMinutes() value	4.0	4.0
getUTCMonth()	Returns the UTC getMonth() value	4.0	4.0
getUTCSeconds()	Returns the UTC getSeconds() value	4.0	4.0
getUTCTime()	Returns the UTC getTime() value	4.0	4.0
getUTCYear()	Returns the UTC getYear() value	4.0	4.0
setDate(*date*)	Sets the day of the month to the value specified in *date*	3.0	2.0
setFullYear(*year*)	Sets the year to the four-digit value specified in *year*	4.0	4.0
setHours(*hour*)	Sets the hour to the value specified in *hour*	3.0	2.0
setMilliseconds(*milliseconds*)	Sets the millisecond value to *milliseconds*	4.0	4.0
setMinutes(*minutes*)	Sets the minute to the value specified in *minutes*	3.0	2.0
setMonth(*month*)	Sets the month to the value specified in *month*	3.0	2.0
setSeconds(*seconds*)	Sets the second to the value specified in *seconds*	3.0	2.0
setTime(*time*)	Sets the time using the value specified in *time*, where *time* is a variable containing the number of milliseconds since December 31, 1969, at 18:00:00	3.0	2.0
setYear(*year*)	Sets the year to the value specified in *year*	3.0	2.0
toDateString()	Returns a date as a string value	5.5	
toLocaleDateString()	Returns a date as a string value	5.5	
toTimeString()	Returns a time as a string value	5.5	
toGMTString()	Converts the current date to a text string in Greenwich Mean Time	3.0	2.0
toLocaleString()	Converts a date object's date to a text string, using the date format the Web browser is set up to use	3.0	2.0
toSource	String representing the source code of the object		4.0
toString()	String representation of a Date object	4.0	2.0
toUTCString()	Date converted to string using UTC	4.0	4.0
UTC()	Milliseconds since December 31, 18:00:00, using UTC	3.0	2.0
UTC(*date*)	Returns *date* in the form of the number of milliseconds since December 31, 1969, at 18:00:00 for Universal Coordinated Time	3.0	2.0
setUTCDate(*date*)	Applies the setDate() method in UTC time	4.0	4.0

JavaScript Elements	Description	IE	Netscape
setUTCFullYear(*year*)	Applies the setFullYear() method in UTC time	4.0	4.0
setUTCHours(*hour*)	Applies the setHours() method in UTC time	4.0	4.0
setUTCMilliseconds (*milliseconds*)	Applies the setMilliseconds() method in UTC time	4.0	4.0
setUTCMinutes(*minutes*)	Applies the setMinutes() method in UTC time	4.0	4.0
setUTCMonth(*month*)	Applies the setMonth() method in UTC time	4.0	4.0
setUTCSeconds(*seconds*)	Applies the setSeconds() method in UTC time	4.0	4.0
setUTCTime(*time*)	Applies the setTime() method in UTC time	4.0	4.0
setUTCYear(*year*)	Applies the setYear() method in UTC time	4.0	4.0
`dir`	A directory listing element in the document	4.0	6.0
Properties			
compact	A Boolean indicating whether the listing should be compacted	6.0	6.0
`div`	A `<div>` (block container) element in the document	4.0	6.0
Properties			
align	Alignment of the element	4.0	6.0
`document`	An HTML document (child of Window)	3.0	2.0
Properties			
alinkColor	The color of active hypertext links in the document	3.0	2.0
all[ ]	An array of each of the HTML tags in the document	4.0	
anchors[ ]	An array of the anchors in the document	3.0	3.0
applets[ ]	An array of the applets in the document	3.0	3.0
attributes[ ]	A collection of attributes for the element		6.0
bgColor	The background color of the document	3.0	2.0
body	Reference to the `<body>` element object of the document	3.0	6.0
charset	A string containing the character set of the document	4.0	
characterSet	A string containing the character set of the document		6.0
childNodes[ ]	A collection of child nodes of the object	5.0	6.0
classes.*class.tag.style*	Deprecated; the *style* associated with the element in the document with the class name *class* and the tag name *tag*		4.0
cookie	A text string containing the document's cookie values	3.0	2.0
designMode	Specifies whether design mode is on or off	5.0	
dir	A string holding the text direction of text enclosed in the document	5.0	6.0
doctype	Reference to the DocumentType object for the document	6.0	6.0
documentElement	Reference to the root node of the document object hierarchy	5.0	6.0
domain	The domain of the document	4.0	3.0
embeds	An array of the embedded objects in the document	4.0	3.0
expando	A Boolean dictating whether instance properties can be added to the object	4.0	
fgColor	The text color used in the document	3.0	2.0
firstChild	Reference to the first child node of the element, if one exists	5.0	6.0
form	A form within the document (the form itself is also an object)	3.0	2.0
forms	An array of the forms in the document	3.0	2.0
ids.*id.tag.style*	Deprecated. The *style* associated with the element in the document with the id name *id* and the tag name *tag*		4.0
implementation	An object with method *hasFeature(feature, level)* that returns a Boolean indicating if the browser supports the feature given in the string *feature* at the DOM level passed in the string *level*	6.0	6.0
lastChild	Reference to the last child node of the element, if one exists	5.0	6.0
lastModified	The date the document was last modified	3.0	2.0
layers	An array of layer objects		4.0
linkColor	The color of hypertext links in the document	3.0	2.0
links	An array of the links within the document	3.0	2.0

JavaScript Elements	Description	IE	Netscape
localName	A string indicating the "local" XML name for the object		6.0
location	The URL of the document	3.0	2.0
media	The media for which the document is intended	5.5	
nextSibling	Reference to next sibling of the node		6.0
nodeName	A string containing the name of the node, the name of the tag to which the object corresponds		6.0
nodeValue	A string containing value within the node		6.0
ownerDocument	Reference to the document in which the element is contained		6.0
parentNode	Reference to the parent of the object		6.0
parentWindow	Reference to the window that contains the document		6.0
previousSibling	Reference to the previous sibling of the node		6.0
protocol	A string containing the protocol used to retrieve the document—its full name		4.0
referrer	The URL of the document containing the link that the user accessed to get to the current document	3.0	2.0
security	A string that contains information about the document's certificate		5.5
styleSheets[ ]	Collection of style sheets in the document	4.0	6.0
tags.*tag.style*	The *style* associated with the tag name *tag*		4.0
title	The title of the document	3.0	2.0
URL	The URL of the document	3.0	2.0
vlinkColor	The color of followed hypertext links	3.0	2.0
XMLDocument	Reference to the top-level node of the XML DOM exposed by the document	5.0	
XSLDocument	Reference to the top-level node of the XSL DOM exposed by the document	5.0	
Methods			
addEventListener (whichEvent, handler, direction)	Instructs the object to execute the function *handler* whenever an event of the type stated in *whichEvent* occurs; *direction* is a Boolean telling which phase to fire; use true for capture and false for bubbling		6.0
appendChild(newChild)	Appends *newChild* to the end of the node's childNodes[ ] list	5.0	6.0
attachEvent(whichHandler, theFunction)	Attaches the function *theFunction* as a handler specified by the string *whichHandler*	5.0	
clear()	Clears the contents of the document window	3.0	2.0
cloneNode(cloneChildren)	Clones the node and returns the new clone	5.0	6.0
close()	Closes the document stream	3.0	2.0
createAttribute(name)	Returns a new attribute node of a name given by string *name*	6.0	6.0
createComment(data)	Returns a new comment node with the text given by *data*	6.0	6.0
createElement(tagName)	Returns a new element object that corresponds to *tagName*	4.0	6.0
createEventObject ([eventObj])	Creates and returns a new Event instance to pass to *fireEvent()*	5.5	
createStyleSheet ([url [,index]])	Creates a new styleSheet object from the Stylesheet at the URL in the string *url* and inserts it into the document at index *index*	4.0	
createTextNode(data)	Returns a new text node with value given by *data*	5.0	6.0
detachEvent(whichHandler, theFunction)	Instructs the object to stop executing *theFunction* as a handler given the string *whichHandler*	5.0	
dispatchEvent(event)	Causes *event* to be processed by the appropriate handler; is used to redirect events		6.0
fireEvent(handler [, event])	Fires the event handler given by *handler*	5.5	
focus()	Gives focus to the document and fires *onfocus* handler	5.5	
getElementById(id)	Returns the element with *id* (or *name*) that is equal to *id*	5.0	6.0

JavaScript Elements	Description	IE	Netscape
getElementByName(name)	Gets a collection of elements with *id* (or *name*) that is equal to *name*	5.0	6.0
getElementByTagName (tagname)	Gets a collection of elements corresponding to *tagname*	5.0	6.0
getSelection()	Returns the selected text from the document		4.0
hasAttributes()	Returns a Boolean showing if any attributes are defined for the node		6.0
hasChildNodes()	Returns a Boolean showing if the node has children	5.0	6.0
insertBefore(newChild, refChild)	Inserts the node *newChild* in front of *refChild* in the *childNodes*[ ] list of *refChild*'s parent node	5.0	6.0
isSupported(feature [, version])	Returns a Boolean showing which feature and version identified in the arguments is supported		6.0
normalize()	Merges adjacent text nodes in the subtree rooted at this element	6.0	6.0
open()	Opens the document stream	3.0	2.0
recalc([forceAll])	If *forceAll* is *true*, all dynamic properties are reevaluated	5.0	
removeChild(oldChild)	Removes *oldChild* from the node's children and returns a reference to the removed node	5.0	6.0
removeEventListener (whichEvent, handler, direction)	Removes the function *handler* for the event declared in *whichEvent* for the phase stated in the Boolean *direction*		6.0
replaceChild(newChild, oldChild)	Replaces the node's child node *oldChild* with the node *newChild*	5.0	6.0
setActive()	Sets the document as the current element but does not give it focus	5.5	
write()	Writes to the document window	3.0	2.0
writeln()	Writes to the document window on a single line (used only with preformatted text)	3.0	2.0
Event Handlers			
onClick	Runs when the document is clicked	3.0	2.0
onDblClick	Runs when the document is double-clicked	3.0	2.0
onKeyDown	Runs when a key is pressed down	3.0	2.0
onKeyPress	Runs when a key is initially pressed	3.0	2.0
onKeyUp	Runs when a key is released	3.0	2.0
onLoad	Runs when the document is initially loaded	3.0	2.0
onMouseDown	Runs when the mouse button is pressed down	3.0	2.0
onMouseUp	Runs when the mouse button is released	3.0	2.0
onUnLoad	Runs when the document is unloaded	3.0	2.0
Error	This object gives information about the error that occurred during runtime	5.0	6.0
Properties			
description	Describes the nature of the error	5.0	6.0
lineNumber	The line number that generated the error	6.0	
number	The numeric value of the Microsoft-specific error number	5.0	
File, FileUpload	A file upload element in an HTML form (use the FileUpload box's name)	3.0	2.0
Properties			
accessKey	Indicates the hotkey that gives the element focus	4.0	6.0
disabled	A Boolean signifying if the element is disabled	4.0	6.0
form	The form object containing the FileUpload box	3.0	2.0
name	The name of the FileUpload box	3.0	2.0

JavaScript Elements	Description	IE	Netscape
size	The width in pixels	4.0	6.0
tabIndex	A numeric value of the width in pixels	4.0	6.0
type	The type attribute of the FileUpload box	3.0	2.0
value	The pathname of the selected file in the FileUpload box	2.0	3.0
Methods			
blur()	Removes the focus from the FileUpload box	4.0	3.0
focus()	Gives the focus to the FileUpload box	4.0	3.0
handleEvent(*event*)	Invokes the event handler for the specified *event*	4.0	3.0
select()	Selects the input area of the FileUpload box	3.0	2.0
Event Handlers			
onBlur	Runs when the focus leaves the FileUpload box	4.0	3.0
onChange	Runs when the value in the FileUpload box is changed	4.0	3.0
onFocus	Runs when the focus is given to the FileUpload box	4.0	3.0
Form	An HTML form (use the form's name)	3.0	2.0
Properties			
acceptCharset	Specifies a list of character encodings for input data to be accepted by the server processing the form	5.0	6.0
action	The location of the CGI script that receives the form values	3.0	2.0
autocomplete	Specifies whether form autocompletion is on or off	5.0	
elements[ ]	An array of elements within the form	3.0	2.0
encoding	The type of encoding used in the form	3.0	2.0
enctype	Specifies the MIME type of submitted data		6.0
length	The number of elements in the form	3.0	2.0
method	The type of method used when submitting the form	3.0	2.0
name	The name of the form	3.0	2.0
target	The name of the window into which CGI output should be directed	3.0	2.0
Methods			
handleEvent(*event*)	Invokes the event handler for the specified *event*	4.0	3.0
reset()	Resets the form	3.0	2.0
submit()	Submits the form to the CGI script	3.0	2.0
urns(*urn*)	Retrieves a collection of all elements to which the behavior of string *urn* is attached	5.0	
Event Handlers			
onReset	Runs when the form is reset	4.0	3.0
onSubmit	Runs when the form is submitted	3.0	2.0
Frame	A frame window (use the frame's name)	3.0	2.0
Properties			
document	The current document in the frame window	3.0	2.0
frames	An array of frames within the frame window	3.0	2.0
length	The length of the frames array	3.0	2.0
name	The name of the frame	3.0	2.0
parent	The name of the window that contains the frame	3.0	2.0
self	The name of the current frame window	3.0	2.0
top	The name of the topmost window in the hierarchy of frame windows	3.0	2.0
window	The name of the current frame window	3.0	2.0
Methods			
alert(*message*)	Displays an Alert box with the text string *message*	3.0	2.0
blur()	Removes the focus from the frame	4.0	3.0

JavaScript Elements	Description	IE	Netscape
clearInterval(*ID*)	Cancels the repeated execution *ID*	4.0	4.0
clearTimeout(*ID*)	Cancels the delayed execution *ID*	4.0	4.0
confirm(*message*)	Displays a Confirm box with the text string *message*	3.0	2.0
open(*URL, name, features*)	Opens a URL in the frame with the name *name* and a feature list indicated by *features*	3.0	2.0
print()	Displays the Print dialog box	4.0	4.0
prompt(*message, response*)	Displays a Prompt dialog box with the text string *message* and the default value *response*	3.0	2.0
setInterval(*expression, time*)	Runs an *expression* after *time* milliseconds	4.0	4.0
setTimeout(*expression, time*)	Runs an *expression* every *time* milliseconds	4.0	4.0
Event Handlers			
onBlur	Runs when the focus is removed from the frame	4.0	4.0
onFocus	Runs when the frame receives the focus	4.0	4.0
onMove	Runs when the frame is moved	4.0	4.0
onResize	Runs when the frame is resized	4.0	4.0
h1...h6	Heading level element in the document	4.0	6.0
Properties			
align	The alignment of the element, for example, "right"	4.0	6.0
head	Corresponds to the <head> element in the document	4.0	6.0
Properties			
profile	A list of the URLs for data properties and legal values	6.0	6.0
hidden	A hidden field on an HTML form (use the name of the hidden field)	3.0	2.0
Properties			
form	The name of the form containing the hidden field	3.0	2.0
name	The name of the hidden field	3.0	2.0
type	The type of the hidden field	4.0	3.0
value	The value of the hidden field	3.0	2.0
history	An object containing information about the Web browser's history list	3.0	2.0
Properties			
current	The current URL in the history list	4.0	3.0
length	The number of items in the history list	3.0	2.0
next	The next item in the history list	4.0	3.0
previous	The previous item in the history list	3.0	2.0
Methods			
back()	Navigates back to the previous item in the history list	3.0	2.0
forward()	Navigates forward to the next item in the history list	3.0	2.0
go(*location*)	Navigates to the item in the history list specified by the value of *location*; the *location* variable can be either an integer or the name of the Web page	3.0	2.0
hr	A horizontal rule element in the document	4.0	6.0
Properties			
align	Alignment of the object, for example, "right"	4.0	6.0
color	The color of the rule	4.0	
noShade	A Boolean indicating that the rule is not to be shaded	4.0	6.0
size	The size (height) of the rule in pixels	4.0	6.0
width	The width of the rule in pixels	4.0	6.0

JavaScript Elements	Description	IE	Netscape
html	Corresponds to the <html> element in the document	4.0	6.0
Properties			
version	The DTD version for the document	6.0	6.0
iframe	An inline frame element in the document	4.0	6.0
Properties			
align	The alignment of the object, for example, "right"	4.0	6.0
allowTransparency	A Boolean specifying whether the background of the frame can be transparent	5.0	
border	The width of the border around the frame	4.0	
contentDocument	The document that corresponds to the content of this frame		6.0
contentWindow	The window that corresponds to this frame	5.0	
frameBorder	String of "0" (no border) or "1" (show border)	4.0	6.0
height	The height of the frame in pixels	4.0	6.0
longdesc	The URL of a long description for the frame	6.0	6.0
marginHeight	Vertical margins in pixels	4.0	6.0
marginWidth	Horizontal margins in pixels	4.0	6.0
name	The name of the frame	4.0	6.0
width	The width of the frame in pixels	4.0	6.0
image	An inline image (use the name assigned to the image)	4.0	3.0
Properties			
align	Specifies the alignment of the object, for example, "left", "right", or "center"	4.0	6.0
alt	A string containing alternative text for the image	4.0	6.0
border	The width of the image border in pixels	4.0	3.0
complete	A Boolean value indicating whether the image has been completely loaded by the browser	4.0	3.0
height	The height of the image in pixels	4.0	3.0
hspace	The horizontal space around the image in pixels	4.0	3.0
isMap	A Boolean indicating whether the image is a server-side image map	4.0	6.0
longDesc	The URL for a more detailed description of the image	6.0	6.0
loop	An integer indicating how many times the image is to loop when activated	4.0	
lowSrc	Specifies a URL for a lower-resolution image to display		6.0
lowsrc	The value of the lowsrc property of the <img> tag	4.0	3.0
name	The name of the image	4.0	3.0
nameProp	Indicates the name of the file given in the *src* attribute of the <img>	5.0	
src	The URL of the image	4.0	3.0
style	Reference to the inline *Style* object for the element	4.0	4.0
useMap	Contains a URL to use as a client-side image map	4.0	6.0
vspace	The vertical space around the image in pixels	4.0	3.0
width	The width of the image in pixels	4.0	3.0
Methods			
handleEvent(*event*)	Invokes the event handler for the specified *event*	4.0	4.0
Event Handlers			
onAbort	Runs when the image load is aborted	4.0	3.0
onError	Runs when an error occurs while loading the image	4.0	3.0
onKeyDown	Runs when a key is pressed down	4.0	3.0
onKeyPress	Runs when a key is pressed	4.0	4.0
onKeyUp	Runs when a key is released	4.0	4.0
onLoad	Runs when the image is loaded	4.0	3.0

JavaScript Elements	Description	IE	Netscape
implementation	Information about the DOM technologies the browser supports (child of Document)	6.0	6.0
Methods			
hasFeature(feature [, version])	A Boolean indicating if the browser supports the feature at the DOM level given in version	6.0	6.0
label	A form field label in the document	4.0	6.0
Properties			
accessKey	Indicates the hotkey that gives the element focus	4.0	6.0
form	The form that encloses the label	4.0	6.0
layer	A document layer (use the name of the layer); deprecated in favor of the standard <div> element	4.0	
Properties			
above	The layer above the current layer		4.0
background	The background image of the layer		4.0
below	The layer below the current layer		4.0
bgColor	The background color of the layer		4.0
clip.bottom, clip.height, clip.left, clip.right, clip.top, clip.width	The size and position of the layer's clipping area		4.0
document	The document containing the layer		4.0
name	The value of the *name* or *id* attribute for the layer		4.0
left	The *x*-coordinate of the layer		4.0
pageX	The *x*-coordinate relative to the document		4.0
pageY	The *y*-coordinate relative to the document		4.0
parentLayer	The containing layer		4.0
siblingAbove	The layer above in the zIndex		4.0
siblingBelow	The layer below in the zIndex		4.0
src	The URL of the layer document		4.0
top	The *y*-coordinate of the layer		4.0
visibility	The state of the layer's visibility		4.0
zIndex	The zIndex value of the layer		4.0
Methods			
handleEvent(*event*)	Invokes the event handler for the specified *event*		4.0
load(*source, width*)	Loads a new URL into the layer from *source* with the specified *width*		4.0
moveAbove(*layer*)	Moves the layer above *layer*		4.0
moveBelow(*layer*)	Moves the layer below *layer*		4.0
moveBy(*x, y*)	Moves the *x* pixels in the *x*-direction, and the *y* pixels in the *y*-direction		4.0
moveTo(*x, y*)	Moves the upper-left corner of the layer to the specified (*x, y*) coordinate		4.0
moveToAbsolute(*x, y*)	Moves the layer to the specified coordinate (*x, y*) within the page		4.0
resizeBy(*width, height*)	Resizes the layer by the specified *width* and *height*		4.0
resizeTo(*width, height*)	Resizes the layer to the specified *height* and *width*		4.0
Event Handlers			
onBlur	Runs when the focus leaves the layer		4.0
onFocus	Runs when the layer receives the focus		4.0
onLoad	Runs when the layer is loaded		4.0
onMouseOut	Runs when the mouse leaves the layer		4.0
onMouseOver	Runs when the mouse hovers over the layer		4.0

JavaScript Elements	Description	IE	Netscape
`legend`	A `<legend>` (fieldset caption) element in the document	4.0	6.0
Properties			
accessKey	Indicates the hotkey	4.0	6.0
align	Specifies the alignment of the element, for example, "right"	4.0	6.0
form	The form in which the element is enclosed	4.0	6.0
`link`	A link within an HTML document (use the name of the link)	3.0	2.0
Properties			
accessKey	Indicates the hotkey that gives the element focus	4.0	6.0
charset	The character set of the linked document	6.0	6.0
coords	Defines the coordinates of the object	6.0	6.0
disabled	A Boolean indicating whether the element is disabled	4.0	6.0
hash	The anchor name from the link's URL	3.0	2.0
host	The host from the link's URL	3.0	2.0
hostname	The hostname from the link's URL	3.0	2.0
href	The link's URL	3.0	2.0
hreflang	Indicates the language code of the linked resource	6.0	6.0
media	The media the linked document is intended for		6.0
nameProp	Holds the filename portion of the URL in the *href*	5.0	
pathname	The path portion of the link's URL	3.0	2.0
port	The port number of the link's URL	3.0	2.0
protocol	The protocol used with the link's URL	3.0	2.0
search	The search portion of the link's URL	3.0	2.0
target	The target window of the hyperlinks	3.0	2.0
text	The text used to create the link	4.0	4.0
type	Specifies the media type in the form of a MIME type for the link target	6.0	6.0
Methods			
handleEvent(*event*)	Invokes the event handler for the specified *event*	4.0	4.0
Event Handlers			
onClick	Runs when the link is clicked	3.0	2.0
onDblClick	Runs when the link is double-clicked	4.0	4.0
onKeyDown	Runs when a key is pressed down	4.0	4.0
onKeyPress	Runs when a key is initially pressed	4.0	4.0
onKeyUp	Runs when a key is released	4.0	4.0
onMouseDown	Runs when the mouse button is pressed down on the link	4.0	4.0
onMouseOut	Runs when mouse moves away from the link	4.0	4.0
onMouseOver	Runs when the mouse hovers over the link	4.0	4.0
onMouseUp	Runs when the mouse button is released	4.0	4.0
`location`	The location of the document	3.0	2.0
Properties			
hash	The location's anchor name	3.0	2.0
host	The location's hostname and port number	3.0	2.0
href	The location's URL	3.0	2.0
pathname	The path portion of the location's URL	3.0	2.0
port	The port number of the location's URL	3.0	2.0
protocol	The protocol used with the location's URL	3.0	2.0
Methods			
Assign(*url*)	Assigns the URL in the string *url* to the object	3.0	2.0
reload()	Reloads the location	4.0	3.0
replace(*url*)	Loads a new location with the address *url*	4.0	3.0

JavaScript Elements	Description	IE	Netscape
map	Corresponds to a <map> (client-side image map) element in the document	4.0	6.0
Properties			
Areas[ ]	A collection of *areas* enclosed by the object	4.0	6.0
Name	String holding the name of the image map	4.0	6.0
Math	An object used for advanced mathematical calculations	3.0	2.0
Properties			
E	The value of the base of natural logarithms (2.7182...)	3.0	2.0
LN10	The value of the natural logarithm of 10	3.0	2.0
LN2	The value of the natural logarithm of 2	3.0	2.0
LOG10E	The base 10 logarithm of E	3.0	2.0
LOG2E	The base 2 logarithm of E	3.0	2.0
PI	The value of pi (3.1416...)	3.0	2.0
SQRT1_2	The square root of $\frac{1}{2}$	3.0	2.0
SQRT2	The square root of 2	3.0	2.0
Methods			
abs(*number*)	Returns the absolute value of *number*	3.0	2.0
acos(*number*)	Returns the arc cosine of *number* in radians	3.0	2.0
asin(*number*)	Returns the arc sine of *number* in radians	3.0	2.0
atan(*number*)	Returns the arc tangent of *number* in radians	3.0	2.0
atan2()	Returns the arc tangent of the quotient of its arguments	3.0	2.0
ceil(*number*)	Rounds *number* up to the next-highest integer	3.0	2.0
cos(*number*)	Returns the cosine of *number*, where *number* is an angle expressed in radians	3.0	2.0
exp(*number*)	Raises the value of E (2.7182...) to the value of *number*	3.0	2.0
floor(*number*)	Rounds *number* down to the next-lowest integer	3.0	2.0
log(*number*)	Returns the natural logarithm of *number*	3.0	2.0
max(*number1, number2*)	Returns the greater of *number1* and *number2*	3.0	2.0
min(*number1, number2*)	Returns the lesser of *number1* and *number2*	3.0	2.0
pow(*number1, number2*)	Returns the value of *number1* raised to the power of *number2*	3.0	2.0
random()	Returns a random number between 0 and 1	3.0	2.0
round(*number*)	Rounds *number* to the closest integer	3.0	2.0
sin(*number*)	Returns the sine of *number*, where *number* is an angle expressed in radians	3.0	2.0
sqrt(*number*)	Returns the square root of *number*	3.0	2.0
tan(*number*)	Returns the tangent of *number*, where *number* is an angle expressed in radians	3.0	2.0
toString(*number*)	Converts *number* to a text string	3.0	2.0
menu	A <menu> (menu list) element in the document	4.0	6.0
Properties			
compact	A Boolean signifying whether the list should be compacted	6.0	6.0
navigator	An object representing the browser currently in use	3.0	2.0
Properties			
appCodeName	The code name of the browser	3.0	2.0
appName	The name of the browser	3.0	2.0
appVersion	The version of the browser	3.0	2.0
cookieEnabled	A Boolean signifying whether persistent cookies are enabled	4.0	6.0
language	The language of the browser	4.0	4.0
mimeTypes	An array of the MIME types supported by the browser	4.0	4.0
oscpu	A string containing the operating system		6.0
platform	The platform on which the browser is running	4.0	4.0

JavaScript Elements	Description	IE	Netscape
plugins	An array of the plug-ins installed on the browser	4.0	3.0
preference	Allows a signed script to get and set certain Navigator preferences		4.0
userAgent	The user-agent text string sent from the client to the Web server	3.0	2.0
Methods			
javaEnabled()	Indicates whether the browser supports Java	4.0	3.0
plugins.refresh()	Checks for newly installed plug-ins	4.0	3.0
taintEnabled()	Specifies whether data tainting is enabled	5.5	3.0
Option	An option from a selection list (use the name of the option or the index value from the options array)	3.0	2.0
Properties			
defaultSelected	A Boolean indicating whether the option is selected by default	4.0	3.0
disabled	A Boolean indicating whether the element is disabled	4.0	6.0
index	The index value of the option	3.0	2.0
label	Alternate text for the option as specified in the *label* attribute		6.0
selected	A Boolean indicating whether the option is currently selected	3.0	2.0
text	The text of the option as it appears on the Web page	3.0	2.0
value	The value of the option	3.0	2.0
param	Corresponds to an occurrence of a <param> element in the document	4.0	6.0
Properties			
name	The name of the parameter	4.0	6.0
type	The type of the value when *valueType* is "ref"	6.0	6.0
value	The value of the parameter	6.0	6.0
valueType	Provides more information about how to interpret value; usually "data", "ref", or "object"	6.0	6.0
Password	A password field in an HTML form (use the name of the password field)	3.0	2.0
Properties			
defaultValue	The default password	3.0	2.0
name	The name of the password field	3.0	2.0
type	The type value of the password field	3.0	2.0
value	The value of the password field	3.0	2.0
Methods			
focus()	Gives the password field the focus	3.0	2.0
blur()	Leaves the password field	3.0	2.0
select()	Selects the password field	3.0	2.0
Event Handlers			
onBlur	Runs when the focus leaves the password field	3.0	2.0
onFocus	Runs when the password field receives the focus	3.0	2.0
plugin	A plug-in object in the Web page	4.0	3.0
Properties			
description	The description of the plug-in	4.0	3.0
filename	The plug-in filename	4.0	3.0
length	The number of MIME types supported by the plug-in	4.0	3.0
name	The name of the plug-in	4.0	3.0
popup	A popup window object created by using the createPopup() method in IE	5.5	
Properties			
document	Reference to the window's document	5.5	
isOpen	A Boolean indicating if the window is open	5.5	

JavaScript Elements	Description	IE	Netscape
Radio	A radio button in an HTML form (use the radio button's name)	3.0	2.0
Properties			
accessKey	Indicates the hotkey that gives the element focus	4.0	6.0
align	A string specifying the alignment of the element, for example, "right"	4.0	6.0
alt	Alternative text for the button		6.0
checked	A Boolean indicating whether a specific radio button has been checked	3.0	2.0
defaultChecked	A Boolean indicating whether a specific radio button is checked by default	3.0	2.0
defaultValue	The initial value of the button's *value* attribute	3.0	6.0
disabled	A Boolean indicating whether the element is disabled	4.0	6.0
form	The name of the form containing the radio button	3.0	2.0
name	The name of the radio button	3.0	2.0
type	The type value of the radio button	4.0	3.0
value	The value of the radio button	3.0	2.0
Methods			
blur()	Gives the radio button the focus	3.0	2.0
click()	Clicks the radio button	3.0	2.0
focus()	Gives focus to the radio button	3.0	2.0
handleEvent(*event*)	Invokes the event handler for the specified *event*	4.0	4.0
Event Handlers			
onBlur	Runs when the focus leaves the radio button	3.0	2.0
onClick	Runs when the radio button is clicked	3.0	2.0
onFocus	Runs when the radio button receives the focus	3.0	2.0
RegExp	An object used for searching regular expressions	4.0	4.0
Properties			
global	Specifies whether to use a global pattern match	4.0	4.0
ignoreCase	Specifies whether to ignore case in the search string	4.0	4.0
input	The search string	4.0	4.0
lastIndex	Specifies the index at which to start matching the next string	4.0	4.0
lastMatch	The last matched characters	4.0	4.0
lastParen	The last parenthesized substring match	4.0	4.0
leftContext	The substring preceding the most recent match	4.0	4.0
multiline	Specifies whether to search on multiple lines	4.0	4.0
rightContext	The substring following the most recent match	4.0	4.0
source	The string pattern	4.0	4.0
Methods			
compile()	Compiles a regular search expression	4.0	4.0
exec(*string*)	Executes the search for a match to *string*	4.0	4.0
test(*string*)	Tests for a match to *string*	4.0	4.0
Reset	A reset button in an HTML form (use the name of the reset button)	3.0	2.0
Properties			
accessKey	Indicates the hotkey that gives the element focus	4.0	6.0
align	Specifies the alignment of the element, for example, "right"	4.0	6.0
alt	Alternative text for the button		6.0
defaultValue	Contains the initial value of the button	3.0	6.0
disabled	A Boolean indicating whether the element is disabled	4.0	6.0
form	The name of the form containing the reset button	3.0	2.0

JavaScript Elements	Description	IE	Netscape
name	The name of the reset button	3.0	2.0
type	The type value of the reset button	4.0	3.0
value	The value of the reset button	3.0	2.0
Methods			
blur()	Removes the focus from the reset button	3.0	2.0
click()	Clicks the reset button	3.0	2.0
focus()	Gives the focus to the reset button	3.0	2.0
handleEvent(*event*)	Invokes the event handler for the specified *event*	4.0	4.0
Event Handlers			
onBlur	Runs when the focus leaves the reset button	3.0	2.0
onClick	Runs when the reset button is clicked	3.0	2.0
onFocus	Runs when the reset button receives the focus	3.0	2.0
screen	An object representing the user's screen	4.0	4.0
Properties			
availHeight	The height of the screen, minus toolbars or any other permanent objects	4.0	4.0
availWidth	The width of the screen, minus toolbars or any other permanent objects	4.0	4.0
colorDepth	The number of possible colors in the screen	4.0	4.0
height	The height of the screen	4.0	4.0
pixelDepth	The number of bits per pixel in the screen	5.0	4.0
width	The width of the screen	4.0	4.0
Script	Corresponds to a <script> element in the document	4.0	6.0
Properties			
charset	The character set used to encode the script	6.0	6.0
defer	A Boolean indicating whether script execution may be deferred	4.0	6.0
src	The URL of the external script	4.0	6.0
text	The contents of the script	4.0	6.0
type	The value of the type attribute	4.0	6.0
Select	A selection list in an HTML form (use the name of the selection list)	3.0	2.0
Properties			
disabled	A Boolean indicating whether the element is disabled	4.0	6.0
form	The name of the form containing the selection list	3.0	2.0
length	The number of *options* in the selection list	3.0	2.0
multiple	A Boolean indicating whether multiple *options* may be selected	4.0	6.0
name	The name of the selection list	3.0	2.0
options[ ]	An array of options within the selection list; see the options object for more information on working with individual selection list options	3.0	2.0
selectedIndex	The index value of the selected option from the selection list	3.0	2.0
size	The number of options that are visible at one time	4.0	6.0
tabIndex	Numeric value that indicates the tab order for the object	4.0	6.0
type	The type value of the selection list	4.0	3.0
value	The *value* of the currently selected option	4.0	6.0
Methods			
add(element, before)	Adds the *option* referenced by the *element* to the list of options before the *option* referenced by *before*; if *before* is null, it is added at the end	5.5	6.0
blur()	Removes the focus from the selection list	3.0	2.0

JavaScript Elements	Description	IE	Netscape
focus()	Gives the focus to the selection list	3.0	2.0
handleEvent(*event*)	Invokes the event handler for the specified *event*	4.0	4.0
remove(index)	Removes the option at index *index* from the list of *options*	5.5	6.0
Event Handlers			
onBlur	Runs when the focus leaves the selection list	3.0	2.0
onChange	Runs when focus leaves the selection list and the value of the selection list is changed	3.0	2.0
onFocus	Runs when the selection list receives the focus	3.0	2.0
String	An object representing a text string	3.0	2.0
Properties			
length	The number of characters in the string	3.0	2.0
Methods			
anchor(*name*)	Converts the string into a hypertext link anchor with the name *name*	3.0	2.0
big()	Displays the string using the <big> tag	3.0	2.0
blink()	Displays the string using the <blink> tag	3.0	2.0
bold()	Displays the string using the <b> tag	3.0	2.0
charAt(*index*)	Returns the character in the string at the location specified by *index*	3.0	2.0
charCodeAt(position)	Returns an unsigned integer of the Unicode value of the character at index *position*	5.5	4.0
concat(*string2*)	Concatenates the string with the second text string *string2*	4.0	4.0
fixed()	Displays the string using the <tt> tag	3.0	2.0
fontColor(*color*)	Sets the color attribute of the string	3.0	2.0
fontSize(*value*)	Sets the size attribute of the string	3.0	2.0
indexOf(*string, start*)	Searches the string, beginning at the *start* character, and returns the index value of the first occurrence of the string *string*	3.0	2.0
italics()	Displays the string using the <i> tag	3.0	2.0
lastIndexOf(*string, start*)	Searches the string, beginning at the *start* character, and locates the index value of the last occurrence of the string *string*	3.0	2.0
link(*href*)	Converts the string into a hypertext link pointing to the URL *href*	3.0	2.0
match(*expression*)	Returns an array containing the matches based on the regular expression *expression*	4.0	4.0
replace(*expression, new*)	Performs a search based on the regular expression *expression* and replaces the text with *new*	4.0	4.0
search(*expression*)	Performs a search based on the regular expression *expression* and returns the index number	4.0	4.0
slice(*begin, end*)	Returns a substring between the *begin* and the *end* index values; the *end* index value is optional	4.0	4.0
small()	Displays the string using the <small> tag	3.0	2.0
split(*separator*)	Splits the string into an array of strings at every occurrence of the *separator* character	4.0	4.0
strike()	Displays the string using the <strike> tag	3.0	2.0
sub()	Displays the string using the <sub> tag	3.0	2.0
substr(*begin, length*)	Returns a substring starting at the *begin* index value and continuing for *length* characters; the *length* parameter is optional	4.0	4.0
substring(*begin, end*)	Returns a substring between the *begin* and the *end* index values; the *end* index value is optional	3.0	2.0
sup()	Displays the string using the <sup> tag	3.0	2.0
toLowerCase()	Converts the string to lowercase	3.0	2.0
toUpperCase()	Converts the string to uppercase	3.0	2.0

JavaScript Elements	Description	IE	Netscape
style	This corresponds to an instance of a <style> element in the page	4.0	6.0
Properties			
disabled	A Boolean indicating whether the element is disabled	4.0	6.0
sheet	The styleSheet object corresponding to the element		6.0
styleSheet	The styleSheet object corresponding to the element	4.0	
type	The value of the *type* attribute for the style sheet	4.0	6.0
Submit	A submit button in an HTML form (use the name of the submit button)	3.0	2.0
Properties			
accessKey	String indicating the hotkey that gives the element focus	4.0	6.0
alt	Alternative text for the button	6.0	
defaultValue	The initial value of the button's *value* attribute	3.0	6.0
disabled	A Boolean indicating whether the element is disabled	4.0	6.0
form	The name of the form containing the submit button	3.0	2.0
name	The name of the submit button	3.0	2.0
tabIndex	Numeric value that indicates the tab order for the object	4.0	6.0
type	The type value of the submit button	4.0	3.0
value	The value of the submit button	3.0	2.0
Methods			
blur()	Removes the focus from the submit button	3.0	2.0
click()	Clicks the submit button	3.0	2.0
focus()	Gives the focus to the submit button	3.0	2.0
handleEvent(*event*)	Invokes the event handler for the specified *event*	4.0	4.0
Event Handlers			
onBlur	Runs when the focus leaves the submit button	3.0	2.0
onClick	Runs when the submit button is clicked	3.0	2.0
onFocus	Runs when the submit button receives the focus	3.0	2.0
Text	An input box from an HTML form (use the name of the input box)	3.0	2.0
Properties			
accessKey	A string indicating the hotkey that gives the element focus	4.0	6.0
defaultValue	The default value of the input box	3.0	2.0
disabled	A Boolean indicating whether the element is disabled	4.0	6.0
form	The form containing the input box	3.0	2.0
maxLength	The maximum number of characters the field can contain	4.0	6.0
name	The name of the input box	3.0	2.0
size	The width of the field in characters	4.0	6.0
tabIndex	The numeric value that indicates the tab order for the object	4.0	6.0
type	The type value of the input box	4.0	3.0
value	The value of the input box	3.0	2.0
Methods			
blur()	Removes the focus from the input box	3.0	2.0
focus()	Gives the focus to the input box	3.0	2.0
handleEvent(*event*)	Invokes the event handler for the specified *event*	4.0	4.0
select()	Selects the input box	3.0	2.0
Event Handlers			
onBlur	Runs when the focus leaves the input box	3.0	2.0
onChange	Runs when the focus leaves the input box and the input box value changes	3.0	2.0

JavaScript Elements	Description	IE	Netscape
onFocus	Runs when the input box receives the focus	3.0	2.0
onSelect	Runs when some of the text in the input box is selected	3.0	2.0
Textarea	A text area box in an HTML form (use the name of the text area box)	3.0	2.0
Properties			
accessKey	Indicates the hotkey that gives the element focus	4.0	6.0
cols	The number of columns of the input area	4.0	6.0
defaultValue	The default value of the text area box	3.0	2.0
enabled	Indicates whether a text area field is enabled using a Boolean	3.0	3.0
form	The form containing the text area box	3.0	2.0
name	The name of the text area box	3.0	2.0
rows	The number of rows of the input area	4.0	6.0
tabIndex	Numeric value that indicates the tab order for the object	4.0	6.0
type	The type value of the text area box	4.0	3.0
value	The value of the text area box	3.0	2.0
Methods			
blur()	Removes the focus from the text area box	3.0	2.0
focus()	Gives the focus to the text area box	3.0	2.0
handleEvent(*event*)	Invokes the event handler for the specified *event*	4.0	4.0
select()	Selects the text area box	3.0	2.0
Event Handlers			
onBlur	Runs when the focus leaves the text area box	3.0	2.0
onChange	Runs when the focus leaves the text area box and the text area box value changes	3.0	2.0
onFocus	Runs when the text area box receives the focus	3.0	2.0
onKeyDown	Runs when a key is pressed down	4.0	4.0
onKeyPress	Runs when a key is pressed	4.0	4.0
onKeyUp	Runs when a key is released	4.0	4.0
onSelect	Runs when some of the text in the text area box is selected	3.0	2.0
window	The document window	3.0	2.0
Properties			
clipboardData	Provides access to the OS's clipboard	5.0	
defaultStatus	The default message shown in the window's status bar	3.0	2.0
directories	A Boolean specifying whether the Netscape 6 "directories" button is visible.		6.0
document	The document displayed in the window	3.0	2.0
frameElement	The *Frame* in which the window is enclosed	5.5	
frames	An array of frames within the window (see the frames object for properties and methods applied to individual frames)	3.0	2.0
history	A list of visited URLs	4.0	3.0
innerHeight	The height of the window's display area	4.0	4.0
innerWidth	The width of the widow's display area	4.0	4.0
length	The number of frames in the window	3.0	2.0
location	The URL loaded into the window	3.0	2.0
locationbar.visible	A Boolean indicating the visibility of the window's location bar	4.0	4.0
menubar.visible	A Boolean indicating the visibility of the window's menu bar	4.0	4.0
name	The name of the window	3.0	2.0
opener	The name of the window that opened the current window	4.0	3.0
outerHeight	The height of the outer area of the window	4.0	4.0
outerWidth	The width of the outer area of the window	4.0	4.0
pageXOffset	The *x*-coordinate of the window	4.0	4.0

JavaScript Elements	Description	IE	Netscape
pageYOffset	The *y*-coordinate of the window	4.0	4.0
parent	The name of the window containing this particular window	3.0	2.0
personalbar.visible	A Boolean indicating the visibility of the window's personal bar	4.0	4.0
screen	The browser's *screen* object	4.0	6.0
screenLeft	The *x*-coordinate in pixels of the left edge of the client area of the browser window	5.0	
screenTop	The *y*-coordinate in pixels of the top edge of the client area of the browser window	5.0	
scrollbars.visible	A Boolean indicating the visibility of the window's scroll bars	4.0	4.0
scrollX	How far the window is scrolled to the right		6.0
scrollY	How far the window is scrolled down		6.0
self	The current window	3.0	2.0
status	The message shown in the window's status bar	3.0	2.0
statusbar.visible	A Boolean indicating the visibility of the window's status bar	4.0	4.0
toolbar.visible	A Boolean indicating the visibility of the window's toolbar	4.0	4.0
top	The name of the topmost window in a hierarchy of windows	3.0	2.0
window	The current window	3.0	2.0
Methods			
alert(*message*)	Displays the text contained in *message* in a dialog box	3.0	2.0
back()	Loads the previous page in the window	4.0	4.0
blur()	Removes the focus from the window	4.0	3.0
captureEvents()	Sets the window to capture all events of a specified type	4.0	4.0
clearInterval(*ID*)	Clears the interval for *ID*, set with the SetInterval method	4.0	4.0
clearTimeout()	Clears the timeout, set with the setTimeout method	3.0	2.0
close()	Closes the window	3.0	2.0
confirm(*message*)	Displays a confirmation dialog box with the text *message*	3.0	2.0
createPopup(*arg*)	Creates a popup window and returns a reference to the new popup object	5.5	
disableExternalCapture	Disables external event capturing	4.0	4.0
enableExternalCapture	Enables external event capturing	4.0	4.0
find(*string, case, direction*)	Displays a Find dialog box, where *string* is the text to find in the window, *case* is a Boolean indicating whether the find is case-sensitive, and *direction* is a Boolean indicating whether the find goes in the backward direction (all of the parameters are optional)	4.0	4.0
focus()	Gives focus to the window	4.0	3.0
forward()	Loads the next page in the window	4.0	4.0
handleEvent(*event*)	Invokes the event handler for the specified *event*	4.0	4.0
moveBy(*horizontal, vertical*)	Moves the window by the specified amount in the *horizontal* and *vertical* directions	4.0	4.0
moveTo(*x, y*)	Moves the window to the *x*- and *y*-coordinates	4.0	4.0
open()	Opens the window	3.0	2.0
print()	Displays the Print dialog box	4.0	4.0
prompt(*message, default_text*)	Displays a Prompt dialog box with the text *message* (the default message is: *default_text*)	3.0	2.0
releaseEvents(*event*)	Releases the captured events of a specified *event*	4.0	4.0
resizeBy(*horizontal, vertical*)	Resizes the window by the amount in the *horizontal* and *vertical* directions	4.0	4.0
resizeTo(*width, height*)	Resizes the window to the specified *width* and *height*	4.0	4.0
routeEvent(*event*)	Passes the *event* to be handled natively	4.0	4.0
scroll(*x, y*)	Scrolls the window to the *x, y* coordinate	4.0	3.0

JavaScript Elements	Description	IE	Netscape
scrollBy(*x, y*)	Scrolls the window by *x* pixels in the *x*-direction and *y* pixels in the *y*-direction	4.0	4.0
scrollTo(*x, y*)	Scrolls the window to the *x, y* coordinate	4.0	4.0
setActive( )	Sets the window to be active but does not give it focus	5.5	
setCursor(*type*)	Changes the cursor to *type*		6.0
setInterval(*expression, time*)	Evaluates the *expression* every *time* milliseconds have passed	4.0	4.0
setTimeout(*expression, time*)	Evaluates the *expression* after *time* milliseconds have passed	3.0	2.0
sizeToContent( )	Resizes the window so all contents are visible		6.0
stop()	Stops the windows from loading	4.0	4.0
Event Handlers			
onBlur	Runs when the window loses the focus	4.0	3.0
onDragDrop	Runs when the user drops an object on or within the window	4.0	4.0
onError	Runs when an error occurs while loading the page	4.0	3.0
onFocus	Runs when the window receives the focus	4.0	3.0
onLoad	Runs when the window finishes loading	3.0	2.0
onMove	Runs when the window is moved	4.0	4.0
onResize	Runs when the window is resized	4.0	4.0
onUnload	Runs when the window is unloaded	3.0	2.0

JavaScript

Operators, Keywords, and Syntactical Elements

The following table lists some of the important JavaScript operators, keywords, and syntactical elements. It also identifies their compatibility with Microsoft Internet Explorer and Netscape browsers.

Operators	Description	IE	Netscape
Assignment	**Operators used to assign values to variables**		
=	Assigns the value of the variable on the right to the variable on the left ($x = y$)	3.0	2.0
+=	Adds the two variables and assigns the result to the variable on the left ($x += y$ is equivalent to $x = x + y$)	3.0	2.0
-=	Subtracts the variable on the right from the variable on the left and assigns the result to the variable on the left ($x- = y$ is equivalent to $x = x - y$)	3.0	2.0
*=	Multiplies the two variables together and assigns the result to the variable on the left ($x *= y$ is equivalent to $x = x * y$)	3.0	2.0
/=	Divides the variable on the left by the variable on the right and assigns the result to the variable on the left ($x /= y$ is equivalent to $x = x / y$)	3.0	2.0
&=	Combines two expressions into a single expression ($x \&= y$ is equivalent to $x = x \& y$)	3.0	2.0
%=	Divides the variable on the left by the variable on the right and assigns the remainder to the variable on the left ($x \%= y$ is equivalent to $x = x \% y$)	3.0	2.0
Arithmetic	**Operators used for arithmetic functions**		
+	Adds two variables together ($x + y$)	3.0	2.0
-	Subtracts the variable on the right from the variable on the left ($x - y$)	3.0	2.0
*	Multiplies two variables together ($x * y$)	3.0	2.0
/	Divides the variable the left by the variable on the right (x / y)		
%	Calculates the remainder after dividing the variable on the left by the variable on the right ($x \% y$)	3.0	2.0
++	Increases the value of a variable by 1 ($x ++$ is equivalent to $x = x + 1$)	3.0	2.0
&	Combines two expressions ($x \& y$)	3.0	2.0

Operators	Description	IE	Netscape
Arithmetic	**Operators used for arithmetic functions**		
--	Decreases the value of variable by 1 (x -- is equivalent to $x = x - 1$)	3.0	2.0
-	Changes the sign of a variable (- x)	3.0	2.0
Comparison	**Operators used for comparing expressions**		
==	Returns true when the two expressions are equal ($x == y$)	3.0	2.0
!=	Returns true when the two expressions are not equal ($x != y$)	3.0	2.0
!==	Returns true when the values of the two expressions are equal ($x !== y$)	5.0	5.0
>	Returns true when the expression on the left is greater than the expression on the right ($x > y$)	3.0	2.0
<	Returns true when the expression on the left is less than the expression on the right ($x < y$)	3.0	2.0
>=	Returns true when the expression on the left is greater than or equal to the expression on the right ($x >= y$)	3.0	2.0
<=	Returns true when the expression on the left is less than or equal to the expression on the right ($x <= y$)	3.0	2.0
Conditional	**Operators used to determine values based on conditions that are either true or false**		
(condition) ? value1 : value2	If *condition* is true, then this expression equals *value1*, otherwise it equals *value2*		
Keywords	**JavaScript keywords are reserved by JavaScript**		
infinity	Represents positive infinity (often used with comparison operators)	5.0	4.0
this	Refers to the current object	3.0	2.0
var	Declares a variable	3.0	2.0
with	Allows the declaration of all the properties for an object without directly referencing the object each time	3.0	2.0
Logical	**Operators used for evaluating true and false expressions**		
^	The XOR (exclusive OR) operator	3.0	2.0
!	Reverses the Boolean value of the expression	3.0	2.0
&&	Returns true only if both expressions are true (also known as an AND operator)		
||	Returns true when either expression is true (also known as an OR operator)	3.0	2.0
|	Returns true if the expression is false and false if the expression is true (also known as a NEGATION operator)	3.0	2.0
Syntax	**Syntactical elements**		
;	Indicates the end of a command line	3.0	2.0
/* comments */	Used for inserting *comments* within a JavaScript command line	3.0	2.0
// comments	Used to create a line of *comments*	3.0	2.0

Working with Cookies

Introducing Cookies

A **cookie** is a piece of information stored in a text file that a Web browser places on a user's computer. Typically, cookies contain data to be accessed the next time a user visits a particular Web site. For example, many online stores use cookies to store users' addresses and credit card information. This enables a store to access previously entered information from a cookie the next time a repeat user makes a purchase, freeing the user from reentering this material.

Where a browser places a cookie file depends on the browser. Netscape stores cookies in a single text file named "cookie.txt." Internet Explorer stores cookies in a separate text file, typically in the Windows/Cookies folder. Browsers limit each cookie to 4 kilobytes in size, and a computer can generally not store more than 300 cookies at one time. If a browser tries to store more than 300 cookies, the oldest cookies are deleted to make room.

Cookies, the Web Server, and CGI Scripts

The first implementation of cookies was with a CGI script running on a Web server. A CGI script can retrieve the cookie information and perform some action based on the information in the file. The process works as follows:

1. A user accesses the Web site and sends a request to the CGI script on the Web server, either by filling out an order form or by some other process that calls the CGI script.
2. The CGI script determines whether a cookie for the user exists.
3. If no cookie is detected, the Web server sends a form, or page, for a user to enter the information needed by the cookie. This information is then sent to the CGI script for processing.
4. If a cookie is found, the CGI script retrieves that information and creates a new page, or modifies the current page, based on the information contained in the cookie.

Information is exchanged using the same Hypertext Transfer Protocol (HTTP) used for retrieving the contents of the Web page. This is because each transfer includes a header section that contains information about the document (such as its MIME data type) and allows for general information in the form

```
field-name: field-value
```

These field-name/field-value pairs contain information that can be stored in a user's cookie.

To store this information on a Web server, a Web programmer must add the Set-Cookie statement to the header section of the CGI script. The Set-Cookie statement is used the first time the user accesses the Web page. Four parameters are often set with cookies: name, expires, path, and domain. The syntax is

```
Set-Cookie: name=text; expires=date; path=text; domain=text; secure
```

The name parameter defines the name of the cookie, and its value cannot contain spaces, commas, or semicolons. The expire parameter indicates the date the information expires; if no expire parameter is included, the cookie expires when the user's browsing session ends. The path parameter indicates the URL path portion to which that cookie applies; setting this value to "/" allows the cookie to be accessed from any folder within the Web site. The domain parameter specifies the URL domain portion to which the cookie applies (usually the domain name of the current document). Finally, the secure parameter indicates that the data should be transferred over a secure link—one that uses file encryption.

Once the initial cookie is created, the browser sends the Cookie statement in the header section of the transfer the next time the user accesses the Web page. The syntax of this statement is

```
Cookie: name1:value1; name2:value2; ...
```

where *name1* is the first field name (whatever that might be), and *value1* is the value of the first field. The statement can contain as many field/value pairs as needed by the Web page so long as the total size of the cookie doesn't exceed 4 kilobytes.

Once the Web server retrieves the cookie field names and values, the CGI script processes them. Because CGI programming is beyond the scope of this book, you will focus on working with cookies on the client side with JavaScript.

Working with the Cookie Property

JavaScript uses the cookie property of the document object to retrieve and update cookie information. The cookie property is simply a text string containing all of the field/value pairs used by the cookie, with each pair separated by a semicolon. To set a value for a cookie, you would use the document.cookie property as follows:

```
document.cookie='cookie1=OrderForm; expires=Mon, 08-Apr-
2006 12:00:00 GMT; path="/"; secure';
```

where the cookie contains the cookie1 field with the value "OrderForm". This particular cookie expires at noon on Monday, April 8, 2006. Because the path value equals "/", this cookie is accessible from any folder within the Web site. The secure property has been set, so any transfer of information involving this cookie must use file encryption. Note that this is a long text string, with the string value enclosed in single quotation marks.

If your Web page had an online form named "Orders", you could create additional field/value pairs using the form names and values as follows:

```
document.cookie='cookie1=OrderForm; name='+document.Orders.Name.
value+'; custid=+'document.Orders.CustId.value;
```

Here, two additional fields have been added to the cookie: name and custid. The values for these fields are taken respectively from the Name field and the CustId field in the Orders form.

Reading a Cookie

One of the challenges of working with cookies in JavaScript is reading the cookie information. To do this you need to extract the appropriate information from the cookie's text string and place that information in the appropriate JavaScript variables. You can use several of JavaScript's string functions to help with this task. To start, create a function named "readCookie(fname)", where "fname" is the name of the field whose value you want to retrieve. The initial code looks as follows:

```
function readCookie(fname) {
    var cookies=document.cookie;
}
```

where the text string of the cookie is stored in the "cookies" variable. In the text string, each field name is followed by an equal sign, so you can use the indexOf( ) method (see Appendix G) to locate the occurrence of the text string "*fname=*", where *fname* is the field name you want to retrieve. You'll store this location in a variable named "startname." The command is:

```
startname=cookies.indexOf(fname+"=");
```

For example, if fname="custid" in the text string below, startname would have a value of 33, because "custid" starts with the thirty-third character in the text string.

```
cookie1=OrderForm; name=Brooks; custid=20010; type=clothes
```

What if the field name is not found in the cookie? In this case, startname has a value of -1, and you can create an If...Else conditional statement to handle this contingency. To simplify things for this example, you'll assume that this is not a concern, and continue.

Next you need to locate the field's value. This value is placed after the equal sign and continues until you reach a semicolon indicating the end of the field's value, or until you reach the end of the text string. The field's value then starts one space after the first equal sign after the field's name. You'll locate the beginning of the field value, using the same indexOf( ) method, and store that location in the startvalue variable. The command is

```
startvalue=cookies.indexOf("=", startname)+1;
```

Here, you locate the text string "=", starting at the point "startname" in the cookies text string. You add one to whatever value is returned by the indexOf() method. In the text string

```
cookie1=OrderForm; name=Brooks; custid=20010; type=clothes
```

the value of the startvalue variable is 40, because the "2" in "20010" is the fortieth character in the string.

Next you locate the end of the field's value, which is the first semicolon after the startvalue character. If the field is the last value in the text string, there is no semicolon at the end, so the indexOf( ) method returns a value of -1. If that occurs, you'll use the length of the text string to locate the value's end. Once again, using the indexOf( ) method, you'll store this value in the endvalue variable. The JavaScript command is

```
endvalue=cookies.indexOf(";",startvalue);
if(endvalue==-1) {
    endvalue=cookies.length;
}
```

In the text string below, the value of the endvalue variable for the custid field is 45.

```
cookie1=OrderForm; name=Brooks; custid=20010; type=clothes
```

To extract the field's value and store it in a variable named "fvalue", use the substring( ) method (see Appendix D) as follows:

```
fvalue=cookies.substring(startvalue, endvalue);
```

where the startvalue indicates the start of the substring and the endvalue marks the substring's end. The complete readCookie(fname) function looks as follows:

```
function readCookie(fname) {
   var cookies=document.cookie;
   var startname=cookies.indexOf(fname+"=");
   var startvalue=cookies.indexOf("=", startname)+1;
   var endvalue=cookies.indexOf(";",startvalue);
   if(endvalue==-1) {
     endvalue=cookies.length;
   }
   var fvalue=cookies.substring(startvalue, endvalue);
return fvalue;
}
```

In a JavaScript program, calling the function

```
readCookie("custid");
```

would return a value of 20010, which is the customer id value stored in the cookie file. You should review this example carefully, paying close attention to the use of the indexOf( ) method and the substring( ) method.

Encoding Cookies

Values in the cookie text string cannot contain spaces, semicolons, or commas. This can be a problem if you are trying to store phrases or sentences. The solution to this problem is to encode the value, using the same type of encoding scheme that is used in URLs (which also cannot contain spaces, commas, and semicolons) or in the mailto action. JavaScript includes the escape( ) method for encoding your text strings. Encoding replaces blank spaces, semicolons, and commas with special characters. For example, if you want to insert an Address field in your cookie that contains a street number and an address, you could use the following JavaScript command:

```
document.cookie='Address='+escape(document.Orders.Address.value);
```

To read a text string that has been encoded, you use JavaScript's unescape( ) method. For example, you could replace the command that stores the field value in the fvalue variable in the readCookie( ) function with the following command:

```
var fvalue=unescape(cookies.substring(startvalue, endvalue));
```

This command removes any encoding characters and replaces them with the appropriate spaces, semicolons, commas, and so forth.

Objectives

Creating Dynamic Web Pages with Netscape 4

Case

Introducing Netscape 4

As JavaScript and browsers have evolved, their ability to create dynamic Web pages has also evolved. Currently, most browsers strive to match the most recent standards of HTML, XHTML, and the JavaScript language. Earlier browser versions are less successful in this regard, however. Thus, programmers must decide how compatible the Web page code they write will be with earlier browsers.

One of the landmark browser releases was Netscape version 4.0 (and later version 4.7). In this version, Netscape added support for several dynamic features, including the first model for handling events and event objects, an element for storing dynamic content, and methods for working with dynamic styles. Many of Netscape 4's features were either part of the current JavaScript and DHTML standards, or they were later adopted into the working standard. However, several features of this browser version were not adopted by the wider browser community. This forced Netscape to decide whether to continue to support the dynamic features unique to Netscape 4 in version 6.0 of their browser, or to drop those features, supporting only the current standard. In order to build a more efficient and compact browser engine, Netscape 6 and more recent releases, do not support the dynamic features of Netscape 4.

Thus, even though both Netscape 4 and more recent versions of the Netscape browser share the same name, you need to treat them as entirely different browsers when creating dynamic Web pages and working with JavaScript. Because Netscape 4 was widely used when it was first released and is still used in some areas today, it is worthwhile to explore the features of this browser version.

Student Data Files

There are no student Data Files needed for this tutorial.

Working with Layers

One of the chief innovations in Netscape 4 was the introduction of the layer element. The **layer element** was designed to store content in a generic block-level element, similar to the div element. The general syntax of the layer element is

```
<layer id="id" attributes>
    content
</layer>
```

where *id* is the id of the layer, *attributes* is a list of HTML attributes that define the appearance, behavior, and placement of the layer, and *content* is the content contained within the layer. This content can contain text, inline images, and so forth. For example, the following layer element contains content for a page's heading:

```
<layer id="heading">
    <h1>Pixal Products</h1>
    <p>Quality digital cameras and peripherals</p>
</layer>
```

Setting the Layer Size

Figure J-1 describes some of the major attributes associated with the layer element.

| Figure J-1 | Attributes of the layer element |

Attribute	Description
clip="*top, left, bottom, right*"	Specifies the coordinates of the viewable region of the layer
height="*value*"	Specifies the height of the layer, in pixels
left="*value*"	Specifies the horizontal offset of the layer, in pixels
pagex="*value*"	Specifies the horizontal position of the layer
pagey="*value*"	Specifies the vertical position of the layer
src="*url*"	Specifies the URL of the document displayed in the layer
top="*value*"	Specifies the vertical offset of the layer, in pixels
visibility="*option*"(hide | inherit | show)	Specifies whether the layer is hidden, shown, or inherits its visibility from the layer that contains it
width="*value*"	Specifies the width of the layer, in pixels
z-index="*value*"	Specifies the stacking order of the layer, relative to the other layers

For example, the code

```
<layer id="heading" width="200" height="150">
    <h1>Pixal Products</h1>
    <p>Quality digital cameras and peripherals</p>
</layer>
```

places the heading layer in a block that is 200 pixels wide by 150 pixels high. If there is more content than can be fit into the specified width and height, Netscape 4 increases the height of the layer to compensate. If you need to keep a layer to specified dimensions regardless of content, you add the clip property to the layer element using the syntax

```
<layer id="id" clip="top, left, bottom, right">
    content
</layer>
```

where *top, left, bottom,* and *right* are the coordinates for the clipping region within the layer. To fix the heading layer at a width of 300 pixels and a height of 100 pixels, you would use the attributes

```
<layer id="heading" width="300" height="150" clip="0,0,300,100">
```

If the content exceeds the dimensions of the layer, Netscape 4 truncates the excess content.

Displaying an External Document in a Layer

The layer element differs from the div element in its ability to display content from external documents. In that sense, layer elements act like inline frames. The syntax to link a layer to an external document is

```
<layer id="id" src="url"></layer>
```

where *url* is the URL of the external file. For example, to display the contents of the heading.htm file in the heading layer, you would use the following code:

```
<layer id="heading" src="heading.htm"></layer>
```

As with inline frames, you can specify the size of a layer element. However, a layer does not automatically display scrollbars if the content of the external document exceeds the layer size. Either the layer increases in size to match the file's content, or the layer is truncated (if you use the clip attribute).

Using Inline Layers and Working with Non-Layer Content

Netscape 4 treats layers like block level elements that float on the top-left corner of the page. If a document contains two layer elements, their content overlaps unless you: (1) place them at different locations using absolute positioning in an attached style sheet, or (2) separate their content using non-layer elements such as the br element. If you want to use relative positioning so that the layers flow alongside each other and along other Web page content, you use the **ilayer element** (ilayer stands for "inflow layer"). The syntax of the ilayer element is

```
<ilayer id="id" attributes>
    content
</ilayer>
```

The ilayer element can also be used to display content from external documents.

Working with Non-Layer Content

When browsers other than Netscape 4 encounter a layer or ilayer element, they ignore the <layer> and <ilayer> tags, but display the content of those tags. This means you can nest layer and ilayer elements within other, more standard elements. For example, the following code nests a layer element within a span element. Netscape 4 browsers recognize the div element and ignore the effects of the span element; other browsers ignore the <layer> tag, but display the span content correctly.

```
<span><layer id="heading">Pixal Products</layer></span>
```

For external documents, you can place an inline frame within a layer element as follows:

```
<layer src="heading.htm"><iframe src="heading.htm" /></layer>
```

Once again, Netscape 4 browsers recognize the external layer element and ignore the inline frame, while other browsers ignore the layer and display the inline frame.

Another way to handle non-Netscape 4 browsers is to place any content that you don't want Netscape 4 to process within a nolayer element. The syntax of the nolayer element is

```
<nolayer>
   Non-Netscape 4 content
</nolayer>
```

Netscape 4 ignores any content placed within the <nolayer> tag, but other browsers ignore the <nolayer> tags and process the content.

Working with Netscape 4 Objects

The document object model for Netscape 4 differs in several important respects from the DOMs for both Internet Explorer and the W3C. In most cases, programmers have to write separate code to perform the same actions in Netscape 4 as in the IE and W3C DOMs. It's therefore important to perform object detection to determine whether a user is running a Netscape 4 browser. Netscape 4 organizes all layers within a document in the document.layers collection. Thus, the following commands create Boolean variables to determine whether a user's browser supports the Netscape 4, Internet Explorer, or W3C DOMs:

```
var NS4DOM = document.layers ? true : false;
var IEDOM = document.all ? true : false;
var W3CDOM = document.getElementById ? true : false
```

If the active browser is Netscape 4, the NS4DOM variable has the Boolean value true; otherwise, it has the value false.

Next, you'll explore how the Netscape 4 document object model differs from the IE and W3C DOMs.

Referencing Page Objects

In the Netscape 4 DOM, a document object can be referenced using the expression

```
document.id
```

where *id* is the id value of the object. In the W3C and IE DOMs, the equivalent expression is

```
document.getElementById(id)
```

You can use the following function to resolve these cross-browser differences:

```
function getObject(id) {
   if (NS4DOM) return eval("document."+id);
   else return document.getElementById(id);
}
```

For example, to create a variable pointing to the Web page object

```
<div id="heading"> … </div>
```

you can run the command

```
headingObj = getObject("heading")
```

This command works under any of the three DOMs.

Referencing Nested Objects

There is one case for which the getObject() function does not work: when an object is nested within another page object (other than the body element). In this situation, the Netscape 4 DOM assumes that the object is a direct child of the body element. To reference such an object, you must use the expression

```
document.id1.document.id2.document.id3 …
```

where *id1*, *id2*, *id3*, etc. are the ids of objects nested within the document hierarchy. If you have a long string of nested objects, the expression to reference the element at the bottom of hierarchy can be quite long and complicated. In the IE and W3C DOMs you don't have to worry about the location of the nested object; using the expression

```
document.getElementById(id3)
```

references the object with the id *id3* no matter where it's located in the document hierarchy.

Referencing Objects by their Tag Name

Finally, the Netscape 4 DOM has a different object method for creating collections of objects with specified tag names. In the Netscape 4 DOM, the expression is

```
document.tags(tagName)
```

while in the W3C DOM it's

```
document.getElementsByTagName(tagName)
```

Thus, to create an object array of all paragraphs in a document, use

```
document.tags("p")
```

in Netscape 4 and

```
document.getElementsByTagName("p")
```

in Internet Explorer and browsers that support the W3C document object model.

Working with Object Styles

Netscape 4 differs from the Internet Explorer and W3C DOMs in how it references style attributes. In some cases the values it assigns to style attributes differ, but in all cases the syntax for referencing the style attributes is different. In the Netscape 4 DOM, style attributes are referenced using the form

```
object.attribute
```

where *object* is a reference to an object in the document and *attribute* is a style attribute. The equivalent expression in the Internet Explorer and W3C DOMs is

```
object.style.attribute
```

For example, to set the font size of an object whose id name is heading, you would run the following command for Netscape 4 browsers:

```
document.heading.fontSize="14pt";
```

For browsers using the other DOMs, you would run the command

```
document.getElementById("heading").style.fontSize="14pt";
```

The following function illustrates a general font size function that works with any of the three document object models:

```
function setFontSize(object,size) {
    if (NS4DOM) object.fontSize=size;
    else object.style.fontSize=size;
}
```

Thus, to set the font size of text within the heading element, you could run the following commands:

```
headObj=getObject("heading");
setFontSize(headObj,"14pt")
```

Stacking Objects on a Web Page

All three DOMs support the z-index style to determine the stacking order of objects on a Web page. In the Netscape 4 DOM, the expression to set the z-index value is

```
object.zIndex
```

while the W3C and Internet Explorer DOMs use

```
object.style.zIndex
```

In addition to the zIndex style property, the Netscape 4 DOM also supports two additional properties named above and below, which are used to reference objects stacked above and below another object. For example, if the subheading object is stacked below the heading object, the expression

```
document.heading.below
```

returns the subheading object. Similarly, the expression

```
document.subheading.above
```

returns the heading object. No similar property is found in either the W3C or Internet Explorer document object models.

Controlling Object Visibility

All three DOMs use the visibility style property to hide or to display objects, but they differ in the values they assign to that property. To display an object, the expressions are

Netscape 4 DOM	`object.visibility="show"`
W3C/IE DOM	`object.style.visibility="visible"`

To hide an object, the expressions are

Netscape 4 DOM	`object.visibility="hide"`
W3C/IE DOM	`object.style.visibility="hidden"`

When you hide or display objects in a dynamic Web page, you need to consider these differences if you want to support the Netscape 4 DOM.

Overflow and Clipping

Figure J-2 describes the properties used to set the width, height, content overflow, and clipping values for document objects.

Overflow and clipping attributes ◀ **Figure J-2**

DOM	Property	Description (all measurements in pixels)
Netscape 4	*object*.width	The width of *object*
	object.height	The height of *object*
	object.clip.top	The position of the top edge of the clipping rectangle
	object.clip.right	The position of the right edge of the clipping rectangle
	object.clip.bottom	The position of the bottom edge of the clipping rectangle
	object.clip.left	The position of the left edge of the clipping rectangle
	object.clip.width	The width of the clipping rectangle
	object.clip.height	The height of the clipping rectangle
Internet Explorer and W3C	*object*.style.width	The width of *object*
	object.style.height	The height of *object*
	object.style.overflow	The way the browser handles content overflow ("visible", "hidden", "scroll", or "auto")
	object.style.clip	A text string specifying the dimensions of the clipping rectangle

As you can see, there are important differences between the document object models, especially in constructing the clipping rectangle. The Netscape 4 DOM places the clipping rectangle settings in six properties: clip.top, clip.right, clip.bottom, clip.left, clip.width, and clip.height. To set the size of the clipping rectangle, you use the following set of commands:

```
object.clip.top=top;
object.clip.right=right;
object.clip.bottom=bottom;
object.clip.left=left;
```

where *top*, *right*, *bottom*, and *left* are the coordinates of the edge of the clipping rectangle. To create the same effect in the W3C or Internet Explorer DOMs, you modify the string value of the style.clip property. The equivalent expression in those DOMs is

```
object.style.clip="rect("+top+" "+right+" "+bottom+" "+left+")";
```

When a clipping rectangle is applied to an object, you can manage the content using the style.overflow property in the W3C and Internet Explorer DOMs. There is no equivalent property to handle content overflow in the Netscape 4 DOM.

Netscape 4 Layer Methods

In addition to the different style properties, the Netscape 4 DOM includes methods for gaining greater control over the size and placement of objects on a Web page. These methods are summarized in Figure J-3.

Figure J-3 | **Netscape 4 layer methods**

Method	Description
load(*url, width*)	Changes the source of the layer to the URL specified by *url*, and changes the width of the layer to *width*
moveAbove(*layer*)	Moves the layer above the *layer* object
moveBelow(*layer*)	Moves the layer below the *layer* object
moveBy(*dx, dy*)	Moves the layer *dx* pixels to the right and *dy* pixels down
moveTo(*x, y*)	Moves the layer to the (*x, y*) coordinates within the parent object
moveToAbsolute(*x, y*)	Moves the layer to the (*x, y*) coordinates on the Web page
resizeBy(*dx, dy*)	Resizes the layer by *dx* pixels horizontally and *dy* pixels vertically
resizeTo(*width, height*)	Resizes the layer to *width* pixels by *height* pixels

For example, the object

```
<div id="heading" style="position: absolute; left: 50px; top: 100px">
   Pixal Products
</div>
```

can be moved to the page coordinates (200, 250) under the Netscape 4 DOM using the JavaScript command

```
document.heading.moveTo(200,250)
```

By default, the moveTo() method assumes that pixels is the unit of distance.

Limits to Changing Styles

There are severe limitations on Netscape 4's dynamic content model. You cannot change the appearance of most page elements after a page is loaded. You cannot, for example, change the display style of an object to create expandable/collapsible content. Neither can you change font size, color, or font family *after* the page is loaded. Those types of modifications can only occur during the period when the page loads.

Writing Dynamic Content in the Netscape 4 DOM

The Netscape 4 DOM does not support document nodes or the node tree. To create dynamic content, you are limited to using the document.write() method. However, the Netscape 4 DOM does allow you to write HTML code into any page object that can be referenced. The general form of the command is

```
object.document.write(content)
```

where *object* is an object on the page and *content* is the HTML code you want placed in the object. Netscape 4's use of the document.write() method is similar to the innerHTML property employed by the Internet Explorer DOM. When you use the document.write() method under the Netscape 4 DOM, it opens input into the object. The document.write() method replaces whatever content was in the object, with succeeding document.write() methods adding additional lines of content. Whenever you open an input stream with the document.write() method, you must also close it. If you do not close the input stream, the new content does not appear in the browser window. The command to close an input stream is

```
object.document.close();
```

where *object* is an object on the page and *content* is the HTML code you want placed in the object. For example, the following command writes content to an element whose id is "heading":

```
document.heading.document.write("<i>Pixal Products</i>");
document.heading.document.close();
```

Note that you must include the document.close() method after the document.write() method is run.

Changing the Source of a Layer

As indicated earlier, Netscape 4 layers can also display the contents of external documents. To change the source of a layer to a new document, run the command

```
object.src="url"
```

where *object* is the layer object in the Web page and *url* is the URL of the document to be displayed in the layer. If you wanted to change the source of the layer element with the id "heading" to the file newhead.htm, for example, you could run the following command:

```
document.heading.src="newhead.htm";
```

Beyond the document.write() method and the properties and methods of the layer object, there are no other ways of creating dynamic content for Web pages under the Netscape 4 DOM.

Text Rollovers with Netscape 4

Because Netscape 4 does not allow you to change the appearance of most page objects after a Web page is loaded, text rollovers can only be created using the document.write() method. For example, the following code uses the document.write() method to change the font color during the mouseover event:

```
<head>
<script language="JavaScript">
function Over() {
    document.heading.document.write("<font color='red'>Pixal
Products</font>");
    document.heading.document.close();
}
function Out() {
    document.heading.document.write("Pixal Products");
document.Globe.document.close();
}
</script>
</head>
<body>
<layer name="heading" onmouseover="Over()" onmouseout="Out()">
    Pixal Products
</layer>
</body>
```

Exploring the Netscape 4 Event Model

As with the document object models, the syntax and structure of the Netscape 4 event model differs greatly from that employed in the Internet Explorer and W3C event models.

Event Handlers

Under the W3C and Internet Explorer event models, just about any object can be the source of an event and can have an event handler. In Netscape 4, event handlers can be added only to a select few elements. Figure J-4 lists the HTML elements that support event handlers under Netscape 4.

Figure J-4	Netscape 4 tags that support event handlers

Event Handler	HTML Tags
onclick	<a>, <area>, <input (type="checkbox", "radio", "reset", "submit")>
ondblclick	<a>
onkeydown	<input (type="password", "text")>, <textarea>
onkeypress	<input (type="password", "text")>, <textarea>
onkeyup	<input (type="password", "text")>, <textarea>
onmousedown	<a>, <input (type="checkbox", "radio", "reset", "submit")>
onmouseout	<a>, <area>, <layer>
onmouseover	<a>, <area>, <layer>
onmouseup	<a>, <input (type="checkbox", "radio", "reset", "submit")>, <layer>

Thus, if you're trying to create a cross-browser Web site that uses event handlers, you have to take into account Netscape 4's limitations. One way to get around this problem is to place those elements that do not support event handlers under the Netscape 4 event model within <a> tags (since the <a> tag supports several different event handlers). You have to include the href attribute in the <a> tag and set the destination of the link to "#" (the current Web page). For example, in the W3C or Internet Explorer DOM, you could add an event handler to a paragraph simply by adding the attribute to the <p> tag:

```
<p onmouseover="showBanner()">
   Display banner
</p>
```

In Netscape 4, you could do this with the code

```
<p><a onmouseover="showBanner()" href="#">
   Display banner
</a></p>
```

When you use this technique, you should employ a style sheet to remove the underlining from the link.

Event Propagation in Netscape 4

In the Netscape 4 event model, events propagate down from the top of a document to the lowest document elements (see Figure J-5).

Event propagation in Netscape 4 ◄ **Figure J-5**

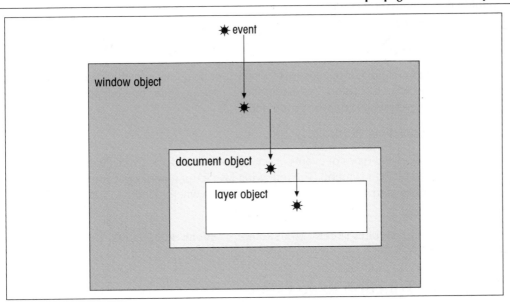

Event propagation in Netscape 4 ◄ **Figure J-5**

For example, the action of moving the mouse is first processed by the browser window, next by the document window, then by an object within the document, and so forth down the hierarchy of objects. If you want a Netscape 4 Web browser to take an action in response to an event, you must capture the event at a particular level of the hierarchy.

Capturing an Event

To capture an event in Netscape 4, you use the JavaScript method

```
object.captureEvents(Event.EVENT_TYPE)
```

where *object* is the object in which the event is captured, and EVENT_TYPE_ is the type of event. Note that the name of the event must be in all capital letters. Figure J-6 lists the various events that can be captured in the Netscape 4 event model.

Event types in Netscape 4 ◄ **Figure J-6**

Event.ABORT	Event.KEYDOWN	Event.MOUSEUP
Event.BLUR	Event.KEYPRESS	Event.MOVE
Event.CHANGE	Event.KEYUP	Event.RESET
Event.CLICK	Event.LOAD	Event.RESIZE
Event.DBLCLICK	Event.MOUSEDOWN	Event.SCROLL
Event.DRAGDROP	Event.MOUSEMOVE	Event.SELECT
Event.ERROR	Event.MOUSEOUT	Event.SUBMIT
Event.FOCUS	Event.MOUSEOVER	Event.UNLOAD

For example, to capture the event when a user double-clicks the mouse anywhere within the browser window, you enter the command

```
window.captureEvents(Event.DBLCLICK);
```

Here, *window* is the object and *DBLCLICK* is the event type. If you want to capture only the double-clicks within the first <layer> tag, you would capture the event at a different level in the object hierarchy:

```
document.layers[0].captureEvents(Event.DBLCLICK);
```

Any double-clicks that occur outside this layer would be ignored by this command.

Finally, if you want to capture the event of the mouse pointer moving across the Web page document, you would use the command:

```
document.captureEvents(Event.MOUSEMOVE)
```

You can capture several types of events at once by separating the events with the OR operator (represented by the | symbol). The following JavaScript command captures the mousedown, mousemove, and mouseup events occurring anywhere within a Web page document:

```
document.captureEvents(Event.MOUSEDOWN | Event.MOUSEMOVE |
Event.MOUSEUP)
```

Assigning a Function to an Event

After Netscape 4 has captured an event, a function can be assigned to run in response to that event's occurrence. For example, to run a function named "grabIt()" when a user presses the mouse pointer down anywhere within a Web document, you first capture the mousedown event and then use the object property method to assign the grabIt() function to the event. The JavaScript code would look as follows:

```
document.captureEvents(Event.MOUSEDOWN);
document.onmousedown=grabIt;
```

Releasing an Event

You can turn off event capturing in Netscape 4 by using the releaseEvents() method. For example, if you want the browser to initially capture the mousemove event, but then at a later point in your script you do not need to capture that event anymore, you can turn off the capture using the command

```
document.releaseEvents(Event.MOUSEMOVE);
```

Events can be released and then recaptured multiple times within your program code.

Routing Events to their Targets

To handle nested objects, the Netscape 4 event model allows you to route an event down the object hierarchy. For example, you might create an onclick event handler for both a Web page document and a layer object in that document. When you click the layer object, the click event starts at the top of the object hierarchy and is first captured by the document's event handler. At that point, two things happen: (1) the function associated with the event handler is run, and (2) the click event stops being propagated down the object hierarchy, never reaching the layer object.

To force the Netscape 4 browser to continue propagating such an event down the object hierarchy, you have to call the routeEvent() method at the end of the function. The code might look as follows:

```
document.captureEvents(Event.CLICK);
document.layers[0].captureEvents(Event.CLICK);
document.onclick=handleClick1;
document.layers[0].handleClick2;

function handleClick1(e) {
...
    document.routeEvent(e);
}
```

In this example, Netscape 4 runs the handleClick1() function when a user clicks any location in the document. If the user happens to click a location within the first layer object, the browser first runs the handleClick1() function, and then routes the event down the object hierarchy, running the handleClick2() function. If the routeEvent() method were not applied, this would not happen and the event propagation would stop at the document level.

Redirecting Events

Another method in Netscape 4 that you can apply to events is the handleEvent() method. While the routeEvent() method passes an event down the object hierarchy to its intended target, the handleEvent() method passes an event to a specified target. For example, the following code demonstrates how to pass the click event to the first link in a document:

```
document.captureEvents(Event.CLICK);
document.onclick=handleAllClicks;
...

function handleAllClicks(e) {

...

    document.links[0].handleEvent(e);
}
```

The effect of this code is that the first link is activated no matter where a user clicks in the document.

The Netscape 4 Event Object

In both the Netscape 4 and the W3C event models, the event object is the parameter of the function assigned to the event (unlike the Internet Explorer event model, which uses the event or window.event object). For example, in the following code:

```
function handleClick1(e) {
...
    document.routeEvent(e);
}
```

the event object is the parameter "e". The Netscape 4 event object supports many of the same properties found in the W3C event model, but there are some differences in the property names. Figure J-7 lists the properties of the Netscape 4 event object.

Figure J-7 | **Properties of the Netscape 4 event object**

Description	Netscape 4 Event Property
Element in which event occurred	target
Type of event that has occurred	type
The (x, y) coordinates of the event within the entire computer screen	screenX, screenY
The (x, y) coordinates of the event within the page	pageX, pageY
The (x, y) coordinates of the event within an object on the page	layerX, layerY x, y
An integer representing the modifier key (Alt, Ctrl, or Shift) pressed by the user	modifiers
Keyboard key that caused the event	which
Mouse button that caused the event	which

For example, to determine the screen coordinates of an event in the Netscape 4 event model, you would use the object properties

```
evt.screenX
evt.screenY
```

where *evt* is the parameter in the event function.

One very useful property in both the W3C and Internet Explorer event models enables you to determine which object initiated an event. In the W3C event model, this is the currentTarget or target property, while in the Internet Explorer event model, it is the srcElement property. The Netscape 4 event model includes no such property. The target property is part of the Netscape 4 model, but it only applies to the mouseover and mouse-out events. Using the target property for any other event results in an error.

Keyboard Keys and Buttons

The Netscape 4 event model also differs from the W3C and Internet Explorer models in the way that a script determines which mouse button or keyboard key a user has pressed. In Netscape 4, the button or key is returned by the property

```
evt.which
```

where *evt* is once again the parameter of the event function. For example, to resolve the differences between browsers, you can use the following function to return the keyboard key:

```
function getKey(e) {
   if (NS4DOM) return e.which;
   else if (IEDOM) return event.keyCode;
   else if (W3CDOM) return e.keyCode;
}
```

Note that this function uses the Boolean variables NS4DOM, IEDOM, and W3CDOM. The cross-browser function that determines which mouse button was clicked has a similar structure:

```
function getButton(e) {
   if (NS4DOM) return e.which;
   else if (IEDOM) return event.button;
   else if (W3CDOM) return e.button;
}
```

Netscape 4's button values differ from those of the W3C or Internet Explorer event models. The Netscape 4 event model does not support the middle button, and as indicated in Figure J-8, the left button has a value of 1 and the right button a value of 3.

Button values in the three event models   **Figure J-8**

Event Model	Event Property	Left	Middle	Right
Netscape 4	e.which	1	n/a	3
Internet Explorer	event.button	1	4	2
W3C	e.button	0	1	2

If you need to capture whether a modifier key, such as the Ctrl, Shift, or Alt key, is being pressed, you need to use Netscape 4's modifiers property. The syntax of the property is

```
evt.modifiers
```

Figure J-9 shows the value of the modifiers property when different combinations of modifier keys are being pressed.

Values of the modifiers property   **Figure J-9**

e.modifiers Value	Modifier Key(s) Being Pressed
0	None
1	Alt
2	Ctrl
3	Alt+Ctrl
4	Shift
5	Alt+Shift
6	Ctrl+Shift
7	Alt+Ctrl+Shift

For example, if the modifiers property returns a value of 5, you know that a user is pressing both the Alt and Shift keys.

Summary

As each year passes, fewer and fewer users run the Netscape 4 browser. At the time of this writing, about 0.2% of browsers in use are Netscape 4. Creating a cross-browser page that supports Netscape 4 can be an exercise in acute frustration—particularly if you are working with the event model or with dynamic content. However, if you are designing Web sites for a population of people who typically use older browsers, such as users in developing or third world countries, then the number of Netscape 4 users among your audience may be much higher. In such cases, you may decide it's important to ensure that your Web pages support Netscape 4 and all of its features.

Glossary/Index